The
SEED SEARCH
1997

Devised, compiled and edited by
Karen Platt

Published by Karen Platt

KP

The first edition of the Seed Search is dedicated to Joshua

British Library Cataloguing in publication Data.
A Catalogue record of this book is available from the British Library.

ISBN 0 9528810 0 4
ISSN 1365-9863

First Edition: Dec 1996

Compiled, Edited, Typeset and Published by:
Karen Platt
37 Melbourn Rd
Crookes
Sheffield
S10 1NR

Front Cover:
Corydalis flexuosa

Back Cover:
Viola 'Bowles Black'
Eschscholtzia californica

Cover Design:
Alan Coventry Design
Sheffield

TABLE OF CONTENTS

Preface - 1997 Edition

This is the first edition of The Seed Search I have compiled and published. It is a unique directory of seed catalogues to enable the gardener to access the vast array of seeds available from sources around the world.

The suppliers in The Seed Search offer a wide range of seeds from the common to the rare, from open-pollinated to F1's. One issue which I feel strongly about is the limitations put on our choice of vegetables by the existence of the National List. Thanks to the HDRA, vegetables not on the National List have been included here, as well as many sources of organic seeds. So, you can make the choice - hand-pollinated F1 seed or organically grown and open-pollinated types. F1 seed is usually far more expensive and seed which is saved from F1's will not breed true.

Similarly, I believe we should all be aware of CITES (Convention on International Trade in Endangered Species of Wild Fauna and Flora) which regulates trade in wild plants and forbids the import and export of those species which are listed as endangered as well as restricting trade in those which are at risk.

There exists a wider choice of seeds than many people would imagine and I hope the book will open your eyes and entice you to contact the suppliers and get growing. I aim to include as many small suppliers as possible together with their specialities in the exotic, unusual and rare.

This first Edition lists over 33,000 seeds and over 100 suppliers. As I write, my mind is already on the Second Edition, and I look forward to many more suppliers sending their information to me.

As a nurserywoman I know that growing from seed is one of the most satisfying pleasures and I hope The Seed Search will make it easier for you to find the seeds you have been searching for and have not been able to find in the past.

Karen Platt
November 1996

Acknowledgements

I am eternally grateful to Ralph Wheatley for his advice, help and expertise when I ran into difficulties with the database and also for his understanding, patience and support, without which I would never have managed to complete the Seed Search 1997.

My thanks also go to Ray Brown of Plant World, and to Dirk Van Der Werff of Plants for their support and to all the seed suppliers who, by sending in their catalogues and information have made the book possible in the first place.

I would also like to acknowledge Chris Philip and the invaluable work he has done over the past ten years in producing The Plant Finder, which formed the inspiration for The Seed Search.

Abbreviations

coll	collection
coll.ref	collector's references
c.s.	coated seed
cv(s)	cultivar(s)
cw	collected wild
dbl	double
d.m.p.	dried mycelium preparation
dw	dwarf
f	forma (botanical form)
fl	flower(ed)
fl.pl.	flore pleno
g	germinated
Gr	group
h-p	hand pollinated
hyb(s)	hybrid(s)
imp	improved
(o)	organic
o-p	open pollinated
poll	pollenless
p.s	pelleted seed
pr.s	primed seed
r-v	revegetation
sel	selected
s-c	separate colours
sp	species
sp.s	sprinter seed
ssp	subspecies
st	stratified
(u-g)	unknown genus
v(ars)	varietas (botanical variety)
(V)	variegated plant
w.a.	widely available
x witt	x wittrochiana (Pansy)

IMPORTANT NOTE TO USERS

To avoid disappointment, I suggest you always:

Check the information given on each supplier you wish to contact and note their method of trading i.e. wholesale or retail. Most retail suppliers are mail order only, some have retail outlets and others welcome callers - always ring first. Details of opening times are given in the Code-Supplier index.
Where the supplier requests stamps or payment for their catalogue please honour their request.
Early orders i.e. Jan/Feb will avoid disappointment where stocks are low.

THE SEED SEARCH exists to put you, the grower, in touch with suppliers. It does not offer value judgments on those included nor intend any reflection on those not included in this edition. In some cases, suppliers sent their information in too late, in many others it is possible I simply did not know of the existence of the supplier, although I have made every effort to make the SEED SEARCH as comprehensive as possible.

I have attempted to make cross-references to the only correct and valid name, and I will continue to do this in future years. It is clearly the responsibility of suppliers to check what they are selling and ensure seeds are accurately named in their catalogues. Unfortunately, many suppliers have not done this.

Disclaimer
As the compiler and Editor of THE SEED SEARCH I have taken every care, in the time available, to check all the information supplied to me by the seed suppliers. Nevertheless, in a work of this nature, containing many thousands of records, errors and omissions are likely to occur. The compiler and editor of THE SEED SEARCH cannot be held responsibile for any consequences arising from any such errors. Please let me know if you do find any errors, so that I may correct them for the next edition.

HOW TO USE THE DIRECTORY

Code-Supplier Index
Codes have been allocated to suppliers as their information was received. At present in this first edition, suppliers have either a one or two letter code.
Codes are given for each seed supplied, except where the number of suppliers exceeds 25, where you will find the words widely available.
In the Code-supplier index on page 270, you will find codes listed for each supplier in alphabetical order, together with detailed information on each supplier.

Supplier-Code Index
For ease of use, a reverse supplier-code index is included on page 277, giving the names of seed suppliers in alphabetical order of their name followed by their code.

Societies
Societies and other horticultural groups which offer seed exchanges have been included here on the understanding that seed exchanges are only offered to members.

Searching for Seeds
If you cannot immediately find the seeds you want, look through the complete listing of that genera and note where reference has been made to name changes. If you still cannot find what you want I am happy to answer any requests provided you send an sae.

Cross references
I have started cross-referencing deletions I have made owing to plant name changes to enable you to find seeds that are still listed by synonyms in seed catalogues. The list of synonyms and common names will also be of use.
There are separate lists for vegetable, herbs and green manures which contain entries for suppliers who have these seeds listed individually, please also refer to the main list for suppliers who do not list these seeds separately.

Suppliers' Details
The details given for each supplier will, I hope, prove useful. The information is compiled from a questionnaire which was sent to each supplier. I have made no personal comment on this. If information is not included here it is because that section was left blank by the supplier. In the case of minimum order, if the information is not given it is because the supplier has no minimum order and will supply one packet. Opening times, where stated will mostly refer to telephone lines for mail order. A charge for catalogues is given where appropriate and the time of year you can expect a new catalogue to be issued. If postage is charged on orders this is also shown. If the supplier gives a seed count on the seed packet, or in their catalogue, this is indicated along with whether you can expect information on growing from seed. I have noted specialities, seed collections (e.g. sweet pea collection/wildflower collection. i.e. a mixture of seeds) and any other information the supplier wished to be included. Days of the week have been abbreviated. So

too, have the credit card organisations' names.

Import and Export
The Plant Health Order 1993 rules over import and export of plant material. Check with seed suppliers for any necessary photosanitary certificates etc.

Plant Breeders' Rights
If you are raising from seed and come across something different, and are intersted in Plant Breedes' Rights, for further information contact:
Mrs. M. Vaughan at the Plant Variety Rights Office, White House Lane, Huntingdon Rd, Cambridge. CB3 0LF. Telephone (01223) 342350. Fax (01223) 342386.

New Entries
If you are a supplier wishing to be included in THE SEED SEARCH 1998, and are not already included, please send sae for details to:
Karen Platt. 37 Melbourn Rd. Crookes. Sheffield. S10 1NR.
Closing date for new entries 15 September 1997.

Collector's References
Where possible, I have indicated seeds collected with the reference. This has not been possible in every case. Please refer to individual catalogues for full references.

Nomenclature
I have followed the Rules of Nomenclature set out in the International Code of Botanical Nomenclature 1994 (ICBN) and the International Code of Nomenclature for Cultivated Plants 1995 (ICNCP), perhaps with the exception of Chrysanthemum.
The use of botanical names avoids confusion. There is only one valid name, although many seeds are listed under synonyms in catalogues. Other catalogues use common names, and these can lead to confusion as the common name may refer to more than one plant.
I would like to see more suppliers keeping their catalogues and naming up-to-date and I know the recent name changes have made this difficult. Hopefully, suppliers will check their lists against the book and make the necessary amendments.

Karen Platt
November 1996

SEED - CULTURAL NOTES

GROWING FROM SEED

Seed is a sexual method of propagation and the commonest way of reproduction found in nature. Resulting seedlings can be variable owing to the variety of genetic combinations. Such variation allows for the breeding and selection of cultivars with combinations of the most desirable characteristics of each parent plant.

Collecting and storing seed

Seed should be collected as soon as it is ripe and stored in a dry, dark, airy place at 1-5°C (34-41°F) until it is used. Some seeds have special requirements.

Viability - Those which are only viable for short periods need to be sown as soon as possible.

Fleshy Fruits - Soften fleshy fruits by soaking them in water, remove the seed and air dry at 10-20°C (50-68°F). Harvest fruits that split to release their seed, if not quite mature, dry in clean paper bags before separating out the seeds.

Wind Disribution - Seeds distributed by the wind can be collected by covering the seed heads.

Storing - The length of time for which seed is viable varies greatly. and depends on the species and the storage conditions. Oily seeds do not store well and should be sown soon after collection. Parsnip seed also needs to be used quickly. The viability of seed may be prolonged if stored at 3-5°C (37-41°F) in sealed containers.

Dormancy

Scarification is used to break down the hardened seed coat to enable water to penetrate and therefore speed up the process of germination. Carefully nick the hard-coated seed with a sharp knife. Alternatively, rub the seed between two sheets of abrasive paper.

Warm stratification is used for hard-coated seeds of many woody species. Place the seed in a plastic bag in equal amounts of sand and leaf mould, or peat substitute and sand. Store for 4-12 weeks at 20-25°C (68-77°F). This method is normally followed by a period of cold stratification.

Cold stratification is used following warm stratification and for many alpines. Put the seeds in a plastic bag in a mixture of 50/50 peat or peat substitute and sand, place in the fridge, not the freezer, for 4-12 weeks until germination starts. You will need to check the seeds regularly for germination and sow as soon as germination has occurred. Alternatively, plunge the seeds outdoors in a pot, covering to keep out mice, and check regularly for signs of germination. Sow seeds immediately this occurs.

Germination

The necessary requirements for germination are water, air, warmth and for some species - light.
Use a fine compost, lightly firmed but not compressed. Check the temperature as low temperatures will inhibit the germination of some seeds and high temperatures will inhibit others. Heated propagators will maintain an even temperature, however seeds can also be successfully raised on a windowsill. A small pot or seed try covered with a plastic bag to conserve the right atmosphere, shaded from strong sunlight.

There is no way of distinguishing which seeds need dark and which need light to germinate. If the requirement is unknown, sow the seed in the dark, if germination does not occur after a number of weeks, place it in the light. Some seeds germinate erratically, prick out germinated seedlings, whilst trying not to disturb those which have not germinated. Be prepared to keep pots for up to two years before discarding the contents.

Pelleted or coated seed is available to enable sowing of very tiny seed such as Begonia or Lobelia.

Aftercare

After sowing do not allow compost to dry out or become waterlogged. Cover the seeds to maintain the appropriate environment. When the seedlings are large enough to handle, prick out to avoid weak growth. Gradually harden off by placing in cooler conditions.

Pollination

Open pollination occurs naturally in nature and is the transfer of pollen from the anthers to the stigma.

Cross pollination is the transfer of pollen from the anther of a flower on one plant to the stigma of a flower on another plant.

Self pollination is the transfer of pollen from the anthers to the stigma of the same flower, or to another flower on the same plant.

Open-pollinated varieties are often better adapted to the home garden and small farm. They deliver the performance, flower and nutrition that is lacking in many selected hybrids.

Hybrids

When hybridising it is important to prevent self-pollination. Petals, sepals and stamens are removed from the proposed female parent and the denuded flower is protected by a plastic or paper bag until the stigmas are sticky and receptive. Pollen is then transferred to the stigmas and the flowers protected again until fertilisation has occurred. The seed can then be collected when ripe.

The attraction of hybrids lies in their vigour and uniformity which I feel is not always a necessity to the home gardener.

True From Seed

A listing in the directory is not a guarantee that seeds will come true. Some cultivars will come true from seed, many will not. Some genera are not normally propagated from seed, coming much better from vegetative propagation, and therefore you may find that seed is not available.

F1 Hybrids will not breed true from seed collected.

SEED DIRECTORY

Abarema grandiflora	AU
Abelia biflora	SA
Abelia chinensis	B
Abelia floribunda	B
Abelia koreana	B
Abelia mosanensis	B
Abelia x grandiflora	B
Abeliophyllum distichum	B
Abelmoschus ficulneus	B
Abelmoschus manihot	G
Abelmoschus man. 'Sunset Grandiflora'	B
Abelmoschus moschatus	B,JE,SA
Abelmoschus moschatus 'Pacific' mix	BS,C
Abelmoschus moschatus ssp palustris	B
Aberia caffra	B
Abies alba	B,SA,T
Abies amabilis	A,B,SA
Abies balsamea	A,B,C,SA
Abies balsamea 'Cook's Blue Improved'	B
Abies borisii regis	B,SA
Abies bornmulleriana	SA
Abies bracteata	B,SA
Abies cephalonica	B,CG,SA
Abies chinensis	B
Abies cilicica	B,SA
Abies concolor	B,C,CG,N,SA,SG
Abies concolor f atroviolacea	SG
Abies concolor ssp lowiana	B,SA
Abies concolor 'Swift's Silver'	B
Abies delavayi	B,SA,SG
Abies densa	B
Abies ernestii	SA
Abies fabri	B
Abies fargesii	B,SA
Abies firma	B,SA
Abies forrestii	B
Abies fraseri	B,SA,SG
Abies georgii v smithii CNW1005	X
Abies grandis	A,B,C,G,SA
Abies holophylla	B,SA
Abies homolepis	B,C,CG,G,N,SA
Abies kawakamii	B
Abies koreana	AP,B,C,CG,I,N,SA,SC,SG, X
Abies lasiocarpa	B,C,SA
Abies lasiocarpa ssp arizonica	B,N,SA
Abies magnifica	B,SA
Abies magnifica v shastensis	B,SA
Abies mariesii	B
Abies mayriana	SA
Abies nephrolepis	B,SA,SG
Abies nordmanniana	B,CG,N,T
Abies nordmanniana 'Ambrolauri'	B,SA
Abies nordmanniana ssp equitrojani	B
Abies numidica	B
Abies pindrow	B,C,G,HA,SA
Abies pinsapo	B,N,SA
Abies pinsapo 'Glauca'	B,C,SA
Abies procera	B,C,G,SA
Abies procera 'Glauca'	B
Abies recurvata	B
Abies recurvata v ernestii	B
Abies religiosa	B
Abies sachalinensis	B,SA
Abies sibirica	B,SA
Abies sibirica 'Argentea'	B

Abies sp mix	C
Abies veitchii	B,SA,SG
Abroma augusta	B
Abroma fastuosa	B
Abronia fragrans v fragrans	B,SW
Abronia latifolia	B
Abronia maritima	B
Abronia villosa	AV,B,SW
Abronia villosa 'Milka'	B
Abrus precatorius	B,HA,SA,SI
Abrus precatorius, white seeded	B
Abutilon amplum	B,SA
Abutilon andrewsianum	AU
Abutilon arboreum	B
Abutilon auritum	B
Abutilon 'Benary's Giant'	B,BS,C
Abutilon 'Canary Bird'	B
Abutilon 'Choice mix'	L
Abutilon geranioides	B
Abutilon hyb 'Feuerglocke'	CG
Abutilon hyb 'Maximum' mix	BS,CL,SA,V
Abutilon hybrida 'Large Flowered mix'	D,F,O,T
Abutilon hybridum	G
Abutilon indicum	B
Abutilon leucopetalum	AU
Abutilon megapotamicum	B
Abutilon mix	DT,J
Abutilon muticum	B,SA
Abutilon 'Nabob'	B
Abutilon otocarpum	AU,B,RS
Abutilon oxycarpum	B
Abutilon pink mix	E
Abutilon sonneratianum	B,SI
Abutilon theophrasti	AP,B,CC,CG,G
Abutilon vitifolium	AP,B,C,JE,LG,RH,SA, SC,T
Abutilon vitifolium 'Album'	C,LG,SC
Abutilon vitifolium 'Ralph Gould'	C
Abutilon white flowers	N
Abutilon x suntense	AP,B,RH,SC
Acacia acanthoclada	B
Acacia acinacea	B,HA,O,SA
Acacia acradenia	AU,B,O
Acacia acuminata	AU,B,HA,O
Acacia acuminata 'Inland Form'	B
Acacia acutaetissima	CG,HA
Acacia adsurgens	B,HA,O
Acacia adunca	B,HA,O
Acacia aestivalis	B
Acacia alata	B,CG
Acacia albida	SA
Acacia amoena	B,HA,O
Acacia ampliceps	B,O
Acacia anaticeps	B
Acacia anceps	B,AU
Acacia anceps v angustifolia	B
Acacia ancistrocarpa	B,O
Acacia andrewsii	B
Acacia aneura	B,HA,O
Acacia angusta	B
Acacia angustissima	B,RE
Acacia anthochaea	B
Acacia aphylla	B
Acacia arabica	SA
Acacia araneosa	AU
Acacia arenaria	B,SI

8

ACACIA

Acacia argyrophylla	B,AU
Acacia arida	B
Acacia arrecta	B
Acacia ashbyae	B
Acacia asparagoides	AU
Acacia aspera	B
Acacia assimilis	B
Acacia ataxacantha	B,SI
Acacia atkinsiana	B
Acacia aulacocarpa	B,HA,O
Acacia aulacophylla	B
Acacia auriculiformis	B,HA,O,SA
Acacia ausfeldii	B,HA
Acacia baileyana	AU,B,C,HA,O,RE,SA,SH
Acacia baileyana 'Purpurea'	B,C,HA,O,SA,SH
Acacia bancroftii	AU,B,HA,O
Acacia barattensis	B
Acacia baxteri	AU,B
Acacia beauverdiana	B
Acacia beckleri	AU,B
Acacia betchei	AU,B,HA
Acacia bidwillii	B
Acacia biflora	B
Acacia binata	B
Acacia binervata	B,HA
Acacia binervia	B,HA,O,SA,SH
Acacia bivenosa	AU,B
Acacia blakei	B,HA
Acacia blakelyi	B
Acacia blue foliage mix	C
Acacia boormanii	AU,B,HA,O,SA
Acacia botrycephala	AU,B,HA,O,SA
Acacia brachybotrya	AU,B,HA
Acacia brachystachya	B
Acacia brassii	O
Acacia browniana v browniana	B
Acacia browniana v endlicheri	B
Acacia browniana v intermedia	B
Acacia brownii	HA
Acacia brunioides	AU,B
Acacia burkei	B,SI
Acacia burkittii	AU,B
Acacia burrowii	B,O
Acacia buxifolia	B,HA,O,SH
Acacia buxifolia ssp pubiflora	B,HA
Acacia caerulescens	AU
Acacia caesia	B
Acacia caesiella	B,HA
Acacia caffra	B,SI
Acacia calamifolia	AU,B,HA
Acacia cambagei	B,O
Acacia cardiophylla	AU,B,C,HA,SA
Acacia caroleae	B
Acacia catechu	B,SA
Acacia celastrifolia	B
Acacia cheelii	AU,B
Acacia chinchillensis	AU,B
Acacia chisholmii	B
Acacia chrysella	B
Acacia chrysocephala	AU,B
Acacia cibaria	B
Acacia cincinnata	B,O
Acacia citrinoviridis	B
Acacia cochlearis	AU,B
Acacia cognata	B,HA,O
Acacia colei	B

Acacia colletioides	B
Acacia complanata	B,HA,O
Acacia concinna	B
Acacia concurrens	B,HA
Acacia conferta	B,HA,SA
Acacia constricta	B
Acacia continua	AU,B
Acacia convenyi	HA
Acacia coolgardiensis	B
Acacia coriacea	B,HA,O
Acacia cowleana	B,HA,O
Acacia craspedocarpa	B
Acacia crassa	B
Acacia crassicarpa	B,O
Acacia crassiuscula	AU
Acacia cultriformis	AU,B,HA,SA
Acacia cunninghamii	B,SA
Acacia cupularis	AU,B
Acacia curranii	B
Acacia curvata	AU,B
Acacia curvinervia	B
Acacia cuthbertsonii	B,HA,O
Acacia cyclops	AU,B,HA,O,SA
Acacia cyperophylla	B
Acacia davyi	B,SI
Acacia dawsonii	B,HA,SH
Acacia dealbata	AU,B,BS,C,HA,N,O,SA, SH,T,V
Acacia deanei	AU,B,HA,O
Acacia declinata	B
Acacia decora	B,C,HA,O,SA
Acacia decurrens	B,HA,O,SA
Acacia delphina	B
Acacia dempsteri	B
Acacia denticulosa	B,O
Acacia dentifera	B,CG
Acacia dictyoneura	B
Acacia dictyophleba	B
Acacia dielsii	B
Acacia dietrichiana	B
Acacia difficilis	B,O
Acacia difformis	B
Acacia discolor	C,HA
Acacia divergens	B
Acacia dodonaeifolia	B
Acacia donaldsonii	B
Acacia dorotoxylon	AU,B,HS
Acacia drepanocarpa	B
Acacia drepanolobium	B
Acacia drewiana	AU
Acacia drummondii	AU,B,C,HA,SA
Acacia drummondii 'Grossus'	B
Acacia drummondii ssp affinis	B,O
Acacia drummondii ssp candolleana	B,O
Acacia drummondii ssp drummondii	O
Acacia drummondii ssp elegans	B,O
Acacia dudgeonii	B
Acacia dunnii	B,C,HA,O
Acacia dystyla	B
Acacia elata	AU,B,HA,O
Acacia elongata	AU,B,HA,SA
Acacia empelioclada	B
Acacia enterocarpaa	AU
Acacia eremaea	B
Acacia eremophila	B
Acacia ericifolia aff	AU,B

ACACIA

Acacia erinacea	AU,B	Acacia hemignosta	B
Acacia erioloba	B,SI	Acacia hemiteles	AU,B
Acacia erioloba giraffae	SA	Acacia hemsleyi	B
Acacia eriopoda	B	Acacia heteroclita	AU,B
Acacia erubescens	B,SI	Acacia heteroneura	B
Acacia estrophiolata	AU,B,O	Acacia heterophylla	B
Acacia euthycarpa	AU,B	Acacia hilliana	B
Acacia everestii	B	Acacia hockii	B
Acacia excelsa	B	Acacia holosericea	B,HA,O
Acacia exilis	B	Acacia homalophylla	HA
Acacia exocarpoides	B	Acacia horridula	B
Acacia extensa	AU,B	Acacia howittii	AU,B,CG,HA,O
Acacia falcata	B,HA,SA	Acacia hubbardiana	B
Acacia falciformis	B,HA,O	Acacia idiomorpha	B
Acacia farnesiana	B,HA,O,SA,SH	Acacia imbricata	AU,B
Acacia fasciculifera	B	Acacia implexa	AU,B,HA,O
Acacia fauntleroyi	AU,B,CG,O	Acacia inaequilatera	B
Acacia ferruginea	B	Acacia inaequiloba	B
Acacia filicifolia	AU,B,HA	Acacia incurva	B
Acacia filifolia	AU,B	Acacia ingramii	AU
Acacia fimbriata	B,C,HA,O,SA	Acacia irrorata	HA
Acacia fimbriata v perangusta	HA	Acacia irrorata ssp irrorata	B
Acacia flagelliformis	B	Acacia iteaphylla	AU,B,HA,O,SH
Acacia flavescens	B	Acacia ixiophylla	B,HA,O
Acacia fleckii	B,SI	Acacia ixodes	B
Acacia flexifolia	B,HA	Acacia jamesiana	B
Acacia floribunda	AU,B,HA,O,SA,SH	Acacia jennerae	B,O
Acacia fragilis	AU	Acacia jensenii	B
Acacia frigescens	B,HA	Acacia jibberdingensis	B
Acacia galpinii	B,SA,SI	Acacia jonesii	AU,B
Acacia genistifolia	AU,B	Acacia julifera	AU,B
Acacia georginae	B,O	Acacia julifera ssp julifera	O
Acacia gerrardii	B,SI	Acacia juncifolia	B,HA
Acacia gilbertii	B	Acacia juncunda	HA
Acacia gillii	AU,B	Acacia juniperina	HA
Acacia giraffae	C	Acacia karroo	B,C,SA,SI
Acacia gittinsii	B	Acacia kempeana	B
Acacia gladiiformis	B,HA	Acacia kirkii	SI
Acacia glandulicarpa	AU	Acacia koa	B
Acacia glaucescens see binervia		Acacia kybeanensis	AU,B,HA,O,SA,SH
Acacia glaucissima	B	Acacia laccata	B
Acacia glaucocarpa	B,O	Acacia lachnophylla	AU
Acacia glaucoptera	B,C,O	Acacia lanigera	AU,B,HA
Acacia gnidium	B	Acacia lanuginophylla	AU
Acacia gnidium v latifolia	HA	Acacia lasiocalyx	B
Acacia gonoclada	B	Acacia lasiocarpa	AU,B,SA
Acacia gonophylla	B	Acacia lasiocarpa v sedifolia	AU,B
Acacia gracilifolia	AU,B	Acacia lateriticola	B
Acacia grandicornuta	B,SI	Acacia latescens	B
Acacia granitica	AU,B,HA	Acacia latisepala	B
Acacia grasbyi	B	Acacia leichhardtii	B
Acacia greggii	B	Acacia leiocalyx	B,HA
Acacia gregorii	AU,B	Acacia leiocladia ssp argentifolia	HA
Acacia guinetii	AU,B	Acacia leioderma	B
Acacia gunnii	HA	Acacia leiophylla	AU,B,HA
Acacia hadrophylla	B	Acacia leptocarpa	B,HA
Acacia haematoxylon	B,SI	Acacia leptoneura	AU,B
Acacia hakeoides	B,HA	Acacia leptospermoides	AU
Acacia halliana	B	Acacia leucoclada	B,HA
Acacia hamersleyensis	B	Acacia leucophloea	B
Acacia hamiltoniana	HA	Acacia ligulata	AU,B,HA,O
Acacia harpophylla	B,HA,O	Acacia ligustrina	B
Acacia harveyi	B	Acacia linearifolia	AU,B,SA
Acacia hastulata	B	Acacia lineata	AU,B,HA
Acacia havilandii	AU,B	Acacia linifolia	AU,B,HA
Acacia hebeclada v tristis	B,SI	Acacia linophylla	B

ACACIA

Acacia littorea	B
Acacia loderi	B
Acacia longifolia	B,C,HA,O,SA,SC
Acacia longiphyllodinea	B
Acacia longispicata	B
Acacia longispicata ssp longispicata	B
Acacia longissima	B,HA,O
Acacia luteola	B
Acacia lysiphloia	B
Acacia mabellae	B,O
Acacia macdonelliensis	B
Acacia macradenia	B,HA,N,O
Acacia macrothyrsa	SI
Acacia maidenii	B,HA,O
Acacia maitlandii	B
Acacia mangium	B,HA,O
Acacia maslinii	B
Acacia 'Maxwellii'	B
Acacia mearnsii	AU,B,CG,HA,O,SA
Acacia meisneri	AU,B
Acacia melanoxylon	AU,B,C,HA,O,SA,SG
Acacia melleodora	B
Acacia mellifera	B,SI
Acacia mellifera detinens	SI
Acacia melvillei	AU
Acacia menzelii	AU,B
Acacia merinthophora	B,O
Acacia merrallii	AU,B
Acacia microbotrya	AU,B
Acacia microcarpa	B
Acacia mimula	B
Acacia mitchellii	B
Acacia modesta	SA
Acacia moirii ssp dasycarpa	AU,B
Acacia mollifolia	AU,B
Acacia mollisima see mearnsii	
Acacia montana	B,HA
Acacia monticola	B
Acacia montis-usti	B
Acacia mucronata	AU,B,O,SA
Acacia muellerana	B,HA
Acacia multispicata	AU,B
Acacia murrayana	B,HA
Acacia myrtifolia	AU,B,HA,O,SA
Acacia myrtifolia v angustifolia	B
Acacia nanodealbata	AU
Acacia nematophylla	B
Acacia neriifolia	B,C,CG,HA,O
Acacia nervosa	B
Acacia neurophylla	B
Acacia nigrescens	B,SA,SI
Acacia nigricans	AU,B
Acacia nilotica	B
Acacia nilotica ssp adansonii	B
Acacia nilotica ssp indica	B
Acacia nilotica ssp kraussiana	SI
Acacia nilotica ssp tomentosa	B
Acacia nodiflora v ferox	B
Acacia notabilis	AU,B,HA,O
Acacia nyssophylla	B
Acacia obliquinervaa	AU
Acacia obovata	B
Acacia obtecta	B
Acacia obtusata	B,HA
Acacia obtusifolia	B,HA,O
Acacia oldfieldii	B

Acacia olsenii	B,HA
Acacia omalophylla	B
Acacia oncinocarpa	B
Acacia oraria	O
Acacia orthocarpa	B
Acacia oswaldii	B,HA,O
Acacia oxycedrus	AU,B
Acacia oxyclada	B
Acacia pachycarpa	B
Acacia palustris	B
Acacia papyrocarpa	AU,B,O
Acacia paradoxa	B,HA,SA
Acacia paraneura	B
Acacia parramattensis	AU,B,HA
Acacia parvipinnula	AU,B,HA
Acacia patagiata	B
Acacia pellita	B
Acacia pendula	B,C,HA,O,SA
Acacia pennata	B
Acacia pennatula	B
Acacia penninervis	B,HA,O
Acacia pentadenia	B
Acacia perangusta	B,HA
Acacia phlebopetala	B
Acacia pilligaensis	B
Acacia pinguifolia	B
Acacia platycarpa	B
Acacia podalyriifolia	AU,B,C,HA,O,SA,SC,SH
Acacia polyacantha	B,SI
Acacia polybotrya	AU,B,HA,O
Acacia polystachya	B
Acacia prainii	B
Acacia pravissima	B,HA,N,O,SA,SH
Acacia prominens	B,HA,O
Acacia pruinocarpa	B,O
Acacia pruinosa	B,HA,O
Acacia pubescens	HA
Acacia pubicosta	B
Acacia pubifolia	B
Acacia pulchella	B,SA
Acacia pulchella v glaberrima	AU,B
Acacia pulchella v goadbyi	B
Acacia pustula	B
Acacia pycnantha	AU,B,HA,O,SA
Acacia pyrifolia	B
Acacia quadrimarginea	B
Acacia quadrisulcata	B
Acacia quornensis	AU
Acacia raddiana	B
Acacia ramulosa	AU,B
Acacia redolens	B,O
Acacia redolens 'Prostrata'	B
Acacia reficiens	B,SI
Acacia rehmanniana	B,SI
Acacia retinodes	AU,C,CG,HA,O,SA
Acacia retinodes blue leaf	B
Acacia retivenia	B
Acacia rhigiophylla	AU,B
Acacia rhodophloia	B
Acacia riceana	AU,B,C,N,O,SA,SG
Acacia rigens	AU
Acacia rivalis	B
Acacia robusta	B,SI
Acacia rossei	AU,B
Acacia rostellifera	AU,B
Acacia rotundifolia	B

ACACIA

Acacia rubida	B,HA,O,SH
Acacia rupicola	B
Acacia saliciformis	B
Acacia salicina	B,HA,O
Acacia saligna	AU,CG,HA,O,SA
Acacia saligna desert form	B
Acacia scirpifolia	B
Acacia sclerophylla	B,C
Acacia sclerophylla v lissophylla	B
Acacia sclerophylla v teretiuscula	AU
Acacia sclerosperma	AU,B
Acacia semilunata	B,HA,O
Acacia semirigida	B
Acacia senegal	B
Acacia senegal v rostrata	B,SI
Acacia sessilis	B
Acacia sessilispica	B
Acacia seyal	B
Acacia shirleyi	B
Acacia shuttleworthii	AU
Acacia sibina	B
Acacia siculiformis	AU,B,HA
Acacia sieberana	B
Acacia sieberana v woodii	B,SI
Acacia signata	AU,B
Acacia silvestris	AU,B
Acacia simsii	B,O
Acacia sophorae	AU,B,HA,O
Acacia sp dwarf mixed	C
Acacia sp mixed	C
Acacia spathulifolia	B
Acacia spectabilis	B,HA,O,SA,SH
Acacia spinescens	AU
Acacia spondylophylla	B,O
Acacia steedmanii	B
Acacia stenophylla	B,HA,O
Acacia stenoptera	B
Acacia stereophylla	B
Acacia stipuligera	B
Acacia stricta	B,HA
Acacia strongylophylla	AU
Acacia suaveolens	B,HA,O,SA
Acacia subcaerulea	B
Acacia subflexuosa	B
Acacia subglauca	B
Acacia subulata	AU,B
Acacia sulcata	AU,B
Acacia sulcata v platyphylla	AU,B
Acacia suma	SA
Acacia sylvestris	HA
Acacia tanumbirinensis	B
Acacia tenuissima	B
Acacia teretifolia	AU,B
Acacia terminalis see botrycephala	
Acacia tetragonocarpa	B
Acacia tetragonophylla	AU,B
Acacia torta	B
Acacia tortilis	B,SA,SI
Acacia torulosa	B
Acacia trachycarpa	B
Acacia trachyphloia	B,HA
Acacia translucens	B
Acacia trigonophylla	B
Acacia trineura	AU,B
Acacia triptera	B
Acacia triptycha	B

Acacia triquetra	B
Acacia truncata	AU,B
Acacia tumida	B
Acacia tysonii	B
Acacia ulicifolia	AU,B,HA
Acacia ulicifolia v brownei	AU,B,O
Acacia ulicina	B
Acacia umbellata	B
Acacia uncinata	AU,B,HA
Acacia uncinella	B
Acacia urophylla	B
Acacia validinervia	B
Acacia venulosa	B,HA
Acacia verniciflua	AU,B,C,HA,SA
Acacia verticillata	AU,B,C,CG,HA,SA
Acacia vestita	AU,B,HA,O,SA,SH
Acacia victoriae	AU,B,HA,O,SA
Acacia viscidula	B,HA
Acacia visite	B
Acacia wanyu	B
Acacia wattsiana	B
Acacia wilhelmiana	AU,B
Acacia willdenowiana	B
Acacia williamsonii	AU,B,HA
Acacia xanthina	B
Acacia xanthocarpa	B
Acacia xanthophloea	B,SI
Acacia xiphophylla	B
Acaena anserinifolia	AP,B,JE,SC,SS
Acaena argentea	G
Acaena 'Blue Haze'	AP,C,I,SC
Acaena buchananii	AP,B,C,JE
Acaena caesiglauca	AP,AU,JE,SA,SC,SG
Acaena fissistipula	B,CG
Acaena glabra	B,SC,SS
Acaena glauca	C
Acaena inermis	B,C,JE,SC,SG,SS
Acaena lucida	AU
Acaena magellanica	JE,SA
Acaena magellanica ssp laevigata	E
Acaena microphylla	AP,AU,B,C,G,KI,SA,SC, SG
Acaena microphylla 'Copper Carpet'	E,JE,SC,T
Acaena microphylla 'Green/Purple Carpet'	ST
Acaena minor	AP,B,SC
Acaena montana	AU
Acaena myriophylla	B,BS,C,P
Acaena novae-zelandiae	AP,B,C,G,I,JE,RH,SA, SC,T
Acaena ovalifolia	AP,B,C,SC
Acaena pinnatifida	RH
Acaena saccaticupula	AU,CC,SC,SG,SS
Acaena sericea	AP,B,CG,P,SC
Acaena sp Tas	AU
Acaena splendens	AU
Acaena viridior	SS
Acalypha hispida	B
Acalypha indica	B
Acalypha peduncularis	B,C,SI
Acanthocalycium catamarcense	B,Y
Acanthocalycium glaucum	B,Y
Acanthocalycium klimpelianum	B,BC,Y
Acanthocalycium peitscherianum	B
Acanthocalycium sp mix	C
Acanthocalycium spiniflorum	B, Y
Acanthocalycium thionanthum	BC

ACANTHOCALYCIUM

Acanthocalycium variifolium	BC
Acanthocarpus preissii	B
Acantholimon acerosum	AP,B
Acantholimon acer. v brachystachium	B
Acantholimon albanicum	AP,SC
Acantholimon alberti	B
Acantholimon armenum	B
Acantholimon armenum v armenum	B
Acantholimon bracteatum ssp bracteatum	B
Acantholimon caryophyllaceum	AP,B,SC
Acantholimon glumaceum	B
Acantholimon hohenackeri	B,I
Acantholimon litvinovii	B
Acantholimon olivieri	G
Acantholimon puberulum	B
Acantholimon sp	JE
Acantholimon ulicinum	PM
Acantholimon ulicinum ssp ulicinum	B
Acantholimon ulicinum v lycaonicum	B
Acantholimon venustum	AP,B,SC
Acanthophoenix crinita	O
Acanthophoenix rubra	B,O
Acanthosicyos naudinianus	B,SI
Acanthospermum hispidum	B
Acanthostachys strobilaceae	SG
Acanthus hungaricus	B,G,JE,SA,SC,T
Acanthus mollis	B,BD,BS,C,CL,DT,F,G, JE,L,O,SA,SU,T
Acanthus mollis latifolius	U
Acanthus peringii	JE
Acanthus spinosus	AP,G,SA,SC
Acanthus syriacus	JE
Acca sellowiana	B,C,CG,SA,T
Acca sellowiana 'Magnifica'	B
Aceitillo amarillo	B
Aceitillo blanco	B
Acer aconitifolium	X
Acer acuminatum	B
Acer argutum	B,N,SA
Acer 'Autumn Coloured Hybrids'	DT
Acer barbatum	SA
Acer barbinerve	B,SA,SG
Acer buergeranum	B,C,CG,G,HA,N,SA
Acer caesium	B,SA
Acer cambelii ssp wilsonii	N
Acer campestre	A,B,C,CG,N,SA,SG
Acer capillipes	CG,N,SA,SG,X
Acer cappadocicum	CG,SA,X
Acer cappadocicum 'Aureum'	B,N,SA
Acer carpinifolium	B,SA
Acer cinnamomifolium	B,SA
Acer circinatum	AP,B,C,CG,N,SA,X
Acer cissifolium	AP,B,SA
Acer cissifolium ssp henryii	B
Acer crataegifolium	CG,N
Acer davidii	B,C,N,SA
Acer davidii ssp grosseri	AP,B,C,N,SA,X
Acer diabolicum	B,CG,SA
Acer divergens	G,SG
Acer drummondii	SA
Acer elegantulum	B,SA
Acer erianthum	N
Acer fabri	SA
Acer glabrum	B,C,SA,SG
Acer glabrum v douglasii	B
Acer granatense	SG

Acer griseum	AP,B,G,N,SA
Acer heldreichii	B,N,SA
Acer heldreichii ssp trautvetteri	B
Acer henryi	SA
Acer hyrcanum	B,SA
Acer japonicum	B,CMN,SA,SG
Acer japonicum 'Aconitifolium'	B,CG,N
Acer japonicum 'Aureum'	AP,SC
Acer kawakamii	N
Acer komarovii	SA
Acer lobelii	SA
Acer longipes	SA
Acer macranthum	CG
Acer macrophyllum	A,B,SA
Acer mandschuricum	B,C,G,SA
Acer maximowiczianum	CG,N,SA
Acer metcalfii	SA
Acer micranthum	N
Acer mono	B,C,SA,SG
Acer monspessulanum	B,CG,HA,SA,SG
Acer negundo	A,B,C,CG,HA,SA,SG
Acer negundo v interius	SG
Acer negundo v pseudocalifornicum	SG
Acer negundo 'Variegatum'	B
Acer nigrum	SA
Acer oblongum	B,SA
Acer obtusatum	SA
Acer oliverianum	B,N,SA
Acer opalus	B,CG,SA
Acer opalus ssp obtusatum	B
Acer palmatum	B,C,CG,G,HA,N,RE,SA, SG,T
Acer palmatum 'Atropurpureum'	B,C,CG,HA,N,SA,V
Acer palmatum 'Dissectum'	B,C,SA,SC
Acer palmatum 'Diss. Atropurpureum'	B,C,N,SA
Acer palmatum 'Dissectum Viridis'	B,N
Acer palmatum 'Hessei'	N
Acer palmatum 'Linearilobum'	N
Acer palmatum 'Matsumurae'	B,C
Acer palmatum 'Osakazuki'	N,SA,SC,X
Acer palmatum 'Roseo Marginatum'	CG
Acer palmatum 'Sanguineum'	N
Acer palmatum 'Sazanami'	N
Acer palmatum 'Senkaki'	N
Acer palmatum 'Shigitatsu sawa'	N
Acer palmatum sp mix	N
Acer palmatum ssp palmatum	N
Acer palmatum 'Tsukomo'	N
Acer palmatum v heptalobum 'Lutescens'	B,N
Acer palmatum v koreanum	N
Acer pectatum ssp laxiflorum	SA
Acer pensylvanicum	B,N,SA,SG
Acer platanoides	A,B,C,CG,SA
Acer platanoides 'Columnare'	B
Acer platanoides 'Crimson King'	N
Acer platanoides 'Laciniatum'	CG
Acer platanoides 'Schwedleri'	B
Acer pseudo-sieboldianum	B,N
Acer pseudo-sieb. v macrocarpum	SG
Acer pseudoplatanus	A,B,CG,SA
Acer pseudoplatanus 'Atropurpureus'	B,HA,RS,SA
Acer pseudoplatanus f. variegatum	RS
Acer pseudosieboldianum	AP,SA,SC
Acer robustum	SA
Acer rubrum	A,B,C,G,SA
Acer rufinerve	AP,B,C,CG,G,N,SA

13

ACER

Acer saccharinum	B,N,SA
Acer saccharum	A,B,C,CG,SA
Acer saccharum ssp grandidentatum	B,SA
Acer saccharum ssp nigrum	B
Acer schwedleri	SA
Acer semenovii	CG,SA
Acer shirasawanum 'Junihitoe'	N
Acer shirasawanum 'Microphyllum'	N
Acer shirasawanum 'Palmatifolium'	N
Acer sieboldianum	B,N
Acer sikkimense ssp metcalfii	N
Acer sinense	B
Acer snake bark varieties mix	C,N
Acer sp CNW1294	X
Acer sp collection	N
Acer sp mix	C
Acer spicatum	B,N,SA,SG
Acer tataricum	B,C,CG,G,RS,SA,SG
Acer tataricum ssp ginnala	A,AP,B,C,CG,N,SA,SG
Acer tataricum ssp ginnala 'Flame'	SA
Acer tataricum v semenovii	B,N
Acer tegmentosum	B,C,SA,SG
Acer trautvetteri	C,N,RH,SA
Acer triffidum	CG
Acer triflorum	B,C,SA
Acer truncatum	B,C,N,SA
Acer tschonoski	B,N
Acer tschonoski var koreanum	N
Acer turkestanicum	CG
Acer ukurunduense	B,C,SA
Acer velutinum	B,SA
Acetosa alpestris	CG
Acetosella tenuifolia	SG
Achillea abrotanoides	G
Achillea acuminata	SG
Achillea ageratum	B,G,MA,T
Achillea ageratum 'Golden Princess'	B
Achillea ageratum 'Moonwalker'	B,BS,C,JE,SA
Achillea asiatica	SG
Achillea asplenifolia	B
Achillea atrata	B,SA
Achillea cartilaginea 'Silver Spray'	B,C
Achillea chrysocoma	SG
Achillea clavennae	B,C,G,JE,SC,T
Achillea clypeolata	B,BS,JE
Achillea coarctaca	B,T
Achillea collina	B
Achillea depressa	B
Achillea distans	B
Achillea erba-rotta ssp moschata	B,JE
Achillea filipendulina	B,CP,G
Achillea filipendulina 'Cloth Of Gold'	B,BS,CL,CO,D,F,J,KS,KI, SE,ST,SU,T,V
Achillea filipendulina 'Parker's Variety'	C,JE,SA,SG
Achillea fraasii	JE,SA
Achillea glaberrima 'Gold Spray'	B
Achillea grandifolia	B,P
Achillea holosericea	AP,B,SC,SG
Achillea impatiens	SG
Achillea lanulosa	B
Achillea macrophylla	B,G,SC
Achillea millefolium	B,C,CP,G,HW,JE,LA,NT, SA,SG,Z
Achillea millefolium 'Colorado'	C,JE
Achillea millefolium F2 'Summer Pastels'	BD,BS,C,CL,D,DT,F,G,J, L,S,SA,SE,T,U,V

Achillea millefolium 'Red Beauty'	B
Achillea millefolium 'Reine Cerise'	B,BS,C,CL,DT,JE,L,KS, SA,SU,T
Achillea millefolium 'Rosea'	B
Achillea millefolium 'Rubra'	B
Achillea millefolium 'Silver Queen'	B
Achillea nana	B,C
Achillea nobilis	G,JE,SA
Achillea nobilis ssp neilreichii	B
Achillea ptarmica	B,SG
Achillea ptarmica 'Ballerina'	B,BS,CO,JE,KI,SA
Achillea ptarmica 'Mother of Pearl'	D
Achillea ptarmica 'Snowball'	B
Achillea ptarmica 'The Pearl'	B,BS,C,CL,DT,J,JE,L,KS, O,SA,SE,T
Achillea ptarmica 'The Pearl Superior'	B,C,JE
Achillea pyrenaica	B,G
Achillea setacea	SG
Achillea sibirica	AP,G,JE,MA,SC,SG,T
Achillea 'Tickled Pink'	BS,KI
Achillea tomentosa	G
Achillea tomentosa 'Aurea'	B,BS,C,CL,JE,L,SA
Achillea umbellata	G,SG
Achimenes f1 'Carmencita'	B,BS,C
Achimenes f1 'Cupid's Bower' mix	V
Achimenes f1 'Palette' mix	BS,C,CL,D,L,N,S,T
Achimenes f1 'Prima Donna'	B,BS,C
Achyrachaena mollis	CG
Achyranthes aspera	B
Achyranthes bidentata	B,CP
Achyrophorus maculatus	SG
Acianthus caudatus	B
Acinos alpinus	AP,B,FH,SC,SG
Acinos arvensis	B,SG
Aciphylla aurea	AP,B,C,CG,SA,SC,SS
Aciphylla colensoi	AP,B,SA
Aciphylla crenulata	AP,B,SS
Aciphylla crosby-smithii	SS
Aciphylla dieffenbachii	B
Aciphylla dissecta	B
Aciphylla dobsonii	AP,SC,SS
Aciphylla hookeri	B,SS
Aciphylla horrida	B,C
Aciphylla kirkii	AP,SS
Aciphylla monroi	AP,B,SC,SS
Aciphylla montana	AP,B,SS
Aciphylla pinnatifida	AP,SA,SC
Aciphylla polita	B
Aciphylla scott-thomsonii	B,SS
Aciphylla similis	B,SS
Aciphylla squarrosa	B,SS
Aciphylla subflabellata	AP,CG,SC
Ackama rosaefolia	B
Acmadenia alternifolia	B
Acmella oleracea	B
Acmella oppositifolia	B
Acmena brachyandra	B
Acmena hemilampra	B
Acmena smithii	B,HA,O,SA,SH
Acmena smithii purple	SH
Acnatherum brachytricum	JE,SA
Acnatherum calmagrostis	JE,SA
Acoelorraphe wrightii	B,HA,O,SA
Acokanthera oblongifolia	CG,SA
Acokanthera oppositifolia	B,SI
Aconitum altaicum	SG

ACONITUM

Aconitum anglicum — AP,I,SC
Aconitum anthora — AP,B,C,G,JE,SA
Aconitum anthoroideum — SG
Aconitum arcuatum — G
Aconitum arendsii — SA
Aconitum barbatum — SG
Aconitum carmichaelii — AP,B,C,P,SC,T
Aconitum carmichaelii 'Arendsii' — B,C,G,JE
Aconitum carmichaelii 'Latecrop' — B
Aconitum carmichaelii wilsonii — G,JE,SA
Aconitum carneum — C
Aconitum columbianum — C,SG
Aconitum czekanovskyi — CG,G,SG
Aconitum delphinifolium delphinifolium — SG
Aconitum firmum — CG,SG
Aconitum forrestii — SG
Aconitum heterophyllum — G,SC
Aconitum 'Ivorine' — AP,B,C,JE,P,SC
Aconitum komarovii — G
Aconitum krylovii — SG
Aconitum lasiostomum — CG,G
Aconitum loczyanum — SG
Aconitum lycoctonum — AP,B,C,G,JE,SA,SG,T
Aconitum lycoctonum ssp — B,G
Aconitum lycoctonum ssp neapolitanum — JE,SC
Aconitum lycoctonum ssp vulparia — AP,C,G,SC
Aconitum moldavicum — SG
Aconitum napellus — AP,B,BS,C,G,JE,KI,RH, SA,SC,SG,ST,SU,T,V,W
Aconitum napellus 'Album' — B,G,JE
Aconitum napellus 'Carneum' — B,G
Aconitum napellus 'Newry Blue' — B,BS,C,CL,JE,L
Aconitum napellus ssp napellus — B
Aconitum napellus var. bicolor — C
Aconitum noveboracensis — G
Aconitum pubiceps — SG
Aconitum septentrionale — C,JE,SG
Aconitum soongaricum — SG
Aconitum variegatum — G,JE,SG
Aconitum volubile — AP,B,SC,SG,T
Aconitum vulparia/orientalis
see A. lyconitum
Aconitum wardii — SG
Acorellus pannonicus — B
Acorus calamus — B,JE,PR,SG
Acorus calamus 'Variegatus' — B
Acorus gramineus — B
Acorus gramineus 'Variegatus' — B
Acosmium panamensis — B
Acridocarpus natalitius — B,C,SI
Acrocarpus fraxinifolius — B,SA
Acrocomia aculeata — B
Acrocomia chunta — B
Acrocomia totai — B
Acrocomia viniferar — B
Acrodon subulatus — B
Acrostichum aureum — B
Actaea acuminata — SG
Actaea alba — AP,B,C,CC,FH,G,JE,P, RS,SA,SC,SG,T
Actaea arguta — SG
Actaea erythrocarpa — AP,B,SA,SG
Actaea pachypoda see A.alba
Actaea rubra — AP,B,C,CG,FH,G,JE,SC, SG
Actaea rubra f neglecta — AP,B,SC

Actaea rubra ssp arguta — B
Actaea spicata — AP,B,C,FH,G,JE,RH,RS, SA,SC,SG
Actinidia arguta — A,B,C,CG,RS,SA
Actinidia arguta 'Issai' — B
Actinidia arguta MW132R — X
Actinidia callosa — CG
Actinidia chinensis — B,C,CG,SA,SG,T,V
Actinidia chinensis 'Bruno' — B
Actinidia chinensis 'Hayward' — B
Actinidia kolomikta — A,B,C,SA,SG
Actinidia melanandra — B
Actinidia polygama — B,RS
Actinidia purpurea — B
Actiniopteris radiata — B
Actinomeris alternifolia — PR
Actinorhytis calapparia — O
Actinostrobus acuminatus — B,O
Actinostrobus arenarius — B,O,SA
Actinostrobus pyramidalis — B,O,SA
Actinotus forsythii — AU
Actinotus helianthi — AU,B,C,HA,O,SA,SH
Actinotus leucocephalus — B,C,O
Actinotus minor — HA
Adansonia — B,SI
Adansonia digitata — B,C,SA,SI,T
Adansonia fony — SI
Adansonia gregorii — B,O,SA
Adansonia madagascariensis — SI
Adenandra brachyphylla — B,SI
Adenandra marginata — B
Adenandra uniflora — B,C
Adenanthera pavonina — B,HA,O,SA
Adenia digitata — B,SI
Adenia glauca — B,Y
Adenia globosa v pseudoglobosa — B,SI
Adenia hastata — B,SI
Adenia keramanthus — B
Adenium obesum — B,C,CH,SA,Y
Adenium obesum 'Multiflorum' — B
Adenium obesum ssp somalense — B
Adenium obesum ssp swazicum — B
Adenocarpus decorticans — SA
Adenolobus gariepensis — B,SI
Adenolobus pechuellii — B,SI
Adenophora aurita — W
Adenophora aurita stricta — SA
Adenophora bulleyana — AP,B,C,G,PM,T,W
Adenophora forrestii — MA
Adenophora himalayana — G,HH
Adenophora hyb — B
Adenophora khasiana — B,P
Adenophora koreana — AP,B,PM,SC
Adenophora liliifolia — AP,B,C,CG,G,HH,JE,SA, SC,T
Adenophora nikoensis — AP,G,SC
Adenophora pereskiifolia — AP,B,G,RS,SC
Adenophora polyantha — AP,P,SG
Adenophora potaninii — B,C
Adenophora remotiflora — CC
Adenophora stricta — SG
Adenophora takedae — B,CC,JE,SA
Adenophora takedae alba — JE
Adenophora tashiroi — AP,CG
Adenophora triphylla — AP,CC,SC
Adenophora triphylla v hakusanensis — AP,B

15

Adenophora triphylla v japonica	G,SG
Adenophora x confusa?	T
Adenopodia spicata	B,SI
Adenostoma fasciculatum	B
Adenostoma sparsifolium	B
Adenostyles alliariae	B,CG,SG
Adenostyles alpina	C,CG,JE,SC
Adiantum aethiopicum	B,C,HA,SA
Adiantum ancens	SG
Adiantum capillus fimbriatum	SG
Adiantum capillus veneris	SG
Adiantum caudatum	B,SG
Adiantum cuneatum see raddianum	
Adiantum edgeworthii	B
Adiantum formosum	B,SG
Adiantum fulvum	B,SG
Adiantum grossum	SG
Adiantum hispidulum	B,HA,SA
Adiantum hyb 'Harlequin'	B
Adiantum imbricata	B
Adiantum macrophyllum	SG
Adiantum peruvianum	B,SA
Adiantum pubescens	B
Adiantum raddianum	B,SA,SG
Adiantum raddianum named cvs	B,C,SA
Adiantum raddianum v majus	B
Adiantum tenerum	SG
Adiantum tenerum 'Bessoniae'	B
Adiantum tenerum 'Fergusonii'	B
Adiantum tenerum 'Scutum Roseum'	B,SA
Adiantum tenerum 'Sleeping Beauty'	B
Adiantum trapeziforme	SG
Adiantum trapeziforme 'Kuranda'	B
Adlumia fungosa	AP,C,SC
Adonis aestivalis	AP,B,C,G,IKS,SC,SG, SU,T,V
Adonis altaicus	B
Adonis amurensis	B
Adonis annua	AP,B,CO
Adonis davurica	SG
Adonis flammea	SG
Adonis vernalis	AP,B,CG,G,,JE,SA,SC, SG,T
Adoxa moschatellina	B
Adriana quadripartita	B
Adriana tomentosa	B
Aechmea aquilegia	B,CG
Aechmea bromeliifolia	B,CG
Aechmea coelestis	B,SG
Aechmea melinonii	SG
Aechmea mertensa	B,CG
Aechmea sp	B
Aechmea tillandsioidea	B,CG
Aegilops geniculata	CG,G
Aegilops neglecta	SG
Aegilops ovata	B
Aegilops ventricosa	G
Aeginetia indica	C,SG
Aegle marmelos	B,HA,SA
Aegopodium podagraria	B
Aeluropus lagopodoides	B
Aeolanthus parvifolius	B
Aeollanthus parvifolius	B
Aeollanthus suaveolens	B
Aeoniopsis cabulica	B
Aeonium arboreum v holochrysum	B

Aeonium glutinosum	B
Aeonium haworthii	B
Aeonium sp. mix	C
Aeranthes grandiflora	B
Aerva lanata	B
Aesculus californica	B,N,SA
Aesculus chinensis	B
Aesculus flava	B,N
Aesculus glabra	B
Aesculus glabra v arguta	B
Aesculus hippocastanum	B,SA
Aesculus indica	B,SA
Aesculus parviflora	G,SA
Aesculus pavia	B,N,SA
Aesculus sylvatica	B
Aesculus turbinata	B
Aesculus wilsonii	B
Aesculus x carnea	B,SA
Aesculus x carnea 'Briotti'	B
Aesculus x hybrida	N
Aesculus x woerlitzensis	B
Aethionema anititaurus	SG
Aethionema arabicum	B,SG
Aethionema armenum	AP,B,FH,SC,SG
Aethionema armenum 'Warley Rose'	AP,FH,G
Aethionema cappadocium	CG
Aethionema coridifolium	B,BS,C,JE,SA,SC,SG
Aethionema creticum	CG
Aethionema glaucescens	B
Aethionema grandiflorum	AP,C,CG,FH,G,I,JE,PM, SC,SG
Aethionema iberideum	B
Aethionema oppositifolium	B,SG
Aethionema saxatile	AP,B,G,SC,SG
Aethionema schistosum	AP,JE,SC,SG
Aethusa cynapium	B
Aethyrium spicatum	B
Afrocarpus falcatus v elongatus	B
Afrocarpus gracilior	B
Afrocarpus usambarensis	B
Afromomum thonneri	B
Afzelia quanzensis	B,SA,SI
Afzelia rhomboidea	B
Agalinis besseyana	B
Agalinis purpurea	PR
Agalinis tenuifolia	B
Agapanthus africanus	B,C,G,I,JE,SA,SI,T
Agapanthus africanus 'Albus'	B,JE,SA
Agapanthus africanus 'Albus Nanus'	B,HA
Agapanthus africanus 'Getty White'	B,HA
Agapanthus angustifolius	CG
Agapanthus 'Best New White hybrids'	C
Agapanthus campanulatus	AP,C,G
Agapanthus campanulatus 'Isis'	PM
Agapanthus campanulatus ssp camp.	B,SI
Agapanthus campanulatus ssp patens	B,SI
Agapanthus campanulatus 'White Form'	T
Agapanthus caulescens ssp angustifolius	B,SI
Agapanthus caulescens ssp caulescens	B,SI
Agapanthus coddii	B,SI
Agapanthus comptonii	CG
Agapanthus comptonii ssp comptonii	SI
Agapanthus comptonii ssp longitubus	B,SI
Agapanthus 'Headbourne Hybrids'	AP,BS,C,G,N,JE,L,SA, SC,T,V
Agapanthus hybrid	B

AGAPANTHUS

Agapanthus hybrid miniature	N	Agastachys odorata	B,O
Agapanthus inap. ssp holl. 'Lydenburg'	B,SI	Agathis australis	B,SA
Agapanthus inapertus ssp hollandii 'Sky'	B,SI	Agathis robusta	B,HA,O,SA
Agapanthus inapertus ssp inapertus	B,SI	Agathosma betulina	SI
Agapanthus inapertus ssp intermedius	B,SI	Agathosma cerefolium	B
Agapanthus inapertus ssp pendulus	G	Agathosma ciliaris	B,SI
Agapanthus 'Lilliput'	G,PM	Agathosma ciliata	SI
Agapanthus minor alba	C	Agathosma crenulata	B,SA,SI
Agapanthus 'Mooreanus minor hybrids'	C	Agathosma ovata	B,SI
Agapanthus 'New Hybrids'	T	Agathosma serpyllacea	B
Agapanthus nutans	B,SI	Agave americana	B,HA,SA
Agapanthus 'Peter Pan'	B,HA,JE,SA	Agave angustifolia	B,SA
Agapanthus praecox	CG,G,SG,SI	Agave angustifolia 'Marginata'	B,SA
Agapanthus praecox 'Blue Baby'	B,HA,T	Agave attenuata	B,SA
Agapanthus praecox 'Grey Pearl'	B	Agave celsius	SA
Agapanthus praecox 'Medium White'	B,SI	Agave desertii	B,SW
Agapanthus praecox ssp minimus	B,C,CG,SI	Agave ferdinandi-regis	Y
Agapanthus praecox ssp min. 'Adelaide'	B,SI	Agave ferox	B
Agapanthus praecox ssp min. 'Forma'	SI	Agave filifera	B,Y
Agapanthus praecox ssp m.'Storms River'	B,SI	Agave havardiana	B
Agapanthus praecox ssp orientalis	CG,LG,SI	Agave lechuguilla	B,Y
Agapanthus praecox ssp orientalis blue	HA,O,SA,SH	Agave mckelveyana	B
Agapanthus praecox ssp o.'Dw White'	B	Agave neomexicana see parryi	
Agapanthus praecox ssp o. 'Mt.Thomas'	B,G	Agave palmeri	B
Agapanthus praecox ssp o. 'Weaver'	B	Agave parryi	B,C,SA,SW,Y
Agapanthus praecox ssp orientalis white	HA,N,O,SA,SH	Agave parryi ssp cousei	B,SW
Agapanthus praecox ssp praecox	B,SI	Agave parryi ssp huachucensis	B,SW
Agapanthus praecox ssp praecox 'Azure'	B,CG,G,SI	Agave parryi ssp parryi	B,SW
Agapanthus praecox ssp pr.'Floribunda'	B,CG,SI	Agave parviflora 'Flexiflora Minima'	B
Agapanthus 'Purple Cloud'	C	Agave schavii	CH
Agapanthus 'Queen Anne'	B,HA	Agave schidigera	B,SW
Agapanthus sp. mix	C,FH	Agave schottii	B,SG
Agapanthus umbellatus	BS,JE	Agave shawii v goldmanniana	B
Agapanthus umbellatus 'Albus'	BS,JE	Agave sisalana	B
Agapanthus walshii	B,SI	Agave sp mix	HA,T
Agapanthus 'Wavy Navy'	B	Agave striata	B
Agapetes serpens	B	Agave stricta	B,GC,Y
Agaricus campestris d.m.p.	B	Agave toumeyana	B,CH
Agastache anisata see foeniculum		Agave utahensis	B
Agastache barberi	B,SW	Agave utahensis v discreta	B
Agastache 'Camphor Hyssop'	B	Agave utahensis v kaibabensis	B,G
Agastache cana	B,SW,T	Agave utahensis v nevadensis	B
Agastache foeniculum	AP,B,C,CP,DT,F,G,JE,KS	Agave victoriae-reginae	B,C,CG,N,SA,SG
	P,PR,RH,SC,SG,T	Agave vilmoriniana	B
Agastache foeniculum 'Alabaster'	E	Agave zebra	B
Agastache foeniculum 'Album'	AP,B,C,SC	Ageratum 'Atlantic Plus'	BS,DT
Agastache 'Fragrant'	D,J,SE,T,V	Ageratum 'Blue Blanket'	BS
Agastache 'Liquorice Blue'	BD,BS,C,KI,L	Ageratum 'Blue Cap'	BS
Agastache 'Liquorice White'	BD,BS,C,L	Ageratum conyzoides	SG
Agastache mexicana	B,C,G	Ageratum houstonianum	SG
Agastache mexicana 'Carlisle Carmine'	B	Ageratum houstonianum 'Bavaria'	B,BS,C,DT,J,O,U
Agastache mexicana 'Champagne'	B,T,KS	Ageratum houstonianum 'Blue Ball'	BS,CO,KI,ST
Agastache micrantha	B,SW	Ageratum houstonianum 'Blue Bouquet'	C,J,V
Agastache 'Neapolitan Mix'	F	Ageratum houstonianum 'Blue Mink'	B,BD,BS,CL,D,DT,F,J,L,
Agastache nepetoides	AP,B,C,CG,CP,G,PR		M,O,R,S,SE,SG,SU,T,
Agastache pallidiflora ssp neomexicana	B,SW		TU,U,V,VH,YA
Agastache pallidiflora ssp pallidiflora	B,SW	Ageratum houstonianum 'Capri'	F,T
Agastache pringlei	B,SW	Ageratum houstonianum 'Dondoblue'	B
Agastache rugosa	AP,B,C,G,JE,SA,SG	Ageratum houstonianum 'Dondowhite'	B
Agastache rugosa alba	JE,SA	Ageratum houstonianum f1 'Adriatic'	B,BD,BS,C,D,DT,KI,
Agastache rugosa B&SWJ 735	E		L,O,S,T,YA
Agastache rupestris	B,SW	Ageratum houstonianum f1 'Blue Blazer'	B,BS,J,KI,ST,TU
Agastache scrophulariifolia	AP,B,G,PR	Ageratum houst. f1 'Bl.Danube' ps	B,BD,BS,CL,D,DT,F,M,S,
Agastache sp	AP,C,CP,G		SE,T,YA
Agastache urticifolia	AP,B,C,SW	Ageratum houstonianum f1 'Blue Horizon'	B,BS,C,CL,D
Agastache wrightii	B,SW	Ageratum houstonianum f1 'Blue Swords'	S

AGERATUM

Ageratum houst. f1 'Champion' s-c	CL
Ageratum houst. f1 'Champion' s-c p.s	CL
Ageratum houstonianum f1 'Hawaii Blue'	B,BD,L
Ageratum houstonianum f1 'Hawaii Mix'	DT
Ageratum houstonianum f1 'Hawaii Royal'	B,BD,BS,L
Ageratum houst. f1 'Hawaii White'	B,BD,BS,DT,KI,L,O,S,YA
Ageratum houstonianum f1 'Madison'	B,BS
Ageratum houstonianum f1 'Mauritius'	BS,KI
Ageratum houstonianum f1 'Neptune Blue'	CL
Ageratum houst. f1 'Neptune Blue' p.s	CL
Ageratum houstonianum f1 'North Sea'	BS,D,J
Ageratum houstonianum f1 'Pacific'	BS,CL,DT,J,L,T
Ageratum houstonianum f1 'Snowball'	F
Ageratum houst. f1 'Summer Snow'	T,VH
Ageratum houstonianum f1 'Summit'	BS,F,S,T
Ageratum houstonianum f1 'Swing'	BS,F,KI,T
Ageratum houstonianum f1 'White Raven'	B
Ageratum houstonianum 'Florists Blue'	B,BS,DT
Ageratum houstonianum 'Pink Beauty'	J,V
Ageratum houst. 'Pink Powder Puffs'	BS,F,KI,SE,TU
Ageratum houstonianum 'Pinky Imp'	T
Ageratum houstonianum 'Snowdrop'	KI
Ageratum houstonianum 'Southern Cross'	SE,T
Ageratum 'Wedgewood'	BS
Aglaia roxburghiana v courtallensis	B
Aglaomorpha meyeriana	SG
Aglaonema commutatum	B
Aglaonema commutatum 'Tricolor'	B
Aglaonema commutatum v maculatum	B
Aglaonema commutatum 'White Rajah'	B
Aglaonema crispum	B
Aglaonema modestum	B
Aglaonema 'Purple Stem'	B
Agonis flexuosa	B,HA,O,SA
Agonis floribunda	B
Agonis hypericifolia	B
Agonis juniperina	B,O,SA
Agonis linearifolia	B,O
Agonis marginata	B
Agonis obtusissima	B
Agonis parviceps	B,O
Agonis spathulata	B
Agoseris cuspidita	PR
Agoseris grandiflora	B
Agrimonia eupatoria	B,C,JE,LA,SA,SG
Agrimonia eupatoria 'Topaz'	B
Agrimonia pilosa	SG
Agrimonia procera	G,SG
Agrimonia sp	SG
Agropyron cristatum	B,SG
Agropyron magellanica	CG
Agropyron pectinatum	B,SG
Agropyron pubiflorum	AP,B,SC
Agropyron repens	B
Agropyron smithii	B
Agropyron trachycaulum	PR
Agropyron trichophorum	B
Agrostemma 'Atrosanguinea'	V
Agrostemma githago	AP,B,C,CO,G,LA,LG,SG, SU,V
Agrostemma githago coeli rosea	KS
Agrostemma githago 'Milas'	B,BS,C,D,J,KS,L,SG,T
Agrostemma githago 'Purple Queen'	B,C
Agrostemma githago 'Rose Queen'	B
Agrostemma gracilis	B,SG
Agrostemma linicola	B

Agrostemma 'Rose of Heaven'	KI
Agrostis alpina	G
Agrostis canina	SG
Agrostis canina 'Silver Needles'	B
Agrostis canina ssp canina	B
Agrostis castellana	B
Agrostis delicatula	SG
Agrostis geminata	SG
Agrostis gigantea	SG
Agrostis nebulosa	B,BS,C,KI,SU
Agrostis rupestris	SG
Agrostis sp	SG
Agrostis stolonifera	B
Agrostis stolonifera 'Cobra'	B
Agrostis tenuis	B
Agrostocrinum scabrum	B,C
Aichryson laxum	B
Ailanthus altissima	A,B,C,N,SA
Ailanthus excelsa	B,SA
Ailanthus giraldii	CG
Ainsliae acerifolia	B
Ainsworthia trachycarpa	B
Aiphanes caryotifolia	B,O
Aiphanes erosa	B
Aira elegantissima	T
Aizoon paniculatum	SI
Aizoon rigidum	B
Ajuga chamaepitys	B,SC
Ajuga chamaepitys v glareosa	B
Ajuga genevensis	B,JE,SA
Ajuga laxmannii	B
Ajuga reptans	B,BS,C,G,JE,L,RH,SA, SC,SU
Ajuga reptans atropurpurea	JE,SA
Akebia quinata	A,B,C,G,SA
Akebia trifoliata	A,B,C,G,SA
Alangium chinensis	SA
Alangium plantanifolium	G,SA,SG
Alangium salviifolium	B
Alaskan wild flower sp	B
Alberta magna	B,SA,SI
Albizia adianthifolia	B,C,SA,SI
Albizia amara	B
Albizia anthelmintica	B
Albizia bermudiana	B
Albizia caribaea	B
Albizia chinensis	B
Albizia falcataria	B
Albizia forbesii	B
Albizia guachepele	B,RE
Albizia gummifera	B
Albizia harveyi	B,SI
Albizia julibrissin	B,C,CG,G,HA,O,SA,SC,T
Albizia julibrissin 'E H Wilson'	B
Albizia julibrissin v rosea	B,C,N,SA
Albizia kalkora	B
Albizia lebbeck	B,HA,O,SA
Albizia lophantha	B,C,HA,JE,O,SA,SG
Albizia lucida	B
Albizia procera	B
Albizia richardiana	B
Albizia saman	B
Albizia sinensis	SA
Albizia stipulata	B
Albizia tanganyicensis	B
Albuca acuminata	B

ALBUCA

Albuca altissima	B,C,SI	Alchemilla mollis 'Robustica'	B,C,F
Albuca angolensis	B,G	Alchemilla mollis 'Select'	B,JE,T
Albuca canadensis	AP,B,LG,SC,SI	Alchemilla mollis 'Thriller'	B,KS,T
Albuca humilis	AP,HH,LG,PM,SC	Alchemilla monticola	B,JE,SA
Albuca juncifolia	MN	Alchemilla saxatilis	B,C,JE,SG
Albuca nelsonii	B,C,SC,SI	Alchemilla sericea	B
Albuca setosa	B,SI,T	Alchemilla vulgaris	B
Albuca shawii	AP,B,G,LG,SC,SG,SI	Alchemilla xanthochlora	B,JE,SG
Albuca sp	AP,SC,SI	Alchryson dichotomum	SG
Albuca sp nova	SI	Alciope tabularis	B
Albuca spiralis	B,C,SI	Alectra sessiliflora	SI
Alcea 'Black Beauty'	P	Alectra sp	SI
Alcea cetosa	B	Alectryon excelsus	B
Alcea ficifolia 'Cottage Mix'	P	Alepidia amatymbica	SI
Alcea ficifolia 'Golden Eye'	P	Alepidia natalensis	B,SI
Alcea ficifolia hybrids mix	AP,C,DT,JE,PG,SA	Aletris farinosa	B
Alcea froloviana	SG	Aleurites fordii	B,HA,S
Alcea pallida	JE,SG	Aleurites moluccana	B,HA,O,SA
Alcea 'Reds & Pinks'	P	Alfedia cernus	SG
Alcea rosea	B,I,SG,V	Alisma gramineum	SG
Alcea rosea annual 'Double' mix	F,J,ST	Alisma lanceolatum	B,JE,SA
Alcea rosea annual 'Single' mix	BS,C,F,J,KI,KS,ST,SU,T	Alisma parviflora	C,JE,SA
Alcea rosea 'Apricot'	AP,B,P	Alisma plantago-aquatica	B,C,G,JE,RH,SA,SC,SG
Alcea rosea 'Chater's Double'	BD,BS,C,CL,CO,D,DT,	Alisma plantago-aquatica v parviflorum	B
	JE,KI,L,R,SA,TU, U,YA	Alisma subcordatum	PR
Alcea rosea 'Chater's Double,apricot'	B,DT,SE,T,V	Alkanna orientals	CG
Alcea rosea 'Chater's Double,ch. Brown'	B,JE	Alkanna tinctoria	B
Alcea rosea 'Chater's Double,pink,bright'	B,F,JE,SE	Allamanda blanchetii	B
Alcea rosea 'Chater's Double,purple'	B,JE	Allamanda blanchetii 'Chocolate Swirls'	B
Alcea rosea 'Chater's Double' s-c	B	Allamanda cathartica	B
Alcea rosea 'Chater's Double,salmon-pink'	B,F,JE	Allamanda neriifolia	SA
Alcea rosea 'Chater's Double,scarlet'	B,JE	Allamanda schottii	B
Alcea rosea 'Chater's Double,white'	B,JE	Allanblackia stuhlmanii	B
Alcea rosea 'Chater's Double,yellow'	B,JE	Alliaria petiolata	B,C,G,LA,SG
Alcea rosea 'Chater's Double,yellow,soft'	B,JE	Allionia incarnata	B
Alcea rosea 'Chater's' mix	JE,S	Allium acuminatum	AP,B,C,JE
Alcea rosea 'East Coast Hybrids'	PG,SE	Allium acuminatum v album	B,JE
Alcea rosea 'Indian Spring' wh/pnk shades	B	Allium aflatunense	AP,B,C,G,FH,I,JE,
Alcea rosea 'Lemon Light'	B,P		LG,RS,SA,SC
Alcea rosea 'Majorette'	BS,C,KS,T,U	Allium aflatunense 'Purple Sensation'	AP,B,LG,SC,T
Alcea rosea 'Nigra'	AP,B,BS,C,CO,G,JE,KI,	Allium akaka	AP,SG
	KS,PG,SA,SE,SU,T,V	Allium altaicum	B,G,SG
Alcea rosea 'Old Fashioned mix'	DT,PG,U	Allium altissimum	G
Alcea rosea 'Powder Puffs'	C,T	Allium amethystinum	B,JE,LG
Alcea rosea 'Simplex'	C,JE,V	Allium ampeloprasum	B
Alcea rosea single colours	G,PG	Allium ampeloprasum v babingtonii	SG
Alcea rosea 'Summer Carnival'	BD,BS,C,CL,D,DT,J,M,	Allium angulosum	AP,B,SC,SG
	KS,L,S,SE,T,V	Allium atropurpureum	AP,B,G,JE,LG
Alcea rosea v nigra plena 'Negrita'	JE	Allium atroviolaceum	B
Alcea rosea 'Watchman'	L,SE	Allium babingtonii	NS
Alcea rosea 'Watermelon'	PG	Allium basticum	SG
Alcea rugosa	AP,HH,JE,PG,SA	Allium beesianum	AP,B,SC
Alchemilla alpina	AP,B,C,I,JE,SA,SG	Allium bodeanum	AP,SG,SC
Alchemilla anisiaca	SG	Allium bucharicum	B
Alchemilla arvensis	B	Allium buriatum	G
Alchemilla caucasica	SG	Allium caeruleum	AP,B,G,JE,SC
Alchemilla conjuncta	B,SG	Allium callimischon	B,SC,SG
Alchemilla epipsila	G,JE,SG	Allium campanulatum	AP,B,SC,SW
Alchemilla erythropoda	B,C,JE,T	Allium canadense	AP,B,G,PR
Alchemilla fulgens	B	Allium carinatum	AP,B,I
Alchemilla glaucescens	SG	Allium carinatum ssp pulchellum	AP,B,C,G,I,JE,LG,MN,
Alchemilla gracilis	SG		PA,RS,SC,SG,T
Alchemilla hoppeana	JE	Allium carinatum ssp pulchellum 'Album'	AP,B,G,HH,PM
Alchemilla mollis	AP,BD,BS,C,CL,F,G,JE,	Allium carinatum ssp pulchellum 'Pink'	C
	KI,L,RH,SC,ST,SU,T,V	Allium cernuum	AP,B,C,FH,G,JE,LG,MN,
Alchemilla mollis 'Auslese'	C,JE		PA,PM,PR,SC,SA,SG,

19

ALLIUM

	SW,T
Allium chamaemoly v littoralis	B
Allium chamaemoly v littoralis A.B.S438	MN
Allium chrysonemum	B
Allium chrysonemum HMS379	MN
Allium cristophii	AP,B,C,FH,G,I,JE,LG,RH,SA,SC,SG,T
Allium cyaneum	AP,SG,SC
Allium cyathophorum	AP,FH,SC
Allium cyathophorum v farreri	AP,B,C,FH,G,JE,LG,SC,SG
Allium cyrillii	G
Allium decipens	SG
Allium denudatum	B
Allium dichlamydeum	AP,B,MN,SC
Allium dregeanum	B,SI
Allium ellisii	B
Allium ellisii PF2571 Iran	MN
Allium ericetorum	B
Allium falcifolium	AP,G
Allium flavum	AP,B,C,FH,G,I,JE,LG,MN,SC,SG
Allium flavum (blue leaf)	PM,SC
Allium flavum v minus	AP,B,G,MN,SC
Allium geyeri	AP,B,SC,SW
Allium giganteum	AP,B,G,JE,SA,SC
Allium globosum	G,SG
Allium haematochiton	B
Allium hierochuntinum	B,MN
Allium hymenorrhizum	CG
Allium insubricum	AP,B,SC
Allium jesdianum	B,CG,G
Allium karataviense	AP,B,C,E,FH,G,I,JE,PM,RS,SA,SC,SG
Allium ledebourianum	SG
Allium libani	AP,G,RS
Allium macleanii	B,G
Allium macropetalum	B,SW
Allium mairei amabile	I
Allium moly	AP,B,C,G,JE,SA,SC,SG
Allium montanum	FH,JE,SG
Allium moschatum	B
Allium narcissiflorum	AP,B,C,JE,SC
Allium neapolitanum	AP,B,C,FH,G,JE,SC,SG
Allium neapolitanum v cowanii	AP,B,SC
Allium nigrum	B,JE,SA
Allium nutans	AP,B,G,LG,SC,SG
Allium obliquum	AP,B,C,RS,SC
Allium ochroleucum	B
Allium odorum	SA
Allium oleraceum	AP,B
Allium oliganthum	SG
Allium oreophilum	AP,B,C,G,JE,LG,SC,SG
Allium oreophilum 'Zwanenberg'	PM
Allium oreoprasum	SG
Allium paradoxum	B
Allium paradoxum PF5085 Iran	MN
Allium peninsulare	AP,B,SC,SW
Allium peninsulare v crispum	B
Allium pyrenaicum	CG
Allium ramosum	B,G,JE,RS,SC,SG
Allium rock garden mix	C
Allium rosenbachianum	AP,B,G,JE,PM
Allium rosenbachianum 'Album'	B,JE
Allium roseum	AP,B,G,SC
Allium rotundum	AP,B
Allium rubrovittatum	B
Allium rubrovittatum C.Barclay	MN
Allium sativum	G
Allium sativum v ophioscorodon	B,CP
Allium scabriscapum	B,MN
Allium schoenoprasum	AP,B,CP,G,JE,KS,RH,SC,SG
Allium schoenoprasum f1 'Hylau Cut'	B
Allium schoenoprasum v sibericum	SG
Allium schubertii	B,C,FH,G,LG,SC,SG
Allium scorodoprasum	AP,B,G,SG
Allium senescens	AP,B,G,JE,LG,SC
Allium senescens ssp montanum	B,I,JE,RH
Allium sikkimense	AP,B,FH,G,RS,SC,SG
Allium sp mix	C,G,SC
Allium sp orange	RS,SG
Allium sphaerocephalum	AP,B,C,G,JE,RS,SA,SC
Allium splendens	AP,FH,SC
Allium stellatum	AP,B,JE,PR,SG
Allium stipitatum	AP,B,FH,G,JE,SC
Allium stipitatum 'album'	G
Allium strictum	SG
Allium subtilissimum	G,SG
Allium tanguticum	B
Allium telavivense	B
Allium textile	AP,B,SG,SW
Allium tricoccum	AP,B,PR,SC
Allium trifolium	B
Allium trifolium L/Cu 124/1 Cyprus	MN
Allium trifolium S.L53 Jordan	MN
Allium tuberosum	AP,B,CP,G,KS,SG
Allium turkestanicum	B
Allium unifolium	AP,B,C,FH,G,LG,MN,SC,SG
Allium ursinum	A,B,C,FH,G,JE,SC
Allium victorialis	B,C,G,JE,SG
Allium vineale	AP,B,SC
Allium vineale v compactum	G
Allium violaceum	AP,G
Allium wallichii	B,SC,SG
Allium winklerianum	LG
Allium zebdanense	AP,B,G,SG
Allium zebrina	B
Allmania nodiflora	B
Allocasuarina campestris	O
Allocasuarina decaisneana	O
Allocasuarina distyla	AU,HA,O
Allocasuarina huegeliana	O
Allocasuarina littoralis	HA
Allocasuarina muellerana	AU,HA
Allocasuarina nana	HA
Allocasuarina paludosa	HA
Allocasuarina pusilla	HA
Allocasuarina sp	AU
Allocasuarina stricta	HA,O
Allocasuarina torulosa	HA,N,O
Allophylus africanus	SI
Allophylus dregeanus	B,SI
Allophylus natalensis	B,C,SI
Allophylus serratus	B
Alloplectus dodsonii	B
Alloteropsis cimicina	B
Alnus acuminata	B
Alnus acuminata ssp arguta	SG
Alnus acuminata ssp glabrata	SG
Alnus cordata	A,B,C,SA,SG

ALNUS

Alnus cremastogyne	B
Alnus firma	SG
Alnus formosana	B,SA
Alnus fruticosa MW313R	X
Alnus glutinosa	A,B,C,RH,SA
Alnus glutinosa v barbata	B
Alnus hirsuta	SG
Alnus incana	A,B,C,CG,RH,SA
Alnus incana f aurea	SG
Alnus japonica	B,RH,SA
Alnus jorullensis	B
Alnus maximowiczii	SG
Alnus nepalensis	B,SA,SG
Alnus nepalensis CNW778	X
Alnus nitida	B,SA
Alnus orientalis	B
Alnus pendula	SG
Alnus rhombifolia	B,RH,SA
Alnus rubra	A,B,C,RH,SA,SG
Alnus rugosa	B
Alnus serrulata	B,CG
Alnus sieboldiana	SG
Alnus sinuata	A,B,C,RH,SG
Alnus tenuifolia	B,RH,SA,SG
Alnus viridis	A,B,CG,RH,SA,SG
Alnus viridis ssp crispa	B,RH,SG
Alnus x mayrii	RH
Alocasia macrorrhiza	B,HA,O
Alocasia sanderana	B
Aloe abyssinica JBG12358	BC
Aloe aculeata	B,SI
Aloe affinis	B
Aloe africana	B,SA,SI
Aloe alferdii	SI
Aloe ammophila	B
Aloe arborescens	B,C,SA,SI,Y
Aloe aristata	B
Aloe asperifolia	B,SI
Aloe bainesii	B,SI
Aloe bakeri	SI
Aloe bellatula	B
Aloe bowiea	SI
Aloe boylii	SI
Aloe bracteata	B,Y
Aloe branddraaiensis	B,SI
Aloe brevifolia	SI
Aloe broomii	B,SI
Aloe buhrii	B,SI
Aloe burgersfortensis	B,SI
Aloe camperi	SI
Aloe camperi 'Maculata'	B
Aloe capitata v cipolinicola	B,SI
Aloe castanea	B,SI,Y
Aloe chabaudii	B,SI
Aloe claviflora	B,SI,Y
Aloe comosa	B,SI,Y
Aloe compressa v schistophylla	B
Aloe comptonii	B,SI
Aloe conifera	SI
Aloe cooperi	B,C,SI
Aloe cryptopoda	SI
Aloe davyana	B,Y
Aloe davyana v subulifera	B,Y
Aloe dichotoma	B,CH,SA,SI
Aloe distans	B
Aloe dolomitica	B

Aloe dominella	B,SI
Aloe erinacea	B,SA,SI
Aloe excelsa	SI
Aloe falcata	B,SI
Aloe ferox	B,SA,SI,Y
Aloe fosteri	B,SI,Y
Aloe framesii	B,SI
Aloe gariepensis	B,SI,Y
Aloe glauca	SI
Aloe globuligemma	B,SI,Y
Aloe graciliflora	B,BC
Aloe graminicola	B
Aloe grandidentata	B,SI
Aloe greatheadii	B
Aloe greatheadii ssp davyana	SI
Aloe greenii	B
Aloe haemanthifolia	SI
Aloe harlana	B
Aloe haworthoides	B
Aloe hereroensis	B,SI
Aloe humilis	B,SI
Aloe immaculata	B
Aloe inyangensis	SI
Aloe jacksonii	B,SI,Y
Aloe karasbergensis	B
Aloe khamiesensis	B,SI
Aloe krapohliana	B,SI,Y
Aloe kraussii	SI
Aloe lineata	B,SI
Aloe lineata v muirii	B,SI
Aloe littoralis	B,SI,Y
Aloe littoralis v rubro-lutea	B,Y
Aloe longibracteata	B
Aloe lutescens	B,Y
Aloe maculata	SI
Aloe madecassa	B,SI
Aloe marlothii	B,SI
Aloe melanacantha	B,SI,Y
Aloe microstigma	B,SI,Y
Aloe minima	SI
Aloe mitis	B
Aloe mitriformis	B,SI
Aloe modesta	SI
Aloe mutabilis	B,Y
Aloe pachygaster	BC
Aloe parvibracteata	B,SI,Y
Aloe peglerae	B,SI
Aloe pictifolia	SI
Aloe pirottae	B
Aloe plicatilis	B,SI
Aloe pluridens	B,SI
Aloe pratensis	B,SA,SI
Aloe pretoriensis	B,SI
Aloe prinslooi	B
Aloe ramosissima	B,SI
Aloe rauhii	B
Aloe reitzii	B
Aloe rupestris	B,SI,Y
Aloe saponaria	B
Aloe sinkatana	SI
Aloe sp mix	C,SI
Aloe speciosa	B,SI
Aloe spectabilis	B,Y
Aloe spicata	SI
Aloe squarrosa	SI
Aloe striata	B,BC,SA,SI,Y

21

ALOE

Aloe striata ssp karasbergensis	SI
Aloe striatula	B,SI
Aloe succotrina	B,SI
Aloe suprafoliata	B,SI
Aloe thraskii	B,CH,SI
Aloe tidmarshii	B
Aloe transvaalensis	SI
Aloe vacillans	B
Aloe vahombe	SI
Aloe vanbalenii	B,Y
Aloe variegata	B,C,CH,SA,SI,Y
Aloe vera	B,SA,SI
Aloe vigueri	SI
Aloe vogtsii	SI
Aloe zebrina	B,SI
Aloinopsis hilmarii	B
Aloinopsis jamesii	B,Y
Aloinopsis lodewykii	Y
Aloinopsis luckhoffii	B,GC,SI,Y
Aloinopsis malherbei	B,SI,Y
Aloinopsis mix	Y
Aloinopsis orpenii	B,SI
Aloinopsis peersii	B,SI
Aloinopsis rosulata	B,SI,Y
Aloinopsis rubrolineata	B
Aloinopsis schooneesii	B,GC,Y
Aloinopsis schooneesii ssp schooneesii	SI
Aloinopsis setifera	B,SI,Y
Aloinopsis spathulata	B,Y
Aloinopsis thudichumi	B
Aloinopsis villetii	B,SI,Y
Alonsoa albiflora	P
Alonsoa albiflora 'Snowflake'	C
Alonsoa hyb new mix	J
Alonsoa linearis	B,C,T
Alonsoa meridionalis	B,C,FH,G,JE,SA,V
Alonsoa meridionalis 'Fire Opals'	F
Alonsoa meridionalis 'Firestone Jewels'	T
Alonsoa meridionalis mix	JE
Alonsoa meridionalis 'Pink Beauty'	B,I,P
Alonsoa meridionalis 'Salmon Beauty'	T
Alonsoa meridionalis 'Shell Pink'	JE
Alonsoa warscewiczii	AP,B,BS,C,DT,SG,T
Alopecurus arundinaceus	SG
Alopecurus geniculatus	B
Alopecurus myosuroides	B
Alopecurus pratensis	B,SG
Alopecurus pratensis 'Aureovariegatus'	B
Aloysia triphylla	B
Alphitonia excelsa	B,HA,O,SA
Alphitonia petriei	B,O
Alphitonia philippinensis	B
Alpine compositae B&SWJ 1659 (u-g)	E
Alpinia caerulea	B,SA
Alpinia calcarata	B
Alpinia galanga	B
Alpinia japonica	B
Alpinia malaccensis	B
Alpinia modesta	B
Alpinia officinarum	B
Alpinia purpurata	SA
Alpinia purpurata red	B
Alpinia rhomburghiana	B
Alpinia vittata 'Oceanica'	B
Alpinia zerumbet	B,O,SA
Alpinia zerumbet 'Variegata'	B

Alstonia macrophylla	B
Alstonia scholaris	HA,SA
Alstroemeria angustifolia	AP,B,SC
Alstroemeria aurea	AP,B,C,G,JE,P,SA,SC,SG
Alstroemeria aurea 'Moorheim Orange'	C,T
Alstroemeria aurea 'Orange King'	AP,B
Alstroemeria brasiliensis	RS,SC,SG
Alstroemeria 'Butterfly Pink'	B
Alstroemeria diluta	AP,B
Alstroemeria exserens	B
Alstroemeria garaventae	B
Alstroemeria 'Hawera'	B
Alstroemeria hookeri	AP,B,SC
Alstroemeria 'Ligtu Hybrids'	AP,BD,BS,C,CL,D,F,FH, G,JE,KI,LG,N,S,SA,SC, SE,SG,SU,SY,T
Alstroemeria ligtu ssp incarnata	B
Alstroemeria ligtu ssp simsii	B
Alstroemeria ligtu x 'Dr Salter's Hybrids'	AP,B,J,L,T,V
Alstroemeria 'Los Andes Hybrids'	B
Alstroemeria magenta	B
Alstroemeria magnifica	B,P
Alstroemeria magnifica ssp maxima	B
Alstroemeria 'Mona Lisa'	B,JE
Alstroemeria mutabilis	B
Alstroemeria pallida	AP,B,SC
Alstroemeria paupercula	B
Alstroemeria pelegrina	AP,MN,SC,SG
Alstroemeria polyphylla	B
Alstroemeria pseudospathulata	B,P
Alstroemeria psittacina	AP,B,CG,MA,PA,SC
Alstroemeria pulchra	B,P
Alstroemeria revoluta	B
Alstroemeria schizanthoides	B
Alstroemeria umbellata	B,SC
Alstroemeria versicolor	AP,B
Alternanthera denticulata	B
Alternanthera ficoidea v amoena 'Sessilis'	B
Alternanthera sessilis	B
Althaea armeniaca	JE
Althaea cannabina	B,C,JE,P
Althaea hispida	B,NS
Althaea officinalis	B,C,CG,CO,CP,JE,KS, SA,SG,T,Z
Althaea officinalis 'Alba'	B,P,PG
Alvaradoa amorphoides	B
Alyogyne cuneiformis	AU
Alyogyne hakeifolia	AU,B,O,SA
Alyogyne huegelii	B,C,O,SA
Alysicarpus monilifer	B
Alysicarpus rugosus	B
Alyssoides utriculata	AP,B,C,G,JE,KI,SC,SG
Alyssoides utriculata 'Lost April'	B
Alyssoides utriculata 'Tinkerbells'	B,KS
Alyssoides utriculata var graeca	FH,SC
Alyssum alpestre	B,CGG,
Alyssum alpestre ssp serpyllifolium	B
Alyssum alyssoides ssp conglobata	B
Alyssum alyssoides tortuosum	B
Alyssum alyssoides t. ssp heterophyllum	B
Alyssum argenteum	B,C,CG,FH,JE,RH,SA, SG
Alyssum armenum	SG
Alyssum borzeanum	SG
Alyssum caespitosum	B
Alyssum cuneifolium	B,JE

Alyssum desertorum	B
Alyssum lesbicum	B
Alyssum maritimum see Lobularia maritima	
Alyssum montanum	AP,B,BS,C,G,SA,SC,SG, T
Alyssum montanum 'Mountain Gold'	AP,BD,D,JE,L,R
Alyssum montanum ssp brymi	B
Alyssum murale	AP,G,SC,SG
Alyssum poderi v poderi	B
Alyssum pulvinare	P
Alyssum repens	B,JE
Alyssum saxatile see Aurinia saxatilis	
Alyssum serpyllifolium	AP,B,C,JE,SC
Alyssum spinosum	AP,B,C,G,JE
Alyssum spinosum 'Roseum'	T
Alyssum wulfenianum	AP,G,SC,SG
Alyxia buxifolia	B
Alyxia ruscifolia	B
Amaranthus acutilobus	CG
Amaranthus albus	B
Amaranthus biltoides	B,SG
Amaranthus caudatus	B,BS,C,CG,CO,DT,F,G,J, O,S,SG,SU,T,TU,V,YA
Amaranthus caudatus 'Albiflorus'	CG
Amaranthus caudatus 'Crimson'	D,F
Amaranthus caudatus 'Flavus'	SG
Amaranthus caudatus 'Grunschwanz'	V
Amaranthus caudatus 'Kiwicha'	B
Amaranthus caudatus 'Red'	BD,KS,ST,V
Amaranthus caudatus 'Red/Green Tassels'	U
Amaranthus caudatus 'Viridis'	B,BS,C,KS
Amaranthus chlorostachys	B,SG
Amaranthus cruentus	C,CG,RH
Amaranthus cruentus 'Alegria'	B
Amaranthus cruentus 'Bronze Standard'	B
Amaranthus cruentus 'Chihuahuan Orn.'	B
Amaranthus cruentus ecuador	B
Amaranthus cruentus 'Foxtail'	B,BS,CL
Amaranthus cruentus 'Golden Giant'	B
Amaranthus cruentus 'Mayo Grain'	B
Amaranthus cruentus 'Mayo Red'	B
Amaranthus cruentus 'Mexican Grain'	B,C
Amaranthus cruentus 'Mtain Pima Greens'	B
Amaranthus cruentus 'Multicolor'	B
Amaranthus cruentus 'Oeschberg'	B
Amaranthus cruentus 'Paiute'	B
Amaranthus cruentus 'Popping'	B
Amaranthus cruentus 'Red'	BS,J,SE
Amaranthus cruentus 'Red Cathedral'	B
Amaranthus cruentus 'Red Cathedral Sup'	B
Amaranthus cruentus 'Rodale Multiflora'	B
Amaranthus cruentus 'Split Personality'	F
Amaranthus c.x 'Hopi Red Dye Amaranth'	B, C
Amaranthus cruentus x powellii	CP
Amaranthus dubius	B
Amaranthus 'Golden Giant'	T
Amaranthus 'Green Thumb'	B,BD,BS,C,KS,T
Amaranthus groecizans v sylvestris	B
Amaranthus 'Hopi Red Dye'	C
Amaranthus hybridus	SG
Amaranthus hybridus 'Burgundy'	B
Amaranthus hybridus 'Dreadicus'	B
Amaranthus hypochondriacus	B,C,CP,SG
Amaranthus hyp. 'Guarijio Grain'	B
Amaranthus hyp.'New Mexico'	B
Amaranthus hyp. 'Pigmy Torch'	B,BS,C,KS,T

Amaranthus hyp. 'Prima Nepal'	B
Amaranthus hyp.'Rio San Lorenzo'	B
Amaranthus lividus	SG
Amaranthus lividus ssp ascendens	B
Amaranthus lividus ssp oleraceus	B
Amaranthus orientalis	B
Amaranthus paniculatus	SG
Amaranthus paniculatus 'Oeschberg'	KS,V
Amaranthus paniculatus 'Red Cathedral'	C
Amaranthus powellii	CG
Amaranthus 'Quintonil'	B
Amaranthus 'Red Fox'	BS,KI
Amaranthus retroflexus	B
Amaranthus spinosus	B,SG
Amaranthus tricolor	B,BD,SE,T,V
Amaranthus tricolor 'Amar Kiran'	B
Amaranthus tricolor 'Amar Peet'	B
Amaranthus tricolor 'Blood Red'	B
Amaranthus tricolor 'Early Splendour'	B,BS,C,J
Amaranthus tricolor 'Elephant's Head'	B
Amaranthus tricolor 'Flaming Fountain'	B
Amaranthus tricolor 'Hartman's Giant'	B
Amaranthus tricolor 'Illumination'	B,BS,KI,U
Amaranthus tricolor 'Lotus Purple'	B
Amaranthus tricolor 'Merah'	B
Amaranthus tricolor 'Molten Fire'	B,KI
Amaranthus tricolor 'Pinang'	B
Amaranthus tricolor 'Puteh'	B
Amaranthus tricolor 'Splendens'	B,BS,L
Amaranthus tricolor 'Splendens Perfecta'	C
Amaranthus tricolor 'White Leaf'	B
Amaranthus viridis	B,KI,ST,SU,T
Amaryllis belladonna	B,C,SA
Amaryllis belladonna v purpurea major	B,C
Amberboa moschata 'Crown' mix	CO
Amberboa moschata 'Dairy Maid'	T
Amberboa moschata 'Imperialis' mix	BS,C,D,V
Amberboa moschata 'Imperialis' s-c	B
Amberboa moschata mix	DT,F,J,KS,SU,T,TU
Amberboa moschata ssp suaveolens	B
Amberboa m. ssp suaveolens 'Magnus'	B
Amberboa moschata 'The Bride'	B,T
Ambrometiella brevifolius	B
Ambrosia artemisiifolia	CG,SG
Ambrosia chamissonis	B
Ambrosia dumosa	B
Ambrosia maritima	B
Amelanchier alnifolia	A,AP,B,SA,SC,SG
Amelanchier arborea	B,N
Amelanchier bartramiana	SG
Amelanchier canadensis	AP,B,C,N,SA
Amelanchier florida	SG
Amelanchier humilis	SG
Amelanchier laevis	B,SA,SC
Amelanchier lamarckii	A,B,SA
Amelanchier oblongifolia	SG
Amelanchier ovalis	SA,SG
Amelanchier pumila	AP,B,G,SC,SG
Amelanchier sanguinea	CG
Amelanchier spicata	B,SG
Amelanchier utahensis	B
Amellus asteroides	B,SI
Amethystea caerulea	AP,C
Amethystea caerulea 'Turquoise'	B
Ammannia baccifera	B
Ammi majus	B,BS,C,CP,KS,V

AMMI

Ammi majus 'Snowflake'	B
Ammi visnaga	B,CG,CP,KS
Ammobium alatum	B,BD,BS,C,CO,DT,J,KI, L,O,TU,V
Ammobium alatum 'Bikini'	BS,C,CL,O
Ammobium alatum 'Grandiflorum'	B,KS,T,SU
Ammodendon conollyi	B
Ammophila arenaria	B,JE,SA
Ammophila littoralis	B
Amoreuxia palmatifida	B,SW
Amorpha californica	B
Amorpha canescens	B,C,G,JE,PR,SA
Amorpha cyanostachys	B
Amorpha fruticosa	A,C,CG,PR,SA
Amorpha fruticosa pods	B
Amorpha nana	PR
Amorpha paniculata	B
Amorphophallus bulifer	SG
Amorphophallus konjac	B
Ampelodesmos mauritanicus	B,C,JE,SA
Ampelopsis arborea	B
Ampelopsis brevipedunculata	B,SA
Ampelopsis megalophylla	SA
Amsonia ciliata	B,G,JE,T
Amsonia elliptica	B
Amsonia tabernaemontana	B,C,CC,CG,G,JE,T
Amsonia tabernaemontana v salicifolia	B,SA
Amsonia tomentosa	B,SW
Anacampseros affinis	B
Anacampseros albissima	B,C
Anacampseros alstonii	B,BC
Anacampseros arachnoides	B,C
Anacampseros comptonii	B
Anacampseros crinita	B
Anacampseros filamentosa	B
Anacampseros gracilis	B
Anacampseros meyeri	B
Anacampseros quinaria	B
Anacampseros recurvata	B
Anacampseros retusa	B,SI
Anacampseros rufescens	AP,B,Y
Anacampseros sp	SI
Anacampseros telephiastrum	B
Anacampseros tomentosa	B,Y
Anacampseros ustulata	SI
Anacamptis pyramidalis	B
Anacardium excelsum	B
Anacardium occidentale	B,HA,RE
Anacistrocactus scheeri	BC
Anacyclus maroccanus	JE
Anacyclus officinarum	SG
Anacyclus pyrethrum	B,CG
Anacyclus pyrethrum v depressus	AP,B,BS,CG,CL,FH,G,L, SA,SC,SG,T
Anacyclus pyr. v dep. 'Garden Gnome'	BS,C,D,JE,KI
Anacyclus pyr. v dep. 'Silberkissen'	JE
Anadenanthera colubrina	B
Anadenanthera peregrina	B
Anagallis arvensis	B,C,SG,SU,V
Anagallis arvensis v caerulea	B,C
Anagallis blue	C,S,U
Anagallis 'Blue Light'	C,KS
Anagallis monellii	AP,CL,SE,SG,T
Anagallis monellii 'Gentian Blue'	J,KS,T,V
Anagallis monellii ssp linifolia	B,SE,T
Ananas comosus	B
Anapalina caffra	SI
Anaphalis alpicola	AP,B,CC,SG
Anaphalis margaritacea	AP,B,BS,KS,MA,SA,SC, SG,SU,T,U
Anaphalis 'New Snow'	B,BS,C,CL,JE,KI
Anarcardium occidentalis	SA
Anchusa americanus	PR
Anchusa arvensis	B
Anchusa azurea	C,JE,SA
Anchusa azurea 'Dropmore'	B,BS,C,KI,SU,T,V
Anchusa capensis	B,G,SI
Anchusa capensis 'Blue Angel'	B,BS,CL,CO,D,J,KI,KS, S,SU,T,TU,U,V
Anchusa capensis 'Blue Bird'	B,BS,C,T
Anchusa capensis dwarf mix	KS
Anchusa 'Dawn'	D,DT,J,S
Anchusa 'Feltham Pride'	BS,CL
Anchusa officinalis	B,C,CP,JE,SA,SG
Anchusa undulata	AP,B,SC
Ancistrocactus brevihamatus	B
Ancistrocactus megarhizus	B
Ancistrocactus scheeri	B,Y
Ancistrocactus tobuschii	B
Andersonia involucrata	B,SA
Andersonia lehmanniana	B
Andira inermis	B
Androcymbium capense	B,SI
Androcymbium ciliolatum	B,SI
Androcymbium cunonis	B
Androcymbium dregei	B
Androcymbium europaeum	B
Androcymbium europaeum MS510 Spain	MN
Androcymbium gramineum	B
Androcymbium gramineum S.F13	MN
Androcymbium melanthoides f striatum	AP,B,SC
Androcymbium pulchrum	B,SI
Andrographis paniculata	B
Andromeda polifolia	C,CC,CG
Andropogon gerardii	B,C,JE,SA
Andropogon gerardii 'Roundtree'	B
Andropogon glomeratus	NT
Andropogon hallii	PR
Andropogon ischaemum	C
Androsace albana	AP,B,G,SC,SG
Androsace alpina	AP,B,C,CG,G,JE,SA,SC
Androsace arachnoides	SG
Androsace caduca	B
Androsace carnea	AP,B,C,CG,JE,SC,SG
Androsace carnea ssp brigantiaca	AP,B,CG,G,JE,SC,SG
Androsace carnea ssp laggeri	AP,CG,SC
Androsace carnea ssp rosea	AP,G,SG
Androsace carnea x pyrenaica	AP,PM,SC
Androsace chaixii	AP,CG,G,SC,SG
Androsace chamaejasme	B,C,JE,SW
Androsace ciliata	AP,SC,SG
Androsace cylindrica	AP,SG,SC
Androsace fedtschenkoi	SG
Androsace foliosa	B
Androsace hediseantha	PM
Androsace hedraeantha	AP,SG,SC
Androsace helvetica	B,C,CG
Androsace hirtella	AP,G,SC
Androsace lactea	AP,G,JE,SC
Androsace lactiflora	AP,CG,JE,SA
Androsace lanuginosa	B
Androsace mathildae	AP,G,SC,SG

24

ANDROSACE

Androsace maxima	CG
Androsace mix	JE
Androsace montana	B,SW
Androsace muscoidea	SG
Androsace obtusifolia	B,C,G,JE,SC
Androsace primuloides	B
Androsace pubescens	AP,CG,SC
Androsace pyrenaica	AP,B,CG,G,SC
Androsace rotundifolia	AP,C,SC
Androsace sarmentosa	B,SG
Androsace sarmentosa v chumbyi	SG
Androsace sempervivoides	AP,B,SC,SG
Androsace septentrionalis	AP,B,CG,G,SC,SG
Androsace septentrionalis 'Stardust'	B,BS,HH,JE
Androsace strigillosa	B,SC
Androsace vandellii	AP,B,CG,SC,SG
Androsace villosa	B,C,CG,G,JE,SA,SC
Androsace villosa v congesta	B
Andryala aghardii	AP,FH,G,SC,SG,T
Anemathele lessoniana	B
Anemocarpa podolepidium	B,O
Anemone altaica	AP,B,C,G,JE,LG,SC
Anemone apennina	B,SC
Anemone baldensis	AP,B,C,CG,G,JE,SA,SC
Anemone biarmiensis	B,SC
Anemone blanda 'New hybrids mix'	C
Anemone blanda 'White Splendour'	B
Anemone canadensis	AP,B,CG,G,JE,P,PR,SG
Anemone caroliniana	AP,CG,G,PM,SC
Anemone coronaria 'De Caen French'	AP,C,D,G,J,S,V
Anemone coronaria 'De Caen Hollandia'	B
Anemone coronaria 'De Caen Mrs. Fokker'	B
Anemone coronaria 'De Caen Sylphide'	B,C
Anemone coronaria 'De Caen The Bride'	B,C
Anemone coronaria f1 'Mona Lisa' mix	BD,BS,CL,DT,L,T
Anemone coronaria 'Gloria Mix'	F
Anemone coronaria hyb 'Cleopatra'	BS
Anemone coronaria hyb 'St Brigid'	BS,C,J,KI,V
Anemone c. hyb 'St Brigid Lord Lieut.'	B
Anemone c. hyb 'St Brigid Mt Everest'	B
Anemone c. hyb 'St Brigid The Governor'	B,C
Anemone coronaria white, ex Turkey	G
Anemone crinita	AP,SC,SG
Anemone cylindrica	AP,B,G,JE,PR,SC,SG
Anemone daurica	SA
Anemone dichotoma	SG
Anemone drummondi	AP,B,P,SC
Anemone elongata	B,SC
Anemone f1 'Cleopatra' mix	C
Anemone fannini	B,SI
Anemone fasciculata	CG
Anemone hortensis	B,C,JE
Anemone hupehensis	G,JE,SA,SG
Anemone hupehensis v japonica	B,BS,C,SG,V
Anemone leveillei	AP,B,BS,C,CG,F,G,JE,P,SC,SG,T
Anemone magellanica see multifida	
Anemone multifida	AP,B,C,CG,G,HH,P,RH,SC,SG
Anemone multifida 'Major'	AP,FH,G,JE,SC
Anemone multifida 'Red Form'	B,F,SC
Anemone multifida 'Rubra'	G,JE
Anemone narcissiflora	AP,B,BS,C,G,I,JE,SA,SC,T,V
Anemone narcissiflora v nipponica	B
Anemone nemorosa	B,C,G,JE,PM,RH,SA,SU,T

Anemone nemorosa 'Alba Plena'	B
Anemone palmata	AP,B,CG,G,JE,PM,SC
Anemone patens	PR,SG
Anemone pavonina	AP,B,G,MN
Anemone pavonina S.L165/3 Greece	MN
Anemone polyanthes	AP,B,JE,SC
Anemone racemosa	RS
Anemone ranunculoides	B,C,G,JE,SC,SG
Anemone reflexa	SG
Anemone rivularis	AP,B,C,CC,G,JE,NG,P,PM,RH,SC,SG,T,V
Anemone rupicola	AP,B,SC
Anemone sp China	SG
Anemone stellata MS938 France	MN
Anemone sylvestris	B,C,CG,CL,G,JE,SA,SG,T,Z
Anemone tenuifolia	B,SI
Anemone tomentosa	B,C,JE
Anemone tuberosa	B,SW
Anemone vernalis	SA
Anemone virginiana	B,C,G,JE,NT,SG,T
Anemone vitifolia	AP,C,SG
Anemone x fulgens	B,G,SC
Anemone x lesseri	B,C,G,HH,LG,SG,T,V
Anemopsis californica	B
Anemopsis macrophylla	AP,G,JE,SC
Angelica archangelica	AP,B,JE,KS,RH,SA,SC,SG
Angelica arguta	B
Angelica atropurpurea	JE,PR,T
Angelica decurrens	SG
Angelica gigas	AP,B,C,JE,SA,SC
Angelica pachycarpa	KS
Angelica paniculata	B
Angelica pinnata	B
Angelica sylvestris	B,C,CG,LA,SA,SG,SS
Angelica sylvestris 'Naini's Wood'	B
Angelica 'Taiwaniana'	T
Angelica ursina	T
Angianthus cunninghamii	B
Angianthus milnei	B
Angianthus tomentosus	B,C,SA
Angophora bakeri	B,HA,O,SA
Angophora costata	B,HA,O
Angophora floribunda	B,HA,O,SA
Angophora hispida	B,HA,O
Angophora melanoxylon	HA
Anigozanthos bicolor	B,C,O,SA,SH
Anigozanthos flavidus	AP,AU,C,HA,O,SA,SC,SH
Anigozanthos flavidus orange & red	B,SH
Anigozanthos flavidus red	HA,O,SA
Anigozanthos gabrielae	B,O
Anigozanthos humilis	B,C,O,SH
Anigozanthos manglesii	AU,B,HA,O,SA,SG,SH,V
Anigozanthos onycis	B,O
Anigozanthos preissii	B,C,O,SH
Anigozanthos pulcherrimus	B,O
Anigozanthos rufus	B,O,SH
Anigozanthos sp mix	C
Anigozanthos viridis	B,C,O,SA,SH
Anisochilus carnosus	B
Anisodontea anomala	B,SI
Anisodontea biflora	B,SA,SI
Anisodontea elegans	SI

ANISODONTEA

Anisodontea julii	B,P,SA,SI	Anthemis cretica ssp cretica	AP,B,SC
Anisodontea scabrosa	AP,B,SC,SI	Anthemis leucanthemifolia	B
Anisodontea sp	SI	Anthemis maritima	JE
Anisodontea triloba	B,SI	Anthemis palaestinus	B
Anisomeles indica	B	Anthemis pseudocotula	B
Anisomeles malabarica	B	Anthemis punctata	SG
Anisotome aromatica	B,SC,SS	Anthemis ruthenica	B
Anisotome filifolia	B,SS	Anthemis sancti-johannis	B,C,G,JE,SA,T
Anisotome flexuosa	B	Anthemis sosnovskyana	SG
Anisotome haastii	AP,B,SA,SC,SS	Anthemis sp Turkey	I
Anisotome intermedia	B	Anthemis tinctoria	B,C,CG,CP,F,G,JE,SC, SG,V
Anisotome pilifera	AP,B,SC,SS		
Annona atemoya	SA	Anthemis tinctoria 'Kelwayii'	B,BS,C,CL,DT,JE,O,SA,T
Annona aurantiaca	B	Anthemis tinctoria ssp subtinctoria	B
Annona cherimola	B,C,G,SA	Anthemis triumfetii	CG
Annona diversifolia	B	Anthemis tuberculata	I
Annona glabra	B	Anthericum angulicaule	B,SI
Annona hyb 'Atemoya'	B	Anthericum baeticum	AP,LG,SC
Annona montana	B	Anthericum floribundum	SG
Annona muricata	B,C	Anthericum liliago	AP,B,C,G,I,JE,LG,MN, RH,SA,SC
Annona reticulata	B		
Annona senegalensis	B	Anthericum ramosum	AP,B,C,G,JE,LG,MA,MN, RH,SC,SG
Annona sp	RE		
Annona squamosa	B,C,SA	Anthericum saundersiae	B,SI
Annonidium mannii	B	Anthocephalus chinensis	B
Anoda cristata	G	Anthocercis littorea	B,C,SA
Anoda cristata 'Opal Cup'	B,C,J,KS	Anthocleista grandiflora	B,SI
Anoda cristata 'Silver Cup'	C	Anthocleista zambesiaca	C
Anoda cristata 'Snow Cup'	B	Anthotium humile	B
Anoda cristata v violacea	B	Anthoxanthum alpinum	SG
Anoda wrightii 'Butter Cup'	B	Anthoxanthum odoratum	B,C,JE,SA,SC
Anogeissus leiocarpus	B	Anthriscus sylvestris	B,C,JE,KS,LA,P,SA,SG,V
Anomatheca fistulosa	B,SI	Anthriscus sylvestris 'Ravenswing'	B
Anomatheca grandiflora	AP,SC,SI	Anthropodium candidum	SG
Anomatheca laxa	AP,B,G,LG,PM,RH,SC, SG,SI	Anthropodium cirrhatum	SG
		Anthurium coriaceum	B
Anomatheca laxa 'Alba'	AP,B,G,HH,PM,SC	Anthurium gracile	B
Anomatheca laxa 'Joan Evans'	AP,PM	Anthurium hookeri	B
Anomatheca viridis	AP,B,C,SC,SI	Anthurium imperiale	B
Anopterus glandulosus	B,C,SA	Anthurium pallidiflorum	B
Anredera cordifolia	B	Anthurium scandens	B
Antegibbaeum fissoides	B	Anthurium scherzeranum	B
Antennaria alpina	SG	Anthurium schlechtendalii	B
Antennaria carpatica	CG,JE	Anthurium wildenovii	SG
Antennaria dioica	AP,B,C,CL,G,JE,SA,SC, SG,T	Anthyllis cytisoides	SA
		Anthyllis dillenii	B
Antennaria dioica red	I	Anthyllis montana	AP,B,BS,SA,SC
Antennaria dioica 'Rosea'	AP,B,BS,JE,SA,SC	Anthyllis montana 'Carminea'	B,C
Antennaria dioica 'Rubra'	JE	Anthyllis montana 'Rubra'	AP,B,JE,SC,SG
Antennaria dioica ssp borealis	CG	Anthyllis polyphylla	B
Antennaria howellii	JE,SC	Anthyllis vulneraria	AP,B,BS,C,FH,HH,I,JE, LA,SA,SC,SG,SU
Antennaria magellanica	B,C,JE		
Antennaria nebrascensis	B	Anthyllis vulneraria red & orange	FH
Antennaria neglecta	B,JE	Anthyllis vulneraria ssp coccinea	AP,B,G,HH,JE,P,RS,SC, SG
Antennaria neodioica	B		
Antennaria 'New Hybrids' mix	C,JE	Anthyllis vulneraria ssp vulneraria	T
Antennaria nitida	B	Anthyllis vulneraria v alpestris	CG
Antennaria parvifolia	AP,B,SG	Anthyllis vulneraria v rubra	AP,FH,SC
Antennaria plantaginifolia	AP,B	Antidesma bunius	B
Antennaria 'Red Hybrids' mix	JE	Antidesma dallachyanum	B
Antennaria rosea	SG	Antidesma venosum	B
Anthemis arabica 'Criss Cross'	KI,T	Antigonon leptopus	B,C,G,HA,O,SA
Anthemis arvensis	B	Antigonon leptopus 'Album'	B,SA
Anthemis austriaca	B,G	Antigonon leptopus v alba 'White Bride'	C
Anthemis carpatica 'Karpatenschnee'	JE	Antimima 'Nelii'	B
Anthemis cotula	B	Antimima pulchella	SI

26

ANTIRRHINUM

Antirrhinum 'Appleblossom'	C
Antirrhinum asarina	AP,B,C,FH,I,JE,P,PM, RH,SA,SC,SG,T
Antirrhinum asarina 'Iberian Trail'	C
Antirrhinum asarina 'Sierra Nevada'	B
Antirrhinum 'Bizarre'	J,V
Antirrhinum braun-blanquetii	AP,B,C,G,FH,HH,JE,P,SC
Antirrhinum 'Brighton Rock'	F
Antirrhinum 'Candyman' mix	S
Antirrhinum 'Carioca'	BS
Antirrhinum 'Choice' mix	DT
Antirrhinum colours mix	S
Antirrhinum 'Crown' mix	BS,CO
Antirrhinum 'Dwarf' bedding mix	T
Antirrhinum 'Dwarf' lg fl mix	J
Antirrhinum f1 hyb 'Bells' mix	BS,D,DT,J
Antirrhinum f1 hyb 'Bells' s-c	CL
Antirrhinum f1 hyb 'Blue Bird'	JE
Antirrhinum f1 hyb 'Blue Jay'	JE
Antirrhinum f1 hyb 'Bright Butterflies'	B,BS,J,KI
Antirrhinum f1 hyb 'Bunting'	JE
Antirrhinum f1 hyb 'Caerulea Het. Musik'	JE
Antirrhinum f1 hyb 'Caerulea Het. Olympia'	JE
Antirrhinum f1 hyb 'Cardinal'	JE
Antirrhinum f1 hyb 'Chimes' mix	BS,J
Antirrhinum f1 hyb 'Chimes' s-c	CL
Antirrhinum f1 hyb 'Coronette Bronze'	B,BS
Antirrhinum f1 hyb 'Coronette Cherry'	B,BS
Antirrhinum f1 hyb 'Coronette Crimson'	B,BS
Antirrhinum f1 hyb 'Coronette' mix	CL,DT,J,KI,S,SE
Antirrhinum f1 hyb 'Coronette Orchid'	B,BS
Antirrhinum f1 hyb 'Coronette Pink'	B,BS
Antirrhinum f1 hyb 'Coronette Rose'	B,BS
Antirrhinum f1 hyb 'Coronette Scarlet'	B,BS
Antirrhinum f1 hyb 'Coronette White'	B,BS
Antirrhinum f1 hyb 'Coronette Yellow'	B,BS
Antirrhinum f1 hyb 'Dove'	JE
Antirrhinum f1 hyb 'Floral Carpet'	C,CL,L
Antirrhinum f1 hyb 'Fl.Showers Crimson'	B,BS
Antirrhinum f1 hyb 'Fl Sh Dp Bronze'	B,BS
Antirrhinum f1 hyb 'Fl Showers Fuchsia'	B
Antirrhinum f1 hyb 'Fl Sh Lavender 2-tone'	B,BS
Antirrhinum f1 hyb 'Floral Showers Lilac'	B,BS
Antirrhinum f1 hyb 'Floral Showers' mix	BD,DT,KI,SE,ST,T,YA
Antirrhinum f1 hyb 'Fl Showers Purple'	B,BS
Antirrhinum f1 hyb 'Floral Showers Rose'	B,BS
Antirrhinum f1 hyb 'Fl Showers Rose Pink'	B,BS
Antirrhinum f1 hyb 'Fl Showers Scarlet'	B,BS
Antirrhinum f1 hyb 'Fl Showers White'	B,BS
Antirrhinum f1 hyb 'Fl Showers Yellow'	B,BS
Antirrhinum f1 hyb 'Florist Mix'	CL
Antirrhinum f1 hyb 'Forerunner'	C,T
Antirrhinum f1 hyb 'Goldfinch'	JE
Antirrhinum f1 hyb 'Jewel Blue'	JE
Antirrhinum f1 hyb 'Jewel Pink'	JE
Antirrhinum f1 hyb 'Jewel Purple'	JE
Antirrhinum f1 hyb 'Jewel White'	JE
Antirrhinum f1 hyb 'Liberty Series' mix	F,T
Antirrhinum f1 hyb 'Liberty Series' s-c	CL
Antirrhinum f1 hyb 'Madame Butterfly'	B,BD,BS,CL,D,DT,F,J,M, O,S,SE,T,U,
Antirrhinum f1 hyb 'Pixie'	BS,CL,D,L,YA
Antirrhinum f1 hyb 'Princess'	B,BS,CL,KI,L,U
Antirrhinum f1 hyb 'Robin'	JE
Antirrhinum f1 hyb 'Sonnet Bronze'	B,BS,YA
Antirrhinum f1 hyb 'Sonnet Burgundy'	B,BS,YA
Antirrhinum f1 hyb 'Sonnet Carmine'	B,BS,YA
Antirrhinum f1 hyb 'Sonnet Crimson'	B,BS,YA
Antirrhinum f1 hyb 'Sonnet' mix	BD,D,DT,KI,L,YA
Antirrhinum f1 hyb 'Sonn.Orange-scarlet'	B,BS,YA
Antirrhinum f1 hyb 'Sonnet Pink'	B,BS,YA
Antirrhinum f1 hyb 'Sonnet Rose'	B,BS,YA
Antirrhinum f1 hyb 'Sonnet White'	B,BS,YA
Antirrhinum f1 hyb 'Sonnet Yellow'	B,BS,YA
Antirrhinum f1 hyb 'Supreme' Dbl giant	C
Antirrhinum f1 hyb 'Tetra Ruffled Giants'	C,T
Antirrhinum f1 'Royal Carpet' mix	BS,S,T
Antirrhinum f1 'Royal Carpet' white	BS
Antirrhinum f1 'Sweetheart' mix	BS,D,DT,F,L,M,S,T
Antirrhinum f1 'Tahiti' mix	BS,F,S
Antirrhinum f2 'Cheerio'	BD,BS,C,DT,L
Antirrhinum f2 'Corona' mix	BS,CL,S
Antirrhinum f2 'Popette'	T,V
Antirrhinum f2 'Vanity Fayre' mix	BS,D,J
Antirrhinum 'Giant Fl. Bedding' mix	D,M
Antirrhinum 'Glamour Shades'	BS,VH
Antirrhinum 'Kelvedon Pride'	BS,KI,SU
Antirrhinum 'Kimosy'	F
Antirrhinum 'Lavender Bicolour'	T
Antirrhinum 'Liberty' s-c	M
Antirrhinum 'Lipstick Gold'	F,T,V
Antirrhinum 'Lipstick' mix	J
Antirrhinum 'Lipstick Silver'	F,S,V
Antirrhinum 'Little Darling Mix'	BS,CL,T
Antirrhinum 'Lollipop'	SE
Antirrhinum 'Madonna' dw	BS
Antirrhinum 'Magic Carpet'	BD,BS,C,D,F,J,S,TU,V
Antirrhinum major	B
Antirrhinum majus	AP,G,SG
Antirrhinum majus 'Maximum' mix	T
Antirrhinum majus 'Maximum' old gold	B
Antirrhinum majus 'Rosovyi'	SG
Antirrhinum majus sempervirens	SG
Antirrhinum majus ssp linkianum	RS
Antirrhinum maximum	V
Antirrhinum molle	AP,PM,RS,SC
Antirrhinum 'Monarch Mix'	BS,DT,F,T
Antirrhinum 'Monarch' s-c	BS,L,T
Antirrhinum multiflorum	B
Antirrhinum nanum	V
Antirrhinum nanum 'Black Prince'	F,L,SE,T
Antirrhinum nanum 'Rust Resistant'	BS,L
Antirrhinum 'Night & Day'	C,F,V
Antirrhinum orontium	C
Antirrhinum 'Peaches & Cream'	BS,D,DT,SE,T
Antirrhinum pendula 'Chinese Lanterns'	T
Antirrhinum pendula 'Lampion'	R
Antirrhinum 'Picturatum'	DT
Antirrhinum 'Powys Pride'	B,P
Antirrhinum pulverulentum	RS
Antirrhinum pumila 'Tom Thumb'	B,BS,CO,D,DT,F,J,KI,L, M,O,ST,V,VH
Antirrhinum 'Purity'	L
Antirrhinum 'Purple King'	T
Antirrhinum 'Rainbow'	BS,R
Antirrhinum 'Rembrandt'	BS,F
Antirrhinum 'Sawyer's Old-Fash. Snaps'	C,SU
Antirrhinum 'Scarlet Giant'	C
Antirrhinum sempervirens	AP,FH,G,SC
Antirrhinum siculum	P
Antirrhinum 'Snap Happy'	KI,ST
Antirrhinum sp	RS

ANTIRRHINUM

Antirrhinum 'Tall' mix	BS,KI,SE
Antirrhinum 'Torbay Rock'	P
Antirrhinum 'Trumpet Serenade' mix	D,F,J,S,T,VH
Antirrhinum 'Welcome'	BS
Antirrhinum 'White' dw	BS
Antirrhinum 'White Wonder'	C,T
Antisdesma venosum	SI
Aotus 'Diffusa'	B,SA
Aotus ericoides	AU,B,HA,SA
Aotus lanigera	B
Aotus preissii	B
Apeiba aspera	B,RE
Apera spica-venti	B
Aphanes arvensis	B
Aphloia theiformis	B
Aphyllanthes monspeliensis	B,C,SC
Apios americana	B
Apium graveolens	B,C
Aplectrum hyemale	B
Apluda mutica	B
Apocynum androsaemifolium	B
Apocynum cannabinum	B,CP
Apodytes dimidiata	C,SI
Apodytes dimidiata ssp dimidiata	B
Apollonias barbujana	B
Aponogeton distachyus	B
Apophyllum anomalum	HA
Aporocactus sp mix	C
Aptenia cordifolia	B,CG
Aptenia lancifolia	B
Aptosimum indivisum	B,SI
Aptosimum procumbens ssp procumbens	B,SI
Aptosimum spinescens	B,SI
Aquilegia 'Aline Fairweather'	B
Aquilegia alpina	AP,B,BS,C,CG,CO,F,G, JE,KS,P,SA,SC,SG,SU,V
Aquilegia alpina 'Alba'	AP,B,C,P,SC
Aquilegia atrata	AP,B,C,CG,G,JE,SA,SC, SG
Aquilegia atrata 'Carl Ziepke'	B
Aquilegia atropurpurea	SG
Aquilegia baikalensis	AP,SC,SG
Aquilegia 'Ballerina'	B,P
Aquilegia barnebyi	AP,B,P
Aquilegia 'Beidermeier'	BS,CG,JE,KS,S,SA
Aquilegia bernardii	CG
Aquilegia bertolonii	AP,B,C,FH,G,PM,SC,SG
Aquilegia borodinii	SG
Aquilegia brevicalcarata	P
Aquilegia buergeriana	AP,B,CC,P,RS,SC
Aquilegia caerulea	AP,B,C,G,JE,SC,SW,T
Aquilegia caerulea 'Blue Star'	JE,SA
Aquilegia caerulea 'Crimson Star'	B,C,JE,SA
Aquilegia caerulea 'Koralle'	B,JE,SA
Aquilegia caerulea 'Snow Queen'	B,SA,T
Aquilegia caerulea v ochroleuca	B
Aquilegia caerulea v pinetorum	B,SW
Aquilegia canadensis	AP,B,BS,C,CC,F,G,HW, JE,KS,NT,P,PR,SA,SC, SE,SW,T
Aquilegia canadensis 'Corbett'	JE
Aquilegia canadensis 'Nana'	AP,B,G,P,SC
Aquilegia 'Celestial Queen'	B
Aquilegia chrysantha	AP,B,C,CG,G,KS,MA,SA, SC,SW
Aquilegia chrysantha (wild form)	JE
Aquilegia chrysantha 'Yellow Queen'	F,JE,SA
Aquilegia 'Cottage Garden' mix	P
Aquilegia 'Cream Dainty'	V
Aquilegia 'Crystal Star'	B
Aquilegia desertorum	AP,B,SC,SW
Aquilegia discolor	AP,B,C,G,P,SC,SG
Aquilegia 'Double Blue'	C
Aquilegia 'Double Pleat'	SE,T
Aquilegia 'Double Quilled Purple'	B,P
Aquilegia 'Double Rubies'	B,P
Aquilegia 'Dragonfly Hybrids'	BS,C,CL,DT,F,JE,L,R,S, SA,SC,YA
Aquilegia 'Dw Fantasy Series' s-c	T
Aquilegia einseleana	B,C,G,SA,SG
Aquilegia 'Elegantissima'	B,P
Aquilegia elegantula	AP,RS,SC,SW
Aquilegia f1 'Music Harmony'	BS,C,D,J,U
Aquilegia f1 'Music Series' mix	CL
Aquilegia f1 'Olympia'	C
Aquilegia f1 'Olympia' mix	C
Aquilegia f1 'Olympia' Red, gold	C
Aquilegia f1 'Songbird' s-c	B,CL,SE
Aquilegia flabellata	AP,B,C,CG,CT,G,SC,SG, T,V
Aquilegia flabellata 'Blue Angel'	B,JE,SA
Aquilegia flabellata 'Ministar'	B,CL,G,JE
Aquilegia flabellata nana	AP,FH,SC
Aquilegia flabellata pink	P
Aquilegia flabellata v pumila	AP,B,C,CC,CG,G,I,RS,SC
Aquilegia flabellata v pumila 'Alba'	B,G,JE,SC
Aquilegia flabellata v pumila 'Alba Fl. Pl.'	AP,B,C
Aquilegia flabellata v pumila 'Kurilensis'	B,JE
Aquilegia flabellata v pumila 'Mini-Star'	AP,BS,C,SC
Aquilegia flabellata v pumila 'Rosea'	B,SC
Aquilegia flabellata v pumila 'Selection'	B,JE
Aquilegia flab.v pum. 'Shimmering Breeze'	SE
Aquilegia flabellata v pumila 'Silver Edge'	B,P
Aquilegia flabellata 'White Angel'	SA
Aquilegia flavescens	B,SA,SG,SW
Aquilegia formosa	AP,AV,B,C,CG,G,JE,SC, SG
Aquilegia formosa v formosa	CC
Aquilegia formosa v truncata	B,SC,SW
Aquilegia fragrans	AP,B,C,CC,P,SC,T
Aquilegia glandulosa	AP,B,P,SC,SG
Aquilegia glandulosa v transsilvanica	B
Aquilegia grata	AP,B,P,SC,T
Aquilegia hyb 'Jewel Dwarf'	AP,PM
Aquilegia hyb tall	I
Aquilegia hybrida 'Dw Fairyland' mix	T
Aquilegia 'Iceberg'	P
Aquilegia 'Irish Elegance'	B,P,SE
Aquilegia 'Isabel Allen'	B
Aquilegia 'Jane Hollow'	P
Aquilegia kitaibelii	CG
Aquilegia 'Kristall'	C,JE
Aquilegia laramiensis	AP,B,SC
Aquilegia 'Long Spurred Hybrids'	D,S,SE,U
Aquilegia longissima	AP,B,CG,CT,P,SA,SC
Aquilegia 'Magpie' see William Guiness	
Aquilegia 'Mckana Giant Hybrids'	AP,BD,BS,C,CG,CO,DT, F,G,J,JE,KS,L,M,SA,SC, ST,T,TU,V,VH
Aquilegia 'Mellow Yellow'	B,P,S
Aquilegia 'Melton Rapids'	T
Aquilegia micrantha	C,SW

AQUILEGIA

Aquilegia 'Miss M.I.Huish' B
Aquilegia 'Mrs Scott Elliott's Variety' B,BS,C,CL
Aquilegia 'Nosegay' C
Aquilegia olympica AP,B,C,G,JE,P,SA,SG
Aquilegia oxysepala B,CG,SA,SG,T
Aquilegia parviflora SG
Aquilegia 'Petticoats' U
Aquilegia pink tall I
Aquilegia 'Pom-poms Crimson' B,P
Aquilegia 'Pom-poms,mix' AP,C,P
Aquilegia 'Pom-poms Rose' B,P
Aquilegia 'Pom-poms Violet' B,P
Aquilegia 'Pom-poms,White & Pink' B,P
Aquilegia pyrenaica AP,B,CG,G,SC,SG
Aquilegia 'Red Hobbit' C
Aquilegia rockii ex KGB176 I
Aquilegia 'Roman Bronze' B,P
Aquilegia 'Royal Purple' P
Aquilegia 'Ruby Port' T
Aquilegia saximontana AP,B,FH,G,SC,SG
Aquilegia 'Schneekonigen' HH
Aquilegia schokleyi G,SG
Aquilegia scopularium AP,FH,RS,SC,SG
Aquilegia scopularium perplexans SG
Aquilegia secundiflora C,RS
Aquilegia sibirica B,CG,SG
Aquilegia 'Silver Edge' P
Aquilegia skinneri B,F,P,SA,SE,SW,T
Aquilegia 'Snow Queen' T
Aquilegia 'Snowlight White' T
Aquilegia sp AP,RS,SC,SW
Aquilegia sp 'Double White' PM
Aquilegia sp mix, cultivars & forms BL,C,PA
Aquilegia 'Star Blue' B,BS,KS
Aquilegia 'Star Crimson' BS
Aquilegia 'Star Gold' B
Aquilegia 'Star' mix BS,F,KI
Aquilegia 'Star Red' AP,B,BS,KS,SC,T
Aquilegia 'Star White' B,BS,KS
Aquilegia 'Star Yellow' SE,T
Aquilegia 'Strawberry Ice-cream' B,P
Aquilegia 'Sweet Lemon Drops' P
Aquilegia 'Sweet Surprise' B,P
Aquilegia thalictrifolia AP,CG,G,SC,SG
Aquilegia 'The Bride' B,P
Aquilegia triternata AP,B,P,SC,SW
Aquilegia vernardii SA
Aquilegia verv. 'Woodside Blue' (V) B,P
Aquilegia vervaeneana 'Woodside Red' (V) P
Aquilegia vervaeneana 'Woodside' (V) AP,CG,I,LG,SC,SE,V
Aquilegia verv. 'Woodside White' (V) B,P
Aquilegia viridiflora AP,B,C,F,G,KS,LG,SC,
SG,T
Aquilegia viridiflora 'Chocolate Soldier' SE,V
Aquilegia vulgaris AP,B,BS,C,FH,G,HW,JE,
LG,RS,SA,SC,SG,V
Aquilegia vulgaris 'Adelaide Addison' AP,B,SC
Aquilegia vulgaris 'Alba' AP,F,JE,SA,SC
Aquilegia vulgaris 'Altrosa' JE
Aquilegia vulgaris 'Anemonaeflora' JE,SA
Aquilegia vulgaris 'Black Barlow' C,SA
Aquilegia vulgaris 'Blue Barlow' C,SA
Aquilegia vulgaris 'Brno' B
Aquilegia vulgaris 'Christa Barlow' C,SA
Aquilegia vulgaris dk purple E
Aquilegia vulgaris fl.pl C,SC

Aquilegia vulgaris 'Gisela Powell' B
Aquilegia vulgaris 'Grandmother's Garden' JE,T
Aquilegia vulgaris 'Heidi' BS,JE,KI
Aquilegia vulgaris light pink E
Aquilegia vulgaris 'Michael Strominger' B,T
Aquilegia vulgaris 'Munstead White' C,P
Aquilegia vulgaris 'Nivea' AP,B,HH
Aquilegia vulgaris 'Nora Barlow' w.a.
Aquilegia vulgaris 'Nora Barlow' mix BS,F,J,KS,SE
Aquilegia vulg 'Nora Barlow's Relatives' C
Aquilegia v. 'Old-fash. Granny's Bonnets' C
Aquilegia v. pale mauve/blue bicolour C
Aquilegia vulgaris 'Patricia Zavros' B
Aquilegia vulgaris 'Red Giant' CT
Aquilegia vulgaris 'Rose Barlow' C,SA
Aquilegia vulgaris 'Ruby Port' B,C,JE,T
Aquilegia vulgaris semi-dbl maroon FH
Aquilegia vulgaris semi-dbl pink FH
Aquilegia vulgaris v clematiflora see stellata
Aquilegia vulgaris v stellata AP,SC
Aquilegia vulgaris v stellata 'Alba' P
Aquilegia vulgaris v stellata Fl.pl. s-c B,P
Aquilegia vulgaris v stellata 'Hybrids' JE
Aquilegia vulgaris v stellata s-c B,P,SA
Aquilegia vulgaris vervaeneana blue PM
Aquilegia vulgaris vervaeneana group AP,B,BS,C,DT,F,FH,HH
,J,KS
Aquilegia vulgaris vervaeneana pink B,FH,PM
Aquilegia vulgaris 'White Barlow' SA
Aquilegia vulgaris 'William Guiness' B,BD,BS,C,CT,D,DT,F,I,
KS,L,LG,P,PM,SC,SE,
T,V
Aquilegia vulgaris 'Yellow Hammer' CT
Aquilegia 'Westfield' C
Aquilegia x cultorum 'Blue Shades' JE
Aquilegia x cultorum 'Heavenly Blue' JE
Aquilegia x cultorum 'Maxi' JE
Aquilegia x cultorum 'Red Hobbit' JE
Aquilegia x cultorum 'Spezialrasse' JE
Aquilegia x hybrida SG
Aquilegia yabeana B,G,SA
Arabidopsis thaliana B,BS
Arabis alpina AP,B,BS,JE,KI,SA,SC,
SG,T
Arabis alpina 'Pink Pearl' J,S,T,V
Arabis alpina pure white BS,J,S,V,YA
Arabis alpina 'Snow Cap' BD,BS,C,D,L
Arabis alpina 'Snowdrop' CL
Arabis alpina 'Snowpeak' T
Arabis alpina v rosea BD,BS,C,CL,SU,T
Arabis androsacea AP,G,SC
Arabis aubrietoides AP,B,G,SC
Arabis blepharophylla AP,C,G,KS,SA,SC,SG
Arabis blepharophylla 'Frulingszauber' AP,B,BS,C,CL,D,JE,L
Arabis blepharophylla 'Rote Sensation' JE,R,S,SE,V
Arabis blepharophylla 'Spring Charm'
see 'Fruhlingszauber'
Arabis bryoides B,SC
Arabis caucasica B,T
Arabis caucasica compacta 'Schneehaube' JE
Arabis caucasica compacta 'Snowball' B,JE,SA
Arabis caucasica 'Compinkie' B,BS,C,CO,D,JE,KI,ST,
YA
Arabis caucasica 'Rosea' B,L,SA
Arabis caucasica 'Rosea,la Fraicheur' B,JE
Arabis cypria SG

29

ARABIS

Arabis hirsuta	B,G,SG	Arctotis gumbletonii	B,SI
Arabis lyallii	C,JE	Arctotis hirsuta	C,SI
Arabis procurrens	B	Arctotis hirsuta orange	B
Arabis procurrens 'Glacier'	JE	Arctotis laevis	B,SI
Arabis pumila	AP,B,G,SC	Arctotis revoluta	B
Arabis scopoliana	JE	Arctotis sp mix	SI
Arabis soyerii	G,SG	Arctotis sp white	SI
Arabis soyerii ssp jaquinii	B	Arctotis special mix	S
Arabis stelleri v japonica	AP,SG	Arctotis stoechadifolia see venusta	
Arabis stricta	SG	Arctotis venusta	B,C,G,SE,SG,SI
Arabis turrita	B,G,SG	Arctotis venusta v grandis	SG
Arachis hypogaea	B,C,SA,SE,V	Ardisia crenata	B,G,SA,SG
Arachis hypogaea 'Tennessee Red'	B	Ardisia crenata 'Porcelain'	B
Arachis pintoi	B	Ardisia crispa	B,C,HA,O,SA
Arachnoides adiantiformis	B	Ardisia crispa 'Alba'	SA
Arachnoides standishii	G	Ardisia escallonoides	CG
Aralia californica	B,G,JE	Ardisia humilis	B,HA,O
Aralia cashmeriana	JE,SA	Ardisia humilis 'Aurea'	B
Aralia chinensis see elata		Ardisia littoralis	B
Aralia continentalis	B	Ardisia macrocarpa	B
Aralia cordata	JE,SA,SG	Ardisia polycephala	B
Aralia elata	A,B,C,N,SA	Ardisiandra wettsteinii	CG
Aralia elata v palmata	B	Areca catechu	B,O,SA
Aralia nudicaulis	SG	Areca ipot	O
Aralia racemosa	B,C,JE,PR,SG	Areca triandra	B,O
Aralia sp CNW373	X	Areca vestiaria	B
Aralia spinosa	B	Arenaria aculeata	B
Araucaria angustifolia	B	Arenaria aggregata	B
Araucaria araucana	B,C,CG,HA,N,SA	Arenaria balearica	AP,C,I,SC,SG
Araucaria bidwillii	B,CG,HA,O,SA	Arenaria blepharophylla v parviflora	B
Araucaria columnaris	B,O	Arenaria congesta v liphophila	SG
Araucaria cunninghamii	B,HA,O,SA	Arenaria erinacea	C
Araucaria heterophylla	B,HA,N,O,SA,SH	Arenaria glomerata	B
Araujia sericofera	AP,B,C,CG,SC,T	Arenaria gracilis	B,JE,SG
Arbutus andrachne	B,SA	Arenaria graminea	B
Arbutus arizonica	B,SW	Arenaria grandiflora	AP,B,SC,SG
Arbutus menziesii	B,C,SA	Arenaria hookeri	B
Arbutus menziesii 'Madrona'	N	Arenaria kingii	G,SG
Arbutus unedo	A,B,C,CG,HA,O,RE,SA,T	Arenaria ledebouriana	B
Arbutus xalapensis	B,SA,SW	Arenaria longifolia	SG
Archontophoenix alexandrae	B,C,HA,O,SA	Arenaria lychnidea	B
Archontophoenix alexandrae v beatricea	B	Arenaria montana	AP,B,BD,BS,C,CO,J,JE,
Archontophoenix cunninghamiana	B,C,HA,N,O,SA		S,SA,SC,T,V
Archontophoenix cunn. 'Illawarra'	B	Arenaria norvegica	AP,SC,SG
Archontophoenix 'Mount Lewis'	O	Arenaria nuttallii	B
Arctanthemum arcticum	B,G	Arenaria procera	B,FH
Arctium lappa	B,C,CP,SG	Arenaria procera ssp glabra	B,CG,JE,SG
Arctium minus	B,SG	Arenaria purparescens	AP,C,JE,SC,SG
Arctogeron gramineum	SG	Arenaria recurva ssp oreina	B
Arctopus echinatus	B,SI	Arenaria serpyllifolia	SG
Arctostaphylos alpina	C	Arenaria serpyllifolia ssp leptocladus	CG
Arctostaphylos glauca	CG,SA	Arenaria stricta	B,PR
Arctostaphylos manzanita	A,B,SA	Arenaria tmolea	B,SC
Arctostaphylos nevadensis	B,C	Arenga ambong	O
Arctostaphylos patula	B,C,SA	Arenga caudata	B,O,SA
Arctostaphylos pungens	B	Arenga engleri	B,O,SA
Arctostaphylos uva-ursi	A,B,C,CG,FH,JE,SA	Arenga pinnata	B,O,SA
Arctostaphylos viscida	B	Arenga tremula	B,O,SA
Arctotheca calendula	B,SG,SI	Arenga undulatifolia	O
Arctotis acaulis	B,C,SI,V	Arenifera pillansii	B
Arctotis acaulis 'Harlequin New Hybrids'	BS,C,D,J,KI,TU	Arequipa erectocylindrica	B
Arctotis acaulis 'New Hybrids'	B,DT,T	Arequipa weingartiana	B
Arctotis aspera	B	Argemone glauca	B
Arctotis auriculata	B,C,SI	Argemone grandiflora	B
Arctotis fastuosa	B,BD,BS,C,F,SI,T	Argemone hispida	B
Arctotis fastuosa v alba 'Zulu Prince'	B,DT,KS,SE,T,V	Argemone mexicana	B,C,G,SG

ARGEMONE

Argemone mexicana 'White Lustre'	B,C
Argemone mexicana 'Yellow Lustre'	B,C,T
Argemone munita	B
Argemone platyceras	G
Argemone platyceras 'Silver Charm'	B
Argemone pleiacantha	B
Argemone polyanthemos	B,T,V
Argemone squarrosa ssp glabrata	T
Argyranthemum frutescens	B
Argyranthemum frutescens 'Whity'	B
Argyreia nervosa	B,C,CP,SA
Argyroderma congregatum	B,SI
Argyroderma crateriforme	B,SI
Argyroderma delaetii	GC,SI,Y
Argyroderma delaetii 'Aureum'	B,SI,Y
Argyroderma delaetii f delaettii	SI
Argyroderma delaetii hybrids	B
Argyroderma delaetii 'Roseum'	B,SI,Y
Argyroderma fissum	B,SI,Y
Argyroderma fissum 'Brevipes'	B
Argyroderma fissum 'Littorale'	B
Argyroderma framesii	B,SI
Argyroderma framesii 'Hallii'	B,SI
Argyroderma framesii 'Minus'	B,BC
Argyroderma patens	B,SI,Y
Argyroderma pearsonii	B,GC,SI,Y
Argyroderma pearsonii 'Luckhoffii'	B,SI
Argyroderma ringens	B,SI,Y
Argyroderma sp mix	C
Argyroderma subalbum	B,SI,Y
Argyroderma subalbum 'Villetii'	B,BC
Argyroderma testiculare	B,SI
Argyrolobium pilosum	B
Argyrolobium zanonii	B
Ariocarpus agavoides	B,Y
Ariocarpus fissuratus	B,BC,CH,GC,Y
Ariocarpus fissuratus v hintonii	B,BC
Ariocarpus fissuratus v intermedius	B
Ariocarpus fissuratus v lloydii	B
Ariocarpus furfuraceus	CH,B,Y
Ariocarpus furfuraceus v rostratus	B,Y
Ariocarpus kotschoubeyanus	B,CH,Y
Ariocarpus kotschoubeyanus v albiflorus	B,Y
Ariocarpus kotsch.v macdowelli	B,BC
Ariocarpus lloydii	CH
Ariocarpus retusus	B,Y
Ariocarpus retusus v elongatus	B,GC,Y
Ariocarpus trigonus	B,CH,Y
Ariocarpus trigonus v elongatus	B,GC,Y
Arisaema amurense	AP,C,G,LG,PM,SC,SG
Arisaema anatolicum	MN
Arisaema ciliatum	G,N,SC
Arisaema concinnum	G,B
Arisaema consanguineum	B
Arisaema flavum	AP,B,C,CC,G,I,LG,MN, SC
Arisaema griffithii	B,CC,FH,G
Arisaema jacquemontii	AP,B,G,SC
Arisaema kishidai	B
Arisaema nepenthoides	C
Arisaema propinquum	B,CC
Arisaema ringens	AP,B,G,SC
Arisaema serratum	B,CG,G
Arisaema sikokianum	B
Arisaema sp	SC,SG
Arisaema speciosum	C,CC,PM

Arisaema tortuosum	AP,B,C
Arisaema triphyllum	AP,B,G,JE,SA,SC
Arisaema yamatense	B
Arisarum proboscideum	AP,B
Arisarum vulgare	B
Aristea africana	B,SA,SI
Aristea angolensis	B,SI
Aristea cognata	SI
Aristea confusa	B,SI
Aristea ecklonii	AP,B,C,G,SC,SG,SI
Aristea ensifolia	SI
Aristea juncifolia	B
Aristea lugens	B,SI
Aristea macrocarpa	B,SI
Aristea major	B,C,SI
Aristea monticola	B,SI
Aristea pusilla ssp pusilla	B
Aristea sp	SI
Aristea spiralis	B,SA,SI
Aristea woodii	B,SG,SI
Aristida hystrix	B
Aristida purpurea	B
Aristida setacea	B
Aristolochia argentina	CG
Aristolochia baetica	B
Aristolochia bodemae	CG
Aristolochia bracteolata	B
Aristolochia californica	C
Aristolochia clematitis	B,C,CG,G,JE,SG
Aristolochia debilis	B
Aristolochia fimbriata	B,CG
Aristolochia gibbosa	CG
Aristolochia grandiflora	B,CG
Aristolochia imbriata	CG
Aristolochia indica	B
Aristolochia kaempferi	B
Aristolochia labiata	B,CG
Aristolochia littoralis	AP,B,C,CG,HA,SA,SG
Aristolochia macrophylla	B,CG,SA
Aristolochia maxima	B
Aristolochia peucinervis	CG
Aristolochia pistolochia	B
Aristolochia ringens	B
Aristolochia rotunda	B
Aristolochia sempervirens	B,CG
Aristolochia tomentosa	B
Aristolochia trilobata	B
Aristolochia watsonii	B
Aristotelia fruticosa	B,SS
Aristotelia peduncularis	B
Aristotelia serrata	B,SS
Armatocereus arboreus	B
Armatocereus matucanensis	B
Armeniaca sibirica	SG
Armeria alliacea	AP,B,G,JE,SA,SC,SG
Armeria alliacea v leucantha	B,FH,G,JE,SA,SG
Armeria alpina	AP,B
Armeria filicaulis	SG
Armeria formosa hybrids	BS,C,L,S,SA,T
Armeria giraldii	PM
Armeria hybrida 'Ornament'	BS,C,CL,G,J,JE,KI,U
Armeria juniperifolia	AP,B,G
Armeria juniperifolia 'Bevan's Variety'	AP,PM,SC,SG
Armeria juniperifolia x maritima	I
Armeria maritima	AP,B,C,CO,D,R,SC,SG
Armeria maritima 'Alba'	AP,B,BD,BS,CL,D,G,JE,

ARMERIA

Armeria maritima alpina	PM,RS,SA,SC
	SG
Armeria maritima 'Carlux Rose'	B
Armeria maritima 'Carlux White'	B
Armeria maritima 'Pink Lusitanica'	B,JE
Armeria maritima 'Sea Spray'	U
Armeria maritima 'Splendens'	B,BD,BS,CL,JE,L,SA,SU
Armeria maritima ssp sibirica	SG
Armeria maritima var laucheana	AP,C
Armeria mix dwarf	S
Armeria morisii	SG
Armeria pseudarmeria	AP,FH,G,JE,SC,V
Armeria pseudarmeria 'Bee's Hybrids'	AP,B,C,SC,SE,T
Armeria pseudarmeria hybs	B,BS,KI
Armeria pungens	G,SC,SG
Armeria setacea	SG
Armeria sp ex Patagonia	PM
Armeria tweedyi	AP,B,P,PM,SC
Armillaria mellea d.m.p	B
Arnica alpina	B,G,I
Arnica chamissonis	BS,CG,G,JE,SC
Arnica cordifolia	B,RS
Arnica foliosa	SG
Arnica latifolia	B,SC
Arnica lessingii	FH,SC
Arnica mollis	CG,SG
Arnica montana	AP,B,BS,C,CG,G,JE,KI, SA,SC,SG,T
Arnica nevadensis	B,SC
Arnica parryi	B
Arnica unalascensis v tschonoskyi	CC
Aronia arbutifolia	RH,SA
Aronia 'Brilliant'	B
Aronia melanocarpa	B,RH,SA,SG
Aronia x prunifolia	B,RH,SA
Arrhenatherum elatius	B
Arrhenatherum e. ssp bulbosum 'V'	B
Arrojadoa albiflora	B
Arrojadoa reflexa	BC
Arrojadoa rhodantha	B,CH,Y
Artabotrys hexapetalus	B,CG
Artemisia abrotanum	B
Artemisia absinthium	B,C,JE,KS,SA,SG
Artemisia afra	B,C,SI
Artemisia alba ssp saxatilis	B
Artemisia annua	B,C,CP,KS,T
Artemisia arborescens	AP,B
Artemisia arborescens 'Powis Castle'	B
Artemisia assoana	I
Artemisia californica	B
Artemisia campestris	G
Artemisia campestris ssp borealis	B
Artemisia campestris ssp campestris	B
Artemisia campestris ssp maritima	B
Artemisia cana	C,SA
Artemisia canariensis	CG
Artemisia caucasica	B
Artemisia chamaemelifolia	B,CG,G,SA
Artemisia douglasiana	B
Artemisia dracunculus	B,JE,KS,SG
Artemisia filifolia	B
Artemisia frigida	B,SG
Artemisia genipi	B,CG,JE
Artemisia glacialis	C,CG,SC
Artemisia glauca	SG
Artemisia gmelinii	B

Artemisia gmelinii 'Viridis'	B
Artemisia herba-alba	B
Artemisia lactiflora 'Green Form'	B,PA
Artemisia lactiflora 'Guizo' group	G,P
Artemisia ludoviciana	B,C,JE,PR
Artemisia monosperma	B
Artemisia mutellina	C,JE
Artemisia nova	B
Artemisia pontica	B
Artemisia pycnocephala	B
Artemisia rupestris	SG
Artemisia thuscula	B
Artemisia umbelliformis	B,CG,G
Artemisia valesiaca	C
Artemisia viridis	B
Artemisia vulgaris	B,CP,JE,SG
Arthropodium candidum	AP,AU,B,G,PM,SC,SS
Arthropodium candidum purpureum	HH
Arthropodium capillipes	SA
Arthropodium cirratum	AP,AU,B,C,G,SA,SC,SG, SS
Arthropodium milleflorum	AP,AU,HA,SC
Arthropodium sp	AU
Artocarpus altilis	B
Artocarpus heterophyllus	B
Artocarpus hyb	B
Artocarpus lakoocha	B
Artocarpus odoratissimus	B
Arum concinnatum	B,C,G,MN,SC
Arum concinnatum NL1234 Iran	MN
Arum creticum	AP,C,G,JE,SA,SC
Arum dioscoridis	B,JE
Arum dioscoridis S.L570/1 Turkey	MN
Arum hygrophilum	B
Arum italicum	B,G,JE,SA,SC,SG
Arum italicum marmoratum	AP,G,I,N
Arum italicum pictum	AP,SC
Arum italicum S.F336 Morocco	MN
Arum italicum ssp italicum	B,PM
Arum maculatum	B,C,CG,JE,SA,SC,SG
Arum orientale	B,G
Arum orientale orientale	SG
Arum pictum	B,C,FH,P,MN,SC,SG
Arum purpureospathum	AP,B,SC
Arum purpureospathum PB49 Crete	MN
Arum rupicola v rupicola	B
Aruncus aethusifolius	AP,B,BS,C,G,I,JE,RH,SA, SC,SG
Aruncus asiaticus	SG
Aruncus chinensis	SA
Aruncus dioicus	AP,B,BS,C,G,JE,KI,SA, SC,SG,T,V
Aruncus dioicus kneiffii	SG
Aruncus sinensis	B,JE
Aruncus sinensis 'Zweiweltenkind'	B,JE
Aruncus sylvester see A. dioicus	
Aruncus vulgaris	SG
Arundo donax	B
Arytera divaricata	O
Asarina scandens	AP,B,SC,SE,V
Asarina scandens 'Amethyst Pink'	SE
Asarina scandens 'Bride's White'	T
Asarina scandens 'Jewel MIx'	T
Asarina scandens 'Joan Loraine'	B,BD
Asarina scandens 'Mystic Rose'	B,BD,SE
Asarina scandens 'Pink'	B

ASARINA

Asarina scandens 'Pink Ice'	I,T
Asarina scandens 'Sky Blue'	B
Asarina scandens 'Snowwhite'	B
Asarina scandens 'Summer Snow'	BD
Asarina scandens 'Violet Glow'	SE
Asarina sp	F,SG
Asarum canadense	B
Asarum caudatum	B,JE,SG
Asarum europaeum	B,C,G,JE
Asarum lemmonii	SG
Asarum shuttleworthii	JE
Asclepias albens	B,SI
Asclepias amplexicaulis	B
Asclepias asperula	B
Asclepias brevipes	SI
Asclepias burchellii	B
Asclepias cancellata	B,SI
Asclepias crispa	SI
Asclepias curassavica	AP,B,BS,C,CP,G,J,JE,KI,
	KS,SA,SG,V
Asclepias curassavica aff 'Rejalgar Rojo'	B
Asclepias curassavica 'Red Butterfly'	C
Asclepias curassavica 'Serenade'	B
Asclepias curassavica 'Silky Gold'	B
Asclepias eriocarpa	B
Asclepias 'Gay Butterflies'	B,JE,SA,T
Asclepias hirtella	PR
Asclepias incarnata	B,BS,CC,G,JE,NT,PR,SA,
	SC
Asclepias incarnata 'Cinderella'	U,V
Asclepias incarnata 'Iceballet'	AP,C,JE
Asclepias incarnata 'Soulmate'	C
Asclepias purpurascens	C,G
Asclepias sp	SI
Asclepias speciosa	B
Asclepias sullivantii	PR
Asclepias syriaca	B,C,CC,CG,CP,G,JE,PR,
	SA,SG
Asclepias tuberosa	AP,B,BS,C,CP,HW,JE,PR,
	SA,SC,SW
Asclepias tuberosa 'Hello Yellow'	JE
Asclepias verticillata	B,JE,PR
Asclepias viridiflora	B
Asimina triloba	A,B,C,G,N,SA
Asimina triloba 'Improved'	B
Askidiosperma chartaceum	SI
Askidiosperma esterhuyseniae	B,SI
Askidiosperma paniculatum	B,SI
Aspalathus elliptica	B,SA,SI
Aspalathus nivea	B,SI
Aspalathus sp	SI
Asparagus cooperi	SA
Asparagus davuricuus	SG
Asparagus deflexus scandens	B,SA
Asparagus densiflorus	B
Asparagus densiflorus 'Cwebe'	B
Asparagus densiflorus 'Mazeppa'	B
Asparagus densiflorus 'Meyeri'	B,BS,C,CL,HA,SA,V
Asparagus densiflorus 'Sprengeri'	B,BD,BS,C,CL,HA,L,SA,
	V,YA
Asparagus dens. 'Sprengeri Compacta'	B,SA
Asparagus dens. 'Sprengeri Variegatus'	B,BS,L
Asparagus falcatus	B,SA
Asparagus ferns mix	T
Asparagus hybridus	B
Asparagus laricinus	B

Asparagus medeloides	HA
Asparagus myricladus	SA
Asparagus officinalis	CG,SG
Asparagus officinalis 'Spitzenschleier'	C,JE
Asparagus plumosus see setaceus	
Asparagus pseudoscaber	B
Asparagus racemosus	B,SA
Asparagus retrofractus	B
Asparagus sarmentosus	B
Asparagus scandens	C
Asparagus setaceus	B
Asparagus setaceus 'Nanus'	B,BD,BS,C,CL,KI,L,S,SA,
	ST,V,YA
Asparagus setaceus 'Pyramidalis'	B,SA
Asparagus setaceus 'Robustus'	B
Asparagus sp	SI
Asparagus umbellatus	B
Asparagus verticillatus	B,C,G,JE,SA
Asparagus virgatus	B,SA
Asperula orientalis	B,BS,C,J,KI,KS,S,SG,T,V
Asperula orientalis 'Blue Mist'	U
Asperula taurina	B
Asperula tinctoria	B,G
Asphodeline liburnica	AP,B,C,G,JE,LG,SA,SC
Asphodeline lutea	AP,B,BS,C,CH,CL,G,JE,
	KI,MN,PA,PM,SA,SC,
	SG
Asphodeline taurica	B,JE
Asphodelus acaulis	B
Asphodelus acaulis S.F. 156 Morocco	MN
Asphodelus aestivus see microcarpus	
Asphodelus albus	AP,B,C,CG,G,JE,LG,SA,
	SC,SG,T
Asphodelus cerasiferus	AP,C,SG
Asphodelus fistulosus see tenuifolius	
Asphodelus microcarpus	AP,B,G,JE,SC,SG
Asphodelus ramosus	AP,B,CG,G,JE,MN,SC
Asphodelus tenuifolius	SG
Asplenium australasicum	B,HA
Asplenium bulbiferum	B,SG
Asplenium dimorphum	SG
Asplenium marinum	B
Asplenium nidus	B,C,SA
Asplenium ruta-muraria	B
Asplenium scolopendrum f marginatum	SG
Asplenium septentrionale	B,CG,G
Asplenium trichomanes	AP,B,CG,G
Asplenium viride	B,G
Asrtophytum capricornis	B,CH,Y
Astartea ambigua	AU,B,O,SA
Astartea fascicularis	AP,B,C,SA,SS
Astelia fragrans	B,SS
Astelia linearis	B,SS
Astelia nervosa	AP,B,SA,SS
Astelia nervosa v chathamica	B,SA
Astelia nivicola	B,SS
Aster 'All Change'	T
Aster 'Allsorts'	F
Aster alpigenus	U
Aster 'Alpine Fairy Mix'	U
Aster alpinus	AP,B,BS,C,CG,CL,F,FH,
	G,I,JE,L,SA,SC,SG,ST,
	T,V
Aster alpinus 'Albus'	AP,B,FH,G,JE,SC,SG
Aster alpinus 'Dark Beauty'	C,JE
Aster alpinus fl.pl 'Marchenland'	AP,C,JE

33

ASTER

Aster alpinus 'Goliath'	B,FH,JE,SA
Aster alpinus 'Happy End'	C,G,JE
Aster alpinus lilac	FH
Aster alpinus mix	BD,JE,KI
Aster alpinus 'Rose'	AP,B,SA
Aster alpinus 'Trimix'	BS,C,CL,D,FH,J,JE,R,T
Aster alpinus v speciosus	SG
Aster alpinus 'Wartburgstern'	BS
Aster alpinus white	SA
Aster alpinus 'White Beauty'	C
Aster altaicus	SG
Aster amellus	AP,B,C,CG,CO,G,JE,SA, SG
Aster amellus hyb mix	BS,JE,KI,T
Aster amellus 'Rudolf Goethe'	B,C,JE
Aster 'Andrella'	D,T
Aster 'Apricot Delight'	S
Aster 'Apricot Giant'	F
Aster azureus	G,JE,PR,SA
Aster bakeranus	B,SI
Aster bellidiastrum	CG
Aster bigelovii	JE
Aster bigelovii 'Happiness'	T
Aster 'Blue Magic'	U
Aster 'Blue Skies'	T
Aster 'Burpeeana'	BS
Aster 'Candy Stripe' mix	BS,DT
Aster 'Carousel' mix	BS,KI
Aster 'Carpet Ball' mix	T,VH
Aster chinensis	B,DT,F
Aster 'Chrysanthemum Fl' mix	S
Aster ciliolatus	SG
Aster 'Colour Carpet'	BS,DT,F,J,L
Aster 'Colour Star'	L
Aster cordifolius	B,CG,G,PR
Aster cordifolius ssp sagittifolius	B
Aster 'Crimson Sunset'	T
Aster 'Cut Flower' mix	D,DT,M,T
Aster 'Devon Riviera' mix	S
Aster divaricatus	AP,B,CG,G,JE,NT
Aster drummondii	PR
Aster dubius v glabratus	B
Aster dumosus	B
Aster 'Dwarf Bedding' s-c	D
Aster 'Dwarf Queen'	BS,CO,KI,M,ST,U
Aster 'Dwarf Starlet'	U
Aster 'Early Charm'	BS
Aster ericoides	B,G,I,PR
Aster falcatus	SG
Aster farreri	AP,B,CG,JE,SC
Aster flaccidus	AP,B,HH,SC
Aster 'Florette Champagne'	T
Aster 'Germannia'	D
Aster 'Giant' single	BS,KI,ST,SU,TU,VH
Aster 'Giants of California'	BS,CO,F,KI,ST,TU,U
Aster grandiflorus	B
Aster 'Gusford Supreme'	T
Aster 'Harz' mix	BS
Aster himalaicus	AP,CG,SC,SG
Aster hyb 'Crego Giants'	B
Aster 'Koningin der Hallen'	V
Aster laevis	B,G,JE,PR,SG
Aster lanceolatus ssp simplex	B
Aster lateriflorus	B,CG,G,PR
Aster 'Lg Fl Imp' mix	BS
Aster linariifolius	B

Aster linosyris	B,C,G,JE
Aster 'Love Me'	U
Aster 'Lutins' mix	BD,BS
Aster macrophyllus	B,G,JE,NT,SC
Aster 'Madeleine' mix	BS,CL
Aster 'Matador' mix	BS,CL,KI,SU,YA
Aster 'Meteor'	BS,U
Aster modestus	B,SG
Aster 'Moraketa'	SE,T
Aster nepalensis	FH
Aster 'Nova'	D
Aster novae-angliae	B,BD,G,HW,J,JE,PR,V
Aster novae-angliae 'Autumn Splendour'	CL
Aster novae-angliae 'Benary's Comp.'	C,F,J,JE
Aster novae-angliae 'Composition Mix'	DT,T,U
Aster novae-angliae 'Dr Eckener'	B
Aster novae-angliae lge fl	S
Aster novae-angliae 'Lucida'	B
Aster n.-a. 'Marshall's Autumn Flowering'	M
Aster novae-angliae 'September Rubin'	B,JE
Aster novi-belgii	G,JE,KS,SG,SU
Aster oblongifolius	NT
Aster oolentangiensis	B
Aster 'Operetta' mix	T
Aster 'Opus'	SE
Aster 'Paeony Pulling'	L
Aster 'Pastel' mix	T
Aster patens	B,G,NT
Aster 'Petite Bedders' mix	YA
Aster petite mix	S
Aster pilosus	B,PR
Aster pilosus v demotus	B
Aster 'Pink Magic'	U
Aster pinnatisectus	SG
Aster 'Pot 'n' Patio'	SE
Aster 'Powderpuffs' mix	BS,L,YA
Aster prenanthoides	PR
Aster 'Prinette' mix	S
Aster 'Prinette Pink'	T
Aster 'Pruhonicer' dw	T
Aster ptarmicoides	B,C,CC,JE,KS,PR,T
Aster puniceus	G,JE,PR,SG
Aster pyrenaeus	AP,JE,SC,SG
Aster 'Queen of the Market'	BS,L
Aster 'Ribbon' mix	BS,KI
Aster 'Riviera'	F
Aster 'Roundabout' mix	CL
Aster scopulorum	B
Aster sedifolius	B
Aster sedifolius ssp canus	B
Aster 'Serene' Light Blue	C
Aster 'Serene' Rose	C
Aster sericeus	B,PR
Aster sibiricus	B,G,JE,SG
Aster sinensis mix	S
Aster sinensis super mix	S
Aster 'Single Giant Mix'	BS,J,U,V
Aster sp & hyb mix	T
Aster squamatus	CG
Aster 'Starburst'	U
Aster 'Starlet' mix	BS,CO,KI
Aster 'Starwort'	J
Aster subcaeruleus	SG
Aster subcaeruleus 'Lavender Star'	C
Aster subspicatus	SC,SG
Aster tataricus	SG

ASTER

Aster 'Teisa Stars'	F,J,S
Aster thomsonii	G,SG
Aster tibeticus	SG
Aster tibeticus v albus	SG
Aster 'Tiger Paw' mix	BD,BS,D,SE
Aster tongolensis	AP,B,G,SA,SC,SG
Aster tongolensis 'Dunkelviolett'	C
Aster tongolensis 'Wartburgstern'	G,JE,KI
Aster tripolium	B
Aster tripolium ssp polonius	B
Aster 'Truffaunt's Paeony Mix'	DT
Aster uliginosus	SG
Aster umbellatus	B,C,G,JE,PR
Aster undulatus	NT
Aster vahlii	AU,SC
Aster x frikartii	AP,AV,G,PA,SC
Asteridea athrixioides	B
Asteridea chaetopoda	B
Asteridea pulverulenta	B
Asteriscus graveolens	B
Asteriscus maritimus	AP,PM,SC
Asterogyne martiana	B,RE
Asteromyrtus magnifica	B
Asters & Stripes	SE
Astilbe biternata	JE
Astilbe chinensis	CG,JE,RH,SG
Astilbe chinensis japonica hyb	JE
Astilbe chinensis v davidii	G,JE,SG
Astilbe chinensis v pumila	B,BS,C,CO,G,JE,KI,SG, SU,T
Astilbe chinensis v taquettii hyb	C,CG,JE,RH
Astilbe chinensis v taquettii 'Superba'	B,C,P
Astilbe grandis	SG
Astilbe koreana	SG
Astilbe microphylla	SG
Astilbe myriantha	JE,SG
Astilbe simplicifolia mix	JE
Astilbe sp AC1262	X
Astilbe sp China	SG
Astilbe sp CNW1225	X
Astilbe thunbergii v congesta	CG,SG
Astilbe x arendsii 'Bunter Zauber'	JE
Astilbe x arendsii 'Garden Delight'	J,SE,T,V
Astilbe x arendsii hybrids mix	D,S
Astilbe x arendsii mix	BD,BS,C,CL,DT,L
Astilbe x arendsii 'New Hybrids'	B
Astilbe x arendsii pink	JE
Astilbe x arendsii red	JE
Astilbe x arendsii 'Roman Dancers'	F
Astilbe x arendsii 'Showstar'	B,C,CL,DT,JE,YA
Astilboides tabularis	AP,B,BS,C,G,JE,SA,SC
Astragalus aboriginum	SG
Astragalus allochrous	B
Astragalus alopecuroides	C,G,SG
Astragalus alpinus	B,C
Astragalus amblytropis	B
Astragalus antisellii	B,CG
Astragalus arnottianus	AP,RS,SC
Astragalus australis	B
Astragalus callichrous	B
Astragalus calycosus	B
Astragalus canadensis	B,G,PR,SG
Astragalus centralpinus	B,SG
Astragalus ceratoides	SG
Astragalus cicer	B,RH,SG
Astragalus crassicarpus	B,PR

Astragalus danicus	SG
Astragalus fruticosusus	SG
Astragalus gilviflorus	B
Astragalus glycyphyllos	A,AP,B,C,G,JE,LA,SA, SC,SG
Astragalus lentiginosus	B
Astragalus macrocarpus	B
Astragalus melilotoides	SG
Astragalus membranaceus	B
Astragalus monspessulanus	AP,B,SC
Astragalus onobrychis	B,SG
Astragalus palenae	AU
Astragalus parryi	B
Astragalus penduliflorus	AP,B,SG
Astragalus plattensis	PR
Astragalus ponoensis	CG
Astragalus purpureus	C
Astragalus purshii	B
Astragalus schelichowii	SG
Astragalus simplicifolius	B
Astragalus sinicus	B
Astragalus spatulatus	B
Astragalus sulcatus	SG
Astragalus tephroides	B
Astragalus thurberi	B
Astragalus uliginosus	SG
Astragalus utahensis	AP,B,SC,SW
Astragalus varius	B
Astragalus vesicarius ssp albidus	B
Astragalus wootonii	B
Astrantia bavarica	SG
Astrantia carniolica	AP,G,RH,SC
Astrantia carniolica 'Rubra'	AP,B,JE,SC,SG
Astrantia carniolica v major	SG
Astrantia hybrida 'Rainbow'	B,JE
Astrantia major	AP,B,BS,C,CG,FH,G,I,JE, KI,PA,RH,SA,SC,SG,ST, T,V
Astrantia major 'Alba'	B,C,G,JE,SA
Astrantia major f rubra	AP,SG
Astrantia major hyb 'Rosensinfonie'	B,C,JE
Astrantia major hyb 'Ruby Cloud'	JE
Astrantia major 'Moyra Reid'	C
Astrantia major 'Primadonna'	B,BS,C,CL,JE
Astrantia major 'Rosea'	B,JE,SA
Astrantia major 'Ruby Wedding Series'	LG,P
Astrantia m.ssp involucrata 'Margery Fish'	AP,B
Astrantia major ssp involucrata 'Shaggy'	AP,P
Astrantia major ssp major	SG
Astrantia major 'Sunningdale'	I
Astrantia major 'Variegata'	G,SG
Astrantia maxima	AP,B,C,G,JE,SA,SC,SG
Astrantia maxima 'Extra Lg Fl'	T
Astrantia minor	AP,B,C,SC
Astrantia 'Rose Symphony'	SA
Astrebla lappacea	B,HA
Astrebla pectinata	B
Astridia alba	B
Astridia citrina aff	B
Astridia dinteri	B
Astridia hallii	B
Astridia hillii	B
Astridia longifolia	B
Astrocaryum alatum	B
Astrocaryum standleyanum	B
Astroloba spiralis	B

ASTROLOMA

Astroloma ciliatum	B
Astroloma epacridis	B
Astroloma foliosum	B
Astroloma glaucescens	B
Astroloma pallidum	B
Astronium graveolens	B
Astrophytum asterias	B,CH,GC,Y
Astrophytum capricornis f aureum	B
Astrophytum capricorn.v crassispinoides	B
Astrophytum capricornis v major	Y
Astrophytum capricornis v minor	B,Y
Astrophytum capricornis v niveum	B,Y
Astrophytum hyb capricornis x asterias	B
Astrophytum myriostigma	B,CH,Y
Astrophytum myriostigma v columnare	B,BC,Y
Astrophytum myriostigma v jamauvense	B
Astrophytum myriostigma v nudum	B,Y
Astrophytum myriostigma v potosinum	B,Y
Astrophytum myr. v quadricostatum	B,GC,Y
Astrophytum myr. v strongylogonum	B
Astrophytum myriostigma v tulense	B,BC
Astrophytum ornatum	B,CH
Astrophytum ornatum v glabrescens	B
Asyneuma canescens	AP,B,C,JE,P,SG
Asyneuma limonifolium ssp pestalozae	T
Atalantia monophylla	B
Atalaya hemiglauca	B,HA,O,SA
Atalaya variifolia	B
Athamanta cretensis	B,JE,SA
Athanasia crithmifolia	B,SI
Athanasia parviflora	C
Athanasia trifurcata	B,SA,SI
Atherosperma moschatum	B,SA
Athrixia fontana	SI
Athrixia phylicoides	B,SI
Athrotaxis cupressoides	B
Athrotaxis x laxifolia	B,SA
Athyrium cristatum	B
Athyrium filix-femina	AP,B,G
Atractylis phaeolepis	B
Atriplex amnicola	B,O
Atriplex amnicola 'Rivermor'	B,O
Atriplex angulata	B
Atriplex bunburyana	B,O
Atriplex canescens	A,B,C,O,SA
Atriplex cinerea	B
Atriplex codonocarpa	B
Atriplex confertifolia	B
Atriplex glabriuscula	FH
Atriplex glauca	B,O
Atriplex halimus	A,B,SA
Atriplex holocarpa	B
Atriplex hortensis	B,KS,SG,V
Atriplex hortensis 'Crimson Plume'	B
Atriplex hortensis cupreata	T
Atriplex hortensis 'Gold Plume'	B,G
Atriplex hortensis 'Green Plume'	B,BS
Atriplex hortensis 'Plumes' mix	C
Atriplex hortensis 'Red Plume'	B,BS,G,SG
Atriplex hortensis 'Rubra'	AP,RH
Atriplex hortensis v purpurea	C
Atriplex hymenelytra	B
Atriplex isatidea	B,O
Atriplex lentiformis	B,O
Atriplex lentiformis ssp breweri	B
Atriplex leucoclada	B

Atriplex lindleyi	B
Atriplex muelleri	B
Atriplex nummularia	B,C,HA,O,SA
Atriplex nummularia 'De Kock'	B
Atriplex nummularia ssp spathulata	B
Atriplex nuttallii	B,SA
Atriplex paludosa	B,O
Atriplex patula	B
Atriplex 'Pintharuka'	B
Atriplex polycarpa	B
Atriplex prostrata	B
Atriplex semibaccata	B,O
Atriplex semilunaris	B
Atriplex undulata	B,O
Atriplex vesicaria	B,HA.O
Atriplex vesicaria v sphaerocarpa	B
Atropa belladonna	B,C,CP,SG
Atropa belladonna 'Lutea'	B,C
Atropanthe sinensis	B
Atylosia scarabaeoides	B
Aubrieta 'Bengal'	BD,BS,C,JE
Aubrieta 'Campbellii'	B,DT,JE,SA
Aubrieta 'Carnival' s-c & mix'	BS
Aubrieta 'Cascade Blue'	B,JE,SA
Aubrieta 'Cascade Lilac'	BS
Aubrieta 'Cascade' mix	BD,BS,CL
Aubrieta 'Cascade Purple'	B,BD,JE,R,SA,ST,T,U
Aubrieta 'Cascade Red'	B,BD,JE,R,SA,ST,U
Aubrieta 'Cascade Rose'	B,BD
Aubrieta 'Dbl & Semi-Dbl'	YA
Aubrieta 'Double Manon'	U,V
Aubrieta f1 'Novalis Blue'	B,C,JE,YA
Aubrieta 'Galaxy Large Flowered'	YA
Aubrieta 'Graeca'	B,BS
Aubrieta 'Grandiflora'	JE
Aubrieta 'Hendersonii'	B,BS,JE,L,SA
Aubrieta 'King Blue'	J,V
Aubrieta 'King Red'	J,V
Aubrieta 'Large Flowered Hybrids' mix	BS,C,CO,FJ,L,M,S,SE,T, TU,U,V,VH
Aubrieta 'Leichtlinii'	B,BS,JE,L,KI,SA
Aubrieta 'Light Series' s-c	YA
Aubrieta 'Monarch'	DT
Aubrieta purpurea	BS,KI
Aubrieta 'Rich Rose'	F,S
Aubrieta 'Royal Blue'	B,BS,CL,J°,SA
Aubrieta 'Royal Cascade'	T
Aubrieta 'Royal' mix	BS
Aubrieta 'Royal Red'	B,BS,C,CL,JE,SA
Aubrieta 'Royal Violet'	B,BS,CL,JE,KI,SA
Aubrieta 'Semi-Dbl'	T
Aubrieta 'Semi-Double Flowered'	D
Aubrieta 'Spring Charm'	D
Aubrieta 'Spring Falls'	KI,ST
Aubrieta 'Whitewell Gem'	B,BS,CG,JE,L,SA
Aubrieta x cultorum	AP,B,CG,SA,SC,SU
Aucuba japonica	B,C,G,SA
Aucuba japonica variegata	SA
Augea capensis	B,SI
Aulacospermum anomalum	SG
Aulax cancellata	B,O,SI
Aulax pallasii	B,SI
Aulax umbellata	B,O,SI
Aureolaria grandiflora	B
Aureolaria virginica	B
Aurinia corymbosa	B,P,T

AURINIA

Aurinia saxatilis	B,BS	Babiana ambigua	B
Aurinia saxatilis 'Citrinum'	CG	Babiana angustifolia	B,G,SI
Aurinia saxatilis compactum	BD,BS,CG,CO,J,JE,KI,	Babiana attenuata	B
	RH,SA,SG,ST,V	Babiana blanda	B
Aurinia saxatilis compactum 'Gold Ball'	CL,JE,L	Babiana curviscapa	B,SI
Aurinia saxatilis compactum 'Gold Dust'	BS,C,F,R	Babiana dregei	B,G,SC,SI
Aurinia saxatilis comp. 'Mountain Gold'	BS,CL,F	Babiana ecklonii	B
Aurinia saxatilis 'Coupe D'or'	B	Babiana fimbriata	B,SI
Aurinia saxatilis 'Golden Queen'	DT,S,T	Babiana leipoldtii	B
Aurinia saxatilis 'Goldkugel'	B	Babiana nana	B,CG,SI
Aurinia saxatilis 'Sulphureum'	B,JE,SA	Babiana odorata	B,SI
Aurinia saxatilis 'Alpinum'	CG	Babiana patersoniae	B,CG,SI
Austrocedrus chilensis	C,SA	Babiana plicata	B,SI
Austrocephalocereus dolichospermaticus	B,Y	Babiana purpurea	B
Austrocephalocereus dybowski	B,Y	Babiana pygmaea	B,MN
Austrocephalocereus estevesii	B,Y	Babiana 'Queen Fabiola'	PM
Austrocephalocereus purpureus	B,Y	Babiana ringens	B
Austrocylindropuntia haematacantha	B	Babiana rubrocyanea	AP,B,C,CG,SI
Austrocylindropuntia inarmata	B	Babiana salteri	B
Austromyrtus dulcis	B	Babiana sambucina	B,SI
Avena fatua	CG,G	Babiana scabrifolia	B
Avena nuda	B	Babiana scariosa	B
Avena persica	SG	Babiana secunda	B
Avena sativa	B,T	Babiana sinuata	B
Avena sativa 'French Black'	B	Babiana sp mix	C,SC,SI
Avena sterilis	B	Babiana spathacea	B,SI
Avena strigosa	B	Babiana stricta	B,SI
Avenula pratensis	B	Babiana thunbergii	B,SI
Avenula pubescens	B	Babiana truncata	SI
Averia javanica	B	Babiana tubulosa	G,SC
Averrhoa bilimbi	B,RE	Babiana tubulosa v tubiflora	AP,B
Averrhoa carambola	B,RE,SA	Babiana tubulosa v tubulosa	B,SI
Avicennia germinans	B	Babiana vanzyliae	B,SI
Axonopus affinis	B	Babiana villosa blue	B,SA,SI
Axyris amaranthoides	B,SG	Babiana villosa red	SA,SI
Aylostera albipilosa	Y	Babiana villosa v grandis	B
Aylostera archibuiningiana	Y	Babiana villosula	B,SI
Aylostera cajasensis	Y	Baccharis emoryi	B
Aylostera carminifilamentosa	Y	Baccharis halimifolia	B,JE,S,SA
Aylostera cintiensis	Y	Baccharis microphylla	B
Aylostera deminuta	Y	Baccharis pilularis ssp pilularis	B
Aylostera fiebrigii	Y	Baccharis pilularis v consanguinea	B
Aylostera flavistyla	Y	Baccharis salicifolia	B
Aylostera fulviseta	Y	Baccharis sarothroides	B,SA
Aylostera fusca	Y	Backhousia anisata	HA
Aylostera muscula	SO,Y	Backhousia citriodora	HA,O
Aylostera narvaecensis	Y	Backhousia myrtifolia	B,HA
Aylostera nitida	Y	Bactris cubensis	B
Aylostera pulvinosa	Y	Bactris gasipaes	B,O
Aylostera spegazziniana	Y	Bactris sp	RE
Aylostera spinosissima	Y	Baeckea camphorosmae	B,C,O
Aylostera tamboensis	Y	Baeckea corynophylla	B
Aylostera tuberosa	Y	Baeckea crispiflora	B
Azadarichta indica	HA,SA	Baeckea densifolia	B,HA
Azanza garckeana	B	Baeckea floribunda	B
Azara integrifolia	SA	Baeckea linifolia	B
Azara microphylla	B,SA	Baeckea preissiana	B
Azara serrata	SA	Baeckea thryptomenoides	B
Azima tetracantha	B	Baeckea virgata	B,HA,O,SA,SH
Azolla filiculoides	B	Baeometra uniflora	B,SC,SI
Azorella filamentosa	AU	Baileya multiradiata	B,C,KS,SA,SW
Azorina vidalii	AP,B,G,JE,KS,SC,SG	Baileya pleniradiata	B
Azorina vidalii 'Alba'	B	Balanites aegyptiaca	B,SA
Azorina vidalii 'Rose Fern'	T	Balanites pedicellaris	B
Azorina vidalii 'Rosea'	B,JE,V	Balaustion pulcherrimum	B,O,SA
Aztekium ritteri	B,CH,GC,Y	Baldellia ranunculoides	B,JE,SA

BALLOTA

Ballota africana	B,SI
Ballota nigra	B,LA,SG
Ballota nigra 'Archer's Variety' (V)	B,P
Ballota rupestris	SG
Ballota saxatilis	SG
Balsamorhiza sagittata	AV,B,C,JE,SA
Bambusa arundinacea	C,SA
Bambusa nutans	SA
Banisteriopsis caapi	B
Banksia aculeata	B,O
Banksia aemula	B,O
Banksia ashbyi	B,O,SA
Banksia aspenifolia	HA,SA,SH
Banksia attenuata	O
Banksia attenuata dw	B,O
Banksia audax	B,O
Banksia baueri	B,C,O
Banksia baxteri	B,O
Banksia benthamiana	B,O
Banksia blechnifolia	B,O
Banksia brownii	B,O
Banksia burdettii	B,O
Banksia caleyi	B,C,O,SA
Banksia candolleana	B,O
Banksia canei	AU,B,C,O
Banksia coccinea	B,O,SA
Banksia collection	C
Banksia collina	C,SA,SH
Banksia conferta ssp penicillata	AU
Banksia conferta v conferta	B,O
Banksia cunninghamii	B
Banksia dentata	B,O
Banksia dryandroides	B,O
Banksia elderana	B,O
Banksia 'Ellisonii'	B,SH
Banksia ericifolia	B,HA,N,SA,SH
Banksia ericifolia ericifolia	O
Banksia ericifolia v macrantha	B,O
Banksia gardneri v gardneri	B,O
Banksia gardneri v hiemalis	B
Banksia grandis	B,O,SA
Banksia grossa	B,O
Banksia hookerana	B,O,SA,T
Banksia ilicifolia	B,O
Banksia incana	B,O
Banksia integrifolia	B,HA,O,SA,SH
Banksia laevigata v fuscolutea	B,O
Banksia laevigata v laevigata	B,O
Banksia lanata	B,O
Banksia laricina	B,O
Banksia lemanniana	B,O
Banksia leptophylla	B,O
Banksia lindleyana	B,O
Banksia littoralis	B,O
Banksia lullfitzii	B,O
Banksia marginata	AU,B,HA,O,SA,SH
Banksia media	B,O,SA
Banksia meisneri	B,O
Banksia menziesii	O
Banksia menziesii dw.f	B,O
Banksia nutans v cernuella	B,O
Banksia nutans v nutans	B,O
Banksia oblongifolia	B,O
Banksia occidentalis	B,O,SA
Banksia oreophila	B,O
Banksia ornata	B,HA,O,SA

Banksia paludosa	B,HA,O,SA,SH
Banksia petiolaris	B,O
Banksia pilostylis	B,O
Banksia praemorsa	B,O,SA
Banksia prionotes	B,O,SA
Banksia pulchella	B,O
Banksia quercifolia	B,O
Banksia repens	B,O
Banksia robur	B,C,HA,O,SA
Banksia saxicola	B,O
Banksia scabrella	B,O
Banksia sceptrum	B,O
Banksia seminuda	B,O
Banksia serrata	B,C,N,O,SA,SH
Banksia serratifolia	C,HA
Banksia solandri	B,O
Banksia sp	AU
Banksia speciosa	B,C,O
Banksia sphaerocarpa v caesia	B,O
Banksia sphaerocarpa v sphaerocarpa	B,O
Banksia spinulosa	SA,SH
Banksia spinulosa v collina	B,HA,O
Banksia spinulosa v neoanglica	O
Banksia spinulosa v spinulosa	B,HA,O
Banksia telmatiaea	B,O
Banksia tricuspis	B,O
Banksia verticillata	B,O
Banksia victoriae	B,O
Banksia violaceae	B,SA,O
Baphia massaiensis	B,SI
Baptisia australis	AP,B,BS,C,CG,G,JE,LG, PR,SA,SC,SE,T
Baptisia bracteata	B
Baptisia lactea	B
Baptisia leucantha	JE,PR,SA,SG
Baptisia leucophaea	JE
Baptisia pendula	B,JE,NT,SA
Baptisia sphaerocarpa	B
Baptisia tinctoria	B
Barbarea intermedia	B
Barbarea stricta	SG
Barbarea verna	B,KS
Barbarea vulgaris	B,G
Barbarea vulgaris variegata	AP,B,C,FH,HH,I,P
Barklya syringifolia	AU,B,O
Barleria buxifolia	B
Barleria cristata	B
Barleria longiflora	B
Barleria obtusa	B,C,SC,SI
Barleria prionitis	B
Barnardiella spiralis	SI
Barringtonia aculatangula	B,HA
Bartlettina sordida	B
Bartschella schumannii	BC,Y
Bartschella schumannii globosa	BC
Bartsia alpina	B,C,FH
Basella alba	B
Basella alba 'Rubra'	B
Bassia scoparia 'Evergreen'	B,BS,T
Bassia scoparia f trichophylla	B,BD,BS,C,CL,D,F,J,KI, KS,L,S,ST,T,TU,V,YA
Bauhinia acuminata	B
Bauhinia alba	HA,O,RE,SA
Bauhinia carronii	HA
Bauhinia galpinii	B,C,HA,RS,O,SA,SI
Bauhinia grandidiae	B

BAUHINIA

Bauhinia hookeri	HA,SA
Bauhinia monandra	B
Bauhinia natalensis	B,O,SI
Bauhinia petersiana	B,SI
Bauhinia petersiana ssp serpae	B
Bauhinia petiolata	B
Bauhinia purpurea	B,SA
Bauhinia purpurea variegata	HA,O
Bauhinia racemosa	B,HA,SA
Bauhinia retusa	B,HA,SA
Bauhinia rufescens	B
Bauhinia scandens	B
Bauhinia sp	RE,T,V
Bauhinia tomentosa	B,O,SI
Bauhinia vahlii	B
Bauhinia variegata	B,HA,SA
Bauhinia variegata 'Candida'	B,C,SA
Bauhinia x blakeana	B
Bauhinia yunnanensis	B
Beaucarnea gracilis	O,SA
Beaucarnea guatamalensis	O,SA
Beaucarnea recurvata	B,HA,O,SA,T
Beaucarnea stricta	HA,O
Beaucarnea texana	O
Beaufortia elegans	B
Beaufortia heterophylla	B
Beaufortia incana	B,O,SA
Beaufortia macrostemon	B
Beaufortia micrantha	B,O
Beaufortia micrantha v empetrifolia	B,O
Beaufortia orbifolia	B,O
Beaufortia purpurea	B
Beaufortia schaueri	B,O
Beaufortia sparsa	B,C,O,SA
Beaufortia squarrosa	B,O
Beaumontia grandiflora	B,C,SA
Beccariophoenix madagascariensis	B
Beckmannia eruciformis	B,CG
Beckmannia syzigachne	B,SG
Begonia conchaefolia	CG
Begonia 'Container/Hanging Basket Mix'	T
Begonia dregei	SG
Begonia elatior f1 'Charisma' s-c	CL,YA
Begonia f1 'All Round Series' s-c	BS,YA
Begonia f1 hyb 'Marshall's Fantasy'	M
Begonia f1 'Illumination Apricot'	CL,SE
Begonia f1 'Illumination' mix	L,T
Begonia f1 'Illumination Orange'	BS,C,CL,KI,SE,V,YA
Begonia f1 'Illumination Pink'	BS,C,CL,KI,SE,YA
Begonia f1 'Inferno Series' s-c	DT,YA
Begonia fib f1 'Devil' mix	CL
Begonia fib f1 'Devil Series's-c	CL
Begonia fib mix o-p	S
Begonia fib 'Sunshine Carpet'	CO,KI
Begonia fuchsoides v rosea	B
Begonia grandis ssp evansiana	B,C,I,SC
Begonia grandis ssp evansiana v alba	AP,C,I
Begonia incana	CG
Begonia leptotricha	CG
Begonia lindleyana	CG
Begonia masoniana	C
Begonia partita 'Bonsai'	C,T
Begonia pendula f1 'Finale' mix	CL
Begonia pendula f1 'Musical' mix	BD,CL,YA
Begonia pendula 'Happy End'	BD,BS,C,R,V
Begonia pendula mix h-p	BL

Begonia pendula 'Picotee' mix h-p	BL
Begonia petisitifolia	CG
Begonia rex	B,DT,F,V
Begonia rex f1 hyb 'Colorvision'	BD,BS,C,L
Begonia rex hyb 'Imperial'	CL
Begonia sanguinea	CG
Begonia schmidtia	CG
Begonia semp 'Atlanta' s-c p.s	U
Begonia semp 'Crown Mix'	BS
Begonia semp 'Dwarf Mix'	D
Begonia semp f1 'Alfa Series' s-c, mix	BS,YA
Begonia semp f1 'Ambassador' mix	BS,D
Begonia semp f1 'Ambassador' mix p.s	D
Begonia semp f1 'Ambassador Series' s-c	BS,YA
Begonia semp f1 'Ambra Mix'	BS,YA
Begonia semp f1 'Ambra Mix' s-c	BS
Begonia semp f1 'Bellavista Mix'	BS,YA
Begonia semp f1 'Bellavista' s-c	BS
Begonia semp f1 'Coco Mix'	T
Begonia semp f1 'Expresso' s-c/mix	BS,YA
Begonia semp f1 'Frilly Dilly Mix'	T
Begonia semp f1 hyb 'Bella Vista'	J,TU
Begonia semp f1 hyb 'Cocktail' c.s	BS,DT,S
Begonia semp f1 hyb 'Cover Girl' c.s	S
Begonia semp f1 hyb 'Devon Gems' c.s	S
Begonia semp f1 hyb 'Excel' mix	F,J,T
Begonia semp f1 hyb 'Kalinka'	CL
Begonia semp f1 hyb 'Lorraine Love-Me'	BS,CL
Begonia semp f1 hyb 'New Generation'	D
Begonia semp f1 hyb 'Olympia' mix	CL,DT,J,KI,L,SE
Begonia semp f1 hyb 'Olympia' s-c	CL,D,DT,L
Begonia semp f1 hyb 'Olympia' s-c c.s	CL,S
Begonia semp f1 hyb 'Olympia' white	CL,D,U
Begonia semp f1 hyb 'Organdy' mix	BD,BS,CL,D,DT,F,J,L,R, SE,V
Begonia semp f1 hyb 'Organdy' p.s	BD,CL
Begonia semp f1 hyb 'Partyfun' mix	C,J,U
Begonia semp f1 hyb 'Royale' p.s	CL
Begonia semp f1 hyb 'Treasure Trove'	S
Begonia semp f1 hyb triploid 'Rusher Red'	C
Begonia semp f1 hyb 'Vision' s-c, mix	BS
Begonia semp f1 hyb 'Viva'	T
Begonia semp f1 hyb white,rose edge	CC
Begonia semp f1 hyb 'Wings'	KI
Begonia semp f1 'Lotto' mix	BS
Begonia semp f1 'Lotto' s-c	BS,U
Begonia semp f1 'Options'	T
Begonia semp f1 'Senator Series' s-c	YA
Begonia semp f1 'Symphony Mix'	YA
Begonia semp f1 'The President Mix'	T,YA
Begonia semp f1 'Total Victory Series' p.s	CL
Begonia semp f1 'Total Victory Series' s-c	CL
Begonia semp f1 'Victory Series' s-c, gr	CL
Begonia semp 'Festival Dw'	BS
Begonia semp 'Happy Choice'	BS
Begonia semp 'Indian Maid'	BS
Begonia semp 'Mardi Gras'	U
Begonia semp mix	C,DT,VH
Begonia semp mix o-p	DT,SU
Begonia semp 'Paint Splash' (V)	DT
Begonia semp 'Pink Sundae'	F
Begonia semp 'Roselyn'	U
Begonia semp 'Scarlet Bedder'	D
Begonia semp 'Summer Rainbow'	F
Begonia semp 'Supernova Mix'	CL
Begonia semp f1 'Colorita Mix'	YA

BEGONIA

Begonia semp f1 'Danica Scarlet'	T
Begonia semp f1 hyb 'Cocktail'	BS,C,D,DT,F,J,KI,L,SE,V
Begonia semp f1 hyb 'Kalinka' s-c	YA
Begonia semp f1 hyb 'Royale' mix	BS,CL,YA
Begonia semp f1 hyb 'Stara'	S
Begonia semp f1 hyb 'Thous. Wonders'	KI
Begonia semp f1 'Victory Series' s-c, br.	CL
Begonia 'Sunshine Carpet'	ST
Begonia sutherlandii	C,I,P,SI
Begonia tub 'Choice Prize Double'	DT,L
Begonia tub, f1 'Clips' mix	BS,CL,L,T
Begonia tub, f1 'Clips' s-c	T
Begonia tub, f1 'Fortune Series' s-c	YA
Begonia tub, f1 'Galaxy'	BS,YA
Begonia tub f1 'Giant Hyb' mix	C
Begonia tub, f1 hyb 'Chanson' mix	DT
Begonia tub. f1 hyb 'Memory'	BS,CL
Begonia tub f1 hyb 'Musical'	BS,L
Begonia tub f1 hyb 'Nonstop' mix	BS,C,CL,D,DT,J,KI,L,R, SE,T,V,YA
Begonia tub, f1 hyb 'Nonstop' mix p.s	BD,CL,S
Begonia tub, f1 hyb 'N.st. Ornament' mix	BS,CL,DT,F
Begonia tub, f1 hyb 'N.st. Orn.' mix p.s	CL,D,L
Begonia tub, f1 hyb 'N.st. Ornament' s-c	BS,CL
Begonia tub, f1 hyb 'Nonstop' s-c	BS,L,SE,T
Begonia tub f1 hyb 'Panorama'	BS,CL
Begonia tub f1 hyb 'Panorama' p.s	CL
Begonia tub f1 hyb 'Party'	BS
Begonia tub f1 hyb 'Pin-Up'	BS,C,CL,KI,L,O,T,V
Begonia tub f1 hyb 'Pin-Up' c.s	S
Begonia tub f1 hyb 'Royal Harlequin'	BS,L,SE
Begonia tub f1 hyb 'Royal Picotee'	BS,DT,L,T
Begonia tub, f1 hyb 'Show Angels' mix	BS,DT,SE,T
Begonia tub, multiflora dbl 'Fiesta' mix	S
Begonia un-named sp ex-Sabah	C
Begonia vernosa	CG,SG
Begonia vitifolia	CG
Behria tenuiflora	SW
Beilschmiedia tawa	B
Belamcanda chinensis	AP,B,C,CC,CG,E,FH,G, JE,LG,KS,NT,SA,SC
Belamcanda 'Leopard Lily Mix'	T
Bellardia trixago	B
Bellendena montana	B,O,SA
Bellevalia dalmatica	B
Bellevalia dubia	AP,B,LG,MN
Bellevalia hackelii	B
Bellevalia hackelii MS439 Portugal	MN
Bellevalia paradoxa	HH,PM,SC
Bellevalia romana	AP,B,G,SC,SG
Bellevalia romana JCA523	MN
Bellevalia sp mixed ex- Jordan	MN
Bellevalia sp S.L42 Jordan	MN
Bellevalia sp S.L86/1 Jordan	MN
Bellida graminea	B,O
Bellidiastrum michellii	SG
Bellis annua 'White Stars'	B
Bellis caerulescens 'Lilac Pixie'	B
Bellis perennis	AP,B,C,JE,SU,V
Bellis perennis 'Buttons Box' s-c	YA
Bellis perennis 'Buttons mix'	BS,CO,DT,ST
Bellis perennis 'Carpet Bright'	C,T
Bellis perennis 'Carpet' dbl mix	BS,CL,KI,S,SU
Bellis perennis 'Carpet' s-c	B,BS,C,CL,T
Bellis perennis 'Clutch of Pearls'	U
Bellis perennis 'Crown Double Mix'	KI

Bellis perennis 'Giant Mix'	D,U
Bellis perennis 'Goliath'	F,S,T
Bellis perennis 'Habanera' mix	CL,D,DT,KI,L,T,U
Bellis perennis 'Habanera' s-c	B,CL
Bellis perennis 'Habanera White,red Tips'	B,CL
Bellis perennis 'Kito Cherry Pink'	B,T
Bellis perennis 'Lipstick'	SE
Bellis perennis 'Medici Button'	BS,F,TU
Bellis perennis 'Medicis Red'	BS,KI
Bellis perennis 'Medicis' s-c	BS,YA
Bellis perennis 'Miniature Buttons' s-c	L
Bellis perennis 'Monstrosa Double' mix	BS,CL,J,TU,V
Bellis perennis 'Monstrosa' s-c	BS,CL,YA
Bellis perennis 'Pomponette' mix	BD,BS,C,CL,J,JE,T,V
Bellis perennis 'Pomponette Pink Buttons'	D
Bellis perennis 'Pomponette' s-c	B,BS,CL,JE
Bellis perennis 'Radar' mix	BD,BS
Bellis perennis 'Radar' s-c	B,BS
Bellis perennis 'Red Tips'	U
Bellis perennis 'Robella'	B,BS,O
Bellis perennis 'Rosina'	SE
Bellis perennis 'Spring Star'	S
Bellis p. 'Super Enorma Ball Salmon'	B,C
Bellis perennis 'Super Enorma' mix	BS,DT,L,R
Bellis perennis 'Super Enorma' s-c	BS
Bellis perennis 'Super Giant Flowering'	M
Bellis perennis 'Swift'	BS
Bellis perennis 'Tasso' mix	B,BS,CL
Bellis perennis 'Tasso' s-c	B,BS,CL
Bellis sylvestris	SG
Bellium bellidioides	B
Bellium minutum 'Fairy Princess'	B
Benincasa hispida	B
Benincasa hispida v chieh-que	B
Benkara malabarica	B
Bensoniella oregana	G,SC,SG
Bentinckia nicobarica	B
Berardia subacaulis	B,C,JE
Berberidopsis corallina	SA
Berberis aetnensis	CG
Berberis aggregata	A,AP,B,C,SA,SG
Berberis amurensis	CG,SG
Berberis angulosa	SG
Berberis aquifolium	SG
Berberis arido-calida	RH
Berberis aristata	A,RH,SA
Berberis asiatica	A,SA
Berberis beanianii	CG,SG
Berberis bergmanniae	SA
Berberis bidentata	B
Berberis brachypoda	CG,SG
Berberis bretschneideri	SG
Berberis buchananii tawangensis	SG
Berberis buxifolia	AU,SA
Berberis centiflora	SG
Berberis chengii	SA
Berberis chinensis	B,CG
Berberis'chitra	SG
Berberis congestiflora	SA
Berberis consimilis	SG
Berberis coxii	SA
Berberis crataegina	SG
Berberis darwinii	A,B,C,RH,SA,T
Berberis dasystachya	SG
Berberis dictiophylla	RH
Berberis dictiophylla v epruinesa	SG

BERBERIS

Berberis dielsiana	SG
Berberis dolichobotrys	B
Berberis edgeworthiana	SG
Berberis faxoniana	SG
Berberis francisci-ferdinande	B
Berberis fremontii	B,SW
Berberis fremontii x haematocarpa	B,SW
Berberis gagnepainii v lanceifolia	B,C,CG,SA,SG
Berberis georgei	SG
Berberis gilgiana	CG
Berberis globosa	SG
Berberis hakodate	CG
Berberis henryana	SG
Berberis heteropoda	SG
Berberis honanensis	SG
Berberis hookeri	CG,SG
Berberis hypokerina	SG
Berberis integerrima	SG
Berberis jaeschkeana v jaeschkeana	SG
Berberis jaeschkeana v usteriana	SG
Berberis jamesiana	CG,RH,SA,SG
Berberis julianae	B,C,CG,G,SA,T
Berberis julianae 'Nana'	B
Berberis kansuensis	B
Berberis kewensis	CG
Berberis koreana	B,CG,SG
Berberis lepidifolia	SG
Berberis linearifolium	SA
Berberis lycium	A,SA
Berberis mitifolia	B,CG
Berberis montana	SA
Berberis oblonga	SG
Berberis phanera	SG
Berberis prattii	B
Berberis pruinosa	SG
Berberis regeliana	SG
Berberis repens	SW
Berberis sherriffii	CG,RH,SG
Berberis sibirica	SG
Berberis ssp	SG
Berberis stiebritziana	SG
Berberis talliensis	SG
Berberis thunbergii	B,BS,SA,SG
Berberis thunbergii 'Atropurpurea'	B,C,CG,N,SA,T
Berberis thunbergii v maximowiczii	B
Berberis valdiviana	SA
Berberis veitchii	CG
Berberis vernus	CG
Berberis vulgaris	A,B,C,SA,SG
Berberis vulgaris 'Atropurpurea'	B,SA
Berberis wilcoxii	B,SW
Berberis wilsoniae	A,B,RH,SA,SG
Berberis wilsonii v subcaulialata	B
Berberis wisonii v stapfiana	SG
Berberis x mistabilis	SG
Berberis x ottawnsis	SG
Berchemia discolor	SI
Berchemia flavescens	SA
Berchemia zeyheri	B,SI
Bergenia ciliata	B
Bergenia ciliata ligulata	CC
Bergenia cordifolia	B,BS,C,CL,JE,L,SA
Bergenia cordifolia 'New Hybrids'	JE
Bergenia cordifolia 'New Winter Fl'	B,D,JE,T,V
Bergenia cordifolia 'Red Start'	B,T,V
Bergenia cordifolia 'Rotblum'	JE

Bergenia crassifolia	B,SG
Bergenia hybrida 'Glockenturn'	SG
Bergenia purpurascens	B,C,JESA
Bergenia x schmidtii	B,SG
Bergeranthus artus	B
Bergeranthus glenensis	B
Bergeranthus longisepalus	B,SI
Bergeranthus multiceps	B
Bergerocactus emoryi	B
Berkheya latifolia	SI
Berkheya macrocephala	SI
Berkheya maritima	B,C,SI
Berkheya setifera	SI
Berkheya speciosa	B,SI
Berlandiera lyrata	B,JE,SA,SW,T
Berrya cordifolia	B
Berrya javanica	B
Berula erecta	B
Berzelia abrotanoides	B,O,SI
Berzelia commutata	B,SI
Berzelia galpinii	B,SC,SI
Berzelia incurva	B,SI
Berzelia intermedia	B,SI
Berzelia lanuginosa	B,O,SA,SI
Berzelia rubra	B,SI
Berzelia sp	SI
Berzelia squarrosa	SI
Bessera elegans	B,SW
Bessera tuitensis	B,SW
Besseya alpina	SW
Besseya bullii	B
Beta trigyna	CG
Beta vulgaris ssp cicla 'Bull's Blood'	B,BS
Beta vulgaris ssp maritima	B
Beta vulgaris 'Strap Leaved'	BS
Betula alba	T
Betula albosinensis	B,C,N,SA,SG
Betula alleghaniensis	B,C,RH,SG
Betula apoiensis	SG
Betula 'Attractive Bark' sp	C
Betula chichibuensis	SG
Betula davurica	B,SA,SG
Betula divaricataa	SG
Betula ermanii	B,C,SA
Betula ermanii 'Grayswood Hill'	B,N,SA
Betula fontinalis	B,RH,SA,SG
Betula fruticosa	SG
Betula glandulifera	SG
Betula glandulifera v glandulifera	SG
Betula globispica	SG
Betula grossa	SG
Betula humilis	RH
Betula insignis	B,N,SG
Betula lenta	B,RH,SA,SG
Betula litwinowii	SA,SG
Betula maximowicziana	B,C,SA
Betula medwediewii	RH,SG
Betula megrelica	SG
Betula microphylla	SG
Betula nana	C,CG,FH,SC,SG
Betula neoalaskana	B
Betula nigra	B,C,N,RH,SA
Betula obscura	B,G,SG
Betula occidentalis	SA
Betula ovalifolia	SG
Betula papyrifera	A,B,C,CG,N,RH,SA,SG,T

BETULA

Betula pendula	A,B,C,CG,HA,SA,SG,V
Betula pendula 'Dalecarlica'	B
Betula pendula 'Purpurea'	B,SA
Betula pendula 'Youngii'	B
Betula platyphylla	B,SG
Betula platyphylla v japonica	B,C,SA,SG
Betula platyphylla v kamchatica	B,N,SA
Betula populifolia	B,RH,SA,SG
Betula potaninii	SG
Betula procurva	SG
Betula pubescens	A,B,SA,SG
Betula pubescens ssp carpatica v munthii	RH
Betula raddeana	SG
Betula rotundifolia	SG
Betula schmidtii	B
Betula sp CNW 285	X
Betula sp (not utilis) CNW 154	X
Betula szechuanica	B,SG
Betula tatewakiana	SG
Betula tianshanica	B,N,SA
Betula tuskesanica	CG
Betula uber	B
Betula utilis	B,C,CG,N,SA,SG
Betula utilis v jacquemontii	B,N,SA,SC
Betula x aschersoniana	SG
Biarum bovei	B
Biarum bovei S.B.L199 Morocco	MN
Biarum carratracense	AP,B
Biarum carratracense S.B.L217 Morocco	MN
Biarum carratracense S.F226 Spain	MN
Biarum carratracense S.F236 Spain	MN
Biarum dispar	B
Biarum dispar A.B.S4455 Morocco	MN
Biarum dispar A.B.S4613 Morocco	MN
Biarum dispar S.F265 Morocco	MN
Biarum dispar S.L261 Tunisia	MN
Biarum dispar S.L282 Tunisia	MN
Biarum dispar S.L290/2 Tunisia	MN
Biarum dispar S.L294 Tunisia	MN
Biarum dispar v hispanica	B
Biarum dispar v hispanica B.S465 Spain	MN
Biarum dispar v hispanica S.F226 Spain	MN
Biarum dispar v hispanica S.F235 Spain	MN
Biarum frassianum	B
Biarum frassianum PB64 Greece	MN
Biarum idomenaeum	B
Biarum idomenaeum MS698 Crete	MN
Biarum idomenaeum MS758 Crete	MN
Biarum pyrami	B
Biarum pyrami PB238 Turkey	MN
Biarum pyrami PB253 Turkey	MN
Biarum sp S.L185 Greece	MN
Biarum tenuifolium	AP,B,SC
Biarum tenuifolium PB154 Greece	MN
Biarum tenuifolium S.B.L228 Morocco	MN
Biarum zeleborei	B
Biarum zeleborei L/T 1 Turkey	MN
Biarum zeleborei PB243 Turkey	MN
Bidens aurea 'Bit Of Sunshine'	B,BS,S
Bidens cernua	PR
Bidens connata	PR
Bidens coronata	PR
Bidens ferulifolia	FH,SG
Bidens ferulifolia 'Golden Goddess'	AP,B,BS,C,DT,F,J,T,U,V
Bidens frondosa	SG
Bidens parviflore	SG
Bidens pilosa	B,CG
Bidens tripartita	B,CG,SG
Bignonia capreolata	B
Bignonia tweediana	HA
Bijlia cana	B,SI,Y
Bijlia tugwelliae	B
Billardiera bicolor	B,C,O,SA
Billardiera candida	B
Billardiera coeruleo-punctata	B
Billardiera coriacea	B
Billardiera cymosa	B
Billardiera drummondiana	B
Billardiera erubescens	B,C,SA
Billardiera floribunda	B,,OSA
Billardiera granulata	B
Billardiera lehmanniana	B
Billardiera longiflora	AU,B,O,P,SA,SC,SG
Billardiera ringens	O
Billardiera sp prostrate	SA
Billardiera variifolia	B
Billardiera variifolia blue	SA
Billbergia magnifica v escuticephala	SG
Billbergia sp,cvs,&vars	B
Billtanthus beuckeri	B
Bischofia javanica	B,HA,SA
Bischofia racemosaa	SA
Biscutella coronopifolia	AP,B,SC
Biscutella laevigata	B,G,JE,SC
Bismarckia nobilis	B,HA,O
Bixa orellana	B,C,HA,O,RE,SA,T
Blackstonia serotina	B
Blaeria ericoides	B,SI
Blancoa canescens	B,O
Blandfordia grandiflora	B,C,HA,O,SA,T
Blandfordia nobilis	O
Blandfordia punicea	AU,B,C,O
Blechnum brasiliense	B
Blechnum capense	B,G
Blechnum cartilagineum	B,SA
Blechnum gibbum	B,SA
Blechnum moorei	B
Blechnum nudum	HA
Blechnum occidentale	B
Blechnum orientale	B
Blechnum patersonii	B,SA
Blechnum spicant	B
Blechnum tabulare	C
Blepharis maderaspatensis	B
Blepharocarya involucrigera	O
Blephilia ciliata	B,PR
Blephilia hirsuta	PR
Bletilla striata	AP,B,SG
Bletilla striata 'Alba'	B
Blighia sapida	B
Bloomeria crocea	AP,B,SC,SW
Blossfeldia fechseri	Y
Blossfeldia flocculosa	Y
Blossfeldia grandiflora	BC
Blossfeldia liliputana	B,CH,GC,Y
Blossfeldia liliputana alba	BC
Blossfeldia minima	Y
Blossfeldia pedicellata	Y
Blossfeldia sp mix	C
Blossfeldia subterranea	Y
Blumea obliqua	B
Blumenbachia insignis	B

BLUMENBACHIA

Blumenbachia laterita	SG	Boscia senegalensis	B
Blysmus compressus	SG	Bossiaea aquifolium	B,SA
Bobartia indica	B,SI	Bossiaea dentata	B,SA
Bobartia longicyma v longicyma	B,SI	Bossiaea ensata	B,HA
Bobartia robusta	B,SI	Bossiaea eriocarpa	B
Bobartia sp	SI	Bossiaea foliosa	B,HA
Boehmeria nivea	B	Bossiaea heterophylla	B,HA
Boehmeria penduliflora	B	Bossiaea laidlawiana	B
Boerhavia diffusa	B	Bossiaea linophylla	B,C,SA
Boerhavia erecta	B	Bossiaea obcordata	HA
Boisduvalia densiflora	CG	Bossiaea ornata	B,SA
Bolboschoenus maritimus	SG	Bossiaea preissii	B
Bolivicereus	Y	Bossiaea pulchella	B,SA
Boltonia asteroides	G,PR,SA	Bossiaea rhombifolia	B,HA
Boltonia asteroides v laisquama	G,JE	Bossiaea scolopendria	HA
Boltonia asteroides v latisquama 'Nana'	C,JE	Bossiaea walkeri	B
Boltonia decurrens	PR	Bossiaea webbii	B
Bolusafra bituminosa	B,SI	Bothrichloa decipiens	HA
Bolusanthus speciosus	B,C,O,SA,SI	Bothrichloa ischaemum	B
Bomarea caldasii	B,C	Bothrichloa macra	HA
Bomarea edulis	SG	Bothrichloa petusa	B
Bomarea lobbiana	B,C	Bothriochloa insculpta	B
Bomarea salsilla	B,P,SG	Bothriochloa pertusa	B
Bomarea 'Senorita'	B	Botryostege bracteata	SG
Bombacopsis glabra	B	Bouea macrophylla	B
Bombacopsis quinata	B,RE	Bouteloua aristidoides	B
Bombax ceiba	B,HA,O,SA	Bouteloua curtipendula	B,C,JE,PR,SA
Bonafousia longituba	B	Bouteloua gracilis	B,C,JE,PR,SA
Bonamia pannosa	B	Bouteloua hirsuta	PR
Boophone disticha	C	Bouvardia glaberrima	B,SW
Boophone guttata	B	Bowenia serrulata	B,C,HA,O
Borago officinalis	B,CG,CP,KS,SG,SU	Bowenia spectabilis	B,O
Borago officinalis 'Alba'	B	Bowenia 'Tinaroo'	O
Borago officinalis 'Bill Archer' (V)	NS	Bowiea volubilis	B,G,SG,SI,Y
Borago pygmaea	B,G,SG,T	Bowkeria citrina	SI
Borassus flabellifer	B	Bowkeria verticillata	B,SI
Borojoa patinoi	B	Boykinia aconitifolia	AP,B,G,P,SC,SG
Boronia alata	AU	Boykinia jamesii	AP,B,JE,SC,SW
Boronia caerulescens	B	Boykinia rotundifolia	B,CG,SC
Boronia citriodora	AU	Brabejum stellatifolium	SI
Boronia crenulata	AU,B,O,SA	Brachiaria decumbens	B
Boronia crenulata v gracilis	B,O	Brachiaria humidicola	B
Boronia cymosa	AU,B,O	Brachiaria miliiformis	B
Boronia denticulata	B,O,SA	Brachiaria mutica	B
Boronia dichotoma	B	Brachycarpaea juncea	B
Boronia falcifolia	B,O	Brachycereus nesiocactus	B
Boronia fastigiata	AU,B	Brachychiton acerifolius	B,C,HA,O,SA
Boronia glabra	B	Brachychiton acuminatus	O
Boronia heterophylla	B,C,O,SA	Brachychiton australis	B,O,SA
Boronia inornata	B,O	Brachychiton bidwillii	B,O
Boronia ledifolia	B,O,SH	Brachychiton discolor	B,C,HA,O,SA
Boronia ledifolia v glabra	HA	Brachychiton diversifolius	B,O
Boronia megastigma	AU,B,C,O,SA	Brachychiton gregorii	B,O,SA
Boronia microphylla	HA	Brachychiton paradoxum	O
Boronia molloyae	B	Brachychiton populneus	B,HA,SA
Boronia ovata	B	Brachychiton rupestris	B,C,HA,O,SA
Boronia pinnata	B,HA,O,SH	Brachyglottis bellidioides	AU,B,SS
Boronia ramosa	B,O,SA	Brachyglottis bidwillii	B,SS
Boronia rosmarinifolia	B,O,SA	Brachyglottis cassinioides	B,SS
Boronia spathulata	B,O	Brachyglottis greyii	B,FH,SC,SS
Boronia stricta	B,O	Brachyglottis haasti	B,SS
Boronia ternata v elongata	B,O	Brachyglottis kirkii	B,SA
Boronia viminea	B,O	Brachyglottis lagopus	B,SS
Borrichia frutescens	B	Brachyglottis monroi	AU,B,SS
Boscia albitrunca	B,C,SA,SI	Brachyglottis repanda	B
Boscia salicifolia	B	Brachylaena discolor	B,SA,SI

43

BRACHYLAENA

Brachylaena elliptica	B
Brachylaena neriifolia	B,SI
Brachylaena rotundata	B,SI
Brachyloma daphnoides	HA
Brachypodium pinnatum	B,SG
Brachypodium sylvaticum	B,JE,SA,SG
Brachyscome ciliaris ssp ciliaris	B,O
Brachyscome dentata	B
Brachyscome diversifolia v diversifolia	AU
Brachyscome iberidifolia	B,BD,BS,C,CO,D,DT,KI, L,O,SA,SG,ST,SU,T,TU
Brachyscome iberidifolia 'Blue Star'	B,BD,BS,CL,D,F,HA,KS, M,T,U
Brachyscome iberidifolia 'Brachy Blue' dw	B,BS,C,HA,KI,ST,YA
Brachyscome iberidifolia 'Bravo'	D,F
Brachyscome iberidifolia 'Gleam Blue'	C
Brachyscome iberidifolia 'Splendour Blue'	B,HA
Brachyscome iberidifolia 'Splendour mix'	BS,J,KS,V
Brachyscome iberid. 'Splendour Purple'	B,BS,C,DT,F,HA,J,T,V,VH
Brachyscome iberidifolia 'Splendour Sky'	B
Brachyscome iberid 'Splendour Violet'	B,C
Brachyscome iberid 'Splendour White'	B,BD,BS,CL,D,DT,F,HA,T
Brachyscome iberidifolia 'Starshine' mix	HA
Brachyscome iberidifolia 'Summer Skies'	F
Brachyscome latisquamata	B,C,O
Brachyscome ptychyocarpa	AU
Brachyscome rigidula	B,SC,SG
Brachyscome sinclairii	B,SS
Brachysema latifolium	B,SA
Brachystegia spiciformis	B,SI
Bracteantha bracteata	AU,B,CG,HA,O,R,SG
Bracteantha bracteata alba	SG
Bracteantha bracteata 'Bikini Bright'	BS,C,CL,CO,D,DT,HA,KI, S,T,YA
Bracteantha bracteata 'Bikini Crimson'	C
Bracteantha bracteata 'Bikini Golden'	C
Bracteantha bracteata 'Bikini Hot'	C,S,T
Bracteantha bracteata 'Bikini' mix	KS
Bracteantha bracteata 'Bikini' s-c	B,C
Bracteantha bracteata dbl	BS,CO,DT,HA,J,ST,TU
Bracteantha bracteata 'Drakkar Pastel'	BS,DT,F,M
Bracteantha bracteata dw mix	BS,DT,F
Bracteantha b. 'Frosted Sul & Sil Rose'	F,T,V
Bracteantha bracteata 'Golden Sun'	BS
Bracteantha bracteata 'Icicle Mix'	SE
Bracteantha bracteata 'King Size' mix	BD,BS,HA,KS,O
Bracteantha bracteata 'King Size New' s-c	B,BS,C
Bracteantha bracteata 'King Size' s-c	B,BS,C,KS
Bracteantha b.'King Size Tall Choice mix'	BS,C,F,S
Bracteantha b.'Marshall's Dbl Swiss Giant'	M
Bracteantha bracteata 'Monstrosum Dbl '	D,YA
Bracteantha bracteata 'Monstrosum Mix'	BS,L,T
Bracteantha bracteata 'Monstrosum' s-c	BS,KI,L,SU,T
Bracteantha b. 'Mon. Tet. Dbl Mix' s-c	T
Bracteantha bracteata 'New Select' s-c	BS
Bracteantha bracteata 'Pastel'	D,KS,S,T
Bracteantha bracteata 'Pastel Sombrero'	U
Bracteantha bracteata 'Rosa'	V
Bracteantha b. 'Standard Series' s-c	B
Bracteantha bracteata 'Sultane' s-c	BS
Bracteantha bracteata 'Swiss Giants'	BS,U
Bracteantha bracteata v albidum	B
Bracteantha bracteata v macranthum	B
Bracteantha bracteata v viscosum	B
Bracteantha bracteatam 'Paper Daisy'	BS,KI
Bracteantha subundulata	AU

Brahea armata	B,O
Brahea dulcis	CG
Brahea edulis	B,O
Brasilicactus graessneri	Y
Brasilicactus graessneri v albisetus	Y
Brasilicactus haselbergii	B,Y
Brasilicactus hasel. v pseudograessneri	Y
Brasilicactus haselbergii v stellatus	Y
Brassica oleracea f1 'O.C.,Bright Lights'	B
Brassica oleracea f1 'O. C., Cherry Sundae'	T
Brassica oleracea f1 'O. C Tokyo'	B,BD,BS,CL,F,KI,YA
Brassica oleracea f1 'O. Kale Chidori' s-c	BS
Brassica oleracea f1 'O. Kale Kamone'	CL
Brassica oleracea f1 'Orn. Kale' mix	L,M,S,ST
Brassica oleracea f1 'Orn. Kale Nagoya'	BS,C,CL,YA
Brassica oleracea f1 'O.K. North.Lights' s-c	CL,T
Brassica oleracea f1 'Orn. Kale Peacock'	BD,T,U,V,VH
Brassica oleracea f1 'O. Kale Peacock Red'	B,BS,CL,KS,L,
Brassica oleracea f1 'O. K Peacock White'	BS,CL,KS,L
Brassica oleracea f1 'O. Kale Pidgeon' mix	BD,BS,U
Brassica oleracea f1 'O. kale Pidgeon pink'	B,BS
Brassica oleracea f1 'O. Kale Pidgeon Red'	B,BS
Brassica oleracea f1 'O. Kale Sparrow' mix	BD
Brassica oleracea f1 'O. Kale Sparrow Red'	B,BS
Brassica oleracea f1 'O. K Sparrow White'	B,BS
Brassica oleracea f1 'Orn. Kale Sunrise'	KS
Brassica oleracea f1 'Orn. Kale Sunset'	KS
Brassica oleracea f1 'Orn. Osaka mix'	BS,F,J,TU
Brassica oleracea 'O. C. Delight mix'	BS
Brassica oleracea 'Orn. Cabbage, mix'	B,C,CO,D,KI,R,ST,SU,T, VH
Brassica oleracea 'O. C.,white/green'	B
Brassica oleracea 'O. K,Decorative Fringe'	CO,BS
Brassica oleracea 'Orn. Kale Feather'	CL
Brassica oleracea 'Orn. Kale,Tassels'	KI,SU
Brassica oleracea 'O. Kale Winter Beauty'	DT
Braunsia apiculata	B,SI
Braunsia geminata	B
Breonadia salicina	SA
Bretschneideri sinensis	B
Breynia retusa	B
Breynia vitis-idaea	B
Bridelia micrantha	B
Bridelia mollis	B
Bridelia retusa	B
Briggsia muscicola	AP,C,SC
Brimeura amethystina	AP,B,G,MN,PM,SC,SG
Brimeura amethystina alba	AP,HH,SC,SG
Brionia dioica	B
Briza maxima	AP,B,C,DT,G,I,KI,KS,L, PM,SC,SU,T,V
Briza media	B,C,G,LA,JE,SA,SC,SG, SU
Briza minor	B,C,KS,L,SG,T
Briza triloba	SG
Brodiaea albus roseus	MN
Brodiaea amoenas USA	MN
Brodiaea californica	B
Brodiaea californica ssp leptandra	B
Brodiaea clavatus v avius	MN ·
Brodiaea coronaria	AP,B,JE,SG,SW
Brodiaea douglasii	C,JE
Brodiaea elegans	B,LG,MN
Brodiaea minor violet	B
Bromelia antiacantha	B
Bromelia balansae	B

44

BROMELIA

Bromelia karatas	B
Bromelia pinguin	B
Bromopsis bebekenii	SG
Bromopsis inermis	SG
Bromopsis pumpelliana	SG
Bromus benekenii	SG
Bromus breviaristatus	B
Bromus briziformis	SG
Bromus canadensis	B
Bromus carinatus	B
Bromus catharticus	SA
Bromus ciliatus	PR
Bromus erectus	B
Bromus inermis	B
Bromus interruptus	SG
Bromus kalmii	PR
Bromus lanceolatus	V
Bromus macrostachys	B,C,L,SG
Bromus madritensis	B
Bromus marginata	B
Bromus mollis	B
Bromus monocladus	SG
Bromus purgans	PR
Bromus ramosus	B,C
Bromus rubens	B
Bromus secalinus	B
Bromus secalinus v velutinus	B
Bromus squarrosus	AP,B
Bromus sterilis	SG
Bromus tectorum	NS
Bromus unioloides	B
Brosimum alicastrum	B
Brosimum utile	B
Broussonetia papyrifera	B,C,HA
Browallia americana	G
Browallia americana 'Skyblue'	B
Browallia americana 'Snowwhite'	B
Browallia 'Bluetta'	YA
Browallia speciosa 'Amethyst'	B,C
Browallia speciosa 'Blue Bells'	C
Browallia speciosa 'Blue Troll'	B,BS,CL,D,L,S,T,V
Browallia speciosa 'Daniella'	CL
Browallia speciosa 'Heavenly Bells'	B,BS,DT
Browallia speciosa 'Jingle Bells'	S
Browallia speciosa 'Violetta'	CL
Browallia speciosa 'White Troll'	B,BS,C,CL,S
Browallia viscosa	SG
Browallia viscosa 'Sapphire'	B,D,J
Browallia viscosa 'Sapphire Reselected'	B
Browallia viscosa 'Starlight' mix	BS
Browallia viscosa 'Starlight' s-c	BS,CO,KI
Browningia hertlingianus	B,C,Y
Brucea macrophylla	B,C,JE,SC,SG
Bruckenthalia spiculifolia	B,C,JE,SC,SG
Brugmansia arborea	B,C,SA,V
Brugmansia aurea	C
Brugmansia 'Hairy Yellow Tree Datura'	B
Brugmansia insignis x 'Pink'	B
Brugmansia sanguinea	B,C,T
Brugmansia suaveolens	F,JE,SC,T
Brugmansia versicolor	B
Brugmansia x candida pink	B,C
Brugmansia x candida white	B,C,SA
Brunfelsia americana	B
Brunfelsia australis	B
Brunfelsia grandiflora ssp schultesii	

Brunfelsia jamaicensis	B
Brunfelsia lactea	B
Brunfelsia latifolia	B,C,HA
Brunfelsia pauciflora	B,SA
Brunfelsia pauciflora 'Floribunda'	B,C
Brunfelsia sp	SG
Brunfelsia undulata	B
Brunia albiflora	B,SA,SI
Brunia alopecuroides	B,SI
Brunia laevis	B,SI
Brunia nodiflora	B,SI
Brunia stokoei	B,SI
Brunnera macrophylla	B
Brunnichia cirrosa	B
Brunonia australis	B,C,O,SA
Brunsvigia appendiculata	B
Brunsvigia bosmanii	B
Brunsvigia comptonii	B
Brunsvigia minor	B
Brunsvigia orientalis	B
Bryonia alba	G,SG
Bryonia dioica	B,G
Buchaniana axillaris	B
Buchaniana obovata	B
Buchloe dactyloides	AV,B,PR
Bucida buceras	B
Buckinghamia celsissima	B,HA,O,SA
Buddleja albiflora	G
Buddleja alternifolia	SA
Buddleja asiatica	B
Buddleja australis	SG
Buddleja colvilei	B
Buddleja davidii	B,C,F,J,RH,SA,SU,T,V
Buddleja fallowiana	B
Buddleja globosa	B,SA,SG
Buddleja glomerata	B
Buddleja hybrid 'Butterfly'	B,BD,BS,L
Buddleja lindleyana	B,CG,SA
Buddleja longiflora	SA
Buddleja loricata	B,SI
Buddleja saligna	B,SI
Buddleja salviifolia	B
Buddleja sp AC1200	X
Buglossoides purpureocaeruleum	B,JE,SA
Buiningia aurea	B,Y
Buiningia brevicylindrica	B,Y
Buiningia brevicylindrica v longispina	Y
Buiningia purpurea	B,Y
Bulbine abyssinica	B,SI
Bulbine bulbosa	AP,B,SC
Bulbine caulescens see frutescens	
Bulbine frutescens	AP,B,C,P,SC,SI
Bulbine glauca	AP,AU
Bulbine haworthioides	B
Bulbine lagopus	SI
Bulbine latifolia	B,C,SI
Bulbine margarethae	B,CH,SI,Y
Bulbine praemorsa	B
Bulbine sedifolia	SI
Bulbine semibarbata	CG,G,SC
Bulbine semibarbata 'Stargazer'	C
Bulbine sp	SI
Bulbine wiesei	B
Bulbinella angustifolia	AP,B,CG,SA,SC,SS
Bulbinella cauda-felis	B,SI
Bulbinella caudata	B

45

BULBINELLA

Bulbinella floribunda	B
Bulbinella gibbsii	B,SS
Bulbinella graminifolia	B
Bulbinella hookeri	AP,B,C,CG,G,P,PM,SA, SC
Bulbinella latifolia	B,SA
Bulbinella latifolia ssp doleritica	B,SI
Bulbinella latifolia ssp latifolia	B,SI
Bulbinella nutans	B,C,SI
Bulbinella nutans v turfosicola	B,SI
Bulbinella punctulata	B,SI
Bulbinella triquetra	B,SI
Bulbocodium vernum	B,G
Bulbophyllum bracteatum	B
Bulbophyllum elisae	B
Bumelia celastrina	B
Bumelia lycioides	CG
Bumelia tenax	B
Bunchosia argentea	B
Bunias orientalis	B,CG,G,SG
Bunium bulbocastanum	B,C,G
Buphthalmum salicifolium	B,C,G,JE,SG,V
Buphthalmum salicifolium 'Alpengold'	B,JE
Bupleurum falcatum	AP,B,G,JE,SC,SG
Bupleurum fruticosum	C,SA
Bupleurum gibraltaricum	SA
Bupleurum longifolium	B,G,SC,SG
Bupleurum longifolium ssp aureum	JE,SA
Bupleurum multinerve	C,SG
Bupleurum petraeum	AP,B
Bupleurum ranunculoides	B,JE,SA
Bupleurum rotundifolium	AP,B,G,LG,SG,V
Bupleurum rotundifolium 'Garibaldi'	B
Bupleurum rotundifolium 'Green Gold'	B,F,KS,T
Bupleurum rotundifolium 'Griffithii'	B,BS
Bupleurum rotundifolium 'Griffithii Decor'	C
Bupleurum stellatum	B
Bupthalmum salicifolium	T
Bupthalmum salicifolium 'Sunwheel'	SA
Burbidgea schizocheila	B
Burchardia multiflora	B
Burchellia bubalina	B,C,SA,SI
Burkea africana	B,SI
Bursaria spinosa	AU,B,HA,SA
Bursaria spinosa r-v	HA
Bursera fagaroides	B,BC,GC,Y
Bursera grandifolia	CH
Bursera microphylla	B,SW
Burtonia hendersonii	Sa
Burtonia scabra	SA
Butea frondosa see monosperma	
Butea monosperma	B,HA,SA
Butia capitata	B,C,HA,O,SA
Butia eriospatha	CG
Butia yatay	B,C,HA,SA
Butomis umbellatus	SG
Buxus microphylla v koreana	B,SA
Buxus sempervirens	B,C,G,SA
Buxus sempervirens 'Elegantissima'	B
Buxus sempervirens 'Suffruticosa'	B
Byblis gigantea	B
Byblis liniflora	B
Byblis liniflora ssp liniflora	B
Byblis liniflora ssp occidentalis	B
Byrsonima crassifolia	B,RE
Byrsonima spicata	B

Caccinia strigosa	B
Cactus Chilean mix	CH
Cactus columnar	C
Cactus 'Crown' mix	BS
Cactus mix	BD,C,DT,L,S,SO,T,Y
Cactus 'Old Man' mix	C
Cactus sp	V
Cactus 'Superfine' mix	BS,J,U
Cadaba aphylla	B,SI
Cadaba fruticosa	B
Cadia purpurea	B
Caesalpinia ferrea	B,HA,O,SA
Caesalpinia gilliesii	B,C,CG,JE,O,SA,SW
Caesalpinia pulcherrima	B,C,HA,O,RE,SA,SW
Caesalpinia regia	HA
Caesalpinia sp	B
Cajanus cajan	B
Cajanus cinereus	B
Cajophora acuminata 'Orange Supreme'	T
Cajophora coronata	RS
Cajophora laterita 'Frothy'	T,V
Cakile maritima	B
Caladenia sp	B
Calamagrostis arundinacea	B,SG
Calamagrostis brachytricha	B
Calamagrostis canadensis	B,PR
Calamagrostis epigioides	B
Calamagrostis sp Canada	SG
Calamagrostis varia	SG
Calamagrostis villosa	SG
Calamintha cretica	AP,G,SC,SG
Calamintha grandiflora	AP,B,C,G,JE,P,SC,SG,T
Calamintha grandiflora 'Variegata'	B
Calamintha nepeta	B,CP,G,JE,SA,SC,T,V
Calamintha nepeta ssp glandulosa	B
Calamintha officinalis	CP
Calamintha sp	C
Calamintha sylvatica	B,C,G,JE
Calamus australis	B,O
Calamus caryatoides	B,O
Calamus discolor	B,O
Calamus moti	B,O
Calamus radicales	B,O
Calamus rotang	B
Calamus tenuis	SA
Calandrinia ciliata	I
Calandrinia compressa	B,SC
Calandrinia grandiflora	AP,B,C,SC,SG,T
Calandrinia grandiflora 'Rosemarie'	D
Calandrinia 'Neon'	U
Calandrinia sericea alba	B,P
Calandrinia umbellata	AP,B,BS,CL,G,J,JE,KI, S,SC,SG,V
Calandrinia umbellata 'Amaranth'	AP,C,SC,T
Calathea crotalifera	B
Calathea inocephala	B
Calathea lancefolia	B,RE
Calathea lutea	B
Calceolaria biflora	AP,C,CC,FH,G,HH,SC, SG
Calceolaria biflora 'Goldcap'	B,JE
Calceolaria biflora 'Goldcrest Amber'	AP,D,SC,T,V
Calceolaria chelidonioides	AP,C,I
Calceolaria crenatiflora 'Goldcut'	B
Calceolaria cymbiflora	B,P
Calceolaria darwinii	AP,C,SG

46

CALCEOLARIA

Calceolaria dw 'Tigered' mix	C
Calceolaria ericoides	RS
Calceolaria f1 'Dainty'	CL,KI,T,YA
Calceolaria f1 hyb 'Anytime'	BD,BS,C,CL,D,DT,F,J,S, T,V
Calceolaria f1 hyb 'Bright Bikini'	C
Calceolaria f1 hyb 'Melody'	CL
Calceolaria f1 'Memory'	L
Calceolaria falklandica	AP,C,JE,SC
Calceolaria fiebrigiana	CG,JE
Calceolaria filicaulis	PM
Calceolaria fothergillii	AP,AU,RS,SC,SG
Calceolaria gracilis	PM
Calceolaria 'Grandiflora'	BS,KI
Calceolaria helianthemoides	RS
Calceolaria hyssopifolia	RS
Calceolaria integrifolia f1 'Cinderella'	BS
Calceolaria integrifolia f1 'Dainty Mix'	BS
Calceolaria integrifolia f1 'Goldari'	BS,V
Calceolaria integrifolia f1 'Goldari' p.s	B,J
Calceolaria integrifolia f1 'Golden Bunch'	B,BS,CL
Calceolaria integrifolia f1 'Sunset'	BS,CL,D,J,L,PM,S,V,YA
Calceolaria integrifolia f1 'Sunshine'	B,BS,CL,DT,L,S,YA
Calceolaria integrifolia f1 'Sunshine' p.s	CL
Calceolaria integrifolia 'Litle Sweeties'	T
Calceolaria integrifolia 'Sweetheart'	J
Calceolaria 'Jewel Cluster'	S,T
Calceolaria lagunae-blancae	RS
Calceolaria lanigera	B,P,RS
Calceolaria mendocina	RS
Calceolaria mexicana	AP,B,RS,SC
Calceolaria nivalis	RS
Calceolaria picta	B
Calceolaria purpurea	B,RS
Calceolaria sp	AP,RS,SC
Calceolaria tenella	AP,B,I,PM,RS,SC
Calceolaria tripartita	AP,CG,RS,SC
Calceolaria volckmannii	RS
Calceolaris scabiosifolia	SG
Calea zacatachichi	B
Calendula arvensis	C,G,SG
Calendula mix	C
Calendula musellii	T
Calendula officinalis	A,B,CG,CO,F,G,JE,RH, SG,T,V
Calendula officinalis 'Apricot Bon Bon'	T
Calendula officinalis 'Apricot Pygmy'	SE
Calendula officinalis 'Art Shades'	BD,BS,C,CO,DT,F,J,KI, KS,L,ST,T,V
Calendula officinalis 'Balls Apricot'	B
Calendula officinalis 'Balls Imp Orange'	B,BD,BS
Calendula officinalis 'Balls Lemon'	B
Calendula officinalis 'Balls Long Orange'	B
Calendula officinalis 'Beauty Apricot'	C
Calendula officinalis 'Beauty Lemon'	C
Calendula officinalis 'Beauty Pacific'	C,D,F,U
Calendula officinalis 'Black Eyes'	F
Calendula officinalis 'Bon Bon'	SE
Calendula officinalis 'Campfire'	DT
Calendula officinalis 'Dbl Lemon Coronet'	T
Calendula officinalis dbl mix	BS
Calendula officinalis dw mix	KS
Calendula officinalis 'Fiesta Gitana'	BD,BS,C,CL,CO,D,DT,J, L,M,S,T,U,V,YA
Calendula officinalis 'Geisha Girl'	F
Calendula officinalis 'Gitana Orange'	S

Calendula officinalis 'Gitana Yellow'	S
Calendula officinalis 'Greenheart Gold'	B
Calendula officinalis 'Greenheart Orange'	B,F,T
Calendula officinalis 'Gypsy Festival'	BS,KI,TU
Calendula officinalis 'Hen & Chickens'	B,C,KS
Calendula officinalis 'Kablouna Golden'	B,KS
Calendula officinalis 'Kablouna' mix	J
Calendula officinalis 'Kablouna Orange'	B,KS
Calendula officinalis 'King Golden'	BS
Calendula officinalis 'King Orange'	BS,CO,J,KI,R,S,ST,V
Calendula officinalis 'Pacific Apricot'	S,T
Calendula officinalis 'Pacific' mix	T
Calendula officinalis 'Pink Surprise'	D
Calendula officinalis 'Prince Golden'	B
Calendula officinalis 'Prince Indian'	B,D
Calendula officinalis 'Prince Orange'	B
Calendula officinalis 'Princess Golden'	C
Calendula officinalis 'Princess mix'	C
Calendula officinalis 'Prolifera'	B,C,P
Calendula officinalis 'Pygmy mix'	F
Calendula officinalis 'Queen Lemon'	S
Calendula officinalis 'Radio'	BS,C,KS,SE,T
Calendula officinalis single	KS
Calendula officinalis 'Touch Of' s-c	DT,F,KS,SE,T
Calibanus hookeri	B
Calla palustris	B,I
Calliandra anomala	B
Calliandra calothyrsus	B,RE,SA
Calliandra emarginata	B
Calliandra eriophylla	B,C,SW
Calliandra haematocephala	B
Calliandra hyb 'Rosea'	B
Calliandra surinamensis	B,SA
Callicarpa americana	B,SA
Callicarpa americana 'Lactea'	B
Callicarpa dichotoma	B,SA
Callicarpa japonica	B
Callicarpa japonica 'Leucocarpa'	B
Callicarpa mollis	B
Callicarpa pedunculata	B
Callicoma serratifolia	B,C,HA
Calligonum comosum	B
Callilepis laureola	B
Callirhoe involucrata	AP,B,G,JE,SC,T
Callirhoe triangulata	PR
Callistachys lanceolata	B
Callistemon brachyandrus	AP,B,HA,O,SA,SC
Callistemon 'Buranda Station'	B
Callistemon 'Burgundy Supreme'	B
Callistemon candy pink	AU
Callistemon chisholmi	AU
Callistemon citrinus	B,C,HA,O,RH,SA,SG, SH,V
Callistemon citrinus 'Splendens'	AP,AU,B
Callistemon comboynensis	B
Callistemon flavovirens	B
Callistemon formosus	B,HA,O
Callistemon glaucus	AU,B,O
Callistemon 'Injune Pink'	B
Callistemon 'Jeffersii'	B
Callistemon linearifolius	B,O
Callistemon linearis	AU,B,C,HA,N,RH,SA,SG
Callistemon macropunctatus	HA
Callistemon montanus	B,HA,O
Callistemon pachyphyllus	AU,B,HA,O
Callistemon pachyphyllus 'Green'	B

47

CALLISTEMON

Callistemon pallidus	AU,B,HA,,OSA
Callistemon pearsonii	AU
Callistemon phoeniceus	AU,B,HA,O,SA,SH
Callistemon pinifolius green	AU,HA
Callistemon pinifolius red	AU,B,SA
Callistemon pityoides	AU,B,SG
Callistemon polandii	AU,B,HA,O,SH
Callistemon pungens 'Gilesii'	B
Callistemon 'Pygmy Pink'	B
Callistemon recurvus	AU
Callistemon rigidus	B,CG,HA,RH,SA
Callistemon rugulosus	AU,B
Callistemon salignus	B,C,HA,O,SA,SH
Callistemon salignus 'Rubra'	B,SA,SH
Callistemon sieberi	B,C,HA,O
Callistemon sieberi pink	B
Callistemon sp 'Austraflora Firebrand'	AU
Callistemon sp 'Emu Creek'	AU
Callistemon sp mix	C,SG
Callistemon speciosus	HA,O
Callistemon subulatus	AU,B,C,HA,SG,T
Callistemon teretifolius	AU,B,HA
Callistemon viminalis	AU,B,C,HA,O,SA,SH
Callistemon viminalis 'Captain Cook'	B,HA,N,SH
Callistemon viminalis 'Dawson River'	B
Callistemon viminalis nanus	SA
Callistemon violaceus	AU,B,O
Callistemon viridiflorus	AP,AU,B,HA,O,P
Callistephus chinensis	G,SG
Callistephus chinensis 'Kamo' red	B
Callistephus chinensis 'Lilliput' s-c	B
Callistephus chinensis 'Starlight Rose'	O
Callistephus 'Comet' dw mix	BS,D,F,J,L,SE,T
Callistephus 'Comet' dw s-c	B,BS,CL
Callistephus 'Compliment' mix	BS
Callistephus 'Compliment' s-c	B,BS
Callistephus 'Duchess' mix	BD,BO,BS,CL,D,DT,F,J, KI,M,R,S,Sm,T,TU,U,YA
Callistephus 'Dw Thousand Wonders' mix	C,U
Callistephus 'Giant Comet'	BS,KI
Callistephus 'Giant Princess' special mix	C
Callistephus 'Ivica'	C
Callistephus 'Lilliput'	BS,CO,KI,S,ST,T
Callistephus 'Matsumoto' mix	B,BD,BS,C,J,L,S,YA
Callistephus 'Matsumoto' s-c	C
Callistephus 'Matsumoto' White	C,DT
Callistephus 'Milady' mix	BD,BS,D,DT,J,KI,L,M,S, SE,SU,T,TU,U,YA
Callistephus 'Milady' s-c	CL
Callistephus 'Olga'	C
Callistephus 'Ostrich Plume'	C
Callistephus 'Ostrich Plume' mix	BD,BO,BS,CL,CO,D,DT, F,J,KI,L,M,R,S,ST,T,TU, U,VH,YA
Callistephus 'Pinocchio'	BS,D,DT,F,J,KI,L,S,SE, V,VH
Callistephus 'Pompom' s-c	C
Callistephus 'Pompon'	BS,D,DT,F,J,T,TU,U
Callistephus 'Princess' mix	BS,KI,ST,T,U,V
Callistephus 'Quadrille' mix	C
Callistephus 'Starlight' mix	BS,M
Callistephus 'Starlight' s-c	B,BS
Callistephus 'Starlight Scarlet'	B,BS,M
Callistephus 'Turandot'	C
Callistephus Waldersee 'Starlet'	B
Callitris canescens	B,O

Callitris columellaris	B,HA,O
Callitris drummondii	B,O
Callitris endlicheri	AU,B,HA,O,SA
Callitris glaucophylla	O
Callitris hugelii	B
Callitris intratropica	B,O
Callitris macleayana	B
Callitris monticola	B,C,O,SA
Callitris muelleri	O
Callitris oblonga	B,C,O
Callitris preissii	B,HA,O,SA
Callitris preissii ssp murrayensis	B,O
Callitris preissii ssp preissii	O
Callitris preissii ssp verrucosa	B,O
Callitris rhomboidea	AU,B,C,HA,O
Callitris roei	B,O
Calluna vulgaris	A,B,C,JE,SA,V
Calmagrostis varia	SA
Calocedrus decurrens	B,C,SA
Calocedrus formosana	SA
Calochilis holtzei	B
Calochortus albus	AP,B,SC,SW
Calochortus albus v rubellus	B
Calochortus ambiguus	B,RS,SW
Calochortus amoenus	B
Calochortus apiculatus	B,RS
Calochortus aureus	B,SW
Calochortus barbatus	B,G,PM,SW
Calochortus catalinae	B,SW
Calochortus clavatus	AP,CG,PM,SC
Calochortus clavatus v avius	B
Calochortus concolor	B,SW
Calochortus davidsonianus	PM
Calochortus eurycarpus	B,RS,SW
Calochortus exilis	B,RS,SW
Calochortus flexuosus	B,SW
Calochortus gunnisonii	B,SW
Calochortus invenustus	B,SW
Calochortus kennedyi	B,SW
Calochortus kennedyi munzii	SW
Calochortus kennedyi v aurea	B
Calochortus luteus	AP,B,SC
Calochortus nitidus	C
Calochortus nuttallii	B,SW
Calochortus purpureus	B,RS,SW
Calochortus splendens	AP,B,PM,SC
Calochortus uniflorus	AP,PM,SC
Calochortus venustulus	B,SW
Calochortus venustus	B,G
Calochortus weedii	B,SW
Calodendrum capense	B,HA,SA
Calomeria amaranthoides	AU,B,SG
Calophyllum brasiliense	B
Calophyllum inophyllum	B
Calothamnus aridus	B
Calothamnus asper	B,HA
Calothamnus blepharospermus	AU,B
Calothamnus chrysantherus	B,HA,O,SA
Calothamnus gilesii	B,C,HA,O
Calothamnus gracilis	B
Calothamnus graniticus	B
Calothamnus hirsutus	B
Calothamnus homalophyllus	AU,B,O
Calothamnus lehmannii	B
Calothamnus pinifolius	B,O,SA
Calothamnus planifolius	B

CALOTHAMNUS

Calothamnus quadrifidus	AU,B,HA,O,SA	Campanula alaskana	CG
Calothamnus rupestris	AU,B,SA	Campanula alliariifolia	AP,B,C,CG,F,G,JE,P,SA,
Calothamnus sanguineus	AU,B,HA		SC,SG
Calothamnus tuberosus	B	Campanula allionii	C,JE
Calothamnus validus	B,C,O,SA	Campanula alpestris	AP,B,CG,SC
Calothamnus villosus	B,HA,O,SA	Campanula alpina	AP,B,C,CG,SC
Calotis cuneifolia	B	Campanula alsinoides	SG
Calotis erinacea	B	Campanula americana	B,PR
Calotis lappulacea	B	Campanula anchusifolia	FH
Calotis multicaulis	B	Campanula angustifolia	SG
Calotropis gigantea	B	Campanula aucheri	AP,JE,SC,SG
Calotropis procera	B	Campanula autraniana	CG
Calpurnia aurea	SA	Campanula barbata	AP,B,C,CG,F,G,JE,RS,
Calpurnia aurea ssp aurea	B,SI		SA,SC,SG
Calpurnia villosa v intrusa	B	Campanula barbata 'Alba'	AP,B,G,SC
Caltha leptosepala	AP,C,SC,SW	Campanula bellidifolia	G,JE,SC,SG
Caltha obtusa	B,SS	Campanula betulifolia	AP,B,G,I,P,SC
Caltha palustris	B,BS,C,CG,CO,FH,G,JE,	Campanula 'Blue Basket'	S
	KI,PR,SA,SG,SU,T	Campanula bononiensis	AP,B,CG,G,SC
Caltha palustris 'Flore Pleno'	B	Campanula 'Border Sp Mix'	T
Caltha palustris v alba	AP,B,C,G,JE,SC	Campanula caespitosa	B
Caltha palustris v palustris	B,G,JE	Campanula calaminthifolia	FH,MA,SC
Caltha sagittata	AU	Campanula carpatica	AP,B,BD,BS,C,CG,CO,
Calycanthus floridus	A,B,C,CG,G,SA		FH,G,JE,L,SC,SG
Calycanthus occidentalis	C,CG,HA,RH,SA	Campanula carpatica 'Alba'	AP,B,BS,FH,JE,ST
Calycotome villosa	B	Campanula carpatica blue	BS,F,J,KI,SA,ST,V
Calyptridium umbellatum	AP,FH,SC	Campanula carpatica 'Blue Gem'	S
Calyptrogyne dulcis	B	Campanula carpatica 'Blue Moonlight'	FH
Calyptrogyne sarapiquensis	B,RE	Campanula carpatica 'Chewton Joy'	FH
Calystegia sepium	B	Campanula carpatica 'Clips Blue'	B,BS,C,CL,DT,G,JE,SA
Calytrix acutifolia	B	Campanula carpatica 'Clips Deep Blue'	B,BS,CL,JE
Calytrix angulata	B	Campanula carpatica 'Clips Light Blue'	B,BS,CL,JE
Calytrix aurea	B	Campanula carpatica 'Clips' mix	BS
Calytrix exstipula	B,SA	Campanula carpatica 'Clips White'	AP,B,BS,C,CL,DT,G,JE,
Calytrix flavescens	B		SA
Calytrix fraseri	B	Campanula carpatica 'Dwarf Hybrids'	D
Calytrix glutinosa	AU,B	Campanula carpatica f1 'Bellissimo' mix	SE,T
Calytrix leschenaultia	B	Campanula carpatica f1 'Bellissimo' s-c	B,T
Calytrix tenuifolia	B	Campanula carpatica f1 'Uniform Blue'	B,JE
Calytrix tetragona	B,HA,SA	Campanula carpatica f1 'Uniform White'	B,JE
Camassia cusickii	AP,B,CG,G,RH,SC	Campanula carpatica 'Isobel'	CG,FH,G,SG
Camassia leichtlinii	AP,B,C,CC,FH,G,JE,RH,	Campanula carpatica 'Jingle Bells'	T
	SA,SC,SG	Campanula carpatica mix	FH
Camassia leichtlinii v alba	AP,B,C,G,LG,SC	Campanula carpatica 'New Hybrids'	B
Camassia quamash	AP,B,C,JE,SA,SC,SG,	Campanula carpatica 'Riverslea'	FH
	SW	Campanula carpatica 'Silberschale'	JE
Camassia quamash v utahensis	B	Campanula carpatica 'Star Blue'	YA
Camassia scilloides	B,PR	Campanula carpatica 'Star White'	YA
Camassia sucksdorfii	SG	Campanula c. carpatica v turbinata	CG,JE,SC
Camassia viridiflora	AP	Campanula c. v turbinata 'Arends Form'	B
Camelina microcarpa	B	Campanula c. v turbinata 'Wheatley Violet'	B,FH
Camelina sativa	B,SG	Campanula carpatica white	F,J,KI,V
Camellia japonica	B,BS,C,CG,SA	Campanula cashmeriana	AP,FH,G,I,SC,SG,T
Camellia japonica named cvs	B	Campanula cenisia	B,C,JE
Camellia oleifera	B,SA	Campanula cephallenica	FH
Camellia rosiflora	B	Campanula cervicaria	AP,G,SG
Camellia saluenensis	B	Campanula cochleariifolia	AP,B,C,CG,CL,G,I,JE,L,
Camellia sasanqua	B,CG,SA		SA,SC,U
Camellia sinensis	B,V	Campanula cochleariifolia 'Alba'	B,I,JE,SA,T
Camellia x williamsii 'Wilber Foss'	B	Campanula coch. 'Baby Series' s-c	B,F
Camissonia bistorta	B,KS	Campanula cochleariifolia 'Bavaria Blue'	JE
Camissonia californica	B,BS,L,SE	Campanula cochleariifolia 'Bavaria White'	JE
Camissonia cheiranthifolia	B	Campanula collina	AP,B,BS,C,CG,G,JE,SA,
Camissonia claviformis	B		SC,SG
Camissonia subacaulis	B	Campanula collina v abschasica	CC
Campanula acaulis	B	Campanula cordifolia	B

CAMPANULA

Campanula 'E.H.Frost'	FH	Campanula medium 'Bella Series' s-c	F
Campanula elatines v elatinoides	B,C,SC	Campanula medium 'Bells of Holland'	BD,BS,C,S
Campanula elatines v fenestrellata	B,F	Campanula medium 'Calycanthema'	B,BS,CL,D,DT,F,KI,L,SE,
Campanula 'Elizabeth'	PM		SU,T,U,YA
Campanula erect border mix	C	Campanula m. 'Calyc. Ringing Bells'	C
Campanula erinus	CG	Campanula medium 'Chelsea Pink'	B,BS,C,CL,DT,F,SE,U,V
Campanula excisa	B,C,SC	Campanula m. 'Cup & Saucer' special	CO,J,S,V
Campanula excisa 'Alba'	B	Campanula medium 'Dean's Hybrids'	L
Campanula fenestrellata	CG,JE	Campanula medium 'Double' Mix	BS,L,TU
Campanula formanekiana	AP,B,C,CG,FH,SSC,G	Campanula medium 'Dwarf Bedding'	D
Campanula fragilis	AP,B,BS,L,SC	Campanula medium 'Dwarf Bell Tower'	U
Campanula fragilis 'Jewel'	C,T	Campanula medium 'Fl.Pl. finest mix	C
Campanula garganica	AP,B,BS,C,CL,D,FH,G,	Campanula medium 'Fl.Pl. Violet-blue'	B
	JE,L,SA,SC,T	Campanula medium 'Fl.Pl. White'	B
Campanula glomerata	AP,B,C,CG,G,LA,MA,SA,	Campanula medium 'Rosea'	D
	SG,SU,T,V	Campanula medium 'Russian Pink'	T
Campanula glomerata 'Acaulis'	AP,B,C,CL,FH,JE,PM,SC	Campanula medium 'Single Blue'	B,C,JE
Campanula glomerata 'Alba'	B,C,G,JE,MA,SA	Campanula medium 'Single Lilac'	B
Campanula glomerata ssp elliptica	SG	Campanula medium 'Single' Mix	BS,KI,L,ST,TU
Campanula glomerata 'Superba'	B,L,P,SA,T	Campanula medium 'Single Rose'	B,C,JE
Campanula glomerata v dahurica	BS,C,F,G,JE	Campanula medium 'Single White'	B,JE
Campanula grossekii	B,CC,FH,G,RS,SC	Campanula moesiaca	AP,C,P
Campanula grossheimii	G,SG	Campanula moravica	CG
Campanula hawkinsiana	T	Campanula ochroleuca	B,G,T
Campanula herzegovina	G,I	Campanula olympica	SG
Campanula hierosolymitana	B	Campanula orphanidea	CG
Campanula hohenackeri	CG	Campanula patula	AP,B,C,G,JE,SC,V
Campanula hondoensis	SG	Campanula persicifolia	A,AP,B,CG,CL,FH,G,I,
Campanula incurva	AP,B,C,CG,G,P,SC		KI,SA,SC,SG,SU,V,W
Campanula incurva 'Blue Ice'	T	Campanula persicifolia 'Alba'	AP,B,F,G,I,SA,SC,SG
Campanula isophylla 'Alba'	B	Campanula persicifolia 'Blue Bell'	C,KS
Campanula isophylla 'Caerulea'	B	Campanula persicifolia grandiflora	JE
Campanula isophylla f1 'Top Star'	YA	Campanula persicifolia grandiflora 'Alba'	B,JE
Campanula isophylla 'Improved' s-c	T	Campanula p. grandiflora 'Caerulea'	G,JE
Campanula isophylla 'Kristal' s-c	T	Campanula persicifolia 'New Giant Hybs'	T
Campanula isophylla mix	T	Campanula persicifolia 'Telham Beauty'	B,BS,C,F,SA
Campanula isophylla 'Stella Blue'	C,CL,DT,L	Campanula persicifolia v planiflora	B
Campanula isophylla 'Stella mix'	C	Campanula persicifolia 'White Bell'	C,KS
Campanula isophylla 'Stella White'	C,CL,DT,L	Campanula persicifolia 'White Queen'	S
Campanula justiniana	B,CG	Campanula petraea	CG
Campanula kemulariae	B,FH,G,JE	Campanula petrophila	CC
Campanula kolenatiana	B,C,SC	Campanula polymorpha	CG
Campanula lactiflora	A,B,CG,F,G,JE,MA,RS,	Campanula portenschlagiana	AP,B,C,F,FH,JE,SA,SC
	SA,SC,SG,T	Campanula poscharskyana	AP,B,BS,C,CG,CL,I,JE,
Campanula lactiflora 'New Hybrids'	B,C,JE		SA,U
Campanula lanata	AP,B,CG,G,P,SG	Campanula poscharskyana 'Stella'	FH
Campanula lasiocarpa	AP,CC,G,SC	Campanula primulifolia	AP,B,CG,G,P,SC,T
Campanula latifolia	A,AP,B,C,CG,G,JE,LA,	Campanula pulla	AP,B,G,SC,T
	PA,PM,SA,SC,SG	Campanula punctata	AP,B,C,CC,F,G,JE,PA,
Campanula latifolia 'Alba'	AP,B,C,JE,SC		SA,SC,SG,T
Campanula latifolia 'Amethyst'	T	Campanula punctata hondoensis	P
Campanula latifolia 'Brantwood'	T	Campanula punctata 'Nana Alba'	AP,B,P,SC
Campanula latifolia v macrantha	AP,B,C,CG,G,JE,SA,SC,	Campanula punctata 'Rubriflora'	AP,B,C,F,P,SA
	SG	Campanula pyramidalis	B,C,F,G,JE,KI,S,SA,T,U,V
Campanula latifolia v macrantha 'Alba'	B,G,JE,SA,SC,T	Campanula pyramidalis 'Alba'	B,BS,C,CG,JE,SA
Campanula l. v macrantha 'Blue Master'	B	Campanula pyramidalis f caerulea	CG
Campanula l. v macrantha 'Snow Master'	B	Campanula pyramidalis mix	BS,C,DT,JE,L
Campanula latiloba	W	Campanula raineri	AP,B,C,CG,JE,SC
Campanula latiloba 'Alba'	B,MA	Campanula rapunculoides	A,B,C,CG,JE,SA,SG
Campanula lingulata	CG	Campanula rapunculus	B,C,G,JE,SG
Campanula linifolia	B	Campanula retrorsa	B
Campanula lusitanica	CG	Campanula rhomboidalis	AP,B,C,SC,SG
Campanula macrostachya	B	Campanula 'Rock Garden Mix'	C,JE,P,T
Campanula malacitana	I	Campanula rotundifolia	AP,B,BD,BS,C,CG,CO,D,
Campanula medium	B,BD,C,CG,G,KS,R,ST,		F,G,KI,LA,JE,PR,SA,SC,
	VH		SE,SG,SU,V,Z

50

CAMPANULA

Campanula rotundifolia 'Olympica'	B,C,HH	Cannomois virgata	B,SI
Campanula rotundifolia v Marchsettii	T,W	Canthium dicoccum	B
Campanula rupestris	AP,SC,W	Canthium inerme	B,SI
Campanula rupestris anchusifolia	PM	Canthium odoratum	B
Campanula sarmatica	AP,B,C,CG,G,P,SC,SG,T	Canthium oleifolium	HA
Campanula sartorii	AP,FH,SC,SG,T,W	Canthium parviflorum	B
Campanula saxifraga	SC,SG	Capparis brevispina	B
Campanula scheuchzeri	CG,JE	Capparis corymbosa	B
Campanula sibirica	AP,C	Capparis mitchellii	B
Campanula sp Turkey	CC	Capparis spinosa	B,C,SA
Campanula speciosa	B,C,CG,G,JE,SC,T	Capparis spinosa v inermis	B,SA
Campanula spicata	AP,B,G,HH,SC	Capparis sp. v inermis 'Spineless Select'	B
Campanula stellaris	B	Capparis spinosa v nummularia	B
Campanula strigosa	B	Capparis tomentosa	B
Campanula sulphurea	B	Capparis zeylanica	B
Campanula takesimana	AP,B,HH,F,G,JE,P,PM,	Capsella bursa-pastoris	B,SG
	SC,T	Capsicum annuum 'Ornamental mix'	BS,KI
Campanula takesimana 'Alba'	B	Caragana arborescens	A,B,C,G,SA,SC,SG
Campanula tatrae	CG,SG	Caragana arborescens v crasseaculeata	B
Campanula thessala	AP,B,FH,RS,SC	Caragana aurantiaca	SA,SG
Campanula thyrsoides	AP,B,C,CG,F,G,JE,SC,SG	Caragana boisii	SA,SG
Campanula thyrsoides ssp carniolica	AP,CG,FH,G,SC,SG,W	Caragana brevispina	AP,CC
Campanula tommasiniana	AP,B,I,G,JE,SC,SG	Caragana frutex	SA,SG
Campanula tommasiniana hyb	I	Caragana microphylla	B,N,SA
Campanula trachelium	AP,B,C,CG,G,LA,JE,PM,	Caragana pekinensis	B
	SA,SC,SG,SU,TU	Caragana pygmaea	SA,SG
Campanula trachelium 'Alba'	SC,SG	Caragana rosea	SA
Campanula trachelium 'Bernice'	AP,B,P	Caragana spinosa	SG
Campanula trachelium 'Faichem Lilac'	C,P	Caragana tragacanthoides	SA
Campanula tridentata	AP,B,C,G,JE,SC,SG	Caralluma sp mix	C
Campanula versicolor	AP,B,C,G,JE	Carapa grandiflora	B
Campanula waldsteiniana	B,C,CG,JE	Carapa procera	B
Campanula x psuedoraineri	FH,G	Cardamine alpina ex Tyrol	G
Campanula x pulloides	B,G	Cardamine asarifolia	CG
Campanula xylocarpa	B	Cardamine bulbifera	B,C,I
Campomanesia lineatifolia	B	Cardamine heptaphylla	B,C,G
Campsis grandiflora	B,G,SA	Cardamine hirsuta	B
Campsis radicans	AP,B,C,CP,G,O,SA,T	Cardamine kitaibellii	B
Campsis x tagliabuana 'Mdm Galen'	B,RS	Cardamine oligosperma	B
Camptotheca acuminata	B,CG,SA	Cardamine opizii	SG
Cananga odorata	B,SA	Cardamine polyphylla	C
Canarium madagascariensis	B	Cardamine pratensis	B,C,CO,JE,SU
Canarium schweinfurthii	B	Cardaria draba	B,SG
Canavalia cathartica	B	Cardiocrinum cordatum	B,CC,CG
Canavalia ensiformis	B	Cardiocrinum giganteum	AP,B,C,G,JE,LG,P,PA,
Canavalia 'Gallito Del Rio'	B		RS,SA,SC,SG,T
Canavalia maritima	HA,SA	Cardiocrinum giganteum v yunnanense	C
Canavalia rosea	AU,B	Cardiocrinum glehnii	C,SA,SG
Canistrum sp	B	Cardiospermum grandiflorum	B
Canna altensteinii	G	Cardiospermum halicacabum	B,C,G,KS,V
Canna americana	B	Carduncellus mitissimus	B,G,SC
Canna coccinea	CG	Carduncellus monspeliensis	B,C
Canna 'Colour Carnival'	O	Carduncellus rhaponticoides	AP,PM
Canna 'Crozy's New Hybrids'	B,BS	Carduus acaulis	B
Canna flaccida	B,G	Carduus benedicyus	SU
Canna glauca	CG	Carduus carlinoides ssp carlinoides	CG
Canna indica	B,BS,C,CG,HA,LG,O,RE,	Carduus crispus	SG
	SA,SG	Carduus dahuricus	SG
Canna indica hyb	T	Carduus nutans	B,C
Canna indica 'Tropical Rose'	B,T,V	Carduus tenuiflorus	B
Canna 'Lg Fl Mix'	F	Cardwellia sublimis	B,O
Canna limbata	B	Carex acuta	B,JE
Canna 'New Hybrids' mix	BS	Carex acutiformis	B,JE
Canna 'Seven Dwarfs Cherry' s-c	B	Carex alba	B,JE,SG
Cannanga odorata	RE	Carex alopecoidea	PR
Cannomois sp	SI	Carex annectens xanthocarpa	PR

CAREX

Carex appressa	B
Carex arenaria	B,JE,SA,SG
Carex atrata ssp aterrima	SG
Carex baccans	SG
Carex bergrenii	AP,AU,B,JE,PM,SG
Carex bicknelii	B
Carex buchananii	AP,B,G,JE,SA,SC
Carex buchananii 'Viridis'	B,JE
Carex caespitosa	SG
Carex capillaris	SG
Carex caryophyllea	B
Carex comans	AP,B,C,G,SA,SC,SG
Carex comosa	PR
Carex crinita	PR
Carex dallii	SG
Carex dipsacea	B,SA
Carex disticha	SG
Carex elata 'Aurea'	B
Carex flacca	B,JE,SA
Carex flagellifera	AP,B,SG
Carex flava	B,G,SG
Carex folliculata	JE
Carex 'Frosted Curls'	AP,B,P,PM
Carex gracilis	G,SA
Carex grayi	AP,B,G,JE,SA,SC,SG
Carex hirta	B
Carex lacustris	PR
Carex leersiana	JE
Carex lupilina	PR
Carex lurida	JE
Carex macrocephala	B,JE
Carex media	SG
Carex melanathiformis	SG
Carex muhlenbergii	PR
Carex muricata	SG
Carex muricata ssp pairaei	SG
Carex muskingumensis	G,JE,SC,T
Carex otrubae	B,G,SG
Carex paniculata	B,JE
Carex pendula	AP,B,C,G,E,LA,JE,SA, SC,SG
Carex petriei	AP,B,G,SC,SS
Carex prairea	PR
Carex pseudocyperus	AP,B,G,JE,SA,SC
Carex remota	JE,SG
Carex retrorsa	PR
Carex rhyncophysa	SG
Carex riparia	B,JE,SG
Carex riparia 'Variegata'	B
Carex rostrata	CG
Carex scoparia	PR
Carex secta	B,SA,SG
Carex secta v tenuiculmis	JE,SC
Carex sempervirens ssp tatrorum	SG
Carex solandri	B
Carex sp China	SG
Carex sp 'Majken'	JE
Carex sprengellii	PR
Carex stenophylla	B
Carex stipata	PR
Carex stricta	PR
Carex sylvatica	G,JE,SA
Carex tenuisecta 'Bronzina'	B
Carex testacea	AP,B,P,SC
Carex trifida	B,SA,SG
Carex tuckermani	PR

Carex vesicaria	B,SG
Carex vulpina	B,JE
Carex vulpinoidea	PR
Carica chrysopetala	B
Carica goudoutiana	B
Carica papaya	C,G,RE,SA,V
Carica papaya 'Ceylon'	B
Carica papaya 'Coorg Honeydew'	B,SA
Carica papaya dwarf	B
Carica papaya hyb 'Red'	B
Carica papaya 'Mammoth'	B
Carica papaya 'Ranchi'	B
Carica papaya 'Solo'	B,C
Carica papaya 'Sunrise'	B
Carica papaya 'Sunset'	B
Carica papaya 'Waimanolo'	B
Carica papaya 'Washington'	B
Carica pentagona	B
Carica pubescens	B
Carica quercifolia	B,CG
Carica stipulata	B
Cariniana pyriformis	B
Carissa bispinosa	B,SI
Carissa carandas	B
Carissa edulis	B
Carissa haematocarpa	B,SI
Carissa macrocarpa	B,C,O,SA,SI
Carissa spinarum	B
Carlina acanthifolia	B,C,JE,SA,T
Carlina acaulis	AP,B,BS,G,SC,T
Carlina acaulis 'Bronze Form'	B,C,G,JE,SA
Carlina acaulis 'Caulescens'	AP,B,C
Carlina acaulis 'Simplex'	FH,JE,SA,SC,SG,V
Carlina vulgaris	B,C,G,JE,SA,SG
Carlina vulgaris 'Silver Star'	B,JE,SA
Carlina vulgaris ssp intermedia	B
Carlina vulgaris ssp vulgaris	CG
Carludovica palmata	B
Carmichaelia aligera	B,SA,SS
Carmichaelia angustata	CG
Carmichaelia australis	SG
Carmichaelia enysii	AP,B,CC,SC,SS
Carmichaelia glabrata	B,SS
Carmichaelia grandiflora	B,SS
Carmichaelia kirkii	B,SS
Carmichaelia monroi	B,SA,SS
Carmichaelia ovata	B
Carmichaelia petriei	SG,SS
Carmichaelia rivulata	B
Carmichaelia robusta	B,SS
Carmichaelia subulata	G,SG
Carmichaelia violacea	SA
Carmichaelia williamsii	SS
Carmona retusa	B
Carnegiea euphorbioides	CG
Carnegiea gigantea	B,C,CH,Y
Carpanthea pomeridiana	B,C,DT,F,SG,SI,Y
Carpanthea pomeridiana 'Golden Carpet'	J,SE,V
Carpentaria acuminata	B,C,HA,N,O,SA
Carpenteria californica	AP,B,C,SA
Carpha alpina	B,SS
Carpinus betulus	B,C,I,N,SA
Carpinus bitrilus	CG
Carpinus caroliniana	B,G,N,SA
Carpinus caucasica	N,SA
Carpinus cordata	CG,SA

CARPINUS

Carpinus coreana	B,N	Casimiroa tetrameria	B
Carpinus japonica	SA	Cassia abbreviata	SI
Carpinus laxiflora	B,N,SA	Cassia absus	B
Carpinus laxiflora Korean form	N	Cassia afrofistula	B
Carpinus orientalis	B,N,SA	Cassia afrofistula 'Beareana'	B
Carpinus polyneura	N	Cassia angustifolia	O
Carpinus schisiensis	N	Cassia arborescens	B
Carpinus turczaninowii	C,N,SA	Cassia australis	HA,SA
Carpinus viminea	N	Cassia barclayana	O
Carpinus x schuschuensis	B	Cassia brewsteri	B,HA,O
Carpobrotus aequilaterus	B	Cassia candolleana	HA,O,SA
Carpobrotus deliciosus	B,SI	Cassia covesii	SW
Carpobrotus edulis	B,C,SA,SI	Cassia eremophylla	HA,SA
Carpobrotus edulis v parviflora	B,SI	Cassia fasciculata	HW,PR
Carpobrotus glaucescens	B	Cassia fistula	B,HA,O,RE,SA
Carpobrotus muirii	B,SI	Cassia glauca	HA,SA
Carpobrotus quadrifidus	SI	Cassia grandis	B,HA,O,RE,SA
Carpobrotus sauerae	SA,SI	Cassia hebecarpa	C,CP,PR
Carpobrotus virescens	B	Cassia helmsii	C
Carpodetus serratus	B,SS	Cassia javanica	B,HA,O,SA
Carrierea calycina	B	Cassia 'John Bull'	B
Carruanthus peersii	B	Cassia laevigata	SG
Carruanthus ssp	B	Cassia leptophylla	B
Carthamus lanatus	B,G	Cassia marginata	HA,O,SA
Carthamus tinctorius	B,C,CP,KS,SU,T,V	Cassia marilandica	JE,PR,SA,SC
Carthamus tinctorius 'Goldtuft'	BS,CO,KI,ST	Cassia moschata	B
Carthamus tinctorius 'Grenade' s-c	B,L	Cassia multijuga	HA,O,SA
Carthamus tinctorius 'Kinko' orange	B,BS	Cassia nodosa	B,HA,O,SA
Carthamus tinctorius 'Lasting Orange'	BS,DT	Cassia occidentalis	O
Carthamus tinctorius 'Lasting White'	BD,BS,C	Cassia pumila	B
Carthamus tinctorius 'Lasting Yellow'	BS	Cassia renigera	B,HA,O,SA
Carthamus tinctorius 'Orange & Cream'	T	Cassia reticulata	RE
Carthamus tinctorius 'Orange-Gold'	U	Cassia roxburghii	B
Carthamus tinctorius 'Shiro' yellow	B,BS	Cassia spectabilis	O,RE
Carthamus tinctorius 'Zanzibar'	B	Cassia sturtii	C,JE,SA
Cartonema spicatum	AU	Cassia tomentella	B
Carum carvi	CG,CP,KS,SG	Cassine aethiopica	B,SI
Carum carvi 'Annua'	B	Cassine crocea	B,SI
Carum roxburgianum	B	Cassine transvaalensis	B
Carya aquatica	B,SA	Cassinia aculeata	B,HA
Carya cathayensis	B,SA	Cassinia arcuata	B,HA,SA
Carya cordiformis	B	Cassinia aureonitens	AU
Carya glabra	B,SA	Cassinia laevis	B
Carya hunanesis	B	Cassinia leptophylla	B
Carya illinoiensis	B,SA	Cassinia leptophylla ssp fulvida	SS
Carya illinoiensis 'Improved'	B	Cassinia leptophylla ssp vauvilliersii	AP,CC,SS
Carya laciniosa	B,CG,SA	Cassinia longifolia	HA
Carya myristicaeformis	SA	Cassinia quinquefaria	B,HA
Carya ovata	B,SA	Cassinia sp	AP,AU
Carya texana	B	Cassinia uncata	B
Carya tomentosa	B,SA	Cassinopsis ilicifolia	B,SI
Caryopteris incana	AP,SA,SC	Cassiope hypnoides	C
Caryopteris mongolica	SA	Cassytha filiformis	B
Caryopteris odorata	B,C	Castalis nudicaulis	B,SI
Caryopteris x bungei	T	Castalis tragus	B,SI
Caryopteris x clandonensis	E,SA,T	Castalis tragus v pinnatifida	B,SI
Caryopteris x clandonensis 'New Hybrids'	B	Castanea dentata	SA
Caryopteris x cl. 'Worcester Gold'	E	Castanea mollissima	B,SA
Caryota cummingii	O	Castanea sativa	B,HA,SA
Caryota maxima	O	Castanopsis cuspidata	SA
Caryota mitis	B,C,O,SA	Castanopsis eyeri	B,SA
Caryota no	O	Castanopsis sempervirens	SA
Caryota ochlandra	B,O,SA	Castanopsis tibetana	B,SA
Caryota rumphiana	O	Castanospermum australe	B,HA,O,SA
Caryota urens	B,O,SA	Castanospora alphandii	B
Casimiroa edulis	B	Castellanosia caineana	Y

CASTILLA

Castilla elastica	B	Catharanthus pusillus	B
Castilleja coccinea	AV,B,PR	Catharanthus roseus	B,C,HA,KI,SA
Castilleja foliolosa	B	Catharanthus roseus 'Albus'	B
Castilleja indivisa	B	Catharanthus roseus 'Apricot Delight'	BS,T
Castilleja integra	B,SW	Catharanthus roseus 'Cooler' s-c	B,BS,T
Castilleja linariifolia	B	Catharanthus roseus 'Grape Cooler' mix	BD,BS
Castilleja martinii	B	Catharanthus roseus 'Ice Cool Mix'	SE
Castilleja miniata	C,JE,SC	Catharanthus roseus 'Kermesina'	B
Castilleja miniata v miniata	B	Catharanthus roseus 'Little Blanche'	B
Castilleja sessiflora	PR	Catharanthus roseus 'Little Bright Eyes'	B
Castilleja stenantha	B	Catharanthus roseus 'Little Delicata'	B
Casuarina acuaria	B	Catharanthus roseus 'Little Linda'	B
Casuarina acutivalvis	B	Catharanthus roseus 'Little Pinkie'	B
Casuarina campestris	B	Catharanthus roseus 'Magic Carpet mix'	J,V
Casuarina corniculata	B	Catharanthus roseus mix	BS
Casuarina cristata	B,SA	Catharanthus roseus 'Ocellatus Albus'	B
Casuarina cristata ssp cristata	HA,O	Catharanthus roseus 'Pacifica' mix	BS
Casuarina cunninghamiana	B,HA,O,SA	Catharanthus roseus 'Pacifica' s-c	CL,T
Casuarina decaisneana	B,HASA	Catharanthus roseus 'Parasol'	B,T
Casuarina decussata	B	Catharanthus roseus 'Petit'	F
Casuarina distyla	B,SA	Catharanthus roseus 'Pretty In Series'	B,BS,T
Casuarina equisetifolia	B,HA,O,SA	Catharanthus roseus 'Tall Crimson'	B
Casuarina equisetifolia v incana	B	Catharanthus roseus 'Tall Rose'	B
Casuarina erecta	B	Catharanthus roseus 'Terrace Vermillion'	T
Casuarina fraserana	B	Catharanthus roseus 'Tropicana'	BS,C,CL,SE,T
Casuarina glauca	B,HA,O,SA	Cathartolinum catharticum	SG
Casuarina helmsii	B	Catophractes alexandri	B,SI
Casuarina huegeliana	B	Catopsis sessiliflora	B
Casuarina humilis	B	Cattleya aurantiaca	CG
Casuarina inophloia	B	Cattleya maxima	B
Casuarina lehmanniana	B,HA	Catunaregam spinosa	B
Casuarina littoralis	B,C,SA	Cautleya spicata	BS
Casuarina luehmannii	B	Ceanothus americanus	AP,B,PR
Casuarina monilifera	B	Ceanothus arboreus	C
Casuarina muellerana	B	Ceanothus cordulatus	B
Casuarina nana	B,C,SA	Ceanothus crassifolius	B
Casuarina paludosa	B,SA	Ceanothus cuneatus	B,SA
Casuarina pauper	B,O	Ceanothus cyaneus	B
Casuarina pinaster	B	Ceanothus greggii	B
Casuarina pusilla	B	Ceanothus griseus	B
Casuarina rigida	B	Ceanothus impressus	B,SC
Casuarina scleroclada	B	Ceanothus integerrimus	B,C,SA
Casuarina sp mix	C	Ceanothus leucodermis	B,SW
Casuarina stricta	SA	Ceanothus megacarpus	B
Casuarina tesselata	B	Ceanothus ovatus	PR
Casuarina thuyoides	B	Ceanothus prostratus	AP,B,SA
Casuarina torulosa	B	Ceanothus ramulosus	B
Casuarina trichodon	B	Ceanothus sanguineus	B,C,SA
Casuarina verticillata	B	Ceanothus spinosus	B
Catalpa bignonioides	B,C,CG,G,HA,N,SA	Ceanothus thyrsiflorus	AP,B
Catalpa bungei	G,SA	Ceanothus thyrsiflorus v repens	C
Catalpa ovata	B,CG,SA	Ceanothus tomentosus	B
Catalpa ovata CNW1297	X	Cecropia palmata	B
Catalpa speciosa	B,CG,G,N,SA	Cedrela chinensis	SA
Catalpa x hybrida	B	Cedrela mexicana	B
Catananche bicolor	T	Cedrela microcarpa	B
Catananche caerulea	AP,B,BS,C,CG,CL,DT,F,	Cedrela montana	B
	G,J,JE,KS,MA,PA,S,SA,	Cedrela odorata	B,RE
	SC,SU,T,TU,V	Cedrela serrata	B
Catananche caerulea v alba	C,JE,KS	Cedrela tonduzzi	B
Catananche 'Stargazer'	SE	Cedronella triphylla	AP,B,C,CP,G,SG
Catasetum violascens	B	Cedrus atlantica	B,HA,SA
Catha edulis	B	Cedrus atlantica 'Argentea'	B
Catharanthus lanceus	B,SI	Cedrus atlantica f glauca	B,C,N,V
Catharanthus 'Morning Mist'	BD	Cedrus brevifolia	B,N,SA,SG
Catharanthus ovalis	B	Cedrus deodara	B,C,HA,N,SA

CEDRUS

Cedrus deodara 'Aurea'	B	Celosia plumosa 'Fairy Fountains'	BD,BS,KS,T
Cedrus libani	B,C,N,SA,X	Celosia plumosa 'Fontana' orange	B
Cedrus libani ssp stenocoma	B	Celosia plumosa 'Forest Fire'	B
Ceiba pentandra	B,HA,RE,SA	Celosia plumosa 'Forest Fire' imp	B
Celastrus orbiculatus	B,C,SA,SG	Celosia plumosa 'Golden Triumph'	B
Celastrus scandens	B,C,PR,SA,SG	Celosia plumosa 'Kimono' mix	BS,CL,CO,J,KI,L,S,T,YA
Celmisia allanii	PM	Celosia plumosa 'Kimono' s-c	BS
Celmisia alpina	AP,B,SS	Celosia plumosa 'Lilliput' mix	BS
Celmisia angustifolia	AP,AU,B,SC,SS	Celosia plumosa 'Lilliput' orange	B
Celmisia angustifolia (Mt.Hutt form)	PM	Celosia plumosa mix	J
Celmisia angustifolia (s.leaf form)	PM	Celosia plumosa 'Rondo'	CL
Celmisia armstrongii	B,SS	Celosia 'Rocket Series' s-c	B
Celmisia bellidioides	AP,B,SC,SS	Celosia spicata 'Flamingo Feather'	BS,C,CO,KI,KS,L,S,T,V
Celmisia dallii	B,PM,SS	Celosia spicata 'Flamingo Pink Feather'	B,U
Celmisia densiflora	AP,AU,B,SC,SS	Celosia spicata 'Flamingo Purple Feather'	B,BS,C,KS,SE
Celmisia discolor	B,SC,SS	Celosia spicata 'Xanthippe'	B
Celmisia du-rietzii	B,SC,SS	Celosia thompsonii 'Magnifica'	BS
Celmisia glandulosa	B,SS	Celtis africana	B,C,SI
Celmisia gracilenta	AP,B,SC,SG,SS	Celtis australis	B,C,HA,SA
Celmisia graminifolia	B,SS	Celtis caucasica	SG
Celmisia haastii	AU,PM,SS	Celtis chinensis	SA
Celmisia hectori	AP,AU,B,CC,SC	Celtis glabrata	SA
Celmisia hookeri	AP,B,C,SC,SS	Celtis laevigata	B,SA
Celmisia incana	AP,PM,SC	Celtis occidentalis	B,C,CG,SA
Celmisia lanceolata	SS	Celtis reticulata	B
Celmisia laricifolia	B,SS	Celtis sinensis	B,C,V
Celmisia lateralis	B	Celtis tournefortii	SA
Celmisia longifolia	AP,G,PM,SC,SG	Cenarrhenes nitida	B
Celmisia lyallii	AP,AU,B,SC,SS	Cenchrus ciliaris	B
Celmisia mackauii	AP,SA,SS	Cenchrus ciliaris 'Biloela'	B
Celmisia monroi	PM,SC	Cenchrus ciliaris 'Gayndah'	B
Celmisia petiolata	B,SS	Cenchrus ciliaris 'Molopo'	B
Celmisia petriei	AP,SS	Cenchrus ciliaris 'Numbank'	B
Celmisia prorepens	AP,B,SS	Cenchrus ciliaris 'U.S.A.'	B
Celmisia semicordata	AP,AU,B,C,CC,PM,SA,	Cenchrus incertus	B
	SC,SS	Cenchrus setigerus	B
Celmisia sericophylla	PM,SG	Cenia turbinata	B,SI
Celmisia sessiliflora	B,SC,SS	Centaurea americana 'Aloha'	B
Celmisia spectabilis	AP,AU,B,PM,SC,SS	Centaurea americana 'Jolly Joker'	C
Celmisia spectabilis v argentea	SG	Centaurea americana 'Lilac Charm'	B
Celmisia spectabilis v magnifica	B,PM,SC,SS	Centaurea arenaria	B
Celmisia stricta	AU	Centaurea atropurpurea	CG
Celmisia traversii	B,PM,SS	Centaurea bella	AP,FH,SC
Celmisia viscosa	AU,B,SC,SS	Centaurea calcitrapa	B
Celmisia walkeri	AP,AU,SC	Centaurea cana rosea	FH
Celmisia webbii	AP,SG	Centaurea cineraria	B,G,JE
Celosia argentea	B,G	Centaurea collina	B
Celosia argentea cristata 'Bombay Purpe'	CL,O	Centaurea crocodylum	B
Celosia argentea 'Sparkler Carmine'	C	Centaurea cyanoides	B
Celosia cristata 'Coral Garden'	C,KS	Centaurea cyanus	AP,B,C,CO,F,G,HW,LA,
Celosia cristata 'Crest' pink	B		SG,SU,TU
Celosia cristata 'Fire Chief'	C	Centaurea cyanus 'Baby Blue'	B,BD,BS,D,L
Celosia cristata 'Jewel Box'	BS,D,J,KS,S,SE,T	Centaurea cyanus 'Baby Pink'	B
Celosia cristata 'Kurume Corona'	KS	Centaurea cyanus 'Ball Giant mix'	M
Celosia cristata 'nana'	V	Centaurea cyanus 'Ball Series' s-c	BS,F,T,V
Celosia 'New Look'	F	Centaurea cyanus 'Black Boy'	B
Celosia 'Olympia' mix	CL,L	Centaurea cyanus 'Blue Boy'	B,BS,KS
Celosia 'Olympic' s-c	B	Centaurea cyanus 'Blue Diadem'	B,D,DT,S,T
Celosia plumosa	KI,V	Centaurea cyanus 'Blue Double'	BD,BS,CO,J,KI,ST,TU,
Celosia plumosa 'Apricot Brandy'	B,BS,SE		YA
Celosia plumosa 'Castle' mix	BS,TU	Centaurea cyanus 'Choice mix'	C
Celosia plumosa 'Castle' s-c	B,BS	Centaurea cyanus 'Cut Fl Mix'	T
Celosia plumosa 'Century' mix	BD,BS,C,CL,S,T	Centaurea cyanus 'Deep Damson'	SE
Celosia plumosa 'Century' s-c	BS,CL	Centaurea cyanus 'Emperor William'	B
Celosia plumosa 'Dw Crown'	BS	Centaurea cyanus 'Florence Lavender'	CL
Celosia plumosa 'Dw Geisha'	BS,D,SE	Centaurea cyanus 'Florence' mix	BD,CL,D,DT,J,SE,U

CENTAUREA

Centaurea cyanus 'Florence Pink'	B,BS,CL,D,KS,O,S,V
Centaurea cyanus 'Florence Pink & White'	U
Centaurea cyanus 'Florence Red'	B,BS,CL,D,KS,U
Centaurea cyanus 'Florence Violet'	CL
Centaurea cyanus 'Florence White'	B,BS,CL,D,KS,O,S,V
Centaurea cyanus 'Frosty' mix	DT,F,J,KS,S,T,V
Centaurea cyanus 'Jubilee Gem'	B,L,S,T
Centaurea cyanus 'King Size mix'	C
Centaurea cyanus 'King Size' s-c	B
Centaurea cyanus 'Mauve Queen'	B,F
Centaurea cyanus 'Midget' mix	F,S
Centaurea cyanus 'Midget' s-c	F
Centaurea cyanus 'Pinkie'	B,BS
Centaurea cyanus 'Polka Dot'	BD,C,CL,CO,DT,F,KI,KS, S,SE,T,VH
Centaurea cyanus 'Red Boy'	B,BS
Centaurea cyanus 'Snowman'	B,BS,C,KS
Centaurea cyanus 'Tall'	F
Centaurea cyanus 'Tall' dbl mix	BD,BS,CO,J,KI,KS,L,R, S,SE,ST,TU,U,YA
Centaurea cyanus 'Tall' dbl mix p.s	S
Centaurea cyanus 'Tall' dbl s-c	BD
Centaurea cyanus 'Ultra Dw'	T
Centaurea cyanus 'Victoria Blue'	B
Centaurea cyanus 'Victoria White'	B
Centaurea cyanus 'Wild Blue Dwarf'	B
Centaurea dealbata	B,BS,C,JE,SA,T
Centaurea jacea	B,CC,JE,SG,V
Centaurea macrocephala	AP,B,BS,C,G,JE,KI,KS, P,RS,SA,SC,SG,ST,SU, T,V
Centaurea micranthos	B
Centaurea montana	AP,B,BS,C,CG,E,G,I,JE, SA,T,V
Centaurea montana 'Alba'	B,JE,PA,SA
Centaurea montana 'Ochroleuca'	E
Centaurea moschata see Amberboa	
Centaurea nervosa	C
Centaurea nigra	B,C,CO,LA,JE,SA,SG
Centaurea nigra ssp nemoralis	CG
Centaurea nigra v rivularis	B,JE,SA
Centaurea orientalis	B,G,JE,SA
Centaurea ornata	I
Centaurea paniculata v henryi	B
Centaurea pannonica	B
Centaurea phrygia	B,SG,T
Centaurea pulcherrima	B,C,F,G,JE,SA
Centaurea pulchra 'Major'	SG
Centaurea rothrockii	B,SW
Centaurea rupestris	B,G,JE
Centaurea ruthenica	B,CG,G,SG
Centaurea sadlerana	B,SG
Centaurea scabiosa	AP,B,C,CG,G,LA,JE,SA, SG
Centaurea scabiosa alba	NS
Centaurea scabiosa 'Alpestris'	B
Centaurea scilloides	B
Centaurea sibirica	SG
Centaurea uniflora	CG
Centaurea uniflora ssp nervosa	AP,B,F,JE,SC
Centaurium chloodes	AP,SC,SG
Centaurium confertum	B,G
Centaurium erythraea	AP,B,C,G,JE,LA,SA,SC
Centaurium muhlenbergii	B
Centaurium pulchellum	SG
Centaurium scilloides	AP,B,C,G,SC,T
Centella asiatica	B
Centranthus angustifolius	AP,C
Centranthus calyptrata	B,KS,SG
Centranthus macrosiphon	B,V
Centranthus m. 'Tumbling Spurs'	F
Centranthus ruber	AP,B,C,DT,E,G,L,PM,SC, SU
Centranthus ruber 'Albus'	B,E,G,JE,KS,MA,SA
Centranthus ruber 'Betsy'	L
Centranthus ruber 'Coccineus'	E,G,JE,SA
Centranthus ruber red	S
Centranthus ruber 'Rosenrot'	JE
Centranthus ruber 'Roseus'	B,C,SE
Centranthus ruber 'Snowcloud'	C,L,SE
Centranthus ruber 'Star'	T
Centrosema pubescens	B
Cephalanthera rubra	B
Cephalanthus occidentalis	B,C,PR,SA
Cephalaria alpina	AP,B,C,FH,G,JE,SA,SC
Cephalaria dipsacoides	AP,CG,G
Cephalaria gigantea	AP,B,BS,C,CL,G,I,JE,P, SA,SC,SG,T
Cephalaria leucantha	B,C,T
Cephalaria natalensis	B,SI
Cephalaria oblongifloia	SI
Cephalaria tchihatchewii	SG
Cephalipterum drummondii	C,O,T
Cephalipterum drummondii white	B
Cephalipterum f major	O
Cephalipterum f minor	O
Cephalocereus chrysacanthus	B,BC
Cephalocereus palmeri	B
Cephalocereus royenii	B
Cephalocereus senilis	B,Y
Cephalocleistocactus ritteri	Y
Cephalocleistocactus schattatianus	Y
Cephalophora aromatica	B,SG
Cephalophyllum alstonii	B,C,SI,Y
Cephalophyllum aureorubrum	B,SI,Y
Cephalophyllum caespitosum	B,SI
Cephalophyllum caespitosum v spissum	B
Cephalophyllum compactum	B
Cephalophyllum diversiphyllum	B
Cephalophyllum franciscii	B,Y
Cephalophyllum littlewoodii	B,SI
Cephalophyllum loreum	B
Cephalophyllum parvibracteatum	B
Cephalophyllum pillansii	B,Y
Cephalophyllum pulchrum	B
Cephalophyllum purpureo-album	B
Cephalophyllum regali	B
Cephalophyllum sp mix	C,SI
Cephalophyllum spongiosum	B,GC,Y
Cephalophyllum staminodiosum	B
Cephalophyllum subulatoides	B,SI
Cephalophyllum 'Supreem'	B
Cephalotaxus fortunei	A,B,CG,SA
Cephalotaxus harringtonia	CG
Cephalotaxus harringtonia v drupacea	A,B,C,SA
Cephalotaxus oliveri	B
Cephalotaxus sinensis	B
Cerastium alpinum	AP,FH,SG
Cerastium alpinum ssp lanatum	B,FH,G,HH,JE,SC
Cerastium articum edmonstonii	SG
Cerastium arvense	B,JE
Cerastium arvense ssp ciliatum	B

CERASTIUM

Cerastium biebersteinii	B,C,JE,SA
Cerastium boissieri	SG
Cerastium brachypetalum	SG
Cerastium dahuricum	B
Cerastium fontanum	B
Cerastium grandiflorum	B,JE
Cerastium ponticum	B
Cerastium tomentosum	B,BD,BS,F,J,L,S,SA,SC, SG,ST,SU,T,U,V
Cerastium tomentosum v columnae	B,C,KS
Cerastium t. v columnae 'Silberteppich'	BS,JE
Cerastium tomentosum 'Yo-Yo'	CL
Cerasus mahaleb	SG
Cerasus maximowiczii	SG
Ceratonia siliqua	B,C,HA,KS,O,SA
Ceratopetalum apetalum	B,HA,O
Ceratopetalum gummiferum	B,C,HA,O,SA,SH
Ceratostigma willmottianum	FH
Ceratotheca sp	SI
Ceratotheca triloba	AP,G,SI
Ceratotheca triloba 'Alba'	B
Ceratotheca triloba mauve	B,C
Ceratozamia hildae	O
Ceratozamia latifolia	O
Ceratozamia mexicana	O
Ceratozamia mexicana v latifolia	B
Ceratozamia robusta	B,O
Cerbera manghas	B
Cercidiphyllum japonicum	B,CG,N,SA
Cercidium microphyllum	B
Cercis canadensis	A,B,N,SA,SC
Cercis chinensis	B,C,SA
Cercis occidentalis	A,B,C,SA,SW
Cercis racemosa	B
Cercis siliquastrum	A,AP,B,C,CG,G,O,RH, SA,SC,T
Cercis siliquastrum 'Afghan'	SA
Cercis siliquastrum f albida	B,C,N,SA
Cercis yunnanensis	SG
Cercocarpus ledifolius	B,C,SA
Cercocarpus montanus	B,C,SA
Cercocarpus montanus v glaber	B
Cereus aethiops	B,CH
Cereus azureus	B
Cereus cochabambensis	B,Y
Cereus comarapanus	B,Y
Cereus grandicostatus	B,CH
Cereus hankeanus	B,GC,Y
Cereus jamacura	B,CH,Y
Cereus peruviana x azureus	Y
Cereus sp mix	C,Y
Cereus uruguayanus 'Peruvianus'	B,CH
Cereus uruguayensis 'Monstrosus'	B,GC,Y
Cereus validus	B,CH,GC,Y
Cereus xanthocarpus	B,BC,Y
Cerinthe glabra	B,C,G,JE,SA
Cerinthe major	T
Cerinthe major v purpurascens	AP,F,KS,P,T
Cerinthe minor	B
Cerochlamys pachyphylla	B
Cerochlamys pachyphylla v albiflora	B
Ceropegia ampliata	B,C
Ceropegia linearis ssp woodii	B,SI
Ceropegia sandersonii	SI
Ceropegia stapeliformis	B,SI
Ceroxylon quindiuense	B

Cestrum auriculatum	B
Cestrum diurnum	B
Cestrum nocturnum	B,C,HA,SA
Cestrum parqui	B
Chaenactis fremontii	B
Chaenactis glabriuscula	B
Chaenactis xantiana	B
Chaenomeles cathayensis	CG,SG
Chaenomeles japonica	A,B,CG,RS,SA,T,V
Chaenomeles sp & cv mix	C
Chaenomeles speciosa	B,C,CG,N,SA
Chaenomeles x californica	C
Chaenorrhinum glareosum	AP,B,SC
Chaenorrhinum glareosum 'Blue Dreams'	T
Chaenorrhinum minus	B
Chaenorrhinum origanifolium	AP,G,SG
Chaerophyllum aromaticum	SG
Chaerophyllum bulbosum	B
Chaerophyllum hirsutum	G,SG
Chaerophyllum hirsutum roseum	P
Chaerophyllum prescottii	SG
Chaerophyllum temulentum	B
Chaetosciadium trichospermum	B
Chamaebatiaria millefolium	B,SW
Chamaecrista fasciculata	B
Chamaecyparis lawsoniana	B,BS,C,HA,RH,SA,SG
Chamaecyparis lawsoniana 'Allumii'	B,BS,C,RS,SG
Chamaecyparis lawsoniana 'Argentea'	B,CG,SA
Chamaecyparis lawsoniana 'Aurea'	B,SA
Chamaecyparis lawsoniana 'Blue Jacket'	RS
Chamaecyparis lawsoniana 'Fletcheri'	B
Chamaecyparis laws. 'Pendula Glauca'	B,SA
Chamaecyparis lawsoniana 'Pyramidalis'	B,SA
Chamaecyparis l. 'Triumph Of Boskoop'	B,SA
Chamaecyparis nootkatensis	RH
Chamaecyparis obtusa	B,C,SA
Chamaecyparis pisifera	RH,SA
Chamaecyparis pisifera 'Filifera'	B
Chamaecyparis pisifera 'Plumosa Aurea'	CG
Chamaecyparis pisifera 'Squarrosa'	CG
Chamaecyparis thyoides	RH
Chamaecyparis thyoides 'Glauca'	B,C,SA
Chamaecytisus austriacus	SG
Chamaecytisus hirsutus	G,SG
Chamaecytisus palmensis	B
Chamaecytisus proliferus	HA,O,SA
Chamaecytisus ruthenicus	AP,G,SG
Chamaedaphne calyculata	B
Chamaedorea cataractarum	B,O
Chamaedorea costaricana	B,O,SA
Chamaedorea elegans	B,HA,O,SA,V
Chamaedorea ernesti-augusti	O
Chamaedorea erumpens	B,O
Chamaedorea geonomiformis	B,O
Chamaedorea glaucifolia	B
Chamaedorea hyb 'Florida'	B
Chamaedorea microspadix	B
Chamaedorea neurochlamys	O
Chamaedorea oblongata	B,CG,SA
Chamaedorea pacaya	B
Chamaedorea radicalis	B,O,SA
Chamaedorea seifrizii	B,C,HA,O
Chamaedorea stolonifera	B
Chamaedorea tenellaa	B,O
Chamaedorea tepejilote	B,CG,O,SA

Chamaelaucium megalopetalum	O
Chamaelaucium micranthum uncinatum	O
Chamaelaucium uncinatum	HA,O,SH
Chamaelopsis mix	CH,Y
Chamaemelum nobile	B,CG,CP,JE,KS,SA,T
Chamaerops humilis	B,C,O,SA,V
Chamaescilla corymbosa	B,C
Chamaescilla corymbosa v latifolia	B
Chamaescilla spiralis	B
Chambeyronia macrocarpa	B
Chamelaucium conostigmum	B
Chamelaucium megalopetalum	B
Chamelaucium micranthum	B
Chamelaucium uncinatum	B,C,SA
Chamerion angustifolium	SG
Chasmanthe aethiopica	B,C,SI
Chasmanthe bicolor	B,C,G,MN
Chasmanthe floribunda	B,C,SI
Chasmanthe floribunda v duckitti	B,SI
Chasmanthium latifolium	B,C,CP,G,JE,LG,NT,SA, SC
Chasmatophyllum braunsii	B
Chasmatophyllum musculinum	B
Cheiranthera filifolia	B
Cheiridopsis acuminata	B
Cheiridopsis aspera	B
Cheiridopsis aurea	B,GC,SI,Y
Cheiridopsis borealis	Y
Cheiridopsis brownii	B,SI
Cheiridopsis brownii-robusta	B
Cheiridopsis carinata	B
Cheiridopsis caroli-schmidtii	B
Cheiridopsis cigarettifera	B,SI
Cheiridopsis cuprea	B,Y
Cheiridopsis denticulata	B,SI,Y
Cheiridopsis derenbergiana	B,SI
Cheiridopsis dilatata	B
Cheiridopsis duplessii	SI,Y
Cheiridopsis excavata	B
Cheiridopsis herrei	B
Cheiridopsis imitans	B
Cheiridopsis marlothii	B,SI,Y
Cheiridopsis meyeri v minor	B
Cheiridopsis peculiaris	B,SI,Y
Cheiridopsis pillansii	B,SI
Cheiridopsis pillansii v crassa	B
Cheiridopsis pulverulenta	B
Cheiridopsis purpurea	B
Cheiridopsis robusta	B,SI
Cheiridopsis roodiae	B,Y
Cheiridopsis rostrata	B
Cheiridopsis sp mix	C
Cheiridopsis speciosa	B
Cheiridopsis turbinata	B
Cheiridopsis vanbredai	B
Cheiridopsis vanzylii	B,SI,Y
Cheirodendron trigynum	B
Chelidonium japonicum	AP,B,P,SC
Chelidonium majus	B,C,CG,CP,G,RH,SG
Chelidonium majus 'Fl.Pl.'	AP,B,C,CP,JE,P
Chelidonium majus semi-plena	SG
Chelidonium majus v laciniatum	CG
Chelidonium m. v l. 'Bowles Variety'	T
Chelone glabra	AP,B,CC,JE,NT,PR,SA
Chelone lyonii	B,JE,NT,SA
Chelone obliqua	B,BS,CG,F,G,JE,SA,T

Chenopodium album	B,CP
Chenopodium ambrosioides	B,C,CP,KS
Chenopodium atro-virens	B
Chenopodium berlandieri 'Chual'	B
Chenopodium berlandieri 'Huizontle'	B
Chenopodium berlandieri 'Quelite'	B
Chenopodium berlandieri v nuttaliae	B
Chenopodium bonus-henricus	B,SG
Chenopodium botrys	B,C,CP,SG
Chenopodium botrys 'Green Magic'	B
Chenopodium capitatum	B,SG
Chenopodium desertorum	B
Chenopodium foliosum	AP,B,C,T
Chenopodium giganteum	B,C,CP
Chenopodium murale	B
Chenopodium nuttaliae	B
Chenopodium quinoa	B,C,KS
Chenopodium quinoa 'Andean Hybrids'	BT
Chenopodium quinoa named hyb	B
Chenopodium urbicum	B
Chiastophyllum oppositifolium	AP,B,C,G,P,SA,SC,T
Chiastophyllum o. 'Goldtropfchen'	JE
Chileorebutia aerocarpa	BC
Chileorebutia napina	BC
Chilopsis linearis	RS,SW
Chilopsis linearis dark purple	B
Chimaphila umbellata	B,C
Chimonanthus praecox	AP,B,BS,C,CG,G,HA,N, SA
Chionanthus foveolata	B
Chionanthus retusus	B,C,SA
Chionanthus virginicus	B,C,G,SA
Chionochloa beddiei	B,SA
Chionochloa conspicua	B,SA,SS
Chionochloa flavescens	B,C,SA,SS
Chionochloa pallens	AP,B
Chionochloa pallida	AU
Chionochloa rigida	AP,SS
Chionochloa rubra	AP,B,SC,SS
Chionodoxa luciliae	AP,B,G
Chionodoxa sardensis	AP,B,G,SC
Chionohebe pulvinaris	B,SS
Chiranthodendron pentadactylon	B
Chirita lavandulacea	SG
Chirita micromusa	C
Chirita sericea	C
Chironia baccifera	B,SI
Chironia laxa	SI
Chironia linoides ssp linoides	B,SI
Chironia melampyrifolia	SI
Chironia peglerae	B,SI
Chironia tetragona	B,SI
Chloris barbata	B
Chloris gayana	HA
Chloris gayana 'Callide'	B
Chloris gayana 'Katambora'	B
Chloris gayana 'Mbah'	B
Chloris gayana 'Pioneer'	B
Chloris gayana 'Samford'	B
Chloris truncata	HA
Chlorogalum pomeridianum	B,MN
Chlorophytum capense	B,SI
Chlorophytum crassinerve	B,SI
Chlorophytum hoffmanii	B
Chlorophytum inornatum	B
Chlorophytum krookianum	B,SI

CHLOROPHYTUM

Chlorophytum macrophyllum	B
Chlorophytum madagascariense	B
Chlorophytum nepalense	B
Chlorophytum orchidastrum	B,SG
Chlorophytum sparsiflorum	B
Chlorophytum undulatum	B,SI
Choisya arizonica	B,SW
Chondrilla juncea	B
Chondropetalum ebracteatum	B,SI
Chondropetalum hookerianum	SI
Chondropetalum mucronatum	B,SI
Chondropetalum sp nova	SI
Chondropetalum tectorum	B,O,SA,SI
Chordospartium stevensonii	AP,B,SA,SC,SS
Chorisia insignis	B,SA
Chorisia speciosa	B,HA,SA,Y
Chorizema aciculare	B
Chorizema cordatum	B,O,RS,SA
Chorizema dicksonii	B,C,SA
Chorizema diversifolium	B,O,SA
Chorizema ilicifolium	B,C,O,RS,SA
Chorizema nervosum	B
Chorizema reticulatum	B
Chorizema rhombeum	B
Chosena arbutifolia	SG
Chosmanthe floribunda	CG
Christella patens v lepida	B
Christia vespertilionis	B
Chrysalidocarpus ankaizinensis	B
Chrysalidocarpus cabadae	B,O
Chrysalidocarpus catechu	HA
Chrysalidocarpus decipiens	B
Chrysalidocarpus fibrosus	O
Chrysalidocarpus lucubensis	O,SA
Chrysalidocarpus lutescens	B,HA,O,SA
Chrysalidocarpus lutescens (g)	B,N
Chrysalidocarpus madagascariensis	B
Chrysalidocarpus m. v lucubensis	B
Chrysalidocarpus 'Mahajanga'	B
Chrysalidocarpus monimony	O
Chrysalidocarpus tsaravotsira	O
Chrysanthemoides incana	SI
Chrysanthemoides monilifera	B,SI
Chrysanthemoides monilifera ssp pisifera	B,SI
Chrysanthemum 'Antwerp Star'	C
Chrysanthemum arcticum	JE
Chrysanthemum carinatum	B,HW,SG
Chrysanthemum c. annual special mix	S
Chrysanthemum carinatum 'Bridal Robe'	S
Chrysanthemum carinatum 'Chameleon'	B
Chrysanthemum carinatum 'Court Jesters'	DT,T
Chrysanthemum c. 'Dunnettii Luteum'	B,KS
Chrysanthemum c. 'Flame Shades'	B
Chrysanthemum carinatum 'John Bright'	B
Chrysanthemum carinatum 'Merry Mix'	C
Chrysanthemum carinatum 'Polar Star'	B,KS,T
Chrysanthemum cinerariifolium	C,CP,JE,KS
Chrysanthemum coronarium	B,CP,G,SG
Chrysanthemum c. 'Cream Bonnet'	B
Chrysanthemum coronarium 'Fl. Pl.'	B,BS
Chrysanthemum c. 'Golden Bonnet'	B
Chrysanthemum c. 'Golden Gem'	B,T
Chrysanthemum c. 'Golden Glory'	B
Chrysanthemum c. 'Primrose Gem'	B,T
Chrysanthemum coronarium 'Shungiku'	SG
Chrysanthemum corymbosum	C,JE

Chrysanthemum discoideum	B
Chrysanthemum f1 'Fanfare'	B,BS,C,CL,DT,F,JE,L,T
Chrysanthemum f1 hyb 'Fashion mix'	C
Chrysanthemum gruppenstolz	SG
Chrysanthemum Incurved fl, mix	C
Chrysanthemum indicum 'Cascade'	DT,T
Chrysanthemum i. 'Charm Early Fashion'	T
Chrysanthemum i. f1 'Autumn Glory Mix'	BS,CL,DT,SE,T,U
Chrysanthemum i. 'Spiders/Spoons imp'	T
Chrysanthemum 'Korean Hybrids'	B,BS,C,D,F,JE,S,SA
Chrysanthemum macrophyllum	C,JE
Chrysanthemum multicaule	C,V
Chrysanthemum multicaule 'Goblin'	DT
Chrysanthemum multicaule 'Gold Plate'	T
Chrysanthemum multicaule 'Moonlight'	BS,F,T
Chrysanthemum nipponicum	JE
Chrysanthemum nivellii 'Snowstorm'	T
Chrysanthemum 'Rainbow'	D,KI,SU
Chrysanthemum sebatense	B
Chrysanthemum sebatense 'Silver Carpet'	C
Chrysanthemum segetum	B,C,CO,G,LA,SU,TU,Z
Chrysanthemum segetum 'Eastern Star'	B
Chrysanthemum segetum 'Eldorado'	B
Chrysanthemum segetum 'German Flag'	B
Chrysanthemum segetum 'Gloria'	B
Chrysanthemum segetum 'Helios'	B
Chrysanthemum segetum 'Paradiso'	B
Chrysanthemum segetum 'Prado'	C,T
Chrysanthemum Spider type, mix	C
Chrysanthemum spray forms	PT
Chrysanthemum tenuiloba 'Golden Fleck'	T
Chrysanthemum tianschanicum	SG
Chrysanthemum x spectabile 'Annette'	B
Chrysanthemum x spectabile 'Cecilia'	B
Chrysanthemum x spectabile 'Mogul'	B
Chrysanthmum 'Fashion Mix'	SE
Chrysanthmum 'Tricolor'	BS,D,F,KI,M,U
Chrysobalanus icaco	B
Chrysocephalum apiculatum	B,O
Chrysocoma coma-aurea	AP,B,C,SI
Chrysolepis chrysophylla	SA
Chrysolidocarpus lutescens	RE
Chrysophyllum cainito	B,RE
Chrysophyllum oliviforme	B
Chrysopog gryllus	JE
Chrysosplenium alternifolium	C,JE
Chrysothamnus friedrichsthaliana	C
Chrysothamnus hyb mix	C
Chrysothamnus nauseosus	B,C,SA
Chrysothamnus n. ssp bernardinus	B
Chrysothamnus viscidiflorus ssp pumilus	B
Chytranthus macrobotrys	B
Cibotium chamissoi	B
Cibotium glaucum	B
Cicer arietinum 'Black Kabuli'	B
Cicer arietinum 'Dolores De Hidalgo'	B
Cicer arietinum 'Garbanzo Channa'	B
Cicer arietinum 'Mayo Winter Bean'	B
Cicerbita alpina	B,C,JE
Cichorium intybus	AP,B,C,CO,CP,HW,JE, KS,LA,SA,SG
Cicuta maculata	B,PR
Cilia capitata	SG
Cima mexicana	B
Cimbotium chamissoi	B
Cimbotium glaucum	B

CIMICIFUGA

Cimicifuga americana	B,C,G,JE,PA
Cimicifuga cordifolia	SA
Cimicifuga dahurica	B,C,JE,SA
Cimicifuga foetida	B,JE,SG
Cimicifuga japonica	B,SG
Cimicifuga racemosa	B,C,CG,SA,SC,SG,T
Cimicifuga ramosa	G,JE,SA
Cimicifuga ramosa 'Atropurpureum'	B,G,JE,PA
Cimicifuga rubifolia	B,C,G,JE
Cimicifuga simplex	B,JE
Cimicifuga simplex 'Atropurpurea'	T
Cinchona pubescens v succirubra	B
Cineraria saxifraga	B,FH
Cipadessa baccifera	B
Cipocereus minensis	CH
Circaea alpina	SG
Circaea lutetiana	B,C,JE
Cirsium acaule	AP,B,C,G,JE
Cirsium arvense	B
Cirsium brachycephalum	B
Cirsium canum	B,G,SG
Cirsium carolinianum	B
Cirsium discolor	B
Cirsium dissectum	B
Cirsium eriophorum	AP,B,G,SC,SG
Cirsium flodmanii	SG
Cirsium helenoides	B
Cirsium heterophyllum	C,JE,SA,SG
Cirsium japonicum	AP,DT,F,SA,SC,V
Cirsium japonicum 'Lilac Beauty'	B
Cirsium japonicum 'Pink Beauty'	B,BS,C,CL,JE,KS
Cirsium japonicum 'Rose Beauty'	B,BS,C,CL,JE,KS,L
Cirsium japonicum 'Snow Beauty'	B
Cirsium japonicum 'Strawberry Ripple'	U
Cirsium japonicum 'White Puff'	JE
Cirsium kamtschaticum	SG
Cirsium muticum	B
Cirsium oleraceum	C,SG
Cirsium palustre	B
Cirsium setosum	SG
Cirsium spinosissimum	AP,B
Cirsium texanum	B
Cirsium undulatum	B
Cirsium vulgare	B
Cissampelos tropaeolifolia	B
Cissus antarctica	B,C,HA,O,SA,SH,V
Cissus hypoglauca	B,C,HA,O,SH
Cissus quadrangularis	B,SI
Cissus rhombifolia	B,O
Cissus setosa	B
Cistus albidus	B,G,SA,SG
Cistus clusii	SA
Cistus creticus	AP,RH,SC,T
Cistus crispus	SA
Cistus heterophyllus	RH
Cistus hirsutus	SG
Cistus incanus	AP,B
Cistus incanus ssp corsicus	B
Cistus ladanifer	B,G,SA,SC,SG
Cistus laurifolius	AP,B,C,CG,G,JE,RH,SA, SC,SG
Cistus libanotis	SA
Cistus lusitanicus 'Decumbens'	SG
Cistus monspeliensis	AP,C,CG,G,SA,SC,SG
Cistus palhinhae	AP,P
Cistus parviflorus	AP,RH,SG

Cistus populifolius	AP,C,SA,SC,SG
Cistus psilosepalus	AP,G,RH,SC,SG
Cistus salviifolius	AP,B,C,CG,G,SA,SC,SG
Cistus sp Portugal	SG
Cistus varius	SG
Cistus vars mix	T
Cistus villosus	C,SA
Citharexylum fruticosum	B
Citrullus colocynthis	B
Citrullus ecirhhosus	B,SI
Citrullus lanatus	SI
Citrullus lanatus 'Charleston Grey'	B
Citrullus lanatus 'Cream Of Saskatchewan'	B
Citrullus lanatus 'Early Moonbeam'	B
Citrullus lanatus f2 'Wanli'	B
Citrullus lanatus 'Hopi Red'	B
Citrullus lanatus 'Hopi Yellow'	B
Citrullus lanatus hort.	B
Citrullus lanatus hyb f1 'Candida'	B
Citrullus lanatus hyb f1 'Nova'	B
Citrullus lanatus 'Ice Cream'	B
Citrullus lanatus 'Kenya'	B
Citrullus lanatus 'Long Dragon'	B
Citrullus lanatus 'Mayo'	B
Citrullus lanatus 'Mayo Sandia'	B
Citrullus lanatus 'Moon & Stars'	B
Citrullus lanatus 'Navajo Winter'	B
Citrullus lanatus 'Northern Sweet'	B
Citrullus lanatus 'Otume'	B
Citrullus lanatus 'Rio Mayo Sakobari'	B
Citrullus lanatus 'Rio San Miguel'	B
Citrullus lanatus 'San Juan'	B
Citrullus lanatus 'Sugar Baby'	B
Citrullus lanatus 'Sunset Pink'	B
Citrullus lanatus 'Tohono O'odham Yellow'	B
Citrullus lanatus v citroides 'Calif. Wild'	B
Citrullus lanatus v citroides 'Chinese Wild'	B
Citrullus lanatus v citroides round	B
Citrullus lanatus 'Yellow Doll'	B
Citrullus melo 'Blenheim Orange'	B
Citrullus melo 'Canary Honeydew'	B
Citrullus melo 'Harvest Queen'	B
Citrullus melo 'Iroquois'	B
Citrullus melo 'Jenny Lind'	B
Citrullus melo 'Nutmeg'	B
Citrullus melo 'Oregon Delicious'	B
Citrullus melo 'Stutz Supreme'	B
Citrullus melo 'Swanlake'	B
Citrus aurantifolia	B
Citrus aurantium	B
Citrus calomondia	SA
Citrus citrange	SA
Citrus 'Citronelle'	B,SA
Citrus jambhiri	B
Citrus kumquat	SA
Citrus limequat	SA
Citrus limetta	B
Citrus limettoides	B
Citrus limon	B
Citrus limon 'Villafranca'	B
Citrus macrophylla	SA
Citrus maxima	B
Citrus medica	B
Citrus 'Orangelo'	B
Citrus paradisi x 'Golden Special'	B
Citrus reticulata	B

CITRUS

Citrus sinensis	B	Clarkia rubicunda	B,BS,T
Citrus sinensis 'Washington'	B	Clarkia rubicunda 'Kermesina'	DT
Citrus sp	RE	Clarkia rubicunda 'Lilacina'	F
Citrus volkamericna	SA	Clarkia rubicunda shamini	T
Citrus x limonia	B	Clarkia 'Salmon Princess' dw	B,BS,F,T
Citrus x paradisi	B	Clarkia single mix	CO,TU
Cladanthus arabicus	B,J,T	Clarkia 'Sybil Sherwood'	B,BS,S,T
Cladanthus arabicus 'Criss-Cross'	C	Clarkia 'Tall Dbl Mix'	BS,T
Cladium mariscus	B,C,JE	Clarkia tenella	AP,B
Cladrastis lutea	B,C,N,SA	Clarkia tenella 'Blue Magic'	C,F
Cladrastis sinensis	SA	Clarkia unguiculata	B,BD,C,CG,G,SG,ST,V
Clappertonia ficifolia	B	Clarkia unguiculata 'Apple Blossom'	B,C,T,V
Clarisia racemosa	B	Clarkia unguiculata 'Brilliant' dbl	S
Clarkia amoena	AP,B,SG	Clarkia unguiculata 'Chieftain'	C
Clarkia amoena 'Aurora'	B	Clarkia unguiculata 'Enchantress'	DT
Clarkia amoena 'Azaleaflora' dbl	B,BS,C,CL,DT,F,KI,L,M,	Clarkia unguiculata 'Love Affair'	D
	R,S,T,U,VH,YA	Clarkia unguiculata mix dbl	BS,J,M,TU,U,VH
Clarkia amoena 'Bornita Mix'	F,T	Clarkia unguiculata 'Rhapsody'	S
Clarkia amoena 'Dream Double'	KI	Clarkia unguiculata 'Royal Bouquet'	B,T
Clarkia amoena 'Dw Bedding' mix	D,DT,F	Clarkia unguiculata 'Salmon Queen'	C
Clarkia amoena 'Dw Gem'	BS	Clarkia unguiculata 'Special Dbl Mix'	DT
Clarkia amoena 'Dw Mix'	BS,U	Clarkia 'White Bouquet' dbl	B,BS
Clarkia amoena 'Dw Selected'	S,TU	Clausena anisata	B,SI
Clarkia amoena f1 'Grace Lavender'	B	Clausena domesticum	B
Clarkia amoena f1 'Grace Lavender Eye'	B	Clausena lansium	B
Clarkia amoena f1 'Grace' mix	BS,C,CL,D,KI	Claytonia australasica	SS
Clarkia amoena f1 'Grace' s-c	B	Claytonia megarrhiza	AP,B,SW
Clarkia amoena f1 'Satin' mix	BS,C,CL,D,DT,S,T,YA	Claytonia megarrhiza v nivalis	AP,HH,SC
Clarkia amoena f1 'Satin' s-c	SE,T	Claytonia nivalis	I
Clarkia amoena 'Furora'	B	Claytonia perfoliata	B
Clarkia amoena 'Gloriana'	B,DT	Claytonia sibirica	AP,C,CG,JE,SA
Clarkia amoena 'Lilac Lady'	V	Cleistanthus collinus	B
Clarkia amoena 'Memoria'	B	Cleistocactus angosturensis	B,BC,Y
Clarkia amoena 'Precious Gems'	S,SE	Cleistocactus aureispinus	B
Clarkia amoena 'Raw Silk' s-c	U	Cleistocactus baumannii	B,CH,Y
Clarkia amoena 'Schamini'	F,SE	Cleistocactus baumannii v flavispinus	B,Y
Clarkia amoena single mix	BS,SU	Cleistocactus brookei	BC,CH,Y
Clarkia amoena ssp whitneyi	B	Cleistocactus bruneispinus	Y
Clarkia bottae	B,G	Cleistocactus buchtienii	B,Y
Clarkia bottae 'Amethyst Glow'	T	Cleistocactus candelilla	B,Y
Clarkia bottae 'Lady in Blue'	T	Cleistocactus chacoanus	B,Y
Clarkia bottae 'Lilac Blossom'	C,CO,J,KI,U	Cleistocactus hildegardiae v flavirufus	Y
Clarkia bottae 'Lilac Pixie'	F	Cleistocactus luribayensis	B,Y
Clarkia bottae 'Pink Joy'	S,V	Cleistocactus parviflorus	B,Y
Clarkia breweri	B	Cleistocactus parviflorus v. aiquilensis	Y
Clarkia breweri 'Pink Ribbons'	C,T	Cleistocactus potosinus	Y
Clarkia 'Cattleya'	T	Cleistocactus ritteri	B
Clarkia concinna	B	Cleistocactus samaipatanus	B
Clarkia 'Crown' mix	CO	Cleistocactus smaragdiflorus	B
Clarkia 'Dbl Nain Cherie Sweetheart'	T	Cleistocactus sp mix	C,CH,Y
Clarkia deflexa	B	Cleistocactus strausii	B,BC,C,CH,Y
Clarkia 'Double Delight'	KI	Cleistocactus tarijensis	B,Y
Clarkia 'Duchess of Albany'	T	Cleistocactus tupizensis	B
Clarkia dw show mix	C,M	Cleistocactus vallegrandensis	Y
Clarkia 'Dwarf Asterix'	U	Cleistocactus villamontesii	Y
Clarkia imbricata	B	Cleistocactus viridiflorus	Y
Clarkia 'Imp Dw Mix'	T	Cleistocactus vulpis cauda	CH,Y
Clarkia 'Jewel' dwarf	J	Clematis addisonii	AP,BR,G,IC,SC
Clarkia 'Monarch' dwarf mix	C	Clematis aethusifolia	AP,BR,CG,IC,SC
Clarkia pulchella 'Alba'	V	Clematis afoliata	AU,B,C
Clarkia pulchella dbl 'Choice' mix	C,F,L	Clematis akeboides hort. orientalis	BR,G
Clarkia pulchella 'Filigree'	D,F	Clematis aljonushka	BR
Clarkia pulchella mix	J,S,SG,T	Clematis alpina	AP,B,C,FH,G,IC,JE,SA,
Clarkia pulchella 'Snowflake'	B,T		SC,SE,T
Clarkia purpurea	B,SW	Clematis alpina blue	IC
Clarkia 'Rosy Morn re-selected'	C	Clematis alpina 'Frances Rivis'	AP,B,BR,C,IC,SC

61

Clematis alpina 'Pamela Jackman'	AP,BR,IC,SC
Clematis alpina pink	IC
Clematis alpina 'Rubra'	JE
Clematis alpina 'Ruby'	BR,IC
Clematis alpina 'Willy'	IC
Clematis annamieke	BR
Clematis arabella	BR
Clematis aristata	AU,B,HA,O,SA,SH
Clematis aristata cw Tasmania	IC
Clematis armandii	AP,B,SC,SG
Clematis australis	AP,B,SC,SS
Clematis balearica 'Freckles'	RS
Clematis barbellata	BR,SC
Clematis 'Bill Mackenzie'	AP,B,BR,C,RS,SC,T
Clematis brachiata	B,SI
Clematis brachyura	IC
Clematis brevicaudata	CG,SG
Clematis buchananiana	B,C,CG,SA
Clematis campaniflora	AP,BR,C,CG,G,I,IC,JE, N,SC,SG
Clematis chiisanensis	AP,N,SC
Clematis chrysocoma	BR,G
Clematis cirrhosa	AP,SA,SC
Clematis cirrhosa balearica 'Freckles'	AP,BR
Clematis cirrhosa 'Wisley Cream'	AP,BR
Clematis coactilis	BR,IC
Clematis columbiana	AP,B,C,IC,SC
Clematis connata	C
Clematis crispa	BR,CG,G
Clematis crispa cw W.Virginia	IC
Clematis cylindrica	BR
Clematis davidiana	SA
Clematis 'Duchess of Albany'	BR
Clematis durandii	BR
Clematis eriostemon	BR
Clematis eriostemon x 'Hendersonii'	RS
Clematis 'Etoile Rose'	BR
Clematis fargesii	AP,BR
Clematis fargesii 'Souljet'	AP,CG,SC
Clematis fauriei x sibirica 'Pansy'	IC
Clematis flammula	AP,B,BR,C,CG,JE,RS, SA,SC
Clematis flammula v rotundifolia	BR
Clematis foetida	AP,B
Clematis forsteri	AP,B,PM,SA,SC
Clematis forsteri 'Lunar Lass'	BR
Clematis forsteri petriei	BR
Clematis fusca	AP,BR,IC,SG
Clematis fusca (In Vladivostok) cult	IC
Clematis fusca v kamtschatica	IC
Clematis fusca v mandschurica	IC
Clematis fusca violacea	AP,BR
Clematis fusijamana	IC
Clematis gentianoides	AP,BR,SC
Clematis glauca	IC,SG
Clematis glaucophylla	AP,BR,IC
Clematis glycinoides	B,C,HA,O,SA
Clematis glycinoides cw Australia	IC
Clematis 'Gravetye Beauty'	BR
Clematis 'Helios'	B,BS
Clematis heracleifolia	AP,CG,G,JE,SA
Clematis heracleifolia v davidiana	BR,IC
Clematis hexapetala	BR,IC,SG
Clematis hiliariae	BR
Clematis hirsutissima	AP,B,C,SC,SW
Clematis hookeriana	B,C
Clematis 'Hybrids'	SE
Clematis integrifolia	AP,B,BR,C,CG,G,IC,JE, RS,SA,SC,SG,T
Clematis integrifolia 'Alba'	AP,BR
Clematis integrifolia 'Olgae'	BR,G,IC
Clematis integrifolia (Prannohybrid blue)	IC
Clematis integrifolia (Prannohybrid red)	IC
Clematis integrifolia 'Rosea'	AP,B,BR,IC
Clematis integrifolia v viticella 'Eriostemon'	IC
Clematis intricata	BR,IC
Clematis ispahanica	BR
Clematis japonica	G
Clematis 'Kermisina'	BR,IC
Clematis kirilowii	CG,IC,SA
Clematis koreana	BR,G
Clematis koreana v fragrans	IC
Clematis koreana yellow	BR,SC
Clematis ladakhiana	BR,CC
Clematis lasiantha	AP,B,RS,SW
Clematis ligusticifolia	B,C,CG,IC,SA
Clematis 'Lunar Lass'	PM
Clematis mackaui	CG
Clematis macropetala	B,C,FH,G,IC,SA,SC,SG
Clematis macropetala hyb	JE
Clematis macropetala 'Jan Lindmark'	IC
Clematis macropetala 'Rosy o' Grady'	BR,IC
Clematis mandschurica	B,BR,CG,RS,SG
Clematis marata	AP,B,SA,SS
Clematis marmoraria	AP,AU,G,PM,SC
Clematis marmoraria hyb	PM,SC
Clematis mauritiana	B
Clematis microphylla	B,C,HA,O,RS,SA
Clematis 'Minuet'	AP,BR,IC
Clematis monroi	CG
Clematis montana	AP,B,BR,G,SA,SC,V
Clematis montana 'Elizabeth'	B
Clematis montana 'Snowflake'	B
Clematis montana v rubens	AP,B,BR,IC,SC
Clematis montana v wilsonii	BR,IC
Clematis napaulensis	AP,B,BR,C,CG,IC,SA,SC
Clematis 'Nelly Moser'	B
Clematis obscura	IC
Clematis occidentalis	B,SG
Clematis occidentalis v dissecta	IC
Clematis occidentalis v grosseserrata	IC
Clematis ochroleura	AP,BR
Clematis orientalis	AP,B,C,BR,RS,SA,SC, SG
Clematis orientalis 'Burford Variety'	BR
Clematis 'Pagoda'	BR
Clematis paniculata cw New Zealand	IC
Clematis parviflora	BR
Clematis patens	B
Clematis petriei	AP,B,PM,SC,SS
Clematis pitcherii	BR,G,IC
Clematis potaninii	AP,B,BR,IC,P,SC
Clematis potaninii v potaninii	G,LG
Clematis pubescens	B,C,O
Clematis purpureostriata x aljonushka	BR
Clematis quadribracteolata	B,SS
Clematis recta	AP,B,BR,C,CG,G,IC,JE, N,SA,SC,SG
Clematis recta 'Purpurea'	AP,B,BR,G,JE,LG,RS, SA,SC
Clematis rehderiana	BR,E,G,SC,SG
Clematis serratifolia	AP,BR,G,IC,SC

CLEMATIS

Clematis sibirica	IC,RS,SG	Clerodendrum trichotomum v fargesii	CG
Clematis simsii	BR	Clethra acuminata	B
Clematis songarica	RS	Clethra alnifolia	B,SA
Clematis sp Ecuador	RS	Clethra alnifolia 'Rosea'	B
Clematis sp mix	C	Clethra arborea	B,SG
Clematis speciosa	SG	Clethra barbinervis	A,AP,B,SA
Clematis stans	C,CG,G,I	Clethra tomentosa	CG
Clematis 'Sun Star'	SE,U	Cleyera japonica	B,SA
Clematis tangutica	AP,B,BR,BS,C,CG,DT,F, FH,G,IC,JE,LG,N,S,SA, SC,SG,T,V	Clianthus formosus Clianthus puniceus Clianthus puniceus 'Albus'	C,F,HA,O,SA,T B,C,CG,SA,SC,SG,SS,V B,C,SA
Clematis tangutica 'Aureolin'	IC	Clianthus puniceus v roseus	AU,C
Clematis tangutica 'Radar Love'	C,L	Cliffortia cuneata	B,SI
Clematis tangutica vernayi	IC	Cliftonia monophylla	B
Clematis 'Tentel'	IC	Clinopodium vulgare	B,C,G,LA,SG,SU
Clematis tenuiloba	SG	Clintonia udensis	SC,SG
Clematis terniflora	AP,AU,B,BR,CG,JE,RS, SA,SC,SG,SS	Clintonia udensis MW34R Clintonia uniflora	X AP,C
Clematis terniflora v robusta	SG	Clitoria mariana	B,RS,SW
Clematis texensis	G,SC	Clitoria ternatea	B,C,SA
Clematis tibetana	AP,B,CG,RS,SC	Clitoria ternatea fl pl 'Blue Sails'	RS,T
Clematis tibetana ssp vernayi Tibet	BR	Clitoria ternatea 'Semi-double'	B
Clematis tubulosa	CG	Clitoria ternatea 'Ultra Alba'	B
Clematis versicolor	AP,B,BR,G,SC	Clitoria ternatea 'Ultra Marina'	B
Clematis viorna	AP,BR,CG,G,IC,RS	Clivia gardenii	B
Clematis virginiana	B,BR,CG,PR	Clivia hybrids	C,HA
Clematis virginiana cw Ontario	IC	Clivia miniata	B,O,SA,SC,SI
Clematis viscosa	CG	Clivia miniata 'Aurea'	B
Clematis vitalba	A,B,C,C,G,JE,RS,SA,SG, Z	Clivia miniata 'California Hybrids' Clivia miniata 'Mammoth'	B B
Clematis viticella	AP,B,BR,BS,CG,DT,G, IC,JE,KI,N,SA,SC,ST	Clivia miniata 'New Hybrids' Clivia miniata 'Twins'	B B
Clematis wilsonii	IC	Clivia miniata 'Variegated'	B
Clematis x clematopsis	B,SI	Clusia major	B
Clematopsis scabiosifolia	B,C,SI	Cneoridium dumosum	B
Cleome angustifolia	SI	Cneorum tricoccon	AP,CG,SC,SG
Cleome foliosa	SI	Cnicus benedictus	B,CP
Cleome gynandra	B	Cobaea scandens	B,BS,C,CO,D,DT,F,J,KI, KS,L,S,SA,ST,T,V
Cleome hasslerana	B,C,CC,G,HW,J,RH,V		
Cleome hasslerana 'Cherry Queen'	B,C,T	Cobaea scandens f alba	B,BS,C,SE,T
Cleome hasslerana 'Colour Fountain'	BS,F	Coccinia grandis	B
Cleome hasslerana 'Helen Campbell'	B,C,KS,T	Coccinia palmata	SI
Cleome hasslerana 'Pink Queen'	B,BS,C,SU,V	Coccinia quinqueloba	B,SI
Cleome hasslerana 'Rose Queen'	B,BD,BS	Coccinia rehmannii	B,SI
Cleome hasslerana 'Violet Queen'	B,C,T,V	Coccoloba uvifera	B,C,SA,T
Cleome hasslerana 'White Queen'	V	Coccothrinax alexandri	B
Cleome hirta	SI	Coccothrinax alta	B,O
Cleome isomeris	B	Coccothrinax argentata	B,O
Cleome lutea	B	Coccothrinax argentea	C,O,SA
Cleome marshallii	B	Coccothrinax bermudezii	B
Cleome monophylla	B	Coccothrinax crinita	B,O
Cleome rosea	B	Coccothrinax cupularis	B
Cleome serrulata	B,SG	Coccothrinax fragrans	B,O
Cleome serrulata 'Orchid Festival'	B	Coccothrinax littoralis	B
Cleome sp	SI	Coccothrinax miraguama	B,O
Cleome viscosa	B,C,SA	Coccothrinax miraguama ssp roseocarpa	B
Cleretum papulosum	B	Coccothrinax rigida	B
Cleretum papulosum v schlechteri	B,SI	Coccothrinax salvatoris	B
Clerodendrum colebrookianum	B	Cochemiea halei	BC
Clerodendrum floribundum	B	Cochemiea maritima	Y
Clerodendrum glabrum	B,SI	Cochemiea pondii	Y
Clerodendrum kaempferi	B	Cochemiea poselgeri	BC,Y
Clerodendrum speciosum	B,CG	Cochemiea setespina	Y
Clerodendrum thomsonae	B	Cochlearia anglica	B
Clerodendrum tomentosum	B,O,SA	Cochlearia glastifolia	B
Clerodendrum trichotomum	AP,B,C,CG,SA,SG	Cochlearia officinalis	B

COCHLOSPERMUM

Cochlospermum fraseri	B,O,SA	Colchicum kotschyi	B,MN
Cochlospermum religiosum	B	Colchicum levieri	B
Cochlospermum vitifolium	B,RE	Colchicum levieri MS937 France	MN
Cocos nucifera	B	Colchicum longiflorum	B
Codariocalyx motorius	B	Colchicum lusitanicum v algeriense	B
Coddia rudis	B,SI	Colchicum l. v algeriense A.B.S4353	MN
Codiaeum bonplandianus	B	Colchicum l. v algeriense A.B.S4362	MN
Codiaeum californicus	B	Colchicum l. v algeriense A.B.S4422	MN
Codiaeum glabellus	B	Colchicum l. v algeriense S.B.L181	MN
Codiaeum macrostachys	B	Colchicum luteum	BS,CC
Codiaeum megalobotrys	B,SI	Colchicum macrophyllum	B,CG,JE,SC
Codiaeum megalocarpus	B	Colchicum neapolitanum PF5014	MN
Codiaeum sylvaticus	B,SI	Colchicum pelopponesiacum S.L191	MN
Codiaeum variegatum hyb	B	Colchicum psaridis S.L200 Greece	MN
Codonanthe crassifolia	B	Colchicum pusillum	B,SC
Codonocarpus cotinifolius	B,C	Colchicum pusillum MS699 Crete	MN
Codonocarpus pyramidalis	B	Colchicum pusillum MS745 Crete	MN
Codonopsis bhutanica	CC,SC	Colchicum pusillum MS803 Crete	MN
Codonopsis bulleyana	P	Colchicum sp & hyb mix	C
Codonopsis cardiophylla	SC,SG	Colchicum sp ?neapolitanum Yugoslavia	MN
Codonopsis clematidea	AP,B,BS,C,CC,F,G,JE,KI,	Colchicum sp nova S.B.L122 Jordan	MN
	P,PM,RS,SA,SC,SG,ST,	Colchicum speciosum	AP,B,G,MN,PM,SC,SG
	T,V	Colchicum speciosum JCA Iran	MN
Codonopsis convolvulacea	AP,HH,SC,SG	Colchicum speciosum PF dwarf	MN
Codonopsis dicentrifolia	CG,SC	Colchicum speciosum v bornmuelleri	CG,MN
Codonopsis mollis	B,JE,SC	Colchicum speciosum v illyricum	AP,MN
Codonopsis ovata	AP,C,CG,G,FH,PM,SC,	Colchicum troodii L/Cu105 Cyprus	MN
	SG	Colchicum umbrosum	MN
Codonopsis pilosula	AP,B,C,G,RS,SC	Colchicum variegatum	B
Codonopsis rotundifolia	G,SC	Coldenia procumbens	B
Codonopsis rotundifolia v angustifolia	RS	Coleocephalocereus goebelianus	B,CH
Codonopsis tabulosa	C	Coleocephalocereus pluricostatus	B,BR
Codonopsis tangshen	AP,B,CC,P,RS,SC	Coleogyne ramosissima	B
Codonopsis ussuriensis	AP,CC	Coleonema album	B,SI
Codonopsis vinciflora	AP,C,SC	Coleonema pulchellum	B,SA,SI
Codonopsis viridiflora	AP,B,F	Coleonema pulchrum	B,SI
Codonopsis viridis	BS,C	Coleostephus myconis 'Goblin'	B
Coeloglossum viride	CG	Coleostephus myconis 'Moonlight'	B
Coffea arabica	B,BS,CG,HA,SG	Coleostephus myconis 'Sunlight'	B
Coffea arabica 'Nana'	B,C,SA,V	Collections 'Wedding Bouquet'	U
Coffea sp	RE	Colletia ferox	SA
Coffea sp & cv	B	Colletia hystrix	SA,SG
Coix lacryma-jobi	B,BS,C,CG,G,SG,SU,V	Colletia spinosa	SA
Cola acuminata	B	Collinsia bicolor	B,C,KS,RS,SW,T,V
Cola digitata	B	Collinsia bicolor 'Blushing Bride'	T
Cola urceolata	B	Collinsia bicolor 'Pink Surprise'	B
Colchicum alpinum	AP,SC,SG	Collinsia grandiflora	B
Colchicum atropurpureum	G	Collinsia verna	NT
Colchicum autumnale	AP,B,C,G,JE,MN,PM,SA,	Collomia biflora	AP,B,C
	SC	Collomia coccinea 'Neon'	B,T
Colchicum baytopiorum	B,G,SC	Collomia grandiflora	AP,B,P,SC
Colchicum baytopiorum PB224 Turkey	MN	Collomia involucrata	SG
Colchicum bornmuelleri	G,PM	Collybia velutipes d.m.p	B
Colchicum cilicium	AP,JE	Colobanthus acicularis	AP,B,SC,SS
Colchicum corsicum	AP,B,C,LG,MN,SC	Colobanthus apetalous v alpinus	B,SS
Colchicum cupanii	AP,B	Colobanthus wallii	CC
Colchicum cupanii MS969 Italy	MN	Colocasia affinis	B
Colchicum cupanii MS977 Italy	MN	Colocasia affinis v jenningsii	C
Colchicum cupanii S.L163 Evvia	MN	Colocasia esculenta	B
Colchicum cupanii S.L454 Greece	MN	Colocasia gigantea	SG
Colchicum cupanii v bertolonii	B	Colophospermum mopane	B,SI
Colchicum cupanii v bertolonii S.L259	MN	Colpias mollis	B,SI
Colchicum cupanii v bertolonii S.L289/6	MN	Colpoon compressum	B,SI
Colchicum cupanii v pulverulentum	B	Colpothrinax wrightii	B
Colchicum c. v pulverulentum S.L250	MN	Colquhounia coccinea	SA
Colchicum giganteum	B	Colquhounia mollis	SA

COLUBRINA

Colubrina arborescens	B
Colubrina asiatica	B
Columnea kienastiana	B
Colutea arborescens	A,AP,B,C,G,SA,SC,SG
Colutea istria	G,SG
Colutea laxmannii	SG
Colutea orientalis	SA
Colvillea racemosa	B,HA,SA,SI
Combretum aculeatum	B
Combretum apiculatum	B,SI
Combretum bracteosum	B,SI
Combretum caffrum	SI
Combretum collinum	B,SI
Combretum elaeagnoides	SI
Combretum erythrophyllum	B,SI
Combretum hereroense	B,SA,SI
Combretum imberbe	B,SI
Combretum kraussii	B,SI
Combretum micranthum	B
Combretum microphyllum	SI
Combretum molle	B,SI
Combretum nigricans	B
Combretum obovatum	B,SI
Combretum padoides	B
Combretum zeyheri	B,SI
Comesperma calymega	B
Comesperma ciliatum	B
Comesperma ericinum	B
Comesperma virgatum	B
Commelina attenuata	B
Commelina benghalensis	B
Commelina coelestis	AP,B,C,FH,G,JE,SA,SC, SG,T
Commelina coelestis 'Sleeping Beauty'	C,F,KS
Commelina dianthifolia	AP,B,SC,SW,T,W
Commelina graminifolia	JE
Commelina tuberosa	AP,C,FH,G,HH,JE,RS, SC,SG
Commelina virginica	C,G
Commersonia bartramia	B
Commicarpus pentandrus	B
Commiphora africana	B
Commiphora glaucescens	B
Commiphora pyracanthoides	B,SI
Compositae 'Flor Olorosa'	B
Compositae 'Hoja Del Pescado'	B
Compositae 'Oreja De Perro'	B
Compositae 'Palo De Sal'	B
Compositae 'Santa Teresa Montes'	B
Conanthera bifolia	AP,B,MN
Condalia globosa v pubescens	B
Conicosia alborosea	B
Conicosia elongata	SI
Conicosia pugioniformis	B,SI,Y
Conicosia pugioniformis ssp alborosea	SI
Conicosia p. ssp pugionoformis	SI
Conioselinum schugnanicum	SG
Conium maculatum	B,G,NS,SG
Conoclinium coelestinum	B
Conophytum altum	B,SI
Conophytum bilobum	B,SI
Conophytum breve	B,SI
Conophytum calculus	B,SI,Y
Conophytum concavum	B,BC
Conophytum crassum	SI
Conophytum dissimile	SI

Conophytum elishae	B,SI
Conophytum fibuliforme	Y
Conophytum minusculum v leipoldtii	B,SI
Conophytum minutum	B,SI,Y
Conophytum minutum v pearsonii	B,SI
Conophytum obcordellum f mundum	B,Y
Conophytum o. ssp obcordellum	B,SI
Conophytum ornatum	B,SI
Conophytum pellucidum	B,BC
Conophytum pellucidum 'Pardicolor'	BC
Conophytum pillansii	B,SI,Y
Conophytum praesectum	SI
Conophytum quaesitum	B,BC
Conophytum sp	GC,SI,Y
Conophytum sp,ssp & v	B
Conophytum subfenestratum	B,SI
Conophytum truncatum	B,SI
Conophytum uvaeforme	B,Y
Conophytum uvaeforme v hillii	BC
Conophytum uvaeforme v subincanum	B,SI
Conophytum uvaeforme v uvaeforme	SI
Conophytum velutinum	B,BC
Conopodium majus	B
Conospermum amoenum	B,O
Conospermum bracteosum	B
Conospermum brownii	B
Conospermum caerulescens	B
Conospermum caeruleum	B,O,SA
Conospermum densiflorum	B
Conospermum distichum	B
Conospermum huegelii	B,O
Conospermum incurvum	B,O,SA
Conospermum mitchellii	B
Conospermum stoechadis	B,O
Conospermum triplinervium	SA
Conospermum triplinervium v minor	B,O
Conostomium natalense v glabrum	B,SI
Conostylis sp	B
Conothamnus aureus	B
Conringia orientalis	SG
Consolida ajacis	AP,B,C,G,T
Consolida ajacis 'Dwarf'	B,BD,BS,KI,KS,ST,TU,V
Consolida ajacis 'Earlybird Resistant'	B
Consolida ajacis 'Hyacinth Flowered' dw	BS,D,DT,F,T,U
Consolida ajacis 'Hyacinth Flowered' tall	B,BD,BS,D,DT,KI,KS,L, R,T,TU,V
Consolida 'Audace'	M
Consolida 'Blue Rocket'	V
Consolida 'Blue Spire'	L,SU
Consolida 'Cloud Blue'	B,C,D,J,KS,YA
Consolida 'Cloud Snow'	D
Consolida 'Eastern Blues'	B
Consolida 'Formula Mix'	L
Consolida 'Frosted Skies'	B,BS,DT,F,SE,T,U,V
Consolida 'Giant'	CO
Consolida 'Imperial' mix	BS,D,DT,F,J,KI,KS,SE, ST,SU,U,VH,YA
Consolida 'Imperial' s-c	B,BS,T,KS
Consolida 'Improved'	T
Consolida minus	B
Consolida orientalis	CG
Consolida 'Q Series' s-c	B
Consolida 'Regal' s-c	BS
Consolida regalis	CG,G,SG
Consolida 'Rocket'	CO,HW,S,Sm,Z
Consolida 'Rosalie'	L

65

Consolida 'Salmon Beauty'	L
Consolida 'Sky Blue'	D
Consolida 'Stock Fl Special' mix	BS,S
Consolida 'Sublime' mix	BS,T
Consolida 'Sublime' s-c	B,BS,T
Consolida 'White Spire'	L
Convallaria majalis	B,JE,SG
Convallaria majalis v keiskei	SG
Convolvulus althaeoides	AP,B,SA
Convolvulus arvensis	B
Convolvulus betonicifolius	B
Convolvulus cantabricus	B,C,JE,SA
Convolvulus capensis	B,SI
Convolvulus chilensis	B,P
Convolvulus dorycnium	B
Convolvulus erubescens	B
Convolvulus major mix	D,S
Convolvulus pentapetaloides	B
Convolvulus remotus	RS
Convolvulus sepium	SG
Convolvulus 'Star of Yelta'	T
Convolvulus tricolor	BS,C,CO,D,DT,F,G,J,KS SU,W,V
Convolvulus tricolor 'Ensign Blue'	S,T
Convolvulus tricolor 'Ensign Dark Blue'	S
Convolvulus tricolor 'Ensign' mix	S,KS,T
Convolvulus tricolor 'Ensign Red'	F,KS,SE,T
Convolvulus tricolor 'Ensign Rose'	T
Convolvulus tricolor 'Ensign Royal'	B,C,F,KS,SE,V
Convolvulus tricolor 'Ensign White'	KS,T
Convolvulus tricolor 'Erecta Blue Flash'	B
Convolvulus tricolor 'Erecta Red Flash'	B
Convolvulus tricolor 'Flagship'	F,SE
Convolvulus tricolor 'Rainbow Flash'	T
Convolvulus tricolor red	B
Convolvulus verecundus	CC
Conyza canadensis	B
Conyza cardaminifolia	B
Coopernookia polygalacea	B
Copaifera langsdorfii	B
Copaifera mildbraedii	B
Copernicia alba	B
Copernicia baileyana	O
Copernicia glabrescens ssp glabrescens	B
Copernicia glabrescens ssp hav.	B
Copernicia hospita	B
Copernicia pruinifera	O
Copiapoa bridgesii	B,BC
Copiapoa cinerea v gigantea	B,Y
Copiapoa coquimbana	B
Copiapoa cupreata	B
Copiapoa echinoides	Y
Copiapoa humilis	B,CH,Y
Copiapoa hypogaea	B,CH,GC,Y
Copiapoa lembcke	B,Y
Copiapoa longispina	B
Copiapoa magnifica	B
Copiapoa marginata	B
Copiapoa montana	B
Copiapoa multicolor	B
Copiapoa pseudocoquimbana	B
Copiapoa pseudocoquimbana v vulgata	B
Copiapoa sp mix	C
Copiapoa tenuissima	B,CH,Y
Copiapoa wagenknechtii	B
Coprinus comatus d.m.p	B

Coprosma acerosa	B,SC,SS
Coprosma antipoda	B,SS
Coprosma areolata	B
Coprosma atropurpurea	B,SS
Coprosma australis	SS
Coprosma banksii	SS
Coprosma brunnea	B,SS
Coprosma cheesemanii	B,CG,SS
Coprosma colensoi	B,SS
Coprosma crassifolia	B
Coprosma crenulata	B,SS
Coprosma depressa	B,SS
Coprosma foetidissima	B
Coprosma grandifolia	B
Coprosma hirtella	B,HA
Coprosma linearifolia	SS
Coprosma lucida	B,SS
Coprosma macrocarpa	B,SS
Coprosma moorei	AU
Coprosma nitida	B,C,O
Coprosma parviflora	B,SS
Coprosma petriei	AP,B,SS
Coprosma polymorpha	SS
Coprosma propinqua	B,SS
Coprosma pseudocuneata	B,SS
Coprosma pumila	B,SS
Coprosma quadrifida	B,O
Coprosma repens	B,SA
Coprosma rhamnoides	AP,SS
Coprosma rigida	B,SS
Coprosma robusta	B,SA
Coprosma rotundifolia	SS
Coprosma rugosa	B,SA,SS
Coprosma serrulata	B,SS
Coprosma sp	AP,AU,CC
Coprosma virescens	SS
Coprosma x cunninghamii	B
Coptis japonica	B,C
Corallocarpus bainesii	B,SI
Corallocarpus disectus	SI
Corallospartium crassicaule	B,SS
Corchorus aestuans	B
Corchorus walcottii	B
Cordia abyssinica	B
Cordia alliodora	B,RE
Cordia amplifolia	B
Cordia boussieri	SA
Cordia caffra	B
Cordia dentata	B
Cordia dichotoma	B
Cordia monoica	B
Cordia myxa	B
Cordia obliqua	B
Cordia sebestena	B,SA
Cordia subcordata	B
Cordia superba	B
Cordia wallichii	B
Cordyla africana	B
Cordyla madagascariensis	B
Cordylanthus parviflorus	SW
Cordyline australis	AP,B,BS,C,CL,HA,O,SA, SS,T,YA
Cordyline australis 'Purple Tower'	T
Cordyline australis 'Purpurea'	B,C,HA,O,SA
Cordyline australis 'Red Robyn'	B,SA
Cordyline banksii	B,C,SA,SS

CORDYLINE

Cordyline banksii 'Purpurea'	B
Cordyline baueri	B
Cordyline baueri 'Purpurea'	B
Cordyline bicolor	B,SA
Cordyline indivisa	AU,B,BS,C,KI,O,SA,SS, ST,X
Cordyline petiolaris	B,O,SA
Cordyline pumilio	AP,B,SA,SC
Cordyline rubra	B,HA
Cordyline stricta	B,C,HA,O,SA
Cordyline terminalis	B,HA,SA,SH
Cordyline terminalis 'Bicolor'	B
Cordyline terminalis 'Dwarf Red'	B
Cordyline terminalis 'Hawaiian Red'	SA
Cordyline terminalis 'Hawaiian Ti'	B
Cordyline terminalis hybrids	C,O,T
Cordyline terminalis 'Rubra'	B
Cordyline terminalis 'Special Pink'	B
Cordyline terminalis 'Tricolor'	SA
Cordyline terminalis 'Variegata'	B,SA
Cordyline terminalis 'White'	B
Cordyline trilocular	B
Coreopsis 'American Dream'	F,PA
Coreopsis basalis 'Gold King'	B,C
Coreopsis basalis 'Golden Crown'	KS,T
Coreopsis bigelovii	B
Coreopsis gigantea	B
Coreopsis grandiflora	AP,B,BS,CG,CO,G,KI, SC,SG,ST
Coreopsis grandiflora 'Domino'	JE
Coreopsis grandiflora 'Early Sunrise'	B,BD,BS,CL,D,DT,F,J, JE,KI,KS,L,R,S,SE,T,TU, V
Coreopsis grandiflora 'Louis D'or'	B
Coreopsis grandiflora 'Mayfield Giants'	B,BD,BS,L,T,V
Coreopsis grandiflora 'Roi Soleil'	B
Coreopsis grandiflora 'Schnittgold'	JE
Coreopsis grandiflora 'Sunray'	B,BD,BS,C,G,JE,SA
Coreopsis grandiflora 'Tetra Giants'	JE
Coreopsis lanceolata	B,C,CC,CG,G,HW,JE,NT, PR,SG
Coreopsis lanceolata 'Baby Gold'	B
Coreopsis lanceolata 'Baby Sun'	B,C,JE,SA
Coreopsis lanceolata 'Cutting Gold'	CL
Coreopsis lanceolata 'Sterntaler'	B,JE,SA
Coreopsis lanceolata 'Sunburst'	B,BS,C,JE,KI,VH
Coreopsis maritima	B
Coreopsis palmata	B,G,JE,PR,SG
Coreopsis radiata 'Tiger Stripes'	DT
Coreopsis rosea	JE
Coreopsis stillmanii 'Golden Fleece'	B,C
Coreopsis tinctoria	B,G,HW,KS,NT,SG,V
Coreopsis tinctoria 'Double Golden'	B
Coreopsis tinctoria dwarf	C,DT,J,T
Coreopsis tinctoria 'Fiery Beam'	C
Coreopsis tinctoria 'Gold Star'	B,BS,D
Coreopsis tinctoria 'Mahogany Midget'	B,BS,D,DT,F
Coreopsis tinctoria tall	C
Coreopsis 'Treasure Trove'	U
Coreopsis tripteris	B,C,JE,PR
Coreopsis verticillata	AV,B
Corethrogyne californica	
Coriaria arborea N.Zealand	SG
Coriaria kingiana	B,SA,SG
Coriaria microphylla	B,SG
Coriaria myrtifolia	SA,SG

Coriaria nepalensis	SG
Coriaria plumosa	SS
Coriaria pottsiana	SG
Coriaria pteridoides N.Zealand	SG
Coriaria ruscifolia	SG
Coriaria sarmentosa	B,SG
Coriaria sinica	B,SA
Coriaria terminalis v xanthocarpa	AP,I,SC,SG
Coridothymus capitatus	B
Corispermum hyssopifolium	CG
Corispermum nitidum	B
Cornus alba	A,B,C,CG,SA
Cornus alba 'Sibirica'	B,SA
Cornus alternifolia	B,CG,SA
Cornus amomum	B,SA
Cornus amomum obliqua	PR
Cornus australis	SG
Cornus baileyii	CG
Cornus bretschneideri	SA
Cornus canadensis	A,AP,B,BS,C,CG,JE,SA, SG,T
Cornus capitata	B,C,CG,HA,SA
Cornus controversa	A,B,C,SA
Cornus darvasica	SG
Cornus drummondii	SA
Cornus florida	A,B,C,SA
Cornus florida 'Pendula'	B
Cornus florida 'Rubra'	B,C,N,SA
Cornus florida 'Variegated'	B
Cornus hongkongensis	B
Cornus kousa	B,G,SA
Cornus kousa 'Milky Way'	B,SA
Cornus kousa v angustata	B,N,SA
Cornus kousa v chinensis	A,B,C,N,SA
Cornus kousa v chinensis 'Imp'	B
Cornus kousa 'Weeping Form'	B
Cornus mas	A,B,C,CG,SA,SG
Cornus mas variegata	C
Cornus nuttallii	B,C,N,SA
Cornus obliqua	SG
Cornus officinalis	B,SA
Cornus pumila	CG
Cornus racemosa	B,CG,G,SA
Cornus rugosa	B,SA
Cornus sanguinea	A,B,C,CG,SA
Cornus sessilis	B
Cornus stolonifera	B,C,CG,PR,SA,SG
Cornus stricta	B
Cornus suecia	C
Cornus walteri	B,C,SA
Corokia cotoneaster	AP,B,CG,SA,SS
Corokia x virgata	B,C,SA
Coronilla cappadocica	AP,FH,SC
Coronilla coronata	AP,B,SC
Coronilla emerus	B,C,G,SA
Coronilla minima	AP,B,G,SC
Coronilla orientalis	SG
Coronilla vaginalis	B,G
Coronilla valentina ssp glauca	C,SA
Coronilla valentina ssp valentina	SG
Coronilla varia	B,C,JE,KS,SA
Corryocactus melanotrichus	B,Y
Corryocactus melanotrichus v caulescens	Y
Corryocactus quadrangularis	B
Corryocactus tarijensis	Y
Corryocactus urmiriensis	B,Y

Cortaderia fulvida	B,C
Cortaderia richardii	B,SC,SG
Cortaderia selloana	B,BD,C,JE,KI,L,SA,ST, SU,T,V
Cortaderia selloana 'Pink Feather'	CL,L
Cortaderia selloana 'Rosea'	B,C,JE,SA,V
Cortaderia selloana 'White Feather'	CL,F
Cortaderia toetoe	SA
Cortusa matthioli	AP,B,CG,G,SA,SC,SG
Cortusa matthioli 'Alba'	AP,B,G,JE,SC
Cortusa matthioli f pekinensis	AP,B,C,G,JE,SC,SG
Cortusa pekinensis	CG
Cortusa turkestanica	AP,CG,G,SC,SG
Cortusa turkestanica 'Alba'	B,P
Coryanthera flava	O
Corycium magnum	B
Corydalis aquae-gelidae	B
Corydalis aurea	AP,B,SC,SW
Corydalis bracteata	SG
Corydalis caseana	SW
Corydalis cava	AP,B,C,G,JE,SA,SC
Corydalis cava f albiflora	AP,NG
Corydalis cheilanthifolia	AP,B,C,FH,G,I,JE,P,RH, SC,SG,T
Corydalis flexuosa	AP,B,P,SC
Corydalis fumariifolia	PM
Corydalis incisa	B
Corydalis intermedia	B
Corydalis lutea	B,BS,C,CG,CL,F,G,I,JE, P,RH,SA,T
Corydalis nobilis	B,C,CG,G,JE,SA
Corydalis ochotensis	B,P
Corydalis ochroleuca	AP,B,C,CG,G,I,JE,P,PM, RH,SC,SG,T
Corydalis ophiocarpa	P
Corydalis rosea	C,MN,SC
Corydalis saxicola	PM
Corydalis sempervirens	AP,B,C,CG,P,PM,SC,T
Corydalis sempervirens 'Alba'	B,P,T
Corydalis solida	AP,B,C,F,G,JE,PM,SC
Corydalis solida MS881 Spain	MN
Corydalis tomentella	AP,C,I,SC
Corydalis wilsonii	AP,FH,HH,I,JE,SC,SG
Corylopsis goloana	CG
Corylopsis pauciflora	B,CG,N
Corylopsis platypetala	B
Corylopsis sinensis	B,N
Corylopsis spicata	N,SG
Corylus americana	B
Corylus avellana	B,C,SA
Corylus chinensis	SA
Corylus colurna	B,SA
Corylus cornuta	B,G,SA,SG
Corylus heterophylla	B,SA,SG
Corylus mandschurica	SA
Corylus maxima	SA
Corymbium africanum	SI
Corymbium glabrum	SI
Corymbium laxum ssp laxum	SI
Corymbium theileri	SI
Corynanthera flava	B,C,O,SA
Corynephorus canescens	B,C,JE,SA
Corynocarpus laevigata	B
Corypha elata	O
Corypha umbraculifera	B,O
Corypha utan	B

Coryphantha andreae	Y
Coryphantha asterias	B
Coryphantha bergerana	B
Coryphantha breviformis	Y
Coryphantha bumamma	B,Y
Coryphantha calipensis	B,Y
Coryphantha chihuahuensis	B
Coryphantha clava	B
Coryphantha compacta	BC
Coryphantha cornifera	B,Y
Coryphantha delaetiana /c salm-dyckiana	B
Coryphantha difficile	B
Coryphantha durangensis	B
Coryphantha echinoidea	B
Coryphantha echinus	B
Coryphantha echinus SB377	Y
Coryphantha erecta	B
Coryphantha gladiispina	B,Y
Coryphantha greenwoodii	B
Coryphantha hendricksoni	B
Coryphantha indensis	B
Coryphantha longicornis	B
Coryphantha macromeris	B
Coryphantha maiz-tablasensis	Y
Coryphantha nickelsae	B
Coryphantha obscura SB714	Y
Coryphantha pallida	B,Y
Coryphantha palmeri	B,BC,Y
Coryphantha pectinata	B,Y
Coryphantha poselgerana v valida	B
Coryphantha poselgeria	B
Coryphantha poselgeriana	B
Coryphantha potosina	B
Coryphantha pseudechinus	B
Coryphantha pseudonickelsa	B
Coryphantha pulleineana	B
Coryphantha pusilliflora	B
Coryphantha pycnacantha	B
Coryphantha radians	B,Y
Coryphantha ramillosa	B
Coryphantha recurvata	B
Coryphantha reduncuspina	Y
Coryphantha retusa	B,Y
Coryphantha roederana	B
Coryphantha runyonii /c macromeris	B
Coryphantha salm-dyckia	B
Coryphantha scheeri	B
Coryphantha scheeri v robustispina	B
Coryphantha scheeri v valida	B
Coryphantha scheerii	B
Coryphantha sp mix	B,Y
Coryphantha sulcata	B,Y
Coryphantha sulconata	Y
Coryphantha unicornis	B,Y
Coryphantha vaupeliana	B
Coryphantha villarensis	B,Y
Cosmelia rubra	B
Cosmidium burridgeanum 'Brunette'	DT,F,KS,T,U
Cosmos atrosanguineus	B
Cosmos bipinnatus	AV,B,G,HW,SG
Cosmos bipinnatus 'Candy Stripe'	B,KS,L,SE
Cosmos bipinnatus 'Collarette'	KS
Cosmos bipinnatus 'Daydream'	B,BD,BS,DT,F,KS,T,V
Cosmos bipinnatus 'Dazzler'	C
Cosmos bipinnatus 'Frosty Rose'	J
Cosmos bipinnatus 'Giant Series'	B

COSMOS

Cosmos bipinnatus 'Gloria'	T
Cosmos bipinnatus 'Picotee'	B,DT,F,SE,T
Cosmos bipinnatus 'Pied Piper Red'	T
Cosmos bipinnatus 'Psyche Mix'	T
Cosmos bipinnatus 'Purity'	C,KS,T
Cosmos bipinnatus 'Sea Shells'	BD,BS,C,D,DT,F,J,KS,L, S,SE,T,V
Cosmos bipinnatus 'Sensation Early mix'	AP,BD,BS,C,CO,D,DT,F, J,KI,KS,L,S,ST,T,TU,U,V
Cosmos bipinnatus 'Sensation Early' s-c	B
Cosmos bipinnatus 'Sonata Dw White'	B,C,CL,D,KS,O,T
Cosmos bipinnatus 'Sonata' mix	BS,CL,D,DT,F,J,KS,L,M, S,SE,T,U,V
Cosmos bipinnatus 'Sonata' s-c	BS,CL
Cosmos bipinnatus 'Sweet Dreams'	SE
Cosmos bipinnatus 'Versailles'	C,KS,L,T
Cosmos bipinnatus 'Versailles' Carmine	C
Cosmos bipinnatus 'Yellow Garden'	B
Cosmos diversifolius	SG
Cosmos 'Imperial Pink'	S
Cosmos sulphureus	AP,B,G,HW,SG
Cosmos sulphureus 'Bright Lights'	B,BS,DT,KS,L
Cosmos sulphureus 'Diablo'	B,G
Cosmos sulphureus 'Goldcrest'	B
Cosmos sulphureus 'Ladybird Dwarf mix'	BS,CL,CO,KI,T,TU,VH
Cosmos sulphureus 'Ladybird Dwarf' s-c	B,BS,CL,T
Cosmos sulphureus 'Lemon Twist'	B,T
Cosmos sulphureus 'Sunny Gold'	S,T,V
Cosmos sulphureus 'Sunny Red'	B,S,T
Cosmos sulphureus 'Sunset'	B,C,V
Costus afer	B
Costus barbatus	B
Costus dinklagei	B
Costus guanaiensis v macrostrobilus	B
Costus guanaiensis v tarmicus	B
Costus igneus	B
Costus lima	B
Costus lucanusianus	B
Costus malortieanus	B
Costus megalobracteatus	B
Costus pictus	B
Costus speciosus	B,C,SA
Costus spectabilis	B
Costus spicatus	B
Costus spiralis	B
Costus warzearum	B
Cotinus coggyria	A,B,C,G,SA
Cotinus coggyria purpurea	SA
Cotinus obovatus	SA
Cotoneaster acuminatus	SG
Cotoneaster acutifolius	B,SA
Cotoneaster adpressus	B,SG
Cotoneaster amoenus	RH,SG
Cotoneaster apiculatus	B,CG,SA
Cotoneaster ascendens	SG
Cotoneaster assamensiss	SG
Cotoneaster Bonsai mix	C
Cotoneaster bullatus	B,RH,SA,SG
Cotoneaster bullatus v floribundus	B,SG
Cotoneaster buxifolius	B
Cotoneaster buxifolius v vellaeus	SG
Cotoneaster cambricus	SG
Cotoneaster cavei	SG
Cotoneaster cinerascens	SG
Cotoneaster cochleatus of gdns	SG
Cotoneaster dammeri	AP,B,FH,SG

Cotoneaster dielsianus	B,RH,SA,SG
Cotoneaster diganthus	CG
Cotoneaster divaricatus	B,SA,SG
Cotoneaster duthianus	SG
Cotoneaster falconeri	SG
Cotoneaster faveolatus	CG,SG
Cotoneaster franchettii	B,C,RH,SA,SG
Cotoneaster franchettii v cinerascens	B,RH
Cotoneaster frigidus	B,SG
Cotoneaster glaucophyllus	B,RH,SG
Cotoneaster glaucophyllus v meiophyllus	SG
Cotoneaster glaucophyllus v serotinus	RH
Cotoneaster harrovianus	RH
Cotoneaster hebephyllus	RH
Cotoneaster horizontalis	B,SA
Cotoneaster horizontalis 'Prostratus'	AP,B
Cotoneaster horizontalis 'Saxatilis'	RS
Cotoneaster hupehensis	SG
Cotoneaster ignavus	SG
Cotoneaster integerrimus	SA,SG
Cotoneaster integrifolius	AP,B,SA,SG,V
Cotoneaster kitaibelii	SG
Cotoneaster kweischoviensis	SG
Cotoneaster lacteus	AP,B,RH,SA
Cotoneaster lindleyi	SG
Cotoneaster linearifolius	B
Cotoneaster lucidus	B,SA,SG
Cotoneaster marquandii	SG
Cotoneaster melanocarpus	RH,SG
Cotoneaster melanocarpus v altaicus	SG
Cotoneaster melanocarpus v laxiflorus	SG
Cotoneaster melanocarpus x multiflorus	SG
Cotoneaster multiflorus	B,SA
Cotoneaster multiflorus v calocarpus	B,SG
Cotoneaster nanshan	B,SA,SG
Cotoneaster niger	RS
Cotoneaster nitens	B
Cotoneaster nitidus	SG
Cotoneaster obscurus	SG
Cotoneaster oliganthus	SG
Cotoneaster pannosus	B,C,SG
Cotoneaster perpusillus	B
Cotoneaster polyanthemus	SG
Cotoneaster przewalskii	SG
Cotoneaster racemiflorus	B,SG
Cotoneaster racemiflorus v nummularius	B,SG
Cotoneaster racemiflorus v songoricus	SG
Cotoneaster racemiflorus v veitchii	B
Cotoneaster roborovskii	SG
Cotoneaster roseus	SG
Cotoneaster rotundifolius	SG
Cotoneaster salicifolius	B,RH,SA
Cotoneaster salicifolius 'Repens'	B
Cotoneaster salicifolius v floccosus	B
Cotoneaster salicifolius v rugosus of gdns	B
Cotoneaster sandakphuensis	SG
Cotoneaster sauvis	SG
Cotoneaster saxatilis	SG
Cotoneaster scandinavicus	SG
Cotoneaster shansiensis	SG
Cotoneaster sikangensis	SG
Cotoneaster simonsii	B,SA,SG
Cotoneaster sp China	SG
Cotoneaster sp mix	AP,C
Cotoneaster splendens	SG
Cotoneaster staintonii	SG

Cotoneaster tomentosus	SG
Cotoneaster veitchii	SG
Cotoneaster wardii	RH,SG
Cotoneaster x watereri	B
Cotoneaster zabellii	CG,SG
Cotoneaster zeravschanicus	SG
Cotula alpina	B,P
Cotula barbata	B,KI
Cotula coronopifolia	B,SI
Cotula duckittae	B
Cotula hispida	AP,I,SC,SI
Cotula plumosa	FH
Cotula turbinata 'Select'	B
Cotula 'Yellow Marbles'	BS,C,CO
Cotyledon adscandens	CG
Cotyledon barbeyi	CG
Cotyledon campanulata	SI
Cotyledon orbiculata	B,C,SI,Y
Cotyledon orbiculata v flanaganii	B,Y
Cotyledon orbiculata v oblonga	B,Y
Cotyledon orbiculata v orbiculata	B,SI
Cotyledon sp mix	C,SI
Cotyledon tomentosa	B
Cotyledon umbilicus	B
Cotyledon velutina	B
Couroupita guianensis	B
Cowania mexicana	B,SW
Cowania mexicana v stansburiana	B
Cowania stansburiana	C,SA
Crabbea reticulata	B
Crabia zimmermannii	B
Crambe abyssinica	B,KS
Crambe abyssinica 'Funfare'	B
Crambe abyssinica 'Serenata'	C
Crambe cordifolia	AP,B,C,CG,G,JE,P,SA,T
Crambe maritima	B,C,JE,SA,SG
Crambe maritima 'Lily White'	B
Crambe tatarica	B,C,CG,JE,SG
Craspedia globosa	BS,CO,DT,HA,KI,KS,L, S,ST,SU,T,TU,U,V
Craspedia incana	AP,B,SC,SS
Craspedia lanata	AP,SS
Craspedia uniflora	B,PM,SG,SS
Crassula acinaciformis	SI
Crassula alba v alba	B,SI
Crassula arborescens	B,SI
Crassula arborescens v arborescens	B,SI
Crassula barklyi	B
Crassula capensis	B
Crassula capensis v capensis	SI
Crassula capitella	SI
Crassula ciliata	SI
Crassula coccinea	B,SI,Y
Crassula columnaris	B,SI
Crassula congesta ssp laticephala	B
Crassula cultrata	Y
Crassula cymosa	B,SI
Crassula dejecta	B,SI,Y
Crassula dependens	SI
Crassula dichotoma	B,SI
Crassula dubia	Y
Crassula elegans	B
Crassula fascicularis	B,SI
Crassula lactea	B,SG
Crassula lanuginosa	SG
Crassula multicava	B,SI,Y

Crassula multiflora	B,SI,Y
Crassula muscosa tetragona	SG
Crassula muscosa v pseudolicopodioides	SG
Crassula muscosa v purpurii	SG
Crassula nudicaulis	Y
Crassula nudicaulis v nudicaulis	B,SI
Crassula nudicaulis v platyphylla	B
Crassula obovata	B
Crassula obtusa	SI
Crassula orbicularis	B,SI
Crassula ovata	C,SA,SI,Y
Crassula pellucida ssp brachypetala	SI
Crassula pellucida ssp marginalis	B,SI,Y
Crassula perfoliata	Y
Crassula perfoliata v minor	B,C,SG,SI,Y
Crassula perfoliata v perfoliata	B
Crassula perforata	SI
Crassula pruinosa	B,SI
Crassula pubescens ssp radicans	B,Y
Crassula pyramidalis	B,SI
Crassula rogersii	B,SI
Crassula rubricaulis	B,SI,Y
Crassula rupestris	B,SI
Crassula sarcocaulis	B,SC,SI
Crassula sarcocaulis ssp rupicola	B,Y
Crassula scabra	B,SI
Crassula sp mix	C,SG,SI,Y
Crassula spathulata	B,SI
Crassula susannae	B
Crassula swaziensis	B,SI
Crassula tetragona	B,SI,Y
Crassula tetragona ssp acutifolia	B,Y
Crassula tetragona ssp robusta	B,SA,Y
Crassula tomentosa	B,SI
Crassula umbellata	B
Crassula vaginata	SI
Crataegus alemanniensis	SG
Crataegus alemanniensis 'Lacinata'	SG
Crataegus alemanniensis v orientobaltica	SG
Crataegus altaica	SG
Crataegus ambigua	SG
Crataegus apiifolia	B
Crataegus apiomorpha	SG
Crataegus armena	SG
Crataegus arnoldiana	SA,SG
Crataegus azarolus	A,B,C,SA
Crataegus basilica	Sg
Crataegus beata	SG
Crataegus brachyacantha	B
Crataegus calpodendron	SG
Crataegus canadensis	SG
Crataegus canbyi	SG
Crataegus caucasica	SG
Crataegus cerronis	SA
Crataegus chlorosarca	B,SA,SG
Crataegus coccinea	SA
Crataegus coccinoides	B
Crataegus coleae	SG
Crataegus columbiana	B,C,SA
Crataegus crus-galli	B,C,SA
Crataegus crus-galli 'Inermis'	B
Crataegus dahurica	SG
Crataegus delawarensis	SG
Crataegus densiflora	SG
Crataegus douglasii	A,B,C,SA,SG
Crataegus faxonii	SG

CRATAEGUS

Crataegus fecunda	SG
Crataegus flabellata	SG
Crataegus foetida	SG
Crataegus gravis	SG
Crataegus grayana	SG
Crataegus hajastana	SG
Crataegus horrida	SG
Crataegus horrida v aboriginum	SG
Crataegus intricata	B,C
Crataegus iracunda	SG
Crataegus iracunda v populnea	SG
Crataegus irrasa	SG
Crataegus jesupii	SG
Crataegus jonesiae	C
Crataegus korolkowii	SG
Crataegus laevigata	A,B,SA,SG
Crataegus laevigata 'Rosea'	B
Crataegus laneyi	SG
Crataegus laurentiana	SG
Crataegus lettermanii	SG
Crataegus lindmanii	SG
Crataegus macrantha	SG
Crataegus macrantha 'Scimitar'	C
Crataegus macrosperma	SG
Crataegus maximowiczii	SG
Crataegus maximowiczii MW103R	X
Crataegus mollis	A,B,C,SG
Crataegus monogyna	A,B,SA,SG
Crataegus nigra	SG
Crataegus orientalis	A,SA
Crataegus osiliensis	SG
Crataegus pedicellata	SG
Crataegus pennsylvanica	SG
Crataegus pentagyna	B,SG
Crataegus phaenopyrum	B,C,SA
Crataegus pinnatifida	B,SG
Crataegus pinnatifida major	SA
Crataegus praecoqua	SG
Crataegus pringlei	SG
Crataegus pringlei v exclusa	SG
Crataegus prona	SG
Crataegus pruinosa	SG
Crataegus pseudoheterophylla	SG
Crataegus pubescens	B
Crataegus punctata	B,SA,SG
Crataegus punctata f aurea	SG
Crataegus putnamiana	SG
Crataegus roanensis	SG
Crataegus russanovii	SG
Crataegus sanguinea	SG
Crataegus sanguinea v chlorocarpa	SG
Crataegus scabrida	SG
Crataegus sp mix	C
Crataegus stankovii	SG
Crataegus stevenii	SG
Crataegus submollis	SG
Crataegus suborbiculata	SG
Crataegus succulenta	B
Crataegus tanacetifolia	C
Crataegus turcomanica	SG
Crataegus uniflora	B
Crataegus vailliae	SG
Crataegus viridis 'Winter King'	B
Crataegus vulsa	B
Crataegus x calycina	SG
Crataegus x curonica	SG

Crataegus x degenii	SG
Crataegus x dsungarica	SG
Crataegus x dunensis	SG
Crataegus x kyrtostyla	SG
Crataegus x luzinii	SG
Crataegus x maritima	SG
Crataegus x ovalifolia	SG
Crataegus x persimilis	SG
Crataegus x prunifolia	B,C,SA
Crataegus x schneideri	SG
Craterostigma plantagineum	SI
Craterostigma wilmsii	B,SI
Crateva magna	B
Cremanthodium delavayii	CC
Cremanthodium retusum	SG
Crepis aurea	AP,B,G,SC,T
Crepis biennis	B
Crepis capillaris	B
Crepis 'Coconut Ice'	U
Crepis conyzifolia	SG
Crepis conyzifolia ssp conyzifolia	SG
Crepis incana	AP,I,PA,SC
Crepis paludosa	SG
Crepis pygmaea	AP,B,C
Crepis rhoeadifolia	B
Crepis rubra	AP,BS,C,D,DT,F,KI,KS, RH,S,SC,SE,T,TU,W
Crepis rubra 'Alba'	B,KS
Crepis rubra 'Rosea'	B,J,SG,V
Crepis rubra 'Snowplume'	T
Crepis sancta	B
Crepis sibirica	SG
Crepis vesicaria	SG
Crescentia alata	B,RE
Crescentia cujete	B,SA
Crinodendron hookerianum	B,P,SG
Crinum asiaticum	B,G
Crinum bulbispermum	B,SG
Crinum moorei	B
Crinum pedunculatum	B,C,HA,O
Crinum x powellii	B
Crithmum maritimum	B,C
Crocosmia aurea	B,SI
Crocosmia 'Bressingham Hybrids'	C
Crocosmia 'Emberglow'	B
Crocosmia hyb	BS,SA,T,W
Crocosmia hyb 'Orangerot'	JE
Crocosmia 'Lucifer'	AP,B,C,E,HH,LG,MA,PA, PM,SC
Crocosmia masonorum	C,G,I,JE,SC,T
Crocosmia paniculata	B,I,sa,SI
Crocosmia pottsii	B,SI
Crocosmia 'Solfatarre'	B,I
Crocosmia variegata	B
Crocosmia x crocosmiiflora	B,E
Crocus abantensis	AP,B,JE,SC
Crocus aleppicus L.B101 Jordan	MN
Crocus aleppicus L.B59 Jordan	MN
Crocus angustifolius	G,SC
Crocus banaticus	AP,G,PM,SC
Crocus baytopiorium	JE,SC
Crocus biflorus v biflorus B.S378 Italy	MN
Crocus biflorus v biflorus MS957 Italy	MN
Crocus boryi	CC,SC
Crocus byzantinus	CG
Crocus cambessedesii PB91 Majorca	MN

CROCUS

Crocus cancellatus	CG
Crocus cancellatus v mazziaricus PB258	MN
Crocus chrysanthus	AP,B,SC
Crocus chrysanthus 'Advance'	B
Crocus chrysanthus 'Lady Killer'	B
Crocus dalmaticus	CG
Crocus etruscus MS949 Italy	MN
Crocus flavus	AP,B,CG,SC
Crocus flavus M.T4578 Turkey	MN
Crocus fleischeri	AP,CG,G,SC
Crocus goulimyi	AP,B,G,SC
Crocus goulimyi S.L197 Greece	MN
Crocus hadriaticus	AP,B,SC
Crocus hadriaticus S.L470 Greece	MN
Crocus hyemalis S.B.L124 Jordan	MN
Crocus imperatii v suaveolens MS962 It.	MN
Crocus kotschyanus	AP,B,CG,G,SC,SG
Crocus kotschyanus A.C.W2413 Turkey	MN
Crocus kotschyanus C.M.W2724 Turkey	MN
Crocus kotschyanus leucopharynx	SG
Crocus kotschyanus M.T4532 Turkey	MN
Crocus longiflorus	B
Crocus longiflorus MS967 Italy	MN
Crocus longiflorus MS968 Italy	MN
Crocus longiflorus MS974 Italy	MN
Crocus minimus	B
Crocus napolitanus	CG
Crocus niveus	AP,B
Crocus niveus MS Greece	MN
Crocus nudiflorus	AP,B,C,CG,SC
Crocus pallasii	PM
Crocus pallasii ssp dispathaceus	JE
Crocus pallasii v haussnechtii S.B.L146	MN
Crocus pulchellus	G,PM,SG
Crocus pulchellus M.T4582 Turkey	AP,MN
Crocus sativus	B
Crocus scepusiensis	CG
Crocus serotinus v ?clusii PB209 Port.	MN
Crocus serotinus v clusii PB375 Portugal	MN
Crocus serotinus v salzmannii A.B.S4324	MN
Crocus serotinus v salzmannii A.B.S4326	MN
Crocus serotinus v salzmannii A.B.S4411	MN
Crocus serotinus v salzmannii S.F218	MN
Crocus serotinus v salzmannii S.F242	MN
Crocus serotinus v salzmannii S.F343	MN
Crocus serotinus v serotinus PB167	MN
Crocus ?serotinus v serotinus S.F237	MN
Crocus sp mix	AP,C,MN
Crocus speciosus	AP,B,CG,G,PM,SC
Crocus speciosus 'Albus'	B
Crocus speciosus v albus hort.	MN
Crocus thomasii B.S364 Italy	MN
Crocus tommasinianus	AP,B,C,CG,SC
Crocus tommasinianus PF6584	MN
Crocus vernus ssp vernus	JE,SC
Crocus vernus v albiflorus	C
Crossandra infundibuliformis	B,BS,SA
Crossandra 'Tropic Flame'	T
Crotalaria barnabassii	B,SI
Crotalaria benthamiana	B
Crotalaria brachycarpa	SI
Crotalaria capensis	B,SI
Crotalaria 'Chepil De Burro'	B
Crotalaria cunninghamii	B,C,O,SA
Crotalaria eremaea	B
Crotalaria globifera	SI

Crotalaria grahamiana	B
Crotalaria juncea	B
Crotalaria laburnifolia	B
Crotalaria longirostrata	B
Crotalaria medicaginea	B
Crotalaria meyerana	B
Crotalaria novae-hollandiae	B,O
Crotalaria pallida	B
Crotalaria paniculata	B
Crotalaria retusa	B
Crotalaria sagittalis	PR
Crotalaria semperflorens	B,O,SA
Crotalaria sessiliflora	B
Crotalaria verrucosa	B
Crowea angustifolia	B,O,SA
Crowea angustifolia v dentata	B,O
Cruciata laevipes	B
Crupina crupinastrus	B
Cryptandra arbutiflora	B
Cryptanthus sp	B
Cryptocarya glaucescens	B
Cryptocarya liebertiana	B
Cryptocarya mackinnoniana	O
Cryptolepis oblongifolia	B
Cryptomeria japonica	B,C,CG,G,HA,N,RH,SA, T,V
Cryptomeria japonica 'Lobbii'	B
Cryptomeria japonica v sinensis	B,SA
Cryptostegia grandiflora	B,C,SA
Cryptostephanus vansonii	B
Cryptotaenia japonica	B
Crysophyllum mexicanum	B
Ctenium concinnum	B,SI
Ctenolepis garcinii	B
Cucubalus baccifer	B,G
Cucumis metuliferus	B,C,SA,SI
Cucumis myriocarpus	B,SI
Cucumis saggitatus	SI
Cucurbita ornamental gourd	BS,C,D,DT,F,G,KI,KS,L, SG,SU,V,VH
Cucurbita o. g. 'Choose Your Weapons'	T
Cucurbita o. gourd 'Crown of Thorns'	BS
Cucurbita o. gourd 'Large Bottle'	B,T
Cucurbita o. gourd 'Luffa'	T
Cucurbita o. gourd small fruited	BS,D,T,U
Cucurbita o. gourd 'Turks Turban'	B,BS,T
Cucurbita ornamental gourd warted	BS
Cumarinia odorata	B,BC
Cunninghamia konishii	SA
Cunninghamia lanceolata	B,C,N,SA
Cunonia capensis	B,O,SA,SI
Cupaniopsis anacardioides	B,HA,O
Cuphea hyssopifolia	CG,G
Cuphea ignea	B,BD,BS,C,CL,DT,G,J, KI,LSA,U,V
Cuphea lanceolata 'Firefly'	C
Cuphea llavea 'Bunny Ears Mix'	T
Cuphea llavea 'Purpurea'	B,F
Cuphea llavea v miniata	B,F
Cupressus anjouce	CG·
Cupressus arizonica	B,C,CG,HA,SA
Cupressus arizonica v glabra	B,HA,RH
Cupressus arizonica v nevadensis	B
Cupressus arizonica v stephensonii	B
Cupressus bakeri	B,SA
Cupressus chengiana	B

CUPRESSUS

Cupressus duclouxiana	B,SG	Cycas couttsiana	O
Cupressus funebris	B,C,HA,RH,SA,SG	Cycas furfuracea	B,O
Cupressus goveniana	B	Cycas guizhouensis	B
Cupressus goveniana v pygmaea	B,SA	Cycas inermis	B
Cupressus guadalupensis ssp forbesii	B,SA	Cycas kennedyana	HA
Cupressus himalaica ssp darjeelingensis	B	Cycas 'Kimbleton'	O
Cupressus knightiana	CG	Cycas lane-poolei	B
Cupressus lusitanica	B,CG,SA	Cycas 'Lichfield Park'	O
Cupressus lusitanica v benthamii	B	Cycas machonochii	B,O
Cupressus macnabiana	B,SA	Cycas 'Marlborough Blue'	C
Cupressus macrocarpa	A,BS,C,HA,SA	Cycas media	B,C,HA,SA,O
Cupressus sargentii	B,SA	Cycas megacarpa	C,O
Cupressus sempervirens	HA,RH	Cycas micholitzii	B
Cupressus sempervirens cereiformis	B	Cycas neo-calidonicae	O
Cupressus sempervirens f horizontalis	B,SA	Cycas nitida	B
Cupressus sempervirens pyramidalis	SA	Cycas normanbyana	B
Cupressus sempervirens 'Stricta'	B,C,SC	Cycas ophiolitica	O
Cupressus torulosa	B,C,HA,SA	Cycas orientalis	O
Cupressus torulosa 'Cashmeriana'	C,HA,N,SA	Cycas panzhihuaensis	B
Cupulanthus bracteolasus	AU	Cycas papuana	B
Curcuma inodora	B	Cycas pectinata	O
Curcuma longa	B	Cycas platyphylla	O
Curtisia dentata	B,SI	Cycas 'Port Keats'	O
Cuscuta campestris	B	Cycas pruinosa green & blue	B,O
Cuscuta chinensis	B	Cycas revoluta	B,C,CG,HA,O,SA
Cussonia natalensis	B	Cycas riamensis	O
Cussonia paniculata	B,C,O,SA,SI,Y	Cycas rumphii	O
Cussonia paniculata v sinuata	B	Cycas segmentifida	B
Cussonia spicata	B,O,SA,SI,Y	Cycas sp mix	T
Cyamopsis tetragonolobus	B	Cycas sylvestris	O
Cyanella alba	B,SI	Cycas taiwaniana	B
Cyanella hyacinthoides	B,SI	Cycas thouarsii	B,O
Cyanella lutea	B,SI	Cycas wadei	O
Cyanella orchidiformis	B,G,SI	Cycas yunnanensis	B
Cyanotis foecunda	B,SI	Cyclamen africanum	AP,AS,B,C,CG,LG,P,PM,
Cyanotis somaliensis	SG		SC,SG
Cyanotis speciosa	SI	Cyclamen africanum JCA855	MN
Cyathea australis	B,C,HA,SA	Cyclamen africanum S.L277 Tunisia	MN
Cyathea brownii	B	Cyclamen 'Albadonna'	B,BS
Cyathea cooperi	B,HA,SA	Cyclamen balearicum	AP,C,G,MN,SC
Cyathea cunninghamii	B,C	Cyclamen balearicum 'Silvery Leaf forms'	C
Cyathea dealbata	B,C,SA	Cyclamen 'Beautiful Helena'	KI
Cyathea leichardtiana	B,HA,SA	Cyclamen 'Blended Mix'	BS
Cyathea medullaris	B,C,SA	Cyclamen 'Cantorial' mix o-p	CL
Cyathea smithii	B,SA	Cyclamen 'Cardinal'	B,BS
Cyathodes colensoi	B,C,SS	Cyclamen 'Cascade'	J
Cyathodes empetrifolia	B,SS	Cyclamen 'Christmas Scarlet'	U
Cyathodes fasciculata	B,C	Cyclamen cilicium	AP,AS,B,C,CG,CT,JE,
Cyathodes glauca	B,O		LG,MN,N,PM,SC,SG
Cyathodes juniperina	B,SS	Cyclamen cilicium f album	AP,CT,PM,SC
Cyathodes parviflora	B,HA,O	Cyclamen cilicium v cilicium	SG
Cyathodes pumila	B,SS	Cyclamen cilicium v intaminatum	SG
Cyathula officinalis	B	Cyclamen coum	w.a
Cybistax donnell-smithii	B	Cyclamen coum best patterns	CT
Cycas angulata	O	Cyclamen coum 'Broadleigh Silver'	CT
Cycas arenticola	O	Cyclamen coum BS 8927	CT
Cycas armstrongii	B,O,SA	Cyclamen coum f albissimum	C,G,JE,SE
Cycas arnhemica	O	Cyclamen coum lge fl mix	CT
Cycas basaltica	B,O	Cyclamen coum 'Linett Jewel'	CT
Cycas brunnea	O	Cyclamen coum 'Linett Rose'	CT
Cycas 'Bynoe/Fog Bay'		Cyclamen coum mass fl	CT
Cycas cairnsiana	B,O,SA	Cyclamen coum mass fl clear light pink	CT
Cycas calcicola	B,O	Cyclamen coum mass fl deep rich pink	CT
Cycas canalis	O	Cyclamen coum mass fl white	CT
Cycas circinalis	B,O	Cyclamen coum 'Maurice Dryden'	AP,CT,SC
Cycas conferta	B,O	Cyclamen coum Pewter Group	C,CT,PM,SE,SG

73

CYCLAMEN

Cyclamen coum propeller shape — CT
Cyclamen coum 'Rubrum' — JE,SC
Cyclamen coum 'Show' mix — C
Cyclamen coum silver leaf — AP,CT,G,JE,SC
Cyclamen coum 'Silver Star' — CT
Cyclamen coum ssp caucasicum — AP,C,G,NG,PM,SC,SG
Cyclamen coum ssp coum — SG
Cyclamen coum 'Turkish Princess' — CT
Cyclamen creticum — AS,G
Cyclamen cyprium — AP,AS,B,C,MN,SC
Cyclamen 'Dainty Ballerina' — BS
Cyclamen 'Dresden' mix — CL
Cyclamen 'Esprit' mix — D,J
Cyclamen 'Esprit' s-c — B
Cyclamen f1 'Butterfly' — L
Cyclamen f1 'Fairytales Mix' — YA
Cyclamen f1 'Firmament' mix — BS,S
Cyclamen f1 'Firmament' s-c — BS
Cyclamen f1 'Halios' s-c — B
Cyclamen f1 'Laser' mix — CL
Cyclamen f1 'Miracle' mix — CL
Cyclamen f1 'Miracle' s-c — CL
Cyclamen f1 'New Wave' — CL
Cyclamen f1 'Romance' s-c, mix — BS
Cyclamen f1 'Sierra' mix — CL
Cyclamen f1 'Sierra' s-c — CL
Cyclamen f1 'Zodiac' — L
Cyclamen 'Fancy free' — O-P
Cyclamen 'Fringed' o-p — CL
Cyclamen graecum — AP,AS,B,C,CG,P,SC,SG
Cyclamen graecum Greece — AP,MN
Cyclamen graecum MS772 Crete — MN
Cyclamen graecum S.L165/2 Evvia — MN
Cyclamen 'Green Leaf Form' — C
Cyclamen 'Hardy Species Mix' — C,CL
Cyclamen hederifolium — w.a
Cyclamen hederifolium 'Album' — B,BS,C,G,P,PM,RS,SA, SG,T
Cyclamen hederifolium 'Bowles' Apollo' — C,NG
Cyclamen hederifolium 'Fairy Rings' — CT
Cyclamen hederifolium 'Island' scented — C
Cyclamen hederifolium mix — AP,BS,C,SE,T
Cyclamen hederifolium 'Perlenteppich' — CT,JE
Cyclamen hederifolium 'Rosenteppich' — JE
Cyclamen hederifolium 'Roseum' — B,BS,SA
Cyclamen hederifolium S.France — CT
Cyclamen hederifolium 'Silver Cloud' — C,CT
Cyclamen hederifolium silver leaf — AP,CT,SC
Cyclamen hederifolium 'Silver Swan' — NG
Cyclamen intaminatum — AP,AS,G,HW,SC
Cyclamen 'Junior' — U
Cyclamen libanoticum — AP,AS,B,C,HW,P,SC
Cyclamen lightly marked leaf form — C
Cyclamen mirabile — AP,AS,C,G,JE,MN,SC
Cyclamen 'New Giants Mix' — BS
Cyclamen parviflorum — AP,C,HW,SC
Cyclamen 'Pastel Compacta' mix — YA
Cyclamen 'Pastel Decora' mix — YA
Cyclamen persicum — AP,AS,BD,CG,G,SC,V
Cyclamen persicum 'Benary's Special' — C
Cyclamen persicum 'Crown' mix — KI,ST
Cyclamen persicum g. 'Flamenco Frills' — T
Cyclamen persicum g. 'Fringed & Ruffled' — T
Cyclamen persicum g. 'Fuzzy Wuzzy' — T
Cyclamen persicum g. 'Gold Medal' — T
Cyclamen persicum g. 'Pink Delight' — T

Cyclamen persicum giganteum 'All Sorts' — T
Cyclamen persicum 'Mozart' — V
Cyclamen persicum Polunin — MN
Cyclamen persicum polypetalum — C
Cyclamen persicum Rhodes — AP,MN
Cyclamen persicum S.L55 Jordan — MN
Cyclamen persicum v album — C
Cyclamen persicum 'Victoria' — B,T
Cyclamen persicum wild form — C
Cyclamen 'Petite Wonder Series' s-c — YA
Cyclamen pseudibericum — AP,AS,C,G,HW,JE,PM, SC
Cyclamen pseudibericum & p. roseum — CT
Cyclamen purpurascens — AP,AS,B,C,CT,G,JE,SA, SC,T,V
Cyclamen purpurascens silver leaf — NG
Cyclamen repandum — AP,AS,C,CT,G,JE,SC,SE
Cyclamen repandum PB111 Italy — MN
Cyclamen repandum v peloponnesiacum — C,CT
Cyclamen r. v p. 'Balearic Hybrids' — C
Cyclamen rholfsianum — AP,AS,G,MN,SC
Cyclamen 'Rose Beauty' — B,BS
Cyclamen 'Rubin' — B,BS
Cyclamen 'Salmon Beauty' — BS,B
Cyclamen 'Scented Silver Leaf' — U
Cyclamen 'Scentsation' mix — C,T
Cyclamen 'Schone Helena' — C
Cyclamen seed autumn fl. — CT
Cyclamen seed starter pack — CT
Cyclamen seed winter fl. — CT
Cyclamen 'Silvery Leaf Form' mix — BS,C
Cyclamen 'Super Puppet' mix — S
Cyclamen 'Sweet Scented' mix — BS,D,S
Cyclamen 'Tiny Mites' — BS,T
Cyclamen 'Treasure Chest' — C,S
Cyclamen 'Treasure Trove' — J,T
Cyclamen 'Triumph Special' — S
Cyclamen trochopteranthum — AP,AS,C,CG,G,HW,PM, SC
Cyclamen trochopteranthum 'Red Devil' — CT
Cyclamen 'Wellensiek' — C
Cyclamen 'Winter Cheer' — U
Cyclamen 'Zodiac Mix' — DT
Cyclanthera 'Fat Baby' — C
Cyclanthera 'Lady's Slipper' — C
Cyclanthera pedata — B,CG
Cyclanthus bipartitus — B
Cyclopia intermedia — B,SI
Cyclopia maculata — B,SI
Cyclopia sp — SI
Cyclosorus pennigera — B
Cycnium racemosum — B
Cydonia oblongata — SA
Cylindrophyllum calamiforme — B
Cylindrophyllum comptoni — B,SI
Cylindrophyllum tugwellii — B
Cymbalaria aequitrilobata — SG
Cymbalaria hepaticifolia — CG
Cymbalaria muralis — AP,B,C,G,JE,SA
Cymbalaria pallida — B
Cymbidium aloifolium — B
Cymbidium canaliculatum — B
Cymbidium suave — B
Cymbopogon ambiguus — B,SA
Cymbopogon bombycinus — B
Cymbopogon citratus — B

CYMBOPOGON

Cymbopogon excavatus	B,SI	Cyphostemma simulans	B
Cymbopogon flexuosus	B	Cypripedium calceolus	AP,B,G
Cymbopogon martinii	B	Cypripedium macranthum	AP,SC
Cymbopogon nardus	B	Cyrilla racemiflora	B,SA
Cymbopogon obtectus	B	Cyrtanthus angustifolius	B,SI
Cymbopogon refractus	HA	Cyrtanthus brachyscyphus	B,G
Cynanchum floribundum	B	Cyrtanthus breviflorus	B,C,SI
Cynanchum laeve	B	Cyrtanthus clavatus	SI
Cynanchum obtusifolium	B	Cyrtanthus elatus	B,SG
Cynanchum vincetoxicum	B	Cyrtanthus euculus	B
Cynara cardunculus	B,C,CG,CP,FH,JE,SC,	Cyrtanthus helictus	B,SI
	SA,T,V	Cyrtanthus herrei	B,SI
Cynara scolymus	CG,G,SA	Cyrtanthus loddigiesanus	B,SI
Cynodon dactylon	B	Cyrtanthus mackenii	C,SI
Cynodon dactylon 'Numex Sahara'	B	Cyrtanthus mackenii v mackenii	B
Cynoglossum amabile 'Avalanche'	B,KS,T	Cyrtanthus macowanii	SG
Cynoglossum amabile blue	AP,S,SC	Cyrtanthus obliquus	B,SI
Cynoglossum amabile 'Blue Bird'	BS,L	Cyrtanthus obrienii	B,SI
Cynoglossum amabile 'Firmament'	B,J,KS	Cyrtanthus sanguineus	AP,B,SI
Cynoglossum amabile 'Mystery Rose'	B,BS,D,J,KS,T	Cyrtanthus speciosus	B,SI
Cynoglossum amabile 'Shower Blue'	B,T,V	Cyrtanthus spiralis	SI
Cynoglossum amabile 'Shower Pink'	V	Cyrtanthus tuckii v viridilobus	B,C,SI
Cynoglossum creticum	B	Cyrtomium acculeatum	B
Cynoglossum glochidiatum	CC	Cyrtomium caryotideum	B
Cynoglossum macrostylum	SG	Cyrtomium falcatum	AP,B,SA,SC
Cynoglossum nervosum	AP,B,G,JE	Cyrtomium falcatum 'Rochefordianum'	B
Cynoglossum officinale	AP,B,G,JE,SA,SC,SG	Cyrtomium fortunei	B,G
Cynoglossum viridiflorum	SG	Cyrtostachys lakka	O,SA
Cynoglossum wallichii	B	Cyrtostachys lakka g	B
Cynosurus cristatus	B	Cyrtostachys renda	RE
Cynosurus echinatus	SG	Cysticapnos vesicaria	B,SI
Cypella herbertii	AP,B,CG,G,MN,SC	Cytharexylum subflavescens	B
Cyperus alternifolius	B,BS,C,CL,SA,SG	Cytisus austriacus	AP,SA
Cyperus alternifolius nanus	SA	Cytisus battandieri	AP,C,G,N,SA,SC,T
Cyperus compactus	SA	Cytisus decumbens	AP,B
Cyperus corymbosus	B	Cytisus emeriflorus	SG
Cyperus eragrostis	JE,SA	Cytisus grandiflorus	C
Cyperus esculentus v sativus	B	Cytisus hyb mix	D,DT,L,S,V
Cyperus fuscus	B	Cytisus madeiriensis	SA
Cyperus glaber	CL,JE,SA	Cytisus 'Monarch' mix	BD,BS
Cyperus gymnocaulos	B	Cytisus monspessulanus	AP,SA
Cyperus longus	B	Cytisus multiflorus	AP,B,C,SA
Cyperus nanus v compactus	B,C	Cytisus 'New Hybrids' mix	BS,C,CL,KI
Cyperus natalensis	SG	Cytisus nigricans	B,SA,SG
Cyperus obtusiflorus	SI	Cytisus procumbens	AP,SG
Cyperus obtusiflorus v flavissimus	B,SI	Cytisus scoparius	A,C,CP,SA,SG
Cyperus obtusiflorus v sphaerocephalus	SI	Cytisus scoparius f andreanus	B
Cyperus papyrus	B,C,G,JE,SA,SG,V	Cytisus scoparius southern	C
Cyperus profiler	B	Cytisus sessilifolius	AP,B,SC,SG
Cyperus reflexus	HA	Cytisus sp & hyb mix	T
Cyperus schweinitz	PR	Cytisus striatus	SG
Cyperus ustulatus	B,SA	Cytisus supranubius	C
Cyperus 'Zumila'	B	Cytronium falcatum	CG
Cyphia elata	SI	Daboecia cantabrica	C,RH,SC
Cyphia phyteuma	B,SI	Daboecia cantabrica hyb	C,JE
Cyphia sp	SI	Dacrycarpus dacrydoides	B,SA,SS
Cyphia volubilis	B,SI	Dacrydium cupressinum	B,SS
Cyphomandra betacea	B,C,CG,O,SA,SG	Dacryodes edulis	B
Cyphomandra betacea 'Fragrans'	B	Dactylis glomerata	B
Cyphomandra betacea 'Large Fruit'	B	Dactylis glomerata 'Currie'	B
Cyphomandra betacea 'Red Fruit'	B	Dactylis pokygama	B
Cyphomandra betacea 'Virus-free Red'	B	Dactylis sp Spain	SG
Cyphomandra hartwegii	B	Dactyloctenium aegyptium	B
Cyphophoenix nucele	B	Dactyloctenium radulans	B
Cyphostemma bainesii	B,CH,Y	Dactylopsis digitata	B,C,SI,Y
Cyphostemma juttae	B,CH,SI,Y	Dactylorhiza fuchsii	AP,I,SC

Dactylorhiza 'Hardy sp & Hyb'	C	Dalbergia armata	B,SI
Dactylorhiza 'Lydia'	I	Dalbergia assamica	HA
Dactylorhiza maculata	AP,CG,G,SC	Dalbergia greveana	B
Dactylorhiza majalis	AP,CG,SC	Dalbergia latifolia	B,HA
Dactylorhiza sambucina	B	Dalbergia melanoxylon	B
Daemonorops mollis	B	Dalbergia obovata	B,SI
Dahlia 'Bambino' mix	T	Dalbergia paniculata	B
Dahlia 'Bedding'	BS,PT	Dalbergia purpurascens	B,SI
Dahlia 'Burnished Bronze'	U	Dalbergia retusa	B,RE
Dahlia 'Cactus' mix	BS,C,DT,F,KI,L,ST,T,V,VH	Dalbergia sissoo	B,HA,SA
Dahlia 'Chi-Chi'	BS	Dalbergiella nyasae	SI
Dahlia coccinea	B	Dalea candida	B
Dahlia 'Collarette Dandy'	BS,C,CL,D,DT,KI,L,SE,	Dalea gattingeri	B
	SU,T	Dalea purpurea	B
Dahlia 'Coltness' hyb mix	BD,BS,C,CL,CO,D,DT,F,	Dalea spinosa	SW
	S,ST,T,TU,U,VH,YA	Dalea 'Toronjil'	B
Dahlia 'Dapper' mix	BS	Damaeonorops mollis	B,O
Dahlia 'Decorative' mix	BD,BS,F,KI,R,SE,ST	Damasonium alisma	B,SG
Dahlia 'Diablo' mix	BD,BS,C,CL,D,DT,F,J,L,	Dampiera sacculata	B
	YA	Danae racemosa	B,SA
Dahlia 'Disco'	T	Daniellia oliveri	B
Dahlia 'Dw Amore'	D	Danthonia californica	B
Dahlia 'Dw' border mix	S	Danthonia decumbens	B
Dahlia 'Dw' dbl quilled	S	Danthonia longifolia	B
Dahlia 'Dw Delight'	D,DT	Danthonia pallida	B
Dahlia 'Dw' hyb dbl	D,F	Danthonia sp	HA
Dahlia 'Dw' hyb semi-dbl	C,T	Danthonia spicata	B
Dahlia 'Early Bird' mix	BS,C,CL,KI,YA	Daphne albowiana	AP,G,NG,SC
Dahlia 'Exhibition'	M,PT	Daphne alpina	AP,B,CG,SA,SC
Dahlia f1 'Sunny Red'	B,BS	Daphne blagayana	SA
Dahlia f1 'Sunny Yellow'	B,BS,C	Daphne cneorum	B,G,SA
Dahlia f2 'Sunny White'	B,BS	Daphne giraldii	AP,B,G,JE,SC,SG
Dahlia 'Figaro'	F,J,L,R,SE,T,V	Daphne gnidium	B,SA
Dahlia 'Figaro' imp	BS,C,DT,KI,YA	Daphne laureola	AP,B,CG,G
Dahlia 'Figaro' s-c	B,BS,CL	Daphne mezereum	AP,B,BS,C,CG,G,JE,LG,
Dahlia 'Giant Decorative' hyb special dbl	C,DT		NG,P,SA,SC,SG
Dahlia 'Giant Hybrids' mix	T	Daphne mezereum v alba	AP,B,C,FH,G,NG,P,SC,
Dahlia 'Hammett'	YA		SG
Dahlia 'Harlequin mix'	J	Daphne mezereum v rubra	NG
Dahlia 'Heirloom Border Dahlias'	T	Daphne oleoides	AP,CG,FH,G,NG,SA,SC
Dahlia imperialis	B	Daphne papyracea	B
Dahlia mammoth fl mix	S	Daphne sericea	CG
Dahlia 'Masterpiece mix' dbl	J	Daphne striata	AP,B,C,SC
Dahlia merckii	AP,CG,SG	Daphne tangutica	AP,FH,G,NG,PM,SC,SG,
Dahlia 'Mignon' mix	BD,BS,G,V		W
Dahlia 'Mignon' s-c	B,T	Daphniphyllum macropodum	SA
Dahlia 'Monarch' mix	BS	Darlingia darlingiana	B,O
Dahlia 'Morada'	B	Darlingia ferruginea	O
Dahlia 'Naranja'	B	Darlingtonia californica	B,BA,C,SC,Y
Dahlia 'Piccolo' mix	J	Darmera peltatum	B,C,G,JE,P,RH,SA,T
Dahlia pinnata	B,SG	Darwinia diosmoides	SA
Dahlia 'Pompon' mix	C,CO,D,DT,F,KI,L,R,S,	Darwinia purpurea	B
	ST,T,U	Dasispermum suffruticosum	SI
Dahlia 'Promenade' hyb	BS	Dasylirion durangensis	B
Dahlia 'Redskin' mix	BD,BS,C,CL,F,J,S,SE,	Dasylirion heteiacanthium	B
	SU,T,TU,V,VH,YA	Dasylirion leiophyllum	B,SW
Dahlia 'Rigoletto'	BS,F,M,S,SE	Dasylirion longissimum	B,C,SA
Dahlia scapigera	CG	Dasylirion texanum	BC
Dahlia sherffii	B,P,MN,SW	Dasylirion wheeleri	B,BC,SA,SW
Dahlia 'Showpiece Hybrids' mix	T	Dasypogon bromeliifolius	B,O,SA
Dahlia 'Southbank Hybrids'	CL	Datisca cannabina	C,SG
Dahlia 'Sunny Yellow'	CL	Datisca glomerata	B
Dahlia 'Unwin's Dwarf Hybrids'	B,BS,DT,J,KI,L,Sm,ST,	Datura ceratocaula	B
	TU,U,V,YA	Datura discolor	B
Dais cotinifolia	B,C,SA,SI	Datura 'Double Golden'	B,SE
Dalanum ladanum	SG	Datura 'Double Purple'	B

DATURA

Datura fastuosa 'Cherub'	DT,F
Datura innoxia	B,CP,DT,LG,N
Datura innoxia ssp innoxia	B
Datura 'La Fleur Lilac'	AP,B,C,T
Datura 'Lavender'	SE
Datura metel	B,C,CP,F
Datura metel 'Belle Blanche'	B,C,F,U
Datura metel 'Black'	B,CP
Datura metel 'Cornucopea'	B
Datura metel fl pl 'Petticoat'	JE
Datura metel 'Golden Queen'	B
Datura meteloides	AP,C,CP,T,V
Datura quercifolia	AP,B
Datura stramonium	AP,B,BS,C,CP,FH,G,LG,
	SG,SU,W
Datura stramonium v inermis	B,C
Datura un-named v	C
Daubenya aurea	B,SI
Daubenya aurea v coccinea	B
Daucus carota	B,C,CP,HW,KS,LA,NT,
	SG,Z
Daucus littoralis	B
Davallia fejeensis	B
Davallia pyxidata	SG
Davallia solida	SG
Davallia tyermannii	B,SG
Davidia involucrata	B,C,N,SA
Davidia involucrata v vilmoriana	G
Davidsonia pruriens	B
Daviesia acicularis	B,C,HA
Daviesia angulata	B
Daviesia benthamii	B
Daviesia cordata	B,O,SA
Daviesia corymbosa	B,HA
Daviesia flexuosa	B
Daviesia genistifolia	B,HA
Daviesia horrida	B
Daviesia juncea	B
Daviesia latifolia	B,HA
Daviesia longifolia	B
Daviesia mimosoides	B,HA
Daviesia obtusifolia	AU
Daviesia polyphylla	B
Daviesia revoluta	B,C
Daviesia rhombifolia	B
Daviesia teretifolia	B
Daviesia ulicifolia	B,HA
Daviesia umbellulata	B
Daviesia virgata	B,HA
Daviesia wyattiana	B
Decaisnea fargesii	A,AP,B,C,CG,G,SA,SG
Deckenia nobilis	B,O
Decodon verticillatus	B,PR
Degenia velebitica	AP,G,SC,SG
Deinbollia oblongifolia	B
Delairea odorata	B
Delonix adansioides	SI
Delonix boivinii	SI
Delonix elata	B
Delonix pumila	SI
Delonix regia	B,C,HA,O,RE,SA,SI,T
Delosperma aberdeenense	AP,B
Delosperma abyssinica	SI
Delosperma annulare	B
Delosperma ashtonii	B,SI,Y
Delosperma asperulum	B

Delosperma britteniae	B
Delosperma cooperi	AP,B,C,JE,SC
Delosperma echinatus	B
Delosperma hallii	B
Delosperma harazianum	B
Delosperma leendertzia	B
Delosperma lehmannii	B
Delosperma littorale	B,SI
Delosperma lydenburgense	B,C,Y
Delosperma madagascariensis	B
Delosperma pergamentaceum	B
Delosperma pruinosum	B
Delosperma sp mix	C,SI
Delosperma sutherlandii	B,JE,Y
Delosperma tradescantoides	B
Delphinium altaicum	CG
Delphinium amabile	SW
Delphinium andesicola	B,RS,SW
Delphinium barbeyi	B,SW
Delphinium belladonna group mix	SA,SE
Delphinium belladonna 'Imp'	T
Delphinium 'Bellamosum'	B,BS,JE,SA
Delphinium bicolor	B,SW
Delphinium 'Blue Shadow'	B
Delphinium brunonianum	AP,C,G,I,SC
Delphinium bulleyanum	AP,G,SC,SG
Delphinium cardinale	B,C,JE,SA,SW,T
Delphinium c. 'Beverly Hills Salmon'	F,U
Delphinium cardinale 'Butterfly' hyb mix	T
Delphinium cardinale 'Butterfly' s-c	B
Delphinium carolinianum	RS
Delphinium 'Casablanca'	B,C,JE,SA,T
Delphinium cashmerianum	AP,CG,G,SC,SG
Delphinium 'Centurion Sky Blue'	CL,F,O,U
Delphinium 'Centurion White'	F
Delphinium chamissonsis	SG
Delphinium cheilanthum	B,T
Delphinium 'Cliveden Beauty'	B,BS,JE
Delphinium 'Connecticut Yankees'	C,S
Delphinium 'Cottage Gdn Mix'	P
Delphinium 'Crown' mix	BS,KI,ST,VH
Delphinium cuneatum	SG
Delphinium delavayi	AP,B
Delphinium dipterocarpum	B,SG
Delphinium drepanocentrum	SG
Delphinium 'Dw. Blue Heaven'	T
Delphinium 'Dw. Snowhite'	T
Delphinium 'Dwarf Pacific' mix	D
Delphinium 'Dwarf Pacific' s-c	B
Delphinium elatum	B,CG,G,JE,SA,SC,SG
Delphinium exaltatum	B,C,G,JE
Delphinium f2 'Dreaming Spires'	BS,D,F,J,SE,V
Delphinium fissum	B
Delphinium 'Foerster's Hybriden'	JE
Delphinium geranifolium	B,SC,SW
Delphinium glaucum	SG
Delphinium grandiflorum	AP,B,FH,G,PM,RS,SC,
	SG
Delphinium grandiflorum 'Blauer Zwerg'	C,G,JE,SC
Delphinium grandiflorum 'Blue Butterfly'	AP,B,BS,C,KI,S,SC,SE,
	ST
Delphinium grandiflorum 'Blue Mirror'	AP,B,C,F
Delphinium g. 'Butterfly Compactum'	B,JE
Delphinium g. 'Gentian Blue Dw'	B
Delphinium grandiflorum 'Sky-blue Dw'	B,J,SA
Delphinium g. 'Snow-white Dw'	B,V

DELPHINIUM

Delphinium hybridum special mix	S	Delphinium virescens	B,PR
Delphinium leptophyllum	B	Delphinium virescens wootoni	RS,SW
Delphinium luteum	AP,RS	Delphinium x cultorum	G,SG
Delphinium 'Magic Fountains' mix	BD,BS,CL,CO,DT,F,JE,	Delphinium x cultorum 'Pygmy'	T
	KI,S,SE,T,TU,YA	Dendranthema mongolicum	G,SG
Delphinium 'Magic Fountains' s-c	B,BS,JE,L	Dendranthema x grandiflorum	B
Delphinium 'Magic Fountains' white	B,JE	Dendranthema zawadskii	G,SG
Delphinium menziesii	AP,B,SC	Dendrobium canaliculatum	B
Delphinium mix finest named vars	BL	Dendrocalamus giganteus	SA
Delphinium mix finest named vars dw	BL	Dendrocalamus strictus	B,SA
Delphinium nelsonii	B,SW	Dendrocereus nudiflorus	B
Delphinium nudicaule	AP,B,BS,C,F,JE,SA,SC,	Dendromecon rigida	B,SW
	SG	Denmoza rhodacantha	B,BC,Y
Delphinium nuttallianum	C	Denrophthoe falcata	B
Delphinium occidentale	B,RS	Deschampsia caespitosa	B,C,JE,SA,SC,SG
Delphinium 'Oriental Blue'	B,F	Deschampsia flexuosa	B,C,PM,SA
Delphinium oxysepalum	AP,CG,G,SC,SG	Deschampsia rubra	B
Delphinium 'Pacific Astolat'	B,BS,C,CL,JE,SA	Descurainia pinnata	B
Delphinium 'Pacific Black Knight'	B,BS,C,CL,JE,SA	Descurainia sophia	SG
Delphinium 'Pacific Blue Bird'	B,BS,C,CL,JE,SA	Desfontainea spinosa	SA
Delphinium 'Pacific Blue Dawn'	B,JE	Desmanthus illinoensis	B,PR
Delphinium 'Pacific Blue Fountains'	AP,BS,F,J,KS,M,U	Desmanthus virgatus	B
Delphinium 'Pacific Blue Jay'	B,BS,JE,SA	Desmodium calycantha	SA
Delphinium 'Pacific Blue Springs'	BS,CG,JE,V	Desmodium canadense	B,PR,SA
Delphinium 'Pacific Camelliard'	B,BS,CL,E,JE,SA	Desmodium canescens	PR
Delphinium 'Pacific Clear Springs' mix	JE,KI,M,U	Desmodium elegans	B,SA,SG
Delphinium 'Pacific Deluxe mix'	JE	Desmodium gangeticum	B
Delphinium 'Pacific Galahad'	B,BS,C,CL,JE,SA	Desmodium glutinasum	PR
Delphinium 'Pacific Giants' mix	BS,CL,CO,D,F,J,KI,M,R,	Desmodium illinoiense	B
	SE,Sm,ST,SU,T,TU,U,YA	Desmodium intortum	B
Delphinium Pacific Giants 'Round Table'	BD,C,DT,KS	Desmodium ooieinense	B
Delphinium 'Pacific Guinevere'	B,BS,C,CL,DT,JE,SA	Desmodium paniculatum	B
Delphinium 'Pacific Hybrids'	RS	Desmodium pulchellum	B
Delphinium 'Pacific King Arthur'	B,BS,C,CL,JE,SA	Desmodium rensonii	B
Delphinium 'Pacific Lancelot'	B,C,JE	Desmodium triflorum	B
Delphinium 'Pacific Percival'	B,C	Desmodium uncinatum	B
Delphinium 'Pacific Summer Skies'	B,BS,CL,JE	Desmoschoenus spiralis	B
Delphinium 'Pacific Tafelrunde'	JE	Deuterocohnia longipetala	CG
Delphinium parishii	B	Deutzia scabra	B
Delphinium parryi	AP,B,SC,SW	Deutzia sp CNW1108	X
Delphinium peregrinum	B	Deutzia x magnifica	B
Delphinium 'Pink dream'	V	Dialium englerianum	SI
Delphinium pogonanthum	RS	Dialium pachyphyllum	B
Delphinium przewalskii	AP,PM,SC	Dialium schlechteri	B,SI
Delphinium pylzowii	AP,B,RS,SC,SG	Dianella brevipedunculata	B
Delphinium requienii	AP,C,CG,LG,RS,SC,T	Dianella caerulea	AP,AU,B,HA
Delphinium requienii 'Variegata'	B,P	Dianella caerulea v protensa	B
Delphinium retropilosum	SG	Dianella congesta	B
Delphinium 'Rose & Pink'	SE	Dianella ensifolia	G
Delphinium scaposum	B,RS,SW	Dianella intermedia	B
Delphinium schmalhausenii	CG	Dianella intermedia v norfolkensis	SG
Delphinium scopulorum	B,RS,SW	Dianella laevis	B,HA
Delphinium 'Seafoam'	SE	Dianella nigra	AU,B,SA,SC,SG,SS
Delphinium semibarbatum	AP,B,BS,C,D,F,G,RS,SA,	Dianella revoluta	AU,B,HA
	SE,T	Dianella revoluta v revoluta	RS
Delphinium 'Southern Deputant'	T	Dianella sp	SG
Delphinium 'Southern Jesters'	T	Dianella tasmanica	AU,B,C,CG,MN,T
Delphinium 'S. Nobleman' series, s-c h-p	T	Dianthus albus	T
Delphinium speciosum	B,SC	Dianthus 'Allwoodii Alpinus'	AL,AP,B,BD,C,CG,CL,D,
Delphinium staphisagria	AP,B,CG,LG		G,GI,JE,SA,SC,T
Delphinium 'Steichen'	B,BS,DT	Dianthus alpinus	AP,B,BS,CG,G,J,JE,KI,S,
Delphinium tatsienense	AP,G,RS,SC,SG		SA,SC,ST,VH
Delphinium tatsienense album	AP,RS	Dianthus alpinus 'Joan's Blood'	AP,I,SC
Delphinium triste	CG,SG	Dianthus amurensis	AP,B,G,JE,P
Delphinium vestitum	B	Dianthus amurensis 'Siberian Blue'	B,T
Delphinium villosum	B	Dianthus amurensis 'Siberian Snow'	B

DIANTHUS

Name	Codes
Dianthus anatolicus	AP,B,C,G,JE,SC,SG
Dianthus angulatus	CC
Dianthus arenarius	AP,B,BD,C,CL,FH,JE,K S,L,SA,SC,SG
Dianthus arenarius ssp pseudoserotinus	B
Dianthus armeria	AP,B,C,G,SC,SU
Dianthus armeria 'Annual Form'	B
Dianthus barbatus	AP,AV,G,I,JE,LG,V,VH
Dianthus barbatus 'Albus'	C
Dianthus barbatus 'Auricula-Eyed'	BD,BS,CL,D,F,KI,SU,T, TU,YA
Dianthus barbatus 'Beauty' s-c & mix	BS
Dianthus barbatus 'Bright Eyes'	D
Dianthus barbatus dbl mix	BD,BS,TU,V,VH
Dianthus barbatus 'Diadem'	BS
Dianthus barbatus 'Diadem' Imp	BS
Dianthus barbatus 'Dunnets'	BS
Dianthus barbatus 'Dunnets Dk Crimson'	BS,T
Dianthus barbatus 'Duplex Super Dbl Mix'	BS,DT,L,YA
Dianthus barbatus dw mix	I,U
Dianthus barbatus 'Early Bird Mix'	YA
Dianthus barbatus f1 'Hollandia' mix	BBS
Dianthus b. f1 'Hollandia' s-c Homeland'	B
Dianthus barbatus f1 'Telstar Crimson'	B
Dianthus barbatus f1 'Telstar Magic Pinks'	B
Dianthus barbatus f1 'Telstar Picotees'	B
Dianthus barbatus fl pl 'Blaupunkt' mix	JE
Dianthus barbatus fl pl mix	C,CO,JE
Dianthus barbatus fl pl nanus	B,JE
Dianthus barbatus 'Forerunner'	D,KS
Dianthus barbatus 'Gemstones'	BS,KI
Dianthus barbatus 'Harlequin'	B,F,KS,SE,T
Dianthus barbatus 'Homeland'	B,C
Dianthus barbatus 'Indian Carpet'	B,BS,CL,CO,D,J,JE,KI, KS,L,R,ST,T,U,V,YA
Dianthus barbatus 'Kurokawa Extra Early'	C
Dianthus b. 'Marshall's Giant Single' mix	M
Dianthus b. 'Marshall's Super Double' mix	M
Dianthus barbatus 'Messenger'	BS,CL,DT,TU
Dianthus barbatus 'Monarch'	F
Dianthus barbatus 'New Era' mix	C,T
Dianthus barbatus 'Nigrescens'	BS
Dianthus barbatus 'Oeschberg'	B,BS,C,JE,KI
Dianthus barbatus 'Pinnochio' mix	T
Dianthus barbatus 'Prelude' s-c	B
Dianthus barbatus 'Prettiness'	KI
Dianthus barbatus 'Roundabout' mix	BD,BS,C,CL,D,DT,F,I,J, T,YA
Dianthus barbatus 'Scarlet Beauty'	C
Dianthus barbatus 'Single' mix	BD,BS,C,F,J,ST,TU
Dianthus barbatus 'Single Super Mix'	CL
Dianthus barbatus 'Sooty'	B,P
Dianthus barbatus 'Special mix'	D,DT
Dianthus barbatus ssp compactus	CG
Dianthus barbatus 'Standard Albus'	B
Dianthus barbatus 'Standard Series' s-c	B
Dianthus barbatus 'Summer Beauty'	BS,T
Dianthus barbatus tall mix	KS
Dianthus barbatus tall scarlet	KS
Dianthus barbatus tall white	BS,KS
Dianthus barbatus 'Unwins Choice' mix	U
Dianthus barbatus 'Wee Willie' mix	BS,C,CL,M,TU,YA
Dianthus barbatus x superbus	G
Dianthus basuticus	B
Dianthus brevicaulis	B,G
Dianthus caespitosus	B,SI
Dianthus caitatus v andrzejowskianus	CC
Dianthus campestris	G,SG
Dianthus capitatus	SG
Dianthus carthusianorum	AP,B,C,CG,G,JE,SA,SC, SG,V
Dianthus carthusianorum v humilis	B
Dianthus caryophyllus	CG
Dianthus c. 'Chabaud Enchantment'	D
Dianthus c. 'Chabaud Giant Double' mix	BD,BS,CL,J,KI,L,M,R, SE,SU,T,U,V,VH
Dianthus c. 'Chabaud Giant Superb' mix	C,CO,DT,S,ST
Dianthus caryophyllus 'Choice Dbl Mix'	F
Dianthus caryophyllus 'Clove Pinks'	KS
Dianthus caryophyllus 'DblTriumph' mix	C
Dianthus caryophyllus 'Du Tyrol'	AL,B
Dianthus caryophyllus 'Dw Dbl'	BS
Dianthus caryophyllus 'Dw Fragrance'	AL,BD,BS,DT,F,R,SU
Dianthus caryophyllus 'Enfant De Nice	BD,BS,CL
Dianthus caryophyllus f1 'Knight'	BD,BS,KI,S
Dianthus caryophyllus f1 'Lillipot' mix	BS,C,DT,L,SE,T
Dianthus caryophyllus f1 'Lillipot' s-c	BS,CL,T
Dianthus caryophyllus f1 'Luminette' mix	T
Dianthus caryophyllus f1 'Minarette'	KI
Dianthus caryophyllus f1 'Mini Spice Mix'	BS,F
Dianthus caryophyllus f1 'Mini Spice' s-c	BS
Dianthus caryophyllus f1 'Monarch' mix	CL,U
Dianthus caryophyllus f1 'Monarch' s-c	CL
Dianthus caryophyllus fl pl 'Orion'	SG
Dianthus caryophyllus 'Floristan'	BS,D,DT,J,L,U
Dianthus caryophyllus 'Floristan Red'	T
Dianthus c. 'Grenadin Dark Red'	B,JE
Dianthus caryophyllus 'Grenadin' mix	JE,V
Dianthus c. 'Grenadin Pale Gold'	B,JE
Dianthus caryophyllus 'Grenadin Pink'	B,JE
Dianthus caryophyllus 'Grenadin Scarlet'	B,JE
Dianthus caryophyllus 'Grenadin White'	B,JE
Dianthus caryophyllus 'Hardy Border' mix	AL,BD,BS,CL,GI,KI,M ,ST,U
Dianthus caryophyllus 'King of the Blacks'	C,V
Dianthus caryophyllus 'Margarita'	BS,KI
Dianthus caryophyllus 'Peach Delight'	T
Dianthus caryophyllus 'Perpetual Choice'	AL,BS,C,GI,KI,ST
Dianthus caryophyllus picotee	AL
Dianthus caryophyllus 'Red Riding Hood'	T
Dianthus caryophyllus 'Sprite'	KI
Dianthus caryophyllus 'Stripes/Picotees'	F,SE,T
Dianthus caryophyllus 'Superb'	BS,TU
Dianthus caryophyllus 'Tige de Fer'	BS,D
Dianthus caryophyllus 'Trailing'	DT,F,KS,T,V,VH
Dianthus caryophyllus 'Vienna' mix	BS,C,JE
Dianthus chinensis	AP,CO,J,SC,SG,SE,V
Dianthus chinensis 'Baby Doll'	BD,BS,CL,D,DT,F,J,KI, M,S,TU,V,YA
Dianthus chinensis 'Bl & Wh Minstrels'	DT,KS,SE,T
Dianthus chinensis 'Bravo'	B
Dianthus chinensis 'Chianti'	B,BD
Dianthus chinensis dbl mix	BS,D,KI,ST,VH
Dianthus chinensis f1 'Carpet Mix'	BS,YA
Dianthus chinensis f1 'Carpet Persian'	BS,C,R
Dianthus chinensis f1 'Carpet' s-c	B,BS
Dianthus chinensis f1 'Festival Carmine'	B,BS
Dianthus chinensis f1 'Festival Ch. Picotee'	B,BS
Dianthus chinensis f1 'Fire Carpet'	BS,T
Dianthus chinensis f1 'First Love'	BS,L
Dianthus chinensis f1 'Ideal Carmine'	B,BS,YA
Dianthus chinensis f1 'Ideal Ch. Picotee'	B,BS,YA

Dianthus chinensis f1 'Ideal Crimson'	B,BS,YA
Dianthus chinensis f1 'Ideal' Mix	BS,TU,YA
Dianthus chinensis f1 'Ideal Pink'	BS,YA
Dianthus chinensis f1 'Ideal Raspberry'	YA
Dianthus chinensis f1 'Ideal Red'	YA
Dianthus chinensis f1 'Ideal Rose'	B,BS,YA
Dianthus chinensis f1 'Ideal Violet'	B,BS,YA
Dianthus chinensis f1 'Ideal Violet Picotee'	B,BS,YA
Dianthus chinensis f1 'Magic Charms'	BS,C,CL,DT,L,YA
Dianthus chinensis f1 'Magic Charms' s-c	B,BS,CL
Dianthus chinensis f1 'Miss Japan Series'	B,BS
Dianthus chinensis f1 'Panda' mix	CL
Dianthus chinensis f1 'Panda' s-c	CL
Dianthus chinensis f1 'Parfait Raspberry'	B,BS,CL,DT,F,KI,L,O,T
Dianthus chinensis f1 'Parfait Strawberry'	B,BS,CL,DT,F,L,U
Dianthus chinensis f1 'Pink Flash'	U
Dianthus chinensis f1 'Princess' mix	CL,D,S
Dianthus chinensis f1 'Princess' s-c	CL
Dianthus ch. f1 'Rosem. Velv. Lavender'	B,BS
Dianthus chinensis f1 'Rosemarie White'	B,BS
Dianthus chinensis f1 'Snowfire'	CL,CO,DT,KI,L,S,T,U
Dianthus chinensis f1 'Telstar' mix	BS,DT,L,M
Dianthus chinensis f1 'Telstar' s-c	BS
Dianthus chinensis 'Heddewigii,Dbl'	B,BS
Dianthus chinensis 'Heddew.,Dbl Gaiety'	BS,F
Dianthus chinensis 'Heddew.,dbl Salmon'	B
Dianthus chinensis 'Heddewigii Frosty'	T
Dianthus chinensis. 'H.,Snowball Dbl'	B
Dianthus chinensis 'Merry-go-round'	B,C,F
Dianthus chinensis mix superb single	BS
Dianthus chinensis 'Splendour'	T
Dianthus chinensis 'Welcome Crimson'	B,BS
Dianthus chinensis 'White Carpet'	T
Dianthus ch. x D.barbatus f1 hyb 'Telstar'	J
Dianthus ciliatus ssp dalmaticus	B
Dianthus cinnabarinus	SG
Dianthus 'Colour Magician'	BS,D,O,U
Dianthus cruentus	B,G,JE,SC
Dianthus cruentus ssp tauricus	SG
Dianthus deltoides	AL,AP,B,BS,C,CG,CO,G, J,KI,LG,SA,SC,SG,ST, SU,V
Dianthus deltoides 'Albus'	AP,B,C,FH,G,JE,RS,SA, SC
Dianthus deltoides 'Arctic Fire'	C,SA
Dianthus deltoides 'Bicolor'	B
Dianthus deltoides 'Brilliancy'	B,BD,BS,FH,JE,SA,T,U
Dianthus deltoides 'Brilliant'	B,C,CG,JE,L,SC
Dianthus deltoides 'Broughty Blaze'	B
Dianthus deltoides 'Erectus'	B,BD,BS,JE
Dianthus deltoides f2 'Canta Libre'	BS,C,CL
Dianthus deltoides 'Fanal'	SA
Dianthus deltoides 'Leuchtfunk'	B,BS,C,CL,JE,KI,SC
Dianthus deltoides 'Lueur'	B,JE
Dianthus deltoides 'Microchip'	B,CL,SC
Dianthus deltoides 'Nelli'	B,JE
Dianthus deltoides pink forms	FH
Dianthus deltoides 'Roseus'	B,JE
Dianthus deltoides 'Samos'	B,JE,SC
Dianthus deltoides 'Spring Beauty'	U
Dianthus deltoides 'Steriker'	B
Dianthus deltoides 'Vampire'	AP,B
Dianthus deltoides 'Wisley Variety'	B
Dianthus deltoides 'Zing'	B
Dianthus erinaceus	AP,SC,SG
Dianthus fragrant village pinks	AL
Dianthus furcatus	B,G
Dianthus gallicus	B,SG
Dianthus gdn pinks mix	AL
Dianthus giganteus	AP,B,G,SC,SG
Dianthus giganteus ssp banaticus	SG
Dianthus glacialis	AP,B,C,G,JE,SC
Dianthus gratianopolitanus	AL,AP,B,BS,C,FH,JE,L, SA,SC,SG,SU
Dianthus gratianopolitanus 'Grandiflora'	JE
Dianthus gratianopolitanus red, dk eye	JE
Dianthus gratianopolitanus rose	CL
Dianthus gratianopolitanus 'Rose Feather'	B,JE
Dianthus gratianopolitanus 'Splendens'	B,JE
Dianthus gratianopolitanus 'Star Cushion'	B
Dianthus gratianopolitanus 'Sternkissen'	JE
Dianthus haematocalyx	AP,CG,SC
Dianthus hoeltzeri	B
Dianthus hungaricus	AP,B,CG,SC,SG
Dianthus hybrida 'Rainbow Loveliness'	B,DT,J,S,SE,T,U
Dianthus 'Ipswich Pinks'	BD,T
Dianthus japonicus	CC
Dianthus japonicus 'Ginza' mix	C
Dianthus japonicus 'Ginza Red'	B,BS
Dianthus japonicus 'Ginza White'	B,BS
Dianthus knappii	AL,AP,B,BS,C,CG,DT,F, G,JE,P,S,SA,SC,SE,T,U, V
Dianthus 'Lady Seymour'	SE
Dianthus laingsburgensis	B,SI
Dianthus lilaceus	CG
Dianthus lumnitzeri	CG,G,SC
Dianthus lusitanus	CG,G
Dianthus maroon shades	FH
Dianthus 'McMurtrie Seedlings'	FH
Dianthus membranaceus	B
Dianthus microlepis	AP,B,JE,SC
Dianthus micropetalus	SI
Dianthus monspessulanus	B,C,G,JE,SA,SC
Dianthus monspessulanus ssp sterbergii	CG,SC
Dianthus nardiformis	B,G,JE
Dianthus neglectus hyb	PM
Dianthus nitidus of gdns	AP,B,JE,SC
Dianthus pallens	SG
Dianthus pavonius	AP,B,CG,G,JE,SA,SC
Dianthus pavonius 'Neglectus'	B
Dianthus petraeus	B,C,G,JE,SG
Dianthus petraeus ssp integer	B,SC
Dianthus petraeus ssp noeanus	B,G,SC,SG
Dianthus petraeus ssp orbelicus	CG
Dianthus petraeus v bebius	B
Dianthus pinifolius	B,G
Dianthus pinifolius ssp lilacinus	B,G
Dianthus plumarius	AP,B,CG,F,G,JE,KS,SA, SG,V
Dianthus plumarius 'Double Mix'	D
Dianthus plumarius fl pl 'Albus'	B,G,JE
Dianthus plumarius fl pl 'Nanus Pink'	B,JE
Dianthus plumarius fl pl 'Roseus'	B,JE
Dianthus plumarius fl pl 'Spring Charm'	JE
Dianthus plumarius 'Highland Hybrids'	BS,T
Dianthus plumarius 'Lumnitzeri'	B
Dianthus plumarius 'Single Mix'	BS,CL,DT
Dianthus plumarius 'Sonata'	T
Dianthus plumarius 'Spring Beauty'	BD,BS,C,DT,KI,L
Dianthus plumarius ssp praecox	B
Dianthus plumarius ssp regis-stephani	B

DIANTHUS

Dianthus pontederae	B,CG,JE,SG
Dianthus pontederae giganteiformis	SG
Dianthus pungens	B,SA
Dianthus pyrenaicus	AP,CG
Dianthus 'Queen of Henri'	AP,HH
Dianthus seguieri	AP,B,CG,SC,SG
Dianthus 'Select Mix'	P
Dianthus serotinus	AP,B,G,SC
Dianthus shinanensis	SG
Dianthus sp	AP,G,SG,SI
Dianthus sp 'Rock Gdn Mix'	BS,C,DT,FH,T
Dianthus speciosus	SG
Dianthus spiculifolius	G,SG
Dianthus squarrosus	AP,FH
Dianthus strictus v bebius	JE
Dianthus subacaulis	B,C,G,JE,SC,SG
Dianthus superbus	AP,B,C,CG,G,JE,SA,SC, SG
Dianthus superbus alpestris	SG
Dianthus superbus 'Arc En Ciel'	B
Dianthus superbus 'Crimsonia'	B
Dianthus superbus 'Primadonna'	B,JE
Dianthus superbus 'Snowdonia'	B
Dianthus superbus 'Spooky'	B
Dianthus superbus ssp longicalycinus	B
Dianthus sup. ssp longicalycinus f albus	B
Dianthus superbus ssp speciosus	B
Dianthus superbus 'Super Fantasy' mix	T,V
Dianthus 'Swiss Balcony'	SE
Dianthus sylvestris	B,CG,G,JE,SA,SG
Dianthus sylvestris ssp siculum	B
Dianthus sylvestris ssp tergestinus	B,JE
Dianthus tatrea	CG
Dianthus tenuifolium	B,CG,G
Dianthus tristis	CG
Dianthus 'Twinkletoes'	S
Dianthus uralensis	SA
Dianthus versicolor	SG
Dianthus webbianus	CG
Dianthus x arvernensis	B,G,JE,SC
Dianthus x roysii	JE
Dianthus zeyheri	B,SI
Diapensia lapponica	C
Diapensia lapponica v obovata	CC
Diascia barberae	AP,V
Diascia barberae 'Apricot Queen'	B,BS,C
Diascia barberae 'Pink Queen'	B,BD,BS,C,CL,D,DT,F, SE,SI,U
Diascia elongata	B,SI
Diascia integerrima	B,SI
Diascia longicornis	B
Diascia sp	SI
Diastema affine	B
Dicentra 'Bacchanal'	B,P
Dicentra chrysantha	B,C
Dicentra eximia	AP,B,C,JE,SA,SC
Dicentra formosa	AP,B,C,JE,SA,SC,SG
Dicentra formosa 'Luxuriant'	G,HH
Dicentra formosa ssp formosa	SG
Dicentra macrocapnos	RS
Dicentra ochroleuca	B
Dicentra peregrina	AP,JE,SC
Dicentra peregrina 'Alba'	JE,SC
Dicentra scandens	B,C,CC,G,JE,P,SA
Dicentra sp China	SG
Dicentra spectabilis	B,BD,BS,C,CL,D,DT,F,G,
	JE,KI,L,RS,S,SA,SE,ST, T
Dicentra spectabilis f alba	AP,B,BS,G,JE,SA,SC,T
Dicentra torulosa	T
Dicentra uniflora	B
Dicentra uniflora 'White Heart'	C
Dicerma biarticulatum	B
Dicerocaryum eriocarpum	SI
Dicerocaryum senecioides	B,SI
Dicerocaryum zanguebarium	B
Dichanthium aristatum	B
Dichanthium sericeum	B,HA
Dichelostemma capitatum	B,SW
Dichelostemma ida-maia	AP,G,LG
Dichelostemma multiflorum	B
Dichelostemma pulchellum	AP,B,SC,SW
Dichodon cerastoides	SG
Dichondra micrantha	B
Dichondra repens	BS,HA
Dichopogon capillipes	B
Dichopogon strictus	B
Dichorisandra thyrsiflora	B
Dichrostachys cinerea	B
Dichrostachys cinerea nyassana	SI
Dichrostachys spicata	B
Dicksonia antarctica	B,C,G,HA,N,SA,SH
Dicksonia fibrosa	B,C,SA
Dicksonia squarrosa	B,C
Dicoma anomala	B,SI
Dicoma grandididieri	SI
Dicoma zeyheri	C
Dicranopteris linearis	B
Dicranostigma franchetianum	AP,B,CC,G
Dicranostigma franchetianum 'Aristocrat'	C
Dicranostigma lactucoides	AP,CC,SC,W
Dicranostigma leptopodum	B,CG
Dicrastylis exsuccosa v elliptica	B
Dicrastylis fulva	B
Dicrastylis microphylla	B
Dicrocaulon spissum	B
Dictamnus albus	AP,B,BS,C,CG,G,JE,RS, SA,SC,SG,T,U
Dictamnus albus 'Albiflorus'	G,JE
Dictamnus albus v purpurea	AP,B,BS,G,LG,RS,SC, SG,T
Dictyolimon macrorrhabdos	AP,SC,SG
Dictyosperma album	B,C,SH
Dictyosperma album v rubrum	O
Didelta carnosa	B,SI
Didelta spinosa	B,SI
Didiera madagascariensis	SI
Didymaotus lapidiformis	B,C,SI,Y
Didymochlaena truncatula	B
Dierama dracomontanum	AP,B,C,LG,P,SA,SC,SI
Dierama floriferum	SI
Dierama hyb dw	C
Dierama igneum	B,P,SI
Dierama latifolium	B,SI
Dierama medium	B,C,SI
Dierama pendulum	AP,B,C,SC,SI
Dierama pulcherrimum	AP,B,C,G,I,JE,LG,MA,N, P,PA,RH,SA,SC,SG,T,V
Dierama pulcherrimum 'Donard' hyb	C,P,SC,T
Dierama pulcherrimum 'Snowbells'	B,P
Diervilla splendens	B
Dietes bicolor	B,HA,O,SA,SI

81

DIETES

Dietes butcheriana	B,O,SI
Dietes flavida	B,SI
Dietes grandiflora	AP,B,MN,SC,SE,SI,T
Dietes iridioides	AP,B,G,HA,O,SC,SG,SI
Dietes robinsoniana	AU
Digitalis alba	SA,SU
Digitalis davisiana	AP,G,HH,RS,SC
Digitalis dubia	AP,B,C,P,SC,SG
Digitalis ferruginea	AP,B,C,CP,F,G,LG,SA,T
Digitalis ferruginea 'Gigantea'	B,JE
Digitalis ferruginea 'Yellow Herald'	C,JE
Digitalis grandiflora	AP,B,BS,C,CG,CO,CP,G, HH,I,JE,RH,RS,KS,SA, SC,SG,T
Digitalis grandiflora 'Carillon' dw	B,BS,C,JE,KI,KS,RS,SA, SE,ST
Digitalis 'John Innes Tetra'	B,F,KS,T
Digitalis laevigata	AP,B,C,F,JE,RS,SA,SC
Digitalis laevigata ssp graeca	C,T
Digitalis lamarckii	C,SA,SC
Digitalis lanata	AP,B,BS,C,CP,E,F,G,HH, JE,KI,LG,P,RH,RS,SA, SC,SG,SU,T,V
Digitalis lanata 'Berggold'	B
Digitalis lanata 'Krajovy'	B
Digitalis leucophragma S3198	E
Digitalis lutea	AP,B,C,CP,E,F,FH,G,HH, JE,LG,P,RH,SA,SC,SG, SU,T,W
Digitalis 'Marshalls Superior Hybrids'	M
Digitalis micrantha	C
Digitalis mix selected	CO,S
Digitalis obscura	AP,B,C,JE,P,SA,SC,SG, T,V,W
Digitalis parviflora	AP,B,C,F,G,HH,LG,P,SA, SC,T
Digitalis purpurea	B,BS,C,CO,CP,E,F,FH,G, HW,I,JE,KI,LA,RH,SG, SU,T,TU,W,Z
Digitalis purpurea 'Apricot'	AP,B,BS,C,F,G,I,JE,KI, KS,L,P,SA,SE,ST,T,V
Digitalis purpurea 'Chedglow'	NS
Digitalis purpurea 'Excelsior Dw. Purple'	B,SG
Digitalis purpurea 'Excelsior Hybrids'	BD,BS,C,CL,D,DT,F,J, KI,KS,L,R,SA,ST,SU,T, TU,U
Digitalis purpurea 'Excelsior' red	B,JE
Digitalis purpurea f albiflora	AP,B,C,F,FH,JE,KS,L,P, SC,T,V
Digitalis purpurea 'Fairy'	B
Digitalis purpurea 'Foxy'	B,BD,BS,C,CL,CO,D,DT, F,JE,KI,KS,SA,SE,TU
Digitalis purpurea 'Giant Spotted'	B,BS,DT,F,L
Digitalis purpurea 'Glittering Prizes'	SE,T,V
Digitalis purpurea 'Isabellina'	B
Digitalis purpurea mix	FH
Digitalis purpurea 'Monstrosa'	B
Digitalis purpurea 'Peloric'	F,T
Digitalis purpurea 'Primrose'	F
Digitalis purpurea ssp heywoodii	AP,B,G,SC,T
Digitalis purpurea ssp purpurea	B,SA
Digitalis purpurea 'Strawberry Crush'	SE
Digitalis purpurea v gloxiniiflora	P,JE,SA
Digitalis purpurea v glox. 'The Shirley'	B,BS,C,T
Digitalis sibirica	AP,G,RS,SC
Digitalis sp 'Brown Flowers'	PM
Digitalis sp & forms mix	C,P
Digitalis 'Suttons Excelsior Hybrids'	S
Digitalis thapsi	AP,B,P,RS,SG
Digitalis viridiflora	AP,B,C,F,G,LG,P,RS,SA, SC
Digitalis x heywoodii	E,P
Digitalis x mertonensis	AP,B,C,F,I,G,JE,L,P,SA, SC,SG,T
Digitalis x mertonensis 'Strawberry'	KS
Dilatris corymbosa	B,SA,SI
Dilatris ixioides	B,SI
Dilatris pillansii	B,SI
Dilatris viscosa	B,SI
Dillenia indica	B,C,SA
Dillwynia cinerascens	B
Dillwynia floribunda	HA,SA
Dillwynia floribunda v floribunda	B
Dillwynia floribunda v teretifolia	HA
Dillwynia glaberrima	B,HA
Dillwynia juniperinum	B,HA
Dillwynia phylicoides	B
Dillwynia retorta	B,HA
Dillwynia uncinata	B
Dimocarpus longan	B
Dimorphotheca aurantiaca see sinuata	
Dimorphotheca cuneata	B,SA,SI
Dimorphotheca hybrida 'Giant Mix'	T
Dimorphotheca minor	SG
Dimorphotheca pluvialis	AP,B,SG,SI,TU
Dimorphotheca pluvialis 'Glistening Wh'	B,BS,C,J,S,SE,T
Dimorphotheca pluvialis mix special	S
Dimorphotheca pluvialis 'Tetra Polar Star'	B,T,V
Dimorphotheca sinuata 'Apollo'	V
Dimorphotheca sinuata hyb 'Imp'	C
Dimorphotheca sinuata hybrids	AP,B,BS,C,CO,D,DT,F,J, KI,KS,L,SG,SI,ST,SU
Dimorphotheca sinuata 'Orange Glory'	B
Dimorphotheca sinuata 'Salmon Queen'	DT,SE,T,V
Dimorphotheca sinuata 'Starshine'	T,V
Dimorphotheca sinuata 'Sunshine Hyb'	U
Dimorphotheca sinuata 'Tetra Goliath'	B
Dimorphotheca sinuata 'White'	B
Dimorphotheca sp	SI
Dinteranthus inexpectatus	B,SI
Dinteranthus microspermus	B
Dinteranthus microsp. ssp puberulus	B,SI,Y
Dinteranthus pole-evansii	B,C,GC,SI,Y
Dinteranthus puberulus	SI
Dinteranthus vanzylii	B,SI,Y
Dinteranthus wilmotianus	B,SI,Y
Dinteranthus wilmotianus ssp impunctata	B
Dionaea muscipula	B,C,G,SE,T
Dionysia aretioides	JE
Dionysia involucrata	AP,JE,SC
Dioon edule	B,C,SA
Dioon edule 'Queretaro'	O
Dioon edule 'Rio Verde'	O
Dioon edule 'Tamaulipas'	O
Dioon edule v edule	O
Dioon edule v palma solo	O
Dioon mejiae	B,O
Dioon rzedowskii	O
Dioon spinulosum	B,O
Dioscorea dregeana	C,SI
Dioscorea dumetorum	SI
Dioscorea elephantipes	B,C,CH,SI,Y

DIOSCOREA

Dioscorea oppositifolia	B
Dioscorea schimperiana	SI
Dioscorea sp	SI
Dioscorea sylvatica	B,SA,SI
Dioscorea villosa	PR
Diosma hirsuta	B,SI
Diosporum lanuginosum	B
Diospyros austroafricana	B,SI
Diospyros dichrophylla	B,SI
Diospyros digyna	B
Diospyros discolor	B
Diospyros ebenum	B
Diospyros exsculpta	B
Diospyros ferrea	B
Diospyros glabra	B,SI
Diospyros kaki	B,C,SA
Diospyros lotus	A,B,C,SA
Diospyros lycioides	SI
Diospyros lycioides ssp guerkei	B
Diospyros lycioides ssp lycioides	B
Diospyros mannii	B
Diospyros melanoxylon	B
Diospyros mespiliformis	B
Diospyros ramulosa	B,SI
Diospyros scabrida	B,SI
Diospyros simii	B,C,SI
Diospyros virginiana	A,B,C,CG,SA
Diospyros whyteana	B,C,SI
Dipcadi crispum	B,SI
Dipcadi fulvum	AP,B
Dipcadi fulvum S.F90 Morocco	MN
Dipcadi marlothii	SI
Dipcadi serotinum	AP,B,CG,G,LG,SA,SC
Dipcadi serotinum MS877 France	MN
Dipcadi serotinum S.L449/1 Spain	MN
Dipcadi serotinum v lividum	B
Dipcadi serotinum v lividum A.B.S4409	MN
Dipcadi serotinum v lividum S.F230 Spain	MN
Dipcadi serotinum v lividum S.F279/1	MN
Dipcadi serotinum v lividum S.F322	MN
Dipcadi viride	B,SC,SI
Dipelta yunnanense CNW366	X
Diphysa robinoides	B
Diplarrena moraea	AP,B,C,SC,SG
Diplarrhena latifolia	AP,AU,SC
Diplocyclos palmatus	B
Diploglottis campbellii	B
Diploglottis cunninghamii	B
Diploglottis diphyllostegia	B
Diplolaena angustifolia	B,C,O
Diplolaena dampieri	B
Diplopeltis eriocarpa	B
Diplopeltis huegelii	B,SA
Diplorhynchus condylocarpon	B
Diplosoma luckhoffii	B
Diplotaxis erucoides	B
Diplotaxis muralis	G,SG
Dipogon lignosus	B,SA,SI
Dipsacus fullonum	AP,B,BS,C,CO,CP,G,JE, KI,LA,NS,S,SA,SC,SG, ST,SU,TU,V,W,Z
Dipsacus gmellinii	SG
Dipsacus inermis	C
Dipsacus japonicus	SG
Dipsacus laciniatus	B,G
Dipsacus pilosus	B,JE,SG

Dipsacus sativus	B,F,I,JE,SA
Dipterronia sinensis	N,SA,SG
Dirca palustris	B
Disa atricapilla	B,SI
Disa bivalvata	B
Disa cardinalis	B
Disa caulescens	SI
Disa cornuta	B,SI
Disa crassicornis	B,SI
Disa draconis	B,SI
Disa ferruginea	B
Disa obtusa	B
Disa patens	B
Disa racemosa	B,SI
Disa tripetaloides	B
Disa tripetaloides ssp aurata	B
Disa uniflora	C,SI
Disa uniflora pink	B
Disa x diores	B
Disa x kewensis	B
Disanthus cercidifolius	B
Discaria toumatou	B,SS
Dischisma ciliatum	SI
Discocactus albispinus	B
Discocactus catingcola HU392	Y
Discocactus crystallophilus	B,Y
Discocactus ferricola	B
Discocactus horstii	B
Discocactus insignis	B
Discocactus insignis HU347	Y
Discocactus latispinus	Y
Discocactus magnimammus	B,Y
Discocactus placentiformis	Y
Discocactus pugionanthus	CH
Discocactus sp nova HU527	Y
Discocactus sp nova HU543	Y
Discocactus sp nova HU544	Y
Discocactus sp nova HU639	Y
Discocactus sp nova HU646	Y
Discocactus subviridigriseus form 438	Y
Discocactus subviridigriseus form 633	Y
Diselma archeri	B,O,SA
Disperis capensis	B,SI
Disphyma clavellatum	B,SA
Disporum hookeri	C
Disporum smithii	AP,PM,SC
Disporum trachycarpum	B,C,SG,SW
Dissotis canescens	B,C,SI
Dissotis princeps	B,C,SI
Dissotis sp	SI
Distylium racemosa	SA
Dithyrea wislizenii	B
Diuris concinna	B
Diuris corymbosa	B
Diuris magnifica	B
Doatia novazelandae	AU
Dodecatheon alpinum	AP,B,SW
Dodecatheon clevelandii	AP,B,SC,SW
Dodecatheon clevelandii ssp insulare	SG
Dodecatheon conjugens	B,SC,SW
Dodecatheon ellisae	B,SW
Dodecatheon hendersoni	AP,PA,SC,SG
Dodecatheon jeffreyi	AP,B,CG,G,SC,SG,SW
Dodecatheon meadia	AP,B,BD,BS,C,CG,D,G, JE,L,LG,NT,PA,PR,SA, SC,ST,SU

DODECATHEON

Dodecatheon meadia album	AP,G,JE,PA,SC
Dodecatheon meadia 'Goliath'	C,JE
Dodecatheon meadia 'Red Colours'	C,G,JE,PA
Dodecatheon pulchellum	AP,B,CG,FH,,JE,PR,SG, SC,SW
Dodecatheon pulchellum 'Red Wings'	AP,B,P,SC
Dodecatheon tatrandum	SG
Dodecatheon tatrandum 'Red Light'	C,JE
Dodonaea angustifolia	B,HA,SI
Dodonaea aptera	B
Dodonaea baueri	B
Dodonaea boroniifolia	B
Dodonaea ceratocarpa	B
Dodonaea concinna	B
Dodonaea coriacea	B
Dodonaea cuneata	HA
Dodonaea divaricata	B
Dodonaea eriocarpa	B
Dodonaea falcata	B
Dodonaea filifolia	B
Dodonaea 'Giant Lantern'	B
Dodonaea hackettiana	AU,B
Dodonaea hirsuta	B
Dodonaea humilis	B
Dodonaea lanceolata	B
Dodonaea lobulata	B,HA
Dodonaea madagascariensis	B
Dodonaea multijuga	B
Dodonaea oxyptera	B
Dodonaea peduncularis	B
Dodonaea petiolaris	B
Dodonaea physocarpa	B
Dodonaea pinifolia	B
Dodonaea ptarmicaefolia	B
Dodonaea rigida	B
Dodonaea rupicola	B
Dodonaea sinuolata	B
Dodonaea stenozyga	B
Dodonaea triangularis	B
Dodonaea triquetra	B,HA
Dodonaea truncatiales	B
Dodonaea viscosa	AP,HA,O,SA,SC,SS
Dodonaea viscosa 'Purpurea'	B,HA,SA
Dodonaea viscosa ssp	B
Dodonaea viscosa v linearis	B
Dolichandrone spathacea	B
Dolichoglottis lyallii	B,SS
Dolichoglottis scorzoneroides	B,SS
Dombeya autumnalis	SI
Dombeya burgessiae	B,C,SA,SI
Dombeya calantha	B,SA
Dombeya cymosa	B,SI
Dombeya goetzenii	B
Dombeya macranthae	SI
Dombeya pulchra	B,SI
Dombeya rotundifolia	B,SI
Dombeya tiliacea	B,SI
Dombeya wallichii	B
Dombeya x cayeuxii	CG
Doronicum austriacum	AP,B,P,SC,SG
Doronicum catarractae	C
Doronicum columnae	J
Doronicum grandiflorum	JE,SG,ST
Doronicum orientale	AP,B,G,JE,KI,SA,SC,V
Doronicum orientale 'Finesse'	C,JE
Doronicum orientale 'Goldcut'	B,JE

Doronicum orientale 'Magnificum'	B,BS,C,CL,D,JE,L,SA
Doronicum pardalianches	G,JE,SG
Doronicum plantagineum	SG
Doronicum styriacum	SG
Dorotheanthus bellidiformis	B,C,CO,D,F,J,KS,L,M,R, ST,TU,U,V,VH,Y
Dorotheanthus bellidiformis p.s	J
Dorotheanthus bellidiformis 'Sparkles'	S
Dorotheanthus bellidi. ssp bellidiformis	SI
Dorotheanthus bidouwensis	B
Dorotheanthus booysenii	B
Dorotheanthus 'Gelato Dark Pink'	B,CL,DT,SE
Dorotheanthus 'Gelato White'	B,C,CL,DT
Dorotheanthus gramineus	B,C,CG,F,SI,Y
Dorotheanthus 'Harlequin' mix	DT,J
Dorotheanthus 'Lunette'	B,BD,C,CL,D,DT,F,KI,S, V,VH
Dorotheanthus 'Magic Carpet'	BD,CL,KI,SE,SU,T,YA
Dorotheanthus 'Pomeridiana Sunshine'	D
Dorotheanthus rourkei	SI
Dorotheanthus sp	SI
Dorstenia carnulosa	Y
Dorstenia foetida	Y
Doryanthes excelsa	B,C,HA,O,SA,SH
Doryanthes palmeri	B,RS
Doryopteris pedata	B,SA
Doryphora sassafras	B
Dovea macrocarpa	B,SI
Dovyalis caffra	B,SI
Dovyalis hebecarpa	B
Dovyalis hyb	B
Dovyalis zeyheri	B,SI
Downingia elegans	C,CC,G
Downingia yina v major	B
Draba aizoides	AP,B,BD,BS,C,CG,CL, JE,L,SA,SC,SG
Draba alpina	AP,B,SC
Draba alpina v glacialis	SG
Draba asprella	B,SW
Draba borealis	SG
Draba bruniifolia	AP,B,G,JE
Draba cappadocica	AP,FH,SC
Draba crassifolia	SG
Draba daurica	SC,SG
Draba dedeana	AP,C,G,SC,SG
Draba densifolia	AP,SC,SG
Draba dubia	AP,C
Draba hispanica	AP,B,HH,JE,SC,SG
Draba incana	SC,SG
Draba incerta	SG
Draba languinosa	SG
Draba lasiocarpa	AP,B,G,JE,SC
Draba linearis	SG
Draba loiseleurii	AP,B,G,JE,SG
Draba longisiliqua	AP,I,SC
Draba muralis	CG
Draba norvegica	AP,G,SC,SG
Draba oligosperma	AP,G,SC,SG
Draba polytricha	AP,SC,SG
Draba ramosissima	B,JE
Draba rigida	SG
Draba 'Rock Gdn' mix	C,JE
Draba sakurai	AP,CC,G,JE
Draba sendtneri	SG
Draba stellata	B
Draba tomentosa	AP,G,SC,SG

DRABA

Draba ussuriensis	AP,FH,SC	Drosera andersoniana	B
Draba ventosa	AP,I,SC,SG	Drosera anglica	B,SI
Dracaena draco	B,C,CG,CL,HA,O,SA,T,V	Drosera arcturi	SS
Dracaena fragrans	B	Drosera auriculata	SI
Dracaena fragrans 'Massangeana'	B	Drosera banksii	B
Dracaena hookeriana	B,SA,SI	Drosera binata	B,C,CG,SI
Dracaena multiflora	B	Drosera binata v multifida	Y
Dracaena thalioides	CG	Drosera brevifolia	B
Dracaena umbraculifera	B	Drosera bulbosa	B
Dracocephalum argunense	AP,CC,FH,SC,T	Drosera bulbosa ssp bulbosa	B
Dracocephalum forrestii	AP,SC,SG	Drosera bulbosa ssp major	B
Dracocephalum grandiflorum	AP,JE,SA,SG	Drosera burkeana	B,SI
Dracocephalum imberbe	T	Drosera burmanni	B
Dracocephalum mairei	SG	Drosera capensis	AP,C,CG,SC,SG,SI,Y
Dracocephalum moldavica	B,C,CG,G,SG,SU,T,V	Drosera capensis red	Y
Dracocephalum mold. 'Dragonhead Blue'	KS	Drosera capillaris	B
Dracocephalum mold. 'Snow Dragon'	B	Drosera capillaris v brasiliensis	B
Dracocephalum nutans	AP,C,JE,SC,SG	Drosera caucasica	CG
Dracocephalum purdomii	SG	Drosera cistiflora	B,C,SI
Dracocephalum ruyschiana	B,C,G,JE,SA,SG	Drosera cistiflora v zeyheri	B
Dracocephalum ruyschiana 'Blue Drips'	F	Drosera coccicaulis	B
Dracocephalum tanguticum	JE	Drosera coccicaulis x D.'Magaliesberg'	B
Dracophilus delaetianus	B	Drosera communis	B
Dracophilus montis-draconis	B	Drosera cuneifolia	B
Dracophilus proximus	B,Y	Drosera dielsiana	B,Y
Dracophyllum acerosum	B,SS	Drosera dielsiana x D.'Magaliesberg'	B
Dracophyllum kirkii	B,SS	Drosera dilatato-petiolaris	B
Dracophyllum latifolium	B	Drosera ericksonae	B
Dracophyllum longifolium	B,SS	Drosera erythrogyne	B
Dracophyllum menziesii	SS	Drosera erythrorhiza	B,C
Dracophyllum pronum	B,SS	Drosera erythrorhiza ssp collina	B
Dracophyllum prostratum	SS	Drosera erythrorhiza ssp magna	B
Dracophyllum traversii	B,SS	Drosera erythrorhiza ssp squamosa	B
Dracopis amplexicaulis	B,NT	Drosera esmereldae	B
Dracunculus muscivorus	B	Drosera falconeri	B
Dracunculus vulgaris	AP,C,G,JE,SC	Drosera falconeri x D.dilatato-petiolaris	B
Drakaea glyptodon	B	Drosera filiformis v filiformis	B,SI
Drapetes dieffenbachii	B,SS	Drosera filiformis v tracyi	B
Drapetes lyallii	SS	Drosera 'Floating'	B
Drapetes villosus	SS	Drosera gigantea	B
Dregea volubilis	B	Drosera gigantea ssp geniculata	B
Drimia altissima	B,SI	Drosera glabripes	B,SI
Drimia elata	B,C,SI	Drosera glanduligera	B
Drimia robusta	B,SI	Drosera graniticola	B
Drimys lanceolata	A,AU,B,C,SA	Drosera hamiltonii	B
Drimys winterii	A,AP,SA	Drosera heterophylla	B
Drosanthemum barwickii	B	Drosera hilaris	B,SI
Drosanthemum bellum	B,SI,Y	Drosera hirtella	B
Drosanthemum bicolor	B,SI,Y	Drosera indica	B
Drosanthemum eburneum	B	Drosera intermedia	B,SI
Drosanthemum floribundum	B,C,SI,Y	Drosera lanata	B
Drosanthemum godmaniae	B	Drosera linearis	B
Drosanthemum hallii	B	Drosera lowriei	B
Drosanthemum hispidum	B,SI,Y	Drosera macrantha 'Gravel Form'	B
Drosanthemum intermedium	Y	Drosera macrantha ssp planchonii	B
Drosanthemum micans	B,SI,Y	Drosera macrophylla	B
Drosanthemum sp mix	C,Y	Drosera macrophylla ssp monantha	B
Drosanthemum speciosum	B,C,SI,Y	Drosera madagascarensis	B
Drosanthemum striatum	B,SI,Y	Drosera menziesii ssp	B
Drosanthemum subalbum	B	Drosera modesta	B
Drosanthemum tuberculiferum	B,SI,Y	Drosera montana	CG
Drosera acaulis	B	Drosera peltata	B,C
Drosera adlinsiae	B	Drosera planchonii	C
Drosera admirabilis	B	Drosera pygmaea	B,CG
Drosera alba	B,SI	Drosera regia	B,SI
Drosera aliciae	B,C,SI	Drosera rotundifolia	B,G,SI

DROSERA

Drosera sp mix	C,SI
Drosera sp,ssp, v, hyb	B
Drosera spathulata Kanto	Y
Drosera stenopetala	CG
Drosera trinervia	B,SI
Drosera whittakeri	B,C
Drosophyllum lusitanicum	B,CG
Dryandra arborea	B
Dryandra arctotidis	B,O
Dryandra armata	B,C,O
Dryandra ashbyi	B,O
Dryandra baxteri	B,O,SA
Dryandra bipinnatifida	B
Dryandra calophylla	B,O
Dryandra carduacea	B,O
Dryandra carlinoides	B,O
Dryandra cirsioides	B,O
Dryandra comosa	B,O
Dryandra conferta	B,O
Dryandra cuneata	B,O,SA
Dryandra drummondii	B,O
Dryandra erythrocephala	B,O
Dryandra ferruginea	B,O
Dryandra foliosissima	B,O
Dryandra formosa	B,C,O,SA
Dryandra fraseri	B,O
Dryandra hewardiana	B,O
Dryandra horrida	B,O
Dryandra kippistiana	B,O
Dryandra longifolia	B
Dryandra mucronulata	B,O
Dryandra nivea	B,O
Dryandra nobilis	B,O
Dryandra obtusa	B,O
Dryandra polycephala	B,O
Dryandra praemorsa	B,O
Dryandra preissii	B,O
Dryandra proteoides	B,O
Dryandra pteridifolia	B,O
Dryandra pulchella	B,O
Dryandra quercifolia	B,C,O,SA
Dryandra seneciifolia	B,O
Dryandra serra	B,O
Dryandra serratuloides	B,O
Dryandra sessilis	B,O
Dryandra shuttleworthiana	B,O
Dryandra speciosa	B,O,SA
Dryandra speciosa 'Tammin'	B
Dryandra stuposa	B,O
Dryandra subpinnatifida	B,O,
Dryandra tenuifolia	B,O
Dryandra tridentata	B,O
Dryandra vestita	B,O
Dryas drummondii	AP,SC,SG
Dryas integrifolia	AP,B,SG
Dryas octopetala	AP,B,BS,C,FH,G,I,JE, KI,SA,SC,SG,ST
Dryas octopetala ssp hookeriana	SG
Dryas x suendermanni	AP,B,G,SC
Drymophila cyanocarpa	AP,B,SC
Dryopteris erthrosora	AP,N
Dryopteris filix-mas	AP,C
Drypetes sepiaria	B
Dterocarya hupehensis	B
Duchesnea indica	AP,B,F,JE,SC,SG
Duchesnea indica 'Harlequin'	B,P

Dudleya albiflora	B
Dudleya brittonii	B
Dudleya caespitosa	B
Dudleya candida	B
Dudleya cymosa	AP,B,SC
Dudleya pulverulenta	B
Dudleya saxosa v collomiae	B
Dunalia australis	B
Duranta erecta	B,C,HA,O,SA
Duranta erecta 'Alba'	B
Duranta erecta 'Variegata'	B
Durio zibethinus	B
Duschekia fruticosa	SG
Duvalia polita v transvaalensis	SI
Duvalia pubescens	SI
Dyckia altissima	B
Dyckia brevifolia	B
Dyckia chaguar	B
Dyckia distachia	B
Dyckia encholiroides	B,BC
Dyckia floribunda	B,SA
Dyckia fosterana	B
Dyckia fosterana 'Silver Queen'	B
Dyckia frigida	B
Dyckia glomerata	B
Dyckia goiana	B
Dyckia leptostachya	B
Dyckia maritima	B
Dyckia marnier-lapostollei estevesii	BC
Dyckia rariflora	B
Dyckia remotiflora	B
Dyckia sulphurea	B,CG
Dyckia tuberosa	B
Dyckia velascana	B
Dyerophytum africanum	B,SI
Dypsis nodifera	SI
Dypsis pinnatifrons	B,O
Dysoxylum fraseranum	B
Dysoxylum muelleri	B
Dysoxylum rufum	O
Dysoxylum spectabile	B
Dysphania rhadinostachys	B
Eberlanzia disarticulata	B
Eberlanzia spinosa	B,Y
Ebracteola montis-moltkei	B,Y
Ecballium elaterium	B,CG
Ecbolium ligustrinum	B
Eccremocarpus scaber	AP,BS,C,FH,G,I,KI,LG, N,SA,SC,SG,X
Eccremocarpus scaber 'Anglia Hyb' s-c	T
Eccremocarpus scaber apricot	LG
Eccremocarpus scaber aurantiacus	HH
Eccremocarpus scaber 'Carnival Time'	F
Eccremocarpus scaber cherry red	C
Eccremocarpus scaber f aureus	AP,FH,SC
Eccremocarpus scaber f carmineus	AP,FH,SC,SG,W
Eccremocarpus scaber f roseus	AP,I
Eccremocarpus scaber 'Fireworks'	AP,U
Eccremocarpus scaber orange	B
Eccremocarpus scaber 'Tresco Gold'	B
Eccremocarpus scaber 'Tresco' mix	C,D,DT,J,S,V
Eccremocarpus scaber 'Tresco Rose'	B
Eccremocarpus scaber 'Tresco Scarlet'	B,SC
Eccremocarpus scaber yellow	P
Ecdeiocolea monostachya	B,O
Echeandia flavescens	B,SW

ECHEANDIA

Echeandia flavescens v stenocarpa	B,SW
Echeveria affinis	B
Echeveria angustifolia	B
Echeveria chihuahuaensis	B
Echeveria ciliata	B
Echeveria derenbergii	B
Echeveria erubescens	B
Echeveria laui	B,BC,CH
Echeveria lilacina	BC
Echeveria nodulosa	B
Echeveria paniculata	B
Echeveria peacockii	B,C,T,U
Echeveria rubromarginata	B
Echeveria sp mix	C,CH
Echeveria strictiflora	B
Echeveria strictiflora v nova	B
Echeveria subsessilis	B
Echeveria tenuifolia	B
Echeveria tenuis	B
Echeveria tolimanensis	B
Echeveria turgida	B
Echeveria walpoleana	B
Echinacea angustifolia	B,JE,PR
Echinacea atrorubens	B
Echinacea laevigata	B
Echinacea pallida	B,C,CP,G,HW,JE,PR,SA, T
Echinacea paradoxa	B,JE,PR
Echinacea purpurea	AP,AV,B,BS,C,CG,CL, CO,CP,DT,F,G,HW,JE, KI,KS,L,N,PR,SA,ST,T, TU,W
Echinacea purpurea 'Alba'	B,JE
Echinacea purpurea 'Bravado'	B
Echinacea purpurea 'Brilliant Star'	C,S
Echinacea purpurea hyb	T
Echinacea purpurea 'Leuchtstern'	B,JE,SA
Echinacea purpurea 'Lustre Hybrids'	B
Echinacea purpurea 'Magnus'	B,JE,LG,T
Echinacea purpurea 'Pink Flamingo'	J,V
Echinacea purpurea 'Satellite Mix'	U
Echinacea purpurea 'White Swan'	AP,F,J,KS,PA,PM,SA,T,V
Echinacea simulata	B
Echinacea tennesseensis	B
Echinocactus coahuilense	B,BC,GC,Y
Echinocactus electracanthus	B
Echinocactus grusonii	C,CH,Y
Echinocactus horizonthalonius	B,BC,Y
Echinocactus hyb	GC
Echinocactus mix	T,Y
Echinocactus parryi	B
Echinocactus platyacanthus	B,Y
Echinocactus senile	Y
Echinocactus senile f aureum	BC
Echinocactus sp /hyb mix	C,SO,Y
Echinocactus texensis	B,BR,C,Y
Echinocactus xeranthemoides	B
Echinocereus adustus	B
Echinocereus adustus v schwarzi	B,BC
Echinocereus berlandieri	B,CH,Y
Echinocereus boyce-thompsonii	Y
Echinocereus brandegeei	B
Echinocereus bristolii	B
Echinocereus bristolii v pseudopectinatus	B,BC
Echinocereus castaneus	Y
Echinocereus chisoensis	B,BC

Echinocereus chisoensis v fobeanus	B
Echinocereus chloranthus	B,Y
Echinocereus chloranthus v cylindricus	B
Echinocereus chl. v cylindricus 'Corelli'	B
Echinocereus chloranthus v neocapillus	B
Echinocereus chloranthus v nov	B
Echinocereus cinerascens septentrionalis	B
Echinocereus coccineus	B,BC
Echinocereus coccineus v arizonica	B
Echinocereus coccineus v arizonicus	B
Echinocereus coccineus v guerneyi	B
Echinocereus coccineus v paucispinus	B
Echinocereus conglomeratus	B
Echinocereus cylindricus	B
Echinocereus dasyacanthus	B,Y
Echinocereus das. v neomexicanus	B
Echinocereus davisii	B,BC,Y
Echinocereus delaetii	B
Echinocereus delaetii v freudenbergeri	B
Echinocereus engelmannii	B,Y
Echinocereus engelmannii v acicularis	B
Echinocereus engelmannii v bonkerae	B,BC
Echinocereus engel. v boyce-thompsonii	B
Echinocereus engel. v chrysocentrus	B,BC,CH
Echinocereus engelmannii v fasciculatus	B
Echinocereus engelmannii v variegatus	B
Echinocereus enneacanthus	B,Y
Echinocereus enneac. sarissophorus	BC
Echinocereus enneac. v brevispinus	B
Echinocereus fasciculatus	B,Y
Echinocereus fendleri	B,BC
Echinocereus fendleri v kuenzleri	B
Echinocereus fendleri v rectispinus	B
Echinocereus ferreirianus v lindsayi	Y
Echinocereus fitchii	B,Y
Echinocereus fitchii v albertii	B
Echinocereus fitchii v armatus	B
Echinocereus gentryi	GC,Y
Echinocereus grandis	B,BC
Echinocereus knippelianus	B
Echinocereus knippelianus v kruegeri	B
Echinocereus knippelianus v reyesi	B
Echinocereus knippelianus v reyesii	B
Echinocereus laui	B,CH
Echinocereus ledingii	B
Echinocereus leonensis	B
Echinocereus longisetus	B
Echinocereus maritimus	B
Echinocereus melanocentruus	Y
Echinocereus neo-mexicanus	Y
Echinocereus nicholii	B
Echinocereus ochoterenae	B,Y
Echinocereus octacanthus	B,Y
Echinocereus palmeri	B
Echinocereus pamanesiorus	B
Echinocereus papillosus	B
Echinocereus papillosus v angusticeps	B
Echinocereus parkeri	B
Echinocereus parkerii	B
Echinocereus pectinatus	B,C
Echinocereus pectinatus rigidissimus	CH
Echinocereus pectinatus v wenigeri	B
Echinocereus pentalophus	B,Y
Echinocereus perbellus	Y
Echinocereus polyacantha	B
Echinocereus polyacanthus	B

ECHINOCEREUS

Echinocereus polyacanthus v densus	B
Echinocereus poselgeri	B
Echinocereus primolanata	B
Echinocereus primolanatus	B
Echinocereus pulchella	B
Echinocereus pulchellus	B
Echinocereus pul. v amoenus 'Albiflorus'	B
Echinocereus pulchellus v weinbergii	B
Echinocereus purpureus	Y
Echinocereus reichenbachii	B,BC
Echinocereus reichenbachii v albispinus	B
Echinocereus reichenbachii v baileyi	B,Y
Echinocereus reichenbachii v caespitosus	B
Echinocereus reichenbachii v castaneus	B
Echinocereus reichenbachii v perbellus	B,BC
Echinocereus rigidissimus	Y
Echinocereus rigidissimus v rubrispinus	Y
Echinocereus rigidissimus v rufispinus	GC
Echinocereus rigidissimus varieties	B
Echinocereus roetteri	B
Echinocereus rufispinus	B
Echinocereus russanthus	B
Echinocereus russanthus sp Nova	BC
Echinocereus russanthus v cowperi	B
Echinocereus russanthus v fiehnii	BC
Echinocereus russanthus 'Weedenii'	B
Echinocereus scheeri	B
Echinocereus scheeri obscuriensis	BC
Echinocereus schmollii	B,Y
Echinocereus sciurus	B
Echinocereus sciurus v floresii	B
Echinocereus sp mix	C,CH,T,Y
Echinocereus spinigemmatus	B
Echinocereus stoloniferus	B
Echinocereus stramineus	B,CH,Y
Echinocereus stramineus parkeri	BC
Echinocereus stramineus v ochoterenae	B
Echinocereus subinermis	B,Y
Echinocereus triglochidiatus	B,Y
Echinocereus trig. v gonacanthus	B
Echinocereus trig. v mohavensis	B,BC
Echinocereus trig. v paucispinus	Y
Echinocereus troglochidiatus	B
Echinocereus viereckii	B
Echinocereus viereckii v morricalii	B,Y
Echinocereus viridiflorus	B,BR,CH,Y
Echinocereus viridiflorus montanus	BC
Echinocereus websterianus	C
Echinocereus x lloydi	B
Echinocereus x roetteri	B
Echinochloa crus-galli	SG,T
Echinochloa crus-galli v frumentacea	B
Echinocystis lobata	B,PR,SG
Echinomastus acunensis /neolloydia	B
Echinomastus dasyacanthus	B,BC
Echinomastus durangensis	B
Echinomastus durangensis v minor	B
Echinomastus erectocentrus	B
Echinomastus intertextus	B,BC
Echinomastus johnsonii	B
Echinomastus johnsonii v lutescens	B
Echinomastus laui	B
Echinomastus mariposensis	B
Echinomastus unguispinus	B
Echinomastus warnockii	B
Echinops adenocaulos	B

Echinops bannaticus	B,G
Echinops bannaticus 'Blue Globe'	B
Echinops bannaticus 'Blue Glow'	C,JE,SA
Echinops bannaticus 'Taplow Blue'	B
Echinops exaltus	T
Echinops latifolius	SG
Echinops ritro	AP,B,BS,C,CL,CO,D,DT, F,JE,KI,KS,L,S,SA,SC, SE,SG,SU,T,V
Echinops ruthenicus	T
Echinops setifer	B
Echinops sphaerocephalus	B,C,G,JE,SA,SG
Echinops strigosus	T
Echinops tschimganicus	T
Echinopsis ancistrophora	B,Y
Echinopsis ancist. ssp cardenasiana	B
Echinopsis ancistrophora v densiseta	B
Echinopsis ancistrophora v hamatacantha	B
Echinopsis ancistrophora v kratochviliana	B
Echinopsis ancistrophora v polyancistra	B
Echinopsis aurea	Y
Echinopsis backebergii	B
Echinopsis bac. v hertrichiana 'Allegriana'	B
Echinopsis backebergii v larae	B
Echinopsis boiyubensis	B
Echinopsis bridgesii	Y
Echinopsis camarapana	B
Echinopsis camarguensis	B
Echinopsis camarguensis v robustior	B
Echinopsis cardenasia	BC,CH,Y
Echinopsis chacoana	B
Echinopsis chamaecereus f crassicaulis	Y
Echinopsis cinnabarina	B,Y
Echinopsis cinnabarina v draxleriana	B
Echinopsis cinnabarina v walterspeilii	B
Echinopsis cochabambensis	B
Echinopsis cordobensis	Y
Echinopsis denudatum	Y
Echinopsis eyriesii	B,Y
Echinopsis ferox	B,Y
Echinopsis ferox v longispina	B,BC
Echinopsis grandiflora v inermis	Y
Echinopsis herbasii	B
Echinopsis histrichoides	Y
Echinopsis 'Holly Gate' new hyb	C
Echinopsis huascha	B,Y
Echinopsis huottii	B
Echinopsis hyb	BC
Echinopsis hyb 'Paramount'	GC
Echinopsis ibicuatensis	B
Echinopsis kermesina	Y
Echinopsis lageniformis	B,Y
Echinopsis leucantha	B,BC,Y
Echinopsis loti	Y
Echinopsis macrogona	B
Echinopsis mamillosa	B,Y
Echinopsis mammilosa v kermesina	B
Echinopsis mirabilis	B,G
Echinopsis multiplex	B
Echinopsis 'New Abbeybrook' f1 & f2 hyb	T
Echinopsis obrepanda	B,Y
Echinopsis obrepanda 'Calliantholilacina'	B
Echinopsis obrepanda v calorubra	B
Echinopsis obrepanda v mizquensis	B
Echinopsis pachanoi	B
Echinopsis pachanoi x peruvianus	B

ECHINOPSIS

Echinopsis paraguayensis	Y
Echinopsis pasacana	B
Echinopsis pentlandii	B,Y
Echinopsis pentlandii v hardeniana	B
Echinopsis peruvianus	B
Echinopsis rhodotricha	B,BC,Y
Echinopsis roseo-lilacina	Y
Echinopsis schickendantzii	B,BC,Y
Echinopsis silvestrii	B
Echinopsis smrzianus	B
Echinopsis sp mix	C,Y
Echinopsis spachiana	B,BC,Y
Echinopsis spiniflora	B
Echinopsis subdenudata	B
Echinopsis tapecuna v tropica	B
Echinopsis tarijensis	B
Echinopsis terscheckii	B
Echinopsis thionantha	B,Y
Echinopsis turbinata	B
Echinopsis validus	B
Echinopsis vallegrandensis	B
Echinopsis werdermanii	B,Y
Echium albicans	SA
Echium angustifolium	B
Echium boisseri	SA
Echium candicans	B,C,SA,SC,T
Echium hyb mix	CO,KI,SU
Echium italicum	B
Echium nervosum	B
Echium pininana	B,C,P,SA,SG,T
Echium plantagineum 'Bedder mix'	J,V
Echium plantagineum 'Blue Bedder Dw'	B,BD,BS,C,KS,L,S,T
Echium plantagineum 'Crown Hybrids'	BS
Echium plantagineum 'Dw Hybrids'	B,D,DT,F,KS,L,T,TU,V
Echium plantagineum 'Moody Blues'	U
Echium plant. 'Suttons Dw. Bedding mix'	S
Echium plantagineum 'White Bedder Dw.'	B
Echium russicum	B,JE,SA
Echium simplex	B
Echium vulgare	B,C,CG,CP,G,JE,P,SA, SC,SG
Echium vulgare 'Drake's Form'	B,D
Echium vulgare dw hyb	C
Echium wildpretii	AP,B,C,SG
Echium wildpretii x pininana hyb	C
Eclipta prostrata	B
Edible fungus nutrient substrate	B
Edithcolea grandis	B
Edmondia sesamoides	SI
Edraianthus graminifolius	B,C,CG,G,JE,SC,SG
Edraianthus graminifolius 'Albus'	JE,SC
Edraianthus jugoslavicus	CG
Edraianthus kitaibeli	CG,G
Edraianthus pumilio	AP,CG,G,JE,SC
Edraianthus serbicus	AP,B,G,PM
Edraianthus tenuifolius	AP,B,C,G,SC,SG
Ehretia dicksonii	SA
Ehretia pubescens	B
Ehretia rigida	B,SI
Ehrhata thunbergii	SI
Einadia nutans	B
Ekebergia capensis	B,SI
Ekebergia pterophylla	B
Elaeagnus angustifolia	A,B,C,SA
Elaeagnus commutata	A,B,C,SA,SG
Elaeagnus macrophylla	B

Elaeagnus multiflora	A,B,CG,SA
Elaeagnus pungens	B,C
Elaeagnus umbellata	A,B,C,SA
Elaeagnus umbellata 'Cardinal'	B
Elaeis guineensis	B,O,SA
Elaeis oleifera	B
Elaeocarpus angustifolius	B,HA,O
Elaeocarpus dentatus	B
Elaeocarpus foveolatus	O
Elaeocarpus hookerianus	B
Elaeocarpus reticulatus	C,HA
Elaeocarpus reticulatus 'Flamingo'	B
Elaeocarpus reticulatus pink	B,HA
Elegia caespitosus	B,SI
Elegia capensis	B,O,SA,SI
Elegia cuspidata	B,C,O,SI
Elegia equisetacea	B,SA,SI
Elegia fenestrata	B
Elegia filacea	B,SI
Elegia grandis	B,SI
Elegia grandispicata	B,SI
Elegia thyrsoidea	B,SI
Eleiotis monophylla	B
Eleocharis acicularis	PR
Elephantopus tomentosus	B
Eleusine coracana	B
Eleutherococcus henryi	CG
Eleutherococcus lasiogyne	B
Eleutherococcus senticosus	B,SA
Eleutherococcus sessiliflorus	B,SA,SG
Eleutherococcus sieboldianus	SG
Elisanthe noctiflora	SG
Elmera racemosa	AP,FH,SC
Elsholtzia ciliata	G,SG
Elsholtzia cristata	CG
Elsholtzia densa	B
Elsholtzia fruticosa	SA
Elsholtzia stauntonii	B,C,G,JE,SA
Elymus arenarius	C,JE,SA
Elymus canadensis	B,JE,PR,SA
Elymus caninus	SG
Elymus condensatus	B,SA
Elymus fibrosus	SG
Elymus glaucus	C
Elymus hispidus	B
Elymus magellanicus	E,SC
Elymus mutabilis	SG
Elymus pycnanthus	B
Elymus riparius	PR
Elymus sibiricus	SG
Elymus trachycaulos	B
Elymus trichophora	SG
Elymus villosus	PR
Elymus virginicus	B,PR
Elytrigia repens	SG
Elytropus chilensis	SA
Embothrium coccineum	AU,B,C,SA,SC
Embothrium coccineum v lanceolatum	C
Embothrium grandifolium	B
Emilia atriplicifolia	B,PR
Emilia coccinea	B,SG,T
Emilia coccinea 'Golden Magic'	B
Emilia coccinea 'Scarlet Magic'	B
Emilia glabra	B
Emilia hastata	SG
Emilia muhlenbergii	PR

Emilia robusta	SG
Emilia sonchifolia mix	C
Emilia suaveolens	G,PR
Emmenopterys henryi	B,SA
Empetrum nigrum	B,C,FH,JE,SA,SG
Empleurum unicapsulare	B
Empodium namaquensis	B
Encelia californica	B
Encelia farinosa	B,SA
Encelia virginensis	B
Encephalartos friderici-guilielmi	B
Encephalocarpus sp	O
Encephalocarpus strobiliformis	BC
Enchylaena tomentosa	B,C,SA
Enchylaena tomentosa v tomentosa	AU
Endiandra palmerstonii	O
Endiandra sieberii	B
Engelhardia roxburghiana	B
Enicostema axillare	B
Enkianthus campanulatus	AP,B,C,SA,SG
Enkianthus campanulatus v palibinii	B,C,N,SA
Enkianthus cernuus v rubens	G,N
Enkianthus chinensis	B,N,SA
Enkianthus chinensis C&H7084	X
Enkianthus perulatus	B
Enneapogon avenaceus	B
Enneapogon intermedius	B
Enneapogon nigricans	B
Enneapogon oblongus	B
Ensete ventricosum	B,C,RE,SA,ST,T,V
Entada abyssinica	B,SI
Entada gigas	B
Entada pusaetha	B
Entandrophragma caudatum	B,SI
Entandrophragma excelsum	B
Entelea arborescens	B,SA
Enterolobium contortisiliquum	B
Enterolobium cyclocarpum	B,RE
Enterolobium timbouva	SA
Enteropogon dolichostachyus	B
Epacris obtusifolia	B
Ephedra equisetina	SA
Ephedra monosperma	B,SC,SG
Ephedra nevadensis	B,C,CP
Ephedra viridis	B,C,CP
Epiblema grandiflorum	B
Epidendrum ibaguense	B
Epidendrum imatophyllum	B
Epidendrum nocturnum	B
Epidendrum parkinsonianum	B
Epidendrum rigidum	B
Epidendrum secundum	B
Epidendrum warasii	B
Epilobium anagallidifolium	B
Epilobium angustifolium	B,BS,G,JE,PR,SA,SG
Epilobium angustifolium f album	C,P
Epilobium canum ssp latifolium	B
Epilobium chloriifolium	B,SS
Epilobium cinereum	SG
Epilobium crassum	AP,B,G,FH,SC,SS
Epilobium dodonaei	AP,B,BS,C,G,JE,SC,SG,T
Epilobium fleischeri	AP,B,G,JE,SA,SC
Epilobium glabellum of gdns	AP,SS
Epilobium glandulosum	PR
Epilobium hirsutum	B,JE
Epilobium hyemalis	SG

Epilobium lanceolatum	B
Epilobium leptophyllum	B
Epilobium luteum	AP,B,SC
Epilobium macrocarpus	SS
Epilobium marginatum	SS
Epilobium melanocaulon	B,SS
Epilobium microphyllum	AP,B,SS
Epilobium montanum	B,SG
Epilobium nummularifolius	B
Epilobium parviflorum	SG
Epilobium pedunculare	SG
Epilobium pynostachyum	AP,B,SS
Epilobium rostratum	B,SS
Epilobium tasmanicum	B,P
Epilobium tetragonum	B,SG
Epipactis atrorubens	CG
Epipactis gigantea	B,G,SC
Epipactis heleborine	CG
Epipactis palustris	AP,B,CG,G,SC
Epiphyllum, hyb lg mix	C,CH,T
Episcia, hyb mix	C
Epithelantha bokei	B
Epithelantha greggii	B,BC
Epithelantha micromeris	B
Epithelantha micromeris v neomexicana	BC
Epithelantha pachyrhiza	B
Equisetum laevigatum	B
Equisetum palustrum	CG
Eragrostis abyssinica	L
Eragrostis brownii	HA
Eragrostis capensis	SI
Eragrostis cilianensis	B
Eragrostis curvula	C,HA,JE
Eragrostis eriopoda	B
Eragrostis falcata	B
Eragrostis interrupta	B
Eragrostis nutans	B
Eragrostis setifolia	B
Eragrostis spectabilis	B,PR
Eragrostis tef	B,C
Eragrostis tenella	B,T
Eragrostis trichodes	JE,SA
Eranthis cilicica	B,G,PM,SC
Eranthis hyemalis	AP,B,BS,C,CO,F,G,KI, SA,SC,SU,T
Eranthis hyemalis ciliciaca group	NG
Ercilla volubilis	SA
Eremaea beaufortioides	AU,B
Eremaea fimbriata	B
Eremaea pauciflora	B
Eremaea purpurea	B
Eremaea violacea	B
Eremocrinum albomarginatum	B
Eremophila alternifolia	B
Eremophila bignoniiflora	B
Eremophila cuneifolia	B
Eremophila densifolia	B
Eremophila desertii	B
Eremophila divaricata	B
Eremophila duttonii	B
Eremophila foliosissima	B
Eremophila freelingii	B
Eremophila gilesii	B
Eremophila glabra	B
Eremophila ionantha	B
Eremophila laanii	B

EREMOPHILA

Eremophila longifolia	B,O	Erica conferta	B,SI
Eremophila macdonnellii	B	Erica conica	B,SI
Eremophila maculata	B,C,O,SA	Erica conspicua	B
Eremophila pachyphylla	B	Erica coriifolia	B,SI
Eremophila polyclada	B	Erica cruenta	B,SI
Eremophila racemosa	B	Erica cubica	B,SI
Eremophila scoparia	B	Erica curviflora	B,O,SI
Eremophila serrulata	B	Erica curviflora 'Splendens'	B
Eremophila spectabilis	B	Erica curvirostris	B,O
Eremophila youngii	B	Erica daphniflora	B,SI
Eremurus altaicus	SG	Erica decora	B,SI
Eremurus bungei	AP,G,JE,MN,SG	Erica deliciosa	B,SI
Eremurus 'Erfo Hybrids'	C,JE	Erica demissa	B,O,SI
Eremurus himalaicus	AP,B,G,RH,SC,SG	Erica densifolia	B,O,SI
Eremurus 'Hybrids'	D,F,SC	Erica denticulata	B,SI
Eremurus olgae	B,G,SA	Erica desmantha	B,SI
Eremurus robustus	AP,B,C,G,JE,RH,RS,SC	Erica diaphana	B,O,SI
Eremurus 'Shelford' hyb	BS,C,KI,SA	Erica discolor	B,C,O,SI
Eremurus spectabilis	B,G	Erica drakensbergensis	B,SI
Eremurus stenophyllus	B,C,CG,G,SC,T	Erica elimensis	B,SI
Eremurus stenophyllus 'Cathedral Mix'	T	Erica fascicularis	B,SI
Eremurus stenophyllus x 'Perfectus'	B,JE,SA	Erica fastigiata	B,SI
Eremurus tauricus	G,JE,SA	Erica fastigiata v coventryana	B,SI
Eremurus x isabellinus 'Ruiter's Hybrids'	B,E	Erica filamentosa	B
Erepsia bracteata	B,SI	Erica filipendulina	SI
Erepsia heteropetala	B	Erica foliaceae	B
Erepsia inclaudens	SI	Erica fontana	B,SI
Erepsia mutabilis	B	Erica formosa	O,SI
Eriachne aristidea	B	Erica fourcadei	B,SI
Eriachne benthamii	B	Erica gallorum	B
Erianthus contortus	JE,SA	Erica georgica	SI
Erianthus giganteus	NT	Erica gibbosa	O,SI
Erianthus ravennae	AV,B,C,JE,SA	Erica gilva	B,O
Erianthus strictus	JE,NT	Erica glandulosa	B,O,SI
Erica abietina	B,SI	Erica glauca v elegans	B,SI
Erica acuta	B,SI	Erica glauca v elegans 'Alba'	B,SI
Erica affinis	B,SI	Erica glauca v glauca	B,SI
Erica algida	B,SI	Erica glomiflora	B,O,SI
Erica alopecurus	B,SI	Erica glutinosa	B,SI
Erica arborea	B,C,JE,RH,SA	Erica gracilis	B,SI
Erica ardens	B,SI	Erica grandiflora	B,O,SI
Erica atrovinosa	SI	Erica grandiflora v exsurgens	B,SI
Erica axilliflora	B	Erica granulosa	SI
Erica baccans	B,CG,O,SI	Erica grata	B,SI
Erica bauera	B,O,SI	Erica hebecalyx	B,O,SI
Erica bergiana	B,SI	Erica heliophila	SI
Erica bicolor	B	Erica hibbertia	B,SI
Erica blandfordia	B,SI	Erica hirtiflora	B,O,SI
Erica blenna	B,SI	Erica hispidula	B
Erica bolusiae	B,SI	Erica holosericea	B,SI
Erica brachialis	B,O,SI	Erica imbricata	O,SI
Erica bracteolaris	B,SI	Erica inflata	B,SI
Erica breviflora	B,SI	Erica infundibuliformis	B,SI
Erica bruniades	B,SI	Erica intervallaris	B,SI
Erica caffra	B,O,SI	Erica irbyana	SI
Erica calcareophila	B,SI	Erica laeta	B,O,SI
Erica calycina	B,SI	Erica lanipes	B,SI
Erica cameronii	B,SI	Erica lateralis	O,SI
Erica carnea	B,RH	Erica leucantha	B,SI
Erica cerinthoides	B,SI	Erica leucotrachela	B,O,SI
Erica chloroloma	B	Erica longifolia	B,O,SI
Erica chrysocodon	B,SI	Erica lucida	B,O,SI
Erica ciliaris	RH	Erica lutea	B,O,SI
Erica cinerea	B,RH,SI	Erica macowanii	B,SI
Erica coccinea	B,O,SI	Erica mammosa	B,C,O,SI
Erica colorans	B,SI	Erica marifolia	B,SI

Erica mauritanica	B
Erica maximiliani	B
Erica melanthera	B,SI
Erica mollis	B,SI
Erica monsoniana	B
Erica multumbellifera	B,SI
Erica nana	B,O,SI
Erica nevillei	B,SI
Erica nudiflora	B,SI
Erica oatesii	B,SI
Erica oblongiflora	B,O,SI
Erica occulta	B
Erica onosmiflora	B,SI
Erica parilis	B,SI
Erica parviflora	B,SI
Erica patersonia	B,O,SI
Erica pectinifolia	B,SI
Erica perspicua	B,O,SI
Erica petraea	B,SI
Erica phylicifolia	B,SI
Erica physodes	B,SI
Erica pillansii	B,SI
Erica pinea	B,C,O,SI
Erica plukenetii	B,SI
Erica polifolia	B,SI
Erica praecox	B,SI
Erica propinqua	B,O,SI
Erica pulchella	B,SI
Erica quadrangularis	O,SI
Erica racemosa	B,SI
Erica regerminans	B,SI
Erica regia	B,SI
Erica savillea	B,SI
Erica savillea v grandiflora	B,SI
Erica scabriuscula	B,SI
Erica selaginifolia	SI
Erica senilis	B,SI
Erica sessiliflora	B,O,SI
Erica sitiens	B,O
Erica sp mix	C,O,SI
Erica sparsa	O,SI
Erica speciosa	B,O,SI
Erica sphaerocephala	B,SI
Erica spheroidea	O,SI
Erica straussiana	B,SI
Erica subdivaricata	B
Erica swinnertonii	SI
Erica syngenesia	B,SI
Erica taxifolia	B,O,SI
Erica tenella	B,SI
Erica tenuis	B
Erica terminalis	C,RH
Erica tetralix	B,C,JE,RH,SA
Erica thomae	B
Erica thunbergii	SI
Erica triflora	B,SI
Erica urna-viridis	B,SI
Erica vagans	RH
Erica verecunda	B,SI
Erica versicolor	B,O,SI
Erica verticillata of gdns	B,O
Erica vestita	B,SI
Erica viridescens	SI
Erica viridescens v viridescens	B,O
Erica walkeria	B,SI
Ericameria parishii	B

Erigeron acer	B
Erigeron acris	SG
Erigeron alpinus	AP,B,G,SC
Erigeron andicola	SG
Erigeron atticus	AP,B,G
Erigeron aurantiacus	AP,B,BS,C,CL,G,JE,KI
Erigeron aurantiacus hyb	SA
Erigeron aureus 'Canary Bird'	AP,C,PM
Erigeron bellidifolius	SG
Erigeron borealis	AP,FH,SC
Erigeron canadensiss	SG
Erigeron chrysopsidis 'Grand Ridge'	AP,G,PM,SC
Erigeron compositus	AP,C,G,FH,SC,SG
Erigeron compositus 'Rocky'	B,BS,FH
Erigeron compositus v discoideus	B,SG
Erigeron flettii	AP,G,I,SC
Erigeron gaudinii	B
Erigeron glabellus	SC,SG
Erigeron glaucus	AP,B,C,G,JE,SC
Erigeron glaucus 'Albus'	AP,JE
Erigeron humilis	AP,SC,SG
Erigeron hybrida 'Jewel Mix'	T
Erigeron hybrida 'Jewel Pink'	BS
Erigeron hybridus x 'Strahlenriese'	SG
Erigeron karvinskianus	AP,B,G,FH,HH,I,L,MA, SC
Erigeron karvinskianus 'Blutenmeer'	JE
Erigeron multiradiatus	AP,CC,SC,SG
Erigeron nanus	AP,B,G,SC
Erigeron peregrinus	B
Erigeron 'Profusion'	BS,C,CL,CO,D,DT,F,J, KI,SU,T,U,V,YA
Erigeron pulchellus	B
Erigeron pumilis	SG
Erigeron roylei	SG
Erigeron simplex	AP,CC,SC,SG
Erigeron speciosus 'Azure Beauty'	T
Erigeron speciosus 'Azure Fairy'	B,BS,C,CL,JE,L,SA
Erigeron speciosus 'Blue Shades'	B
Erigeron speciosus fl pl 'Blue Beauty'	B,JE,SA
Erigeron speciosus 'Grandiflorus'	JE,V
Erigeron speciosus 'Lilac Beauty'	B
Erigeron speciosus 'Pink Jewel'	B,BD,C,CL,DT,JE,KI,L, SA
Erigeron speciosus ssp macranthus	B
Erigeron trifidus	AP,C,JE,SC
Erigeron unalaschkensis	SG
Erigeron uniflorus	AP,SC,SG
Erinus alpinus	AP,B,BS,C,CL,FH,G,I, JE,L,RH,SA,SC,T,W
Erinus alpinus 'Albus'	AP,B,C,FH,G,I,JE,SC
Erinus alpinus 'Dr.Hahnle'	AP,B,C,G,JE,SC
Eriobotrya deflexa	B,SA
Eriobotrya japonica	B,C,G,SA
Eriocephalus africanus	B,SA,SI
Eriocephalus duttonii	SA
Eriocephalus ericoides	B,SI
Eriocephalus ionantha	SA
Eriocephalus nivea	SA
Eriocephalus racemosus	B
Eriocephalus sp	SI
Eriocephalus spectabilis	SA
Eriocereus bonplandii	Y
Eriodictyon californicum	B
Eriodictyon crassifolium	B
Eriodictyon lanatum	B

ERIODICTYON

Eriodictyon trichocalyx	B
Eriodictyon trichocalyx v lanatum	SW
Eriogonum arborescens	B,SA
Eriogonum cinereum	B
Eriogonum fasciculatum	C,JE
Eriogonum fasciculatum ssp fasciculatum	B
Eriogonum fasciculatum ssp polifolium	B
Eriogonum giganteum	B,C
Eriogonum niveum nanum	I
Eriogonum ovalifolium	AP,SC,SG
Eriogonum parvifolium	B
Eriogonum saxatile	SC,SG
Eriogonum sphaerocephalum	SG
Eriogonum umbellatum	B,JE,SG
Eriogonum umbellatum v subalpinum	SG
Eriophorum alpinum	B
Eriophorum angustifolium	B,G,JE,SC
Eriophorum polystachon	SG
Eriophorum sp	PR
Eriophorum vaginatum	B,G
Eriophyllum confertiflorum	B,SA
Eriophyllum lanatum	AP,B,BS,G,JE,KI,SA,SC,SG
Eriophyllum lanatum 'Bella'	JE
Eriophyllum lanatum 'Pointe'	B,C,JE,SG
Eriophyllum stoechadifolium	B
Eriophyllum 'Sunkiss'	U
Eriosema distinctum	B
Eriosema salignum	B
Eriosema squarrosum	B,SI
Eriospermum abyssinicum	SI
Eriospermum bayerii	B
Eriospermum natalense	B,SI
Eriospermum porphyrovalve	SI
Eriospermum sp	SI
Eriospermum tenellum	SI
Eriostemon australasius	B,HA,SH
Eriostemon difformis v difformis	HA
Eriostemon spicatus	B,SA
Eriosyce ihotzkyana Talahuen	BC
Eriosyce sandillon de Vicuna	BC
Eriosyce sp mix	C
Eritrichium nanum	B,C,CG,SC
Eritrichium nanum 'Himmelsherold'	JE
Eritrichium sibiricum	AP,B,P,SC
Erodium acaule	FH
Erodium botrys	CG
Erodium castellanum	AP,CG,G,SC
Erodium ciconium	CG
Erodium cicutarium	B,CG,SG
Erodium cicutarium ssp cicutarium	CG
Erodium danicum	CG
Erodium gruinum	AP,B,C,G,P,SC
Erodium hirtum	B,CG
Erodium malacoides	CG
Erodium manescavii	AP,B,C,G,HL,JE,P,SA,SC
Erodium moschatum	CG
Erodium pelargoniiflorum	AP,B,CG,FH,HH,P,SC
Erodium telavivense	B
Erodium trifolium	C,I
Eruca sativa	B,SG
Eruca vesicaria	B,CP
Erucaria hispanica	B
Ervatamia angustisepala	B
Erymophyllum ram. ssp involucratum	B,O
Erymophyllum ramosum ssp ramosum	B,O
Erymophyllum tenellum	O
Eryngium agavifolium	AP,B,C,G,JE,LG,P,SA,SC,SG,T
Eryngium alpinum	AP,B,C,FH,G,J,PA,SC,T
Eryngium alpinum 'Blue Dwarf'	PA
Eryngium alpinum 'Blue Lace'	B
Eryngium alpinum 'Etiole Bleu'	B,C,JE,SA,U,V
Eryngium alpinum 'Superbum'	AP,B,BS,C,CL,D,F,JE,KI,KS,L,SA,ST
Eryngium amethystinum	AP,B,C,CG,F,JE,SA,SC
Eryngium anethipteum	CG
Eryngium biebersteinianum	CC
Eryngium billardieri	AP,B
Eryngium bourgatii	AP,B,BS,C,CG,CL,FH,G,J,JE,LG,P,RS,SA,SC
Eryngium bourgatii 'Oxford Blue'	PA
Eryngium caeruleum	AP,CG,G,SC
Eryngium campestre	B,C,JE,SA
Eryngium campestris	CG
Eryngium canigallii	CG
Eryngium caucasicum	B
Eryngium dichotomum	B
Eryngium eburneum	T
Eryngium foetidum	CP
Eryngium giganteum	AP,B,C,G,JE,LG,PA,RH,SA,SC,SE,T
Eryngium gig. 'Miss Willmott's Ghost'	AP,C,FH,G,P,PM,SA,SC,SG
Eryngium horridum	B,P,SA
Eryngium maritimum	AP,B,C,G,JE,SA,SC
Eryngium oliverianum	C
Eryngium pandanifolium	B,P,SA
Eryngium planum	B,BS,C,CL,JE,KS,P,SA,SC,SG,SU
Eryngium planum 'Azureum'	B
Eryngium planum 'Blaukappe'	C,JE
Eryngium planum 'Fluella'	AP,SA
Eryngium planum 'Seven Seas'	B
Eryngium planum 'Tetra Petra'	B
Eryngium proteiflorum	T
Eryngium sp mix	AP,C,P,PA,T
Eryngium spinalba	B,C,JE
Eryngium tricuspidatum	C,G,JE,SA
Eryngium tripartitum	AP,C,F,FH,G,JE,SA,SC
Eryngium variifolium	B,FH,P,SA,SC,SG,T
Eryngium yuccifolium	B,C,CG,CP,F,G,JE,NT,PR,RH,SA
Erysimum 'Apricot Delight'	B
Erysimum 'Bedder Golden'	B,BS,CL,DT,J,L,S,U
Erysimum 'Bedder Ivory White'	U
Erysimum 'Bedder' mix	BS,CL,DT,F,L,M,R,S,T,U,VH
Erysimum 'Bedder Orange'	B,BS,CL,J,KI,L,M,S,ST,T,U
Erysimum 'Bedder Primrose'	B,BS,CL,J,L,M,S,V
Erysimum 'Bedder Scarlet'	B,BS,CL,DT,J,L,M,S,T,U
Erysimum 'Blood Red'	B,BD,BS,CL,D,FJ,KI,M,S,ST,SU,T,TU,V,VH,YA
Erysimum capitatum	B,SC,SW
Erysimum 'Carmine King'	BS
Erysimum cheiri	B,C,CO,F,IG,SG,SU
Erysimum cheiri 'Aurora'	T
Erysimum 'Cloth Of Gold'	B,BD,BS,C,CL,D,F,KI,M,S,ST,T,TU,VH
Erysimum concinnum 'Orange & Cream'	T
Erysimum 'Covent Garden'	C

ERYSIMUM

Erysimum 'Crown'	BS
Erysimum 'Double Dwarf Branching'	L,T
Erysimum 'Eastern Queen'	T,VH
Erysimum 'Fair Lady'	BS,C,CL,DT,F,J,KI,L,M, Sm,SU,T,TU,U,V
Erysimum 'Fire King'	B,BD,BS,C,CL,DT,KI,S, ST,SU,T,TU,VH,YA
Erysimum 'Fire King Imp'	D
Erysimum 'Giant Pink'	BD,BS
Erysimum 'Glasnost Mix'	T
Erysimum 'Gold King'	BS
Erysimum 'Golden Monarch'	B,BD,BS,CL,YA
Erysimum 'Golden Yellow'	J
Erysimum 'Goliath'	BS
Erysimum grandiflorum	CG
Erysimum 'Harlequin'	BS,D
Erysimum helveticum	AP,B,G,JE,PM,SC,SG
Erysimum helveticum ssp wahlenbergii	SG
Erysimum hieraciifolium	B,G,JE
Erysimum hieraciifolium 'Golden Gem'	B,FH,G,I,V
Erysimum hybridum 'Marengo'	F
Erysimum 'Ivory White'	BS,CL,S,YA
Erysimum 'Lemon Delight'	B
Erysimum leptostylum	SG
Erysimum linifolium	AP,B,BS,C,D,KI,L,SU
Erysimum linifolium 'Variegatum'	B
Erysimum mix dbl, dw	BS,C
Erysimum mix dbl, tall	C
Erysimum mix, fine	C
Erysimum mix, special stock	BS,D
Erysimum 'Moonlight'	AP,PM,SC
Erysimum mutabilis	B
Erysimum ochroleucum	B
Erysimum odoratuum	SG
Erysimum 'Orange King'	BS
Erysimum 'Orange Monarch'	B
Erysimum 'Pastel Shades'	D
Erysimum perofskianum	AP,B,SA
Erysimum perofskianum 'Gold Shot'	C
Erysimum 'Persian Carpet'	BD,BS,CO,KI,L,ST,TU, YA
Erysimum 'Pink Monarch'	YA
Erysimum 'Plantworld Series'	P
Erysimum 'Primrose Dame'	B,BS,KI,SU
Erysimum 'Primrose Monarch'	B,BD,CL,S
Erysimum 'Prince Golden'	CL,D,S
Erysimum 'Prince Mix'	BD,BS,CL,D,F,S
Erysimum 'Prince Orange'	CL,D,S
Erysimum 'Prince Primrose'	CL,D,S
Erysimum 'Prince Red'	CL,D,S
Erysimum 'Prince Violet'	CL,D,S
Erysimum pumilum	AP,B,C
Erysimum 'Ruby Gem'	B,BD,BS,CL,DT,KI,S,YA
Erysimum 'Scarlet Emperor'	BD,BS
Erysimum scoparium	B,P
Erysimum 'Siberian'	CO
Erysimum 'Simplicity mix'	KI
Erysimum 'Single' mix	BS,CO,J,ST,Z
Erysimum 'Spring Jester'	D
Erysimum suffrutescens	B,HH,SC
Erysimum 'Sulphur Delight'	B
Erysimum 'Super mix'	CL
Erysimum 'Suttons Persian Carpet'	S
Erysimum 'Tom Thumb' mix	BS,C,CL,CO,D,DT,J,KI, L,R,ST,TU,V
Erysimum 'Turkish Bazaar'	JE

Erysimum 'Vulcan'	B,BS,C,CL,J,KI,YA
Erysimum 'Vulcan Imp'	D
Erysimum wheeleri	B,FH,SC,SG,SW,T
Erysimum 'White Dame'	B,BD,BS,T,TU,VH
Erysimum 'World Hybrids'	B
Erysimum x allionii	BS,D,F,G,J,JE,KI,SU,TU, V
Erysimum x allionii imp	BS,L
Erysimum x allionii orange	B,BS,ST
Erysimum x allionii 'Orange Queen'	CL
Erysimum x allionii 'Spring Tapestry'	J,V
Erysimum 'Yellow Bird'	JE
Erythea armata	C,SA
Erythea edulis	SA
Erythrina abyssinica	B,SA
Erythrina amazonica	B
Erythrina americana	B
Erythrina berteroana	B,RE,SA
Erythrina caffra	B,SA,SI
Erythrina corallodendrum	B,C
Erythrina costaricensis	B,SA
Erythrina crista-galli	AP,B,C,CG,HA,JE,N,O, SA,SC,T,V
Erythrina dominguezii	B
Erythrina edulis	B
Erythrina falcata	B
Erythrina flabelliformis	B,SW
Erythrina fusca	B,RE,SA
Erythrina herbacea	B
Erythrina humeana	B,SI
Erythrina indica	HA,SA,V
Erythrina lanceolata	B
Erythrina latissima	B,SI
Erythrina livingstoniana	B,SA,SI
Erythrina lysistemon	B,C,RE
Erythrina poeppigiana	B,RE,SA
Erythrina princeps	SA
Erythrina rubrinervia	B
Erythrina senegalensis	B
Erythrina smithiana	B
Erythrina speciosa	B
Erythrina speciosa v rosea	B
Erythrina stricta	C
Erythrina variegata	B
Erythrina verna	B
Erythrina vespertilio	B,C,HA,O,SA
Erythrina zeyheri	B,SI
Erythrina 'Zompantlillo'	B
Erythrochiton brasiliense	CG
Erythronium californicum	AP,G,LG,NG,SC
Erythronium californicum 'White Beauty'	B,G,I,LG,PA
Erythronium 'Citronella'	B
Erythronium dens-canis	AP,B,C,CG,G,JE,SA,SC
Erythronium grandiflorum	AP,B,C,JE,SA,SW
Erythronium hendersonii	AP,B,G,SC
Erythronium montanum	B,C,JE
Erythronium multiscapoideum	AP,G,NG,SC
Erythronium oregonum	AP,B,JE,PA,SC
Erythronium revolutum	AP,B,JE,LG,SC,SG
Erythronium revolutum v johnsonii	AP,LG,SC,SG
Erythronium revolutum v smithii	C
Erythronium sp mix	AP,C,PA,SC
Erythrophleum africanum	SI
Erythrophleum chlorostachys	B,O
Erythrophleum fordii	B
Erythrophysa alata	B,SI

ERYTHROXYLON

Erythroxylon coca	CG
Escallonia alpina	SA
Escallonia florida	SA
Escallonia rosea	SA
Eschscholzia caespitosa	AP,B,SC
Eschscholzia caespitosa 'Sundew'	AP,B,C,J,KS,PM,T
Eschscholzia californica	AV,B,C,FH,G,HW,J,PM, RH,SG,VH
Eschscholzia californica, 8 types sep.pk	B
Eschscholzia californica 'Alba'	B,C,KS
Eschscholzia californica 'Apricot Bush'	F
Eschscholzia californica 'Apricot Chiffon'	B,C,F,KS
Eschscholzia cal. 'Apricot Flambeau'	DT,SE,T
Eschscholzia californica 'Aurantiaca'	KS
Eschscholzia cal. 'Aurantiaca Orange King'	B
Eschscholzia californica 'Ballerina' mix	BS,C,DT,KS,L,T
Eschscholzia californica 'Carmine King'	B,DT,KS
Eschscholzia californica 'Dalli'	B,BS,C,CL,D,J,O,T,U,V
Eschscholzia californica 'Golden Values'	F
Eschscholzia californica 'Golden West'	B
Eschscholzia californica 'Inferno'	F,SE,T
Eschscholzia californica 'Ivory Castle'	B,C
Eschscholzia californica 'Jersey Cream'	SE
Eschscholzia californica 'Mahogany Red'	B
Eschscholzia californica 'Mikado'	B,F,SE
Eschscholzia californica 'Milky White'	T
Eschscholzia californica 'Mission Bells'	BD,BS,C,CO,KI,ST,SU, T,TU
Eschscholzia californica mix single	DT,F
Eschscholzia californica mix special	S
Eschscholzia cal. 'Monarch Art Shades'	F,T,U
Eschscholzia californica 'Moonglow'	B
Eschscholzia californica 'Orange'	KS
Eschscholzia californica 'Pink Shades'	T
Eschscholzia californica 'Prima Ballerina'	F
Eschscholzia californica 'Purple Gleam'	B,C,KS,V
Eschscholzia californica 'Purple Violet'	T
Eschscholzia californica 'Red Chief'	B,C
Eschscholzia californica 'Rose Bush'	F,KS
Eschscholzia californica 'Rose Chiffon'	F,SE
Eschscholzia cal. 'Sugared Almonds'	SE
Eschscholzia californica 'Sundew'	V
Eschscholzia californica 'Thai Silk Apricot'	B
Eschscholzia californica 'Thai Silk Fire'	B
Eschscholzia californica 'Thai Silk' mix	D,J,T
Eschscholzia californica 'Thai Silk Orange'	B
Eschscholzia californica 'Thai Silk Rose'	B
Eschscholzia californica 'Unwins Superb'	U
Eschscholzia californica v maritima	B
Eschscholzia lobbii	SG
Eschscholzia lobbii 'Moonlight'	F
Eschscholzia mexicana	B,SW
Escobaria aguirreana	B
Escobaria albicolumnaria	B
Escobaria asperispina	Y
Escobaria bibeana	BC
Escobaria chaffeyi	B,BC
Escobaria cubensis	B
Escobaria dasyacantha	B,Y
Escobaria duncanii	B
Escobaria guadalupensis	B
Escobaria hester	B
Escobaria hesteri	B
Escobaria laredoi	B
Escobaria leei	B
Escobaria lloydii	B

Escobaria minima	B,BC,Y
Escobaria missouri. v asperispina	B
Escobaria missouri. v caespitosa	B
Escobaria missouriensis	B
Escobaria muehibaueriana	Y
Escobaria orcuttii	B
Escobaria orcuttii v koenigii	B
Escobaria orcuttii v macraxina	B
Escobaria organensis	B
Escobaria robbinsorum	B
Escobaria roseana	B,BC,Y
Escobaria runyonii	B
Escobaria sandbergii	B
Escobaria sneedii	B,BC
Escobaria tuberculosa	B
Escobaria tuberculosa v varicolor	B
Escobaria villardii	B
Escobaria vivipara	B,Y
Escobaria vivipara v arizonica	B,Y
Escobaria vivipara v desertii	B
Escobaria vivipara v kaibabensis	B
Escobaria vivipara v neomexicana	B
Escobaria vivipara v radiosa	B
Escobaria vivipara v rosea	B
Escobaria vivipara v zilziana	B
Escobaria zilziana	B
Escobaria zilziana chariacantha	BC
Escontria chiotilla	B
Esobe gooseberry	B
Espostoa cantaensis	CH,Y
Espostoa churinensis	BC,Y
Espostoa hylea	BC
Espostoa lanata	B,C,Y
Espostoa lanata rubrispina	BC
Espostoa laticormis	Y
Espostoa melanostele	B
Espostoa mirabilis	B,CH,Y
Espostoa mirabilis v primigena	Y
Espostoa nana	B,Y
Espostoa ritteri	CH,Y
Espostoa sp mix	C,Y
Etlingera elatior	B,RE
Etlingera hieroglyphica	B
Eucalyptus acaciiformis	B,C,HA
Eucalyptus accedens	B
Eucalyptus acies	AU,B
Eucalyptus acmenioides	B,C,HA,O
Eucalyptus 'Affinis'	B
Eucalyptus agglomerata	AU,B,HA,O
Eucalyptus aggregata	B,C,HA,O,SA,SH
Eucalyptus alba	B,HA,O
Eucalyptus albens	B,HA
Eucalyptus albida	B
Eucalyptus alpina	B,C,HA,O
Eucalyptus amplifolia	HA
Eucalyptus amplifolia v amplifolia	B
Eucalyptus amplifolia v sessiliflora	B
Eucalyptus amygdalina	AU,B,HA,O,SA
Eucalyptus anceps	B,O
Eucalyptus andrewsii	B
Eucalyptus andrewsii ssp andrewsii	O
Eucalyptus andrewsii ssp campanulata	B
Eucalyptus angulosa	B
Eucalyptus angustissima	B
Eucalyptus annulata	B
Eucalyptus apiculata	B

Eucalyptus arachnaea	B
Eucalyptus archeri	B,HA,O,RH,SA
Eucalyptus argillacea	B
Eucalyptus argophloia	B
Eucalyptus arnhemensis	B
Eucalyptus aromaphloia	B,HA,O
Eucalyptus aspera	B
Eucalyptus astringens	B,HA
Eucalyptus baileyana	B
Eucalyptus bakeri	B,HA
Eucalyptus balladoniensis	AU,B
Eucalyptus bancroftii	B,O
Eucalyptus banksii	B
Eucalyptus bauerana	B
Eucalyptus baxteri	B
Eucalyptus behriana	B,C
Eucalyptus benthamii	B
Eucalyptus beyeri	B
Eucalyptus bicostata	HA,SA,SH
Eucalyptus bigalerita	B,O
Eucalyptus blakelyi	B,C,HA
Eucalyptus blaxlandii	AU
Eucalyptus bleeseri	B,O
Eucalyptus bosistoana	B,HA
Eucalyptus botryoides	AU,C,HA,O,SA
Eucalyptus botryoides c.s	B
Eucalyptus botryoides v nana	B,O
Eucalyptus brachycorys	B
Eucalyptus brachyphylla	B
Eucalyptus brassiana	B
Eucalyptus brevifolia	B,O
Eucalyptus bridgesiana	B,C,HA,O,SA,SH
Eucalyptus brockwayi	B,O
Eucalyptus brookerana	B,O
Eucalyptus brownii	B
Eucalyptus brunnea	B
Eucalyptus buprestium	B
Eucalyptus burdettiana	AU,B,HA
Eucalyptus burgessiana	B
Eucalyptus burracoppinensis	B,O
Eucalyptus caesia	AU,C,HA,SA
Eucalyptus caesia ssp caesia	O
Eucalyptus caesia ssp magna	O
Eucalyptus caesia ssp magna c.s	B
Eucalyptus caesia weeping	B,SA
Eucalyptus calcareana	B
Eucalyptus calcicola	AU,B
Eucalyptus caleyi	B,O
Eucalyptus caliginosa	B,HA
Eucalyptus 'Callanii'	B
Eucalyptus calophylla	B,HA,O,SA
Eucalyptus calophylla 'Rosea'	B,HA,O
Eucalyptus calycogona	B,C,O
Eucalyptus camaldulensis	B,HA,O,SA
Eucalyptus camaldulensis ssp subcinerea	HA
Eucalyptus camaldulensis v brevirostris	B
Eucalyptus camaldulensis v obtusa	HA,O
Eucalyptus camaldulensis x rudis	AU,B
Eucalyptus cambageana	B
Eucalyptus camfieldii	B
Eucalyptus campaspe	B,HA,O
Eucalyptus camphora	B,HA,O,SA
Eucalyptus canaliculata	B,HA
Eucalyptus cannonii	AU
Eucalyptus capillosa ssp capillosa	B
Eucalyptus capillosa ssp polyclada	B

Eucalyptus capitellata	B
Eucalyptus carnei	B
Eucalyptus celastroides	B
Eucalyptus celastroides ssp virella	B
Eucalyptus centralis	B
Eucalyptus cephalocarpa	B,O
Eucalyptus ceratocorys	B
Eucalyptus cinerea	C,CP,HA,O,SA,SH
Eucalyptus cinerea c.s	B
Eucalyptus cinerea 'Pendula'	B
Eucalyptus cinerea ssp cephalocarpa	HA
Eucalyptus citriodora	B,BS,C,CL,CP,HA,KS,N, O,SA,T
Eucalyptus cladocalyx	B,HA,O,SA
Eucalyptus cladocalyx 'Nana'	AU,HA,O,SA
Eucalyptus cladocalyx 'Nana' c.s	B
Eucalyptus clelandi	B
Eucalyptus cloeziana	B,HA,O
Eucalyptus cneorifolia	AU,B,HA
Eucalyptus coccifera	AU,B,C,HA,N,O,SA,SH
Eucalyptus concinna	AU,B
Eucalyptus conferruminata	AU,B
Eucalyptus confluens	B
Eucalyptus conglobata	B
Eucalyptus conglomerata	B
Eucalyptus conica	B
Eucalyptus 'Conservatory' mix	U,V
Eucalyptus consideniana	B,C,HA
Eucalyptus coolabah	B
Eucalyptus cooperana	B
Eucalyptus cordata	AU,B,C,HA,O,SA,SH
Eucalyptus cornuta	AU,B,C,SA
Eucalyptus coronata	B
Eucalyptus corrugata	B
Eucalyptus cosmophylla	B,C,HA
Eucalyptus crebra	B,HA,O,SA,SH
Eucalyptus crenulata	B,HA,O,SA
Eucalyptus crucis	AU,SA
Eucalyptus crucis ssp crucis	B,O
Eucalyptus curtisii	B,HA,O
Eucalyptus cyanophylla	B
Eucalyptus cylindriflora	B
Eucalyptus cylindrocarpa	B
Eucalyptus cypellocarpa	B,C,HA,O,SA
Eucalyptus dalrympleana	AU,B,C,HA,N,O,SA
Eucalyptus dalrympleana ssp heptantha	B
Eucalyptus dawsonii c.s	B
Eucalyptus dealbata	B,HA
Eucalyptus deanei	B,HA,O
Eucalyptus debeuzevillei	SA
Eucalyptus decaisniana	B
Eucalyptus decipiens	B,O
Eucalyptus decorticans	B,HA
Eucalyptus decurva	AU,B
Eucalyptus deglupta	B,O
Eucalyptus delegatensis	AU,B,C,HA,O,SA
Eucalyptus dendromorpha	B
Eucalyptus desmondensis	B,O
Eucalyptus dicromophloia	B
Eucalyptus dielsii	B
Eucalyptus diptera	B
Eucalyptus diversicolor	B,O
Eucalyptus diversifolia	AU,B,HA
Eucalyptus dives	AU,B,HA,O,SA
Eucalyptus doratoxylon	B
Eucalyptus drepanophylla	B,O

EUCALYPTUS

Eucalyptus drummondii	B
Eucalyptus drysdalensis	B
Eucalyptus dumosa	AU,B,HA
Eucalyptus dundasii	B,O
Eucalyptus dunnii	HA,O
Eucalyptus dunnii c.s	B
Eucalyptus dwyeri	B,C
Eucalyptus ebbanoensis	B
Eucalyptus effusa	B
Eucalyptus elata	B,HA,O
Eucalyptus elata andreana	SH
Eucalyptus eremophila	AU,B,HA,O,SA
Eucalyptus eremophila red	SA
Eucalyptus erythranda	O
Eucalyptus erythrocorys	AU,B,C,HA,O,SA
Eucalyptus erythronema	AU,B,C,HA,O
Eucalyptus erythronema red	HA
Eucalyptus erythronema v marginata	O
Eucalyptus erythronema v marg. yellow fl	AU,B
Eucalyptus eudesmioides ssp eudes.	B
Eucalyptus eugenioides	B,HA
Eucalyptus ewartiana	B
Eucalyptus exilis	B
Eucalyptus eximia	B,HA
Eucalyptus eximia v nana	B,C,HA,O,SA,SH
Eucalyptus exserta	B,HA
Eucalyptus falcata	B
Eucalyptus famelica	B
Eucalyptus fasciculosa	B,HA
Eucalyptus fastigata	AU,B,HA,O
Eucalyptus ferruginea	B
Eucalyptus fibrosa	B
Eucalyptus fibrosa ssp fibrosa	HA
Eucalyptus fibrosa ssp nubila	B
Eucalyptus ficifolia	B,C,HA,O,SA
Eucalyptus fl mix	C
Eucalyptus flavida	B
Eucalyptus flocktoniae	AU,B,O
Eucalyptus foecunda	AU,B,HA
Eucalyptus formanii	B
Eucalyptus forrestiana	B,C,HA,O,SA
Eucalyptus forrestiana ssp dolichorhyncha	B,O
Eucalyptus forrestiana ssp stoatei	B
Eucalyptus fraseri	B
Eucalyptus fraxinoides	AU,B,C,HA,O
Eucalyptus froggattii	B
Eucalyptus 'Frost Resistant Sp Mix'	T
Eucalyptus fruticetorum	C
Eucalyptus gamophylla	AU,B,C,O,SA
Eucalyptus gardneri	AU,B,HA,O
Eucalyptus georgei	B
Eucalyptus gillenii	B
Eucalyptus gillii	AU,B,HA,SA
Eucalyptus gittinsii	B
Eucalyptus glaucescens	AU,B,C,HA,O,SA,SH
Eucalyptus globoidea	B,HA
Eucalyptus globulus	BD,BS,C,CL,CP,L,O,RE, SA,SH,V
Eucalyptus globulus ssp bicostata	B,HA,O
Eucalyptus globulus ssp globulus	HA,O
Eucalyptus globulus ssp globulus c.s	B
Eucalyptus globulus ssp glob. 'Compacta'	B,HA,O,SA
Eucalyptus globulus ssp maidenii	B,HA,O
Eucalyptus gomphocephala	AU,B,HA,O,SA
Eucalyptus gongylocarpa	B
Eucalyptus goniantha ssp goniantha	B

Eucalyptus goniocalyx	B,HA,O
Eucalyptus gracilis	B,HA
Eucalyptus grandis	HA,O
Eucalyptus grandis c.s	B
Eucalyptus gregsoniana	AU,B,C,HA,O,RH,SA,SH
Eucalyptus griffithsii	B
Eucalyptus grossa	B,C,HA,RE,SA
Eucalyptus guilfoylei	B
Eucalyptus gullickii	SH
Eucalyptus gummifera	HA,O
Eucalyptus gummifera c.s	B
Eucalyptus gunnii	AU,BD,BS,C,F,HA,KI,L, N,O,SA,SH,YA
Eucalyptus gunnii c.s	B,CL
Eucalyptus gunnii 'Silver Drop'	T
Eucalyptus haemastoma	B,HA
Eucalyptus haematoxylon	B
Eucalyptus halophila	B
Eucalyptus henryi	B
Eucalyptus herbertiana	B
Eucalyptus hypochlamydea ssp hypo.	B
Eucalyptus incerata	B
Eucalyptus incrassata	B,HA
Eucalyptus indurata	B
Eucalyptus intermedia	B,HA,O
Eucalyptus intertexta	B,HA,O
Eucalyptus jacksonii	B
Eucalyptus johnstonii	AU,B,C,O,SA
Eucalyptus jucunda	B
Eucalyptus jutsonii	B
Eucalyptus kartzoffiana	B,HA
Eucalyptus kessellii	B
Eucalyptus kingsmillii	B
Eucalyptus kitsoniana	B,C,HA
Eucalyptus kochii ssp kochii	B
Eucalyptus kochii ssp plenissima	B,O
Eucalyptus kondinensis	B,HA,O
Eucalyptus kruseana	AU,B,HA,O,SA,SH
Eucalyptus kybeanensis	AU,B,C
Eucalyptus laeliae	B
Eucalyptus laevopinea	AU,B
Eucalyptus lane-poolei	B,O
Eucalyptus lansdowneana	AU
Eucalyptus lansd. ssp albopurpurea	B,O
Eucalyptus lansd. ssp lansdowneana	B,O
Eucalyptus laophila	AU
Eucalyptus largiflorens	B,HA
Eucalyptus lateritica	B
Eucalyptus lehmannii	AU,B,HA,O
Eucalyptus leptocalyx	AU,B
Eucalyptus leptophleba	HA
Eucalyptus leptophylla	AU,B
Eucalyptus leptopoda	B
Eucalyptus lesouefii	B
Eucalyptus leucophloia	B
Eucalyptus leucoxylon	AU,HA,SA
Eucalyptus leucoxylon rosea	HA,SA
Eucalyptus leucoxylon ssp leucoxylon	B,O
Eucalyptus leucoxylon ssp megalocarpa	B,HA,O,SA
Eucalyptus leucoxylon ssp petiolaris	B
Eucalyptus leuc. ssp pruinosa 'Rosea'	B,O
Eucalyptus leuc. v macrocarpa rosea	HA
Eucalyptus leuhmanniana	HA
Eucalyptus ligulata	AU
Eucalyptus ligustrina	B
Eucalyptus linearis	C

Eucalyptus 'Little Boy Blue'	B,SA,SH
Eucalyptus littorea	AU
Eucalyptus livida	B
Eucalyptus longicornis	B
Eucalyptus longifolia	B
Eucalyptus loxophleba	B
Eucalyptus loxophleba ssp gratiae	B
Eucalyptus loxophleba ssp lissophloia	B
Eucalyptus luehmanniana	B
Eucalyptus macarthurii	AU,B,HA,O,SA
Eucalyptus mackintii	B
Eucalyptus macrandra	AU,B,O
Eucalyptus macrocarpa	C,HA,O,SA,T
Eucalyptus macrocarpa c.s	B
Eucalyptus macrocarpa ssp elachantha	B
Eucalyptus macrorhyncha	HA
Eucalyptus macrorhyncha ssp cannonii	B
Eucalyptus macrorhyncha ssp macror.	B
Eucalyptus maculata	B,HA,O
Eucalyptus maidenii	SA
Eucalyptus mannensis	B,HA
Eucalyptus mannifera	HA,SH
Eucalyptus mannifera ssp maculosa	B,HA,O
Eucalyptus mannifera ssp mannifera	B
Eucalyptus mannifera ssp praecox	B
Eucalyptus marginata	B,O
Eucalyptus marginata v thalassica	B
Eucalyptus mckieana	B
Eucalyptus megacarpa	B
Eucalyptus megacornuta	B
Eucalyptus melanophloia	B,HA,SH
Eucalyptus melanoxylon	B
Eucalyptus melliodora	B,HA
Eucalyptus merrickiae	B
Eucalyptus micranthera	B
Eucalyptus microcarpa	B,HA
Eucalyptus microcorys	HA,SA
Eucalyptus microcorys c.s	B
Eucalyptus microtheca	AU,B,HA,O
Eucalyptus miniata	B
Eucalyptus misella	B
Eucalyptus mitchelliana	B,O
Eucalyptus moluccana	B,HA,O
Eucalyptus 'Moon Lagoon'	O
Eucalyptus moorei	B,HA,SH
Eucalyptus moorei nana	AU,C,N,O,SA
Eucalyptus morrisbyi	B
Eucalyptus morrisii	B,HA
Eucalyptus muellarana	B,C,HA
Eucalyptus neglecta	B,O,SA
Eucalyptus newbeyi	B
Eucalyptus nicholii	C,HA,O,SA
Eucalyptus nicholii c.s	B
Eucalyptus nigra	B
Eucalyptus nigrifunda	B
Eucalyptus nitens	AU,B,C,HA,O,SA
Eucalyptus nitida	B,C,O,SA
Eucalyptus nortonii	B,HA
Eucalyptus notabilis	B
Eucalyptus nova-anglica	B,HA,O,SA,SH
Eucalyptus nutans	B,HA,O,SA
Eucalyptus obliqua	B,HA,O,SA
Eucalyptus oblonga	B
Eucalyptus obtusiflora	B,O,SA
Eucalyptus occidentalis	AU,B,HA,O
Eucalyptus occidentalis v stenantha	B
Eucalyptus ochrophloia	B,O
Eucalyptus odontocarpa	B
Eucalyptus odorata	B,HA
Eucalyptus oldfieldii	B
Eucalyptus oleosa	HA
Eucalyptus oleosa v oleosa	B
Eucalyptus olsenii	AU,HA
Eucalyptus orbifolia	AU,B,O,SA
Eucalyptus oreades	AU,B,O
Eucalyptus orgadophila	B
Eucalyptus ovata	HA,O
Eucalyptus ovata v ovata c.s	B
Eucalyptus ovularis	B
Eucalyptus oxymitra	AU,B,HA
Eucalyptus pachycalyx	B
Eucalyptus pachyloma	B
Eucalyptus pachyphylla	AU,B,O
Eucalyptus paliformis	AU
Eucalyptus paniculata	HA
Eucalyptus paniculata c.s	B
Eucalyptus papuana	B,O
Eucalyptus parramattensis	B,HA
Eucalyptus parvifolia	B,C,HA,O,RH,SA
Eucalyptus patellaris	B
Eucalyptus patens	B
Eucalyptus pauciflora	B,C,HA,SH
Eucalyptus pauciflora 'Pendula'	B,SA
Eucalyptus pauciflora ssp debeuzevillei	AU,B
Eucalyptus pauciflora ssp niphophila	AU,B,BS,C,HA,N,O,RH, SA,T
Eucalyptus pauciflora ssp pauciflora	AU,O
Eucalyptus pellita	B,O
Eucalyptus peltata	B
Eucalyptus pendens	B
Eucalyptus perfoliata	B
Eucalyptus perriniana	AU,C,N,O,RH,SA,SH
Eucalyptus perriniana c.s	B
Eucalyptus perriniana Tas	AU
Eucalyptus petraea	B
Eucalyptus phaeotricha	HA
Eucalyptus phoenicia	AU,B
Eucalyptus pileata	B
Eucalyptus pilligaensis	B
Eucalyptus pilularis	B,HA,O
Eucalyptus pimpiniana	B
Eucalyptus piperita	B,HA,O
Eucalyptus piperita ssp urceolaris	B,HA
Eucalyptus planchoniana	B,HA,O
Eucalyptus platycorys	B
Eucalyptus platyphylla	B
Eucalyptus platypus	AU,B,HA
Eucalyptus platypus v heterophylla red fl	B
Eucalyptus platypus v platypus	O
Eucalyptus pluricaulis ssp porphyrea	B,O
Eucalyptus polita	B
Eucalyptus polyanthemos	B,C,HA,O,SA,SH
Eucalyptus polybractea	B
Eucalyptus polycarpa	B,O
Eucalyptus populnea	B,HA,O
Eucalyptus populnea x crebra 'Rariflora'	B
Eucalyptus porosa	B,HA
Eucalyptus porrecta	B
Eucalyptus preissiana	AU,B,HA,O
Eucalyptus preissiana x staeri	B
Eucalyptus propinqua	B,HA
Eucalyptus pruinosa	B

EUCALYPTUS

Eucalyptus pryoriana	AU,B,HA	Eucalyptus sp mix foliage	O
Eucalyptus pseudoglobulus	HA,SA	Eucalyptus sp tropical mix	C
Eucalyptus pterocarpa	B	Eucalyptus spathulata	HA,O
Eucalyptus ptychocarpa	B,HA,O	Eucalyptus spathulata c.s	B
Eucalyptus pulchella	AU,B,HA,O	Eucalyptus spathulata v grandiflora	B
Eucalyptus pulverulenta	AU,C,HA,O,SA,SH	Eucalyptus staeri	B
Eucalyptus pulverulenta c.s	B	Eucalyptus staigerana	B
Eucalyptus pumila	B	Eucalyptus steedmanii	AU,B,HA
Eucalyptus punctata	HA	Eucalyptus stellulata	AU,B,C,HA,N,O,SA,SH
Eucalyptus punctata c.s	B	Eucalyptus stoatei	HA,O
Eucalyptus punctata v didyma	B	Eucalyptus stowardii	B
Eucalyptus punctata v longistrata	B,HA	Eucalyptus striaticalyx	B
Eucalyptus pyriformis	O	Eucalyptus stricklandii	AU,B,C,HA,O
Eucalyptus pyriformis pink fl	B	Eucalyptus stricta	B,C,HA,SA
Eucalyptus pyrocarpa	B	Eucalyptus stricta v subcampanulata	B
Eucalyptus quadrangulata	B	Eucalyptus sturgissiana	B,C,O,SH
Eucalyptus radiata	AU,C,HA,SA,SH	Eucalyptus subcrenulata	AU,B,C,O,SA
Eucalyptus radiata ssp radiata	B,O	Eucalyptus talyuberlup	AU,B
Eucalyptus radiata ssp robertsonii	B	Eucalyptus tenuipes	B,HA
Eucalyptus radiata v australiana	B,O	Eucalyptus tenuiramis	AU,B,C,O,SA
Eucalyptus raveretiana	B	Eucalyptus tereticornis	HA,O
Eucalyptus recondita	B	Eucalyptus tereticornis c.s	B
Eucalyptus redacta	B	Eucalyptus terminalis	B
Eucalyptus redunca	B	Eucalyptus tessellaris	B,HA,O
Eucalyptus regnans	B,C,HA,O,SA	Eucalyptus tetragona	B,O,SH
Eucalyptus remota	B	Eucalyptus tetraptera	AU,B,C,HA,O
Eucalyptus resinifera	B,HA,O,SA	Eucalyptus tet. x angulosa 'Erythrandra'	B
Eucalyptus rhodantha	AU,B,O	Eucalyptus tetrodonta	B
Eucalyptus rigens	B	Eucalyptus thozetiana	B
Eucalyptus rigidula	B	Eucalyptus 'Tinghaensis'	B
Eucalyptus risdonii	AU,B,C,HA,N,O,SA,SH	Eucalyptus todtiana	B
Eucalyptus robusta	AU,B,HA,O,SA	Eucalyptus torelliana	HA,O
Eucalyptus rodwayi	AU,B,O	Eucalyptus torelliana c.s	B
Eucalyptus rossii	B,C,HA	Eucalyptus torquata	AU,B,C,HA,O,RE,SA
Eucalyptus rubida	C,HA,O,SA,SH	Eucalyptus tor. x woodwardii 'Torwood'	AU,B,O
Eucalyptus rubida c.s	B	Eucalyptus 'Trabuti'	B
Eucalyptus rudis	AU,B,O	Eucalyptus trachyphloia	B,HA
Eucalyptus rugosa	B,O	Eucalyptus transcontinentalis	AU,B
Eucalyptus rummeryi	B	Eucalyptus 'Tricarpa'	B
Eucalyptus salicola	B	Eucalyptus triflora	O
Eucalyptus saligna	B,HA,O,SA	Eucalyptus trivalvis	B
Eucalyptus salmonophloia	B,HA,O	Eucalyptus uceolaris	O
Eucalyptus salubris	AU,B,HA,O	Eucalyptus umbra	HA
Eucalyptus salubris v glauca	B	Eucalyptus umbra ssp umbra	B
Eucalyptus sargentii	AU,B,O	Eucalyptus uncinata	AU,B
Eucalyptus sclerophylla	B	Eucalyptus urnigera	B,C,O,SA
Eucalyptus scoparia	B,HA,O,SA,SH	Eucalyptus urophylla	B
Eucalyptus seeana	B,HA	Eucalyptus vernicosa	AU,O
Eucalyptus sepulcralis	B,O	Eucalyptus victrix	B
Eucalyptus sessilis	B	Eucalyptus viminalis	B,C,HA,O,SA
Eucalyptus setosa	AU,B,O	Eucalyptus viminalis ssp cygnetensis	B
Eucalyptus sheathiana	B	Eucalyptus viridis	B,HA,SA
Eucalyptus shirleyi	B	Eucalyptus wandoo	B,O
Eucalyptus siderophloia	B,HA	Eucalyptus watsoniana	B
Eucalyptus sideroxylon	AU,B,HA,O,SA	Eucalyptus websterana	AU,B,SA
Eucalyptus sideroxylon 'Rosea'	B,HA,SA	Eucalyptus websterana ssp norsemanica	O
Eucalyptus sideroxylon ssp tricarpa	B,HA	Eucalyptus whitei	B
Eucalyptus sieberi	AU,B,HA,O,SA	Eucalyptus willisii	B
Eucalyptus signata	B,HA	Eucalyptus woodwardii	AU,B,HA,O,RE,SA
Eucalyptus 'Silver Plate'	CL	Eucalyptus woollsiana	B
Eucalyptus 'Silver Spoon'	B	Eucalyptus xanthonema	B
Eucalyptus similis	B	Eucalyptus yalatensis	B
Eucalyptus smithii	B,HA,O,SA	Eucalyptus youmanii	B,O,SA
Eucalyptus socialis	B,HA,O	Eucalyptus youngiana	B,O
Eucalyptus sp dw mix	C	Eucalyptus yumbarrana	AU,B
Eucalyptus sp mix	C,S	Eucalyptus zygophylla	B

EUCLEA

Euclea acutifolia	B	Eupatorium altissimum	PR
Euclea crispa ssp crispa	B	Eupatorium cannabinum	B,C,CG,CO,G,JE,LA,SA
Euclea natalensis	B,SI		,SC,SG
Euclea pseudabenus	B,SI	Eupatorium coelestinum	JE,PR
Euclea racemosa	B,SI	Eupatorium dubium	B
Euclea tomentosa	B,SI	Eupatorium hyssopifolius	B,PR
Euclea undulata	SI	Eupatorium ligustrinum	SA
Euclinia longiflora	B	Eupatorium maculatum	B,JE,SG
Eucnide bartonioides	B,CG,T	Eupatorium maculatum 'Glow'	B
Eucodonia hyb & var mix	C	Eupatorium maculatum v atropurpureum	B,JE,PR,SA,T
Eucomis autumnalis	B,C,SI	Eupatorium perfoliatum	B,CP,JE,P,PR,SA
Eucomis bicolor	AP,B,C,E,G,PM,SI	Eupatorium purpureum	B,BS,C,CP,G,JE,KI,NT,
Eucomis bicolor v alba	C,G		SA,SC,SG
Eucomis comosa	C,G,LG,SG	Eupatorium rotundifolium	C,PR
Eucomis montana	SI	Eupatorium rugosum	B,C,G,JE,SC
Eucomis pole-evansi	B,G,SC,SI	Eupatorium semiserratum	B
Eucommia ulmoides	B,C,SA	Euphorbia amygdaloides	B,JE,RH,SA
Eucryphia cordifolia	N,SA	Euphorbia amygdaloides 'Purpurea'	B,JE,P,SA,T
Eucryphia glutinosa	AU,N,SA,SG	Euphorbia amygdaloides v robbiae	B,P,RH,SA
Eucryphia lucida	B,N,O,SA	Euphorbia angularis	SG
Eucryphia moorei	B,SA	Euphorbia antiquorum	CG
Eugenia aggregata	B	Euphorbia 'Borde sp & Fl Arranging Mix'	T
Eugenia bracteata	B	Euphorbia bothii	CH
Eugenia brasiliensis	B	Euphorbia brittingeri	B,CG,G
Eugenia buxifolia	B	Euphorbia caput-medusae	B,SI
Eugenia cumini	HA	Euphorbia characias	AP,B,C,F,JE,RH,SA
Eugenia leuhmannii	B,HA,O	Euphorbia characias ssp wulfenii	B,F,JE,P,RH,T,W
Eugenia myrtifolia	HA,O,SA,SH	Euphorbia c. ssp wulfenii 'Jimmy Platt'	C
Eugenia reinwardtiana	B	Euphorbia c. ssp wulfenii 'John Tomlinson'	C
Eugenia stipitata	B	Euphorbia c. ssp wulfenii 'Lambrook Gold'	W
Eugenia uniflora	B,HA	Euphorbia clandestina	B
Eugenia uniflora 'Adams Concord'	B	Euphorbia clava	B
Eugenia uniflora 'My Fancy'	B	Euphorbia clavaroides v truncata	B
Eugenia uvalha	B	Euphorbia cognata	CC
Eugenia victoriana	B	Euphorbia coralloides	AP,B,C,G,JE,P,SA,SC
Eulophia clavicornis	SI	Euphorbia cornigera	P,SA
Eulophia livingstoniana	B	Euphorbia corollata	B,JE,PR
Eulophia sp	SI	Euphorbia cotinifolia	B
Eulophia speciosa	SI	Euphorbia cyathophora	B,J,KS,V
Eulophia streptopetala	B	Euphorbia cyparissias	B,C,F,JE,SA,W
Eulychnia castanea	Y	Euphorbia drummondii	B
Euonymus alatus	B,G,RH,SA,SG	Euphorbia dulcis 'Chameleon'	B,P,SC
Euonymus americanus	B	Euphorbia enopla	CH
Euonymus atropurpureus	B,SG	Euphorbia exigua	CG
Euonymus bungeanus	SA	Euphorbia ferox	CH
Euonymus bungeanus 'Pink Lady'	B	Euphorbia fischerana	SG
Euonymus europaeus	B,C,CG,RH,SA,SG	Euphorbia 'Golden Foam'	B,P
Euonymus europaeus 'Albus'	SG	Euphorbia grandialata	SI
Euonymus europaeus v intermedius	RH	Euphorbia grandicornis	B,C
Euonymus fortunei	B	Euphorbia griffithii	JE
Euonymus fortunei 'Vegetus'	B	Euphorbia griffithii 'Fireglow'	B,P
Euonymus fortunei 'Vegetus Sarcoxi'	B	Euphorbia hamata	B,Y
Euonymus hamiltonianus	B	Euphorbia helioscopia	B,CG
Euonymus hamilt.ssp sieboldianus	B,RH,SA,SG	Euphorbia heterophylla see cyathora	
Euonymus japonicus	B,CG	Euphorbia hirta	B
Euonymus latifolius	CG	Euphorbia horrida	CH
Euonymus leiophloeus	SG	Euphorbia hyberna	P
Euonymus maackii	SG	Euphorbia inermis	Y
Euonymus maximowiczianus	SG	Euphorbia ingens	B
Euonymus myrianthus	RH	Euphorbia ipecacuanha	CG
Euonymus oxyphyllus	C,SC	Euphorbia komponii	SI
Euonymus phellomanus	SC,SG	Euphorbia lathyris	AP,B,BS,C,CP,G,JE,KI,
Euonymus planipes	B,C,G,RH,SA		SA,SG
Euonymus sachalinensis see planipes		Euphorbia leucocephala	B,C
Euonymus sacrosanctus	SG	Euphorbia lophogona	SG
Euonymus verrucosus	SG	Euphorbia 'Magic Flute'	U

EUPHORBIA

Euphorbia marginata 'Early Snow'	B,J
Euphorbia marginata 'Kilimanjaro'	B
Euphorbia marginata 'Late Snow'	B
Euphorbia marginata 'Snow Top'	B
Euphorbia marginata 'Summer Icicle'	B,BD,BS,T,VH
Euphorbia marginata (V)	B,BS,C,HW,KS,L,S,V
Euphorbia mellifera	AP,B,C,P,SA
Euphorbia meloformis	Y
Euphorbia milii	B
Euphorbia multiceps	B
Euphorbia myrsinites	AP,B,BS,C,CL,F,FH,G,
	JE,SA,SC,SG
Euphorbia nicaeensis	B,C,JE,SA
Euphorbia obesa	B,BC,SI,Y
Euphorbia palustris	B,G,JE,SA
Euphorbia palustris 'Zauberflote'	C
Euphorbia pendula	SG
Euphorbia pilosa	B,NS
Euphorbia pinea	SA
Euphorbia pithyusa	P
Euphorbia platyphyllos	B,CG,SG
Euphorbia polychroma	B,BD,BS,C,CL,F,G,JE,
	SA,V
Euphorbia pulcherrima 'Santa Catarina'	B
Euphorbia ramipressa	SG
Fuphorbia regis-jubae	C
Euphorbia rigida	B
Euphorbia salicifolia	B
Euphorbia schoenlandii	B,C,GC,SI,Y
Euphorbia seduduniensis	SG
Euphorbia seguieriana	B,CG,JE,SA
Euphorbia shillingii	SA
Euphorbia sikkimensis	B,FH,P
Euphorbia sp 'Hardy Mix'	C,P
Euphorbia sp 'Succulent Mix'	C
Euphorbia spinosa	JE
Euphorbia tirucallii	SG
Euphorbia trigona	SG
Euphorbia tuberculata	B,SI,Y
Euphorbia tuberculatoides	B,Y
Euphorbia villosa	B
Euphorbia virosa	B,SI
Euphorbia wallichii	AP,JE,SC,T
Euphorbia wallichii 'T&M Form'	T
Euphrasia cockayniana	SS
Euphrasia monroi	SS
Euphrasia revoluta	SS
Euphrasia salisburgensis	SG
Euphrasia stricta	B
Euphrasia zelandica	SS
Eurea lacinata	RE
Eurotia lanata	B
Eurya japonica	CG
Eurya marginata	CG
Eurycorymbus cavalieri	B
Euryops abrotanifolius	B,SI
Euryops brevipapposus	B,SI
Euryops chrysanthemoides	B,SI
Euryops decipiens	B,SI
Euryops dregeanus	B,SI
Euryops erectus	B,SI
Euryops lateriflorus	B,SI
Euryops linearis	B,SI
Euryops othonoides	B,SI
Euryops pectinatus	B,SI
Euryops rehmannii	B,SI

Euryops speciosissimus	B,SI
Euryops tenuissimus	B,SA,SI
Euryops transvaalensis	SI
Euryops tysonii	B,SI
Euryops virgineus	B,C,SI
Euryops wagnerii	B,SI
Eustoma exaltatum	B,SW
Eustoma grandiflorum	V
Eustoma grandiflorum 'Dbl Edge Mix'	T
Eustoma grandiflorum 'Dbl Pink Picotee'	SE
Eustoma grandiflorum f1 hyb 'Blue Lisa'	BS
Eustoma grandiflorum f1 hyb 'Echo' mix	C
Eustoma grandiflorum f1 hyb 'Echo' s-c	C,T
Eustoma grandiflorum f1 hyb 'Heidi'	D,S
Eustoma grand. f1 hyb 'Mermaid Blue'	CL
Eustoma grand. f1 hyb 'Mermaid Mix'	T
Eustoma grandiflorum f1 hyb 'Mickey'	T
Eustoma grandiflorum f1 hyb 'Mix'	T
Eustoma grandiflorum f1 hyb 'Yodel' mix	C
Eustoma grandiflorum f1 hyb 'Yodel' s-c	C
Eustoma grandilforum 'Primrose Dbl'	SE
Eustoma grandilforum 'Rainy Orange'	SE
Eustrephus latifolius	B,HA,SA
Eutaxia epacridioides	B
Eutaxia parvifolia	B,SA
Euterpe dominicana	B
Euterpe edulis	B,O,SA
Euterpe globosa	B
Euterpe macrospadix	O,RE
Evodiopanax innovans	CG
Evolvulus alsinoides	B
Evolvulus arizonicus	B,SW
Exacum affine	BS,KI
Exacum affine 'Midget' blue	BD,BS,C,CL,J,L
Exacum affine 'Midget' white	B,BD,BS,C,CL
Exacum affine 'Starlight Fragrance'	S
Exacum 'Best Blue Improved'	YA
Exacum 'Best Rose'	U
Exacum 'Best White Imp'	YA
Exacum pedunculatum	B
Exacum 'Royal Dane'	YA
Exacum 'Sweet Star'	U
Exacum 'Tiddywinks'	BS
Exocarpos bidwillii	SS
Exocarpos sparteus	B
Exochorda giraldii	B,SA
Exochorda giraldii v wilsonii	B
Exochorda racemosa	B,CG,SA
Fadogia agrestis	B
Fadogia caessneri	B
Fagara zanthoxyloides	B
Fagonia mollis	B
Fagopyrum esculentum	G,KS,SU
Fagopyrum tataricum	CG
Fagraea berterana	B
Fagus crenata	B,N,SA
Fagus engleriana	B
Fagus grandifolia	B,SA
Fagus longipetiolata	B
Fagus lucida	N
Fagus orientalis	B,SA
Fagus sylvatica	B,C,SA
Fagus sylvatica 'Atropurpurea'	B,C,N,RS,SA
Fagus sylvatica heterophylla	N
Faidherbia albida	B,SI
Falcaria vulgaris	B

FALCATUM

Falcatum variegatum	CG
Fallopia aubertii	C
Fallopia cuspidatum	B
Fallopia cuspidatum v compactum	B
Fallopia dumetorum	B
Fallugia paradoxa	B,SA,SW
Falsa conejera	B
Fargesia murieliae	JE
Faroa axillaris	B
Farsetia aegyptica	B
Fascicularia bicolor	SA
Fatsia japonica	B,BS,C,CG,CL,KI,LG,N, S,SG,ST,T
Faucaria albidens	B
Faucaria bosscheana	B,CH,Y
Faucaria bosscheana v haagei	B
Faucaria britteniae	B,CH,Y
Faucaria candida	B
Faucaria felina ssp felina	B
Faucaria felina v jamesii	B
Faucaria kingiae	B
Faucaria longifolia	B
Faucaria lupina	B
Faucaria mix	Y
Faucaria paucidens	B
Faucaria peersii	B
Faucaria plana	B
Faucaria speciosa	B
Faucaria subintegra	B,CH,Y
Faucaria tigrina	B,SI
Faucaria tuberculosa	B,SI,Y
Faurea speciosa	B
Fedia cornucopiae	AP,B,C,G
Felicia aethiopica	B,C,SA,SI
Felicia aethiopica ssp aethiopica	B
Felicia amoena	AP,FH
Felicia australis	SI
Felicia bergerana	B,DT,FH,S,SE,T
Felicia bergerana 'Cub Scout'	C,KS
Felicia dregei	B,SI
Felicia echinata	B,SA,SI
Felicia elongata	SI
Felicia filifolia	B,SI
Felicia filifolia ssp bodkinii	B,SI
Felicia fruticosa	B,SI
Felicia heterophylla	CO,SG,SI
Felicia heterophylla pink	B
Felicia heterophylla 'Spring Marchen'	CL
Felicia heterophylla 'The Blues'	BS,C,FH,KS,L,S,V
Felicia heterophylla 'The Rose'	BS,C,KS,V
Felicia hyssopifolia	B,SI
Felicia minima	B,SI
Felicia rosulata	FH,SG
Felicia sp	SI
Felicia tenella	B,SI
Felicia uliginosa	AP,FH,SC
Fendlera rupicola	B,SW
Fenestraria aurantiaca f rhopalophylla	B,SI,Y
Fenestraria aur. f rhopalophylla CM99	Y
Fenestraria aur. f rhopalophylla 'Fireworth'	B,SI
Fenestraria aur. f rhopalophylla hybs.	B
Fenestraria sp mix	C
Feretia apodanthera	B
Ferocactus acanthodes see cylandraceus	
Ferocactus alamosanus	Y
Ferocactus corniferus	B

Ferocactus cylindraceus	B,CH,Y
Ferocactus cylindraceus tortulospinus	BC
Ferocactus cylindraceus v eastwoodiae	B,Y
Ferocactus cylindraceus v lecontei	B,Y
Ferocactus diguettii	B
Ferocactus echidne	B
Ferocactus echidne v aurispina	GC,Y
Ferocactus emoryi	B,CH,Y
Ferocactus flavispinus	B
Ferocactus flavovirens	B,Y
Ferocactus fordii	Y
Ferocactus gatesii	B
Ferocactus glaucescens	B,BC,Y
Ferocactus gracilis	B,CH
Ferocactus gracilis v coloratus	B,BC
Ferocactus hamatacanthus	B,Y
Ferocactus herrerae	B,CH
Ferocactus histrix	B,CH,Y
Ferocactus latispinus	B,BC,CH,Y
Ferocactus latispinus v flavispinus	Y
Ferocactus latispinus v spiralis	B
Ferocactus lindsayi	B
Ferocactus macrodiscus	B,BC,Y
Ferocactus novilis	B,Y
Ferocactus peninsulae	B
Ferocactus peninsulae v santa-maria	B
Ferocactus peninsulae v townsendianus	B
Ferocactus peninsulae v viscainensis	B
Ferocactus pilosus	B,GC,Y
Ferocactus rectispinus	B,BC
Ferocactus robustus	B,Y
Ferocactus santa-maria	B
Ferocactus schwarzii	CH,Y
Ferocactus sinuatus	B
Ferocactus sinuatus v papyracanthus	B
Ferocactus sp mix	C,CH,Y
Ferocactus stainesi	B,CH
Ferocactus viridescens	B,BC,CH,Y
Ferocactus wislizenii	B,Y
Ferocactus wislizenii v herrerae	Y
Ferraria crispa	AP,B,MN,SC,SI
Ferraria densepunctulata	B
Ferraria divaricata	B,SI
Ferraria sp	SI
Ferula assa-foetida	B,C,CP
Ferula communis	AP,B,C,JE,SA
Ferula sadlerana	B
Ferula soogarica	SG
Festuca altissima	SG
Festuca amethystina	AP,B,C,G,JE,SA,SC
Festuca elatior	B
Festuca elatior 'Demeter'	B
Festuca gautieri	B,G
Festuca gigantea	B,JE,SA,SG
Festuca glauca	B,BD,JE,KI,L,SA,V
Festuca glauca 'Sea Urchin'	B
Festuca glauca 'Select'	JE
Festuca incrassata	B
Festuca juncifolia	B
Festuca longifolia	B
Festuca mairei	AP,B,G,SA
Festuca megalura	B
Festuca novae-zelandiae	JE,SA,SS
Festuca occidentalis	B,SA
Festuca ovina	B,JE
Festuca ovina 'Elijah Blue'	I,PM

FESTUCA

Festuca ovina glauca	AV,C,SC
Festuca ovina v novae-zelandiae	B
Festuca pacifica	B
Festuca pratensis	B,SG
Festuca pseudovina	B,SG
Festuca pulchella	JE
Festuca punctoria	G,PM
Festuca rubra	B,SG
Festuca rubra 'Ensylva'	B
Festuca rubra ssp commutata	B
Festuca rubra ssp commutata 'Frida'	B
Festuca rubra ssp littoralis	B
Festuca rubra ssp rubra	B
Festuca rubra v pruinosa	B
Festuca scoparia	B,JE,SA
Festuca tatrae	SG
Festuca tenuifolia	B
Festuca valesiaca glaucantha	B,JE
Festuca valesiaca 'Silver Sea'	I
Fibigia clypeata	AP,B,BS,C,G,JE,SC
Ficalhoa laurifolia	B
Ficinia radiata	B,SI
Ficus auriculata	B
Ficus benghalensis	B,C,HA,SA
Ficus benjamina	B,C,HA,O,SA
Ficus benjamina 'Exotica'	B
Ficus benjamina v nuda	B
Ficus burtt-davyi	B,SI
Ficus capensis	C
Ficus carica	G,SA
Ficus cordata	B,C,SI
Ficus cordata ssp salicifolia	B
Ficus coronata	B
Ficus elastica	B,KI,SA
Ficus elastica 'Decora'	B,BS,C,L
Ficus fraseri	B
Ficus glumosa	SI
Ficus hillii	B,O,SA
Ficus hispida	B
Ficus ingens	B,SI
Ficus lutea	SI
Ficus lyrata	B
Ficus macrophylla	B,C,HA,O,SA
Ficus microcarpa	HA
Ficus natalensis	B,C,SI
Ficus nigropunctata	SI
Ficus obliqua	B,HA
Ficus obliqua v obliqua	O
Ficus petiolaris	CH,Y
Ficus platypoda	B
Ficus platypoda v nana	O
Ficus pumila	B
Ficus racemosa	B,HA,SA
Ficus religiosa	B,HA,SA
Ficus 'Rubber Plant sp Mix'	T
Ficus ruginosa	B,O
Ficus sp mix	C
Ficus superba v henneana	B
Ficus sur	B,SI
Ficus sycomorus	B,SI
Ficus thonningii	B
Ficus virens	B,O
Ficus virens ssp sublanceolata	B
Ficus watkinsoniana	B,HA,O
Fieldia australis	AU
Filipendula kamtschatica	SG

Filipendula palmata	B,G,SG
Filipendula rubra	JE
Filipendula ulmaria	AP,B,BS,C,CO,G,JE,KI, KS,LA,SASG
Filipendula ulmaria aurea	FH,G
Filipendula vulgaris	AP,B,C,G,JE,LA,SA,SC, SG,SU
Firmiana simplex	B,C,SA
Fitzroya cupressoides	SA
Flacourtia euphlebia	B
Flacourtia indica	B
Flacourtia jangomans	B,HA,SA
Flaveria australasica	B
Flemingia macrophylla	B
Flemingia strobilifera	B
Flindersia australis	B,HA,O,SA
Flindersia brayleyana	B,O
Flindersia maculosa	B,O
Flindersia schottiana	B
Flindersia xanthoxyla	B,O
Fockea edulis	C,SI
Foeniculum dulce	CP
Foeniculum vulgare	B,G,LA,SG
Foeniculum vulgare 'Purpurascens'	AP,B,CP,E,FH,G,JE,KS, SA,SG
Foeniculum vulgare 'Smokey'	AP,B,T
Foeniculun 'Bronze' see Purpurascens	CP,FH,KS,SG
Fokienia hodginsii	B,SA
Fontanesia fortunei	SA
Forestiera neomexicana	B,SA
Forestiera segregata	B
Forstera sedifolia	B,SS
Forstera tenella	B,SS
Forsythia giraldiana	CG
Forsythia japonica	B
Fortunearia sinensis	SA
Fortunella crassifolia	B
Fortunella japonica	B
Fosterella penduliflora	B
Fothergilla major	B,SA
Fouquieria burragei	B
Fouquieria columnaris	B
Fouquieria diguetii	B
Fouquieria splendens	B,BC,C,CH,SW,Y
Foveolina tenella	SI
Fragaria vesca	B,C,JE,V
Fragaria virginiana	B
Frailea castanea	B
Frailea columbiana	B
Frailea friedrichii	Y
Frailea grahliana	B,Y
Frailea horstii	BC
Frailea klusacekii	Y
Frailea knippeliana	B
Frailea lepida	BC
Frailea mammifera	B,Y
Frailea pseudograhliana	B,Y
Frailea pumila	Y
Frailea pygmaea	B,Y
Frailea pygmaea v boyansis	Y
Frailea pygmaea v lorencoensis	Y
Frailea pygmaea v phaeodisca	Y
Frailea schilinzkyana	B
Frailea sp mix	C
Frailea uhligiana	Y
Frailea ybatense	B

FRANCOA

Francoa appendiculata	AP,C,SC
Francoa ramosa	B,C,SC
Francoa sonchifolia	AP,B,C,G,I,JE,LG,P,RH, SA,SC,SG
Francoa sonchifolia 'T&M Form'	T
Frangula alnus	SG
Frankenia connata	B
Frankenia laevis	SG
Frankenia serpyllifolia	B
Franklinia alatamaha	B,SA
Frasera albicaulis	B
Frasera parryi	B
Frasera speciosa	B,SW
Fraxinus americana	B,C,CG,HA,SA
Fraxinus angustifolia	B,HA,SA,SG
Fraxinus angustifolia 'Raywood'	B
Fraxinus anomala	B,SW
Fraxinus bungeana	B,SA
Fraxinus caroliniana	B
Fraxinus chinensis	B,SA
Fraxinus cuspidata v macropetala	B,SW
Fraxinus dipetala	B
Fraxinus excelsior	A,B,C,SA
Fraxinus excelsior 'Jaspidea'	SG
Fraxinus excelsior 'Pendula'	B,RS
Fraxinus griffithii	B,HA
Fraxinus insularis	B
Fraxinus latifolia	CG
Fraxinus mandshurica	B,SA,SG
Fraxinus ornus	A,B,C,HA,SA
Fraxinus pallisus	CG
Fraxinus pennsylvanica	B,C,SG
Fraxinus pennsylvanica lanceolata	SA
Fraxinus potamophila	CG
Fraxinus uhdei	B
Fraxinus velutina	B,C,SA
Fraxinus velutina v coriacea	B
Freesia alba of gdns	B,CG,SI
Freesia andersonii	MN
Freesia blue	BS
Freesia caryophyllacea	B,SI
Freesia corymbosa	B
Freesia elimensis	B,C,SC,SI
Freesia fergusonae	B,MN
Freesia hyb choice mix	D,VH
Freesia hyb fragrant	U
Freesia hybrida 'Florist Hybrids'	B
Freesia hybrida 'Parigo's' mix	BD
Freesia hybrida 'Parigo's' s-c	B,BS
Freesia leichtlinii	B
Freesia muirei	MN
Freesia occidentalis	B
Freesia 'Royal Crown'	KI,L,YA
Freesia 'Royals' mix	S
Freesia sp	SI
Freesia 'Super Giants' mix	C,CL,F,M,T
Freesia 'Superior 'mix	J,V
Fremontodendron californicum	AP,B,C,G,SA
Fremontodendron mexicanum	B,CG,SA
Freylinia lanceolata	B,SI
Frithia pulchra	B,SI,Y
Frithia pulchra v minor	B
Fritillaria acmopetala	AP,B,CG,G,LG,MN,PA, PM,SC
Fritillaria affinis	AP,B,CG,JE,LG,SC
Fritillaria atropurpurea	B,SW

Fritillaria aurea	AP,PM,SC
Fritillaria biflora	AP,B,LG
Fritillaria bithynica	AP,B,CG,LG,MN,PM,SC
Fritillaria camschatcensis	AP,B,CG,FH,G,SC
Fritillaria caucasica	CG,SC
Fritillaria citrina	AP,SG
Fritillaria crassifolia	AP,LG,PM,SC
Fritillaria crassifolia ssp kurdica	AP,B,CG,JE,LG,PM,SC
Fritillaria davisii	AP,CG,G,PM,SC
Fritillaria epirotica	AP,PM
Fritillaria gracilis	AP,CG,SC
Fritillaria graeca	AP,G,LG,SC
Fritillaria graeca ssp thessala	AP,C,G,LG,PM,SC
Fritillaria gussichiae	AP,CG,G
Fritillaria hermonis ssp amana	AP,CG,G,SC
Fritillaria imperialis	AP,B,CG,G,JE,LG,RH, SC,T
Fritillaria imperialis 'Fasciata'	CG
Fritillaria imperialis 'Lutea'	AP,CG,PM,SC
Fritillaria involucrata	AP,B,CG,G,LG,PM,SC
Fritillaria kurdica	AP,CG
Fritillaria latifolia	AP,PM,SC
Fritillaria latifolia nobilis	PM
Fritillaria lusitanica	CG,G
Fritillaria maximowiczii	SG
Fritillaria meleagris	AP,B,C,CG,CO,FH,G,I, JE,LG,MN,N,PA,PM,RH, SC,SG,SU,T
Fritillaria meleagris f alba	AP,B,G,JE,LG,PM,SC, SG
Fritillaria meleagris 'Jupiter'	PM
Fritillaria meleagris 'Poseidon'	AP,PM
Fritillaria meleagris 'Saturnus'	PM
Fritillaria messanensis	AP,B,C,G,LG,PM,SC
Fritillaria messanensis Greece	MN
Fritillaria messanensis ssp gracilis	AP,CG,G,SC
Fritillaria messanensis ssp gussichiae	CG
Fritillaria michailovskyi	AP,B,C,G,LG,PM,SC
Fritillaria mix	P
Fritillaria pallidiflora	AP,B,C,CG,G,JE,LG,N, PA,PM,SC,SG,T
Fritillaria persica	AP,JE,LG,SC
Fritillaria pinardi	CG,SC
Fritillaria pontica	AP,B,C,G,JE,LG,MN,PA, PM,SC
Fritillaria pudica	B,CG,JE,SW
Fritillaria pyrenaica	AP,B,CG,G,LG,SA,SC
Fritillaria raddeana	B,G,LG,SC
Fritillaria rhodocanakis	G,PM
Fritillaria ruthenica	AP,G,SC,SG
Fritillaria sp & forms mix	AP,C,G,SC
Fritillaria thessala	CG
Fritillaria tubiiformis	AP,B,C,CG,G,JE,SC
Fritillaria uva-vulpis	AP,CG,G,MN,PM,SC
Fritillaria verticillata	AP,PA
Fritillaria walujawii	PM,SC
Fritillaria whitallii	AP,PM,SC
Froelichia floridana	B,CG,PR
Fuchsia 'Ballerina' mix	J,T
Fuchsia boliviana	C,SG
Fuchsia 'Crown Supreme'	BS
Fuchsia excorticata	B,C,SA,SS
Fuchsia f1 hyb 'Chimes'	BD,D,F,KI,M,S,SE,T,U
Fuchsia f1 hyb 'Florabelle'	BD,C,CL,D,DT,J,L,M,O, S,SE,T,V,YA
Fuchsia 'Fete Florale'	U

FUCHSIA

Fuchsia 'Flucia Montes' — B
Fuchsia 'Fuchsoides' — SE
Fuchsia hyb mix — C,JE,V
Fuchsia loxensis red form — B
Fuchsia magellanica — C,G,JE,SA
Fuchsia perscandens — SS
Fuchsia procumbens — AP,B,C,CC,FH,I,SC,SG, SS
Fuchsia regia — SG
Fuchsia 'Supreme' mix — CO,ST
Fumana ericoides — SG
Fumana nudifolia — FH
Fumana procumbens — AP,B,C,G,JE,SC,SG
Fumana thymifolia — B
Fumaria bastardii — CG
Fumaria officinalis — B,C,SG
Funastrum crispum — B
Furcraea foetida — B
Furcraea longaeva — SA
Gagea granulose — SG
Gagea mauretanica — B
Gagea mauretanica A.B.S4376 Morocco — MN
Gahnia aspera — B,HA
Gahnia clarkei — B
Gahnia grandis — AU,B
Gahnia melanocarpa — HA
Gahnia microstachya — B
Gahnia setifolia — B
Gahnia sieberana — AU,B,HA,SA
Gahnia subaequiglumis — AU,B,HA,SA
Gaillardia amblyodon — B
Gaillardia aristata — AP,AV,B,C,HW,JE,KS, SC,SG
Gaillardia aristata dw — SA
Gaillardia aristata 'Fackelschein' — JE
Gaillardia aristata 'Indian Yellow' — T
Gaillardia aristata 'Maxima Aurea' — JE,SA
Gaillardia aristata 'Tokajer' — JE,T
Gaillardia 'Gaiety' — C
Gaillardia 'Lollipops' — U
Gaillardia mix dbl — S
Gaillardia 'Monarch Mix' — U
Gaillardia pulchella — AV,B,G,HW,NT,SG,V
Gaillardia pulchella 'Dbl Mix' — T
Gaillardia pulchella 'Picta' — B,C
Gaillardia pulchella 'Red Plume' — B,BS,D,DT,F,L,SE,T
Gaillardia pulchella 'Sherbet Plume' — U
Gaillardia pulchella 'Yellow Plume' — B,BS,D,DT,L
Gaillardia 'Summer Fire' — U
Gaillardia x grandiflora 'Aurea Pura' — B
Gaillardia x grandiflora 'Bremen' — B,JE,SA
Gaillardia x grandiflora 'Burgunder' — B,BS,G,JE,SA,T,W
Gaillardia x grandiflora 'Dazzler' — B,BD,BS,JE,KI,R,ST
Gaillardia x grandiflora 'Giant Hybrids' — BS,CL,D,DT
Gaillardia x grandiflora 'Goldkobold' — B,JE,T
Gaillardia x grandiflora 'Kobold' — B,BD,BS,C,CL,D,FH,JE, KI,PA,S,SE,ST
Gaillardia x grandiflora mix — BS,CO,F,J,KI,TU,V
Gaillardia x grandiflora 'New Giant Hyb' — BD,L
Gaillardia x gr. 'T&M Reselected Hybrids' — T
Gaillardia x grandiflora 'Torch' — B
Gaillardia x grandiflora 'Torchlight' — C,F
Gaillardia x grandiflora 'Wirral Flame' — PA
Galactites tomentosa — B,P
Galanthus allenii — B
Galanthus caucasicus — G,NG

Galanthus elwesii — AP,JE,NG,SC
Galanthus elwesii 'Casaba' — NG
Galanthus gracilis — B,JE,NG
Galanthus ikariae ssp ikariae 'Butt's Form' — NG
Galanthus nivalis — AP,B,G,JE,PM,SC,SG
Galanthus nivalis S.forms — NG
Galanthus plicatus — NG
Galanthus plicatus late fl forms — NG
Galanthus plicatus ssp byzantinus — NG
Galanthus rare mix — NG
Galanthus reginae-olgae ssp reginae-olgae — NG
Galanthus reginae-olgae ssp vernalis — NG
Galanthus sp & hyb choice mix — NG
Galanthus sp & hyb mix — C,CT
Galatella biflora — SG
Galaxia alata — B
Galaxia ciliata — B
Galaxia fugacissima — B,SI
Galaxia luteoalba — B,SI
Galaxia ovata — B,SC,SI
Galaxia sp — SI
Galaxia variabilis — B,SI
Galaxia versicolor — B,SI
Galega officinalis — AP,BS,C,G,JE,KI,SA,SC
Galega officinalis 'Alba' — AP,B,G,LG
Galega officinalis 'Bicolor' — B,T,V,W
Galeopsis ladanum — B
Galeopsis speciosa — AP,B
Galeopsis tetrahit — B,LA
Galium aparine — B,SG
Galium boreale — B,PR,SG
Galium elongatum — B
Galium glaucum — B
Galium mollugo — B,JE,LA,SG
Galium odoratum — B,JE,SA,SG
Galium palustre — B
Galium saxatile — B
Galium schultesii — SG
Galium triflorum — SG
Galium uliginosum — SG
Galium verum — B,C,JE,LA,SA,SG,V,Z
Gallito rojo — B
Galphimia glauca — B,C
Galpinia transvaalica — B,C,SA,SI
Galtonia candicans — AP,B,C,CG,G,JE,LG,RH, SA,SC,SG,SI,T
Galtonia princeps — AP,B,C,G,LG,SC,SG
Galtonia viridiflora — AP,C,G,RH,SC,SE,T,V
Garcinia sp — B
Gardenia augusta — B,SA
Gardenia augusta named vars — B
Gardenia carinata — B
Gardenia cornuta — B,C,SI
Gardenia resiniflua — SI
Gardenia spathulifolia — B,C
Gardenia ternifolia — B
Gardenia thunbergii — B,C,O,RE,SA,SI
Gardenia volkensii — B
Garidella nigellastrum 'Blue Butterflies' — B
Garidella nigellastrum 'Summer Stars' — T
Garrya buxifolia — B,SA
Garrya elliptica — A,SA,SG
Garrya fremontii — C,SG
Garrya wrightii — B
Gasteria acinacifolia — B,SI
Gasteria armstrongii — Y

GASTERIA

Gasteria batesiana	SI
Gasteria baylissiana	B,SI
Gasteria bicolor ssp bicolor	B,SI
Gasteria bicolor ssp liliputana	SI
Gasteria brachyphylla	SI
Gasteria brachyphylla ssp brachyphylla	B
Gasteria carinata	B
Gasteria croucheri	B
Gasteria disticha	B
Gasteria ellaphieae	SI
Gasteria huttoniae	B
Gasteria nitida	SI
Gasteria nitida v armstrongii	B
Gasteria obliqua	SI
Gasteria sp mix	C,Y
Gasteria transvaalensis	B
Gasteria vlokii	B
Gastrococos crispa	B
Gastrolobium sp	B
Gaultheria adenothrix	AP,B,CC,G,SC
Gaultheria alpina	SS
Gaultheria antipoda	AP,B,CG,SA,SS
Gaultheria apressa	AU
Gaultheria crassa	AU,B,C,CG,SS
Gaultheria cuneata	SG
Gaultheria depressa	AU,B,SA,SC,SS
Gaultheria depressa v novazelandae	AU
Gaultheria hispida	AU,B,C,O,SA
Gaultheria itoana	CC,G
Gaultheria lanceolata	AU
Gaultheria leucocarpa	CC
Gaultheria macrostigma	B,SA,SS
Gaultheria miqueliana	JE,SG
Gaultheria nana	B,SS
Gaultheria paniculata	B,SA
Gaultheria parvifolia	B
Gaultheria parvula	AU
Gaultheria procumbens	B,C,JE,SA
Gaultheria pumila	SA
Gaultheria rupestris	B
Gaultheria shallon	A,B,C,G,JE,SA
Gaultheria shallon 'Select'	B
Gaultheria sp (white fruits) CNW487	X
Gaultheria tasmanica	B
Gaura biennis	AP,B,G,PR
Gaura coccinea	B
Gaura lindheimeri	B,BS,C,G,JE,KI,SA,SC,T
Gaura lindheimeri 'The Bride'	F,J,V
Gaura longiflora	PR
Gaussia maya	B
Gaussia princeps	B
Gazania 'Chansonette'	BS,D,DT,FJ,U,V
Gazania 'Daybreak Bright Orange'	O,U
Gazania 'Daybreak' mix	BD,BS,CL,DT,R,TU
Gazania 'Daybreak Series' s-c	BS,CL,L,YA
Gazania 'Harlequin Hybrids'	T
Gazania krebsiana	B,SA,SI
Gazania krebsiana 'Orange Peacock'	B,F
Gazania liechtensteinii	B,SI
Gazania maritima	B,SI
Gazania 'Mini-Star' mix	BD,BS,C,CL,DT,F,KI,S, SE,T,YA
Gazania 'Mini-Star' s-c	BS,CL
Gazania 'Mini-Star' white	BS,C,CL
Gazania 'Orange Surprise'	S
Gazania rigens	B

Gazania rigens 'Bronze Red'	B
Gazania rigens 'Grandiflora'	B
Gazania rigens 'Red Shades'	B
Gazania rigens v uniflora	B
Gazania sp	SI
Gazania splendens	BS,CO,KI,SG,ST
Gazania 'Sundance Mix'	T
Gazania 'Sunshine'	F
Gazania 'Sunshine' mix	C,KS,SE
Gazania 'Sunshine' s-c	BD
Gazania 'Sunshine White'	B
Gazania 'Suttons Hybrids' mix	S
Gazania 'Talent' mix	BS,C,CL,D,DT,L,S,T,TU, U,YA
Gazania 'Talent' yellow	BS,CL
Geijera linearifolia	B
Geijera parviflora	B,HA,O,SA
Geissorhiza aspera	B,MN,SC,SI
Geissorhiza bonae-spei	B
Geissorhiza confusa	B,SI
Geissorhiza darlingensis	B,SI
Geissorhiza heterostyla	B,SI
Geissorhiza humilis	B,SI
Geissorhiza imbricata	B,SI
Geissorhiza inaequalis	AP,B,MN
Geissorhiza inflexa	B,SI
Geissorhiza mathewsii	B
Geissorhiza monantha	B,SC,SI
Geissorhiza ovalifolia	SI
Geissorhiza ovata	B,SI
Geissorhiza purpureolutea	B
Geissorhiza radians	AP,B,C,SI
Geissorhiza silenoides	B,SI
Geissorhiza sp	SI
Geissorhiza splendidissima	B,SC
Geissorhiza tulbaghensis	B,SI
Gelasine azurea	AP,C,MN,SC
Gelasine azurea v orientalis	MN
Gelasine elongata	B
Gelasine elongata v orientalis	B
Gelasine uruguainensis v orientalis	B
Geleznowia verrucosa	B,O
Gelsemium sempervirens	B
Genipa americana	B
Genista aethnensis	AP,B,C,SA,T
Genista anglica 'Cloth of Gold'	FH
Genista florida	SA,SG
Genista germanica	B
Genista hispanica ssp occidentalis	B
Genista maderensis	B
Genista monspessulana	B,SC
Genista radiata	SG
Genista sagittalis	AP,B,C,JE,SA,SC,SG
Genista scorpius	SA
Genista tenera	SG
Genista tinctoria	A,AP,B,C,G,HA,JE,RS, SA,SG
Genista umbellata	SA
Genlisea sp	B
Gentaurium tenuiflorum	B
Gentiana acaulis	AP,B,BD,BS,C,CL,CO,F, FH,G,I,JE,KI,L,S,SA,SC, SG,ST,T,U,V
Gentiana acaulis 'Blue Gem'	J
Gentiana adsurgens	B
Gentiana affinis	B,SC,SW

106

GENTIANA

Gentiana alba	B,FH	Gentiana nivalis	CG,FH,RS
Gentiana algida	B,F,JE,SW	Gentiana oliverei	AP,SC,SG
Gentiana algida v igarashii	CC	Gentiana ornata	CG
Gentiana alpina	B,C	Gentiana pannonica	CG,G,SC,SG
Gentiana amarella	C	Gentiana paradoxa	AP,B,G,P,SC
Gentiana andrewsii	AP,B,CC,G,JE,PR,SC	Gentiana paradoxa 'Blauer Herold'	JE
Gentiana andrewsii 'Cream'	B	Gentiana parryi	AP,B,SC,SG,SW
Gentiana angulosa	C	Gentiana phlogifolia	CG
Gentiana angustifolia	AP,B,JE,SC,SG	Gentiana pneumonantha	AP,B,C,CG,JE,SA,SC
Gentiana angustifolia 'Frei Hybrid'	JE	Gentiana puberulenta	B
Gentiana asclepiadae	AP,B,C,F,FH,G,JE,P,PA,	Gentiana punctata	B,C,F,G,JE,SG
	RH,RS,SA,SC,SG,T	Gentiana purpurea	B,C,CG,G,JE,SA,SC
Gentiana asclepiadae 'Nymans'	AP,G,I	Gentiana purpurea 'Nana'	B,C,JE
Gentiana asclepiadae 'Whitethroat'	B,P	Gentiana pyrenaica	B
Gentiana asclepiadea 'Alba'	AP,B,C,G,JE,P,SC,SG	Gentiana quinquefolia	PR
Gentiana asclepiadea 'Knightshayes'	C	Gentiana rochelii	AP,SG
Gentiana asclepiadea 'Phyllis'	B,P	Gentiana saponaria	B,CG,SG
Gentiana asclepiadea 'Snowcloud'	BS,KI	Gentiana saxosa	AP,B,CG,FH,P,SC,SG
Gentiana asclepiadea turquiose	AP,C	Gentiana scabra	B,CG,G,SC
Gentiana axiliflora	CG	Gentiana scabra v buergeri	B,C
Gentiana bavarica	B,C,JE	Gentiana septemfida	AP,B,BS,C,CG,F,FH,G,I,
Gentiana bavarica ssp subcaulis	CG		KI,SC,SG,ST,W
Gentiana bellidifolia	SS	Gentiana septemfida flatifolia	SG
Gentiana bigelovii	AP,CG,G,SC	Gentiana septemfida v lagodechiana	AP,B,C,CL,FH,JE,SA,
Gentiana brachyphylla	AP,B,C,CG,JE,SC		SC,SG,T,V
Gentiana bracteosa	SG	Gentiana septemfida v lagod. 'Select'	JE
Gentiana burseri	CG,G,SG	Gentiana serotina	B,SS
Gentiana burseri ssp villarsii	CG	Gentiana sikokiana	CC
Gentiana cachemirica	AP,SC,SG	Gentiana sino-ornata 'Blauer Edelstein'	JE
Gentiana campestris	CG	Gentiana sino-ornata 'New Hybrids'	B
Gentiana catesbaei	C	Gentiana siphonantha	B,G,SC
Gentiana clusii	AP,B,BS,C,CG,G,JE,SC	Gentiana sp China	SG
Gentiana clusii f alboviolacea	G,JE	Gentiana sp mix	AP,C,I,SC
Gentiana corymbifera	AP,B,CG,SS	Gentiana speciosa	C,CC
Gentiana cruciata	AP,B,BS,CG,G,JE,KI,SC,	Gentiana straminea	AP,G,JE,SG
	SG	Gentiana tergestina	C
Gentiana cruciata ssp phlogifolia	CG,SG	Gentiana terglouensis	AP,B,C
Gentiana dahurica	B,BS,C,CG,G,JE,SA,SG	Gentiana tianschanica	AP,SC,SG
Gentiana dalmatica	SG	Gentiana tibetica	AP,B,BS,CC,CG,G,JE,
Gentiana decumbens	AP,B,RS,SC		SC,SG
Gentiana dendrologii	CG,SG	Gentiana triflora	AP,B,P,SC
Gentiana dinarica	AP,B,C,JE,SC	Gentiana triflora 'Alba'	AP,B,P,SC
Gentiana divisa	AP,CG,SC,SS	Gentiana triflora v japonica	AP,B,CC,JE,SC
Gentiana fetisowii	AP,CG,G,SG	Gentiana triflora v japonica 'Alba'	AP,B,C,SC
Gentiana flavida	PR	Gentiana trinervis	B,P
Gentiana freyniana	AP,G,SC,SG	Gentiana utriculosa	CG
Gentiana gelida	AP,B,G,SC	Gentiana verna	AP,B,BS,C,FH,G,JE,SA,
Gentiana germanica	CG		SC,SG
Gentiana gracilipes	B,C,CG,G,JE,SC	Gentiana verna v angulosa	AP,G,I,JE,SC
Gentiana grisebachii	SS	Gentiana waltonii	I
Gentiana grombczewskii	SG	Gentiana walujewis	AP,B,SA,SC
Gentiana grossheimii	AP,B,G,P,SC	Gentiana wutaiensis	AP,B,CG,SC,SG
Gentiana imbricata	JE	Gentiana x hascombensis	FH,SC
Gentiana kesselringii	I,SG	Gentiana x hexafarreri	B,JE,P
Gentiana kurroo	AP,C,JE	Gentianella campestris	B
Gentiana lagodechiana		Gentianella detonsa elegans	SW
see septemfida v lagodechiana		Gentianella diemensis	AU
Gentiana lutea	AP,B,C,CG,F,G,JE,P,SA,	Gentianella germanica	B,G
	SC,SG	Gentianella lutescens	SG
Gentiana macrophylla	SG	Gentianella quinquefolia	B
Gentiana makinoi	AP,G,RS	Gentianella tenella	B
Gentiana makinoi 'Alba'	JE	Gentianella utriculosa	B
Gentiana makinoi 'Royal Blue'	B,SA	Gentianopsis crinita	B,PR
Gentiana montana	B,SS	Gentianopsis detonsa v elegans	B
Gentiana 'Moorcroftiana'	T	Geonoma congesta	B
Gentiana newberryi	CG	Geonoma schottiana	B

GERANIUM

Geranium albanum	CG,SA	Geranium pratense 'Rose Queen'	B,HL,P
Geranium andersonii	B	Geranium pratense 'Silver Queen'	C,HL,P
Geranium aristatum	AP,B,CG,JE,P,SA,SC	Geranium pratense stewartianum	CC
Geranium asphodeloides	AP,B,CG,G,HL,P,SC	Geranium pratense striatum	AP,SG
Geranium bicknelli	SG	Geranium psilostemon	AP,B,HL,JE,P,SC
Geranium biuncinatum	AP,B,P,SC	Geranium pulchrum	B,P
Geranium bohemicum	AP,B,C,CG,FH,HL,P,SC,T	Geranium purpureum	CG
Geranium 'Border Varieties Mix'	T	Geranium pusillum	B,CG
Geranium caffrum	B,P,SC	Geranium pyrenaicum	AP,B,C,CG,SA,SC,SG
Geranium canariense	B,P	Geranium pyrenaicum 'Bill Wallis'	AP,B,P
Geranium carolinianum	CG	Geranium pyrenaicum f albiflorum'	B,P
Geranium cinereum	CG,SC	Geranium reflexum	CG,G
Geranium clarkei 'Kashmir Purple'	HL	Geranium regelii	CC,SC
Geranium columbinum	B,CG	Geranium richardsonii	B,P,SG
Geranium dalmaticum	CG,SC	Geranium rivulare	P
Geranium dissectum	B,SU	Geranium robertianum	B,C,CG,SA,SU
Geranium endressii	C,CG	Geranium robertianum 'Celtic White'	B,HL,P
Geranium endressii hybs	B,JE	Geranium robustum	AP,B,P
Geranium erianthum	B,CG,G,P,SG	Geranium rotundifolium	CG
Geranium eriostemon	AP,P,SC,SG	Geranium rubescens	B,C,G,P
Geranium farreri	AP,B,P,SC,T	Geranium ruprechtii	AP,B,P
Geranium fremontii	CG,SC	Geranium sanguineum	AP,B,BD,BS,C,CG,CL,F,
Geranium 'Geranos' sp hardy mix	C		G,JE,L,PM,SA,SC,SG,
Geranium gracile	P		SU
Geranium 'Hardy Mix'	HL,JE,P	Geranium sanguineum 'Nanum'	B,JE,SC
Geranium harveyi	P	Geranium sanguineum 'Sara'	HL
Geranium himalayense	HL	Geranium sanguineum v striatum	AP,B,G,HL,I,JE,SC,SG
Geranium himalayense 'Gravetye'	AP,B,P	Geranium sessiliflorum	B,CG,SC,SS
Geranium himalayense 'Plenum'	B	Geranium sessiliflorum 'Nigricans'	AP,B,P,SC
Geranium ibericum	B,JE,RS	Geranium sessiliflorum 'Rubrum'	B,P
Geranium incanum	AP,C,SC,SI	Geranium sibiricum	B,CG
Geranium incanum white	B,SI	Geranium sinense	B,P,SC
Geranium lanuginosum	B,CG,P	Geranium sp Russia	SG
Geranium lucidum	B,CG,P	Geranium swatense	HH
Geranium luganense	CG	Geranium sylvaticum	AP,B,C,CG,F,G,JE,SA,
Geranium macrorrhizum	AP,B,C,CG,G,JE,SA,SG		SC,SG
Geranium macrorrhizum 'Bevan's Variety'	B,P	Geranium sylvaticum 'Mayflowr'	P
Geranium macr. 'Ingwersen's Variety'	C	Geranium sylvaticum white & lace veins	C
Geranium macrorrhizum purple-red	JE	Geranium thunbergii	B,CG,I,P,SG
Geranium macrorrhizum v album	C,SC,SG	Geranium transbaicalicum	C
Geranium maculatum	AP,B,G,JE,PR,SG	Geranium traversii	AP,B,P,SC,SS
Geranium maderense	AP,B,C,P,SC,SG	Geranium tuberosum	B
Geranium molle	B,CG	Geranium versicolor	B,C,G,P
Geranium napuligerum	AP,CG	Geranium viscosissimum	B,C,JE,SG
Geranium nepalense	B,CG,SA	Geranium wallichianum 'Buxton's Variety'	AP,C,CC,G,HL,SC,T
Geranium nepalense v thunbergii	JE	Geranium wilfordii	CG
Geranium nervosum	P,SG	Geranium 'Winscombe'	P
Geranium 'Nimbus'	P	Geranium wlassovianum	CG
Geranium nodosum	B,JE	Geranium x oxonianum	C,P
Geranium ocellatum	CG	Geranium x oxonianum 'Claridge Druce'	AP,B,HL,G
Geranium ornithopodon	B	Geranium x oxonianum 'Thurstonianum'	HL
Geranium palmatum	AP,B,C,CG,D,P,SC	Gerardia tenuifolia	PR
Geranium palustre	G,SG	Gerbera ambigua	SI
Geranium 'Pastel Clouds'	P	Gerbera 'Blackheart' mix	T
Geranium phaeum	AP,B,C,CG,F,G,HL,JE,P,	Gerbera 'Californian Giants' mix	J,SE,V
	SA,SC	Gerbera cordata	C,SI
Geranium phaeum f album	AP,SG	Gerbera 'Dw Frisbee' mix	T
Geranium platypetalum	CG,SG	Gerbera 'Dw Pandora' mix	T
Geranium pratense	AP,B,BS,C,CC,CG,CO,F,	Gerbera 'Dw Parade' mix	J,V
	FH,G,HH,HL,JE,KI,LA,	Gerbera f1 'Festival'	YA
	P,SA,SC,SG,SU,V,Z	Gerbera f1 hyb 'Skipper'	CL
Geranium pratense f albiflorum	AP,B,C,CG,G,HL,JE,P,	Gerbera f1 hyb 'Tempo' dw mix	BS,C,CL
	SC,SG	Gerbera f1 'Living Colours' dw	B
Geranium pratense hyb 'Spinners'	C	Gerbera f1 'Mardi Gras' mix	T
Geranium pratense 'Mrs Kendall Clarke'	AP,B,C,G,HL,SC	Gerbera f1 'Masquerade Mix'	YA
Geranium pratense pale azure	C,HL	Gerbera jamesonii	B,BD,BS,C,CL,F,KI,L,S

GERBERA

Gerbera viridifolia	B,SI	Gilia capitata	B,C,G,J,KS,SC,V
Gesneria cardinalis v compacta	C	Gilia capitata abrontanifolia	T
Gesneria cuneifolia 'Quebradillas'	C	Gilia capitata 'Alba'	B
Gesneria macrantha compacta	CL,L	Gilia diegensis	B,SW
Gesneria 'Sundrop'	C	Gilia leptantha	G,KS
Gesneriads sp & hyb mix	C	Gilia leptantha ssp purpusii	B
Geum album	CG	Gilia longiflora	B,SW
Geum aleppicum	B,G,PR,RS,SG	Gilia macombii	B
Geum bulgaricum	CG	Gilia milefoliata	SG
Geum calthaefolium	CC,P,SC	Gilia rigidula	B,SW
Geum canadense	B	Gilia rubra	C,V
Geum chiloense	G,SC,T	Gilia spicata	SW
Geum chiloense 'Lady Stratheden'	AP,B,BD,BS,C,CL,CO,	Gilia subnuda	B,SW
	DT,F,J,JE,KI,L,MA,SA,	Gilia tenuituba	B,SW
	ST,SU,V	Gilia thurberi	B,SW
Geum chiloense 'Mrs. J.Bradshaw'	AP,B,BD,BS,C,CL,CO,F,	Gilia tricolor	B,BS,G,KS,SG,T,V
	G,J,JE,KI,L,MA,S,SA,	Gilia tricolor 'Snow Queen'	B,V
	SC,ST,SU,V	Gillenia trifoliata	B,C,G,I,JE,SC,T
Geum chiloense 'Mrs. J.Bradshaw' Imp	DT	Gingidia montana	B,SC
Geum coccineum	AP,B,JE,P,SA,SC,SG	Ginkgo biloba	A,B,BS,C,CG,HA,N,RE,
Geum 'Gold Ball' see 'Lady Stratheden'			SA,T,V
Geum japonicum	AP,B,SC	Gladiolus abbreviatus	SI
Geum leiospermum	B,P,SC,SS	Gladiolus alatus	SI
Geum macrophyllum	B,C,JE,SC,SG	Gladiolus alatus v alatus	B
Geum macrophyllum perincisum	SG	Gladiolus alatus v meliusculus	B
Geum magellanicum	C,P,SC	Gladiolus angustus	B,SI
Geum montanum	AP,B,BD,BS,C,CG,FH,G,	Gladiolus aurantiacus	B,SI
	JE,RS,SA,SC,SG,T	Gladiolus aureus	B
Geum parviflorum	B,G,RS,SC,SS	Gladiolus bonae-spei	B,SI
Geum pentapetalum	CC	Gladiolus bonae-spei v merianellus	B
Geum peruvianum	SG	Gladiolus brevifolius v brevifolius	B,SI
Geum pyrenaicum	B,G,JE,SC,SG,T	Gladiolus callianthus	B,G
Geum reptans	AP,B,BS,C,G,I,JE,SA,SC	Gladiolus cardinalis	B,SI
Geum rhodopeum	AP,B	Gladiolus carinatus ssp carinatus	B,SI
Geum rivale	AP,B,C,CG,FH,G,JE,LA,	Gladiolus carinatus ssp parviflorus	B,SI
	RH,SA,SC,SG,SU	Gladiolus carmineus	AP,SC,SI
Geum rivale 'Album'	FH,SC,T	Gladiolus carneus	AP,B,C,CG,RS,SC,SI
Geum rivale 'Leonard's Variety'	P	Gladiolus carneus f 'Tradouwspass'	B
Geum 'Scarlet & Gold'	D	Gladiolus carneus v albidus	B,SC
Geum triflorum	AP,B,JE,PR,SC,SG	Gladiolus carneus v macowanii	B
Geum triflorum v ciliatum	B	Gladiolus caryophyllaceus	B,SC,SI
Geum 'Two Ladies'	BD,SE,U	Gladiolus citrinus	AP,SI
Geum uniflorum	B,SS	Gladiolus citrinus x alatus	SI
Geum urbanum	B,C,G,JE,LA,SA,SC,SG,	Gladiolus communis	AP,B,G,LG,SC
	Z	Gladiolus communis ssp byzantinus	AP,C,I
Geum x borisii of gdns see coccineum		Gladiolus comm. ssp byz. A.B.S4662	MN
Gevuina avellana	B,SA	Gladiolus crassifolius	SI
Gibbaeum album	B,SI,Y	Gladiolus cunonius	B,SI
Gibbaeum comptonii	B,SI,Y	Gladiolus dalenii	B,SI
Gibbaeum cryptopodium	B,SI,Y	Gladiolus dalenii v primulinus	B,SI
Gibbaeum dispar	B,SI,Y	Gladiolus debilis	B
Gibbaeum esterhuyseniae	B	Gladiolus ?dubius S.F301 Spain	MN
Gibbaeum geminum	B	Gladiolus ecklonii	B,SI
Gibbaeum gibbosum	B	Gladiolus equitans	B,SI
Gibbaeum haagei	Y	Gladiolus floribundus ssp floribundus	AP,B,SI
Gibbaeum heathii	B,SI,Y	Gladiolus floribundus ssp miniatus	B
Gibbaeum petrense	B,SI,Y	Gladiolus fourcadei	SI
Gibbaeum pilosulum	B	Gladiolus garnieri	AP,B
Gibbaeum pubescens	B,SI	Gladiolus gracilis ssp gracilis	B,SI
Gibbaeum schwantesii	B	Gladiolus gracilis v latifolius	B,SC,SI
Gibbaeum shandii	B	Gladiolus gueinzii	B,SI
Gibbaeum velutinum	B,Y	Gladiolus huttonii	B,SI
Gilia achilleifolia	B,C	Gladiolus hyalinus	B,SI
Gilia aggregata	C,SW	Gladiolus illyricus	AP,B,G,JE,MN,SC,SG
Gilia aggregata arizonica	SW	Gladiolus imbricatus	AP,CG,G,MN,SC,SG
Gilia aggregata macrosiphon	SW	Gladiolus inflatus	B,SI

109

GLADIOLUS

Gladiolus italicus	B,CG,G,JE,SC	Globba marantiana	C
Gladiolus kamiesbergensos	B,SI	Globba winitii	B
Gladiolus kotschyanus	MN,RS	Globularia cordifolia	AP,B,BS,CG,G,JE,KI,SA,
Gladiolus liliaceus	B,SI		SC,SG
Gladiolus maculatus	SI	Globularia incanescens	AP,FH,SC
Gladiolus maculatus v maculatus	B	Globularia nudicaulis	AP,B,C,JE,SA,SC,T
Gladiolus marlothii	B,SI	Globularia punctata	AP,B,G,JE,SC,SG,T
Gladiolus monticola	B,SI	Globularia repens	AP,B,C,SC
Gladiolus nerineoides	SI	Globularia trichosanthes	AP,CC,SC
Gladiolus ochroleucus	B,SC	Globularia vulgaris	HA,SG
Gladiolus ochroleucus v macowanii	B,SI	Glochidion ferdinandi	B
Gladiolus ochroleucus v ochroleucus	SI	Gloriosa dbl mix	BS
Gladiolus odoratus	B,SI	Gloriosa single mix	BS
Gladiolus orchidiflorus	B,SI	Gloriosa superba	B,C,O,SA,SE,SI,T,V
Gladiolus palustris	AP,B,G,,JE,SA,SC	Gloriosa superba 'Rothschildiana'	B,G,SA,SC
Gladiolus pappei	B,SI	Gloriosa superba 'Simplex'	B,SC,SG
Gladiolus patersonii	B,SI	Gloriosa verschuuri	C
Gladiolus permeabilis	B	Glottiphyllum depressum	B,SI
Gladiolus permeabilis v wilsonii	B	Glottiphyllum fragrans	B
Gladiolus priorii	B,SI	Glottiphyllum herrei	B
Gladiolus pritzelii	B,SI	Glottiphyllum linguiforme	Y
Gladiolus punctulatus	B,SI	Glottiphyllum longum	B,CG,SI
Gladiolus quadrangulus	B,SI	Glottiphyllum muirii	B
Gladiolus recurvus	B,SI	Glottiphyllum nelii	B,Y
Gladiolus rogersii	B	Glottiphyllum oligocarpum	B
Gladiolus saccatus	B,SI	Glottiphyllum parvifolium	B
Gladiolus saundersii	B,SI	Glottiphyllum pygmaeum	B
Gladiolus scullyi	B,SI	Glottiphyllum regium	B
Gladiolus sericeo-villosus	B,SI	Glottiphyllum salmii	B
Gladiolus sp	SI	Glottiphyllum semicylindricum	B
Gladiolus splendens	B	Glottiphyllum sp mix	C
Gladiolus stefaniae	SI	Gloxinia 'Crown' mix	BS,KI
Gladiolus tenellus	AP,B,SI	Gloxinia f1 'Avanti'	YA
Gladiolus teretifolius	SI	Gloxinia f1 hyb 'Brocade'	C,CL,L,T
Gladiolus tristis	AP,B,LG,SC,SI	Gloxinia f1 hyb 'Empress' mix	BS,CL,D,DT,L,T
Gladiolus tristis v concolor	B,C,SI	Gloxinia f1 hyb 'Fanfare' mix	CL
Gladiolus undulatus	B,SI	Gloxinia f1 hyb 'Glory' mix	CL
Gladiolus venustus	B,SI	Gloxinia f1 hyb 'Glory' s-c	CL
Gladiolus violaceo-lineatus	B,SI	Gloxinia f1 hyb 'Gregor Mendal'	BS
Gladiolus virescens	B,SI	Gloxinia f1 hyb 'Ultra' mix	C
Gladiolus virescens v roses-venosus	B	Gloxinia f2 hyb 'Jester' mix	BS,J,SE,T,V
Gladiolus watermeyeri	B,SI	Gloxinia 'Giant Flowered' mix	BD
Gladiolus watsonius	B,SI	Gloxinia named vars mix h-p	BL
Gladiolus watsonoides	B	Gloxinia perennis	B,C
Glandulicactus wrightii	B,Y	Gloxinia racemosa	C
Glaucidium palmatum	AP,B,CC,CG,JE,SA,SC	Glumicalyx goseloides	B,SI
Glaucium corniculatum	B,C,G,P,SA,SC	Glyceria canadensis	PR
Glaucium elegans	B,CC,P	Glyceria fluitans	B
Glaucium flavum	AP,B,C,CG,G,JE,SA,SC,	Glyceria grandis	PR
	SG,SU,T,W	Glyceria maxima	B,JE,SA
Glaucium flavum v aurantiacum	B,BS,C,JE,KI	Glyceria striata	PR
Glaucium grandiflorum	AP,B	Glycine canescens	B
Glaucium sp	CC	Glycine max	B
Glaucium vitellianum	T,W	Glycine tabacina	B
Glechoma hederacea	B,C,JE	Glycosmis pentaphylla	B
Gleditsia caspica	B,SA	Glycyrrhiza acanthocarpa	B
Gleditsia chinensis	SA	Glycyrrhiza echinata	A,B,C,JE
Gleditsia japonica	B,SA	Glycyrrhiza glabra	A,B,C,CP,G,JE,SA
Gleditsia macrantha	SA	Glycyrrhiza glabra 'Poznan'	B
Gleditsia triacanthos	A,B,C,G,HA,SA	Glycyrrhiza lepidota	B,PR,SG
Gleditsia triacanthos inermis	HA,SA	Glycyrrhiza uralensis	B,SG
Gleditsia triacanthos v inermis	B,N	Glyptostrobus pensilis	B
Gleditsia triacanthos v inermis imp	B	Gmelina arborea	B,C,RE,SA
Gleditsia triacanthos v sinensis	B	Gmelina asiatica	B
Gliricidia sepium	B,HA,RE,SA	Gmelina leichardtii	B,O
Glischrocaryon aureum	B	Gmelinii v japonica	CG

GNAPHALIUM

Gnaphalium 'Fairy Gold'	V
Gnaphalium mackayi	SS
Gnaphalium obtusifolium	PR
Gnaphalium sylvaticum	B
Gnaphalium traversii	SS
Gnetum gnemon	B
Gnidia squarrosa	B,SA,SI
Gomphocarpus fruticosus	B,SI,SG
Gomphocarpus physocarpa	B,C,SI
Gompholobium aristatum	B
Gompholobium baxteri	B
Gompholobium capitatum	B
Gompholobium confertum	B
Gompholobium knightianum	B,SA
Gompholobium latifolium	B,C,HA,SA
Gompholobium marginatum	B
Gompholobium ovatum	B
Gompholobium polymorphum yellow fl	AU,B
Gompholobium preissii	B
Gompholobium scabrum	B
Gompholobium shuttleworthii	B
Gompholobium tomentosum	B
Gompholobium venustum	B
Gompholobium villosum	B
Gompholobium virgatum	B,HA
Gomphostigma virgatum	SI
Gomphrena affinis	B,O
Gomphrena canescens	B,O,SA
Gomphrena cunninghamii	B,O
Gomphrena decumbens	B
Gomphrena diffusa	B
Gomphrena dispersa 'Pink Pinheads'	B,BS,C,KS
Gomphrena globosa	BS,CG,DT,F,KI,L,SU,V
Gomphrena globosa 'Aurea-superba'	B
Gomphrena globosa 'Buddy'	BS,C,T
Gomphrena globosa 'Choice Soft Pink'	B
Gomphrena globosa 'Dwarf Buddy'	B,KS
Gomphrena globosa 'Dwarf Cissy'	B,KS
Gomphrena globosa 'Dw.Dolly' cs	B
Gomphrena globosa 'Gemini Mix'	D
Gomphrena globosa 'Lavender Lady'	B,BS
Gomphrena globosa 'Q formula mix'	C,KI
Gomphrena globosa 'Q Lavender Lilac'	C
Gomphrena globosa 'Q Lilac'	B
Gomphrena globosa 'Q Pink'	B,C
Gomphrena globosa 'Q Purple'	B,C
Gomphrena globosa 'Q Rose'	B,C
Gomphrena globosa 'Q White'	B,C
Gomphrena globosa 'Rose Bicolour'	KS
Gomphrena globosa 'Strawberry Fair'	B
Gomphrena globosa 'Sunburst' mix	BD,BS
Gomphrena globosa 'Sunburst' s-c	BS
Gomphrena globosa tall s-c	KS
Gomphrena globosa 'White Gnome'	T
Gomphrena haageana	C
Gomphrena haageana 'Orange Globe'	C,CO,SGKS
Gomphrena haageana 'Q s-c'	B
Gomphrena haageana 'Sunburst' s-c	BS
Gomphrena hybrida 'Full Mix'	T
Gomphrena 'Strawberry Fields'	B,BS,C,KI,KS,U,V
Goniolimon speciosum	SG
Goniolimon tataricum	B,BD,C,CG,CL,JE,KS, SA,V
Goniolimon tataricum 'Woodcreek'	B
Goniophlebium subauriculatum	B,SG
Goodenia havilandii	B

Goodenia incana	B
Goodenia pinnatifida	B
Goodenia pterygosperma	B
Goodenia scaevolina	B,O,SA
Goodenia scapigera	B,O
Goodenia stelligera	B
Goodenia viscida	B
Goodenia watsonii	B
Goodia latifolia	AU,B,HA,SA
Gordonia axillaris	B
Gordonia lasianthus	B
Gorteria diffusa	B,SI
Gorteria personata	B,SI
Gossypioides kirkii	SI
Gossypium arboreum	B
Gossypium australe	B
Gossypium barbadense	B
Gossypium bickii	B
Gossypium herbaceum	B,C,V
Gossypium herbaceum africanum	SI
Gossypium hirsutum	B,C
Gossypium hirsutum 'Peruvian Brown'	B
Gossypium h. v punctatum	B
Gossypium h. v p. 'Hopi Short Staple'	B
Gossypium nanking	B
Gossypium palmeri	B
Gossypium raimondii	B
Gossypium robinsonii	B,SA
Gossypium soilana	B
Gossypium sturtianum	B,O,SA
Gossypium thurberi	B
Gossypium tomentosum	B
Gossypium wigthianum	B
Gotu kola	B
Graptopetalum bellum	B,C,SE,V
Grass, 'Alsike Clover'	CD
Grass, 'Bowling Green'	YA
Grass, 'Chalky Soil'	CO,SU
Grass, 'Cocksfoot'	CD
Grass, 'Creeping Red Fescue'	CD
Grass, 'Early Bite'	CD
Grass, 'Exposed Clay Subsoil'	CO,PR
Grass, 'Gallop Mixture'	CD
Grass, 'Herbal' mix	CO
Grass, 'Horse Leys'	CD
Grass, 'Intensive Dairy Graze'	CD
Grass, 'Landscape'	YA
Grass, lawn mix, 'All-purpose'	D
Grass, lawn mix, 'Fine'	CO,KI,YA
Grass, lawn mix, 'Hardwearing'	CD,D
Grass, lawn mix, 'Ornamental'	AV,BD,BS,CD,D,DT,KI, T,V
Grass, lawn mix, 'Practical'	KI
Grass, lawn mix, 'Shady'	D,KI
Grass, 'Light Land'	CD
Grass, 'Loam/Alluvial Soil'	CO
Grass, 'Low Maintenance' mix	CO
Grass, 'Lucerne'	CD
Grass, 'Maximum D-Value'	CD
Grass, 'Maximum Early'	CD
Grass, 'Maximum Yield'	CD
Grass, 'Meadow Fescue'	CD
Grass, 'Meadow Sedge Short'	PR
Grass, 'Meadow Sedge Tall'	PR
Grass, 'Medium to Heavy Soil'	SU
Grass, 'Over-Seeding Mix'	CD

111

GRASS

Grass, 'Paddock' mix	CO,KI
Grass, 'Permanent'	CD
Grass, 'Pochon High Clover Ley'	CD
Grass, 'Prairie' short	PR
Grass, 'Prairie' tall	PR
Grass, 'Quick Bulk'	CD
Grass, 'Quickturf'	YA
Grass, 'Red Clover'	CD
Grass, 'Red Clover Ley'	CD
Grass, 'Ryegrass'	CD
Grass, 'Sainfoin'	CD
Grass, 'Sandy Soil'	CO,SU
Grass, 'Set-Aside Mixtures'	CD
Grass, 'Sportsturf'	YA
Grass, 'Suburban'	YA
Grass, 'Timothy'	CD
Grass, 'Tufflawn' mix	CO
Grass, 'Under Trees' mix	CO
Grass, 'Westerwolds Bulk'	CD
Grass, 'Wet Soil'	CO
Grass, 'White Clover'	CD
Grass, 'Woodland'	PR,SU
Grass, 'Woods Edge Savanna Short'	PR
Grass, 'Woods Edge Savanna Tall'	PR
Grass, 'Your Own Mix'	CD
Grasses, 'Ornamental'	CO,F,J,ST
Gratiola officinalis	B,C,G,JE
Grayia spinosa	B
Greenovia aurea	C
Grevillea agrifolia	B,O
Grevillea annulifera	O
Grevillea aquifolium	B,O
Grevillea baileyana	B
Grevillea banksii	B,HA,SA,SH
Grevillea banksii 'Alba'	B,HA,O,SA
Grevillea banksii 'Forsterii'	O
Grevillea bipinnatifida	B,O
Grevillea biternata	O
Grevillea brownii	O
Grevillea candelabroides	B,O
Grevillea 'Coochin Hills'	HA,O
Grevillea crithmifolia	B,O
Grevillea decurrens	B
Grevillea didymobotrya	B
Grevillea drummondii	B
Grevillea dryandri	B,O
Grevillea endlicherana	B,O
Grevillea eriobotrya	B,O
Grevillea eriobotryoides	B
Grevillea eriostachya	B,O
Grevillea eriostachya ssp excelsior	B
Grevillea excelsior	O
Grevillea fasciculata	O
Grevillea floribunda	B,O
Grevillea formosa	O
Grevillea glauca	B,O,SA
Grevillea goodii ssp decora	B,O
Grevillea goodii ssp goodii	B,O
Grevillea hakeoides	B
Grevillea heliosperma	B,O
Grevillea hookerana	B,O
Grevillea insignis	O
Grevillea integrifolia	O
Grevillea juncifolia	B,O
Grevillea leucopteris	B,O
Grevillea monticola	B,O

Grevillea nudiflora	B,O
Grevillea paradoxa	B,O
Grevillea petrophiloides	B,O
Grevillea pilulifera	B,O
Grevillea plurijuga	B,O
Grevillea polybotrya	B,O
Grevillea pteridifolia	B,O
Grevillea pterosperma	B,O
Grevillea pulchella	B,O
Grevillea pyramidalis	B,O
Grevillea quercifolia	B,O
Grevillea ramosissima	B,O
Grevillea refracta	B,O
Grevillea robusta	B,BS,C,CL,HA,KI,O,RE, S,SA,SH,T,V
Grevillea 'Sandra Gordon'	B,HA
Grevillea sp mix	C
Grevillea stenobotrya	B,HA,O
Grevillea stenostachya	B
Grevillea striata	B,HA,O
Grevillea synapheae	B
Grevillea teretifolia	B,O
Grevillea thelemanniana	AU
Grevillea venusta	B
Grevillea whiteana	B
Grevillea wickhamii	B,O
Grevillea wilsonii	B,O
Grewia asiatica	B
Grewia bicolor	B,SI
Grewia breviflora	B
Grewia caffra	B
Grewia carpinifolia	B
Grewia flava	B,SI
Grewia flavescens	SI
Grewia flavescens v flavescens	B
Grewia hirsuta	B
Grewia occidentalis	B,C,SI
Grewia oppositifolia	B,SA
Grewia polygama	B
Grewia robusta	B,SI
Greyia radlkoferi	B,SI
Greyia sutherlandii	B,C,SI
Grielum grandiflorum	B,SI
Grielum humifusum	B,SI
Grielum sp	SI
Grindelia aphanactis	B
Grindelia integrifolia	B
Grindelia nana	B
Grindelia robusta	B,G,JE,SA,SG
Grindelia stricta ssp venulosa	B
Griselina littoralis	B,SA,SS
Gronophyllum microcarpum	B,O
Gronophyllum ramsayi	B,O
Guaiacum officinale	B
Guaiacum sanctum	B
Guazuma ulmifolia	B
Guibourtia coleosperma	B,SI
Guichenotia ledifolia	B,C,SA
Guichenotia macrantha	B,SA,SC
Guiera senegalensis	B
Guizotia abyssinica	B
Gulubia costata	O
Gunnera dentata	SS
Gunnera flavida	B,P,SS
Gunnera magellanica	B,P
Gunnera manicata	B,BS,C,G,JE,N,SA,T

GUNNERA

Gunnera monoica	AP,B,SS
Gunnera prorepens	AP,B,P,PM,SC,SS
Gunnera tinctoria	B,JE,SA,SG
Gunniopsis quadrifida	B
Gutierrezia sarothrae	B
Guzmania sp	B
Gymnadenia conopsea	B,CG
Gymnadenia odoratissima	B
Gymnelaea lanceolata	B
Gymnocactus beguinii	B,Y
Gymnocactus gielsdorfianus	Y
Gymnocactus horripilus	B
Gymnocactus knuthianus	B
Gymnocactus subterraneus v zaragosae	B
Gymnocactus viereckii	B
Gymnocactus viereckii LAU1159	CH,Y
Gymnocactus viereckii v. major	B
Gymnocactus viereckii v. major LAU730	Y
Gymnocalycium achirasense	Y
Gymnocalycium alboareolatum	B
Gymnocalycium andreae	Y
Gymnocalycium andreae v grandiflorum	Y
Gymnocalycium andreae v. longispinum	B
Gymnocalycium anisitsii	B,Y
Gymnocalycium asterium	B
Gymnocalycium baldianum	B,Y
Gymnocalycium bald. x venturianum	CH
Gymnocalycium bayrianum	B,BC
Gymnocalycium bicolor	B
Gymnocalycium bicolor v simplex	Y
Gymnocalycium bodenbenderianum	B,Y
Gymnocalycium bozsingianum	B,Y
Gymnocalycium bruchii	Y
Gymnocalycium bruchii /g.lafaldense	B,CH
Gymnocalycium buenekeri	Y
Gymnocalycium calochlorum	B
Gymnocalycium caloch. v. proliferum	B,Y
Gymnocalycium capillaense	B
Gymnocalycium capillaensis	B
Gymnocalycium cardenasianum	B,Y
Gymnocalycium carminanthum	Y
Gymnocalycium castellanosii	B,Y
Gymnocalycium chiquitanum	B
Gymnocalycium chubutense	B,Y
Gymnocalycium damsii	B
Gymnocalycium damsii v. centrispinum	Y
Gymnocalycium damsii v. rotundulum	B,Y
Gymnocalycium damsii v. torulosum	B
Gymnocalycium damsii v. tucavocense	B,BC,Y
Gymnocalycium deeszianum	B,Y
Gymnocalycium delaetii	B
Gymnocalycium denudatum	B
Gymnocalycium denud. v wagnerianum	B
Gymnocalycium eurypleurus	B,Y
Gymnocalycium eytianum	B
Gymnocalycium ferrari	B,Y
Gymnocalycium friedrichii	B
Gymnocalycium friedrichii v. moserianum	B
Gymnocalycium friedrichii v. piraretaense	B
Gymnocalycium fucarocence	CH
Gymnocalycium gibbosum	B,Y
Gymnocalycium gibbosum v. caespitosum	B
Gymnocalycium gibbosum v. ferox	B,Y
Gymnocalycium gibbosum v. gerardii	B
Gymnocalycium gibbosum v. nigrum	B
Gymnocalycium gibbosum v. nobile	B,Y

Gymnocalycium gib. v. pleurocostatum	Y
Gymnocalycium gib. v. schlumbergeri	B,Y
Gymnocalycium glaucum	GC,Y
Gymnocalycium guerkeanum	Y
Gymnocalycium hamatum	Y
Gymnocalycium horridispinum	B,Y
Gymnocalycium hybopleurum	B
Gymnocalycium hyptiacanthum	Y
Gymnocalycium intertextum	Y
Gymnocalycium kozelskyanum	B,Y
Gymnocalycium lagunillasense	B,BC
Gymnocalycium leeanum	B
Gymnocalycium leptanthum	B
Gymnocalycium marquezii	B,GC,Y
Gymnocalycium mazanense	B,Y
Gymnocalycium mazanense v. ferox	B
Gymnocalycium megatae	B,Y
Gymnocalycium michoga	B
Gymnocalycium mihanovichii	B,Y
Gymnocalycium mihanov. v. filadelfiense	B,Y
Gymnocalycium mihanovichii v. friedrichii	Y
Gymnocalycium m. v. fried. f albiflorum	Y
Gymnocalycium m. v. melocactiforme	B
Gymnocalycium m. v. pirarettaense	Y
Gymnocalycium m. v. rysanekianum	B
Gymnocalycium m. v. stenogonum	B
Gymnocalycium m. v. st. f albiflorum	Y
Gymnocalycium millaresii	Y
Gymnocalycium mix	Y
Gymnocalycium monvillei	B,Y
Gymnocalycium moserianum	B,Y
Gymnocalycium mostii	B,Y
Gymnocalycium mostii v. kurtzianum	B
Gymnocalycium multiflorum	B,Y
Gymnocalycium multiflorum v. parisiense	B
Gymnocalycium nidulans	B
Gymnocalycium ochoterenae	B
Gymnocalycium ochoterenae FR734	Y
Gymnocalycium och. v variispinum	B
Gymnocalycium ourselianum	Y
Gymnocalycium parag. v. wagnerianum	B
Gymnocalycium pflanzii	B,Y
Gymnocalycium pflanzii v albipulpa	Y
Gymnocalycium pflanzii v. eytianum	B
Gymnocalycium pflanzii v. lagunillasense	B
Gymnocalycium pflanzii v. marquezii	B
Gymnocalycium pflanzii v. tominense	B
Gymnocalycium platense	Y
Gymnocalycium pungens	B,Y
Gymnocalycium quehlianum	B,Y
Gymnocalycium qu. v. albispinum	B
Gymnocalycium qu. v. flavispinum	B
Gymnocalycium quehlianum v. rolfianum	Y
Gymnocalycium qu. v. zantnerianum	Y
Gymnocalycium ragonesii	B,Y
Gymnocalycium riograndense	B
Gymnocalycium riojense	Y
Gymnocalycium ritterianum	B
Gymnocalycium saglione	B,Y
Gymnocalycium saglione v albispinum	Y
Gymnocalycium saglione v tilcarense	Y
Gymnocalycium schatzlianum	B
Gymnocalycium schickendantzii	B,BC,Y
Gymnocalycium schickendantzii v. delaetii	B,Y
Gymnocalycium schroederianum	B
Gymnocalycium schuetzianum	Y

GYMNOCALYCIUM

Gymnocalycium sp mix	C,CH
Gymnocalycium spegazzini	B,BC,Y
Gymnocalycium stellatum	B,Y
Gymnocalycium stellatum v. albispinum	Y
Gymnocalycium stellatum v. cinerium	Y
Gymnocalycium stellatum v. paucispinum	B,Y
Gymnocalycium stuckertii	B
Gymnocalycium sutterianum	Y
Gymnocalycium tilcarense	BC
Gymnocalycium tillianum	B,Y
Gymnocalycium tudae	B,Y
Gymnocalycium uruguayense	B,Y
Gymnocalycium vallegrandense	Y
Gymnocalycium valnicekianum	B,GC,Y
Gymnocalycium vatteri	B,Y
Gymnocalycium wagnerianum	Y
Gymnocalycium weissianum	B
Gymnocalycium zegarrae	B,Y
Gymnocladus chinensis	SA
Gymnocladus dioica	A,B,C,SA
Gynandriris cedarmontana	B
Gynandriris pritzeliana	B,SI
Gynandriris setifolia	AP,B,MN,SC,SI
Gynandriris sisyrinchium MS509/1 Spain	MN
Gynandriris sisyrinchium Pol36 Lebanon	MN
Gynandriris sis. v purpurea S.B.L4/1 .	MN
Gynandriris sis. v purpurea S.F7 Morocco	MN
Gypsophila altissima	B
Gypsophila bicolor	CG
Gypsophila cerastioides	CC,T,V
Gypsophila elegans	C,HW,J,SG,U,V
Gypsophila elegans 'Carmine & Rose'	T
Gypsophila elegans 'Carminea'	B,BS
Gypsophila elegans 'Colour Blend'	D
Gypsophila elegans 'Covent Garden'	B,BD,BS,C,CO,D,DT,J, KI,L,M,S,SE,ST,SU,T, TU,U,V,VH,YA
Gypsophila elegans 'Crimson'	B,L,SE
Gypsophila elegans 'Giant White'	T
Gypsophila elegans 'Imp Mix'	T
Gypsophila elegans 'Lady Lace'	B
Gypsophila elegans 'Rose Charm'	VH
Gypsophila elegans 'Rosea'	B,BD,BS,F,KI,KS,SG, ST,U
Gypsophila elegans 'White Elephant'	B,D,DT
Gypsophila elegans 'White Monarch'	B,F
Gypsophila fastigiata ssp arenaria	B
Gypsophila 'Kermesina'	C
Gypsophila latifolia alba	SG
Gypsophila muralis	B,CG
Gypsophila muralis 'Garden Bride'	B,BD,CL,SE,T,U,YA
Gypsophila muralis 'Gypsy'	F
Gypsophila oldhamiana	B,T
Gypsophila pacifica	B,BS,C,JE,KI,KS,SA
Gypsophila pacifica 'Rose'	U
Gypsophila paniculata	B,BS,C,CP,G,JE,KI,KS, L,S,SA,SG,ST,SU,T
Gypsophila paniculata dbl	DT,KS,L,M,S
Gypsophila paniculata 'Diamond Spray'	U
Gypsophila paniculata 'Flocon De Neige'	B,BS,C,CL,D,F,JE,SE,T,V
Gypsophila paniculata 'Virgo'	B
Gypsophila patrinii	SG
Gypsophila repens	AP,B,BS,C,CG,G,JE,SC, SG,V
Gypsophila repens 'Alba'	B,BD,BS,CL,SA
Gypsophila repens 'Rosea'	AP,B,BD,BS,C,CL,JE,L,

	SA,T
Gypsophila 'Snow Fountain'	F
Gypsophila tenuifolia	AP,FH,SC
Gypsophila tenuifolia v gracilipes	B
Gyrocarpus americanus	B
Gyrostemon ramulosus	B
Haageocereus aureispinus	Y
Haageocereus chosicensis	Y
Haageocereus chrysacanthus	Y
Haageocereus decumbens v acinacispinus	Y
Haageocereus lachayensis	B
Haageocereus limensis	Y
Haageocereus limensis v netachrous	Y
Haageocereus olowinskianus	Y
Haageocereus pseudoacranthus	Y
Haageocereus sp mix	C
Haageocereus subtilispina	Y
Haageocereus versicolor	Y
Haastia recurva	SS
Haastia sinclairii	B,SS
Haberlea rhodopensis	B,G,JE,PA,SC
Hablitzia tamnoides	B,C
Habranthus andersonii & texanus see tubispathus	
Habranthus gracilifolius	AP,B,I,LG,MN,SC
Habranthus robustus	AP,B,G,LG,MN,SG
Habranthus tubispathus	AP,B,C,CG,G,I,LG,MN, PM,SC,SG
Habranthus tubispathus cupreus	FH
Habranthus tubispathus Cutler 4/41	MN
Habranthus verecunda	I
Hackelia floribunda	G,SG
Hacquetia epipactis	AP,B,SC
Haemanthus albiflos	B,SG
Haemanthus amarylloides	B
Haemanthus coccineus	B
Haemanthus humilis ssp humilis	B
Haemanthus pumilis	B
Haemanthus sanguineus	B
Haematoxylum brasiletto	B
Haematoxylum campechianum	B
Haemodorum laxum	B,SA
Haemodorum paniculatum	B
Haemodorum planifolium	AU,HA
Haemodorum simplex	B
Haemodorum spicatum	B
Hakea adnata	B,O
Hakea amplexicaulis	B,O
Hakea angustifolia	B
Hakea arborescens	O
Hakea bakeriana	HA
Hakea baxteri	B,O
Hakea brachyptera	B,O
Hakea brooksiana	B,O
Hakea brownii	B
Hakea bucculenta	AU,B,C,O,SA
Hakea ceratophylla	B,O
Hakea cinerea	B,O
Hakea clavata	B,O
Hakea commutata	B,O
Hakea conchifolia	B,O
Hakea coriacea	B,O
Hakea corymbosa	B,O
Hakea costata	B,O
Hakea crassifolia	B,O
Hakea cucullata	B,O

HAKEA

Hakea cyclocarpa	B,O	Hakea undulata	B,O
Hakea cyclocloptera	O	Hakea varia	B,O
Hakea dactyloides	B,HA,O	Hakea varia v florida	B
Hakea decurrens	B,O	Hakea verrucosa	B,O
Hakea elliptica	B,O	Hakea victoriae	AU,B,O
Hakea epiglottis	B,O	Haleria corniculata	AP,B,P
Hakea erecta	B,O	Halesia carolina	B,CG,SA
Hakea eriantha	B,HA,O	Halesia diptera	B,SA
Hakea erinacea	B,O	Halesia monticola	B,N,SA
Hakea eyreana	B,O	Halesia monticola f rosea	B
Hakea ferruginea	B,O	Halgania argyrophylla	B
Hakea flabellifolia	B,O	Halgania cyanea	B
Hakea florulenta	B,O	Halimium atriplicifolium	SA
Hakea francisiana	B,O	Halimium lasianthum	CG
Hakea gibbosa	B,HA,O,SA	Halimium ocymoides	AP,SG
Hakea gilbertii	B	Halimodendron halodendron	SA
Hakea grammatophylla	B,HA,O	Halleria elliptica	B,SI
Hakea incrassata	B,O	Halleria lucida	B,SI
Hakea invaginata	B	Halmoorea trispatha	B
Hakea lasianthoides	B	Haloragis erecta	B
Hakea laurina	AU,B,HA,O,SA	Haloragis erecta 'Wellington Bronze'	B,C,P
Hakea lehmanniana	B,O	Haloragodendron glandulosum	B
Hakea leucoptera	B,HA,O	Halosarcia pergranulata	B
Hakea lissocarpha	B,O	Haloxylon ammodendron	B
Hakea lissosperma	AU,B,HA,O,SA	Haloxylon persicum	B
Hakea lorea	B,O	Hamamelis japonica	B,C,SA,T
Hakea macraeana	B,O	Hamamelis japonica arborea	N,SG
Hakea macrocarpa	B	Hamamelis mollis	B,C,G,SA
Hakea meisnerana	B	Hamamelis mollis 'Pallida'	G,N
Hakea microcarpa	AU,HA,O	Hamamelis vernalis	B
Hakea minyma	B,O	Hamamelis virginiana	A,B,C,CG,SA
Hakea multilineata	B,O	Hamamelis x intermedia	B,N
Hakea neurophylla	BO	Hamatocactus sinuatus	B
Hakea nitida	B,O	Hamelia patens	B,SA
Hakea nodosa	B,O	Hannonia hesperidum	B
Hakea obliqua	B,O	Hannonia hesperidum S.F.273 Morocco	MN
Hakea obliqua v brooksiana	B	Haplocarpha scaposa	AP,B,SC,SI
Hakea obtusa	B,O	Haplopappus glutinosus	AP,FH,G,I,SC
Hakea oldfieldii	B	Haplopappus linearifolius	B
Hakea oleifolia	B	Haplopappus pinifolius	B
Hakea orthorrhyncha	B,O	Haplopappus RB 94063	I
Hakea pandanicarpa	B,O	Haplopappus rehderii	AP,B
Hakea petiolaris	BO	Haplophytum crooksii	SW
Hakea platysperma	B,O	Hardenbergia comptoniana	B,C,O,RS,SA,SC,V
Hakea plurinervia	B,O	Hardenbergia violacea	AP,B,HA,O,SA,SH,T
Hakea preissii	B,O	Hardenbergia violacea 'White Crystal'	B,HA
Hakea prostrata	B,O	Hardwickia binata	B
Hakea purpurea	B,HA,O	Harpagophytum zeyheri	B,SI
Hakea pycnoneura	B,O	Harpephyllum caffrum	B,C,CL,HA,O,SA,SI
Hakea recurva	B,O	Harpullia pendula	B,HA,O,SA
Hakea rostrata	B,O	Harrisia bonplandi	B,BC,Y
Hakea ruscifolia	B	Harrisia bonplandii	BC
Hakea salicifolia	B,C,HA,O,SA	Harrisia brookii	B
Hakea scoparia	B,O	Harrisia eriophora	B
Hakea sericea of gdns see lissosperma		Harrisia jusbertiiii	Y
Hakea smilacifolia	B,O	Hartogiella schinoides	B,SI
Hakea sp mix	C	Harungana madagascariensis	SI
Hakea stenocarpa	B,O	Haworthia angolensis	SI
Hakea stenophylla	B	Haworthia arachnoidea	B
Hakea strumosa	B,O	Haworthia attenuata	B,SI
Hakea suaveolens	B,HA,O	Haworthia bolusii	SI
Hakea sulcata	B,O	Haworthia comptoniana	B,SI
Hakea teretifolia	B,HA,O	Haworthia decipiens	B
Hakea teretifolia r-v	HA	Haworthia emelyae	B,SI
Hakea trifurcata	B,O	Haworthia emelyae v multifolia	B
Hakea ulicina	B,O	Haworthia herbacea	SI

Haworthia koelmaniorum	SI
Haworthia longiana	B,SI
Haworthia maughanii	B,Y
Haworthia mutica	SI
Haworthia nigra	SI
Haworthia nortieri	B
Haworthia pumila	B,CH,SI,Y
Haworthia pygmeae	SI
Haworthia reticulata v reticulata	SI
Haworthia retusa	B,SI
Haworthia retusa v multilineata	B
Haworthia scabra	B
Haworthia semiviva	B
Haworthia sp mix	C
Haworthia truncata	B,CH,Y
Hebe acutiflora	CG
Hebe albicans	AP,B,SG
Hebe allanii	B,C
Hebe amplexicaulis	B,SS
Hebe barkeri	B
Hebe buchananii	B
Hebe canterburiensis	B
Hebe chathamica	AP,B,SS
Hebe ciliolata	SS
Hebe coarctata	B
Hebe cupressoides	B,SS
Hebe dieffenbachii	B
Hebe diosmifolia	B
Hebe epacridea	B,SS
Hebe glaucophylla	SS
Hebe haastii	AP,B,SS
Hebe hectoris	B
Hebe hulkeana	AP,B,C,SA,SC
Hebe lavaudiana	SS
Hebe lyallii	SG
Hebe lycopodioides	B,G,SS
Hebe macrantha	B,SS
Hebe ochracea	B,SS
Hebe odora	B,SC,SS
Hebe pauciramosa	SS
Hebe pimeleoides	B,SG,SS
Hebe pinguifolia	AP,B,SS
Hebe raoulii	AP,SA,SC,SS
Hebe raoulii v raoulii	B
Hebe raoulii v macgaskillii	B
Hebe recurva	B,SA
Hebe salicifolia	AP,LG,SS
Hebe sp mix	B
Hebe speciosa	B,C,SA
Hebe stricta	SA
Hebe stricta v stricta	B
Hebe subalpina	B,SG,SS
Hebe tetrasticha	AP,B,SS
Hebe topiaria	B,SS
Hebe toriganii	CG
Hebe traversii	AP,SG,SS
Hebe vernicosa	B,SS
Hebenstretia comosa	SI
Hebenstretia comosa 'Attraction'	B,V
Hebenstretia dentata	B,C
Hebenstretia dura	B,SI
Hebenstretia fastigiosa	SI
Hebenstretia sp	SI
Hedeoma nana	B
Hedeoma pulegioides	B,C,CP
Hedera colchica	SG

Hedera helix	B,SA
Hedera hibernica	SA
Hedycarya arborea	B
Hedychium coccineum	B
Hedychium coccineum v aurantiacum	B
Hedychium coronarium	B
Hedychium cylindricum	B
Hedychium flavescens	B,SA
Hedychium flavum	B
Hedychium gardneranum	B
Hedychium horsfieldii	B,SG
Hedychium roxburghii	B
Hedychium sp	SG,V
Hedychium spicatum	B
Hedyotis crouchiana	B
Hedysarum alpinum	SG
Hedysarum arcticum	SG
Hedysarum boreale	B
Hedysarum boreale ssp mackenzii	SG
Hedysarum boreale v boreale	SG
Hedysarum boutignyanum	B
Hedysarum consanguineum	SG
Hedysarum coronarium	B,BS,C,KI,SA,T,V
Hedysarum ferganense	SG
Hedysarum flavescens	SG
Hedysarum hedysaroides	B,JE
Hedysarum neglectum	SG
Hedysarum obscurum	C
Hedyscepe canterburyana	B,O
Heimia myrtifolia	B
Heimia salicifolia	B,C,I,CP
Helenium amarum	B,T
Helenium amarum 'Sunny Boy'	B
Helenium autumnale	B,BS,DT,F,G,JE,PR,SC
Helenium autumnale 'New Hybrids'	B,JE
Helenium autumnale 'Praecox'	B,JE
Helenium autumnale 'Sunshine Hybrid'	T
Helenium bigelovii	B,SA
Helenium flexuosum	B
Helenium hoopesii	B,BD,BS,C,CL,CO,JE, KI,SA,SG,ST
Helenium 'Rotgold'	B,BD,C,CL,D,JE,L,SA
Heliabravoa chende	Y
Heliamphora heterodoxa	B
Helianthella quinquenervis	B,JE
Helianthella uniflora	C
Helianthemum apenninum	B,C,CG,G,JE,SA,SG
Helianthemum apenninum v roseum	CG,SG
Helianthemum canadense	B
Helianthemum canum	AP,B,RS,SC
Helianthemum caput-felis	CG
Helianthemum 'Choice Mix'	SU
Helianthemum 'Crown Mix'	KI
Helianthemum grandiflorum	SG
Helianthemum hybridum	B,T
Helianthemum ledifolius	B
Helianthemum mix	BS,FH,I,S
Helianthemum nummularium	AP,B,C,CG,D,G,J,JE,SA, SC,ST,U,V
Helianthemum nummularium mutabile	DT,JE,L
Helianthemum nummularium 'New Hyb'	B
Helianthemum numm. ssp grandiflorum	B,JE
Helianthemum numm.'Sunshine Mix'	F
Helianthemum nuttallii	SG
Helianthemum oelandicum ssp alpestre	AP,B,JE
Helianthemum ovatum	CG

HELIANTHEMUM

Helianthemum pilosus	B
Helianthemum 'Rock' mix	CL
Helianthemum salicifolius	B
Helianthemum scoparium	B,SW
Helianthemum scoparium v aldersonii	B
Helianthemum stipulatum	B
Helianthocereus antezanae	Y
Helianthocereus bertramianus	Y
Helianthocereus crassicaulis	Y
Helianthocereus escayachensis	Y
Helianthocereus grandiflorus	Y
Helianthocereus herzogianus	Y
Helianthocereus huascha	Y
Helianthocereus narvaecensis	Y
Helianthocereus orurensis	Y
Helianthocereus pasacana	Y
Helianthocereus poco	Y
Helianthocereus poco v fricianus	Y
Helianthocereus randallii	Y
Helianthus angustifolius	JE
Helianthus annuus	AV,C,HW,PR
Helianthus annuus 'African Sunset'	SE
Helianthus annuus 'Apache Br.Striped'	B
Helianthus annuus 'Autumn Beauty'	B,C,J,KS
Helianthus annuus 'Big Smile' dw	B,BS,CO,D,SE
Helianthus annuus 'Dunblane'	U
Helianthus annuus 'Dwarf'	B
Helianthus annuus 'Evening Sun'	B,KS
Helianthus annuus f1 'Full Sun' pol	B
Helianthus annuus f1 hyb 'Sunspot'	B,BD,BS,CL,KS,SE,T
Helianthus annuus f1 'Sunbeam'	B,KS,T,V
Helianthus annuus f1 'Sunbright' pol	B,L
Helianthus annuus 'Floristan'	B,BD,BS,KS,L
Helianthus annuus 'Full Sun'	S
Helianthus annuus 'Giant Single'	B,BD,BS,C,CO,D,DT,F,J, KI,KS,L,M,S,ST,T,TU,U, V,VH
Helianthus annuus 'Gloriosa Red'	B
Helianthus annuus 'Gold Bouquet'	M
Helianthus annuus 'Gold & Silver'	F
Helianthus annuus 'Hallo'	B,KS
Helianthus annuus 'Havasupai Striped'	B
Helianthus annuus 'Henry Wilde'	B,C,KS
Helianthus annuus 'Holiday'	B,BS,C,KS
Helianthus annuus 'Hopi Black Dye'	B
Helianthus annuus 'Incredible' dw	B,F,KI,ST,V
Helianthus annuus 'Israeli Single'	B
Helianthus annuus 'Lemon Moon'	B,V
Helianthus annuus 'Lemon Queenn'	F
Helianthus annuus 'Lion's Mane Golden'	B
Helianthus annuus 'Lion's Mane Yellow'	B
Helianthus annuus 'Moonwalker'	SE,T,V
Helianthus annuus 'Music Box'	B,BD,BS,C,D,J,KI,KS,M, S,T,TU,U,VH
Helianthus annuus 'Orange Double'	BS
Helianthus annuus 'Orange Sun'	B,T
Helianthus annuus 'Pacino'	F
Helianthus annuus 'Pastiche'	SE,T
Helianthus annuus 'Prado Red'	B,T,V
Helianthus annuus 'Prado Yellow'	B,T
Helianthus annuus 'Red Sun'	SE
Helianthus annuus 'Sonja'	B,BD,BS,C,DT,F,KS
Helianthus annuus 'Stella'	DT
Helianthus annuus 'Summer Days'	F
Helianthus annuus 'Sunburst'	F,S,T
Helianthus annuus 'Sungold'	B,BS,C,F,KS,L,V

Helianthus annuus 'Taiyo'	B,C,T
Helianthus annuus 'Tarahumara White'	B
Helianthus annuus 'Teddy Bear' dw	B,BD,BS,C,CL,DT,F,KS, T,U
Helianthus annuus 'The Sun'	B
Helianthus annuus 'Titan'	F
Helianthus annuus 'Valentine'	B,BD,BS,J,KS,L,SE,T
Helianthus annuus 'Van Gogh Gloriosa'	B
Helianthus annuus 'Velvet Queen'	B,C,F,KS,SE,T
Helianthus annuus 'Velvet Tapestries'	SE
Helianthus annuus 'Zebulon'	B
Helianthus argophyllus	B
Helianthus atrorubens	B,NT
Helianthus debilis	C,KS
Helianthus debilis 'Italian White'	B,T,V
Helianthus debilis 'Piccolo'	KS
Helianthus debilis ssp cucumerifolius	BS,CO,V
Helianthus debilis 'Vanilla Ice'	B,BD,BS,C,SE
Helianthus divaricatus	B,JE
Helianthus giganteus	B
Helianthus grosse-serratus	B,PR
Helianthus hirsuta	PR
Helianthus maximiliani	AV,B,C,JE,PR,SA
Helianthus mollis	B,JE,PR
Helianthus nuttalii	B,C,JE
Helianthus occidentalis	B,JE,PR
Helianthus simulans	NT
Helianthus strumosus	B,JE
Helianthus x laetiflorus	B,C,JE,PR
Helichrysum adenocarpum	SI
Helichrysum albidum	O
Helichrysum allioides	SI
Helichrysum appendiculatum	SI
Helichrysum arenarium	B,C,JE,SA,SG
Helichrysum argyrosphaerum	SI
Helichrysum aureonitens	SI
Helichrysum aureum ssp aureum	B,SI
Helichrysum bellidioides	AP,B,PM,SC,SS
Helichrysum bellidioides prostratum	SG
Helichrysum bellum	G,PM
Helichrysum cassinianum	BS,KI,ST,T
Helichrysum cassinianum 'Gabriele'	C
Helichrysum cassinianum 'Pink Bedder'	U
Helichrysum cassinianum 'Rose Beauty'	BD,J,KS
Helichrysum cassinianum 'Tanner's Pride'	T
Helichrysum confertifolium	SI
Helichrysum dasyanthum	B,C,SI
Helichrysum davenportii	B,C
Helichrysum dendroidum	HA
Helichrysum depressum	B,SS
Helichrysum diosmifolium	B,HA,O
Helichrysum elatum	B
Helichrysum felinum	B,SI
Helichrysum filicaule	B,SS
Helichrysum foetidum	B,SI
Helichrysum glomeratum	SS
Helichrysum grandiflorum	B,SI
Helichrysum heldreichii	I
Helichrysum herbaceum	SI
Helichrysum hookeri	I
Helichrysum italicum	B,C,G,JE
Helichrysum lepidophyllum	CG,O
Helichrysum leucopsideum	B
Helichrysum lindleyii	B,O
Helichrysum milfordae	AP,G,I,SC
Helichrysum nitens	SI

HELICHRYSUM

Helichrysum orientale	I,SG
Helichrysum pandurifolium	B,SI
Helichrysum petiolare	B,SI
Helichrysum pet. 'Dargan Hill Monarch'	T
Helichrysum petiolare 'Limelight'	B
Helichrysum petiolare 'Variegatum'	B
Helichrysum podolepideum	C
Helichrysum sanguineum	T
Helichrysum scorpioides	B,SG,O
Helichrysum semipapposum	B,O
Helichrysum sessiloides	AP,I,SC
Helichrysum setosum	C,T
Helichrysum sibthorpii	AP,FH,I,SC
Helichrysum sp	SC,SI
Helichrysum splendidum	B,SC
Helichrysum stoechas	B,C
Helichrysum subulifolium	AU,B,C,D,U
Helichrysum subulifolium 'Golden Sun'	B,BS,J,T
Helichrysum 'Summer Solstice'	T
Helichrysum sutherlandii	B,SI
Helichrysum thianschanicum	AP,G,SA,SC
Helichrysum thianschanicum 'Goldkind'	B,BS,C,CL,D,FH,JE,KI,U
Helichrysum 'Tom Thumb' mix	J
Helichrysum umbraculigerum	SI
Helichrysum wilmsii	B,SI
Heliconia aemygdiana ssp transandina	B
Heliconia bihai	B
Heliconia bourgaeana	B
Heliconia caribaea	B
Heliconia chartacea	B
Heliconia longiflora	B
Heliconia platystachys	B
Heliconia schiedeana	B
Heliconia sclerotricha	B
Heliconia sp	RE
Heliconia stricta 'Dwarf Jamaican'	B
Heliconia wagnerana	B,SA
Helicteres isora	B
Helictotrichon sempervirens	B,G,JE,SA
Heliophila longifolia	B,C,SI
Heliophila longifolia 'Atlantis'	B
Heliophila longifolia 'Blue Bird'	B,F
Heliophila longifolia 'Mediterranean Blue'	V
Heliophila rigidiuscula	B,SI
Heliophila scoparia	B,SI
Heliophila sp	SI
Heliophila suavissima	B,SI
Heliopsis 'Border Varieties Mix'	T
Heliopsis helianth. v scabra 'New Hyb mix'	C,JE
Heliopsis helianthoides	B,JE,PR,SG
Heliopsis hel ssp scabra 'Sommersonne'	B,BS,C,CL,D,JE,KI,KS, L,V
Heliopsis orientalis flavida	SA
Heliopsis scabra	SA
Heliopsis scabra 'Goldspitz'	T
Heliotropium arborescens	B,TU,V
Heliotropium arborescens 'Marine'	B,BD,BS,C,CL,F,J,KI,L, S,T,YA
Heliotropium arborescens 'Mini-Marine'	B,BS,D,T
Heliotropium europaeum	CG
Heliotropium finest mix	C
Heliotropium indicum	B
Heliotropium paniculatum	B
Heliotropium 'Regale mix'	BS,CO,KI
Heliotropum europaeum	B
Helipterum argyropsis	B

Helipterum canescens	B
Helipterum milleflorum	B
Helipterum muelleri 'Snowflake'	B
Helipterum sandfordii	BS,J,KI,KS,SU
Helipterum stipitatum	HA,O
Helleborus argutifolius	AP,AS,B,BS,C,CG,CT,F, FH,G,I,JE,LG,PH,RH, SA,SC,SG,W
Helleborus 'Ashwood Garden Hybrids'	AS
Helleborus atrorubens f cupreus	B
Helleborus atrorubens WM9617	NG,PH
Helleborus croaticus	B,JE,PH
Helleborus croaticus WM9628	NG
Helleborus cyclophyllus	B,C,JE,NG,PH,SA,T
Helleborus cyclophyllus WM9560	NG
Helleborus dumetorum	AS,B,C,JE,PH
Helleborus dumetorum ssp atrorubens	AP,B,JE,SC
Helleborus dumetorum WM9276	NG
Helleborus dumetorum WM9629	NG
Helleborus dumetorum WM9631	NG
Helleborus foetidus	AP,AS,B,BS,C,CG,CT,G, JE,MN,PH,SA,SC,SG,T, W
Helleborus foet. 'Bowles Cabbage Stalk'	AP,NG
Helleborus foetidus England	MN
Helleborus foetidus 'Gertrude Jekyll'	PH
Helleborus foetidus italian form	AS
Helleborus foetidus 'Pontarlier'	PH
Helleborus foetidus 'Ruth'	NG,PH
Helleborus foetidus 'Sienna'	PH .
Helleborus foetidus 'Sopron'	CT,PH
Helleborus foetidus 'Tros-os-Montes'	CT,PH
Helleborus foetidus (v)	PH
Helleborus foetidus 'Wester Flisk'	AP,AS,B,C,CT,JE,NG, PH,SC
Helleborus guttatus	AP,CG,SC
Helleborus lividus	CT,MN,PH,SC
Helleborus lividus Majorca	AS
Helleborus multifidus	AP,B,JE,SA
Helleborus multifidus ssp hercegovinus	NG,PH
Helleborus multifidus ssp istriacus	AP,NG,PH
Helleborus multifidus ssp istriacus	NG
Helleborus multifidus ssp multifidus	NG,PH
Helleborus niger	B,BD,BS,C,CG,D,DT,F,G, JE,KI,L,S,SA,SC,SE,SG, ST,T,V
Helleborus niger Europe	AS
Helleborus niger 'Grandiflorus'	B
Helleborus niger 'Maximus'	B,JE
Helleborus niger ssp macranthus	B,C,JE,SA
Helleborus niger ssp macranthus 'Roseus'	B,C,JE,SA
Helleborus niger 'Sunrise' WM9519	NG,PH
Helleborus niger 'Sunset'	PH
Helleborus niger x H.lividus	AS
Helleborus niger x H.sternii (Eric smithii)	AS
Helleborus odoratus Ukraine	NG
Helleborus odoratus WM9460	NG
Helleborus odoratus WM9624	NG
Helleborus odorus	AS,B,C,CG,CT,F,JE,PH
Helleborus orientalis selected forms	P
Helleborus orientalis ssp guttatus	AP,B,SC,T
Helleborus orientalis ssp orientalis	JE
Helleborus orientalis/caucasicus	PH
Helleborus purpurascens	AS,B,C,F,JE,NG,PH,SA, SC,
Helleborus purpurascens WM9644	NG

HELLEBORUS

Helleborus sp fragrant	P
Helleborus sp mix	PA
Helleborus 'Thoroughbred' mix	C
Helleborus torquatus	B,NG,PH
Helleborus torquatus hyb	G
Helleborus torquatus WM9637	NG
Helleborus vesicarius	JE,NG,PH
Helleborus viridis	AP,B,C,G,JE,SA
Helleborus viridis MS473 Spain	MN
Helleborus viridis ssp occidentalis	NG,PH
Helleborus 'Winter fl. imp Mix'	T
Helleborus x hybridus	AP,B,BS,C,G,JE,MA,SA, SC,SE,T
Helleborus x hybridus 'Amethyst'	NG
Helleborus x hybridus 'Best Picotees'	NG
Helleborus x hybridus 'Clear Colours'	CT
Helleborus x hybridus 'Dark'	PA,PH
Helleborus x hybridus 'Eric's Best'	NG
Helleborus x hybridus 'Helen Ballard'	P,PH
Helleborus x hybridus 'Netta's Famous'	NG
Helleborus x hybridus 'Netta's Pink'	NG
Helleborus x hybridus 'New Hybrids'	B,JE
Helleborus x hybridus s-c	B,C,CT,JE,NG,PH
Helleborus x hybridus 'Spotted,Speckled'	CT,PH
Helleborus x hybridus 'Stripey Child'	NG
Helleborus x hybridus 'Sylvia'	NG
Helleborus x hybridus 'Unspotted'	PH
Helleborus x hybridus 'Ushba'	NG
Helleborus x hybridus 'Very Best Mix'	NG
Helleborus x hybridus 'White'	C,CT,G
Helleborus x nigercors	AS
Helleborus x sternii	AS,B,C,CT,G,JE,P,PH
Helleborus x sternii 'Blackthorn Strain'	AP,AS,SC
Helleborus x sternii 'Boughton Beauty'	AS,NG
Helleborus x sternii 'Bulmer's Strain'	AS
Heloniopsis orientalis v flavida	C
Hemerocallis citrina	AP,B,SC
Hemerocallis dumortieri	SG
Hemerocallis fulva	B
Hemerocallis 'Hyb' mix	AP,C,SC
Hemerocallis lilioasphodelus	B,C,G,JE,SG
Hemerocallis lilioasphodelus minor	SG
Hemerocallis middendorfii	SG
Hemerocallis middendorfii v exaltata	B,JE
Hemerocallis minor	B,G,SG
Hemerocallis 'New Hybrids'	B,BS,JE
Hemerocallis 'New Miniature Hybrids'	BS,C,CL,JE,L
Hemerocallis 'Novelties Mixed'	BS,CL,F,T
Hemerocallis 'Summer Trumpets'	U
Hemerocallis 'Wichford'	E
Hemiandra pungens	B,SA
Hemidesmus indicus	B
Hemigenia eutaxoides	AU
Hemigenia pritzelii	B
Hemigenia ramosissima	B
Hemigenia sericea	B
Hemionitis arifolia	B
Hemiphragma heterophyllum	CC,SG
Hemispherica 'Helani Tulip Ginger'	B
Hemitelia smithii	C
Hemizygia canescens	SI
Hemizygia elliotii	B,SI
Hemizygia obermeyerii	B,SI
Hemizygia sp	B,SI
Hemizygia transvaalensis	SI
Hepatica nobilis	AP,B,C,CG,G,SC,SG

Heracleum dissectum	SG
Heracleum lanatum	JE,SG
Heracleum lehmannianum	B,C,JE
Heracleum mantegazzianum	B,I,JE
Heracleum maximum	PR
Heracleum minimum	AP,SC,SG
Heracleum sibiricum	SG
Heracleum sphondylium	B,C,LA,SG
Heracleum sphondylium ssp montanum	B
Heracleum sphondylium v roseum	B,NS
Heracleum stevenii	SG
Herbertia lahue	AP,MN
Herbertia platensis	AP,C,SC
Herbertia pulchella	AP,LG,SC
Hereroa herrei	B
Hereroa hesperantha	B
Hereroa incurva	B
Hereroa muirii	B
Hereroa odoratum	B,Y
Hereroa puttkameriana	B
Hereroa teretifolia	B
Hereroa uncipetala	B
Hermannia flammea	SI
Hermannia grandiflora	B,SI
Hermannia hyssopifolia	B,SI
Hermannia multiflora	B,SI
Hermannia pinnata	B,SI
Hermannia saccifera	B,C,SA,SI
Hermannia ssp	SI
Hermannia stricta	B,SA,SI
Hermas sp	SI
Hermas villosa	B
Hermbstaedtia glauca	B,SI
Hermodactylus tuberosus	B,RS
Hermodactylus tuberosus B.S348 Italy	MN
Hermodactylus tuberosus Crete	MN
Hermodactylus tuberosus Greece	MN
Hermodactylus tuberosus MS821 Crete	MN
Herniaria glabra	B,BS,C,CL,JE,SA
Herpolirion novae-zelandiae	B,SS
Herrania pulcherrima	B
Herrea elongata	B
Herrea robusta	B
Herreanthus meyeri	B
Herschelia barbata	B
Herschelianthe graminifolia	SI
Hesperaloe funifera	B
Hesperaloe parviflora	B,SA,SW
Hesperaloe parviflora 'Rubra'	B
Hesperaloe pavia	B
Hesperantha angusta	B
Hesperantha bachmannii	AP,B,G,SC,SI
Hesperantha baurii	AP,SC,SI
Hesperantha cucullata	AP,B,C,G,SC,SI
Hesperantha erecta	B,SI
Hesperantha falcata	AP,B,G,SC,SI
Hesperantha humilis	B
Hesperantha latifolia	SI
Hesperantha pauciflora	AP,B,MN,SI
Hesperantha rivulicola	B
Hesperantha sp	SC,SI
Hesperantha vaginata	B,C,SI
Hesperis lutea	JE
Hesperis matronalis	AP,B,C,CO,F,G,HW,JE, KI,KS,I,RH,SA,SE,SG, SU,T,TU,U,V

119

HESPERIS

Hesperis matronalis 'Purpurea'	B,C
Hesperis matronalis v albiflora	AP,B,C,FH,JE,T
Hesperis steviniana	B,C,HH,T
Hesperocallis undulata	B,SW
Hesperocallis undulata dwarf	SW
Hesperochiron pumilus	B,SC,SW
Hessia chaplinii	B
Hessia discifera	B
Hessia dregeana	B
Hessia gemmata	B
Hessia unguiculata	B
Hessia zeyheri	B
Heterodendron oleifolium	B
Heterolepis aliena	B,SA,SI
Heterolepis peduncularis	SI
Heteromorpha arborescens	B,SI
Heteromorpha trifoliata	B,SI
Heteropappus altaicus	B,C,SG
Heteropogon contortus	B
Heteropterys nitida	B
Heteropterys salicifolia	B
Heteropyxis natalensis	B,SI
Heterospathe elata	B,O
Heterospathe philippensis	B,O
Heterotheca camporum	PR
Heterotheca graminifolia	NT
Heterotheca mariana	B,NT
Heterotheca mucronata	CC
Heterotheca subaxillaris	B
Heterotheca villosa	AP,B,G,JE,SA,SG
Hetropyxis natalensis	O
Heuchera americana	B,CC,JE,PA
Heuchera 'Autumn Leaves'	B,P
Heuchera bracteata	SG
Heuchera chlorantha	AP,SG
Heuchera cylindrica	AP,B,CC,JE,PA,SC,SG
Heuchera cylindrica 'Greenfinch'	B,C,G,P,T
Heuchera 'Emperor's Cloak'	P
Heuchera 'Firefly'	B,BS,C,CL
Heuchera 'Green Ivory'	B
Heuchera hartwegii	SG
Heuchera himalayensis	SG
Heuchera hybrida	B
Heuchera micrantha	AP,B,SC
Heuchera micrantha 'Palace'	SA
Heuchera mic. v diverifolia 'Purple Palace'	AP,B,BS,C,CL,D,F,FH,G, P,T,V
Heuchera micrantha v diversifolia	SG
Heuchera mic. v div. 'Purple Palace Select'	JE
Heuchera parvifolia	B
Heuchera pilosa	SG
Heuchera 'Pluie De Feu'	B
Heuchera pubescens	B,SG
Heuchera pulchella	AP,T,SC
Heuchera richardsonii	B,JE,PR,SG
Heuchera sanguinea	B,BS,G,S,SG,SW,V
Heuchera sanguinea 'Bressingham Hyb'	AP,B,BS,C,D,JE,KI,L, SA,T
Heuchera sanguinea 'Crimson'	SA
Heuchera sanguinea 'Fackel'	SA
Heuchera sanguinea 'Sioux Falls'	B,JE
Heuchera sanguinea 'Splendens'	B,JE
Heuchera sanguinea 'Super Hybrids'	CL
Heuchera sanguinea 'White Cloud'	B,JE
Heuchera sanguinea 'Widar'	B,JE
Heuchera 'Titania'	B

Heuchera x pruhoniciana 'Dr.Sitar's Hyb'	B,C,T
Hevea brasiliensis	B
Hewittia sublobata	B
Hexaglottis lewisiae	B
Hexalobus crispiflorus	B
Hibbertia amplexicaulis	B,SA
Hibbertia aurea	B
Hibbertia commutata	B
Hibbertia cuneiformis	B
Hibbertia hypericoides	B
Hibbertia lasiopus	B
Hibbertia ovata	B
Hibbertia scandens	B,C,HA,O
Hibbertia serrata	B,SA
Hibbertia vaginata	B
Hibiscadelphus giffardianus	B
Hibiscus acetosella 'Red Shield'	B
Hibiscus 'Baltimore' mix	JE
Hibiscus biseptus	B,SW
Hibiscus burt-davyii	SI
Hibiscus calyphyllus	B,SI
Hibiscus cameronii	B
Hibiscus cannabinus	B,C,CG
Hibiscus 'Charles September'	B
Hibiscus coccineus	B,C,CG,JE,SC,SA
Hibiscus 'Cooperi'	B
Hibiscus coulteri	B,RS
Hibiscus 'Cream Cup'	B,BS
Hibiscus denisonii	B
Hibiscus denudatus	B,RS
Hibiscus denudatus v involucellatus	B,SW
Hibiscus diversifolius	B,C,SI
Hibiscus elatus	B
Hibiscus engleri	B,SI
Hibiscus f1 hyb 'Disco Belle' mix	BS,C,CL,DT,JE,T,V
Hibiscus f1 hyb 'Disco Belle Pink'	JE
Hibiscus f1 hyb 'Disco Belle Red'	B,JE
Hibiscus f1 hyb 'Disco Belle White'	B,JE,SA
Hibiscus f1 hyb 'Southern Belle' mix	BD,BS,JE
Hibiscus f1 'Les Belles'	D
Hibiscus ficilifolius	B
Hibiscus fragilis	B
Hibiscus genevii	B
Hibiscus 'Gina Marie'	B
Hibiscus 'Golden Dust'	B
Hibiscus grandiflora	FS
Hibiscus hamabo	B
Hibiscus 'Harvest Moon'	B
Hibiscus insignus	B
Hibiscus 'Joan Kinchen'	B
Hibiscus lasiocarpos	B
Hibiscus 'Lavender Lady'	B
Hibiscus ludwigii	B,SI
Hibiscus makinoi	B
Hibiscus manihot	JE,SA
Hibiscus manihot 'Cream Cup'	T
Hibiscus meersianus	B
Hibiscus militaris	B,PR
Hibiscus mutabilis	B,C,SA
Hibiscus 'Okinawan'	B
Hibiscus ovalifolius	B
Hibiscus panduriformis	B,C,SA
Hibiscus paramutabilis	B
Hibiscus pedunculatus	B,SI
Hibiscus pusillus	C,SI
Hibiscus radiatus	B

HIBISCUS

Hibiscus rockii	B	Hoffmanseggia jamesii	B
Hibiscus 'Ross Estey'	B	Hohenbergia augusta	B
Hibiscus sabdariffa	B,C	Hohenbergia correia - araujei	B
Hibiscus schizopetalus	B	Hohenbergia disjuncta	B
Hibiscus sororius	B	Hohenbergia megalantha	B
Hibiscus sp	LG,SI	Hohenbergia membranostrobilis	B
Hibiscus surattensis	B	Hohenbergia portoricensis	B
Hibiscus syriacus	A,AP,B,G,N,SA	Hohenbergia ridleyi	B
Hibiscus syriacus v album	B,C,SA	Hohenbergia stellata	B
Hibiscus syriacus 'Woodbridge'	C	Hoheria angustifolia	SA
Hibiscus taiwanensis	B	Hoheria glabrata	SS
Hibiscus tiliaceus	B,HA,O,SA,SI	Hoheria lyallii	AP,LG,SS
Hibiscus trionum	AP,B,C,G,RS,SA,SC,SI, W	Hoheria populnea	B,SS
		Holacantha emoryi	B
Hibiscus trionum 'Luyona'	B	Holarrhena pubescens	B
Hibiscus trionum 'Simply Love'	B,C,DT,T	Holcus lanatus	B
Hibiscus trionum 'Sunnyday'	B,T	Holodiscus discolor	B,C,SA,SG
Hibiscus trionum 'Vanilla Ice'	U,V	Holodiscus dumosus	B,SW
Hibiscus vitifolius	B	Holoschoenus romanus holoschoenus	B
Hicksbeachia pinnatifolia	B	Holothrix aspera	B
Hieracium alpinum	B,JE,SG	Holothrix sp	SI
Hieracium amplexicaule	RH	Holubia saccata	B,SI
Hieracium argenteum	SG	Homalanthus populifolius	B
Hieracium bombycinum	AP,FH,JE,SC,SG	Homeria breyniana	AP,MN,SC,SI
Hieracium bupleuroides	SG	Homeria collina	B,C,G,SI
Hieracium canadense	B,PR	Homeria comptonii	B,SI
Hieracium chondrillifolium	B,G,JE	Homeria cookii	SI
Hieracium intybaceum	B,G,JE	Homeria elegans	B
Hieracium korschynskyi	SG	Homeria flaccida	B
Hieracium lanatum	AP,B,C,G,RH,SC,SG	Homeria marlothii	B,MN
Hieracium longipilum	B,PR	Homeria miniata	B
Hieracium maculatum	AP,FH,I,PM,RH,SC	Homeria ochroleuca	AP,B,SI
Hieracium maculatum 'Leopard'	B,G,JE,SA	Homeria pendula	Si
Hieracium olafii	FH	Homeria ramosissima	SI
Hieracium pilosella	AP,G,JE,SC,SG,SU	Homeria sp	SI
Hieracium prenanthoides	SG	Homeria tricolor	B
Hieracium ssp	LA	Homogyne alpina	B,G,SG
Hieracium tomentosum	AP,JE	Honkenya peploides	B
Hieracium umbellatum	B,JE,SG	Hoodia bainsii	B,SI
Hieracium villosum	AP,B,C,G,HH,I,JE,SA, SC,SG,V	Hoodia gordonii	B,C,Y
		Hoodia lugardii	B,SI
Hieracium vulgatum	B	Hoodia sp	SI
Hieracium wetteranum	SG	Hoplophyllum spinosum	B,SI
Hierochloe alpina	SG	Hordelymus europaeus	B
Hierochloe occidentalis	B	Hordeum brevisubulatum	SG
Hierochloe odorata	AP,G,SG	Hordeum californicum	B
Hilaria jamesii	B	Hordeum distichum	B
Hilaria rigida	B	Hordeum hystrix	B
Hildewintera aureispina	BC,Y	Hordeum jubatum	AP,B,C,KI,SC,SG,SU,T,V
Hippeastrum 'Appleblossom'	B	Hordeum junceum	AP,P
Hippeastrum bicolor	B	Hordeum murinum	B
Hippeastrum hyb mix	AP,C,SG	Hordeum polystichum	B
Hippeastrum 'Picotee'	B	Hordeum pyrenaicum	SG
Hippeastrum 'Red Lion'	B	Hordeum secalinum	B
Hippeastrum sp BCW 5038	AP,SC	Hordeum vulgare	B
Hippeastrum 'United Nations'	B	Hordeum vulgare 'Kanzaki'	B
Hippeastrum vittatum	B,SA	Horminum pyrenaicum	B,FH,G,I,JE,P,SA,SC
Hippeastrum vittatum f1 hyb s-c	B	Horridocactus aconcaguensis	Y
Hippeastrum white, red striped	C	Horridocactus choapenensis	BC
Hippia frutescens	B,SI	Horridocactus curvispinus petorcensis	BC
Hippobroma longiflora	B	Horridocactus heinrichianus Tambillos	BC
Hippocrepis comosa	B,SU	Horridocactus tuberisulcatus	Y
Hippophae rhamnoides	A,B,C,SA,SG	Hosta caerulea	B,G
Hippophae salicifolia	SA	Hosta 'Decorative Foliage Mix'	T,V
Hiptage benghalensis	B	Hosta elata	JE,SG
Hirpicium alienatum	B,SI	Hosta fortunei	B,C

121

HOSTA

Hosta fortunei 'Aurea'	CG
Hosta gracillima	AP,SC,SG
Hosta minor	B,JE
Hosta montana	B
Hosta 'New Hybrids'	B,BD,BS,JE,SA
Hosta plantaginea	B
Hosta rectifolia	JE
Hosta sieboldiana	AP,B,BS,C,G,SC,SG,T
Hosta sieboldiana 'Elegans'	B,C,JE,L,SA
Hosta sieboldii	DT,F,JE,SG
Hosta sp mix	C,I,J,N,PA
Hosta 'Tall Boy'	B
Hosta tokudama	FH,G
Hosta 'True Blue'	PM
Hosta ventricosa	AP,B,C,E,JE,SA,SC,SG,T
Houstonia longifolia	PR
Houttuynia cordata	B,CC
Hovea acanthoclada	B
Hovea acutifolia	B,HA
Hovea chorizemifolia	B
Hovea elliptica	B,C,HA,SA
Hovea lanceolata	B,HA,SA
Hovea linearis	B,SA
Hovea longifolia	B
Hovea pungens	B,SA
Hovea purpurea v rosmarinifolia	B
Hovea rosmarinifolia	HA
Hovea trisperma	B
Hovenia acerba	B
Hovenia dulcis	A,B,C,CGSA
Howea belmoreana	B,HA,O,SA
Howea forsterana	B,HA,O,SA,SH,T
Hoya australis	B
Hoya australis ssp bandaensis	B
Hoya carnosa	B
Hoya purpureofusca	B,C
Huernia hystrix	B,SI
Huernia kirkii	SI
Huernia pillansii	B
Huernia quinta	SI
Huernia whitesloaneana	SI
Huernia zebrina	SI
Huernia zebrina v magniflora	B,SI
Hugonia mystax	B
Hugueninia tanacetifolia	B,CG
Hugueninia tanacetifolia v suffruticosa	C,JE
Humulus japonicus	B,BS,C,V
Humulus lupulus	B,C,CG,DT,JE,SG
Humulus lupulus 'Aureus'	B
Hunnemannia fumariifolia 'Sunlite'	B,KS,T
Hura crepitans	B
Hurungana madagascariensis	B
Hyacinthoides hispanica	B,C,G,SC
Hyacinthoides hispanica MS467 Portugal	MN
Hyacinthoides hispanica v algeriense	B
Hyacinthoides hispanica v algeriense	MN
Hyacinthoides hispanica v algeriense	MN
Hyacinthoides non-scripta	AP,B,C,CO,KI,LA,LG, SA,SU,Z
Hyacinthoides non-scripta pink	RS
Hyalosperma cotula	B,O
Hyalosperma glutinosum	B
Hyalosperma glutinosum ssp venustum	O
Hyalosperma praecox	B,O
Hybanthus calycinus	B
Hybanthus enneaspermus	B

Hybanthus floribundus	B,C,SA
Hybanthus floribundus ssp adpressus	B
Hydrangea arborescens	B,CG
Hydrangea heteromalla	B,SG
Hydrangea heteromalla Bretschneideri Gr	SA
Hydrangea heteromalla CNW376	X
Hydrangea indochinensis	SG
Hydrangea macrophylla	B
Hydrangea paniculata	B,SA
Hydrangea petiolaris	B,C,SA
Hydrangea quercifolia	B,C,SA
Hydrangea sargentiana	B
Hydrangea sp CNW818	X
Hydrangea sp CNW871	X
Hydrangea sp CNW885	X
Hydrangea villosa	SA,SG
Hydrangea xanthoneura	SA
Hydrastis canadensis	B
Hydriastele wendlandiana	B,O
Hydrophilus rattrayii	B,SI
Hydrophyllum capitatum	SW
Hygrophila auriculata	B
Hylomecon japonicum	AP,JE,SC
Hymenaea courbaril	B,RE
Hymenocallis littoralis	JE
Hymenocallis narcissiflora 'Sulphur Qu.'	B
Hymenocardia ulmoides	B,SI
Hymenogyne glabra	B,SI
Hymenolepis parviflora	B,SI
Hymenorebutia mix	Y
Hymenosporum flavum	B,C,HA,O,SA,SC,SH
Hymenoxys subintegra	AP,SG
Hyophorbe indica	O
Hyophorbe lagenicaulis	B,O
Hyophorbe verschaffelti	B,O,SA
Hyoscyamus albus	B,C,G
Hyoscyamus aurus	SA
Hyoscyamus niger	AP,B,C,G,SG
Hypericum aethiopicum	B,SI
Hypericum androsaemum	B,C,E,G,JE,LA,SA,SG
Hypericum andros. 'Gladys Brabazon'	C
Hypericum ascyron	AP,B,JE,SC,SG
Hypericum athoum	AP,G,I,SC
Hypericum balearicum	SG
Hypericum buckleyi	I
Hypericum calycinum	B,BD,BS,C,CL,D,HA,JE, L,SA
Hypericum cerastoides	AP,B,I,JE,RH,SC,SG
Hypericum choisianum	SG
Hypericum cistifolium	B
Hypericum coris	AP,B,C,G,I,JE,RH,SC
Hypericum delphicum	I
Hypericum erectum	B
Hypericum forrestii	RH
Hypericum fragile	B,C,JE
Hypericum frondosum	AP,B
Hypericum galioides	B
Hypericum henryi ssp henryi	B
Hypericum henryi ssp uraloides	RH
Hypericum 'Hidcote'	RS
Hypericum hircinum	RH
Hypericum hirsutum	B,SG
Hypericum hyssopifolium	B,C,JE,RH
Hypericum japonicum	B,SS
Hypericum kamtschaticum	RH
Hypericum kouytchense	RH,SA

HYPERICUM

Hypericum lalandii	B,SI	Hypoestes phyllostachya 'Desert Pink'	BS
Hypericum lancasteri	SG	Hypoestes phyllostachya 'Pink Splash' sel.	B,BS,CL,HA,J,L,T,V
Hypericum linarifolium	B	Hypoestes phyllostachya 'Red Splash' sel.	CL
Hypericum maculatum	B,CG	Hypoestes phyllostachya 'Rose Sp.' sel.	B,BS,CL,HA
Hypericum montanum	B,SG	Hypoestes phyllostachya 'Splash' mix	L
Hypericum oblongifolium	AP,B	Hypoestes phyllostachya 'White Sp.' sel.	B,BS,CL,HA
Hypericum olympicum	AP,B,C,FH,G,I,JE,RH,SA,	Hypoxis angustifolia	SI
	SC,SG,T	Hypoxis aquatica	B,SI
Hypericum olympicum 'Grandiflorum'	B	Hypoxis capensis	B,SI
Hypericum olympicum minus	HH	Hypoxis colchicifolia	B,SI
Hypericum orientale	AP,B,SC	Hypoxis decumbens	CG
Hypericum pallens	AP,SG	Hypoxis hemerocallidea	B,C,SI
Hypericum patulum	B,JE	Hypoxis hirsuta	PR
Hypericum perforatum	AP,B,C,CP,G,LA,JE,RH,	Hypoxis hygrometrica	G,PM,SC
	SC,SG	Hypoxis iridifolia	B,SI
Hypericum perforatum 'Pharma'	B	Hypoxis multiceps	SI
Hypericum perforatum 'Topas'	B	Hypoxis neocanaliculata	B
Hypericum polyphyllum	C,CG,SG	Hypoxis rigidula	B,SI
Hypericum polyphyllum 'Grandiflorum'	CL,JE,L	Hypoxis rigidula v pilosissima	B
Hypericum proliferum	B,JE	Hypoxis sp	SI
Hypericum pseudohenryi	RH	Hypoxis villosa	B
Hypericum pseudopetiolatum yak.	P,SC	Hypoxis woodii	B,SI
Hypericum pulchrum	AP,B,JE	Hyptis emoryi	B
Hypericum punctatum	CP,PR	Hyptis suaveolens	B
Hypericum pyramidatum	PR	Hyssopus fergonensis	SG
Hypericum repens	I	Hyssopus officinalis	AP,B,CP,FH,G,KS,RH,
Hypericum revolutum	AP,B,C,SI		SC,SG
Hypericum richeri	B	Hyssopus officinalis blue	SA
Hypericum roeperianum	B	Hyssopus officinalis f albus	B,E,G,JE,SA
Hypericum sp 2m shrubs CNW769	X	Hyssopus officinalis f roseus	AP,B,P,JE,SA
Hypericum sp China	SG	Hyssopus officinalis 'Ruber'	E
Hypericum sp CNW848	X	Hyssopus officinalis 'Sprite Blue'	B
Hypericum sp coll Murren	W	Hyssopus officinalis 'Sprite Pink'	B
Hypericum subsessile	SG	Hyssopus officinalis 'Sprite Snow'	B
Hypericum tenuicaule	SG	Hyssopus officinalis ssp aristatus	G,RH,SG
Hypericum tetrapterum	AP,B,G,JE,LA,SU	Hyssopus officinalis v canescens	B
Hypericum triquetrifolium	B	Hystrix patula	B,G,JE,PR,SA
Hypericum uralum	C	Iberis amara	B,G,SG
Hypericum x inodorum	RH	Iberis amara 'Empress' hyacinth fl	KS
Hypericum x inodorum 'Albury Purple'	E	Iberis amara 'Iceberg'	B,C,J
Hypericum yakusimense	AP,B,FH	Iberis amara 'Iceberg Superior'	B,BS
Hypericum yezoense	B,P	Iberis amara 'Mount Hood'	B
Hypertelis salsoloides	B,SI	Iberis amara 'White Pinnacle'	B
Hyphaene coriacea	B,O	Iberis coronaria 'Hyacinth Fl'	DT,T
Hyphaene natalensis hybrid	B	Iberis crenata	T
Hyphaene parvula	B	Iberis 'Crown' mix	BS
Hyphaene petersiana	B,O	Iberis 'Fantasia'	S
Hyphaene shadron	B	Iberis gibraltarica	AP,B,BD,C,CO,JE,KI,L,
Hyphaene shatan	B		SA
Hypocalymma angustifolium	B,O,SA	Iberis hybrida	B
Hypocalymma robustum	B,O	Iberis 'Improved White Spiral'	S
Hypocalymma strictum	B	Iberis saxatilis	B,C,JE
Hypocalymma xanthopetalum	B	Iberis sempervirens pink	S
Hypocalyptus sophoroides	B,SA,SI	Iberis sempervirens 'Snowflake'	AP,B,C,JE,KS,SE,T,U
Hypochoeris radicata	B,C	Iberis sempervirens white	AP,CG,CL,D,JE,KI,L,S,
Hypochoeris uniflora	AP,B,JE,SA,SC		SA,SC,ST,SU,TU,V
Hypodiscus aristatus	B,SI	Iberis 'Spangles'	KI
Hypodiscus synchrolepis	B,SI	Iberis 'Special mix'	CO,DT,L
Hypoested phyllostachya	C,KI	Iberis umbellata	G,SG
Hypoestes aristata	B	Iberis umbellata 'Fairy' mix	BD,BS,C,D,F,J,M,S,SE,
Hypoestes phyllostachya 'Arctic White'	BS		SU,T,U,V
Hypoestes phyllostachya 'Confetti' mix	S,T,YA	Iberis umbellata 'Flash' mix	C,F,J,KS,T
Hypoestes phyllostachya 'Confetti Red'	B,BS,YA	Iberis umbellata 'Flash' s-c	B,BS
Hypoestes phyllostachya 'Confetti Rose'	B,BS,YA	Iberis umbellata 'Flash White'	B,KS
Hypoestes phyllostachya 'Confetti White'	B,BS,YA	Iberis umbellata 'Super' mix	C
Hypoestes phyllostachya 'Conf. Wine Red'	B,BS,YA	Ibervillea sonorae	B

IBICELLA

Ibicella lutea	B,G
Ichnocarpus frutescens	B
Idesia polycarpa	B,C,G,SA
Ilex aquifolium	A,B,C,G,RH,SA
Ilex aquifolium 'Fructo Luteo'	C
Ilex aquifolium variegated	C
Ilex cassine	B
Ilex chinensis of gdns	B,SA
Ilex cornuta	B,SA
Ilex crenata	B,SA
Ilex decidua	B,SA
Ilex geniculata	SG
Ilex glabra	B
Ilex laevigata	SG
Ilex latifolia	B
Ilex mitis	B,SI
Ilex montana	B
Ilex opaca	B,C,SA
Ilex paraguariensis	B
Ilex pedunculosa	B
Ilex pernyi	G,SG
Ilex serrata	B
Ilex verticillata	B,SA,SG
Ilex vomitoria	B,SA
Ilex x altaclerensis	RH
Iliamna remota	C,PR
Iliamna rivularis	B,C
Illicium anisatum	B,SA
Imitaria muirii	B
Impatiens 'Baby' mix	J
Impatiens balfourii	CG
Impatiens balsamina	B,C,CG,G
Impatiens balsamina 'Bush Fl'	BS,CO,ST
Impatiens balsamina 'Camellia Fl' mix	BD,BS,D,F,J,T,V
Impatiens balsamina 'Tom Thumb'	BD,C,D,DT,L,S,SE,T,YA
Impatiens balsamina 'Topknot' mix	BS,D,R
Impatiens balsamina 'Topknot' s-c	B,BS
Impatiens brachcentra	CG
Impatiens burtonii	B
Impatiens capensis	PR
Impatiens cristata	CG
Impatiens dwarf mix	CO,SU,VH
Impatiens edgeworthii	C
Impatiens f1 'Accent Apricot'	CL,M,U,VH
Impatiens f1 'Accent Bright Eye'	DT,T
Impatiens f1 'Accent Burgundy Star'	B,BS,CL,DT
Impatiens f1 'Accent Lavender Blue'	CL,D,DT,M,VH
Impatiens f1 'Accent' mix	BS,CL,D,DT,F,J,M,S,SE
Impatiens f1 'Accent Orange Star'	BS,B,CL
Impatiens f1 'Accent Pink'	CL,D,DT,M,VH
Impatiens f1 'Accent Red'	BS,CL,D,DT,M,VH
Impatiens f1 'Accent Red Star'	B,CL
Impatiens f1 'Accent Rose'	BS,CL,D
Impatiens f1 'Accent Rose Star'	B,CL
Impatiens f1 'Accent Salmon'	CL,D
Impatiens f1 'Accent Violet'	BS,CL,D
Impatiens f1 'Accent Violet Star'	B,CL
Impatiens f1 'Accent White'	,CLD,M,VH
Impatiens f1 'Babylon Series' s-c	YA
Impatiens f1 'Bellizzy Colourballs' dbl mix	C
Impatiens f1 'Blitz Jumbo'	D
Impatiens f1 'Blitz' mix	BS,J,U
Impatiens f1 'Blitz' s-c	BS,SE,T
Impatiens f1 'Bright Shades'	U
Impatiens f1 'Bruno'	F
Impatiens f1 'Busy Lizzie Accents'	M

Impatiens f1 'Chelsea Girl'	F
Impatiens f1 'Cherry Blush'	U,V
Impatiens f1 'Circus'	F
Impatiens f1 'Cleopatra'	T
Impatiens f1 'Confection' mix	BS,J,U
Impatiens f1 'Dble Confection' mix	DT,T
Impatiens f1 'Dble Confection' s-c	SE,T
Impatiens f1 'Deco Burgundy'	B,CL
Impatiens f1 'Deco Crystal'	B,CL,U
Impatiens f1 'Deco Daydream'	D
Impatiens f1 'Deco' mix	CL,DT,KI,M,ST,T,U,YA
Impatiens f1 'Deco' s-c	B,CL,T
Impatiens f1 'Emperor Mixed'	U
Impatiens f1 'Expo' mix	D,F,S
Impatiens f1 'Expo Picotee'	F
Impatiens f1 'Expo' s-c	B
Impatiens f1 'Eye-Eye' mix	D
Impatiens f1 'Florette Stars' mix	BS,J,TU
Impatiens f1 'Futura' mix	BS
Impatiens f1 'Imp' mix	M
Impatiens f1 'Impact' mix	BS,C
Impatiens f1 'Impact's-c	BS,C
Impatiens f1 'Impulse Appleblossom'	BD,TT
Impatiens f1 'Lavender Blush'	U
Impatiens f1 'Lilac Pearl'	T,U
Impatiens f1 'Mega Orange Star'	B,C,CL,D,DT,L,O,SE,T,U, YA
Impatiens f1 'Mosaic Lilac'	CL,D,DT,SE,T,U
Impatiens f1 'Mystic'	U
Impatiens f1 'Neon'	U
Impatiens f1 'New Guinea Borneo Bold'	BS
Impatiens f1 'New Guinea Spectra'	BD,BS,C,CL,DT,F,J,KI, L,M,R,S,SE,T,U,V,YA
Impatiens f1 'New Guinea Tango'	B,BS,C,CL,D,DT,J,KI,L, S,SE,T,V
Impatiens f1 'Novette Star' mix	D,S
Impatiens f1 'Pantomime'	F
Impatiens f1 'Petticoat'	V
Impatiens f1 'Plum Sorbet'	U
Impatiens f1 'Revue' s-c	V
Impatiens f1 'Rosette' mix	BD,BS,D,F,KI,L,S,SE
Impatiens f1 'Special' mix	DT
Impatiens f1 'Starbright'	BD,BS,CL,CO,DT,F,KI, L,M,R,SE,T,U,V,YA
Impatiens f1 'Sunrise' mix	DT
Impatiens f1 'Super Elfin Apricot'	B,BS,CL,YA
Impatiens f1 'Super Elfin Blue Pearl'	B,BS,CL,KI,S,SE,YA
Impatiens f1 'Super Elfin Blush'	B,BS,CL,YA
Impatiens f1 'Super Elfin Cherry'	B,BS,CL,KI,S,YA
Impatiens f1 'Super Elfin Coral'	B,BS,CL,YA
Impatiens f1 'Super Elfin Lavender'	B,BS,CL,YA
Impatiens f1 'Super Elfin Lilac'	B,BS,CL,YA
Impatiens f1 'Super Elfin Lipstick'	B,BS,CL,F,S,YA
Impatiens f1 'Super Elfin' mix	BD,BS,CL,D,DT,F,J,KI, L,R,S,SE,ST,T,TU,VH,YA
Impatiens f1 'Super Elfin Mother of Pearl'	F
Impatiens f1 'Super Elfin Orange'	B,BS,CL,KI,S,YA
Impatiens f1 'Super Elfin Pastel'	BD,BS,CL,DT,J,KI,S,V, YA
Impatiens f1 'Super Elfin Pearl'	B,BS,CL,F,YA
Impatiens f1 'Super Elfin Picotee'	T
Impatiens f1 'Super Elfin Pink'	B,BS,CL,KI,YA
Impatiens f1 'Super Elfin Red'	B,CL,KI,S
Impatiens f1 'Super Elfin Red Velvet'	B,CL,F,YA
Impatiens f1 'Super Elfin Rose'	B,BS,CL,S,YA
Impatiens f1 'Super Elfin Salmon'	B,BS,CL,KI,YA

IMPATIENS

Impatiens f1 'Super Elfin Salmon Blush'	B,BS,CL,S,YA
Impatiens f1 'Super Elfin Scarlet'	B,BS,CL,YA
Impatiens f1 'Super Elfin Violet'	B,BS,CL,YA
Impatiens f1 'Super Elfin White'	B,BS,CL,KI,S,YA
Impatiens f1 'Swirl Coral'	B,BS,S,SE
Impatiens f1 'Swirl' mix	BS,CL,S,SE,M,T,VH,U,YA
Impatiens f1 'Swirl Peach'	B,BS,SE
Impatiens f1 'Swirl Pink'	B,BS,SE,YA
Impatiens f1 'Symphony Red Star'	F
Impatiens f1 'Tempo Blackpool Rock'	DT
Impatiens f1 'Tempo Burgundy'	B,BS,L,T,U
Impatiens f1 'Tempo' mix	BD,BS,CL,DT,L,T
Impatiens f1 'Tempo Series' s-c	B,BS,DT,F,L,T
Impatiens f1 'Tiara' mix	T
Impatiens f1 'Unwins Pride Mix'	U
Impatiens f1 'Unwins Pride Red Glow'	U
Impatiens f1 'Unwins Pride Tahiti'	U
Impatiens f2 'Action Series'	T
Impatiens f2 'Dainty Maid'	D
Impatiens f2 'Dwarf' mix	BS,L,S
Impatiens f2 'Imagination' mix	CL
Impatiens f2 'Safari'	B,BS,F,J,KI,R,TU,V,YA
Impatiens 'Gem'	BS
Impatiens glandulifera	B,C,CG,G,SG
Impatiens glandulifera alba	CG
Impatiens hochstetleri ssp hochstetteri	B,SI
Impatiens 'Holstii' hyb	BS
Impatiens hyb	I
Impatiens hyb 'Rainbow Shower'	B
Impatiens 'Improved' formula mix	BS
Impatiens 'Little Lizzie'	BS,KI,Sm,ST
Impatiens niamniamensis	B
Impatiens noli-tangere	AP,B,SG
Impatiens oncidioides 'Malaysia Gold'	T
Impatiens pallida	PR
Impatiens platypetala	C
Impatiens scabrida	CG
Impatiens 'Sultani Scarlet'	BS,KI,ST
Impatiens sylvicola	SI
Impatiens textori	B
Impatiens walleriana	CG
Impatiens walleriana 'Sultana'	C
Impatiens zombensis	B,SI
Imperata cylindrica	G,HA
Imperata cylindrica v major	B
Incarvillea arguta	AP,FH
Incarvillea compacta	AP,G,SC,SG
Incarvillea delavayi	AP,B,BS,C,CG,CL,G,HH,JE,KI,L,LG,PM,S,SA,SC,SG,T
Incarvillea delavayi 'Alba'	AP,B,G,JE,P,SA,SC
Incarvillea mairei	AP,B,CC,CG,JE,SA,SC,SG
Incarvillea mairei 'Nyoto Sama'	FH,SC
Incarvillea mairei v grandiflora	AP,B,CG,G,SC,SG
Incarvillea olgae	AP,B,G,JE,SC,SG
Incarvillea sinensis	AP,B,SC
Incarvillea sinensis 'Cheron'	AP,BS,C,D,DT,T,V
Incarvillea sin. ssp variabilis f prizewalskii	SG
Incarvillea sp	AP,SC,SG
Incarvillea sp ex CLD233	CC
Indigofera amblyantha	B,SA
Indigofera aspalathoides	B
Indigofera australis	AU,B,C,HA,O,SA,SH
Indigofera brevidens	B

Indigofera cylindrica	C
Indigofera cytisoides	B,SA,SI
Indigofera decora	B
Indigofera dosua	B
Indigofera enneaphylla	B
Indigofera filicaulis	B,SI
Indigofera filifolia	B,SI
Indigofera foliosa	SI
Indigofera frutescens	B,SI
Indigofera glabra	B
Indigofera hamulosa	B,SI
Indigofera hedyantha	SI
Indigofera heterantha	AP,B,C,SA,G
Indigofera hilaris	SI
Indigofera hirsuta	B
Indigofera kirilowii	SA
Indigofera langebergensis	B,SI
Indigofera linifolia	B
Indigofera linnaei	B
Indigofera monophylla	B
Indigofera natalensis	B,SI
Indigofera pendula	SG
Indigofera pseudotinctoria	AP,B,SA
Indigofera sp	SI
Indigofera suffruticosa	B
Indigofera tinctoria	B,C,CP
Indigofera trita	B
Indigofera woodii	SI
Indoneesiella echioides	B
Inga edulis	B
Inga fuillei	B
Inga spectabilis	B
Inula acaulis	FH,SC
Inula britannica	B,SG
Inula candida	B,JE
Inula conyzae	B
Inula crithmoides	B
Inula ensifolia	AP,B,BS,C,CG,G,I,JE,SC,SG,V
Inula ensifolia 'Compacta'	AP,B,G,SC
Inula ensifolia 'Mediterranean Sun'	U
Inula ensifolia 'Star Gold'	CL
Inula ensifolia 'Star Oriental'	CL
Inula germanica	B
Inula grandiflora	PS
Inula helenium	AP,B,BS,C,CP,G,JE,RS,SA,SC,SG
Inula helenium 'Goliath'	B,C
Inula hirta	B,G,JE
Inula hookeri	AP,G,SC
Inula magnifica	AP,B,C,CG,FH,G,JE,PA,SA,SC,SG
Inula montana	B
Inula oculus-christi	B
Inula orientalis	AP,B,C,F,G,SA,T
Inula orientalis 'Grandiflora'	B,JE
Inula pulicaria	B
Inula racemosa	B,CC
Inula racemosa 'Sonnenspeer'	JE
Inula rhizocephala	AP,B,G,JE,SC
Inula royleana	AP,B,G,SA,SC
Inula salicina	B,SG
Inulanthera calva	B,SI
Iochroma cyanea	B
Ionopsidium acaule	B,C,J,T,V
Iostephane heterophylla	SW

IPHEION

Ipheion uniflorum	AP,B,G	Ipomopsis aggregata v macrosiphon	B
Ipheion uniflorum 'Album'	AP,PM	Ipomopsis longiflora	B
Ipheion uniflorum 'Froyle Mill'	AP,PM	Ipomopsis rubra	B,HW,KS,V
Ipomoea adenoides	SI	Ipomopsis rubra 'Red Arrow'	B
Ipomoea alba	B,C,F,KS,T	Ipomopsis spicata	B
Ipomoea aquatica	B	Iriartea deltoides	B
Ipomoea arborescens	B	Iriartea gigantea	B,O,RE
Ipomoea batatas	B	Iriartea ventricosa	B
Ipomoea brasiliensis	C	Iris aphylla	B,G,JE
Ipomoea cairica	B	Iris aphylla ssp hungarica	B
Ipomoea carnea ssp fistulosa	B	Iris attica, Greece	MN
Ipomoea coccinea	B,C,SW	Iris barbata	JE
Ipomoea conzattii aff 'Jicama Montes'	B	Iris barbata elatior hyb	G
Ipomoea costata	B,C	Iris barbata nana 'New Hybrids'	JE
Ipomoea 'Dbl Blue Picotee'	SE	Iris biglumis	SG
Ipomoea hederacea	B,CG,G,SG	Iris bracteata	AP,I,SC
Ipomoea hederacea 'Roman Candy'	T	Iris bucharica (orchioides)	AP,B,G,LG,SC,SG
Ipomoea heterophylla	B	Iris bulleyana	AP,B,JE,SA,SC
Ipomoea holubii	CG	Iris carthaliniae	G,SG
Ipomoea involucrata	SI	Iris chrysographes	AP,B,G,JE,LG,SC,SG
Ipomoea leptophylla	B,SC	Iris chrysographes 'Black Forms'	AP,B,C,F,FH,LG,PA,SC
Ipomoea leptotoma	B	Iris chrysographes 'Black Night'	T
Ipomoea lobata	B,C,CG,CL,DT,F,FH,G,J,	Iris chrysographes hyb	I,SC
	KS,L,S,V	Iris clarkei	AP,B,G,JE,SC,SG
Ipomoea lobata 'Citronella'	DT,SE,U	Iris crocea	B,CC
Ipomoea lobata 'Exotic Love'	SE	Iris decora	AP,B,G,SC
Ipomoea lobata 'Mexican Fiesta'	U	Iris delavayi	B,CG,G,I,SC
Ipomoea mix	FH	Iris dichotoma	CG,SG
Ipomoea muelleri	B	Iris douglasiana	AP,B,C,CG,JE,LG,SC
Ipomoea nil	B,C,KS	Iris ensata	AP,B,G,P,SA,SC,SG
Ipomoea pennata	C,RS	Iris ensata 'Higo'	T
Ipomoea pes-caprae	B,SA	Iris ensata hyb	BS,JE,L,SA
Ipomoea pes-tigridis	B	Iris ensata 'New Hybrids'	B
Ipomoea platensis	B,CH,Y	Iris ensata 'Prize Winning Mix'	P
Ipomoea 'Platycodon Fl. Picotee'	T	Iris foetidissima	B,C,CG,FH,G,I,JE,LG,
Ipomoea 'Platycodon Fl.' white	T		RH,RS,SA,SC,SG,W
Ipomoea pubescens	B	Iris foetidissima 'Citrina'	AP,C,SC,SG
Ipomoea purpurea	AP,B,C,CG,F,SG,T,W	Iris forrestii	AP,B,CG,G,I,JE,SA,SC,T
Ipomoea purpurea 'Kniola's Purple-black'	B	Iris forrestii armene	FH
Ipomoea quamoclit	B,F,SA,V	Iris fulva	AP,B
Ipomoea 'Quebraplata'	B	Iris germanica cvs mix	C
Ipomoea sepiaria	B	Iris germanica 'Florentina'	B,CG
Ipomoea setosa v campanulata	B	Iris gracilipes	AP,B,CC
Ipomoea tricolor	G,V	Iris graminea	AP,B,C,G,JE,LG,SA,SC
Ipomoea tricolor 'Blue Star'	B	Iris graminea ssp pseudocyperus	B
Ipomoea tricolor 'Cardinal'	BS,S	Iris hartwegii	B
Ipomoea tricolor 'Crimson Rambler'	F	Iris hoogiana	B,G
Ipomoea tricolor 'Early Call'	T,U	Iris humilis	CG,SG
Ipomoea tricolor 'Flying Saucers'	B,D,F	Iris innominata 'Broadleigh Rose'	P
Ipomoea tricolor 'Heavenly Blue'	B,BD,BS,C,CL,CO,D,DT,	Iris innominata hyb	FH,I,SG
	F,J,KI,KS,L,S,ST,T,U,V	Iris J437	P
Ipomoea tricolor 'Magenta Climber'	B	Iris japonica	B,SG
Ipomoea tricolor 'Mini Sky Blue'	SE,T	Iris kamaonensis	JE,SG
Ipomoea tricolor mix	J,SE	Iris kerneriana	AP,CG,G,SC
Ipomoea tricolor 'Pearly Gates'	B,BS,V	Iris lactea	AP,G,SC,SG
Ipomoea tricolor 'Scarlet O'Hara'	B,BS,C,L	Iris laevigata	B,CG,G,JE,SA,SC,SG
Ipomoea tricolor 'Scarlet Star'	T	Iris laevigata f alba	JE
Ipomoea tricolor 'Sunrise Serenade'	B	Iris latifolia	AP,B,G,HH,JE,LG,RS,SC
Ipomoea tricolor 'Super Garland'	C	Iris latifolia LG340 Spain	MN
Ipomoea tricolour 'Moonflower'	SE	Iris longipetala	B
Ipomoea 'Variegated Leaf Mix'	BS	Iris luriola	CG
Ipomoea verbascoidea	SI	Iris lutescens	AP,C,JE,MN,SC
Ipomoea villosa	B	Iris lutescens B.S337 Italy	MN
Ipomoea violacea	SG	Iris lutescens B.S389 France	MN
Ipomoea x multifida	B	Iris lutescens L/E171 Spain	MN
Ipomopsis aggregata	AP,B	Iris lutescens MS515 France	MN

IRIS

Iris lutescens MS524 Spain	MN
Iris lutescens 'Nana'	B
Iris maackii	B,G,SA,SG
Iris macrosiphon	AP,B,PM,SC
Iris magnifica	AP,B,G,JE,LG,PM,SC
Iris missouriensis	AV,B,C,G,JE,SC,SG,SW
Iris missouriensis v arizonica	B,SW
Iris musulanica	SG
Iris neglecta	CG
Iris notha	G,SG
Iris orientalis	AP,B,G,JE,SC
Iris oristata	B
Iris 'Pacific Coast Hyb'	AP,SC,T
Iris palaestina	B
Iris pallida	B,CG,,JE,SA
Iris paradoxa f choschab	JE
Iris plicata	CG
Iris polakii	B,CG,SG
Iris prismatica	AP,B,CG,SC,SG
Iris pseudacorus	B,C,CG,FH,G,I,JE,LA,LG, RH,SA
Iris pseudacorus aureus	PM
Iris pseudacorus 'New Hybrids'	B
Iris pseudacorus 'New Varieties'	JE
Iris pseudacorus 'Sulphur Queen'	B
Iris pumila	AP,B,SC
Iris purpureobractea	PM
Iris regius uzziae S.B.L160 Jordan	MN
Iris reichenbachii	AP,B,JE,SC
Iris reticulata	B,G,SC
Iris ruthenica	B,CG,G
Iris sanguinea	AP,B,CG,G,JE,SA,SG
Iris sanguinea 'Snow Queen'	B,G,JE,SA
Iris sari	B,JE
Iris setosa	AP,B,G,JE,RH,SA,SC,SG
Iris setosa 'Alba'	B,G,I,P,SG
Iris setosa 'Blue Light'	B,BD,BS,C,CL,JE,KI,L, ST
Iris setosa major	I
Iris setosa nana see canadensis	
Iris setosa ssp canadensis	AP,B,CG,G,JE,SA,SC,SG
Iris setosa v arctica	B,G,P
Iris sibirica	AP,B,CG,FH,G,JE,LG, RH,RS,SA,SC,SG
Iris sibirica cult mix	C
Iris sibirica f alba	AP,B,CC,FH,G,JE,SA, SC,SG
Iris sibirica 'New Hybrids'	AP,JE,SA,T
Iris sibirica 'Plant World' hyb	C,P
Iris sibirica 'Red Flare'	T
Iris sikkimensis	AP,CG,SC
Iris sintenisii	AP,B,CG,G,JE,SC,SG
Iris sp mix	AP,C,JE,P,SC
Iris spuria	AP,B,G,JE,SC,SG
Iris spuria maritima	I
Iris spuria notha	CC
Iris spuria ssp muselmanica	SG
Iris spuria v halophila	CG,FH,G,MN,SC,SG
Iris suaveolens	JE,PM
Iris subbiflora	CG
Iris tectorum	AP,B,G,JE,SC
Iris tenax	AP,B,C,CG,FH,G,JE,SA, SC
Iris tigrida	SG
Iris tingitana v fontanesii A.B.S4211	MN
Iris tingitana v fontanesii A.B.S4452	MN
Iris unguicularis cretensis	CG,SC
Iris uniflora	SG
Iris variegata	B,G,JE,SA
Iris ventricosa	SG
Iris versicolor	AP,B,G,JE,PM,PR,SA, SC,SG
Iris versicolor 'Kermesina'	B,JE
Iris virginica	B,G
Iris virginica v shrevei	PR
Iris wilsonii	CG
Iris winogradowii	B
Iris x monnieri	B,JE,MN,SA
Iris x sambucina	B
Iris xiphium	B,MA
Iris xiphium B.S411 Portugal	MN
Iris xiphium MS437 Portugal	MN
Iris xiphium MS502 Spain	MN
Irvingia gabonensis	B
Irvingia grandifolia	B
Irvingia smithii	B
Irvingia wombulu	B
Isatis glauca	JE
Isatis lusitanica	B
Isatis tinctoria	AP,B,C,CP,G,JE,LA,KS, RH,SA,SG
Ischryolepis ocreata	B,SI
Ischryolepis subverticillata	B,SI
Iseilema membranaceum	B
Islaya solitaria	Y
Islaya sp mix	C
Isolatocereus dumortiera	CH
Isolepis canariensis	SA
Isolepis cernua	B
Isolepis cernuus	SG
Isolepis nodosa	B
Isoplexis canariensis	AP,CG,G,SC
Isoplexis canariensis ssp lamarkii	SG
Isoplexis sceptrum	C,T
Isopogon alcicornis	B
Isopogon anemonifolius	B,C,HA,O,SA,SH
Isopogon anethifolius	B,HA,O,SA,SH
Isopogon attenuatus	B
Isopogon axillaris	B
Isopogon baxteri	B,O
Isopogon buxifolius	B,O
Isopogon cuneatus	B,O
Isopogon dawsonii	AU
Isopogon divergens	B,O
Isopogon dubius	B,O
Isopogon formosus	B,O,SA
Isopogon latifolius	B
Isopogon polycephalus	B,O
Isopogon scabriusculus	B,O
Isopogon sp	AU
Isopogon sphaerocephalus	B,O
Isopogon teretifolius	B,O
Isopogon tridens	B
Isopogon trilobus	B,O
Isopogon villosus	O
Isopyrum thalictroides	JE
Isotropis cuneifolia	B,SA
Itea illicifolia	G,SA
Itea virginica	B,SA
Iva hayesiana	B
Ixerba brexioides	B
Ixia campanulata	B

Ixia capillaris	B,SI
Ixia conferta	B
Ixia dubia	B,SI
Ixia flexuosa	B,SI
Ixia latifolia v angustifolia	B,SI
Ixia 'Lavender Pink'	C
Ixia maculata	B,C,SI
Ixia marginifolia	B,SI
Ixia odorata	B,SI
Ixia pauciflora	B
Ixia polystachya	B,SI
Ixia pumilio	C
Ixia rapunculoides	B,SI
Ixia rouxii	B,SI
Ixia scillaris	B,SI
Ixia sp	SC,SI
Ixia thomasiae	SI
Ixia vanzijliae	B
Ixia viridiflora	AP,B,C,SC,SI
Ixiochlamys cuneifolia	B
Ixiodia achillaeoides ssp achilaeoides	O
Ixiodia achillaeoides ssp alata	O
Ixiodia achillaeoides ssp arenicola	O
Ixiolirion tataricum	AP,CG,G,JE,PA,SC
Ixiolirion tataricum Ledebourii Gr	B,G
Ixora arborea	B
Ixora coccinea	B
Ixora pavetta	B
Ixora pusilla	SG
Jacaranda acutifolia	B
Jacaranda caucana	B
Jacaranda copaia	B
Jacaranda mimosifolia	B,BS,C,CG,CL,HA,KI,O, RE,SA,ST,T,V
Jacaranda obtusifolia	B
Jacksonia furcellata	B
Jacksonia lehmannii	B
Jacksonia scoparia	B,HA,SA
Jacksonia sternbergiana	B
Jacksonia thesioides	B
Jacobsenia hallii	B
Jacobsenia kolbei	B
Jacquemontia pentantha	B
Jacquemontia pringlei	SW
Jacquinia pungens	B
Jagera pseudorhus	B,O
Jamesia americana	B,SW
Jasione crispa	JE,SC,T
Jasione crispa ssp crispa	SG
Jasione heldreichii	AP,B,C,FH,I,SC,SG
Jasione montana	AP,B,BS,C,CG,JE,KI,NS, RS,SC,SU
Jasione perennis	B,CG,G,SA,SC,SG
Jasione perennis 'Blue Buttons'	B
Jasione perennis 'Blue Light'	BS,C,CL,JE,L,V
Jasminum abyssinicum	SI
Jasminum 'Angustifolium'	B
Jasminum beesianuum	SG
Jasminum floridum	B
Jasminum fruticans	B,CG,SA
Jasminum humile 'Revolutum'	B,SA
Jasminum lineare	B
Jasminum mesnyi	B
Jasminum nudiflorum	SA
Jasminum officinale	B,I,SA
Jasminum polyanthum	B

Jatropha cinerea	B
Jatropha curcas	B,SA,SI
Jatropha gossypifolia	B,CH
Jatropha macrorrhiza	B
Jatropha panduriifolia	B
Jatropha podagrica	B
Jatropha tanjorensis	B
Jeffersonia diphylla	AP,B,CG,G,SC
Jensenobotrya lossowiana	B
Jessenia bataua	B
Johnsonia lupulina	B,C
Johnsonia pubescens	B
Jovellana sinclairii	B
Jovibarba hirta	B
Jovibarba hirta ssp arenaria	B
Jovibarba hueffellii	AP,JE,SC
Jovibarba sobolifera	B
Jubaea chilensis	B,CG,O,SA
Jubaeopsis caffra	B
Juglans ailanthifolia	B,SA,SG
Juglans ailanthifolia v cordiformis	B,SA
Juglans alanchanum	B
Juglans californica	B
Juglans cathayensis	SA
Juglans cinerea	B,CG,SA
Juglans hindsii	B,SA
Juglans hyb	B
Juglans major	B,SA
Juglans mandshurica	B,SA,SG
Juglans microcarpa	B,SA
Juglans neotropica	B
Juglans nigra	B,CG,HA,SA
Juglans regia	C,N,SA
Juglans regia hardy carpathian	B
Juglans regia 'Improved'	B
Juncus antarcticus	B,SS
Juncus brachycarpus	PR
Juncus compressus	B,SG
Juncus conglomeratus	B
Juncus decipiens 'Curly-Wurly'	JE
Juncus effusus	AP,C,CG,JE,PR,SA
Juncus ensifolius	AP,C,G,JE,SA,SC
Juncus inflexus	A,JE,SA
Juncus interior	PR
Juncus nodosus	PR
Juncus pallidus	B
Juncus tenuis	PR
Juncus torreyi	PR
Juncus usitanus	HA
Juncus xiphoides	B
Juniperus cedrus	B
Juniperus chinensis	B,C,SA,V
Juniperus communis	A,B,C,SA,SG
Juniperus communis 'Bush Form'	B
Juniperus communis ssp nana	CG,SG
Juniperus communis v depressa	B
Juniperus conferta	HA,SG
Juniperus deppeana	B
Juniperus deppeana v glauca	B
Juniperus deppeana v pachyphlaea	C,SA
Juniperus excelsa	SA
Juniperus flaccida	B
Juniperus foetidissima	SA
Juniperus formosana	B,SA
Juniperus horizontalis	SA
Juniperus monosperma	B,SA

JUNIPERUS

Juniperus nana	B,SA	Kennedia beckxiana	B,O,SA
Juniperus osteosperm~	B	Kennedia carinata	B
Juniperus oxycedrus	SA	Kennedia coccinea	AU,B,C,O,. -.
Juniperus oxycedrus ssp macrocarpa	B	Kennedia eximia	B,C,HA,O
Juniperus phoenicea	B CG,SA,SG	Kennedia glabrata	B
Juniperus pinchotii	B	Kennedia macrophylla	B,HA,O
Juniperus rigida	B,SA,V	Kennedia microphylla	B
Juniperus rigida prostrata	SA	Kennedia nigricans	B,C,HA,O,SA,SH
Juniperus sabina	SA,SG	Kennedia prorepens	B
Juniperus sabina v tamariscifolia	CG	Kennedia prostrata	AP,AU,B,C,HA,O,SA,SH
Juniperus scopulorum	B,C,SA	Kennedia retrorsa	B
Juniperus scopulorum 'Glauca'	B	Kennedia rubicunda	AU,B,C,HA,O,SA,SH
Juniperus silicicola	B,SA	Kennedia sp mix	C
Juniperus squamata 'Meyeri'	CG	Kensitia pillansii	B
Juniperus thurifera	SA	Keraudrenia integrifolia	B
Juniperus virginiana	A,B,C,CG,SA,SG	Kernera saxatilis	AP,B
Juniperus vulgaris	B	Kerria japonica	A,B,SA
Jurinea mollis	B,C,JE	Kerria japonica 'Albescens'	B
Justicia aconitiflora	B	Keteleeria davidiana	CG,SA
Justicia adhatoda	B	Keteleeria evelyniana	B
Justicia betonica	B	Khadia acutipetala	B,SI
Justicia carnea	B	Khaya madagascariensis	B,SI
Justicia prostrata	B	Khaya nyasica	B,SA,SI
Juttadinteria albata	B	Khaya senegalensis	B
Juttadinteria ausensis	B	Kickxia elatine	SG
Juttadinteria decumbens	B	Kickxia elatine ssp elatine	CG
Juttadinteria deserticola	B	Kickxia sieberi	B
Juttadinteria kovismontana	B	Kickxsia spuria	AP,B
Juttadinteria simpsoni	B,SI	Kigelia africana	B,C,SI
Juttadinteria suavissima	B	Kigelia pinnata	HA,O,RE,SA
Kadsura japonica	CG	Kiggelaria africana	B,SA,SI
Kalanchoe blossfeldiana	CG	Kirengeshoma palmata	B,JE,SA,SC
Kalanchoe blossfeldiana 'Pot Gold Hyb'	T	Kirkia acuminata	B,SA,SI
Kalanchoe blossfeldiana 'Swiss Hybrids'	V	Kirkia wilmsii	B,SI
Kalanchoe blossfeldiana 'Tetra Vulcan'	B,BD,BS,CL	Kirkianella novar-zelandiae	SS
Kalanchoe bloss. 'Tom Thumb Scarlet'	BS,L	Kissenia capensis	B,SI
Kalanchoe bloss. 'Tom Thumb Yellow'	B	Kitaibela vitifolia	B,C,G,JE,SA,SC
Kalanchoe brachyloba	B,Y	Kleinedoxa gabonensis	B
Kalanchoe lanceolata	B,SI	Kleinhovia hospita	B
Kalanchoe lugardii	CG	Kleinia fulgens	SI
Kalanchoe paniculata	SI	Kleinia grandiflora	B
Kalanchoe rotundifolia	CH,Y	Kleinia longiflora	B
Kalanchoe sexangularis	SI	Knautia arvensis	B,C,CG,CO,G,JE,LA,SA
Kalanchoe sp mix	C	Knautia macedonica	AP,B,BS,C,G,I,JE,P,RS,
Kalanchoe 'Swiss' hyb mix	C,J,S		SA,SC,SE,T
Kalanchoe thyrsiflora	B,CH,GC,SI,Y	Knautia macedonica 'Melton Pastels'	B,T
Kalimeris incisa	C,G	Knautia saragavensis 'Pink Stars'	B,C
Kallstroemia grandiflora	B,SW	Knightia excelsa	B,SA
Kallstroemia platyptera	C	Kniphofia 'Border Ballet'	JE,U
Kalmia angustifolia	B,C,SA,SG	Kniphofia breviflora	SI
Kalmia latifolia	C,CG,SA	Kniphofia buchananii	B,SI
Kalmia latifolia 'Rubra'	B,C	Kniphofia caulescens	AP,B,P,SI
Kalmia latifolia white	B	Kniphofia citrina	JE,SI
Kalmia microphylla	B,SW	Kniphofia 'Crown Hybrids'	BS,N
Kalmia occidentalis	B	Kniphofia ensifolia	B,G,JE,RH
Kalmia poliifolia	CG	Kniphofia foliosa	AP,B,RH
Kalmia sp mix	T	Kniphofia hirsuta	B,SI
Kalopanax septemlobus	B,CG,G,SA	Kniphofia hybrid	B,CG,KI,SA
Karomia speciosa ssp speciosa	SI	Kniphofia hybrida 'Fairyland' mix	C,DT
Keckiella antirrhinoides ssp antirrhinoides	B	Kniphofia hybrida mix	BD,C,F
Keckiella antirrhinoides ssp microphylla	B,SW	Kniphofia ichopensis	B,SC,SI
Keckiella cordifolia	B,SW	Kniphofia laxiflora	B,SI
Keckiella ternata	B,SW	Kniphofia linearifolia	B,C,SC,SI,T
Kedrostis africana	AP,B,SI	Kniphofia littoralis	B,SI
Kedrostis punctata	CH	Kniphofia multiflora	B
Keetia gueinzii	B	Kniphofia natalensis	RH

KNIPHOFIA

Kniphofia northiae	B,LG,SI
Kniphofia praecox	AP,SC,SI
Kniphofia pumila	B,G
Kniphofia rituralis	SI
Kniphofia rooperi	B,C,SI
Kniphofia sarmentosa	B,SI
Kniphofia sp	AP,SI
Kniphofia splendida	SI
Kniphofia stricta	B,SI
Kniphofia thompsonii v snowdenii	RH
Kniphofia triangularis	C,JE,RH,SI
Kniphofia triangularis hyb	JE
Kniphofia uvaria	B,CG,G,J,RH,SI
Kniphofia uvaria hybs 'Express'	JE
Kniphofia uvaria hybs 'Royal Castle'	B,V
Kniphofia uvaria 'New Hybrids'	B,JE,CL,L,T
Kniphofia uvaria 'Special Hybrids'	T
Kniphofia uvaria v grandiflora	B,JE
Knowltonia sp	SI
Knowltonia vesicatoria	B,SI
Kochea laniflora	B
Koeleria glauca	AP,B,BS,C,G,JE,SA,SC
Koeleria macrantha	B,JE,PR,SA,SG
Koelreuteria bipinnata	B
Koelreuteria elegans	B
Koelreuteria integrifolia	SA
Koelreuteria paniculata	A,B,C,CG,G,HA,N,O,SA, SC
Kolkwitzia amabilis	B,C,CG,N,SA,SG,T
Komatsuna senposai	B
Kosteletskya virginica	JE,NT
Krainzia longiflora	BC
Kraussia floribunda	B,C
Kuhnia eupatorioides	B,PR
Kunzea ambigua	B,C,HA,O,SA
Kunzea baxteri	AU,B,C,HA,O,SA
Kunzea capitata	AU,B,C,HA,O,SH
Kunzea ericifolia	B
Kunzea ericoides	AP,AU,B,HA,SA,SH,SS
Kunzea flavescens	B,O
Kunzea 'Mauve Mist'	B
Kunzea micromera	B
Kunzea opposita	B
Kunzea parvifolia	B,C,HA,O,SA,SH
Kunzea pomifera	B
Kunzea preissiana	B
Kunzea pulchella	B
Kunzea recurva	B,O
Kunzea sp mix	C
Labichea lanceolata	SA
Labichea lanceolata ssp brevifolia	B
Labichea lanceolata ssp lanceolata	B
Labichea punctata	B
Lablab fabiiformis	B
Lablab lignosus	C
Lablab purpureus	B,C,F
Lablab purpureus named vars	B
Laburnum alpinum	B,SA,SG
Laburnum anagyroides	A,B,CG,SA,SG
Laburnum anagyroides 'Quercifolium'	SG
Laburnum bonsai types mix	C
Laburnum watereri	SA
Laburnum watereri x 'Vossii'	B
Laccospadix australasica	B,HA,O,SA
Lachenalia algoensis	B,SC
Lachenalia aloides	B,SC,SI

Lachenalia aloides 'Nelsonii'	B
Lachenalia aloides v aurea	B
Lachenalia aloides v luteola	B
Lachenalia aloides v quadricolor	B
Lachenalia ameliae	B
Lachenalia bulbifera	B,SA,SC,SI
Lachenalia bulbifera 'Agulhas' form	B
Lachenalia capensis	AP,B,SI
Lachenalia carnosa	B,SA,SI
Lachenalia comptonii	B,SI
Lachenalia concordiana	SI
Lachenalia congesta	B,SI
Lachenalia contaminata	B,C,SI
Lachenalia elegans	AP,B,MN,SI
Lachenalia elegans v flava	B,SI
Lachenalia elegans v suaveolens	B
Lachenalia fistulosa	AP,B,C,O,SI
Lachenalia framesii	B
Lachenalia gillettii	AP,B,SC,SI
Lachenalia haarlemensis	AP,B
Lachenalia hirta	B,SI
Lachenalia juncifolia	B,SI
Lachenalia kliprandensis	SI
Lachenalia latifolia	AP,B,SC
Lachenalia liliiflora	AP,B,MN,SI
Lachenalia longibracteata	B
Lachenalia mathewsii	AP,B,SI
Lachenalia mediana	AP,B,SC,SI
Lachenalia minima	B
Lachenalia mutabilis	B,SI
Lachenalia namaquensis	B,C,O,SI
Lachenalia namibensis	B,O
Lachenalia neilii	SI
Lachenalia orchioides	AP,B,SC,SI
Lachenalia orchioides v glaucina	B,SI
Lachenalia orchioides v glaucina var.1	B
Lachenalia orchioides v glaucina var.2	B
Lachenalia orchioides v orchioides	B,SI
Lachenalia orthopetala	AP,B,O,SI
Lachenalia pallida	AP,SC,SI
Lachenalia pallida blue	B
Lachenalia patula	B,SI
Lachenalia peersii	AP,SI
Lachenalia polyphylla	SI
Lachenalia purpureo-caerulea	AP,B,C,MN,SI
Lachenalia pusilla	B,C,SI
Lachenalia pustulata	AP,C,SI
Lachenalia pustulata white	B
Lachenalia reflexa	AP,B,C,MN,SC,SI
Lachenalia rosea	B,G,SC
Lachenalia rubida	B
Lachenalia salteri	B
Lachenalia sp	MN,SI
Lachenalia splendida	B,SI
Lachenalia thomasiae	SI
Lachenalia trichophylla	B
Lachenalia undulata	B
Lachenalia unicolor	AP,B,C,MN,SI
Lachenalia unifolia	B,SI
Lachenalia unifolia wrightii	SI
Lachenalia van rhynsdorp form	B
Lachenalia variegata	B,SI
Lachenalia violacea	B,SA,SI
Lachenalia viridiflora	B,C,O,SI
Lachenalia zeyheri	B,MN
Lachnaea capitata	B

LACHNOSPERMUM

Lachnospermum imbricatum	B,SI
Lachnostachys eriobotrya	B,SA
Lactuca perennis	AP,B,SC
Lactuca saligna	B,NS
Lactuca sativa v angustana	B
Lactuca sativa v asparagina	B
Lactuca serriola	B
Lactuca virosa	B
Lafoensia punicifolia	B
Lagenaria siceraria	KS,V
Lagenaria siceraria 'Acoma Rattle Gourd'	B
Lagenaria siceraria 'Apache Dipper Gourd'	B
Lagenaria siceraria 'Bule De Pescuezo'	B
Lagenaria sic. 'Bule Redondo Mediano'	B
Lagenaria siceraria 'Hernandez Bule'	B
Lagenaria siceraria 'Hernandez Snake'	B
Lagenaria siceraria 'Hopi Rattle Gourd'	B
Lagenaria siceraria 'Long Dipper Gourd'	B
Lagenaria siceraria 'Mayo Giant Bule'	B
Lagenaria siceraria 'Mayo Gooseneck'	B
Lagenaria siceraria 'Mayo Warty Bule'	B
Lagenaria siceraria 'O'odham Dipper'	B
Lagenaria siceraria 'O'odham Sm. Bilobal'	B
Lagenaria siceraria 'Peyote Ceremonial'	B
Lagenaria siceraria 'San Juan Snake'	B
Lagenaria sic. 'Santo Domingo Dipper '	B
Lagenaria sic. 'Santo Domingo Str. Dipper'	B
Lagenaria sic. 'Tarahumara Canteen'	B
Lagenaria siceraria 'Tepehuan Canteen'	B
Lagenaria siceraria v clavatina	SG
Lagenaria sic. 'Yaqui Deer Dance Rattle'	B
Lagenaria sp	SI
Lagenaria sphaerica	B,SI
Lagenophora cuneata	B,SS
Lagenophora petiolata	SS
Lagerstroemia archerana	B,HA
Lagerstroemia duperreana	B
Lagerstroemia floribunda	B,HA,SA
Lagerstroemia flos reginae	HA,SA
Lagerstroemia hyb dwarf	B
Lagerstroemia indica	B,HA,JE,SA
Lagerstroemia indica 'Alba'	JE
Lagerstroemia ind. 'Basham's Party Pink'	B
Lagerstroemia indica 'Little Chief'	BS,HA,T
Lagerstroemia lanceolata	HA,SA
Lagerstroemia loudonii	B
Lagerstroemia microcarpa	B
Lagerstroemia reginae	B
Lagerstroemia rosea	HA
Lagerstroemia speciosa	B,RE
Lagerstroemia thorellii	HA,SA
Lagerstroemia villosa	B
Lagotis glauca	CC
Lagunaria patersonii	B,C,HA,O,SA
Lagurus ovatus	AP,B,C,CG,CL,DT,F,G,J, KI,KS,SG,T,U,V
Lagurus ovatus 'Florist Select'	B
Lagurus ovatus 'Nanus'	B
Lamarchea hakeifolia	B
Lamarckia aurea	B
Lamarckia aurea 'Golden Shower'	C
Lambertia formosa	B,HA,O,SA
Lambertia multiflora	B
Lambertia propinqua	B,O
Lamiastrum galeobdolon	JE,SU
Lamium album	B

Lamium galeobdolon	B
Lamium maculatum	C,JE
Lamium moschatum	B
Lamium purpureum	B,JE
Lamourouxia dasyantha	B
Lampranthus amoenus	B,SA,SI,Y
Lampranthus arbuthnotiae	B
Lampranthus aureus	B,C,SI,Y
Lampranthus bicolor	B,SI
Lampranthus blandus	B
Lampranthus cedarbergensis	B,SI
Lampranthus compressus	B
Lampranthus copiosus	B,SI,Y
Lampranthus corolliflorus	SI
Lampranthus deltoides	B,SI
Lampranthus emarginatus	B,SI
Lampranthus explanatus	B,SI,Y
Lampranthus falcatus	SI
Lampranthus franciscii	B
Lampranthus godmaniae v grandiflorus	B
Lampranthus haworthii	B,SI
Lampranthus hoerleianianus	B,SI
Lampranthus maximilianus	B,SI
Lampranthus multiradiatus	B,SA,SI,Y
Lampranthus primavernus	B,SI,Y
Lampranthus productus	SI
Lampranthus promontorii	B
Lampranthus roseus	B,SI,Y
Lampranthus scaber	B,SI
Lampranthus sp mix	C,SI,T,Y
Lampranthus spectabilis	B,C,SA,SI,Y
Lampranthus stayneri	B
Lampranthus stenus	B,SI
Lampranthus tegens	B,SI,Y
Lampranthus violaceus	B
Lanaria lanata	B,SI
Lannea coromandelica	B
Lansium domesticum	B
Lantana camara	B,JE,SA,SC,SG
Lantana camara hyb	G,T
Lantana camara v splendens	B
Lantana 'Crown Hybrids'	BS,KI
Lantana hybrida nana mix	C
Lantana lilacina	B
Lantana montevidensis	AP,B
Lapageria rosea	B,C,P,SA,SC,SE,T
Lapageria rosea v albiflora	B
Lapeirousia anceps	AP,B,G,SI
Lapeirousia azurea	B
Lapeirousia barklyii	B
Lapeirousia corymbosa	B,SI
Lapeirousia cruenta	MN
Lapeirousia cruenta forms mix	C
Lapeirousia cruenta v alba	MN
Lapeirousia cruenta viridis	MN
Lapeirousia divaricata	AP,B,SC,SI
Lapeirousia fabricii	B,SI
Lapeirousia jacquinii	AP,B,G,SI
Lapeirousia laxa	SG
Lapeirousia laxa v alba	C
Lapeirousia micrantha	SI
Lapeirousia montana	B
Lapeirousia neglecta	B,SI
Lapeirousia oreogena	B,SC,SI
Lapeirousia plicata	B,SI
Lapeirousia pyramidalis	B,SI

LAPEIROUSIA

Lapeirousia rhodesiana	B
Lapeirousia silenoides	B,SI
Lapeirousia sp	SI
Lapidaria margaretae	B,BC,SI,Y
Lapo...a canadensis	B
Lapsana communis	B,CG
Lapsana communis 'Inky'	NS
Lapsana communis 'Patchy' (V)	NS
Lardizabala biternata	B,SA
Larix decidua	B,C,RH,SA,SG
Larix decidua v sudetica	B
Larix gmelinii	B,RH,SA,SG
Larix gmelinii v olgensis	B
Larix kaempferi	B,C,CG,G,N,RH,SA,SG,T
Larix laricina	B,SG
Larix occidentalis	B,C,SA
Larix olgensis	SA
Larix pricipis	SA
Larix sibirica	B,SA,SG
Larix sukaczewi	SA
Larix x czekanowskii	SG
Larrea tridentata	B
Laserpitium gallicum	B,JE
Laserpitium halleri	B
Laserpitium hispidum	SG
Laserpitium latifolium	B,JE,SG
Laserpitium peucedanoides	B
Laserpitium siler	B,G,JE
Lasiopetalum baueri	B
Lasiopetalum behrii	B,SA
Lasiopetalum bracteatum	B
Lasiopetalum indutum	B
Lasiopetalum schulzenii	B
Lasiospermum bipinnatum	B,SI
Lasthenia glabrata	B
Latania loddigesii	B,O
Latania lontaroides	B,O
Latania verschaffeltii	B,O
Lathyraea squamaria	CG
Lathyrus angulatus	RS
Lathyrus angustifolius RB94068	P
Lathyrus annuus	PG,RS
Lathyrus annuus red	RS
Lathyrus aphaca	B,RS
Lathyrus articulatus	RS
Lathyrus aureus	AP,LG,PG,SC
Lathyrus blepharicarpus	B
Lathyrus 'Bushy & Climbing Sp Mix'	T
Lathyrus chilensis	C
Lathyrus chloranthus	AP,C,MS,PG,RS
Lathyrus chloranthus 'Lemonade'	T
Lathyrus clymenum	AP,CG,PG,RS
Lathyrus clymenum articulatus	PG
Lathyrus clymenum 'Chelsea'	PG
Lathyrus filiformis	RS,SC
Lathyrus fremontii	B,P
Lathyrus gmelinii	B,JE,SA
Lathyrus gorgonii	PG
Lathyrus grandiflorus	AP,B,C,G,JE,SA
Lathyrus graysonii	PG
Lathyrus heterophyllus	B,C,F,JE,PG,SA
Lathyrus hierosolymitanus	B,PG,RS
Lathyrus hirsutus	PG
Lathyrus japonicus	AP,B,G,SA,SC
Lathyrus laetiflorus v alefeldii	B,RS,SW
Lathyrus laevigatus	AP,B,JE

Lathy.. ~ latifolius	w.a.
Lathyr.. ...folius 'Albus'	AP,G,LG,SC
Lathyrus la...olius 'Apple Blossom'	PG
Lathyrus latifolius deep pink	RS
Lathyrus latifolius finest mix	BO,JE
Lathyrus latifolius pale pink	I,LG,PG,RS
Lathyrus latifolius 'Pearl' mix	BS,KS
Lathyrus latifolius 'Pearl Pink'	B,BS,C,JE,SA
Lathyrus latifolius 'Pearl Red'	B,BS,C,JE,KS
Lathyrus latifolius 'Pearl White'	AP,B,BS,C,G,I,JE,KS, LG,P,PG,SA,T
Lathyrus latifolius 'Pink Blush'	B,P
Lathyrus latifolius purple	PG
Lathyrus latifolius two tone pink	I
Lathyrus laxiflorus	P,PG
Lathyrus linifolius v montanus	B,G,SC
Lathyrus luteus	B,C
Lathyrus maritimus	C,SG
Lathyrus nervosus	AP,C,HH,SE,SG
Lathyrus neurolobus	AP,RS
Lathyrus niger	AP,B,CG,JE,NS,RS,SA
Lathyrus nissolia	AP,B,G,RS
Lathyrus ochrus	B,CG,PG,RS
Lathyrus odoratus	AP,LG,SC,SG
Lathyrus odoratus 'Aerospace'	B,BS,KI
Lathyrus odoratus 'Air Warden'	B,BD,BS,KI,M,PG
Lathyrus odoratus 'Alan Titchmarsh'	B,BO,BS,KI,TU
Lathyrus odoratus 'Alan Williams'	B,KI,MS
Lathyrus odoratus 'Albatross'	PG
Lathyrus odoratus 'Alice Hardwick'	B,BO,BS,KI
Lathyrus odoratus 'America'	B,BO,BS,DT,F
Lathyrus odoratus 'American Beauty'	L
Lathyrus odoratus 'Angela Ann'	B,BS,KI,MS
Lathyrus odoratus 'Annabelle'	BO,T
Lathyrus odoratus 'Anne Vestry'	BS
Lathyrus odoratus 'Annie B Gilroy'	PG
Lathyrus odoratus 'Annie Good'	BS,KI
Lathyrus odoratus 'Anniversary'	B,BS,KI,MS,T
Lathyrus odoratus 'Anthea Turner'	T
Lathyrus odoratus 'Antique Fantasy Mix'	T
Lathyrus odoratus 'Apricot Sprite'	B,BS,KI
Lathyrus odoratus 'Arbor Low'	BS,KI
Lathyrus odoratus 'Arthur Hellyer'	U
Lathyrus odoratus 'Ascot'	B,BS
Lathyrus odoratus 'Avon Beauty'	BS
Lathyrus odoratus 'Ballerina'	M
Lathyrus odoratus 'Band Aid'	B,BS,KI,U
Lathyrus odoratus 'Barry Dare'	U
Lathyrus odoratus 'Batheaston'	BS,KI
Lathyrus odoratus 'Beacon'	BS
Lathyrus odoratus 'Beaujolais'	B,BD,BS,D,KI,S,TU
Lathyrus odoratus 'Beauty Queen'	BS
Lathyrus odoratus 'Bijou'	BS,DT,F,KI,T
Lathyrus odoratus 'Black Diamond'	BS,KI,PG
Lathyrus odoratus 'Black Knight'	F,PG
Lathyrus odoratus 'Black Prince'	B,BS,KI,U
Lathyrus odoratus 'Blanche Ferry'	PG
Lathyrus odoratus 'Blaze'	BS
Lathyrus odoratus 'Blue Danube'	B,BO,BS,KI,T,U
Lathyrus odoratus 'Blue Heaven'	BS,KI
Lathyrus odoratus 'Blue Ice'	M
Lathyrus odoratus 'Blue Mantle'	BS,U
Lathyrus odoratus 'Blue Riband'	BS
Lathyrus odoratus 'Blue Triumph'	BO,BS
Lathyrus odoratus 'Blue Velvet'	B,BD,BS,KI,PG
Lathyrus odoratus 'Blushing Bride'	BS,KI

LATHYRUS

Lathyrus odoratus 'Bolton's Unequalled'	BO
Lathyrus odoratus 'Bouquet mix'	BS,D,DT,F,KI,M,S,SE
Lathyrus odoratus 'Bouquet' s-c	S
Lathyrus odoratus 'Br.Cupani's Original'	PG
Lathyrus odoratus 'Brampton'	PG
Lathyrus odoratus 'Brian Clough'	B,KI,M,MS,U
Lathyrus odoratus 'Bridget'	U
Lathyrus odoratus 'Bristol Cream'	KI
Lathyrus odoratus 'Brother Cadfael'	PG
Lathyrus odoratus 'Buccaneer'	BS,KI,PG
Lathyrus odoratus 'Bulldog'	PG
Lathyrus odoratus 'Burnished Bronze'	KI,MS
Lathyrus odoratus 'Burpee's Patio mix'	MS
Lathyrus odoratus 'Bushby'	C,PG,T
Lathyrus odoratus 'Butterfly'	PG
Lathyrus odoratus 'Calamity Jayne'	PG
Lathyrus odoratus 'Cambridge Blue'	BS,KI,U
Lathyrus odoratus 'Camilla'	U
Lathyrus odoratus 'Candy Frills'	BO
Lathyrus odoratus 'Candyman'	F
Lathyrus odoratus 'Captain of The Blues'	BS,PG
Lathyrus odoratus 'Captain Scott'	BO
Lathyrus odoratus 'Carlotta'	BS,J,KI
Lathyrus odoratus 'Cascade'	L
Lathyrus odoratus 'Catherine'	B,U
Lathyrus odoratus 'Celebration'	B
Lathyrus odoratus 'Champagne Bubbles'	U
Lathyrus odoratus 'Charles Unwin'	B,U
Lathyrus odoratus 'Charlie's Angel'	BS,KI,MS,U
Lathyrus odoratus 'Charlotte Riley'	PG
Lathyrus odoratus 'Chesire Blue'	MS,PG
Lathyrus odoratus 'Claire Elizabeth'	BO,BS,KI
Lathyrus odoratus 'Colin Unwin'	B,U
Lathyrus odoratus collections	BO,D,U
Lathyrus odoratus 'Concorde'	BS,KI
Lathyrus odoratus 'Continental'	BD,BS,CL,DT,KI,KS
Lathyrus odoratus 'Corinne'	BO,BS,KI
Lathyrus odoratus 'Countess Cadogan'	PG
Lathyrus odoratus 'Countess of Radnor'	PG
Lathyrus odoratus 'Cream Beauty'	BS
Lathyrus odoratus 'Cream Delight'	BS
Lathyrus odoratus 'Cream Southbourne'	B,BO,BS,KI,T,U
Lathyrus odoratus 'Cubar Edge'	BS
Lathyrus odoratus 'Cupani'	C,DT,F
Lathyrus odoratus 'Cupid Pink'	T
Lathyrus odoratus 'Cupid Pink Improved'	CL,S,V
Lathyrus odoratus 'Cuthbertson'	BS,F
Lathyrus odoratus 'Daily Mail'	U
Lathyrus odoratus 'Daleman'	BO
Lathyrus odoratus 'Daphne'	L,U
Lathyrus odoratus 'Dawn'	MS
Lathyrus odoratus 'Dean's Scarlet'	BO,BS,KI
Lathyrus odoratus 'Denis Compton'	BO,BS,KI
Lathyrus odoratus 'Denise Tanner'	PG
Lathyrus odoratus 'Diamond Wedding'	BS,KI,U
Lathyrus odoratus 'Diana'	BS,U
Lathyrus odoratus 'Dobies Giant Waved'	D
Lathyrus odoratus 'Dolly Varden'	PG
Lathyrus odoratus 'Donna Jones'	PG
Lathyrus odoratus 'Dorothy Eckford'	B,BO,C,MS,PG
Lathyrus odoratus 'Douglas McArthur'	L
Lathyrus odoratus 'Dr. Robert Uvedale'	PG
Lathyrus odoratus 'Dragonfly'	PG
Lathyrus odoratus 'Duke of York'	C,PG
Lathyrus odoratus 'Dynasty'	BS,KI,MS
Lathyrus odoratus 'Early Spencer' s-c	B
Lathyrus odoratus 'Eckford's Mix'	DT
Lathyrus odoratus 'Eclipse'	BS,MS
Lathyrus odoratus 'Edward Unwin'	U
Lathyrus odoratus 'Edwardian Collection'	U
Lathyrus odoratus 'Elaine Paige'	B
Lathyrus odoratus 'Elizabeth'	PG
Lathyrus odoratus 'Elizabeth Taylor'	B,BD,BO,BS,J,KI,PG,S, TU
Lathyrus odoratus 'Ella'	BS
Lathyrus odoratus 'Ena Margaret'	BS
Lathyrus odoratus 'Esther Rantzen'	B,KI
Lathyrus odoratus 'Ethel Grace'	BO,MS,PG
Lathyrus odoratus 'Evening Glow'	KI
Lathyrus odoratus 'Evensong'	U
Lathyrus odoratus 'Exhibition Collection'	U
Lathyrus odoratus 'Explorer'	BS,D,DT,F
Lathyrus odoratus 'Fairy Queen'	PG
Lathyrus odoratus 'Fanny Adams'	PG
Lathyrus odoratus 'Fantasia' mix	F,S,T
Lathyrus odoratus 'Fatima'	BS,KI,U
Lathyrus odoratus 'Felicity Kendal'	B,BS,KI
Lathyrus odoratus 'Fiona'	BS
Lathyrus odoratus 'Firebrand'	BS,KI
Lathyrus odoratus 'Firecrest'	BO,BS,KI,T
Lathyrus odoratus 'Fireglow'	BS
Lathyrus odoratus 'First Lady'	BS,KI
Lathyrus odoratus 'Flagship'	J
Lathyrus odoratus 'Flashlight'	BS
Lathyrus odoratus 'Flora Norton'	B,BO,F,PG
Lathyrus odoratus 'Floral Tribute'	T
Lathyrus odoratus 'Floriana'	V
Lathyrus odoratus 'Flower Arrangers'	T,U
Lathyrus odoratus 'Fragrantissima'	T
Lathyrus odoratus 'Frolic'	BS,KI
Lathyrus odoratus 'Gaiety'	BO,BS,KI
Lathyrus odoratus 'Galaxy'	BO,BS,CL,D,F,KI,M,R,S, ST,YA,U
Lathyrus odoratus 'Gardener's Favourite'	U
Lathyrus odoratus 'Geranium Pink'	B,BD,J
Lathyrus odoratus 'Geranium Pink Im'	BS,KI
Lathyrus odoratus 'Gertrude Tingay'	BS
Lathyrus odoratus 'Giant Exhibition Mix'	SE
Lathyrus odoratus 'Giant Hybrids Mix'	BS
Lathyrus odoratus 'Giant Waved Mix'	J,V
Lathyrus odoratus 'Gipsy Queen'	BO,BS,KI,PG
Lathyrus odoratus 'Glow'	U
Lathyrus odoratus 'Gorleston'	BO
Lathyrus odoratus 'Grace Of Monaco'	B,BS,KI
Lathyrus odoratus 'Grayson Gr. 300's mix'	PG
Lathyrus odoratus 'Great Expectations'	BS,KI
Lathyrus odoratus 'Hampton Court'	B,BS,KI
Lathyrus odoratus 'Hanslope Gem'	BS,KI
Lathyrus odoratus 'Harvest Time'	BS
Lathyrus odoratus 'Harvey's Blush'	KI
Lathyrus odoratus 'Hazel Tasker'	BS
Lathyrus odoratus 'Henry Eckford'	BS,PG
Lathyrus odoratus 'Her Majesty'	U
Lathyrus odoratus 'Herald'	BS
Lathyrus odoratus 'Honeymoon'	BS,KI,MS,TU
Lathyrus odoratus 'Hunters Moon'	BS,KI,TU
Lathyrus odoratus 'Ice Butter Grandiflora'	KI
Lathyrus odoratus 'Ice Cream'	J
Lathyrus odoratus 'Ice Vanilla Grandiflora'	KI
Lathyrus odoratus 'Indigo King'	PG
Lathyrus odoratus 'Ivory Queen'	PG
Lathyrus odoratus 'Janet Scott'	B,BO,BS,C,F,PG

LATHYRUS

Lathyrus odoratus 'Jayne Amanda' BO,KI,MS
Lathyrus odoratus 'Jemma' PG
Lathyrus odoratus 'Jet Set' BS,D,DT,F,J,S
Lathyrus odoratus 'Jill Walton' MS
Lathyrus odoratus 'Jilly' B,KI,MS,U
Lathyrus odoratus 'John Ness' BS
Lathyrus odoratus 'Joker' BO,BS,KI
Lathyrus odoratus 'Judy Gaunt' PG
Lathyrus odoratus 'Judyth Macleod' PG
Lathyrus odoratus 'Juliana' BS
Lathyrus odoratus 'Karen Reeve' B,MS
Lathyrus odoratus 'Ken Colledge' U
Lathyrus odoratus 'King Edward V11' B,BO,BS,C,F,PG
Lathyrus odoratus 'King's Bounty' BS,KI
Lathyrus odoratus 'King's Bride' BS,KI
Lathyrus odoratus 'King's Cloak' BS,KI
Lathyrus odoratus 'King's Frill' BS
Lathyrus odoratus 'Kingfisher' PG
Lathyrus odoratus 'Kings Reach' KI
Lathyrus odoratus 'Kings' Scented Coll' KI
Lathyrus odoratus 'Kings' Special' KI
Lathyrus odoratus 'Kiwi Bicolours Mix' DT,F,YA
Lathyrus odoratus 'Knee-Hi' BO,BS,C,KI,KS,L,ST
Lathyrus odoratus 'Lady Diana' BS,KI
Lathyrus odoratus 'Lady Fairburn' BS,KI
Lathyrus odoratus 'Lady Grisel Hamilton' C,F,PG
Lathyrus odoratus 'Lady Penny' BO
Lathyrus odoratus 'Lady Serena James' PG
Lathyrus odoratus 'Lady Turral' PG
Lathyrus odoratus 'Larkspur' BS,KI
Lathyrus odoratus 'Leamington' B,BD,BS,D,J,KI,M,PG,S
Lathyrus odoratus 'Liberty Belle' PG
Lathyrus odoratus 'Lilac Queen' PG
Lathyrus odoratus 'Lilac Ripple' PG,T
Lathyrus odoratus 'Lilac Silk' BO,BS,KI
Lathyrus odoratus 'Lilac Time' B,BS,KI
Lathyrus odoratus 'Little Sweetheart' BS,KI,KS,V
Lathyrus odoratus 'Liz Bolton' BO,BS
Lathyrus odoratus 'Lizbeth' KI,MS
Lathyrus odoratus 'Loch Lomond' PG
Lathyrus odoratus 'Lord Nelson' B,BO,C,PG
Lathyrus odoratus 'Louise' BS,T
Lathyrus odoratus 'Love Match' D
Lathyrus odoratus 'Lovejoy' B,BO,KI
Lathyrus odoratus 'Lustre' BS
Lathyrus odoratus 'Macmillan Nurse' U
Lathyrus odoratus 'Maggie May' T
Lathyrus odoratus 'Majesty' BS
Lathyrus odoratus 'Mammoth' mix BD,BS,C,KI
Lathyrus odoratus 'Mammoth' s-c BS
Lathyrus odoratus 'Margot' BO,BS
Lathyrus odoratus 'Marilyn Barlow' PG
Lathyrus odoratus 'Marion' BS,KI,MS
Lathyrus odoratus 'Mars' SE,U
Lathyrus odoratus 'Marti Caine' MS
Lathyrus odoratus 'Mary Malcolm' BO
Lathyrus odoratus 'Mary Rose' BO
Lathyrus odoratus 'Matucana' PG,SE,T
Lathyrus odoratus 'Maudie Best' BS,KI
Lathyrus odoratus 'Mauve King' BS,KI
Lathyrus odoratus 'Mauve Queen' PG
Lathyrus odoratus 'Memories' T
Lathyrus odoratus 'Midnight' B,BS,KI,U
Lathyrus odoratus 'Milestone' BS,U
Lathyrus odoratus 'Miss Truslove' KI
Lathyrus odoratus 'Miss Willmott' F,PG

Lathyrus odoratus 'Mix, 10 Varieties' T
Lathyrus odoratus 'Mollie Rilstone' KI,MS
Lathyrus odoratus 'Mr. President' PG
Lathyrus odoratus 'Mrs Bernard Jones' B,BO,BS,MS,PG,TU,U
Lathyrus odoratus 'Mrs C Kay' BS,KI,PG
Lathyrus odoratus 'Mrs Collier' B,BO,C,F,MS,PG
Lathyrus odoratus 'Mrs R Bolton' B,BD,BS,KI,M,PG,S
Lathyrus odoratus 'Mrs Walter Wright' B,BO,BS
Lathyrus odoratus multiflora mix BS
Lathyrus odoratus 'Myrtle Mann' BS,KI
Lathyrus odoratus 'Nancy Colledge' U
Lathyrus odoratus 'Nanette Newman' B,BS,KI
Lathyrus odoratus 'Negro' PG
Lathyrus odoratus 'Nelly Viner' PG
Lathyrus odoratus 'Nimbus' U
Lathyrus odoratus 'Noel Edmonds' B,BS,KI
Lathyrus odoratus 'Noel Sutton' B,BD,BO,BS,D,J,KI,M,
  MS,S
Lathyrus odoratus 'Nora Holman' KI,MS
Lathyrus odoratus 'North Shore' BS,T
Lathyrus odoratus 'Oban Bay' BO
Lathyrus odoratus 'Old Spice' mix C,F,J,M,SE
Lathyrus odoratus 'Old Times' U
Lathyrus odoratus 'Old-Fashioned' mix C,CO,D,J,KI,MS,Sm,ST,
  V
Lathyrus odoratus 'Old-Fash.Scented' mix S,TU
Lathyrus odoratus 'Orange Dragon' BO,BS
Lathyrus odoratus 'Orange Surprise' BS,KI
Lathyrus odoratus 'Our Jenny' B,BO
Lathyrus odoratus 'Ouse Valley' BS,KI
Lathyrus odoratus 'Painted Lady' BS,C,DT,F,KI,MS,PG,
  SE,SU,T
Lathyrus odoratus 'Pall Mall' BS,KI
Lathyrus odoratus 'Pamela' KI,MS
Lathyrus odoratus 'Patio' D,F,KI,S,U
Lathyrus odoratus 'Patio Collection' 6 pk BS
Lathyrus odoratus 'Peach Sundae' BS
Lathyrus odoratus 'Pearl's Buck' L
Lathyrus odoratus 'Peerless Pink' BS
Lathyrus odoratus 'Percy Thrower' B,BO,BS,KI
Lathyrus odoratus 'Perfume Delight' BS,KI,KS
Lathyrus odoratus 'Phantom of The Opera' SE
Lathyrus odoratus 'Philip Miller' PG
Lathyrus odoratus 'Pink Bouquet' U
Lathyrus odoratus 'Pink Expression' U
Lathyrus odoratus 'Pink Leamington' BS
Lathyrus odoratus 'Pluto' BO,BS
Lathyrus odoratus 'Pocahontas' PG
Lathyrus od. 'Poi de Senteur Sauvage' PG
Lathyrus od. 'Pre-Spencer Grandiflora' PG
Lathyrus odoratus 'Premier Collection' DT
Lathyrus odoratus 'Pretty Polly' B,BO,KI
Lathyrus odoratus 'Prima Donna' BS,C,PG
Lathyrus odoratus 'Prince Edward of York' C,PG
Lathyrus odoratus 'Princess Elizabeth' B,BD,BS,J,KI,PG,S
Lathyrus odoratus 'Princess Juliana' U
Lathyrus odoratus 'Princess of Wales' C,PG
Lathyrus odoratus 'Prize Strain' T
Lathyrus odoratus 'Pulsar' U
Lathyrus odoratus 'Purple Prince' C,PG
Lathyrus odoratus 'Purple Velvet' BS
Lathyrus odoratus 'Queen Alexandra' B,BO,BS,PG
Lathyrus odoratus 'Queen Mother' MS,U
Lathyrus odoratus 'Queen of the Isles' C,PG
Lathyrus odoratus 'Quito' C
Lathyrus odoratus 'Razamataz' PG

LATHYRUS

Lathyrus odoratus 'Red Arrow'	B,BS,PG,U	Lathyrus odoratus 'Terry Wogan'	B,BS,KI,M,TU,U
Lathyrus odoratus 'Red Ensign'	BO,KI	Lathyrus odoratus 'The Doctor'	BS,KI,U
Lathyrus odoratus 'Restormal'	KI,MS	Lathyrus odoratus 'The Exhibitor's Coll'	KI,ST
Lathyrus odoratus 'Romance'	S	Lathyrus odoratus 'The Small Grower Coll'	KI,ST
Lathyrus odoratus 'Rosalind'	U	Lathyrus odoratus 'Thomas Bradley'	U
Lathyrus odoratus 'Rosalyn Morris'	BS	Lathyrus odoratus 'Titan'	B
Lathyrus odoratus 'Rosanna Alice'	U	Lathyrus odoratus 'Top 6'	V
Lathyrus odoratus 'Rosemary Padley'	BO	Lathyrus odoratus 'Tovah Martin'	PG
Lathyrus odoratus 'Rosemary Verey'	T	Lathyrus odoratus 'Treasure Island'	L
Lathyrus odoratus 'Rosina'	MS	Lathyrus odoratus 'Uncle Albert'	PG
Lathyrus odoratus 'Rosy Frills'	BS,KI	Lathyrus odoratus 'Unique'	BS,PG
Lathyrus odoratus 'Roy Castle'	BO	Lathyrus odoratus 'Unwins Mixed Hybrids'	U
Lathyrus odoratus 'Roy Phillips'	BS	Lathyrus odoratus 'Unwins Mixed Stripes'	U
Lathyrus odoratus 'Royal Baby'	U	Lathyrus o. Unwins Sriped 'Butterfly'	C
Lathyrus odoratus 'Royal Blue'	BS,C,V	Lathyrus o. 'Unwins Superscent Old Fash'	U
Lathyrus odoratus 'Royal Crimson'	BS,C	Lathyrus odoratus 'Velvet Night'	BS
Lathyrus odoratus 'Royal Family' mix	BD,C,J	Lathyrus odoratus 'Vera Lynn'	BS,KI
Lathyrus odoratus 'Royal Flush'	BO,BS	Lathyrus odoratus 'Violet Queen'	BS,PG
Lathyrus odoratus 'Royal Lavender'	BS,C,J,KS	Lathyrus odoratus 'Virginia'	PG
Lathyrus odoratus 'Royal Maroon'	BS,J	Lathyrus odoratus 'W.J.Unwin'	U
Lathyrus odoratus 'Royal Navy Blue'	BS,C,J,V	Lathyrus odoratus 'Waved Standards'	YA
Lathyrus odoratus 'Royal Pink'	J,V	Lathyrus odoratus 'Welcome'	BS,J,KI,PG,TU
Lathyrus odoratus 'Royal Rose Pink'	BS,C	Lathyrus odoratus 'White Ensign'	B,BD,BS,KI
Lathyrus odoratus 'Royal Scarlet'	BS,C,J,B	Lathyrus odoratus 'White Royal'	J
Lathyrus odoratus 'Royal Wedding'	B,BS,KI,MS,T,TU,U	Lathyrus odoratus 'White Supreme'	BO,BS,KI,MS,PG,T
Lathyrus odoratus 'Royal White'	BS,C,J,KS,V	Lathyrus odoratus wild form	C
Lathyrus odoratus 'Royals mix' multiflora	BS,CL,S,SE,KS,YA	Lathyrus odoratus 'Willies Red'	BS
Lathyrus odoratus 'Ruffled mix'	BS	Lathyrus odoratus 'Wiltshire Ripple'	BS,KI,T,V
Lathyrus odoratus 'Sandringham'	B,BS,KI	Lathyrus odoratus 'Wings'	T
Lathyrus odoratus 'Sarah'	B,BS,KI	Lathyrus odoratus 'Winner'	BS,KI
Lathyrus odoratus scented coll	CO	Lathyrus odoratus 'Winston Churchill'	B,BD,BS,D,J,KI,PG,S
Lathyrus odoratus 'Scented Collection'	U	Lathyrus odoratus 'Winter Elegance'	BS
Lathyrus odoratus 'Sea Wolfe'	BS,KI	Lathyrus odoratus 'Wisteria'	BS
Lathyrus odoratus 'Senator'	PG	Lathyrus odoratus x 'Quito'	B
Lathyrus odoratus 'Sheila Mcqueen'	BS,U	Lathyrus odoratus 'Xenia Field'	BO,BS,KI
Lathyrus odoratus 'Shirley Pink'	BS,KI	Lathyrus odoratus 'Yankie Doodle'	PG
Lathyrus odoratus 'Shirley Temple'	L	Lathyrus odoratus 'Yardley'	BS,KI
Lathyrus odoratus 'Sicilian Fuchsia'	MS,PG	Lathyrus odoratus 'Yasmin Khan'	B,BO,BS,KI
Lathyrus odoratus 'Sicilian Pink'	B,BO	Lathyrus palustris	B,C,JE
Lathyrus odoratus 'Skylon'	BS	Lathyrus pisiformis	SG
Lathyrus odoratus 'Small' coll	CO	Lathyrus pratensis	B,C,PG,RS,SG,SU
Lathyrus odoratus 'Snoopea'	B,BO,BS,CO,KI,SU,T,	Lathyrus roseus	B
	TU,VH	Lathyrus rotundifolius	AP,C,RS,SC
Lathyrus odoratus 'Snowdonia Park'	BS,KI	Lathyrus sativus	AP,B,C,I,RS,T
Lathyrus odoratus 'Sonia'	BO	Lathyrus sativus mix	PG
Lathyrus odoratus 'South Atlantic'	BS,KI	Lathyrus sativus v albo-azuri	PG
Lathyrus odoratus 'Southampton'	BO,BS,PG	Lathyrus sativus v albus	C,PG
Lathyrus odoratus 'Southbourne'	B,BO,BS,D,KI,U	Lathyrus sativus v azureus	AP,C,F,G,PG,SE,W
Lathyrus odoratus 'Special Collection'	BS,DT	Lathyrus sp purple	P
Lathyrus odoratus 'Special mix'	S	Lathyrus sphaericus	RS
Lathyrus odoratus 'Spencer Choice Mix'	BD,C,CL,DT,KI,MS	Lathyrus splendens	B,SA
Lathyrus o. 'Spencer Special Highly Scent'	MS,PG	Lathyrus sylvestris	AP,B,C,CG,CO,F,LG,NS,
Lathyrus odoratus 'Spencer Waved'	BS,CO,KI,R,ST,TU,VH		P,PG,SA,SG,SU
Lathyrus odoratus 'Splendour'	BS	Lathyrus tingitanus	AP,C,F,I,LG,PG,RS,T
Lathyrus odoratus 'Steve Davis'	BS,KI,U	Lathyrus tingitanus 'Flame'	RS
Lathyrus odoratus 'Stylish'	B,BD,BS,J,KI	Lathyrus tingitanus 'Harmony'	PG
Lathyrus odoratus 'Su Pollard'	B,BS,KI	Lathyrus tingitanus salmon pink form	C
Lathyrus odoratus 'Summer Breeze'	SE,T	Lathyrus tuberosus	AP,B,G,LG,SG
Lathyrus o.'S.S. Unwins Special Mix' c.s	U	Lathyrus venetus	B,JE
Lathyrus odoratus 'Supersnoop'	B,BD,D,J,KS,ST,YA	Lathyrus venosus	B,SG
Lathyrus odoratus 'SuperStar'	T	Lathyrus vernus	AP,B,C,CG,F,G,JE,P,PG,
Lathyrus o. 'Suttons Exhibitor's Coll'	S		SA,SC,SG
Lathyrus odoratus 'Swan Lake'	BS,J,KI,M	Lathyrus vernus cyaneus	RS
Lathyrus odoratus 'Sylvia Mary'	BO,BS	Lathyrus vernus f albus	SG
Lathyrus odoratus 'Tall'	F	Lathyrus vernus f roseus	B
Lathyrus odoratus 'Tell Tale'	BS,KI	Lathyrus vernus forms mix	C

LATHYRUS

Lathyrus vernus 'Rosenelfe'	HH,JE
Lathyrus vernus v albo-roseus	C
Lathyrus vestitus	B,SC
Launea angustifolia	B,JE
Laurelia novae-zelandiae	B
Laurelia sempervirens	SA
Laurentia axillaris 'Stars Blue'	CL,L,SE,T
Laurocerasus officinalis	SG
Laurophyllus capensis	B,SI
Laurus nobilis	A,B,C,N,SA
Lavandula angustifolia	AP,B,BD,C,CG,CP,G,KS, RH,SA,SG,T
Lavandula angustifolia 'Alba'	FH
Lavandula angustifolia 'Folgate'	FH
Lavandula angustifolia 'Hidcote'	AP,B,BD,BS,C,CL,G,JE, L,SA,T,TU,YA
Lavandula angustifolia 'Hidcote Pink'	FH
Lavandula angustifolia 'Lady'	B,BD,BS,C,CL,D,JE,KS, S,SE,T
Lavandula angustifolia 'Loddon Blue'	FH
Lavandula angustifolia 'Munstead'	w.a.
Lavandula angustifolia 'Nana Alba'	AP,E,G,RS,SC
Lavandula angustifolia 'Rosea'	B,C,G,JE,RS
Lavandula angustifolia 'Twickel Purple'	FH
Lavandula canariensis	RS
Lavandula cretica	I
Lavandula dentata	FH,G,KS,RS
Lavandula 'Dw' vars mix	C
Lavandula hybrida	SG
Lavandula lanata	AP,B,C,RS,SA,SC
Lavandula latifolia	B,CG,SG,JE
Lavandula multifida	B,G,RS,SG
Lavandula multifida dentata	SA
Lavandula pedunculata	P
Lavandula 'Princess Blue'	FH
Lavandula 'Royal Purple'	FH
Lavandula spica see angustifolia	
Lavandula ssp mix	KS
Lavandula stoechas	AP,B,C,F,G,JE,RS,SA, SC,SG,T
Lavandula stoechas f leucantha	RS
Lavandula stoechas ssp pedunculata	AP,B,CG,SA,SC
Lavandula viridis	B,C,CG,P
Lavatera arborea	B,SA,SG
Lavatera arborea 'Variegata'	AP,B,C,G,HH,P,SG
Lavatera assurgentiflora	B
Lavatera cachemiriana	AP,B,CC,G,HH,SG,T
Lavatera 'Candy Floss'	I
Lavatera maritima	SA
Lavatera oblongifolia	SA
Lavatera olbia	AP,CG
Lavatera plebeia	B,RS
Lavatera punctata	B
Lavatera 'Snowcap'	I
Lavatera tauricensis	T
Lavatera thuringiaca	B,JE,SA,SG,V
Lavatera thuringiaca 'Ice Cool'	HH
Lavatera thuringiaca 'Rose'	T
Lavatera triloba	SA
Lavatera trimestris	AP,BS,G,HW,R,SG,T,V
Lavatera trimestris 'Beauty' mix	CL,D,S
Lavatera trimestris 'Beauty Pink'	B,CL,F,J,T,U,V
Lavatera trimestris 'Beauty Rose'	B,CL,T
Lavatera trimestris 'Beauty White'	B,CL
Lavatera trimestris 'Loveliness'	B,BS,CO,KI,S,ST,T,VH
Lavatera trimestris 'Mont Blanc'	AP,B,BD,BS,CO,D,DT,F,

	G,J,KI,KS,L,S,ST,SU,T, TU,U,V,VH,YA
Lavatera trimestris 'Parade' mix	BD,C,DT,F,KS,M,SE,U
Lavatera trimestris 'Pastel' mix	J
Lavatera trimestris 'Ruby Regis'	B,BD,C,F,KS,T,V,W
Lavatera trimestris 'Silver Cup'	B,BD,BS,C,CO,D,DT,F,G, J,KI,KS,L,S,ST,SU,T,TU, U,V,YA
Lavatera trimestris 'Tanagra'	B,BS
Lavatera trimestris 'White Cherub'	D,T
Lavigera macrocarpa	B
Lawrencella davenportii	B,O
Lawrencia berthae	B
Lawrencia viridigrisea	B
Lawsonia inermis	B,SA
Laxmannia gracilis	B
Laxmannia minor	B
Laxmannia paleacea	B
Layia chrysanthemoides	B
Layia platyglossa	B,C,D,SG,T,V
Lebeckia plukenetiana	B,SI
Lebeckia sericea	B,SI
Lebeckia simsiana	B,SI
Lebeckia sp	SI
Lecythis minor	B
Lecythis pisonis	B
Ledebouria cooperi	B,SI
Ledebouria ovalifolia	B,SI
Ledebouria socialis	SG
Ledum decumbens MW317R	X
Ledum groenlandicum	G,X
Ledum palustre	SG
Leea coccinea	B,SA
Leea coccinea v rubra	B
Leea guineensis	B
Leea indica	B
Leea rubra	SA
Leersia oryzoides	PR
Legousia 'Blue Carpet'	D,S
Legousia pentagonia	T
Legousia speculum-veneris	B
Leipoldtia amplexicaulis	B
Leipoldtia britteniae	B
Leipoldtia jacobseniana	B
Leipoldtia weigangiana	B
Lemaireocereus eburneus	B,Y
Lemaireocereus griseus	BC
Lemaireocereus montanus	Y
Lemaireocereus pruinosus	B,Y
Lemaireocereus queretaroense	B
Lemaireocereus thurberi	B,Y
Lenophyllum guttatum	B
Lenophyllum reflexum	B
Lens culinaris 'Masoor'	B
Lens culinaris 'O'odham Lentil'	B
Lens culinaris 'Tarahumara Pink'	B
Lens esculenta	C
Lentinus edodes d.m.p	B
Leonotis leonurus	B,C,SA,SI
Leonotis nepetiifolia	B
Leonotis ocymifolia	C,G,SA
Leonotis ocymifolia ssp ocymifolia	B,SI
Leonotis ocymifolia ssp raineriana	B,SI
Leonotis 'Staircase'	BS,C,F
Leontodon autumnalis	B,CG,JE,LA
Leontodon hispidus	B,C,G,SG

LEONTODON

Leontodon hispidus ssp glabratus	SG
Leontodon hispidus ssp hispidus	SG
Leontodon rigens	JE
Leontopodium alpinum	AP,B,BS,C,CG,CL,FH,G, J,JE,KI,L,S,SA,SC,SG, ST,T,V
Leontopodium alpinum ssp nivale	AP,B
Leontopodium discolor	B,G,SC
Leontopodium fauriei	CC,SC
Leontopodium hyachinense	CC
Leontopodium jacotianum	B
Leontopodium leontopodiodes	B,C,G,SC,SG
Leontopodium linearifolia	CG
Leontopodium ochroleucum v campestre	B,G,JE,SC,SG
Leontopodium shinanenense	CC
Leontopodium soulei	AP,G,SC,SG
Leontopodium stracheyi	CG
Leontopodium wilsonii	B
Leonurus artemisia	B
Leonurus cardiaca	AP,B,C,CG,CP,G,JE,SA, SG
Leonurus sibiricus	B,F,G,SG,T
Leonurus tataricus	SG
Leopoldia maritima S.L258 Tunisia	MN
Lepechinia fragrans	B
Lepidagathis cristata	B
Lepidium attraxa	SG
Lepidium campestre	B,SG
Lepidium densiflorum	SG
Lepidium fremontii	B
Lepidium leptopetalum	B
Lepidium menziesii	B
Lepidium pholidogynum	B
Lepidium ruderale	BS,C
Lepidium strongylophyllum	B
Lepidospartium squamatum	B
Lepidosperma costale	B
Lepidothamnus laxifolius	B,SS
Lepidozamia hopei	B,O
Lepidozamia peroffskyana	B,C,O
Lepisanthes tetraphylla	B
Leptadenia pyrotechnica	B
Leptadenia reticulata	B
Leptinella atrata	B,SS
Leptinella dendyi	B,SS
Leptinella pectinata	B,SS
Leptinella pyrethrifolia	B,SS
Leptinella squalida	B
Leptodactylon californicum	B,SW
Leptomeria empetriformis	B
Leptopteris superba	B
Leptosema chambersii	B
Leptosiphon hyb	C,V
Leptosiphon 'Rainbow Mix'	D
Leptosiphon 'Stardust Hybrids Mix'	T
Leptospermum arachnoides	AU,B,HA,O
Leptospermum 'Beach'	B
Leptospermum blakeleyi	AU
Leptospermum brachyandrum	B,HA,O
Leptospermum brevipes	B,HA
Leptospermum continentale	AU,HA
Leptospermum 'Copper Glow'	SH
Leptospermum coriaceum coastal strain	B
Leptospermum emarginatum	B,HA
Leptospermum epacridoideum	B,HA,SA
Leptospermum erubescens	AU,B

Leptospermum glaucescens	B
Leptospermum grandiflorum	AU,B,HA,O,RH,SA
Leptospermum horizontalis	HA
Leptospermum juniperinum	AU,B,HA
Leptospermum laevigatum	AU,B,HA,O,SA
Leptospermum lanigerum	AU,B,HA,O,RH
Leptospermum lanigerum v macrocarpum	HA
Leptospermum liversidgei	B,RH,O,SA
Leptospermum micromyrtus	RH
Leptospermum minutifolium	AU,B,O
Leptospermum morrisonii	AU
Leptospermum myrsinoides	B,HA
Leptospermum myrtifolium	AU,B,HA
Leptospermum nitidum	AU,B,O,SA
Leptospermum obovatum	AU,B,HA,SG
Leptospermum oligandrum	B
Leptospermum parvifolium	HA
Leptospermum petersonii	C,HA,O,RE,SA,SH
Leptospermum peters. ssp lanceolatum	B
Leptospermum 'Pink Lady'	AP,FH
Leptospermum polyanthum	AU
Leptospermum polygalifolium	B,HA,O,SA
Leptospermum polygal. 'Copper Glow'	O
Leptospermum rotundifolium	B,HA,O,SA,SH
Leptospermum rotundifolium 'Jervis Bay'	B
Leptospermum rotundi. 'Pink Beauty'	B,SH
Leptospermum rotundifolium v alba	B
Leptospermum rupestre	AU,B,HA,O
Leptospermum rupestre 'Roseum'	B
Leptospermum scoparium	AU,B,HA,O,RH,SS
Leptospermum scoparium 'Horizontalis'	B
Leptospermum scoparium 'Roseum'	B,SA
Leptospermum scoparium v nanum	C,I
Leptospermum scoparium v nicholsii	AP,C,SC
Leptospermum scoparium v rotundifolium	HA,O
Leptospermum semibaccatum	B,HA
Leptospermum sericeum	AU
Leptospermum sp mix	C
Leptospermum speciosum	B
Leptospermum sphaerocarpum	AU
Leptospermum spinescens	B
Leptospermum squarrosum	AU,B,HA,O
Leptospermum trinervium	AU,B,HA
Leptospermum trivalvum	B,HA
Leptospermum whiteii	HA
Leschenaultia biloba	B,O,SA
Leschenaultia floribunda	B,C,SA
Leschenaultia formosa	B,O,SA
Leschenaultia linarioides	B
Leschenaultia macrantha	AU,B,O
Lespedeza bicolor	A,B,C,SG
Lespedeza bicolor japonica	SA
Lespedeza capitata	B,PR
Lespedeza cuneata	B
Lespedeza thunbergii	G,SA,SC
Lespedeza virginica	PR
Lesquerella arctica	AP,HH
Lesquerella arizonica	AP,HH
Lesquerella fendleri	B,SW
Lesquerella gordonii	B
Lesquerella intermedia	B,SW
Lesquerella purpurea	B,SW
Lesquerella wardii	SW
Lessertia diffusa	B
Lessertia perennans	SI
Lessertia sp	SI

137

LESSERTIA

Lessertia spinescens	B,SI
Leucadendron album	B,O,SI
Leucadendron arcuatum	B,O,SI
Leucadendron argenteum	B,C,O,SA,SI
Leucadendron barkerae	SI
Leucadendron brunioides	B,O,SI
Leucadendron chamelaea	B,O,SI
Leucadendron cinereum	SI
Leucadendron comosum	B,SI
Leucadendron conicum	B,SI
Leucadendron coniferum	B,O,SI
Leucadendron corymbosum	B,SI
Leucadendron daphnoides	B,O,SI
Leucadendron discolor	B,O,SI
Leucadendron dregei	SI
Leucadendron dubium	B,SI
Leucadendron elimense	B,SI
Leucadendron elimense ssp elimense	O
Leucadendron elimense ssp salteri	O
Leucadendron eucalyptifolium	B,OMSI
Leucadendron flexuosum	SI
Leucadendron floridum	B,O
Leucadendron galpinii	B,O,SA,SI
Leucadendron gandogeri	B,O,SI
Leucadendron gydoense	SI
Leucadendron hypophyllocarpodendron	SI
Leucadendron lanigerum	B,SI
Leucadendron laureolum	B,O,SI
Leucadendron laxum	B,SI
Leucadendron levisanus	B,SI
Leucadendron linifolium	B,SI
Leucadendron loeriense	B,O
Leucadendron loranthifolium	B,SI
Leucadendron macowanii	B,O
Leucadendron meridianum	B,O,SI
Leucadendron microcephalum	B,SI
Leucadendron modestum	B,O,SI
Leucadendron nervosum	B,SI
Leucadendron nobile	B,SI
Leucadendron platyspermum	B,SI
Leucadendron procerum	B,SI
Leucadendron pubescens	B,SI
Leucadendron pubibracteolatum	B,SI
Leucadendron remotum	B,SI
Leucadendron roodii	B
Leucadendron rubrum	B,O,SI
Leucadendron salicifolium	B,SI
Leucadendron salignum	B,O,SA,SI
Leucadendron sessile	B,O,SI
Leucadendron sheliae	B
Leucadendron sp mix	C,V
Leucadendron spissifolium	B,SI
Leucadendron spissifolium ssp fragrans	B,SI
Leucadendron spissifolium ssp oribinum	SI
Leucadendron spissifolium ssp phillipsii	B,O
Leucadendron spissifolium ssp spiss.	SI
Leucadendron stellare	SI
Leucadendron strobolinum	B,O,SI
Leucadendron teretifolium	B,O,SI
Leucadendron thymifolium	B,O,SI
Leucadendron tinctum	B,O,SI
Leucadendron uliginosum ssp uliginosum	B,O,SI
Leucadendron uliginosum v glabratum	B,SI
Leucadendron verticillatum	B,SI
Leucadendron xanthoconus	B,O,SI
Leucaena cunninghamii	B,HA,SA

Leucaena glauca	SA
Leucaena 'Guaje'	B
Leucaena 'Guaje Costeno'	B
Leucaena leucocepha	B,O,RE
Leucaena leucocephala 'K636'	B
Leucaena leucocephala 'K8'	B,HA
Leucaena leucocephala 'Peru'	B
Leucaena salvadorensis	B
Leucaena shannoni	B
Leucanthemella serotinum	JE
Leucanthemopsis alpina	B,C,JE,SA,SC
Leucanthemopsis pectinata	SG
Leucanthemum maximum	AV,B,JE,SG,SU,TU,Z
Leucanthemum maximum 'Coconut Ice'	BS,KI
Leucanthemum paludosum	C,D,T,V
Leucanthemum paludosum 'Giganteum'	B
Leucanthemum paludosum 'Snowland'	B,CL,KI
Leucanthemum paludosum 'Sterling'	B
Leucanthemum paludosum 'White Ring'	B,L
Leucanthemum sx uperbum f1 'Nordlicht'	B,JE
Leucanthemum vulgare	B,C,CO,G,JE,LA,SA,SG, V
Leucanthemum vulgare 'May Empress'	B
Leucanthemum vulgare 'May Queen'	B,JE,V
Leucanthemum vulgare 'Paris White'	U
Leucanthemum vulgare 'Rhine View'	B,JE
Leucanthemum waldsteinii	SG
Leucanthemum x superbum	B,F,SG,T
Leucanthemum x superbum 'Alaska'	B,F,JE,SA
Leucanthemum x superbum 'Amelia'	B,JE
Leucanthemum x sup. 'Antwerp Star'	B,C
Leucanthemum x s. 'Diener's Dbl Giants'	B
Leucanthemum x s. 'Etoile D'anvers'	B
Leucanthemum x superbum 'Exhibition'	B
Leucanthemum x s. f1 'Snow Lady Dw'	B,BD,C,CL,F,JE,L,S,SE, YA
Leucanthemum x superbum f1 'Starburst'	B,T
Leucanthemum x s. fl pl 'Snowdreft'	JE
Leucanthemum x s. 'Little Silver Princess'	B,BS,C,JE,S,SA,V
Leucanthemum x s. 'Mayfield Giant'	CO,KI
Leucanthemum x superbum 'Polaris'	B,C,JE
Leucanthemum x s. 'Rijnsburg Glory'	B,JE
Leucanthemum x s. 'Snow Banquet'	SE
Leucanthemum x superbum 'Supra'	B,JE
Leucanthemum x s. 'White Iceberg'	KI
Leucanthemum x s. 'White Knight'	B,BS
Leucanthemum x s. 'Wild Shasta Daisy'	B,VH
Leucas aspera	B
Leuchtenbergia principis	B,BC,C,CH,GC,Y
Leucochrysum albicans	O
Leucochrysum fitzgibbonii	B,HA,O
Leucochrysum molle	B,O
Leucocoryne hybrida x 'New Hybrids'	B
Leucocoryne ixioides	B
Leucocoryne ixioides 'The Bride'	B
Leucocoryne narcissoides	SI
Leucocrinum montanum	SW
Leucogenes grandiceps	B,SS
Leucogenes leontopodium	AP,SC,SS
Leucojum aestivum	AP,B,G,MN
Leucojum autumnale	AP,LG,SC,SG
Leucojum autumnale v oporanthum	AP,B,G
Leucojum autumnale v oporanthum	MN,PM
Leucojum autumnale v pulchellum	AP,B,PM,SC
Leucojum autumnale v pulchellum	MN
Leucojum nicaeensis	AP,C,FH,G,PM,SC,SG

LEUCOJUM

Leucojum roseum	AP,I,PM,SC
Leucojum trichophyllum	AP,B,LG
Leucojum trichophyllum B.S.409 Portugal	MN
Leucojum trichophyllum B.S.449/1	MN
Leucojum vernum	AP,B,C,G,JE,PM,SC
Leucojum vernum Nancy Lindsay's form	NG
Leucojum vernum v carpathicum	B,G,NG,SC
Leucophyta brownii	AU,B,O
Leucophyta citreus	AU
Leucopogon capitellatus	B
Leucopogon ericioides	HA
Leucopogon fraseri	AP,AU,B,SS
Leucopogon nutans	B
Leucopogon obovatus	B
Leucopogon ovalifolius	B
Leucopogon propinquus	B
Leucopogon pulchellus	B
Leucopogon rubicundus	B
Leucopogon strictus	B
Leucopogon suaveolens	B
Leucopogon verticillatus	B,C
Leucorchis albida	CG
Leucosidea sericea	B,SI
Leucospermum bolusii	B,O,SI
Leucospermum catherinae	B,O,SI
Leucospermum conocarpodendon ssp c.	O,SI
Leucospermum conocarp. ssp viridum	B,SI
Leucospermum conocarpodendron	B
Leucospermum cordifolium	B,O,SA,SI,V
Leucospermum cord. 'Yellow Bird' o.p.	B,SI
Leucospermum cuneiforme	B,O,SI
Leucospermum erubescens	B,O,SI
Leucospermum formosum	B,O,SI
Leucospermum glabrum	B,O,SI
Leucospermum glabrum 'Helderfontein'	B,SI
Leucospermum grandiflorum	B,SA
Leucospermum guenzii	B,O,SI
Leucospermum 'High Gold'	SI
Leucospermum hyb mix	O
Leucospermum hypophyllocarpodendron	B
Leucospermum incisum	B
Leucospermum lineare	B
Leucospermum muirii	B,O,SI
Leucospermum oleifolium	B,O
Leucospermum patersoni	B,O,SI
Leucospermum praecox	B,SI
Leucospermum praemorsum	SI
Leucospermum reflexum	B,O
Leucospermum reflexum 'Rocket'	O
Leucospermum reflexum v luteum	B
Leucospermum rodolentum	B
Leucospermum 'Scarlet Ribbon'	B,SI
Leucospermum sp mix	C,V
Leucospermum 'Tango'	SI
Leucospermum tomentosum	B,SI
Leucospermum tottum	B,O
Leucospermum vestitum	B,SI
Leucothoe catesbaei of gdns	B,C
Leucothoe grayana	B
Leucothoe racemosa	B
Leuzea australis	B
Leuzea conifera	B,SC
Leuzea rhapontica	B,G,JE
Levenhookia chippendalei	B
Levenhookia pauciflora	B
Levenhookia preissii	B

Levenhookia pulcherrima	B
Levenhookia pusilla	B
Levenhookia stipitata	B
Levisticum apiifolium	B
Levisticum officinale	B,CP,G,KS,SA,SC,SG
Levisticum officinale 'Magnus'	B
Lewisia 'Ashwood Hybrids'	AP,AS
Lewisia 'Ashwood Ruby'	AS
Lewisia 'Ashwood Strain'	AP,AS,C,D,S,SC
Lewisia 'Ballet Royale'	SE
Lewisia 'Birch hybrids'	C,I
Lewisia brachycalyx	AP,AS,C,G,SC,SG,SW
Lewisia brachycalyx pink	B,SC,SW
Lewisia cantelovii	AP,AS,C,SC
Lewisia cantelovii o-p	FH
Lewisia columbiana	AP,AS,B,C,CG,G,I,JE,SC
Lewisia columbiana hyb o-p	FH
Lewisia columbiana 'Rosea'	AP,AS,SC,SG
Lewisia columbiana ssp rupicola	AP,AS,SC
Lewisia columbiana ssp wallowensis	AP,AS,CG,SC
Lewisia congdonii	SG
Lewisia cotyledon	AP,AS,BP,BS,CG,CL,G,
	HH,L,P,PA,PM,SC,SG
Lewisia cotyledon f alba	AP,JE,SC,SG
Lewisia cotyledon 'Fransi'	AP,JE
Lewisia cotyledon hyb	AP,CG,JE,SC,SG
Lewisia cotyledon hyb o-p	FH
Lewisia cotyledon hyb selected	PM
Lewisia cotyledon 'Praline'	JE
Lewisia cotyledon 'Regenbogen'	BS,C,JE
Lewisia cotyledon 'Rondo'	JE
Lewisia cotyledon 'Soranda Hyb' resel.	B,J,V
Lewisia cotyledon 'Sunset Strain'	AP,B,BD,BS,CG,G,JE,
	SA,SC
Lewisia cotyledon v heckneri	AP,B,CG,JE,SC,SG
Lewisia cotyledon v howellii	AP,SC,SG
Lewisia 'Howellii Hybrids'	BS,T
Lewisia leeana	AP,AS,G,SC
Lewisia longipetala	AP,AS,G,I,SC,SG
Lewisia longiscapa	AP,AS
Lewisia mix	CH
Lewisia mix vars	JE
Lewisia nevadensis	AP,AS,B,BS,C,CG,G,JE,
	PM,SA,SC
Lewisia nevadensis o-p	FH
Lewisia nevadensis rosea	AS,SC
Lewisia oppositifolia	AP,AS,SC
Lewisia pygmaea	AP,AS,B,C,CG,G,I,JE,SC,
	SW
Lewisia rediviva	SP,AS,B,C,JE,SC,SW
Lewisia rediviva alba	AP,AS,SC
Lewisia rediviva Jolon Strain	AS
Lewisia rediviva o-p	FH
Lewisia 'Rock Garden Mix'	U
Lewisia 'Rose Splendour'	AP,AS
Lewisia serrata	AS
Lewisia sierrae	AP,AS,G,I,JE,SC
Lewisia triphylla	AP,AS,C,G,SC
Lewisia tweedyi	AP,AS,B,C,G,JE,SC,SG
Lewisia tweedyi 'Alba'	AP,AS,G,SC
Lewisia tweedyi 'Elliotts Variety'	AP,AS
Lewisia tweedyi lemon	AS
Lewisia tweedyi 'Lovedream'	C,JE
Lewisia tweedyi 'Rosea'	AP,AS,SC
Lewisia 'White Splendour'	AS,I
Leycesteria crocothyrsos	B,P

LEYCESTERIA

Leycesteria formosa	B,C,JE,P,RH,SA,T	Ligularia wilsoniana	B,G
Leymus arenarius	B,C,JE,SA	Ligusticum ferrulaceum	B
Leymus condensatus	B	Ligusticum porteri	B
Leymus secalinus	B	Ligusticum scoticum	B,G,SG
Leysera gnaphaloides	B	Ligustrum acutissimum	CG
Leyssera gnaphaloides	B,SI	Ligustrum chenaultii	SA
Lhotzkya ericoides	C	Ligustrum ibota	B
Liatris aspera	B,JE,PR,T	Ligustrum japonicum	B,C,SA
Liatris cylindracea	B,CG,JE,PR	Ligustrum lucidum	B,C,G,SA
Liatris earleyi	B	Ligustrum obtusifolium	B,SA
Liatris elegans	JE	Ligustrum ovalifolium	B,SA
Liatris graminifolia	B	Ligustrum sinense	B,SA
Liatris ligulistylis	B,CG,JE,PR	Ligustrum tschonoskii	CG
Liatris microcephala	NT	Ligustrum vulgare	B,SA,SG
Liatris punctata	B,PR	Lilium albanicum	LG
Liatris pycnostachya	B,C,CG,G,HW,JE,PR,S,	Lilium alexandrae	LG
	SA,SG,T	Lilium amabile	LG,SC
Liatris scariosa	B,G	Lilium amabile v luteum	C,LG
Liatris scariosa 'Alba'	B,JE	Lilium Asiatic hyb mix	C
Liatris scariosa 'Gracious'	T	Lilium 'Asiatic Hyb' mix h-p	T
Liatris scariosa 'September Gory'	JE	Lilium 'Asiatic Hyb' s-c	B
Liatris spicata	B,BS,CL,CO,FH,G,HW,	Lilium auratum	AP,B,LG
	JE,L,LG,KI,KS,NT,PR,	Lilium 'Bright Star'	B
	SA,SG,SU,TU	Lilium brownii	LG
Liatris spicata 'Floristan Violet'	B,BS,C,JE	Lilium bulbiferum	CG,G,SC
Liatris spicata 'Floristan White'	B,BS,C,G,JE,KI	Lilium bulbiferum ssp bulbiferum	B
Liatris spicata 'Kobold'	B,BS,C,G,JE,PM,SA,U,V	Lilium bulbiferum v croceum	B,G,JE,LG,SC
Liatris spicata 'Picador'	JE	Lilium callosum	LG
Liatris spicata 'Purple Torch'	B	Lilium canadense	AP,B,CC,G,LG,SC
Liatris spicata voilet	SA	Lilium candidum	C,G,JE,LG
Liatris spicata white	SA	Lilium candidum L/Y Yugoslavia	MN
Liatris spicata 'White Torch'	B	Lilium carniolicum	AP,B,JE,LG
Liatris squarrosa	B,NT,PR	Lilium cernuum	LG,SC
Libanotis pyrenaica	SG	Lilium chalcedonicum	LG
Libertia caerulescens	AP,B,C,P	Lilium columbianum	AP,C,G,JE,SC
Libertia formosa	AP,C,FH,RH,SC,SG	Lilium concolor v partheneion	PM
Libertia grandiflora	AU,B,C,I,JE,MN,RS,SA	Lilium concolor v strictum	B
Libertia ixioides	AP,B,SA,SC,SG,SS	Lilium dauricum	LG
Libertia peregrinans	AP,B,C	Lilium dauricum v alpinum	LG
Libertia peregrinans 'Gold Leaf'	B,P	Lilium davidii	AP,B,C,LG,SC
Libertia pulchella	AP,AU	Lilium davidii v willmottiae	B,C,JE,LG
Libocedrus plumosa	B	Lilium duchartrei	AP,G,LG,SC
Licuala grandis	B,C,O,SA	Lilium formosanum	AP,B,C,G,LG,SC
Licuala pacifica	B	Lilium formosanum 'Little Snowwhite'	AP,B,C,SC
Licuala paludosa	B	Lilium formosanum 'Little Snowwhite' h-p	T
Licuala ramsayi	B,O,SA	Lilium formosanum v pricei	AP,B,G,LG,P,PA,RS,SC,
Licuala sp	RE		SG
Licuala spinosa	B,O,SA	Lilium grayi	LG
Lignocarpus carnosulus	AP,B,SS	Lilium hansoniii	AP,G,LG,SC
Ligousia pentagonia	B	Lilium henryi	AP,B,C,G,LG,SC
Ligularia altaica	SG	Lilium humboldtii	B,LG
Ligularia amplexicaulis	B	Lilium humboldtii bloomerianum	SW
Ligularia dentata	B,C,FH,JE,SA,SC	Lilium hyb Aurelian mix	C
Ligularia dentata 'Dark Beauty'	B,C,JE,SA	Lilium hyb Aurelian 'Reflexed Yellow'	C
Ligularia dentata 'Desdemona'	B,P,SC,SG	Lilium hyb - bulbiferum x 'Brismark'	B
Ligularia dentata 'Othello'	T	Lilium hyb - martagon x pumilum	B
Ligularia fischeri	B,JE,SC	Lilium hybrids	G,LG
Ligularia glauca	SG	Lilium japonicum	LG
Ligularia hodgsonii	B,SA	Lilium kelleyanum	LG
Ligularia japonica	JE	Lilium kelloggii	LG
Ligularia macrophylla	SG	Lilium 'Kiwi Fanfare'	C
Ligularia przewalskii	B,C,G,JE,L,SA,SC,T	Lilium lancifolium	CG,LG,SC
Ligularia sachalinensis	G,SC,SG	Lilium lancifolium 'Fl.Pl.'	AP,B,P
Ligularia sibirica	B,CG,G,JE,SG	Lilium lankongense	LG,SC
Ligularia stenocephala hyb	B,JE	Lilium ledebourii	AP,LG,SC
Ligularia veitchiana	B,SG	Lilium leucanthum v centifolium	C,G,LG

LILIUM

Lilium 'Lily World' sp & cvs mix — C
Lilium longiflorum — AP,LG,SC
Lilium longiflorum f1 hyb 'Snow Trumpet' — B,BD,C,CL,T
Lilium longiflorum 'Trumpet Hybrids' — B,V
Lilium 'Mabel Violet' o-p — C
Lilium mackliniae — AP,B,LG,P,SC
Lilium maculatum — CC,LG
Lilium martagon — AP,B,C,CG,G,I,JE,LG, MN,N,P,PM,RS,SA,SC, SG,T,V
Lilium martagon hyb mix — AP,SC,T
Lilium martagon v album — AP,B,C,G,JE,LG,MN,RS, SC,SG
Lilium martagon v cattaniae — AP,G,LG,SC,SG
Lilium medeoloides — CC,G,SC
Lilium michiganense — PR
Lilium monadelphum — AP,B,C,G,JE,LG,SC,SG
Lilium nanum — AP,B,G,LG,SC
Lilium nepalense — C
Lilium pardalinum — G,LG
Lilium parryi — B,LG
Lilium parvum — LG,SG
Lilium pensylvanicum — SG
Lilium philadelphicum — PR
Lilium philippinense — B,C,LG
Lilium pomponium — AP,G,LG,PM,SC,SG
Lilium pumilum — AP,B,C,JE,LG,RS,SC,SG
Lilium pyrenaicum — AP,C,G,JE,LG,SA,SC,SG
Lilium regale — AP,B,BS,C,CL,G,JE,KI, LG,MA,N,RS,SA,SC,SG, T
Lilium regale 'Pink Picotee' — T
Lilium regale v album — AP,G,LG
Lilium rubellum — B,LG,SC
Lilium rubescens — B
Lilium sacchalinense — SA
Lilium sargentiae — LG,SG
Lilium sp CNW1129 — X
Lilium sp mix — PA,T
Lilium speciosum v speciosum — LG
Lilium sulphureum — LG
Lilium superbum — B,LG,SC
Lilium szovitsianum see monadelphum
Lilium tigrinum see lancifolium
Lilium Trumpet Hyb mix h-p — T
Lilium Trumpet Hyb New Zealand s-c mix — C
Lilium Trumpets 'Wyoming' mix — C
Lilium umbellatum — B,SW
Lilium washingtonianum — B
Lilium x aurelianense 'Copper King' — C
Lilium x aurelianense 'First Love' — C
Lilium x testaceum — B
Limnanthes douglasii — A,AP,B,BD,BS,C,CO,D, FH,G,I,J,KI,KS,L,S,SC, SE,SG,ST,SU,T,TU,V,VH
Limnanthes douglasii v sulphurea — C
Limonia acidissima — B
Limonium aureum 'Sahin's Gold' — B
Limonium aureum 'Supernova' — T
Limonium bellidifolium — AP,FH,I,SC
Limonium bellidifolium 'Spangle' — B
Limonium binervosum — T
Limonium bonduelli — B,C,T
Limonium caspia 'Dazzling Blue' — B,SA,U
Limonium cosyrense — AP,I,SC
Limonium dumosum — T

Limonium fortunei 'Confetti' — T
Limonium gmelinii — B,C,G,JE,KS
Limonium gmelinii hungaricum — SA
Limonium gougetianum — AP,G,JE,SC
Limonium latifolium — AP,B,C,DT,FH,JE,KI,KS, L,SA,SU,T
Limonium 'Marshall's Super Mix' — M
Limonium minutum — AP,FH,G,PM,SC
Limonium otolepis 'Lavender Lace' — B,C
Limonium otolepis 'Select' — T
Limonium peregrinum — B,SI
Limonium perezii — AP,B,JE,KS,SA,SC,T,V
Limonium perezii 'Atlantis' — B
Limonium pruinosum — B
Limonium puberulum — B
Limonium purpuratum — B,SI
Limonium sinensis — JE
Limonium sinensis 'Stardust' — CL,KI
Limonium sinuatum — B,CL,SU
Limonium sinuatum 'American Beauty' — B,C,T
Limonium sinuatum 'Apricot' — C
Limonium sinuatum 'Apricot Beauty' — B,T
Limonium sinuatum 'Art Shades mix' — CO,J,ST,TU,V,VH
Limonium sinuatum 'Art Shades' s-c — KI
Limonium sinuatum 'Azure' — T
Limonium sinuatum 'Beldermeier mix' — D,J,T,V
Limonium sinuatum 'Blue Peter' — CL
Limonium sinuatum 'Blue River' — B
Limonium sinuatum 'Chamois' — B
Limonium sinuatum 'Compindi' — C
Limonium sinuatum 'Compindi Rose' — C
Limonium sinuatum 'Forever Blue' — B
Limonium sinuatum 'Forever Gold' — B,BD,CL,KS,O
Limonium sinuatum 'Forever Happy' — KS
Limonium sinuatum 'Forever Lavender' — B,KS
Limonium sinuatum 'Forever' mix — C,F
Limonium sinuatum 'Forever Moonlight' — B,DT,KS,T
Limonium sinuatum 'Forever Pink' — B
Limonium sinuatum 'Forever Rose' — B,KS
Limonium sinuatum 'Forever Silver' — B,KS
Limonium sinuatum 'Formula mix' s-c — D,T
Limonium sinuatum 'Gold Coast' — C,CL,T
Limonium sinuatum 'Heavenly Blue' — CL
Limonium sinuatum hyb mix — U
Limonium sinuatum 'Iceberg' — C,CL,T,V
Limonium sinuatum 'Kaleidoscope' s-c — YA
Limonium sinuatum 'Lavender' — C,KS
Limonium sinuatum 'Market Blue' — T
Limonium sinuatum 'Midnight Blue' — C
Limonium sinuatum 'Pacific' mix — C,KS
Limonium sinuatum 'Pacific' s-c — KS
Limonium sinuatum 'Pacific' white — B
Limonium sinuatum 'Petite Bouquet' mix — BD,C,CL,CO,KI,KS,R,TU
Limonium sinuatum 'Petite Bouquet' s-c — KS
Limonium sinuatum 'Purple Attraction' — C
Limonium sinuatum 'Purple Monarch' — T
Limonium sinuatum 'Q' mix — DT
Limonium sinuatum 'Q' s-c — L
Limonium sinuatum 'Q' white — B
Limonium sinuatum 'Rose Light' — C,CLV
Limonium sinuatum 'Salmon Shades' — KS
Limonium sinuatum 'Sky Blue' — C
Limonium sinuatum 'Soft Pastel' mix — C,KS,SE,T,U
Limonium sinuatum 'Special' mix — F,S
Limonium sinuatum 'Sunset Shades Mix' — B,BD,C,CL,DT,F,KS,SE, T,V

LIMONIUM

Limonium sinuatum 'Twilight'	C	
Limonium speciosus 'Blue Diamond'	JE	
Limonium 'Sunburst Dark Blue'	S	
Limonium 'Sunburst Golden'	U	
Limonium 'Sunburst' mix	S	
Limonium 'Sunburst Pale Blue'	S	
Limonium 'Sunburst Rose'	S	
Limonium 'Sunburst White'	S	
Limonium 'Sunburst Yellow'	S	
Limonium tetragonum 'Confetti'	B	
Limonium tetragonum 'Stardust'	B	
Linanthus floribundus	B	
Linanthus grandiflorus	AP,B,C,KS,SC,T	
Linanthus grandiflorus 'Princess Blush'	V	
Linanthus nuttallii	B,JE,SW	
Linaria aeruginea	AP,RS,SC	
Linaria aeruginea ssp nevadensis	HH,SG	
Linaria alpina	AP,B,BS,C,CG,FH,G,JE, RS,SA,SC,SG,T	
Linaria alpina hyb	I	
Linaria amethystea	B	
Linaria broussonetii	C	
Linaria 'Excelsior mix'	J	
Linaria 'Fantasia Series' s-c	F	
Linaria genistifolia	AP,B,CG,T	
Linaria genistifolia ssp dalmatica	AP,B,C,G,JE,SC,SG	
Linaria halaeva	B	
Linaria joppensis	B	
Linaria maroccana	B,I,KS	
Linaria maroccana 'Excelsior Mixed'	V	
Linaria maroccana 'Fairy Bouquet Mixed'	B,C,CO,D,DT,F,KI,L,S, SU,T,TU,U	
Linaria maroccana 'Northern Lights Mix'	B,KS,T	
Linaria nevadensis 'Elfin Delight'	CG,V	
Linaria purpurea	B,BS,JE,MA,SA,SC,SU, V,W	
Linaria purpurea 'Alba'	B,JE,SA	
Linaria purpurea 'Bowles' Mauve'	B	
Linaria purpurea 'Canon J.Went'	AP,B,C,JE,SA,SC,T	
Linaria purpurea 'Rev. C.E.Bowring'	B	
Linaria repens	B,G,JE	
Linaria reticulata 'Aureopurpurea'	B,T	
Linaria reticulata 'Flamenco'	C	
Linaria supina	AP,B,FH,G,JE,SC	
Linaria tonzigii	B,CG	
Linaria triornithophora	AP,B,G,P,T	
Linaria vulgaris	B,C,CO,F,JE,LA,SA,SG,V	
Lindelofia longiflora	AP,B,CC,G,JE,SA	
Lindera benzoin	A,B,SA	
Lindera glauca	SA	
Lindera obtusiloba	B,N,SA	
Lindheimera texana	B,KS,T	
Linospadix minor	B,O,SA	
Linospadix monostachya	B,C,HA,O,SA	
Linum africanum	B,SI	
Linum alpinum	AP,JE,SA	
Linum arboreum	AP,SC,T	
Linum austriacum	B,G,W	
Linum bienne	B	
Linum blue	S	
Linum capitatum	AP,B,JE,SC	
Linum dolmiticum	CC,JE	
Linum flavum	AP,B,BS,SC	
Linum flavum 'Compactum'	AP,B,C,CL,G,JE,SA,SC, SG,T	
Linum flavum v comp. 'Golden Cushion'	V	

Linum grandiflorum	G,HW,SG	
Linum grandiflorum 'Album'	T	
Linum grandiflorum 'Bright Eyes'	B,C,J,KS,T,V	
Linum grandiflorum 'Rubrum'	B,C,D,KS,L,T	
Linum hirsutum	AP,JE,SA	
Linum komarovii 'Blue Ice'	T	
Linum lewisii	AP,SG,SW,W	
Linum marginale	RS	
Linum monogynum	AP,B,SC,SS	
Linum narbonense	AP,B,C,FH,G,JE,SA,SC	
Linum narbonense 'Heavenly Blue'	T	
Linum perenne	AP,AV,B,BS,C,CO,DT,G, HW,JE,KI,KS,L,SA,SC, SG,V	
Linum perenne 'Album'	AP,B,C,CG,JE,SA	
Linum perenne 'Himmelszelt'	JE	
Linum perenne 'Jewels Mix'	U	
Linum perenne nanum 'Alba Diamant'	B,BD,BS,C,JE,KI,KS, SA,T	
Linum perenne nanum 'Blue Saphyr'	B,BD,BS,C,CL,JE,S,SA ,T,TU	
Linum perenne ssp alpinum	B,C	
Linum perenne ssp anglicum	NS	
Linum perenne ssp lewisii	AP,B,C,RS	
Linum pubescens	B	
Linum rhodopeum	SG	
Linum rubrum	BS,CO,KI,ST,V	
Linum scarlet	DT,J,S,U	
Linum sp blue Chile	P	
Linum suffruticosum ssp salsoloides	AP,B,C,JE,SC	
Linum sulcatum	PR	
Linum trigynum	CG	
Linum usitatissimum	B,BS,C,CP,G,KS,SG,V,W	
Linum usitatissimum cvc,vars	B	
Linum virginianum	B	
Liparia splendens	B,SI	
Lippia dulcis	B,C,CP	
Liquidambar acalycina	B	
Liquidambar formosana	B,N,SA	
Liquidambar styraciflua	A,B,BS,C,CG,HA,N,SA,T	
Liriodendron chinense	B,SA	
Liriodendron tulipifera	A,B,C,CG,HA,RH,SA	
Liriope muscari	C	
Liriope muscari 'Big Blue'	JE	
Liriope muscari 'Gigantea'	B	
Listera ovata	B	
Litchi chinensis	B	
Lithocarpus densiflorus	B,SA	
Lithocarpus sclerophylla	B	
Lithodora arvensis	SG	
Lithops alpina	CG	
Lithops aucampiae	B,CH,SI	
Lithops aucampiae 'Kuruman'	B,Y	
Lithops aucampiae ssp auc. v aucampiae	Y	
Lithops aucampiae ssp auc. v koelmanii	Y	
Lithops aucampiae ssp eunicae v eunicae	Y	
Lithops aucampiae ssp eun. v fluminalis	Y	
Lithops aucampiae v euniceae	B	
Lithops aucampiae v fluminalis	B,BC	
Lithops aucampiae v koelemanii	B	
Lithops aucampiae v 'Kuruman'	B	
Lithops bromfieldii	B	
Lithops bromfieldii v bromfieldii	Y	
Lithops bromfieldii v glaudinae	B	
Lithops bromfieldii v glaudinae	Y	
Lithops bromfieldii v insularis	B	

LITHOPS

Lithops bromfieldii v insularis C42 & C57	Y
Lithops bromfieldii v insularis 'Sulphurea'	B,Y
Lithops bromfieldii v mennellii	B
Lithops bromfieldii v mennellii C44	Y
Lithops comptonii	B,SI
Lithops comptonii v comptonii C125	Y
Lithops comptonii v weberi	B
Lithops dinteri	B,CG
Lithops dinteri ssp dinteri v brevis C84	Y
Lithops dinteri ssp dinteri v dinteri C206	Y
Lithops dinteri v brevis	B
Lithops dinteri v friederichii	B,Y
Lithops dinteri v multipunctata	B,BC,Y
Lithops divergens	B,CG
Lithops divergens v amethystina	B,BC,Y
Lithops divergens v divergens C202	Y
Lithops dorotheae	B,Y
Lithops elevata	CG
Lithops erniana	B
Lithops erniana v witputzensis /l.kara.ssp	B
Lithops francisci	B,CG,Y
Lithops fulleri v brunnea	B
Lithops fulleri v rouxii	B
Lithops fulleri v rouxii /julii ssp fu.v.rou.	B
Lithops fulleri var	B
Lithops fulviceps	B,CG,SI
Lithops fulviceps v aurea	B
Lithops fulviceps v fulviceps coll ref	Y
Lithops fulviceps v fulviceps 'Lydiae'	B
Lithops fulviceps v lactinea	B,Y
Lithops gesinae	B,CG,SI
Lithops gesinae v annae	B,Y
Lithops gesinae v gesinae C207	Y
Lithops geyeri	B,CG,Y
Lithops gracilidelineata	B,BC,CG
Lithops gracilid. ssp brandbergensis	B,Y
Lithops gracilid. ssp gr. 'Fritz White Lady'	Y
Lithops gracilidelineata ssp gracil v gracil	Y
Lithops gracilidelineata v waldroniae	B,Y
Lithops hallii	B,BC,CG,SI
Lithops hallii 'Salicola Reticulata'	B,Y
Lithops hallii v 'Brown'	B
Lithops hallii v hallii C22 & C45	Y
Lithops hallii v ochracea	B,Y
Lithops hallii v ochr. 'Green Soapstone'	Y
Lithops hallii v 'White Form'	B
Lithops harlequin	CH
Lithops heimutii	B,CG,Y
Lithops herrei	B,Y
Lithops herrei v 'Translucens'	B
Lithops hookeri	B,CG
Lithops hookeri v dabneri	B,Y
Lithops hookeri v elephina	B,Y
Lithops hookeri v hookeri	Y
Lithops hookeri v hookeri 'Turbiniformis'	B
Lithops hookeri v hookeri 'Vermiculata'	B,Y
Lithops hookeri v lutea	B,Y
Lithops hookeri v marginata	B,Y
Lithops hookeri v marginata 'Cerise'	B,Y
Lithops hookeri v marginata 'Red-brown'	B,Y
Lithops hookeri v subfenestrata	B,Y
Lithops hookeri v subf. 'Brunneoviolacea'	B,Y
Lithops hookeri v suzannae	B,Y
Lithops julii	B,CG,SI
Lithops julii 'Pallid'	B
Lithops julii 'Reticulata'	B
Lithops julii ssp fulleri	B,BC,Y
Lithops julii ssp fulleri v brunnea	B,Y
Lithops julii ssp fulleri v rouxii	B,Y
Lithops julii ssp julii	Y
Lithops julii ssp julii 'Chrysocephala'	B,Y
Lithops julii ssp julii 'Fuscous'	B
Lithops julii ssp julii 'Littlewoodii'	B,Y
Lithops julii ssp julii 'Reticulata''	Y
Lithops karasmontana	B,CG
Lithops karasmontana 'Jacobseniana'	B,Y
Lithops karasmontana 'Mickbergensis'	B,Y
Lithops karasmontana 'Opalina'	B,Y
Lithops karasmontana 'Signalberg'	B,Y
Lithops karasmontana ssp bella	B,Y
Lithops karasmontana ssp eberlanzii	B,Y
Lithops karas. ssp eb. 'Avocado Cream'	B
Lithops karas.ssp eberlanzii 'Erniana'	B,Y
Lithops karas. ssp eb. 'Witputzensis'	B,Y
Lithops karasmontana ssp karas v karas	Y
Lithops karasmontana v aiaisensis	B,Y
Lithops karasmontana v lericheana	B,Y
Lithops karasmontana v lerichiana	B
Lithops karasmontana v tischerii	B,Y
Lithops kunjasensis	CG
Lithops lesliei	B,CG,SI
Lithops lesliei 'Albiflora'	B,Y
Lithops lesliei 'Albinica'	B,Y
Lithops lesliei 'Albinigold'	Y
Lithops lesliei 'Kimberley'	B,Y
Lithops lesliei 'Luteoviridis'	B,Y
Lithops lesliei 'Pietersburg'	B,Y
Lithops lesliei 'Prince Albert'	B
Lithops lesliei ssp burchellii	B,Y
Lithops lesliei ssp lesliei	Y
Lithops lesliei v hornii	B,Y
Lithops lesliei v mariae	B,Y
Lithops lesliei v minor	B,Y
Lithops lesliei v minor 'Witblom'	B,Y
Lithops lesliei v rubrobrunnea	B,Y
Lithops lesliei v venteri	B,Y
Lithops lesliei v venteri 'Maraisii'	B
Lithops lesliei 'Warrenton'	B,Y
Lithops marginata	CG
Lithops marmorata	B,SI
Lithops marmorata 'Framesii'	B,CH,Y
Lithops marmorata ssp marmorata	CH,Y
Lithops marmorata ssp marm. 'Diutina'	B,Y
Lithops marmorata 'Umdausensis'	B
Lithops marmorata v elisae	B,Y
Lithops meyeri	B,Y
Lithops naureeniae	B,Y
Lithops olivacea	B,CH
Lithops olivacea v nebrownii	B,Y
Lithops olivacea v olivacea	Y
Lithops optica	B,SI,Y
Lithops optica 'Maculata'	B,Y
Lithops optica 'Rubra'	B,CH,Y
Lithops otzeniana	B,CH,Y
Lithops 'Pebble Plants Mix'	T
Lithops pseudotruncatella	B,SI
Lithops pseudotruncatella 'Alpina'	B,Y
Lithops pseudotruncatella 'Mundtii'	B,Y
Lithops pseudotruncatella pallid form	Y
Lithops pseudotruncatella ssp archerae	B,Y
Lithops pseudotruncatella ssp dendritica	B,Y
Lithops pseudot. ssp dendritica 'Farinosa'	B,Y

LITHOPS

Lithops p. ssp dendritica 'Pulmonuncula.	B,Y
Lithops pseudot. ssp groendraaiensis	B,Y
Lithops pseudot. ssp pseudo v pseudo	Y
Lithops pseudotruncatella ssp volkii	B,CG,Y
Lithops pseudotruncatella v elisabethiae	B,Y
Lithops pseudotruncatella v riehmerae	B,Y
Lithops rugosa	CG
Lithops ruschiorum	B
Lithops ruschiorum 'Nellii'	B,Y
Lithops ruschiorum v ruschiorum coll ref	Y
Lithops salicola	B,SI,Y
Lithops salicola 'Maculata'	B,Y
Lithops schwantesii	B,BC
Lithops schwantesii 'Grey'	B,Y
Lithops schwantesii 'Gulielmi'	B,Y
Lithops schwantesii 'Kuibisensis'	B,Y
Lithops schwantesii ssp gebseri	B,Y
Lithops schwantesii ssp sch v sch	Y
Lithops schwantesii 'Triebneri'	B
Lithops schwantesii v marthae	B,Y
Lithops schwantesii v rugosa	B,Y
Lithops schwantesii v urikosensis	B,Y
Lithops sch. v urikosensis 'Christinae'	B,Y
Lithops sch. v urikosensis 'Kunjasensis'	B,Y
Lithops sch. v urikosensis 'Nutupsdrift'	B
Lithops sp mix	C,J,L,SI,SO,Y
Lithops 'Sunstone'	CH
Lithops 'Talisman'	CH
Lithops terricolor	B,SI,Y
Lithops terricolor d 'Localis'	B,Y
Lithops terricolor 'Peersii'	B,Y
Lithops terricolor 'Prince Albert'	B,Y
Lithops vallis-mariae	B
Lithops vallis-mariae 'Margarethae'	B,Y
Lithops vallis-mariae v groendraaiensis	B
Lithops verruculosa	B,SI,Y
Lithops verruculosa 'Inae'	B
Lithops verruculosa v glabra	B,Y
Lithops verruculosa v verruculosa	Y
Lithops villetii	B
Lithops villetii ssp deboeri	B,Y
Lithops villetii ssp villetii	Y
Lithops villetii v kennedyi	B,Y
Lithops viridis	B
Lithops werneri	B,Y
Lithospermum canescens	B
Lithospermum caroliniense	B,JE
Lithospermum erythrorhizon	CG
Lithospermum incisum	B
Lithospermum officinale	B,G,SG
Litsea leefeana	O
Littonia modesta	B,C,MN,SG,SI
Littorella uniflora	SS
Living Stones & Other Succ. exc Lithops	C
Livistona alfredii	B,C,O,SA
Livistona australis	B,C,HA,O,SA
Livistona benthamii	B,O
Livistona chinensis	B,C,HA,O,SA
Livistona decipiens	B,HA,O,SA
Livistona drudei	B,O
Livistona eastonii	B,O
Livistona humilis	B,O,SA
Livistona inermis	B,O
Livistona jenkensiana	HA,O,SA
Livistona loryphylla	B,O
Livistona mariae	B,HA,O

Livistona muelleri	B,O
Livistona rigida	B,O
Livistona robinsoniana	B,O
Livistona rotundifolia	B,O
Livistona saribus	B,O,RE
Livistona 'Victoria River'	B,O
Lloydia serotina	B,C,SW
Loasa triphylla	SG,T
Loasa triphylla v volcanica	AP,B,C,FH,I,SG
Lobelia anatina	B,SW,T,V
Lobelia cardinalis	AP,B,C,CC,CG,CP,FH, HW,JE,NT,PR,SA,SW,T, W
Lobelia cardinalis 'Bees Flame'	U
Lobelia cardinalis multiflora	SW
Lobelia chamaepitys	SI
Lobelia comosa	B,CG,SI
Lobelia 'Complexion'	T
Lobelia coronopifolia	B,SI
Lobelia erinus	I
Lobelia erinus 'Blue Gown'	BS
Lobelia erinus 'Blue Moon'	T
Lobelia erinus 'Blue Pearl'	BD,L
Lobelia erinus 'Blue Stone'	U
Lobelia erinus 'Blue Wings'	D
Lobelia erinus 'Cambridge Blue'	B,BD,BS,C,CL,CO,D,DT, F,J,KI,L,M,R,SE,ST,T, TU,V,VH,YA
Lobelia erinus 'Cambridge Blue' c.s	S
Lobelia erinus 'Cascade Blue'	B,BS,F,J,SE,T,U,V,YA
Lobelia erinus 'Cascade Crimson'	T
Lobelia erinus 'Cascade Lilac'	B,D,SE,T,VH,YA
Lobelia erinus ' Cascade' mix	BD,BS,CO,DT,F,J,KI,KS, L,M,R,S,SE,Sm,ST,T,U, V,VH,YA
Lobelia erinus 'Cascade' mix p.s	BD,U,YA
Lobelia erinus 'Cascade Red'	B,BS,D,F,J,S,T,V,YA
Lobelia erinus 'Cascade Rose'	B
Lobelia erinus 'Cascade Ruby'	B,BS,T,U,YA
Lobelia erinus 'Cascade Sapphire'	B,BD,CL,D,F,KI,L,S,SE, ST,U
Lobelia erinus 'Cascade Sapphire' p.s	YA
Lobelia erinus 'Cascade White'	B,BS,SE,T,YA
Lobelia erinus 'Cobalt Blue'	B,BD,BS,F,KI
Lobelia erinus 'Crystal' c.s	S
Lobelia erinus 'Crystal Palace'	B,BD,BS,C,CL,CO,D,DT, F,J,KI,L,M,R,SE,ST,SU, T,TU,U,V,VH,YA
Lobelia erinus 'Crystal Palace' p.s	BD,S,YA
Lobelia erinus 'Early Dwarf Blue Mink'	B
Lobelia erinus 'Early Dwarf Snow Mink'	B
Lobelia erinus 'Emperor William'	B,BD,BS,CL,L,T
Lobelia erinus 'Fountains Blue'	B,BD,C,CL,CO,D,DT,KS, TU
Lobelia erinus 'Fountains Crimson'	B,BD,BS,C,CL,DT,F,KS, TU
Lobelia erinus 'Fountains Lilac'	B,BD,BS,C,CL,D,DT,F, KS,M,TU,V
Lobelia erinus 'Fountains' mix	BS,C,CL,D,DT,F,KI,SE, Sm,ST,SU,TU
Lobelia erinus 'Fountains Rose'	B,BD,BS,C,CL,D,DT,TU
Lobelia erinus 'Fountains' Select	CL
Lobelia erinus 'Fountains White'	B,BD,BS,C,CL,CO,D,DT, F,KS,S,TU,V
Lobelia erinus 'Half Moon'	M
Lobelia erinus 'Hamburgia'	B

LOBELIA

Lobelia erinus 'Kaleidoscope'	U
Lobelia erinus 'Lilac Time'	B
Lobelia erinus 'Mixed Shades'	D
Lobelia erinus 'Mrs.Clibran'	B,BD,BS,C,CL,J,KI,L,S, SE,V,YA
Lobelia erinus 'Mrs.Clibran Imp'	D,DT,F,T,U
Lobelia erinus 'Mrs.Clibran' p.s	YA
Lobelia erinus 'Palace Blue'	B,YA
Lobelia erinus 'Palace Blue With Eye'	B,F,YA
Lobelia erinus 'Palace Royal'	B
Lobelia erinus 'Palace White'	B,YA
Lobelia erinus 'Rapid Blue' p.s	D
Lobelia erinus 'Rapid White' p.s	D
Lobelia erinus 'Regatta Blue Splash'	BS,CL,DT,F,SE,T
Lobelia erinus 'Regatta Lilac'	BS,C,CL,YA
Lobelia erinus 'Regatta Marine Blue'	B,BS,C,CL,F,YA
Lobelia erinus 'Regatta Midnight Blue'	BS,CL
Lobelia erinus 'Regatta' mix	BS,C,CL,DT,L,YA
Lobelia erinus 'Regatta Sky Blue'	BS,C,CL,YA
Lobelia erinus ' Regatta White'	BS,CL
Lobelia erinus 'Ripples'	U
Lobelia erinus 'Riviera Blue Eyes'	BS,CL,L
Lobelia erinus 'Riviera Blue Splash'	B,BS,CL,DT,F,KI,KS,L, SE,T,U,YA
Lobelia erinus 'Riviera Lilac'	B,BS,C,CL,DT,F,KI,KS, L,SE,T,TU,V,YA
Lobelia erinus 'Riviera Lilac' c.s	D,S,SE
Lobelia erinus 'Riviera Marine Blue'	BS,CL
Lobelia erinus 'Riviera Midnight'	BS,CL,YA
Lobelia erinus 'Riviera' mix	BD,BS,CL,DT,YA
Lobelia erinus 'Riviera Sky Blue'	B,BS,C,CL,D,KS,YA
Lobelia erinus 'Riviera White'	BS,CL,L
Lobelia erinus 'Rosamond'	B,BD,BS,C,CL,DT,F,J,KI, L,R,S,SE,ST,T,TU,U,V, YA
Lobelia erinus 'Rosamond' p.s	YA
Lobelia erinus 'Sapphire'	C,DT,F,J,M,R,TU,V,VH
Lobelia erinus 'Sapphire' p.s	BD
Lobelia erinus 'Sky Blue'	CL
Lobelia erinus 'Snowball'	BD,M,R,T,YA
Lobelia erinus 'Snowball' p.s	YA
Lobelia erinus 'String of Pearls'	BD,BS,C,F,ST,J,KI,L,M, R,SE,ST,T,TU,V,VH,YA
Lobelia erinus 'String of Pearls' p.s	BD,S,YS
Lobelia erinus 'Sutton's Blue'	B
Lobelia erinus 'White Lady'	B,BS,CL,CO,D,F,J,KI,SE, ST,TU,U,V,VH
Lobelia erinus 'White Lady' c.s	S
Lobelia erinus 'White Perfection'	DT,L
Lobelia excelsa	C
Lobelia heterophylla	B
Lobelia holstii	SI
Lobelia inflata	B,C,CP,PR
Lobelia 'Light Blue Basket'	S
Lobelia linnaoides	AP,B,SC,SS
Lobelia pinifolia	B,SI
Lobelia 'Pink Flamingo'	C,F,T
Lobelia pteropoda	B,SI
Lobelia 'Queen Victoria'	AP,B,BD,BS,C,CL,DT,F ,I,KI,L,R,T
Lobelia rhombifolia	B
Lobelia rhytidosperma	B
Lobelia roughii	AP,B,SC,SS
Lobelia sessilifolia	AP,B,C,JE,P,SA,SG
Lobelia siphilitica	AP,B,BS,C,CG,CP,KI, LG,NT,P,PR,SA,SG,T,W

Lobelia siphilitica 'Blue Select'	B,JE,T
Lobelia siphilitica f albiflora	AP,B,C,G,JE,NT,SA
Lobelia sp	I,SI
Lobelia spicata	B,PR
Lobelia splendens 'Blinkfeuer'	B
Lobelia splendens 'Elmfeuer'	JE
Lobelia tenuior	B,O
Lobelia tenuior 'Blue Wings'	B,C,J,T
Lobelia tupa	AP,B,C,P,SA,T
Lobelia valida	B,C,SI
Lobelia valida 'African Skies'	B
Lobelia valida 'Blue Ribbons'	V
Lobelia valida 'South Seas'	T
Lobelia x gerardii	G,T
Lobelia x gerardii 'Vedrariensis'	AP,B,BD,BS,JE,SA,SC
Lobelia x speciosa 'Compliment Blue'	B,BS,D,JE,KI,YA
Lobelia x speciosa 'Compliment Dp Red'	B,BS,CL,JE
Lobelia x speciosa 'Compliment' mix	BS,CL,J,U
Lobelia x speciosa 'Compliment Scarlet'	B,BS,CL,JE,KI,V,YA
Lobelia x speciosa f1 'Fan Cinnabar Pink'	B,JE
Lobelia x speciosa f1 'Fan Cinnabar Rose'	B,BS,CL,CO,D,DT,KI,U
Lobelia x speciosa f1 'Fan Deep Red'	B,BS,C,CL,DT,JE,KI
Lobelia x speciosa f1 'Fan' Mix	DT,L
Lobelia x speciosa f1 'Fan Orchid Rose'	B,BS,CL,U
Lobelia x speciosa f1 'Fan Scarlet'	B,BS,CL,JE,O,S,SE,U, YA
Lobelia x s. f1 'Fan Scarlet/Cinnabar Rose'	T
Lobelia x speciosa hyb	T
Lobelia x speciosa 'Pink Flamingo'	B,V
Lobivia acanthophlegma	B,Y
Lobivia acanthophlegma v. oligotricha	B
Lobivia acanthophlegma v. patula	Y
Lobivia atrovirens	B
Lobivia atrovirens v ritteri	B
Lobivia aurantiaca	Y
Lobivia aurea	B,BC
Lobivia aurea v leucomalla	B
Lobivia aurea v schaferi	B
Lobivia binghamiana	Y
Lobivia caineana	B
Lobivia cardenasiana	B,Y
Lobivia chrysantha	B,Y
Lobivia cintiensis	B,Y
Lobivia culpinensis	Y
Lobivia draxleriana	Y
Lobivia drijveriana	Y
Lobivia einsteinii v aureiflora	Y
Lobivia emmae	Y
Lobivia famatimensis	Y
Lobivia famatimensis v leucomalla	Y
Lobivia guinesensis	Y
Lobivia haageana v chrysantha	Y
Lobivia haagei	B
Lobivia haematantha v amblayensis	B
Lobivia haematantha v densispina	B
Lobivia haematantha v elongata	B
Lobivia haematantha v kuehnrichii	B
Lobivia haematantha v rebutioides	B
Lobivia hertrichiana	B
Lobivia hertrichiana v laui	B
Lobivia horrida	B,Y
Lobivia jajoiana	B,Y
Lobivia jajoiana v fleischerana	B,Y
Lobivia jajoiana v nigrostoma	B
Lobivia jajoiana v paucicostata	B
Lobivia lateritia	B,Y

LOBIVIA

Lobivia leucorhodon	Y
Lobivia longispina	Y
Lobivia marsoneri	B
Lobivia marsoneri iridescens	BC
Lobivia maximilliana	Y
Lobivia maximilliana v caespitosa	B
Lobivia maximilliana v charazanensis	B
Lobivia maximilliana v corbula	B
Lobivia maximilliana v intermedia	B
Lobivia maximilliana v westii	B
Lobivia napina	Y
Lobivia obrepanda	Y
Lobivia oligotricha	Y
Lobivia omasuyana	Y
Lobivia oyonica	Y
Lobivia pachycantha	Y
Lobivia peeslianum	Y
Lobivia pugionacantha v rossii	B
Lobivia pusilla	Y
Lobivia pygmaea	B
Lobivia rossii	Y
Lobivia rossii v salmonea	Y
Lobivia saltensis	B
Lobivia saltensis v pseudocachensis	B
Lobivia sanguiniflora	B
Lobivia schieliana v quiabayensis	B
Lobivia schreiteri	B
Lobivia sp mix	C,Y
Lobivia steinmannii	B
Lobivia steinmannii v costata	B
Lobivia sublimiflora v krausii	Y
Lobivia tegeleriana	B
Lobivia tenuispina	B,Y
Lobivia thionantha	B
Lobivia thionantha v aurantiaca	B
Lobivia thionantha v glauca	B
Lobivia tiegelana	Y
Lobivia tiegelana v cinnabarina	B
Lobivia tiegelana v pusilla	B
Lobivia tiegelana v ruberrima	Y
Lobivia winteriana	Y
Lobivia wrightiana	B
Lobivia zecheri	B
Lobivopsis 'Paramount Hybrids'	Y
Lobostemon fruticosus	B
Lobostemon glaucophyllus	B,SI
Lobularia 'Aphrodite mix'	BS,F,SE
Lobularia 'Apricot Shades'	SE,T
Lobularia 'Delight Purple' s-c	CL
Lobularia 'Easter Basket'	DT
Lobularia 'Easter Bonnet' mix	BD,BS,D,J,L,M,SE,T,TU, V,YA
Lobularia 'Easter Bonnet' s-c	B,BS,YA
Lobularia 'Golf'	CL,F
Lobularia 'Little Dorrit'	F,J,M
Lobularia maritima	B,SG
Lobularia maritima 'Carpet Of Snow'	B,BS,C,D,DT,F,J,KI,L,R, S,SE,ST,T,U,V,VH
Lobularia maritima 'Creamery'	B,BD,BS,CL,F,KS
Lobularia maritima 'Easter Bonnet'	B,BS,D,YA
Lobularia maritima 'Minimum'	B,BS,D,L,YA
Lobularia maritima 'Navy Blue'	B
Lobularia maritima 'New Apricot'	B,BD,BS,L
Lobularia maritima 'New Red'	B,BD,BS,F
Lobularia maritima 'Rosario'	B,BS,L
Lobularia maritima 'Rosie O'Day'	B,BD,BS,C,CL,DT,J,KI,

	L,R,S,T,TU,V,YA
Lobularia maritima 'Royal Carpet'	B,BS,C,D,DT,F,J,KI,O,S, ST,V
Lobularia maritima 'Snow Crystals'	B,BD,BS,CL,D,DT,F,L,O, S,SE,T,U,YA
Lobularia maritima ssp benthamii	B
Lobularia maritima 'Violet Queen'	B,BS,CL
Lobularia maritima 'Wonderland Purple'	B,BS,YA
Lobularia maritima 'Wonderland White'	B,BS
Lobularia 'Morning Mist'	S
Lobularia 'New Lemon'	BD
Lobularia 'New Purple'	B,BD,BS,L
Lobularia 'New Salmon'	BD
Lobularia 'Oriental Night'	C,D,J,S,T
Lobularia 'Pastel Carpet'	BD,BS,C,CL,KI,KS,Sm,T
Lobularia 'Rosebud'	BS
Lobularia 'Snowcloth'	B,BS,F,KS,M,YA
Lobularia 'Snowdrift'	B,BD,BS,CL,KS,S
Lobularia 'Sweet White'	T
Lobularia 'Tiny Tim'	B
Lobularia 'Trailing Rosy Red'	BS,DT,F,T
Lobularia 'Wonderland' mix	BS,T
Lobularia 'Wonderland Red'	BS,S,T
Lodoicea maldivica	B
Logania obovata	B
Logania stenophylla	B
Loiseleuria procumbens	AP,B,C,FH,JE
Lolium multiflorum	B
Lolium multiflorum 'Barcoo'	B
Lolium multiflorum 'Paroa'	B
Lolium perenne	B
Lolium perenne 'Gator'	B
Lolium perenne 'Hermes'	B
Lolium perenne 'Kangaroo Valley'	B
Lolium perenne 'Loretta'	B
Lolium perenne 'Lorina'	B
Lolium perenne 'Matilda'	B
Lolium perenne 'Victorian'	B
Lomandra hastilis	B
Lomandra longifolia	AU,B,HA,SA
Lomandra obliqua	B
Lomatia frazeri	B,HA,O,SA
Lomatia ilicifolia	HA
Lomatia myricoides	AU,B,HA,O,SA
Lomatia polyforma	AU
Lomatia silaifolia	B,O
Lomatia tinctoria	B
Lomatium californicum	B
Lomatium dissectum	B
Lomatium macrocarpum	B
Lomatium nudicaule	B
Lomatium triternatum	B
Lomatium utriculatum	B
Lonas annua	B
Lonas annua 'Gold Rush'	B,BS,CL,CO,KI,L
Lonas annua 'Golden Yellow'	J,V
Lonas inodora	BS,C,D,KI,KS,SU,T
Lonchocarpus capassus	B,SI
Lonchocarpus eriocalyx	SI
Lonchocarpus sericeus	B
Lonchostoma monogynum	B,SI
Lonicera albiflora	B,SW
Lonicera alpigena	B,G,SG
Lonicera altmannii	B
Lonicera canadensis	SG
Lonicera chrysantha latifolia	SG

LONICERA

Lonicera chrysantha v longipes	SG
Lonicera ciliosa	C
Lonicera demissa	B
Lonicera dioica	B,SG
Lonicera edulis	SG
Lonicera etrusca	B,SA,SG
Lonicera fragrantissima	B
Lonicera gibbiflora	SG
Lonicera glabra	B
Lonicera henryi	SG
Lonicera hispida	SG
Lonicera involucrata	SG
Lonicera japonica	B,SA
Lonicera korolkowii	SG
Lonicera maackii	B,CG,SA,SG,X
Lonicera maackii f podocarpa	B
Lonicera maximowiczii	SG
Lonicera maximowiczii v sachalinensis	SG
Lonicera morrowii	SG
Lonicera nigra	G,SG
Lonicera pallasii	SG
Lonicera periclymenum	B,CO,RS
Lonicera periclymenum 'Serotina'	B
Lonicera pileata	SG
Lonicera praeflorens	B
Lonicera pseudochrysantha	SG
Lonicera ruprechtiana	SG
Lonicera sempervirens	B
Lonicera strusca	CG
Lonicera tatarica	B,C,SA,SG
Lonicera trichosantha	SG
Lonicera vesicaria	SG
Lonicera xylosteum	AP,B,CG,SA,SC,SG
Lopezia racemosa	V
Lopezia racemosa 'Pink Brush'	B,C
Lopezia racemosa 'Pretty Rose'	B
Lophocereus schottii	B,CH,Y
Lophomyrtus obcordatus	B
Lophomyrtus x ralphii	B
Lophophora diffusa	B
Lophophora echinata v diffusa	CH,GC,Y
Lophophora frichii	CH,Y
Lophophora williamsii	B,CH,T,Y
Lophophora williamsii v decipiens	Y
Lophospermum erubescens	AP,B,C,D,DT,G,HH,J,JE, P,S,SC,SG,V
Lophostemon confertus	B,C,HA,O,SA
Loranthus europaeus	B
Loropetalum chinense	B,SA
Lotononis bainesii	B
Lotononis corymbosa	B,SI
Lotus berthelotii	B
Lotus corniculatus	AP,B,C,CO,G,JE,LA,SA, SC,SU
Lotus corniculatus 'Kalo'	B
Lotus creticus	B
Lotus cruentus	B
Lotus discolor	SI
Lotus frondosus	SG
Lotus halophilus	B
Lotus herbaceus	B
Lotus hirsutum	B,C,FH,HH,I,JE,SA
Lotus maritimus	AP,B
Lotus maritimus ssp siliquosus	B
Lotus scoparius	B
Lotus sessilifolius	B

Lotus tetragonolobus	B,G
Lotus uliginosus	B,C
Lotus wrightii	B
Loxanthocereus eulalianus	B
Loxostylis alata	B,SI
Luchea candica	B
Luculia grandifolia	B
Luculia gratissima v rosea	B,SA
Luculia tsetensis	B,SA
Ludwigia alternifolia	B,PR
Ludwigia hexapetala	B
Ludwigia octovalvis	B
Luffa acutangula	B
Luffa aegyptica	CP,KS
Luffa cylindrica	B,C,CG,HA,SA,SG
Luffa operculata	B
Lunaria annua	AP,BD,C,DT,E,F,FH,G,JE, L,KI,KS,S,SA,ST,SU,T,V
Lunaria annua 'Alba'	B,C,E,HH,SA,T,V
Lunaria annua 'Atrococcinea'	B
Lunaria annua mix	CO,D,J,KS,T,TU
Lunaria annua 'Munstead Purple'	B
Lunaria annua 'Sissinghurst White'	B,KS
Lunaria annua 'Variegata Purple'	AP,B,C,T
Lunaria annua 'Variegata White'	AP,B,C
Lunaria annua 'Violet'	B
Lunaria rediviva	AP,B,C,HH,G,JE,LG,RS, SA,SG
Lupinus albicaulis	B
Lupinus albicaulis 'Hederma'	B
Lupinus albifrons	AP,B
Lupinus albifrons v collinus	FH
Lupinus albus	B,C
Lupinus angustifolius	B,RS
Lupinus angustifolius 'Blue'	B
Lupinus angustifolius 'Chittick'	B
Lupinus angustifolius 'Illyarrie'	B
Lupinus angustifolius 'Yandee'	B
Lupinus arboreus	AP,B,BS,CG,JE,KI,P,SA, SC,T
Lupinus arboreus hyb mix	C,D
Lupinus arboreus true wild form	A,C,E,JE,SA,SG
Lupinus arcticus	AP,SC,SG
Lupinus argenteus	AP,SA
Lupinus benthami	B
Lupinus bicolor	AP,B
Lupinus 'Carnival Mix'	JE
Lupinus caudatus	B
Lupinus 'Chepilillo'	B
Lupinus densiflorus v aureus	B,RS
Lupinus elegans	CG
Lupinus excubitus v austromontanus	B
Lupinus 'Gallery Blue'	B,BS,JE,L,SA
Lupinus 'Gallery' mix	BD,BS,C,CL,J,JE,L,T,U, YA
Lupinus 'Gallery Pink'	B,BS,JE,L,SA
Lupinus 'Gallery Red'	B,BS,JE,L,SA
Lupinus 'Gallery White'	B,BS,JE,L,SA
Lupinus 'Gallery Yellow'	B,BS,JE,L,SA
Lupinus hartwegii	V
Lupinus hartwegii 'Biancaneve'	F,T
Lupinus hartwegii ssp cruickshankii	F,RS
Lupinus hart. ssp cruickshankii 'Sunrise'	T
Lupinus hirsutissimus	B,CG
Lupinus latifolius	B,C
Lupinus lepidus	JE

Lupinus lepidus 'Panache Bleu'	B
Lupinus lepidus v lepidus	B
Lupinus littoralis	AP,B,JE,SA,SC,SG
Lupinus longifolius	B
Lupinus 'Lulu' mix	BS,S,T
Lupinus luteus	B,BS,C,LG,RS,T
Lupinus micranthus	SG
Lupinus microcarpus	P
Lupinus mutabilis	SG
Lupinus nanus	AP,B,CG,SC,V
Lupinus nanus 'Pixie Delight' mix	B,C,D,F,KS,S,T,V
Lupinus nootkatensis	AP,SC,SG
Lupinus palaestinus	B
Lupinus perennis	A,B,HW,JE,PR,SA
Lupinus pilosus	B
Lupinus polyphyllus	AV,B,CG,LA,SG
Lupinus polyphyllus 'Band of Nobles'	C,CL,DT
Lupinus polyphyllus 'Band of Nobles' s-c	T
Lupinus polyphyllus 'Flamme Rouge'	B,BS,JE,ST
Lupinus polyphyllus 'Garden Gnome'	BS,C,CO,JE,ST,SU,TU
Lupinus polyphyllus 'Minarette'	BS,J,JE,L,SA,V
Lupinus 'Rising Sun'	SE
Lupinus 'Russell Chandelier'	B,BS,C,CL,JE,KI,SA,SU
Lupinus 'Russell Hyb' dw	B,D,SA
Lupinus 'Russell Hyb' mix	BD,CO,DT,F,I,J,JE,KI,L, R,S,SA,ST,SU,TU,U,V, VH,YA
Lupinus 'Russell My Castle'	B,BS,C,CL,JE,KI,SA,SU
Lupinus 'Russell Noble Maiden'	B,BS,CL,KI,KS,SA
Lupinus 'Russell Reselected'	D
Lupinus 'Russell The Chatelaine'	B,BS,C,CL,JE,KI,SA
Lupinus 'Russell The Governor'	B,BS,C,CL,JE,KI,SA
Lupinus 'Russell The Pages'	B,BS,C,CL,JE,KI,SA
Lupinus sericeus	B,C,JE,RS,SA
Lupinus subcarnosus	C
Lupinus succulentus	B,RS,SA
Lupinus texensis	B,F,HW,KS,RS,T
Lupinus varius	B,F
Lupinus versicolor	AP,B,P,SC
Lupinus versicolor hyb	P
Luzula albida	SA
Luzula alpinopilosa	JE,SG
Luzula crinita	SS
Luzula glabrata	B
Luzula luzuliodes	G,JE,SG
Luzula nivea	AP,B,C,CL,G,JE,PA,SA, SC
Luzula pallescens	SG
Luzula parviflora	SG
Luzula rufa	B,SS
Luzula sylvatica	B,G,SA
Luzula sylvatica 'Select'	JE
Luzula ulophylla	AP,B,G,JE,SC,SS
Luzuriaga parviflora	SS
Luzuriaga radicans	SA
Lychnis alpina	AP,B,BS,C,CG,CL,FH,G, JE,SA,SC,SG
Lychnis alpina alba	AP,SC,SG
Lychnis alpina 'Drake's Form'	B
Lychnis alpina 'Rosea'	AP,B,SC
Lychnis alpina v oelandica	CG
Lychnis 'Blue Angel'	BD,BS,J,KS
Lychnis 'Brilliant' mix	S
Lychnis chalcedonica	AP,B,BD,BS,C,CL,DT,F, G,JE,KI,KS,L,PM,RH,S, SA,SC,SG,SU,T,V

Lychnis chalcedonica 'Alba'	AP,B,BD,C,G,SC,SG
Lychnis chalcedonica 'Morgenrot'	JE
Lychnis chalcedonica 'Raureif'	JE
Lychnis chalcedonica 'Rosea'	AP,B,C,G,RH,SC,SG
Lychnis chalcedonica 'Summer Sparkle'	U,V
Lychnis 'Cherry Blossom'	KS
Lychnis coronaria	AP,B,BS,C,CP,FH,HH,I, JE,KS,PA,RH,SC,SG,SU
Lychnis coronaria 'Alba'	AP,B,C,G,I,JE,MA,PA, RH,RS,SC,SG,T
Lychnis coronaria 'Angel Blush'	B
Lychnis coronaria 'Atrosanguinea'	AP,B,KS,SC,T
Lychnis coronaria 'Atrosanguinea' cerise	T
Lychnis coronaria 'Flottbek'	JE
Lychnis coronaria v oculata	AP,C,KS
Lychnis 'Dancing Ladies' mix	C,T,V
Lychnis 'Dancing Ladies Series'	T
Lychnis flos-cuculi	AP,B,C,CO,FH,G,JE,LA, SA,SC,SG,SU,V,Z
Lychnis flos-cuculi 'Alba'	B,C,I
Lychnis flos-cuculi 'Little Robin'	AP,FH
Lychnis flos-cuculi 'Nana'	AP,HH,JE,SC
Lychnis flos-jovis	AP,B,C,JE,SA,SC,SG,Z
Lychnis flos-jovis 'Alba'	I
Lychnis flos-jovis nana 'Peggy'	JE
Lychnis fulgens	SG
Lychnis 'Heavenly Mixed'	J
Lychnis miqueliana	AP,C,RS,SC,SG
Lychnis oculata	C,F,KS
Lychnis oculata candida	KS
Lychnis 'Rose Angel'	BD,BS,J,KS
Lychnis 'Rose Pearl'	BS
Lychnis 'Royal Celebration'	D
Lychnis sieboldii	AP,CC,SC
Lychnis sp mix	PA
Lychnis sp 'Terry's Pink'	JE
Lychnis viscaria	AP,B,C,FH,G,JE,RH,SA, SC,SG
Lychnis viscaria 'Alba'	AP,B,G,SG
Lychnis viscaria 'Firebird'	B,JE,SA
Lychnis viscaria 'Snowbird'	JE,SA
Lychnis viscaria 'Splendens Plena'	B,SG
Lychnis viscaria ssp atropurpurea	B,SG
Lychnis wilfordii	P
Lychnis x arkwrightii	AP,C,G,SC
Lychnis x arkwrightii 'Orange Zwerg'	C,JE
Lychnis x arkwrightii 'Vesuvius'	B,BD,C,G,JE,SA,T
Lychnis x haageana	AP,C,G,I,JE,L,RS,SC,T
Lychnis x haageana 'Molten Lava'	B,BD,BS,CL,D,DT,F,S,SE
Lychnis x haageana 'New Hybrids'	B,SA
Lychnis x walkeri 'Abbotswood Rose'	T
Lychnis yunnanensis	AP,B,C,CC,FH,G,JE,SA, SC,SG
Lycium barbarum	A,B,SA
Lycium chinense	B,SA
Lycium ferocissimum	B
Lycium pallidum	B
Lycopus europaeus	B,LA,SA,SG
Lycopus exaltatus	B
Lycoris sanguinea	B
Lycoris squamigera	B
Lygodium japonicum	SG
Lygodium scandens	CG
Lymania alviimii	B
Lymania smithii	B
Lyonia sp CNW1116	X

LYONIA

Lyonia sp CNW621	X
Lyonothamnus floribundus v asplenifolius	B,SA
Lyperanthus antarcticus	SS
Lyperanthus nigricans	B,SA
Lyperanthus serratus	B
Lysichiton americanus	AP,C
Lysiloma bahamensis	B
Lysiloma microphylla	B,SA
Lysimachia atropurpurea	B,JE
Lysimachia atropurpurea 'Geronimo'	C
Lysimachia barystachys	B,JE
Lysimachia ciliata	B,JE,SG
Lysimachia clethroides	B,C,G,JE,SG
Lysimachia clethroides 'Lady Jane'	C,T
Lysimachia clethroides MW159R	X
Lysimachia clethroides MW82R	X
Lysimachia ephemerum	AP,B,CG,G,JE,SC,T
Lysimachia hybrida	PR
Lysimachia japonica minutissima	I
Lysimachia lichiangensis	B,C,G,P,SG
Lysimachia minoricensis	B,HH,JE,P,T
Lysimachia nemorum	B
Lysimachia punctata	B,BS,C,CL,JE,KI,SA,SG, SU,T,V
Lysimachia pyramidalis	SG
Lysimachia quadriflora	B,PR
Lysimachia terrestris	B
Lysimachia vulgaris	B,C,CP,G,JE,RH,SA,SG
Lysinema ciliatum	B
Lysiphyllum carronii	B,O
Lysiphyllum cunninghamii	B,O
Lysiphyllum gilvum	B
Lysiphyllum hookeri	B,O
Lythrum salicaria	B,BS,C,CO,F,G,JE,KI,LA, SG,V,Z
Lythrum salicaria Red hyb	C,JE
Lythrum salicaria 'Rosy Gem'	B,BS,C,CL,SA
Lythrum salicaria x 'Robert'	D
Lythrum virgatus	B
Lythrum x hybrida	T
Lytocarium weddellianum	O
Lytocarium weddellianum g	B
Maackia amurensis	A,B,C,N,SA,SG
Maackia amurensis v buergeri	B
Maackia chinensis	B,N
Maba chrysocarpa	B
Macadamia integrifolia	B,O,RE
Macadamia integrifolia 'Beaumont'	B
Macadamia integ. 'Mullimbimby Marvel'	B
Macadamia ternifolia	B,SA
Macadamia tetraphylla	B,O
Macfadyena unguis-cati	B,C,SA
Machaeranthera bigelovii	B
Machaeranthera tanacetifolia	B,T
Machaerina sinclairii	CG
Machaerocereus gummosus	B
Machairophyllum albidum	B
Mackaya bella	B,CG,SI
Mackaya gangetica	B
Macleania popenoei	B
Macleaya cordata	B,C,G,JE,SA,SG
Macleaya frutescens	CG
Macleaya microcarpa	T,W
Maclura pomifera	A,B,C,SA
Macropidia fuliginosa	B,O
Macropiper excelsum	B,SS

Macroptilium atropurpureum	B
Macrotyloma axillare	B
Macrotyloma uniflorum	B
Macrozamia communis	B,C,HA,O,SA,SH
Macrozamia conferta	O
Macrozamia cranei	O
Macrozamia crassifolia	O
Macrozamia diplomera	B,O
Macrozamia douglasii	O
Macrozamia dyeri	O
Macrozamia fawcettii	B,O
Macrozamia fearnsdei	O
Macrozamia flexuosa	O
Macrozamia fraseri	O
Macrozamia heteromera	B,O
Macrozamia heteromera blue	O
Macrozamia hyb	B
Macrozamia johnsonii	O
Macrozamia lomandroides	O
Macrozamia lucida	B,O
Macrozamia macdonnellii	B,O
Macrozamia machinii	O
Macrozamia miquellii	B,C,HA,O,SH
Macrozamia moorei	B,HA,O,SA
Macrozamia mountperriensis	B,O
Macrozamia 'Northern Pilliga'	O
Macrozamia occidua	O
Macrozamia parcifolia	O
Macrozamia pauli-guilielmi	HA,O
Macrozamia pauli-guilielmi ssp p.-g	B
Macrozamia platyrachis	O
Macrozamia plurinervia	O
Macrozamia riedlei	B,C,O,SA
Macrozamia secunda	B,O
Macrozamia 'Southern Pilliga'	O
Macrozamia spiralis	B,C,HA,O,SA
Macrozamia stenomera	B,O
Macrozamia viridis	O
Madhuca longifolia	B
Madia elegans	B,DT
Madia sativa	B
Maerua juncea	B
Maerua oblongifolia	B
Maerua schinzii	B,SI
Maesa lanceolata	B,SI
Maesopsis eminii	B
Magnolia acuminata	B,SA
Magnolia biondii	SA
Magnolia campbellii	X
Magnolia 'Charles Raffil'	X
Magnolia cylindrica	N
Magnolia denudata	B,N,SA,X
Magnolia 'Frank Gladney'	X
Magnolia grandiflora	B,C,CG,N,SA
Magnolia hypoleuca 1995	X
Magnolia kobus	A,B,C,G,SA
Magnolia liliiflora	B,SA
Magnolia macrophylla	B,SA
Magnolia 'Manchu Fan'	X
Magnolia officinalis	B,SA
Magnolia 'Pickards Opal'	X
Magnolia sargentiana var robusta	X
Magnolia sieboldii	B,C,N,SA,SC,SG,X
Magnolia sinensis	AP,C,N,SC
Magnolia 'Spectrum'	X
Magnolia stellata	B,N,SA

MAGNOLIA

Magnolia tripetala	B,C,CG	Malope trifida 'Pink Queen'	B,F,KS,T
Magnolia virginiana	A,B,C,CG,SA	Malope trifida 'Red Queen'	B
Magnolia 'Wada's Picture Giant'	X	Malope trifida 'Tetra Vulcan'	B,C,DT,G,T
Magnolia wilsonii	AP,B,C,N,SC,SG,T	Malope trifida 'White Queen'	B,C,KS,T
Magnolia wilsonii 1995	X	Malosma laurina	B
Magnolia x highdownensis	C	Malpighia coccigera	B
Magnolia x soulangeana 'Rustic Rubra'	N	Malpighia emarginata	B
Magnolia x soulangiana	B,C,CG,N,SA,X	Malpighia glabra	B
Magnolia x soulangiana 'Alba Superba'	X	Malus angustifolia	B
Magnolia x soulangiana 'Alexandrina'	X	Malus baccata	B,C,SA,SG
Magnolia x soulangiana 'Brozzoni'	X	Malus baccata v mandshurica	B
Magnolia x soulangiana 'Lennei'	B,N,SA	Malus 'Bittenfelder'	B
Magnolia x soulangiana 'Lennei Alba'	X	Malus communis	SA
Magnolia x s. 'Robusta' (Nymans form)	X	Malus coronaria	B
Mahonia aquifolium	A,B,C,CG,SA,SG	Malus domestica 'Antonovka'	SA
Mahonia fremontii	SA	Malus domestica 'Bittenfelder'	SA
Mahonia haematocarpa	B	Malus domestica 'Delicious'	SA
Mahonia japonica	B,SA	Malus domestica ssp cerasifera	SG
Mahonia japonica 'Bealei'	B,SA	Malus domestica ssp prunifolia	SG
Mahonia lomariifolia	B,C,SA	Malus floribunda	B,C,N,SA
Mahonia nervosa	A,B,C,G,SA,SG	Malus honanensis	B,SA
Mahonia nevinii	B	Malus hupehensis	B,SA,SG
Mahonia 'Pinnacle' pinnata of gdns	SA	Malus hupehensis 'Rosea'	B
Mahonia pumila	SA	Malus kansuensis	SG
Mahonia repens	A,B,C,CG,G,SA	Malus mandschurica	SG
Maianthemum bifolium	B,C,JE,SG	Malus micromalus	B
Maianthemum canadense	CC	Malus mix	C
Maianthemum kamtschaticum	SG	Malus prunifolia	B,SA,SG
Maihuenia poeppigii	B,P,Y	Malus pumila 'Antonovka'	B
Maihueniopsis glomerata	B	Malus pumila northern prov.(u.s.a.)	B
Maireana aphylla	B	Malus sargentii	B,SA,SG
Maireana appressa	B	Malus sieboldii	B,SA
Maireana astrotricha	B	Malus sieboldii v arborescens	B
Maireana atkinsiana	B	Malus 'Small Fruited Hybrids'	T
Maireana brevifolia	B,HA,SA	Malus sp	SG
Maireana carnosa	B	Malus sylvestris	B,SA
Maireana convexa	B	Malus toringoides	B,N,SG
Maireana eriantha	B	Malus x zumi	B
Maireana erioclada	B	Malus yunnanensis	SG
Maireana georgei	B,HA	Malus zumi x v calocarpa	B
Maireana melanocoma	B	Malva alcea	AP,G,JE
Maireana pentatropis	B	Malva alcea v fastigiata	AP,B,C,HH,JE,SA
Maireana platycarpa	B	Malva crispa	SG
Maireana polypterygia	B	Malva 'Gibbortello'	B,P
Maireana pyramidata	B,HA	Malva moschata	AP,B,C,G,JE,LA,SC,SG,
Maireana schistocarpa	B		V,Z
Maireana tomentosa	B	Malva moschata 'Alba'	AP,B,C,G,I,JE,KS,LG,P,
Maireana triptera	B		RS,SA,SC,U
Maireana turbinata	B	Malva moschata 'Pirouette'	HL,T,V
Maitenus boaria	SA	Malva moschata 'Rosea'	B,KS,SA,T
Maitenus disticha	SA	Malva neglecta	B,C,SA,SG
Malacothamnus densiflorus	B	Malva officinalis	SG
Malaxis spicata	B	Malva parviflora	B
Malcolmia maritima	B,BS,C,D,DT,F,J,KI,KS,	Malva pusilla	SG
	SU,T,U	Malva robusta	SG
Maleophora crocea	SI,Y	Malva sylvestris	B,C,CG,CO,G,JE,LA,SA,
Maleophora crocea v purpureocrocea	B,Y		SG
Maleophora lutea	SI	Malva sylvestris 'Brave Heart'	B,C,P,T
Malleostemon hursthousei	B,SA	Malva sylvestris v mauritiana	AP,HH,F,G,JE,KS,V
Malleostemon roseus	B	Malva sylvestris v mauritiana 'Bibor Felho'	T
Mallotus japonicus	CG	Malva sylvestris v mauritiana 'Moravia'	B
Mallotus philippensis	B	Malva sylvestris 'Zebrina'	AP,B,C,DT,F,G,KS,SE,T,V
Mallotus rhamnifolius	B	Malva verticillata v crispa	B,C
Malope trifida 'Crown' mix	BS	Malva 'Windsor Castle'	SE
Malope trifida grandiflora 'Choice' mix	C,CO,F,T	Malvastrum coromandelianum	B
Malope trifida mix	G,J,KS,V	Malvaviscus 'Fire Darts'	B

MAMMEA

Mammea africana	B
Mammea americana	B
Mammilaria albata sanciro	BC
Mammilaria albiarmata	B
Mammilaria albicans	B,Y
Mammilaria albicoma	B
Mammilaria albilanata	B,Y
Mammilaria angelensis	B
Mammilaria arida	CH,Y
Mammilaria armillata	B,Y
Mammilaria aureilanata	B
Mammilaria aureilanata v. alba	B
Mammilaria aurihamata	B,Y
Mammilaria backebergiana	B,Y
Mammilaria backebergiana v. ernestii	B
Mammilaria barbata	B,GC
Mammilaria baumii	B,Y
Mammilaria baxteriana	B,Y
Mammilaria bella	B
Mammilaria bicornuta	Y
Mammilaria blossfeldiana	B,BC,Y
Mammilaria bocasana	B,CH,Y
Mammilaria bocasana v Ed Hummel	Y
Mammilaria bocasana v multilanata	Y
Mammilaria bocasana v roseiflora	CH,Y
Mammilaria bocasana v splendens	Y
Mammilaria bocensis	B,Y
Mammilaria bombycina	B,BC,CH,Y
Mammilaria boolii	B,CH,Y
Mammilaria brandegeei	B,Y
Mammilaria brandegei	B
Mammilaria brauneana	B,Y
Mammilaria bravoae	B
Mammilaria bullardiana	B
Mammilaria caerulea	BC
Mammilaria calacantha	B
Mammilaria camptotricha	CH
Mammilaria canalensis	B,CH,Y
Mammilaria candida	B
Mammilaria candida v caespitosa	B
Mammilaria capensis (m.armillata)	B,Y
Mammilaria capensis pallida	BC
Mammilaria carmenae	B,GC,Y
Mammilaria carnea	B,Y
Mammilaria carretii	B,BC,Y
Mammilaria celsiana	B,CH,Y
Mammilaria centraliplumosa	B
Mammilaria cerralboa	B
Mammilaria chionocephala	B,Y
Mammilaria coahuilensis	B
Mammilaria colina	B,Y
Mammilaria collinsii	B
Mammilaria columbiana	B,CH,Y
Mammilaria compressa	B,Y
Mammilaria craigii	B
Mammilaria crassior	BC
Mammilaria crinita	B
Mammilaria crinita cowperae	Y
Mammilaria crucigera aff	B
Mammilaria dawsonii	CH
Mammilaria decipiens	B
Mammilaria deherdtiana v dodsonii	B
Mammilaria densispina	B,Y
Mammilaria denudata (m.lasiacantha)	B,Y
Mammilaria dioica	B,Y
Mammilaria discolor	B

Mammilaria discolor f. esperanzaensis	B
Mammilaria dixanthocentron	B,BC,Y
Mammilaria dixanthocentron f flavicentra	B
Mammilaria dixanthrocentron	B
Mammilaria dumetorum	B
Mammilaria duoformis	B,Y
Mammilaria durispina	B
Mammilaria duwei	B,Y
Mammilaria egregia	B
Mammilaria elegans	B,Y
Mammilaria elongata	B,Y
Mammilaria elongata v. echinata /-aria	B
Mammilaria erectacantha	B
Mammilaria erythrosperma	B
Mammilaria eschanzieri	Y
Mammilaria esseriana	Y
Mammilaria estebanensis	B
Mammilaria euthele	Y
Mammilaria evermanniana	B,Y
Mammilaria fera-rubra	Y
Mammilaria fittkaui	B,CH,GC,Y
Mammilaria flavicentra	B
Mammilaria formosa	B,Y
Mammilaria fraileana	B,Y
Mammilaria freudenbergeri	BC
Mammilaria fuscata	B,Y
Mammilaria fuscohamata	Y
Mammilaria garessii	B
Mammilaria gasseriana	B
Mammilaria gasterantha	B,BC,Y
Mammilaria gaumeri	B
Mammilaria geminispina	CH,Y
Mammilaria gigantea	B,Y
Mammilaria gilensis	B,GC,Y
Mammilaria ginsa maru	CH,Y
Mammilaria glareosa	B
Mammilaria glassii	B,CH,Y
Mammilaria glassii siberiensis	BC
Mammilaria glassii v. ascensionis	B
Mammilaria glassii v. nominis dulcis	Y
Mammilaria goodridgii	B,BC
Mammilaria graessneriana	B
Mammilaria grahamii	B,Y
Mammilaria grahamii f. oliviae	B
Mammilaria guelzowiana	B,CH,Y
Mammilaria guerreronis	B
Mammilaria gummifera	B,CH,Y
Mammilaria haageana	B,Y
Mammilaria haageana f conspicua	B
Mammilaria haageana v. schmollii	B
Mammilaria hahniana	B,CH,Y
Mammilaria hahniana v albiflora	B
Mammilaria hahniana v 'Superba'	Y
Mammilaria hahniana v woodsii	B
Mammilaria halbingeri	BC
Mammilaria halei	B
Mammilaria heeriana	CH
Mammilaria heidiae	B,Y
Mammilaria hernandezii	Y
Mammilaria herrerae	B
Mammilaria herrerae v. albiflora	B
Mammilaria heyderi	B,CH,Y
Mammilaria heyderi v applanata	B,Y
Mammilaria heyderi v bullingtoniana	B,BC
Mammilaria heyderi v hemispherica	B,Y
Mammilaria hirsuta REP1236	Y

MAMMILARIA

Mammilaria huitzilopochtli	B
Mammilaria huitzilopochtli v niduliformis	BC
Mammilaria humboldtii	Y
Mammilaria hutchisoniana	B,GC,Y
Mammilaria insularis	B,Y
Mammilaria jaliscana	B
Mammilaria johnstonii	B,Y
Mammilaria johnstonii v. guaymensis	B,Y
Mammilaria johnstonii v. sancarlensis	B,BC
Mammilaria karwinskiana	B,Y
Mammilaria kelleriana	Y
Mammilaria kewensis	B,Y
Mammilaria kladiwae	BC,CH,Y
Mammilaria klissingiana	B
Mammilaria knebeliana	B
Mammilaria kunthii	Y
Mammilaria lasiacantha	B,Y
Mammilaria lenta	B,Y
Mammilaria leucantha	B
Mammilaria lewisiana	B,BC,
Mammilaria lindsayii	B
Mammilaria lloydii	B,Y
Mammilaria longicoma	Y
Mammilaria longiflora	B,Y
Mammilaria longiflora Krainzia	Y
Mammilaria longiflora v. stampferi	B,Y
Mammilaria longimamma	B,Y
Mammilaria louisae	B,Y
Mammilaria macrocarpa	B
Mammilaria magallanii	B
Mammilaria magallanii v. hamatispina	B
Mammilaria magallanii v. ham. 'Chica'	B
Mammilaria magnifica	B,Y
Mammilaria magnifica v. minor	B
Mammilaria magnimamma	B,Y
Mammilaria magnimamma v bockii	B
Mammilaria magnimamma v macrantha	Y
Mammilaria mainiae	B,BC
Mammilaria mammilaris	B,CH
Mammilaria maritima	B
Mammilaria marksiana	B,Y
Mammilaria martinezii	GC,Y
Mammilaria mathildae	B
Mammilaria matudae	B,GC,Y
Mammilaria matudae v. serpentiformis	B
Mammilaria matudae v. spinosior	B
Mammilaria mazatlanensis	B,Y
Mammilaria mazatlanensis v. monocentra	Y
Mammilaria mazatlanensis v. patonii	B
Mammilaria meiacantha	B
Mammilaria meigiana	B
Mammilaria melanocentra	B,Y
Mammilaria mercadensis	B
Mammilaria meridiorosei	B
Mammilaria meyranii	B,CH
Mammilaria meyranii v. michoacana	B,Y
Mammilaria microcarpa	B,Y
Mammilaria microcarpa v. arizonica	Y
Mammilaria microcarpa v. auricarpa	B,Y
Mammilaria microhelia	B,Y
Mammilaria microhelia v microheliopsis	Y
Mammilaria microthele	B
Mammilaria mitlensis	B
Mammilaria moellerana	B,Y
Mammilaria mollendorffiana	B
Mammilaria monancistracantha	Y

Mammilaria montensis	B
Mammilaria morganiana	B,Y
Mammilaria morricalii	B
Mammilaria muehlenpfordtii	B
Mammilaria multidigitata	B,Y
Mammilaria multiseta	BC
Mammilaria mundtii	B
Mammilaria mystax	B,BC,CH,Y
Mammilaria nana	B,Y
Mammilaria nana v. 'Trichacantha'	B
Mammilaria napina	B,BC
Mammilaria nejapensis	B,BC,CH,Y
Mammilaria neomystix	Y
Mammilaria neopalmeri	B,Y
Mammilaria neopotosina	B
Mammilaria neoschwarziana	B
Mammilaria nivosa	B
Mammilaria obconella	B
Mammilaria obscura	B
Mammilaria occidentalis	B
Mammilaria ocotillensis	CH
Mammilaria ortiz-rubiona	Y
Mammilaria oteroi	B,Y
Mammilaria pachycylindrica	B
Mammilaria pachyrhiza	B
Mammilaria painteri	B,Y
Mammilaria parkinsonii	B,CH,GC,Y
Mammilaria pectinifera	B,Y
Mammilaria peninsularis	B,GC,Y
Mammilaria pennispinosa	B,BC,GC,Y
Mammilaria pennispinosa v. nazasensis	B
Mammilaria perbella	B,CH,Y
Mammilaria petrophila	B
Mammilaria petterssonii	B,Y
Mammilaria phitauiana	B
Mammilaria picta	B
Mammilaria pilcayensis	Y
Mammilaria pilcayensis v chrysothele	Y
Mammilaria pilispina	B
Mammilaria pilosa	B
Mammilaria pitcayensis	C,CH
Mammilaria plumosa	B,CH,GC,Y
Mammilaria polyedra	B
Mammilaria polythele	B
Mammilaria poselgeri	B
Mammilaria pottsii	B
Mammilaria preissnitzii	BC
Mammilaria pringlei	B
Mammilaria prolifera	B
Mammilaria prolifera v. texana	B,Y
Mammilaria pseudoperbella	B,GC,Y
Mammilaria pygmaea	B
Mammilaria rekoi	B,Y
Mammilaria rekoi v. aureispina	B,Y
Mammilaria rekoi v. leptacantha	B
Mammilaria rettigiana	B
Mammilaria rhodantha	B,Y
Mammilaria rhodantha v ruberrima	B
Mammilaria ritterana	B
Mammilaria roseo - alba	B
Mammilaria roseocentra	B
Mammilaria rubrograndis	B
Mammilaria rubrum	B
Mammilaria ruestii	B,Y
Mammilaria saetigera	B,Y
Mammilaria santaclarensis	Y

MAMMILARIA

Mammilaria scheidweileriana	Y
Mammilaria schiedeana	B,CH,Y
Mammilaria schiedeana f plumosa	B
Mammilaria schumannii (bartschella)	B
Mammilaria scrippsiana	B,Y
Mammilaria scrippsiana v. autlanensis	B
Mammilaria sempervivi	B,Y
Mammilaria senilis	B
Mammilaria setispina	B
Mammilaria sheldonii	B,Y
Mammilaria sheldonii f. inaiae	B
Mammilaria simplex	BC
Mammilaria sinistrohamata	B
Mammilaria slevinii	B,Y
Mammilaria solisioides	B,BC
Mammilaria sonorensis	B,Y
Mammilaria sonorensis v. 'Tesopacensis'	B
Mammilaria sp mix	C,CH,T,Y
Mammilaria sphaerica	B
Mammilaria spinosissima	B,CH,GC,Y
Mammilaria spinosissima v. auricoma	B
Mammilaria standleyi	B
Mammilaria supertexta	B,BC
Mammilaria surculosa	B
Mammilaria swinglei	B
Mammilaria tayloriorum	B
Mammilaria tepexicensis	BC
Mammilaria tetracantha v galeottii	B
Mammilaria tetrancistra	B,BC
Mammilaria thornberi	B
Mammilaria tiegeliana	Y
Mammilaria tlalocii	B
Mammilaria tolimensis	Y
Mammilaria uncinata	B,Y
Mammilaria vaupelii v flavispina	B
Mammilaria vaupelis	B
Mammilaria vetula	B
Mammilaria viereckii	B
Mammilaria viperina	B
Mammilaria virginis	B
Mammilaria viridiflora	B
Mammilaria wagnerana / m. obscura	B
Mammilaria weingartiana	B
Mammilaria wiesingeri	B,Y
Mammilaria wildii	B
Mammilaria winterae	B
Mammilaria wohlschlageri	B
Mammilaria woodsii	B
Mammilaria wrightii	B,Y
Mammilaria wrightii v wilcoxii	Y
Mammilaria wrightii v wolfii	B
Mammilaria xaltianguensis	B,Y
Mammilaria yucatanensis	B,BC,Y
Mammilaria zacatecasensis	B
Mammilaria zahniana	Y
Mammilaria zeilmanniana	B,CH,GC,SO,Y
Mammilaria zeilmanniana v alba	CH,BC,Y
Mammilaria zephyranthoides	B,BC
Mammilaria zeyeriana	B
Mammilaria zuccariniana	B
Mammillaria centricirrha	CH
Mammillaria melaleuca	Y
Mammillopsis senilis	Y
Mammilloydia candida	Y
Mandevilla laxa	B,C,SA,T
Mandragora autumnalis	B,JE

Mandragora officinarum	AP,JE,SA,SC
Manfreda maculata	B
Mangifera foetida	B
Mangifera indica	B
Mangifera indica 'Manzana'	B
Manglietia insignis	SA
Manihot esculenta	B
Manihot glaziovii	B
Manihot palmata	CG
Manilkara hexandra	B
Manilkara roxburghiana	B
Manilkara zapodilla	B,RE
Manochlamys albicans	B,SI
Mansoa alliacea	B
Manulea altissima	B
Manulea benthamiana	B,SI
Marah fabaceus	B
Marah macrocarpus	B
Maresia pulchella	B
Margaretha weisei	B
Marginatocereus marginatus	Y
Margyricarpus pinnatus	AP,B,SG
Marica gracilis	MN
Markhamia acuminata	B,SA
Markhamia lutea	B
Markhamia zanzibarica	SI
Marojejea beranitso	B
Marojejea darianii	B
Marojejya darianii	B
Marrubium incanum	B,JE,SA
Marrubium peregrinum	B
Marrubium supinum	C
Marrubium vulgare	B,CP,G,JE,KS,SA,SG
Marrubium vulgare 'Green Pompon'	C,T
Marrubium vulgare 'Pompon'	B,JE
Marsiprospermum gracile	SS
Marsiprospermum grandiforum	AU
Martynia annua	B
Massonia depressa	B,SC,SI
Massonia pustulata	AP,B,SC,SI
Massonia sp	AP,SI
Matelea sp	B
Matricaria grandiflora 'Gold Pompoms'	T
Matricaria grandiflora 'Pincushion'	C
Matricaria inodorum 'Bridal Robe'	C,T
Matricaria matricarioides	B,CP
Matricaria perforata	SG
Matricaria recutita	B
Matricaria recutita 'Bodegold'	B,BD
Matteuccia struthiopteris	B,C
Matthiola aspera	B
Matthiola 'East Lothian Stocks' mix	BD,C,D,S
Matthiola fruticulosa	AP,B
Matthiola incana	AP,B,CG,CO,FH,I,J,SC, ST,VH
Matthiola incana 'Anthony Series' s-c/mix	BS,YA
Matthiola incana 'Austral' mix	YA
Matthiola incana 'Batavia' apple-blossom	B,SE,T,V
Matthiola incana 'Beauty of Nice'	BD,BS,S
Matthiola incana 'Brompton'	BS,DT,F,KI,L,M,SU,T,U, YA
Matthiola incana 'Brompton Lady' mix	BD,BS,C,CL,R,TU
Matthiola incana 'Cinderella' dark blue	B,BS,CL
Matthiola incana 'Cinderella' mix	BS,CL,D,J,L,S,T,YA
Matthiola incana 'Cinderella' s-c	B,BS,CL,T
Matthiola incana 'Cleopatra' s-c, mix	BS

153

Matthiola incana 'Double Flash' med blue	B
Matthiola incana 'Floral Delight'	SE
Matthiola incana 'Forcing Wonder'	L
Matthiola incana 'Giant Column' s-c	B,T
Matthiola incana 'Giant Excelsior Colum'	BS,C,T,U
Matthiola incana 'Giant Exc. Valour' s-c	BS
Matthiola incana 'Giant Imperial mix'	C,F,SE
Matthiola incana 'Giant Perfection mix'	BS,S,U
Matthiola incana 'Gladiator' s-c, mix	BS
Matthiola incana 'Happistock' mix	T
Matthiola incana 'Imperial Crown'	BS
Matthiola incana 'Legacy mix'	BS,DT,SE,T
Matthiola incana 'Mammoth Column' mix	YA
Matthiola inc. 'Mammoth Ex. Column' wh	B
Matthiola incana 'Marshall's Special Mix'	M
Matthiola incana 'Midget Series'	BS,KI
Matthiola incana mix	S
Matthiola incana 'Nordic' s-c	YA
Matthiola incana 'Pacific Column' mix	CL
Matthiola incana 'Park' mix	T,U
Matthiola incana 'Park' red	B
Matthiola incana 'Queen Astrid'	BS
Matthiola incana 'Record Series' mix	CL
Matthiola incana 'Regal' mix	J,V
Matthiola incana 'Sentinel' mix	B,BS
Matthiola incana 'Sentinel' s-c	BS
Matthiola incana 'Seven Week Formula'	C
Matthiola incana 'Superb Bedding mix'	S
Matthiola incana 'Tartan' mix	CL
Matthiola incana 'Ten Week' 100% dbl	KI
Matthiola incana 'Ten Week' mix	BD,BS,C,CL,CO,D,DT,F, J,KI,L,M,R,ST,T,TU,U,V, YA
Matthiola incana 'Tristar' s-c, mix	BS
Matthiola incana 'Viking' yellow	B
Matthiola incana white perennial	C,FH
Matthiola longipetala	B
Matthiola longipetala ssp bicornis	BS,C,CO,D,F,J,KI,KS,L, S,ST,SU,T,TU,V,VH
Matthiola sinuata	B
Matthiola 'Starlight Scentsation'	U
Matthiola tricuspidata	B
Matthiola 'Virginian' mix	S
Matucana aureiflora	B
Matucana aureiflora v elata	B
Matucana caespitosa	B
Matucana hystrix	Y
Matucana madisoniorum	B
Matucana madisoniorum v horridispinum	B
Matucana oreodoxa	B
Matucana paucicostata	B
Matucana paucicostata 'Senilis'	B
Matucana ritteri	B
Matucana roseo-alba	B,Y
Matucana variabilis	B
Matucana weberbaueri	B,Y
Matucana weberbaueri v flammels	Y
Matucana winteri	B
Maughaniella luckhoffii	GC,SI,Y
Maurandella antirrhiniflora	AP,B,SG,SW,T
Maurandella antirrhiniflora 'Coccinea'	B,C
Maurandya barclayana	AP,B,C,CG,SC,SG,T
Maurandya barclayana f alba	SG
Maurandya purpusii	SC,SG
Maurandya purpusii 'Victoria Falls'	AP,B,BD,C,DT,T
Maurandya 'Red Dragon'	P

Maurandya scandens	AP,C
Maurandya wislizenii	B,SW
Maxillaria crassifolia	B
Maxillaria tenuifolia	B
Maytenus acuminata	B,SI
Maytenus boaria	B,C
Maytenus emarginata	B
Maytenus heterophylla	B,SI
Maytenus oleoides	B,SI
Maytenus procumbens	B,SI
Maytenus undata	B,SI
Mazus pumilio	B
Mazus radicans	B,SS
Mazus reptans	AP,B,JE,SC
Meconopsis aculeata	AP,B,SC
Meconopsis betonicifolia	w.a.
Meconopsis betonicifolia v alba	AP,B,G,P,JE,SA,SC,SE,T
Meconopsis cambrica	w.a.
Meconopsis cambrica 'Aurantiaca'	AP,B,C,I,JE,SA,SC
Meconopsis cambrica 'Aurantiaca Fl.pl.'	AP,B,FH,JE,SC
Meconopsis cambrica dbl yellow	P
Meconopsis cambrica 'Fl Pl'	AP,B,C,HH,P,PM,SC
Meconopsis cambrica 'Frances Perry'	AP,B,C,G,P,PM,SC,T
Meconopsis cambrica 'Muriel Brown'	AP,B,P
Meconopsis cambrica 'Rubra'	JE,SA
Meconopsis chelidonifolia	MA
Meconopsis delavayi CLD1093	AP,LG
Meconopsis dhwoji	AP,B,SC,SG
Meconopsis grandis	AP,B,C,G,JE,LG,P,SA, SC,SE,SG,T
Meconopsis horridula	AP,B,G,JE,LG,P,SA,SC, SG
Meconopsis horridula 'Fl Pl'	P
Meconopsis horridula ssp prattii	SG
Meconopsis mix	JE
Meconopsis napaulensis	AP,B,BS,C,CG,JE,P,PM, SA,SC,SE,SG,T
Meconopsis napaulensis (pink)	SC,SE
Meconopsis paniculata	AP,P,SC,SG
Meconopsis punicea	AP,LG,SC
Meconopsis quintuplinervia	AP,SC,SG
Meconopsis regia	AP,B,C,G,JE,SC,T
Meconopsis regia bicolor	B,P
Meconopsis robusta	AP,SC,SG
Meconopsis simplicifolia	AP,B,LG,SC
Meconopsis sp mix	AP,SC,T
Meconopsis superba	AP,B,JE,SA,SC,SG
Meconopsis villosa	AP,B,C,JE,P,SC,SG
Meconopsis x musgravei	SG
Medicago arabica	SG
Medicago arborea	SA
Medicago falcata	SG
Medicago lupulina	B,C,SG
Medicago minima	SG
Medicago orbicularis	AP,B
Medicago sativa	B,C,SU
Medicago sativa cvs	B
Medicago scutellata	B
Medicago tornata 'Tornafield'	B
Medinilla magnifica	B,SA
Mediolobivia aureiflora	Y
Mediolobivia aureiflora v albilongiseta	Y
Mediolobivia aureiflora v rubriflora	Y
Mediolobivia brachycantha	Y
Mediolobivia diersiana	Y
Mediolobivia elegans	Y

MEDIOLOBIVIA

Mediolobivia eucaliptana	Y
Mediolobivia gracilispina FR1118	Y
Mediolobivia ithyacantha	Y
Mediolobivia margaretae	Y
Mediolobivia nigracans	Y
Mediolobivia pectinata v digitiformis	Y
Mediolobivia pectinata v neosteinmannii	Y
Mediolobivia pygmaea	Y
Mediolobivia ritteri	Y
Megacodon sp CNW1190	X
Meiostemon tetrandus	SI
Melaleuca acerosa	AU,B,O
Melaleuca acuminata	AU,B,HA,O
Melaleuca alternifolia	AU,B,HA,O
Melaleuca arcana	B
Melaleuca argentea	B,HA
Melaleuca armillaris	AU,B,C,HA,O
Melaleuca baxteri	B
Melaleuca bracteata	B,C,HA,O
Melaleuca brevifolia	AU,B,HA
Melaleuca brevifolia 'Neglecta'	B
Melaleuca calycina ssp dempta	B
Melaleuca capitata	B,SH
Melaleuca cardiophylla	B
Melaleuca cardiophylla v parviflora	B
Melaleuca ciliosa	B
Melaleuca citrina	B,O
Melaleuca coccinea	B,O
Melaleuca coccinea ssp coccinea	AU
Melaleuca conothamnoides	B,O
Melaleuca cordata	B
Melaleuca cornucopiae	B
Melaleuca cucculata	B
Melaleuca cuneata	B
Melaleuca cuticularis	AU,B,O
Melaleuca decora	AU,B,HA
Melaleuca decussata	B,C,HA,O
Melaleuca densa	B
Melaleuca depressa	B
Melaleuca diosmatifolia	B,HA
Melaleuca diosmifolia	B
Melaleuca eleuterostachya	B
Melaleuca elliptica	AU,B,HA,O,SA
Melaleuca ericifolia	AU,B,C,HA,O,SA
Melaleuca ericifolia nana	HA,SA
Melaleuca filifolia	AU,B
Melaleuca fulgens	AU,B,HA,O
Melaleuca fulgens ssp steedmanii	AU,B
Melaleuca fulgens v corrugata	B
Melaleuca gibbosa	B
Melaleuca glaberrima	B,O
Melaleuca globifera	B
Melaleuca glomerata	B,HA
Melaleuca halmaturorum	B,HA
Melaleuca halmaturorum ssp halm.	AU
Melaleuca hamulosa	B
Melaleuca holosericea	AU,B
Melaleuca huegelii	AU,B,HA,SA
Melaleuca huegelii ssp pristicensis	AU
Melaleuca hypericifolia	AU,B,HA,SH
Melaleuca incana	B,HA,O
Melaleuca irbyana	HA
Melaleuca lanceolata	B,HA,O
Melaleuca lanceolata ssp lanceolata	AU
Melaleuca lanceolata ssp occidentalis	B
Melaleuca lateriflora	B

Melaleuca lateritia	B,HA,O,SH
Melaleuca laxiflora	B
Melaleuca leptospermoides	B
Melaleuca leucadendron	B,HA,O
Melaleuca linariifolia	AU,B,HA,O,SH
Melaleuca macronychia	AU,B
Melaleuca megacephala	B,HA
Melaleuca microphylla	B
Melaleuca nematophylla	O
Melaleuca nesophila	AU,B,HA,O
Melaleuca nodosa	AU,B,HA,O
Melaleuca oldfieldii	B
Melaleuca pauciflora	B,HA
Melaleuca pauperiflora	B
Melaleuca pentagona	AU,B
Melaleuca platycalyx	AU,B
Melaleuca preissiana	B
Melaleuca pulchella	B,HA,O
Melaleuca pungens	B
Melaleuca pustulata	B
Melaleuca quadrifaria	B
Melaleuca quinquenervia	B,HA
Melaleuca quinquenervia red	B
Melaleuca radula	B,HA
Melaleuca rhaphiophylla	B
Melaleuca scabra aff 'Concinna'	B
Melaleuca scabra 'Bicolor'	B
Melaleuca sheathiana	B
Melaleuca sieberi	HA
Melaleuca sp mix	C
Melaleuca spathulata	AU,B,SA
Melaleuca spicigera	B
Melaleuca squamea	AU,B,HA
Melaleuca squarrosa	AU,B,C,HA,SA,SH
Melaleuca steedmanii	HA
Melaleuca striata	B
Melaleuca stypheloides	B,HA,O
Melaleuca suberosa	B
Melaleuca subfalcata	B
Melaleuca tamariscina	B
Melaleuca teretifolia	B
Melaleuca thymifolia	AI,B,HA,O,SH
Melaleuca thymoides	AU,B
Melaleuca thyoides	B
Melaleuca trichophylla	B
Melaleuca trichostachya	B,HA
Melaleuca uncinata	B,HA
Melaleuca undulata	B
Melaleuca viminea	B
Melaleuca violacea	AU,B,O
Melaleuca viridiflora	B
Melaleuca viridiflora 'Red Cloud'	B
Melaleuca viridiflora v rubriflora	B
Melaleuca wilsonii	AU,B,HA,O,SA
Melampodium paludosum	AP,C,S,V
Melampodium paludosum 'Showstar'	B,BS,CL
Melanthium virginicum	PR
Melasphaerula ramosa	AP,B,C,G,HH,MN,SC,SI
Melastoma sanguineum	B
Melhania oblongifolia	B
Melia azedarach	B,C,HA,RE,SA
Melia azedarach 'Floribunda'	B
Melia azedarach 'Umbraculiformis'	B
Melia azedarach v australasica	O
Melia toosendan	B,CG,SA
Melianthus comosus	B,SA,SI

MELIANTHUS

Melianthus major	B,SA,SI
Melianthus minor	B,SA,SI
Melianthus pectinatus	B,SA,SI
Melianthus villosus	B,SA,SI
Melica altissima	SG
Melica altissima 'Atropurpurea'	AP,B,G,JE,P,SA,SC,T
Melica californica	B
Melica ciliata	AP,B,C,CG,FH,G,JE,SG, SA,SC,T
Melica imperfecta	B
Melica nutans	B,G,JE,SA
Melica torreyana	B
Melica transsilvanica	B,JE,SA,SC
Melica transsilvanica atropurpurea	AP,SA
Melica uniflora	B,JE,SA
Melica uniflora albida	SG
Melica uniflora variegata	I
Melicoccus bijugatus	B
Melicope ellergana	O,SA
Melicope simplex	B
Melicope ternata	B
Melicytus alpinus	AU,B,SS
Melicytus crassifolius	AU,B,CG,SG
Melicytus lanceolatus	B,C,SA
Melicytus obovatus	B
Melicytus ramiflorus	B,C
Melilotus alba	B,C,G,LA,SG,SU
Melilotus altissima	B
Melilotus indica	B
Melilotus officinalis	B,C,SG
Melilotus suaveolens	SG
Melinis repens	B,SA,SI
Melinus minutiflora	B
Meliosma parviflora	CG
Melissa officinalis	A,B,CP,G,KS,RH
Melittis melisophyllum	B,C,I,JE,SA
Melocactus amoenus	B,Y
Melocactus arcuatispinus	B
Melocactus azulensis	B
Melocactus azureus	B,CH,Y
Melocactus bahiensis	B,Y
Melocactus cabescens	Y
Melocactus caesius	B,BC,Y
Melocactus concinnus	B
Melocactus conoideus	B,Y
Melocactus curvispinus	B,Y
Melocactus delessertianus	B,Y
Melocactus depressus	Y
Melocactus ernestii	B,CH,Y
Melocactus glaucescens	B
Melocactus glauxianus	B
Melocactus grisoleoviridis	B
Melocactus guitarta	B
Melocactus holguinensis	BC
Melocactus itaberensis	Y
Melocactus loboguerreroi	Y
Melocactus longispinus	Y
Melocactus matanzanus	B,T,Y
Melocactus maxonii	B,Y
Melocactus melocactoides	Y
Melocactus morrochapensis	Y
Melocactus neglectus	B
Melocactus neglectus v diamantinensis	B
Melocactus neryi	B,Y
Melocactus oreas	B
Melocactus peruvianus	B,G,Y

Melocactus rubrisaetosus HU137	BC
Melocactus rubrispinus	B,Y
Melocactus ruestii	Y
Melocactus salvadorensis	B,Y
Melocactus saxicola	Y
Melocactus sp	BC,Y
Melocactus uebelmannianus	Y
Melocactus violaceus	BC
Melocactus zehntneri	B
Melochia corchorifolia	B
Melochia nodiflora	B
Melothria pendula	B
Memecylon umbellatum	B
Menispermum canadense	B
Menispermum dahuricum	SA,SG
Menodora juncea	B,SI
Mentha aquatica	A,B,C
Mentha arvensis	B,SG
Mentha gentilis variegata	B
Mentha longifolia	B,C,JE
Mentha longifolia ssp capensis	B,SI
Mentha longifolia ssp wissii	B,SI
Mentha pulegium	C,CP,SA
Mentha spicata	C,JE
Mentha spicata 'Crispa'	B,G
Mentha spicata viridis	KS,SA
Mentha suaveolens	B
Mentha suaveolens 'Variegata'	B
Mentha x piperita	B,C,JE,KS,SA
Mentha x piperita f citrata	B,T
Mentha x piperita variegata	B
Mentyanthes trifoliata	B,C
Mentzelia decapetala	B,SW
Mentzelia laevicaulis	B,SC
Mentzelia lindleyi	AP,B,C,D,J,S,T,V
Mentzelia pumila	B
Mercurialis perennis	B
Merendera filifolia A.B.S4665 Morocco	MN
Merendera filifolia S.F300 Spain	MN
Merendera montana	AP,B,G,SA,SC
Merendera montana MS900/1 Spain	MN
Merendera montana MS909 Spain	MN
Merendera montana MS913/3 Spain	MN
Merendera montana S.F221 Spain	MN
Merendera trigyna	PM
Merremia sibirica	B
Merremia tridentata	B
Merremia tuberosa	B,C
Mertensia arizonica	B,SW
Mertensia maritima	AP,B,SC
Mertensia sibirica	AP,B,SC
Mertensia simplissima	AP,B,P
Mertensia virginica	P
Mertensia viridis	B,SW
Merxmuellera arundinacea	B,SI
Meryta sinclairii	B,SA
Mesembryanthemum crystallinum	B
Mesembryanthemum guerichianum	B,SI
Mesembryanthemum longipapillatum	B
Mesembryanthemum nodiflorum	B
Mesembryanthemum pellitum	B
Mesembryanthemum speciosum	B,SI
Mesomelaena tetragona	B
Mespilus germanica	B,C,SA,SG
Mestoklema arboriforme	B
Mestoklema tuberosa	B

MESUA

Mesua ferrea	B
Metalasia cephalotes	B,SI
Metalasia muricata	B,SI
Metasequoia glyptostroboides	B,C,CG,N,SA
Metrosideros angustifolia	B,SI
Metrosideros diffusa	SS
Metrosideros excelsus	B,C,HA,SA
Metrosideros fulgens	B
Metrosideros robusta	B
Metrosideros umbellata	B,SS
Metroxylon rumphii	B
Meum athamanticum	B,G,JE,SA,SC
Meyerophytum meyeri	B
Michauxia campanuloides	C,G,SE,T
Michauxia tchihatcheffii	SF,T,V
Michelia champaca	B,HA,SA
Michelia doltsopa	B
Michelia figo	B
Michelia maudiae	B,SA
Michelia sinensis	B
Michelia wilsonae	SA
Micranthocereus auri-azureus	B,Y
Micranthocereus densiflorus	B,Y
Micranthocereus polyanthus	B,Y
Micranthocereus streckerii	B,Y
Micranthocereus villianus	B
Micranthus alopecuroides	B,SI
Micranthus junceus	B,SI
Micranthus sp	SI
Micranthus tubulosus	B,SI
Micrococca mercurialis	B
Microderis 'Girandole'	BS,KI
Microlaena avenacea	B
Microlaena stipoides	HA
Microlepia speluncae	SA
Microloma sagittatum	B,SI
Microloma sp	SI
Microloma tenuifolium	B
Micromeles alnifolia	SG
Micromeria dalmatica	B
Micromeria 'Emperor's Mint'	B
Micromeria fruticosa	B
Micromeria thymifolia	AP,B,C,JE,FH
Micropterum papulosum	Y
Micropterum schlechteri	B
Microseris ringens	SA
Microseris ringens 'Girandole'	B,T
Microsorium punctatum	SG
Microsperma tasseloides 'Golden Tassel'	B
Microtis media ssp densiflora	B
Microtis oligantha	SS
Microtis unifolia	SS
Mila caespitosa	B
Mila caespitosa v churinensis	B
Mila cereoides	B
Mila fortalezensis	B
Mila maritima	B
Mila nealeana	B
Mila pugionifera	B
Milicia excelsa	B
Milium effusum	B
Milium effusum v aureum	AP,B,C,G,I,JE,P,SA,SC, SG
Milla biflora	B,SW
Millettia dura	B
Millettia grandis	B,SI

Millettia laurentii	B
Millettia ovalifolia	B,SA
Millingtonia hortensis	B
Mimetes cucullatus	B,O,SI
Mimosa biuncifera	B
Mimosa dysocarpa	B
Mimosa hostilis	B
Mimosa intsia	B
Mimosa pigra	B
Mimosa polycarpa	B
Mimosa pudica	B,BD,BS,C,CG,D,F,G,HA, KI,KS,S,SA,ST,T,V
Mimosa quitoense	B
Mimosa scabrella	B,RE
Mimosa tenuiflora	B
Mimulus 'Andean Nymph'	AP,B,BS,CL,FH,SC,SE,T, V
Mimulus aurantiacus	SW
Mimulus 'Bonfire'	BS
Mimulus brevipes	B,SW
Mimulus cardinalis	AP,B,C,CG,G,JE,SA,SC, SG,SW,
Mimulus cardinalis 'Siskiyou Gold'	B
Mimulus 'Crown Jewels'	BS,KI
Mimulus 'Extra Choice Mix'	F
Mimulus f1 hyb 'Calypso'	B,BD,BS,CL,D,DT,R,S, SE,T
Mimulus f1 hyb 'Magic' mix	CL,D,F,J,L,YA
Mimulus f1 hyb 'Magic Pastel' mix	DT,J,S
Mimulus f1 hyb 'Magic' s-c	B,CL,YA
Mimulus f1 hyb 'Malibu'	BD,BS,C,D
Mimulus f1 hyb 'Malibu 92'	M
Mimulus f1 hyb 'Malibu' orange	S
Mimulus f1 hyb 'Malibu Sunshine'	U
Mimulus f1 hyb 'Sparkles'	U
Mimulus f1 hyb 'Viva'	B,BS,C,D,F
Mimulus f1 'Mystic' mix	CL
Mimulus guttatus	AP,B,C,CG,G,JE,SA,SG
Mimulus guttatus variegata	P
Mimulus 'Highland Fling'	BD,BS
Mimulus 'Highland Series' s-c	B,BS
Mimulus lewisii	AP,B,C,G,JE,SA,SC,SG, SW,T
Mimulus longiflorus	B
Mimulus luteus	B,C,G,JE,SA,SC,T
Mimulus luteus 'Tigrinus Grandiflorus'	B,BS,C,CO,JE,KI,L,ST, SU,V
Mimulus minima	AP,JE
Mimulus moschatus	B
Mimulus primuloides	AP,B,G,SW
Mimulus puniceus	B
Mimulus 'Queen's Prize' mix	BS,DT
Mimulus 'Red Emperor'	B,JE,T
Mimulus ringens	B,C,G,JE,P,PR,SA,SC
Mimulus 'Roter Kaiser'	B
Mimulus 'Shade Loving Mix'	T
Mimulus tilingii	AP,B,JE,SC
Mimulus 'Whitecroft Scarlet'	AP,B,BS,SC
Mimusops coriacea	B
Mimusops elengi	B,HA,SA
Mimusops hexandra	B,HA,SA
Mimusops obovata	B
Mimusops obtusifolia	B
Mimusops zeyheri	B
Minuartia capillacea	B,JE,RS
Minuartia kashmirica	AP,CC

MINUARTIA

Minuartia langii	SG	Monarda bradburniana	G,JE
Minuartia laricifolia	AP,B,C,G,JE	Monarda bradburniana ssp russeliana	F
Minuartia recurva	B	Monarda citriodora	B,BS,CP,F,G,HW,JE,KS,
Minuartia verna	B,C,I,JE,SG		SA,T
Minuria denticulata	B,SA	Monarda didyma	B,G,KI,SA,ST,V
Minuria leptophylla	B	Monarda didyma 'Alba'	JE,SA
Mirabilis dichotoma	B	Monarda didyma 'Cambridge Scarlet'	CG,T
Mirabilis hirsuta	SG	Monarda didyma 'Goldmelisse'	JE
Mirabilis jalapa	AP,C,F,FH,G,KS,LG,RH,	Monarda didyma 'New Hybrids'	B
	S,SG,V	Monarda didyma 'Panorama'	B,BD,BS,C,CL,D,DT,F,J,
Mirabilis jalapa '4 0' Clock Special'	T		JE,L,SE
Mirabilis jalapa 'Afternoon Delight'	U	Monarda didyma 'Red Bergamot'	B,CO,F,JE,V
Mirabilis jalapa 'Crown Mix'	BS	Monarda didyma vars mix	BS,JE
Mirabilis jalapa 'Fellow's Pastels'	B	Monarda didyma 'Violacea'	B
Mirabilis jalapa prov.	B	Monarda fistulosa	B,C,CC,CP,G,JE,PR,SG
Mirabilis jalapa 'Red'	B,G	Monarda 'Lambada'	B,C,SA
Mirabilis jalapa 'Rose'	B,G	Monarda menthifolia	B,SW,T
Mirabilis jalapa 'Teatime'	BS,DT,F	Monarda punctata	B,C,CP,JE,PR,T
Mirabilis jalapa 'White'	B,G	Monarda 'Superb Mix'	T
Mirabilis jalapa 'Yellow'	B,G	Monardella lanceolata	B,SW
Mirabilis longiflora	B	Monardella macrantha ssp nana	B
Mirabilis multiflora	B	Monardella nana nana	SW
Mirabilis pumila	B	Monardella odoratissima	B,JE,SW
Mirabilis viscosa	F	Monilaria chrysoleuca v polita	B
Mirbelia dilatata	B,SA	Monilaria chrysoleuca v salmonea	B
Mirbelia pungens	B,SA	Monilaria moniliformis	SI,Y
Miscanthus nepalensis	B	Monilaria pisiformis	SI,Y
Miscanthus sinensis	AV,B,C,JE,SA,SC	Monimia rotundifolia	B
Miscanthus sinensis CNW11	X	Monochather paradoxa	B
Miscanthus sinensis 'Late Hybrids'	JE,V	Monocostus uniflorus	B
Miscanthus sinensis 'New Hybrids'	B,C,JE,SA	Monolena primuliflora	CG
Miscanthus sinensis 'Zebrinus'	AV,B	Monopsis debilis	SI
Miscanthus transmorrisonensis	B,JE	Monopsis lutea	B,C,SI
Misopates orontium	B	Monopsis sp	SI
Mitchella repens	A,B	Monopsis unidentata	SI
Mitella breweri	AP,B,FH,MA,SC,SGP,	Monsonia angustifolia	B,SI
Mitella caulescens	SG	Monsonia emarginata	SI
Mitella pentandra	B,SG	Monstera deliciosa	B,C,HA,SA
Mitragyna inermis	B	Monstera deliciosa 'Seidel'	B
Mitragyna parvifolia	B	Monstera deliciosa 'Tauer Strain'	CL
Mitraria coccinea	SA	Monstera friedrichsthalii	B
Mitrophyllum grande	B	Montinia caryophyllacea	B,SI
Mitrophyllum ripense	B	Montonoa bipinnatifida	B
Moehringia muscosa	AP,B,SC	Montonoa grandiflora	B
Moehringia pendantra	CG	Monvillea vallegrandensis	Y
Molinia arundinacea	JE,SA	Moraea algoensis	B
Molinia caerulea	B,JE,SA,SG	Moraea afticola	AP,B,LG,SI
Molinia caerulea ssp arundinacea	B	Moraea ardesiaca	SI
Molinia caerulea variegata	I	Moraea aristata	AP,B,SI
Mollugo disticha	B	Moraea atropunctata	B
Mollugo pentaphylla	B	Moraea bellendenii	B,SC,SI
Mollugo verticillata	B	Moraea bicolor	SA
Molopospermum peloponnesiacum	B,C,JE,SA	Moraea bipartita	B,SI
Moltkia petraea	AP,B,BS,C,G,JE,SA,SC	Moraea bituminosa	AP,B,SI
Moltkia suffriticosa	CG,SC	Moraea ciliata	B,SI
Molucella laevis	B,BD,BS,C,CO,D,DT,F,J,	Moraea cooperi	B,SI
	KI,KS,L,O,S,ST,SU,T,TU,	Moraea crispa	B
	U,V	Moraea falcifolia	B,SI
Momordica balsamina	B,SI	Moraea fugax	B,SC,SI
Momordica charantia	B	Moraea fugax yellow	B,MN
Momordica charantia 'Hong Kong'	B	Moraea gawleri	B,MN,SI
Momordica charantia 'Taiwan Large'	B	Moraea gigandra	B
Momordica charantia 'Thailand'	B	Moraea gracilenta	AP,B,SI
Momordica cochinchinensis	B	Moraea huttonii	AP,B,SC,SI
Monadenia bracteata	B	Moraea inclinata	B,SI
Monarda austromontana	AP,B,G,SW,T	Moraea inconspicua	B,SI

MORAEA

Moraea irioides	SA	Musa velutina	B,C,CG,SA
Moraea longiaristata	B	Musa violacea	B,C,SA
Moraea loubseri	AP,B,G,MN	Musa x paradisiaca	B,CG
Moraea macrocarpa	AP,B,SI	Muscari armeniacum	AP,B,G,RH,SC,SG
Moraea moggii	C	Muscari aucheri	AP,B,RH,SC
Moraea natalensis	AP,SC,SG	Muscari azureum	AP,B,G,HH,RH
Moraea neglecta	B	Muscari botryoides	B
Moraea neopavonia	B,SI	Muscari bourgaei S.L586 Turkey	MN
Moraea papilionacea	AP,B,SC,SI	Muscari chalusicum B.S.B.E842 Iran	MN
Moraea polyanthes	B,G,SI	Muscari comosum	AP,B,C,CG,G,SG
Moraea polystachya	B,SC,SI	Muscari comosum A.B.S4368 Morocco	MN
Moraea ramosissima	B,SI	Muscari comosum LG163 Spain	MN
Moraea serpentina	B,SI	Muscari conicum	G,SG
Moraea sp mix	C,SI	Muscari grandiflorum v populeum	MN
Moraea spathulata	AP,B,MN,P,SC,SI	Muscari inconstrictum S.L15 Jordan	MN
Moraea stricta	AP,B,SI	Muscari inconstrictum S.L20 Jordan	MN
Moraea tortilis	B	Muscari inconstrictum S.L56/1 Jordan	MN
Moraea tricolor	B	Muscari latifolium	AP,B,G,MN,SA,SC
Moraea tricuspidata	B	Muscari muscarimi	JE
Moraea trifida	SI	Muscari neglectum	AP,B,CG,SC,SG
Moraea tripetala	AP,B,SI	Muscari pseudomuscari	MN,SC
Moraea unguiculata	B,SI	Muscari racemosum	SG
Moraea vegeta	B,SC,SI	Muscari racemosum B.S349 Italy	MN
Moraea villosa	B,C,SC,SI	Muscari sp mix	AP,C,SC
Moricandia arvensis	B,C,T	Muscari spritzenhoferi MS707 Crete	MN
Moricandia nitens	B	Muscari spritzenhoferi SL702 Crete	MN
Morina kokanica	SG	Muscari steupii	SG
Morina longifolia	AP,B,BS,G,JE,P,T,SA,	Muscari tenuiflora S.L90 Jordan	MN
	SC,SG	Muscari tenuifolium	SC,SG
Morina persica	B,C,G,JE,T,SG	Muscari tubergentianum	AP,SC,SG
Morinda citrifolia	B	Mussaenda incana	B
Morinda coreia	B	Mutisia coccinea	SG
Moringa oleifera	B,SI	Mutisia decurrens	SA
Moringa ovalifolia	B,SI	Mutisia ilicifolia	AP,B,C,P,SC
Moringa pterygosperma	SA	Mutisia latifolia	P
Morus alba	A,B,C,N,SA,SG	Mutisia oligodon	AP,SA,SC,T
Morus alba v tatarica	A,B,SA	Mutisia retusa	SA,SC
Morus australis	SG	Mutisia spinosa	AP,SA,SC
Morus nigra	A,B,C,N,SA	Mutisia subulata	P
Morus rubra	B	Myagrum perfoliatum	CG
Mucuna bennettii	B,SA	Myoporum acuminatum	B,HA
Mucuna derringiana	SA	Myoporum apiculatum	B
Mucuna pruriens	B	Myoporum caprarioides	B
Mucuna pruriens v utilis	B	Myoporum insulare	B,HA,SA
Mucuna sempervirens	B	Myoporum laetum	AP,B,SA,SC
Muehlenbeckia axillaris	B,SS	Myoporum montanum	SA
Muehlenbeckia complexa	AU	Myoporum parviflorum	SG
Muehlenbeckia hastulata	SA	Myoporum platycarpum	B
Muhlenbergia mexicana	JE	Myoporum serratum	B
Muhlenbergia rigens	B	Myoporum tetrandrum	B
Mukia maderaspatana	B	Myosotidium hortensia	AP,B,SC,SS
Mundia spinosa	B,C	Myosotis alpestris	B,CG,G,SC
Mundulea sericea	B,SI	Myosotis alpestris 'Pink Posies'	B,P
Muntingia calabura	B	Myosotis alpestris 'Tall' s-c	KS
Murraya exotica	C,HA,O,SA,SG	Myosotis arvensis	B,C,SU
Murraya koenigii	B	Myosotis australis	AP,AU,B,SC,SS
Murraya paniculata	B	Myosotis azorica 'Maria Luisa'	B
Musa acuminata	B	Myosotis 'Blue Spire'	BS
Musa baccara	B	Myosotis colensoi	B,SC,SS
Musa balbisiana	B	Myosotis 'Compindi'	BS,D,DT
Musa basjoo	C	Myosotis dissitiflora 'Blue-Bird'	B
Musa bicolor	B	Myosotis drucei	SS
Musa coccinea	B,C,SA	Myosotis 'Dw Blue'	J
Musa ornata	SG	Myosotis explanata	B
Musa sp	RE,SE,T	Myosotis 'Light Blue'	KI
Musa troglodytarum	B	Myosotis macrantha	B,SS

MYOSOTIS

Myosotis mix	DT,F,J	Myrtus lechleriana	SA
Myosotis 'Nina' s-c	BS	Myrtus luma	B,SA
Myosotis palustris	B,JE,SA	Nageia nagi	B
Myosotis pygmaea v minutiflora	B,SS	Namaquanthus vanheerdii	B,Y
Myosotis rakiura	AP,SG	Nananthus broomii	B
Myosotis 'Rose Pink'	D	Nananthus transvaalensis	B
Myosotis scorpioides	B,C	Nananthus vittatus	B
Myosotis scorpioides 'Pinkie'	B,P	Nananthus wilmaniae	B
Myosotis sp	AP,SG	Nandina domestica	B,C,CG,HA,N,SA,SG
Myosotis stricta	SG	Nandina domestica nana	N,SA
Myosotis sylvatica	B,R,ST,TU,V	Nandina domestica 'Richmond'	B
Myosotis sylvatica 'Ball Blue'	B,BS,CL,D,SU,T,V,YA	Nandina domestica v leucocarpa	B,C
Myosotis sylvatica 'Ball Marine'	B	Nani petiolata	B
Myosotis sylvatica 'Ball Pink'	B	Napaea dioica	G,PR
Myosotis sylvatica 'Ball Snow'	B	Narcissus albidus ssp.kesticus S.F 70	MN
Myosotis sylvatica 'Blue'	CO,U	Narcissus albidus v occidentalis S.F.15	MN
Myosotis sylvatica 'Blue Basket'	B,BS,CL	Narcissus apertus	B
Myosotis sylvatica 'Bobo' s-c	B,L	Narcissus atlanticus S.B.L.270 Morocco	MN
Myosotis sylvatica 'Carmine King'	B,BS,T	Narcissus bertolonii	CG
Myosotis sylvatica 'Indigo Compacta'	B,BS,CL,F	Narcissus bicolor B.S.402 Spain	MN
Myosotis sylvatica 'Miniature Blue'	S	Narcissus bicolor B.S.448 Spain	MN
Myosotis sylvatica 'Music'	B,BS,CL,KI	Narcissus bulbocodium	AP,B,CG,G,RH,SC
Myosotis sylvatica 'Pink Princess'	B	Narcissus bulb. genuinus x albidus	MN
Myosotis sylvatica 'Pompadour'	B,BS	Narcissus bulbocodium 'Nylon'	PM
Myosotis sylvatica 'Rosie'	U	Narcissus bulbocodium ssp genuinus	MN
Myosotis sylvatica 'Rosylva'	CL,O,T,U	Narcissus bulbocodium ssp mairei	MN
Myosotis sylvatica 'Royal Blue'	B,BS,CL,J,S,VH	Narcissus bulbocodium ssp mix	MN
Myosotis sylvatica 'Royal Blue Imp'	T	Narcissus bulbocodium ssp obesus	AP,PM,SC
Myosotis sylvatica 'Snow Queen'	B	Narcissus bulbocodium ssp obesus hort.	MN
Myosotis syl. 'Spring Symphony Blue'	S	Narcissus bulb. ssp obesus MS.451	MN
Myosotis sylvatica 'Spring Symphony'	S	Narcissus bulb. ssp romieuxii 'Atlas Gold'	PM
Myosotis sylvatica 'Ultramarine'	B,BS,C,KS	Narcissus bulb. ssp rom.'Treble Chance'	PM
Myosotis sylvatica 'Unwins Special Mix'	U	Narcissus bulbocodium ssp tenuifolius	PM
Myosotis sylvatica 'Victoria Dw Azurea'	B,BD,BS,C,CL	Narcissus bulb. ssp tenuifolius S.B.214	MN
Myosotis sylvatica 'Victoria Dw' mix	BD,BS,C,KI,T,V,YA	Narcissus bulb. ssp viriditubus MS.411	MN
Myosotis sylvatica 'Victoria Dw Rosea'	B,BD,BS,C,CL	Narcissus bulb. ssp viriditubus MS.448	MN
Myosotis sylvatica 'Victoria Dw White'	B,BD,BS,C,CL	Narcissus bulb.ssp viriditubus MS.453	MN
Myosotis traversii	AP,AU,B,SC,SS	Narcissus bulb. ssp viriditubus S.B.204	MN
Myosotis white	C	Narcissus bulb. ssp vulgaris MS.412 Sp.	MN
Myosurus minimus	B	Narcissus bulbocodium 'Taffeta'	B
Myrcianthes leucoxyla	B	Narcissus bulbocodium v conspicuus	AP,B,SC
Myrciaria cauliflora	B	Narcissus bulb. v conspicuus S.F.391 Sp.	MN
Myrciaria edulis	B	Narcissus calcicola	AP,CG,SC
Myrciaria floribunda	B	Narcissus cantabricus	AP,PM,SC
Myrciaria glomerata	B	Narcissus cant. ssp cantabricus MS.424	MN
Myrianthus arboreus	B	Narcissus cant. ssp cantabricus S.F.395	MN
Myrica cerifera	A,B,C,SA	Narcissus cant. ssp eualbidus S.F.354/2	MN
Myrica gale	B,SG	Narcissus cant. ssp monophyllus B.S.416	MN
Myrica pensylvanica	A,B,C,SA	Narcissus cant. ssp monophyllus B.S457	MN
Myrica rubra	B	Narcissus cant. ssp monophyllus MS558	MN
Myriocephalus guerinae	O	Narcissus cant. ssp monophyllus MS657	MN
Myriocephalus stuartii	B,C,O	Narcissus cant. ssp monophyllus S.F.385	MN
Myrospermum sousanum	B	Narcissus cant. ssp monophyllus S.L432	MN
Myroxylon balsamum	B,SA	Narcissus cant. ssp monophyllus S.S.120	MN
Myrrhis odorata	B,C,CG,E,JE,LA,SA,SC	Narcissus citrinus ssp belinensis B.S391	MN
Myrsine africana	B,SI	Narcissus citrinus ssp belinensis MS579	MN
Myrsine australis	B	Narcissus citrinus ssp citrinus MS567 Sp.	MN
Myrsine divaricata	B,SS	Narcissus citrinus ssp citrinus MS577 Sp.	MN
Myrsine nummularia	B,SS	Narcissus citrinus ssp graellsii MS399 Sp.	MN
Myrsiphyllum asparagoides	B,SI	Narcissus cordubensis MS434 Spain	MN
Myrsiphyllum scandens	B,SI	Narcissus elegans ssp elegans A.B.S.4301	MN
Myrtillocactus geometrizans	B,BC,GC,Y	Narcissus 'Far North' mix	C
Myrtillocactus geom. v grandiareolatus	Y	Narcissus fernandesii MS414 Spain	MN
Myrtus communis	A,B,C,CG,SA,SG,T,V	Narcissus fernandesii MS449 Portugal	MN
Myrtus communis 'Compacta'	B,C	Narcissus fernandesii MS547 Spain	MN
Myrtus communis ssp tarentina	B,SG	Narcissus fernandesii MS660 Spain	MN

NARCISSUS

Narcissus fernandesii S.S.105 Spain	MN
Narcissus hedreanthus MS543 Spain	MN
Narcissus hispanicus ssp bujei MS853 Sp.	MN
Narcissus hisp. ssp pinetorum B.S470 Sp.	MN
Narcissus humilis ssp humilis S.F.14	MN
Narcissus hum ssp mauretanica S.F.268	MN
Narcissus jonquilla	AP,B,RS,SC
Narcissus jonquilla B.S420 Spain	MN
Narcissus juncifolius	AP,PM,SG
Narcissus longispathus S.S134 Spain	MN
Narcissus luteolentus S.S127 Spain	MN
Narcissus minor	AP,B,SC
Narcissus nobilis ssp primagenus MS905	MN
Narcissus pallidiflorus ssp macrolobus	MN
Narcissus pallid. ssp pallidiflorus B.S442	MN
Narcissus pallid. ssp pallidiflorus B.S482	MN
Narcissus pallid ssp pallidiflorus MS576	MN
Narcissus papyraceus	MN,SC
Narcissus papyraceus ssp papyraceus PB	MN
Narcissus papyraceus ssp papy. S.B.L48	MN
Narcissus perez-chiscanoi MS560	MN
Narcissus poeticus	C,JE
Narcissus poeticus v recurvus	B
Narcissus pseudonarcissus	AP,B,C,CO,SC,SG,Z
Narcissus pseudonarcissus moschatus	MN
Narcissus pseudonarcissus Trade	MN
Narcissus redinganorum MS434 Spain	MN
Narcissus requienii ssp minutus MS570	MN
Narcissus requienii ssp requienii B.S481	MN
Narcissus romieuxii HC2522 ex Morocco	LG
Narcissus romieuxii ssp riffanus B8928	MN
Narcissus rupicola	AP,FH,PM,SC,SG
Narcissus serotinus MS813/1 Crete	MN
Narcissus serotinus PB141 Crete	MN
Narcissus serotinus S.F169 Morocco	MN
Narcissus serotinus S.F257 Morocco	MN
Narcissus serotinus S.F278 Morocco	MN
Narcissus serotinus ssp grandiflorus	MN
Narcissus serotinus ssp gr. S.L298 Spain	MN
Narcissus serotinus ssp gr. S.L457 Spain	MN
Narcissus serotinus ssp orientalis MS740	MN
Narcissus serotinus ssp orientalis S.L487	MN
Narcissus sp mix	MN
Narcissus tazetta	G
Narcissus tazetta ssp grandicrenatus	MN
Narcissus triandrus ssp pallidulus	MN
Narcissus triandrus ssp triandrus	G,RS
Narcissus triandrus ssp triandrus MS915	MN
Narcissus triandrus ssp triandrus PB376	MN
Narcissus viridiflorus MS498 Spain	MN
Narcissus viridiflorus MS500 Spain	MN
Narcissus viridiflorus MS639 Spain	MN
Narcissus watieri	AP,PM,SC
Narcissus zaianicus S.B.L82 Morocco	MN
Narcissus zaianicus S.F371 Morocco	MN
Narcissus zaianicus S.F377 Morocco	MN
Narcissus zaianicus S.F379 Morocco	MN
Narcissus zaianicus v albus S.B.L85	MN
Nardus stricta	B,C
Narthecium ossifragrum	B,C,G,JE,SC
Nassella trichotoma	E
Nasturtium officinale	B
Nauclea orientalis	B,O,SA
Nauclea wadurata	B
Nebelia fragarioides	B,SI
Nebelia paleacea	B,SI

Nebelia sphaerocephala	B,SA,SI
Nectandra globosa	B
Nectaroscordum siculum	AP,B,C,FH,G,I,LG,PA, SC,SG,T
Nectaroscordum siculum ssp bulgaricum	AP,C
Nelia schlechteri	B
Nelumbo lutea	B
Nelumbo nucifera	B,C,SA,V
Nelumbo nucifera 'Alba Grandiflora'	B
Nemastylis tenuis ssp pringlei	B,SW
Nemcia capitata	B
Nemcia coriacea	B
Nemcia ilicifolia	B,SA
Nemcia reticulata	B
Nemcia spathulata	B
Nemesia caerulea	AP,B,P,PM,SI
Nemesia caerulea 'Pallida'	B,BS,DT,F
Nemesia 'Carnival' mix	B,BD,BS,C,CL,CO,D,DT, F,J,KI,L,M,R,S,SE,Sm, ST,T,TU,VH,YA
Nemesia cheiranthus	B,SI
Nemesia floribunda	B
Nemesia 'Funfair'	CT
Nemesia 'Galaxy' mix	BS,DT,L,YA
Nemesia melissifolia	CG,SG
Nemesia nana compacta 'Orange King'	T
Nemesia sp	SI
Nemesia 'St.George'	J
Nemesia strumosa	B,SI
Nemesia strumosa 'Blue Gem'	B,BS,S,V
Nemesia strumosa 'Blue Gem Superior'	B
Nemesia strumosa 'Blue & White'	SE
Nemesia strumosa 'Carmine Queen'	B
Nemesia strumosa 'Danish Flag'	B,BD,BS,DT,KI,L
Nemesia strumosa 'Fire King'	B,F,SE
Nemesia strumosa 'KLM'	BD,BS,C,CL,DT,F,J,KI, KS,L,T,U,V,YA
Nemesia strumosa 'KLM' p.s	B
Nemesia strumosa 'Mello White'	T
Nemesia strumosa 'National Ensign'	F,KS
Nemesia strumosa 'Orange Prince'	B,BS,CL
Nemesia strumosa 'Pastel Shades'	DT,F,U
Nemesia strumosa 'Red Ensign'	CL
Nemesia strumosa 'Red & White'	C,SE,T
Nemesia strumosa 'Snow Princess'	B,D,KS
Nemesia strumosa 'Unwins Hybrids'	U
Nemesia 'Tapestry' mix	T,VH
Nemesia 'Triumph'	BS,F,J,KI,TU
Nemesia versicolor	B,CG,SG,SI
Nemesia versicolor 'Blue Bird'	B
Nemesia versicolor 'Blue Gem'	T
Nemopanthus mucronatus	B
Nemophila atomaria 'Snowstorm'	B,C,KS,L,SE,T,V
Nemophila 'Freckles'	B,BD,BS
Nemophila maculata 'Five Spot'	B,BS,C,DT,F,HW,J,KS,L, T,TU,U,V
Nemophila menziesii	B,BS,C,D,HW,JS,KI,L, ST,SU,TU
Nemophila menziesii 'Baby Blue Eyes'	BD,CO,DT,F,KS,T,V
Nemophila 'Penny Black'	AP,B,BD,BS,C,DT,KS, SE,T,V
Neobinghamia climaxacantha	B,Y
Neobuxbaumia euphorbioides	Y
Neobuxbaumia polylopha	B,Y
Neobuxbaumia tetetzo	B
Neocardenasia herzogiana	B,Y

NEOCARDENASIA

Neocardenasia palos blancos	B	Nepeta nervosa	B,C,F,FH,G,JE,SA,SC,SG
Neochilenia aerocarpa	Y	Nepeta nervosa 'Blue Carpet'	B,U
Neochilenia aspillagai	Y	Nepeta nuda	AP,SG
Neochilenia crispa	Y	Nepeta parnassica	P
Neochilenia deherdtiana	BC	Nepeta sibirica	B,CG,JE,SA,SG
Neochilenia floccosa	Y	Nepeta 'Six Hills Giant'	B,P
Neochilenia glaucescens	BC	Nepeta sp woolly	B,P,SG
Neochilenia odoriflora	B,Y	Nepeta stewartiana	P
Neochilenia paucicostata	Y	Nepeta subsessilis	B,G,JE,P,SG
Neochilenia sp mix	C,Y	Nepeta sulphurea	SG
Neochilenia subikii	BC	Nepeta teydea	B
Neochilenia taltalensis	Y	Nepeta troodii	B,P
Neochilenia wagenknechtii	Y	Nepeta tuberosa	B,G,P
Neochilenia wagenknechtii v napina	Y	Nepeta x faassenii	B,G,JE,KS
Neodypsis baronii	B,O	Nepeta x faassenii 'Alba'	B,JE
Neodypsis darianii	B	Nepeta x faassenii 'Select'	B,JE
Neodypsis decaryi	B,HA,O	Nepeta x f. 'Souvenir D'andree Chaudron'	B
Neodypsis lastelliana	B,O	Nephelium lappaceum	B
Neodypsis leptocheilos	O	Nephrolepis cordata	B
Neoevansia diguetii	B	Nephrolepis cordata compacta	SA
Neohenricia sibbetti	B	Nephrolepis cordifolia	B,SG
Neolitsea dealbata	O	Nephrolepis cordifolia 'Plumosa'	B,SA
Neolloydia conoidea	B	Nephrolepis exaltata	B,SA,SG
Neolloydia conoidea v grandiflora	B	Nephrolepis exaltata 'Bornstedt'	B,SA
Neolloydia conoides	B	Nephrolepis exaltata 'Erecta'	B
Neolloydia dasyacantha	B	Nephrolepis exaltata 'Fluffy Ruffles'	SG
Neolloydia intertexta	B	Nephrolepis exaltata 'Teddy Junior'	SG
Neolloydia odorata	Y	Nephrolepis exaltata 'Whitmanii'	CG,SG
Neolloydia schmiedickeana	B,Y	Nephrolepis imbricata	B,SA
Neomarica gracilis	B	Neptunia dimorphantha	B
Neonicholsonia watsonii	B,O	Neptunia monosperma	B
Neopatersonia uitenhagensis	B	Neptunia oleracea	B
Neopaxis australasica	B	Nerine angulata	B
Neoportera chilensis	Y	Nerine bowdenii	B,C
Neoporteria atrispinosa	B,Y	Nerine bowdenii 'Fenwick's Variety'	PM
Neoporteria castaneoides	Y	Nerine filamentosa	B,MN
Neoporteria cephalophora	Y	Nerine filifolia	AP,B,MN
Neoporteria coimasensis	B,Y	Nerine humilis	B
Neoporteria gerocephala	B,Y	Nerine humilis v tulbaghensis	B
Neoporteria mammillaroiides	Y	Nerine krigei	B
Neoporteria microsperma	B,Y	Nerine masionorum	AP,B
Neoporteria multicolor	B,Y	Nerine sarniensis	B
Neoporteria nidus f. senilis	B,Y	Nerine undulata	B
Neoporteria nigrihorrida	B,Y	Nerium oleander	C,HA,G,JE,SA
Neoporteria pseudolaniceps	Y	Nerium oleander 'Fiesta' s-c	B
Neoportera sp	B	Nerium oleander mix	B,C
Neoporteria sp mix	CH,Y	Nerium oleander 'Variegata'	B
Neoporteria subgibbosa	B,Y	Nertera balfouriana	B,CC,SS
Neoporteria wagenknechtii	B,Y	Nertera depressa	SS
Neoraimondia arequipensis	B	Nertera granadensis	B
Neorautanenia mitis	B	Nestegis cunninghamii	B
Neoregelia sp	B	Nestegis lanceolata	B
Nepenthes khasiana	B,C	Neurachne alopecuroides	B
Nepenthes sp & hyb	B	New Mexico Native Shrub Seed	AV
Nepeta camphorata	B,C,CP,SG,T,V	Newcastelea sp	B
Nepeta cataria	B,C,CP,F,JE,KS,SA,SG,T	Newtonia buchananii	B
Nepeta cataria 'Citriodora'	B,C,CP,G,JE,P,T,V	Newtonia hildebrantii	SI
Nepeta grandiflora	B,C,G,SG	Nicandra physaloides	AP,B,BS,C,CC,CO,CP,F,
Nepeta italica	SG		G,I,P,S,SG,T,V
Nepeta kokanica	B,SG	Nicandra physaloides 'Alba'	B,C,P
Nepeta lanceolata	B,C	Nicandra physaloides 'Black Rod'	B
Nepeta latifolia	B,P	Nicandra physaloides 'Lg Fl'	T
Nepeta mussinii	BD,BS,C,CL,D,DT,F,KI,	Nicandra rustica	CP
	L,S,SA,SG,ST,T,V	Nicotiana acuminata	B
Nepeta nawaschinii	SG	Nicotiana affinis o-p	CL
Nepeta nepetella	AP,CG,FH,G,SC	Nicotiana affinis see alata	

NICOTIANA

Nicotiana alata	BD,BS,CO,D,G,S,SG
Nicotiana alata grandiflora	C,V
Nicotiana alata 'Sweet White'	B
Nicotiana alata 'Tabaco Blanco'	B
Nicotiana antennaria	B
Nicotiana 'Breakthrough Mix'	T
Nicotiana 'Canasta'	BD
Nicotiana 'Evening Fragrance'	S
Nicotiana f1 'Hippy'	D,S
Nicotiana f1 hyb 'VIP' s-c	C
Nicotiana f1 'Merlin Magic'	F
Nicotiana f1 'Metro' mix	BS,KI
Nicotiana f2 'Mannequin' mix	BS
Nicotiana f2 'Roulette'	BS,D,DT,F,J,KI,L,YA
Nicotiana f2 'Top Arts'	BS
Nicotiana 'Fragrant Cloud'	SE,T
Nicotiana glauca	B,C,JE,SG
Nicotiana 'Havana Appleblossom'	BS,CL,D,DT,F,M,O,R,SE, T,U,V,VH,YA
Nicotiana 'Havana Appleblossom' p.s	YA
Nicotiana 'Havana Series' s-c	BS,F,YA
Nicotiana knightiana	C,P,RS
Nicotiana langsdorfii	AP,B,C,F,G,KS,P,SG,T,V
Nicotiana langsdorfii 'Cream-Splash' (V)	P
Nicotiana 'Lime Green'	B,BS,CO,DT,F,J,KI,L,S, SE,ST,T,V,VH
Nicotiana 'Lime Green Unwins Strain'	U
Nicotiana 'Mop-Cap'	P
Nicotiana rustica	B,C,FH,PR,RS,SG,T
Nicotiana rustica named vars	B
Nicotiana 'Sensation' mix	BD,BS,CO,D,F,J,KI,ST, T,TU,SU,V,VH
Nicotiana sylvestris	AP,BS,C,DT,F,HH,G,I,KS, L,RH,SC,T,V
Nicotiana sylvestris 'Only The Lonely'	B,BD,C
Nicotiana tabacum	B,BS,CP,SG,SU
Nicotiana tabacum 'Burley' tn90	B,C
Nicotiana tabacum named varieties	B,BS
Nicotiana tabacum 'Virginian'	B,V
Nicotiana trigonophylla	B
Nicotiana velutina	B
Nicotiana x sanderae 'Bedder Crimson'	B,BS
Nicotiana x sanderae 'Bedder White'	B,BS
Nicotiana x s. f1 hyb 'Domino Crimson'	B,BS,CL,D,L,YA
Nicotiana x s. f1 hyb 'Domino Lime Green'	B,BS,CL,D,DT,F,L,M,YA
Nicotiana x s. f1 hyb 'Domino' mix	BD,BS,CL,D,DT,F,J,L,M, R,S,SE,T,TU,U,YA
Nicotiana x s. f1 hyb 'Domino' Pink Bicol	B,BS,CL,L,YA
Nicotiana x s. f1 hyb 'Domino Purple'	B,BS,CL,YA
Nicotiana x s. f1 hyb 'Domino Red'	B,BS,CL,YA
Nicotiana x s. f1 hyb 'Domino Rose Picot'	B
Nicotiana x s. f1 hyb 'Domino' s-c p.s	U
Nicotiana x s. f1 hyb 'Domino Salm. Pink'	BS,CL,D,DT,F,L,M,S,SE, T,U,V,YA
Nicotiana x s. f1 hyb 'Domino White'	B,CL,D,DT,F,L,M,T,YA
Nicotiana x sanderae f1 'Nicki' mix	BS,CL,S
Nicotiana x sanderae f1 'Nicki' s-c	B,BS,T
Nicotiana x s. f1 'Starship Lime Green'	B,BS,CL
Nicotiana x sanderae f1 'Starship' mix	BS
Nicotiana x sanderae f1 'Starship Pink'	B,BS,CL
Nicotiana x sanderae f1 'Starship Red'	B,BS,CL
Nicotiana x s. f1 'Starship Rose Pink'	B,BS,CL
Nicotiana x sanderae f1 'Starship White'	B,BS,CL
Nicotiana x sanderae 'Fragrant Delight'	B
Nicotiana x sanderae 'Tania' red,dwarf	B
Nidorella auriculata	SI
Nidularium angraensis	B
Nidularium sp	B
Nierembergia caerulea 'Mont Blanc'	B,BS,CL,D,F,KI,O,SE,T, V,YA
Nierembergia caerulea 'Purple Robe'	C,S,T,V
Nierembergia caerulea 'White Robe'	BS,C
Nierembergia caeruleaa v violacea	B,SC
Nierembergia solanacea	B
Nigella arvensis	B
Nigella ciliaris	B
Nigella ciliaris 'Pinwheel'	KS
Nigella damascena	AP,B,G,I,RH,SG
Nigella damascena 'Albion'	B
Nigella damascena 'Blue Cambridge'	B
Nigella damascena 'Blue Midget'	KS
Nigella damascena 'Blue Oxford'	B,BS,T
Nigella damascena 'Dw Moody Blue'	T
Nigella damascena f nana	SG
Nigella damascena fl pl mix	C
Nigella damascena 'Miss Jekyll Dark Blue'	B,BD,BS,KS
Nigella damascena 'Miss Jekyll' mix	KS,V
Nigella damascena 'Miss Jekyll Rose'	B,BD,BS,KS
Nigella damascena 'Miss Jekyll Sky Blue'	AP,B,BS,C,CO,D,DT,F,J, KI,KS,L,S,ST,SU,T
Nigella damascena 'Miss Jekyll White'	B,BD,BS,KS,T
Nigella damascena 'Mulberry Rose'	B,C,T,V
Nigella damascena 'Persian Indigo'	KS
Nigella damascena 'Persian Jewels'	B,BD,BS,C,CO,D,DT,F,G, J,KI,KS,L,M,S,ST,SU,T, TU,U,V
Nigella damascena 'Persian Red'	B,SE
Nigella damascena 'Persian Violet'	B
Nigella damascena 'Shorty Blue'	B,BS,C,KI
Nigella hispanica	AP,B,BS,G,T,V
Nigella hispanica 'Curiosity'	C,KS
Nigella orientalis	RH
Nigella orientalis 'Transformer'	AP,B,BS,C,F,KI,T,V
Nigella sativa	B,C,KS,SG
Nigella sp mix	F
Nigritella nigra	CG
Nissolia fruticosa	CG
Nitraria billardieri	B,SA
Nivenia binata	SI
Nivenia corymbosa	B,SI
Nivenia stokoei	B,SI
Nolana humifusa	B,BS,DT,KS
Nolana napiformis	AP,B,SC
Nolana paradoxa	AP,FH,SC,SG
Nolana paradoxa 'Blue Bird'	B,BD,BS,C,CO,D,DT,F, KI,KS,L,S,T,U,V
Nolana paradoxa 'Little Bells'	BS
Nolana paradoxa 'Shooting Star'	D,S,V
Nolana paradoxa 'Snow Bird'	B,BD,BS,D,KS,T,U,V
Nolina beldingii	B
Nolina bigelowii	B,SW
Nolina durangensis	B
Nolina gracilis	B
Nolina guatemalensis	B
Nolina microcarpa	B,CH,SW
Nolina parryi	B
Nolina sp mix	C
Nolina stricta	B
Nolina texana	B,RS
Nomocharis aperta	AP,LG,SC,SG
Nomocharis mix	P
Nomocharis oxypetala v insigne	SG

NOMOCHARIS

Nomocharis pardanthina	AP,G,N,SC
Nomocharis pardanthina punctulata	AP,PM,SC
Nomocharis saluenensis	AP,SC,SG
Nonea pulla	B,JE
Normanbya normanbyi	B,HA,O
Noronhia emarginata	B
Nothofagus alessandri	B,SA
Nothofagus antarctica	B,SA
Nothofagus cunninghamii	B,N,O,SA
Nothofagus dombeyi	B,SA
Nothofagus fusca	B
Nothofagus obliqua	B,C,N,SA
Nothofagus procera	B,C,SA
Nothofagus pumilio	B,N,SA
Nothofagus solandri v cliffortioides	AP,SS
Nothofagus truncata	B
Notholirion bulbiferum	AP,B,LG,SC
Notholirion campanulatum	AP,C,SC,T
Notholirion macrophyllum	B,SC
Notholirion sp CNW448	X
Nothoscordum bivalve	SG
Nothoscordum gracile	AP,CG,G,HH,I,SC
Nothoscordum gracile v macrocarpum	MN
Nothoscordum inodorum see gracile	
Nothoscordum minarum (Yellow)	MN
Nothoscordum sp Castillo 8264 Argentina	MN
Nothoscordum texanum	B
Notobasis syriaca	B
Notospartium carmichaeliae	B,SC,SW
Notospartium glabrescens	B,SW
Notospartium torulosum	B,SW
Notothlaspi rosulatum	B,SW
Nuphar lutea	B,SA
Nuxia congesta	B,SI
Nuxia floribunda	B,SI
Nuxia oppositifolia	SI
Nuytsia floribunda	B,O,SA
Nyctanthes arbortristis	B,HA,SA
Nycteranthus noctiflorum	B
Nylandtia spinosa	B,SI
Nymania capensis	B,C,SI
Nymphaea capensis	B,C
Nymphaea lotus v dentata	C
Nymphaea micrantha	C
Nymphaea 'Sir Galahad'	C
Nypa fruticans	B
Nyssa aquatica	B,SA
Nyssa ogeche	B
Nyssa sinensis	B,SA
Nyssa sylvatica	B,C,CG,HA,N,SA
Obregonia denegrii	B,BC,C,CH,GC,Y
Ochna kirkii	B,SG
Ochna natalita	B,SI
Ochna obtusata v gamblei	B
Ochna pulchra	B
Ochna serrulata	B,C,HA,SA,SG,SI
Ochroma lagopus	B,RE
Ochrosia sandwichensis	B
Ocimum adscendens	B
Ocimum americanum	B,SI
Ocimum basilicum	CP
Ocimum basilicum 'Dark Opal'	BS,C,CO,ST,T
Ocimum basilicum micranthemum	B
Ocimum basilicum 'Ruffles' green	B
Ocimum basilicum 'Ruffles' purple	B,L,S,T
Ocimum gratissimum	B

Ocimum kilimandscharicum	CP
Ocimum micranthum	CP
Ocimum tenuiflorum	B,CP
Ocimum viride	CP
Odontites lutea	B
Odontites verna	B
Odontites vulgaris	B,SG
Odontophorus angustifolius	B
Odontophorus marlothii	B
Odontophorus nanus	B
Oedera imbricata	B,SI
Oemleria cerasiformis	B,CG,SA
Oenanthe aquatica	B
Oenanthe crocata	B,G
Oenanthe sarmentosa	B
Oenanthe silaifolia	B
Oenothera acaulis	AP,C,F,FH,SA,SC
Oenothera acaulis 'Aurea'	AP,B,JE,SC
Oenothera 'Afternoon Beauty'	B
Oenothera 'Apricot Delight'	B,P
Oenothera argillicola	B
Oenothera biennis	B,C,CP,E,B,I,JE,LA,PR, SG,TU
Oenothera biennis 'Saguin'	B
Oenothera brachycarpa	B
Oenothera brevipes	B,RS,SW
Oenothera 'C.Porter'	C,P
Oenothera caespitosa	AP,B,BS,C,J,JE,RS,SC, SG,SW,V
Oenothera cardiophylla	B,SW
Oenothera cheiranthifolia	FH
Oenothera childsii	AP,FH
Oenothera deltoides	B,SW
Oenothera d. v howellii 'Antioch Dunes'	T
Oenothera drummondii	B
Oenothera elata	SW
Oenothera elata ssp hookeri	AP,B,C,SW
Oenothera erythrosepala	AP,C,G,JE,KI,SC,V
Oenothera flava	AP,SC,SG
Oenothera flava ssp taraxacoides	B,SW
Oenothera fruticosa	G,SG
Oenothera fruticosa ssp glauca	AP,B,C,G,JE,SA,SC
Oenothera fruticosa 'Youngii'	JE
Oenothera glazioviana	B
Oenothera hartweggii	SW
Oenothera kunthiana	AP,HH,JE,RH,RS,SC
Oenothera 'Lemon Sunset'	T,V
Oenothera macrocarpa	AP,B,BD,BS,C,CG,CL, DT,F,I,HW,J,JE,KS,L,SA, SC,SG,V
Oenothera mollis	P
Oenothera odorata	AP,C,E,F,G,JE,SC,SG
Oenothera pallida	B,JE,KS,SA,T
Oenothera pallida 'Innocence'	C,CO,KI,L,S,TU
Oenothera patagonica	HH
Oenothera perennis	AP,G,I,JE,SG
Oenothera rosea	AP,CC,CG,G
Oenothera sp	AP,SC,T
Oenothera speciosa	AP,B,BS,DT,HW,JE,SC
Oenothera speciosa 'Pink'	B,KS,T
Oenothera speciosa 'Silky Orchid'	F
Oenothera stricta	AP,B,I,RH,SC,SG
Oenothera stricta 'Moonlight'	I
Oenothera syrticola	JE
Oenothera tetragona fraseri	SC,SG
Oenothera versicolor 'Sunset Boulevard'	P,T

OENOTHERA

Oenothera 'Wedding Bells'	U	Onoclea sensibilis	PR
Oldenlandia herbacea	B	Ononis alopecuroides	B
Oldenlandia umbellata	B	Ononis arvensis	SG
Olea africana	SA	Ononis cenisia	B
Olea cuspidata	B	Ononis fructicosa	C,FH,SA
Olea europaea	B,C,N,SA,T,V	Ononis natrix	AP,B,G,SC
Olea europaea ssp africana	C,SI	Ononis repens	B,FH
Olea exasperata	SI	Ononis rotundifolia	AP,C,FH,G,JE,SC,SG
Olea hochstetteri	B	Ononis speciosus	SA
Olearia albida	AU,B	Ononis spinosa	B,BS,G,JE,KI,SA,SG,SU
Olearia allomii	B	Onopordum acanthium	AP,C,CP,G,HH,JE,KI,P,
Olearia angustifolia	AU		SA,SC,SG,ST,SU,T
Olearia arborescens	B	Onopordum nervosum	AP,B,BS,C,SC
Olearia avicenniaefolia	SS	Onosma arenaria	B,G
Olearia axillaris	B,HA,O	Onosma brignetii	SG
Olearia ciliata	B,O	Onosma echioides	FH,SC,SG
Olearia colensoi	B,SS	Onosma helvetica	AP,SC,SG
Olearia cymbifolia	CG	Onosma heterophylla	SG
Olearia frostii	RS	Onosma nanum	SC,SG
Olearia furfuracea	B,CG	Onosma rupestre	SG
Olearia gravis	B	Onosma seranschinica	JE
Olearia 'Henry Travers'	AU	Onosma stellulatum	AP,C,G,JE,SA,SG
Olearia ilicifolia	SS	Onosma tornensis	B,G
Olearia lacunosa	B	Onosmodium mollis	PR
Olearia lessoniana	B	Onychium japonicum	B
Olearia lirata	AP,AU,HA	Oophytum nanum	B,SI,Y
Olearia lyallii	B	Oophytum oviforme	B,C,SI,Y
Olearia macrodonta	AP,B,SC,SG,SS	Opercularia echinocephala	B
Olearia magniflora	B	Operculina brownii	B
Olearia microphylla	HA,O	Ophiopogon jaburan	B,SC
Olearia moschata	B,SS	Ophiopogon jaburan 'Vittatus'	B
Olearia myrsinoides	SG	Ophiopogon planiscapus 'Nigrescens'	AP,B,JE,SA
Olearia nummularifolia	AP,B,I,SS	Ophrys apifera	B
Olearia nummularifolia v cymbifolia	SS	Ophrys holosericea	B
Olearia paniculata	SC,SS	Ophthalmophyllum dinteri	BC,Y
Olearia passerinoides	B	Ophthalmophyllum friedrichiae	Y
Olearia paucidentata	B	Ophthalmophyllum haramoepense	B
Olearia phlogopappa	AU	Ophthalmophyllum herrei	B
Olearia pimeleoides	B,O	Ophthalmophyllum latum	B,Y
Olearia ramosissima	B	Ophthalmophyllum littlewoodii	B
Olearia rudis	B	Ophthalmophyllum longum	B
Olearia sp	AU	Ophthalmophyllum maughanii	B
Olearia tilicifolia	B	Ophthalmophyllum praesectum	B,Y
Olearia traversii	B,SW	Ophthalmophyllum pubescens	B
Olearia virgata	B,CG,SW	Ophthalmophyllum schlechteri	B,Y
Olearia x haastii	CG,G,SC	Ophthalmophyllum schuldtii	B
Olinia emarginata	B,C	Ophthalmophyllum triebneri	B
Olinia ventosa	B	Ophthalmophyllum verrucosum	B,BC
Olsynium douglasii	AP,B,JE,SC,SG	Oplismenus compositus	B
Olysnium biflora ssp biflora	AU	Oplopanax horridus	SG
Omalanthus populifolius	HA,O	Opophytum aquosum	B
Omalotheca norvegica	SG	Opuntia acanthocarpa v thornberi	B
Omalotheca sylvatica	SG	Opuntia alta	B
Omphalodes kuzinskyana	B,PM	Opuntia ammophila	B
Omphalodes linifolia	AP,B,C,FH,HH,I,LG,SC,V	Opuntia arizonica	BC
Oncidium altissimum	B	Opuntia atrispina	B
Oncidium cebolleta	B	Opuntia basilaris	B,CH
Oncidium macranthum	B	Opuntia bermichiana	BC
Oncidium sphacelatum	B	Opuntia chisosensis	B
Oncoba spinosa	B	Opuntia chlorotica	CH
Oncosiphon grandiflorum	B,SI	Opuntia chlorotica v santa-rita	B
Oncosiphon grandiflorum 'Pincushion'	B	Opuntia clavata	B
Oncosperma tigillarium	B,O	Opuntia cochenillifera	B
Onixotis triquetrum	B,MN,SI	Opuntia compressa	B,JE,PR
Onobrychis sibirica	SG	Opuntia compressa v rafinesqui	B
Onobrychis viciifolia	B,C,G,LA,SU	Opuntia cymochila	B

165

OPUNTIA

Opuntia decumbens	B
Opuntia dulcis	BC
Opuntia erinacea	CH
Opuntia ficus-indica	C
Opuntia ficus-indica v dillei	B
Opuntia huajuapensis	B
Opuntia imbricata	B
Opuntia imbricata v vexans	B
Opuntia joconostele	B
Opuntia kleinia	B
Opuntia laevis /o.phaecantha v l.	B
Opuntia leptocaulis	B
Opuntia leucotricha	CH
Opuntia lindheimeri	B
Opuntia lindheimeri v linguiformis	B
Opuntia loomisii aff	B
Opuntia mackensii	BC
Opuntia macrocentra	B,BC
Opuntia macrorhiza	B
Opuntia microdasys	B
Opuntia microdasys v rufida	B
Opuntia nopalea	B
Opuntia oricola	B
Opuntia phaeacantha	B,BC,JE
Opuntia phaeacantha v albispina	BC
Opuntia phaeacantha v brunnea	B
Opuntia phaeacantha v charlestonensis	BC
Opuntia phaeacantha v discata	BC,G
Opuntia phaeacantha v major	B
Opuntia phaeacantha v minor	BC
Opuntia phaeacantha v rubra	BC
Opuntia phaeacantha v tortispina	B
Opuntia pilifera	B
Opuntia polyacantha	B
Opuntia polyacantha v hystricina	B
Opuntia polyacantha juniperina	BC,G
Opuntia quimilo	B
Opuntia rhodantha	BC
Opuntia rhodantha salmonea	BC
Opuntia robusta	B
Opuntia rosea	B
Opuntia sp mix	C,CH
Opuntia spinosior	B
Opuntia spinulifera	B
Opuntia stenopetala	B
Opuntia stricta	B
Opuntia strigil	B
Opuntia sulphurea	B
Opuntia tardospina	BC
Opuntia tortispina	B
Opuntia tuna	B
Opuntia velutina	B
Opuntia viridiflora	B
Opuntia whipplei	B
Opuntia winter hardy mix	C,JE
Orbea tapscottii	B,SI
Orbea variegata	B,SI
Orbea woodii	B,SI
Orbeanthus hardyi	B
Orbeopsis caudata	B,SI
Orbeopsis caudata ssp rhodesiaca	SI
Orbeopsis lutea ssp lutea	B,SI
Orbeopsis melanantha	B,SI
Orbignya polysticha	B
Orchis mascula	AP,B,CG,SC
Orchis militaris	B

Orchis morio	B
Orchis sancta	B
Oreobilus pectinatus	B,SW
Oreocereus aequatorialis	B
Oreocereus arboreus	Y
Oreocereus aurantiacus	B
Oreocereus celsianus	B
Oreocereus culpinensis	Y
Oreocereus fossulatus	B,Y
Oreocereus giganteus	B,BC,Y
Oreocereus gracilis	B
Oreocereus haynei	B
Oreocereus haynei vars	B
Oreocereus hendriksenianus	B,Y
Oreocereus hendrik. v densilanatus	Y
Oreocereus hendriksenianus v gracilior	B,Y
Oreocereus intertexta	B
Oreocereus magnificus	B,Y
Oreocereus maximus	B,Y
Oreocereus neocelsianus	Y
Oreocereus potosinus	B,Y
Oreocereus seracata	Y
Oreocereus sp mix	C,Y
Oreocereus trollii	B,BC,Y
Oreocereus trollii v mayor	Y
Oreocereus urmiriensis	B,Y
Oreomyrrhis colensoi	B,SW
Oreomyrrhis rigida	SS
Oreopanax xalapensis	B
Oriana sylvicola	B,O
Orianopsis appendiculata	B,O
Origanum creticum	T
Origanum laevigatum	AP,C,I,JE,T
Origanum laevigatum album	T
Origanum laevigatum 'Herrenhausen'	PA
Origanum laevigatum 'Hopley's'	HH,I,PA,T
Origanum rotundifolium	CC,SC
Origanum vulgare 'Album'	JE
Origanum vulgare 'Aureum'	B
Origanum vulgare 'Gold Tip'	B
Origanum vulgare ssp hirtum	B,CG,SG
Origanum vulgare v prismaticun	SG
Orites acicularis	AU
Orites diversifolia	B,O
Orlaya grandiflora	B
Ormocarpum kirkii	B,SI
Ormosia henryi	B
Ornithogalum arcuatum	G,MN
Ornithogalum comosum	B
Ornithogalum dubium	B,O,SA,SI,T
Ornithogalum exscapum	AP,MN
Ornithogalum fimbriatum	PM
Ornithogalum fimbrimarginatum	B
Ornithogalum glandulosum	B
Ornithogalum graminifolium	B,SI
Ornithogalum hispidum	B,SI
Ornithogalum juncifolium	SI
Ornithogalum longibracteatum	AP,B,CG,G,SC,SG,SI
Ornithogalum maculatum	B,C,SI
Ornithogalum magnum	AP,G,MN
Ornithogalum montanum	B,SG
Ornithogalum multifolium	B,SC,SI
Ornithogalum narbonense	AP,RS,SA,SC
Ornithogalum nutans	AP,B,FH,SG
Ornithogalum pilosum	B
Ornithogalum polyphyllum	B

ORNITHOGALUM

Ornithogalum prasinum	B
Ornithogalum pruinosum	B
Ornithogalum pyramidale	AP,B,C,G,SG
Ornithogalum pyramidalis aff S.L93	MN
Ornithogalum pyrenaicum	AP,B,C,JE,PA,SA,SC
Ornithogalum pyrenaicum A.B.S4368A	MN
Ornithogalum pyrenaicum v flavescens	G,MN
Ornithogalum rogersii	B
Ornithogalum saundersiae	AP,B,SC,SI
Ornithogalum secundum	B
Ornithogalum seineri	B,SI
Ornithogalum sessiliflorum A.B.S4619	MN
Ornithogalum sp	G,SI
Ornithogalum spicatum B.S404 Portugal	MN
Ornithogalum suaveolens	B,SI
Ornithogalum thyrsoides	AP,B,C,O,SA,SC,SI
Ornithogalum umbellatum	B,C,CG,JE,SG
Ornithogalum unifolium	B
Ornithoglossum viride	B,SI
Ornithopus compressus 'Pitman'	B
Ornithopus compressus 'Uniserra'	B
Ornithopus sativus	CG
Orobanche hederae	AP,C,G
Orobanche ramosa	SG
Oroxylum indicum	B
Orphium frutescens	B,C,SA,SI
Orphium frutescens 'Select'	B
Orthocarpus purpurascens	B
Orthophytum foliosum	B
Orthopterum coeganum	B
Orthosiphon serratus	B
Orthrosanthus chimboracensis	AP,B,SC
Orthrosanthus laxus	AP,AU,P,SA,SC,SG
Orthrosanthus multiflorus	AP,B,C,SC
Orthrosanthus polystachyus	AU,P
Orychophragmus violaceus	B,T
Oryza sativa	B,SG
Oryzopsis hymenoides	B
Osmanthus fragrans	B,SA
Osmanthus heterophyllus	B
Osmitopsis asteriscoides	SI
Osmitopsis osmitoides	B,SI
Osmorhiza claytonii	B,PR
Osmunda regalis	AP,B,N,SC
Osteocarpum acropterum ssp acropterum	B
Osteocarpum acrop. ssp dipterocarpum	B
Osteomelis schwerinae v microphylla	SG
Osteospermum acutifolium	SI
Osteospermum barberiae Of gdns	AP,I,SG
Osteospermum clandestinum	B,SI
Osteospermum ecklonis	AP,B,F,SA,SC,SI
Osteospermum hyoseroides	C,SI
Osteospermum hyoseroides 'Pot Pourri'	F,J,U
Osteospermum microcarpum	B,SI
Osteospermum oppositifolium	B,SA,SI
Osteospermum pinnatum	B,SI
Osteospermum 'Silver Sparkler'	B
Osteospermum 'Sky & Ice'	BD,BS
Osteospermum tripterus 'Gaiety'	B
Ostrowskia magnifica	B,SC
Ostrya carpinifolia	B,CG,N,SA
Ostrya japonica	N,SA
Ostrya virginiana	B,G,N,SA
Osyris alba	B
Osyris quadripartita	SA
Otatea acuminata	B

Otholobium fruticans	B,SI
Otholobium hirtum	B,SI
Otholobium sericeum	B,SI
Otholobium sp	SI
Otholobium striatum	B
Othonna arborescens	B,SA,SI
Othonna cheirifolia	AP,FH,SC
Othonna clavifolia	B
Othonna cuneata	B
Othonna filicaulis	B,SI
Othonna lobata	B
Othonna sp	SI
Ourisia caespitosa	AP,B,SW
Ourisia macrocarpa	B,SW
Ourisia macrophylla	AP,JE,P,SC
Ourisia macrophylla v lactea	SG
Ourisia sessilifolia	B,SW
Owenia acidula	B,SA
Owenia reticulata	B
Oxalis acetosella	AP,B
Oxalis corniculata	B
Oxalis deppei see tetraphylla	
Oxalis lactea	B,SW
Oxalis megalorrhiza	B
Oxalis oregana	B,G
Oxalis purpurea	B
Oxalis stricta	B
Oxalis tetraphylla	B,G
Oxalis tetraphylla 'Iron Cross'	B
Oxalis valdiviensis	P
Oxipolis rigidior	B
Oxydendrum arboreum	A,B,C,I,N,SA
Oxygonum sinuatum	B
Oxylobium arborescens	B,HA
Oxylobium ellipticum	AU,B
Oxylobium ilicifolium	HA
Oxylobium lanceolata	SA
Oxylobium microphyllum	B
Oxylobium procumbens	B,HA
Oxylobium robustum	B
Oxyria digyna	A,B,C,FH,I,SG
Oxytropis amethystea	B
Oxytropis campanulata	SG
Oxytropis campestris	B,G,JE,SA,SC,SG
Oxytropis campestris v johannensis	SG
Oxytropis gaudinii	CG
Oxytropis halleri	AP,SC,SG
Oxytropis japonica	CC
Oxytropis lagopus	B,SW
Oxytropis lapponica	JE
Oxytropis megalantha	CC
Oxytropis middendorffii	SG
Oxytropis myriophylla	SG
Oxytropis pilosa	B,SC
Oxytropis sericea	B
Oxytropis setida	CG
Oxytropis songorica	SG
Oxytropis splendens	SG
Oxytropis strobilacea	SG
Oxytropis teres	SG
Oxytropis urumovii	AP,SG
Oxytropis viscida	AP,SG
Ozoroa dispar	B,SI
Ozoroa mucronata	B,SI
Ozothamnus lepidophyllus	AP,B
Ozothamnus sediformis	FH

OZOTHAMNUS

Ozothamnus selago	B,SG,SS
Pachira aquatica	B
Pachira fendleri	B
Pachira insignis	B
Pachira quinatum	SA
Pachycarpus campanulatus	SI
Pachycarpus grandiflorus	SI
Pachycarpus sp	SI
Pachycereus chrysomalus	BC
Pachycereus hollianus	B
Pachycereus pecten-aboriginum	B,Y
Pachycereus pringlei	B,Y
Pachycymbium keithii	B,SI
Pachycymbium lugardii	B,SI
Pachycymbium rogersii	B,SI
Pachygone ovata	B
Pachyphragma macrophyllum	C
Pachyphytum compactum	B
Pachypleurum mutellinoides	SG
Pachypodium baronii	B,O,SI
Pachypodium baronii v windsorii	B
Pachypodium bispinosum	BC,SI
Pachypodium decaryi	B,O
Pachypodium densiflorum	B,BC,O
Pachypodium geayi	B,O,SI
Pachypodium horombense	B,O
Pachypodium lamerei	B,CH,O,SA,SI,V
Pachypodium lealii	B,O
Pachypodium namaquanum	B
Pachypodium rosulatum	B,CH,O,V
Pachypodium saundersii	B,O,SI
Pachyrhizus erosus	B
Pachyrhizus tuberosus	B
Pachysandra terminalis	B
Pachystegia insignis	AP,B,SA,SC,SG,SS
Pachystegia minor	AP,SS
Pachystegia rufa	AU,B,SC
Packera aurea	B
Packera paupercula	B
Padus asiatica	SG
Padus avium	SG
Padus maackii	SG
Padus virginiana x P. avium	SG
Paeonia anomala	AP,B,G,PH,SG
Paeonia anomala v intermedia	SG
Paeonia arborea	CG
Paeonia broteroi	AP,CG,G,PH,SC,SG
Paeonia brownii	PH
Paeonia brownii maroon sepal	PH
Paeonia californica	B,PH,SW
Paeonia cambessedesii	AP,MN,PH,SC,SG
Paeonia caucasica	CG,PH
Paeonia chamaeleon	PH
Paeonia coriacea	PH,SA
Paeonia delavayi	AP,B,C,CG,G,I,LG,P,PH, SA,SC
Paeonia delavayi v ludlowii	AP,B,C,JE,LG,P,PH,SA, SC,SG
Paeonia delavayi v lutea	G,N,X
Paeonia emodi	B,PH,SC
Paeonia European sp, ex bot. gdns mix	PH
Paeonia hybridum	B,SG
Paeonia kartalinika	PH
Paeonia lactiflora	AP,B,G,PH,SA,SG
Paeonia lactiflora hyb	JE,PH
Paeonia lagodechiana	PH

Paeonia lutea see delavayi	
Paeonia mascula	AP,B,CG,G,JE,LG,SC,SG
Paeonia mascula ssp arietina	CG,PH,SC,SG
Paeonia mascula ssp mascula	PM
Paeonia mascula ssp russoi	PH
Paeonia mascula ssp triternata	AP,CG,PH,SC
Paeonia mlokosewitschii	AP,B,C,CG,G,JE,PH,SC, SG
Paeonia moutan	SA
Paeonia obovata	AP,B,G,PH,SA
Paeonia officinalis	AP,B,C,CG,G,PH,SA,SC, SG
Paeonia officinalis ssp banatica	B,CG,JE,SG
Paeonia officinalis ssp humilis	AP,SC,SG
Paeonia officinalis ssp villosa	CG
Paeonia oreogoton	PH
Paeonia peregrina	AP,B,CG,G,JE,PH,SA, SC,SG
Paeonia ruprectii	PH
Paeonia 'Special Border Mix'	T
Paeonia suffruticosa	B,G,PH,SC
Paeonia tenuifolia	B,CG,G,JE,PH,SC,SG
Paeonia tenuifolia ssp biebersteiniana	PH
Paeonia tenuifolia ssp lithophila	PH
Paeonia tomentosa	PH,SG
Paeonia veitchii	AP,B,CG,G,JE,PH,SA, SC,SG
Paeonia veitchii alba	PH
Paeonia veitchii v woodwardii	AP,G,SC,SG
Paeonia wittmanniana macrophylla	PH
Paeonia wittmanniana nudicarpa	PH,SG
Palafoxia hookerana	B
Palisota barteri	CG
Palisota bracteosa	SG
Paliurus spina-christi	B,C,SA
Palura paniculata	B
Pamburus missionis	B
Panax ginseng	B,SA
Panax ginseng (st)	JE,SA
Panax japonicus	B
Panax quinquefolius	B,CG
Pancratium maritimum	B,C,CG,T
Pancratium maritimum Tunisia	MN
Pancratium tenuifolium	B
Panda oleosa	B
Pandanus aquaticus	B,O
Pandanus basedowii	B,O
Pandanus furcatus	B,O
Pandanus montana	B,O
Pandanus spiralis	B,O,SA
Pandanus tectorius	B
Pandanus utilis	B
Pandanus vandermeerchii	B
Pandorea doratoxylon	SH
Pandorea jasminoides	AP,AU,B,C,HA,O,SA,SC, SE,SH,T
Pandorea pandorana	AP,AU,B,C,HA,O,SA,SC, SH
Pandorea pandorana v doratoxylon	B
Panicum antidotale	B
Panicum capillare	B
Panicum coloratum 'Bambatsi'	B
Panicum coloratum v makarikariense	B
Panicum decompositum	B,HA
Panicum hamil	B
Panicum maximum 'Colonaio'	B

PANICUM

Panicum maximum v trichoglume	B
Panicum miliaceum	I,SG
Panicum miliaceum 'Violaceum'	B,BS,C,SU,T,V
Panicum psilopodium	B
Panicum ruderale	B
Panicum sonorum 'Guarijio'	B
Panicum turgidum	B
Panicum virgatum	AP,B,NT,PR,SA
Panicum virgatum red hyb	JE,SA
Papaver aculeatum	B,SI
Papaver albo roseum	AP,SC,SG
Papaver alpinum	AP,B,BD,BS,C,CL,G,I,J,
	JE,L,S,SA,SC,SG,T,V
Papaver alpinum ssp kerneri	CG
Papaver alpinum ssp sendteri	CG
Papaver anomalum	AP,B,JE,RS
Papaver anomalum 'Album'	AP,B,G,T
Papaver argemone	B,C,CG
Papaver atlanticum	AP,B,C,G,JE,SA,SC,SG
Papaver atlanticum dbl form	AP,C
Papaver atlanticum 'Semi-pl'	B
Papaver bracteatum	AP,B,G,SC,T
Papaver burseri	AP,B,CG,G,I,JE,SC
Papaver carmeli	B
Papaver commutatum	AP,B,C,D,J,KS,LG,P,PM,
	SC,SE,T,V,W
Papaver 'Danebrog Laced'	T
Papaver degenii	AP,T
Papaver dubium	B,C,CG,F,G,LA,SG
Papaver ecoanense	T
Papaver 'Eighth Wonder'	SE
Papaver fauriei	AP,C,CC,G,SC,SG
Papaver fauriei 'Pacino'	AP,BS,C,F,FH,JE
Papaver heldreichii	B,C,SC,T
Papaver hybridum	CG
Papaver laciniatum 'Carmine'	B
Papaver laciniatum 'Crimson'	B,C,T
Papaver laciniatum fimbriatum	W
Papaver laciniatum fl pl	JE
Papaver laciniatum 'Fluffy Ruffles' mix	C,KS
Papaver laciniatum 'Lilac'	B
Papaver laciniatum 'Pink'	B,T
Papaver laciniatum 'Pink' dark	W
Papaver laciniatum 'Pink' dbl	W
Papaver laciniatum 'Rose'	B,T
Papaver laciniatum 'Salmon'	B,T
Papaver laciniatum 'White Swansdown'	B,C,T
Papaver 'Ladybird Hybrids'	P
Papaver lapponicum	AP,SC,SG
Papaver lateritium	AP,C,G
Papaver lateritium 'Fl.Pl.'	B
Papaver miyabeanum of gnds see fauriei	
Papaver nudicaule 'Artists Glory'	BS
Papaver nudicaule 'Aurora Borealis'	B
Papaver nudicaule 'Ballerina mix'	J,V
Papaver nudicaule deluxe mix	JE
Papaver nud. 'Sunbeam Art Shades'	D
Papaver nudicaule dwarf	F,SA
Papaver nudicaule 'Excelsior'	B
Papaver nud. f1 'Champagne Bubbles'	AP,B,BD,BS,C,CL,KS,U
Papaver nud. f1 hyb 'Summer Breeze'	B,BD,CL,D,J,S,YA
Papaver nudicaule f1 'Illumination'	C
Papaver nudicaule f1 'Matador'	C
Papaver nudicaule f2 'Wind Song' mix	B
Papaver nudicaule f2 'Windsong'	JE,SA
Papaver nudicaule 'Garden Gnome'	BS,C,CL,HH,JE,L,T

Papaver nudicaule 'Giant Coonara Mix'	U
Papaver nudicaule 'Giganteum'	SA,ST
Papaver nudicaule 'Giganteum Matador'	B,JE
Papaver nudicaule hybridum	CG
Papaver nudicaule 'Kelmscott Giants'	BS
Papaver nudicaule 'Lge Fl Special'	S
Papaver nudicaule 'Meadow Pastels'	B,C,JE
Papaver nudicaule of gdns	AP,AV,B,CC,CO,G,KI,SC,
	SG,VH
Papaver nudicaule 'Oregon Rainbows'	B,T
Papaver nudicaule 'Pacino'	B,CL,HH
Papaver nudicaule 'Partyfun'	B,C,CL,JE
Papaver nudicaule 'Red Sails'	B,D,F,SE,T,U,V
Papaver nudicaule 'Rubro Aurantiacum'	SG
Papaver nudicaule 'Ruffled Chief'	R
Papaver nudicaule 'San Remo'	B,DT,JE,SA
Papaver nudicaule 'Wonderland' mix	C,CO,JE,KI,T
Papaver nudicaule 'Wonderland Orange'	B,JE
Papaver nudicaule 'Wonderland Pink'	B,JE
Papaver nudicaule 'Wonderland White'	B,JE
Papaver nudicaule 'Wonderland Yellow'	B,JE
Papaver oreophilum	CG
Papaver orientale	AP,CG,G,KI,ST,TU,W
Papaver orientale 'Allegro'	BD,BS,CL,SA,T,V
Papaver orientale 'Allegro Vivace'	U
Papaver orientale 'Beauty Of Livermere'	B,BS,JE,SU
Papaver orientale 'Benary's Special' mix	C,KS
Papaver orientale 'Border Vars Mix'	T
Papaver orientale 'Brilliant'	B,F,JE,SA,V
Papaver orientale 'Carneum'	B,JE,SA
Papaver orientale fl.pl.'Red Shades'	B,JE
Papaver orientale 'Harenstraum'	JE
Papaver orientale mix	F,P,PM,S,SG
Papaver orientale 'Nana Allegro'	B,J,JE,L
Papaver orientale 'New Hybrids'	B,KI
Papaver orientale 'Pizzicato'	B,BD,BS,C,CL,D,DT,F,
	JE,KS,M,O,S,SA,T,U,V,
	YA
Papaver orientale 'Prince of Orange'	SA
Papaver o. 'Princess Victoria Louise'	B,JE,KS,SA
Papaver orientale 'Queen Alexandra'	B,JE,SA
Papaver orientale 'Royal Wedding'	JE
Papaver paeony	BS,F,S,TU
Papaver paeony 'Flemish Antique'	F
Papaver paeony 'Guinness'	F
Papaver paeony 'Oasis'	B,C
Papaver paeony 'Paeony Black'	B,C,DT,KS,SE,T,V
Papaver paeony 'Paeony' mix	T,U
Papaver paeony 'Paeony Pink Chiffon'	C
Papaver paeony 'Paeony' s-c	F,KS,T
Papaver paeony 'Paeony White Cloud'	B,KS,SE,T
Papaver paeony 'Taffeta'	D
Papaver persicum	SG
Papaver pilosum	AP,B,C,F,G,JE,SA,SC,SG
Papaver pilosum 'Orange Crepe'	KS
Papaver radicatum	AP,B,C,G,JE,SC,SG
Papaver radicatum pink form	AP,C
Papaver radicatum white form	C
Papaver rhaeticum	AP,B,C,CG,G,JE,SA,SC
Papaver rhoeas	AP,B,CO,E,FH,G,HW,LA,
	SC,SG,TU,V,W
Papaver rhoeas 'American Legion'	B
Papaver rhoeas 'Angel Wings'	B,F,KS
Papaver rhoeas 'Angels Choir'	BD,T
Papaver rhoeas 'Cedric Morris'	AP,RS
Papaver rhoeas 'Double Mix'	C,J,V

PAPAVER

Papaver rhoeas 'Fairy Wings'	J
Papaver rhoeas 'Mother of Pearl'	SE,T,V,VH
Papaver rhoeas selected single mix	F,S
Papaver rhoeas 'Shirley'	B,BD,BS,CO,DT,F,J,KI, L,ST,SU,T,V
Papaver rupifragum	AP,B,C,CG,JE,P,RS,SA, SC,SG,T,V
Papaver rupifragum fl pl	AP,C
Papaver schinzianum	SG
Papaver sendtneri	AP,B,C,G,JE,SC
Papaver somniferum	AP,B,CG,FH,G,I,KI,L,P, SG,ST,W
Papaver somniferum 'Breadseed'	B
Papaver somniferum 'Danish Flag'	B,C,F,S,SE,V
Papaver somniferum 'Double Pink'	CG
Papaver somniferum 'Double Purple'	B
Papaver somniferum 'Double Scarlet'	B
Papaver somniferum 'Giganteum'	B,BD,BS
Papaver somniferum 'Hen & Chickens'	B,BD,BS,C,KS,SE,T
Papaver somniferum 'Igor'	NS
Papaver somniferum 'Lilac Single'	B
Papaver somniferum 'Maximum'	B,C,KS
Papaver somniferum 'Minimum'	B,C,KS
Papaver somniferum mix	CG
Papaver somniferum 'Oase'	C
Papaver somniferum 'Pepperbox'	B
Papaver somniferum 'Raj Red'	B
Papaver somniferum 'Single White'	B
Papaver somniferum 'White Cloud'	BS,C,KI
Papaver s. 'White Persian Breadseed'	B
Papaver sp, forms & cult	B,C
Papaver special offer	C
Papaver spicatum spicatum	SG
Papaver subpiriforme	B
Papaver syriacus	B
Papaver triniifolium	AP,B,C,SC
Papaver 'Victoria Cross'	DT
Papaver x hybridum f1 'Summer Blaze'	F
Pappea capensis	B
Paradisea liliastrum	AP,B,C,G,MN,RS,SA,SC, T
Paradisea liliastrum 'Major'	JE
Paradisea lusitanicum	AP,B,C,G,JE,P,SC
Paragonia pyramidata	B
Parahebe canescens	SS
Parahebe catarractae	AP,SG,SS
Parahebe decora	AP,B,CC,SA,SC,SS
Parahebe derwentiana	AU
Parahebe linifolia	AP,B,SC,SS
Parahebe lyallii	AP,B,CC,SS
Parahebe 'Mervyn'	FH
Parahebe perfoliata	AU,AP,B,P
Parajubaea torallyi	B
Paranomus bracteolaris	B,SI
Paranomus reflexus	B,O
Paranomus spicatus	B,SI
Paraquilegia anemonoides CNW522	X
Pararchidendron pruinosa	AU
Parentucellia viscosa	B
Parinari excelsa	B
Paris polyphylla	AP,B,SG
Paris quadrifolia	AP,B,C,G,SC
Parkia africana	B
Parkia biglandulosa	B,CG,SA
Parkia biglobosa	B
Parkia pedunculata	B

Parkinsonia aculeata	B,C,HA,SA
Parkinsonia africana	B,SI
Parkinsonia florida	B
Parmentiera aculeata	B
Parmentiera cereifera	B
Parmentiera edulis	B
Parnassia nubicola	B
Parnassia palustris	B,C,FH,JE,SC,SG
Parnassia sp	CC,SG
Parochetus africana	AP,LG
Parodia acutus	B,Y
Parodia agnetae	B,Y
Parodia agnetae v aureispinus	B
Parodia allosiphon	B
Parodia arachnites	Y
Parodia arechavaletai	Y
Parodia arechavaletai v aureus	B,Y
Parodia arechavaletai v limiticola	B,Y
Parodia arnostianus	Y
Parodia aureicentra	B
Parodia aureispina	B,CH,GC,Y
Parodia aurisetus	B,Y
Parodia aurisetus v longispinus	B
Parodia betaniana	B
Parodia blaauwianus	B,Y
Parodia bommeljei	B
Parodia brevihamatus f conjugens	B
Parodia buenekeri	B
Parodia buenekeri v conjugens	B
Parodia buenekeri v intermedia	B
Parodia buiningii	B,Y
Parodia caespitosus	B
Parodia camargensis	B,BC,CH,Y
Parodia camargensis v castanea	B
Parodia campestrae	B
Parodia caraparina	B
Parodia cardenasii	B,SG
Parodia cardenasii v applanata	B
Parodia carrerana	B,Y
Parodia catamarcensis	Y
Parodia catamarcensis v rubriflorens	B
Parodia catarinensis	B
Parodia cephalophora	Y
Parodia chrysacanthios	B,CH,Y
Parodia chrysocomus v rubrispinus	B
Parodia claviceps	B,CH,Y
Parodia cobrensis	B
Parodia comarapana	B,BC
Parodia comosa	Y
Parodia concinna	B,Y
Parodia concinna f tolomban	B
Parodia concinna v brevispinus	Y
Parodia concinna v cunarpiruensis	Y
Parodia concinna v flavispinus	Y
Parodia concinna v joadii	B
Parodia concinna v parviflorum	Y
Parodia concinna v piriapolisensis	B
Parodia crassigibbus	B,BC
Parodia culpinensis	B
Parodia dextrohamata	BC
Parodia dichroantha	B
Parodia eremiticus	B,Y
Parodia erinacea	B,Y
Parodia erubescens	Y
Parodia erythracanthus	Y
Parodia erythrantha	B

PARODIA

Parodia escayechensis	B,YB
Parodia eugeniae	B,Y
Parodia faustiana	B
Parodia ferrugineus	Y
Parodia floricomus	B
Parodia floricomus Rivera	Y
Parodia floricomus v flavispinus	B
Parodia floricomus v rubrispinus	B,BC,Y
Parodia floricomus v spinosissimus	Y
Parodia floricomus v velenovsky	B,Y
Parodia fricii	Y
Parodia fuscus	Y
Parodia gibbulosa	B
Parodia glaucinus	B
Parodia glaucinus v depressus	B,BC
Parodia glaucinus v gracilis	B
Parodia glischrocarpa	B
Parodia gracilis	B,Y
Parodia graessneri	B
Parodia graessneri v albisetus	B
Parodia graessneri v flaviflorus	B
Parodia grandis	Y
Parodia grossei	B,Y
Parodia haselbergii	B,CH
Parodia hausteiniana	B
Parodia herteri	B,Y
Parodia horstii	B,BC,Y
Parodia idiosa	B
Parodia incomptus	B,Y
Parodia intermedius	Y
Parodia koehresiana	B
Parodia kovaricii	Y
Parodia laetivirens	B
Parodia lecorensis v longispina	B
Parodia lecoriensis	B
Parodia leninghausii	B,CH,Y
Parodia leprosorum	Y
Parodia linkii	B
Parodia linkii v buenekeri	B
Parodia linkii v guaibensis	Y
Parodia maassii	B,Y
Parodia maassii v albescens	B,Y
Parodia maassii v intermedia	B,Y
Parodia maassii v multispina	B,Y
Parodia maassii v rectispina	Y
Parodia macroacanthus	B,Y
Parodia magnifica	B,Y
Parodia mairanana	B,GC,Y
Parodia mammulosa	B,CH,Y
Parodia mammulosa 'Lemon Ball'	T
Parodia mammulosa v albispinus	B
Parodia mammulosa v arbolitoensis	B
Parodia mammulosa v brasiliensis	B,Y
Parodia mammulosa v curtinensis	B
Parodia mammulosa v gracilior	Y
Parodia mammulosa v masollerensis	B,Y
Parodia mammulosa v meldiensis	Y
Parodia mammulosa v multiflorus	B
Parodia mammulosa v nigrispinus	B
Parodia mammulosa v pampeanus	B
Parodia mammulosa v paucicostatus	Y
Parodia mammulosa v rubrispinus	B,Y
Parodia mammulosa v tureczakianus	BC
Parodia mannii	Y
Parodia maxima	B,Y
Parodia megalanthus	B,Y

Parodia megapotamicus	B
Parodia megapotamicus v crucicentrus	B
Parodia mercedesiana	B
Parodia microsperma	B,SG,Y
Parodia microsperma v cafayatensis	B
Parodia microthele	B
Parodia militaris	B
Parodia minimus	B,Y
Parodia muegelianus	B,Y
Parodia mueller-melchersii	B
Parodia mueller-melchersii v longispinus	B
Parodia mueller-moelleri	B,Y
Parodia multicostata	B,Y
Parodia muricatus	B,Y
Parodia mutabilis	D,Y
Parodia mutabilis v ferruginea	B
Parodia neoarechavaletai v kovarikii	B
Parodia neohorstii W34	Y
Parodia nivosa	B,Y
Parodia notabilis	Y
Parodia obtusa	B
Parodia ocampoi	Y
Parodia orthacanthus	B
Parodia otaviana	B
Parodia ottonis	B,CH,Y
Parodia ottonis v blossfeldianus	B
Parodia ottonis v janousekianus	B
Parodia ottonis v minasensis	Y
Parodia ottonis v nugualensis	Y
Parodia ottonis v paraguayensis	B,Y
Parodia ottonis v rufispinus	B
Parodia ottonis v schuldtii	B
Parodia ottonis v tenuispinus	B
Parodia ottonis v tortuosus	B
Parodia ottonis v vencluianus	B
Parodia otuyensis	B
Parodia oxycostatus	B
Parodia paraguyensis	CH
Parodia pauciareolatus	B
Parodia paulus	Y
Parodia penicillata	B,Y
Parodia penicillata v nivosa	B,Y
Parodia potosina	B,Y
Parodia procera	B
Parodia pseudorutilans	B
Parodia pseudostuemeri	B
Parodia punae	B
Parodia purpureus v meugelianus	B
Parodia rauschii	B,Y
Parodia rechensis	B,Y
Parodia riojensis	B
Parodia ritteri	B
Parodia roseoluteus	B,Y
Parodia rubida	B,Y
Parodia rubistaminea	B
Parodia rubricostata	Y
Parodia rubriflora	B,Y
Parodia rubrispina	B
Parodia rutilans	B,Y
Parodia saint pieana	Y
Parodia sanagasta	Y
Parodia sanguiniflora	B,CH,GC,Y
Parodia schlosseri	B
Parodia schuetziana	B
Parodia schumannianus	B,Y
Parodia schumannianus v brevispinus	Y

PARODIA

Parodia schwebsiana	B
Parodia schwebsiana v applanata	B
Parodia scopa	B,CH,Y
Parodia scopa v brunispinus	B
Parodia scopa v daenikerianus	Y
Parodia scopa v elachisanthus	Y
Parodia scopa v erythinus	B
Parodia scopa v glauserianus	B
Parodia scopa v longispinus	Y
Parodia scopa v murielii	Y
Parodia scopaoides	B
Parodia securituberculatus	B
Parodia sellowii	B
Parodia setosa	B
Parodia sotomayorensis	B
Parodia sp mix	C,CH,Y
Parodia splendens	Y
Parodia steumeri	B,Y
Parodia subterranea	B,BC
Parodia succineus	B
Parodia succineus v albispinus	B,Y
Parodia sulphureus	B
Parodia suprema	B
Parodia tabularis	B,Y
Parodia tabularis v nigrispinus	Y
Parodia tabularis v splendens	Y
Parodia tarabucina	B
Parodia taratensis	Y
Parodia tephracantha	Y
Parodia tilcarensis	B
Parodia tredecimcostata	B
Parodia uebelmanniana	B,BC,CH,Y
Parodia uebelmannianus v flaviflorus	B
Parodia vanvlietii	B,Y
Parodia vanvlietii v gracilior	B,Y
Parodia vanvlietii v rubrispinus	B
Parodia variicolor	B,Y
Parodia veenianus	B,Y
Parodia veerbekianus	Y
Parodia vorwerkiana	B,Y
Parodia warasii	B,BC,CH,Y
Parodia weberiana	B
Parodia werdermannianus	B,Y
Parodia winkleri	B
Parodia yamparaezi	B,Y
Parodia yunpiensis	Y
Paronychia argentea	B,FH
Paronychia fastigiata	B
Paronychia kapela	AP,JE,SC
Paronychia kapela ssp serpyllifolia	B,C
Parrotia persica	B,SA
Parrotiopsis jacquemontiana	B,CG,G,SA
Parsonsia capsularis	B,SW
Parsonsia columella	B
Parsonsia eucalyptophylla	HA
Parsonsia heterophylla	B,C,SW
Parsonsia multiflora	B
Parsonsia praemorsa	B
Parsonsia schrankii	B
Parsonsia sepium	B
Parsonsia spinifex	B
Parsonsia ureus	B
Parsonsia ventricosa	SA
Parsonsia zeylanica	B
Parthenium integrifolium	B,C,CP,JE,PR
Parthenocissus henryae	B,SA

Parthenocissus quinquefolia	A,C,F,SA
Parthenocissus tricuspidata	B,C,SA,V
Parthenocissus tricuspidita 'Veitchii'	BS,KI,S,SA
Paspalum ciliatifolium	PR
Paspalum dilatatum	B,HA
Paspalum notatum	B
Paspalum plicatulum 'Bryan'	B
Paspalum plicatulum 'Rodd's Bay'	B
Paspalum wettsteinii	B
Passerina falcifolia	B,SI
Passerina vulgaris	B,SI
Passiflora actinia	B
Passiflora adenopoda	B
Passiflora 'Adularia'	B,NP,T
Passiflora alata	B,C,NP,SA,T
Passiflora alata 'Shannon'	NP
Passiflora 'Amethyst'	NP
Passiflora amethystina	B
Passiflora ampullacea	B,C,T
Passiflora anfracta	B
Passiflora antioquiensis	B,T
Passiflora aurantia	B,NP
Passiflora auriculata	B,NP
Passiflora biflora	B,NP
Passiflora bryonoides	CG
Passiflora caerulea	w.a.
Passiflora caerulea 'Constance Elliott'	B,NP
Passiflora capsularis	B,C,NP,SG,T
Passiflora cinnabarina	B,C,O,SA
Passiflora citrina	B,NP
Passiflora coccinea	B,NP,SA,SE,T,V
Passiflora coriacea	B,NP
Passiflora coriacea cw Costa Rica	NP
Passiflora cuneata	B,NP
Passiflora deciasneana	NP
Passiflora edulis	B,BS,C,HA,NP,O,SA,T,V
Passiflora edulis f flavicarpa	B,NP
Passiflora edulis f flavicarpa 'Golden Giant'	B
Passiflora edulis 'Hawaiian Gold'	B,HA
Passiflora edulis yellow	C
Passiflora eichleriana	CG
Passiflora filipes	NP
Passiflora flavicarpa	SA
Passiflora foetida	B,C,CG,SA
Passiflora foetida hirsuta	NP
Passiflora foetida hirsutissima	NP
Passiflora foetida orinocensis	NP
Passiflora foetida v galapagensis	B
Passiflora gibertii	B,NP
Passiflora gracilis	B,C,NP,T
Passiflora guatemalensis	B,NP
Passiflora hahnii	B,C
Passiflora helleri	B
Passiflora herbertiana	B,C,NP,T
Passiflora incarnata	B,CG,NP,T
Passiflora indica	B
Passiflora involucrata	B
Passiflora kalbreyerii	B,NP
Passiflora laurifolia	B,NP,SA
Passiflora ligularis	B,C,NP,SA,T
Passiflora lindeniana	B,C,NP
Passiflora lutea	B
Passiflora macrophyllum	B
Passiflora maliformis	B,C,NP,SA,T
Passiflora manicata	B,C,NP
Passiflora mixta	B,C,NP

PASSIFLORA

Passiflora mollissima	B,C,HA,O,SA,SE,T,V	Pedalium murex	B
Passiflora morifolia	B,C,NP,SA,T	Peddiea africana	B
Passiflora 'Norfolk'	B	Pedicularis bracteata v flavida	B
Passiflora oerstedii	B,C,NP	Pedicularis canadensis	PR
Passiflora organensis marmorata hyb	NP	Pedicularis foliosa	C
Passiflora pallens	NP	Pedicularis groenlandica	B,C
Passiflora 'Passion Fruits of The World'	T	Pedicularis kerneri	CG
Passiflora phoenicia hyb	NP	Pedicularis lanceolata	B,PR
Passiflora platyloba	B,C,NP	Pedicularis palustris	B
Passiflora puncata hyb	NP	Pedicularis sudetica	SG
Passiflora quadrangularis	B,C,NP,O,SA,T,V	Pedilanthus macrocarpus	B
Passiflora quadrangularis v macrocarpa	B	Pedilanthus tithymaloides	SG
Passiflora quadrifolia	NP	Pediocactus bradyi	B
Passiflora racemosa	B,NP	Pediocactus despainii	B
Passiflora rubra	B,C,NP	Pediocactus knowltonii	B
Passiflora rubra pink fruited	NP	Pediocactus paradinei	B
Passiflora sanguinolenta	B,NP	Pediocactus peeblesianus	B
Passiflora seemanii	B,NP,SA	Pediocactus peeblesianus v fickeisenii	B
Passiflora serratifolia	B,NP	Pediocactus peebles. v fickeisenii 'Maia'	B
Passiflora serrulata	NP	Pediocactus simpsonii	B
Passiflora sp mix	C,RE,T	Pediocactus simpsonii v minor	B
Passiflora suberosa	B,C,CG,NP	Pediocactus simpsonii v nigrispinus	B
Passiflora subpeltata	B,C,NP,SA,SE,T	Pediocactus simpsonii v robustior	B
Passiflora 'Sunburst'	B	Pediocactus winkleri	B
Passiflora tridactylites	NP	Peganum harmala	B,C,CP
Passiflora violacea	B	Pegolettia baccharidifolia	B
Passiflora vitifolia	B,C,T	Pelargonium abrotanifolium	B
Passiflora vitifolia 'Sacralet Flame'	NP	Pelargonium acetosum	B,G,SI
Passiflora warmingii	CG	Pelargonium acraeum	B
Passiflora x allardii	B	Pelargonium album	B
Passiflora x exoniensis	CG	Pelargonium alchemilloides	B,G,I,SC,SI
Passiflora x hyb	B	Pelargonium alternans	B,SI
Passiflora x kewensis	B	Pelargonium andlicheranium	PM
Passiflora x piresii	NP	Pelargonium anethifolium	B,SI
Passiflora zamorana	B,C	Pelargonium antidysentericum	SI
Pastinaca sativa	B,C,LA,SG	Pelargonium appendiculatum	B
Pastinaca sativa 'Hollow Crown'	B	Pelargonium aridum	B,CH,G,SI,Y
Pastinaca sativa 'Oatney'	B	Pelargonium auritum	B,SI
Pastinaca sativa ssp pratensis	B	Pelargonium auritum v auritum	MN
Pastinaca sativa ssp sylvestris	SG	Pelargonium australe	AP,B,C,G,MN,SC,SI
Patersonia fragilis	HA	Pelargonium barklyi	AP,B,MN
Patersonia glabrata	B,HA	Pelargonium betulinum purple	AP,B,C,SI
Patersonia juncea	B	Pelargonium betulinum white	SI
Patersonia longifolia	B	Pelargonium bowkeri	SI
Patersonia occidentalis	AU,B,C,SA	Pelargonium brevipetalum	B
Patersonia sericea	B,HA	Pelargonium caffrum	B,SI
Patersonia umbrosa	B,SA	Pelargonium candicans	B,SI
Patersonia umbrosa 'Xanthina'	B	Pelargonium capitatum	AP,AU,B,C,G,SI
Patrinia gibbosa	C,G,JE	Pelargonium carnosum	B,CH,GC,MN,Y
Patrinia intermedia	SG	Pelargonium caucalif. v convolvulifolium	B,SI
Patrinia scabiosifolia	JE,SG	Pelargonium caylae	B
Patrinia scabiosifolia MW250R	X	Pelargonium ceratophyllum	B
Paulownia elongata	B,C,SA	Pelargonium chamaedrifolium	AP,B,SC,SI
Paulownia fortunei	B,N,SA	Pelargonium citronellum	B,C,SI
Paulownia sp	SG	Pelargonium columbinum	B,SI
Paulownia tomentosa	B,C,CG,G,HA,N,SA,T	Pelargonium cordifolium	B,C,SI
Pavetta lanceolata	B,SI	Pelargonium coronopifolium	SI
Pavetta revoluta	SI	Pelargonium cortusifolium	B
Pavetta zeyheri	B	Pelargonium 'Country Garden'	CO,KI,Sm,ST
Pavonia columella	SI	Pelargonium crassicaule	B
Pavonia hastata	B,SA	Pelargonium crithmifolium	B,MN
Pavonia missionum	B	Pelargonium cucullatum	C
Pavonia praemorsa	B,C,SI	Pelargonium cucullatum ssp cucullatum	SI
Pavonia schrankii	B	Pelargonium cucullatum ssp strigifolium	B,SI
Pavonia spinifex	B	Pelargonium cucullatum ssp tabulare	B,SI
Pavonia zeylanica	B	Pelargonium dasyphyllum	B,G,SI

PELARGONIUM

Pelargonium denticulatum	B,G,SI
Pelargonium desertorum	B
Pelargonium dichondrifolium	B,SI
Pelargonium dipetalum	B
Pelargonium dolomiticum	B,SI
Pelargonium echinatum	B,SI
Pelargonium elongatum	B,SI
Pelargonium endlicherianum	G,JE
Pelargonium engleranum	B,SI
Pelargonium exhibens	B,SI
Pelargonium exstipulatum	B,SI
Pelargonium f1 'Atlanta' s-c, mix	BS
Pelargonium f1 'Avanti' mix	BS,KI,T
Pelargonium f1 'Avanti' s-c	BS,T,YA
Pelargonium f1 'Bedding Mix'	DT
Pelargonium f1 'Breakaway Red'	B,BD,BS,CL,D,DT,F,S
Pelargonium f1 'Breakaway Red' p.s	S
Pelargonium f1 'Breakaway Salmon'	B,BD,BS,CL,DT,S,T
Pelargonium f1 'Cascade Orange'	U
Pelargonium f1 'Cascade Salmon'	BS,U
Pelargonium f1 'Century' mix	BS,CL,F
Pelargonium f1 'Century' s-c	BS,B,CL,F
Pelargonium f1 'Century' s-c, mix	BS
Pelargonium f1 'Challenge'	BS,J
Pelargonium f1 'Cheerio Cherry'	BS,U
Pelargonium f1 'Cheerio Series' s-c, mix	BS,YA
Pelargonium f1 'Cherie'	BS,J
Pelargonium f1 'Cherry Diamond'	BS
Pelargonium f1 'Classic Scarlet'	T
Pelargonium f1 'Container Mix'	DT
Pelargonium f1 'Elite' mix	CL
Pelargonium f1 'Elite Red'	B,BD,BS,CL,J,L
Pelargonium f1 'Elite' s-c	BS,CL,J
Pelargonium f1 'Eyes Right'	BS,T
Pelargonium f1 'Freckles'	B
Pelargonium f1 'Gala'	J
Pelargonium f1 'Gala White'	U
Pelargonium f1 'Hollywood Star'	B,BD,BS,J,KI,T,U,YA
Pelargonium f1 'Horizon Deep Scarlet'	S
Pelargonium f1 'Horizon' mix	DT,L
Pelargonium f1 'Horizon Series' s-c	YA
Pelargonium f1 'Ivy Leaved Mix'	U
Pelargonium f1 'L'Amour' mix	T
Pelargonium f1 'Leo'	U
Pelargonium f1 'Maverick' mix	CL
Pelargonium f1 'Maverick' s-c	CL
Pelargonium f1 'Maverick Star'	BD,BS,CL,S,SE
Pelargonium f1 'Multibloom Bright Rose'	B,BS,C,CL,U
Pelargonium f1 'Multibloom Collection'	M,U
Pelargonium f1 'Multibloom Lavender'	B,BS,CL
Pelargonium f1 'Multibloom' mix	BS,C,CL,DT,F,M,SE,T,U
Pelargonium f1 'Multibloom Pink'	B,BS,C,CL
Pelargonium f1 'Multibloom Red'	B,BS,CL
Pelargonium f1 'Multibloom Salmon'	B,BS,C,CL,DT,M,T
Pelargonium f1 'Multibloom Scarlet'	B,BS,C,CL,DT,M
Pelargonium f1 'Multibloom Scarlet Eye'	B,BS,C,CL
Pelargonium f1 'Multibloom White'	B,BS,C,CL,M
Pelargonium f1 'Musical Mix'	BS
Pelargonium f1 'Orange Appeal'	B,BD,BS,CL,D,DT,F,KI, L,O,S,U
Pelargonium f1 'Orange Blaze'	J
Pelargonium f1 'Orbit' mix	BS,DT,L
Pelargonium f1 'Orbit' s-c	B,BS,T
Pelargonium f1 'Orbit White'	B,BS,S
Pelargonium f1 'Playboy Speckles' s-c	T
Pelargonium f1 'Pulsar Series' mix	BS
Pelargonium f1 'Pulsar Series' s-c	BS,T
Pelargonium f1 'Raspberry Ripple'	BS,CL,DT,F,L,SE,T,U
Pelargonium f1 'Sensation' mix	BS,D,J,L,KI,S,SE,U
Pelargonium f1 'Sensation' mix supastart	S
Pelargonium f1 'Sensation' s-c	B,L,S,SE
Pelargonium f1 'Sheba'	U
Pelargonium f1 'Signal Orange'	YA
Pelargonium f1 'Softly Spftly' mix	T
Pelargonium f1 'Solo'	YA
Pelargonium f1 'Sprinter' mix	BS,J,M,ST,TU
Pelargonium f1 'Sprinter Series' s-c	BS,KI
Pelargonium f1 'Startel' mix	T
Pelargonium f1 'Summer Showers' ivy lf	B,BD,BS,C,CL,CO,D,DT, F,KI,L,SE,ST,T,TU,VH
Pelargonium f1 'Summer Showers' s-c	CL
Pelargonium f1 'Summertime Lilac'	BS,CL,D,T
Pelargonium f1 'Sundance Orange-scarlet'	B,BS
Pelargonium f1 'Sundance Salmon-rose'	B,BS,SE,T
Pelargonium f1 'Tango Orange'	BS,T
Pelargonium f1 'Tornado Lilac Cadix'	SE,T,U
Pelargonium f1 'Tornado White Felix'	SE,T,U
Pelargonium f1 'Unwins Special Mix'	U
Pelargonium f1 'Venus'	BS,DT,F,U
Pelargonium f1 'Video' mix	BD,CL,D,J,S,SE,U,YA
Pelargonium f1 'Video' mix supastart	S
Pelargonium f1 'Video' s-c	B,BD,BS
Pelargonium f1 'Vogue Appleblossom'	T
Pelargonium f1 'White Star'	BD
Pelargonium f2 'Bambi'	DT,KI,ST,VH
Pelargonium f2 'Border Series' s-c	T
Pelargonium f2 'Cabaret'	BS,CL,L
Pelargonium f2 'Carioca Mix'	T
Pelargonium f2 deep rose	J
Pelargonium f2 deep salmon	J
Pelargonium f2 'Fleuriste'	BS
Pelargonium f2 hyb choice mix	C,DT
Pelargonium f2 'Lucky Break'	BS,J,M,SE,T,U
Pelargonium f2 'Lucky Charm'	BD,R
Pelargonium f2 'Lustre Series' s-c, mix	BS,YA
Pelargonium f2 'Matisse'	F
Pelargonium f2 'Paintbox'	BD,BS,SE,TU
Pelargonium f2 'Pastorale'	D,S
Pelargonium f2 'Picasso'	BS
Pelargonium f2 'Pinto' mix	BS,D
Pelargonium f2 'Pinto' s-c	BS
Pelargonium f2 'Scarlet Border'	VH
Pelargonium f2 scarlet red	J
Pelargonium f2 'Speckles'	BS,J
Pelargonium f2 'Sprite'	CL
Pelargonium f2 'Stardust'	BS
Pelargonium f2 'Torbay Colour Mix'	S
Pelargonium f2 'Torbay Colour Mix' p.s	S
Pelargonium f2 'Vista Pale Salmon'	S
Pelargonium f2 'Vista Red'	D,S
Pelargonium f2 'Vista Rose'	D,S
Pelargonium f2 'Vista Salmon'	D
Pelargonium f2 'Vista White'	D,S
Pelargonium fissifolium	B
Pelargonium 'Florist Strain'	BS
Pelargonium frutetorum	B,SI
Pelargonium fruticosum	B,G,SI
Pelargonium fulgidum	B
Pelargonium gibbosum	B
Pelargonium glutinosum	B,C,SI
Pelargonium grandiflorum	B
Pelargonium graveolens	B,C,SI

PELARGONIUM

Pelargonium greytonense	B,SI		Pelargonium suburb. ssp suburbanum	B,SI
Pelargonium griseum	B		Pelargonium tabulare	B,SI
Pelargonium grossularoides	AP,B,C,SC,SI		Pelargonium tenuicaule	SI
Pelargonium hirtum	B,MN,SI		Pelargonium ternatum	B,SI
Pelargonium hispidum	B,SI		Pelargonium tetragonum	B,SI
Pelargonium hystrix	B,SI		Pelargonium tomentosum	B,G,KS,SI
Pelargonium incrassatum	B,C,SI		Pelargonium tongaense	B,SI
Pelargonium inquinans	B,G		Pelargonium tragacanthoides	B
Pelargonium iocastum	B		Pelargonium transvaalense	B
Pelargonium ionidiflorum	B		Pelargonium tricolor mauve	SI
Pelargonium klinghardtense	B,SI		Pelargonium tricolor white & red	B,SI
Pelargonium laevigatum	B		Pelargonium trifidum	B,SI
Pelargonium lanceolatum	B		Pelargonium triste	B,C,SI
Pelargonium laxum	B		Pelargonium vitifolium	B,C,G,SI
Pelargonium lobatum	B		Pelargonium worcesterae	B
Pelargonium longicaule ssp longicaule	B,SI		Pelargonium 'World's Top 6 Mix'	T
Pelargonium longifolium	B,SI		Pelargonium xerophyton	B
Pelargonium luridum	B,SI		Pelargonium zonale	B,SI
Pelargonium luteolum	B		Pelargonium zonale f1 'Hallo Purple'	C
Pelargonium madagascariense	C		Pelargonium zonale f1 'Hallo White'	C
Pelargonium magenteum	B,SI		Pelargonium z. f1 'Sprinter' 'Hallo' mix	C
Pelargonium minimum	B		Pelecyphora asseliformis	B
Pelargonium mollicomum	B,SI		Pelecyphora pseudopectinatus	CH
Pelargonium multibracteatum	B,SI		Pelecyphora strobiliformis	B
Pelargonium multicaule	C		Peliostemon virgatum	B
Pelargonium multicaule ssp multicaule	B,SI		Pellaea atropurpurea	G,SG
Pelargonium mutans	SI		Pellaea falcata	B,HA
Pelargonium myrrh. v coriandrifolium	B		Pellaea hastata	B
Pelargonium myrrhifolium v myrrhifolium	B,SI		Pellaea rotundifolia	B,SA,SG
Pelargonium namaquense	B,MN,SI		Pellaea viridis	B
Pelargonium nanum	B,SI		Pellaea viridis hastata	SA
Pelargonium oblongatum	B,SI		Peltoboykinia tellimoides	B,JE,SA
Pelargonium odoratissimum	B,SI		Peltoboykinia watanabei	AP,C,I,SC
Pelargonium oreophilum	B		Peltophorum africanum	B,C,SA,SI
Pelargonium ovale	B,SI		Peltophorum dubium	B,CG
Pelargonium ovale ssp veronicifolium	B,SI		Peltophorum ferrugineum	B,HA,O,SA
Pelargonium panduriforme	B,SI		Peltoyne purpurea	B
Pelargonium paniculatum	B		Peniocereus greggii	B
Pelargonium papilionaceum	B,G,SI		Pennisetum alopecuroides	B,C,HA,JE,SA
Pelargonium patulum	B,SI		Pennisetum alopecuroides v viridescens	B,JE,SA
Pelargonium peltatum	B,SI		Pennisetum americanum	B,SG
Pelargonium polycephalum	B		Pennisetum clandestinum 'Whittet'	B
Pelargonium praemorsum	B		Pennisetum flaccidum	B,JE
Pelargonium praemorsum ssp praem.	SI		Pennisetum orientale	B,JE,SC
Pelargonium pseudoglutinosum	B		Pennisetum purpureum	SG
Pelargonium pulchellum	B		Pennisetum setaceum	B,C,SA,V
Pelargonium quercifolium	B,SG,SI		Pennisetum villosum	B,G,SG,V
Pelargonium quinquelobatum	B,G,SC,SI		Penstemon albomarginatus	B,SW
Pelargonium radens	B,C,G,SI		Penstemon alpinus	AP,B,C,CG,HH,JE,SC
Pelargonium radulifolium	B,SI		Penstemon aluviorum	CG
Pelargonium rapaceum	B,SI		Penstemon ambiguus	B,JE,SW
Pelargonium reniforme	B		Penstemon angustifolius	AP,B,C,FH,SC,SW
Pelargonium ribifolium	B		Penstemon antirrhinoides	CG
Pelargonium 'Rosy Sunset'	U		Penstemon aridus	B,G
Pelargonium scabroide	B		Penstemon arizonica	CG
Pelargonium scabrum	B,SI		Penstemon attenuatus	B
Pelargonium semitrilobum	B		Penstemon azureus	AP,B,CG,G,SC,SG
Pelargonium senecioides	B,SI		Penstemon baccharifolius	B,SW
Pelargonium sericifolium	B		Penstemon barbatus	AP,B,BS,G,RH,S,SC,SW,
Pelargonium sidoides	B,G			T
Pelargonium 'South Africa' mix	C		Penstemon barbatus 'Coccineus'	B,C,G,JE,SA
Pelargonium sp	SI		Penstemon barbatus 'Petite Bouquet'	B,BD,BS,DT,F
Pelargonium sp aromatic	SI		Penstemon barbatus praecox nanus	B,C,SA
Pelargonium stipulaceum	B		Penstemon barb. praecox nanus 'Rondo'	JE
Pelargonium sublignosum	B		Penstemon barrettiae	B
Pelargonium suburb. ssp bipinatifidum	B		Penstemon breviflorus	B

PENSTEMON

Penstemon bridgesii	B,SW	Penstemon leonensis	AP,CC
Penstemon caesius	B	Penstemon 'Lge Fl' mix	BD,BS,S
Penstemon californicus	CG	Penstemon linaroides	B,G,SW
Penstemon calycosus	I	Penstemon lyallii	AP,B,C,P,SC,SG,SW
Penstemon campanulatus	AP,CC,CG,G,JE,SA,SC,	Penstemon menziesii	AP,CG,G
	SG,T	Penstemon menziesii menziesii	SG
Penstemon campanulatus chihuahuaensis	B,SW	Penstemon menziesii 'Microphyllus'	RS
Penstemon cardinalis	CG	Penstemon montanus	AP,B,FH,SC,SW
Penstemon cardinalis v regalis	B,SW	Penstemon neomexicanus	B,SW
Penstemon cardwellii	AP,B,C,CG,G,SC	Penstemon newberryi	CG,G,FH,SG
Penstemon centranthifolius	B,CG,SW	Penstemon newberryi f humilior	AP,RS
Penstemon clevelandii	B,SW	Penstemon nitidus	B,SW
Penstemon cobaea	JE,SC	Penstemon nudiflorus	B,SW
Penstemon comarrhenus	B,SW	Penstemon oliganthus	B,SW
Penstemon confertus	AP,CG,FH,JE,SC,SG	Penstemon ophianthus	B,SW
Penstemon crandallii	FH,SC	Penstemon ovatus	AP,B,C,JE,P,SC,SG,T
Penstemon cyananthus	C,CG,SW	Penstemon pachyphyllus	B,SW
Penstemon dasyphyllus	B,SW	Penstemon pallidus	AP,CG,PR,SC
Penstemon deustus	B,C,SW	Penstemon palmeri	AP,B,CC,CG,SA,SW,T
Penstemon digitalis	AP,B,C,G,HW,JE,PR,SA,	Penstemon 'Papal Purple'	AP,C,P
	SC	Penstemon parryi	B,JE,SW
Penstemon digitalis 'Albus'	T	Penstemon PCHA148	P
Penstemon digitalis 'Huskers Red'	AP,B,C,F,G,JE,P,SA,SC,	Penstemon perfoliatus	CG
	SE	Penstemon pinifolius	AP,B,G,JE,SC,SW
Penstemon digitalis x calycosus	CG	Penstemon pinifolius 'Mersea Yellow'	AP,JE
Penstemon douglasii	CG	Penstemon platyphyllus	B,SW
Penstemon 'Dw Salmon Red'	B	Penstemon 'Prize Strain'	DT,L
Penstemon eatonii	B,C,JE,SW	Penstemon procerus	B,C,JE,SG
Penstemon eriantherus	AP,B,SW	Penstemon pseudospectabilis	B,SW
Penstemon fendleri	B,SW	Penstemon pubescens	CG
Penstemon 'Firebird'	B,P	Penstemon pygmaea	CG
Penstemon frutescens	CC	Penstemon 'Rainbow' mix	C
Penstemon fruticosus	AP,B,C,HH,SC,SG	Penstemon ramosus	B,SW
Penstemon 'Garnet'	C,JE	Penstemon rattani	B
Penstemon gentianoides	B	Penstemon richardsonii	AP,B,C,G,JE,SC
Penstemon glaber	AP,B,JE,SC,SW	Penstemon roezlii	SG
Penstemon glaber v alpinus	CG	Penstemon rupicola	AP,FH,SC,SG
Penstemon globosus	B	Penstemon scouleri	AP,B,C,JE
Penstemon gloxinoides 'New Hybs' mix	CL	Penstemon scouleri 'Albus'	AP,JE,P
Penstemon gloxinoides 'Sensation' mix	C,SE	Penstemon secundiflorus	CG
Penstemon gormanii	AP,CG,I,SC,SG	Penstemon 'Sensation' mix	D,T
Penstemon gracilis	B,JE,PR,SG	Penstemon sepalulus	SW
Penstemon grandiflorus	B,PR,SC,T	Penstemon serrulatus	AP,B,C,CG,G,JE,SC,SG
Penstemon grinnellii ssp grinnellii	B	Penstemon smallii	AP,CC,FH,NT
Penstemon grinnellii ssp scrophularoides	B	Penstemon sp	AP,RS,SC,T
Penstemon hartwegii 'Earlibird'	B,T	Penstemon spectabilis	B,SW
Penstemon hartwegii 'Scarlet Queen'	C,DT,F	Penstemon stenophyllus	B,SW
Penstemon hartwegii 'Skyline'	BS,V	Penstemon strictus	AP,B,BS,C,F,JE,KI,SA,
Penstemon heterophyllus	AP,B,CG,G,SC,SW		SC,SG,SW,T
Penstemon heterophyllus 'Blue Gem'	FH,I	Penstemon subglaber	AP,B
Penstemon heterophyllus 'Blue of Zurich'	G,JE,SA,SG	Penstemon subulatus	B,SW
Penstemon heterophyllus 'True Blue'	SE	Penstemon superbus	B,SW
Penstemon hirsutus	AP,B,CG,F,FH,G,JE,P,SC	Penstemon superbus x parryi	B
Penstemon hirsutus 'Pygmaeus'	AP,B,C,G,SC	Penstemon thompsoniae	B,SW
Penstemon hirsutus 'Pygmaeus Atropps'	B,P	Penstemon thurberi	B,SW
Penstemon humilis	AP,B,JE,SC	Penstemon un-named sp	T
Penstemon 'Hyacinth Fl'	AP,F	Penstemon utahensis	B,JE,SA,SC,SW
Penstemon hyb 'Cambridge Mix'	SE,U,V	Penstemon utahensis 'Alba'	B,JE,SA
Penstemon hyb 'Crown'	BS	Penstemon venustus	AP,B,C,CG,SC
Penstemon hyb 'Giant'	BS,CO,KI,ST,SU	Penstemon virgatus ssp arizonicus	AP,B,SC,SW
Penstemon jamesii	AP,B,CG,SG,SW	Penstemon virgatus ssp putus	B,SW
Penstemon kunthii	AP,B,G,SW	Penstemon virgatus ssp virgatus	B,SW
Penstemon labrosus	B,SW	Penstemon watsonii	B,SW
Penstemon laevis	B,SW	Penstemon whippleanus	AP,B,CG,G,JE,SA,SC,
Penstemon laxifolius	B		SW
Penstemon leiophyllus	B,SW	Penstemon wislizenii	B,MA,SW

PENSTEMON

Penstemon x edithae	P
Pentachondra pumila	AU,B,SW
Pentaclethra macrophylla	B
Pentadiplandra brazzeana	B
Pentagonia grandiflora aff	B
Pentapeltis peltigera	B
Pentaphylloides davurica	SG
Pentaphylloides fruticosa	SG
Pentas lanceolata 'New Look'	CL,D
Pentas 'New Look'	C,D
Penthorum sedoides	B,PR,SG
Pentzia grandiflora	KS
Pentzia incana	B,SI
Pentzia pilulifera	B,SI
Pentzia 'Pincushion'	BS,KI,SU
Pentzia sp	SI
Pentzia suffruticosa	B,C
Peperomia maculosa	C
Peperomia pellucida	B
Peperomia retusa	B
Pereskia acutifolia	B
Perezia multiflora	SG
Perezia recurvata	AP,AU,PM
Pergularia daemia	B
Pergularia daemia v daemia	B,SI
Pericallis 'Amigo'	B,BS
Pericallis 'Brilliant'	CL
Pericallis 'Chloe'	CL
Pericallis 'Cindy'	CL,D
Pericallis 'Cupid'	BS
Pericallis 'Daruma'	B
Pericallis 'Dutch Master'	B
Pericallis 'Erfut' dw finest mix	C
Pericallis 'Feltham Star'	B
Pericallis 'Gay Mixed'	V
Pericallis 'Giant Rainbow'	B
Pericallis hybridus 'Dw. British Beauty'	T
Pericallis 'Jubilee'	BD,BS
Pericallis lanata	RS
Pericallis 'Melody Picotee'	SE
Pericallis 'Meteor'	YA
Pericallis 'Moll Strain Imp'	T
Pericallis 'Rasse Moll'	BS
Pericallis 'Royalty'	CL
Pericallis 'Sandor'	L
Pericallis 'Sox Blue'	YA
Pericallis 'Sox Pink'	YA
Pericallis 'Spring Glory'	BS,F,M
Pericallis 'Star Wars'	B,CL,YA
Pericallis 'Starbright'	U
Pericallis 'Starlet' mini mix	C,T
Pericallis 'Supernova'	YA
Pericalymma elliptica	B
Perideridia kelloggii	B
Perideridia parishii	B
Perilla frutescens	B,CP
Perilla frutescens 'Atropurpurea'	B,CP,KI,KS
Perilla frutescens 'Green Cumin'	B
Perilla frutescens 'Macrobiotic'	B
Perilla frutescens v crispa	B,YA
Perilla frutescens v crispa laciniata	C,CL
Periploca graeca	C,CG,SA,T
Perityle incana	B
Perotis indica	B
Perovskia atriplicifolia	B,JE,SA
Persea americana	B

Persicaria bistorta	AP,B,C,JE,SA,SG
Persicaria bistorta 'Superbum'	B
Persicaria bistortoides	AP,B
Persicaria capitata	I
Persicaria capitata 'Afghan'	C,J
Persicaria capitata 'Victory Carpet'	B,BS,D
Persicaria macrophyllum	B
Persicaria milletii	B,JE,SA
Persicaria orientale	B,C
Persicaria virginiana	B
Persicaria virginiana 'Variegatum'	B
Persoonia caleyi	B,O
Persoonia comata	B,O
Persoonia cornifolia	B,O
Persoonia curvifolia	O
Persoonia elliptica	B,O
Persoonia gunnii	B,O
Persoonia laevis	B,HA,O,SA
Persoonia lanceolata	B,O
Persoonia linearis	B,HA,O
Persoonia longifolia	B,O
Persoonia mollis	HA
Persoonia oxycoccoides	HA
Persoonia pinifolia	B,HA,O,SA
Persoonia saccata	B
Persoonia sylvatica	HA
Persoonia teretifolia	B,O
Persoonia tortifolia	B,O
Persoonia virgata	HA
Perymenium strigillosum	B
Petalostemon candidum	JE,SA
Petalostemon purpureus	C,JE,PR,SA
Petalostemon villosum	PR
Petalostigma pubescens	B
Petalostigma quadriloculare	B
Petalostylis labicheoides	B,HA
Petasites albus	CG,G
Petasites frigidus	AP,B
Petasites hybridus	B,JE,SG
Petasites rubellus	SG
Petiveria sp	SG
Petopentia natalensis	B
Petrea volubilis	B,RE,SA
Petrocoptis glaucifolia	AP,B,G,HH,JE,SC
Petrocoptis pyrenaica	AP,B,FH,SC
Petrophile biloba	AU,B,O
Petrophile canescens	AU,B,O
Petrophile carduacea	B
Petrophile divaricata	B,O
Petrophile diversifolia	B,O,SA
Petrophile ericifolia	B
Petrophile fastigiata	B
Petrophile heterophylla	B
Petrophile incurvata	B
Petrophile linearis	B
Petrophile longifolia	B,O
Petrophile macrostachya	B
Petrophile pulchella	B,HA,O
Petrophile scabriuscula	B
Petrophile serruriae	B,O
Petrophile sessilis	B,HA,O,SA
Petrophile shuttleworthiana	B
Petrophile squamata	B
Petrophile striata	B
Petrophile teretifolia	B
Petrophile trifida	B

PETROPHYTUM

Petrophytum caespitosum	AP,B,JE,SC,SW
Petrophytum cinerascens	AP,I
Petrorhagia nanteuillii	B,NS
Petrorhagia prolifera	CG,SG
Petrorhagia saxifraga	AP,B,BS,C,G,FH,I,JE,KI, SA,SC,SG
Petroselinum crispum	B,CP
Petteria ramentacea	B,SA
Petunia axillaris 'Rainmaster'	F
Petunia 'Babylon Pink'	R
Petunia 'Babylon Purple'	R
Petunia 'Bedder Series'	B
Petunia 'California Girl'	CL,S
Petunia 'Cavalcade' mix	BS
Petunia 'Cloud Snow'	B,BS,CL,KI
Petunia 'Coral Satin'	BS
Petunia 'Dw' bedding mix	D
Petunia 'Electra'	BS
Petunia f1 'All Double Fanfare' mix	B,BD
Petunia f1 'Birthday Celebration'	S
Petunia f1 'Blue & White Lace'	U
Petunia f1 'Bouquet' mix	T
Petunia f1 'Brass Band'	BS
Petunia f1 'Buttercream'	SE,U
Petunia f1 'Caprice'	T
Petunia f1 'Cascade' hyb mix	CO,KI,M,Sm
Petunia f1 'Celebrity' mix	BS,FL,SE,YA
Petunia f1 'Celebrity' s-c	BS,DT,F,SE,T,YA
Petunia f1 'Cherry Tart' mix	J
Petunia f1 'Chiffon Morn'	DT,SE,V
Petunia f1 'Cloud Blue'	B,BS,KI
Petunia f1 'Cloud' mix	BS,CL,KI,T
Petunia f1 'Cloud Orchid'	B,BS,CL,KI
Petunia f1 'Cloud Pink'	B,BS,CL,KI
Petunia f1 'Cloud Red'	B,BS,CL,KI
Petunia f1 'Cloud Rose'	B,BS,CL
Petunia f1 'Cloud Salmon'	B,BS,CL,KI
Petunia f1 'Delight' mix	J
Petunia f1 'Devon Cream' mix	SE,U
Petunia f1 'Falcon Blue Imp'	B,BS
Petunia f1 'Falcon Burgundy'	B,BS
Petunia f1 'Falcon Lilac'	B,BS
Petunia f1 'Falcon Mid-blue'	B,BS,S
Petunia f1 'Falcon' mix	BS,S
Petunia f1 'Falcon Pastel Salmon'	S
Petunia f1 'Falcon Pink Morn'	B,BS
Petunia f1 'Falcon Red'	B,BS,S
Petunia f1 'Falcon Red Morn'	B,BS,F,S
Petunia f1 'Falcon Red & White'	B,BS
Petunia f1 'Falcon Rose'	B,BS
Petunia f1 'Falcon Salmon'	B,BS,S
Petunia f1 'Falcon White'	B,BS,S
Petunia f1 'Frost Blue'	S
Petunia f1 'Frost Mix'	F
Petunia f1 'Frost Red'	U
Petunia f1 'Garden Party' mix	J
Petunia f1 'Global Grandiflora'	T
Petunia f1 'Gloriosa Double mix'	DT,YA
Petunia f1 'Glorious' mix	KI
Petunia f1 'Hulahoop Series' mix	BS,DT,L,YA
Petunia f1 'Hulahoop Series' s-c	BS,YA
Petunia f1 'International Flag Flying' mix	T
Petunia f1 'Mirage' mix	BS,DT,F
Petunia f1 'Mirage Series' s-c	BS,D,F,YA
Petunia f1 'Niagara Mix'	D,L
Petunia f1 'Petunia Collection'	U

Petunia f1 'Pink Passion Mix'	U
Petunia f1 'Polo Rose Flare'	U
Petunia f1 'Raspberry Blush'	U
Petunia f1 'Reflections' mix	BS,J,KI
Petunia f1 'Rose Star'	KI
Petunia f1 'Serene' mix	S
Petunia f1 'Starfire' mix	J
Petunia f1 'Strawberry Tart'	D
Petunia f1 'Summer Morn'	D
Petunia f1 'Summer Serenade'	J
Petunia f1 'Summer Stars'	U
Petunia f1 'Summertime Carpet'	F
Petunia f1 'Super Cascade' mix	BD,BS,F,KS,SE,ST,T,TU, U,YA
Petunia f1 'Super Cascade' s-c	B,BS,F,T
Petunia f1 'Super Magic'	BS,KI
Petunia f1 'Traum Series'	V
Petunia f1 'Unwins Fine Mix'	U
Petunia f1 'Victoria Falls Mix'	U
Petunia f1 'Wave Pink'	DT,SE,T,U
Petunia f1 'Wave Pink' p.s	D
Petunia f1 'Wave Purple'	DT,S,SE,T,U
Petunia f1 'Wave Purple' p.s	D
Petunia f1 'White Swan'	T
Petunia f2 'Balcony Choice'	DT,F
Petunia f2 'Carnival'	BS,KI,VH
Petunia f2 'Colorama Bedding'	B,BD,BS,DT,L
Petunia f2 'Compact Choice'	BS,S
Petunia f2 'Fancy Pants'	D,S
Petunia f2 'Rainbow'	J,KI,Sm,ST,SU,T,TU,VH
Petunia f2 'Stars & Stripes'	F
Petunia 'Falcon Pink Veined'	B,BS
Petunia 'Festival' mix	CL
Petunia 'Flash'	BS
Petunia floribunda f1 'Mirage Reflections'	BD,D,S
Petunia floribunda f1 'Mirage Refls' p.s	BD
Petunia 'Galaxy mix'	BS,YA
Petunia 'Glitters'	BS
Petunia grandiflora f1 'Aladdin' mix	BD,F
Petunia grandiflora f1 'Aladdin' s-c	BS
Petunia grandiflora f1 'All Double Dwarf'	C
Petunia grandiflora f1 'Colour Parade'	BS,C
Petunia grandiflora f1 'Daddy' mix	BD,BS,CL,D,DT,F,J,KI, L,M,SE,YA
Petunia grandiflora f1 'Daddy' s-c	BS,CL,F,SE,T,VH
Petunia grandiflora f1 'Dreams' mix	BS,DT,J,KI,T
Petunia grandiflora f1 'Dreams' s-c	BS,L
Petunia grandiflora f1 'Express Series'	CL
Petunia grandiflora f1 'Giant Victorious'	F
Petunia grandiflora f1 'Harmony Mix'	CL
Petunia grandiflora f1 'Ice Series'	BS,CL
Petunia grandiflora f1 'Picotee' mix	BS,C,D,J,KI,SE,ST,T,TU
Petunia grandiflora f1 'Picotee' s-c	BS
Petunia grandiflora f1 'Pirouette Purple'	BS,CL,D,T
Petunia grandiflora f1 'Pirouete Rose'	CL,D
Petunia grandiflora f1 'Razzle Dazzle'	BS,CO,D,J,KI,S
Petunia grandiflora f1 'Storm Lavender'	BS,CL,KS,O,S,SE,U
Petunia grandiflora f1 'Storm Pink'	CL,U
Petunia grandiflora f1 'Super Fanfare' dbl	S
Petunia grandiflora f1 'Ultra Series' s-c	BS,DT
Petunia grandiflora f1 'Ultra Star' mix s-c	BS,T
Petunia grandiflora f1 'Windsor Series' s-c	YA
Petunia grandiflora 'Special' mix	CL,DT,U
Petunia grandiflora 'Yellow Magic'	R
Petunia 'Heavenly Lavender'	CL,SE,U
Petunia 'Highlight'	BS

PETUNIA

Petunia hybrida	SG
Petunia integrifolia	B
Petunia 'Marshmallow'	F
Petunia 'Mercury'	BS
Petunia milliflora f1 'Dreamcoat'	BS
Petunia milliflora f1 'Fantasy Blue'	BS,CL,D,S,SE
Petunia milliflora f1 'Fantasy Crystal'	BS,CL,D,KS,S
Petunia milliflora f1 'Fantasy Ivory'	BS,CL,D,KS,S,SE
Petunia milliflora f1 'Fantasy' mix	BS,CL,D,DT,F,KI,KS,J,S,SE,U
Petunia milliflora f1 'Fantasy Pink'	BS,CL,D,S
Petunia milliflora f1 'Fantasy Pink Morn'	BS,CL,D,KS,S,SE,U
Petunia milliflora f1 'Fantasy Red'	BS,CL,D,S,SE,U
Petunia milliflora f1 'Fantasy Salmon'	BS,CL,D,S,SE
Petunia milliflora f1 'Garden Party' s-c /m	BS
Petunia multiflora f1 'Blue Skies'	T
Petunia multiflora f1 'Bonanza'	BD,BS,J,KI,L,R,TU,V,YA
Petunia multiflora f1 'Carpet Buttercream'	BS,D
Petunia multiflora f1 'Carpet' mix	BS,D,DT,F,J,L,S,SE
Petunia multiflora f1 'Carpet' s-c	BS,F,L,T
Petunia multiflora f1 dbl mix	M
Petunia multiflora f1 'Delight' mix dbl	F,S,SE,T
Petunia multiflora f1 'Duo' mix dbl	BS,CL,D,DT,F,KI,S,SE,T,U,YA
Petunia multiflora f1 'Duo Series' s-c	BS,CL,SE
Petunia multiflora f1 formula mix	C,DT,S,SE,ST
Petunia multiflora f1 'Frenzy Series' s-c	CL
Petunia m. f1 'Horizon Lavender Sunrise'	DT
Petunia multiflora f1 'Horizon' mix	T
Petunia multiflora f1 'Joy' mix	BS,SE
Petunia multiflora f1 'Joy' s-c	BS,M
Petunia multiflora f1 'Merlin Picotee' mix	BS,CL,DT,KI,T,U,YA
Petunia multiflora f1 'Merlin' mix/s-c	BS,T
Petunia multiflora f1 'Pastel Salmon'	T
Petunia multiflora f1 'Pearl Series'	BS,KI
Petunia multiflora f1 'Plum Pudding'	BD,D,S,U
Petunia multiflora f1 'Plum' s-c	BS,T
Petunia multiflora f1 'Polo Mix'	T
Petunia multiflora f1 'Primetime' s-c	CL,DT,F
Petunia multiflora f1 'Resisto' mix	CL,CO,DT,J,KI,ST,TU
Petunia multiflora f1 'Satin & Silk'	S
Petunia multiflora f1 'Starship'	SE,T
Petunia multiflora f1 'Summer Sun'	T
Petunia multiflora f2 'Confetti' mix	F
Petunia multiflora f2 'Crown'	BS
Petunia multiflora f2 'Deluxe' blend	BS,C,CL
Petunia multiflora f2 mix	YA
Petunia multiflora f2 'Mosaic' mix	BS
Petunia multiflora f2 'Star' mix	BS
Petunia multiflora f2 'Super' mix	BS
Petunia multiflora o-p 'Celestial Rose'	C
Petunia multiflora o-p 'Fire Chief'	C
Petunia multiflora o-p 'Snowball'	C
Petunia multiflora single mix	BS,R
Petunia 'Nana Compacta Mix'	BD,C,CO,J,V
Petunia 'Orange Bells'	BS
Petunia 'Patio Collection'	U
Petunia pendula mix	BS,C
Petunia 'Pendulina' mix	F
Petunia 'Polaris' mix	BS,R
Petunia 'Polaris' s-c	BS
Petunia 'Polaris' veined s-c	BS
Petunia 'Red Picotee'	CL,S
Petunia 'Resisto' dw	BS
Petunia 'Rosette' mix	CL
Petunia 'Stardust' mix	BS
Petunia 'Superbissima' mix	BS
Peucedanum austriacum	SG
Peucedanum caffrum	B,SI
Peucedanum capense	SI
Peucedanum carvifolium	B
Peucedanum ferulaceum	B,SI
Peucedanum japonicum	B
Peucedanum morisonii	SG
Peucedanum officinalis	B,JE
Peucedanum oreoselinum	SG
Peucedanum ostruthium	B,G,JE,SA
Peucedanum ruthenicum	SG
Peucedanum thodei	B,SI
Peucedanum venutum	B
Peucedanum verticillare	G,JE,SA
Peucephyllum schottii	B
Pfeiffera ianthothele	Y
Pfeiffera multigona	Y
Phacelia bipinnatifida	AP,NT
Phacelia bolanderi	B
Phacelia campanularia	B,BS,C,CG,D,DT,J,KI,KS,S,SU,TU,U,V
Phacelia cicutaria	B
Phacelia distans	B
Phacelia grandiflora	B
Phacelia linearis	CG
Phacelia minor	B
Phacelia parryi	B,SW,V
Phacelia 'Sea Seventeen'	F
Phacelia sericea	AP,B,SC,SW
Phacelia tanacetifolia	B,BS,C,CG,CO,KS,SC,SG,SU,V
Phacelia viscida	B
Phaenocoma prolifera	B,C,SA,SI
Phagnalon helichrysoides	I
Phagnalon rupestre	B
Phagnalon saxatile	I
Phalaris aquatica named cvs	B
Phalaris arundinacea	B,JE,SA
Phalaris arundinacea 'Feesey'	I
Phalaris canariensis	B,C,SG,SU,V
Phalaris minor	B
Pharnaceum croceum	SI
Pharnaceum sp	SI
Phaseolus sp	B
Phebalium filifolium	B
Phebalium tuberculosum	SA
Phebalium tuberculosum ssp tuberc.	B
Phellandrum aquaticum	SG
Phellodendron amurense	A,B,C,CG,RE,SA
Phellodendron chinense	B
Phellodendron lavallei	B
Phellodendron sachalinense	B
Phemeranthus calycinus	B
Phemeranthus longipes	B
Pherosphaera hookerana	B
Philadelphus coronarius	B
Philadelphus inodorum	B
Philadelphus lewisii	B,C,SG
Philadelphus microphyllus	B,SW
Philadelphus 'New Hybrids'	B
Philadelphus tenuifolius MW127R	X
Philippicereus castaneus	Y
Phillyrea angustifolia	SA
Phillyrea latifolia	SG
Phillyrea media	SA

Philodendron adamantinum	B
Philodendron 'Angra Dos Reis'	B
Philodendron 'Barryi'	B
Philodendron bipinnatifidum	B,BS,CCL,HA
Philodendron bipinnatifidum 'Compactum'	B
Philodendron bipinnatifidum 'Sao Paolo'	B
Philodendron bipinnatifidum 'Uruguay'	B
Philodendron cannifolium	B,HA
Philodendron colombianum	B
Philodendron cordatum	B
Philodendron crassinervium	B
Philodendron cymbispathum	B
Philodendron eichleri	B
Philodendron erubescens	B
Philodendron 'Evansii'	B
Philodendron eximium	B
Philodendron fragrans	B
Philodendron giganteum	B
Philodendron hastatum of gdns imp	B,HA
Philodendron hyb	B
Philodendron imbe	B
Philodendron lundii	B,CL
Philodendron mamei	B
Philodendron martianum	B
Philodendron mello-barretoanum	B
Philodendron ornatum	B
Philodendron pseudoradiatum	B
Philodendron radiatum	B
Philodendron rubrinervum	B
Philodendron saxicolum	B
Philodendron scandens	B
Philodendron scandens ssp oxycardium	B
Philodendron speciosum	B
Philodendron tuxla	B,HA
Philodendron undulatum	B
Philodendron wendlandii	B
Philodendron williamsii	B
Philotheca slasolifolia	HA
Phlebodium aureum	B
Phlebodium aureum 'Mandaianum'	B,SG
Phlebodium aureum v areolatum	B,SA,SG
Phleum arenarium	B
Phleum hirsutum	SG
Phleum phleoides	B,SG
Phleum pratense	B,C,SA,SG
Phleum pratense ssp bertolonii	B
Phlomis cashmeriana	B,CC,JE,SA
Phlomis chrysophylla	SA,SG
Phlomis fruticosa	AP,B,BS,C,FH,JE,SA, SC,SG
Phlomis herba-venti	B
Phlomis longifolia	SA
Phlomis lychnitis	AP,B,SA
Phlomis purpurea	B,SA
Phlomis russeliana	AP,B,BS,C,F,G,JE,KI,P, SA,SC,SG
Phlomis samia of gdns see russeliana	
Phlomis tuberosa	AP,B,G,JE,SA,SC,SG
Phlox amoena	B
Phlox carolina	B
Phlox decussata	CO,KI,ST
Phlox decussata hyb	BS
Phlox divaricata	B,SC
Phlox drummondii	B,G,HW,R,SG
Phlox drummondii 'African Sunset'	BS,C,CO,J,KI,KS,S,TU,U
Phlox drummondii 'Beauty' mix	BS,C,CL,DT,L,S,SE,YA

Phlox drummondii 'Blue Beauty'	BS,V
Phlox drummondii 'Bright Eyes'	D,S,SE
Phlox drummondii 'Brilliancy'	F
Phlox drummondii 'Carnival'	D
Phlox drummondii 'Cecily Old/New'	F
Phlox drummondii 'Chanal'	BS,C,CL,D,DT,J,KI,KS, ST,YA
Phlox drummondii 'Choice' mix	C
Phlox drummondii 'Coral Reef'	BS,DT,F,SE
Phlox drummondii 'Crystal'	YA
Phlox drummondii 'Dolly'	BS
Phlox drummondii 'Dw Mix'	J,ST,V
Phlox drummondii f2 'Ethnie' mix	B,BS,CL
Phlox drummondii 'Fantasy' mix	BD,BS,DT,F,SE
Phlox drummondii 'Grandiflora'	BS,TU
Phlox drummondii 'Grandiflora Brilliant'	C
Phlox drummondii 'Grandiflora Cinnabar'	B
Phlox drummondii 'Grandiflora Coccinea'	B
Phlox drummondii 'Grandiflora Leopoldii'	B,DT
Phlox drummondii 'Grand. White Swan'	B
Phlox drummondii 'Hazy Days'	D
Phlox drummondii lge fl	CO,DT,S
Phlox drummondii 'Masterpiece'	BS,KI
Phlox drummondii 'Nana Compacta Mix'	BS
Phlox drummondii 'Palona'	BS,DT,F
Phlox x drummondii 'Phlox of Sheep'	BD,BS,KS,T,V
Phlox drummondii 'Promise Peach'	BS,C
Phlox drummondii 'Promise Pink'	BS,U
Phlox drummondii 'Tapestry'	D,F
Phlox drummondii 'Twinkles'	B,BD,BS,C,DT,J,KI,KS,L, SV,V
Phlox drummondii 'Twinkling Stars'	D,F
Phlox nana compacta	KI,SU
Phlox nivalis	B
Phlox paniculata	C,G,SA,V
Phlox paniculata 'New Hybrids'	B,JE,L
Phlox pilosa	B,JE,PR
Phlox stolonifera	B
Phlox x arendsii 'Newest Hybrids'	JE
Phoenix acaulis	B,HA,O,SA
Phoenix canariensis	B,C,CG,HA,O,S,SA,V
Phoenix dactylifera	B,C,HA,O,SA
Phoenix dactylifera 'Midjool'	B
Phoenix hanceana	O
Phoenix hyb	B
Phoenix paludosa	B,O
Phoenix pusilla	B,O
Phoenix reclinata	B,C,HA,O,SA,SI
Phoenix roebelinii	B,C,HA,O,RE,SA
Phoenix rupicola	B,C,HA,O,SA
Phoenix sylvestris	B,SA
Pholiota aegerita d.m.p	B
Pholistoma auritum	B
Phormium colensoi see cookianum	
Phormium cookianum	A,AP,AU,B,C,LG,SA,SC, SG,SS
Phormium cookianum hyb pink striped	B
Phormium cookianum 'Tricolor'	B,SA
Phormium tenax	A,AP,B,C,HA,RH,SA,SC, SG,SS
Phormium tenax 'Bronze'	B,C
Phormium tenax hyb 'Rainbow'	B,T
Phormium tenax 'Purpureum'	AP,BS,C,HA,KI,SA,T
Phormium tenax 'Purpureum Select Red'	B
Phormium tenax 'Red Edge'	C
Phormium tenax 'Variegatum'	B,BS,HA,N,SA,SC

PHORMIUM

Phormium tenax 'Yellow Wave' — B,C,PM
Photinia amphidoxa — SG
Photinia arbutifolia — B,C,SA,SG
Photinia davidiana — B,SA
Photinia davidsoniae — C,SG
Photinia lasiogyna — SG
Photinia melanocarpa — SG
Photinia serratifolia — B,HA,SA
Photinia villosa — SG
Phragmites australis — B,C,HA,JE,SA
Phuopsis stylosa — B,BS,C,G,JE,KI,SA,SC, SG,V
Phygelius aequalis — AP,B,SA,SG,SI
Phygelius aequalis 'Yellow Trumpet' — B,JE
Phygelius 'African Queen' — C
Phygelius capensis — AP,B,C,CG,G,JE,SA,SI
Phyla nodiflora — B
Phylica buxifolia — B,SI
Phylica callosa — SI
Phylica cryptandroides — SI
Phylica imberbis — SI
Phylica odorata — SI
Phylica oleifolia — SI
Phylica plumosa — AP,B,C,SA,SI
Phylica sp — SI
Phylica stipularis — SI
Phyllacne colensoi — SS
Phyllanthus acidus — B
Phyllanthus amarus — B
Phyllanthus angustifolius — B
Phyllanthus calycinus — B,SA
Phyllanthus emblica — B,HA
Phyllanthus grandifolius — SG
Phyllanthus polyphyllus — B
Phyllanthus reticulatus — B
Phyllocarpus septentrionalis — B
Phyllocladus alpinus — B
Phyllocladus aspleniifolius — B,O,SA
Phyllocladus aspleniifolius v alpinus — AP,AU,SS
Phyllocladus trichomanoides — B
Phyllodoce caerulea — C,FH,SC
Phyllostachys edulis — B
Phymaspermum acerosum — B
Phymatocarpus maxwellii — AU,B
Physalis alkekengi — AP,B,C,CG,CL,F,SG
Physalis alkekengi 'Pygmaea' — B
Physalis franchetii — BD,BS,C,CO,D,DT,J,JE, KI,U
Physalis franchetii 'Gigantea' — JE,L,S,SA,SU,V
Physalis heterophylla — B
Physalis ixocarpa — B,CG,CP
Physalis minima — B
Physalis peruviana — B,C,SG,ST
Physalis peruviana 'Gigantea' — B,T
Physalis philadelphica — W
Physalis philadelphica 'Purple De Milpa' — B
Physalis phil. 'Tarahumara Tomatillo' — B
Physalis phil. 'Tepehuan Tomatillo' — B
Physalis pruinosa — B
Physalis subglabrata — B
Physaria acutifolia — B,SW
Physaria newberryi — SW
Physocarpus malvaceus — B
Physocarpus opulifolius — B,C,PR,SA,SG
Physocarpus ribesifolius — SG
Physochliana orientalis — JE

Physoplexis comosa — AP,C,G,JE,SC
Physopsis lachnostachya — B
Physostegia digitalis — B
Physostegia virginiana — AP,B,BS,KI,PR,SA,KI,T
Physostegia virginiana 'Alba' — CG,G,JE,SA,SC,SG
Physostegia virginiana grandiflora 'Rosea' — JE
Physostegia virginiana 'New Hybrids' — B
Physostegia virginiana 'Rose Crown' — B,C,F
Physostegia virginiana 'Rose Spire' — B
Physostegia virginiana 'Schneekrone' — B,C,CL,D,DT,F,HH,JE,L, U,V
Physostegia virginiana speciosa — PR
Physostegia virginiana 'Summer Snow' — T
Physostegia virginiana 'White Spire' — B
Phytelephas macrocarpa — B
Phyteuma betonicifolium — B,C,G,SC
Phyteuma charmelii — AP,B,C,FH,G,SC
Phyteuma globulariifolius — B
Phyteuma hemisphaericus — AP,B,C,CG,JE,SC
Phyteuma nigrum — AP,C,G,JE,SA,SC,SG
Phyteuma orbiculare — AP,B,CG,G,JE,SA,SC,SG
Phyteuma ovatum — B
Phyteuma scheuchzeri — AP,B,C,CG,FH,G,JE,SC, SG
Phyteuma scheuchzeri ssp scheuchzeri — CG
Phyteuma sieberi — AP,CG,G,SC
Phyteuma spicatum — B,C,CG,G,I,JE,SG
Phyteuma spicatum 'Caeruleum' — B,JE
Phytolacca acinosa — B,C,JE
Phytolacca americana — B,C,JE,RH,SA,Y
Phytolacca americana 'Yellow Berry' — B
Phytolacca dioica — B,C,SA,Y
Phytolacca mexicana — SA
Phytolacca polyandra — B
Piaranthus punctatus — B,C
Picea abies — B,C,CG,SA
Picea ajanensis — SG
Picea asperata — B,CG,SA,SG
Picea breweriana — B,C,N,SA,T
Picea cembra — A
Picea engelmannii — B,C,SA
Picea glauca — A,B,C,SA,SG
Picea glauca 'Densata' — B,C,B,SA
Picea glauca v albertiana — B
Picea glehnii — B,N,SA,SG
Picea jezoensis — B,N,SA,SG
Picea jezoensis v hondoensis — B,N,SA
Picea koraiensis — C,SG
Picea koyamae — AP,B
Picea likiangensis — B
Picea mariana — B,C,SA
Picea meyeri — B,N,SA
Picea morinda — HA
Picea obovata — B,SA
Picea obovata v caerulea — B,N
Picea omorika — B,C,N,SA
Picea omorika 'Fassei' — CG
Picea orientalis — B,C,SA
Picea pungens — B,SG
Picea pungens 'Glauca' — B,BS,C,CG,N,SA,T
Picea purpurea — B
Picea rubens — B,SA
Picea schrenkiana — SA
Picea schrenkiana ssp tianschanica — B
Picea sitchensis — B,C,SA
Picea smithiana — B,CG,N,SA

181

PICEA

Picea wilsonii	B,SA	Pimpinella major	B,SG
Picea x lutzii	B	Pimpinella major 'Rosea'	AP,LG
Pickeringia montana	SA	Pimpinella saxifraga	B,C,CP,G,JE,SA,SG
Picrasma quassioides	B,SA	Pinanga barnesii	B,O
Picris echioides	B,LA,NS	Pinanga coronata	B,O
Picris echioides 'Teras'	B	Pinanga dicksonii	B
Picris hieracioides	SG	Pinanga insignis	B,O
Pieranthus punctatum	CH	Pinanga javana	B,O
Pieris floribunda	B,SA	Pinanga kuhlii	O,RE,SA
Pieris formosa	RH,SG	Pinanga maculata	B,O
Pieris japonica	B,C,CG,RH,SA	Pinanga patula	B,O
Pieris japonica 'Yakushimanum'	B	Pinckneya pubens	B
Pieris sp CNW377	X	Pinellia tripartita	G,PM
Pigafetta filaris	O	Pinguicula 'Agarra Mosca Violeta'	B
Pilea involucrata	B,C	Pinguicula agnata ssp?	B
Pilea involucrata 'Silver Tree'	B	Pinguicula alpina	B,C
Pileanthus filifolius	B	Pinguicula caerulea	B
Pileanthus peduncularis	B,O	Pinguicula corsica	B
Piliostigma reticulatum	B	Pinguicula grandiflora	AP,B,G,PM,SC,Y
Piliostigma thonningii	B,SI	Pinguicula grandiflora f pallida	B
Pilosella aurantiaca	AP,B,C,G,I,JE,SA,SC,SU	Pinguicula grandiflora ssp grandiflora	B
Pilosella officinarum	B	Pinguicula grandiflora ssp rosea	B
Pilosocereus alensis	Y	Pinguicula gypsicola	B
Pilosocereus arrabidae	BC	Pinguicula ionantha	B
Pilosocereus aurilanatus	Y	Pinguicula jaumavensis	B
Pilosocereus azureus	B,BC,Y	Pinguicula leptoceras	C
Pilosocereus bradei	BC,Y	Pinguicula longifolia ssp longifolia	B
Pilosocereus brasiliensis ML407	BC	Pinguicula lusitanica	B
Pilosocereus chryostelle	B	Pinguicula lutea	B
Pilosocereus fulvilanatus	B	Pinguicula moranensis 'Cantil Del Tambor'	B
Pilosocereus glaucescens	B,Y	Pinguicula moranensis 'La Vuelta'	B
Pilosocereus glaucochrous	Y	Pinguicula potosiensis	B
Pilosocereus luetzelburgii	Y	Pinguicula primuliflora	B
Pilosocereus magnificus	B,Y	Pinguicula pumila	B
Pilosocereus pachycladus	Y	Pinguicula villosa	RS
Pilosocereus palmeri	Y	Pinguicula vulgaris	B,C,CG,SG
Pilosocereus pentaedrophorus	Y	Pinguicula vulgaris f bicolor	B
Pilosocereus royenii	Y	Pinus albicaulis	B,N
Pimelea ammocharis	B	Pinus aristata	B,C,N,SA
Pimelea argentea	B	Pinus armandii	B,C,SA
Pimelea brevistyla	B	Pinus attenuata	B,SA
Pimelea ciliata	B	Pinus austriaca	CG
Pimelea cocinna	SS	Pinus ayacahuite	B,SA
Pimelea ferruginea	B,O	Pinus balfouriana	B
Pimelea floribunda	B	Pinus banksiana	B,N,SA
Pimelea glauca	B,SA	Pinus brutia	B,CG
Pimelea holroydii	B,SA	Pinus brutia ssp eldarica	B
Pimelea imbricata	B	Pinus bungeana	B,C,SA
Pimelea imbricata ssp piligera	B	Pinus canariensis	B,C,HA,SA
Pimelea imbricata v baxteri	B	Pinus caribaea	SA
Pimelea lehmanniana	B	Pinus caribaea v bahamensis	B
Pimelea linifolia	HA	Pinus caribaea v caribaea	B
Pimelea longiflora	B,SA	Pinus caribaea v hondurensis	B
Pimelea microcephala	HA	Pinus cembra	B,CG,N,SA
Pimelea oreophylla	B,SS	Pinus cembra ssp sibirica	B,SA
Pimelea physodes	B,C,O,SA	Pinus cembra ssp sibirica 'Glauca'	B
Pimelea prostrata	SS	Pinus cembroides	B
Pimelea rosea	B	Pinus cembroides monophylla	N,SA
Pimelea sericeo-villosa	SS	Pinus clausa	B
Pimelea spectabilis	B,O,SA	Pinus contorta	B,SA
Pimelea suaveolens	B,O	Pinus contorta v latifolia	B,SA,SG
Pimelea sylvestris	B,SA	Pinus contorta v murrayana	B
Pimelea traversii	AP,B,SW	Pinus coulteri	B,C,N,SA
Pimenta dioica	B	Pinus densa	B
Pimenta racemosa	B	Pinus densiflora	C,G,N,SA
Pimpinella anisum	B,CP,KS	Pinus echinata	B,SA

PINUS

Pinus edulis	B	Pinus serotina	B,SA
Pinus edulis v fallax	B	Pinus sibirica	A,SG
Pinus eldarica	SA	Pinus sp mix	C
Pinus elliottii	B,SA	Pinus strobiformis	B,SA
Pinus engelmannii	B,SA	Pinus strobus	B,C,CG,N,SA
Pinus flexilis	B,C,G,SA,SC	Pinus sylvestris	B,C,CG,N,SASG
Pinus flexilis v reflexa	B	Pinus sylvestris v mongolica	B,SA
Pinus gerardiana	A,HA,SA	Pinus sylvestris v rigensis	B
Pinus glabra	B	Pinus szemaonensis	B
Pinus greggii	B,SA	Pinus tabuliiformis	B,C,SA
Pinus halepensis	B,C,CG,G,HA,SA,SG	Pinus taeda	B,SA
Pinus halepensis brutia	SA	Pinus taiwanensis	SA
Pinus halepensis reg	SA	Pinus tecunumanii	B
Pinus heldreichii	B,SA	Pinus thunbergii	B,C,G,N,SA,T,V
Pinus incinata prostrata	CG	Pinus torreyana	B,SA
Pinus jeffreyi	B,SA	Pinus uncinata	CG
Pinus kesiya	B,SA	Pinus virginiana	B,SA
Pinus koraiensis	A,N,SA,SG	Pinus wallichiana	AP,B,CC,CG,N,SC
Pinus lambertiana	B,SA	Pinus yunnanensis	B,N,SA
Pinus leucodermis	SA	Piper angustifolium	B
Pinus massoniana	B,N,SA	Piper augustum	B
Pinus maximartinezii	B	Piper concepsionis	B
Pinus maximinoi	B	Piper guineense	B
Pinus merkusii	B,SA	Piper marginatum	B
Pinus michoacana	SA	Piper nigrum	B,RE,SA
Pinus monophylla	B	Piptanthus nepalensis	C,CG,SA,SG
Pinus montezumae	B,N,SA	Pisolithus tinctorius	B
Pinus monticola	B,C,SA	Pisonia umbellifera	B
Pinus mugo	AP,B,V	Pistacia atlantica	B,SA
Pinus mugo forms mix	N	Pistacia chinensis	B,C,HA,SA
Pinus mugo ssp uncinata	B,SA	Pistacia lentiscus	SA
Pinus mugo v mugo	B,SA	Pistacia palaestina	B
Pinus mugo v pumilio	B,C,SA,T	Pistacia terebinthus	B,CG,SA,SG
Pinus muricata	B,C,SA	Pistacia texana	B
Pinus nelsonii	SA	Pistacia vera	B,SA
Pinus nigra	CG,N	Pitcairnia andreana	CG
Pinus nigra austriaca	SA	Pitcairnia corallina	B
Pinus nigra corsicana	SA	Pitcairnia decidua	B
Pinus nigra ssp nigra	B	Pitcairnia flammea	B
Pinus nigra v calabrica	B,SA	Pitcairnia flammea v floccosa	B
Pinus nigra v caramanica	B	Pitcairnia heterophylla	B,SG
Pinus nigra v maritima	B,C	Pitcairnia integrifolia	B
Pinus nigra v pyramidalis	B	Pitcairnia morelii	B
Pinus nigra 'Villetta Barrea'	B	Pitcairnia seidelii	B
Pinus oocarpa	B,SA	Pitcairnia xanthocalyx	CG
Pinus pallasiana	SA	Pithecellobium arboretum	B
Pinus palustris	B,C,SA	Pithecellobium dulce	B,HA,SA
Pinus parviflora	B,C,N,SA,T,V	Pithecellobium flexicaule	B,CG
Pinus parviflora (ex Ha Tsumari)	X	Pithecellobium mangense	B
Pinus parviflora f glauca (A.M.Form)	X	Pithecellobium saman	SA
Pinus patula	B,C,HA,SA	Pittosporum bicolor	B,O,SA
Pinus peuce	B,SA,SG	Pittosporum crassifolium	B,C,SA
Pinus pinaster	B,C,HA,N,SA,SG	Pittosporum eugenoides	B,C,O,SA,SS
Pinus pinea	A,B,C,HA,KS,N,SA,T	Pittosporum phillyreoides	B,C,HA,O,SA
Pinus pithyusa	B,SA	Pittosporum ralphii	B,C,CG,SA
Pinus ponderosa	B,C,SA	Pittosporum revolutum	B,HA,O
Pinus ponderosa 'Rosebud'	B	Pittosporum rhombifolium	B,HA,O,SA
Pinus ponderosa ssp scopulorum	B,SA	Pittosporum tenuifolium	B,C,SA,SG,SS
Pinus ponderosa timber	B	Pittosporum tenuifolium ssp colensoi	B
Pinus pseudostrobus	B	Pittosporum tobira	B,C,CG,O,SA
Pinus pumila	B,C,N,SA,SG	Pittosporum turneri	CG
Pinus radiata	B,C,HA,RH,SA	Pittosporum undulatum	B,BS,HA,O
Pinus resinosa	B,SA	Pittosporum viridiflorum	B,SA,SI
Pinus rigida	B,G,SA	Pityrodia loxocarpa	B,SA
Pinus roxburghii	B,HA,SA	Pityrodia terminalis	B
Pinus sabiniana	B,SA	Placospermum coriaceum	O,SA

Planchonella australis	B
Planchonella costata	B
Plantago affra	B
Plantago antartica	SG
Plantago argentea	C,SG
Plantago asiatica	B
Plantago asiatica 'Variegata'	AP,B,E,G,P
Plantago coronopus	B,G,SG
Plantago grandiflora	B,P
Plantago indica	B
Plantago insularis	B,SG
Plantago lagopus	B
Plantago lanceolata	B,JE,LA,SG
Plantago lanigera	SS
Plantago latifolia 'Atropurpurea'	JE,SA
Plantago major	B,C,SG,SI
Plantago major 'Atropurpurea'	B,C,SC
Plantago major 'Frills'	NS
Plantago major 'Karmozijn'	E
Plantago major 'Rosularis'	AP,B,C,E,G,SC
Plantago major 'Rosularis' Bowles v	P
Plantago major 'Rubrifolia'	AP,C,E,FH,G,RH,SC,T
Plantago maritima	AP,B,SC,SG
Plantago media	C,SG,SU
Plantago media ssp stepposa	B
Plantago nivalis	AP,B,FH,G,JE,P,SC,SG
Plantago novae-zelandiae	SS
Plantago patagonica	B
Plantago purshii	PR
Plantago salsa	SG
Plantago sempervirens	B,SC
Plantago spathulata	SS
Plantago squalida	SG
Plantago triandra	B,P
Platanthera bifolia	B,SC,SG
Platanus mexicana	B
Platanus occidentalis	B,SA
Platanus orientalis	B,C,HA,SA
Platanus orientalis v digitata	HA
Platanus racemosa	B
Platanus wrightii	B
Platanus x hispanica	B,SA
Platycarya strobilacea	SA
Platycerium alcicorne	SA
Platycerium andinum	B
Platycerium bifurcatum	B
Platycerium grande	B,SA
Platycerium hillii	B
Platycerium mixed	C
Platycerium stemaria	B
Platycerium wilhelminae-reginae	B,SA
Platycodon f1 'Sentimental Blue'	B,BS,C,CL,JE
Platycodon grandiflorus	AP,BS,C,CC,CG,G,I,J, LG,SC,SG,T
Platycodon grandiflorus 'Alpinum'	B
Platycodon gr. apoyama 'Misato Purple'	JE
Platycodon grandiflorus 'Blaue Glocke'	JE
Platycodon grandiflorus f albus	AP,B,G,JE
Platycodon grandiflorus f apoyama	AP,B,G,SC
Platycodon grandiflorus f1 'Astra Blue'	JE,YA
Platycodon grandiflorus f1 'Astra Pink'	JE,YA
Platycodon grandiflorus f1 'Astra White'	JE,YA
Platycodon gr. f1 'Sentimental Blue'	BS
Platycodon grandiflorus 'Florist Blue'	B,C,SA
Platycodon grandiflorus 'Florist' mix	C
Platycodon grandiflorus 'Florist Pink'	B,C,SA

Platycodon grandiflorus 'Florist White'	B,C,SA
Platycodon grandiflorus 'Fuji Blue'	JE
Platycodon grandiflorus 'Fuji' mix	V
Platycodon grandiflorus 'Fuji Pink'	G,JE
Platycodon grandiflorus 'Fuji White'	JE,T
Platycodon grandiflorus 'Hakone Blue'	JE
Platycodon grandiflorus 'Hakone White'	JE
Platycodon grandiflorus 'Komachi'	B
Platycodon grandiflorus 'Mariesii'	AP,B,BS,C,CG,G,JE,KI, SC,SU
Platycodon grandiflorus 'Mariesii Album'	B,SC
Platycodon grandiflorus 'Mini Blue'	B
Platycodon grandiflorus 'Mini White'	B
Platycodon grandiflorus 'Mixed Hybrids'	JE
Platycodon grandiflorus 'Mother of Pearl'	T
Platycodon grandiflorus MW89R	X
Platycodon grandiflorus 'Park's Dbl Blue'	B,C
Platycodon grandiflorus 'Perlmutterschale'	B,JE
Platycodon grandiflorus 'Pygmy Blue'	D,S,T
Platycodon grandiflorus 'Zwerg'	JE
Platylobium formosum	B,HA
Platymiscium pinnatum	B
Platymiscium polystachyum	B
Platysace compressa	B
Platystemon californicus	SG,V
Plectranthus ambiguus	B,SI
Plectranthus ciliatus	B,C,SI
Plectranthus ciliatus 'Drege'	B,SI
Plectranthus dolichopodus	SI
Plectranthus ecklonii	B,SI
Plectranthus ecklonii 'Erma'	B,SI
Plectranthus ecklonii 'Medleywood'	B,SI
Plectranthus ecklonii 'Tommy'	B,SI
Plectranthus elegantulus	B,SI
Plectranthus fruticosus	B,SI
Plectranthus fruticosus 'James'	B,SI
Plectranthus grallatus	SI
Plectranthus hadiensis	B,SI
Plectranthus hadiensis v tomentosus	B,SI
Plectranthus hereroensis	B,SI
Plectranthus laxiflorus	SI
Plectranthus mandalensis	B,SI
Plectranthus oertendahlii	B,SI
Plectranthus rehmannii	B,SI
Plectranthus sp mix	C
Plectranthus spicatus	SI
Plectranthus spicatus 'Nelspruit'	B
Plectranthus verticillatus	B,SI
Plectranthus zuluensis	SI
Pleioblastus auricomus	B
Pleioblastus humilis v pumilus	B
Pleioblastus pygmaeus	B
Pleioblastus variegatus	B
Pleiogynium cerasiferum	HA
Pleiogynium timorense	B,O,SA
Pleione formosana	B,G
Pleione forrestii	B
Pleione limprichtii	AP,G
Pleione 'Oriental Grace'	B
Pleione 'Shantung Ridgeway'	B
Pleione 'Versailles'	B,SC
Pleiospilos bolusii	B,Y
Pleiospilos compactus	B,SI
Pleiospilos compactus ssp canus	B,SI
Pleiospilos compactus ssp minor	B
Pleiospilos compactus ssp sororius	B

PLEIOSPILOS

Pleiospilos fergusonae	B,CH,Y	Podolepis canescens	B
Pleiospilos leipoldtii	B	Podolepis gracilis	B,O
Pleiospilos magnipunctatus	B	Podolepis jaceoides	B,O
Pleiospilos nelii	B,CH,Y	Podolepis nutans	B,O
Pleiospilos prismaticus	B	Podophyllum aurantiacum	SG
Pleiospilos rouxii	B	Podophyllum emodi see hexandrum	
Pleiospilos simulans	B,SI	Podophyllum hexandrum	AP,B,CC,CG,G,JE,RS,
Pleiospilos sp	SI,Y		SA,SC,SG,T
Pleurostemon uralense	SG	Podophyllum hexandrum v chinense	SG
Pleurothallis grobyi	B	Podophyllum peltatum	B,CG,JE
Pleurotus eryngii d.m.p	B	Podospermum laciniatum	CG
Pleurotus ostreatus d.m.p	B	Podotheca gnaphalioides	B
Pluchea purpurascens	B	Podranea brycei	B
Plukenetia volubilis	B	Podranea ricasoliana	B,SI
Plumbago auriculata	B,BS,C,CL,D,HA,JE,KI,	Pogostemon heyneanus	B
	SA,ST,T,V	Polanisia dodecandra	B
Plumbago zeylanica	B	Polaskia chichipe	B,Y
Plumeria frangipanni alba	B,SA,T	Polemonium acutiflorum	AP,SG
Plumeria frangipanni rubra	SA	Polemonium acutiflorum 'Album'	JE
Plumeria hybs 'New Hawaiian'	B	Polemonium 'Apricot Delight'	T,V
Plumeria rubra	B,C,G,V	Polemonium brandegei ssp mellitum	B,P
Plumeria rubra v acutifolia	C	Polemonium caeruleum	AP,B,BS,C,CC,FH,G,HH,
Pneumonanthe asclepiadea	SG		I,JE,KI,KS,PA,SA,SC,
Poa acicularifolia	SS		SG,SU,VH
Poa alpina	G,JE,SG	Polemonium c. 'Album' see v lacteum	
Poa alpina v nodosa	B,C,SA	Polemonium caeruleum v himalayanum	B
Poa alpina v vivipara	B	Polemonium caeruleum v lacteum	AP,B,C,DT,F,FH,G,HH,
Poa angustifolia	SG		JE,SA,SC,T,V
Poa annua	B	Polemonium caeruleum 'White Pearl'	B,BS,C
Poa attenuata	SG	Polemonium carneum	AP,C,JE,SA,SC
Poa chaixii	B,JE,SA,SC	Polemonium cashmerianum	AP,C,JE,SG,T,W
Poa colensoi	SS	Polemonium cashmerianum album	C,JE
Poa compressa	B	Polemonium caucasicum	SG
Poa kirkii	SS	Polemonium delicaticum	G,SG
Poa labillardieri	HA	Polemonium elegans	AP,B
Poa laevis	SS	Polemonium filicinum	SG
Poa laxa	SG	Polemonium foliosissimum	AP,B,G,JE,SW
Poa leptocoma ssp paucispicula	SG	Polemonium foliosissimum 'Album'	B
Poa lindsayii	SS	Polemonium foliosissimum flavum	AP,HH
Poa nemoralis	B	Polemonium 'Golden Showers' (V)	P
Poa poiformis	B	Polemonium pauciflorum	AP,B,C,DT,F,FH,G,HH,
Poa pratensis	SG		JE,P,PM,RS,SA,SC,SE,
Poa scabrella	B		SG,SW
Poa sclerophylla	SS	Polemonium pauciflorum silver leaf form	T
Poa sibirica	SG	Polemonium pulcherrimum	AP,B,C,P,SC,SG,SW
Poa sieberiana	HA	Polemonium 'Purple Rain'	B,P
Poa trivialis	B	Polemonium reptans	AP,B,C,G,PR,SA,SC
Podalyria biflora	B,SI	Polemonium reptans 'Alba'	B
Podalyria calyptrata	B,C,SA,SI	Polemonium reptans 'Blue Pearl'	B,BS,C,JE,S,V
Podalyria canescens	B,SI	Polemonium scopulinum	B,SW
Podalyria myrtillifolia	SI	Polemonium viscosum	AP,B,SC,SG,SW
Podalyria sericea	B,C,SA,SI	Polemonium x richardsonii	B,G
Podalyria sp	SI	Polianthes nelsonii	B,SW
Podalyria zimbabweense	B	Polianthes tuberosa 'The Pearl'	B
Podocarpus elatus	B,HA,O,SA	Polyalthia longifolia 'Pendula'	B,O
Podocarpus elongatus	SI	Polyalthia nitidissima	B
Podocarpus falcatus	HA,SI	Polyalthia obtusifolia	B
Podocarpus henkelii	B,SI	Polyalthia suberosa	B
Podocarpus latifolius	B,SI	Polycalymma stuartii	B
Podocarpus macrophyllus	B,SA	Polycarpaea aurea	B
Podocarpus macrophyllus 'Maki'	B	Polycarpaea longiflora	B
Podocarpus nivalis	B,SS	Polygala chamaebuxus	C
Podocarpus rumphii	B	Polygala hottentotta	SI
Podocarpus salignus	B,SA	Polygala myrtifolia	B,SA,SI
Podocarpus totara	B	Polygala senega	B,PR
Podolepis auriculata	B,O	Polygala virgata	B,C,SA

POLYGONATUM

Polygonatum biflorum	B,JE
Polygonatum falcatum variegatum	CG
Polygonatum hirtum	JE
Polygonatum humile	JE
Polygonatum maximoviczii	SA
Polygonatum multiflorum	B,G,JE,SA,T
Polygonatum odoratum	B,C,G,JE,KI,SA,SG,ST
Polygonatum odoratum v thunbergii	JE
Polygonatum sibiricum	SG
Polygonatum verticillatum	B,JE,SA,SG
Polygonum alpinum	B,CG,SG
Polygonum angustifolium	SG
Polygonum arenarium	B
Polygonum convolvulus	B
Polygonum dibotrys	B
Polygonum divaricatum	SG
Polygonum fagopyrum	B
Polygonum filiforme	G,JE,SC
Polygonum filiforme 'Variegatum'	JE
Polygonum hydropiper 'Fastigiatum'	B
Polygonum lapathifolium	B
Polygonum sachalinense	B
Polygonum saggittatum	PR
Polygonum see also Persicaria/Fallopia	
Polygonum tataricum	B
Polygonum tinctorium	C
Polygonum viviparum	B,C,JE,SA
Polygonum weyrichii	B,JE,SG
Polymeria ambigua	B
Polymnia uvedalya	B
Polypodium punctatum	B
Polypodium vulgare	B,G
Polypogon monspeliensis	B,C,V
Polypompholyx multifida	B
Polypompholyx tenella pink	B
Polypompholyx westonii	B
Polyscias elegans	B,O,SA
Polyscias fulva	B
Polyscias murrayi	B,O
Polystichum erythrosora	B
Polystichum munitum	AP,B,G
Polystichum setiferum	G,N
Polystichum tsussimense	B,G
Polytaenia nuttallii	PR
Polyxena angustifolia	B
Polyxena ensifolia	AP,B,SC,SI
Polyxena odorata	AP,SC,SI
Polyxena sp	SI
Pomaderris elliptica	AU,B
Pomaderris hamiltonii	B
Pomaderris kumeraho	B,SA
Pomaderris myrtilloides	B
Pomaderris obcordata	AU,B,C
Pomaderris oraria v n.z.	B
Pomaderris phylicifolia	B
Pomaderris rugosa	B
Pomaderris sp	HA
Poncirus trifoliata	A,B,C,G,SA,SG
Pongamia pinnata	B,HA,O,SA
Pontederia cordata	JE
Pontederia cordata 'Alba'	JE
Populus alba	B,SA
Populus balsamifera	SG
Populus canescens	SA
Populus fremontii	B
Populus nigra	SA

Populus suaveolens	SG
Populus tremula	B,SA,SG
Porophyllum ruderale ssp macrocephalum	B
Portea fosteriana	B
Portea kermesiana	B
Portea kermesiana v rubra	B
Portea leptantha	B
Portea petropolitana	B
Portea petropolitana v extensa	B
Portea petropolitana v noettigii	B
Portulaca cryptopetala	CG,Y
Portulaca cyanosperma Hawaii	Y
Portulaca dbl mix	B,BS,C,D,F,TU
Portulaca dbl mix imp	S
Portulaca f1 hyb 'Sundial' mix	BS,CL,DT,F,R,SE,U,YA
Portulaca f1 hyb 'Sundial' s-c	B,BS,SE,T,U
Portulaca f2 hyb 'Calypso'	BD,BS,CL,J,V
Portulaca f2 hyb 'Kariba'	B,C,T
Portulaca foliosa	B
Portulaca grandiflora	B,CG,CO,KI,SG
Portulaca grandiflora 'Cloudbeater' mix	T
Portulaca grandiflora 'Swan Lake'	B,T
Portulaca marginata	B
Portulaca 'Minilace' mix	BS
Portulaca mundula DJF1350	Y
Portulaca oleracea	CG
Portulaca oleracea v sativa	B
Portulaca oleracea v sativa 'Aurea'	B
Portulaca oleracea 'Verdolaga Agria'	B
Portulaca philippii	Y
Portulaca pilosa	B
Portulaca single mix	C
Portulaca sp	SI
Portulaca 'Sundance'	D
Portulacaria afra	B
Posoqueria latifolia	B
Potentilla alba	SG
Potentilla alchemilloides	B,SG
Potentilla argentea	AP,B,BS,C,G,JE,SA,SG
Potentilla argentea v calibra	JE
Potentilla arguta	B,PR,SG
Potentilla argyrophylla	AP,F,JE,SA,T
Potentilla atrosanguinea	AP,B,C,F,G,JE,RH,SA, SC,SG,T,V
Potentilla atrosanguinea v argyrophylla	B,CC
Potentilla aurea	B,F,JE,SA,SC
Potentilla calabra	B
Potentilla canescens	B
Potentilla crantzii	AP,B,G,JE,SC,SG
Potentilla diversifolia	SG
Potentilla erecta	B,C,JE,SA,SC
Potentilla 'Etna'	P
Potentilla fragiformis see megalantha	
Potentilla fruticosa	G,SA
Potentilla fruticosa 'Pyrenaica'	B
Potentilla fruticosa v pumila	CC
Potentilla fulgens	B
Potentilla glandulosa ssp pseudorupestris	SG
Potentilla gracilis	AP,B,C,JE,SA,SC,SG
Potentilla grandiflora	B,JE,SA,SC
Potentilla 'Herzblut'	B,JE
Potentilla hippiana	B,G,SG
Potentilla hyb	B
Potentilla hyparctica	SC,SG
Potentilla impolita	B
Potentilla inquinans	SG

POTENTILLA

Potentilla lutea	C
Potentilla megalantha	AP,B,C,FH,G,JE,SA,SC, SG,T
Potentilla 'Melton Fire'	AP,G,T,V
Potentilla meyeri	B
Potentilla 'Monarch's Velvet'	BS,L,SE,T
Potentilla 'Monsieur Rouillard'	T
Potentilla nepalensis	AP,FH,MA,RH,SC,SG
Potentilla nepalensis 'Helen Jane'	B
Potentilla nepalensis 'Miss Willmott'	AP,B,BD,BS,C,CL,DT,F, FH,G,JE,KI,L,P,SA,SC,T
Potentilla nepalensis red	B,JE
Potentilla nepalensis 'Roxana'	B,JE
Potentilla neumanniana	B,SA
Potentilla nitida	AP,B,SC
Potentilla nivalis	AP,G,SC,SG
Potentilla norvegica	B,JE,SG
Potentilla palustris	B,G,SA,SC,SG
Potentilla pamirica	CC
Potentilla pectinisecta	B,SG
Potentilla pensylvanica	JE,SA
Potentilla pyrenaica	AP,SA
Potentilla recta	AP,B,F,FH,G,JE,SC,SG
Potentilla recta 'Alba'	B,F
Potentilla recta 'Macrantha'	B
Potentilla recta ssp pallida	AP,E,I
Potentilla recta sulphurea	AP,NS
Potentilla recta v warrenii	AP,BS,C,G,I,SA
Potentilla rupestris	AP,B,G,JE,SA,SC,SG
Potentilla salesovianum	SG
Potentilla simplex	CC
Potentilla sp mix	AP,SC,T
Potentilla speciosa	AP,B,C,JE,SC
Potentilla sterilis	B
Potentilla strigosa	SG
Potentilla tergemina	SG
Potentilla thurberi	AP,B,SC,SW
Potentilla tridentata	AP,B,JE
Potentilla villosa	AP,G,SG
Potentilla warrenii	CL,SG
Potentilla x hybrida 'Jean Jabber'	T
Pothomorphe peltata	B
Pourouma cecropiifolia	B,RE
Pouteria caimito	B
Pouteria campechiana	B
Pouteria obovata	B
Pouteria sapota	B
Pouteria sericea	B
Prasophyllum colensoi	B,SW
Prasophyllum cypochilum	B
Prasophyllum drummondii	B
Prasophyllum regium	B
Pratia angulata	B,SC,SG,SS
Pratia macrodon	B,SS
Pratia puberula	SG
Premna serratifolia	B
Prenanthes alba	PR
Prenanthes purpurea	SG
Prenanthes racemosa	B
Priestleya myrtifolia	B
Priestleya tomentosa	B,SI
Primula 'Alaska'	BS,CL
Primula algida	AP,CG,G
Primula 'All Sorts'	U
Primula alpicola	AP,B,C,CG,FH,JE,P,SA, SC,SG

Primula alpicola alba	CR,SC
Primula alpicola mix	AP,FH
Primula alpicola v violacea	B,CG,CR,FH,JE,SC,SG
Primula alpicola white & yellow	FH
Primula alpine mix	J
Primula amoena	SC,SG
Primula angustifolia	B,SW
Primula anisodora	AP,B,CG,P,SC
Primula aurantiaca	CG,CR
Primula auricula	AP,BD,BS,C,CO,CR,D, FH,G,J,JE,LG,R,S,SC, U,V
Primula auricula alpina 'Alp. Pastures' h-p	CR
Primula auricula alpina mix	FH,L,SA,ST,V,W
Primula auricula 'Ashwood Auriculas'	AS
Primula auricula 'Beckfoot Strain'	CR
Primula auricula 'Border'	F,M,W
Primula auricula dbl	BP,CR,P
Primula auricula 'Douglas Prize Mix'	T
Primula auricula 'Field House' mix	FH
Primula auricula 'Garden' mix	BP,FH
Primula aur. 'Genuine Old Irish Blue' h-p	CR
Primula auricula hyb	AP,C
Primula auricula 'Old Yellow Dusty Miller'	CR
Primula auricula pubescens	SA
Primula auricula show mix	FH
Primula auricula ssp bauhinii	AP,B,C,CR,JE
Primula beesiana	AP,B,BS,C,CG,CR,F,FH, G,JE,KI,P,SA,SC,SG,SU, U
Primula 'Beidermeier'	BS
Primula bellidifolia	AP,BP,CG,G,SC
Primula 'Bergfruhling Mix'	FH
Primula 'Bergfruhling' s-c	FH
Primula boveana	AP,FH,SC
Primula bulleyana	AP,B,BS,C,CG,CR,FH,I, JE,KI,P,SA,SC,SG,T
Primula burmanica	B,BS,CR,I,JE,SG
Primula candelabra hyb	AP,C,JE,PM,SC,W
Primula candelabra 'Oriental Sunrise'	BP
Primula candelabra 'PW Rainbows'	P
Primula candelabra sp mix	CG,FH,J
Primula candelabra 'T&M Hybrids'	T,V
Primula capitata	AP,CG,FH,SA,SC,SG
Primula capitata ssp mooreana	AP,B,BP,C,CR,FH,JE,SC
Primula cashmeriana	SA
Primula cernua	AP,FH,SC
Primula cernua ex F.Cabot coll	FH
Primula 'Charisma'	CL
Primula chionantha	AP,B,BS,C,CR,FH,JE,KI, SA,SC,T
Primula chungensis	AP,B,BS,C,CR,JE,SA,SC, SG
Primula clusiana	CC
Primula cockburniana	AP,B,C,CR,F,FH,G,HH, JE,SC,SG,W
Primula concholoba	AP,CR,FH,SC
Primula conspersa	SG
Primula cortusoides	AP,B,JE,SA,SC
Primula 'Crown'	BS
Primula daonensis	AP,CG,SC,SG
Primula darialica	CG,G
Primula denticulata	B,BD,C,CG,CR,DT,I,J,JE, KI,S,SC,SG,SU,T,V,YA
Primula denticulata 'Alba'	B,BP,BS,C,CG,CL,FH,JE
Primula denticulata 'Blue Selection'	B,FH,JE

PRIMULA

Primula denticulata 'Dark Colours Mix'	B,FH,JE	Primula f1 'Lucento'	BS
Primula denticulata 'Grandiflora Hybrids'	B,JE	Primula f1 'Meteor Series' s-c	YA
Primula denticulata hyb	D,L,S,ST	Primula f1 'Pageant'	BS,CL,KI,L,SE
Primula denticulata 'Lilac'	CL	Primula f1 'Pastel'	BS
Primula denticulata mix	BP,BS,CL,FH	Primula f1 'Prominent' s-c & mix	BS
Primula denticulata 'Ronsdorf Hybrids'	B,C	Primula f1 'Riviera'	YA
Primula denticulata 'Rubra'	B,CG,JE	Primula f1 'Serenade' s-c, mix	BS
Primula denticulata 'Rubra Selection'	B,JE	Primula f1 'Silver Lining'	T
Primula denticulata 'Ruby'	BS,C,CL,FH	Primula f1 'Spectrum' mix	L
Primula denticulata 'Snowball'	C	Primula f1 'Spectrum' s-c	T
Primula 'Dobies Coloured Hybrids'	D	Primula f1 'Supreme'	BS
Primula elatior	AP,B,C,CG,CO,CR,F,G,I,	Primula f1 'Wanda' mix	BS,D,DT,J,R,SE,t,U,YA
	JE,P,PM,SA,SC,SG,SU,	Primula f1 'Wanda's-c	B,BS,JE,FH
	V,W	Primula 'Fama' mix	BS,R
Primula elatior 'Chartreuse'	BS,F	Primula farinosa	AP,B,C,CC,CG,CR,FH,G,
Primula elatior cordifolia	SG		JE,SA,SC,SU
Primula elatior deep-blue primrose	W	Primula farinosa ex Bavaria	FH
Primula elatior hyb	FH	Primula farinosa ex JCA786.600	FH
Primula elatior hyb 'Alba'	JE	Primula fasciana	CG
Primula elatior hyb 'Aurea'	JE	Primula firmipes	CG,G
Primula elatior hyb 'Gigantea' mix	JE	Primula flaccida	FH
Primula elatior hyb 'Grandiflora' mix	JE	Primula floribunda v isabellina	W
Primula elatior hyb red colours	JE	Primula florindae	AP,B,BS,C,CC,CG,CR,
Primula elatior 'Old Curiosity'	F		FH,G,I,JE,KI,P,SA,SC,
Primula elatior 'Paris 90'	F		SG,T,W
Primula elatior 'Selected Blues'	F	Primula florindae hyb	BP,FH
Primula elatior ssp intricata	AP,CG,FH,SC	Primula florindae 'Keilour Hybrid'	B,JE
Primula elatior ssp leucophylla	I	Primula florindae 'Orange Hybrids'	C
Primula elatior ssp pallasii	AP,SC,SG,W	Primula florindae 'Red & Orange'	B
Primula elatior 'Victorian Mauve'	F	Primula florindae red shades	C,FH,JE,SC
Primula elatior 'Vierlander Gold'	JE	Primula florindae 'Ruby'	B,T
Primula elatior x P.juliae	W	Primula 'Fondant Creams'	U
Primula Elizabethan primr. 'Gallygaskins'	BP	Primula forbesii	W
Primula Elizabethan primr. 'Hose in Hose'	BP	Primula forrestii	AP,SC,SG,W
Primula Elizabethan primr. 'Jack in Green'	BP	Primula 'Forza'	CL
Primula Elizabethan primr. 'Jack/Hose mix'	P	Primula frondosa	B,C,FH,G,HH,JE,SA,SG,
Primula Elizabethan primrose 'Jackanapes'	BP		W
Primula Eliz. pr. 'Jackanapes-on-Horse'	BP	Primula geranifolia	AP,SC,SG
Primula Elizabethan primrose 'Pantaloons'	BP	Primula 'Giant' superb mix	S,T
Primula Elizabethan primrose 'Traditional'	BP	Primula glaucesens	AP,CG,SC
Primula Elizabethan strain	CR	Primula glaucesens ssp calycina	C,CR
Primula ellisae	CR	Primula glomerata	CR
Primula 'English Spring Trio'	C	Primula glutinosa	CG,CR
Primula 'Eskimo' mix	R	Primula 'Gold Lace Doctor's Delight'	CR
Primula 'European' hyb mix	FH	Primula 'Gold Laced'	AP,B,BP,BS,CR,F,FH,G,
Primula 'Exotic Collection' mix	BS,T		P,SE,T,W
Primula 'Exotic Collection' s-c	BS	Primula grandis	AP,CG,SC
Primula f1 'Bi-colour' s-c	BS,KI	Primula halleri	AP,B,CG,CR,FH,G,JE,
Primula f1 'Bright Lights'	U		SA,SC
Primula f1 'Can Can'	BS	Primula 'Hardy Species Mix'	BS,C,DT,F,SE,T
Primula f1 'Dania' mix	U,YA	Primula 'Harlow Carr hyb'	C,CR
Primula f1 'Dania Series' s-c	YA	Primula helodoxa	AP,C,CG,CR,JE,P,SA,SC,
Primula f1 'Daniella' s-c	YA		SG,T,W
Primula f1 'Danova Series' s-c, mix	BS,YA	Primula heucherifolia	AP,SC,SG
Primula f1 'Dreamer'	BS	Primula hirsuta	AP,B,C,CC,CR,FH,G,JE,
Primula f1 'Encore' mix	J		SA,SC
Primula f1 'Fama'	BS	Primula hyllopana	CG
Primula f1 'Finesse' mix	BS,CL,D,J,L,V,YA	Primula ianthina	CC
Primula f1 'Garden Pride' mix	J	Primula 'Inshriach' hyb	C,CG,P
Primula f1 'Grande Series' s-c	YA	Primula integrifolia	B,C,CR,JE,SA
Primula f1 hyb 'Countrywide'	S	Primula ioessa	CR,G
Primula f1 hyb 'Husky' mix	CL,S	Primula japonica	AP,BD,BS,CG,G,L,SA,
Primula f1 hyb 'Show' mix	BS,S		SC,SG
Primula f1 hyb 'Show' s-c	BS	Primula japonica 'Alba'	AP,B,CR,G,JE
Primula f1 'Jackpot' mix	S	Primula japonica 'Carminea'	AP,B,JE
Primula f1 'Lovely'	BS,CL,D	Primula japonica 'Deluxe Mix'	JE

PRIMULA

Primula japonica 'Fuji Hybrids'	P
Primula japonica 'Glowing Embers'	FH
Primula japonica 'Hall Barn Ripple'	CR
Primula japonica hyb mix	C,SC
Primula japonica 'Miller's Crimson'	AP,B,BP,BS,C,CR,JE,P, SA,SC
Primula japonica mix	B,PM,S,T
Primula japonica 'Postford White'	AP,B,BP,CR,G,P,SC,SG
Primula japonica red forms	FH
Primula japonica 'Valley Red'	AP,CG,CR,SC
Primula japonica white forms	FH
Primula jesoana	AP,SC,SG
Primula 'Jewelled Ladies'	M
Primula juliae	B,JE,SC
Primula juliana blue	BP
Primula juliana f1 'Mini'	T
Primula juliana 'Fireflies'	BP
Primula juliana 'Footlight Parade'	BP
Primula juliana mix	B
Primula juliana polyanthus mix	BP,FH
Primula juliana polyanthus s-c	BP
Primula juliana red	BP
Primula juliana 'Wanda' mix	C,T,V
Primula juliana yellow	BP
Primula latifolia	B,CR,SC
Primula laurentiana ex Great Wassi	FH
Primula littoniana	CL
Primula luteola	AP,B,C,F,JE,SG
Primula macrocalyx	G,SG
Primula macrophylla	AP,CR,SC
Primula, Mjr Knocker's 'Black Eyed Reds'	CR
Primula malacoides 'Ballerina mix'	CL,FH
Primula malacoides 'Benary's special mix'	C
Primula malacoides 'Bright Eyes'	T
Primula malacoides 'Classic' mix	BS
Primula malacoides f1 'Prima mix'	YA
Primula malacoides 'Lollipops mix'	YA
Primula malacoides mix	BD,BS,J,L
Primula malacoides 'Special' mix	BS,S
Primula malacoides 'Unwins Formula' mix	U
Primula 'Mardigras' primrose	KI,ST
Primula marginata	AP,CR,G,SC
Primula 'Marshalls Giant Hybrids'	M
Primula melanops	AP,SC,SG
Primula minima	B,CR
Primula mistassinica alba	FH
Primula miyabeana	CC,SC
Primula modesta fauriae	FH
Primula mollis	B,P,SC
Primula 'Morning Star'	CL
Primula 'Mother's Day'	BS,VH
Primula muscarioides	AP,FH,SC
Primula 'Mystery Packet'	BP
Primula nutans	CG
Primula obconica	KI,L,V,YA
Primula obconica 'Blue Agate'	T
Primula obconica 'Chartres' o-p	CL
Primula obconica 'Crown mix'	BS
Primula obconica deep blue	C
Primula obconica f1 'Ariane'	CL,FH
Primula obconica f1 'Cantata' mix	CL,S
Primula obconica f1 'Juno Series'	T
Primula obconica f1 'Libre' mix	CL,D
Primula obconica f1 'Pink Velvet' mix	CL
Primula obconica 'Fashbender Blue'	BS
Primula obconica fimbriata	BS
Primula obconica finest mix	C,J,ST
Primula obconica 'Freedom mix'	J
Primula obconica 'Gigantea Galaxy mix'	BS,YA
Primula obconica 'Special Formula'	CL
Primula obconica 'Suttons Giant fl mix'	S
Primula obconica 'Swift' o-p	CL
Primula palinuri	AP,SG
Primula pallasii	SG
Primula parryi	B,JE,SW
Primula pavianae	CG
Primula pedemontana	CG,SC
Primula petiolaris	AP,B,C,CC
Primula poisonii	G,SC,W
Primula Polyanthus 'Bolton's Sel. Giants'	BO
Primula, Polyanthus, 'Carnation Victorians'	BP
Primula, Polyanthus Cow. 'Amethyst'	BP
Primula, Polyanthus Cowichans 'Blue'	AP,BP
Primula, Polyanthus Cowichans f1	T
Primula, Polyanthus Cowichans 'Garnet'	BP,C
Primula, Polyanthus, Cowichans mix	BP,SC,W
Primula, Polyanthus, Cowichans 'Venetian'	BP
Primula, Polyanthus, Cowichans 'Yellow'	BP
Primula Polyanthus, 'Exhibition Giants'	BD
Primula Polyanthus, f1 'Concorde' s-c	YA
Primula Polyanthus, f1 'Crescendo' mix	AP,BS
Primula Polyanthus, f1 'Crescendo' s-c	BS,CL,D,DTJ,JE,R,S,T, U,YA
Primula Polyanthus, f1 'Harlequin' mix	F,J
Primula Polyanthus, f1 'Rainbow' mix	BS,CL,DT,L
Primula Polyanthus, f1 'Rainbow' s-c	BS,CL
Primula Polyanthus, f1 'Spring Rainbow'	D,S
Primula Polyanthus 'Firefly' hyb	W
Primula Polyanthus, 'Fuchsia Victorians'	BP
Primula Poly, 'Giant Bedding Galaxy Mix'	YA
Primula Polyanthus 'Lge Fl' mix	C,CO,F,J,T,TU,VH
Primula Polyanthus, ' Giant Fenland Strain'	M
Primula Polyanthus, 'Mauve Victorians'	BP
Primula Polyanthus, 'Muted Victorians'	BP
Primula Polyanthus, 'Old Rose Victorians'	BP
Primula Polyanthus, 'Pacific Blue'	KI
Primula Polyanthus, 'Pacific Giants'	BS,CL,F,J,KI,L,M,R,SE, SU,TU,U,YA
Primula Polyanthus, 'Pacific Giants' s-c	BD,BS
Primula Polyanthus, 'Regal mix'	KI
Primula Polyanthus, 'Rumba mix'	CL
Primula Polyanthus, S.D. 'Boys n' Girls'	BP
Primula Polyanthus, S.D. 'Chartreuse'	BP
Primula Polyanthus, S.D. 'Daybreak'	BP
Primula Polyanthus, S.D. 'Desert Sunset'	BP
Primula Polyanthus, S. D. 'Fire Dance'	BP
Primula Polyanthus, S.D. 'Flamingo'	BP
Primula Polyanthus, S.D. 'Fl.Arranger's'	BP
Primula Polyanthus, S.D. 'Grand Canyon'	BP
Primula Polyanthus, S.D. 'Harbour Lights'	BP
Primula Polyanthus, S.D. 'Harvest Yellows'	BP
Primula Polyanthus, S. D. 'Indian Reds'	BP
Primula Polyanthus, S.D. 'Limelight'	BP
Primula Polyanthus, S.D. 'Little Egypt'	BP
Primula Polyanthus, S.D. 'Marine Blues'	BP
Primula Polyanthus, S.D. 'Mexico'	BP
Primula Polyanthus, S.D. 'Midnight'	BP
Primula Polyanthus, S.Dollar strain mix	BP
Primula Polyanthus, S.D. 'New Pinks'	BP
Primula Polyanthus, S.D. 'Oranges/Lems'	BP
Primula Polyanthus, S.D. 'Paris '90'	BP
Primula Polyanthus, S.D. 'Ramona'	BP

PRIMULA

Primula Polyanthus, S.D. 'Reverie'	BP
Primula Polyanthus, S.D. 'Rustic Reds'	BP
Primula Polyanthus, S.D. 'Spice Shades'	BP
Primula Polyanthus, S.D. 'Tinted Shades'	BP
Primula Polyanthus, S.D. 'Vivid Shades'	BP
Primula Polyanthus, S.D 'Winter White'	BP
Primula Polyanthus, 'Southbank Strain'	CL
Primula Polyanthus special mix	CR
Primula Polyanthus 'Superb Mix'	D,DT
Primula Polyanthus 'Unwins Superb mix	U
Primula Polyanthus, 'Valentine Victorians'	BP
Primula Polyanthus, 'Victorians' mix	BP
Primula Polyanthus, 'Violet Victorians'	BP
Primula polyneura	AP,B,BP,C,CR,FH,JE,SA, SC,SG,W
Primula primrose dbl	BP,CR
Primula primrose hyb h-p	W
Primula primrose mix	BD,FH,TU
Primula prolifera	B,G
Primula prolifera v smithiana	B
Primula pruhoniciana f1 'Bergfruhling' s-c	JE
Primula pubescens	CR,DT,G
Primula pulverulenta	AP,B,BP,C,CG,CR,D,FH, G,JE,L,P,PA,SA,SC,SG, V,W
Primula pulverulenta 'Bartley Strain'	BP,CG,SC
Primula 'Quantum Series'	CL
Primula 'Regency' mix	R
Primula reidii	AP,BP
Primula reidii hyb	AP,FH
Primula reidii hyb white	FH
Primula 'Repeat Performance'	SE
Primula rosea	AP,CG,CR,FH,G,SC
Primula rosea 'Gigas'	B,G,JE
Primula rosea 'Grandiflora'	B,BD,BS,C,CL,JE,KI,L, SA,SC,T
Primula 'Rosetta Jones Strain' dbl prim	C,FH,SE
Primula rusbyi	B,SC,SW
Primula saxatilis	AP,B,BP,CG,FH,G,JE,SC, SG,W
Primula scandinavica	AP,C,FH,SC,W
Primula scotica	AP,B,CR,FH,SC,SG,T
Primula secundiflora	AP,B,C,CG,CR,JE,SA, SC,SG
Primula sieboldii	B,CR,FH,G,JE
Primula sieboldii 'Dancing Ladies'	BP
Primula sieboldii 'Galaxy'	BP
Primula sieboldii 'Manakoora'	BP
Primula sieboldii 'Pago-Pago'	BP,G
Primula sieboldii 'Tah-ni'	BP
Primula sieboldii 'Winter Dreams'	BP
Primula sikkimensis	AP,B,BS,CG,CR,FH,JE, KI,SA,SC,SG
Primula sikkimensis crimson & gold	FH
Primula sikkimensis hyb	FH
Primula sikkimensis sect CNW137	X
Primula sikkimensis 'Tilman's No.2'	CR
Primula sikkimensis v hopeana	CG
Primula sinensis	FH
Primula sinensis 'Fanfare'	BS,YA
Primula sinensis single superb mix	J,S
Primula sinoplantaginea	CR,SC
Primula sinopurpurea	AP,B,CR,JE,SG,W
Primula smithiana	C,CR,JE,SA,SC,SG
Primula sp nivalis section	CC
Primula sp nivalis section CNW 287	X

Primula sp sikkimensis section CNW 1157	X
Primula sp sikkimensis section CNW 512	X
Primula spectabilis	CC,CG
Primula 'Spectrum Bi-colour'	BS
Primula specuicola	B,SW
Primula 'Spring Parade'	F
Primula 'Supra'	CL
Primula 'Torino'	SE
Primula veris	w.a.
Primula veris 'Beckfoot Tudor Cowslips'	CR
Primula veris 'Coronation Cowslip'	BP,CR
Primula veris hyb mix	AP,B,C,FH
Primula veris ssp canescens exJCA	FH
Primula veris ssp columnea	AP,B,C,G,JE
Primula veris ssp macrocalyx	SG
Primula veris ssp veris v ampliata	SG
Primula veris Switzerland	FH
Primula verticillata	AP,FH,SC,SG
Primula verticillata ssp boveana	SG
Primula verticillata v simensis	SG
Primula vialii	w.a.
Primula villosa cottia hyb	CR
Primula viscosa	JE,SA
Primula vulgaris	w.a.
Primula vulgaris 'Asteroid'	T
Primula vulgaris 'Barnhaven Blues'	BP
Primula vulgaris 'Barnhaven Gold'	BP
Primula vulgaris 'Butterscotch'	BP
Primula vulgaris 'Candy Pinks'	BP
Primula vulgaris 'Casquet'	BP
Primula vulgaris dbl	T
Primula vulgaris 'Easterbloom' s-c	B
Primula vulgaris 'Ernst Benary' mix	BS,DT,L
Primula vulgaris 'Ernst Benary' s-c	BS,JE
Primula vulgaris f1 'African-violet' dp blue	B
Primula vulgaris f1 'Apple-blossom'	B
Primula vulgaris f1 'Birdseye'	B
Primula vulgaris f1 hyb 'Joker' mix	BS,C,DT,KI
Primula vulgaris f1 hyb 'Joker' s-c	BS
Primula vulgaris f1 hyb 'Orient Star'	BS,C,T
Primula vulgaris 'Harbinger'	BP
Primula vulgaris 'Harmony'	BP
Primula vulgaris 'Langdon's Blue'	B
Primula vulgaris 'Osiered Amber'	BP
Primula vulgaris 'Osterblute' s-c	JE
Primula vulgaris 'Potsdam'	C
Primula vulgaris 'Select Series'	B
Primula vulgaris 'Selection Blue'	JE
Primula vulgaris 'Selection Mixed'	JE
Primula vulgaris 'Selection Red'	JE
Primula vulgaris 'Selection White'	JE
Primula vulgaris 'Springtime mix'	BP
Primula vulgaris 'Tartan Reds'	BP
Primula vulgaris 'Traditional Yellows'	BP
Primula vulgaris 'True Blue'	T
Primula vulgaris 'Yellow Selection'	JE
Primula waltonii	CR,SG
Primula Wanda 'Blue Moon'	CR
Primula Wanda 'Cornish Primrose'	CR
Primula Wanda 'Ember Shadows'	CR
Primula Wanda 'Lilac Time'	CR
Primula Wanda 'Red Riding Hood'	CR
Primula Wanda 'Rosie-Posie'	CR
Primula Wanda 'Snow Shadows'	CR
Primula Wanda 'Supreme Mix'	BS,CL,T
Primula wilsonii	AP,C,SC,SG

PRIMULA

Primula x bullesiana	AP,B,BS,C,CG,DT,FH,G, JE,L,SA,SC
Primula x chunglenta	AP,B,JE,SC
Primula x kewensis	AP,FH,SC,W
Primula x kewensis 'Mountain Spring'	CL,FH
Primula x kewensis 'Thurgold'	BD,BS,C,SA
Primula x pubescens 'Gigantea'	B,JE
Primula x pubescens hyb	FH,JE
Primula x pubescens hyb 'Boothman's V'	FH
Primula x pubescens hyb 'Pink Denim'	CR
Primula yargongensis	B,CG,FH,JE,SC,SG
Prinsepia sinensis	B,SA,SG
Prinsepia uniflora	SA
Printzia polifolia	SI
Prismatocarpus fruticosus	SI
Pritchardia grandis	B
Pritchardia hillebrandii	B
Pritchardia pacifica	O,SA
Pritchardia pacifica g	B
Pritchardia thurstonii	O
Pritchardia thurstonii g	B
Pritzelago alpina	B
Proboscidea fragrans	B
Proboscidea louisianica	B,CP,G
Proboscidea parviflora v hohokamiana	B
Proboscidea parv.v hohokamiana paiute	B
Proboscidea parv.v hohokiama tohono	B
Proboscidea parviflora v parviflora	B
Proboscidea parviflora v sinaloensis	B
Proboscidea sp	CP
Pronaya fraseri	B
Prosopis chilensis	SA
Prosopis glandulosa	B
Prosopis juliiflora	B,SA
Prosopis pubescens	B
Prostanthera baxteri	B,SA
Prostanthera campbellii	AU
Prostanthera cuneata	AP,SG
Prostanthera lasianthos	B,HA,O,P,SA
Prostanthera nivea	B,SA
Prostanthera striatiflora	B
Protasparagus africanus	SI
Protasparagus densiflorus 'Gwebe'	SI
Protasparagus densiflorus 'Meyersii'	SI
Protasparagus natalensis	SI
Protasparagus retrofractus	SI
Protasparagus subulatus	SI
Protasparagus virgatus	SI
Protea acaulos	B,SI
Protea acuminata	B,SI
Protea amplexicaulis	B,O,SI
Protea angolensis	B
Protea arborea	B
Protea aristata	B
Protea aurea	C,SI
Protea aurea ssp aurea	B,O
Protea burchellii	B,O,SI
Protea caffra	B,SI
Protea canaliculata	B,SI
Protea collection of 4	C
Protea compacta	B,O,SA,SI,V
Protea cordata	B,C,SI
Protea coronata	B,O,SI
Protea cynaroides	B,C,O,SA,SI,V
Protea cynaroides named cvs	B
Protea decurrens	B

Protea dracomontana	B,SI
Protea effusa	SI
Protea eximia	B,C,O,SA,SI,V
Protea gaguedi	SI
Protea grandiceps	B,O,SA,SI,V
Protea humiflora	B,SI
Protea hyb	O,SI
Protea inyanganiensis	SI
Protea lacticolor	B,O,SI
Protea lacticolor x mundi	SI
Protea laetans	B
Protea laevis	B,SI
Protea lanceolata	B,SI
Protea laurifolia	B,O,SA,SI
Protea lepidocarpodendron	B,O,SI
Protea longifolia	B,C,O,SI
Protea lorifolia	B,SI
Protea magnifica	C,O,SI,V
Protea magnifica 'Cedarberg'	B
Protea magnifica 'Koo'	B
Protea magnifica white	B
Protea mundii	B,O,SI
Protea namaquana	SI
Protea nana	B,O,SA,SC,SI
Protea neriifolia	B,O,SA,SI,V
Protea neriifolia cream	C
Protea nitida	B,O,SI
Protea obtusifolia	B,O,SI,V
Protea pendula	B,SI
Protea petiolaris	SI
Protea pityphylla	B
Protea pudens	B
Protea pulchra	B,C
Protea punctata	B,O,SI
Protea recondita	B,SI
Protea repens	B,C,O,SI,V
Protea restionifolia	SI
Protea revoluta	SI
Protea roupelliae	B,SI
Protea rupicola	SI
Protea scabra	B
Protea scolopendriifolia	B,SI
Protea scolymocephala	B,C,O,SI
Protea simplex	B,SI
Protea sp mix	T
Protea speciosa	B,O,SI
Protea stokoei	B
Protea subvestita	B,SI
Protea sulphurea	B,O,SI
Protea susannae	B,O,SA,SI
Protea susannae x eximia	B
Protea tenax	B,SI
Protea turbiniflora	B
Protea venusta	SI
Protea welwitschii	B,SI
Protea witzenbergiana	B,SI
Protea witzenbergiana x pendula	B
Protorhus longifolia	B
Prumnopitys andina	B,SA
Prumnopitys ferruginea	B
Prumnopitys taxifolia	B,SS
Prunella grandiflora	AP,B,G,JE,MA,SA,SC
Prunella grandiflora 'Alba'	B,JE,SA
Prunella grandiflora 'Blue Loveliness'	B,P
Prunella grandiflora 'Pagoda'	B,C,I,JE,T,U,V
Prunella grandiflora 'Pink Loveliness'	B,P,RS

PRUNELLA

Prunella grandiflora 'Rosea'	B
Prunella hyssopifolia	RH
Prunella laciniata	SG
Prunella vulgaris	B,C,CP,JE,LA,SA,SG
Prunella vulgaris lilac	FH
Prunella webbiana	JE,PA,SC,SG
Prunella webbiana hort 'Rosea'	SG
Prununs prostrata	JE
Prunus africana	B
Prunus americana	SA
Prunus armeniaca cvs	B,SA
Prunus armeniaca v ansu	B
Prunus avium	B,C,SA
Prunus besseyi	B,N,SA,SG
Prunus capuli	C
Prunus caroliniana	B,SA
Prunus cerasifera	A,B,C,SG
Prunus cerasifera myrobalum	SA
Prunus cerasifera ssp divaricata	RS
Prunus davidiana	B,C,SA
Prunus domestica	SA
Prunus dulcis	B,SA
Prunus fremontii	B
Prunus fruticosa	B,SG
Prunus glandulosa	B,SA
Prunus ilicifolia	B,SA
Prunus incisa	N
Prunus institia	SA
Prunus jamasakura	B
Prunus japonica	B
Prunus laurocerasus	B,C,SA
Prunus lauro. 'Schipkaensis Macrophylla'	C
Prunus lusitanica	SA
Prunus lyonii	B,SA
Prunus maackii	B,N,SA,SG
Prunus mahaleb	A,B,C,SA
Prunus mandshurica	B,N,SA
Prunus maritima	B
Prunus mume	B,N,SA
Prunus nana	SG
Prunus nigra	B
Prunus padus	A,B,C,SA,SG
Prunus pensylvanica	SA,SG
Prunus persica	B,C,SA
Prunus prostrata	B
Prunus prostrata v discolor	N
Prunus pubigera	C
Prunus pumila	B,SG
Prunus salicifolia	B
Prunus salicina	B,SA
Prunus salicina v mandshurica	B
Prunus sargentii	B,SA
Prunus serotina	A,B,C,SA
Prunus serrulata	B,SA
Prunus sp mix	C
Prunus spinosa	A,B,C,SA,SG
Prunus subhirtella	B,SA
Prunus subhirtella 'Pendula'	B,SA
Prunus tangutica	SA
Prunus tenella	B,N,SA
Prunus tomentosa	B,G,SA,SG
Prunus triloba	B,C,SA
Prunus triloba v plena	C
Prunus virginiana	B,C,SA,SG
Prunus virginiana 'Schubert'	B
Prunus x yedoensis	B,SA

Psammophora longifolia	B
Psammophora modesta	B
Psammophora nissenii	B
Psathyrostachys juncea	SG
Pseudarthria viscida	B
Pseudobombax ellipticum	B
Pseudocydonia sinensis	B
Pseudoespostoa melanostele	Y
Pseudoespostoa melanostele v inermis	Y
Pseudognaphalium luteoalbum	B
Pseudognaphalium obtusifolium	B
Pseudolachnostylis maprouneifolia	B
Pseudolarix amabilis	B,C,N,SA
Pseudolobivia ancistrophora	Y
Pseudolobivia aurea	Y
Pseudolobivia aurea v dobeana	BC
Pseudolobivia aurea v fallax	Y
Pseudolobivia aurea v grandiflora	Y
Pseudolobivia callichroma	BC
Pseudolobivia calorubra pojoensis	BC
Pseudolobivia cardenasianum	BC
Pseudolobivia kratochviliana	Y
Pseudolobivia leucorhodantha	Y
Pseudolobivia longispina	Y
Pseudolobivia longispina v nigra	Y
Pseudolobivia obrepanda	Y
Pseudolobivia tapecuana	BC
Pseudolobivia torrecillasensis	Y
Pseudopanax anomalum	SS
Pseudopanax arboreus	B,SA,SS
Pseudopanax colensoi	B,SS
Pseudopanax colensoi v ternatus	B,C
Pseudopanax crassifolius	B,SA,SS
Pseudopanax crassifolius v trifoliatus	B
Pseudopanax ferox	B,SA
Pseudopanax laetus	B
Pseudopanax lessonii hybrids	B,SA
Pseudophoenix sargentii	B
Pseudosamanea guachepele	B
Pseudosbeckia swynnertonii	SI
Pseudotsuga macrocarpa	B,SA
Pseudotsuga menziesii	B,C,G,SA,SG
Pseudotsuga menziesii 'Caesia'	B,SA,SG
Pseudotsuga menziesii v glauca	B,C,SA,SG
Pseudotsuga menziesii 'Viridis'	B,C,SA,SG
Pseudotsuga sinensis	B
Pseudowintera colorata	B,SS
Psidium angulatum	B
Psidium friedrichsthalium	B,RE
Psidium guajava	B,HA,RE,SA
Psidium guajava 'Beaumont'	B
Psidium guajava 'Criolla'	B
Psidium guajava v pyriferum	B,C
Psidium guajava v pyriferum 'Bromar'	B
Psidium guajava 'White'	B
Psidium guajava 'Winter Wonder'	B
Psidium guineense	B
Psidium littorale	SG
Psidium littorale v littorale	B
Psidium littorale v littorale 'Gold'	B
Psidium littorale v longipes	B,C,HA,SA,SG
Psidium sartorium	B
Psilanthus bengalensis	B
Psilliostachys suworowi	C,CL,DT,KI,KS,L,S,SU,V
Psilliostachys suworowi 'Pink Pokers'	T
Psilostrophe sparsiflora	B

Psilostrophe tagetina	T
Psophocarpus tetragonolobus	B
Psoralea aphylla	B,SI
Psoralea australasica	B
Psoralea bituminosa	B,SA
Psoralea cuspidata	PR
Psoralea esculenta	PR
Psoralea lachnostachys	B
Psoralea leucantha	B
Psoralea macrostachya	B
Psoralea parva	B
Psoralea pinnata	B,C,SA,SI
Psoralea pustulata	B
Psoralea spicata	B
Psoralea tenuiflora	B
Psorothamnus spinosus	B
Psychotria capensis	B,C,SI
Psychotria viridis	B
Psydrax obovata ssp obovata	B
Psylliostachys suworowii	B
Ptaeroxylon obliquum	B
Ptelea trifoliata	B,C,G,N,RS,SA,T
Pteleopsis myrtifolia	B,SI
Pteris argyraea	B,SA
Pteris cretica	SG
Pteris cretica 'Albo-lineata'	B,SA,SG
Pteris cretica major	SA
Pteris cretica 'Mayii'	B,SA
Pteris cretica multifida	SA
Pteris cretica 'Parkeri'	B,SA,SG
Pteris cretica 'Rivertoniana'	B,SA
Pteris cretica 'Rowerii'	B,SA
Pteris cretica 'Tricolor'	B
Pteris cretica v alexandrae	SG
Pteris cretica 'Wimsettii'	B,SA
Pteris ensiformis	B,SA,SG
Pteris ensiformis 'Evergemiensis'	B
Pteris longifolia	B,SA,SG
Pteris multifida	B
Pteris multifida 'Ouvardii'	B
Pteris quadriaurita 'Faurei'	B
Pteris tremula	B,SA
Pteris umbrosa	B
Pteris umbrosa 'Berlin'	B
Pteris vittata	B
Pterocarpus angolensis	B,C,SI
Pterocarpus brenanii	SI
Pterocarpus indicus	B
Pterocarpus lucens	B
Pterocarpus marsupium	B,HA,SA
Pterocarpus rotundifolius	B,SI
Pterocarpus santalinus	B
Pterocarya fraxinifolia	A,B,RS,SA,SG
Pterocarya hupehensis	B
Pterocarya rhoifolia	B
Pterocarya stenoptera	B,SA
Pterocaulon sphacelatum	B
Pterocelastrus echinatus	SI
Pterocelastrus tricuspidarus	SI
Pteroceltis tartarinowii	B,SA
Pterocephalus hookeri KGB782	I
Pterocephalus perennis	FH,JE
Pterocephalus perennis ssp perennis	G,I
Pterocephalus plumosus	B
Pterodiscus ngamicus	B,SI
Pterogodium catholicum	SI

Pterogodium magnum	SI
Pterolobium hexapetalum	B
Pteronia camphorata	B,SI
Pteronia glauca	SI
Pteropogon humboldtianum	B,C,O,T
Pterospermum acerifolium	B,HA
Pterospermum suberifolium	B
Pterostylis barbata	B
Pterostylis nana	B
Pterostylis nana 'Gnangarra'	B
Pterostylis recurva	B
Pterostyrax corymbosa	SA
Pterostyrax hispida	B,CG,G,SA
Pterostyrax psilophylla	B,SA
Pterygota alata	B
Ptilostemon afer	AP,B,C,CG,FH,G,JE,SC
Ptilostemon chamaepeuce	CG
Ptilotus aervoides	B
Ptilotus astrolasius	B
Ptilotus auriculifolius	B,SA
Ptilotus axillaris	B
Ptilotus calostachyus	B,SA
Ptilotus carinatus	B
Ptilotus clementii	B,SA
Ptilotus exaltatus	AU,B,HA,O,SA
Ptilotus exaltatus semi-lunatus	HA
Ptilotus gomphrenoides	B
Ptilotus helipteroides	AU,B,O
Ptilotus macrocephalus	B
Ptilotus manglesii	B
Ptilotus obovatus	B,O,SA
Ptilotus obovatus v obovatus	AU
Ptilotus polakii	B
Ptilotus polystachyus	AU,B
Ptilotus rotundifolius	B,O,SA
Ptilotus spathulata	AU
Ptychoraphis augusta	RE
Ptychosperma elegans	B,HA,O,RE,SA
Ptychosperma macarthurii	B,HA,O,RE,SA
Ptychosperma microcarpa	SA
Ptychosperma microcarpa hyb	B,O
Puccinellia ciliata 'Menemen'	B
Puccinellia distans	B
Puccinellia festuciformis	CG
Puccinellia limosa	B
Puccinellia peisonis	B
Pueraria lobata	A,B,C,SA
Pulicaria crispa	B
Pulicaria dysenterica	B,C,G,LA,NS
Pulicaria vulgaris	B
Pulmonaria angustifolia	B
Pulmonaria mollissima	JE,SA,SG
Pulmonaria officinalis	G,JE,SA
Pulsatilla alba	AP,B,SC,SG
Pulsatilla albana	AP,G,RS,SC
Pulsatilla alpina	AP,B,BS,B,C,CG,G,JE, KI,SA,SC,SU,T
Pulsatilla alpina ssp apiifolia	AP,B,BS,G,J,JE,KI,SA, SC,SG,T
Pulsatilla alpina ssp sulphurea see apiifolia	
Pulsatilla ambigua	AP,B,G,RS,SC
Pulsatilla armena	CG
Pulsatilla dahurica	AP,SC,SG
Pulsatilla grandis	JE
Pulsatilla halleri	AP,B,C,CG,G,JE,P,RS, SC,T

PULSATILLA

Pulsatilla halleri ssp grandis	B,C,G
Pulsatilla halleri ssp slavica	AP,G,SC,SG
Pulsatilla halleri ssp taurica	JE
Pulsatilla montana	AP,B,C,CG,JE,SC,SG
Pulsatilla myrrhidifolia	B
Pulsatilla occidentalis	AP,C,JE,SC
Pulsatilla patens	AP,B,C,G,SC,SG,SW
Pulsatilla pratensis	AP,B,CG,G,SC
Pulsatilla pratensis ssp nigricans	B,G,JE,SC
Pulsatilla sulphurea	C,SE,V
Pulsatilla tenuiloba	SG
Pulsatilla turkzaninovii	SG
Pulsatilla vernalis	AP,B,C,G,JE,SC
Pulsatilla vulgaris	B,BS,C,CG,D,FH,G,I,J, JE,KI,PM,RH,SA,SC,SG, ST,T,W
Pulsatilla vulgaris 'Eve Constance'	AP,I
Pulsatilla vulgaris f alba	AP,B,BS,C,G,JE,SC
Pulsatilla vulgaris 'Fringed' mix	AP,C,D,P,SC,SE
Pulsatilla vulgaris 'Fringed' red	PM
Pulsatilla vulgaris 'Heiler Hybrids'	C,F,JE
Pulsatilla vulgaris mix	J,P,S,T,V
Pulsatilla vulgaris 'Papageno'	AP,BS,G,JE,SC
Pulsatilla vulgaris pink	NG
Pulsatilla vulgaris red & blue	N
Pulsatilla vulgaris 'Rode KloKke'	AP,G,JE,SC,SE
Pulsatilla vulgaris 'Rubra'	AP,B,BS,C,FH,G,RS,SA, SG
Pulsatilla vulgaris ssp gotlandica	AP,SC,SG
Pulsatilla vulgaris 'Violacea'	B
Pulsatilla zimmermanii	RH
Pultenaea acerosa	B
Pultenaea blakelyi	HA
Pultenaea canaliculata v latifolia	B
Pultenaea cunninghamii	HA
Pultenaea daphnoides	B,SA
Pultenaea daphnoides v obcordata	B
Pultenaea ericifolia	B
Pultenaea euchila	B,HA
Pultenaea flexilis	B,HA
Pultenaea foliolosa	HA
Pultenaea juniperina	B,HA
Pultenaea microphylla	B,HA,SA
Pultenaea microphylla v cinerescens	B
Pultenaea myrtoides	B
Pultenaea obcordata	B
Pultenaea paleacea v paleacea	B
Pultenaea polifolia	B
Pultenaea reticulata	B
Pultenaea retusa	B,HA
Pultenaea rosmarinifolius	HA
Pultenaea scabra	B
Pultenaea skinneri	B
Pultenaea tenuifolia	B
Pultenaea villosa	AU,B,HA,SA
Pultenaea villulosa	B
Pultenaea viscosa	B,HA
Punica granatum	AP,B,C,HA,SA,V
Punica granatum 'Minima'	B,SA
Punica granatum v nana	B,BD,BS,C,CG,HA,JE,N, SA,V
Punica granatum v nana 'Orange Pygmy'	B
Pupalia lappacea	B
Purshia tridentata	B,C
Puschkinia scilloides	AP,B,G,SC
Puschkinia scilloides 'Alba'	AP,B

Puschkinia scilloides Pol5328	MN
Puschkinia scilloides v libanotica	FH
Putterlickia pyracantha	SI
Puya alpestris	B
Puya berteroniana	B
Puya chilensis	B,SA
Puya coerulea	AP,B,P
Puya coquimbensis	SA
Puya mirabilis	B,BC,C,SA,SG,W,Y
Puya sp mix	C
Pychnostachys urticifolia	B
Pycnanthemum flexuosum	B,C
Pycnanthemum incanum	NT
Pycnanthemum pilosum	B,C,G,JE,PR
Pycnanthemum pycnanthemoides	B,C,CP
Pycnanthemum tenuifolium	CP,PR
Pycnanthemum virginianum	B,PR
Pycnosorus chrysantha	O
Pycnosorus globosus	B,O
Pycnostachys coerulea	SI
Pycnostachys glomerata	B
Pycnostachys reticulata	SI
Pycnostachys urticifolia	SI
Pygmaecereus bylesianus	BC
Pyracantha angustifolia	B,C,HA,SA
Pyracantha aurantiaca	B
Pyracantha coccinea	B,C,SA,SG
Pyracantha coccinea 'Lalandei'	B,C
Pyracantha crenatoserrata	B
Pyracantha crenulata	B,SA
Pyracantha rogersiana	B
Pyracantha rogersiana 'Flava'	B
Pyrola asarifolia	C
Pyrola minor	FH,SG
Pyrola norvegica	C
Pyrola rotundifolia	CG
Pyrrhocactus andreaeana	B
Pyrrhocactus atrispinosus	B
Pyrrhocactus bulbocalyx	B,Y
Pyrrhocactus cachytayensis	Y
Pyrrhocactus catamarcensis	B,Y
Pyrrhocactus dubius	B,Y
Pyrrhocactus megliolli	B
Pyrrhocactus strausianus	B,Y
Pyrrhocactus umadeave	Y
Pyrrhocactus umadeave v marayesensis	B,BC
Pyrrosia rupestris	HA
Pyrus betulifolia	B,SA
Pyrus calleryana	A,B,SA
Pyrus communis	B,SA
Pyrus communis 'Bartlett'	B
Pyrus pyrifolia	B,SA,SG
Pyrus salicifolia	SA
Pyrus ussuriensis	B,SA,SG
Qualea paraensis	B
Quaqua dependens	B
Quaqua mammilaris	B
Quaqua sp	SI
Quararibea mestonii	B
Quercus acutissima	B,HA,N,SA
Quercus agrifolia	B,SA
Quercus alba	B,SA
Quercus arizonica	B
Quercus bicolor	B,HA,N,SA
Quercus canariensis	B,SA
Quercus castaneifolia	B,N,SA

QUERCUS

Quercus cerris	B,C,HA,SA	Quercus variabilis	B,SA
Quercus chapmanii	B	Quercus velutina	B,SA
Quercus chrysolepis	B,SA	Quercus virginiana	B,SA
Quercus cirispula	B	Quercus wislizenii	B,SA
Quercus coccinea	B,N,SA	Quesnelia augusto-coburgii	B
Quercus costaricensis	B	Quesnelia blanda	B
Quercus dentata	B,SA	Quesnelia humilis	B
Quercus douglasii	B,HA,SA	Quesnelia liboniana	B
Quercus dumosa	B,SA	Quesnelia marmorata	B
Quercus durata	B	Quesnelia quesneliana	B
Quercus ellipsoidalis	B,SA	Quesnelia seideliana	B
Quercus emoryi	B	Quesnelia testuda	B
Quercus engelmannii	B	Quillaja saponaria	SA
Quercus faginea	SA	Quinoa	CO
Quercus falcata	B,SA	Quisqualis indica	B
Quercus falcata v pagodifolia	B,SA	Rabdosiella calycina	B,SI
Quercus frainetto	SA	Rabiea albinota	B
Quercus gambellii	B,SA	Rabiea albipunctata	B
Quercus garryana	B,SA	Rabiea lesliei	B
Quercus georgiana	B	Radermachera frondosa	B
Quercus glandulifera	B	Radermachera sinica	B,C,HA,SAO,
Quercus glauca	SA	Radermachera sinica 'China Doll'	HA
Quercus hemispherica	B	Radermachera sinica 'Jumbo'	B,S
Quercus hypoleucoides	B	Radermachera xylocarpa	B
Quercus ilex	A,B,C,HA,N,SA	Radyera farragei	B,SA
Quercus ilicifolia	B,N,SA	Radyera urens	B,SI
Quercus imbricaria	B,SA	Rafinesquia neomexicana	B,SW
Quercus incana	B,SA	Rafnia amplexicaulis	B,SI
Quercus ithaburensis	SA	Rafnia capensis	B,SI
Quercus kelloggii	B,SA	Rafnia sp	SI
Quercus laevis	B	Raimondia quinduensis	B
Quercus laurifolia	B,SA	Ramonda myconi	AP,B,C,CC,CG,FH,G,I,
Quercus leucotrichophora	B		JE,P,PM,SC,SG,T
Quercus lobata	B,HA,SA	Ramonda nathaliae	B,G,JE
Quercus lusitanica	HA,SA	Ramonda serbica	AP,B,G,JE,SC,SG
Quercus lyrata	B,SA	Randia dumetorum	B
Quercus macedonica	SA	Randia formosa	B
Quercus macrocarpa	B,HA,N,SA	Randia megacarpa	B
Quercus marilandica	B,SA	Ranunculus abortinus	B
Quercus mexicana	B	Ranunculus aconitifolius	AP,B,C,JE,SA,SC
Quercus michauxii	B,SA	Ranunculus acris	B,CO,LA,SU,V
Quercus mongolica	SA,SG	Ranunculus acris 'Citrinus'	AP,B,G,P
Quercus muehlenbergii	B,SA	Ranunculus alpestris	AP,C,SC
Quercus myrsinifolia	B,SA	Ranunculus amplexicaulis	AP,B,JE,SC,SG
Quercus myrtifolia	B	Ranunculus aquatilis	B
Quercus nigra	B,SA	Ranunculus arvensis	B
Quercus nuttallii	B,SA	Ranunculus asiaticus 'Elfin'	BS
Quercus oblongifolia	B	Ranunculus asiaticus f1 'Accolade' s-c	CL
Quercus palustris	B,HA,N,SA	Ranunculus a. f1 'Bloomingdale' mix	C,DT,J,T,V
Quercus petraea	B,SA	Ranunculus a. f1 'Bloomingdale' s-c	B,YA
Quercus phellos	B,N,SA	Ranunculus asiaticus 'Giant mix'	BS,KI
Quercus phillyreoides	B,N,SA	Ranunculus asiaticus S.L18 Jordan	MN
Quercus polymorphus	SA	Ranunculus bulbosus	B,SG
Quercus prinoides	B	Ranunculus calandrinioides	AP,SC,SG
Quercus prinus	B,SA	Ranunculus calandrinioides S.F137	MN
Quercus pubescens	B,SA	Ranunculus cortusifolius	SG
Quercus pyrenaica	SA	Ranunculus cortusifolius Canaries	MN
Quercus reticulata	B	Ranunculus crithmifolius	AU,B,SS
Quercus robur	B,C,HA,N,SA	Ranunculus dbl mix	C
Quercus robur 'Fastigiata'	B	Ranunculus enysii	AU,B,SS
Quercus rubra	B,HA,N,SA	Ranunculus eschscholtzii	B,G,SG
Quercus rugosa	B	Ranunculus ficaria	B
Quercus sadlerana	B	Ranunculus flammula	B,G,SG
Quercus shumardii	B,SA	Ranunculus glacialis	B,JE,SA,SC
Quercus stellata	B,SA	Ranunculus godleyanus	AU
Quercus suber	B,HA,N,SA	Ranunculus gracilipes	B,SS

RANUNCULUS

Ranunculus gramineus	AP,B,G,JE,P,PM,SA,SC	Reaumuria hirtella	B
Ranunculus grandis	SG	Rebutia albiareolata	B,Y
Ranunculus haastii	AU,B,SS	Rebutia albipilosa	B
Ranunculus hispid	PR	Rebutia alegraiana	Y
Ranunculus insignis	AP,B,P,SC,SS	Rebutia almeyeri	Y
Ranunculus jovis	B	Rebutia archibuiningiana	B
Ranunculus lappaceus	AP,SC,SS	Rebutia aureicentra	Y
Ranunculus lingua 'Grandiflorus'	B,P	Rebutia aureispina	B
Ranunculus lyallii	AU,B,SA,SS	Rebutia cajasensis	B
Ranunculus marginatus	B	Rebutia calliantha	B,Y
Ranunculus monroi	B,SS	Rebutia canaletas	B
Ranunculus montanus	B	Rebutia chrysacantha	B,Y
Ranunculus multifidus	B,SI	Rebutia chrysacantha v elegans	Y
Ranunculus nepalensis	B	Rebutia cintiensis	B
Ranunculus nivicola	P	Rebutia corroana	B,Y
Ranunculus occidentalis	SG	Rebutia curvispinus	CH
Ranunculus ophioglossifolius	B,NS,SG	Rebutia deminuta	B
Ranunculus parnassifolium	AP,B,JE,SC	Rebutia densipectinata	B
Ranunculus pensylvanicus	PR	Rebutia donaldiana	B,CH,Y
Ranunculus petiveri	B	Rebutia ehretiana	Y
Ranunculus platanifolius	AP,SG	Rebutia erinacea	Y
Ranunculus polyanthemos	B,SC	Rebutia erinacea v catarinensis	B,Y
Ranunculus pyrenaeum	B,C,JE,SA,SC	Rebutia fiebrigii	B
Ranunculus repens	B	Rebutia fiebrigii v densiseta	B
Ranunculus rhomboideus	B,PR	Rebutia fiebrigii v nivosa	B
Ranunculus sceleratus	B	Rebutia flavistyla	B,CH
Ranunculus sp ex Morocco	HH	Rebutia frankii	B
Ranunculus sp mix	AP,SC,T	Rebutia fulviseta	B,CH
Ranunculus thora	AP,B,JE	Rebutia gibbulosa	B
Ranunculus trichophyllum	B	Rebutia glomeriseta	Y
Ranunculus uncinatus	B	Rebutia graciliflora	B,Y
Raoulia australis	AP,SC,SG,SS	Rebutia graciliflora v borealis	B
Raoulia eximia	SS	Rebutia gracilispina	B
Raoulia glabra	AP,B,SC,SG,SS	Rebutia grandiflora	B,BC,Y
Raoulia grandiflora	SS	Rebutia hediniana	B
Raoulia haastii	SS	Rebutia heliosa	B
Raoulia hectori	SS	Rebutia heliosa v cajasensis	B
Raoulia hookeri	AP,B,SC	Rebutia hoffmannii	CH,Y
Raoulia mammillaris	SS	Rebutia HS13	BC
Raoulia monroi	AP,SC,SS	Rebutia HS189	BC
Raoulia subsericea	AP,B,SC,SS	Rebutia ithyacantha	B
Raoulia tenuicaulis	B,PM,SS	Rebutia jujuyana	B
Raoulia youngii	SS	Rebutia krainziana	B,CH,Y
Rapanea howitteana	SA	Rebutia krainziana albiflora	BC
Rapanea melanophloeos	B,SI	Rebutia kupperana	B
Raphia australis	B	Rebutia kupperiana v spiniflora	B
Raphia farinifera	B	Rebutia lanata	B,Y
Raphia gigantica	B	Rebutia lateritia KK1519	Y
Raphia monbuttorum	B	Rebutia lauii	B
Raphiolepsis indica	HA,SA	Rebutia lepida	Y
Raphiolepsis umbellata	SA	Rebutia longigibba	B,Y
Raphiolepsis umbellata var ovata	C,HA	Rebutia mammillosa v australis	Y
Ratibida columnaris	AV,HW,JE,SA	Rebutia mammillosa v orientalis	CH,Y
Ratibida columnifera	B,C,HW,PR,SC,V	Rebutia marsoneri	B,Y
Ratibida columnifera f pulcherrima	B,JE	Rebutia marsoneri v brevispina	B
Ratibida pinnata	B,G,HW,JE,PR	Rebutia maxima	B
Ratibida tagetes	B	Rebutia menesesii	B,Y
Rauvolfia caffra	B,SA,SI	Rebutia middendorfii	SA
Rauvolfia serpentina	B	Rebutia miniscula	B,BC,CH,Y
Rauvolfia tetraphylla	B	Rebutia miniscula f kariusiana	B
Rauvolfia verticillata	B	Rebutia miniscula ssp grandiflora	Y
Rauwenhoffia leichardtii	B	Rebutia miniscula v knuthiana	B,Y
Ravenala madagascariensis	B,C,O	Rebutia minuscula	B
Ravenea glauca	B	Rebutia minuscula v densispina	B
Ravenea madagascariensis	B,SA	Rebutia minuscula v rosea	Y
Ravenea rivularis	B,HA,O,SI	Rebutia multispina	B,Y

REBUTIA

Rebutia narvaecensis	B
Rebutia neocumingii	Y
Rebutia nitida	B
Rebutia patericalyx	Y
Rebutia permutata	Y
Rebutia pilosa	B
Rebutia platygona	Y
Rebutia poecilantha	B,Y
Rebutia polymorpha	Y
Rebutia potosina	B
Rebutia pseudodeminuta	B
Rebutia pseudodeminuta v schneideriana	B
Rebutia pseudodeminuta v schumanniana	B
Rebutia pulquinensis	B
Rebutia pulquinensis v mairananensis	B,Y
Rebutia pygmaea	CH
Rebutia ritteri	B
Rebutia robustispina	B
Rebutia salmonea	CH
Rebutia sanguinea	BC
Rebutia senilis	B,Y
Rebutia senilis v cana	Y
Rebutia senilis v chrysacantha	B
Rebutia senilis v elegans	B,Y
Rebutia senilis v erecta	B
Rebutia senilis v gracilis	Y
Rebutia senilis v iseliana	B,CH,Y
Rebutia senilis v kesselringiana	B,BC,Y
Rebutia s. v kesselringiana 'Rose Of York'	B
Rebutia senilis v lilacino-rosea	Y
Rebutia senilis v longiflora	B
Rebutia senilis v luteospina	Y
Rebutia senilis v schieliana	B
Rebutia senilis v stuemeri	B,Y
Rebutia sp mix	C,CH,SO,Y
Rebutia spegazziniana	B
Rebutia spinosissima	B
Rebutia steinbachii v polymorpha	B
Rebutia sucrensis	B
Rebutia tamboensis	B
Rebutia tiraquensis v electracantha	B,Y
Rebutia tuberosa	B
Rebutia vatteri	CH
Rebutia violaciflora see minuscula	
Rebutia vorwerkii	Y
Rebutia wessneriana	B,Y
Rebutia wessneriana v beryllioides	B
Rebutia xanthocarpa	B,CH,Y
Rebutia xanthocarpa v citricarpa	B
Rebutia xanthocarpa v coerulescens	B
Rebutia xanthocarpa v dasyphrissaa	B,Y
Rebutia xanthocarpa v salmonea	B,Y
Rebutia xanthocarpa v violaciflora	B
Rechsteineria see Sinningia	
Reclamation ground cover,grasses	B
Regelia ciliata	B,SA
Regelia cymbifolia	B
Regelia inops	B
Regelia megacephala	B
Regelia velutina	B,SA
Rehmannia angulata see elata	
Rehmannia elata	AP,B,BS,C,CL,E,F,G,HH, JE,SA,SC,V
Rehmannia elata 'Popstar'	AP,T
Rehmannia glutinosa	C
Rehmannia 'Pink Perfection'	U

Rehmannia sp	RS
Reinhardtia gracilis	O
Reissantia indica	B
Relhania pungens	B,SI
Renealmia alpina	B
Reseda alba	B,G,SC,SG,V
Reseda lutea	B,C,CO,G,LA,RH,SG
Reseda luteola	B,C,CP,LA,NS,RH
Reseda muricata	B
Reseda odorata	CP,F,J,KI,KS,SE,ST,SU,U
Reseda odorata 'Alba'	KS
Reseda odorata 'Fragrant Beauty'	T
Reseda odorata 'Grandiflora'	B,C
Reseda odorata 'Machet'	B,C,D,V
Reseda odorata 'Red Monarch'	B
Reseda orientalis	B
Reseda stenostachya	B
Restio bifarius	B,SI
Restio fimbriatus	O
Restio gracilis	O
Restio pachystachyus	SI
Restio quadratus	SI
Restio tetraphyllus	AP,AU,B,SA
Restio tetraphyllus ssp meiostachys	O
Restio tremulus	B,O
Retama monosperma	B,C,SA
Retama raetam	B,SA
Retama raetam v judaica	B
Retama spaerocarpa	SA
Rhadamanthus namibensis	B,SI
Rhagodia baccata	B
Rhagodia preissii	B
Rhamnus alaternus	SA
Rhamnus alpinus	G
Rhamnus californicus	B
Rhamnus carolinianus	B,SA
Rhamnus catharticus	B,C,SA,SG
Rhamnus davurica	SG
Rhamnus frangula	A,B,SA
Rhamnus frangula 'Columnaris'	B
Rhamnus japonicus	B
Rhamnus koraiensis	B
Rhamnus lycioides	SA
Rhamnus prinoides	B,SI
Rhamnus purshianus	B
Rhamnus saxatilis ssp saxatilis	SG
Rhaphidophora decursiva	B
Rhaphiolepis indica	B
Rhaphiolepis indica 'Clara'	B
Rhaphiolepis x delacourii	B
Rhaphiolepsis umbellata	B
Rhaphiolepsis umbellata v integerrima	CG
Rhaphithamnus spinosus	SA
Rhapis excelsa	B,O,SA
Rhapis subtilis	B,O
Rhaponticum carthamoides	CG,SG
Rhaponticum chamarense	SG
Rhaponticum orientale	SG
Rhaponticum serratuloides	SG
Rheedia macrophylla	B
Rheedia madruno	B
Rheedia magnifolia	B
Rheum altaicum	SG
Rheum australe	B,JE
Rheum compactum	B,SG
Rheum emodi	CG,SA

RHEUM

Rheum officinale	B
Rheum palmatum	B,BS,CG,SC,T
Rheum palmatum 'Atrosanguineum'	B,PA,PM
Rheum palmatum 'Bowles Crimson'	B,BS
Rheum palmatum red	SA
Rheum palmatum v tanguticum	B,JE,P,SA
Rheum palm. v tanguticum 'Red Selection'	JE
Rheum rhaponticum	JE
Rheum tibeticum	JE
Rheum undulatum	SG .
Rheum x cultorum 'Glaskin's Perpetual'	B
Rheum x cultorum 'Victoria'	B
Rhexia virginica	AP,C,JE
Rhigozum brevispinosum	B,SI
Rhigozum obovatum	B,SI
Rhinanthus angustifolius	B
Rhinanthus minor	B,C,CC,LA,RS,SU
Rhinanthus serotinus ssp grandiflorus	B
Rhinephyllum broomii	AP,B,SC,SG
Rhinephyllum macradenium	B
Rhinephyllum muirii	B
Rhipogonum scandens	SS
Rhipsalis baccifera	Y
Rhipsalis cappiliformis	SG
Rhipsalis clavata	SG
Rhipsalis fasciculata	CH
Rhipsalis heptagona	SG
Rhipsalis horrida	CH
Rhipsalis houlletiana	SG
Rhipsalis mesembrianthemoides	SG
Rhipsalis sp mix	C,CH
Rhizobium inoculant	B
Rhodanthe anthemoides	AU,FH
Rhodanthe 'Baby Sun'	U
Rhodanthe charsleyae	B,O
Rhodanthe chlorocephala 'Alba'	KS
Rhodanthe chlorocephala 'Bonnie'	B,D,KS,M
Rhodanthe chlorocephala 'Brilliant'	KS
Rhodanthe chlorocephala dbl mix	BS,CO,J,L,KI,ST,SU,T, TU
Rhodanthe chlorocephala dbl s-c	T
Rhodanthe chlorocephala dbl white	C
Rhodanthe chlorocephala 'Giant Mix'	KS
Rhodanthe chlorocephala 'Goliath'	B,F
Rhodanthe chlorocephala semi-dbl	U
Rhodanthe chlorocephala 'Special'	S
Rhodanthe chlorocephala ssp chloroc.	B,O
Rhodanthe chlorocephala ssp roseum	B,BS,C,DT,F,HA,O,R,SG, SU,V
Rhodanthe citrina	B,O
Rhodanthe 'Ebony Rouge'	SE
Rhodanthe floribunda	B,O
Rhodanthe manglesii	B,BS,C,CO,D,HA,J,KI,L, O,TU,V
Rhodanthe manglesii 'Maculata Album'	B,C,KS
Rhodanthe manglesii 'Maculatum' mix	BS,C
Rhodanthe m. 'Maculatum Roseum'	B,C,KS
Rhodanthe manglesii 'Pinky'	BS,U
Rhodanthe manglesii 'Timeless Rose'	B,C
Rhodanthe polygalifolia	B,O
Rhodanthe sterilescens	B,O
Rhodanthe stricta	B,O
Rhodanthe 'Tetred'	C
Rhodanthemum hosmariense	HH
Rhodiola himalensis v ishidae	B
Rhodiola kirilovii	B,CG

Rhodiola pinnatifida	SG
Rhodiola primuloides v pachyclada	B
Rhodiola rhodantha	AP,B,SC
Rhodiola rosea	B,C,I,JE,SC,SG
Rhodocactus v gran chaco	B
Rhodochiton atrosanguineum	AP,B,BS,C,CL,D,DT,F,G, J,S,SA,SE,SG,T
Rhodocoma arida	B,SI
Rhodocoma fruticosa	B,SI
Rhodocoma gigantea	B,SI
Rhododendron adenogynum	B
Rhododendron aganniphum	B
Rhododendron agastum	B
Rhododendron albiflorum	AP,B
Rhododendron albrechtii	CG,SG
Rhododendron albrechtii h-p	X
Rhododendron alutaceum	X
Rhododendron amamiense	CC
Rhododendron ambiguum	B,SG
Rhododendron ambiguum C&H7025	X
Rhododendron angustinii	SG
Rhododendron anhweiense	X
Rhododendron anthosphaerum	B
Rhododendron arborescens	X
Rhododendron arboreum	B,C,SA
Rhododendron arboreum ssp delavayi	B
Rhododendron asterochnoum C&H7051	X
Rhododendron asterochnoum Leibo	X
Rhododendron asterochnoum Yunnan	X
Rhododendron atlanticum	AP,B,SA
Rhododendron augustinii	N
Rhododendron aureum	B
Rhododendron aureum MW10R	X
Rhododendron auriculatum	X
Rhododendron austrinum	B
Rhododendron barbatum	SA
Rhododendron beesianum	B,SA
Rhododendron 'Boule De Neige'	B
Rhododendron brachycarpum	AP,CC,SG
Rhododendron brachycarpum v tigerstedii	X
Rhododendron 'Briarcliff'	B
Rhododendron bureavii	SG
Rhododendron burmanicum	CG
Rhododendron calendulaceum	B
Rhododendron calophytum C&H7111	X
Rhododendron campanulatum	SA
Rhododendron campanulatum TW34	X
Rhododendron campylocarpum	CC
Rhododendron camtschaticum	AP,B,G,JE,SC
Rhododendron canadense	B
Rhododendron 'Cardinalis'	B
Rhododendron carolinianum see minus	
Rhododendron catawbiense	B,SA
Rhododendron catawbiense 'Album'	B
Rhododendron cat. 'Album Elegans' sel.	B
Rhododendron catawbiense hyb	C
Rhododendron cat. 'Roseum Varieties'	B
Rhododendron catawbiense v compactum	B
Rhododendron cephalanthum	B
Rhododendron ciliicalyx	B,CG
Rhododendron 'Cleopatra'	B
Rhododendron concinnum (Tower Court)	SG,X
Rhododendron coriaceum	CG
Rhododendron crinigerum	B
Rhododendron cubittii	CG
Rhododendron 'Cunningham's White'	B

RHODODENDRON

Rhododendron cyanocarpum	B
Rhododendron dauricum	B,SG
Rhododendron davidsonianum	B,CG
Rhododendron decatros	B
Rhododendron decorum	B,SG,X
Rhododendron decorum CNW602	X
Rhododendron degronianum	B,X
Rhododendron delavayi	CG
Rhododendron delavayi AC911	X
Rhododendron delavayi CNW994	X
Rhododendron denudatum AC1143	X
Rhododendron denudatum C&H7118	X
Rhododendron denudatum EGM334	X
Rhododendron 'Dexter's Pink'	B
Rhododendron dilatatum	X
Rhododendron discolor sdling x	
R. 'Bisciut Box' h-p 1994	X
Rhododendron edgeworthii	CC,CG
Rhododendron edgeworthii CNW896	X
Rhododendron ellipticum	CG
Rhododendron 'Exbury' hyb	B
Rhododendron excellens C&H7180	X
Rhododendron faberi	B
Rhododendron fargesii	SA
Rhododendron fargesii aff AC1104	X
Rhododendron faucium KR3465	X
Rhododendron fauieri MW306R	X
Rhododendron fauieri MW327R pink	X
Rhododendron 'Fedora'	B
Rhododendron ferrugineum	AP,B,C,G,JE,SA,SC
Rhododendron fortunei	B,SA,X
Rhododendron fortunei f1 Lu Shan	B,N
Rhododendron fortunei f1 Lu Shan h-p	C
Rhododendron fortunei ssp discolor	B,SA,X
Rhododendron fulvum	B
Rhododendron fumidum CNW1048	X
Rhododendron fumidum CNW944	X
Rhododendron fumidum CNW974	X
Rhododendron 'Ghent' hyb pink selection	B
Rhododendron glanduliferum C&H7131	X
Rhododendron glaucophyllum	CC,SG
Rhododendron glischrum	B
Rhododendron gongshanensis	B
Rhododendron grande	X
Rhododendron 'Gwyllt King' h-p	X
Rhododendron 'Gwyllt King' o-p	X
Rhododendron 'Gwyllt King' x penjerrick	X
Rhododendron 'Gwyllt King' x sinogrande	X
Rhododendron habrotrichum	CG
Rhododendron haematodes	B
Rhododendron heliolepis	B
Rhododendron heliolepis sp CNW998	X
Rhododendron hemsleyanum	B,X
Rhododendron hirsutum	AP,B,JE
Rhododendron hodgsonii	CC
Rhododendron houlstonii	X
Rhododendron huianum C&H7049	X
Rhododendron huianum C&H7073	X
Rhododendron huianum EGM330	X
Rhododendron hunnewellianum	CG
Rhododendron hyb mix	C
Rhododendron hybridum 'Modern Hybs'	B
Rhododendron irroratum	B
Rhododendron irroratum sp CNW362	X
Rhododendron irroratum sp CNW363	X
Rhododendron irroratum sp CNW365	X

Rhododendron irroratum sp CNW392	X
Rhododendron irroratum sp CNW395	X
Rhododendron irroratum sp CNW555	X
Rhododendron irroratum sp CNW568	X
Rhododendron irroratum sp CNW674	X
Rhododendron irroratum v ningyuense	X
Rhododendron japonicum	B,N
Rhododendron jununegig	B
Rhododendron 'Kettledrum'	B
Rhododendron 'Knap Hill' hyb	C
Rhododendron lacteum	B
Rhododendron lapponicum CNW168	X
Rhododendron latouchae	CG,X
Rhododendron lepidotum	CC
Rhododendron lepidotum TW40	X
Rhododendron leptothrium	B
Rhododendron leucaspis	SG
Rhododendron lindleyi flushed pink	X
Rhododendron linearifolium	B
Rhododendron lutescens C&H7124	X
Rhododendron luteum	B,G,N,RH,SC
Rhododendron macabeanum	X
Rhododendron macrophyllum	B,CG,X
Rhododendron maddenii	SG
Rhododendron makinoi	B,X
Rhododendron maximum	B,SA
Rhododendron 'Maxwellii'	B
Rhododendron metternichii	X
Rhododendron 'Mikado'	B
Rhododendron minus	B,SA,SG,X
Rhododendron minus 'Album'	B
Rhododendron mix	N
Rhododendron mix bonsai	N
Rhododendron mix deciduous	N
Rhododendron molle	B
Rhododendron mollicomum	CG
Rhododendron mollis hyb	B,BS,C,F,SA
Rhododendron monosematum CNW956	X
Rhododendron morii	CG,X
Rhododendron 'Mossiena'	B
Rhododendron moupinense	N
Rhododendron mucronata hyb	B
Rhododendron mucronulatum	B,G,SA,SG
Rhododendron mucronulatum MW109R	X
Rhododendron mucronulatum MW242R	X
Rhododendron nipponicum	AP,SC,X
Rhododendron nudiflorum	B
Rhododendron nuttallii	X
Rhododendron obtusa hyb	B
Rhododendron obtusa kaempferi hyb	B
Rhododendron occidentale	B
Rhododendron occidentalis	B,SA
Rhododendron 'Old Spice'	X
Rhododendron oreodoxa v fargesii	B
Rhododendron oreotrephes	B,SG
Rhododendron parvifolium MW318R	X
Rhododendron phaeochrysum	B
Rhododendron pogonostylum	CG
Rhododendron polylepis	X
Rhododendron ponticum	B,SA
Rhododendron poukhanensis	B,SA
Rhododendron procumbens	SA
Rhododendron prunifolium	B
Rhododendron pumilum	G,SG
Rhododendron purdomii	X
Rhododendron 'Purple Splendour'	B

RHODODENDRON

Rhododendron 'Quadrille'	B
Rhododendron racemosum	B,X
Rhododendron racemosum CNW789	X
Rhododendron reticulata	B,SA
Rhododendron rex ssp arizelum	B
Rhododendron rex ssp rex C&H7003	X
Rhododendron ririei	CG
Rhododendron rosea	B,SA
Rhododendron rubiginosum	B,SG
Rhododendron rubiginosum CNW 1143	X
Rhododendron rubiginosum CNW 352	X
Rhododendron rubiginosum CNW 381	X
Rhododendron rubiginosum CNW 683	X
Rhododendron saluenense	B
Rhododendron sanguineum	B
Rhododendron scabrifolium	B
Rhododendron scabrum	X
Rhododendron schlippenbachii	B,C,CG,G,SA,X
Rhododendron schlippenbachii MW157R	X
Rhododendron schlippenbachii MW241R	X
Rhododendron scottianum	CG
Rhododendron selense	B
Rhododendron selense? CNW6120	X
Rhododendron serotinum	X
Rhododendron sichotense MW243R	X
Rhododendron sidereum	B
Rhododendron siderophyllum	B
Rhododendron siderophyllum aff	X
Rhododendron sikangense aff CNW1060	X
Rhododendron sikangense v exquisitum	X
Rhododendron sikangense v exquisitum	X
Rhododendron simsii	B
Rhododendron simsii CNW816	X
Rhododendron sinofalconeri C&H7183	X
Rhododendron sinogrande	B,X
Rhododendron smirnowii	AP,B,SC
Rhododendron souliei	B
Rhododendron 'Southern Cross' sdling	
x R. 'Bisciut Box' h-p 1994	X
Rhododendron sp CNW1283	X
Rhododendron sp mix	C
Rhododendron spaeroblastum v wum.	X
Rhododendron sperabile	B
Rhododendron spinuliferum CNW1084	X
Rhododendron stewartianum	B
Rhododendron strigillosum C&H7047	X
Rhododendron strigillosum EGM305	X
Rhododendron sutchuenense	X
Rhododendron taggianum	CG
Rhododendron tashiroi	CG
Rhododendron 'Tigerstedtii'	B
Rhododendron traillianum	B
Rhododendron traillianum v dictyotum	B
Rhododendron trichocladum CNW612	X
Rhododendron trichocladum CNW622	X
Rhododendron trichocladum CNW841	X
Rhododendron trichocladum CNW880	X
Rhododendron triflorum KR3388	X
Rhododendron uvarifolium	B
Rhododendron uvarifolium CNW382	X
Rhododendron uvarifolium CNW585	X
Rhododendron valentinum aff C&H7186	X
Rhododendron 'Van Werden Poelman'	B
Rhododendron vaseyi	B,SA,SG,X
Rhododendron vernicosum	B
Rhododendron vernicosum C&H7009	X

Rhododendron vernicosum C&H7027	X
Rhododendron vernicosum CNW641	X
Rhododendron vernicosum f sheltonae?	X
Rhododendron 'Virgin'	B
Rhododendron viscosum	B
Rhododendron wadanum	CG,X
Rhododendron wardii	B,SG,X
Rhododendron williamsianum	AP,B
Rhododendron x obtusum	B,X
Rhododendron yakushimanum	AP,B,C,CG,N,SA,SG,X
Rhododendron yakushimanum f 'F.C.C.'	B,X
Rhododendron yak. x R. 'Pioneer'	X
Rhododendron yedoense v poukhanense	B
Rhododendron yunnanense	B,SG
Rhodohypoxis mix	AP,I
Rhodomyrtus tomentosa	B,HA,SH
Rhodophiala andicola	AP,B,P
Rhodosphaera rhodanthema	B,HA,O
Rhodotypos kerrioides see scandens	
Rhodotypos scandens	AP,B,C,CG,LG,SA,SC,SG
Rhoeo discolor see Tradescantia	
Rhoicissus digitata	B,C,O,SA,SI
Rhoicissus tomentosa	SI
Rhoicissus tridentata	B,SI
Rhombophyllum dolabriforme	B
Rhombophyllum nelii	B,Y
Rhopaloblaste augusta	B
Rhopalostylis baueri	B,HA,O,SA
Rhopalostylis cheesmanii	B,O
Rhopalostylis sapida	HA,O,SA,SS
Rhopalostylis sapida g	B
Rhus angustifolia	B,SI
Rhus aromatica	B,CG,SA
Rhus batophylla	B
Rhus burchellii	SI
Rhus chinensis	B,SA
Rhus chirindensis	B
Rhus choriophylla	B,SW
Rhus ciliata	SI
Rhus copallina	B,C,NT,SA
Rhus coriaria	SA
Rhus crenata	B,SI
Rhus dentata	B,SI
Rhus discolor	SI
Rhus erosa	SI
Rhus glabra	A,B,C,NT,SA
Rhus glauca	B,SI
Rhus gueinzii	B
Rhus incisa	B,SI
Rhus integrifolia	B,C
Rhus laevigata	B,SI
Rhus lancea	B,SI
Rhus leptodictya	B,SI
Rhus lucida	B,SI
Rhus microphylla	B,SW
Rhus ovata	B
Rhus pallens	SI
Rhus pendulina	B,SI
Rhus populifolia	B,SI
Rhus potaninii	SA,SG
Rhus punjabensis	B
Rhus punjabensis v sinica	B
Rhus pyroides	B,SI
Rhus rehmammiana	SI
Rhus succdanea	B,CG
Rhus tomentosa	B,SI

RHUS

Rhus transvaalensis	B	Rodgersia pinnata 'Superba'	B,C,JE,P
Rhus trilobata	B,C,CG,SA,SG	Rodgersia pinnata v elegans	B,C
Rhus typhina	A,B,C,NT,SA	Rodgersia podophylla	B,G,JE
Rhus typhina 'Dissecta'	CG	Rodgersia sambucifolia	B,JE,SA
Rhus undulata	B,SI	Rodgersia sp mix	T
Rhus verniciflua	B,CG,SA,SG	Roella ciliata	B,SI
Rhynchelytrum see Melinis	B,SA	Roella compacta	B,SI
Rhynchocalyx lawsonoides	B,SI	Roella maculata	B,SI
Rhynchosia capitata	B	Roella triflora	B,SI
Rhynchosia caribaea	B	Roemeria refracta	B
Rhynchosia minima	B	Rogeria adenophylla	SI
Rhynchosia phaseoloides	B	Rogeria longifolia	SI
Rhynchosia sordida	SI	Rollinia deliciosa	B
Rhytidophyllum tomentosum	B	Rollinia mucosa	B
Ribes alpinum	A,B,SA,SG	Romanzoffia californica	SG
Ribes alpinum 'Pumilum'	SG	Romanzoffia sitchensis	AP,B,P
Ribes altissima	SG	Romneya coulteri	AP,B,C,JE,SA,T
Ribes aureum	B,SA,SG	Romneya coulteri coulteri	SW
Ribes cereum	B,G	Romneya coulteri v trichocalyx	B,SW
Ribes diacatha	SG	Romulea amoena	B,SI
Ribes fasciculatum	G,SG	Romulea atrandra	B
Ribes fasciculatum v chinense	B	Romulea atrandra ssp atranda	SI
Ribes glandulosum	SG	Romulea austinii	B
Ribes komarowii	SG	Romulea bifrons A.B.S 4351 Morocco	MN
Ribes latifolium	SG	Romulea bifrons A.B.S 4360 Morocco	MN
Ribes magellanicum	SA	Romulea bulbicodium	AP,C,SC,SG
Ribes nigrum	SA,SG	Romulea bulbicodium B.S345 Italy	MN
Ribes odoratum	SG	Romulea bulbicodium (violet)	MN
Ribes oxyacanthoides	SG	Romulea campanuloides	AP,LG,MN,SC
Ribes petraeum	G,SG	Romulea citrina	B,SI
Ribes pubescens	SG	Romulea clusiana	AP,MN,SC
Ribes sanguineum	B	Romulea clusiana S.F327 Morocco	MN
Ribes speciosum	B,SG	Romulea columnae	AP,G,SC
Ribes x holosericeum	SG	Romulea columnae A.B.S4610 Morocco	MN
Richea dracophylla	AU,B,P,O,SA	Romulea columnae Spain	MN
Richea gunnii	AU	Romulea columnae v saccodoana	MN
Richea pandanifolia	O	Romulea crocea L/T19 Turkey	MN
Ricinocarpus pinifolius	B,HA	Romulea cruciata	B,SI
Ricinocarpus tuberculatus	B,O	Romulea cruciata v cruciata	B
Ricinodendron heudelotii	B	Romulea diversiformis	SI
Ricinus communis	B,CG,G,SA	Romulea engleri	MN
Ricinus communis 'Carmencita'	B,C,L,T,YA	Romulea eximia	B,SI
Ricinus communis 'Carmencita Pink'	T	Romulea flava	AP,B,SC,SI
Ricinus communis 'Gibsonii'	B,BS,C,SA,V	Romulea flava v minor	B,SI
Ricinus communis 'Higuerilla Roja'	B	Romulea gaditana PB206 Portugal	MN
Ricinus communis 'Impala'	B,D,T	Romulea gigantea	B
Ricinus communis 'Purple'	B,G	Romulea grandiscapes	B
Ricinus communis 'Sanguineus'	B,BS	Romulea hirsuta	B,SI
Ricinus communis 'Zanzibarensis'	B,BS,C,CP,SA,V	Romulea hirsuta ssp zeyheri	SI
Ricinus sp purple New Zealand	CP	Romulea hirta	AP,B,SC,SI
Ricotia lunaria	B	Romulea hirta S.Africa	MN
Ridolfia segetum	B	Romulea kamisensis	B,SI
Rivea hypocrateriformis	B	Romulea komsberghensis	SI
Rivinea aurantiaca	SG	Romulea leipoldtii	B,SC,SI
Rivinea laevis	SG	Romulea ligustica v rouyana A.B.S4313	MN
Robinia hispida v fertilis	B,C,SA,SH	Romulea linaresii	AP,G,SC
Robinia neomexicana	B,C,SA,SW	Romulea linaresii C.E.H626 Yugoslavia	MN
Robinia pseudoacacia	A,B,C,CG,HA,N,SA,SG,T	Romulea linaresii Corsica	MN
Roceocereus mizquiensis	B	Romulea linaresii L/Sa 65 Sardinia	MN
Roceocereus tephracanthus	B	Romulea luteoflora	B,SC,SI
Rodgersia aesculifolia	AP,B,BS,C,G,JE,SA,SC	Romulea macowani v alticola	AP,MN,SC
Rodgersia henrici hyb	JE,SA	Romulea minutiflora	B
Rodgersia New hyb	C,JE	Romulea monadelpha	B,SI
Rodgersia pinnata	AP,B,BS,C,F,JE,SA,SG,T	Romulea monticola	B,SI
Rodgersia pinnata ? CNW19	X	Romulea monticola S.Africa	MN
Rodgersia pinnata CNW865	X	Romulea namaquensis	B

ROMULEA

Romulea obscura	B
Romulea obscura v campestris	B
Romulea obscura v obscura	B,SC
Romulea pearsonii	SI
Romulea pratensis	AP,B,G,SC,SI
Romulea pratensis S.Africa	MN
Romulea ramiflora France	MN
Romulea ramiflora S.F63 Morocco	MN
Romulea requienii	AP,G,LG,SC
Romulea rosea	AP,B,C,G,SC
Romulea rosea v australis	B
Romulea rosea v reflexa	B,SI
Romulea rosea v rosea	B
Romulea rosea v speciosa	B
Romulea sabulosa	AP,B,MN,SC,SI
Romulea saldanhensis	AP,B,MN,SC,SI
Romulea schlechteri	SI
Romulea setifolia	B,SI
Romulea setifolia v aggregata	B
Romulea sladenii	B,SI
Romulea sp	AP,SC,SI
Romulea sp A.B.S4421 Morocco	MN
Romulea sp MS465 Spain	MN
Romulea sp S.F383 Morocco	MN
Romulea sp S.L12 Jordan	MN
Romulea subfistulosa	B,SI
Romulea syringodeoflora	B,SI
Romulea tabularis	AP,B,C,G,SI
Romulea tabulosa	B
Romulea tempskyana Sardinia	MN
Romulea tetragona	B,SI
Romulea thodei	AP,FH,PM,SC
Romulea tortuosa	B,SI
Romulea tortuosa v aurea	B,SI
Romulea tortuosa v tortuosa	AP,B,SI
Romulea toximontana	B
Romulea triflora	B,SI
Romulea zahnii	AP,MN,SC
Roridula dentata	B
Roridula gorgonias	B
Rorippa islandica	B
Rosa achburensis	SG
Rosa acicularis	B,SG
Rosa acicularis MW45R	X
Rosa alpina	C
Rosa arizonica	B,SW
Rosa arkansana	PR
Rosa arvensis	B
Rosa bella	SG
Rosa blanda	PR,SG
Rosa brunonii	CC
Rosa californica	B,SW
Rosa canina	B,C,RS,SA,SG,Z
Rosa carolina	B,SA
Rosa chinensis	B,SA,V
Rosa chinensis 'Angel Wings'	U
Rosa corymbifera	CG
Rosa davidii	B,SA
Rosa davurica	SA,SG
Rosa dumalia	CG,G,SG
Rosa eglanteria	A,B,C,G,SA
Rosa 'Fairy Rose' dw	B,BD,BS,C,J,KI,L,ST,T
Rosa filipes	RH
Rosa filipes 'Kiftsgate'	C
Rosa forrestiana	SG
Rosa 'Fru Dagmar Hastrup'	C

Rosa gallica	C
Rosa glauca	B,C,FH,G,RH,SC,SG
Rosa gymnocarpa	B,C,SG
Rosa hemsleyana	CG,SG
Rosa laevigata	B
Rosa laxa	B,SA
Rosa laxa alba	SG
Rosa longicuspus CNW411	X
Rosa macrophylla	C
Rosa majalis	RS,SG
Rosa maracandica	SG
Rosa marrettii	SG
Rosa maximowicziana	CC,SG
Rosa maximowiczizna MW186R	X
Rosa moschata	C,SA
Rosa moyesii	A,AP,B,C,CG,LG,RH,SA, SC,SG
Rosa moyesii fargesii	SG
Rosa moyesii 'Geranium'	C
Rosa multibracteata	CG,SG
Rosa multiflora	B,C,SA
Rosa multiflora 'Nana'	B
Rosa multiflora thorny	B
Rosa nanothamnus	CC
Rosa nitidula	G,SG
Rosa nutkana	B,C,SG
Rosa obtusifolia	SG
Rosa old fashioned roses mix	C
Rosa palustris	B
Rosa pendulina	AP,CG,SG
Rosa pomifera	CG
Rosa primula	B,C
Rosa roxburghii	C,G,SG
Rosa rugosa	A,AP,B,C,RH,SA,SC,SG
Rosa rugosa v alba	B,C,SA,SG
Rosa rugosa v rubra	B,SA
Rosa sericea	CC,SA,SG
Rosa setigera	PR
Rosa soulieana	C
Rosa sp mix	C,T
Rosa sp yellow & red hips CNW999	X
Rosa spinosissima	B,C,CG,G,SA,SC,SG
Rosa spinosissima 'Altaica'	SG
Rosa stellata	B
Rosa stellata erlansoniae	SW
Rosa subcanina	RS
Rosa subcollina	RS
Rosa sweginzowii	C,SG
Rosa tomentosa	RS
Rosa ultramontana	SG
Rosa villosa	RS,SG
Rosa virginiana	AP,B,C,G,SA,SG
Rosa vosagiaca	RS
Rosa wichurana	B,CG,SA
Rosa woodsii	B,C,SA,SC,SG
Rosa x alba	RS
Rosa x damascena	B
Rosa xanthina	B,SA
Rosa xanthina f hugonis	B,SA
Roscoea alpina	AP,B,BS,C,G,JE,P,SA,SC
Roscoea alpina pink	P
Roscoea cautleoides	AP,B,C,G,JE,P,RH,SC, SG
Roscoea humeana	AP,G,SC,SG
Roscoea purpurea	B,C,G,JE,SC,SG,T
Roseocereus tephracanthus	B,Y

ROSEOCEREUS

Roseocereus tephracanthus v mizquens	B,Y
Rosmarinus officinalis	B,CG,FH,SA,SG
Rosmarinus officinalis 'Albus'	B
Rosmarinus officinalis 'Prostratus'	B,G
Rostkovia magellanica	AU
Rosularia spathulata	FH
Rothia indica	B
Rothmannia capensis	B,C,O,SA,SI
Rothmannia globosa	B,C,HA,O,SA,SI
Rothmannia manganjae	B
Rothmannia urcelliformis	SI
Rottboellia myurus	B
Roystonea borinquena	B
Roystonea elata	B,O
Roystonea lenis	B
Roystonea oleracea	B,O
Roystonea regia	B,C,HA,O,RE
Roystonea stellata	B
Roystonea violacea	B
Rubia peregrina	B
Rubia tinctoria	B
Rubus alleghaniensis	B
Rubus caesius	SG
Rubus chamaemorus	B,C
Rubus cissoides	SS
Rubus cockburnianus	SG
Rubus crataegifolius	SG
Rubus fruticosus	B
Rubus glaucus	B
Rubus idaeus	B,SG
Rubus illecebrosus	SG
Rubus intercurrens	B,SI
Rubus niveus	C
Rubus odoratus	SG
Rubus parviflorus	AU,B
Rubus parvus	B,SS
Rubus phoenicolasius	B,SG
Rubus procerus	B
Rubus rosifolius	B,SI
Rubus saxatilis	C
Rubus schmidelioides	B,SS
Rubus spectabilis	C
Rudbeckia amplexicaulis	HW
Rudbeckia californica	T
Rudbeckia fulgida	B,G
Rudbeckia fulgida v deamii	JE
Rudbeckia fulgida v speciosa	B,C,F,JE,PM,SA
Rudbeckia fulgida v sullivanti 'Goldsturm'	B,BS,CL,D,G,JE,L,NT,P, PA,SA,T,U,V
Rudbeckia hirta	AP,AV,B,C,G,HW,NT,PR, SG
Rudbeckia hirta 'All Sorts Mix'	T
Rudbeckia hirta 'Autumn Leaves'	B
Rudbeckia hirta 'Becky' mix	BD,BS,J,KI,KS,M,SE,T, TU,U,YA
Rudbeckia hirta 'Giant Double Daisy'	B,BD
Rudbeckia hirta 'Gloriosa Dbl Daisy'	C,F,J,KI,L,SG,T,V
Rudbeckia hirta 'Goldilocks'	B,BS,CL,D,DT,F,M,S,SE, SU,T,TU,V
Rudbeckia hirta 'Indian Summer'	BS,CL,DT,KS
Rudbeckia hirta 'Irish Eyes'	B,BS,C,KI,ST,T
Rudbeckia hirta 'Kelvedon Star'	T
Rudbeckia hirta 'Marmalade'	B,BS,CL,CO,D,DT,F,J, KI,L,S,T,YA
Rudbeckia hirta 'My Joy'	BS
Rudbeckia hirta 'Rustic Dwarf'	B,BD,BS,C,CL,CO,D,DT,

	F,J,KI,L,R,S,ST,SU,T,U, VH,YA
Rudbeckia hirta 'Sonora'	D,F,SE,U,V
Rudbeckia hirta 'Toto'	BS,CL,D,T,U
Rudbeckia hirta x pulcherrima	T
Rudbeckia laciniata	B,JE,PR,SA
Rudbeckia maxima	JE,SA
Rudbeckia occidentalis	AP,B,JE,SA
Rudbeckia occidentalis 'Green Wizard'	P,SE,T
Rudbeckia ritida 'Herbstsonne'	T
Rudbeckia subtomentosa	CC,JE,PR,T
Rudbeckia triloba	B,G,JE,NT,PR
Ruellia humilis	AP,B,PR
Ruellia prostratus	B
Ruellia tuberosa	B
Rulingia platycalyx	B
Rumex acetosa	B,CP,G,KS,SU
Rumex acetosa 'Blonde De Lyon'	B
Rumex acetosa 'Nobel'	B
Rumex acetosella	B,JE
Rumex alpestris	SG
Rumex alpinus	CG
Rumex altimissus	PR
Rumex aquaticus	CG,SG
Rumex confertus	B,SG
Rumex conglomeratus	B,SG
Rumex cordatus	B,SI
Rumex crispus	B,CP,SG
Rumex cyperus	B
Rumex hydrolapathum	B,C,JE
Rumex hymenosepalus	B
Rumex kerneri	B
Rumex madaio	B
Rumex maritimus	B,SG
Rumex obtusifolius	B
Rumex patienta	B
Rumex sagittatus	B,SI
Rumex sanguineus	AP,B,C,CG,I,PA,SC,SG
Rumex scutatus	B,SG
Rumex sibiricus	SG
Rumex stenphyllus	SG
Rumex thyrsiflorus	SG
Rumex venosus	B,SG
Rumex verticillatus	PR
Rumex woodii	SI
Rumohra adiantiformis	B
Rupicapnos africana	AP,PM,SC
Ruschia caroli	B,SI
Ruschia concinna	SI
Ruschia dualis	B,SI
Ruschia elevata	B
Ruschia evoluta	B,SI
Ruschia fredericii	B
Ruschia frutescens	B
Ruschia fulleri	B
Ruschia gemina	B
Ruschia gracillima	B
Ruschia indurata	B
Ruschia intrusa	B
Ruschia lineolata	B,SI
Ruschia macowanii	SI
Ruschia marianae	B,SI
Ruschia maxima	B,SI
Ruschia misera	B,SI
Ruschia multiflora	B,SI
Ruschia pulchella	B,SI

Ruschia pulvinaris	B
Ruschia pungens	B,SI
Ruschia pygmaea	B,SI,Y
Ruschia rigidicaulis	B,SI
Ruschia rubricaulis	B,SI
Ruschia rupicola	B
Ruschia salteri	B
Ruschia sarmentosa	B
Ruschia schlechteri	B
Ruschia schneiderana	B
Ruschia solida	SI
Ruschia sp mix	C,SI
Ruschia stenophylla	B
Ruschia strubeniae	B,SI
Ruschia subpaniculata	B,SI
Ruschia tumidula	B,SI
Ruschia turneriana	B
Ruschia uncinata	B,SI
Ruscus aculeatus	B,SA
Ruspolia hypocrateriformis	B,SI
Russelia equisetiformis	B
Ruta corsica	AP,SC,SG
Ruta graveolens	AP,B,C,CP,G,HH,KS,SA, SC,SG
Ruta graveolens 'Variegata'	B,P,T
Ruta graveolens 'Variegata Harlequin'	B,C
Ruta sp Spain	SG
Rutidosis helichrysoides	B
Ruttya ovata	B
Sabal blackburniana	B,CG
Sabal causiarum	B,O,RE,SA
Sabal etonia	B
Sabal mauritiiformis	B,O
Sabal mexicana	B,HA,O,SA
Sabal minor	B,C,HA,O,SA,SG
Sabal palmetto	B,HA,O,SA
Sabal princeps	B,O
Sabatia angularis	JE
Saccharum officinarum	B
Saccharum officinarum v nigra	B
Saccharum spontaneum	B
Sacropeterium spinosum	B
Sagina saginoides	C
Sagina subulata	B,BS,C,CL,JE,SA,T,V
Sagittaria latifolia	PR
Sagittaria sagittifolia	B,C,JE,SA
Saintpaulia 'Carnival' mix	J,V
Saintpaulia 'Fairytale' s-c	BS
Saintpaulia 'Fondant Creams' mix	T,V
Saintpaulia 'Mistral' mix	CL
Saintpaulia 'Rainbow Falls' mix	T
Saintpaulia 'Selection'	F
Salacca zalacca	B
Salacia chinensis	B
Salacia senegalensis	B
Salazaria mexicana	B
Salix alba	B,SA
Salix arctica	FH
Salix bebbiana	SG
Salix caprea	B,SA
Salix cinerea	B
Salix fragilis	B
Salix glauca	SG
Salix gordejevii	SG
Salix herbacea	FH,SG
Salix hirsuta	B

Salix jacquiniana	SG
Salix kitaibeliana	SG
Salix lanata	AP,FH
Salix microstachya	SG
Salix nigra	B
Salix phylicifolia	FH
Salix pseudopentandraa	SG
Salix schwerinii	SG
Salix vestita	AP,SG
Salmea 'Palito De Chile'	B
Salpiglossis 'Batik'	U
Salpiglossis 'Emperor' mix	BS
Salpiglossis f1 'Casino' mix	BS,CL,DT,L,SE,T,U,YA
Salpiglossis f1 'Festival' mix	D,S
Salpiglossis f1 'Flamenco' mix	F
Salpiglossis f1 'Splash' mix	BS
Salpiglossis f1 'Triumph' mix	S
Salpiglossis f2 'Bolero'	BD,BS,C,F,J,KI,L,ST,T, TU,V
Salpiglossis f2 'Carnival'	D,S
Salpiglossis sinuata	AP,B
Salpiglossis sinuata f1 'Chocolate Pot'	F
Salpiglossis sinuata 'Gloomy Rival'	B,C
Salpiglossis sinuata 'Kew Blue'	B
Salpiglossis 'Superbissima'	DT
Salsola kali	B,SG
Saltera sarcocolla	B
Salvia aethiopis	AP,B,C,FH,G
Salvia africana-caerulea	B,SI
Salvia africana-lutea	B,SI
Salvia agnes	B
Salvia 'Amethyst Blue'	BS,KI
Salvia amplexicaulis	B,G,JE,SA
Salvia apiana	B,KS
Salvia apiana apiana	SW
Salvia argentea	AP,B,C,CG,E,F,G,JE,SA, SC,SG,T
Salvia arizonica	B,SG,SW
Salvia austriaca	B,G
Salvia azurea	AP,C,CP,HW,SA
Salvia azurea ssp pitcheri	B
Salvia azurea v grandiflora	B
Salvia bertolonii	JE,SA
Salvia bicolor	D,SA
Salvia bulleyana	AP,B,FH,JE,P,SA,SC,SG, T
Salvia cacalcifolia	B
Salvia candelabrum	CG,T
Salvia canescens	PM
Salvia carduacea	B,SW
Salvia cleistogama	SC,T
Salvia 'Cleopatra' mix	CO,KI,Sm
Salvia clevelandii	B,C,KS,SW
Salvia coccinea	AP,B,C,CG,CP,G,HW,NT, SA,SG
Salvia coccinea 'Cherry Blossom'	T
Salvia coccinea 'Coral Nymph'	AP,B,BS,D,J,KS,V
Salvia coccinea 'Lady In Red'	B,BS,C,CL,D,J,JE,O,T,U, V
Salvia coccinea 'Pink Pearl'	B
Salvia coccinea 'Red Indian'	B
Salvia coccinea 'Snow Nymph'	B,BS,KS
Salvia coccinea 'Starry Eyed'	KS,V
Salvia coccinea v bicolor	CP
Salvia coccinea 'White Dove'	B
Salvia columbariae	B,C,SW

SALVIA

Salvia davidsonii	B,SW
Salvia dentata	B,SI
Salvia deserta	SG
Salvia disermas	B,SI
Salvia divinorum	B
Salvia dolomitica	SI
Salvia dorrii	B
Salvia dorrii 'Argentea'	SW
Salvia elegans	B,SW
Salvia eremostachya	B,SW
Salvia fallax	B
Salvia farinacea	B,F,G,RH
Salvia farinacea 'Blue Bedder'	B,BS,KI,KS
Salvia f. 'Delft, Porcelain & Warwick Coll.'	T
Salvia farinacea 'Reference'	C
Salvia farinacea 'Rhea'	B,BS,CL
Salvia farinacea 'Silver'	C
Salvia farinacea 'Strata'	BS,CL,DT,J,KS,O,SE,T, U,YA
Salvia farinacea 'Victoria'	BD,BS,CL,CO,D,DT,KI, J,L,S,ST,SU,T,TU,V
Salvia farinacea 'Victoria Blue'	B,C,S,SE
Salvia farinacea 'Victoria Silver'	B
Salvia farinacea 'Victoria White'	BD,BS,CL,S
Salvia forsskaolii	AP,B,C,G,HH,P,SA,SC
Salvia fulgens	B,SW
Salvia gesneriflora	B,SW
Salvia glutinosa	B,G,HH,JE,SA,SC,SG
Salvia henryi	B,SW
Salvia hians	AP,B,JE,SC,SG,T
Salvia icterina	B
Salvia involucrata 'Boutin'	B
Salvia iodantha	B,SW
Salvia judaica	SA
Salvia jurisicii	AP,B,BS,CG,G,JE,KI,SA, SC,SG
Salvia lanceolata	AP,SI
Salvia lavandulifolia	B,CP,G,SA
Salvia leucantha	B
Salvia leucophylla	B,P,SW
Salvia lyrata	B,C
Salvia madrensis	B,SW
Salvia mellifera	B,KS,SW
Salvia mexicana	AP,B
Salvia microphylla	B,RH,SA
Salvia microphylla v wislezenii	B,SW
Salvia moelleri	B,P
Salvia mohavensis	SW
Salvia moorcroftiana	AP,CC,T
Salvia moricana	DT
Salvia munzii	B,SW
Salvia nemorosa	B,CG,FH,G,JE,SA,SC
Salvia nemorosa rose	SA
Salvia nemorosa 'Rosenwein'	B,JE
Salvia nubicola	SA
Salvia nutans	B,CG,G
Salvia officinalis	B,CP,G,JE,KS,SA
Salvia officinalis 'Albiflora'	B,P
Salvia officinalis 'Latifolia'	B
Salvia officinalis 'Purpurascens'	B
Salvia officinalis v minor ssp alba	JE
Salvia patens	AP,B,BD,BS,C,D,G,HH, PM,SA,SC
Salvia patens 'Cambridge Blue'	AP,SC,T
Salvia pratensis	AP,B,C,G,JE,RH,SA,T,V
Salvia pratensis 'Baumgartenii'	B

Salvia pratensis 'Haematodes'	AP,B,C,CP,F,G,JE,RH,T
Salvia pratensis 'Haematodes Indigo'	B,JE
Salvia przewalskii	G,SA,SC
Salvia recognita	AP,JE,SC
Salvia 'Red Rose'	BS
Salvia reflexa	B
Salvia regeliana	B,P
Salvia repens v repens	CP,SI
Salvia ringens	AP,B,G,JE
Salvia 'Scarlet O' Hara'	BS,KI
Salvia sclarea	AP,B,C,CG,CP,E,F,G,JE, KS,RH,SA,SC,SG,V
Salvia sclarea v turkestanica	AP,C,G,HH,RH,SA,SG, SC,T
Salvia sonomensis	B,SW
Salvia sp mix	SC,T
Salvia spathacea	SW,T
Salvia splendens	SG
Salvia splendens 'Blaze Of Fire'	B,BD,BS,CL,CO,D,DT,F, J,KI,L,M,R,S,SE,ST,SU, T,U,V,VH,YA
Salvia splendens 'Carabiniere'	BS,CL,KI,S,YA
Salvia splendens 'Collection'	U
Salvia splendens 'Coral Nymph'	CL,S
Salvia splendens 'Dress Parade'	C,S
Salvia splendens 'Firecracker'	D
Salvia splendens 'Flare'	DT,M,S
Salvia splendens 'Fury'	CL
Salvia splendens 'Inferno' dw	B
Salvia splendens 'Laser Purple'	T
Salvia splendens 'Maestro'	BS,CL,YA
Salvia splendens 'Phoenix Dark Salmon'	B,BD,BS
Salvia splendens 'Phoenix' mix	BD,BS,CL,D,DT,J,SE,T, V,VH
Salvia splendens 'Phoenix Purple'	BD,BS
Salvia splendens 'Phoenix Red'	BS,D
Salvia splendens 'Piccolo Salmon' dw	B
Salvia splendens 'Piccolo Scarlet' dw	B
Salvia splendens 'Purple Beacon'	BS
Salvia splendens 'Rambo'	BS,D
Salvia splendens 'Red Arrow'	B,BS,DT,J,SE,T,TU
Salvia splendens 'Red Riches'	BS,YA
Salvia splendens 'Red River'	S
Salvia splendens 'Red Rum'	YA
Salvia splendens 'Salsa Scarlet Bicolour'	SE
Salvia splendens 'Salsa Series' mix	CL
Salvia splendens 'Scarlet King'	BS,F,L
Salvia splendens 'Scarlet Queen'	BS
Salvia splendens 'Scarlet Signal'	F
Salvia splendens 'Sizzler Burgundy'	BS,T
Salvia splendens 'Sizzler' mix	BS,CL,TU,U,YA
Salvia splendens 'Sizzler Orchid'	U
Salvia splendens 'Sizzler Purple' dw	B,BS
Salvia splendens 'Sizzler Salmon'	BS,KI,U
Salvia splendens 'Splendissima'	T
Salvia splendens 'St. John's Fire'	C
Salvia splendens 'Vanguard'	B,BS,CL,KI
Salvia splendens 'Volcano'	BS
Salvia stenophylla	B,CP
Salvia stepposa	SG
Salvia tachiei	RH
Salvia tesquicola	SG,T
Salvia tiliacea	SA
Salvia tiliifolia	B,C,CP,G,SG
Salvia transylvanica	AP,G,JE,RH,SA,T
Salvia turkestanica	P

205

SALVIA

Salvia uliginosa	B
Salvia vaseyi	B,SW
Salvia verbenaca	AP,B,C,SU
Salvia verticillata	B,F,G,JE,P,SA,SC,SG,T
Salvia verticillata v alba	C,T
Salvia viridis	AP,C,F,G,I,J,KS,L,SG
Salvia viridis 'Blue Bird'	V
Salvia viridis 'Blue Monday'	B,KS
Salvia viridis 'Bouquet' mix	BS,CO,KI,S,V
Salvia viridis 'Claryssa' mix & s-c	T
Salvia viridis 'Colour Blend'	D
Salvia viridis 'Monarch Art Shades'	BS,M,U
Salvia viridis 'Oxford Blue'	BS
Salvia viridis 'Pink Sundae'	B,BS,C,KS
Salvia viridis 'Tricolour'	DT
Salvia viridis 'White Swan'	B,KS
Salvia x superba	AP,B,C,SG
Salvia x superba 'Blue Princess'	B
Salvia x superba 'Blue Queen'	BS,C,CL,F,JE,T,V
Salvia x superba 'May Night'	SG
Salvia x superba 'Rose Princess'	B
Salvia x superba 'Rose Queen'	AP,B,BS,C,JE,T
Salvia x sylvestris	SA
Samanea saman	O,RE
Sambucus caerulea	A,B
Sambucus caerulea v neomexicana	B
Sambucus canadensis	B
Sambucus coreana	SG
Sambucus ebulus	B,C,G,SG
Sambucus glauca	SA
Sambucus hybridum	B
Sambucus latipinna	B
Sambucus nigra	A,B,SA,SU
Sambucus pubens	B
Sambucus racemosa	A,B,C,SA,SG
Sambucus racemosa 'Sutherland Gold'	SG
Sambucus sibirica	SG
Sambucus wightiana	CC
Sandersonia aurantiaca	AP,B,C,G,SA,SC,SI,T
Sandersonia aurantiaca 'Dutch Selection'	B
Sandoricum koetjepe	B
Sanguinaria canadensis	B,G,JE,SA,SC,T
Sanguisorba alpina	SG
Sanguisorba canadensis	B,SC
Sanguisorba dodecandra	B,G
Sanguisorba magnifica	B
Sanguisorba minor	B,G,JE,LA,KS,SA
Sanguisorba minor ssp muricata	B
Sanguisorba officinalis	B,C,G,JE,LA,SA,SG
Sanguisorba parviflora	AP,SG
Sanguisorba tenuifolia	B,C,G,JE,SG
Sanicula europaea	B,JE
Sansevieria aethiopica	B
Sansevieria hyacinthoides	B
Sansevieria roxburghiana	B
Sansevieria stuckyi	CG
Sansevieria zeylanica	B,C
Santalum acuminatum	B,HA,O,SA
Santalum album	B,HA
Santalum spicatum	B,O,SA
Santolina chamaecyparissus	B,C,G,JE,SA,T
Santolina pectinata	SG
Santolina pinnata	B,BD,JE
Santolina rosmarinifolia	B,G,JE,SA
Santolina tomentosus	BS,CL,L,SA
Sanvitalia procumbens	B,BS,C,CG,CL,D,DT,L,

	SG
Sanvitalia procumbens 'Gold Braid'	BS,KI,V
Sanvitalia procumbens 'Irish Eyes'	B,BD,BS
Sanvitalia procumbens 'Mandarin Orange'	B,BD,BS,V
Sapindus drummondii	B,SA
Sapindus laurifolia	B
Sapindus mukorossi	B,HA,SA
Sapindus 'Pipe Negro'	B
Sapindus saponaria	B
Sapium sebiferum	B,C,HA,SA
Saponaria caespitosa	AP,B,G,JE,PM,RH,SC
Saponaria calabrica	B
Saponaria calabrica 'Select'	C
Saponaria lutea	AP,B,C,CG,G,JE,SC,SG
Saponaria ocymoides	AP,B,BD,BS,C,CL,I,J,JE,
	KI,KS,L,SA,SC,SG,ST,T,
	U,V
Saponaria ocymoides 'Snow Tip'	JE
Saponaria officinalis	A,B,C,CG,CP,G,HH,JE,
	KS,SA,SG
Saponaria officinalis 'Rosea Plena'	B
Saponaria pumilio	B,C,JE
Saponaria splendens	B
Saponaria suendermannii	B
Saponaria vaccaria	SU,TU
Saponaria vaccaria 'Alba'	YA
Saponaria vaccaria 'Pink Beauty'	BD,BS,C,J,L,T,YA
Saponaria vaccaria 'White Beauty'	BD,BS
Saponaria x olivana	B,FH,G
Saraca indica	B,C,HA
Saraca thaipingensis	B
Sarcocapnos enneaphylla	AP,PM
Sarcocaulon crassicaule	B
Sarcocaulon herrei	B
Sarcocaulon l-heritieri	B,SI
Sarcocaulon salmoniflorum	B
Sarcocaulon vanderietae	B
Sarcocephalus xanthoxylon	B
Sarcochilus falcatus	B
Sarcococca confusa	B,SA
Sarcococca hookeriana	CG,SA,SG
Sarcococca ruscifolia	B,JE,SA
Sarcopoterium spinosum	B
Sarcostemma intermedium	B
Sarcostemma viminale	SI
Sarracenia alata	B
Sarracenia alata hyb	B
Sarracenia flava	B,BA,SI
Sarracenia flava hyb	B
Sarracenia flava v atropurpurea	B
Sarracenia leucophylla	B,BA,C
Sarracenia leucophylla hyb	B
Sarracenia minor	.B,C,SI
Sarracenia 'Nat. Coll. Hyb' non-anon. mix	BA,C
Sarracenia oreophila	B,BA,C
Sarracenia oreophila hyb	B
Sarracenia psittacina	B
Sarracenia purpurea	B,BA,C,G
Sarracenia purpurea hyb	B,T
Sarracenia purpurea ssp gibbosa	B
Sarracenia purpurea ssp purpurea	B
Sarracenia purp. ssp purp. heterophylla	B,C
Sarracenia purpurea ssp venosa	B
Sarracenia purpurea ssp venosa hyb	B
Sarracenia rubra	B
Sarracenia rubra ssp	B

SARRACENIA

Sarracenia sp & hyb mix	C	Saxifraga cymbalaria	AP,I,SC
Sarracenia x courtii hyb	B	Saxifraga densa	C
Sarracenia x mitchelliana	B	Saxifraga 'Encrusted' mix	AP,BS,FH,SC
Sarracenia x rehderi	B	Saxifraga exarata	B,JE
Sassafras albidum	B,SA	Saxifraga ferdinandi-coburghi	AP,G
Sassafras tsumu	B,SA	Saxifraga ferdinandi-coburghi v pravislawii	SG
Satureja alpina	FH	Saxifraga 'Flower Carpet'	KI
Satureja alternipilosa	JE	Saxifraga frederici-angusti ssp grisebachii	PM,SG
Satureja biflora	B,G	Saxifraga granulata	C,CG,G,JE,SG,SU
Satureja caerulea	B	Saxifraga grisebachii	AP,FH,JE,SC
Satureja hortensis	B,CG,CP,SG	Saxifraga hirculus	FH
Satureja hortensis 'Aromata'	B	Saxifraga hostii	AP,B,C,CG,G,JE
Satureja montana	AP,B,CP,FH,G,JE,SA,SG	Saxifraga hostii ssp hostii	CG
Satureja montana illyrica	G,JE,SG	Saxifraga huetiana	C
Satureja nepeta	SG	Saxifraga hypnoides	B,SC
Satyrium carneum	B,SI	Saxifraga kabschia mix	FH,G
Satyrium coriifolium	B,SI	Saxifraga latepetiolata	SG
Satyrium longicauda v longicauda	B,SI	Saxifraga lingulata see callosa	
Satyrium macrophyllum	SI	Saxifraga longifolia	B,G,JE,SC
Satyrium pumilum	SI	Saxifraga luteoviridis	AP,SC,SG
Satyrium sp	SI	Saxifraga manschuriensis	AP,JE
Saussurea alpina 'Pygmaea'	B	Saxifraga marginata	AP,CG,G,JE,SC
Saussurea amara	SG	Saxifraga mertensiana	B,P
Saussurea controversa	SG	Saxifraga 'Mossy Varieties' mix	AP,BD,BS,C,CL,D,DT,I,
Saussurea gossypiphora	B		J,KI,L,S,U
Saussurea grandiflora	I	Saxifraga mutata	B,C,CC,JE
Saussurea heteromala	B,G	Saxifraga nevadensis	SG
Saussurea pseudotilesii	SG	Saxifraga nivalis	AP,FH,SC
Saussurea riederi v insularis	SG	Saxifraga oppositifolia	AP,BS,C,CG,FH,G,JE,SC
Saussurea sacchaliensis	SA	Saxifraga oppositifolia 'Latina'	B,C,JE
Saussurea tilesii	SG	Saxifraga oppositifolia 'Splendens'	B,SC
Saxegothaea conspicua	B,SA	Saxifraga paniculata	AP,B,C,CL,G,JE,SA,SC,
Saxifraga aizoides	AP,B,CC,CG,FH,JE,SC,		SG
	SG	Saxifraga paniculata hirtifolia	SG
Saxifraga aizoon see paniculata		Saxifraga paniculata ssp brevifolia	G,JE,SC
Saxifraga arendsii	B,C,R,SA	Saxifraga paniculata v sturmiana	CG
Saxifraga arendsii x 'Floral Carpet'	B,BS,JE,V	Saxifraga pedemontana	AP,PM
Saxifraga arendsii x 'Manteau Pourpre'	B,BS	Saxifraga pensylvanica	B,G,PR
Saxifraga arendsii x 'Purpurteppich'	BS,JE	Saxifraga pentadactylis	CG
Saxifraga arendsii x 'Schneeteppich'	B,BS,JE	Saxifraga probynii	SG
Saxifraga aspera	AP,B,G,JE,SC	Saxifraga pubescens ssp iratiana	PM
Saxifraga biflora	B,C,JE	Saxifraga punctata	AP,G,SG
Saxifraga boryi	SG	Saxifraga 'Rock Garden' mix	JE,T
Saxifraga bronchialis	SG,SW	Saxifraga rosacea	B,SG
Saxifraga burserana	B	Saxifraga rosacea 'Sir Douglas Haig'	FH
Saxifraga caesia	AP,B,C,CC,SC,SG	Saxifraga rotundifolia	AP,B,G,JE,SA,SC,SG
Saxifraga caespitosa	FH	Saxifraga sancta	B,FH,G
Saxifraga callosa	AP,B,FH,G,SC	Saxifraga sarmentosa	JE
Saxifraga callosa ssp lantoscana	B,C	Saxifraga sempervivum	AP,JE,SC
Saxifraga callosa v albertiana	SC,SG	Saxifraga silver varieties mix	I
Saxifraga camposii	B	Saxifraga sm rosette varieties mix	JE
Saxifraga cebennensis	AP,CC,I,SC,SG	Saxifraga sp & vars mix	T
Saxifraga chrysosplenifolia	B	Saxifraga spathularis	JE,RH,SG
Saxifraga cochlearis	AP,G,SC,SG	Saxifraga stellaris	C,FH,JE,SC
Saxifraga cochlearis 'Minor'	AP,JE	Saxifraga stribryni	AP,G,PM,SC
Saxifraga conifera	SG	Saxifraga trifurcata	SA
Saxifraga continentalis	CG	Saxifraga umbrosa	AP,B,BD,BS,C,G,JE,RH,
Saxifraga cordifolia rotundifolia	CG		SA,SC,T
Saxifraga cortusifolia v fortunei	G,JE	Saxifraga umbrosa 'Elliott's Variety'	AP,B,C,G,JE,SC
Saxifraga cotyledon	AP,SC,SG,T	Saxifraga vandellii	AP,B,C
Saxifraga cotyledon 'Islandica'	JE	Saxifraga virginensis	JE
Saxifraga cotyledon 'Montafonensis'	AP,CG,SC	Saxifraga 'White Pixie'	B
Saxifraga cotyledon norvegica	SG	Saxifraga 'Whitehill'	AP,FH
Saxifraga cotyledon 'Pyramidalis'	B,G,JE	Saxifraga x apiculata	B,G
Saxifraga cuneifolia	AP,B,G,SC	Saxifraga x urbium	RH
Saxifraga cuneifolia subintegra	SG	Scabiosa africana	B,SI

Scabiosa albanensis	SI
Scabiosa argentea	B
Scabiosa atropurpurea 'Ace of Spades'	T
Scabiosa atropurpurea 'Black Knight'	B
Scabiosa atropurpurea 'Blue Cockade'	B
Scabiosa atropurpurea 'Dw Dbl Mix'	B,F,T
Scabiosa atropurpurea 'Fire King'	B
Scabiosa atropurpurea 'Nana'	B
Scabiosa atropurpurea 'Oxford Blue'	B
Scabiosa atropurpurea 'Salmon Queen'	B
Scabiosa atropurpurea 'Snowmaiden'	B
Scabiosa atropurpurea tall	V
Scabiosa 'Border Hybrids'	U
Scabiosa canescens	SG
Scabiosa caucasica	AP,B,G,SC,SG,T
Scabiosa caucasica 'Compliment'	B,FE
Scabiosa caucasica 'Fama'	B,BS,C,CL,D,JE,T
Scabiosa caucasica 'Goldingensis'	B,BS,SA
Scabiosa caucasica 'House's Hybs'	B,BS,C,CL,D,DT,JE,KI, L,SA,SE,ST,TU,YA
Scabiosa caucasica 'Lavender Blue'	CL
Scabiosa caucasica 'Perfecta Alba'	B,C,JE
Scabiosa caucasica 'Perfecta Blue'	B,JE,V
Scabiosa caucasica 'Perfecta Dk Lavender'	B
Scabiosa caucasica 'Perfecta Lilac'	B
Scabiosa caucasica 'Satchmo'	G
Scabiosa caucasica 'Spielarten'	JE
Scabiosa columbaria	AP,C,CG,LA,JE,SA,SC, SG,SI
Scabiosa columbaria lilac	B
Scabiosa columbaria 'Nana'	AP,JE,RH,SC
Scabiosa columbaria v ochroleuca	G,HH,MA
Scabiosa cretica	AP,SC,T
Scabiosa dbl lge fl mix	S,TU
Scabiosa dw mix	BD,BS,CO
Scabiosa farinosa	AP,SC,SG
Scabiosa fischeri	SG
Scabiosa 'Giant Hyb' mix	C,D,J,KI
Scabiosa graminifolia	AP,B,C,G,HH,JE,LG,RH, SC,SG
Scabiosa incisa	B,SI
Scabiosa japonica	C
Scabiosa japonica v alpina	AP,B,G,JE,P
Scabiosa lucida	AP,B,C,G,JE,SC,SG
Scabiosa maritima	T
Scabiosa ochroleuca	AP,B,JE,SA,SC,SG
Scabiosa perfecta	SA
Scabiosa perfecta alba	SA
Scabiosa prolifera	AP,B
Scabiosa rhizantha	B
Scabiosa rotata	T
Scabiosa silenifolia	SG
Scabiosa stellata	B,D,G,KS
Scabiosa stellata 'Paper Moon'	AP,B,C,F,J,S,SU,T,U,V
Scabiosa stellata 'Ping-pong'	B,BS,CL,CO,DT,KI,L,SU, TU
Scabiosa 'Sunburst' s-c	BS
Scabiosa tall dbl	BS,CO,ST
Scabiosa triandra	G,SG,T
Scabiosa x hybrida	B
Scadoxus membranaceus	B
Scadoxus multiflorus	B
Scadoxus multiflorus ssp katherinae	B,C,CG,SG
Scadoxus puniceus	B
Scaevola calendulacea	B,HA
Scaevola calliptera	B
Scaevola crassifolia	B,C,SA
Scaevola fasciculata	B
Scaevola frutescens	B
Scaevola frutescens v sericea	B
Scaevola globulifera	B
Scaevola koenigii	B
Scaevola nitida	B
Scaevola pilosa	B
Scaevola platyphylla	B
Scaevola plumieri	B
Scaevola spinescens	B
Scaevola stenophylla	B
Scaevola taccada	B
Scaevola thesioides	B
Scandix pecten-veneris	B,G,NS
Sceletium joubertii	B
Sceletium rigidum	B
Sceletium tortuosum	B,SI
Scheelea butyraceae	B
Scheelia rostrata	B,O
Schefflera actinophylla	B,C,CL,HA,O,SA,V
Schefflera actinophylla 'Compact'	B
Schefflera arboricola	B,C,CL,HA,SA
Schefflera digitata	AU,B
Schefflera elegantissima	B,C,HA,SA
Schefflera pueckleri	B
Schefflera venulosa	B,SA
Schima argentea see wallichi	
Schima sp CNW563	X
Schima wallichii	B,SA
Schinus molle	B,C,HA,SA
Schinus patagonicus	SA
Schinus terebinthifolius	B,C,HA,SA
Schinziophyton rautenenii	SI
Schisandra chinensis	A,B,SA,SG
Schisandra grandiflora	B
Schivereckia doerfleri	AP,JE,SC
Schivereckia podolica	B,C,JE
Schizachyrium scoparium	B,C,JE,PR,SA
Schizanthus 'Angel Wings' mix	B,C,F
Schizanthus candidus	B,P
Schizanthus dbl mix	VH
Schizanthus 'Dr. Badger'	BS,CO,KI,ST,V
Schizanthus 'Dw Bouquet' mix	T
Schizanthus f2 'Disco'	T
Schizanthus 'Gay Pansies'	F
Schizanthus gilliesii	AP,RS
Schizanthus 'Hit Parade'	B,BS,C,CL,S,YA
Schizanthus hookeri	B,P,RS,SG
Schizanthus hyb lge fl	J
Schizanthus 'My Lovely'	D
Schizanthus 'Pierrot'	T,U
Schizanthus pinnatus 'Lilac Time'	B
Schizanthus 'Star Parade'	B,BS,C,CL,D,DT,F,J,L,S, T
Schizanthus 'Sweet Lips'	T
Schizanthus x wisetonensis	BS
Schizolobium parahybum	B,HA,RE,SA
Schizonepeta multifida	SG
Schizonepeta tenuifolia	B
Schizopetalon walkeri	B,C,F,RS,T
Schizophragma hydrangeoides	SA
Schizostylis coccinea	AP,B,SI
Schizostylis coccinea 'Major'	C
Schizostylis coccinea 'Sunrise'	B,P
Schizostylis coccinea v alba	AP,B,SG

SCHKUHRIA

Schkuhria pinnata	B
Schkuhria pinnata 'Starry Skies'	C
Schlumbergera hyb mix	CH
Schlumbergera 'Noel' hyb	C,T
Schoenia cassiniana	AU,O
Schoenia cassiniana 'Rose Beauty'	B
Schoenia filifolia ssp subulifolia	AU,O
Schoenia macivorii	B,O
Schoenia pauciflorus	SS
Schoenoplectus lacustris tabernaemontani	B,JE
Scholtzia involucrata	B
Scholtzia laxiflora	B
Scholtzia oligandra	B
Scholtzia spathulata	B
Schotia afra	B,HA,SI
Schotia brachypetala	B,C,HA,SA,SI
Schotia kaffra	SA
Schotia latifolia	B,SA,SI
Schrankia uncinata	PR
Schrebera alata	B
Schrebera trichoclada	SI
Schwantesia acutipetala	B
Schwantesia herrei f major	B
Schwantesia herrei v minor	B
Schwantesia marlothii	B
Schwantesia pillansii	B
Schwantesia ruedebuschii	B
Schwantesia speciosa	B
Schwantesia triebneri	B
Sciadopytis verticillata	B,C,SA
Scilla allionii	MN
Scilla autumnalis	AP,CG,G,MN,SC
Scilla autumnalis Corfu	MN
Scilla autumnalis Greece	MN
Scilla autumnalis MS495 Gibraltar	MN
Scilla autumnalis MS771 Crete	MN
Scilla autumnalis Spain	MN
Scilla autumnalis v fallax A.B.S4345	MN
Scilla autumnalis v gracillima S.L382	MN
Scilla baurii	SI
Scilla bifolia	AP,B,C,G,SG
Scilla bifolia 'Rosea'	B,SC
Scilla cilicica H.Wollin Cyprus	MN
Scilla gruilhuberi	G,MN
Scilla hohenackeri	PM
Scilla hohenackeri B.S.B.E811	MN
Scilla intermedia A.B.S.4410 Morocco	MN
Scilla intermedia A.B.S.4427 Morocco	MN
Scilla intermedia A.B.S.4449 Morocco	MN
Scilla intermedia S.F383 Morocco	MN
Scilla lingulata S.F281 Morocco	MN
Scilla litardierei	AP,B,G,MN,SC
Scilla mauretanica S.F65 Morocco	MN
Scilla mischenkoana	AP,G,MN
Scilla monophylla S.B184 Portugal	MN
Scilla morisii Cyprus	MN
Scilla natalensis	B,C,SI
Scilla nervosa	B,SI
Scilla numidica S.L288 Tunisia	MN
Scilla obtusifolia A.B.S4395 Morocco	MN
Scilla obtusifolia MS509 Spain	MN
Scilla obtusifolia S.B.L41/4 Morocco	MN
Scilla obtusifolia S.F280 Morocco	MN
Scilla obtusifolia S.L252 Tunisia	MN
Scilla obtusifolia v glauca S.L375	MN
Scilla persica B.S.B.E1054	MN
Scilla persica PF	MN
Scilla peruviana	AP,CG,G,SC
Scilla peruviana 'Alba'	AP,B,SC
Scilla peruviana v elegans	MN
Scilla peruviana v gattefossei S.F7	MN
Scilla peruviana v ifnense S.F56 Morocco	MN
Scilla peruviana v venusta	MN
Scilla pratensis	AP,SG
Scilla ramburei	MN,PM
Scilla scilloides	AP,B,G,PM,SC
Scilla siberica	AP,B,G,SC
Scilla siberica 'Alba'	B,SC
Scilla siberica Polunin25 Lebanon	MN
Scilla siberica 'Spring Beauty'	B
Scilla verna	AP,B,G,SC
Scilla verna aff MS467 Portugal	MN
Scilla villosa S.L310 Tunisia	MN
Scilla vincentii MS442 Portugal	MN
Scilla vincentii VH702 Portugal	MN
Scilla vincentii VH719 Portugal	MN
Scirpoides holoschoenus	B,JE,SA
Scirpus acutus	PR
Scirpus atrovirens	PR
Scirpus cyperinus	B,PR
Scirpus mucronatus	B,JE,SA
Scirpus paludosus	B
Scirpus robustus	B
Scirpus sylvaticus	B,JE,SA
Scirpus validus	PR
Scleranthus biflorus	AP,B,C,G,P,SC
Scleranthus biflorus 'Brockiei'	B,SS
Scleranthus biflorus 'Uniflorus'	B,CC,SG,SS
Sclerocactus glaucus	B
Sclerocactus glaucus SB141	Y
Sclerocactus heilii	B
Sclerocactus mesae-verdae	B
Sclerocactus parviflorus	B
Sclerocactus polyancistrus	B
Sclerocactus pubispinus	B
Sclerocactus schleseri	B
Sclerocactus spinosior	B
Sclerocactus uncinatus	B,Y
Sclerocactus wetlandicus	B
Sclerocactus whipplei	B
Sclerocactus whipplei intermedis	CH
Sclerocactus wrightiae	B
Sclerocarya birrea	B
Sclerocarya birrea ssp caffra	B,C,SI
Sclerochiton harveyanus	B
Sclerolaena diacantha	B
Sclerolaena eurotioides	B
Sclerolaena microcarpa	B
Sclerostegia tenuis	B
Scletium concavum	SI
Scolopendrium ssp scolopendrium	CG
Scoparia dulcis	B
Scopelogena gracilis	B
Scopelogena veruculata	B
Scopolia carniolica	AP,G,JE
Scorzonera austriaca	SG
Scorzonera hispanica	SG
Scorzonera hispanica 'Giant Russian'	B
Scorzonera hispanica 'Maxima'	B
Scorzonera humilis	B
Scorzonera papposa	B
Scorzonera radiata	SG

SCROPHULARIA

Scrophularia auriculata	B
Scrophularia californica	B
Scrophularia canina ssp hoppei	C
Scrophularia glabrata	B
Scrophularia grandiflora	JE,SG
Scrophularia lanceolata	B
Scrophularia nodosa	B,C,CG,G,LA,JE,SA,SC, SG
Scutellaria albida	CG,G
Scutellaria alpina	AP,B,C,G,JE,SA,SC,SG
Scutellaria alpina 'Arcobaleno'	JE
Scutellaria alpina 'Fairy Carpet Mix'	F
Scutellaria altissima	AP,B,BS,C,G,JE,P,SA
Scutellaria baicalensis	B,FH,G,JE,SC,SG,T
Scutellaria galericulata	B
Scutellaria incana	AP,B,G,JE
Scutellaria lateriflora	AP,B,CP
Scutellaria minor	B
Scutellaria novae zelandiae	AP,B,P,SC
Scutellaria orientalis	AP,B,SC
Scutellaria orientalis v pinnatifida	AP,G,JE
Scutellaria rubicunde	SG
Scutellaria sp	CC
Scutellaria tessellata	B,SW
Scutellaria woronowii	SG
Scutia myrtina	B
Sebaea exacoides	B,SI
Sebaea minutiflora	B,SI
Sebaea sedoides	B
Sebaea sedoides ssp sedoides	B,SI
Sebaea sp	SI
Sebastiana chamaelea	B
Secale cereale 'Tetra Pectus Rye'	B
Secamone alpini	B
Securidaca longipedunculata	B,SA,SI
Securinega leucopyrus	B
Securinega suffruticosa	B,SG
Sedum acre	B,BD,BS,C,CL,JE,KI,L, SA,ST,V
Sedum aizoon	B,G,I,JE,SA,SG
Sedum aizoon 'Aurantiacum'	AP,T
Sedum aizoon v ramosum	B
Sedum album	B,JE,SC,SG
Sedum album 'Murale'	B
Sedum anacampseros	B,C
Sedum anopetalum	B
Sedum borissovae	SG
Sedum cepaea	B
Sedum 'Crown'	BS
Sedum dasyphyllum	B
Sedum ewersii	B,CC,FH
Sedum floriferum	B
Sedum forsteranum	B
Sedum 'Hidakense'	FH
Sedum hirsutum ssp baeticum	SG
Sedum hispanicum	B,CG
Sedum hybridum	B,SG,T
Sedum kamtschaticum	AP,B,C,JE,SA,SC,SG
Sedum kamt. ssp ellacombianum	B,G,JE
Sedum kamt. ssp middendorffianum	B
Sedum kamtschaticum 'Tricolor'	CG
Sedum lanceolatum	B,JE
Sedum middendoidianum	SG
Sedum oreganum	B,C,JE
Sedum pallescens	SG
Sedum pilosum	AP,FH,G,SC

Sedum popuifolium	B,JE
Sedum purpureum	AP,SG
Sedum reflexum see rupestre	
Sedum 'Rock Garden Mix'	T
Sedum rubens	B
Sedum rupestre	B,BS,C,CG,CL,I,JE,SG, SU
Sedum sediforme	B,CG
Sedum selskianum	B,CL,SA
Sedum sempervivoides	AP,B,FH,G,JE,SC
Sedum sp mix	BD,BS,C,CL,D,JE,L
Sedum spathulifolium	B,C,JE
Sedum spathulifolium ssp pruinosum	B,P
Sedum spectabile 'Autumn Beauty'	B
Sedum spurium	B,CG,SG
Sedum spurium 'Coccineum'	B,BS,C,CL,JE,S,SA,T,V
Sedum stelliferum	B,SC
Sedum stenopetalum	SG
Sedum stoloniferum	B
Sedum telephium	A,B,SC,SG,T
Sedum telephium 'Purpureum'	B
Sedum telephium ssp fabaria	B
Sedum telephium ssp maximum	B,G,JE,SG
Sedum villosum	C,FH,G,SC
Sedum x 'Silvermoon'	I
Selaginella selaginoides	B
Selago corymbosa	B
Selago serrata	B,SI
Selago spuria	B,SI
Selago thunbergii	B
Selenicereus tesudo	B,Y
Selinum carvifolia	CG
Selinum wallichianum	AP,B,SA,SC
Semiaquilegia ecalcarata	AP,B,C,CG,G,JE,SC,SG
Semiaquilegia simultrix	AP,P
Semiaquilegia simultrix 'Early Dw'	P
Semnanthe lacera	B,SI
Sempervivum alatuum	SG
Sempervivum arachnoideum	B,CG,SC,SG
Sempervivum arach. ssp tomentosum	B,JE,SG
Sempervivum atlanticum	SG
Sempervivum ballsii	SG
Sempervivum ciliosum	SG
Sempervivum grandiflorum	C,CG
Sempervivum guiseppii	SG
Sempervivum marmoreum	SC,SG
Sempervivum montanum	CG,SG
Sempervivum montanum braunii	SG
Sempervivum montanum striatum	SG
Sempervivum octopodes apelalum	SG
Sempervivum pitonii	SG
Sempervivum ruthenicum	SG
Sempervivum sp & hyb mix	C,I,V,W
Sempervivum sp mix	BS,DT,F,J,KI,L,R,SA,ST
Sempervivum tectorum	AP,B,C,CG,I,JE,SG
Sempervivum tectorum glaucum	SG
Sempervivum thompsonianum	SG
Sempervivum vincentii	B,SG
Sempervivum winter hardy vars	JE
Sempervivum wulfenii	B,SG
Sempervivum x 'New American Hybrids'	T
Sempervivum zeleborii	SG
Senecio abrotanifolius	AP,SC,SG
Senecio aizoides	SG
Senecio alpinus	JE,SA,SG
Senecio anethifolius	B

210

SENECIO

Senecio angulatus	B,SI	Senna artemisoides	AU,C,HA
Senecio arcticulatus	SG	Senna artemisoides ssp artemisoides	B,O
Senecio arcticus	SG	Senna artemisoides ssp circinnata	B
Senecio barbatus	B,SI	Senna artemisoides ssp coriacea	B
Senecio brachypodus	B,SI	Senna artemisoides ssp filifolia	B,O
Senecio cakilefolius	B,SI	Senna artemisoides ssp hamersleyensis	B
Senecio canus	SG	Senna artemisoides ssp helmsii	B,O
Senecio carniolicus	SG	Senna artemisoides ssp oligophylla	B,O
Senecio chrysanthemoides	B	Senna artemisoides ssp petiolaris	B
Senecio cineraria	SG	Senna artemisoides ssp sturtii	B,O
Senecio cineraria 'Candicans'	AU,B,BS,L	Senna artemisoides ssp zygophylla	B
Senecio cineraria 'Cirrus'	B,BS,CL,D,DT,F,T,U,YA	Senna atomaria	B
Senecio cineraria 'Diamond'	BS,SA	Senna auriculata	B
Senecio cineraria 'Dwarf Silver'	D	Senna barclayana	B,O
Senecio cineraria 'Silver Dust'	w.a.	Senna candolleana	B
Senecio cineraria 'Silver Dust' p.s	B,BD,CL	Senna corymbosa	JE,V
Senecio cineraria 'Silver Lace'	B	Senna costata	B
Senecio cinerascens	B,SI	Senna covesii	B
Senecio coleophyllus	B,SI	Senna didymobotrya	B,C,G,HA,JE,O,SA
Senecio confusus	B	Senna glutinosa ssp chatelainiana	B,O
Senecio cordatus	B,G	Senna glutinosa ssp ferraria	B
Senecio coronatus	B,SI	Senna glutinosa ssp glutinosa	B,O
Senecio doria	B,JE	Senna glutinosa ssp luerssenii	B,O
Senecio doronicum	B,JE,SA	Senna glutinosa ssp pruinosa	B,O
Senecio douglasii	B	Senna hebecarpa	B
Senecio dregeanus	B,SI	Senna hirsuta	B
Senecio elegans	AP,B,C,SI	Senna hirsuta v glaberrima	B
Senecio elegans white	B	Senna marilandica	B
Senecio erucifolius	B,SG	Senna multijuga	B
Senecio glastifolius	B,SI	Senna nemophila	AU
Senecio gregorii	B,O	Senna notabilis	O
Senecio helminthioides	B,SI	Senna obtusifolia	B
Senecio integrifolius	SG	Senna occidentalis	B
Senecio jacobaea	B,SG	Senna odorata	AU,B,O
Senecio jacobaea 'Elegans'	B	Senna pallida	B
Senecio joppensis	B	Senna pendula v glabrata	B
Senecio kleinia	C	Senna petersii	B,SI
Senecio lautus	B,O	Senna planitiicola	AU,B
Senecio macroglossus	SI	Senna pleurocarpa v angustifolia	B
Senecio magnificus	B,O,SA	Senna pleurocarpa v pleurocarpa	B,O
Senecio nemorensis	B,JE,SA,SG	Senna reticulata	B
Senecio nemorensis v fuchsii	B,JE	Senna septemtrionalis	B
Senecio plattensis	PR	Senna siamea	B,HA,O,RE,SA
Senecio platylepis	B	Senna spectabilis	B
Senecio pleistocephalus	B,SI	Senna sturtii	B
Senecio polyodon	P	Senna surattensis	B
Senecio pseudoarnica	SG	Senna venusta	B,O
Senecio radicans	SG	Senna x floribunda	B,HA,O,SA
Senecio resedifolius	SG	Sequoia sempervirens	A,B,C,CG,N,SA,T,V
Senecio scandens	AP,B,P	Sequoiadendron giganteum	A,B,C,CG,N,SA
Senecio scapiflorus	B,SI	Serenoa repens	B,SA
Senecio serpens	SG	Seriphidium canum	B
Senecio sp	SC,SI	Seriphidium maritimum	B
Senecio subalpinus	SG	Seriphidium maritimum ssp monogynum	B
Senecio sylvaticus	B	Seriphidium maritimum ssp patens	B
Senecio tamoides	B,SI	Seriphidium palmeri	B
Senecio tangutica	C,JE,SA	Seriphidium tridentatum	B,C,SA
Senecio triangularis	B	Seriphidium tripartitum v rupicola	B
Senecio umbrosus	SG	Seriphidium vallesiacum	B
Senecio vernalis	B	Seronoa repens	O
Senecio viscosus	B	Seronoa repens blue	O
Senecio vulgaris	B	Serratula centauroides	SG
Senna aciphylla	B	Serratula radiata	B
Senna alata	B,C,HA,O,SA	Serratula seoanii	I,SC
Senna alexandrina	B	Serratula tinctoria	AP,B,G,JE,SG
Senna armata	B	Serratula tinctoria ssp macrocephala	B,C

SERRATULA

Serratula wolfii	G,SC,SG	Sida cordifolia	B
Serruria aemula	SI	Sida echinocarpa	B
Serruria cygnaea	SI	Sida filicaulis	B
Serruria elongata	B,SI	Sida filiformis	B
Serruria flava	O,SI	Sida goniocarpa	B
Serruria florida	B,C,O,SI,V	Sida petrophila	B,C
Serruria glomerata	B	Sida rohlenae	B
Serruria hybrid	SI	Sida schimperiana	B
Serruria leipoldtii	B,SI	Sida subspicata	B
Serruria linearis	SI	Sidalcea campestris	B
Serruria pedunculata	B,SI	Sidalcea canadensis	B
Serruria phylicoides	B,SI	Sidalcea candida	AP,B,C,P,SC
Serruria rostellaris	B	Sidalcea candida 'Bianca'	HH,JE,SA
Serruria trilopha	B	Sidalcea 'Crown'	BS
Sesamum alatum	B,SI	Sidalcea hybrida pink	SA
Sesamum capense	SI	Sidalcea malviflora 'Pink Hybrid'	B
Sesamum indicum	B,C	Sidalcea malviflora 'Stark's Hybrids'	B,C,JE,SA
Sesamum indicum 'Thai Black'	B	Sidalcea neomexicana	B,SA
Sesamum indicum 'Turkish'	B	Sidalcea 'Party Girl'	AP,BD,BS,C,CL,CO,G,
Sesamum sp	SI		JE,KI,KS,L,ST,T,V
Sesbania aculeata	B	Sidalcea 'Purpetta'	C,G,JE
Sesbania agyptica	SA	Sidalcea 'Rosaly'	JE
Sesbania bispinosa	B	Sidalcea 'Rosanna'	C,JE
Sesbania cannabina	AU,B,SA	Sidalcea 'Special Hybrids'	T
Sesbania cannabina v sericea	B	Sideritis cyrenaica	FH
Sesbania formosa	B,C,O,SA	Sideritis hyssopifolia	AP,B,SC,SG
Sesbania grandiflora	B,HA,O,SA	Sideritis montana	B
Sesbania punicea	B,G,SA	Sideritis syriaca	AP,B,JE,SC
Sesbania sesban	B,O	Sideritis syriaca ssp syriaca	AP,T
Sesbania tripetii	AP,B,C,SA,SC	Sideroxylon inerme	B,SI
Sesbania versicaria	B	Siegfriedia darwinoides	B
Seseli buchtormense	SG	Silaum silaus	B
Seseli gummiferum	AP,B,JE	Silene acaulis	AP,B,C,FH,JE,SA,SC
Seseli ledebourii	SG	Silene acaulis pedunculata	SG
Seseli libanotis	G,SG	Silene acaulis ssp exscapa	CG
Sesleria hueffleriana	JE	Silene aegyptiaca	B
Sesleria sadlerana	B,JE,SA	Silene alba	AP,C,CG,LA,JE,SA,SG,
Sessilistigma radians	B		SU
Setaria anceps 'Kazungula'	B	Silene alpestris	AP,B,C,FH,G,JE,SA,SC,
Setaria anceps 'Nandi'	B		SG
Setaria anceps 'Narok'	B	Silene armeria	AP,B,C,G,HW,SC
Setaria chevalieri	B	Silene armeria compacta 'None-so-pretty'	B,BD,BS
Setaria glauca	B,T,V	Silene armeria 'Electra'	B,J,U
Setaria italica	B,SG	Silene asterias	AP,C,G,JE,SC,T
Setaria italica 'Hairy'	B	Silene 'Balletje Balletje'	BS,C,KI
Setaria italica 'Macrochaeta'	B,BS,C	Silene bellidifolia	B
Setaria italica 'Polydactyla'	B	Silene bellidioides	B,SI,T
Setaria italica 'White Wonder'	B	Silene burchellii	AP,B,SI
Setaria macrostachya	B	Silene campanula	T
Setaria palmifolia	B	Silene capensis	B,SI
Setaria pumila	SA	Silene caryophylloides echinus	SG
Setaria sphacelata	SI	Silene clandestina	B,SI
Setaria viridis	B	Silene coeli-rosa 'Blossom' s-c	B,T
Seticereus chlorocarpus	Y	Silene coeli-rosa 'Blue Pearl'	B,V
Seticereus icosagonus	Y	Silene coeli-rosa nana 'Angel' mix	C,T,V
Setiechinopsis mirabilis	CH,SG,Y	Silene coeli-rosa nana 'Blue Angel'	B,C,T
Severinia buxifolia	B	Silene coeli-rosa nana 'Rose Angel'	B,C,T,V
Shepherdia argentea	B,SA,SG	Silene coeli-rosa 'Rose Beauty'	B
Shepherdia canadensis	A,B,SA	Silene compacta	JE
Shortia soldanelloides	A,B,SC	Silene conica hort.	B,C,KS
Shortia uniflora	AP,B	Silene delavayi	AP,PM,SC
Sibbaldia procumbens	AP,B,CC,FH,G,JE,SC	Silene dichotoma	B
Sibiraea laevigata	SG	Silene dinarica	SC,SG
Sicana odorifera	B,C	Silene dioica	B,C,CO,G,JE,LA,SA,SC,
Sida acuta	B		SG,TU,V
Sida cordata	B	Silene dioica et alba	W

SILENE

Silene dioica 'Graham's Delight'	B,P
Silene elisabethae	AP,B,C,G,JE,SC
Silene fimbriata	LG
Silene gallica	B,SG
Silene gallica ssp quinquevulnera	SC,T
Silene hookeri	AP,B,C,JE,SC
Silene italica	AP,B,G,NS
Silene keiskii	AP,SG
Silene laciniata	B,SC,SW
Silene lagascae	CG
Silene latifolia	B
Silene maritima	AP,C,SA
Silene maritima 'Robin White Breast'	AP,BS,C,CL,JE,L
Silene maritima rosea	AP,FH
Silene multiflora	B
Silene multinerva	B
Silene muscipula	SG
Silene nemoralis	B
Silene nigrescens	AP,SC,SG
Silene noctiflora	B,G,SC
Silene nutans	AP,B,G,JE,SA,SG
Silene obtusifolia	SG
Silene orientalis	JE,SA
Silene otites ssp hungarica	B
Silene palaestina	B
Silene pendula	AP,F,I
Silene pendula 'Alba'	B
Silene pendula 'Compacta'	BS,SC,T,V
Silene pendula 'Compacta Peach Blossom'	B,BS,D,DT,KS,SE
Silene pendula 'Compacta Snowball' fl pl	BS,C,KS,T
Silene pendula 'Compacta Triumph'	B
Silene pendula 'Rosea'	B
Silene pendula 'Ruberrima'	B
Silene pendula 'Treasure Island' mix	T
Silene 'Pink Pirouette'	T
Silene procumbens	SG
Silene pusilla	AP,G,JE,SC
Silene regia	B,C,JE,PR
Silene repens latifolia	FH
Silene rupestris	B
Silene saxifraga	AP,B,G,JE,SC,SG
Silene schafta	AP,B,BS,C,CG,CL,G,J, KI,SA,SC,SG,T
Silene schafta 'Splendens'	JE
Silene scouleri v pauciflora	JE
Silene sp	SG,SI
Silene stellata	PR
Silene thessalonica	P
Silene undulata	B,SI
Silene uniflora	B,E,G,T
Silene vallesia	B,C,JE
Silene virginica	AP,C,G,JE
Silene viscosa	B,SG
Silene vulgaris	B,C,LA,JE,KS,SA,SG
Silene vulgaris ssp alpina	B
Silene vulgaris ssp gloriosa	SG
Silene vulgaris ssp macrocarpa	SG
Silene vulgaris ssp maritima	AP,SC,SG
Silene vulgaris ssp maritima 'Rosea'	SG
Silene waldensteinii	JE,SG
Silene wallichiana	SG
Silene 'White Bells'	BS,FH
Silene zawadskii	AP,B,BS,JE,SC,SG
Silphium dentatum	NT
Silphium integrifolium	B,G,JE,PR,SG
Silphium laciniatum	B,C,JE,PR
Silphium perfoliatum	AP,B,G,PR
Silphium terebinthinaceum	B,JE,PR
Silphium trifoliatum	B
Silybum eburneum	B,SG
Silybum marianum	AP,B,C,CG,CP,E,FH,G, HH,JE,PA,SA,SC,SG,SU
Silybum marianum 'Adriana'	B
Simarouba glauca	B
Simmondsia chinensis	B,C,O,SA
Sinningia canescens	B,BC,C,SG
Sinningia cardinalis	B,BC
Sinningia 'Diego'	D
Sinningia eumorpha	C
Sinningia f1 'Empress Mixed'	B
Sinningia 'Mini Hybrids, Cindy ella'	C
Sinningia 'Mini Hybrids Mix'	C,T
Sinningia speciosa f1 'Carmen'	T
Sinningia speciosa 'New Hybrids'	B
Sinningia verticillata	B
Sinocalycanthus chinensis	B
Sinocrassula indica	SG
Sinojackia xylocarpa	B,SA
Sinowilsonia henryi	SA
Siphonochilus kirkii	SI
Sison amomum	B
Sisymbrium alliaria	B
Sisymbrium altissimum	B
Sisymbrium loeselii	SG
Sisymbrium luteum	B
Sisymbrium officinale	B
Sisymbrium orientale	B
Sisymbrium strictissimus	B
Sisymbrium tanacetifolium	B
Sisyndite spartea	B,SI
Sisyrinchium angustifolium/ bermudiana see graminoides	
Sisyrinchium arizonicum	B,SW
Sisyrinchium atlanticum	HH
Sisyrinchium bellum see idahoense	
Sisyrinchium californicum	AP,B,FH,G,I,PM,SA,SC, SG
Sisyrinchium campestre	B,C,JE,PR,SG
Sisyrinchium campestre albiflorum	PR
Sisyrinchium chilense	I
Sisyrinchium commutatum	B,P
Sisyrinchium convolutum	AP,C,FH,SC
Sisyrinchium cuspidatum	MN
Sisyrinchium demissum	B,SW
Sisyrinchium depauperatum	AP,FH,SC
Sisyrinchium douglasii see Olsynium	
Sisyrinchium elmeri	B,SC
Sisyrinchium graminoides	AP,B,BS,CG,F,FH,JE, RH,RS,SA,SC,SG,T
Sisyrinchium graminoides 'Album'	AP,B,G,JE,P,SC,T
Sisyrinchium idahoense	B,BS,C,CL,G,HH,JE,KS, L,SA,SG,SW,U
Sisyrinchium iridifolium	AP,JE,SC,SG
Sisyrinchium littorale	AP,B,HH,JE,RS
Sisyrinchium macrocarpum	AP,B,FH,G,MN,PM,SC, SG
Sisyrinchium macrocephalum	AV
Sisyrinchium micranthum	AP,B
Sisyrinchium mix	AP,HH,P
Sisyrinchium montanum	AP,B,G,SC,SG
Sisyrinchium montanum v crebum	SG
Sisyrinchium 'Mrs. Spivey'	AP,FH,I,SC

Sisyrinchium patagonicum	AP,G,HH,RS,SC,SG
Sisyrinchium 'Pole Star'	C
Sisyrinchium sp mix	AP,C,JE,SC,T
Sisyrinchium striatum	AP,B,BS,C,E,F,FH,G,I,
	JE,LG,P,PM,RH,SA,SC,
	SG,T
Sisyrinchium tenuifolium	AP,B,HH,SC
Sitanion hystrix	B
Sium sisarum	B
Skimmia japonica	B,RH,SA,SG
Smilacina japonica	B
Smilacina racemosa	AP,B,C,CC,G,JE,LG,SA,
	SC,SG,SW,T
Smilacina stellata	B,C,SG,SW
Smilacina trifolia	SG
Smilax aspera	B,CL,L
Smilax bona-nox	B
Smilax herbacea	B
Smilax laurifolia	B
Smilax zarsaparilla	B
Smithiantha zebrina	C
Smodingium argutum	B
Smyrnium olusatrum	B,C,LA,SA,SG
Smyrnium perfoliatum	AP,B,C,CG,NG,SG,T
Soehrensia bruchii	Y
Soehrensia formosa	Y
Soehrensia korethroides	Y
Solanaceae 'Miltomate Criollo'	B
Solanaceae 'Miltomate Montes'	B
Solanaceae 'Miltomate Vallisto'	B
Solandra maxima	B
Solanum aculeatissimum	B
Solanum atropurpureum	B
Solanum aviculare	AU,B,SA,SG
Solanum biflorum	CG
Solanum capsicastrum	B,S,T
Solanum carolinense	B
Solanum carstellatum	CG
Solanum centrale	B
Solanum cithrifolium	SG
Solanum coactiliferum	B
Solanum crispin 'Glasnevin'	I
Solanum diversiflorum	B
Solanum dulcamara	B,SG
Solanum elaeagnifolium	B
Solanum erianthum	B
Solanum ferocissimum	B
Solanum gabrielae	B
Solanum giganteum	SI
Solanum gilo	B
Solanum hindsianum	B
Solanum hirsutissimum	B
Solanum horridum	B
Solanum integrifolium	B
Solanum japonense	B
Solanum khasianum	B
Solanum kitagawe	SG
Solanum laciniatum	AU,B,C,P,SA
Solanum lasiophyllum	B,SA
Solanum mammosum	B
Solanum mauritianum	B,C
Solanum melanocerasum	B
Solanum muricatum	B
Solanum nigrum	B,CP,SG
Solanum persicum	SG
Solanum petrophilum	B

Solanum phlomoides	B
Solanum pseudocapsicum	B,SI,V
Solanum pseudocapsicum 'Ballad'	CL
Solanum pseudocapsicum 'Balloon'	B,YA
Solanum pseudocapsicum 'Big Boy'	B
Solanum pseudocapsicum 'Capital'	CL
Solanum pseudocapsicum 'Cherry Ripe'	BS
Solanum pseudocaps. 'Covent Garden'	BS
Solanum pseudocapsicum 'Dw Red'	D
Solanum pseudocapsicum 'Harlequin'	B
Solanum pseudocaps. 'Joker'	B,BD,BS,J,L,YA
Solanum pseudocaps. New Patterson'	B,C
Solanum pseudocapsicum 'Pearl'	BS
Solanum pseudocapsicum 'Pinocchio'	BS
Solanum ptycanthum	B
Solanum quitoense	B,C,RE,SA
Solanum rigescens	SI
Solanum seaforthianum	B,C
Solanum sessiflorum	B
Solanum simile	B
Solanum sisymbrifolium	T
Solanum sturtianum	B
Solanum surattense	B
Solanum torvum	B
Solanum trilobatum	B
Solanum viarum	B
Solanum 'Vishate'	B
Solanum wrightii	B
Solanum x burbankii	B
Solanum xanthocarpum	B
Solanum xantii	B
Soldanella alpina	AP,B,C,CG,G,JE,SA,SC,T
Soldanella hungarica	AP,B,SC
Soldanella minima	B
Soldanella montana	AP,CG,G,JE,P,SC
Soldanella pusilla	B,C,G,JE
Solena amplexicaulis	B
Solenomelus pedunculatus	AP,B
Solenomelus sisyrinchium	P
Solenopsis axillaris	AP,AU,B,C,DT,F,R,SC,V
Solenopsis axillaris 'Alba'	B,P
Solenopsis axillaris 'Blue Star'	U
Solenopsis axillaris 'Fantasy Blue'	D
Solenopsis axillaris 'Stars Mix'	SE
Solenopsis axillaris 'Stars Shooting'	T
Solenopsis axillaris 'Stars White'	CL
Solenostemon 'Black Dragon'	BS,DT,F
Solenostemon 'Camelot'	F
Solenostemon 'Carefree'	B,BS,DT,L
Solenostemon 'Choice Hybs Superb Mix'	DT
Solenostemon 'Color Pride'	C
Solenostemon f1 'Dragon Sunset/Volcano'	T,V
Solenostemon 'Fairway'	D
Solenostemon 'Fashion Parade' mix	J,M,SE,U
Solenostemon 'Flame Dancers'	F
Solenostemon frederici	SG
Solenostemon hypocrateriformis	B,C
Solenostemon 'Milky Way'	BS
Solenostemon 'Molten Lava'	T
Solenostemon 'Nottingham Lace'	SE
Solenostemon petraea	B
Solenostemon 'Prize Strain'	BS
Solenostemon 'Prize Strain Imp'	T
Solenostemon 'Rainbow' mix	BD,BS,C,D,J,L,S
Solenostemon 'Red Velvet'	C
Solenostemon rotundifolius	B

SOLENOSTEMON

Solenostemon 'Sabre'	B,BS,CL
Solenostemon 'Salmon Lace'	C
Solenostemon 'Scarlet Poncho'	T,U
Solenostemon 'Rainbow Masterblend'	B
Solenostemon 'Superfine Rainbow' mix	C
Solenostemon 'Top Crown'	BS,CO,KI,ST
Solenostemon 'Volcano'	C
Solenostemon 'Wizard Golden'	U
Solenostemon 'Wizard' mix	BS,CL,R,S,T,U,YA
Solenostemon 'Wizard Scarlet'	U
Solidago caesia	G,NT
Solidago canadensis	B,JE,SA
Solidago canadensis 'Golden Baby'	B,BS,C,CL,J,JE,L,U,V
Solidago canadensis 'Yellow Springs'	BS,CO,KI,SU
Solidago cutleri	AP,C,JE,SC
Solidago flexicaulis	PR
Solidago gigantea	CG,JE
Solidago glomerata	B,C,G,JE
Solidago graminifolia	B,G,PR
Solidago hispida	G,SG
Solidago juncea	B
Solidago missouriensis	B,G,SC,SG
Solidago nemoralis	B,NT,PR
Solidago odora	G,NT
Solidago 'Perkeo'	B
Solidago riddellii	B,CG,PR,SG
Solidago rigida	B,G,JE,PR,SG
Solidago rigida v humilis	SG
Solidago rugosa	G,NT
Solidago sempervirens	B,NT
Solidago spathulata nana	FH,SC
Solidago speciosa	B,JE,NT,PR
Solidago sphacelata	NT
Solidago spiraefolia	SG
Solidago tenuifolia	B
Solidago uliginosa	G,JE
Solidago ulmifolia	B,PR
Solidago virgaurea	AP,B,CG,G,JE,SA,SC, SG,SU
Solidago virgaurea ssp gigantea	CG
Solidago virgaurea ssp minuta	G,JE,SC,SG
Solisia pectinata	BC
Sollya heterophylla	AP,C,HA,O,SA,SC,SH,T
Sollya heterophylla pink	SA
Sollya parviflora	B
Sonchus arvensis	B
Sonchus asper	B
Sonchus oleraceus v glabrescens	B
Sonchus palustris	B,G
Sophora chrysophylla	B
Sophora davidii	SA
Sophora formosa	B,SW
Sophora japonica	A,B,C,HA,N,SA,T
Sophora macrocarpaa	SA
Sophora microphylla	B,C,N,SA,SS
Sophora mollis	C
Sophora prostrata	B,SS
Sophora secundiflora	B,C,SA
Sophora stenophylla	B,SW
Sophora tetraptera	AP,B,HA,SA,SS,T
Sophora tetraptera 'Otari Gnome'	B
Sophora tomentosa	B,SA
Sopubia mannii tenuifolia	SI
Sorbaria kirilowii	SA
Sorbaria rhoifolia MW315R	X
Sorbaria sorbifolia	SA,SG

Sorbaria sorbifolia f incerta	SG
Sorbaria sp Russia	SG
Sorbaria tomentosa v angustifolia	SA
Sorbus alnifolia	B,SA
Sorbus americana	B,SA,SG
Sorbus amurensis	SG
Sorbus anglica	NS,SG
Sorbus aria	A,B,SA
Sorbus arranensis	NS
Sorbus aucuparia	A,B,C,SA,SC,SG
Sorbus aucuparia 'Fastigata'	SG
Sorbus aucuparia 'Rossica'	SG
Sorbus aucuparia ssp sibirica	SG
Sorbus aucuparia v edulis	SG
Sorbus bakonyensis	SG
Sorbus bristoliensis	NS,SG
Sorbus cascadensis	SG
Sorbus cashmiriana	AP,C,FH,G,N,SC,SG
Sorbus chamaemespilus	C
Sorbus commixta	B,N,SA,SG
Sorbus commixta v rufoferruginea	SG
Sorbus croceocarpa	NS
Sorbus danubialis	B
Sorbus decora	SG
Sorbus decora mougeotii	SG
Sorbus decora nana	SG
Sorbus decora rupicola	SG
Sorbus devoniensis	SG
Sorbus discolor see commixta	
Sorbus domestica	A,B,C,SA,SG
Sorbus epidendron	SG
Sorbus erubescens	SG
Sorbus essertiauna	SA
Sorbus folliolosa	SG
Sorbus forrestii	SG
Sorbus graeca	SG
Sorbus hibernica	SG
Sorbus hupehensis	B,N,SC,SG
Sorbus hybrida Norway	SG
Sorbus insignis	SG
Sorbus intermedia	A,B,RS,SA
Sorbus 'Joseph Rock'	N
Sorbus koehneana	AP,SC,SG
Sorbus kusnetzovii	SG
Sorbus lancastriensis	B
Sorbus latifolia	B,G
Sorbus laxiflora	SG
Sorbus leptophylla	SG
Sorbus leyana	SG
Sorbus maderensis	SG
Sorbus megalocarpa	N,SG
Sorbus meliosmifolia	SG
Sorbus microphylla	SG
Sorbus minima	SG
Sorbus mougeotii	B,SG
Sorbus munda	SG
Sorbus 'Pink Pearl'	SG
Sorbus pogonpetala	SG
Sorbus pohuashanensis	B,SA,SG
Sorbus porrigentiformis	NS,SG
Sorbus poteriifolia	SG
Sorbus prattii	SC,SG
Sorbus pseudofennica	B,SG
Sorbus randaiensis	SG
Sorbus reducta	AP,N,SC,SG
Sorbus rehderiana	SG

SORBUS

Sorbus rupicola	B,G,NS,SG	Sphaerolobium alatum	B,SA
Sorbus scalaris	SG	Sphaerolobium grandiflorum	B
Sorbus scopulina	B,SA	Sphaerolobium medium	B
Sorbus setschwanensis	SC,SG	Sphaerolobium scabriusculum	B
Sorbus sibirica	SG	Sphaerolobium vimineum	B
Sorbus simonkaiana	SG	Sphaerophysa salsula	SG
Sorbus sitchensis	SG	Sphallerocarpus gracilis	SG
Sorbus sp	SG,T	Sphalmanthus aridum	SI
Sorbus takhtajanii	SG	Sphalmanthus delus	B
Sorbus torminalis	A,B,SA	Sphalmanthus noctiflorus	B,SI
Sorbus vestita	SG	Sphalmanthus prasinus	B,SI
Sorbus vexans	NS	Sphalmanthus procinus	B
Sorbus vilmorinii	AP,SC,SG	Sphalmanthus tenuiflorus	B
Sorbus wardii	SG	Sphedamnocarpus pruriens	B,SI
Sorbus x thuringiaca 'Decurrens'	SG	Sphenotoma gracilis	B,C
Sorghastrum nutans	B,JE,NT,PR,SA	Spinifex littoreus	B
Sorghastrum nutans 'Indian Steel'	B,JE	Spinifex sericeus	HA
Sorghastrum nutans 'Ne-54'	B	Spiraea alba	PR,SG
Sorghum bicolor	B	Spiraea alpina	Sg
Sorghum bicolor named v/cv	B	Spiraea aquilegifolia	SG
Sorghum carneum v nigrum	B,BS,SU,T,V	Spiraea bella	B,SG
Sorghum sudanense	B	Spiraea betulifolia	SG
Sorghum timorense	B	Spiraea bumaldii	SA
Sorghum vulgare	C,CP	Spiraea chamaedrifolia	SG
Sowerbaea juncea	B,HA	Spiraea crenata	SG
Sowerbaea laxiflora	B	Spiraea douglasii	B,C,SG
Sparaxis bulbifera	AP,B,SC,SI	Spiraea humilis	SG
Sparaxis 'Colour Fantasy'	S	Spiraea hypericifolia	SG
Sparaxis 'Colour Mill' hyb	BD,BS,L,T	Spiraea japonica	SG
Sparaxis elegans	B,SI	Spiraea margaritae	SG
Sparaxis fragrans	B	Spiraea media	SG
Sparaxis fragrans ssp grandiflora	B,SI	Spiraea miyabei	B
Sparaxis grandiflora see fragrans		Spiraea nipponica 'Snowmound'	B
Sparaxis parviflora	B	Spiraea salicifolia	SG
Sparaxis sp	SC,SI	Spiraea sericea	SG
Sparaxis tricolor	B,SA,SI	Spiraea sp China	SG
Sparaxis variegata	B,G	Spiraea tomentosa	PR
Sparaxis variegata v meterlekampiae	B	Spiraea trilobata	SG
Sparaxis villosa	B	Spiraea ussuriensis	SG
Sparganium erectum	B,C,JE,SA,SG	Spiraea x schinaboukii	SG
Sparganium eurycarpum	PR	Spiraea x vanhouttei	SG
Sparmannia africana	B,SA,SI	Spiranthes aestivalis	B
Sparmannia ricinocarpa	B,SI	Spiranthes ovalis	B
Spartina cynosuroides	JE,SA	Spodiopogon sibiricus	B,G,JE
Spartina pectinata	B,JE,PR,SA	Spondias dulcis	B
Spartium junceum	B,C,G,SA,SC	Spondias mangifera	B
Spathiphyllum floribundum 'Mauna Loa'	B	Spondias mombin	B,RE
Spathiphyllum 'Tasson'	B	Spondias pinnata	B
Spathiphyllum wallisii	B	Spondias purpurea	B
Spathodea campanulata	B,HA,O,RE,SA	Sporobolus airoides	B
Spergula arvensis	B	Sporobolus aspera	B,PR
Spergularia maritima	B	Sporobolus cryptandrus	B,PR
Spergularia nicaeensis	SG	Sporobolus heterolepis	B,JE,PR,SA
Spergularia rubra	AP,B,C,JE,SA	Sprekelia formosissima	B
Spergularia rupicola	AP,B	Sprengelia incarnata	B
Spermacoce hispida	B	Sprengelia sprengelioides	B
Spermacoce ocymoides	B	Spyridium globulosum	B,C
Spermacoce pusilla	B	Spyridium rotundifolium	B
Sphaeralcea ambigua	SW	Staavia dodii	SG
Sphaeralcea coccinea	JE,SA,SC	Staavia glutinosa	B
Sphaeralcea fendleri v venusta	B,SW,T	Staberoha aemula	B,SI
Sphaeralcea incana	T	Stachys affinis	B
Sphaeralcea munroana	C	Stachys alpina	B,G,NS,SG
Sphaeralcea sp mix	T	Stachys annua	B
Sphaeralcea subhastata	B	Stachys byzantina	AP,B,BS,C,CL,E,F,G,I,JE,
Sphaeranthus indicus	B		RS,SA,SC,SG,T

STACHYS

Stachys candida	AP,I,SC
Stachys coccinea	AP,P,SW
Stachys cretica	AP,B,C
Stachys discolor	HH
Stachys germanica	B,C,G
Stachys grandiflora see micrantha	
Stachys lanata see byzantina	
Stachys linearis	B,SI
Stachys macrantha	AP,B,G,RS,sSA,SC,SG,T
Stachys macrantha 'Superba'	F,JE
Stachys monierii	AP,B,F,G,JE,P,SA,SC
Stachys officinalis	AP,B,C,CO,CP,G,I,JE,LA, SA,SC,SG
Stachys palustris	B,SG
Stachys pillansii	SG
Stachys recta	AP,B,G,SG
Stachys rigida	B,SW
Stachys sylvatica	B,G,JE,LA,SA,SU
Stachys sylvatica 'Husker's Variety'	P
Stachys thireri	SC,T
Stachys tysonii	SI
Stachytarpheta indica	C
Stachytarpheta jamaicensis	B
Stachytarpheta mutabilis	C
Stackhousia huegelii	B,SA
Stackhousia pubescens	B
Stanhopea tigrina	B
Stanleya pinnata	B,SW
Stapelia ambigua	CG
Stapelia desmetiana	B
Stapelia gemniflora	CG
Stapelia gettliffei	B,SI
Stapelia glanduliflora	SI
Stapelia grandiflora	B,SI
Stapelia hirsuta	B,SI
Stapelia kwebensis	B,SI
Stapelia leendertziae	AP,SC,SI
Stapelia lepida	CG
Stapelia longipedicellata	SI
Stapelia nobilis	B,SI
Stapelia pilansii	CG
Stapelia schinzii	SI
Staphylea bumalda	SA
Staphylea colchica	B
Staphylea holocarpa	SA
Staphylea pinnata	A,B,G,SA
Staphylea trifolia	A,B,SA
Stauntonia hexaphylla	C
Stayneria neilii	B
Steganotaenia araliacea	B,SI
Steirodiscus tagetes	B,C,SI
Steirodiscus tagetes 'Goldilocks'	B,BS,T
Stellaria gracelienta	SS
Stellaria graminea	B,SG
Stellaria holostea	B,C,JE,SA,SU
Stellaria media	B
Stellaria nemorum	SG
Stellaria roughii	AP,SS
Stemmadenia donnell-smithii	B,RE
Stemodia floribunda	B
Stenactis annua	B
Stenocactus acroacanthus	Y
Stenocactus albatus	B
Stenocactus caespitosus	B
Stenocactus coptonogonus	B
Stenocactus densispinus	Y

Stenocactus erectocentrus	B
Stenocactus guerraianus	Y
Stenocactus hookeri	BC,Y
Stenocactus kellerianus	Y
Stenocactus lamellosus	B
Stenocactus multicostatus	B,Y
Stenocactus obvallatus	BC
Stenocactus ochoterenaus	B,Y
Stenocactus pentacanthus	Y
Stenocactus phyllacanthus	B
Stenocactus phyllacanthus v tricuspidatus	B
Stenocactus sp mix	C,Y
Stenocactus tetracanthus	BC
Stenocactus violaciflorus	B,Y
Stenocactus zacatecasensis	B
Stenocarpus sinuatus	C,HA,O,SA,SH
Stenocereus eruca	CH
Stenocereus pruinosus	B
Stenocereus stellatus	B
Stenocereus thurberi	B
Stenochlaena tenuifolia	SG
Stenoglottis longifolia	B
Stenomesson aurantiacum	B,C
Stenomesson raui	B,C
Stenomesson sp 'White Parasol'	C
Stenopetalum filifolium	B
Stenotus acaulis	B
Stephanocereus leucostele	Y
Stephanotis floribunda	B,C,HA,SA,SE,T
Sterculia africana	SI
Sterculia alata	HA,SA
Sterculia apetala	B
Sterculia discolor	C
Sterculia foetida	B
Sterculia murex	B,SI
Sterculia quinqueloba	SI
Sterculia rupestris	C
Stereospermum euphoroides	SI
Sternbergia candida	AP,B,JE
Sternbergia clusiana	JE
Sternbergia colchicifolia	AP,G,PM
Sternbergia fischeriana	B,JE
Sternbergia lutea 'Angustifolia'	B,SC
Sternbergia lutea v angustifolia S.L469	MN
Sternbergia lutea v graeca MS802 Crete	MN
Sternbergia lutea v sicula MS977 Italy	MN
Sternbergia lutea v sicula MS981 Italy	MN
Sternbergia sicula	B,G
Sternbergia sicula 'Graeca'	B
Stetsonia coryne	B,CH,Y
Stetsonia coryne v procera	Y
Stevia rebaudiana	B
Stewartia grandiflora	SA
Stewartia malacodendron	B
Stewartia monadelpha	B,SA
Stewartia ovata	B,SA
Stewartia ovata v grandiflora	B
Stewartia pseudocamellia	B,C,SA
Stewartia pseudocamellia Koreana group	B,N,SA
Stewartia sinensis	B,SA
Stictocardia beraviensis	B,C
Stilbe vestita	B
Stipa arundinacea	AP,C,E,RH
Stipa badachshanica	SG
Stipa barbata	AP,B,G,JE,SA
Stipa barbata 'Silver Feather'	C

Stipa calamagrostis	B
Stipa capillata	AP,B,G,JE,SA,SC,SG
Stipa cernua	B
Stipa comata	B
Stipa coronata	B
Stipa elegantissima	AP,B,SA
Stipa extremiorientalis	JE,SA
Stipa gigantea	G,JE,SA
Stipa grandis	JE,SA
Stipa juncea	B
Stipa lepida	B
Stipa nitida	B
Stipa nodosa	B
Stipa pennata	AP,C,JE,SA,SC,SG,T
Stipa pulcherrima	G,SG
Stipa pulcherrima 'Windfeder'	JE
Stipa pulchra	B
Stipa robusta	B
Stipa semibarbata	B
Stipa spartea	B,PR
Stipa splendens	SG
Stipa tenacissima	C,G,JE,SA,V
Stipa tenuissima	AP,C,JE,SA,T
Stipa ucrainicaa	JE
Stipa viridula	G,PR
Stipagrostis raddiana	B
Stirlingia latifolia	B,O,SA
Stirlingia simplex	B
Stirlingia tenuifolia	B
Stoebe plumosa	B,SI
Stoeberia littlewoodii	B
Stokesia laevis	AP,B,BS,C,G,JE,NT,SA, SC,T
Stokesia laevis 'Alba'	AP,B,SA,SE
Stokesia laevis alba v 'Traumeri'	C,JE
Stokesia laevis 'Mischung'	JE
Stomatium beaufortense	B
Stomatium latifolium	Y
Stomatium logani	B
Stomatium meyeri	B
Stomatium niveum	B,SI
Stomatium peersii	B
Stomatium pyrodorum	B
Stomatium suaveolens	B
Strangea cynanchocarpa	B
Strelitzia alba	B,O
Strelitzia juncea	B,C,O,SI
Strelitzia nicolai	B,C,CG,HA,O,SA,SI
Strelitzia reginae	B,CG,HA,O,S,SA,SI,V
Strelitzia reginae dw	T
Strelitzia reginae kirstenbosch gold	SI
Streptocalyx floribundus	B
Streptocalyx longifolius	B
Streptocalyx poeppigii	B
Streptocarpella caulescens pallens	SI
Streptocarpella f1 'Goodhope'	J,V
Streptocarpus candidus	B,C,SI
Streptocarpus compressus	SI
Streptocarpus cooperi	B,C
Streptocarpus 'Crown Hybrids'	KI
Streptocarpus cyaneus	B,SI
Streptocarpus dunii	SI
Streptocarpus eylesii	B,SI
Streptocarpus f1 'Bandwagon'	BS
Streptocarpus f1 'Concord'	BS,S
Streptocarpus f1 'Lipstick'	T

Streptocarpus f1 'Melody'	D
Streptocarpus f1 'Royal mix'	CL,F,L,SE,T,YA
Streptocarpus f1 'Windowsill Magic'	T
Streptocarpus f2 'Fiesta'	J,T,V
Streptocarpus fanniniae	B,C,SI
Streptocarpus fasciatus	B,C,SI
Streptocarpus fenestra dei	SI
Streptocarpus floribundus	C,SI
Streptocarpus formosus	C,SI
Streptocarpus gardenii	B,C,SI
Streptocarpus grandis	B,C,SI
Streptocarpus haygarthii	B,CG,SI
Streptocarpus hyb mix	BS,C,SI,ST
Streptocarpus hyb 'Wahroonga' mix	C
Streptocarpus kentaniensis	B,C
Streptocarpus kentaniensis white	C
Streptocarpus kirkii	B
Streptocarpus modestus	C,SI
Streptocarpus parviflorus	SI
Streptocarpus pentherianus	B,C,SI
Streptocarpus polyanthus	C,SI
Streptocarpus polyanthus ssp comptonii	SI
Streptocarpus polyanthus ssp polyanthus	B,SI
Streptocarpus primulifolius	B,SI
Streptocarpus prolixus	B,SI
Streptocarpus rexii	B,C,SI
Streptocarpus saxorum	B,SI
Streptocarpus sp 'Merrivale' mix	C
Streptocarpus trabeculatus	C,SI
Streptocarpus wendlandii	C,CGSI
Streptocarpus 'Wiesmoor' hyb	C
Streptocarpus wilmsii	B,SI
Streptoglossa decurrens	B
Streptopus amplexifolius	B,C,G,JE
Streptopus roseus	CC
Streptosolen jamesonii	B
Striga asiatica	B
Strobilanthes atropurpurea	G
Strombocactus disciformis	B,C,CH,Y
Strombosia globulifera	B
Strophanthus kombe	C,SI
Strophanthus speciosus	B,C,SI
Stropharia ferrii d.m.p	B
Strumaria rubella	B
Strumaria salteri	B
Strumaria tenella	B
Strumaria truncata	B
Strumaria watermeyeri	B
Strychnos colubrina	B
Strychnos decussata	B,SI
Strychnos nux-vomica	B
Strychnos potatorum	B,SI
Strychnos spinosa	SI
Strychnos wallichiana	B
Stylidium affine	AU,B,SA
Stylidium albolilacinum	B
Stylidium amoenum mauve	B
Stylidium articulatum	B
Stylidium brunonianum	B,SA
Stylidium brunonianum 'Beachboro'	B
Stylidium brunonianum v minor	B
Stylidium calcaratum	B
Stylidium canaliculatum	B
Stylidium caricifolium	B
Stylidium caricifolium v nungarinense	B
Stylidium ciliatum	B

STYLIDIUM

Stylidium cordifolium	B
Stylidium crassifolium	B,C
Stylidium curtum	B
Stylidium dichotomum	B
Stylidium diuroides ssp diuroides	B
Stylidium divaricatum	B
Stylidium diversifolium	B
Stylidium ecorne elliptic	B
Stylidium elongatum	B
Stylidium galioides	B
Stylidium glandulosum	B
Stylidium graminifolium	AP,AU,B,HA
Stylidium guttatum	B
Stylidium hispidum	D
Stylidium imbricatum	B
Stylidium junceum	B
Stylidium laricifolium	B,HA
Stylidium luteum ssp luteum	B
Stylidium macranthum	B,C
Stylidium merrallii	B
Stylidium mimeticum	B
Stylidium multiscapum	B
Stylidium muscicola	B
Stylidium pedunculatum v ericksonae	B
Stylidium piliferum	B
Stylidium piliferum ssp minor	B
Stylidium piliferum ssp piliferum	B
Stylidium pilosum	B
Stylidium plantagineum	B
Stylidium pubigerum	B
Stylidium rigidifolium	B
Stylidium scandens	B
Stylidium schizanthum	B
Stylidium schoenoides	B
Stylidium soboliferum	B
Stylidium spathulatum	B
Stylidium spathulatum ssp acuminatum	B
Stylidium spinulosum	B
Stylidium squamosotuberosum	B
Stylidium striatum pinkish-white	B
Stylidium tepperianum	B
Stylobasium spathulatum	B,SA
Stylomecon heterophyllum	AP,B,C,T
Stylophorum diphyllum	AP,B,BS,C,G,JE,SC
Stylophorum lasiocarpum	AP,B,C,G,JE,SC
Stylosanthes fruticosa	B
Stylosanthes guianensis 'Cook'	B
Stylosanthes guianensis 'Graham'	B
Stylosanthes guianensis 'Oxley'	B
Stylosanthes hamata 'Verano'	B
Stylosanthes scabra 'Fitzroy'	B
Stylosanthes scabra 'Seca'	B
Stypandra caespitosa	HA
Stypandra glauca	HA
Stypandra imbricata	B
Styphelia pulchella	B
Styphelia tenuiflora	B
Styrax americanum	B,SA
Styrax confucus	B
Styrax hemslyana	SA
Styrax japonicum	AP,B,C,N,SA,SC,SG
Styrax obassia	B,N,SA
Styrax odoratissimum	SA
Styrax officinale	C,SA
Styrax officinale v californicum	B
Styrax serrulata	SA

Submatucana aureiflora	B,Y
Submatucana caespitosa	B
Submatucana celendiensis	B
Submatucana grandiflora	B
Submatucana intertexta	Y
Submatucana krahnii	Y
Submatucana madisoniorum	B,Y
Submatucana paucicostata	Y
Submatucana tubercolosa	Y
Succisa pratensis	AP,C,CO,G,LA,JE,SA, SC,SG
Succisella petteri	CG
Sulcorebutia albida	Y
Sulcorebutia arenacea	B,Y
Sulcorebutla breviflora	Y
Sulcorebutia candiae	B,Y
Sulcorebutia crispata	B
Sulcorebutia flavissima	Y
Sulcorebutia frankiana	Y
Sulcorebutia glomerispina	Y
Suregada angustifolia	B
Sutera aurantiaca	SI
Sutera breviflora	B,SI
Sutera grandiflora	B,SI
Sutera sp	SI
Sutera tristis	B,SI
Sutherlandia frutescens	AP,B,C,G,SA,SI,T
Sutherlandia frutescens prostrata	HH,SC
Sutherlandia microphylla	B,SI
Sutherlandia sp	SC,SI
Swainsona burkittii	B
Swainsona canescens	B
Swainsona cyclocarpa	B
Swainsona fissimontana	B
Swainsona formosa see Clianthus	
Swainsona galegifolia	B,HA,O,SA
Swainsona greyana ssp greyana	B
Swainsona kingii	B
Swainsona maccullochiana	B,O,SA
Swainsona microcalyx	O
Swainsona murrayana	B
Swainsona novae-zelandiae	AP,B,SS
Swainsona phacoides	B
Swainsona procumbens	B,O,SA
Swainsona pterostylis	B
Swainsona pubescens	O
Swainsona stenodonta	B
Swainsona stipularis	B,O,SA
Swainsona swainsonoides	B
Swainsona tephrotricha	RS
Swainsona viridis	B
Swartzia madagascariensis	SI
Swertia aucheri	SG
Swertia bimaculata	B
Swertia longifolia	SG
Swertia montana	B
Swertia perennis	B,C,JE,SA,SW
Swertia perennis ssp alpestris	SG
Swertia petiolata	SG
Swietenia humilis	B
Swietenia macrophylla	B
Swietenia mahagoni	B,HA,RE,SA
Swinglia glutinosa	B
Syagrus cocoides	B
Syagrus flexuosa	B
Syagrus romanzoffianum	B,C,HA,N,O,SA

Syagrus schizophylla	B
Symphoricarpos albus	A,B,C,CG,SA,SG
Symphoricarpos albus v laevigatus	B,RS
Symphoricarpos occidentalis	B,SG
Symphoricarpos orbiculatus	B,C,SA
Symphoricarpos oreophilus	B,SG
Symphyandra armena	AP,B,G,P,RS,SC,SE,SG, T,V
Symphyandra cretica	T
Symphyandra hoffmannii	AP,B,C,CG,G,JE,P,RS, SA,SC,SG,T
Symphyandra pendula	AP,B,C,FH,G,JE,RS,SC
Symphyandra wanneri	AP,B,C,G,P,SC,SG
Symphyandra zanzegura	AP,RH,SC
Symphytum officinale	JE
Symphytum officinale white fl.	A,B
Symphytum x uplandicum	B
Symplocos paniculata	B
Synaphea acutiloba	B,O
Synaphea petiolaris	B
Syncarpha affinis	B,SI
Syncarpha argyropsis	B
Syncarpha canescens	B,SI
Syncarpha eximia	B,SI
Syncarpha gnaphaloides	B,SI
Syncarpha milleflora	B,SI
Syncarpha paniculata	B,SI
Syncarpha sp	SI
Syncarpha speciosissima	B,SI
Syncarpha variegata	B,SI
Syncarpha vestita	B,SI
Syncarpia glomulifera	B,C,HA,O
Syncarpia hillii	B
Syncarpia laurifolia	SA
Syncolostemon macranthus	SI
Syncolostemon rotundifolius	SI
Synedrella nodiflora	B
Syneilesis aconitifolia	B
Syngonium podophyllum	SA
Syngonium podophyllum 'Emerald Gem'	B
Syngonium podophyllum 'Variegatum'	B
Syngonium reticulatum	B
Syngonium vellozianum	B
Synnotia parviflora	B,MN,SC,SI
Synnotia variegata	AP,B,SC
Synnotia villosa	AP,B,SC,SI
Synsepalum dulcificum	B
Synsepalum subcordatum	B
Synthyris reniformis	B
Syragus romanzoffianum	O
Syrenia cana	B
Syringa amurensis	SA,SG
Syringa emodi	B
Syringa josikaea	B,SA,SG
Syringa josikaea 'Pallida'	B
Syringa komarowii	B
Syringa oblata	B,SA
Syringa reflexa	AP,B
Syringa reticulata	B
Syringa reticulata ssp pekinensis	B,SA
Syringa reticulata v mandshurica	B
Syringa sp CNW226	X
Syringa taiwania flouseana	SA
Syringa velutina of gdns	SA
Syringa villosa	B,C,CG,SA
Syringa vulgaris	A,B,C,SA
Syringa vulgaris 'Alba'	B
Syringa wolfii	B,C,SG
Syringa x prestoniae	B
Syzygium aqueum	B
Syzygium australis	SA
Syzygium cordatum	B,SI
Syzygium cumini	B
Syzygium forte ssp forte	B
Syzygium francisii	B,O
Syzygium jambos	B
Syzygium luehmannii	B
Syzygium maire	B
Syzygium malaccense	B
Syzygium moorei	B,O
Syzygium oleosum	B
Syzygium paniculatum	B
Syzygium samarangense	B
Syzygium wilsonii ssp cryptophlebia	B
Syzygium wilsonii ssp wilsonii	B
Tabebuia argentea	B,SA
Tabebuia chrysantha	B,RE
Tabebuia chrysotricha	B,SA
Tabebuia guayacan	B
Tabebuia heterophylla	B
Tabebuia impetiginosa	B
Tabebuia rosea	B,C,RE,SA
Tabebuia roseoalba	B
Tabebuia serratifolia	B
Tabernaemontana divaricata	B
Tabernaemontana sananho	B
Tacca chantrieri	B,C,SA,T
Tacitus bellus see Graptopetalum	
Taenidia integerrima	B,PR
Tagetes erecta	B,G,SG,VH
Tagetes erecta 'Calando' mix	BS,DT,J,L,YA
Tagetes erecta 'Calando' s-c	BS
Tagetes erecta 'Crackerjack' mix	BD,BS,CL,DT,F,KI,L,S, SU,T,TU,U,YA
Tagetes erecta 'Crush' mix	SE
Tagetes erecta 'Cupid' mix dw	BS,C
Tagetes erecta dbl mix	CO,J
Tagetes erecta f1 'Antigua Series'	CL,SE
Tagetes erecta f1 'Ball Mix'	V
Tagetes erecta f1 'Ball Orange'	V
Tagetes erecta f1 'Ball Yellow'	V
Tagetes erecta f1 'Beau Brummell'	B
Tagetes erecta f1 'Beau Geste'	B
Tagetes erecta f1 'Climax'	S
Tagetes erecta f1 'Dbl Eagle'	BS
Tagetes erecta f1 'Discovery' mix	BS,T,YA
Tagetes erecta f1 'Discovery Orange'	B,BS,L,R,T,YA
Tagetes erecta f1 'Discovery Yellow'	B,BS,L,R,T,YA
Tagetes erecta f1 'Dubloon'	BS
Tagetes erecta f1 'Excel Gold'	CL,M
Tagetes erecta f1 'Excel' mix	CL,M,U
Tagetes erecta f1 'Excel Soft Primrose'	CL,M
Tagetes erecta f1 'Galore Gold'	B,BS,S,T
Tagetes erecta f1 'Galore' mix	BS,T
Tagetes erecta f1 'Galore Yellow'	B,BS,T
Tagetes erecta f1 'Gay Ladies'	KI,S
Tagetes erecta f1 'Gold Coins'	L,U
Tagetes erecta f1 'Gold 'n' Vanilla'	SE,T,U
Tagetes erecta f1 'Inca Gold'	B,BS,CL,D,DT,L,S,SE,T, YA
Tagetes erecta f1 'Inca' mix	BS,C,CL,D,DT,F,J,KI,L, S,SE,ST,T,TU,YA

TAGETES

Tagetes erecta f1 'Inca Orange' — B,BS,CL,D,DT,L,S,SE,T,U,YA
Tagetes erecta f1 'Inca Yellow' — B,BS,CL,D,DT,L,S,SE,T,U,YA
Tagetes erecta f1 'Jubilee Golden' — B,BS
Tagetes erecta f1 'Jubilee Mix' — BS,D,U
Tagetes erecta f1 'Jubilee Orange' — B,BS
Tagetes erecta f1 'Jubilee Yellow' — B
Tagetes erecta f1 'Lady Gold' — B,BD,BS
Tagetes erecta f1 'Lady Orange' — B,BS
Tagetes erecta f1 'Lady Yellow' — B,BS
Tagetes erecta f1 'Marvel' mix — BS,F
Tagetes erecta f1 'Marvel' s-c — B,BS
Tagetes erecta f1 'Marvellous' mix — D
Tagetes erecta f1 'Perfection Colour Blend' — CL,D,F
Tagetes erecta f1 'Perfection Gold' — CL,D,U
Tagetes erecta f1 'Perfection Orange' — CL,D,F
Tagetes erecta f1 'Perfection Yellow' — CL,D,F
Tagetes erecta f1 'Sumo' mix — BS,KI,S,T
Tagetes erecta f1 'Sumo' s-c — BS,YA
Tagetes erecta f1 'Vanilla' — CL,DT,F,KI,L,SE,V,U,YA
Tagetes erecta f1 'Voyager Orange' — B
Tagetes erecta f1 'Voyager Yellow' — B
Tagetes erecta f1 'Yellow Galore' — S
Tagetes erecta 'Golden Age' dwarf — B,KI
Tagetes erecta 'Golden Trumpets' — B
Tagetes erecta 'Guys & Dolls' mix — BS,CL
Tagetes erecta 'Hawaii' (xanthophyll) — B,BS
Tagetes erecta 'Moonbeam' — T,VH
Tagetes erecta 'Rhapsody' — D
Tagetes erecta 'Sahara' — F
Tagetes erecta 'Snowbird' — BS,TU
Tagetes erecta 'Snowdrift' — B
Tagetes erecta 'Sunset Giants' — BS,C,F,KI,M,Sm,ST
Tagetes erecta 'Sunspot' — D
Tagetes erecta 'Sunspot' mix — CL
Tagetes erecta 'Superjack' mix — BS,R
Tagetes erecta 'Superjack Orange' — S
Tagetes erecta 'Tall Dbl Orange' — B
Tagetes erecta 'Tall Dbl Yellow' — B
Tagetes erecta 'Treasure Trove' mix — CL
Tagetes erecta 'White' — ST
Tagetes filifolia — B
Tagetes lemmoni — AP,B,KS,SW
Tagetes lucida — B,KS
Tagetes lunulata — B,KS
Tagetes 'Marigold Package Deal' — T
Tagetes minuta — C,CO,SU
Tagetes patula — B,G,JE,SG,SU
Tagetes patula 'Alamo Series' — CL
Tagetes patula 'Aurora Primrose' — U
Tagetes patula 'Aurora Series' s-c — BS,CL,DT,T
Tagetes patula 'Bolero' — B,U,V
Tagetes patula 'Bonanza Bee' — B,BD,BS
Tagetes patula 'Bonanza Deep Orange' — B,BD
Tagetes patula 'Bonanza Flame' — B,BD,BS
Tagetes patula 'Bonanza Gold' — B,BD,BS
Tagetes patula 'Bonanza Harmony' — B,BD,BS
Tagetes patula 'Bonanza Orange' — B,BD,BS
Tagetes patula 'Bonanza Yellow' — B,BD,BS
Tagetes patula 'Bonita' mix — BSC,DT,F,J,KI,T,VH,YA
Tagetes patula 'Bonita' s-c — BS
Tagetes patula 'Boy,golden' — B,BS,CL,D,YA
Tagetes patula 'Boy,harmony' — B,BS,CL,D,YA
Tagetes patula 'Boy o Boy mix' — BS,CL,D,DT,F,J,L,R,KI,S,SE,SG,Sm,ST,SU,T,TU,

Tagetes patula 'Boy,orange' — B,BS,CL,D,F,L,S,T,V,YA
Tagetes patula 'Boy,yellow' — B,BS,CL,D,L,T,V,YA
Tagetes patula 'Brocade Red' — B,BS,S
Tagetes patula 'Brocade Spanish' — B,BS,CL,KI,M,SU,T,TU
Tagetes patula 'Butterscotch' — BS
Tagetes patula 'Calico' — B,BS
Tagetes patula 'Carmen' — B
Tagetes patula 'Centenary' — D
Tagetes patula 'Champion Mixed' — BS,KI
Tagetes patula 'Champion' s-c — BS
Tagetes patula 'Choice Single' — SU
Tagetes patula 'Crested Series' — BS,D,YA
Tagetes patula 'Dainty Marietta' — B,BS,D,L
Tagetes patula 'Del Sol' — B
Tagetes patula 'Disco Flame' — B,BS,CL
Tagetes patula 'Disco Golden' — B,BS,CL
Tagetes patula 'Disco Marietta' — B,BS,CL,S
Tagetes patula 'Disco' mix — BS,CL,CO,DT,KI,L,R,TU,YA
Tagetes patula 'Disco Orange' — B,BS,CL
Tagetes patula 'Disco Red' — B,BS,CL,S
Tagetes patula 'Disco Yellow' — B,BS,CL
Tagetes patula dw dbl mix — CO,F,J,TU
Tagetes patula 'Espana Granada' — B,BS
Tagetes patula 'Espana' mix — BD,J
Tagetes patula 'Espana Ole' — B,BS
Tagetes patula 'Espana Red Marietta' — B,BS
Tagetes patula f1 'Vanilla' — KS,R
Tagetes patula 'Fantasia' mix — S
Tagetes patula 'Favourite' mix — BS,DT,J,L,S,T,U,V
Tagetes patula 'Fiesta' — B
Tagetes patula 'Fireflame' — T
Tagetes patula 'Garden Gate' mix — BS,CL,DT,KI,L
Tagetes patula 'Gate,golden' — B,BS,CL,DT,KI,L,T
Tagetes patula 'Gate,orange' — B,BS,CL,DT,L
Tagetes patula 'Gate,yellow' — B,BS,CL,DT,L
Tagetes patula 'Golden Days' — KI,ST
Tagetes patula 'Goldfinch' — D,S,T,U,YA
Tagetes patula 'Goldie' — S
Tagetes patula 'Granada' — YA
Tagetes patula 'Gypsy Sunshine' — T
Tagetes patula 'Harlequin' — SE
Tagetes patula 'Harlequin' dw — SE
Tagetes patula 'Harmony' — KS
Tagetes patula 'Hero Flame' — B,BS,L,YA
Tagetes patula 'Hero Gold' — B,BS,DT,L,YA
Tagetes patula 'Hero Harmony' — B,BS,L,YA
Tagetes patula 'Hero' mix — BS,DT,L,YA
Tagetes patula 'Hero Orange' — B,BS,DT,L,YA
Tagetes patula 'Hero Red' — B,BS,L,T,YA
Tagetes patula 'Hero Spry' — B,BS,DT,L,YA
Tagetes patula 'Hero Yellow' — B,BS,L,YA
Tagetes patula 'Holiday Crested Mix' — T
Tagetes patula 'Honey' mix — D
Tagetes patula 'Honeycomb' — C,CL,D,F,J,S,T,V,YA
Tagetes patula 'Instant' — BS
Tagetes patula 'Jacket,orange' — B,BS,CL,D,J,M,YA
Tagetes patula 'Jacket,yellow' — B,BS,CL,D,F,J,M,U,YA
Tagetes patula 'Jolly Jester' — S
Tagetes patula 'Juliette' — BS,F
Tagetes patula 'Legion of Honour' — BS,C,KI
Tagetes patula 'Lemon Drop' — SE
Tagetes patula 'Lilliput Orange Flame' — C
Tagetes patula 'Marionette Mix' — U
Tagetes patula 'Mischief' mix — BS,D

Name	Codes
Tagetes patula 'Mischief' s-c	BS
Tagetes patula 'Mr. Majestic'	T
Tagetes patula 'Naughty Marietta'	B,BS,CL,D,DT,F,J,KI,ST, T,U,YA
Tagetes patula 'Orion'	B
Tagetes patula 'Pascal'	BS
Tagetes patula 'Petite' mix	BS,KI,M,S
Tagetes patula 'Petite' s-c	BS
Tagetes patula 'Queen Bee'	B,BS,S,T,VH,YA
Tagetes patula 'Queen Sophia'	BS,S,U
Tagetes patula 'Red Cherry'	B,F,SE,YA
Tagetes patula 'Red Marietta'	BD,BS,D,F,YA
Tagetes patula 'Romania Bronze'	SG
Tagetes patula 'Royal Crested' mix	BS,CL,KI,J,S,YA
Tagetes patula 'Royal Crested' s-c	B,BS,U
Tagetes patula 'Royal King'	BS,D
Tagetes patula 'Rusty Red'	BS
Tagetes patula 'Safari Bolero'	B,BS,CL,DT,L,T,YA
Tagetes patula 'Safari Gold'	B,BS,CL,L,YA
Tagetes patula 'Safari' mix	BS,CL,DT,F,J,L,YA
Tagetes patula 'Safari Orange'	B,BS,CL,L,YA
Tagetes patula 'Safari Primrose'	B,BS,CL,D,DT,L
Tagetes patula 'Safari Queen'	B,BS,CL,L,YA
Tagetes patula 'Safari Scarlet'	B,BS,CL,L,YA
Tagetes patula 'Safari Tangerine'	B,BS,CL,D,DT,G,L,O,U, YA
Tagetes patula 'Safari Yellow'	B,BS,CL,KI,L,YA
Tagetes patula 'Silvia'	BS,D
Tagetes patula 'Sophia Classic'	M
Tagetes patula 'Sophia' mix	BS,CG,CL,D,F,J,S
Tagetes patula 'Sophia' s-c	BS,D,T
Tagetes patula 'Sparky'	BS,D,DT
Tagetes patula 'Spice'	BS
Tagetes patula 'Striped Marvel'	KS,T
Tagetes patula 'Sunny'	B
Tagetes patula 'Suzanna'	SG
Tagetes patula 'Tall Scotch Prize'	DT
Tagetes patula 'Tangerine'	B,BS,J,V
Tagetes patula 'Tanja'	YA
Tagetes patula 'Tessy Gold'	BS
Tagetes patula 'Tiger Eyes'	B,BS,CO,F,KI,M,SE,T,U, VH
Tagetes patula 'Valencia' golden-orange	B
Tagetes patula 'Winner' orange	D,S,U
Tagetes pusilla	B
Tagetes tenuifolia	SG
Tagetes tenuifolia 'Carina'	C
Tagetes tenuifolia 'Carina Osena'	C
Tagetes tenuifolia 'Gem' mix	BS,TU
Tagetes tenuifolia 'Golden Gem'	B,BS,CL,CO,DT,F,J,KI, L,S,ST,T,U,V,VH,YA
Tagetes tenuifolia 'Golden Ring'	BS
Tagetes tenuifolia hyb 'Tessy Gold'	B
Tagetes tenuifolia 'Lemon Gem'	BS,C,CL,D,DT,F,J,KI,KS, L,R,S,ST,T,U,V,VH,YA
Tagetes tenuifolia 'Lemon Star'	B
Tagetes tenuifolia 'Lulu'	BS,M
Tagetes tenuifolia 'Luna'	YA
Tagetes tenuifolia 'Orange Gem'	L,V,YA
Tagetes tenuifolia 'Ornament'	C,DT,L
Tagetes tenuifolia 'Paprika'	B,F,J,M,T,V
Tagetes tenuifolia 'Starfire'	BS,C,CL,DT,F,J,KI,KS, L,M,S,T,TU,V,VH,YA
Tagetes tenuifolia 'Sundance'	U
Tagetes tenuifolia 'Tangerine Gem'	B,BS,CL,D,DT,F,KI,KS, R,S
Tagetes tenuifolia 'Ursula'	D
Tagetes triploid 'Beau' s-c, mix	BS
Tagetes triploid 'Little Nell'	B,BS,CL
Tagetes triploid 'Nell Gwyn'	B,BD,BS,CL
Tagetes triploid 'Seven Star'	B,BS,D,T
Tagetes triploid 'Solar Series' s-c, mix	B,BS,CL
Tagetes triploid 'Super Star'	BS,KI
Tagetes triploid 'Super Star Orange'	U
Tagetes triploid 'Suzie Wong'	B,CL,T
Tagetes triploid 'Trinity' mix	T
Tagetes triploid 'Zenith' mix	BS,CL,L
Tagetes triploid 'Zenith' s-c	B,BS,CL,D,U,YA
Tagetes tubiflora	B
Talinum angustissimum	B
Talinum appelachianum	Y
Talinum aurantiacum	B,SW
Talinum brevifolium	B,SW
Talinum caffrum	B,Y
Talinum calycinum	Y
Talinum confertiflorum	Y
Talinum okanoganense	AP,I,SC,Y
Talinum palmeri	Y
Talinum paniculatum	AP,B,C,G
Talinum parviflorum	Y
Talinum parviflorum v nova DJF1425	Y
Talinum parviflorum v nova DJF1426	Y
Talinum portulacifolium	B
Talinum rugospermum	AP,B,JE,SC
Talinum spinescens	AP,CC,I,SC
Talinum teretifolium	AP,B,SC
Talinum 'Zoe'	I
Tamarindus indica	B,HA,RE,SA
Tamarix aphylla	B
Tamarix chinensis	SA
Tamarix gallica	B,SA
Tamarix parviflora	CG
Tamus communis	B,G,SG
Tanacetum balsamita	B
Tanacetum balsamita ssp balsamita	SG
Tanacetum boreale	SG
Tanacetum cinerariifolium	B
Tanacetum coccineum	AP,B,SG
Tanacetum coccineum 'Duro'	B,JE
Tanacetum coccineum 'James Kelway'	B,SASC
Tanacetum coccineum 'Robinson's' mix	JE,SA
Tanacetum coccineum 'Robinson's' s-c	B,BS,JE,SA,T
Tanacetum coccineum 'Silver Princess'	B
Tanacetum coccineum single giant	BD,BS,V
Tanacetum corymbosum	B,RS,SC,SG
Tanacetum dbl mix	J,ST,TU,V
Tanacetum hultenii	B
Tanacetum hyb lge fl	BS,S,ST
Tanacetum macrophyllum	B
Tanacetum niveum	B,C,CP,T
Tanacetum parthenium	B,C,CP,JE,KS,LA,SA,SG, YA
Tanacetum parthenium 'Alba'	CP
Tanacetum parthenium 'Aureum'	B,C,CP,G,I
Tanacetum parthenium 'Ball's Dbl White'	B,D
Tanacetum parthenium 'Butterball'	B,D,DT,F,T,U
Tanacetum parthenium 'Fortuna'	B
Tanacetum parthenium 'Gold Ball'	B,BS,C,CL,D,DT,J,KI,L, S,TU,V,YA
Tanacetum parthenium 'Goldball Imp'	B
Tanacetum parthenium 'Golden Moss'	B,BS,CL,DT,T
Tanacetum parthenium 'Perfection'	B

TANACETUM

Tanacetum parthenium plenum	I
Tanacetum parthenium 'Princess Daisy'	B
Tanacetum parthenium 'Rotary'	B
Tanacetum parthenium 'Roya'	B
Tanacetum parthenium 'Salome'	B
Tanacetum parthenium 'Santana'	CL,F,T
Tanacetum parthenium 'Santana Yellow'	B,CL
Tanacetum parthenium 'Selma Star'	B,BS,KI,ST
Tanacetum parthenium 'Silverball'	B,BS,CO,KI,TU
Tanacetum parthenium 'Snowball'	B,C,DT
Tanacetum parth. 'Tetra White Wonder'	B
Tanacetum parthenium 'Tom Thumb'	SG
Tanacetum parthenium 'Variegatum'	B
Tanacetum parthenium 'White Star'	B,BL,CL,YA
Tanacetum ptarmicaeflorum	BS,DT,S,SG,YA
Tanacctum ptarm. 'Silver Feather'	CL,J,L,T
Tanacetum 'Robinson's Giant Fl'	C,DT,L,SE
Tanacetum roseum	C,CP
Tanacetum roseum 'Duro'	C
Tanacetum roseum 'King Size'	CL,F
Tanacetum single mix	CO,D,J,TU
Tanacetum 'Snow Dwarf'	U
Tanacetum 'Snow Puffs'	D
Tanacetum 'Snowball'	B,BD,BS,L,V
Tanacetum vulgare	B,C,G,JE,KS,LA,SA,SG
Tanacetum vulgare 'Gold-sticks'	B
Tanacetum 'White Gem'	S
Tanacetun 'Superb' mix	T
Tanquana archeri	B
Tanquana hilmarii	B,SI,Y
Tanquana prismatica	B
Tapeinochilus ananassae	B
Taraxacum magellanicum	G,SS
Taraxacum officinale album	SG
Taraxacum serotinum	B
Taraxacum sp	AP,SG
Tarchonanthus camphoratus	B,SI
Tarenna asiatica	B
Tavaresia barklyi	B,SI
Taxodium distichum	B,C,CG,N,SA
Taxodium distichum v imbricarium	B
Taxodium dist. v imbricarium 'Nutans'	B
Taxodium mucronatum	B,HA,SA
Taxus baccata	A,B,C,G,SA
Taxus baccata 'Dovastonii'	CG
Taxus baccata 'Erecta'	B
Taxus baccata 'Fastigiata'	B,SA
Taxus brevifolia	B,C
Taxus chinensis	B,C,SA
Taxus cuspidata	B,SA,V
Taxus cuspidata 'Capitata'	B
Taxus mairei	SA
Taxus x media 'Hicksii'	B
Taxus x media 'Kelseyi'	B
Tecoma capensis	B,SA,SI,SG
Tecoma stans	B,C,JE,HA,O,SA,SW
Tecoma x smithii	B
Tecomanthe hillii	B
Tectaria incisa	B
Tectona grandis	B,C,HA,RE,SA
Teesdaliopsis conferta	CG,SC
Telekia speciosa	AP,B,C,CG,G,JE,P,SA, SC,T
Telekia speciosissima	B,G,SG
Telephium imperata	AP,B,C,SC
Teline monspessulana	SG

Tellima grandiflora	B,C,CC,G,I,JE,P,RH,SA, SC,SG
Tellima grandiflora odorata group	E
Tellima grandiflora odorata 'Howell'	T
Tellima grandiflora v rubra	E,SG
Telopea mongaensis	B,O,SA
Telopea oreades	B,C,HA,O,SA
Telopea speciosissima	AU,B,C,HA,O,SA,SI,V
Telopea truncata	B,C,N,O,SA
Teloxys aristata	B,C,V
Templetonia biloba	B
Templetonia egena	B
Templetonia hookeri	B
Templetonia neglecta	B
Templetonia retusa	AU,C,O,SA
Templetonia stenophylla	B
Tenicroa filifolia	B
Tephrocactus alexanderi bruchii	BC
Tephrocactus articulatus polyacanthus	BC
Tephrocactus asplundtii	BC
Tephrocactus chilecitoensis	CH
Tephrocactus glomeratus	CH
Tephrocactus syringacanthus	CH
Tephrosia candida	B,SI
Tephrosia eriocarpa	B,SA
Tephrosia flammea	B
Tephrosia glomeruliflora	B
Tephrosia grandiflora	B
Tephrosia maxima	B
Tephrosia polystacha	SI
Tephrosia purpurea	B
Tephrosia rosea	B,SA
Tephrosia sp	SI
Tephrosia uniovulata	B
Tephrosia villosa	B
Tephrosia virginiana	PR
Tephrosia vogelii	B
Teramnus labialis	B
Terminalia amazona	B
Terminalia arjuna	O
Terminalia arostrata	O
Terminalia bellirica	B
Terminalia canescens	B
Terminalia carpentariae	B
Terminalia catappa	B,HA,RE,SA
Terminalia cunninghamii	B
Terminalia ferdinandiana	B,O
Terminalia ivorensis	B
Terminalia lucida	B
Terminalia mantaly	B,SI
Terminalia mollis	SI
Terminalia muelleri	B
Terminalia petiolaris	B
Terminalia phanerophlebia	B
Terminalia platyphylla	B
Terminalia platyptera	B
Terminalia porphyrocarpa	B
Terminalia prunioides	B,SI
Terminalia sericea	B,SI
Terminalia sericocarpa	B,O
Terminalia stuhlmannii	SI
Terminalia supranitifolia	B
Terminalia trichopoda	SI
Ternstroemia gymnanthera	B,C,SA
Ternstroemia japonica see gymnanthera	
Testudinaria elephantipes see Dioscorea	

223

Tetracarpidium conophorum	B
Tetracentron sinense	B,SG
Tetraclinis articulata	B
Tetradium danielli	B,C,SA
Tetradium elleryana	B,HA,RE,SA
Tetradium fraxinifolia	C
Tetradium hupehensis	SA
Tetraganolobus purpureus	CG
Tetragonia diptera	B
Tetragonia eremaea	B
Tetragonia tetragonioides	B,CG
Tetragonolobus maritimus	C,SC,SG
Tetranema roseum	B,SG
Tetranema roseum 'Violetta'	C
Tetraneuris grandiflora	B,JE,SW
Tetrapanax papyrifer	C,HA,SA
Tetrapathaea tetrandra	B
Tetrarrhena laevis	B
Tetraselago wilmsii	B,SI
Tetratheca confertifolia	B
Tetratheca hirsuta	B
Tetratheca setigera	B
Tetratheca virgata	B
Teucrium arduinii	AP,C,I,SC
Teucrium asiaticum	SC,SG
Teucrium botrys	AP,B,NS
Teucrium canadense	AP,B,CP,PR
Teucrium chamaedrys	B,BS,C,CG,CL,JE,SA, SC,T
Teucrium flavum	AP,B,C,G,JE,SC
Teucrium hyrcanicum	AP,B,C,CP,E,G,SC
Teucrium massiliense	AP,B,C,CP
Teucrium montanum	AP,B,C,SC
Teucrium polium	B,C,JE,S
Teucrium polium 'Aureum'	B,I
Teucrium pyrenaicum	G,SA,SG
Teucrium racemosum v racemosum	B
Teucrium scorodonia	B,C,CP,E,JE,SA,SG
Teucrium scorodonia 'Crispum'	FH,SC
Teucrium sc. 'Crispum Marginatum' (V)	FH
Thalictrum alpinum	AP,B,G,SC
Thalictrum aquilegiifolium	AP,B,BS,DT,G,JE,KI,SA, SC,SG,SU
Thalictrum aquilegiifolium 'Album'	B,G,JE,SA
Thalictrum aquilegiifolium 'New Hybrids'	B,C,CL,F,T,V
Thalictrum aquilegiifolium 'Purpureum'	B,JE,SA
Thalictrum chelidonii	B,SA,SC,SG
Thalictrum dasycarpum	B,JE,PR
Thalictrum delavayi	AP,B,BS,C,G,JE,MA,SA, SC,T
Thalictrum delavayi 'Album'	B,MA,SC
Thalictrum del. album 'Sternenhimmel'	JE
Thalictrum dioicum	PR
Thalictrum dipterocarpum see delavayi	
Thalictrum fendleri	B,CG
Thalictrum flavum	G,SA,SG,T
Thalictrum flavum ssp flavum	B,JE
Thalictrum flavum ssp glaucum	AP,B,C,JE,P,SG
Thalictrum foetidum	AP,B,JE,SC,SG
Thalictrum 'Hierba De Polen'	B
Thalictrum javanicum	B,SC
Thalictrum lucidum	B,C,G,JE
Thalictrum minus	B,C,CG,G,SA,SC,SG
Thalictrum minus 'Adiantifolium'	B,G,JE
Thalictrum minus ssp minus	JE
Thalictrum petaloideum	G,SG

Thalictrum polycarpum	B
Thalictrum polygamum	B,SG
Thalictrum rhynchocarpum	SI
Thalictrum rochebrunianum	AP,B,G,JE,SA,SC
Thalictrum simplex	SG
Thalictrum sp	AP,FH,SC,SG
Thalictrum sp CNW331	X
Thalictrum speciosissimum	
see flavum ssp glaucum	
Thalictrum venulosum	SG
Thamnocalamus spathaceus	
see Fargesia murieliae	
Thamnochortus acuminatus	B
Thamnochortus bachmannii	B,SI
Thamnochortus cinereus	B,SI
Thamnochortus insignis	B,C,O,SA,SI
Thamnochortus lucens	B,SI
Thamnochortus platypteris	SI
Thamnochortus rigidus	B,SI
Thamnochortus sp nova	SI
Thamnochortus spicigerus	B,O,SI
Thapsia garganica	SA
Thaspium trifoliatum	PR
Thea sinensis	SA
Thelesperma burridgeanum	B
Thelesperma burridgeanum 'Brunette'	C
Thelesperma filifolius	FH
Thelocactus bicolor	B,Y
Thelocactus bicolor v bolansis	B,Y
Thelocactus bicolor v flavidispinum	B
Thelocactus bicolor v pottsii	B
Thelocactus bicolor v schottii	B,Y
Thelocactus bicolor v tricolor	B
Thelocactus bolensis	B
Thelocactus bueckii	B
Thelocactus conothele	B
Thelocactus conothele v argenteus	B
Thelocactus conothele v aurantiacus	B
Thelocactus flavidispinus	Y
Thelocactus hastifer	B
Thelocactus heterochromus	B
Thelocactus hexaedrophorus	B
Thelocactus hexaedrophorus v fossulatus	B,Y
Thelocactus krainzianus	Y
Thelocactus leucacanthus	B,Y
Thelocactus leucacanthus v schmollii	B
Thelocactus lloydii	B,Y
Thelocactus macdowellii	B,BC,GC,Y
Thelocactus matudae	B
Thelocactus nidulans	B,Y
Thelocactus pseudopectinatus	B
Thelocactus rinconensis	B,CH
Thelocactus saussieri	Y
Thelocactus saussieri albiflora	BC
Thelocactus schwarzii	B
Thelocactus setispinus	B,SG,Y
Thelocactus setispinus v hamatus	B
Thelocactus setispinus v setaceus	B
Thelocactus sp mix	C,CH,Y
Thelocactus tulensis	B,Y
Thelocactus wagnerianus	Y
Thelymitra antennifera	B
Thelymitra benthamiana	B
Thelymitra campanulata	B
Thelymitra crinita	B
Thelymitra flexuosa	B

THELYMITRA

Thelymitra graminea	B
Thelymitra holmesii	B
Thelymitra ixioides	B
Thelymitra longifolia	SS
Thelymitra nuda white	B
Thelymitra pauciflora	B
Thelypteris dentata	B
Themeda pilbara	B
Themeda triandra	B,HA
Themeda triandra japonica	JE
Theobroma cacao	B
Theobroma gilleri	B
Thereianthus spicatus	B,SI
Thermopsis caroliniana see villosa	
Thermopsis fabacea	B,JE,SC
Thermopsis lanceolata	AP,B,BS,C,JE,KI,SA,SG, U,V
Thermopsis lupinoides	SG
Thermopsis macrophylla	B
Thermopsis montana see rhombifolia	
Thermopsis rhombifolia	B,CJE,SA,SG,T
Thermopsis villosa	AP,B,C,JE,NT
Thesium alpinum	SG
Thespesia acutiloba	B
Thespesia populnea	B,HA,RE,SA
Thevetia neriifolia see peruviana	
Thevetia peruviana	B,C,HA,RE,SA
Thevetia peruviana 'Alba'	B
Thladiantha speciosa	B
Thlaspi alpestre	B,G
Thlaspi alpestre 'Krodde'	C
Thlaspi alpinum	C,CG,FH,G,JE,SA,SC
Thlaspi arvense	B,CG,LA,SG
Thlaspi bulbosum	SC,SG
Thlaspi ceratocarpum	B
Thlaspi fendleri	AP,B,SW
Thlaspi kovatsii	FH
Thlaspi montanum	B,G,SC
Thlaspi perfoliatum	CG
Thlaspi rotundifolium	AP,B,C,JE,SA,SC
Thomasia angustifolia	B
Thomasia glutinosa	B
Thomasia macrocarpa	B
Thomasia quercifolia	B
Thomasia solanacea	AU
Thomasia triphylla	B
Thorncroftia succulenta	B,SI
Thounidium decandrum	B
Threlkeldia diffusa	B
Thrinax compacta	B
Thrinax excelsa	B
Thrinax morrisii	B,O,SA
Thrinax parviflora	B,O,SA
Thrinax radiata	B
Thrincia tuberosa	B
Thrixanthocereus blossfeldiorum	Y
Thryallis glauca	B
Thryptomene aspera ssp glabra	B
Thryptomene baeckeacea	B
Thryptomene calycina	B
Thryptomene johnsonii	B,SA
Thryptomene kochii	B
Thryptomene maisoneum	B
Thryptomene mucronulata	B
Thryptomene racemulosa	B
Thuja compacta	HA

Thuja koraiensis	B
Thuja occidentalis	A,B,C,SA,SG
Thuja occidentalis 'Cristata'	CG
Thuja occidentalis 'Fastigiata'	B
Thuja occidentalis 'Filiformis'	CG
Thuja occidentalis pyramidalis	SA
Thuja occidentalis 'Rosenthallii'	CG
Thuja occidentalis 'Wareana'	CG
Thuja orientalis	B,C,CG,HA,SA
Thuja orientalis 'Aurea'	B
Thuja orientalis 'Aurea Nana'	B
Thuja orientalis 'Beverleyensis'	B
Thuja orientalis 'Pyramidalis'	B,SA
Thuja orientalis 'Sieboldii'	B
Thuja orientalis v aurea	C,SA
Thuja orientalis v aurea nana	C,SA
Thuja orientalis v compacta	C
Thuja orientalis v compacta nana	SA
Thuja plicata	A,B,C,CG,SA
Thuja standishii	SG
Thujopsis dolobrata	CG,SA
Thunbergia alata	AP,B,BS,C,CO,J,KI,KS, L,R,S,SA,ST,VH
Thunbergia alata 'Susie' mix	BD,BS,CL,D,DT,F,M,SE, T,U,V,YA
Thunbergia alata 'Susie Orange'	V
Thunbergia erecta	B
Thunbergia fragrans	B
Thunbergia fragrans 'Angel Wings'	T
Thunbergia grandiflora	B,SA
Thunbergia grandiflora 'Alba'	B
Thunbergia kirkii	B
Thunbergia lancifolia	B,C
Thunbergia natalensis	SI
Thymophylla tenuiloba	B,BD,BS,DT,G,KS,L,SG
Thymophylla tenuiloba 'Golden Cascade'	J
Thymophylla tenuiloba 'Shooting Star'	BS,C,CL,F
Thymus adamovicii	SG
Thymus argaeus	T
Thymus caespititius	B
Thymus camphorata	B,SG
Thymus carnosus	B
Thymus 'Coconut'	B
Thymus comosus	AP,B,SC,T
Thymus doerfleri 'Bressingham Pink'	B
Thymus 'Doone Valley'	FH
Thymus longiflorus	SA
Thymus 'Longwood'	B
Thymus marschallianus	FH
Thymus mastichiana	AP,SA,SC
Thymus polytrichus	B
Thymus polytrichus ssp arcticus	B,SG,SU
Thymus pseudolanuginosus	B
Thymus pulegioides	B,C,JE
Thymus pulegioides albiflora	SG
Thymus richardii ssp nitidus	SG
Thymus serpyllum	B,BD,BS,C,CL,J,JE,L,S, SA,T,V
Thymus serpyllum 'Aureus'	B
Thymus serpyllum 'Minor'	B
Thymus serpyllum v coccineus	B
Thymus sp Spain	SG
Thymus thracicus	B
Thymus vulgaris 'Silver Posie'	B
Thymus x citriodorus	B
Thymus x citriodorus cvs	B

Thymus zygis	SA	Tillandsia spiculosa v ustulata	B
Thysanotus dichotomus	B	Tillandsia streptocarpa	B
Thysanotus manglesianus	B	Tillandsia stricta	B
Thysanotus multiflorus	B,SA	Tillandsia tenuifolia	B
Thysanotus thyrsoideus	B	Tillandsia tricholepis	B
Tiarella cordifolia	AP,CC,FH,SC	Tillandsia vernicosa	B
Tiarella polyphylla	B,G,P	Tillandsia vestita	B
Tiarella polyphylla 'Filigran'	BS,JE	Tillandsia viridiflora	B
Tiarella sp	PA	Tillandsia xerographica	B
Tiarella wherryi	B,C,CG,JE,NT,SA,T	Tillandsia xiphioides	B
Tibouchina granulosa	B,SE,T	Tinnea barbata	B,SI
Tibouchina holosericea	B	Tinnea rhodesiana	B,SI
Tibouchina macrantha	B	Tinospora smilacina	B
Tibouchina mix	SA	Tipuana tipu	C,HA,O,SA
Tibouchina mutabilis	B	Titanopsis calcarea	B,SI,Y
Tibouchina paratropica	SG	Titanopsis fulleri	B,SI,Y
Tibouchina sellowiana	B	Titanopsis hugo-schlechteri	B,SI,Y
Tibouchina urvilleana	B	Titanopsis hugo-schlechteri v alboviridis	B
Tigridia chrysantha	B,SW	Titanopsis luederitzii	B,SI
Tigridia dugesii	B,SW	Titanopsis primosii	B,SI,Y
Tigridia durangense	B,SC,SW	Titanopsis schwantesii	B,SI
Tigridia multiflora	SW	Titanopsis sp mix	C,Y
Tigridia pavonia	AP,B,LG,SC	Tithonia 'Arla'	B
Tigridia pavonia 'New Hybrids'	B	Tithonia 'Fiesta del Sol'	F
Tilia americana	A,B,SA	Tithonia rotundifolia	B,G,SG,V
Tilia amurensis	B,SA,SG	Tithonia rotundifolia 'Goldfinger'	B,L,S,T
Tilia argentea	SA	Tithonia rotundifolia 'Torch'	B,C
Tilia cordata	A,B,C,SA,SG	Toddalia asiatica	B
Tilia dasystyla of gnds	SA	Tofieldia calyculata	B,C,JE,SG
Tilia japonica	SA	Tofieldia glutinosa	B,C,JE,SG
Tilia mandschurica	SA	Tolmiea menziesii	B,C,G,JE,SA
Tilia miqueliana	C	Tolpis barbata	B,C,D,KS,T
Tilia mongolica	SA	Toona australis	B,HA,O
Tilia oliveri	B,SA	Toona sinensis	B,C,HA,SA
Tilia platyphyllos	A,B,SA,SG	Tordylium aegyptiacum	B
Tilia sibirica	SG	Torenia flava 'Suzie Wong'	B,S
Tilia tomentosa	A,B,C,CG	Torenia fournieri	B,T
Tillandsia aeranthos	B	Torenia fournieri 'Clown' mix	B,C,CL,J,T,V
Tillandsia anceps	B	Torenia fournieri 'Nana Compacta Blue'	B
Tillandsia balbisiana	B	Torenia fournieri 'Pink Panda'	B,BS
Tillandsia bulbosa	B	Torilis arvensis	B,SG
Tillandsia capitata v rubra	B	Torilis japonica	B,LA
Tillandsia dura	B	Torreya grandis	B,SA
Tillandsia gardneri	B	Torreya nucifera	B
Tillandsia geminiflora	B	Toumeya papyracantha	B
Tillandsia geminiflora v gigantea	B	Townsendia exscapa	AP,B,G,SC,SW
Tillandsia geminiflora v incana	B	Townsendia florifera	AP,HH,SC
Tillandsia juncea	B	Townsendia formosa	B,G,SC,SW
Tillandsia loliacea	B	Townsendia incana	AP,B,SC,SW
Tillandsia lorentziana	B	Townsendia montana	AP,CG,SC
Tillandsia mallemontii	B	Townsendia montana v minima	B,SW
Tillandsia paraensis	B	Townsendia parryi	AP,CG,G,SC
Tillandsia pohliana	B	Townsendia rothrockii	AP,G,SC,SG
Tillandsia polystachia	B	Toxicodendron see Rhus	
Tillandsia pruinosa	B	Trachelium caeruleum	B,C,G,SA
Tillandsia punctulata	B	Trachelium caeruleum 'Album'	B,SA
Tillandsia regnellii	B	Trachelium caer. f1 'Passion in Violet'	F
Tillandsia remota	B	Trachelium caeruleum 'Umbrella' mix	U
Tillandsia rubida	B	Trachelium caeruleum 'Umbrella Purple'	BS,JE,V
Tillandsia schiedeana	B	Trachelium caeruleum 'Umbrella White'	BS,JE
Tillandsia schiedeana v minor	B	Trachelium caer. 'Violet Veil of Flowers'	C
Tillandsia schreiteri	B	Trachelium caer. 'White Veil of Flowers'	C
Tillandsia seideliana	B	Trachelium rumelianum	B,T
Tillandsia setacea	B	Trachelospermum asiaticum	B
Tillandsia simulata	B	Trachelospermum jasminoides	B
Tillandsia spiculosa	B	Trachyandra divaricata	B

TRACHYANDRA

Trachyandra falcata	B,SI
Trachyandra hirsuta	SI
Trachyandra hirsutiflora	B,SI
Trachyandra revoluta	B,SI
Trachycarpus fortunei	A,B,C,CG,HA,O,RE,SA, SH,T
Trachycarpus martianus	B,C,O
Trachymene anisocarpa	O
Trachymene coerulea	AU,B,BS,C,F,KS,O,SA, T,V
Trachymene coerulea 'Alba'	B,KS
Trachymene coerulea 'Madonna'	C
Trachymene coerulea 'Rosea'	B,KS
Trachymene glaucifolia	B
Trachymene oleracea	B
Trachys muricata	B
Trachyspermum ammi	B
Trachyspermum ammi 'Bold'	B
Trachyspermum ammi 'Thin'	B
Tradescantia Andersoniana 'Blanca'	JE
Tradescantia Andersoniana 'Blue'	JE
Tradescantia Andersoniana 'Carmine Red'	JE
Tradescantia Andersoniana gr.	JE
Tradescantia Andersoniana 'New Hybrids'	C
Tradescantia bracteata	PR
Tradescantia occidentalis	B,PR
Tradescantia ohiensis	B,JE,PR
Tradescantia spathacea	B,C,SA
Tradescantia subaspera montana	SG
Tradescantia virginiana	B,BD,BS,C,SA
Tradescantia virginiana 'Alba'	B
Tradescantia virginiana 'Caerulea'	B
Tradescantia virginiana 'Rosea'	B
Tragia involucrata	B
Tragia plukenetii	B
Tragopogon balcanicus	B
Tragopogon dubius	B,SG
Tragopogon floccosus	B
Tragopogon orientalis	B,SG
Tragopogon porrifolius	AP,B,CG,G,SC
Tragopogon pratensis	B,G,LA,SC,SG
Tragus roxburghii	B
Treculia africana	B
Trema orientalis	SI
Tremastelma palaestinum	CG
Trevesia palmata	B
Trianthema pilosa	B
Trianthema portulacastrum	B
Trianthema turgidifolia	B
Triaspis nelsonii	B
Tribonanthes australis	C
Tribulus cistoides	B
Tribulus hirsuta	B
Tribulus platyptera	B
Tribulus terrestris	B
Trichilia colimana	B
Trichilia dregeana	B
Trichilia emetica	B
Trichilia glabra	B
Trichocaulon cactiforme	B
Trichocaulon puntatus	CH
Trichocereus atacamensis	B,Y
Trichocereus bruchii	B
Trichocereus camarguensis	Y
Trichocereus catamarcensis	B
Trichocereus cephalomacrostibas	Y

Trichocereus chilensis borealis	BC
Trichocereus chilensis panhoplites	BC
Trichocereus culpinensis	Y
Trichocereus culpinensis v monstrosus	B
Trichocereus escayensis	B
Trichocereus formosus	B
Trichocereus grandiflorus see Echinopsis huascha	
Trichocereus herzogianus	B
Trichocereus lobivioides 'Grandiflorus'	B
Trichocereus lobivioides 'Purpureominiata'	B
Trichocereus macrogonus	B,Y
Trichocereus mix	Y
Trichocereus narvaezensis	B
Trichocereus orurensis	B
Trichocereus pachanoi	Y
Trichocereus poco	B
Trichocereus puquiensis	Y
Trichocereus purpureopilosus	BC
Trichocereus randallii	B
Trichocereus schickendantzii	Y
Trichocereus sc. hybs 'Paramount'	B
Trichocereus scopulicopus	Y
Trichocereus shaferi	B,Y
Trichocereus smrzianus	B
Trichocereus spachianus see Echinopsis	
Trichocereus strigosus	B
Trichocereus tacaquirensis	B,Y
Trichocereus tarijensis v orurensis	B
Trichocereus terschecki	B,Y
Trichocereus thelegonoides	Y
Trichocereus thelegonus	B,Y
Trichocereus totorensis	B,BC
Trichocereus trichosus	Y
Trichocereus tunarensis	B,Y
Trichocereus validus	B,Y
Trichocereus werdermannianus	B,Y
Trichocereus werd. v lecoriensis	B,Y
Trichodesma zeylanicum	B,C
Trichodiadema barbatum	B
Trichodiadema densum	B
Trichodiadema intonsum	B
Trichodiadema mirabile	B,Y
Trichodiadema stellatum	B,BC,SI
Tricholaena rosea	C
Trichopetalum plumosum B.C.W4116	MN
Trichosanthes cucumerina	B,C
Trichosanthes cucumerina v anguina	B
Trichosanthes cucumerina v tricuspidata	B
Trichosanthes kirilowii	B
Trichostema arizonicum	B,SW
Trichostema lanatum	AP,B,SW
Trichostema lanatum v parishii	B,SW
Tricoryne elatior	B
Tricyrtis affinis	B,SG
Tricyrtis bakeri see latifolia	
Tricyrtis flava	B
Tricyrtis formosana	SG
Tricyrtis hirta	B,CG,JE,SA,T,V
Tricyrtis hirta hyb 'Miyazaki'	AP,C,JE
Tricyrtis hirta 'Variegata'	B
Tricyrtis 'Hybrids Mix'	T
Tricyrtis Japanese hyb	JE
Tricyrtis latifolia	CG,G,JE,SC,SG
Tricyrtis macrantha	I
Tricyrtis macrantha ssp macranthopsis	B

TRICYRTIS

Tricyrtis macropoda	AP,C,G,JE,SC,SG	Triodia irritans v laxispicata	B
Tricyrtis maculata	JE	Triodia mitchellii	B
Tricyrtis nana	B	Triodia pungens	B
Tricyrtis ohsumiensis	B	Triodia wiseana	B
Tricyrtis puberula	AP,SC,SG	Triosteum perfoliatum	B
Tricyrtis sp	LG	Triphasia trifolia	B
Tridax procumbens	B	Triplaris weigeltiana	B
Tridax trilobata	B	Tripleurospermum inodorum	B,LA
Tridentea aperta	B	Tripleurospermum inodorum 'Bridal Robe'	B,KS
Tridentea umdausensis	B	Tripleurospermum maritima ssp inodorum	B,G
Tridentia peculiaris	B	Triplochiton zambesiacus	B,SI
Trifolium alexandrinum	AP,B	Tripsacum dactyloides	B,PR
Trifolium alpestris	B	Tripteris 'Gaiety'	T
Trifolium alpinum	B,C,JE,SA	Tripterococcus brunonis	B
Trifolium ambiguum	SG	Tripterygium regelii	B,SA
Trifolium argutum	B	Trisetum altaicum	SG
Trifolium arvense	B,SG	Trisetum flavescens	B,JE
Trifolium aureum	B	Tristania laurina	SA
Trifolium badium	AP,B	Tristania neriifolia	B
Trifolium billardieri	B	Tristaniopsis laurina	C,HA,O
Trifolium campestre	B	Triteleia hyacinthina	AP,B,G,MN,RH,SC,SG
Trifolium clusii	B	Triteleia laxa	AP,C,FH,G,RH,SC
Trifolium dubium	B	Triteleia lemmoni	B,SW
Trifolium fragiferum	B	Triteleia peduncularis	B,MN
Trifolium fragiferum 'O'connors'	B	Triteleia x tubergenii	PM,SC
Trifolium fragiferum 'Palestine'	B	Trithrinax acanthocoma	B
Trifolium hirtum	B	Triticum aestivum	B
Trifolium hirtum 'Hykon'	B	Triticum aestivum 'Baart'	B
Trifolium hirtum 'Kondinin'	B	Triticum aestivum 'Pima Club'	B
Trifolium hybridum	B	Triticum aestivum v spelta	B
Trifolium incarnatum	B,SU	Triticum aestivum 'White Sonora'	B
Trifolium lupinaster	SG	Triticum monococcum	SG
Trifolium macrocephalum	B	Triticum spelta	SG,T
Trifolium medium	SG	Triticum turgidum v durum	B,C
Trifolium montanum	B,SG	Triticum turgidum v durum 'Bidi'	B
Trifolium ochroleucon	B,SG	Tritonia bakeri	B
Trifolium pratense	B,C,SC,SG	Tritonia crispa	B,SI
Trifolium pratense 'Redquin'	B	Tritonia crocata	B,MN,O,SI
Trifolium purpureum	B	Tritonia deusta	B,O,SI
Trifolium repens	B,C,SG,SU	Tritonia deusta ssp miniata	B
Trifolium repens f minus	B	Tritonia disticha ssp rubrolucens	B,C,P
Trifolium repens vars	B	Tritonia dubia	AP,B
Trifolium rubens	A,AP,B,C,JE,SA,T	Tritonia flabellifolia	B
Trifolium semipilosum	B	Tritonia karooica	B,SI
Trifolium semipilosum 'Safari'	B	Tritonia lineata	B,SI
Trifolium stellatum	B,SC	Tritonia pallida	B
Trifolium striatum	B,CG	Tritonia paniculata	B,SC,SI
Trifolium subterraneum named vars	B	Tritonia securigera	MN,SC
Trifolium tomentosum	B	Tritonia sp	SI
Trifolium trichocephalum	SC,SG	Tritonia squalida	B,SI
Trifolium vulgare	SG	Tritoniopsis caffra	B,SI
Triglochin maritima	B,G,SG	Tritoniopsis parviflora	B,SI
Trigonella caerulea	B	Triumfetta appendiculata	B,SA
Trigonella foenum-graecum	B,KS	Triumfetta chaetocarpa	B
Trigonella melelorus caerulea	T	Triumfetta rhomboidea	B
Trigonidium egertonianum	B	Trochetiopsis melanoxylon	SG
Trillium chloropetalum	AP,B,G,P,SC	Trochocarpa thymifolia	B,C
Trillium cuneatum	G,PM	Trochodendron aralioides	SA,SG
Trillium erectum	AP,B,CC,G,P,PM,SC	Trollius acaulis	AP,B,SC,T
Trillium grandiflorum	CG,G,SC	Trollius altaicus	AP,SG
Trillium kamtschaticum	SG	Trollius asiaticus	B,JE,SG
Trillium ovatum	SC,SG	Trollius chinensis	AP,B,CC,CG,G,SA,P,SC, SG
Trillium sessile	B,G,P		
Trimeria trinervis	B,SI	Trollius chinensis 'Golden Queen'	AP,B,BD,BS,C,CL,CO, HH,JE,KI,SC,V
Triodanis perfoliata	PR		
Triodia angusta	B	Trollius 'Choice Mix'	U

TROLLIUS

Trollius europaeus	AP,B,BS,C,CG,F,G,JE, RS,SA,SC,SG,T
Trollius europaeus 'Superbus'	B,JE,SA
Trollius europaeus transilvanicus	SG
Trollius hondoensis	B,P
Trollius hybridus	T
Trollius laxus	B,JE,SW
Trollius ledebourii see chinensis	
Trollius pumilus	AP,B,CC,G,HH,JE,SC,SG
Trollius ranunculinus	B,SC,SG
Trollius x cultorum 'Early Hybrids'	B,JE
Trollius x cultorum 'New Hybrids'	B,C,JE
Trollius x cultorum 'Orange Globe'	B,JE
Trollius yunnanensis	AP,G,SC,SG
Tropaeolum 'Alaska'	BS,C,CL,CO,D,DT,F,J,KI, KS,L,M,S,SE,ST,SU,T, TU,U,V,VH,YA
Tropaeolum azureum	AP,B,J,P,SC,SE,T
Tropaeolum ciliatum	AP,B,P,MN,N,SC
Tropaeolum majus	SG,SU
Tropaeolum majus 'Apricot Trifle'	SE
Tropaeolum majus 'Cherry Rose'	V
Tropaeolum majus 'Collection'	U
Tropaeolum majus 'Dark Leaved' mix	DT
Tropaeolum majus dw semi-dbl mix	U
Tropaeolum majus 'Empress Of India'	BD,BS,C,DT,F,J,KS,S, SU,T,V,YA
Tropaeolum majus 'Gleam Golden'	B,BD,BS,J,KI
Tropaeolum m. 'Gleam Hybrids' semi-dbl	BD,C,D,DT,F,J,KI,L,ST, TU,YA
Tropaeolum majus 'Gleam Scarlet'	B,BD,BS,D,J,KI
Tropaeolum majus 'Glorious Gleam' dbl	BS,C,T,V
Tropaeolum majus 'Golden Emperor'	B,DT
Tropaeolum majus 'Jewel Cherry Rose'	B,C,DT,T
Tropaeolum majus 'Jewel Golden'	B
Tropaeolum majus 'Jewel Mahogany'	B
Tropaeolum majus 'Jewel' mix	BS,CL,D,DT,F,J,KI,M,S, ST,YA
Tropaeolum majus 'Jewel of Africa'	SE,T
Tropaeolum majus 'Jewel Primrose'	B,D,DT
Tropaeolum majus 'Jewel Scarlet'	B
Tropaeolum majus 'Moonlight'	B,F,SE
Tropaeolum majus 'Peach Melba'	B,BD,BS,CL,DT,F,KS,T,U
Tropaeolum majus 'Pineapples & Strawb'	F
Tropaeolum majus 'Queen Of The Dwarfs'	B
Tropaeolum majus 'Raspberry Sorbet'	SE
Tropaeolum majus 'Salmon Baby'	DT,F,KS,U,V
Tropaeolum majus 'Strawberries & Cream'	SE,T,V
Tropaeolum majus 'Strawberry Ice'	SE,T,VH
Tropaeolum majus 'Tall' mix	C,CO,D,J,KI,M,ST,SU,T, U
Tropaeolum majus 'Tip Top Apricot'	B,BD,BS,D,DT,F,T
Tropaeolum majus 'Tip Top Gold'	B,F,T
Tropaeolum majus 'Tip Top Mahogany'	B,T
Tropaeolum majus 'Tip Top' mix	D,DT,J,T
Tropaeolum majus 'Tip Top Scarlet'	B,T
Tropaeolum majus 'Tom Thumb'	BD,BS,C,CO,F,J,KI,R,S, ST,T,TU,VH
Tropaeolum majus 'Top Fl Series'	KS
Tropaeolum majus 'Trailing' mix	DT,F,T
Tropaeolum majus 'Vesuvius'	B,C
Tropaeolum majus 'Whirlybird Cherry'	B,BS,C,SE,T
Tropaeolum majus 'Whirlybird Cream'	B,BS,S,T,V
Tropaeolum majus 'Whirlybird Gold'	B,BS,C,S,V
Tropaeolum majus 'Whirlybird Mahogany'	B,BS,C
Tropaeolum majus 'Whirlybird' mix	B,BD,BS,CL,CO,D,DT,F,

	J,KI,KS,L,S,SE,ST,T,TU, U,VH,YA
Tropaeolum majus 'Whirlybird Orange'	B,BS,C
Tropaeolum majus 'Whirlybird Scarlet'	B,B,BS,S,U
Tropaeolum majus 'Whirlybird Tangerine'	B,BS,S,V
Tropaeolum peltophorum	RS
Tropaeolum peltophorum 'Spitfire'	C
Tropaeolum peregrinum	B,BD,BS,C,CO,D,DT,F,J, KI,KS,L,RS,S,ST,SU,T, U,V
Tropaeolum polyphyllum	AP,B,F,P,PM,SC,SG,T
Tropaeolum speciosum	AP,B,C,N,P,SC,SE,SG,T
Tropaeolum tricolorum	AP,B,F,MN,P,T
Trymalium ledifolium	B,SA
Trymalium myrtillus	B
Trymalium spathulatum	B
Tsuga canadensis	C,CG,G,SA
Tsuga canadensis 'Pendula'	B
Tsuga canadensis prov.southern	B
Tsuga caroliniana	B,SA
Tsuga chinensis	B,SA
Tsuga diversifolia	B,CG
Tsuga heterophylla	AP,B,C,G,SA
Tsuga mertensiana	B,SA
Tsuga sieboldii	B
Tuberaria lignosa	AP,RS,SC
Tulbaghia cepacea	MN
Tulbaghia galpinii	AP,MN,SC
Tulbaghia leucantha	B,SI
Tulbaghia ludwigiana	B,SI
Tulbaghia maritima	B,MN
Tulbaghia natalensis	AP,B,C,I,SC
Tulbaghia simmleri	AP,B,MN,SC,SI
Tulbaghia violacea	AP,B,G,SA,SC,SI
Tulbaghia violacea 'John Rider'	B,BS,C,T
Tulbaghia violacea pallida	I,MN
Tulbaghia violacea v alba	AP,B,MN
Tulipa agenensis ssp boisseri	B
Tulipa australis see sylvestris	
Tulipa batalinii	AP,CG,MN,SC,SG
Tulipa biflora	CG,PM,SG
Tulipa bifloriformis	G,PM,RS
Tulipa butkovii	MN
Tulipa clusiana	FH
Tulipa clusiana 'Cynthia'	PM
Tulipa clusiana v chrysantha	AP,RS,SC
Tulipa didieri	CG
Tulipa iliensis	CG
Tulipa kaufmanniana	G,JE,SC
Tulipa kaufmanniana 'Scarlet Elegance'	PM
Tulipa kolpakowskiana	AP,CG,G,SC
Tulipa montana	AP,SC,SG
Tulipa ostrowskiana	SG
Tulipa platystigma	SG
Tulipa praestans 'Fusilier'	B
Tulipa pulchella	AP,JE,SC
Tulipa pulchella cv 'Humilis'	B,PM
Tulipa pulchella cv 'Violacea'	B
Tulipa sarracenica	CG
Tulipa saxatilis	AP,B,SC
Tulipa sprengeri	AP,B,C,FH,G,JE,LG,MN, PA,PM,RH,SC
Tulipa sylvestris	AP,B,CG,G,I,JE,SC,SG
Tulipa sylvestris ssp australis	CG
Tulipa tarda	AP,B,CG,G,JE,LG,RS, PM,SC,SG

TULIPA

Tulipa turkestanica	AP,CG,G,JE,LG,PM,SC,SG
Tulipa undulatifolia	CG
Tulipa urumiensis	AP,CG,G,JE,SC,SG
Tulipa wedenskyi	AP,LG,PM,SC,SG
Tupidanthus calyptrata	HA,SA
Turbina corymbosa	B
Turbinicarpus dickisoniae	Y
Turbinicarpus flaviflorus	B,GC,Y
Turbinicarpus gracilis	B,Y
Turbinicarpus gracilis v dickisonii	B
Turbinicarpus hoferi	BC,Y
Turbinicarpus jauernigi	Y
Turbinicarpus klinkerianus	B,Y
Turbinicarpus krainzianus	B,Y
Turbinicarpus krainzianus v minimus	Y
Turbinicarpus laui	B,CH,Y
Turbinicarpus lophophoroides	B,Y
Turbinicarpus macrochele	B,Y
Turbinicarpus mix	Y
Turbinicarpus polaskii	B,Y
Turbinicarpus pseudomacrochele	B,Y
Turbinicarpus pseudom. v lausseri	Y
Turbinicarpus pseudopectinatus	B
Turbinicarpus roseiflorus	Y
Turbinicarpus roseiflorus v albiflorus	Y
Turbinicarpus schwarzii	B,Y
Turbinicarpus swobodae	B,Y
Turbinicarpus valdezianus	B
Turbinicarpus valdezianus v albiflorus	B
Turnera ulmifolia v angustifolia	B
Turpinia nepalensis	B
Turraea obtusifolia	B,C,O,SI
Turricula parryi	B
Turritis glabra	B
Tussilago farfara	B,CG
Tweedia caerulea	B,C,CG,G,HH,PM,SA,SC,SG,T,U
Tylecodon buchholtziana	BC
Tylecodon grandiflorus	B,SI
Tylecodon hallii	B,SI
Tylecodon paniculatus	B,CH,SI,Y
Tylecodon papillaris ssp wallichii	B,CH,SI,Y
Tylecodon pearsonii	B
Tylecodon pygmaeus	SI
Tylecodon reticulatus	B,SI
Tylecodon ventricosus	B
Tylophora indica	B
Tylosema esculentum	B,SI
Typha angustifolia	B,C,JE,SA
Typha capensis	B,SI
Typha latifolia	B,C,JE,SA,SG
Typha laxmannii	B,JE,SG
Typha minima	B,G,JE
Typha muelleri	B
Typha orientale	B
Typha shuttleworthii	B,JE
Typhonium diversifolium	B
Uapaca kirkiana	B
Uebelmannia gummifera	CH
Uebelmannia pectinifera	B
Ugni molinae	SA,SG
Ulex europaeus	A,B,C,SA,T
Ulex europaeus nanus	SA
Ulex minor	B
Ulmus americana	B,C,SA

Ulmus davidiana	B,SA
Ulmus glabra	B
Ulmus japonica	SA,SG
Ulmus parvifolia	B,C,N,SA
Ulmus pumila	A,B,N,SA,SG
Umbellularia californica	B,SA
Umbilicus horizontalis	B
Umbilicus rupestris	AP,B,C,PM,SC,SG
Uncarina stellulifera	SI
Uncinia divaricata	B,SS
Uncinia egmontiana	B
Uncinia ferruginea	B
Uncinia rubra	AP,B,SA,SC,SS
Uncinia uncinata	B,SA,SG
Ungnadia speciosa	B,SW
Urena lobata ssp lobata	B
Urena lobata ssp sinuata	B
Urginea fugax	B
Urginea fugax S.F62 Morocco	MN
Urginea maritima	B,SA
Urginea olivieri	B
Urginea olivieri S.L250 Tunisia	MN
Urginea sanguinea	B,SI
Urginea undulata MS529 Spain	MN
Urginea undulata S.F279 Morocco	MN
Urginea undulata S.F321 Morocco	MN
Urginea undulata S.L323/251 Morocco	MN
Urginea undulata S.L340 Morocco	MN
Urochloa mosambicensis	B
Urodon dasyphyllus	B
Urospermum delachampii	AP,LG,SC
Ursinia abrotanifolia	B,SI
Ursinia anthemoides	B,J,SG,SI,T,V
Ursinia cakilefolia	B,SI
Ursinia calenduliflora	B,C,SI
Ursinia chrysanthemoides	B,SI
Ursinia eckloniana	B,SI
Ursinia nana	B,SI
Ursinia paleacea	B,SI
Ursinia pulcherrima 'Solar Fire'	S
Ursinia scariosa	B,SI
Ursinia sericea	B,SI
Ursinia sp mix	C,SI
Ursinia speciosa	B,C,SI,T
Ursinia tenuifolia	B,SI
Ursinia tenuiloba	B,SI
Ursinia tenuiloba var montana	C
Urtica cannabina	SG
Urtica dioica	B,SG,SU
Urtica galeopsifolia	B
Urtica kioviensis	B
Urtica urens	B
Utricularia alpina	B
Utricularia arenaria	B
Utricularia benthamii	B
Utricularia bifida	B
Utricularia biloba	B
Utricularia bisquamata	B
Utricularia caerulea	B
Utricularia calycifida	B
Utricularia capilliflora	B
Utricularia chrysantha	B
Utricularia delicatula	B
Utricularia dichotoma	B
Utricularia dunstaniae	B
Utricularia endressii	B

UTRICULARIA

Utricularia fistulosa	B
Utricularia hamiltonii	B
Utricularia helix	B
Utricularia hispida	B
Utricularia inaequalis	B
Utricularia kamienskii	B
Utricularia kimberleyensis	B
Utricularia lasiocaulis	B
Utricularia lateriflora	B
Utricularia laxa	B
Utricularia leptoplectra	B
Utricularia limosa	B
Utricularia livida	B
Utricularia longifolia	B
Utricularia menziesii	B
Utricularia monanthos	B
Utricularia nigrescens	B
Utricularia novae-zelandiae	B
Utricularia odorata	B
Utricularia parthenopipes	B
Utricularia pusilla	B
Utricularia quinquedentata	B
Utricularia reniformis	B
Utricularia simplex	B
Utricularia simulans	B
Utricularia subulata	B
Utricularia subulata f cleistogama	B
Utricularia tridactyla	B
Utricularia tridentata	B
Utricularia triflora	B
Utricularia uliginosa	B
Utricularia violacea	B
Utricularia volubilis	B
Uvularia grandiflora	B,SC
Uvularia sessilifolia	AP,FH
Vaccaria hispanica	AP,SG
Vaccaria hispanica 'Florist Rose'	B
Vaccaria hispanica 'Florist Snow'	B
Vaccaria hispanica 'Pink Beauty'	B,V
Vaccaria hispanica 'White Beauty'	B
Vaccinium angustifolium	SG
Vaccinium corymbosum	B,SA
Vaccinium macrocarpon	B
Vaccinium membranaceum	B,C
Vaccinium myrtillus	B,C,SA,SG
Vaccinium ovatum	C
Vaccinium padifolium	B
Vaccinium parvifolium	B,C,SG
Vaccinium uliginosum	C,SG
Vaccinium vitis-idaea	B,C,JE,SA,SG
Valeriana coccinea	BS,CO,KI,ST
Valeriana dioica	B
Valeriana montana	B,CG,G
Valeriana officinalis	B,C,G,JE,KS,SA,SG
Valeriana officinalis 'Anthos'	B
Valeriana officinalis 'Select'	B
Valeriana saliunca	B
Valeriana tripteris	B
Vancouveria hexandra	AP,SC,SG
Vanda tricolor	B
Vangueria edulis	SA
Vangueria infausta	SI
Vangueria madagascariensis	B
Vanheerdia angusta	B
Vanheerdia divergens	B,SI,Y
Vanheerdia primosii	B,SI,Y

Vanheerdia roodiae	B,SI,Y
Vanilla planifolia	B
Vatricania guentheri	B,Y
Veitchia macdanielsii	B
Veitchia merrillii	B,O,SA
Veitchia montgomeryana	B,O
Veitchia winin	B
Vella spinosa	CC,SC
Velleia discophora	B,CB,SI
Velleia rosea	B,C,O,SA
Velleia trinervis	B,O
Veltheimia bracteata	B,LG,O,SC,SI
Venegasia carpesoides	B
Ventilago maderaspatana	B
Ventilago viminalis	B,HA,O,SA
Vepris lanceolata	B,SI
Veratrum album	B,BS,C,CG,JE,SA,SC,SG
Veratrum album ssp lobelianum	CG,G
Veratrum californicum	AP,B,G,JE,SC
Veratrum lobelianum	SG
Veratrum nigrum	AP,B,C,G,JE,LG,SA,SC, SG
Veratrum ussuriensis MW56R	X
Veratrum viride	B,C,JE,SA,SG
Verbascum adzurmericum	AP,SC,SE,T
Verbascum agrimanifolia ssp agrimanifolia	T
Verbascum arcturus	G,SC,SG
Verbascum austriacum	B,CG
Verbascum bakerianum	SG
Verbascum blattaria	AP,B,C,CP,E,G,SC,SG,T, V
Verbascum blattaria 'Albiflorum'	AP,B,C,E,V
Verbascum blattaria 'Pink form'	T
Verbascum bombyciferum	C
Verbascum bomb. 'Polar Summer'	B,C,CL,JE,SA,T,V
Verbascum bombyciferum 'Silver Lining'	T
Verbascum chaixii	AP,B,F,G,HH,JE,SC
Verbascum chaixii f album	AP,B,C,FH,G,HH,I,JE, KS,PM,SC,T,V
Verbascum creticum	AP,E,SC
Verbascum densiflorum	AP,B,C,G,JE,SA
Verbascum dumulosum	B,SC,SG
Verbascum eremobium	B
Verbascum f1 'Southern Charm'	T
Verbascum hybridum 'Silberkandelaber'	JE
Verbascum hybridum 'Spica'	JE
Verbascum hybridum 'Wega'	JE
Verbascum longifolium	B,C,JE
Verbascum lychnitis	B,G
Verbascum nigrum	AP,B,C,G,LA,JE,RS,SA, SC,SG,SU
Verbascum nigrum 'Album'	B,C,JE,SA
Verbascum olympicum	AP,B,C,CP,E,F,J,JE,L, SA,SC,T
Verbascum phlomoides	B,HH,RS
Verbascum phoeniceum	AP,B,C,CP,E,F,J,JE,KI, KS,MA,SA,SC,SG,ST, SU,V
Verbascum phoenicium 'Flush of White'	BS,C,F,JE,KI
Verbascum phoenicium 'Hyb' mix	BD,BS,C,CL,DT,L,T
Verbascum phoenicium 'White Bride'	B
Verbascum 'Pink Domino'	B,P
Verbascum pulverulentum	B,SG
Verbascum pyramidatum	B,G,JE,SA,SC
Verbascum roripifolia	B,C,JE,SA
Verbascum 'Silver Candelabrum'	B

VERBASCUM

Verbascum 'Sunset Shades'	D,U
Verbascum thapsus	AP,B,C,CO,CP,E,LA,PM, SA,SG
Verbascum undulatum	B
Verbascum virgatum	B,G,SG
Verbascum 'Wega'	B
Verbascum wiedemannianum	B,KS,T
Verbena 'Adonis Light Blue'	S
Verbena 'Appleblossom'	S
Verbena atenuisecta	HW
Verbena bipinnatifida	B
Verbena bonariensis	AP,B,BS,C,F,G,JE,SA, SC,T,V
Verbena canadensis	B,G
Verbena canadensis 'Compacta'	DT,F,V
Verbena 'Celebration Mix'	U
Verbena 'Derby' mix	BD,BS,CL,J,S,TU,YA
Verbena 'Derby' s-c	BS
Verbena 'Garden Party' mix	CL
Verbena giant mix	S
Verbena gooddingii	B
Verbena hastata	AP,B,C,CP,G,JE,PR,SA, SC,T
Verbena hastata 'Alba'	B,SA
Verbena 'Highlight' mix	S
Verbena 'Ideal Florist mix'	BS,SE
Verbena 'Imagination'	B,BD,BS,CL,CO,DT,F,G, J,KI,L,M,O,S,SE,U,V,YA
Verbena lilacina	B
Verbena 'Misty'	U
Verbena 'Novalis' mix	BD,BS,CL,DT,J,KI,L,R, S,YA
Verbena 'Novalis' s-c	B,BS,CL,DT
Verbena officinalis	B,C,CP,G,KS,SA,SG
Verbena 'Peaches & Cream'	B,BD,BS,C,CL,D,F,T,J, KI,L,O,R,S,SE,U,V,VH, YA
Verbena 'Perfecta'	C,CL
Verbena 'Quartz'	CL
Verbena rigida	AP,B,BS,C,CL,G,T
Verbena rigida 'Lilacina'	B
Verbena rigida 'Venosa'	J,KS,V
Verbena 'Romance Lavender'	SE,V
Verbena 'Romance' mix	BS,F,S
Verbena 'Sandy' mix	BS,KI,YA
Verbena 'Sandy' s-c	B,BS,CL,D
Verbena scabra	B
Verbena 'Showtime'	BS,T
Verbena 'Sparkle' mix	CO,KI,M,TU
Verbena 'Sterling Star' mix	BD,BS
Verbena stricta	B,JE,PR
Verbena tenuisecta	B,C,JE,SA,V
Verbena tridens	AU
Verbena urticifolia	B,CP
Verbena venosa see rigida	
Verbena 'Violet Profusion'	C
Verbena x hybrida 'Amour Light Pink'	T
Verbena x hybrida 'Blaze'	T
Verbena x hybrida 'Blue Lagoon'	B,BS,CL,D,T,U
Verbena x hybrida 'Dw Jewels'	T
Verbena x hybrida 'Mammoth'	BS,C,KI,SG,Sm,ST,VH
Verbena x hybrida 'Olympia'	BD,BS,C,J
Verbena x hybrida pendula 'Elegance'	F
Verbena x hybrida 'Raspberry Crush'	F
Verbena x hybrida 'Sweet Dreams'	F
Verbena x hybrida 'Tropic' dwarf	B

Verbesina alternifolia	B
Verbesina alternifolia 'Goldstrahl'	JE
Verbesina encelioides	B,G,SG
Verbesina helianthoides	CC
Verbesina occidentalis	B
Vernonia altissima	B,NT
Vernonia anthelmintica	B
Vernonia arkansana	NT
Vernonia baldwinii	B
Vernonia cinerea	B
Vernonia crinita	JE
Vernonia fasciculata	JE,PR
Vernonia hirsuta	B,SI
Vernonia mespilifolia	B
Vernonia missurica	PR
Vernonia natalensis	B
Vernonia neocorymbosa	SI
Vernonia noveboracensis	AP,B,C,CP,G,JE,PR
Vernonia noveboracensis 'Albiflora'	JE
Vernonia oligocephala	B,SI
Veronica agrestis	B
Veronica alpina	B,FH,G,SC
Veronica anagalis-aquatica	SG
Veronica arvensis	B
Veronica austriaca	B,SG
Veronica austriaca 'Shirley Blue'	B,BS,C
Veronica austriaca ssp teucrium	BS,KI,SG
Veronica a. ssp teucrium 'Royal Blue'	B,C,JE,L,SA
Veronica a. ssp teucrium 'Crater Lake Blue'	T
Veronica bachofenii	T
Veronica beccabunga	AP,B,SA
Veronica bellidioides	B,JE
Veronica caespitosa	B,JE
Veronica chamaedrys	B,SU
Veronica cymbalaria	B
Veronica dentata	SG
Veronica dillenii	SG
Veronica fruticans	AP,B,C,CG,FH,G,JE,P,SC
Veronica fruticulosa	B,C,G,JE,SG
Veronica gentianoides	AP,C,F,G,JE,SC,SE,SG,T
Veronica gutheriana	B,JE
Veronica hederifolia	B
Veronica longifolia	AP,B,C,G,JE,RH,SA,SC, SG
Veronica longifolia 'Alba'	B,C,JE,SA
Veronica longifolia 'Oxford Blue'	DT,F
Veronica longifolia 'Pink Shades'	B,BS,C,F,JE,KI
Veronica 'Mix Colours'	T
Veronica montana	B
Veronica officinalis	B,C,JE,SG
Veronica ornata	CG
Veronica peregrina	B
Veronica persica	B
Veronica polita	B
Veronica prostrata	JE,SC
Veronica repens	B,BS,C,J,JE,SA
Veronica satureioides	B,C,SC
Veronica schmidtiana	CC,G,SG
Veronica scutellata	B,SG
Veronica selleri	FH
Veronica serpyllifolia	FH,SG
Veronica spicat ssp incana 'Silbersee'	B,JE
Veronica spicata	AP,B,BD,BS,C,F,FH,G, JE,KS,RH,SA,SC,SG, SU,V
Veronica spicata 'Alba'	B,JE,SA

VERONICA

Veronica spicata 'Best Blue'	JE
Veronica spicata 'Blue Bouquet'	CL,D,U
Veronica spicata 'Heidekind'	FH
Veronica spicata 'New Hybrids'	B
Veronica spicata 'Red Variations'	JE
Veronica spicata 'Rosea'	B,C,SA
Veronica spicata 'Rosenrot'	JE
Veronica spicata 'Sightseeing'	B,BD,BS,C,CL,D,DT,F,J, JE,L,U,V
Veronica spicata ssp incana	AP,B,BS,C,CL,F,JE,L,SA, SG,T
Veronica spicata ssp minor	B,JE,SA
Veronica spicata v nana 'Blue Carpet'	BS,C,JE,KI
Veronica subsessilis	G
Veronica subsessilis hyb 'Blue Pyramid'	JE
Veronica teucrium see austriacum ssp	
Veronica urticifolia	B,JE
Veronicastrum sibiricum v japonicum	B
Veronicastrum sib. v japonicum 'Album'	B
Veronicastrum virginicum	B,C,G,JE,P,PR,RH,SA, SG
Veronicastrum virginicum 'Albo-roseum'	B,JE,SA
Veronicastrum virginicum 'Album'	B,G,JE
Veronicastrum virginicum 'Roseum'	B,JE
Verticordia acerosa	B
Verticordia brachypoda	B
Verticordia chrysantha	B
Verticordia chrysantha v preissii	AU,B
Verticordia densiflora	B,O,SA
Verticordia eriocephala	B,O
Verticordia fimbrilepis	B
Verticordia forrestii	B,O
Verticordia grandiflora	B,O
Verticordia grandis	B
Verticordia huegelii	SA
Verticordia huegelii v decumbens	B
Verticordia huegelii v huegelii	B
Verticordia insignis	B
Verticordia lindleyi	B,O
Verticordia monodelpha	B
Verticordia muellerana	B,O
Verticordia nitens	B,O,SA
Verticordia ovalifolia	B
Verticordia pennigera	B
Verticordia pennigera v prostrata	B
Verticordia picta	B,O
Verticordia plumosa	B,O
Verticordia preissii	O
Verticordia roei	B,O
Verticordia serrata	B,O
Vestia foetida	AP,B,LG,P,SG
Viburnum acerifolium	B,SA
Viburnum betulifolium	RRH,SA
Viburnum carlesii	B,SC,SA
Viburnum cassinoides	B,G
Viburnum cotinifolium	A,SA
Viburnum dentatum	B,SA
Viburnum dilatatum	B,G,SA
Viburnum edule	A
Viburnum erubescens	B
Viburnum furcatum	B,SA
Viburnum henryi	B,SA
Viburnum ichangense	B,C,SA
Viburnum lantana	B,C,SA,SU
Viburnum lentago	A,B,SA
Viburnum macrocephalum	SA

Viburnum odoratissimum	B,SA
Viburnum opulus	A,B,C,RH,RS,SA,SC,SU
Viburnum opulus 'Xanthocarpum'	B
Viburnum orientale	B
Viburnum phlebotrichus	B
Viburnum plicatum f tomentosum	B
Viburnum prunifolium	A,B,SA
Viburnum rhytidophyllum	B,C,SA
Viburnum rufidulum	A,B
Viburnum sargentii	B,SA
Viburnum setigerum	B,SA
Viburnum setigerum 'Aurantiacum'	B,SA
Viburnum sieboldii	B,SA
Viburnum tinus	B,C,SA
Viburnum trilobum	A,B,G,SA
Viburnum trilobum 'Wentworth'	B,SA
Viburnum wrightii	B,G,SA
Vicia americana	B
Vicia angustifolia	B,HA
Vicia benghalensis	B
Vicia cracca	B,C,LA,SU
Vicia dasycarpa	B
Vicia ervilia	B
Vicia gigantea	C
Vicia hirsuta	B,LA
Vicia narbonensis	B
Vicia palaestina	B
Vicia peregrina	B
Vicia sativa	B,C,LA
Vicia sepium	B,LA
Vicia sylvatica	B,SU
Vicia tenuifolia	CG
Vicia tetrasperma	B
Vigna aconitifolia	B
Vigna angularis	B
Vigna caracalla	B,HA
Vigna radiata	B
Vigna umbellata	B
Vigna unguiculata	B
Vigna unguiculata named cvs	B
Vigna unguiculata ssp cylindrica	B
Vigna unguiculata ssp sesquipedalis	B
Vigna vexillata	B
Viguiera deltoidea v parishii	B
Viguiera laciniata	B
Viguiera lanata	B
Viguiera multiflora	B,JE
Vila aetolica	JE
Villarsia calthifolia	B
Villarsia capensis	B,SI
Villarsia parnassifolia	B
Viminaria denudata	HA,O,SA
Viminaria juncea	B,C
Vinca minor	B
Vinca minor 'Variegata'	B
Vincetoxicum hirundinaria	CG,G
Vincetoxicum nigrum	CG,G,SC
Vincetoxicum officinale	B
Vincetoxicum pannonicum	B
Vincetoxicum scandens	B
Viola 'Aalsmeer Giant' mix	C
Viola alba	B,C,G,JE,SA
Viola arvensis	B,C,CG,LA
Viola bedding mix	S
Viola betonicifolia	B,O
Viola betonicifolia albescens	P

VIOLA

Viola biflora	AP,CG,SC	Viola declinata	CG
Viola 'Black Star'	J	Viola declinata 'Melton Sapphire'	T
Viola 'Blackjack'	BS,F,L	Viola decumbens	B
Viola 'Bolton's Superb Giant Strain'	BO	Viola dubyana	B,SC
Viola 'Bowles Black'	AP,B,CL,JE,P,SC,SE,SU,	Viola erecta (elatior)	AP,B,C,CG,G,I,P,PA,SC
	T,V	Viola eriocarpa	PR
Viola calcarata	AP,B,JE,SC,SA	Viola 'Evening Glow'	C
Viola canadensis	AP,B,CG,SC,SW	Viola f1 'Alpine Summer'	BS,DT,J,L,V
Viola canina	CG	Viola f1 'Alpine Wing'	BS
Viola celamineria	CG	Viola f1 'Azure Blue'	S
Viola cenisia	B,SC	Viola f1 'Bravissimo'	C
Viola chaerophylloides	CG,SC	Viola f1 'Crystal Bowl'	C
Viola 'Charlotte'	B,P	Viola f1 'Eclipse'	S
Viola 'Columbine'	B,P	Viola f1 'Fanfare Mix'	BS,L,U,YA
Viola comollia	B	Viola f1 'Giant Fancy mix'	S
Viola conspersa	AP,PR	Viola f1 'Maxim'	C
Viola cornuta	B,CG,G,HW,PM,SA	Viola f1 'Penny Series' s-c	CL,SE
Viola cornuta 'Admiration'	C,JE	Viola f1 'Sorbet Series' mix	BS,CL,DT,KS,L,SE,T,YA
Viola cornuta alba	AP,MA,SC	Viola f1 'Sorbet Series' s-c	BS,DT,F,KS,T
Viola cornuta 'Arkwright's Ruby'	B,BS,C,CL,L,SA,T	Viola f2 'Toyland'	BS,C,CL
Viola cornuta 'Azurella'	B,BS,JE	Viola 'Fancy Shades' mix	S
Viola cornuta 'Baby Franjo'	B,BS,C,J,JE,SA,U,V	Viola 'Flame'	C
Viola cornuta 'Baby Lucia'	B,BD,BS,C,J,JE,SA,T,V	Viola 'Glacier Ice'	CO
Viola cornuta 'Bambini'	BD,BS,C,DT,F,J,JE,L,KS,	Viola hederacea	C,JE
	U,V	Viola hirta	C,JE
Viola cornuta 'Bijou'	BS,KI	Viola hybrida 'Blue Shades'	T
Viola cornuta 'Blaue Schonheit'	JE	Viola jaubertiana	CG
Viola cornuta 'Blaue von Paris'	JE	Viola jooi	AP,C,CG,G,I,SA,SC
Viola cornuta 'Blue Gem'	B,SA	Viola jordanii	CG
Viola cornuta 'Blue Perfection'	B,BS,CL,JE,L,SA	Viola kitaibeliana	CG
Viola cornuta 'Bluebird'	T	Viola kleiskei pink	P
Viola cornuta 'Carpathian Spring'	B,C,JE	Viola koreana	AP,B,P,SC
Viola cornuta 'Chantreyland'	B,BS,C,CL,JE,L,SA,T	Viola labradorica	AP,B,C,JE,SA,SC,T
Viola cornuta 'Collection'	U	Viola labradorica v purpurea see riviniana	
Viola cornuta 'Cornetto'	B,C,F,JE,SA	Viola lanceolata	AP,G,RS,SC
Viola cornuta 'Cuty'	B,BS,CL,T,U	Viola lutea	AP,G,SC,W
Viola cornuta 'Felix'	D,DT	Viola macedonica	CG
Viola cornuta 'Funny Face'	D	Viola macloskeyi v pallens	B,P
Viola cornuta 'Johnny-jump-up'	B,BS,C,CL,F,JE,KI,KS,L,	Viola maculata	CG
	SA,SE	Viola mandshurica	AP,SA,SC
Viola cornuta 'King Henry'	B,JE,KS,SA	Viola mandshurica 'Grandiflora'	JE
Viola cornuta 'Lg Fl' mix	F	Viola mirabilis	C,JE,SC
Viola cornuta 'Lutea Splendens'	B,CL,JE	Viola 'Monarch mix'	J
Viola cornuta 'Maroon Picotee'	BS	Viola nephrophylla	B,SW
Viola cornuta 'Monarch Mix'	DT	Viola nigra	G,SA
Viola cornuta 'Painted Black'	B,BS,SA	Viola obliqua	B,JE
Viola cornuta 'Pariser' s-c	JE	Viola obliqua striata 'Alba' (cucullata)	SE,T,V
Viola cornuta 'Pretty'	BS,C,JE,U	Viola odorata	AP,B,BS,C,CG,CO,G,JE,
Viola cornuta 'Prince Henry'	B,BD,BS,C,CL,DT,SU,W,		KI,PA,SA,ST,SU,V
	U,YA	Viola odorata 'Alba'	B
Viola cornuta 'Prince John'	B,BS,C,CL,L,SU,SA,YA	Viola odorata 'Empress Augusta'	B
Viola cornuta 'Prince William'	YA	Viola odorata 'Princess of Wales'	T
Viola cornuta 'Princess' mix	BS,CL,D,DT,KI,KS	Viola odorata 'Queen Charlotte'	B,BS,C,F,JE,S,SA
Viola cornuta 'Princess' s-c	BS,CL,D,JE,L,U,Y	Viola odorata 'Sulphurea'	AP,B,JE,T
Viola cornuta 'Purple Blaze'	B,SA	Viola odorata 'The Czar'	B,C,DT,SA,T
Viola cornuta 'Purple Picotee'	BS	Viola odorata 'Vilmoriniana'	B,C
Viola cornuta 'Ulla'	JE	Viola palmata	CG,G,JE,SA
Viola cornuta v minor	AP,B,G,P,SC	Viola palmata hyb	B
Viola cornuta v minor 'Alba'	AP,B,P	Viola palmata x loveliana	P
Viola cornuta 'White Perfection'	B,BS,C,CL,JE,L,SA,T	Viola palustris	B
Viola cornuta 'Yellow Perfection'	B,JE,L,SA	Viola pedata	AP,B,G,HH,JE,PR,SC
Viola cornuta 'Yellow Prince'	JE	Viola pedatifida	B,C,JE
Viola 'Coronation Gold'	J	Viola pinnata	AP,CG,G,SC
Viola corsica	AP,B,G,JE,P,SC	Viola pubescens	B,P
Viola cotyledon	B,P	Viola 'Raspberry Rose'	CG,JE,V
Viola cunninghamii	B,SS	Viola reichenbachiana	B,C,JE

VIOLA

Viola reichii RB94126-94131	P
Viola riviniana	AP,B,C
Viola riviniana pink	B
Viola riviniana 'Purpurea'	B,C,G,I,P,SC,SU
Viola 'Roccoco' frilled	C,J,V
Viola 'Rodney Davey'	B,G,P,T
Viola rupestris	CG,G
Viola rupestris 'Rosea'	B,JE,P,T
Viola 'Sawyer's Black'	BS,C,SU
Viola 'Scottish Hybrids'	BS,SE
Viola selkirkii	AP,B,P
Viola 'Small Flowered'	BS,L
Viola sororia	B,C,JE,SC,T
Viola sororia 'Albiflora'	B,G,JE,SA
Viola sororia 'Freckles'	B,BD,BS,C,CO,HH,JE,
	KI,L,SA,SE,T,V
Viola sororia 'Rubra'	B,C,JE,T
Viola sp Borohoro Shan	CC
Viola 'Striped'	SE
Viola suavis	CG
Viola 'Sunbeam'	BS,CL,S,SE,V
Viola 'Sunbeam & Blackjack'	SE
Viola 'Symphonia'	KI,ST
Viola tricolor	AP,B,C,CO,F,G,LA,SC,
	SU,T,V
Viola tricolor 'Black'	B,CG
Viola tridentata	AU
Viola 'Trimardeau' mix	C
Viola velutina (gracilis)	B,JE
Viola x witt 'Amsterdam Giants'	BS
Viola x witt 'Aquarelle'	F
Viola x witt 'Black'	C
Viola x witt 'Black Devil'	SE
Viola x witt 'Black Pansy'	C,T,V
Viola x witt 'Brown's Prizewinner'	BS
Viola x witt 'Brunig'	T
Viola x witt 'Celestial Queen'	BS
Viola x witt 'Challenge Improved' s-c	R
Viola x witt 'Clarion' s-c o-p	YA
Viola x witt 'Clear Sky Primrose'	T
Viola x witt 'Crown Exhibition'	BS
Viola x witt 'Dobies Emperor Strain'	D
Viola x witt 'Dream' s-c & mix	BS
Viola x witt 'Dreams'	L
Viola x witt 'Early Flowering'	D,DT,F
Viola x witt 'Eclipse'	F
Viola x witt 'Engelmann's Mix'	BS,DT
Viola x witt f1 'Allegro' mix	DT,F,S
Viola x witt f1 'Banner Series'	CL
Viola x witt f1 'Berries and Buttermilk'	SE
Viola x witt f1 'Bingo'	T
Viola x witt f1 'Black Beauty'	D,S
Viola x witt f1 'Black Star'	BS
Viola x witt f1 'Challenge' s-c, mix	BS
Viola x witt f1 'Clear Crystal' black	B,KS
Viola x witt f1 'Clear Crystals mix'	BS,F,J,KI,S,ST,SU,T,TU,
	U,V
Viola x witt f1 'Crown' mix	B,BS
Viola x witt f1 'Crown' s-c	B,BS,T
Viola x witt f1 'Crystal Bowl' mix	L
Viola x witt f1 'Delia Mix'	U
Viola x witt f1 'Early Giants mix'	BD,BS
Viola x witt f1 'Easter Parade'	U
Viola x witt f1 'Happy Face' mix	BD,BS,S
Viola x witt f1 'Happy Face' s-c	BS
Viola x witt f1 'Imperial Antique Shades'	BS,CL,D,L,T

Viola x witt f1 'Imperial Frosty Rose'	BS,CL,D,KI,L,O,S,T,U
Viola x witt f1 'Imperial Pink Shades'	BS,CL,S,T
Viola x witt f1 'Imperial Princess Gold'	BS,CL,L,O,S,V
Viola x witt f1 'Imperial Series' mix	BS
Viola x witt f1 'Imperial Series' s-c	BS,CL,L,T,U,V
Viola x witt f1 'Lac de Zurich'	T
Viola x witt f1 'Loyal King & Queen' mix	BS,R
Viola x witt f1 'Loyal King & Queen' s-c	BS
Viola x witt f1 'Majestic Giants'	BS,C,CL,D,DT,J,KI,L,M,
	SE,T,U,VH
Viola x witt f1 'Mammoth Giants'	BS,CL
Viola x witt f1 'Maxim Marina'	SE,T
Viola x witt f1 'Maximum'	BS
Viola x witt f1 'Melody Sunrise'	T
Viola x witt f1 'Miss Liberty'	BS
Viola x witt f1 'Psychedelia'	U
Viola x witt f1 'Regal' s-c, mix	BS
Viola x witt f1 'Reveille Series' mix	F
Viola x witt f1 'Reveille Series' s-c	F,YA
Viola x witt f1 'Rippling Waters'	D,S,SE,T,V
Viola x witt f1 'Rococco'	BS
Viola x witt f1 'Scala Series' s-c	YA
Viola x witt f1 'Scimitar White'	BS
Viola x witt f1 'Springtime Black'	BD,BS,CL
Viola x witt f1 'Springtime Lemon Splash'	BS,CL,T
Viola x witt f1 'The Ultimate Blend'	YA
Viola x witt f1 'Turbo Series'	CL
Viola x witt f1 'Tutti Frutti'	BS,F,KI,U,YA
Viola x witt f1 'Ultima' mix	BD,BS,C,CL,D,DT,J,KI,
	TU,U
Viola x witt f1 'Ultima Pastel' mix	D
Viola x witt f1 'Ultima pink'	CL,C
Viola x witt f1 'Ultima Series' s-c	BS,CL,L,YA
Viola x witt f1 'Ultima Silhouette' mix	BD,CL,DT,U
Viola x witt f1 'Universal mix'	D,F,J,T,U
Viola x witt f1 'Universal Plus mix'	CL,DT,S,SE
Viola x witt f1 'Universal Plus' s-c	CL,S,SE
Viola x witt f1 'Velour Blue'	BS,CL,DT,F,O,T,U,YA
Viola x witt f1 'Velour Mix'	F,U
Viola x witt f1 'Velour Purple'	CL,U,YA
Viola x witt f1 'Watercolours'	BS,DT,F,KI,L,SE,T,V
Viola x witt f1 'Winter Garden' mix	BS
Viola x witt f1 'Winter Garden' s-c	BS
Viola x witt f2 'Colour Festival'	BS,CL,S
Viola x witt f2 'Happy Flower Mix'	BS,YA
Viola x witt f2 'Joker Light Blue'	BS,CL,DT,F,KS,S
Viola x witt f2 'Joker' mix	BS,CL,DT,J,L,SE,V
Viola x witt f2 'Joker Series' s-c	BS,CL,D,T,U,YA
Viola x witt f2 'Jolly Joker'	BD,BS,C,CL,D,DT,F,J,
	KI,KS,L,SE,ST,T,U,V,VH
Viola x witt f2 'Northern Lights'	SE
Viola x witt f2 'Padparadja'	BD,BS,C,CL,CO,D,DT,F,
	J,KI,KS,O,S,SE,T,U,V,YA
Viola x witt f2 'Premiere' mix	BD,BS,C,CL,D,L
Viola x witt f2 'Premiere' s-c	CL,S
Viola x witt 'Floral Dance' mix	S,T,U
Viola x witt 'Forerunner' mix	BS,CO,DT,J,L,ST
Viola x witt 'Forerunner' s-c	BS,L
Viola x witt 'Gay Jesters'	D
Viola x witt 'Harlequin Mix'	DT
Viola x witt 'Jupiter'	BS
Viola x witt 'Lace Series' s-c	SE
Viola x witt 'Large Flowered' mix	CL,CO,T,VH
Viola x witt 'Lemon Ice'	BS
Viola x witt 'Love Duet'	BS,D,J,SE,T,U,V
Viola x witt 'Magic Fire'	BS

VIOLA

Viola x witt 'March Beauty'	BS		Vitis coignetiae	B,C,SA
Viola x witt 'Marshall's Nene Giant Strain'	M		Vitis davidii	B
Viola x witt 'Mello 21'	T		Vitis riparia	C,PR,SA
Viola x witt 'Moonlight'	T,U		Vitis rotundifolia	B
Viola x witt 'North Pole'	BS		Vitis thunbergii	B
Viola x witt 'Oliver Twist'	SE		Vitis vinifera	B,SA
Viola x witt 'Paper White'	T,VH		Vitis vinifera 'Black Hamburgh'	B
Viola x witt 'Pastel Butterflies'	T		Vitis vinifera 'Brandt'	B
Viola x witt 'Pink Panther'	F		Vitis vinifera 'Buckland Sweetwater'	B
Viola x witt 'Prizewinner'	DT		Vitis vinifera 'Himrod'	B
Viola x witt 'Querelle'	F		Vitis vinifera 'Leon Millot'	B
Viola x witt 'Rhine Gold'	C,CG,T		Vitis vulpina	B
Viola x witt 'Roggli Giants'	BS,CL,D		Vittadinia australis	AP,SS
Viola x witt 'Romeo and Juliet'	BS,F,J,KS,M,SE,T,V		Voacanga africana	B
Viola x witt 'Rosy Morn Shades'	T		Voandzeia subterranea white	B
Viola x witt S1 'Allegro'	BS		Vriesea altodaserra	B
Viola x witt S1 'Armado'	F		Vriesea atra	B
Viola x witt 'Selection' mix	F		Vriesea barclayana	B
Viola x witt 'Senator Series'	CL		Vriesea barilletii	B
Viola x witt 'Silver Wings'	SE,T		Vriesea biguassuensis	B
Viola x witt 'Spanish Sun'	T		Vriesea bituminosa	B
Viola x witt 'Special Mix'	DT		Vriesea bleheri	B
Viola x witt 'Super Chalon Giants mix'	BD,BS,CL,D,DT,F,L,S,		Vriesea botafogensis	B
	SE,T,U,VH		Vriesea brassicoides	B
Viola x witt 'Superb Giant Strain'	U		Vriesea carinata	B
Viola x witt 'Swiss Giant Alpenglow'	B,BS,J,KI,V		Vriesea chrysostachia	B
Viola x witt 'Sw. Giant Benary's Exhib Str'	L		Vriesea corcovadensis	B
Viola x witt 'Swiss Giant Coronation Gold'	B,BS,KI		Vriesea cv 'Brentwood'	B
Viola x witt 'Swiss Giant Elite'	C		Vriesea cv 'Eico'	B
Viola x witt 'Swiss Giant' mix	BS,CL,CO,DT,F,J,KI,R,		Vriesea cv 'Fascination'	B
	Sm,ST,SU,TU,V		Vriesea cv 'Flammenschwert'	B
Viola x witt 'Swiss Giant Orange Sun'	B,BS,KI		Vriesea cv 'Gemma'	B
Viola x witt 'Swiss Giant' s-c	B,BS,SE		Vriesea cv 'Goldfisch'	B
Viola x witt Swiss Giant 'Ullswater Blue'	J,KI		Vriesea cv 'Komet'	B
Viola x witt Swiss Giants 'Southbank Mix'	CL		Vriesea cv 'Perfecta'	B
Viola x witt Swiss Master Mix'	CL		Vriesea cv 'Poelmannii Selecta'	B
Viola x witt 'Swiss Velvet' mix	J		Vriesea cv 'Rubin'	B
Viola x witt 'Tiara' mix	KI,ST		Vriesea cv 'Sanderiana'	B
Viola x witt 'True Blue'	T		Vriesea cv 'Sceptre D'or'	B
Viola x witt 'Wessel Ice'	L		Vriesea cv 'Splendide'	B
Viola x witt 'Wine Red'	BS		Vriesea cv 'Vigeri'	B
Viola x witt 'Wink'	BS,KI		Vriesea declinata	B
Viola x witt 'Winter Flowering' mix	BS,DT,F,KI,Sm,ST,SU,		Vriesea delicatula	B
	TU,U,VH		Vriesea drepanocarpa	B
Viola x witt 'Winter Sun'	BS		Vriesea duvaliana	B
Viola x witt'Ullswater'	C,T,V		Vriesea ensiformis	B
Viola x witta 'Floral Dance' s-c	T		Vriesea ensiformis v ensiformis	B
Viola x witta 'Queen of The Planets'	T		Vriesea ensiformis v striata	B
Viola x witta 'Rally' s-c	BS		Vriesea erythrodactylon	B
Viola x wittrochiana	CG		Vriesea erythrodactylon v striata	B
Viola 'Yellow Prince'	C		Vriesea fenestralis	B
Virgilia divaricata	O,SI		Vriesea flammea	B
Virgilia oroboides	B,O,SA		Vriesea fluminensis	B
Viscaria see Lychnis			Vriesea fosteriana	B
Vitaliana primuliflora	AP,B,C,JE,SC		Vriesea fosteriana v seideliana	B
Vitaliana primuliflora ssp praetutiana	B,JE		Vriesea fosteriana v seideliana rubra	B
Vitex agnus-castus	A,AP,B,C,CP,JE,SA,SC		Vriesea fosteriana v seideliana-pallida	B
Vitex ciencowkii	B		Vriesea friburgensii	B
Vitex incisa	B		Vriesea friburgensis v paludosa	B
Vitex keniensis	B		Vriesea gigantea	B
Vitex lucens	B,SA		Vriesea gigantea v seideliana	B
Vitex negundo	B,C,CP,SA		Vriesea gladioliflora	B
Vitex payos	SI		Vriesea glutinosa	B
Vitis amurensis	SA		Vriesea graciliscapa	B
Vitis amurensis MW140R	X		Vriesea gradata	B
Vitis californica	B		Vriesea grande	B

236

VRIESEA

Vriesea guttata	B
Vriesea guttata v striata	B
Vriesea heliconioides	B
Vriesea heterostachys	B
Vriesea hieroglyphica	B
Vriesea hieroglyphica v zebrina	B
Vriesea hoehneana	B
Vriesea hyb	B
Vriesea hyb 'Illustris'	B
Vriesea hyb 'Morreniana'	B
Vriesea hyb 'Rex'	B
Vriesea imperialis	B
Vriesea incurvata	B
Vriesea incurvata v longiflora	B
Vriesea inflata	B
Vriesea inflata v seideliana	B
Vriesea itatiaia	B
Vriesea jonghe	B
Vriesea longicaulis	B
Vriesea longiscapa	B
Vriesea lubbersii	B
Vriesea modesta	B
Vriesea neoglutinosa	B
Vriesea oligantha	B
Vriesea ourensis	B
Vriesea paratiensis	B
Vriesea pardalina	B
Vriesea pauperrima	B
Vriesea petropolitana	B
Vriesea petropolitana v virosa	B
Vriesea philippocoburgii	B
Vriesea philippocoburgii v philippocoburgii	B
Vriesea platynema	B
Vriesea platynema v albo - lineata	B
Vriesea platynema v flava	B
Vriesea platynema v rosea	B
Vriesea platynema v striata	B
Vriesea platynema v variegata	B
Vriesea platystachys	B
Vriesea platzmannii	B
Vriesea poenulata	B
Vriesea procera	B
Vriesea procera v debilis	B
Vriesea procera v procera	B
Vriesea procera v rubra	B
Vriesea psittacina	B
Vriesea psittacina v psittacina	B
Vriesea psittacina v rubro-bracteata	B
Vriesea rastrensis	B
Vriesea regina	B
Vriesea regnelli	B
Vriesea retroflexa	B
Vriesea roberto-seidelii	B
Vriesea rodigasiana	B
Vriesea rodigasiana v maculata	B
Vriesea rodigasiana v purpurea	B
Vriesea sanguinea	B
Vriesea saundersii	B
Vriesea scalarii	B
Vriesea sceptrum v flavobracteata	B
Vriesea seideliana	B
Vriesea simplex	B
Vriesea simplex v gigantea	B
Vriesea sparsiflora	B
Vriesea splendens	B
Vriesea splendens v major	B

Vriesea splendens v mortefontanensis	B
Vriesea sucrei	B
Vriesea taritubensis	B
Vriesea triangularis	B
Vriesea unilateralis	B
Vriesea vagans	B
Vriesea weberi	B
Vriesea x mariae	B
Wachendorfia brachyandra	B
Wachendorfia paniculata	B,SI
Wachendorfia sp	SI
Wachendorfia thyrsiflora	B,C,SI
Wahlenbergia albomarginata	AP,B,JE,SS
Wahlenbergia albomarginata v saxicola	B
Wahlenbergia annularis	SI
Wahlenbergia capensis	B,SI
Wahlenbergia cartilagena	AP,AU
Wahlenbergia congesta	AP,C,G,I,PM,SC
Wahlenbergia gloriosa	AP,AU,SC
Wahlenbergia gracilis	CG
Wahlenbergia hederacea	CG
Wahlenbergia krebsii ssp krebsii	B
Wahlenbergia lobelioides	CG
Wahlenbergia mathewsii	CG
Wahlenbergia 'Melton Bluebird'	BD,BS,SE,V
Wahlenbergia pendula	CG
Wahlenbergia procumbens	B
Wahlenbergia pygmaea	B,SS
Wahlenbergia saxicola	AP,CG,G,SC
Wahlenbergia sp	SI
Wahlenbergia undulata	B,SI
Wahlenbergia zeyheri	SI
Waitzia acuminata v acuminata	B,O
Waitzia acuminata v albicans	B,O
Waitzia nitida	C,O
Waitzia suaveolens v flava	B,O
Waitzia suaveolens v suaveolens	B,O
Wallichia densiflora	B,O,SA
Wallichia disticha	B
Walsura trifoliata	B
Waltheria indica	B
Washingtonia filifera	B,C,CG,HA,O,SA
Washingtonia robusta	B,C,HA,O,SA
Washingtonia sonorae	CG
Waterhousea floribunda	SA
Watsonia aletroides	B,C,SI
Watsonia angusta	B,SI
Watsonia angustifolia	B
Watsonia borbonica	CG,SI
Watsonia borbonica ssp ardernei	B,C,CG,SI
Watsonia borbonica ssp borbonica	B
Watsonia brevifolia	B
Watsonia 'Candy Stripes'	B
Watsonia 'Cardinal'	B
Watsonia coccinea	B,SI
Watsonia 'Dawn'	B
Watsonia densiflora	B,SA,SI
Watsonia distans	B,SA,SI
Watsonia 'Flame'	B
Watsonia fourcadei	B,CG,SI
Watsonia fulgens	B,SI
Watsonia humilis	B,SI
Watsonia hybrids	B,CG
Watsonia 'Jewel'	B
Watsonia laccata	B,SI
Watsonia 'Lady Rose'	B

WATSONIA

Watsonia latifolia	SI	Wildflower mix, 'Hedgerow/Shady Glade'	LA
Watsonia marginata	B,C,SI	Wildflower mix, 'Herbaceous'	NA
Watsonia marginata v alba	B	Wildflower mix, 'Leaves/Shoots Salad'	CO
Watsonia marginata v minor	B	Wildflower 'Leaves/Stems/Roots Edible'	CO
Watsonia meriana	B,CG,SI	Wildflower mix, 'Little Bit Shady'	HW
Watsonia meriana v bulbilifera	B	Wildflower mix, 'Long Season Meadow'	NA
Watsonia pillansii	B,LG,SI	Wildflower mix, 'Old Flower Meadow'	LA
Watsonia 'Pink Lady'	B	Wildflower mix, 'Ozark'	HW
Watsonia 'Purity'	B	Wildflower mix, 'Patio'	NA
Watsonia 'Shady Lady'	B	Wildflower mix, 'Pond Edge'	CO,LA,SU
Watsonia sp & hyb mix	C	Wildflower mix, 'Pond/Bog mix'	Z
Watsonia stenosiphon	B,SI	Wildflower mix, 'Queen Anne's Lace'	LA
Watsonia tabularis	B,CG,SA,SI	Wildflower mix, 'Riverside mix'	Z
Watsonia vanderspuyae	B,SI	Wildflower mix, 'Rocky Mountain'	AV
Watsonia versfeldii	SI	Wildflower mix, 'Scented'	NA
Watsonia watsonioides	SI	Wildflower mix, 'Seed Head'	LA
Watsonia wordsworthiana	B	Wildflower mix, 'Short Meadow'	LA
Weberberocereus churinensis	Y	Wildflower mix, 'Southwestern'	AV
Weberberocereus johnsonii	B,Y	Wildflower mix, 'Spring Meadow'	LA
Weberberocereus rauhii	B	Wildflower mix, 'Spring/Woodland mix'	Z
Weberberocereus winterianus	Y	Wildflower mix, 'Summer Meadow'	LA
Wedelia trilobata	B	Wildflower mix, 'Sun & Shade'	AV
Wehlia thryptomenoides	B	Wildflower mix, 'Texas'	AV
Weigela florida	B,SA	Wildflower mix, 'Watermeadow'	SU
Weinmannia racemosa	SA,SS	Wildflower mix, 'Waterside'	NA
Weinmannia sylvicola	B	Wildflower mix, 'Wildlife Garden' (RSPB)	CO
Weinmannia trichosperma	B,SA	Wildflower mix, 'Windowbox'	CO
Welfia georgii	B	Wildflower mix, 'Woodland'	CO,LA,NA,SU
Welwitschia mirabilis	B,SI	Willdenowia incurvata	B,SI
Westringia fruticosa	O,SA	Wisteria brachybotrys ' Murasaki Kapitan'	B
Westringia raleighi	AU	Wisteria brachybotrys 'Shiro Kapitan'	B
Wheat, organic 'Maris Widgeon'	CO	Wisteria floribunda	B,N,SA
Whiteheadia bifolia	B,SI	Wisteria floribunda 'Alba'	B,SA
Wiborgia monoptera	SI	Wisteria floribunda 'Honbeni'	B
Wicoxia schmollii	CH	Wisteria floribunda 'Macrobotrys'	B,C
Widdringtonia cedarbergensis	B,C,SA,SI	Wisteria frutescens	B,N,SA
Widdringtonia cupressoides	C	Wisteria sinensis	B,C,CG,HA,N,SA,T,U
Widdringtonia nodiflora	B,SA,SI	Wisteria sinensis 'Alba'	B,C,HA,SA
Widdringtonia schwarzii	B,SI	Wisteria x formosa	B,C,N
Widdringtonia whytei	SG	Withania somnifera	C,CP
Wigandia caracasana	SG	Witheringia solanacea	B
Wilcoxia australis	Y	Wittrockia amazonica	B
Wilcoxia tamaulipensis deherdtii	BC	Wittrockia bahiana	B
Wild bulb selection	PA	Wittrockia campos - portos	B
Wildenowia incurvata	B	Wittrockia smithii	B
Wildflower meadow mix	ST,Z	Wittrockia superba	B
Wildflower mix, 'Architectural/Bird/Bee'	Z	Wodyetia bifurcata	B,O
Wildflower mix, 'Bats in the garden'	CO	Woodwardia orientalis	B
Wildflower mix, 'Bee'	SU	Wrightia tinctoria	B,SA
Wildflower mix, 'Bird'	NA,SU	Wrightia tomentosa	B
Wildflower mix, 'Bumblebee'	CO,NA	Wrixonia prostantheroides	B
Wildflower mix, 'Butterfly'	CO,LA,NA,TU,SU	Wulfenia carinthiaca	AP,B,G,JE,SA,SC
Wildflower mix, 'Calcareous Meadow'	LA	Wulfenia carinthiaca 'Alba'	JE
Wildflower mix, 'California'	AV	Wurmbea sp	SI
Wildflower mix, 'Continuous Color'	HW	Wurmbea spicata	B,SI
Wildflower mix, 'Cornfield'	CO,LA,NA,TU,SU,Z	Wyethia angustifolia	B
Wildflower mix, 'Cottage Garden'	LA,NA,Z	Wyethia glabra	B
Wildflower mix, 'Damp Meadow'	LA	Wyethia helenioides	B,C
Wildflower mix, 'Derelict Land'	LA	Wyethia helianthoides	B,JE
Wildflower mix, 'Field And Hedgrow'	CO	Wyethia scabra	B
Wildflower mix, 'Flower Arrangers'	CO	X Citrofortunella microcarpa	B
Wildflower mix, 'Flowering Lawn'	CO	X Pardancanda norrisii	B,JE,SA
Wildflower mix, general	KI,Z	X Pardancanda norrisii 'Candy Lilies'	C
Wildflower mix, 'Golden Days' ann	D	Xanthisma texana	B,G,T,U
Wildflower mix, 'Haymeadow'	SU	Xanthisma texana 'Flower Power'	J
Wildflower mix, 'Hedgerow'	NA,SU	Xanthium spinosum	CG,G

XANTHIUM

Xanthium strumarium	B,CG,SG
Xanthoceras sorbifolium	B,G,N,SA
Xanthocercis zambesiaca	B,SI
Xanthorrhiza simplicissima	B
Xanthorrhoea australis	B,C,HA,O,SA,SH
Xanthorrhoea caespitosa	AU
Xanthorrhoea fulva	B,O
Xanthorrhoea gracilis	B,O,SA
Xanthorrhoea johnstonii	B,O
Xanthorrhoea macronema	B,HA,O,SH
Xanthorrhoea media	B,O,SH
Xanthorrhoea minor	AU,HA
Xanthorrhoea preissii	AU,B,O,SA
Xanthorrhoea quadrangulata	AU,B,O
Xanthorrhoea resinifera	AU
Xanthorrhoea resinosa	C,HA,O
Xanthorrhoea semiplana	B,O
Xanthorrhoea semiplana v tateana	AU
Xanthorrhoea thorntonii	B,O
Xanthosia atkinsoniana	B
Xanthosia candida	B,SA
Xanthosia rotundifolia	B,SA
Xanthostemon chrysanthus	B,SA
Xeranthemum annuum	BD,BS,C,CO,D,DT,F,KI, KS,L,S,SG,ST,SU,T,TU
Xeranthemum annuum 'Cherry Ripe' mix	C
Xeranthemum annuum 'Lumina' mix	J,KS,T,U,V
Xeranthemum annuum 'Lumina' s-c	T
Xeranthemum annuum 'Snowlady'	T
Xeranthemum annuum 'Superbissimum'	B
Xeranthemum annuum 'Violet-purple'	B
Xeranthoxylum alatum	SA
Xeranthoxylum americanum	SA
Xeranthoxylum bungeanum	SA
Xeranthoxylum piperitum	SA
Xeroderris stuhlmannii	SI
Xeronema callistemon	B,C
Xerophyllum tenax	B,C,JE,KS
Xerophyta dasylirioides	SI
Ximenia americana	B
Xylococcus bicolor	B
Xylomelum angustifolium	B,O,SA
Xylomelum occidentale	B,O,SA
Xylomelum pyriformis	B,O
Xyris lanata	B,C,SA
Xyris operculata	B
Xyris torta	B
Xysmalobium stockenstromense	B,C,SI
Xysmalobium tysonianum	B,SI
Xysmalobium undulatum	SI
Yakirra australiensis	B
Yucca aloifolia	B,C,HA,SA
Yucca aloifolia 'Marginata'	B,SA
Yucca angustissima	B,SW
Yucca arizonica	B,SW
Yucca baccata	B,C,JE,SA,SW
Yucca baccata v thornberi	B
Yucca brevifolia	B,C,SA,SW
Yucca brevifolia v jaegeriana	B
Yucca campestris	B,SW
Yucca carnerosana	B,SA
Yucca elata	B,C,SW
Yucca elephantipes	B
Yucca faxoniana	B
Yucca filamentosa	B,BS,C,CL,G,JE,L,N,SA, V

Yucca filamentosa 'Bright Edge'	B
Yucca glauca	B,C,JE,PR,SA,SW
Yucca glauca v arkansana	B
Yucca glauca v baileyi	B
Yucca glauca v elata	B
Yucca glauca v gurneyi	B
Yucca glauca v kanabensis	B
Yucca glauca v radiosa	B
Yucca gloriosa	B
Yucca harrimaniae	BC,SW
Yucca kanabensis	SW
Yucca navajoa	B,SW
Yucca neomexicana	B
Yucca 'Outdoor Vars Mix'	T
Yucca rigida	B
Yucca rigida 'Palmita'	SW
Yucca rostrata	B,SA
Yucca rupicola f pallida	B
Yucca schidigera	B
Yucca schottii	B,SW
Yucca sp mix	C
Yucca thompsoniana	B
Yucca torreyi	B,C,SA,SW
Yucca valida	B
Yucca whipplei	B,C,SA,SW
Yucca whipplei ssp caespitosa	B
Yucca whipplei ssp whipplei	B
Yucca whipplei v intermedia	B
Yucca whipplei v parishii	B
Yushania anceps	B
Zaleya decandra	B
Zaluzianskya capensis	SG,SI,V,W
Zaluzianskya capensis 'Midnight Candy'	B,C,F,KS,SE
Zaluzianskya katherinae	B,SI
Zaluzianskya sp	I,SI
Zaluzianskya spathacea	SI
Zaluzianskya villosa	B,SI
Zamia dominiquensis	B
Zamia fischeri	B,C,O
Zamia furfuracea	B,C,HA,O,SA
Zamia integrifolia	B
Zamia loddigesii	B,O
Zamia pumila	B,O
Zamia skinneri	O
Zantedeschia aethiopica	AP,B,C,G,SA,SI
Zantedeschia aethiopica 'Crowborough'	B,LG,SC
Zantedeschia aethiopica 'Giant Vanetti'	B
Zantedeschia aethiopica 'Green Goddess'	B,HA,MN
Zantedeschia aethiopica pink bracted	B
Zantedeschia albomaculata	AP,B,G,MN,SI
Zantedeschia elliottiana	B,G
Zantedeschia 'Giant' s-c	B
Zantedeschia hybs	B
Zantedeschia odorata	B,SI
Zantedeschia 'Rainbow' mix	HA
Zantedeschia rehmannii	B,MN,SI
Zanthoxylum alatum	A,C,SG
Zanthoxylum americanum	A,B,G
Zanthoxylum capense	B,SI
Zanthoxylum molle	B
Zanthoxylum piperitum	A,B
Zanthoxylum simulans	B,G,SG
Zauschneria californica	AP,C,G
Zauschneria californica 'Dublin'	PM
Zauschneria latifolia	SW
Zea diploperennis	B

239

ZEA

Zea gracillima	KS
Zea japonica	KS
Zea japonica 'Red Berry'	L
Zea mays v gracillima	B
Zea mays v gracillima 'Gelbe Beere'	CG
Zea mays v mexicana	B
Zelkova carpinifolia	B,C,N,SA
Zelkova hyrcania	SA
Zelkova schneiderana	B
Zelkova serrata	B,C,HA,N,SA,T,V
Zelkova sinica	B,N,SA
Zenobia pulverulenta	B,CG,N,SC
Zephyranthes atamasco	AP,B
Zephyranthes candida	AP,SG
Zephyranthes citrina	B
Zephyranthes drummondii	AP,B
Zephyranthes grandiflora	AP,B,SC
Zephyranthes lindleyana	SG
Zephyranthes longifolia	B,G,SC,SW
Zephyranthes minima	LG
Zephyranthes rosea	AP,B,SC
Zephyranthes x lancasterae	AP,LG
Ziera smithii	HA
Zigadenus elegans	AP,B,JE,SC,SG
Zigadenus fremontii	AP,B
Zigadenus glaucus	JE
Zigadenus nutallii	AP,JE,SC
Zigadenus venosus	B,JE
Zilla spinosa	B
Zingiber spectabile	B
Zingiber zerumbet	B
Zingiber zerumbet 'Darceyi'	B
Zinnia acerosa	B
Zinnia angustifola see Z.haageana	
Zinnia 'Belvedere'	U
Zinnia 'Burpee's Hybrids'	BS
Zinnia 'Cactus' fl giant mix	C,L,T
Zinnia 'Candy Cane'	C
Zinnia 'Chippendale'	T
Zinnia 'Classic'	U
Zinnia 'Dahlia Flowered' mix	B,BS,C,D,DT,KI,L,SE,ST, TU,VH,YA
Zinnia darwiniana	AP,B
Zinnia 'Dasher' s-c, mix	BS
Zinnia dwarf dbl mix	S,T
Zinnia 'Early Wonder'	C,F
Zinnia elegans	B,G,SG
Zinnia elegans 'Tufted Exemption'	F
Zinnia elegans 'Whirligig'	C,S
Zinnia elegans 'Whirligig Imp'	T
Zinnia 'Envy' green	B,BS,C,F,KS,T
Zinnia f1 'Dreamland Series'	B,BS,SE
Zinnia f1 'Fairyland'	D
Zinnia f1 'Parasol'	T
Zinnia f1 'Peter Pan' s-c	BS,CL,YA
Zinnia f1 'Short Stuff Series'	CL
Zinnia f1 'Small World Cherry'	B,BS
Zinnia f1 'Small World Pink'	B,BS
Zinnia 'Giant Dbl Mix'	J,S,T,V
Zinnia grandiflora	B
Zinnia haageana	B,SG
Zinnia haageana 'Mandarin Orange'	J
Zinnia haageana 'Orange'	B,V
Zinnia haageana 'Persian Carpet Mix'	B,BS,D,DT,F,G,J,KI,S,T
Zinnia haageana 'Star Series'	BS,CL
Zinnia haageana 'Starbright'	BS,CL,F,KI,S

Zinnia haageana 'White'	B
Zinnia 'Hobgoblin'	BS
Zinnia 'Lilliput'	BD,BS
Zinnia linearis	G,KS
Zinnia linearis 'White Star'	KS
Zinnia 'Mammoth'	BS
Zinnia 'Old Mexico'	C
Zinnia peruviana	AP,B
Zinnia peruviana 'Bonita Red'	B
Zinnia peruviana 'Bonita Yellow'	B
Zinnia 'Pink Pinwheel'	V
Zinnia 'Pumila Mix'	BS,YA
Zinnia scabious fl mix	B,T
Zinnia 'Sombrero'	T
Zinnia 'Sprite' mix	J
Zinnia 'State Fair'	B,BD,BS,C
Zinnia 'Sunbow'	T
Zinnia 'Thumbelina'	B,BS,C,CO,D,KI,L,SE, TU,V
Zinnia 'Tropical Snow'	BS,T
Zinnia 'White Star'	M
Zinnia 'Yoga'	BS
Zinnia 'Zebra'	DT
Zizania aquatica	B
Zizia aptera	B,PR,SG
Zizia aurea	B,G,PR,SG
Ziziphus jujuba	A,B,C,HA,SA,SI
Ziziphus lotus	B
Ziziphus mauritanica	B
Ziziphus mucronata	B,C,SA,SI
Ziziphus oenoplia	B
Ziziphus pubescens	SI
Ziziphus rivularis	B,SI
Ziziphus spina-christi	B,HA
Zornia diphylla	B
Zoysia japonica	B,HA,SA
Zygochloa paradoxa	B
Zygophyllum aurantiacum	B
Zygophyllum eremaeum	B,SA
Zygophyllum meyeri	B,SI
Zygophyllum morgsana	B,SI
Zygophyllum sessilifolium	B,SI

GREEN MANURES

Alfalfa	CD,CO,KI,SU,TU,V
Field Beans	CO,SU,TU
Buckwheat	CO,KI,SU,TU,V
Clover Alsike	CD,CO
Clover Red	CO,SU,TU,V
Fenugreek	CO,KI,SU,TU
Lupins	CO,KI,SU,TU,V
Mustard	CO,KI,SU,TU,V
Phacelia	CO,KI,SU,TU,V
Rye,Grazing	CO,KI,SU,TU
Tares	CO,KI,SU
Trefoil	CO,KI,SU,TU
Radish	CO,TU
Clover, Crimson	KI,SU,TU

VEGETABLES

Variety	Code
Argula 'Italian Wild Rustic'	KS
Artichoke, 'Green Globe'	B,BD,BS,C,CO,DT,F,J,KI,L,M,Mc,S,ST,SU,TU,U,V
Artichoke, 'Green Globe Imp'	KS,T,VH
Artichoke, 'Purple de Jesi'	KS
Artichoke, 'Purple Globe'	BS,CO,KI
Artichoke, 'Purple Romanesco'	KS
Artichoke, 'Romagna'	V
Artichoke, 'Selma-Cynara' F1	V
Artichoke, 'Violetto di Chiogga'	B,BS
Asparagus, 'Acell' F1	BS
Asparagus, 'Argenteuil Purple Imp'	BS
Asparagus, 'Connover's Colossal'	B,BD,BS,C,CO,D,KI,L,ST,SU,U,YA
Asparagus, 'Franklim' F1	B,KI,M,SU,V
Asparagus, 'Jersey Knight Improved'	T
Asparagus, 'Limbras Franklim' F1	J
Asparagus, 'Mary Washington'	BS,V,VH
Aubergine, 'Antar' F1	BS,SN,TU
Aubergine, 'Bandera' F1	T
Aubergine, 'Black Beauty'	B,BD,BS,F
Aubergine, 'Black Beauty' o-p	SN
Aubergine, 'Black Bell' F1	J,SN,V,YA
Aubergine, 'Black Emperor'	U
Aubergine, 'Black Enorma' F1	VH
Aubergine, 'Black Magic' hyb	SN
Aubergine, 'Blanca de Menorca' o-p	SN
Aubergine, 'Bonica' F1	BS,D,TU,VH
Aubergine, 'Bride' F1	V
Aubergine, 'Casper'	SN,V
Aubergine, 'Chinese'	HD
Aubergine, 'Classic' hyb	SN
Aubergine, 'Dusky' o-p	SN
Aubergine, 'Easter Egg'	KS
Aubergine, 'Epic'	KI
Aubergine, 'Florence Round Purple'	KS
Aubergine, 'Giullietta' hyb	SN
Aubergine, 'Long Purple'	BS,C,CO,J,ST,TU
Aubergine, 'Long Tom' F1	BS,CO,KS
Aubergine, 'Mini Bambino'	T
Aubergine, 'Moneymaker' F1	B,BD,BS,DT,F,KI,L,R,S,TU,VH
Aubergine, 'New York Round Purple'	BS
Aubergine, 'Onita'	BS,SU
Aubergine, 'Ova' F1	BS,CO,S,TU
Aubergine, 'Pingtung Long' F1	V
Aubergine, 'Prelane' F1	SN
Aubergine, 'Rotunda Bianca di Rosa' o-p	SN
Aubergine, 'Short Tom' F1	BS,SU
Aubergine, 'Slice Rite' F1	TU
Aubergine, 'Slice Rite No.23'	M,U
Aubergine, 'White Egg' F1	B,V
Bean , Adzuki	T
Bean, Asparagus, 'Liana'	V
Bean, Borlotti, 'Fire Tongue'	B,V
Bean, Flageolet	B,V
Bean, Lablab Climbing	V
Bean, Lablab Climbing, 'Ruby Moon'	M
Bean, Red Kidney, 'Bruine Noordhollandse'	V
Bean, Soya, 'Gieso'	V
Bean, Yard Long	CO,KS,SU
Bean, Yard Long, 'Extra Early Ben'	F
Bean, Yard Long, 'Green Pod Kaohsiung'	V
Bean, Yard Long, 'Purple Mart'	V
Beans, Broad, 'Acme'	YA
Beans, Broad, 'Aquadulce'	B,BD,BS,D,DT,F,J,KI,Mc,S,SE,VH
Beans, Broad, 'Aquadulce Claudia'	B,BS,CO,D,KI,L,M,SE,SN,SU,T,TU,YA
Beans, Broad, 'Bunyards Exhibition'	B,BD,BS,CO,DT,F,J,KI,L,Mc,U,VH
Beans, Broad, 'Crimson Flowered'	HD
Beans, Broad, 'Dreadnought'	BS,D,KI,YA
Beans, Broad, 'Driemaal wit'	V
Beans, Broad, 'Express'	B,BS,CO,J,KI,M,Mc,SU,T,TU
Beans, Broad, 'Futura'	B,BD,BS
Beans, Broad, 'Giant Exhibition Longpod'	B,C,K,KI,Mc,S
Beans, Broad, 'Gloster Bounty'	HD
Beans, Broad, 'Hylon'	S,SN,TU
Beans, Broad, 'Imperial Green Longpod'	D,DT,F,R,T
Beans, Broad, 'Imperial Green Windsor'	BS,J,U
Beans, Broad, 'Imperial White Windsor'	S
Beans, Broad, 'Jade'	M,SE
Beans, Broad, 'Jubilee Hysor'	D,M
Beans, Broad, 'Martock'	HD
Beans, Broad, 'Masterpiece Gr. Longpod'	B,BD,BS,C,CO,DT,F,KI,L,S,SU,TU,VH
Beans, Broad, 'Meteor * Vroma'	M
Beans, Broad, 'Metissa'	CO
Beans, Broad, Mix	B
Beans, Broad, 'Optica'	V
Beans, Broad, 'Perovka'	HD
Beans, Broad, 'Red Epicure'	U,V
Beans, Broad, 'Relon'	D,S
Beans, Broad, 'Rognon de Coq'	D,S,SN
Beans, Broad, 'Statissa'	T
Beans, Broad, 'Stereo'	D,DT,YA
Beans, Broad, 'Talia'	C
Beans, Broad, 'The Sutton'	B,BD,BS,CO,D,DT,F,KI,L,M,Mc,S,SU,T,TU,U,V,VH
Beans, Broad, 'Threefold White'	J
Beans, Broad, 'Topic'	C
Beans, Broad, 'Verdy'	D,U,VH
Beans, Broad, 'Windsor Green'	B,CO,KI,SU
Beans, Broad, 'Windsor White'	B,BS,CO,KI
Beans, Broad, 'Witkeim Manita'	B,BD,CO,DT,J,KI,SN,TU
Beans, Broad, 'Witkeim Vroma'	D,F,V
Beans, Broad, 'Witkeim Major'	B,U,VH
Beans, Climbing, 'Borlotto Lingua di Fuoco'	D,KI,SU
Beans, Climbing French, 'Algarve'	D,YA
Beans, Climbing French, 'Blue and White'	HD
Beans, Climbing French, 'Blue Lake'	B,BS,C,CO,D,DT,F,J,KI,L,M,Mc,S,SN,SU,TU
Beans, Cl. Fr., 'Cherokee Trail of Tears'	HD
Beans, Climbing French, 'Coco Bicolour'	HD
Beans, Climbing French, 'Corona D'Oro'	J,KI,L,TU
Beans, Climbing French, 'Cosse Violette'	TU
Beans, Climbing French, 'Crystal'	K,YA
Beans, Climbing French, 'Goldmarie'	S
Beans, Climbing French, 'Hunter'	B,CO,DT,F,J,KI,L,M,S,SU,TU
Beans, Climbing French, 'Jack Edward's'	HD
Beans, Climbing French, 'Kentucky Blue'	CO,K,KI,T,S
Beans, Climbing French, 'Kingston Gold'	RO
Beans, Climbing French, 'Largo'	DT,M
Beans, Climbing French, 'Marvel of Venice'	B,CO,SU
Beans, Climbing French, 'Mix'	T
Beans, Climbing French, 'Musica'	T,VH
Beans, Climbing French, 'Neckargold'	D

BEANS

Beans, Climbing French, 'Oregon Giant' HD
Beans, Climbing French, 'Pea Bean' CO
Beans, Climbing French, 'Purple Giant' HD
Beans, Climbing French, 'Purple Podded' S
Beans, Climbing French, 'Red Robin' HD
Beans, Climbing French, 'Rob Roy' RO
Beans, Climbing French, 'Rob Splash' RO
Beans, Climbing French, 'Romano' T
Beans, Climbing French, 'Selma Zebra' HD
Beans, Climbing French, 'Viola Cornetti' CO,SU
Beans, Climbing French, 'Yugoslavia No.1' HD
Beans, Climbing, 'Goja' J
Beans, 'Coloured Collection' DT
Beans, Dwarf, 'Admires z dr.' J,V
Beans, Dwarf, 'Arranesco' HD
Beans, Dwarf, 'Black Canterbury' HD
Beans, Dwarf, 'Black Prince' BS
Beans, Dwarf, 'Brown Dutch' CO,SU
Beans, Dwarf Bush, 'Label' SN
Beans, Dwarf Bush, 'Marbel' SN
Beans, Dwarf Bush, 'Masai' SN,T
Beans, Dwarf, 'Canadian Wonder' BS,CO,J,KI,SU
Beans, Dwarf, 'Canberra' V
Beans, Dwarf, 'Coquette' CO
Beans, Dwarf, 'Early Warwick' HD
Beans, Dwarf, 'Ernie's Big Eye' HD
Beans, Dwarf French, 'Annabel' D,KI,M
Beans, Dwarf French, 'Aramis' T,TU,U
Beans, Dwarf French, 'Atlanta' K,T
Beans, Dwarf French, 'Baffin' CO
Beans, Dwarf French, 'Bush Blue Lake' B,BD,K
Beans, Dwarf French, 'Capitole' DT,T
Beans, Dwarf French, 'Cascade' BD
Beans, Dwarf French, Collection D
Beans, Dwarf French, 'Contender' BS,CO,SU
Beans, Dwarf French, 'Cropper Teepee' CO,F,J,KI,SU
Beans, Dwarf French, 'Delinel' M
Beans, Dwarf French, 'Deuil Fin Precoce' CO,SU
Beans, Dwarf French, 'Dorabel' SN
Beans, Dwarf French, 'Dutch Princess' VH
Beans, Dwarf French, 'Fin de Bagnol' B,KS,SU
Beans, Dwarf French, 'Golddukat' M,V
Beans, Dwarf French , 'Golden Butter' CO,SU
Beans, Dwarf French , 'Golden Sands' CO,SU
Beans, Dwarf, 'French Horticultural' HD
Beans, Dwarf French, 'Irago' TU
Beans, Dwarf French, 'Kinghorn Wax' S
Beans, Dwarf French, 'Laura' YA
Beans, Dwarf French, 'Loch Ness' BS
Beans, Dwarf French, 'Maradonna' R
Beans, Dwarf French, 'Masterpiece' BS,D,F,J,KI,S,SU
Beans, Dwarf French, 'Masterp. Stringless' D,M,RU
Beans, Dwarf French, 'Milagrow' YA
Beans, Dwarf French, 'Mondeo' D
Beans, Dwarf French, 'Mont d'Or' BS,C,F,M,S,T,U
Beans, Dwarf French, 'Montano' DT,L,YA
Beans, Dwarf French, 'Nassau' CO,DT,L,S
Beans, Dwarf French or Bush, 'Daisy' M,T
Beans, Dwarf French or Bush, Mix T
Beans, Dwarf French or Bush, 'Radar' T
Beans, Dwarf French or Bush, 'Vibel' T
Beans, Dwarf French, 'Primel' M,SE
Beans, Dwarf French, 'Pros' D
Beans, Dwarf French, 'Pros Gitana' SE,U
Beans, Dwarf French, 'Provider' SU
Beans, Dwarf French, 'Purple Queen' F,L,S,U

Beans, Dwarf French, 'Purple Teepee' D,F,SU,T
Beans, Dwarf French, 'Rido'(Kenyan) C,D
Beans, Dwarf French, 'Rocdor' SN
Beans, Dwarf French, 'Roquencourt' DT,SU
Beans, Dwarf French, 'Royalty' C,CO,DT,KI,M,SU,TU
Beans, Dwarf French, 'Safari' K,M,S
Beans, Dwarf French, 'Safran' F
Beans, Dwarf French, 'Sprite' BS,KI
Beans, Dwarf French, 'Sungold' TU
Beans, Dwarf French, 'Sunray' DT,L
Beans, Dwarf French, 'Tendercrop' U
Beans, Dwarf French, 'Tendergreen' B,BD,BS,CO,DT,F,J,KI,
Mc,S,TU
Beans, Dwarf French, 'The Prince' BD,BS,C,CO,DT,F,K,KI,
M,S,T,TU,U
Beans, Dwarf French, 'Top Crop' SU
Beans, Dwarf French, 'Wachs GoldPerle' B,D
Beans, Dwarf, 'Horsehead' CO
Beans, Dwarf, 'Hutterite Soup' HD
Beans, Dwarf, 'Ice/Crystal Wax' HD
Beans, Dwarf, 'Lasso' F
Beans, Dwarf, 'Montano' J,V
Beans, Dwarf, 'Odessa' J
Beans, Dwarf, 'Prelude' J,V
Beans, Dwarf, 'Purple King' J,KI,V
Beans, Dwarf Runner, 'Pickwick' DT,U
Beans, Dwarf, 'Shirokostruczkovnia' HD
Beans, Dwarf, 'Slenderwax' J
Beans, Dwarf, 'Snake Bean' HD
Beans, Dwarf, 'Soldier' HD
Beans, Dwarf, 'Yugoslavian No.4' HD
Beans, Flageolet, 'Chevrier Vert' B,SU
Beans, French, 'Cordoba' V
Beans, 'French Navy' SU
Beans, French, 'Violet Podded Stringless' F
Beans, Haricot, 'Triomphe de Farcy' B,SU
Beans, Runner, 'Achievement' B,BD,J,M,S,SN,TU
Beans, Runner, 'Best of All' S
Beans, Runner, 'Bok' HD
Beans, Runner, 'Crusader' BD,F,KI,L,Mc,U
Beans, Runner, 'Czar' CO,J,SN,SU,TU
Beans, Runner, 'Droitwich Champion' HD
Beans, Runner, 'Enorma' B,BD,BS,DT,F,KI,J,L,M,
Mc,R,S,SE,SN,TU,VH,
YA
Beans, Runner, 'Enorma Elite' K
Beans, Runner, 'Erecta' V
Beans, Runner, 'Hammonds Dw. Scarlet' B,BD,CO,KI,SU,T,U,VH
Beans, Runner, 'Kelvedon Marvel' B,BD,BS,CO,KI,M,SN,
SU,TU,U,YA
Beans, Runner, 'Liberty' RO
Beans, Runner, 'Mrs. Cannell's Black' HD
Beans, Runner, 'Painted Lady' B,CO,D,DT,F,KI,M,Mc,
SN,SU,TU
Beans, Runner, 'Prizetaker' BS,KI
Beans, Runner, 'Prizewinner' BS,C,F,KI,S,SN,TU,U,V
Beans, Runner, 'Red Rum' T
Beans, Runner, 'Scarlet Emperor' B,BS,CO,D,DT,F,J,KI,S,
SE,SN,SU,T,TU,U
Beans, Runner, 'Streamline' B,BD,BS,C,CO,D,DT,F,J,
KI,T,M,TU,U,VH,YA
Beans, Runner, 'Sunset' HD
Beans, Runner, 'White Achievement' S
Beans, Runner, 'White Emergo' B,BD,BS,DT,F,KI,L,U,YA
Beans, Stringless Runner, 'Butler' CO,KI,S
Beans, Stringless Runner, 'Desiree' CO,DT,F,KI,M,Mc,R,T,V,

BEANS

	VH
Beans,Stringless Runner, 'Fergie'	F
Beans, Stringless Runner, 'Gulliver'	D
Beans, Stringless Runner, 'Ivanhoe'	T
Beans, Stringless Runner, 'Kelvedon'	D
Beans, Stringless Runner, 'Lady Di'	DT,F,J,K,KI,L,SE,SN,T, TU,U,VH
Beans, Stringless Runner, 'Mergoles'	D,DT,F,S
Beans, Stringless Runner, 'Pickwick'	BD,F,J,M,Mc,S,TU
Beans, Stringless Runner, 'Polestar'	B,BD,DT,F,J,M,Mc,S,U
Beans, Stringless Runner, 'Red Knight'	B,CO,DT,F,KI,M,Mc,SU, VH
Beans, Stringless Runner, 'Royal Standard'	D,T
Beetroot, 'Albina Vereduna'	T
Beetroot, 'Albina' white	KS
Beetroot, 'Avon Early'	BS,HD
Beetroot, Baby Beet, 'Action'	M
Beetroot, 'Barbabietola di Chiogga'	B,BS,CO,SU
Beetroot, 'Bikores'	B,BS,DT,J,KI,VH
Beetroot, 'Boldet'	BS
Beetroot, 'Boltardy'	w.a.
Beetroot, 'Bonel'	BS,F
Beetroot, 'Boston'	BS
Beetroot, 'Bull's Blood'	BS
Beetroot, 'Burpee's Golden'	BS,C,D,DT,J,L,S,T,TU,V
Beetroot, 'Cheltenham Green Top'	B,BS,KI,SU
Beetroot, 'Cheltenham Green Top Select'	BD,BS,CO
Beetroot, 'Cheltenham Mono'	BS,M
Beetroot, 'Chioggia Pink'	C,SN,T,V
Beetroot, 'Crimson King'	BS,CO,KI,ST
Beetroot, 'Crosby's Egyptian'	B,DT
Beetroot, 'Cylindra'	B,BS,DT,J,KI,L,M,SU,T, TU,U,VH
Beetroot, 'Detroit'	BS,KI,SU,VH
Beetroot, 'Detroit 2'	J,M
Beetroot, 'Detroit 2 - Crimson Globe'	BD,BS,DT,F,T
Beetroot, 'Detroit 2 - Little Ball'	BS,D,M,S
Beetroot, 'Detroit 2 - Nero Mini'	F
Beetroot, 'Detroit 2 - New Globe'	B,BS,CO,D,YA
Beetroot, 'Detroit 2 - Tardel'	BS,T
Beetroot, 'Detroit 6 - Rubidus'	T
Beetroot, 'Detroit Globe'	BS,C,Mc,ST,TU
Beetroot, 'Devoy'	HD
Beetroot, 'Dwergina'	B,BS,C,CO,KI,SN
Beetroot, 'Egyptian Turnip Rooted'	BS
Beetroot, 'Forono'	BS,CO,D,F,KI,S,V,YA
Beetroot, 'Globe 2'	S
Beetroot, 'Golden'	B,CO,KI,KS,Mc,SU
Beetroot, 'Golden Ball'	BS,SN,ST
Beetroot, 'Libero'	BS,KI,SN
Beetroot, 'Little Ball'	KS,ST,TU
Beetroot, Long K's selected	K
Beetroot, 'Mammoth Long'	RO
Beetroot, Mix	T
Beetroot, 'Modena'	DT
Beetroot, 'Monaco' Mini	D
Beetroot, 'Mondella'	BS,F,T
Beetroot, 'Moneta'	BS,KI,S,T,U
Beetroot, 'Monodet' Monogerm	BS
Beetroot, 'Monogram'	BS,J,T,U,V
Beetroot, 'Monopoly' Monogerm	BS,CO
Beetroot, 'Motown' Monogerm	D,M
Beetroot, 'Nobol'	BS
Beetroot, 'Nobolt' (Boltardy Selected)	BS
Beetroot, 'Pablo' F1	BS,DT,K,L,S,TU,VH
Beetroot, 'Perfect 2'	J

Beetroot, 'Perfect 3'	F
Beetroot, 'Pronto'	B,BD,BS,S
Beetroot, 'Pronto' o-p	K
Beetroot, 'Red Ace' F1	F,K,RO,S,SE,T,U
Beetroot, 'Red Arrow' F1	BS
Beetroot, 'Regala'	BS,SU,U
Beetroot, 'Rubigala'	BS
Beetroot, 'Spinel' mini	VH
Beetroot, 'Wodan' F1	K
Bitter Gourd, 'Halflange Groene'	V
Bitter Gourd, 'High Moon' F1	V
Bitter Gourd, 'Long Green'	V
Broccoli, 'Autumn Calabrese'	U
Broccoli, 'Brocoletto'	BS,SU
Broccoli, 'Caravel' F1	T
Broccoli, Chinese, 'Green Lance' F1	SU
Broccoli, 'Christmas Marvel'	M
Broccoli, 'Claret' F1	K,M,T
Broccoli, 'De Cicco'	BS,SU
Broccoli, 'Early Purple Sprouting'	B,BS,D,DT,F,KI,KS,L,R, ST,TU,YA
Broccoli, 'Early Purple Sprouting Blend'	M
Broccoli, 'Early Purple Spr. Red Arrow'	D, J, T
Broccoli, 'Early Romanesco'	C,D,M
Broccoli, 'Early White Sprouting'	B,BS,F,K,KI,M,SU,T,TU, U,VH,YA
Broccoli, 'El Centro'	M
Broccoli, 'Emperor'	U
Broccoli, 'Futura' F1	V
Broccoli, 'Italian Sprouting'	DT,F
Broccoli, 'Late Purple Sprouting'	B,BS,DT,KI,L,M,ST,SU,T
Broccoli, 'Late White Sprouting'	B,BS,D,DT,KI,L,M
Broccoli, 'Late White Sprouting White Star'	T
Broccoli, 'Late Sp. White Star - Tozer Stock'BS	
Broccoli, 'Marshalls Long Season'	M
Broccoli, 'Mix'	T
Broccoli, 'Nine Star Perennial'	BS,C,D,DT,KI,M,S
Broccoli, 'Purple Sprouting'	BD,C,CO,J,Mc,S,SU,U, V,VH
Broccoli, 'Purple Sprouting Red Arrow'	BS,CO
Broccoli, 'Purple Sprouting Redhead'	BS
Broccoli, 'Queen' F1	V
Broccoli, 'Raab'	KS
Broccoli, 'Red Arrow'	K,TU
Broccoli, 'Red Spear' F1	BS, L
Broccoli, 'Romanesco'	BS,CO,DT,KI,KS,SU,TU, VH
Broccoli, 'Royal Banquet'	U
Broccoli, 'Rudolph'	DT,TU
Broccoli, 'Snow Star'	M
Broccoli, 'Special Sprouting Mix'	SE
Broccoli, 'Temple'	T
Broccoli, 'Tribute' F1	VH
Broccoli, 'Trixie' F1	CO,KI,T,TU,M,SU,U,YA
Broccoli, 'White Sprouting'	BD,C,CO,J,Mc,ST,V
Broccoli, 'White Sprouting Imp'	S
Broccoli/Cauliflower, 'Floccoli' F1	T,V
Brussels Sprouts, '2-Pk Peer Gynt/Welland'	M
Brussels Sprouts, 'Acropolis' F1	B,BS
Brussels Sprouts, 'Adonis' F1	T
Brussels Sprouts, 'Ajax' F1	BS
Brussels Sprouts, 'Aries' F1	B,BS
Brussels Sprouts, 'Bedford'	D,DT,VH
Brussels Sprouts, 'Bedford Darkmar 21'	BS,F,J,R,TU
Brussels Sprouts, 'Bedford Fillbasket'	B,BS,T,S,ST,SU,VH

BRUSSELS SPROUTS

Brussels Sprouts, 'Bedford Winter Harvest'	S	Burdock 'Takinogawa'	KS
Brussels Sprouts, 'Blue Vein'	BS,ST	Cabbage, 'Advantage' F1	DT,S,TU
Brussels Sprouts, 'Boxer' F1	B,BS,VH	Cabbage, 'All Year Selection'	M
Brussels Sprouts, 'Cambridge No 5'	BS	Cabbage, 'Amager'	BS
Brussels Sprouts, 'Cascade' F1	BS,D,DT,K,KI	Cabbage, 'Apex' F1	BS
Brussels Sprouts, 'Cavalier' F1	B,BS,T,TU	Cabbage, 'Aquila' F1	BS
Brussels Sprouts, 'Citadel' F1	BS,KI,T,VH	Cabbage, 'Arena' F1	BS,YA
Brussels Sprouts, 'Claudette' F1	BS,CO,KI,M,SE,YA	Cabbage, 'Avonquest'	BS
Brussels Sprouts, 'Collette' F1	BS,KI,M,ST	Cabbage, 'B.G. 283'	BS
Brussels Sprouts, 'Content' F1	BS,M,TU	Cabbage, 'Balbro' F1	BS
Brussels Sprouts, 'Cor' F1	B,BD,BS	Cabbage, 'Bartolo' F1	BS
Brussels Sprouts, 'Darkmar 21'	B,BD,CO,KI	Cabbage, 'Baseball'	BS
Brussels Sprouts, 'Diablo' F1	BS,K,L,TU,VH	Cabbage, 'Bewama'	BS
Brussels Sprouts, 'Dolmic' F1	T	Cabbage, 'Big Ben' F1	BS
Brussels Sprouts, 'Early Half Tall'	BD,BS,CO	Cabbage, 'Bingo' F1	CO,T
Brussels Sprouts, 'Edmund'	BS	Cabbage, 'Bison' F1	BS
Brussels Sprouts, 'Evesham Special'	B,BD,BS,DT,F,J,KI,L,Mc, SU,V	Cabbage, 'Black Tuscany'	D, S
		Cabbage, 'Brunswick'	BS,KI,Mc,VH
Brussels Sprouts, 'Evident'	BS	Cabbage, 'Brunswick' o-p	K
Brussels Sprouts, 'Falstaff'	D,S	Cabbage, 'Cape Horn' F1	BS,F,KI,YA
Brussels Sprouts, 'Fillbasket'	C,KI	Cabbage, 'Carlton' F1	K
Brussels Sprouts, 'Fortress' F1	J,ST,V	Cabbage, 'Carnival' F1	BS
Brussels Sprouts, 'Golfer'	B,BS,KI	Cabbage, 'Castello' F1 Mini	BS,F,M,T
Brussels Sprouts, 'Hamlet'	D,S	Cabbage, 'Celtic' F1	BD,BS,CO,D,DT,F,KI,M,
Brussels Sprouts, 'Hunter'	BS		Mc,S,TU,U,YA
Brussels Sprouts, 'Icarus' F1	T,VH	Cabbage, 'Charmant' F1	YA
Brussels Sprouts, 'Lunet' F1	B,BS,M,TU	Cabbage, Chinese, 'Blues' F1	BD,BS
Brussels Sprouts, 'Mallard'	U	Cabbage, Chinese, 'Bouquet' F1	BS,KI,Mc,SN,TU
Brussels Sprouts, 'Masterline' F1	DT	Cabbage, Chinese, 'China Express' F1	BS,KI,SU
Brussels Sprouts, 'Montgomery' F1	BS,D,L,M	Cabbage, Chinese, 'China King No 14' F1	C
Brussels Sprouts, 'Noisette'	B,BS,CO,SU	Cabbage, Chinese, 'Early Jade Pagoda' F1	BS,KI,SU,YA
Brussels Sprouts, 'Odette' F1	BS,SU,T,TU,YA	Cabbage, Chinese 'Flowering'	KS,SU
Brussels Sprouts, 'Oliver' F1	BS,CO,DT,KI,L,ST,T	Cabbage, Chinese, 'Green Rocket' F1	BS,KI
Brussels Sprouts, 'Peer Gynt' F1	B,BD,BS,CO,D,DT,F,J,KI,	Cabbage, Chinese, 'Kasumi' F1	BS,DT,L,M,TU
	L,M,Mc,S,SE,ST,SU,T,U,	Cabbage, Chinese, 'Mariko' F1	BS
	VH	Cabbage, Chinese, 'Monument' F1	J
Brussels Sprouts, 'Perfect Line' F1	BS	Cabbage, Chinese 'Nagaoka 60 Day' F1	B,BS,F
Brussels Sprouts, 'Predora' F1	B,BS,M	Cabbage, Chinese 'Okido' F1	BS
Brussels Sprouts, 'Prelent' F1	B,BS,TU	Cabbage, Chinese, 'One Kilo SB' F1	YA
Brussels Sprouts, 'Prince Marvel' F1	BS,KI,ST	Cabbage, Chinese, 'Orange Queen' F1	BS,KI,SU,T
Brussels Sprouts, 'Profline' F1	DT	Cabbage, Chinese, 'Pe Tsai'	BS
Brussels Sprouts, 'Rampart' F1	B,BD,CO,D,J,KI,L,ST,	Cabbage, Chinese, 'Ruffles' F1	D,S
	SU,TU,U	Cabbage, Chinese, 'Santo'	BS,KS,SU
Brussels Sprouts, 'Revenge' F1	K	Cabbage, Chinese, 'Serifon'	V
Brussels Sprouts, 'Roger'	BS	Cabbage, Chinese, 'Shaho Tsai'	BS
Brussels Sprouts, 'Roodnerf'	D,S	Cabbage, Chinese, 'Shantung' o-p	C
Brussels Sprouts, 'Rous Lench'	BS	Cabbage, Chinese, 'Tah Tsai'	BS,CO,KS
Brussels Sprouts, 'Rubine'	B,BS,C,CO,F,Mc,SU,V	Cabbage, Chinese, 'Tango'	BS
Brussels Sprouts, 'Saxon' F1	S	Cabbage, Chinese, 'Tip Top No 12' F1	C
Brussels Sprouts, 'Seven Hills'	B,BS,CO,KI,ST,SU	Cabbage, Chinese, 'Tiptop' F1	BS,CO,J,TU,V
Brussels Sprouts, 'Sheriff' F1	B,BS,CO,K,M,SE,T,TU,	Cabbage, Chinese, 'W.R. 60 Days'	BS
	VH	Cabbage, Chinese, 'Wong Bok'	B,BS,CO,KI,SU,ST
Brussels Sprouts, 'Solent' F1	BS	Cabbage, Chinese, 'Wong Bok' o-p	C
Brussels Sprouts, 'Stan' F1	RO	Cabbage, 'Christmas Drumhead'	BS,CO,D,J,KI,L,M,Mc,S,
Brussels Sprouts, 'Stockade' F1	BS		ST,SU,U,VH
Brussels Sprouts, 'Talent' F1	BS,TU	Cabbage, 'CLX 514' F1	YA
Brussels Sprouts, 'Tavernos' F1	BS	Cabbage, 'Colt' F1	D,K
Brussels Sprouts, 'The Wroxton'	BS	Cabbage, 'Copenhagen Market'	BS
Brussels Sprouts, 'Topline'	DT,U	Cabbage, 'Cortina' F1	K
Brussels Sprouts, 'Trimmer' F1	BS	Cabbage, 'Cotswold Queen'	BS,DT
Brussels Sprouts, 'Troika' F1	BS,D,F,J	Cabbage, 'Custodian' F1	BS
Brussels Sprouts, 'United'	BS	Cabbage, 'Decema'	BD,DT
Brussels Sprouts, 'Victor' F1	BS	Cabbage, 'Decema Extra'	BS
Brussels Sprouts, 'Warrior' F1	K	Cabbage, 'Delicatesse'	BS
Brussels Sprouts, 'Welland'	M	Cabbage, 'Delphi' F1	BS
Brussels Sprouts, 'Wellington' F1	BS,F,KI,U	Cabbage, 'Derby Day'	BS,DT,F,L,M,TU

CABBAGE

Cabbage, 'Destiny' F1	K	Cabbage, 'Offenham 3'	BS,R
Cabbage, 'Dorado'	BS	Cabbage, 'Offenham 3 Kempsey'	BD,BS
Cabbage, 'Duchy' F1	BS,DT,K,T	Cabbage, 'Offenham - Flower of Spring 2'	BD,BS,C,D,F,J,S,ST,TU
Cabbage, 'Duncan' F1	BS,DT,M,TU,U,YA	Cabbage, 'Optiko' F1	VH
Cabbage, 'Dynamo' F1	SE	Cabbage, Palm Tree, 'Di Toscana'	KS
Cabbage, 'Elisa' F1	BS,YA	Cabbage, 'Patron' F1	BS
Cabbage, 'Ellam's Early Dwarf'	BS	Cabbage, 'Pedrillo' F1	BS,V
Cabbage, 'Enkutzein Glory'	BS,ST	Cabbage, 'Perfect Ball' F1	T
Cabbage, 'Estron' F1	BS	Cabbage, 'Pixie'	BS,D,DT,L,S,T,U
Cabbage, 'Eureka' F1	YA	Cabbage, 'Pointer' F1	YA
Cabbage, 'Extra Early'	BS	Cabbage, 'Polestar' F1	BS
Cabbage, 'Felix' F1	F	Cabbage, 'Polinius' F1	BS
Cabbage, 'Fidelio' F1	K	Cabbage, 'Primax'	BS
Cabbage, 'First Early Market No.218'	BD,BS,DT,ST,TU,U	Cabbage, 'Primo'	CO,KI,R,ST,U
Cabbage, 'First of June'	BS	Cabbage, 'Princess' F1	BS
Cabbage, 'Flagship' F1	BS,CO,J,K,SU,TU	Cabbage, 'Progress'	BS
Cabbage, 'Freshma' F1	BS,F,KI,YA	Cabbage, 'Prospera' F1	B,BD,V
Cabbage, 'Golden Acre'	B,BS,C,CO,D,F,KI,L,Mc, VH,YA	Cabbage, 'Puma' F1	YA
		Cabbage, 'Quickstep' F1	M,T
Cabbage, 'Golden Acre - Earliana'	D,J	Cabbage, 'Rapid' F1	BS
Cabbage, 'Golden Acre May Express'	S	Cabbage, 'Rapidity'	BS
Cabbage, 'Golden Acre Primo 11'	DT,J,M,S,TU	Cabbage, Red, 'Autura' F1	BD,BS,TU,VH
Cabbage, 'Golden Acre Special'	BS	Cabbage, Red, 'Cicero' F1	K
Cabbage, 'Golden Cross'	B,BS,KI	Cabbage, Red, 'Drumhead'	BD,C,CO,J,KI,Mc,S,ST, SU,TU
Cabbage, 'Gourmet' F1	DT		
Cabbage, 'Green Coronet'	BS	Cabbage, Red, 'Hardoro' F1	BS,J,KI,TU
Cabbage, 'Green Express' F1	KI,YA	Cabbage, Red, 'Huzaro' F1	K
Cabbage, 'Green Wonder'	BS	Cabbage, Red, 'Langedijk Red Late'	BS
Cabbage, 'Greensleeves'	BS	Cabbage, Red, 'Langedijk Red Medium'	D
Cabbage, 'Greyhound'	BD,BS,C,CO,D,DT,F,J,KI, L,M,Mc,R,S,ST,SU,TU, U,VH,YA	Cabbage, Red, 'Metro' F1	M
		Cabbage, Red, 'Niggerhead'	BS
		Cabbage, Red, 'Normiro'	KI
Cabbage, 'Harbinger'	BS,J	Cabbage, Red, 'Primero' F1	K
Cabbage, 'Hardora' F1	BS,CO	Cabbage, Red, 'Primero' F1 Mini	D
Cabbage, 'Hawke' F1	D,S	Cabbage, Red, 'Rodeo' F1	BS,TU
Cabbage, 'Hercules'	V	Cabbage, Red, 'Rodima' F1	BS,T,YA
Cabbage, 'Hidena' F1	BS,U	Cabbage, Red, 'Rodon' F1	BS
Cabbage, 'Hispi' F1	BS,D,DT,F,J,KI,L,Mc,S, SE,ST,SU,T,TU,U,V	Cabbage, Red, 'Rondy' F1	BS
		Cabbage, Red, 'Rookie' F1	BS,F,KS
Cabbage, 'Histona'	U	Cabbage, Red, 'Ruby Ball' F1	BS,F,L,M,U
Cabbage, 'Holland Late Winter'	BS,CO,KI,ST,SU,TU	Cabbage, Red, 'Winner' F1	BS,DT,F,L,M,U,YA
Cabbage, 'Holland Winter White Extra Late'	BS,M,S,TU,U	Cabbage, 'Robinson's Champion'	BS
Cabbage, 'Hyjula' F1	BS,U	Cabbage, 'Robinson's Champion Giant'	RO
Cabbage, 'Impala' F1	K	Cabbage, 'Salarite' F1	F
Cabbage, 'Jersey Wakefield'	BS	Cabbage, 'Savana' F1	BS
Cabbage, 'Julius' F1	T	Cabbage, Savoy, 'Alexander's No 1'	BS,M
Cabbage, 'Kalorama'	DT	Cabbage, Savoy, 'Alex's No 1 Lincoln Late'	BS
Cabbage, 'Kingspi'	M	Cabbage, Savoy, 'Avon Coronet'	BS
Cabbage, 'Krautman'	VH	Cabbage, Savoy, 'Best of All'	BS,CO,D,KI,Mc,ST,SU, TU
Cabbage, 'Langedijk 4 (Holl. Winter E50)'	F,J,KI,V		
Cabbage, 'Langedijk 4 Starski' o-p	YA	Cabbage, Savoy, 'Cantasa' F1	BD,K
Cabbage, 'Langedijk Superstar'	BS	Cabbage, Savoy, 'Capraccio' F1	M
Cabbage, 'Lincoln Improved'	BS	Cabbage, Savoy, 'Chirimen' F1	BS,YA
Cabbage, 'Marabel' F1	K,SE,T,VH	Cabbage, Savoy, 'Colorsa' F1 (red)	T
Cabbage, 'Marathon' F1	K	Cabbage, Savoy, 'Concerto' F1	YA
Cabbage, 'Marnah Allfruh'	BS,KI	Cabbage, Savoy, 'Daphne'	YA
Cabbage, 'Marvellon' F1	BS,T	Cabbage, Savoy, 'Dwarf Green Curled'	BS
Cabbage, 'Meggaton' F1	K	Cabbage, Savoy, 'Famosa' F1	K
Cabbage, 'Minicole' F1	BS,CO,D,DT,F,J,KI,L,S, SE,SU,T,TU,U,VH	Cabbage, Savoy, 'Hamasa' F1	BS,KI
		Cabbage, Savoy, 'January King'	BS,C,CO,KI,J,M,Mc,R, ST,SU,U,VH
Cabbage, 'Mix' F1	T		
Cabbage, 'Multiton' F1	TU	Cabbage, Savoy, 'January King 3'	BD,BS,D,DT,J,L,S
Cabbage, 'Nobilis'	BS,YA	Cabbage, Savoy, 'J.K.3 Hardy Late Stock 3'	M,TU,YA
Cabbage, 'Offenham'	BS	Cabbage, Savoy, 'J.King Imp Extra Late'	BS
Cabbage, 'Offenham 1 Little Kempsey'	BS	Cabbage, Savoy, 'January King Special'	BS
Cabbage, 'Offenham 2 First and Best'	BS	Cabbage, Savoy, 'King' F1	BS,DT,F,KI,SE,T,U

CABBAGE

Name	Codes
Cabbage, Savoy, 'Midvoy' F1	BS,DT,R
Cabbage, Savoy, 'Novum'	BS
Cabbage, Savoy, 'Novusa'	M,TU
Cabbage, Savoy, 'Ormskirk 1'(Early)	BD,BS,KI,SU
Cabbage, Savoy, 'Ormskirk 1(Extra Late)'	BS,TU
Cabbage, Savoy, 'Ormskirk 1(Late)'	BS,C,CO,D,DT,J,L,M,ST, TU,U,VH
Cabbage, Savoy, 'Ormskirk 1(Med)'	BS
Cabbage, Savoy, 'Ormskirk 1 Rearguard'	C,D,J,L,M,U
Cabbage, Savoy, 'Ovasa' F1	VH
Cabbage, Savoy, 'Paravoy' F1	BS
Cabbage, Savoy, 'Paresa' F1	YA
Cabbage, Savoy, 'Perfection Drumhead'	BS
Cabbage, Savoy, 'Polasa' F1	K
Cabbage, Savoy, 'Primavoy' F1	BS
Cabbage, Savoy, 'Protovoy' F1	BS,D,S,VH
Cabbage, Savoy, 'Rhapsody' F1	YA
Cabbage, Savoy, 'Rigoletto' F1	DT,YA
Cabbage, Savoy, 'Silva'	S
Cabbage, Savoy, 'Starski' o-p	BS
Cabbage, Savoy, 'Taler'	M
Cabbage, Savoy, 'Tarvoy' F1	KI,T,TU
Cabbage, Savoy, 'Tombola' F1	BS
Cabbage, Savoy, 'Traviata'	YA
Cabbage, Savoy, 'Tundra' F1	BS,DT,SE
Cabbage, Savoy, 'Winter King 2'	M
Cabbage, Savoy, 'Winter King Harda' o-p	BS
Cabbage, Savoy, 'Winter King Shortie'	BS
Cabbage, Savoy, 'Winter Star' F1	BS
Cabbage, Savoy, 'Winterkoning' o-p	BS,V
Cabbage, Savoy, 'Winterton'	J
Cabbage, Savoy, 'Wintessa' F1	BS,KI,SU
Cabbage, Savoy, 'Wirosa' F1	BS,DT,TU,YA
Cabbage, Savoy, 'Wivoy' F1	BS,D,M,TU
Cabbage, Savoy, Yellow	V
Cabbage, 'Scanbo' F1	YA
Cabbage, 'Scanita' hyb	YA
Cabbage, 'Scanner' F1	YA
Cabbage, 'Scanvi' F1	YA
Cabbage, 'Scarisbrick'	BS
Cabbage, 'Scout' F1	BS
Cabbage, 'Spartan' F1	BS
Cabbage, 'Speedon' F1	BS
Cabbage, 'Spirant' F1	BS
Cabbage, 'Spirit' F1	BS
Cabbage, 'Spitfire' F1	BS,CO,D,KI
Cabbage, Spring, 'April'	BS,KI,S, ST,SU,TU,VH, YA
Cabbage, Spring, 'Cotswold Queen'	CO,YA
Cabbage, Spring, 'Durham Early'	BD,BS,DT,KI,M,ST,TU, U,VH
Cabbage, Spring, 'Durham Elf'	BS,J,K,TU,YA
Cabbage, Spring, 'Durham Elf Elite Strain'	K
Cabbage, Spring, 'Earliest of All'	BD,BS,KI,SU
Cabbage, Spring, 'Early Queen'	BS,KI,SU
Cabbage, Spring, 'Express'	V
Cabbage, Spring 'Fem 218'	YA
Cabbage, Spring, 'Flower of Spring'	CO,KI
Cabbage, Spring, 'Hero' F1	BS,CO,D,F,J,KI,M,SE, ST,SU,TU,U,YA
Cabbage, Spring, 'Offenham 3 Winter Gr'	BS,TU,YA
Cabbage, Sp 'Offenham Myatts Comp' 1	BS,CO,DT,KI,L,M,TU,YA
Cabbage, Spring, 'Pewa'	YA
Cabbage, Spring, 'Pixie'	M
Cabbage, Spring, 'Prospera' F1	BS
Cabbage, Spring, 'Sparkel' F1	D,F,K
Cabbage, Spring, 'Vanguard' F1	SE
Cabbage, Spring, 'Wheeler's Imperial'	BD,BS,C,D,J,KI,S,ST, TU,YA
Cabbage, Spring, 'Wintergreen'	CO,KI,SU
Cabbage, 'Springtime'	BS
Cabbage, 'Standby'	BS
Cabbage, 'Starski'	CO,KI
Cabbage, 'Steppe' F1	BS
Cabbage, 'Stonehead' F1	B,BD,BS,CO,D,DT,F,KI, L,ST,TU,YA
Cabbage, 'Super Action' F1	BS
Cabbage, 'Tundra' F1	B,CO,D,F,J,L,M,SE,T,TU, U,YA
Cabbage, 'Vantage Point' F1	BS,KI
Cabbage, Walking Stick	B,C,F,T,V
Cabbage, 'Wiam'	BS
Cabbage, 'Winchester' F1	K
Cabbage, 'Winnigstadt'	BS,C,CO,D,J,KI,M,ST, SU,VH
Calabrese, 'Arcadia' F1	BS,KI,TU,YA
Calabrese, 'Autumn Spear'	S
Calabrese, 'Cape Queen' F1	BS
Calabrese, 'Citation' F1	D
Calabrese, 'Corvet' F1	B,BS,CO,D,DT,F,KI,SE, SN,ST,SU,TU,U
Calabrese, 'Cruiser' F1	B,BS
Calabrese, 'Dandy' F1	BS
Calabrese, 'Dundee' F1	YA
Calabrese, 'Emerald City' F1	YA
Calabrese, 'Emperor' F1	BS,CO,KI
Calabrese, 'Eusebio' F1	J
Calabrese, 'Express Corona' F1	S
Calabrese, 'Ginga' F1	YA
Calabrese, 'Green Comet'	B,BD,BS,F,ST,T
Calabrese, 'Green Duke'	BS
Calabrese, 'Green Sprouting'	B,BD,BS,C,CO,D,J,Mc, ST,SU,VH
Calabrese, 'Greenbelt' F1	L,YA
Calabrese, 'Jewel' F1 Mini	BS,F
Calabrese, 'Landmark' F1	HD
Calabrese, 'Lord' F1	DT
Calabrese, 'Marathon' F1	BS,DT,K,KI,L,R,SN,TU, YA
Calabrese, 'Mercedes' F1	BS,CO,M
Calabrese, 'Morses 4638'	BS
Calabrese, 'Pacifica'	BS
Calabrese, 'Packman' F1	BS
Calabrese, 'Pinnacle'	BS
Calabrese, 'Pirate'	BS
Calabrese, 'Premium Crop' F1	BS,SN
Calabrese, 'Romanesco Natalino'	F
Calabrese, 'Roxette'	YA
Calabrese, 'S.G.1'	SN
Calabrese, 'S.G. 1 S.C. ' F1	BS
Calabrese, 'Samurai' F1	BS,L,TU,YA
Calabrese, 'Shogun' F1	B,BD,BS,CO,DT,F,J,KI, L,SN,SU,TU,YA
Calabrese, 'Southern Comet' F1	B,BS
Calabrese, 'Stolto' F1	BS
Calabrese, 'Vantage' F1	BS
Calabrese, 'Viking' F1	K
Cape Gooseberry, Physalis Edulis	CO,D,DT,F,J,KS,S,SU,V, VS
Caper	C
Cardoon	C,KS,Mc,S,V
Cardoon, 'Gigante di Romagna'	CO,SU

CARDOON

Cardoon, Spanish	BS
Cardoon, 'White Ivory'	KS
Carrot, 'Allegro' F1	BS
Carrot, 'Amini'	DT,S,YA
Carrot, 'Amsterdam Forcing'	B,BD,BS,CO,D,F,KI,L,M, S,SN,TU
Carrot, 'Amsterdam Forcing 3 - Minicor'	BS,F,KS,SU,V
Carrot, 'Amsterdam Sweetheart'	BS,DT,U
Carrot, 'Astra'	BS
Carrot, 'Autumn King'	B,BD,BS,C,CO,KI,Mc,T, U,VH
Carrot, 'Autumn King 2'	D,F,J,S,T
Carrot, 'Autumn King 2 Vita Longa'	BS,KI,L,M,TU,U
Carrot, 'Autumn King 3'	TU
Carrot, 'Autumn King - Giganta'	BS
Carrot, 'Autumn King Red Winter'	BS
Carrot, 'Autumn King Viking'	BS
Carrot, 'Balin' F1	C
Carrot, 'Bangor' F1	S
Carrot, 'Banta'	BS
Carrot, 'Barbados' F1	K
Carrot, 'Berlanda' F1	BS,VH
Carrot, 'Berlicum'	BS,KI
Carrot, 'Berlicum 2 * Berjo'	B,BD,BS,M,SE,SU,TU,V, VH
Carrot, 'Berlicum 2 Oranza'	BS,DT
Carrot, 'Berlicum Special'	BS
Carrot, 'Berltop'	VH
Carrot, 'Bertan' F1	BS, T
Carrot, 'Bolero' F1	BS
Carrot, 'Boston' F1	J
Carrot, 'Calgary'	K
Carrot, 'Campestra'	BS
Carrot, 'Cardinal' F1	BS
Carrot, 'Carpa'	J
Carrot, 'Cartoga' F1	F
Carrot, 'Chanson'	K
Carrot, 'Chantenay 3 Comet'	BS
Carrot, 'Chantenay Babycan'	B,BS,SU
Carrot, 'Chantenay Canners' Favourite'	BS,YA
Carrot, 'Chantenay Long'	BS
Carrot, 'Chantenay Red Cored'	B,BD,BS,C,CO,KI,Mc, SN,ST,VH
Carrot, 'Chantenay Red Cored 2'	F,J,L,M,U
Carrot, 'Chantenay Red Cored 3 Supreme'	BS
Carrot, 'Chantenay Red Cored Fenman'	BS
Carrot, 'Chantenay Red Cored Gold King'	BS
Carrot, 'Chantenay Red Cored Royal 2'	BS,D,KI,SU
Carrot, 'Cobba' F1	D,YA
Carrot, 'Cordia'	BS
Carrot, 'Danvers'	BS
Carrot, 'Danvers Scarlet Half Long'	DT
Carrot, 'Danvers Scarlet Intermediate'	BS
Carrot, 'Decora'	BS
Carrot, 'Discovery'	K
Carrot, 'Douceur', Baby Carrot	C
Carrot, 'Early French Frame'	BS,DT,S
Carrot, 'Early French Frame 4 * Lisa'	M
Carrot, 'Early Horn'	BS
Carrot, 'Early Market'	J,KI,ST
Carrot, 'Early Market Horn'	TU
Carrot, 'Early Nantes'	B,BD,BS,KI,Mc,ST,SU, T,TU,VH
Carrot, 'Early Nantes 2'	F,J,L,M,TU,U
Carrot, 'Early Nantes 5'	DT,S
Carrot, 'Early Nantes Duke'	BS

Carrot, 'Early Nantes -Gringo'	YA
Carrot, 'Early Nantes Tip Top'	BS
Carrot, 'Early Scarlet Horn'	DT,F,J,U
Carrot, 'Fakkell Mix'	BS
Carrot, 'Fancy'	BS
Carrot, 'Favourite'	K,S
Carrot, 'Fedora'	U
Carrot, 'Flak'	VH
Carrot, 'Flakee'	B,KI,Mc,SU,TU
Carrot, 'Fly Away' F1	BD,BS,CO,K,KI,ST,SU, T,V
Carrot, 'Guerande'	BS
Carrot, 'Ideal' Mini	D
Carrot, 'Ideal Red'	BS,SU
Carrot, 'Imperator'	BS
Carrot, 'Ingot' F1	BS,DT,F,KI,L,SE,T,TU, U,V
Carrot, 'Invictor' F1	K
Carrot, 'James Scarlet Intermediate'	BS,C,CO,F,J,KI,ST,SU, T,TU,U,VH
Carrot, 'Jasper'	D
Carrot, 'Jumbo'	V
Carrot, 'Junior' F1	DT
Carrot, 'Juwarot'	B,BS,J,T
Carrot, 'Kanzan'	K
Carrot, 'Karotan'	BS
Carrot, 'Kingston' F1	DT
Carrot, 'Kudulus' mini	VH
Carrot, 'Lagor' F1	M
Carrot, 'Lange Rote Stumpfe 2 Zino'	T
Carrot, 'Lange Stumpfe Winter - Laros'	BS
Carrot, 'Liberno' F1	T
Carrot, 'London Market'	HD
Carrot, 'Long Red Surrey'	CO,KI
Carrot, Long (reselected)	K
Carrot, Long (St. Valery selected)	RO
Carrot, 'Major' F1	DT,K
Carrot, 'Mokum' F1	T
Carrot, 'Nabora' F1	YA
Carrot, 'Naironi' F1	KI,SU
Carrot, 'Nanco' F1	BS,J,M
Carrot, 'Nandor' F1	DT,RO
Carrot, 'Nantaise 2 -Michel'	BS
Carrot, 'Nantes'	R,V
Carrot, 'Nantes 2 Romosa'	BS,DT
Carrot, 'Nantes 3 TipTop'	CO,D
Carrot, 'Nantes 5 Champion Scarlet Horn'	S
Carrot, 'Nantes 5- Tam Tam'	YA
Carrot, 'Nantes Express'	SE,U
Carrot, 'Nantucket' F1	TU
Carrot, 'Napoli' F1	VH
Carrot, 'Narman' F1	B,BD,BS
Carrot, 'Narova' F1	BS
Carrot, 'Navarre' F1	F
Carrot, 'Nelson' F1	S
Carrot, 'Nelson' F1 pr.s	D
Carrot, 'New Radiance'	BS
Carrot, 'New Red Intermediate'	K,S
Carrot, 'Newmarket' F1	CO,F,KI,SE
Carrot, 'Obtuse de Doubs'	BS
Carrot, 'Oxheart'	B,SU
Carrot, 'Panther'	DT,U
Carrot, 'Parabell'	BS,CO,KI,SN
Carrot, 'Parano' F1	D
Carrot, 'Parmex'	D,J,SU,U,V
Carrot, 'Primo' F1	K

CARROT

Carrot, 'Rapier' F1	BS	Cauliflower, 'Cappacio'	T
Carrot, 'Red Rum' F1	TU	Cauliflower, 'Cargill'	T
Carrot, 'Redca'	BS,CO,KI	Cauliflower, 'Cargill' mini	VH
Carrot, 'Regulus'	BS	Cauliflower, 'Carlos'	BS
Carrot, 'Rocket'	D,DT	Cauliflower, 'Carron' F1	YA
Carrot, 'Romosa'	BS	Cauliflower, 'Castlegrant'	DT,M,U,YA
Carrot, 'Royal Chantenay'	DT,TU	Cauliflower, 'Coleman'	K
Carrot, 'Rubin'	BS,V	Cauliflower, 'Corvilia'	YA
Carrot, 'Scarlet Nantes'	BS	Cauliflower, 'Dinnet' F1	YA
Carrot, 'Senior'	DT,U	Cauliflower, 'Dok'	BS,D,K,S,T
Carrot, 'Sheila' F1	YA	Cauliflower, 'Dok Elgon'	J,L,M,RO,SE,U,VH
Carrot, 'Spalding'	K	Cauliflower, 'Dominant'	B,BS,CO,KI,SU
Carrot, 'St. Valery'	BS,C,CO,D,DT,F,J,KI,M,	Cauliflower, 'Dova' F1	BS, L
	S,SN,ST,SU,TU,U	Cauliflower, 'Dunkeld' F1	YA
Carrot, 'Stelio' F1	YA	Cauliflower, 'Early Feltham'	M
Carrot, 'Suko'	J,M,T	Cauliflower, 'Early Feltham 2'	U
Carrot, 'Supreme'	K	Cauliflower, 'Elby' F1	BS,D,T
Carrot, 'Sytan'	M	Cauliflower, 'Erfu'	BS
Carrot, 'Tamino' F1	BS	Cauliflower, 'Esmeraldo' F1	S,YA
Carrot, 'Thumbelina'	BS	Cauliflower, 'Fargo' F1	K,T
Carrot, 'Top Score'	BS	Cauliflower, 'Firstman'	K,TU
Carrot, 'Turbo' F1	YA	Cauliflower, 'Fleurly'	B,BS,D
Carrot, 'Waltham Hicolour'	BS	Cauliflower, 'Flora Blanca'	S
Carrot, 'White Belgium'	HD	Cauliflower, 'Florian'	YA
Carrot, 'Zino'	V	Cauliflower, 'Fortuna'	BS
Cauliflower, 'A.G. 63'	BS	Cauliflower, 'Fremont' F1	K
Cauliflower, 'Ace Early'	BS,D	Cauliflower, 'Garant'	B,CO
Cauliflower, 'Alban'	YA	Cauliflower, 'Goodman'	VH
Cauliflower, 'Alice Springs'	BS	Cauliflower, 'Grodan'	B,BS
Cauliflower, 'All The Year Round'	B,BD,C,CO,D,DT,F,J,KI,	Cauliflower, 'Hawkesbury' F1	YA
	L,M,Mc,R,S,ST,SU,T,U,	Cauliflower, 'Idol' Mini	D,M,V
	V,VH,YA	Cauliflower, 'Igloo'	DT
Cauliflower, 'Alpha 5'	M	Cauliflower, 'Imp. Majestic'	BS
Cauliflower, 'Alpha Ajubro' F1	BS	Cauliflower, 'Inca'	B,BS,CO,K,KI,SU
Cauliflower, 'Alverda'	B,CO,KI,KS,SU,TU,V	Cauliflower, 'Jaudy'	YA
Cauliflower, 'Angers No 1 - Extra Early'	BS	Cauliflower, 'Jerome'	M
Cauliflower, 'Angers No 4 - Late'	BS	Cauliflower, 'Kestel'	TU
Cauliflower, 'Angers No 5 - Extra Late'	BS	Cauliflower, 'Kibo'	V
Cauliflower, 'April Queen'	BS	Cauliflower, 'King'	B,BS,KI,YA
Cauliflower, 'Arbon'	BS	Cauliflower, 'King' mini	U
Cauliflower, 'Arcade'	M	Cauliflower, 'Late June(EWK)'	BS,KI
Cauliflower, 'Asmer Snowcap March'	M	Cauliflower, 'Lateman'	DT,K,TU,VH
Cauliflower, 'Asterix' F1	BD	Cauliflower, 'Lateman' Mini	F
Cauliflower, 'Aston Purple' F1	YA	Cauliflower, 'Lawyna'	BS
Cauliflower, 'Astral' F1	YA	Cauliflower, 'Leamington'	BS
Cauliflower, 'Aubade'	F	Cauliflower, 'Lecerf'	V
Cauliflower, 'Autumn Giant'	B,BD,BS,C,J,KI,M,Mc,	Cauliflower, 'Lenton Monarch'	BS
	ST,VH	Cauliflower, 'Limelight'	J,M,U
Cauliflower, 'Autumn Giant 3'	BS,T	Cauliflower, 'Lincoln Early'	BS
Cauliflower, 'Aut. Giant 4 Veitch's Self Prot'	BS,D	Cauliflower, 'Marmalade' F1	D,L,YA
Cauliflower, 'Aut. Giant Superlative Prot'	S	Cauliflower, 'May Blossom'	BS
Cauliflower, 'Autumn Glory'	BS,U	Cauliflower, 'Maystar'	BS,CO,KI,SU,TU
Cauliflower, 'Baco'	BS	Cauliflower, 'Mechelse-Carillon'	BS
Cauliflower, 'Balmoral' F1	DT,YA	Cauliflower, 'Medallion'	KI
Cauliflower, 'Bambi'	T	Cauliflower, 'Midsummer'	BS
Cauliflower, 'Barrier Reef'	B,BD,BS,C,DT,J,KI,L,M,	Cauliflower, 'Minaret' F1	TU
	S,SU,ST,TU	Cauliflower, 'Montano'	M
Cauliflower, 'Batsman'	F,TU	Cauliflower, 'Nautilus' F1	DT,K
Cauliflower, 'Beauty' F1	D,K	Cauliflower, 'Nevada'	BS
Cauliflower, 'Belot'	KI	Cauliflower, 'November Heading'	BS
Cauliflower, 'Boston Prize Early'	BS	Cauliflower, 'Orange Bouquet'	KS
Cauliflower, 'Briac'	BS,YA	Cauliflower, 'Oze White Top'	BS
Cauliflower, 'Calan'	BS	Cauliflower, 'Pacific Charm'	BS
Cauliflower, 'Cambridge Early Giant'	BS	Cauliflower, 'Panda'	BS
Cauliflower, 'Cambridge Mid Giant'	BS	Cauliflower, 'Perfection'	B,BS,KI,SU,YA
Cauliflower, 'Candid Charm' F1	B,BS,CO,KI,ST,SU,TU	Cauliflower, 'Plana' F1	M,SE,T,TU,U

CAULIFLOWER

Cauliflower, 'Predial'	B,BS
Cauliflower, 'Predominant'	BS
Cauliflower, 'Profil'	B,BS
Cauliflower, 'Purple Cape'	B,BS,C,CO,D,J,M,SU, TU,U,V
Cauliflower, 'Revito'	YA
Cauliflower, 'Romanesco'	B,BS,V
Cauliflower, 'Rosalind'	M
Cauliflower, 'Saint George'	BS,C,J
Cauliflower, 'Shannon'	J
Cauliflower, 'Snow Cap'	B,BD,BS,CO,KI,TU
Cauliflower, 'Snow Crown' F1	BS,KI,M,U
Cauliflower, 'Snow February'	BS
Cauliflower, 'Snow King'	BS
Cauliflower, 'Snow March'	BS
Cauliflower, 'Snow Prince'	BS,KI,ST
Cauliflower, 'Snowball'	B,BD,BS,D,F,J,KI,Mc,S, ST,SU
Cauliflower, 'Snowbred' F1	BS,C,CO,KI,TU
Cauliflower, 'Snowy River'	BS
Cauliflower, 'Solide'	B,BS
Cauliflower, 'Spalding'	K
Cauliflower, 'Stella' F1	CO,KI
Cauliflower, 'Taroke'	BS
Cauliflower, 'Taymount' F1	DT,YA
Cauliflower, 'Tico' F1	K
Cauliflower, 'Triskel'	YA
Cauliflower, 'Tulchan' F1	S,YA
Cauliflower, 'Valentine'	D
Cauliflower, 'Vidoke'	BS
Cauliflower, 'Vilna'	BS,DT,L
Cauliflower, 'Violet Queen'	BS,CO,KI,S,SU,T,TU,V
Cauliflower, 'Violet Sicilian'	KS
Cauliflower, 'Vision'	L,M
Cauliflower, 'Wainfleet'	K
Cauliflower, 'W.Winter 3 - Armado April'	B,BS,BD,CO,D,DT,F,KI, L,M,SE,ST,T,TU,U,VH
Cauliflower, 'W.Winter 3 - Armado Mayo'	B,BS,DT,KI
Cauliflower, 'W.Winter 3 - Thanet'	S
Cauliflower, 'W.Winter 4 - Markanta'	F,M
Cauliflower, 'W.Winter - Albon No. 10'	BS
Cauliflower, 'W.Winter - Armado Quick'	J,V
Cauliflower, 'W.Winter - Armado Tardo'	B,BD,BS
Cauliflower, 'W.Winter - Arminda'	BS
Cauliflower, 'W.Winter - Atares'	BS
Cauliflower, 'W.Winter - Capella'	BS
Cauliflower, 'W.Winter - Centaurus'	BS
Cauliflower, 'W.Winter - Florissant'	BS
Cauliflower, 'W.Winter - Janus'	BS
Cauliflower, 'W.Winter - Pilgrim'	T
Cauliflower, 'W.Winter - Prestige'	BS
Cauliflower, 'W.Winter - St. Mark'	BS
Cauliflower, 'W.Winter - Trisket No. 22'	BS
Cauliflower, 'W.Winter - Uranus'	BS
Cauliflower, 'Wallaby'	B,BS,CO,F,T,TU,VH,YA
Cauliflower, 'White Ball'	F
Cauliflower, 'White Dove'	YA
Cauliflower, 'White Fox'	BS
Cauliflower, 'White Rock'	B,BS,CO,DT,KI
Cauliflower, 'Winter Selection'	M
Cauliflower, 'Woomera'	YA
Cauliflower, 'Yann'	BS,YA
Cauliflower, 'Yuletide'	S
Cauliflower, 'YX D377' F1	YA
Cauliflower, 'Zara'	BS
Celeriac, 'Alabaster'	BS,F,J,V
Celeriac, 'Balder'	BS,C,CO,KI
Celeriac, 'Brilliant'	D,VH
Celeriac, 'Cesar' F1	L
Celeriac, 'Diament'	K
Celeriac, 'Giant Prague'	BD,BS,DT,KI,KS,Mc,ST, SU,TU
Celeriac, 'Iram'	U
Celeriac, 'Marble Ball'	BS
Celeriac, 'Mentor'	T
Celeriac, 'Monarch'	BS
Celeriac, 'Snevhide'	M
Celeriac, 'Tellus'	S
Celery, 'American Green'	BS
Celery, 'Avon Pearl'	BS
Celery, 'Brydon's Prize Red'	BD
Celery, 'Celebrity'	B,BS,D,DT,L,M,SE,TU, YA
Celery, 'Celery Leaf'	CO
Celery, Chinese	CO,KS
Celery, Chinese, 'Kintsai'	B,D,SU
Celery, 'Clayworth Pink'	B,SU
Celery, Cutting	D,S,SU,V
Celery, 'Giant Green'	BS
Celery, 'Giant Red'	B,BS,C,KI,M,TU,YA
Celery, 'Giant White'	B,BD,BS,C,D,DT,F,KI,ST, TU
Celery, 'Golden Self Blanching'	B,BD,C,CO,KI,ST
Celery, 'Golden Self Blanching 2'	TU
Celery, 'Golden Self Blanching 3'	BS,F,J,S
Celery, 'Golden Spartan'	BS
Celery, 'Green Sleeves'	BS
Celery, 'Green Utah'	B,BS,CO,KI
Celery, 'Greensnap'	BS
Celery, 'Hopkins Fenlander'	BS,L,M,T,VH
Celery, 'Ideal'	K
Celery, 'Ivory Towers'	F, S
Celery, 'Lathom Blanching-Galaxy'	T,VH
Celery, 'Lathom Self-Blanching'	B,BS,R,SU,U
Celery, 'Lathom Self-Blanching - Jason'	BS
Celery, 'Mammoth White and Pink'	RO
Celery, 'Martine'	RO
Celery, 'Multipak'	BS
Celery, 'Pearly Queen'	BS
Celery, 'Pink Champagne'	DT
Celery, 'Ramon' F1	DT
Celery, 'Selfire'	BS
Celery, 'Solid Pink'	CO,S
Celery, 'Solid White'	CO,S
Celery, 'Tall Utah Triumph'	B,J,S,V
Celery, 'Tendercrisp'	BS
Celery, 'Utah 52-70'	BS
Celery, 'Victoria' F1	B,BS,D,DT,M,T
Celery, white K's selection	K
Celery, 'White Pascal'	BS, J,KI,SU
Celtuce	BS,CO,KS,Mc,SU,T,TU
Celtuce, 'Majesty'	V
Chicory, Alouette	F,T
Chicory, 'Apollo'	DT,M
Chicory, 'Bianca di Milano'	BS,SU
Chicory, 'Biondissima di Trieste'	SU
Chicory, 'Brussels Witloof'	B,BD,CO,KI,SU
Chicory, 'Chioggia Giant'	KS
Chicory, 'Cilantro'	S
Chicory, 'Del Veneto'	KS
Chicory, 'Du Pere Vendi'	VS
Chicory, 'Extra Fine de Louvier'	VS

CHICORY

Chicory, 'Gradina'	BS
Chicory, 'Grummolo Biondo'	KS
Chicory, 'Grummolo Verde'	CO,KI,KS,SU,V
Chicory, 'Kristalkopf'	T,V,VH
Chicory, 'Madgeburg' (lge root)	BS,SU
Chicory, 'Puntarella'	KS
Chicory, 'Rubello'	VH
Chicory, 'Spadona'	KS
Chicory, 'Sugar Loaf'	BS,CO,DT,F,KI,S,ST,SU, TU
Chicory, 'Trieste'	KS
Chicory, Winter Fare	D
Chicory, Witloof	BS,C,F,J,ST,TU
Chicory, 'Witloof- Rouge Carla' F1	V
Chicory, 'Witloof -Terosa'	V
Chicory, 'Witloof Zoom' F1	D,SU,V
Chicory, 'Zuckerhut'	KS
Chinese Greens Veg Pack	T
Chinese Melon, bitter	KS,SN
Chinese Melon, winter	KS,SN
Chinese Mustard	BS,K,SU
Chinese Mustard, 'Bao Sin'	V
Chinese Mustard, 'Green in Snow'	CO,Mc,KI,SU,TU
Chinese Mustard, 'Kaisoi'	Su
Chinese Mustard, 'Swollen Stem' F1	V
Chop Suey Greens	BS,C,CO,D,DT,F,KI,L, Mc,SU,TU
Claytonia, Miner's Lettuce(Winter Purslane)	C,S,SU,TU,V
Corn Salad, 'Cavallo'	T,YA
Corn Salad, 'Elan'	T,U
Corn Salad, 'English Broad Leaved'	TU
Corn Salad, 'Grote N-Hollandse'	V
Corn Salad, 'Jade'	F,M
Corn Salad, Lamb's Lettuce	B,J,KS,Mc,SG,ST
Corn Salad, 'Large Leaved'	BS,C,CO,D,KI,S,SU
Corn Salad, 'Valgros'	TU
Corn Salad, 'Verte de Cambrai'	B,BS,CO,K,SU
Corn Salad, 'Vit'	B,DT,KI,SU
Courgette, 'Acceste' F1	K
Courgette, 'All Green Bush'	BD,BS,C,CO,DT,F,J,KI, Mc,SE,ST,T,VH
Courgette, 'Ambassador' F1	B,BD,BS,CO,D,DT,L,M, R,SE,SN,TU,YA
Courgette, 'Ambassador' Mini	F
Courgette, 'Bambino'	BS
Courgette, 'Belor' F1	BS
Courgette, 'Black Jack'	BS
Courgette, 'Botna' F1	C
Courgette, 'Brimmer'	BS
Courgette, 'Burpee Golden Zucchini'	BS,S,ST
Courgette, 'Burpee Zucchini' hyb	SN
Courgette, 'Clarella'	CO
Courgette, 'Clarion' F1	B,KI,SU
Courgette, 'Clarita'	U
Courgette, 'Cocozelle'	B,BS
Courgette, 'Cocozelle v Tripolis' o-p org	SN
Courgette, 'Cora' F1	K,YA
Courgette, 'De Nice'	F,T
Courgette, 'Defender' F1	BS,CO,KI,S,SU,T,TU
Courgette, 'Diamant' F1	B,V
Courgette, 'Early Gem'	B,BD,J,KI,U
Courgette, 'Early Yellow Crookneck'	BS,SU
Courgette, 'Elite' F1	BS,DT,KI
Courgette, 'Excalibur' F1	YA
Courgette, 'French Early White' o-p org	SN
Courgette, 'Giada Blanca' hyb org	SN

Courgette, 'Giada' hyb org	SN
Courgette, 'Gold Rush' F1	B,BS,C,D,DT,F,J,KS,L,M, SN,SU,T,TU,U,V,YA
Courgette, 'Greyzin' F1	BS, T
Courgette, 'Grisette de Provence' hyb	SN
Courgette, 'Hercules'	V
Courgette, 'Jemmy' F1	CO,KI
Courgette, 'Leprechaun'	TU
Courgette, 'Lynx' F1	DT
Courgette, 'Market King' F1	BS
Courgette, 'Moreno' F1	F,YA
Courgette, 'Nice Long'	VS
Courgette, 'Nice Round'	VS
Courgette, 'Opal' F1	DT
Courgette, 'Patriot' F1	B,BD,TU
Courgette, 'Patriot' Mini	M
Courgette, 'President' F1	B,BS,YA
Courgette, 'Raven' F1	F
Courgette, Salad Collection	T
Courgette, 'Saracen' F1	DT
Courgette, 'Sardane' F1	T
Courgette, Selection	M
Courgette, 'Seneca Zucchini' F1	BS,YA
Courgette, 'Spineless Beauty'	BS
Courgette, 'Storr's Green' hyb	SN,YA
Courgette, 'Super Select'	BS
Courgette, 'Supremo' F1	SE,T
Courgette, 'Supremo' F1 Mini	D
Courgette, 'Tarmino'	U
Courgette, 'Taxi'	F
Courgette, 'Tondo di Nizza'	B,BS,CO,KI,ST,SU
Courgette, 'Triple 5'	DT
Courgette, 'Tromboncino'	B,BS,CO,SU
Courgette, 'Zucchini Dark Green'	BS
Courgette, 'Zucchini' F1	B,BS,CO,D,DT,F,KI,M, Mc,S,ST,SU,TU,U,VH
Courgette, 'Zucchini Select'	M
Cress, 'Armada'	M
Cress, 'Curled'	C,J,M,S
Cress, 'Double Curled'	ST
Cress, 'Extra Double Curled'	D
Cress, 'Fine Curled'	B,BS,DT,F,KI,SU,TU,U
Cress, Garden, 'Extra Curled'	T
Cress, 'Greek'	B,BS,CO,SU
Cress, 'Land' (American)	BS,C,CO,D,J,KI,M,Mc,S, ST,SU,T, TU,V,VH
Cress, 'Mega'	T
Cress, 'Moss Curled'	KS
Cress, Plain	BD,BS,KI,L,ST,VH
Cress, Super Salad	D
Cress, Water	BD,BS,C,CO,D,KI,KS, ST,SU
Cress, Water Imp Lge Leaved	BS
Cucumber, 'Aidas' F1	K,T
Cucumber, 'Alert' F1	VH
Cucumber, 'Aramon' F1	B,BS
Cucumber, 'Armenian Yard Long'	KS
Cucumber, 'Athene' F1	M
Cucumber, 'Avanti' F1	BS,KI
Cucumber, 'Bedfordshire Prize Ridge'	BS,C,KI,Mc,ST,YA
Cucumber, 'Bella' F1	S
Cucumber, 'Beta Alphee' f1	SU
Cucumber, 'Bianco Lungo di Parigi'	C
Cucumber, 'Bimbostar' F1	V
Cucumber, 'Birgit' F1	B,BD,BS,D,DT,F,KI,L,SE
Cucumber, 'Brocade'	V

CUCUMBER

Variety	Code
Cucumber, 'Bronco' F1	YA
Cucumber, 'Brunex' F1	B,BS,CO,R,S,YA
Cucumber, 'Burpless Tasty Green' F1	B,BD,BS,CO,DT,F,KI,L, M,S,SE,ST,SU,T,TU,U, V,VH
Cucumber, 'Bush Champion' F1	B,CO,D,DT,F,KI,S,SU,T
Cucumber, 'Bush Crop' F1	B,M
Cucumber, 'Butcher's D.R.'	BS
Cucumber, 'Carmen' F1	B,BS,T,VH
Cucumber, Chinese 'Tseng Gwa'	V
Cucumber, 'Conqueror'	CO,D
Cucumber, 'Corona' F1	V
Cucumber, 'Crystal Apple'	B,BD,BS,C,DT,KI,S,SU
Cucumber, 'Crystal Lemon'	CO,ST
Cucumber, 'Crystal Lemon' o-p org	SN
Cucumber, 'Cumlaud'	K
Cucumber, 'Danimas' F1 Mini	D,T,YA
Cucumber, 'Diana' F1	BS,KI,SN,TU,U
Cucumber, 'Euphya' F1	B,BS,J
Cucumber, 'Experimental TM/MO8'	T
Cucumber, 'Fanfare' hyb	KS
Cucumber, 'Fatum'	U
Cucumber, 'Fembaby' F1	T
Cucumber, 'Femdan' F1	BS,DT
Cucumber, 'Femspot' F1	B,BS,F,S,TU
Cucumber, 'Femunex' F1	B,BS,CO,KI,Mc,ST,SU
Cucumber, 'Fitness' F1	YA
Cucumber, 'Flamingo' F1	BS
Cucumber, 'Gherkin'	KI,SU
Cucumber, 'Hana' F1	BS
Cucumber, 'II57' F1	YA
Cucumber, 'Jamaican' o-p org	SN
Cucumber, 'Janeen' F1 Mini	YA
Cucumber, 'Japanese Yamoto'	BS,CO,KI,Mc,SN,SU
Cucumber, 'Jazzer' F1	T,VH
Cucumber, 'Jessica' F1	K
Cucumber, 'King George'	RO
Cucumber, 'Kyoto'	B,BS
Cucumber, 'Lange Gele Tros'	V
Cucumber, 'Lemon'	B,KS
Cucumber, 'Long Green Ridge'	BD,J,S,V
Cucumber, 'Marketeer'	BS
Cucumber, 'Marketmore'	B,DT,M
Cucumber, 'Masterpiece'	BS,CO,KI,SN
Cucumber & Melon, Chitted Seed	M
Cucumber, 'Mervita'	V
Cucumber, 'Mistral' F1	D
Cucumber, 'Mustang' F1	YA
Cucumber, Oriental 'Soo Yoh'	KS
Cucumber, 'Paska' F1	C,J
Cucumber, 'Passandra' F1	D
Cucumber, 'Pepinex 69' F1	D,DT,J,K,M
Cucumber, 'Perfection'	B,BS,L
Cucumber, 'Petita' F1	B,BD,BS,CO,D,DT,F,J, KI,L,S,SU,U
Cucumber, 'Richmond Green Apple'	
Cucumber, 'Simpson's Sweet Success' F1	SN
Cucumber, 'Slice King' F1	CO,KI,SN,SU
Cucumber, 'Superator'	B,BS,L
Cucumber, 'Support' F1	YA
Cucumber, 'Telegraph'	CO,D,J,R,S,SN
Cucumber, 'Telegraph Imp'	B,BD,DT,F,KI,L,M,S,ST, SU,TU,U,VH
Cucumber, 'Telstar'	DT
Cucumber, 'Tokyo Slicer'	U
Cucumber, 'Topsy'	U
Cucumber, 'Toret'	BS
Cucumber, 'Toro'	BS
Cucumber, 'Tyria' ch.s	M
Cucumber, 'Tyria' F1	B,BS,M
Cucumber, 'Uniflora' F1	VH
Cucumber, 'White Wonder'	B,V
Dandelion, 'Thick Leaved'	C,SU,VS
Dandelion, 'Volhart'	V
Edible Burdock, Mitoya Shirohada	C,CO,SU,V
Edible Flowers Mixed	T,V
Edinle Flower Petal Salad	T
Endive, 'Atria'	YA
Endive, 'Batavian Green'	B,CO,TU
Endive, 'Bossa'	B,V,VH
Endive, 'Brevo'	V
Endive, 'Dolly'	BS
Endive, 'Dorana'	YA
Endive, 'Elysee'	YA
Endive, 'Eminence'	DT
Endive, 'Glory'	YA
Endive, 'Golda'	U
Endive, 'Green Curled'	B,KI,KS
Endive, 'Green Moss Curled'	J,Mc,ST,TU,V
Endive, 'Ione'	D
Endive, 'Italian Fine Curled'	KS
Endive, 'Jeti'	B,BS,KI
Endive, 'Malan'	V
Endive, 'Minerva'	YA
Endive, 'Moss Curled'	C,CO,S
Endive, 'No 52'	BS
Endive, 'Oxalie'	B,BD
Endive, 'Plain leaf En Cornet de Bordeaux'	B,ST
Endive, 'Riccia Pancalieri'	BS,CO,KI,SU
Endive, 'Ruffec'	BS,F,KS
Endive, 'Saint Laurent'	KS
Endive, 'Sally'	BS,M,YA
Endive, 'Tres Fine Maraichere'	KS,SU,T,VH
Endive, 'Wallonne'	SU
Endive, 'White Curled'	KS
Fenugreek, 'T&M Spicy'	T
Florence Fennel	B,C,F,VS
Florence Fennel, 'Cantino'	CO,KI,M,Mc,SU,TU
Florence Fennel, 'Herald'	T
Florence Fennel, 'Perfection'	SU
Florence Fennel, 'Sirio'	S
Florence Fennel, 'Sweet'	CO,KI
Florence Fennel, 'Zefa Fino'	B,BD,BS,D,DT,F,KS,L,U, V
Florence Fennel, 'Zefa Tardo'	KS
Garden Huckleberry o-p	SN
Gherkin, 'Accordia'	B,BD,L
Gherkin, 'Alvin' F1	J
Gherkin, 'Arena' F1	M
Gherkin, 'Bestal' F1	M
Gherkin, 'Boston Green'	BS
Gherkin, 'Conda' F1	DT,U
Gherkin, 'Experimental TM/MO7'	T
Gherkin, 'Fanfare' F1	F
Gherkin, 'Hokus'	BS
Gherkin, 'Liberty' F1	T
Gherkin, 'National Pickling'	BS,C,CO,ST
Gherkin, 'Parisian Pickling'	BS,D,S
Gherkin, 'Pointsett'	BS
Gherkin, 'Venlo Pickling'	BS,D,S
Golden Berry	T
Good King Henry	C,Mc,SU,U,V

GOURD

Gourd, African	VS	Kale, 'Westfalian'	HD
Gourd, Antilles	VS	Kale, 'Westland Autumn'	D
Gourd, Armenian	VS	Kale, 'Winterbor' F1	BS,F,KI,TU,YA
Gourd, 'Blue Hill' F1	V	Kiwano	C
Gourd, Calabash	B,VS	Kohl Rabi, 'Danube Purple'	B,KI
Gourd, Calabash Mini	VS	Kohl Rabi, 'Danube White'	B,CO,KI
Gourd, 'Cou Tors'	VS	Kohl Rabi, 'Gigante'	KS
Gourd, Decorative	VS	Kohl Rabi, 'Lanro'	D,V
Gourd, Decorative 'Amphore'	VS	Kohl Rabi, 'Logo'	S
Gourd, Decorative 'Plate de Course'	VS	Kohl Rabi, 'Rolano'	L
Gourd, Decorative 'Trombolino d'Albinga'	VS	Kohl Rabi, 'Rolano' Mini	D
Gourd, Devil's	VS	Kohl Rabi, 'Rowel'	M,U
Gourd, Edible	KS	Kohl Rabi, 'Superschmelz'	V
Gourd, 'Giant Bottle'	V	Kohl Rabi, 'Trero' F1	T
Gourd, Jointed	V	Kohl Rabi, 'Vienna Green'	B,BD,BS,DT,F,J,KI,Mc,
Gourd, 'Long Green'	VS		ST,SU,TU
Gourd, 'Marenka'	VS	Kohl Rabi, 'Vienna Purple'	B,BD,BS,C,CO,D,DT,J,
Gourd, 'Miniature Bottle'	KS,V		KI,KS,L,Mc, S,ST,SU,
Gourd, 'Paris Long White'	VS		TU,V
Gourd, 'Paris Small Green'	VS	Kohl Rabi, 'White Vienna'	C,CO,S,TU
Gourd, Russian	VS	Leaf Beet, 'Fordbrook Giant'	U
Green Soy Bean	CO	Leaf Beet, Italian	SU
Ground Cherry	C	Leaf Beet, Perpetual Spinach	B,BD,BS,C,CO,D,DT,F,J,
Japanese Greens, Mibuna	CO,KS,SU		KI,KS,L,M,Mc,ST,T,TU,
Japanese Greens, Misome hyb	KS		U,V,VS,YA
Japanese Greens, Mizuna Greens	BS,C,CO,K,KI,KS,Mc,	Leaf Beet, Rhubarb Chard	B,BS,CO,D,J,K,KI,L,Mc,
	SU,TU,V,YA		S,ST,SU,T,TU,V
Japanese Greens, Mizuna Gr 'Tokyo Belle'	KS	Leaf Beet, Rhubarb Chard 'Vulcan'	F
Japanese Greens, Mizuna Gr, 'Youzen'	D	Leaf Beet, Swiss Chard	B,BD,CO,KI,Mc,ST,TU
Japanese greens, Mustard Lettuce	KS	Leaf Beet, Swiss Chard, 'Erbette'	B,BS,SU
Japanese gr., Must. Spinach 'Savannah' F1	KS	Leaf Beet, Swiss Chard, 'Lucullus'	BS, T, V
Japanese greens, Mustard-Horned	KS	Leaf Beet Swiss Chard, 'White Silver'	DT
Japanese greens, Mustard-Salad	KS	Leek, 'Alaska'	BS,TU
Japanese gr., Swatow Mustard Cabbage	KS	Leek, 'Albinstar'	BS,KI,CO,S
Japanese Greens, Tendergreen	C	Leek, 'Alma'	BS
Japanese Greens, Texel Greens	BS,CO,DT,Mc,SU,TU	Leek, 'Ardea'	B,BS
Japanese Greens, Tsai-Hsin	BS,CO, Mc,SU,TU,YA	Leek, 'Argenta'	CO
Japanese Parsley, Mitsuba	BS,KI,KS,Mc,TU	Leek, 'Arial'	DT
Jicama	C	Leek , 'Armor'	YA
Kale, 'Asparagus'	HD	Leek, 'Autumn Giant 2-Argenta'	D,T,TU,V
Kale, 'B.J. 1628' F1	K	Leek, 'Autumn Giant 3 - Rami'	S,YA
Kale, 'Bornic' F1	BS	Leek, 'Autumn Mammoth 2 * Walton'	BS,DT,M,TU
Kale, 'Buffalo' F1	BS,TU	Leek, 'Autumn Mammoth Goliath'	TU
Kale, 'Cavalo Nero'	M	Leek , 'Autumn Mammoth Snowstar 2'	D,F,J
Kale, Chinese, 'Green Lance' F1	BS,C,CO,KI,Mc,SN,V	Leek, 'Autumn Mammoth Startrack'	J
Kale, Chinese, 'Kailaan'	BS,KI,Mc,SU,YA	Leek, 'Autumn Mammoth Verina'	U
Kale, Chinese, 'Kintsai'	B,KI,Mc	Leek, 'Autumn Mammoth Wintra RZ'	BD,TU
Kale, 'Cottagers'	BS	Leek, 'Bandit'	DT
Kale, 'Darkibor' F1	D,DT,L	Leek, 'Bastion'	B,BS
Kale, 'Dwarf Green Curled'	B,BD,BS,CO,D,DT,F,J,	Leek, 'Blizzard'	B,BS,VH
	KI,L,M,S,ST,SU,T,TU,U,	Leek, 'Blue-Green Autumn Cortina'	J,TU,V
	V	Leek, 'Bluestar'	BS
Kale, 'Dwarf Green Curled - Afro'	BS	Leek, 'Bulgaria'	BS
Kale, 'Fribor' F1	BD,BS,CO,KI,TU,VH	Leek, 'Carlton' F1	D,S
Kale, 'Hungry Gap'	M, TU	Leek, 'Catalina'	BS
Kale, 'Pentland Brig'	BS,CO,DT,KI,M,Mc,SU,	Leek, Chinese, Broad Leaf (Chinese Chives)	C,KS
	TU,U	Leek, 'Coloma'	HD
Kale, 'Ragged Jack'	HD	Leek, 'Colossal'	HD
Kale, 'Red Russian'	B,KS	Leek, 'Conora'	CO,KI,YA
Kale, 'Redbore' F1	K	Leek, 'Derrick'	BS,KI,L
Kale, 'Savoy Salad'	KS	Leek, 'Elefant'	BS
Kale, 'Showbor' F1	D,K,S	Leek, 'Elina'	BS
Kale, 'Siberian'	HD	Leek, 'Emperor'	BS
Kale, 'Spurt'	T	Leek, 'Farinto'	C
Kale, 'Tall Green Curled'	B,BD,BS,M,TU	Leek, 'Gavia'	BS
Kale, 'Thousand Head'	S,SU,TU,U	Leek, 'Genita'	V

LEEK

Leek, 'Gennevilliers Splendid'	BS,SU,U
Leek, 'Giant Winter'	CO,KI,Mc,ST
Leek, 'Giant Winter 3'	BS,F
Leek, 'Giant Winter * Carina'	M
Leek, 'Giant Winter * Wila'	M
Leek, 'Goliath'	BS,Mc
Leek, 'Hanniabal'	BS
Leek, 'Jolant'	B,BD,BS,L,TU,VH
Leek, 'Jolant' Mini	M
Leek, 'Kajak'	BS,CO,KI,SU
Leek, 'Kelvedon King'	BS
Leek, 'King Richard'	BS,CO,KI,M,R,SE,SU,T, TU,U,VH,YA
Leek, 'King Richard' Mini	D,S
Leek, 'Lancelot'	K
Leek, 'Laura'	B,KI
Leek, 'Lavi'	BS,YA
Leek, 'Long Blanch'	K
Leek, 'Long Bow'	BS,DT
Leek, 'Longa'	BS
Leek, 'Lyon'	B,BS,DT,J,Mc,ST,T
Leek, 'Lyon 2 - Prizetaker'	BS,F,S
Leek, 'Malabar'	BS
Leek, 'Mammoth Blanch'	RO
Leek, 'Mammoth Pot'	RO
Leek, 'Monstruoso di Carentan'	B,BS,CO,SU
Leek, 'Musselburgh'	B,BD,BS,C,CO,D,DT,F,J, KI,L,M,Mc,S,ST,SU,TU, U,VH
Leek, 'Musselburgh Improved'	T
Leek, 'Odin Longstanton'	BS
Leek, 'Pancho'	BS,D,TU
Leek, 'Poribleu'	D
Leek, 'Poristo' Mini	F
Leek, Pot K's strain	K
Leek, 'Prenora'	DT,KI
Leek, 'Prizetaker'	KI
Leek, 'Romil'	YA
Leek, 'Senora'	YA
Leek, 'Siegfried Frost'	YA
Leek, 'Snowstar B'	BS
Leek, 'St. Victor'	CO,SU
Leek, 'Startrack'	DT
Leek, 'Sterna'	DT
Leek, 'Swiss Giant - Coloma'	BS
Leek, 'Tadorna'	B,BS
Leek, 'The Lyon'	CO,KI
Leek, 'Thor'	BS
Leek, 'Titan'	BS
Leek, 'Toledo'	BS,T
Leek, 'Tropita'	BS,KI
Leek, 'Verina'	BS
Leek, 'Winora'	T,YA
Leek, 'Winter'	B,RO
Leek, 'Winter Crop'	S
Leek, 'Winterreuzen'	BS
Leek, 'Wintra'	B,BS,KI,L,SU
Leek, 'Yates Empire'	BS,U
Lettuce, 'Abba'	K
Lettuce, 'Action'	F,SE
Lettuce, 'All The Year Round'	BS,C,CO,D,DT,F,J,KI,M, Mc,S,ST, T,TU,U,VH
Lettuce, 'Ambassador'	BS
Lettuce, 'Arctic King'	BS,KI,S,ST,TU,VH
Lettuce, 'Attraction'	KI
Lettuce, 'Avoncrisp'	BS,CO,KI,M,ST,TU

Lettuce, 'Avondefiance'	B,BD,BS,CO,D,KI,L,M,S, SU,YA
Lettuce, 'Babylon'	T
Lettuce, 'Balloon'	BS,KI,SN,SU
Lettuce, 'Baltic'	M
Lettuce, 'Bastion'	J
Lettuce, Batavia 'Goutte de Sang'	VS
Lettuce, Batavia 'La Brillante'	VS
Lettuce, Batavia 'Reine des Glaces'	VS
Lettuce, 'Bath Cos'	HD
Lettuce, 'Beatrice'	B,BS,CO,KI,SU,T,VH
Lettuce, 'Bikini'	YA
Lettuce, 'Biscia Rossa'	SU
Lettuce, 'Black Seeded Simpson'	KS,SN
Lettuce, 'Blonde Groene'	V
Lettuce, 'Blush'	D,YA
Lettuce, 'Borough Wonder'	ST
Lettuce, 'British Hilde'	M
Lettuce, 'Brown Goldring'	B,HD
Lettuce, 'Bruna di Germania'	SU
Lettuce, 'Bubbles'	B,D,K,L,T
Lettuce, 'Burgundy Boston'	BS,KI,Mc,SN
Lettuce, 'Buttercrunch'	B,BS,CO,D,J,KI,ST,SU, U,VH
Lettuce, 'Butterscotch'	T
Lettuce, 'Capital'	L
Lettuce, 'Capuccio'	VS
Lettuce, 'Cartan'	BS
Lettuce, 'Catalogna'	CO,SU
Lettuce, 'Challenge'	S
Lettuce, 'Clarion'	B,BS,DT,K,KI,L
Lettuce, 'Cobham Green'	B,BS
Lettuce, 'Cocarde'	CO,SU
Lettuce, collection	KI,M
Lettuce, 'Columbus'	BS,D
Lettuce, 'Conny'	M,TU
Lettuce, 'Continuity'	B,BS,CO,KI,ST,TU
Lettuce, 'Corsair'	BS,D,DT,SE,T
Lettuce, 'Cortina'	SU
Lettuce, 'Cosmic'	BS,D,SE,T
Lettuce, 'Crestana'	F
Lettuce, 'Crispino Mini'	BS,U
Lettuce, 'Cynthia'	B,BS
Lettuce, 'Daphne'	BS
Lettuce, 'Dark Green Cos'	VS
Lettuce, 'De Pologne'	BS
Lettuce, 'Delta'	S
Lettuce, 'Diamant'	KS
Lettuce, 'Diamond Gem'	BS
Lettuce, 'Diana'	U
Lettuce, 'Dolly'	CO,KI,SU
Lettuce, 'Dynasty'	T
Lettuce, 'El Toro'	VS
Lettuce, 'Express'	BS
Lettuce, 'Favourite'	HD
Lettuce, 'Feuille de Chene'	T
Lettuce, 'Fortune'	B,D,J,SE,T,TU,U
Lettuce, Fresh Salad Mix	BS
Lettuce, 'Frisby'	VS
Lettuce, 'Grand Rapids'	B,BS,DT,KI,M,Mc,ST,U
Lettuce, 'Grasse Madrilene'	BS
Lettuce, 'Great Lakes'	KS
Lettuce, 'Great Lakes 659 Mesa'	YA
Lettuce, 'Green Ice'	BS,U,VH
Lettuce, 'Greenway'	
Lettuce, 'Hilde II'	

LETTUCE

Lettuce, 'Hudson' — BS
Lettuce, 'Ibis' — K
Lettuce, 'Iceberg' — B,BD,BS,CO,J,KI,Mc, ST,SU,T,VH
Lettuce, 'Iceberg 2' — TU
Lettuce, 'Iceberg' mini green — VH
Lettuce, 'Imperial Winter' — B,BS,CO
Lettuce, 'Impulse' — K
Lettuce, 'Ithaca' — B,BS
Lettuce, 'Jackpot' — BS
Lettuce, 'Jaguar' — DT
Lettuce, 'Jewel' — BS,DT,S
Lettuce, 'Karola' — V
Lettuce, 'Kelly's' — B,BS,CO,DT,KI,L,M,SU, TU,U,V
Lettuce, 'Kendo' — F
Lettuce, 'King Crown' — BS,SN
Lettuce, 'Kloek' — BS,ST
Lettuce, 'Kwiek' — BS,CO,S,ST
Lettuce, 'La Premiere' — VS
Lettuce, 'Lactuca Angustana' — HD
Lettuce, 'Lake Nyah' — BS
Lettuce, 'Lakeland' — BS,D,DT,F,L,M,SE,U,VH
Lettuce, 'Leopard' — DT
Lettuce, 'Lilian' — BS, D
Lettuce, 'Little Gem' — B,BD,BS,CO,D,DT,F,J, KI,KS,L,M,Mc,R,S,SN, ST,SU,T,TU,U,VH,YA
Lettuce, 'Little Gem Ferro' — K
Lettuce, 'Little Leprechaun' — BS,CO,KI,SN,SU,V
Lettuce, 'Lobjoits Green Cos' — B,BS,CO,F,J,KI,M,R,S, SU,TU,YA
Lettuce, 'Lollo Bionda' — B,BD,BS,CO,D,F,KI,KS, SU,M,YA
Lettuce, 'Lollo Biondo - Lobi' — J,V
Lettuce, 'Lollo' Mix — U
Lettuce, 'Lollo Rossa' — B,BD,BS,C,CO,D,DT,F, KI,KS,L,M,Mc,S,ST,SU, T,TU,VH,YA
Lettuce, 'Lollo Rosso- Atsina' — J,V
Lettuce, 'Loos Tennis Ball' — HD
Lettuce, 'Lovina' — KS,YA
Lettuce, 'Malika' — BS,U
Lettuce, 'Marbello' — D
Lettuce, 'Massa' — BS
Lettuce, 'May King' — BS,CO,D,KI,SU
Lettuce, 'MDQS Chaperon' — J, V
Lettuce, 'Merveille des Quatres Saisons' — B,BD,BS,CO,KI,KS,Mc, SN,SU,TU
Lettuce, 'Mescher' — HD
Lettuce, 'Milva' — KI
Lettuce, 'Minetto' — BS
Lettuce, 'Mini Green' — BS,CO,KI,M,SU
Lettuce, 'Miura' — T
Lettuce, Mixed — S
Lettuce, Mixed Leaf Salad — F
Lettuce, Mixed Salad Leaves — D,F,KI,M, U
Lettuce, 'Musette' — B,BS,CO,KI,S,SN,TU
Lettuce, 'Nancy' — B,BS
Lettuce, 'New Red Fire' — T
Lettuce, 'Novita' — BS,CO,KI,M,SE,SU,TU
Lettuce, 'Oak Leaf' — B,KS
Lettuce, 'Ovation' — VH
Lettuce, 'Pablo' — J
Lettuce, 'Pablo' Red — V
Lettuce, 'Parella, Green' — B,SU

Lettuce, 'Parella, Red' — SU
Lettuce, 'Paris Island' — B,BS,SN
Lettuce, 'Paris White' — BS,C,KI,KS,ST
Lettuce, 'Pasquier' — VS
Lettuce, 'Pedro' — YA
Lettuce, 'Pennlake' — BS
Lettuce, 'Perlane' — BS
Lettuce, 'Plevanos' — BS
Lettuce, 'Polana' — YA
Lettuce, 'Poulton Market' — DT
Lettuce, 'Prado' — V
Lettuce, 'Premier Great Lakes' — BS
Lettuce, 'Prestine' — BS
Lettuce, 'Prize Head' — K
Lettuce, 'Rachel' — B,J,L,YA
Lettuce, 'Raisa' — M
Lettuce, 'Ravel' — B,BS,CO,KI,SU,TU
Lettuce, 'Red Fire' — BS,KI,KS,SN
Lettuce, 'Red Iceberg Sioux' — D
Lettuce, 'Red Lettuce' Mix — T
Lettuce, 'Red Sails' — DT,KS
Lettuce, 'Redina' — M
Lettuce, 'Regina dei Ghiacci' — SU
Lettuce, 'Remus' — K
Lettuce, 'Reskia' — B,BS,KI
Lettuce, 'Ricardo' — BS,KI,TU
Lettuce, 'Ricciolina Bionda' — SU
Lettuce, 'Rigoletto' — V
Lettuce, Roman 'Chicon des Charentes' — VS
Lettuce, Roman 'Pomme en Terre' — VS
Lettuce, 'Romance' — J
Lettuce, 'Rosalita' — KS,SU
Lettuce, 'Rossa Fruilana' — SU
Lettuce, 'Rossimo' — KS
Lettuce, 'Rougette du Midi' — SU
Lettuce, 'Royal Frillice' — J, V
Lettuce, 'Royal Oak Leaf' — KS
Lettuce, 'Rusty' — TU
Lettuce, 'Sabrina' — F
Lettuce, 'Salad Bowl' — BS,CO,D,DT,J,KI,KS,M, S,ST,SU,TU,VH
Lettuce, 'Salad Bowl, Red' — B,BS,CO,D,DT,KI,KS,L, S,ST,SU,TU
Lettuce, Salad Bowl,Red - 'Everest' — J, V
Lettuce, Salad Bowl, Red & Green Mix — DT,F
Lettuce, 'Salad Mix' — DT
Lettuce, 'Saladin' — B,BD,BS,C,CO,D,DT,F,J, K,KI,L,SN,ST,TU,U,YA
Lettuce, 'Saladin Supreme' — BS
Lettuce, 'Saladini' — CO
Lettuce, 'Salvo' — YA
Lettuce, 'Sangria' — KS,S,SE
Lettuce, 'Santiago' — F
Lettuce, 'Sherwood' — T
Lettuce, 'Simpson Elite' — B,KS
Lettuce, 'Soprane' — YA
Lettuce, 'St. Antoine' — VS
Lettuce, 'Stoke' — HD
Lettuce, 'Strada' — K
Lettuce, 'Suzan' — B,BS,DT,KI,S,ST,TU
Lettuce, 'Tango' — KS
Lettuce, 'Tiger' — M
Lettuce, 'Timo' — V
Lettuce, 'Toledo' — M,VH
Lettuce, 'Tom Thumb' — B,BD,BS,C,CO,D,DT,F,J, KI,L,M,S,SN,ST,SU,TU

LETTUCE

Lettuce, 'Triumphator'	V
Lettuce, 'Trocadero Improved'	BD,J,KI,SU
Lettuce, 'Unrivalled'	BS,C,CO,S
Lettuce, 'Valdor'	B,BS,CO,D,KI,S,SU,TU
Lettuce, 'Valeria'	D
Lettuce, 'Valeria (Red)'	F,SN
Lettuce, 'Valmaine'	B,BD,BS,CO,KI,SN,SU, VH
Lettuce, 'Vaux Self-Folding'	CO
Lettuce, 'Warpath'	S
Lettuce, 'Webb's Wonderful'	B,BD,BS,C,CO,D,F,J,KI, M,Mc,S,SE,ST,SU,T,TU, U,VH
Lettuce, 'Windermere'	S
Lettuce, 'Winter Crop'	J,V
Lettuce, 'Winter Density'	B,BD,BS,C,CO,D,DT,F,J, KI,M,S,SN,ST,TU,U,V
Lettuce, 'Winter Imperial'	KI,ST
Lettuce, 'Zodiac'	B,BS
Loofah	F,SU,V,VS
Loofah, 'Large Fruit' Smooth	V
Loofah, 'San-C' F1	V
Loofah, 'Seven Star' F1	V
Maize, Decorative Multicoloured	VS
Malabar Spinach	KS,SU
Mallow, Curled	KS
Mangel, 'Prizewinner'	B,CO,KI,SU
Mangel, 'Wintergold'	BS
Marrow, 'Aristocrat' F1	BS
Marrow, 'Badger Cross' F1	BS,K,M,SE
Marrow, 'Bianco Friulano'	BS
Marrow, 'Clarella' F1	BS
Marrow, 'Clarita' F1	BS
Marrow, 'Cobra' F1	BS
Marrow, 'Cousa'	BS
Marrow, 'Custard Yellow'	BS
Marrow, 'Diament' F1	B,BS
Marrow, 'Emerald Cross' F1	B,BD,BS,KI
Marrow, 'Green Bush' F1	B,BD,C,CO,J,R,S,ST,T, TU,VH,YA
Marrow, 'Green Bush Special'	BS
Marrow, 'Green Gem'	BS
Marrow, 'Jackpot'	BS
Marrow, 'Long Green Bush'	KI,Mc,S
Marrow, 'Long Green Bush 2'	BS,D,F,L,U
Marrow, 'Long Green Bush 2' - Imp	BS,S
Marrow, 'Long Green Bush 3- Cobham '	BS
Marrow, 'Long Green Bush 3' - Smallpack	S
Marrow, 'Long Green Bush 4'	DT,M
Marrow, 'Long Green Striped'	S,VH
Marrow, 'Long Green Trailing'	B,BD,BS,CO,D,J,KI,M, ST,TU,U
Marrow, 'Long White Trailing'	K
Marrow, 'Minipak'	BS,C,CO,KI
Marrow, 'Moreno' F1	BS
Marrow, Neapolitan	VS
Marrow, 'Onyx' F1	BS
Marrow, 'Prepak'	BS,CO,D,KI,ST
Marrow, 'Sundance'	BS
Marrow, 'Table Dainty'	BS,K,S
Marrow, 'Tender and True'	S
Marrow, 'Tiger Cross' F1	B,BS,CO,F,KI,L,S,T,TU
Marrow, 'White Bush'	BS
Marrow, 'Zebra Cross'	B,BS,DT,M,YA
Melon, 'Amber Nectar'	B,T

Melon, 'American Ananas'	B,VS
Melon, 'Berlia'	BS
Melon, 'Blenheim Orange'	B,BS,CO,KI,M,S,ST
Melon, 'Charantais'	BS, F,VH
Melon, Chitted Seed	M
Melon, 'Clipper' F1	J
Melon, 'Early Dawn' F1	B,BS
Melon, 'Early Dew'	BS
Melon, 'Early Sweet'	S
Melon, 'Emerald Gem'	S
Melon, 'Experimental'	T
Melon, 'Fuzzy'	KS
Melon, 'Galia' F1	B,BS,T,YA
Melon, 'Geabel' F1	C
Melon, 'Golden Crown' F1	T
Melon, 'Goldstar' F1	V
Melon, 'Green Nutmeg'	HD
Melon, 'Market Pride'	BS
Melon, 'No Name'	V
Melon, 'Ogen'	B,BD,BS,D,DT,J,KI,L,M, Mc,S,SE,ST,SU,T,TU,V
Melon, 'Oranje Ananas'	V
Melon, 'Pasteque a Confiture'	VS
Melon, 'Rapid'	BS
Melon, 'Rock Sunrise'	KS
Melon, 'Rock Sweet n' Early'	KS
Melon, 'Romeo' F1	M
Melon, 'Sweetheart' F1	B,BD,BS,CO,D,DT,F,J, KI,L,M,S,SE,SU,T,TU,YA
Melon, 'Tropical'	KS
Melon, 'Vieille France'	VS
Melon, Water, 'Charleston Gray'	BD,BS,CO,KI,Mc
Melon, Water, 'Chilton'	VS
Melon, Water, 'Crimson Sweet'	BS,J
Melon, Water, Sin F1	D
Melon, Water, 'Sugar Baby'	BS,SU,V
Melon, Water, 'Tiny Orchid'	V
Melon, Water, 'Wanli'	V
Mesclun	KS,SU
Mesclun, Oriental	KS
Mexican Water Chestnut 'Jicama'	KS
Millet	VS
Miscluglio	SU
Mushroom 'Grey Oyster'	CO
Mushroom Spawn, 'Button'	CO
Mushroom Spawn, 'Cultivated'	DT,M
Mushroom Spawn, 'Darlington's Grain'	S
Mushroom Spawn, 'Darlington's No.1'	ST
Mushroom Spawn, 'Darlington's No.2'	ST
Mushroom Spawn, 'Darlington's No.3'	ST
Mushroom Spawn, 'Darlington's Pelleted'	S
Mushroom Spawn, 'Dobies Grain Spawn'	D
Mushroom Spawn, 'Dobies Pelleted'	D
Mushroom Spawn, 'Oyster'	M
Mustard Greens, 'Miike Giant'	SU
Mustard Greens, 'Red Giant'	B,KS,SU,YA
Mustard , Salad 'Kingston'	B,KI,ST,SU,VH
Mustard Spinach, 'Komatsuna'	B,BS,CO,Mc,SU,TU,YA
Mustard Spinach, 'Rondbladige'	V
Mustard Spinach, 'Summer Feast' F1	V
New Zealand Spinach	BS,C,D,J,KS,M,S,V
Okra	B,CG,L,KS
Okra, 'Artist'	V
Okra, 'Burgundy'	KS
Okra, 'Clemson's Spineless'	B,BD,BS,C,DT,F,J,KI,Mc, T,TU,V

255

Okra, 'Dwarf Green Long Pod'	BS
Okra, 'Green Velvet'	B,U
Okra, 'Long Green'	D,S
Okra, 'Penta Green'	BS
Okra, 'Pure Luck' F1	B,BS,KI,ST,SU
Onion, '8838'	BS
Onion, 'A-1 ' (Sutton's)	BS
Onion, 'Ailsa Craig'	B,BD,BS,C,CO,J,KI,L,M, Mc,ST,SU,TU,U,V,VH
Onion, 'Ailsa Craig' Crosslings Seedlings	BS
Onion, 'Ailsa Craig Prizewinner'	DT,F,S
Onion, 'Ailsa Craig' Selected	BS,S
Onion, 'Albion' F1	DT,F,J,M,SE,T,VH
Onion, 'Amigo'	F
Onion, 'Augusta'	BS
Onion, 'Beacon' F1	SE,T,V
Onion, 'Bedfordshire Champion'	B,BD,BS,C,CO,D,DT,F,J, KI,L,M,Mc,S,ST,SU,U
Onion, 'Bedf. Champ. The Sutton Globe'	S
Onion, 'Brunswick'	F,S
Onion, 'Buffalo' F1	B,BS,D,T,TU
Onion, Bulbing, exhibition type	R
Onion, Bunching, 'Hikari'	B,BD,BS,CO,SU,TU,YA
Onion, Bunching, 'Ishiko'	YA
Onion, Bunching, 'Ishikura'	B,BS,CO,F,J,KI,Mc,S, SU,T,TU,U, V
Onion, Bunching, 'Kyoto Market'	BS,D
Onion, Bunching, 'Laser'	YA
Onion, Bunching, 'Long White Tokyo'	C
Onion, Bunching, 'Multi-Stalk Kujo Green'	B,C
Onion, Bunching, 'Parade'	VH
Onion, Bunching, 'Red'	KS
Onion, Bunching, 'Redbeard'	B,BS,CO,SU
Onion, Bunching, 'Scallion'	SU
Onion, Bunching, 'SY 678'	BS
Onion, Bunching, 'White Spear'	YA
Onion, Bunching, 'Winter White'	T
Onion, 'Caribo' F1	T,VH
Onion, 'Contessa'	T,VH
Onion, 'Daytona'	VH
Onion, 'Downing Yellow Globe'	BS
Onion, 'Duraldo'	BS,KI
Onion, 'Early Yellow Globe'	BS
Onion, 'Ebeneezer'	BS
Onion, 'Extra Early Kaizuka'	BS
Onion, 'Giant Zittau'	BS,CO,KI,M
Onion, 'Golden Bear'	BS,CO,KI,SU
Onion, 'High Keeper' F1	K
Onion, 'Hygro' F1	B,BD,BS,CO,D,DT,J,KI, L,M,ST,TU,U
Onion, 'Hyper' F1	BS
Onion, 'Hyrate' F1	BS
Onion, 'Hysam' F1	B,BS,K
Onion, 'Hyton' F1	BS,VH
Onion, Japanese, 'Express Yellow' F1	B,BS,CO,KI,ST,SU
Onion, Japanese, 'Imai Early Yellow'	B,BD,BS,M,YA
Onion, Japanese, 'Indared'	YA
Onion, Japanese 'Keepwell' F1	BS,KI
Onion, Japanese, 'Senshyu Yellow'	B,BD,BS,CO,J,KI,L,M,S, ST,TU,V,YA
Onion, K's selection	K
Onion, 'Lancastrian'	D,F,J,T
Onion, 'Long Red Florence'	B,BS,SU
Onion, 'Lotus'	K
Onion, 'Mammoth Improved'	RO
Onion, 'Mammoth Red'	RO

Onion, 'Maraton' F1 p.s	D
Onion, 'Oakey'	SU
Onion, 'Oporto'	BS
Onion, 'Owa'	F
Onion, 'Own World Record Strain'	K
Onion, Pickling, 'Barletta'	B,BS,SU
Onion, Pickling, 'Brown SY300'	D,DT,S,YA
Onion, Pickling, 'Giant Rocco Brown'	BS
Onion, Pickling, 'Monkston Exhibition'	BS,KI,ST
Onion, Pickling, 'North Holland Flat Yellow'	BS
Onion, Pickling, 'Paris Silverskin'	B,BD,BS,C,CO,DT,F,J, KI,L,M,S,ST,TU,U,V,VH
Onion, Pickling, 'Pompei'	BS
Onion, Pickling, 'Shakespeare Mini'	D,DT,S,YA
Onion, Pickling, 'The Queen'	D
Onion, 'Purplette'	B,CO,KS,SU
Onion, 'Radar' F1	B,BS,K
Onion, 'Red Baron'	B,BD,BS,D,DT,J,K,SE,T, TU,V,VH
Onion, 'Red Italian'	BS
Onion, 'Red Moon'	L
Onion, 'Reliance'	BS,CO
Onion, 'Rijnsburger'	KI,SE,VH
Onion, 'Rijnsburger 2 Sito'	F
Onion, 'Rijnsburger 4'	F,S
Onion, 'Rijnsburger 5 Balstora'	B,BS,DT,J,M,V
Onion, 'Rijnsburger 5 Jumbo'	BS,D
Onion, 'Rijnsburger 5 -Toro'	BS
Onion, 'Rijnsburger Reinaldo'	BS
Onion, 'Rijnsburger Rocky'	YA
Onion, 'Rijnsburger Tamrock'	YA
Onion, 'Robusta'	BS,CO,KI
Onion, 'Romeo'	F
Onion, 'Rossa di Bassano'	B,C
Onion, 'Royal Oak' F1	BS,F
Onion, Salad, 'Long White Tokyo'	KI
Onion, 'Sentry'	BS
Onion, Shallot, 'Ambition' F1	DT,F,K
Onion, Shallot, 'Atlas' F1	B
Onion, Shallot, 'Creation' F1	D,S,T,V,VH
Onion, Shallot, 'Golden Gourmet' F1	D,S,T,V
Onion, Shallot, 'Matador' F1	S
Onion, 'Sherpa' F1	DT,L
Onion, 'Southport Red'	BS,CO,DT,KI,Mc,ST,SU, U
Onion, 'Southport White'	BS
Onion, Spring, 'Emerald Isle'	DT
Onion, Spring, 'Guardsman'	D,DT,M,TU
Onion, Sp., 'N. Holland Blood - Redmate'	F,S,YA
Onion, Spring , 'Santa Clause'	T
Onion, Spring, 'Savel'	M
Onion, Spring, 'White Lisbon'	w.a
Onion, Spring, 'White Lisbon Winter Hardy'	CO,D,DT,F,J,KI,L,Mc,R, S,ST,U,V,YA
Onion, 'Stunova'	V
Onion, 'Suntan' F1	BS
Onion, 'Super Bear'	BS,KI,ST
Onion, 'Sweet Sandwich' F1	CO,KI,ST,T,V
Onion, 'Tarzan'	BS
Onion, 'Torpedo'	C
Onion, 'Toughball' F1	BS,K,YA
Onion, 'TZ 8825' F1	BS
Onion, 'Unwins Exhibition'	U
Onion, Welsh	B,F,KS,M,Mc,ST,V
Onion, Welsh Red	SU
Onion, 'White Knight'	M

ONION

Onion, 'White Portugal'	BS
Onion, 'White Spanish'	BS
Onion, 'White Spear' F1	BS
Onion, 'Winter White Bunching'	BS,M
Onion, 'Winter-Over'	B,BD,BS,TU
Onion, 'Yellow Globe Danvers'	BS
Orach, Blonde	VS
Orach, Green	V,VS
Orach, Red	V,VS
Oriental greens, 'Chinese Green Giant'	KS
Oriental Greens, 'Giant Purple'	KS
Oriental Greens, 'Green Boy'	Mc,V
Oriental greens, 'Green Rocket' F1	SU
Oriental Greens, 'Indian Mustard'	CO,SU,SY
Oriental Vegetables, 'Purple Choy Sum'	SU
Oriental Vegetables, Tsoi-Sim	L
Pak Choi	BS,C,DT,L,Mc,S,U
Pak Choi, 'Canton Dwarf'	V
Pak Choi, Chingesai	D
Pak Choi, 'Flowering' F1	C,KS
Pak Choi, 'Flowering Purple'	C,KS,Mc,TU
Pak Choi, Hon Sai Tai	SN
Pak Choi, Japanese White Celery Mustard	BS,C,CO,KI,Mc,SU
Pak Choi, Joi Choi F1	CO,J,KI,KS,M,Mc,SN, SU,TU,U,V,YA
Pak Choi, 'Kaneko Cross' Hybrid	D
Pak Choi, 'Mei Qing Choi' F1	KS,SN,V,YA
Pak Choi, 'Pueblo'	D,J
Pak Choi, 'Shanghai'	V
Pak Choi, 'Tatsai'	BS,KI,Mc,SU
Papaya	SU
Papaya, 'K.Y. No.1' F1	V
Paprika 'Mild Californian'	SN
Par-Cel, Plain Leaved	KS,T,V
Parsley, 'Bravour'	B,BS,TU,YA
Parsley, 'Calito'	YA
Parsley, 'Champion Moss Curled '	B,BS,CO,K,R
Parsley, 'Champion Moss Curled 2'	J,SE
Parsley, 'Champion Moss Curled 3'	TU
Parsley, 'Clivi'	BS,L
Parsley, 'Consort'	BS
Parsley, 'Curlina'	B,BS,D,M
Parsley, 'Darki'	B,BS,ST,YA
Parsley, 'Envy'	BS,KI,Mc,V
Parsley, 'Extra Triple Curled'	VH
Parsley, 'Fakir'	S
Parsley, 'Favorit'	CO,KI,SU,V
Parsley, Hamburg	U
Parsley, Hamburg 'Berliner'	D
Parsley, Hamburg 'Omega'	BS,TU
Parsley, Hamburg 'Triple Turnip Rooted'	B,J,M,S,ST
Parsley, Hamburg 'Turnip Rooted'	SN
Parsley, 'Japanese Giant'	D,KI,L,M,S,ST
Parsley, 'Moss Curled 2'	
Parsley, 'Moss Curled 2 * Krausa', Parsnip 'Arrow' Carrot 'Primo' Sp.s	J, M
Parsley, 'Moss Curled 2 * Krausa', Sp.s	M
Parsley, 'Pagoda'	VH
Parsley, 'Plain Leaved'	B,BS,CO,J,KI,M, ST, TU,YA
Parsley, 'Plain Leaved 2'	F,J,M,S
Parsley, 'Regent'	BS
Parsley, 'Robust'	K
Parsley, 'Sparticus'	BS
Parsley, 'Verdi'	BS
Parsnip, 'Alba'	BS

Parsnip, 'Archer'	K
Parsnip, 'Arrow'	K
Parsnip, 'Arrow' Mini	F
Parsnip, 'Arrow', Sp.s	M
Parsnip, 'Avonresister'	BD,BS,CO,DT,F,J,KI,L, T,M,ST,SU, TU,U,V,VH
Parsnip, 'Bayonet'	U
Parsnip, 'Bedford Monarch'	BS
Parsnip, 'Cambridge Imp Marrow'	BS
Parsnip, 'Cobham Improved Marrow'	BS,D,M
Parsnip, 'E.W.K's Imperial Crown'	BS
Parsnip, 'Eversham'	BS
Parsnip, 'Exhibition' (Dobies)	D
Parsnip, 'Exhibition Long'	RO
Parsnip, 'Gladiator' F1	CO,DT,F,K,L,S,SE,SU,U, V,VH
Parsnip, 'Harris Model'	BS
Parsnip, 'Hollow Crown'	BD,BS,C,CO,DT,F,J,KI, L,ST,TU,VH
Parsnip, 'Hollow Crowned Imp'	D,U
Parsnip, 'Imperial Crown'	KI
Parsnip, 'Improved Marrow'	BS,R,YA
Parsnip, Japanese	C
Parsnip, 'Javelin' F1	BS,DT,K,TU
Parsnip, 'Kingship'	DT,KI
Parsnip, 'Lancer'	BS
Parsnip, 'Lancer' Mini	D,M,S
Parsnip, 'Lisbonnais'	BD,BS, F
Parsnip, 'New White Skin'	BS,K,S
Parsnip, 'New White Skin' - pr.s	D
Parsnip, 'Offenham'	BS,KI
Parsnip, 'Tender and True'	BS,CO,D,DT,F,J,KI,M, Mc,S,ST,SU,T,TU
Parsnip, 'The Student'	BS,CO,DT,KI,Mc,ST
Parsnip, 'Viceroy'	BS
Parsnip, 'White Diamond'	BS
Parsnip, 'White Gem'	BS,DT,F,J,KI,M,S,SU, TU,U,VH,YA
Parsnip, 'White King'	BS,CO,ST
Parsnip, 'Yatesnip'	YA
Passion Fruit	SU,V
Pea, Asparagus	BS,C,CO,D,F,KS,KI,Mc, ST,SU,T,TU,V
Pea Bean	BS,Mc,SU
Peas, 'Alderman'	BS,CO,D,DT,J,KI,M,SN, SU,TU,U,VH
Peas, 'Ambassador'	CO
Peas, 'Banff'	CO
Peas, 'Beagle'	B,KI
Peas, 'Carlin'	HD
Peas, 'Cavalier'	DT,F,L,M,S
Peas, 'Champion of England'	HD
Peas, Chick	V
Peas, 'Cockpit'	SN
Peas, 'Daybreak'	F,SE,SN,T
Peas, 'Douce Provence'	B,BS,F,M,TU
Peas, 'Early Onward'	B,BS,C,CO,D,DT,J,KI,M, R,S,TU,U,YA
Peas, 'Eminent'	V
Peas, 'Epicure'	HD
Peas, 'Excellenz'	YA
Peas, 'Feltham Advance'	BS
Peas, 'Feltham First'	B,BD,BS,CO,D,DT,F,J, KI,L,M,Mc,S,SU,TU,U, VH,YA
Peas, 'Fortune'	BS,DT,KI,TU

257

PEAS

Peas, 'Fruher Heinrich'	HD	Peas, 'Show Perfection'	DT,K,RO
Peas, Garden Peas Mix	T	Peas, Spring	M,SE
Peas, 'Gradus'	BS,CO,J,KI,TU	Peas, 'Superb'	BS
Peas, 'Holiday'	S	Peas, 'Table Talk'	HD
Peas, 'Hurst Beagle'	BD,BS,DT,M,U	Peas, 'Television'	TU
Peas, 'Hurst Green Shaft'	B,BD,BS,C,CO,D,DT,F,J,	Peas, 'Top Pod'	K,T,VH
	KI,L,M,Mc,S,SE,SU,T,	Peas, 'Veitch's Western Express'	HD
	TU,U,VH,YA	Pepper, Chili, 'Anaheim'	B,KS,T
Peas, Johnsons Freezer	J	Pepper, Chili, 'Anaheim' o-p	SN
Peas, 'Kelvedon Monarch'	BS	Pepper, Chili, 'Ancho Gigantea'	KS
Peas, 'Kelvedon Triumph'	BS	Pepper, Chili, 'Ancho St. Luis'	B,KS
Peas, 'Kelvedon Wonder'	B,BD,C,CO,D,DT,F,J,KI,	Pepper, Chili, 'Antler'	YA
	L,M,Mc,R,S,SU,T,TU,U,	Pepper, Chili, 'Apache' F1	B,BD,D,DT,J,L,S
	V,VH	Pepper, Chili, 'Cayenne'	B,BD,BS,DT,F,J,KS,SN,
Peas, Leafless Pea Twiggy	T		ST,U,VS
Peas, 'Lincoln'	BD,BS,CO,KI,SN,SU,TU	Pepper, Chili, 'Charleston Hot'	SN
Peas, 'Little Marvel'	BS,CO,D,F,J,KI,M,S,T,U	Pepper, Chili, 'Cherry Bomb' hyb	SN
Peas, 'Lord Chancellor'	BS	Pepper, Chili, 'Chili'	CO,KI,S,Mc
Peas, 'Magnum Bonum'	HD	Pepper, Chili, 'Chili Grande'	V
Peas, Mangetout, 'Bayard'	F	Pepper, Chili, 'Crespin'	SU
Peas, Mangetout, 'Carouby de Maussane'	BD,CO,DT,KI,SN,SU,TU	Pepper, Chili, 'Ethiopian'	SU
Peas, Mangetout, 'Corgi'	BD,CO,KI,SN,SU,TUD	Pepper, Chili, 'Fire Cracker'	KS
Peas, Mangetout, 'Dwarf Sugar Sweet'	B,BD,C,CO,DT,KI,SN,SU	Pepper, Chili, 'Garden Salsa' hyb	SN
Peas, Mangetout, 'Edula'	U	Pepper, Chili, 'Gold Spike' hyb	SN
Peas, Mangetout, 'Honeypod'	T	Pepper, Chili, 'Golden Cayenne'	V
Peas, Mange., 'Lage Grijze Roodbloeiende'	V	Pepper, Chili, 'Habanero' F1	V
Peas, Mangetout, 'Nofila'	D	Pepper, Chili, 'Hero' F1	V
Peas, Mangetout, 'Norli'	T,TU	Pepper, Chili, 'Hot Mexican'	M
Peas, Mangetout, 'Oregon Giant'	B,U	Pepper, Chili, 'Hungarian Wax'	B,CO,KI,KS,SN,SU,V
Peas, Mangetout, 'Oregon Sugar Pod'	BD,DT,KI,M,S,SN,U,VH,	Pepper, Chili, 'Jalapa' F1	YA
	YA	Pepper, Chili, 'Jalapeno'	BS,F,KS,SN,SU
Peas, Mangetout, 'Oregon Sugar Pod II'	B,SN,T	Pepper, Chili, 'Jamaican Hot'	KS
Peas, Mangetout, 'Record'	J	Pepper, Chili, 'Long des Landes' Green	VS
Peas, Mangetout, 'Reuzensuiker'	J	Pepper, Chili, 'Madame Jeanette'	V
Peas, Mangetout, 'Snow'	KS	Pepper, Chili, 'Mulato'	KS
Peas, Mangetout, 'Stam de Grace'	BD,V	Pepper, Chili, 'Mulato Isleno' o-p	SN
Peas, Mangetout, 'Sugar Ann'	J,SE,T,TU	Pepper, Chili, 'Numex 6-4L'	KS
Peas, Mangetout, 'Sugar Bon'	M,S,TU,V	Pepper, Chili, 'Numex Sweet'	KS
Peas, Mangetout, 'Sugar Dw. Sweetgreen'	BS,D,L,TU,U	Pepper, Chili, 'Pasilla Bajio'	KS
Peas, Mangetout, 'Sugar Gem'	S,T,TU	Pepper, Chili, 'Pasilla Bajio' o-p	SN
Peas, Mangetout, 'Sugar Rae'	BS,CO,D,KI,SU	Pepper, Chili, 'Peter Pepper'	KS
Peas, Mangetout, 'Sugar Snap'	BS,C,CO,DT,KI,L,M,Mc,	Pepper, Chili, 'Rawit'	V
	S,SN,SU,T,TU	Pepper, Chili, 'Red Cherry'	S
Peas, 'Markana'	BS,CO,KI,M,TU,YA	Pepper, Chili, 'Serrano'	B,KS,SU,T
Peas, Marrowfat, 'Blauwschok Desiree'	V	Pepper, Chili, 'Serrano' o-p	SN
Peas, Marrowfat, 'Blauwschokkers'	V	Pepper, Chili, 'Serrano Tampiqueno'	KS
Peas, 'Meteor'	B,BD,BS,CO,F,KI,SU,	Pepper, Chili, 'Spaanse' Red	V
	TU,U	Pepper, Chili, 'Super Cayenne' F1	T
Peas, 'Minnow'	D	Pepper, Chili, 'Tabasco-Habernero'	B,KS,T
Peas, 'Miracle'	BS,KI,SN	Pepper, Chili, 'Thai'	KS
Peas, 'Ne Plus Ultra'	HD	Pepper, Decorative	VS
Peas, 'Onward'	B,BD,BS,C,CO,D,DT,F,J,	Pepper, Hot Pepper	C
	KI,L,M,Mc,S,T,TU,U,VH,	Pepper, Purple	VS
	YA	Pepper, Sweet, 'Ace'	M,U
Peas, Petit Pois, 'Darfon'	J	Pepper, Sweet, 'Ariane' F1	B,BS,CO,J,KI,TU,V
Peas, Petit Pois, 'Lynx'	F,SE,TU	Pepper, Sweet, 'Astra' F1	YA
Peas, Petit Pois, 'Waverex'	BS,C,CO,KI,L,M,Mc,S,	Pepper, Sweet, 'Baby Belle'	DT
	SU,TU	Pepper, Sweet, 'Banana Supreme' hyb	SN
Peas, 'Pilot'	BS,CO,KI	Pepper, Sweet, 'Beauty Bell' F1	KI,ST,SU
Peas, 'Poppet'	HD	Pepper, Sweet, 'Bellboy' F1	B,BS,CO,D,DT,L,SN,TU,
Peas, 'Premium'	TU		YA
Peas, 'Progress No.9'	B,BS,D,KI	Pepper, Sweet, 'Bianca' F1	B,TU
Peas, 'Purple Podded'	HD	Pepper, Sweet, 'Big Bertha' F1	T,SN
Peas, 'Robinson'	HD	Pepper, Sweet, 'Bull Nose Red'	BS
Peas, Semi-Leafless, 'Bikini'	J	Pepper, Sweet, 'Californian Wonder'	B,BD,BS,C,F,J,KS,M,U
Peas, 'Senator'	F,S	Pepper, Sweet, 'Cal. Wonder Golden'	KS

PEPPER

Pepper, Sweet, 'Californian Wonder' o-p	SN
Pepper, Sweet, 'Canape' F1	D,SE,T,U,VH
Pepper, Sweet, 'Corne de Bouc Jaune'	SN,VS
Pepper, Sweet, 'Corne de Bouc Rouge'	SN,VS
Pepper, Sweet, 'Cubanelle' o-p	SN
Pepper, Sweet 'Delphin' F1	B,DT,VH
Pepper, 'Sweet Dwarf'	U
Pepper, Sweet, 'Eagle'	DT
Pepper, Sweet, 'Early Prolific' F1	M
Pepper, Sweet, 'Feher'	V
Pepper, Sweet, 'Gambo'	SN
Pepper, Sweet, 'Giant Chinese' o-p	SN
Pepper, Sweet, 'Giant Szegedi' o-p	SN
Pepper, Sweet, 'Golden Bell' F1	SN,V
Pepper, Sweet, 'Golden Calwonder' o-p	SN
Pepper, Sweet, 'Granny Smith'	SE,U
Pepper, Sweet, 'Gypsy' F1	F,T,S,SN
Pepper, Sweet, 'Hybrid Mix F1	J
Pepper, Sweet, 'Jingle Bells' mini	T,VH
Pepper, Sweet, 'Jumbo Sweet' F1	T
Pepper, Sweet, 'Jupiter' o-p	SN
Pepper, Sweet, 'Keystone' o-p	SN
Pepper, Sweet, 'Long Red Marconi'	BS,KI,SU
Pepper, Sweet, 'Long Red Rubens' F1	B,SU
Pepper, Sweet, 'Long Yellow Ringo' F1	B,SU
Pepper, Sweet, 'Luteus' F1	B,KI,L,S,SU
Pepper, Sweet, 'Marconi' o-p	SN
Pepper, Sweet, 'Mavras' F1	B,BS,CO,KI,V
Pepper, Sweet, 'Merit' F1	V
Pepper, Sweet, 'Midway' o-p	SN
Pepper, Sweet, 'Minibel'	M
Pepper, Sweet, 'Mogador' F1	V
Pepper, Sweet, 'New Ace' F1	B,BD,BS,CO,F,J,KI,R,SU
Pepper, Sweet, 'New Carnival Mix' F1	M
Pepper, Sweet, 'Orobelle' F1	KS
Pepper, Sweet, 'Peperoncino' o-p	SN
Pepper, Sweet, 'Pimiento Elite' o-p	SN
Pepper, Sweet, 'Pimiento L' o-p	SN
Pepper, Sweet, 'Purple Beauty'	T
Pepper, Sweet, 'Rainbow' F1	F
Pepper, Sweet, 'Red Cherry L. Sweet' o-p	SN
Pepper, Sweet, 'Redskin' F1	B,BD,CO,DT,KI,L,S
Pepper, Sweet, 'Roumanian Sweet' o-p	SN
Pepper, Sweet, 'Ruby King/Golden Queen'	DT
Pepper, Sweet, 'Salad Festival'	U
Pepper, Sweet, 'Salad Mix'	SE
Pepper, Sweet, 'Slim Pin'	B,CO,SU
Pepper, Sweet, 'Spanish Red and Green'	BS,KI,ST
Pepper, Sweet, 'Summer Salad Mix' F1	SN,T,VH
Pepper, Sweet, 'Sunnybrook' o-p	SN
Pepper, Sweet, 'Super Sweet Banana' F1	V
Pepper, Sweet, 'Sweet Banana' o-p	SN
Pepper, Sweet, 'Sweet Chocolate'	T
Pepper, Sweet, 'Sweet Delight Mix'	DT,F,V
Pepper, Sweet, 'Sweet Green'	BS
Pepper, Sweet, 'Top Banana' Hyb	SN
Pepper, Sweet, 'Topboy'	BD,DT
Pepper, Sweet, 'Topepo Giallo' o-p	SN
Pepper, Sweet, 'Westlandse'	V
Pepper, Sweet, 'Worldbeater'	S
Pepper, Sweet, 'Yellow Banana'	KS
Pepper, Sweet, 'Yolo Wonder'	CO,SN
Pepper, Sweet, 'Yolo Wonder' o-p	SN
Pepper/Tomato Cross	VS
Pepper/Tomato Cross 'Liebsapfel'	V
Pepper/Tomato Cross 'Top Boy'	BS,V

Pepper/Tomato Cross 'Top Girl'	BS
Perilla Green and Purple	KS
Popcorn	VS
Popcorn, 'Peppy' F1	V
Potato, 'Accent'	JM,M,SN,ST,TU
Potato, 'Ailsa'	SN,TU
Potato, 'Almaria'	SN,TU
Potato, 'Aminica'	CO,SN,TU
Potato, 'Arran Banner'	F
Potato, 'Arran Comet'	HE,SN,SU,TU
Potato, 'Arran Consul'	F
Potato, 'Arran Pilot'	DT,HE,JM,SN,ST,TU
Potato, 'Arran Victory'	CO,SU
Potato, 'Avalanche'	CO
Potato, 'Ballydoon'	F
Potato, 'Balmoral'	SN,TU
Potato, 'Belle de Fontenay'	M,SN,TU
Potato, 'Bintje'	M,SN,TU
Potato, 'British Queen'	F
Potato, 'Caesar'	SN,TU
Potato, 'Cara'	D,DT,HE,JM,M,SN,ST, SU,TU
Potato, 'Carlingford'	D,SN,TU
Potato, 'Catriona'	F,HE,JM,SN,ST,TU
Potato, 'Charlotte'	M,SN
Potato, 'Concorde'	JM,M,SN,ST,TU
Potato, 'Desiree'	CO,D,DT,HE,JM,SN,ST, SU,TU
Potato, 'Diana'	SN,TU
Potato, 'Duke of York'	CO,HE,JM,SN,ST,TU
Potato, 'Duke of York' Red	HE,F,JM,SN,ST,TU
Potato, 'Dunbar Rover'	F
Potato, 'Dunbar Standard'	F,SN,TU
Potato, 'Dunluce'	M,SN,TU
Potato, 'Edzell Blue'	F,SN,TU
Potato, 'Epicure'	HE,JM,SN,ST,TU
Potato, 'Estima'	HE,JM,SN,ST,TU
Potato, 'Fiana'	SN,TU
Potato, 'Florette'	SN
Potato, 'Foremost'	HE,JM,M,S,SN,ST,TU
Potato, 'Golden Wonder'	HE,SN,ST,TU
Potato, 'Heather'	M,SN,TU
Potato, 'Home Guard'	HE,JM,SN,ST,TU
Potato, 'Kerrs Pink'	CO,F,HE,SN,ST,TU
Potato, 'Kestrel'	D,DT,HE,JM,M,SN,ST, TU
Potato, 'King Edward'	HE,JM,SN,ST,TU
Potato, 'King Edward' Red	F
Potato, 'Kirsty'	SN,TU
Potato, 'Kondor'	M,SN,ST,TU
Potato, 'Linzer Delikatess'	M,S,SN,TU
Potato, 'Majestic'	HE,JM,SN,ST,TU
Potato, 'Manna'	SN,TU
Potato, 'Marfona'	JM,M,SN,ST,TU
Potato, 'Maris Bard'	D,DT,HE,JM,M,SN,ST, TU
Potato, 'Maris Peer'	D,HE,JM,SN,ST,TU
Potato, 'Maris Piper'	D,DT,HE,JM,SN,ST,TU
Potato, 'Maxine'	JM,M,SN
Potato, 'Mona Lisa'	SN,TU
Potato, 'Nadine'	D,HE,JM,M,SN,ST,TU
Potato, 'Obelix'	SN,TU
Potato, 'Pentland Crown'	HE,JM,SN,ST,TU
Potato, 'Pentland Dell'	HE,SN,ST,TU
Potato, 'Pentland Hawk'	HE
Potato, 'Pentland Javelin'	DT,HE,JM,SN,ST,TU

POTATO

Potato, 'Pentland Squire'	HE,ST
Potato, 'Picasso'	SN,TU
Potato, 'Pink Fir Apple'	CO,D,DT,HE,JM,M,SN, ST,SU,TU
Potato, 'Pomfine'	SN
Potato, 'Pompadour'	SN
Potato, 'Premiere'	SN,TU
Potato, 'Ratte'	F,JM,M,SN,ST
Potato, 'Record'	HE,SN,ST,TU
Potato, 'Remarka'	CO
Potato, 'Rocket'	DT,HE,JM,M,SN,ST,TU
Potato, 'Romano'	HE,JM,SN,ST,TU
Potato, 'Rooster'	HE,JM,SN,ST,TUD
Potato, 'Roseval'	M,SN
Potato, 'Samba'	SN
Potato, 'Sante'	CO,M,SN,TU
Potato, 'Saturna'	CO
Potato, 'Saxon'	SN,TU
Potato Seed,pre-chitted	M
Potato, 'Sharpes Express'	CO,HE,JM,SN,ST,TU
Potato, 'Shula'	SN,TU
Potato, 'Stemster'	HE,JM,SN,ST,TU
Potato, 'Stroma'	HE,JM,S,SN,ST,TU
Potato, 'Swift'	D,DT,HE,JM,M,SN,ST, TU
Potato, 'Symphonia'	SN,TU
Potato, 'Ulster Chieftain'	HE,JM,SN,ST,TU
Potato, 'Ulster Prince'	SN,TU
Potato, 'Ulster Sceptre'	HE,SN,TU
Potato, 'Valdor'	ST
Potato, 'Valor'	DT,JM,M,SN,TU
Potato, 'Vanessa'	D,HE,JM,S,SN,ST,TU
Potato, 'Wilja'	D,DT,HE,JM,SN,ST,TU
Potato, 'Winston'	D,HE,JM,M,SN,ST,TU
Pumpkin	VS
Pumpkin, 'Apollo' F1	BS
Pumpkin, 'Appalachian' F1	BS
Pumpkin, 'Aspen'	BS
Pumpkin, 'Atlantic Giant'	B,BS,DT,F,KS,M,S,SE, SN,T,V
Pumpkin, 'Autumn Gold'	BS, M, S
Pumpkin, 'Baby Boo'	BS, V
Pumpkin, 'Becky'	DT
Pumpkin, 'Big Autumn'	BS
Pumpkin, 'Big Max'	BS
Pumpkin, 'Big Moon'	BS
Pumpkin, 'Buckskin' F1	BS
Pumpkin, 'Cinderella'	BS,TU
Pumpkin, 'Conneticut Field'	BS,SU
Pumpkin, 'Crown Prince' F1	BS, M
Pumpkin, 'Early Price'	CO
Pumpkin, 'Fall Star'	BS
Pumpkin, 'Frosty'	BS,SN
Pumpkin, 'Funny Face'	BS
Pumpkin, 'Ghost Rider'	BS,TU
Pumpkin, 'Half Moon'	BS
Pumpkin, 'Happy Jack'	BS
Pumpkin, 'Harvest Moon'	YA
Pumpkin, 'Howden'	BS
Pumpkin, 'Hundredweight'	KI,S,ST,TU
Pumpkin, 'Jack Be Little'	BS,CO,KI,KS,SU,VS
Pumpkin, 'Jack O Lantern'	BS,KI,SN,ST,TU,VS
Pumpkin, 'Jackpot'	K,U
Pumpkin, 'Janne Gros de Paris'	BS
Pumpkin, 'Kumi-Kumi'	KS
Pumpkin, 'Large'	K

Pumpkin, 'Little Lantern' F1	BS
Pumpkin, 'Mammoth'	BS,C,CO,D,J,L,R
Pumpkin, 'Mammoth Gold'	BS,F
Pumpkin, 'Mammoth Orange'	M
Pumpkin, 'Munchkin'	B,BD,BS
Pumpkin, 'Musquee de Provence'	V
Pumpkin Nuts	C
Pumpkin, 'Prizewinner'	BS,KS,SN
Pumpkin, 'Rebecca'	BS
Pumpkin, 'Rouge Vif d'Etamps'	BS
Pumpkin, 'Show King'	VS
Pumpkin, 'Small Sugar'	B,BS,CO,L,SN,TU,YA
Pumpkin, 'Spellbound'	BS,M
Pumpkin, 'Spirit' F1	B,BD,BS
Pumpkin, 'Spookie'	BS
Pumpkin, 'Spooktacular' F1	BS
Pumpkin, 'Sumo'	BS
Pumpkin, 'Sunny' F1	BS,DT
Pumpkin, 'Sweetie Pie'	BS, V
Pumpkin, 'Tallman'	BS
Pumpkin, 'Tom Fox'	BS
Pumpkin, 'Trickster' F1	YA
Pumpkin, 'Triple Treat'	BS,DT,KI,SU
Pumpkin, 'Uchiki Kuri'	BS,CO,KI,TU,V
Pumpkin, White Large	VS
Pumpkin, 'Young's Variety'	BS
Radicchio, 'Augusto'	F
Radicchio, 'Castelfranco'	KS
Radicchio, 'Cesare'	DT,J,SU,V
Radicchio, 'Fidelio' F1	YA
Radicchio, 'Guilio'	KS,SU
Radicchio, 'Late Rossa di Chioggia'	B,C
Radicchio, 'Palla di Fuoco'	SU
Radicchio, 'Palla Rossa'	BS,KI,M,Mc,ST,TU,U
Radicchio, 'Palla Rossa Bella'	S
Radicchio, 'Palla Rossa Red Devil'	D
Radicchio, 'Red Verona'	BS,KS
Radicchio, 'Rialto' F1	YA
Radicchio, 'Rossa di Treviso'	B,BS,CO,SU,VS
Radicchio, 'Rossa di Verona'	CO,SU
Radicchio, 'Selvatica da Campo'	V
Radicchio, 'Variegata di Castelfranco'	B,BS,C,KI,SU,V
Radicchio, 'Variegata di Chioggia'	SU
Radicchio, 'Varieg. di Sottomarina Precoce'	SU
Radish, '18 Day'	BS,SU
Radish, 'Beacon'	BS
Radish, 'Black Spanish Long'	B,BD,BS,C,CO,KI,KS, SU,V
Radish, 'Black Spanish Round'	B,BS,CO,DT,KI,M,S,ST, SU,TU,V
Radish, 'Caravella'	BS
Radish, 'Cello'	BS
Radish, 'Cherry Belle'	B,BD,BS,CO,D,DT,KI, KS,L,M,R,SU,T,TU,U, VH,YA
Radish, 'China Rose'	B,BD,BS,CO,J,KI,S,SN, ST,SU,TU
Radish, Chinese, 'Cherokee' F1	D,J,T,V
Radish, Chinese, 'Mantanhong' F1	T,V
Radish, 'Crimson Giant'	BS
Radish, 'Crystal Ball'	BS,S
Radish, 'Cyros' F1	BS,KI
Radish, 'D'Avignon'	BS,KS,SU
Radish, 'Easter Egg'	BS,KS,SU
Radish, 'Eterna'	V
Radish, 'Fire Candle'	CO

RADISH

Radish, 'Flair'	BS
Radish, 'Flamboyant Sabina 2'	BS,YA
Radish, 'Fluo' F1	F,SE,SN
Radish, 'Flyer' F1	BS
Radish, 'Fota'	BS
Radish, 'French Breakfast'	B,BD,BS,CO,KI,Mc,ST, VH
Radish, 'French Breakfast 2'	TU
Radish, 'French Breakfast 3'	C,D,DT,F,J,L,M,S,SE,T, U,V
Radish, 'French Breakfast Forcing'	B,BS
Radish, 'French Breakfast- Fusilier'	BS
Radish, 'Fr. Breakfast Large White Tipped'	BS
Radish, 'French Breakfast' o-p	SN
Radish, 'French Breakfast-Rafale'	BS
Radish, 'French Golden'	HD
Radish, Globe Vars Mix	U,V
Radish, 'Helro' (Forcing)	BS,J
Radish, Japanese, 'Aomaru-Koshin'	KS
Radish, Japanese, 'April Cross' F1	BS,DT,M,SE,SN,T,U,V, YA
Radish, Japanese, 'Attila' F1	YA
Radish, Japanese, 'Mino Early'	D,J,S,YA
Radish, Japanese, 'Mooli'	KI,KS,ST,SU
Radish, Japanese, 'Omny' F1	KS
Radish, Japanese, 'Sakurajima Mammoth'	KS
Radish, Japanese, 'Tokinashi'	KS
Radish, 'Jolly'	DT,K
Radish, 'Juliette' F1	T
Radish, 'Jumbo'	BS
Radish, 'Long White Icicle'	B,BD,BS,CO,D,F,J,L,M, S,ST,SU,TU,V
Radish, 'Mantanghong' F1	J, S
Radish, 'Marabelle'	BS
Radish, 'Minowase Summer Cross' F1	KI,TU
Radish, 'Minowase Summer No 2' F1	BS
Radish, 'Misato Green Flesh'	CO
Radish, 'Misato Rose Flesh'	BS,SN
Radish, Mix	D,DT,KI,M,S
Radish, 'Munchien Bier'	B,BS,CO,KI,KS,SU,T
Radish, 'Parat'	F,SN
Radish, 'Pegaso'	BS
Radish, 'Pernot'	DT
Radish, 'Pink Beauty'	BS,CO,D,J,KI,S
Radish, 'Poker' F1	BS
Radish, 'Primella'	BS
Radish, 'Prinz Rotin'	BS,DT,F,KI,M,SE,T,U
Radish, 'Rainbow Salad Mix'	T
Radish, 'Rat's Tail'	HD
Radish, 'Revosa'	VH
Radish, 'Ribella'	BS,M
Radish, 'Robino'	BS, M
Radish, 'Rota'	BD,BS
Radish, 'Round Red Forcing Real'	BS
Radish, 'Rudi'	YA
Radish, 'Saxa'	BS
Radish, 'Scarlet Globe'	B,BS,C,CO,F,J,KI,Mc,S, ST
Radish, 'Scharo'	BS
Radish, 'Short Top Forcing'	BS,S
Radish, 'Shunkyoh' semi-long	SN
Radish, 'Solar' F1	BS
Radish, 'Sora'	KS
Radish, 'Sparkler'	BS,CO,KI,ST
Radish, 'Sparkler 3'	D,F,J,S
Radish, 'Summer Crunch'	BS,KI,SU

Radish, 'Summer Mix'	F
Radish, 'Tama' hyb	SN
Radish, 'Volcano'	F
Radish, 'White Hailstone'	BS
Radish, 'White Icicle'	KI
Radish, 'White Turnip'	BS
Radish, 'Wood's Frame'	HD
Rampion	C,V
Rhubarb, 'Champagne Early'	M
Rhubarb, 'Glaskins Perpetual'	BS,C,KI,ST,SU,T,TU
Rhubarb, 'Holstein Bloodred'	BS
Rhubarb, 'Large Victoria'	BS
Rhubarb, 'Prince Albert'	BS
Rhubarb, 'Redstick'	BS,V
Rhubarb, 'Strawberry'	BS
Rhubarb, 'Timperley Early'	TU
Rhubarb, 'Victoria'	BD,BS,DT,L,S
Rocket	C,KS,S,SU,TU,V
Rocket, 'Rucola'	CO
Rutabuga See Swede	
Salad, American	U
Salad, 'El Toro'	VS
Salad, 'Misticanza'	C
Salad, Mixed Collection	V
Salad Mustard, 'Fine White'	B,C,D,DT,F,J,M,S,SE,ST, SU,TU
Salad, Mustard Tilney	YA
Salad, Rape	B,BS,C,CO,KI,ST,SU,V, YA
Salad, Roman Celtuce	VS
Salad, Roman Green 'Grass'	VS
Salad, Roman Red 'Les Oreilles du Diable'	VS
Salad, Roman 'St. Martha'	VS
Salad, Roman 'St. Vincent'	VS
Salad, Thai	CO,SU
Saladisi	T
Salsify, 'Giant'	S
Salsify, 'Mammoth'	B,M
Salsify, 'Sandwich Island'	B,CO,D,DT,F,KI,KS,Mc, ST,SU,T
Salsify, 'Sandwich Island Mammoth'	BS,C,TU
Salsify, 'Vegetable Oyster'	J,V
Scorzonera	KS,L,T
Scorzonera, 'Giant Rooted'	BS
Scorzonera, 'Habil'	M
Scorzonera, 'Lange Jan'	BS,D,V
Scorzonera, 'Long Black'	C,KI,SU
Scorzonera, 'Maxima'	BS,CO,J,Mc,TU
Scorzonera, 'Russian Giant'	S
Seakale Beet	B,CO,SG
Seakale Beet, 'Fordhook Giant'	M
Seakale Beet, 'Mostruosa d'Ingegnoli'	V
Seakale Beet, Rhubarb Chard*'Feurio'	C,M
Seakale Beet, 'Walliser'	V
Seakale, 'Lily White'	B,C,KI,Mc,ST,SU,T
Seakale, Swiss Chard	BS,C,D,F,L,M,S
Seedling Radish, 'Jaba'	B,BS,SU
Skirret	C,SU
Spinach	BS
Spinach, 'America'	YA
Spinach, 'Atlanta'	BS,KI,Mc
Spinach, 'Bakan'	L
Spinach, 'Bazaroet'	V
Spinach, 'Bergola'	BS,CO
Spinach, 'Bloomsdale'	B,BS,C,KI,M,ST
Spinach, 'Broad Leaf Prickly Standwell'	BS,CO,TU

SPINACH

Spinach, 'Ceylon'	V	Squash, 'Baby Bear'	BS,D,F
Spinach, 'Dash' F1	BS	Squash, 'Baby Delica'	BS
Spinach, 'Dominant'	BS,J	Squash, 'Banana Blue'	VS
Spinach, 'Fabris'	BS	Squash, 'Banana Pink Jumbo'	BS,VS
Spinach, 'Giant New Prickly'	B,BS	Squash, 'Blue Hubbard'	VS
Spinach, 'Giant Thick Leaved'	BS,K	Squash, 'Brazilian Sugar'	VS
Spinach, 'Giant Thick Leaved Prickly'	C	Squash, 'Brodee Galeuse'	VS
Spinach, 'Grodane'	BS,KI,TU,YA	Squash, 'Bubble & Squeak'	U
Spinach, 'Hollandia'	BS	Squash, 'Bushfire' F1	YA
Spinach, Japanese 'Summer Green'	KS	Squash, 'Buttercup'	B,BS,D,SN,SU,VS
Spinach, 'King of Denmark'	BS	Squash, 'Butternut'	B,DT,KI,YA
Spinach, 'Long Standing'	T,VH	Squash, 'Butternut Supreme' F1	SN
Spinach, 'Mazarka' F1	BS	Squash, 'Chioggia'	VS
Spinach, 'Mazarka' F1 Mini	F	Squash, 'Cream of the Crop'	BS
Spinach, 'Medania'	B,BS,CO,DT,KI,L,ST,TU,	Squash, 'Crown Prince' F1	S,YA
	U,YA	Squash, 'Cushaw Striped'	SN,VS
Spinach, 'Melody'	BS	Squash, 'Custard White'	B,BS,CO,KI,SN,ST,TU,V
Spinach, 'Monarch Long Standing'	U	Squash, 'Dawn'	BS
Spinach, 'Monnopa'	BS,CO,KI,KS,T	Squash, 'Delicata'	B,BS,F,KS,SN,V
Spinach, 'New Zealand'	CO,KI,SU	Squash, 'Early Acorn'	BS,CO,KI
Spinach, 'Nobel'	BS	Squash, 'Early Butternut' F1	BD,SN
Spinach, 'Novadane' F1	YA	Squash, 'Futsu'	VS
Spinach, 'Olympia'	BS	Squash, 'Gemstore' F1	BS,D
Spinach, 'Oscar' F1	BS	Squash, 'Gold Nugget'	BS,CO,D,KI,ST,TU
Spinach, 'Polka' F1	BS	Squash, 'Golden Delicious'	BS,SN,TU
Spinach, 'Predane' F1	YA	Squash, 'Golden Hubbard'	S,SN,SU,VS
Spinach, 'Resistofaly Securo'	V	Squash, 'Golden Hubbard' org	CO
Spinach, 'Rico' F1	J	Squash, 'Goldkeeper'	BS
Spinach, 'Samson'	KS	Squash, 'Green Delicious'	SN
Spinach, 'Sigmaleaf' F1	S	Squash, 'Hokkaido'	TU
Spinach, 'Space' F1	B,BD,BS,F,KS	Squash, 'Honey Delight'	SN
Spinach, 'Spartacus'	BS	Squash, 'Hubbard Improved Green'	SN
Spinach, 'Spinoza'	BS	Squash, 'Jersey Golden Acorn'	BS,TU
Spinach, 'Splendour' F1	B,BD,BS,DT,VH	Squash, 'Lady Godiva'	HD
Spinach, 'Spokane' F1	D	Squash, 'Lebanese'	KS
Spinach, 'Sprint' F1	BS	Squash, 'Little Gem'	M,SU
Spinach, 'Sputnik'	BS	Squash, 'Lumina'	BS,V
Spinach, Strawberry	F,U,V,VS	Squash, 'Mandan'	HD
Spinach, 'Teton' Summer Round	TU	Squash, 'Medallion' F1	BS
Spinach, 'Triade' F1	F	Squash, 'Melonette'	SN
Spinach, 'Triathlon' F1	M,TU	Squash, 'Mini Green Hubbard'	SN,V
Spinach, 'Triathlon' &'Trinidad' F1, 2-pack	M	Squash, 'Moschata'	SN
Spinach, 'Tribute' F1	BS	Squash, 'New England Blue'	SN
Spinach, 'Trinidad' F1	M	Squash, 'North Georgia'	VS
Spinach, 'Triptiek' F1	TU	Squash, 'Nutty Delica' F1	V
Spinach, 'Triton' F1	S,SE	Squash, 'Olive'	HD,VS
Spinach, 'Tyee'	BS	Squash, 'Olive' org	SN
Spinach, 'Vienna'	BS	Squash, 'Onion'	BS
Spinach, 'Viking'	BS,F	Squash, 'Pacifica' F1	YA
Spinach, 'Virkade'	BS	Squash, 'Patisson Bunter'	VS
Spinach, 'Viroflav'	BS	Squash, 'Patisson Orange'	VS
Spinach, 'Winterreuzen'	V	Squash, 'Patisson Patty Pan'	KS,VS
Spring Greens, Vanguard	M	Squash, 'Patisson White'	VS
Sprouting, Mung Beans	BS,CO,KI,L,S,SU,TU	Squash, 'Pepita'	VS
Sprouting , Quinoa	SU	Squash, 'Peruvian'	VS
Sprouting , Radish	CO,SU	Squash, 'Peter Pan' F1 Mini	S
Sprouting Salad, T&M	T	Squash, 'Peter Pan' hyb	BS,SN,V
Sprouting Seeds, Alfalfa	BS,CO,D,J,KI,L,M,SU,T,	Squash, 'Pink Jumbo'	SN
	TU,V	Squash, 'Pompeon'	CO,SU
Sprouting Seeds, Chick Peas	CO	Squash, 'Ponca'	BS
Sprouting Seeds, Fenugreek	BS,CO,KI,SU,TU,V	Squash, 'Pontimarron'	SN,VS
Sprouting Seeds, Spicy Fenugreek	J,L	Squash, 'Pontiron Chinese'	VS
Sprouting , Soya Beans	CO	Squash, 'Pontiron Hungarian Blue'	VS
Sprouting , Wheat	CO	Squash, 'Pontiron Rouge Vif d'Etamps'	VS
Squash, 'Alexandria'	S	Squash, 'Prince Regent' F1	BS,YA
Squash, 'Autumn Queen'	SN,U	Squash, 'Queensland Blue'	BS

SQUASH

Squash, 'Red Kuri'	BS	Sweetcorn, 'Banker' F1	YA
Squash, 'Rolet'	BS,DT,TU	Sweetcorn, 'Bullion' F1	YA
Squash, 'Scallop Scallopini'	BS	Sweetcorn, 'Butterscotch' F1	T
Squash, 'Scallop Yellow Bird'	BS	Sweetcorn, 'Challenger' F1	BS,F
Squash, 'Siamese'	VS	Sweetcorn, 'Champ' F1	DT,F,M,T,VH
Squash, 'Stripetti' F1	BS,SN	Sweetcorn, 'Citation' F1	BS
Squash, 'Sugarberry'	VS	Sweetcorn, 'Classic' F1	BS
Squash, 'Sun Drops' hyb	SN	Sweetcorn, 'Cobham Sweet' F1	BS
Squash, 'Sunburst' F1	DT,SN,TU,V	Sweetcorn, 'Conquest' F1	BD,BS,D,DT,T
Squash, 'Supreme Delite' F1	D	Sweetcorn, 'Crisp- n- Sweet' F1	BS,TU
Squash, 'Swan White Acorn'	BS,SN	Sweetcorn, 'Dawn' F1	BS
Squash, 'Sweet Dumpling'	B,BS,C,D,DT,KI,SN,SU,	Sweetcorn, 'Dickson' F1	S,T,VH
	TU,V	Sweetcorn, 'Earlibelle' F1	BS,S,TU
Squash, 'Sweet Mama' F1	BS,CO,KI,Mc,SN,ST,TU	Sweetcorn, 'Earliking' F1	BS,C,CO,L
Squash, 'Sweet Meat'	BS	Sweetcorn, 'Earlivee' F1	BS
Squash, 'Sweet Sensation' F1	S	Sweetcorn, 'Early Cup' F1	BS
Squash, 'Table Ace' F1	B,BD,BS,DT,L,SN,TU	Sweetcorn, 'Early Pak' F1	BS,KI,SU,YA
Squash, 'Table Gold'	SN,VS	Sweetcorn, 'Extra Early Sweet' F1	B,KI
Squash, 'Table King'	SN	Sweetcorn, 'Festival' F1	DT
Squash, 'Table Queen'	BS,SN	Sweetcorn, 'Fiesta' F1	B,BD,BS,F,L,R,TU
Squash, 'Tancheese'	VS	Sweetcorn, 'First of All' F1	S
Squash, 'Tay Bell'	SN	Sweetcorn, 'Florida Stay Sweet' F1	BS
Squash, 'Tivoli' F1	BD,BS,D,L,S,T,M,U,YA	Sweetcorn, 'Golden Bantam' o-p	BD,BS
Squash, 'Triamble'	B,SN,VS	Sweetcorn, 'Golden Sweet' F1	BS,CO,KI
Squash, 'Turk's Hat Small'	VS	Sweetcorn, 'Gourmet' F1	BS,M
Squash, 'Turks Turban'	B,BS,CO,KI,SU,TU	Sweetcorn, 'Herald' F1	B,BS
Squash, 'Ultra Butternut' F1	SN	Sweetcorn, 'Honey and Cream' F1	M
Squash, Vegetable Spaghetti	BS,C,CO,D,F,J,KI,Mc,	Sweetcorn, 'Honey Bantam Bicolor (30)' F1	T
	TU,V,VS	Sweetcorn, 'Honeycomb' F1	BS,KI,ST,SU
Squash, Vegetable Spaghetti 'Orangetti'	BS	Sweetcorn, 'Honeydew' F1	BS
Squash, Vegetable Spaghetti 'Pyjamas'	BS	Sweetcorn, 'Incredible' F1	DT,F
Squash, 'Waltham Butternut'	B,BS,SN	Sweetcorn, 'Indian Dawn' F1	BS
Squash, 'Warted Hubbard'	V	Sweetcorn, 'J.Innes Hyb(Canada Cross)' F1	BS
Squash, 'Winterhorn'	VS	Sweetcorn, 'Joro' Ancient Red	VS
Squash, 'Zapallito di Tronco Redondo'	HD	Sweetcorn, 'Jubilee' F1	B,BS,J,KI,L,SU
Squash, 'Zenith' F1	SN	Sweetcorn, 'Kelvedon Glory' F1	B,BD,BS,CO,F,KI,ST
Strawberry, 'Alpine Alexandria'	B,BD,CO,JE,KI,SU	Sweetcorn, 'Kelvedon Sweetheart' F1	BS
Strawberry, 'Baron Solemacher'	B,J,L,V	Sweetcorn, 'Kodiak' F1	BS
Strawberry, 'Mignonette'	T	Sweetcorn, 'Lariat' F1	BS
Strawberry, 'Sweet Sensation' F1	D	Sweetcorn 'Minipop' F1 Mini	BS,D,KI,S
Strawberry Sweetcorn	VS	Sweetcorn 'Minisweet' F1	CO
Strawberry, 'Sweetheart' F1	CO,J,JE,SU,V	Sweetcorn, 'Minor' F1	F,J,T,V
Strawberry, 'Temptation'	B,BD,DT,J,KI,SE,T,U,V,	Sweetcorn, 'Miracle' F1	BS,ST
	VH	Sweetcorn, 'Morning Sun'	BS
Strawberry, 'Verbesserte Rugen'	B,JE	Sweetcorn, 'North Star' F1	BS
Strawberry, 'Yellow Wonder'	B,J,V	Sweetcorn, 'Northern Bell' F1	B,BS,TU
Swede, 'Angela'	B,BS	Sweetcorn, 'Northern Extra Sweet' F1	BS
Swede, 'Best of All'	B,BD,BS,D,DT,F,J,KI,M,	Sweetcorn, 'October Gold' F1	BS
	Mc,T,U	Sweetcorn, 'Ovation' F1	BS
Swede, 'Blaukop'	VH	Sweetcorn, 'Pinnacle' F1	BS
Swede, 'Champion'	VH	Sweetcorn, 'Prime Pak' F1	BS,KI,Mc
Swede, 'Champion Purple Top'	BS	Sweetcorn, 'Reliance' F1	BS
Swede, 'Devon Champion'	TU	Sweetcorn, 'Reward' F1	BS,J
Swede, 'Garden Purple Top Acme'	BD,BS,C,CO,KI,Mc,ST	Sweetcorn, 'Rosella 425' F1	BS
Swede, 'Joan'	K,YA	Sweetcorn, 'Seneca Horizon' F1	BS
Swede, 'Laurenthian'	BS	Sweetcorn, 'Starlite' F1	BS,C,V
Swede, 'Lizzy'	BS,D,DT,F,J,L,SE,V	Sweetcorn, 'Sugar Boy' F1	BS
Swede, 'Magres'	BS,YA	Sweetcorn, 'Sugar Loaf' F1	BS
Swede, 'Marian'	B,BD,BS,CO,DT,F,KI,M,	Sweetcorn, 'Summer Flavour ® 64Y'	T
	ST,SU,TU,U,VH,YA	Sweetcorn, 'Sun Up' F1	BS
Swede, 'Ruby'	BS,M,S,TU	Sweetcorn, 'Sundance' F1	BS,D,DT,S,SE,U
Swede, 'Ruta Otofte'	B,BS	Sweetcorn, 'Sunrise' F1	BS,D,M
Sweetcorn, 'Amarillo' Ancient Yellow	VS	Sweetcorn, 'Sweet 77' F1	B,BS
Sweetcorn, 'Astarac' Ancient White	VS	Sweetcorn, 'Sweet Mexi' F1	B,BS
Sweetcorn, 'Baby' mini	B,VH	Sweetcorn, 'Sweet Nugget' F1	BS,KI,TU
Sweetcorn, 'Balai'	VS	Sweetcorn, 'Sweet Season' F1	BS

SWEETCORN

Sweetcorn, 'Sweet September' F1	BS
Sweetcorn, 'Tasty Gold' F1	BS,KI
Sweetcorn, 'Tasty Sweet' F1	BS,KI,SU
Sweetcorn 'Tasty Treat' F1	CO,ST
Sweetcorn, 'Terrific'	BS
Sweetcorn, 'Trophy' F1	V
Sweetcorn, 'Two's Sweeter' F1	SE,VH
Sweetcorn, 'Xtra Sweet Early'	BS, U
Sweetcorn, 'Xtra Sweet Improved'	M
Sweetcorn, 'Yukon' F1	BS,KI
Tomatillo	C,KS,VS
Tomatillo 'Chilean Orange' org	SN
Tomatillo 'Mexican Green Husk' o-p org	SN
Tomatillo 'Peruvian Violet' org	SN
Tomato, 'Ace 55'	KI
Tomato, 'Ace 55' o-p	SN
Tomato, 'Ailsa Craig'	B,C,CO,D,DT,F,J,KI,L,M, Mc,R,S,ST,SU,U,VH,YA
Tomato, 'Ailsa Craig' o-p	BS,SN
Tomato, 'Alfresco' F1	BS
Tomato, 'Alicante'	B,BD,CO,D,DT,F,J,KI,L, M,R,S,SE,ST,T,TU,U,VH, YA
Tomato, 'Alicante' o-p	BS,SN
Tomato, 'Altaisky'	VS
Tomato, 'Amish Paste' o-p	KS,SN
Tomato, 'Ananas' o-p EEC reg	SN,VS
Tomato, 'Andine Cornue'	VS
Tomato, 'Angelo' F1	BS
Tomato, 'Arasta' F1	B,BS,DT,KI,SN,ST
Tomato, 'Auriga'	B,KI,SU
Tomato, 'Auriga' o-p	SN
Tomato, 'Azoychka' o-p	SN
Tomato, 'Balconstar' o-p	SN
Tomato, 'Beaute Blanche' o-p	SN,VS
Tomato, 'Beefmaster VFN' F1	BS,SN,V,VS
Tomato, 'Beefsteak Improved'	BS,SN,V,VSVH
Tomato, 'Bernado'	BS
Tomato, 'Better Boy' hyb	SN
Tomato, 'Big Beefie 6737' hyb	SN
Tomato, 'Big Boy' F1	BD,BS,C,CO,DT,F,KI,L, M,R,SN,ST,SU,TU,U,YA
Tomato, 'Big Boy Giant Hybrid 6802'	SN
Tomato, 'Big Early 1200' hyb	SN
Tomato, 'Big Pack 6837' o-p	SN
Tomato, 'Big Rainbow'	KS
Tomato, 'Big Star 1201' o-p	SN
Tomato, 'Black Krim' o-p	SN
Tomato, 'Black Prince' o-p	SN
Tomato, 'Blizzard' F1	BS,F,KI,L,SN,TU
Tomato, 'Bonner Beste 6839' o-p	SN
Tomato, 'Bonset' F1	V
Tomato, 'Brandywine' o-p	KS,SN,VS
Tomato, 'Brasero' Mini	BS, F
Tomato, 'Britain's Breakfast'	RO
Tomato, 'Budai Torpe' o-p	SN,VS
Tomato, 'Buissonante'	VS
Tomato, 'Burpee Supersteak' hyb	SN
Tomato, 'Burpee's Delicious'	VS
Tomato, 'Calypso'	BS
Tomato, 'Camello'	BS
Tomato, 'Campbells 1327' o-p	SN
Tomato, 'Campbells 28' o-p	SN
Tomato, 'Camporosso' o-p	SN
Tomato, 'Caro' o-p	SN
Tomato, 'Cerisette'	VS
Tomato, 'Cerisette Brin de Muguet' o-p	SN
Tomato, 'Cherokee Purple'	KS
Tomato, 'Cherry Belle' F1	D,S,YA
Tomato, 'Cherry Wonder' F1	YA
Tomato, 'Choice' F1	K
Tomato, 'Chonto Mejorado' o-p	SN
Tomato, 'Clementine' o-p	SN
Tomato, 'Cocktail Clementine'	VS
Tomato, 'Cocktail' mix	KS
Tomato, 'Colorado' o-p	SN
Tomato, 'Cossack'	BS
Tomato, 'Costuloto Fiorentino'	F
Tomato, 'Count 11' hyb	SN
Tomato, 'Counter'	U
Tomato, 'Craigella'	DT,KI
Tomato, 'Craigella' o-p	SN
Tomato, 'Cristal' F1	DT
Tomato, 'Cumulus' F1	D
Tomato, 'Currant Red'	KS
Tomato, 'Currant Yellow'	KS
Tomato, 'Cyclon'	BS,U
Tomato, 'Dario'	M
Tomato, 'Delicate' o-p	SN,VS
Tomato, 'Dombello' F1	BS,D,J,S,SN,TU
Tomato, 'Dombito' F1	BS,DT,M,SE,SN,T,YA
Tomato, 'Dona' hyb	SN
Tomato, 'Duke' hyb	SN
Tomato, 'Earliana'	BS
Tomato, 'Earliana' o-p	SN
Tomato, 'Early Fuego' o-p	SN
Tomato, 'Estrella' F1	BS,D,DT
Tomato, 'Eurocross BB' F1	BS,J,KI,YA
Tomato, 'Evergreen' o-p	KS,SN,VS
Tomato, 'Exclusive Collection'	T
Tomato, 'Experimental TM/MO5'	T
Tomato, 'Extase' F1	KI
Tomato, 'Fandango' F1	V
Tomato, 'Firefly' F1	YA
Tomato, 'First in the Field'	B,BD,J,KI,SU
Tomato, 'First in the Field' o-p	BS
Tomato, 'Floradade' o-p	SN
Tomato, 'Fond Red Mini Plum'	SE
Tomato, 'Full Flavour Pack'	T
Tomato, 'Garden Pearl'	DT
Tomato, 'Gardener's Delight'	w.a.
Tomato, 'Gardener's Delight' o-p	BS,SN
Tomato, 'Gemini' F1	V
Tomato, 'Giant, Experimental Variety SEY2'	SE
Tomato, 'Golden Boy' hyb	BS,S,SN
Tomato, 'Golden Jubilee' F1	V
Tomato, 'Golden Nugget'	KS
Tomato, 'Golden Sunrise'	BD,C,CO,D,DT,F,J,KI,L, S,ST,SU,T,TU,VH
Tomato, 'Golden Sunrise' o-p	BS
Tomato, 'Golden Tomboy' F1	CO
Tomato, 'Goldstar' F1	K,KI
Tomato, 'Gourmet'	U
Tomato, 'Gourmet Marmande' o-p	SN
Tomato, 'Great White Beefsteak' o-p	KS,SN
Tomato, 'Green en Grappes'	VS
Tomato, 'Green Grape' o-p	SN
Tomato, 'Green Zebra' o-p	SN,VS
Tomato, Greenhouse Assortment	M
Tomato, 'Grenadier' F1	BS, S
Tomato, 'Harbinger' F1	CO,D,KI,S,SU
Tomato, 'Harbinger' o-p	BS,SN

TOMATO

Tomato, 'Harzfeuer' F1	V
Tomato, 'Hayslip' o-p	SN
Tomato, 'Heinz 1350'	BS
Tomato, 'Herald'	M
Tomato, 'Hillbilly' o-p	SN
Tomato, 'Histon Early'	U
Tomato, 'Homestead' o-p	SN
Tomato, 'Incas' F1	D,S
Tomato, 'Ipsolon' F1	BS,D,S
Tomato, 'Ivory Egg' o-p	SN
Tomato, 'Jackpot' hyb	SN
Tomato, 'Jaune St. Vincent' o-p	SN
Tomato, 'Joie de la Table' o-p	SN,VS
Tomato, 'JR-6' o-p	BS
Tomato, 'Jubilee'	RO
Tomato, 'Kentucky Beefsteak' o-p	SN
Tomato, 'La Carotina' o-p	SN,VS
Tomato, 'Lemon Plum' o-p	SN
Tomato, 'Libra' F1	CO,DT,KI,SU
Tomato, 'Long Red' o-p	SN
Tomato, 'Lylia Cerisette'	VS
Tomato, 'Lylia' o-p	SN
Tomato, 'Madagascar' o-p	SN,VS
Tomato, 'Maja'	SU
Tomato, 'Maja' o-p	SN
Tomato, 'Manhattan' F1	BS
Tomato, 'Marglobe'	BS,RO
Tomato, 'Marglobe' o-p	SN
Tomato, 'Marmande'	BD,C,D,DT,F,J,KI,S,ST, SU,U,V
Tomato, 'Marmande Ancienne'o-p	SN
Tomato, 'Marmande' o-p	BS,SN
Tomato, 'Marmande Super'	CO
Tomato, 'Marmande Super' o-p	BS
Tomato, 'Matador' F1	BS,T
Tomato, 'Megatom'	V
Tomato, 'Mexican'	VS
Tomato, 'Mexican Honey' o-p	SN,VS
Tomato, 'Minibel'	F
Tomato, 'Mirabel'	M
Tomato, 'Mirabelle Blanche' o-p	SN,VS
Tomato, 'Mirror' F1	YA
Tomato, 'Money Cross'	B,BS
Tomato, 'Moneymaker'	B,BD,C,D,DT,F,J,KI,L, Mc,R,S,ST, T,TU,U,V, VH,YA
Tomato, 'Moneymaker' o-p	BS,SN
Tomato, 'Mortgage Lifter'	KS
Tomato, 'Mountain Pride' hyb	SN
Tomato, 'Mr.Stripey	KS
Tomato, 'MS-10 FT-R' F1	V
Tomato, 'Napoli VF' o-p	SN
Tomato, 'Nebraska Wedding' o-p	KS,SN
Tomato, 'Nemastar' hyb	SN
Tomato, 'New Yorker' o-p	SN
Tomato, 'Nimbus'	S
Tomato, 'Noire Charbonneuse' o-p	SN,VS
Tomato, 'Old German' o-p	SN
Tomato, 'Oregon Oxheart' o-p	SN
Tomato, 'Ostona'	BS
Tomato, 'Outdoor Girl'	B,BS,CO,DT,J,KI,M
Tomato, 'Oxheart Giant'	SU
Tomato, 'Oxheart' o-p	BS,SN
Tomato, 'Pannovoy'	K
Tomato, 'Petit Coeur de Boeuf'	VS
Tomato, 'Phyra'	B,C,CO,KI,Mc,SU,V

Tomato, 'Phyra' o-p	BS
Tomato, 'Pineapple'	KS
Tomato, 'Piranto' F1	M
Tomato, 'Pixie' F1	BS,CO,M,ST,SU
Tomato, 'Plaisir d'Ete' o-p	SN
Tomato, 'Plumito'	RO
Tomato, 'Pomme Rouge'	VS
Tomato, 'Ponderosa' o-p	KS,SN
Tomato, 'Potiron Ecarlate' o-p	SN,VS
Tomato, 'Primato' F1	D
Tomato, 'Principe Borghese'	KS
Tomato, 'Prisca' F1	M
Tomato, 'Pritchard' o-p	SN
Tomato, 'Purple Calabash'	VS
Tomato, 'Red Alert'	B,BD,CO,DT,F,J,KI,M, SE,SN,ST,SU,U
Tomato, 'Red Cherry'	RO,SE
Tomato, 'Red Peach' o-p	SN
Tomato, 'Red Pear' o-p	KS,SN
Tomato, 'Red Plum'	VS
Tomato, 'Red Rose'	SN
Tomato, 'Red Star'hyb	SN
Tomato, 'Redskin'	VS
Tomato, 'Reine de Claude Rouge' o-p	SN,VS
Tomato, 'Reine de Sainte Marthe' o-p	SN,VS
Tomato, 'Rocamar'	BS
Tomato, 'Roma' o-p	BS,SN
Tomato, 'Roma VF'	BD,DT,F,KI,M,SN,U
Tomato, 'Roncardo'	BS
Tomato, 'Rose de Berne' o-p	SN,VS
Tomato, 'Round Yellow Sunrise'	RO
Tomato, 'Royale des Guineaux' o-p	SN,VS
Tomato, 'Russe' o-p	SN,VS
Tomato, 'Rutgers'	BS
Tomato, 'Rutgers' o-p	SN
Tomato, 'Saint Pierre'	M,SU
Tomato, 'Saint Pierre' o-p	SN
Tomato, 'Sainte Lucie' o-p	SN,VS
Tomato, 'San Marzano'	B,BS,C,CO,KI,KS,Mc, SN,ST,SU,V
Tomato, 'Santa'	T
Tomato, 'Seville Cross'	S
Tomato, 'Shirley' F1	BO,BS,CO,DT,F,J,KI,L, M,R,S,SE,SN,ST,T,TU, U,VH,YA
Tomato, 'Sigmabush'	S
Tomato, 'Sioux'	U
Tomato, 'Sleaford Abundance'	M,SN
Tomato, 'Snowball' o-p	SN
Tomato, 'Sonatine'	S
Tomato, 'Spectra'	BS
Tomato, 'Stonor Exhibition'	RO
Tomato, 'Stresa' F1	YA
Tomato, 'Sun Baby'	DT,F,K
Tomato, 'Sun Belle'	F,L
Tomato, 'Sun Cherry' F1	KS
Tomato, 'Sungold' F1	BD,BS,L,T
Tomato, 'Super Marmande'	B,M,VH,VS
Tomato, 'Super Roma VF'	T,VH
Tomato, 'Supersonic' hyb	SN
Tomato, 'Supersteak' F1	T,VH
Tomato, 'Supersweet' F1	M,SN,SU
Tomato, 'Sweet 100' F1 mini	B,BS,C,CO,DT,F,J,KI,S, SN,T,U,V,VH
Tomato, 'Sweet Cherry' F1	BS,F
Tomato, 'Sweet Cherry' o-p	SN

TOMATO

Tomato, 'Sweet Million'	KS,SN,U
Tomato, 'Sweet Peel'	SN
Tomato, 'Tangerine' o-p	SN,VS
Tomato, 'Taxi'	U
Tomato, 'The Amateur'	BD,C,KI,S,U
Tomato, 'The Amateur' o-p	BS,SN
Tomato, 'The Chef's Brigade'	T
Tomato, 'The Helen Hawkins' org	SN
Tomato, 'The John Hawkins' org	SN
Tomato, 'Thessaloniki' o-p	SN
Tomato, 'Tigerella'	B,CO,DT,F,KI,M,S,SU,T, U,V,VS
Tomato, 'Tigerella' o-p	BS,SN
Tomato, 'Tiny Tim'	DT,KI,SU,TU
Tomato, 'Tiny Tim' o-p	BS
Tomato, 'Tomboy'	BS
Tomato, 'Tornado' F1	BS,CO,D,F,KI,M,S,TU
Tomato, 'Totem' F1	BS,D,J,KI,Mc,SN,TU,U
Tomato, 'Trio' F1	BS,YA
Tomato, 'Tumbler' F1	BD,BS,D,DT,J,M,R,S, SE,T,U,VH,YA
Tomato, 'Turbo' F1	BS
Tomato, 'Typhoon' F1	BS,D,DT,J,K,L
Tomato, 'Valerie' hyb	SN
Tomato, 'Vanessa'	K,BS
Tomato, 'Virginia'	K,BS
Tomato, 'Vitador' F1	YA
Tomato, 'Walter' o-p	SN
Tomato, 'White Wonder' o-p	SN
Tomato, 'Yellow Canary'	B,BS
Tomato, 'Yellow Cherry' o-p	SN
Tomato, 'Yellow Cocktail'	B,C,KI,SU
Tomato, 'Yellow Cocktail' o-p	BS
Tomato, 'Yellow Currant'	RO
Tomato, 'Yellow Debut' F1	BS,D,YA
Tomato, 'Yellow Peach' o-p	SN
Tomato, 'Yellow Pear' o-p	KS,SN
Tomato, 'Yellow Pearshaped'	V
Tomato, 'Yellow Perfection'	M, U
Tomato, 'Yellow Plum'	VS
Tomato, 'Yellow St. Vincent'	VS
Tomato, 'Yellow Stuffer'	VS
Tronchuda	B,C
Turkish Rocket	C
Turnip, 'Arcoat'	BS,YA
Turnip, 'Arcoat' Mini	S
Turnip, 'Champion Green Top Yellow'	TU
Turnip, 'Golden Ball'	B,BD,BS,CO,D,DT,J,KI, M,S,ST,SU,TU,U
Turnip, 'Green Globe'	S
Turnip, 'Green Top Stone'	B,BS,J,KI,M,ST
Turnip, 'Hakutaka' F1	D
Turnip, 'Manchester Market'	DT,L,YA
Turnip, 'Market Express' F1	KI,YA
Turnip, 'Model White'	BS,D
Turnip, 'Presto' (Tokyo Market Sagami)	C
Turnip, 'Purple Top Milan'	B,BD,BS,D,DT,F,J,KI, Mc,S,ST,SU,TU,U,VH
Turnip, 'Red Milan'	BS
Turnip, 'Red Round'	KS
Turnip, 'Royal Crown' F1	SU
Turnip, 'Snowball'*Early White Stone	B,BD,BS,C,CO,D,DT,F,J, KI,M,Mc, S,ST,SU,T,TU, VH
Turnip, 'Sprinter'	BS
Turnip, 'Stanis'	BS

Turnip, 'Tokyo Cross' F1	BS,CO,KS,SE,SU,T,TU
Turnip, 'Tokyo Cross' F1 Mini	D,F,S
Turnip, 'Tokyo Market' Second Early	C
Turnip, 'Tokyo Top' F1'	BS
Turnip, 'Veitch Red Globe'	BS,CO,KI,TU
Turnip, 'White Milan'	BS,L,KS
Turnip, 'White Milan Forcing'	BS
Vegetable Amaranth	CO,SU
Vegetable Amaranth,'Groenbladig type'	SU,V
Vegetable Amaranth, 'Roodbladig type'	V
Vegetable Amaranth, 'White leaf'	SU
Vegetable Chinese/Oriental Collection	F
Vegetable Collection 1	F
Vegetable Collection 2	F
Vegetable Collections	BD
Vegetable Mini Collection	D,M
Vegetable Seed Collection, 13 Varieties	D
Vegetable Seed Collection , 26 Varieties	D
Vegetable Seed Collection , 'Mediterranean'	U
Vegetable 'Stir-Fry Collection'	D
Water Pepper	KS
Water Spinach	KS,SU
Watercress	VH

HERBS

Agrimony	CE,H,JV,SU
Ajwain	C,SU
Alexanders	CE,SU
Alkanet	H,SU
Angelica	BD,BS,C,CE,CO,J,JE, KI,Mc,R,ST,SU,U,V
Anise	BD,BS,C,CE,CO,H,JE, JV,KI,Mc,R,ST,SU,V
Anise Hyssop	SU
Annual Herb Mixture	M
Arnica Chamissonis	CE,JV,SU
Arnica Montana	SU
Aromatic Seasonings	SE,T
Artichoke, Globe	H
Balm	BS,C,J,L,JE,Mc,R,S,V
Balm, Lemon	BD,CE,CO,CP,F,JV,KI, KS,M,ST,SU,T,VH
Basil, Anise	B,BS,CE,JV,KS,SU
Basil, Bush (Greek)	B,BD,BS,CE,CO,CP,H, JE,JV,KI,KS,M,Mc,R,S, ST,SU,T
Basil, Bush (Gr) 'Finissimo verde a palla'	C,Mc
Basil, 'Cinnamon'	B,BD,BS,C,CE,CP,D,JV, KI,KS,SU,T
Basil, 'Dark Opal'	BD,BS,C,CO,KS,Mc,ST, SU
Basil 'Fino Verde'	B,CP,KS
Basil, 'Genovese'	B,C,KS,L,SU
Basil, 'Genovese Giant'	KS
Basil, 'Greek Mini'	KS,SU
Basil, 'Green Globe'	SU
Basil, Holy	CE,V,KS,S,SU,V
Basil, 'Horapha'	B,CE,SU,V
Basil, Italian	CE,V
Basil, Lemon	B,BS,CP,CE,CO,H,JV, KS,SU,V
Basil, 'Lettuce Leaved'	B,C,CO,CP,H,JV,KS
Basil, 'Liquorice'	B,C,CP

BASIL

Basil, 'Mexican'	C
Basil 'Napoletano'	B,BS,C,CP,KS,SU
Basil 'New Guinea'	B,CP
Basil, 'Opal'	H,JV
Basil, 'Piccolo'	B
Basil, 'Purple'	B,CE,CP
Basil, 'Purple' dw	B
Basil, 'Red Rubin'	B,CE,D,KS,SU,V
Basil, 'Ruffles Green'	B,BD,BS,CE,JV,KS,SU
Basil, 'Ruffles' Mixed	U
Basil, 'Ruffles Purple'	B,BS,CE,H,JV,K,KS,S,SU
Basil, 'Siam Queen'	F
Basil, 'Spice'	B,CE,SU
Basil, 'Spicy Globe'	B,C,KS,SU
Basil, Sweet	w.a.
Basil, 'Sweet Green Bouquet'	B,D,SU
Basil, Thai	B,C,CE,CP,D,DT,KS,SE
Basil 'Yeome Awaaka'	B
Bergamot, Lemon	BS,CE,JV,Mc,S,SU
Bergamot, Mint	V
Bergamot, Oswego tea	BD,JE
Bergamot, Wild	JV,KI,SU
Betony	CE,JV,SU
Borage	BD,BS,C,CE,CO,F,H,J,JE,JV,KI,L,M,Mc,S,SE,ST,SU,V,VH
Borage, White	CE,SU
Bugle	CE
Burdock	CE
Calamint	C,CE,JV,SU,V
Campion, Bladder	CE,SU
Campion, Red	CE,SU
Caraway	BD,BS,C,CE,CO,H,J,JE,JV,KI,L,Mc,ST,SU,T,U,V
Cardoon	H,KI
Catmint	CE,H
Catmint, 'Faassenii'	JV
Catmint, Lemon	JV
Catnip	CE,JV,SU
Catnip, Lemon	CE,SU
Celandine, Greater	CE,SU,V
Celandine, Lesser	CE
Celery, Cutting	M
Celery, Par-cel	H,M,U
Celery Parcel, 'Zwolsche Krul'	C,T
Centaury	CE,SU
Chamomile, Dyers	CE,JV,SU
Chamomile, German (Wild)	C,CE,H,SU,V
Chamomile, Matricaria	BD,CO,JE
Chamomile, Roman	C,BD,BS,CE,CO,F,H,JV,KI,L,Mc,R,ST,SU,T,U,V,VH
Chervil	B,BD,BS,CE,CO,CP,F,G,H,J,JE,JV,KS,L,ST,SU,T,U,V
Chervil, Curled	C,H,KI,Mc,S,SU
Chicory	CE,H,JV,SU,V
Chives	w.a.
Chives, Fine Leaved	H,SU
Chives, Forcing	SU
Chives, Garlic	BD,C,CE,CO,D,DT,H,J,JV,KI,KS,M,Mc,R,S,SE,SU,T,U,V
Chopsuey Green	JV
Choy Sum	JV
Cicely, Sweet	BD,BS,C,CE,CO,H,JV,Mc
Clary	CO
Comfrey	C,ST,SU,V
Coriander	BD,BS,C,CE,CO,DT,F,J,JV,K,KI,L,Mc,R,S,ST,SU,V,VH
Coriander, Cilantro,Chinese Parsley	B,C,CO,D,M,SE,T,U
Coriander, Moroccan	KI,SU
Coriander, Roman	C,D,SU
Coriander, 'Santo'	H
Corn Salad	H
Cowslip	H,JV
Cumin	B,BD,BS,C,CO,KI,Mc,R,ST,SU,V
Cumin, Black	BS,SU
Dandelion	B,BS,CO,SU
Dill	w.a.
Dill, Bouquet	B,BS,G,KI,KS,SU,U
Dill, Dukat	B,BS,K,SU
Dill, Indian	SU
Dill, Mammoth	BS,SU
Dill, 'Sari'	T,V
Dill, Vierling	B,C,SU
Dog Rose	CO
Dropwort	CE
Dyers Greenwood	CE,SU
Dyers Weld	CE
Elecampane	CE,H,JE,JV,SU
Endive, 'Tres Fine'	SE
Eucalyptus, Lemon	H,SU
Eucalyptus, Peppermint	SU
Evening Primrose	CE,JV,KS,SU
Fennel, 'Cantino'	BS
Fennel, Sweet	w.a.
Fennel, Sweet Bronze	BD,C,CE,CO,F,JV,K,KI,S,SU,V
Fenugreek	C,SU
Feverfew	BD,BS,C,CE,CO,J,JV,KI,L,Mc,S,ST,SU,V
Feverfew, Golden	BS,CE,JV
Figwort	CE
Flax	CE,SU
Flax, Red	CE
Fleabane	CE,SU
Foxglove, ambigua	H,JV
Foxglove, lanata	H
Foxglove, lutea	H
Foxglove, purpurea	SU
Garlic Mustard	BS,CO,SU,T
Garlic, Wild Ramsons	SU
Gayfeather	CE,SU
Ginseng, Asiatic	SU
Ginseng, Panax stratified seed	JE
Goats Rue	CE,SU
Good King Henry(Mercury)	BS,CE,CO,JV,KI,R,T
Greater Knapweed	CE
Greater Knapweed, Golden	CE
Greater Stitchwort	CE
Gypsywort	CE
Heartsease	CE,JV,SU
Henbane	CE
Herb Bennet	CE,SU
Herb Collection, Culinary	JV
Herb Collection, Edible Flower	JV
Herb Collection, Herbal Tea	JV

267

Herb Collection, Herbal Wild Flower	JV
Herb Collection, Salad Herb	JV
Herb Collections	BD
Herb Robert	CE
Herbs, Companion Plants	T
Herbs, Culinary Mixed	C
Hollyhock	H,KI,SU,V
Hop	ST,SU
Horehound	BD,BS,C,CE,CO,JE,JV, KI,Mc,SU,V
Horehound, Black	SU
Horseradish Tree	SU
Hungarian Blue Breadseed Poppy	C
Hyssop	BD,BS,C,CE,CO,D,J,JE, L,Mc,S,ST,SU,V
Hyssop, Blue Flowered	CE,H,JV,KI,SU
Hyssop, Pink Flowered	BS,C,CE,JV,SU
Hyssop, White Flowered	BS,C,CE,JV,SU
Incense Plant	JV
Jacob's Ladder	CE,JV,SU
Jacob's Ladder, White	CE
Japanese Green, Mizuna	JV
Japanese Parsley, Mitsuba	CE,JV
Kidney Vetch	CE
Ladies Mantle	CE,KS,SU
Lady's Bedstraw	CE,SU
Lavender, angustifolia	BD,CO,JV,KI,ST,SU,V, VH
Lavender, French	CE,SU
Lavender, 'Hidcote'	CE,H,JV,SU
Lavender, latifolia	JE
Lavender, 'Munstead'	CE,JV,SU
Lavender, officinalis	JE
Lavender, spica	CO,Mc,SU
Lavender, Woolly	CE,SU
Lovage	BD,BS,C,CE,CO,H,JE, JV,K,KI,M,Mc,ST,SU,V
Madder	SU
Mallow, Common	CE,JV,SU
Mallow, 'Crispa'	CE
Mallow, Field	CE
Mallow, Marsh	BS,CE,H,JE,JV,SU
Mallow, Musk	CE,JV,SU
Mallow, Musk White	CE
Mamang	C
Marigold, 'Fiesta'	JV
Marigold, Pot	BS,C,H,JE,JV,ST,SU,T
Marjoram, Pot	BD,BS,C,CE,CO,JE,JV, KI,MC,R,ST,SU,T,V
Marjoram, Sweet	w.a
Meadowsweet	CE,JV,SU,T
Mexican Tea	C
Mint	J,M,S,T,VH
Mint, Apple	SU
Mint, Emperor's	C,JV,SU
Mint, Korean	JV,SU
Mint, Lemon	C
Mint, Mountain	C,SU
Mint, Peppermint	BS,C,CO,L,JE,Mc,R,SE, SU,V
Mint, Spearmint	BS,C,CO,F,JE,KI,R,ST, SU,V
Mint, Water	SU
Monkshood	CE
Motherwort	CE,SU
Mountain tobacco	JE

Mugwort	C,CE,JE,SU,V
Mullein, Greater	CE,H,SU,V
Myrrh	JE,SU,T
Nasturtium	JV,SU,VH
Onion, Welsh	BD,CO,H,JV,KI,ST,SU
Onion, Welsh red	SU
Orach, Gold	BS,CE,SU,
Orach, Green	SU
Orach, Red	BS,CE,JV,SU
Oregano	w.a.
Oregano, Greek	BS,C,JV,KI,KS,SU
Oregano, Showy	C
Oregano, white	JV
Ox-Eye Daisy	CE,SU
Parsley, Bravour	BD,DT,U
Parsley, 'Champion Moss Curled'	C,DT,VH
Parsley, 'Curlina'	F,KS
Parsley, Curly	CE,JV,SU
Parsley, 'Envy'	S
Parsley, French	CE,JV,K,R,SU
Parsley, Genovese	KS
Parsley, Hamburg	BD,F,KS
Parsley, Italian	CE,KS,SU
Parsley, Moss Curled	BD,F,H
Parsley, Neapolitan	C
Parsley, Plain Leaved	BD,H,JE,U
Parsley, 'Triple Curled'	C,KS,VH
Parsley, 'Unicurl'	KS
Parsley, 'Verbo'	DT
Parsley, Wild	T
Pennyroyal	BS,CE,CO,F,H,JV,KI,Mc, SU
Perilla Frutescens	H,KS
Pimpernel	V
Plantain	JE
Pleurisy Root	CE,SU
Pokeroot	CE,SU
Poppy	H,SU,V
Purple Loosestrife	CE,SU
Purslane	BD,BS,C,CE,H,JV,Mc
Purslane, Golden	BS,C,CE,CO,JV
Purslane, Green	C,CO,JV
Pyrethrum	JV,SU
Rampion	JE,SU
Rhubarb	JE
Rocket	BD,BS,CE,J,JV,K,KI,M, Mc,SE,ST,SU,T,U,VH
Rocket, Wild	JV,SU
Rosemary	w.a
Rue	BD,BS,CE,CO,JE,JV,KI, Mc,S,SU,V
Safflower	CE,SU
Sage	w.a.
Sage, Clary	BS,CE,JV,SU
Sage, Painted	BS,CE,SU
Salad Burnet	BD,C,CE,CO,H,JE,JV, KI,T,Mc,S,SU,V˙
Savory, Broad Leaved	CE
Savory, Creeping	CE
Savory, Summer	BD,BS,C,CE,CO,H,JE, JV,KI,KS,Mc,S,ST,SU, T,V
Savory, Winter	BD,BS,C,CE,CO,H,JE, JV,KI,KS,M,Mc,S,ST,SU, V
Scabious, Devils Bit	CE,SU

SCABIOUS, FIELD

Scabious, Field	CE,SU
Scabious, Sheeps	CE
Scabious, Small	CE,SU
Scurvy Grass	SU,V
Self Heal	CE,SU
Sesame	BS,SU
Shiso, Green	CE,JV
Shiso, Purple	JV
Skullcap	CE,JV,SU
Soapwort	CE,CO,JV,SU
Sorrell	C,CE,CO,J,JE,JV,M,Mc,ST,V
Sorrell, Buckler Leaved	CE,CO,H,JV,SU
Sorrell, French (lge leaf)	BD,H,K,KI,S,SU
St.John's Wort	CE,JE,SU
St.Mary's Thistle	V
Stone Orpine	JE
Strawberry, Alpine	CE
Strawberry, Sticks	KI,SU
Strawberry, Wild	JV,SU
Sweet Rocket	CE,JV,KS
Tansy, Common	BD,BS,C,CE,CO,JV,KI,KS,Mc,S,SU,V
Tarragon	BD,BS,C,CO,J,JE,KI,KS,L,Mc,R,S,SU,T,V
Teasel	CE,SU
Thyme	w.a.
Thyme, Broad Leaved	U
Thyme, Old English	B,DT,K,SE,T
Thyme, Wild Creeping	CE,H,JV,KS,R,SU
Toadflax	CE,JV,KS,SU
Toadflax, Purple	CE
Tormentil	CE,SU
Valerian	CE,H,JE,JV,SU,V
Valerian, Red	JV,SU
Vervain	CE,H,JV,SU
Vervain, Blue	CE,SU
Viper's Bugloss	CE,H,JV,SU
Vitex	CE,SU
Watercress	JE,V
Weld	H,SU
Woad	CE,H,JV,KS,SU
Woodruff, Sweet	BS,JE,KS,SU,V
Woodsage	CE,JV,SU
Wormwood	BD,BS,CE,CO,JE,JV,KS,SU,V
Yarrow	H,JE,JV,KS,SU
Yellow Melilot	CE

CODE-SUPPLIER INDEX

A   Agroforestry Research Trust, 46 Hunters Moon, Dartington, Totnes, Devon. TQ9 6JT   CONTACT: Mr.M.Crawford CAT.COST:3x 1st class stamps   CAT OUT:Jan '97 POSTAGE ON ORDERS:£1 for orders under £10 RETAIL/WHOLESALE:Retail   CULTURAL NOTES:Yes SEED COUNT:Yes   EXPORT:Yes SPECIALITIES:Trees, shrubs, perennials   OTHER INFO:Profits go to research projects

AL   Allwood Bros. Mill Nursery. Hassocks. W.Sussex. BN6 9NB. TEL: 01273 844229   FAX:01273 846022 CAT COST: 2x 1st class stamps   CAT OUT:Dec WHOLESALE/RETAIL: Retail   CULTURAL NOTES: Yes EXPORT: Yes   CREDIT CARDS: Yes

AP   Alpine Garden Society, AGS Centre, Avon Bank, Pershore. Worcs. WR10 3JP   CONTACT; Mr. W.J.Simpson TEL: 01386 554790   FAX: 01386 554801 CAT COST:Membership fee   CAT OUT:Dec POSTAGE ON ORDERS: £3   CULTURAL NOTES: Yes EXPORT: Seed exchange with overseas members OTHER INFO: Seed available to members only

AS   Ashwood Nurseries Ltd, Greensforge, Kingswinford. W.Midlands. DY6 0AE   CONTACT; Mr. T.D. Baulk TEL: 01384 401996   FAX: 01384 401108 OPENING TIMES: Everyday, except Xmas & Boxing Day. CAT COST: 4x 1st class stamps   CAT OUT:Autumn 1997 POSTAGE FOR ORDERS: Yes   WHOLESALE/RETAIL: Both CULTURAL NOTES: Yes   SEED COUNT:Yes EXPORT: Yes   CREDIT CARDS:A,V,AE SPECIALITIES: Auricula, Cyclamen, Hellebores, Lewisias.

AU   Australasian Plant Society. Stonecourt. 74 Brimstage Rd, Heswall, Wirral. L60 1XQ CONTACT: J.Irons   CAT COST:Membership   CAT OUT:May CULTURAL NOTES: Yes SPECIALITIES: Australian & New Zealand sp. OTHER INFO: List may change from year to year. Seed available to members only.

AV   Agua Viva Seed Ranch, R&I, Box 8, Taos, New Mexico 87571. U.S.A. TEL: (505) 758-4520   FAX: 505 758 1745 OPENING TIMES: M-F 9-5, Sat 10-4   CAT COST: $3 CAT OUT: Jan '97   WHOLESALE/RETAIL : Retail CULTURAL NOTES:Yes SPECIALITIES: Wildflower & Native Perennials EXPORT:Yes   CREDIT CARDS:Amex,Mc,V OTHER INFO: Pack by weight E-MAIL: aguaviva@taos.newmex.com

B   B&T World Seeds. Rue des Marchandes. Paguignan, 34210 Olonzac. France   CONTACT: Mr.R.Wheatley TEL:01278 733209   FAX: 01278 733209 E-M:r@thesys.demon.co.uk. OPENING TIMES: Dawn-Dusk 365 days   MIN ORDER: £5 CAT COST:Europe £10, Elsewhere £14. Sublists 50p +.Disc £5. CAT OUT: Feb '97. Published quarterly. Sub-lists/discs ad hoc. POSTAGE ON ORDERS: Upto £20 -£1, £20-£50 -£2, £50+ qu. DISCOUNTS: Trade terms available, occasional special offers. WHOLESALE/RETAIL: Both. Limited stock held. Callers welcome   CULTURAL NOTES: (Yes) SEED COUNT:Rarely given   SEED COLLECTIONS: Australian native flowers & shrubs in pictorial pks.   EXPORT: Yes CREDIT CARDS: A,Eu,Ma,V   SPECIALITIES: The exotic, obscure and/or hard to get.   OTHER INFO:Over 30,000 seeds listed, divided into 187 sub-lists e.g. Erosion control plant seed list. Grasses. Primulaceae. Orchidaceae. Cactaceae etc.

BA   J & J Ainsworth. Bank Farm. Bank Head Ln, Bamber Bridge, Preston. PR5 6YR TEL: 01772 321557   CONTACT: J. Ainsworth OPENING TIMES:By appt. One open day.   No cat. POSTAGE ON ORDERS: 26p. CULTURAL NOTES: Yes   SEED COUNT:Min. SPECIALITIES: Sarracenia seed. OTHER INFO: Limited quantities, sp & hyb, harvested Oct.

BC   British Cactis & Succulent Society. Mr.P.Lewis, The Membership Secretary. 'Firgrove', 1 Springwoods, Courtmoor, Fleet, Hants. GU13 9SU CONTACT: Mr. P.Lewis CAT COST:Free to members   CAT OUT:Nov EXPORT: Overseas members   SPECIALITIES:Cactus OTHER INFO: Seeds available to members only

BD   Basically Seeds. Risby Business Park. Newmarket Rd. Risby. Bury St. Edmunds. IP11 8AS   CONTACT: V.Dahl TEL: 01284 811001   FAX:01284 811021 CAT COST: Free   CAT OUT:Sept   POSTAGE: Free OPENING TIMES:By arrangement. DISCOUNTS; Special offers in Mar.   WHOLESALE/RETAIL:Both SEED COUNT: Yes   EXPORT:Yes

BL   Blackmore & Langdon. Pensford. Nr Bristol. BS18 4JL TEL:01275 332300   CONTACT:R.A.Langdon OPENING TIMES: M-Sa 9-5, Su 10-4 CAT OUT:Mar   DISCOUNTS:Occasionally WHOLESALE/RETAIL:Retail   CULTURAL NOTES: Yes SEED COUNT: On request   EXPORT:Yes SPECIALITIES: Begonias,Delphiniums

BO   Robert Bolton & Son. Birdbrook. Halstead. Essex. CO9 4BQ TEL: 01440 785246   FAX:01440 788000 CAT COST:Free   CAT OUT:August POSTAGE ON ORDERS: Free over £10, Overseas £1.75 WHOLESALE/RETAIL: Retail   CULTURAL NOTES: Yes SEED COUNT:Yes   SEED COLLECTIONS:Yes EXPORT:Yes   CREDIT CARDS: Mc,V

BP   Barnhaven Primroses. Langerhouad 22420. Plouzelambre. France CONTACT: A.Bradford   E-MAIL:Bradford@wanadoo.fr TEL: (+33) 02 96 35 31 54   FAX:(+33) 96 35 31 55 CAT COST: £7 col cat., £1 seed list   CAT OUT: Oct POSTAGE ON ORDERS:£1   WHOLESALE /RETAIL: Retail CULTURAL NOTES: Yes   SEED COUNT: Yes EXPORT: Worldwide   CREDIT CARDS: MA,V SPECIALITIES: Primulas, Barnhaven Polyanthus.

BR   British Clematis Society. 4 Springfield. Lightwater. Surrey. GU18 5XP   CONTACT: R.J.Stothard. (Sec) TEL: 01276 476387   CAT COST:Membership fee. CAT OUT: Spring   POSTAGE:Free EXPORT: Overseas members OTHER INFO: Annual seed exchange available to members only.

BS   Seeds-By-Size, 45 Crouchfield, Boxmoor, Hemel Hempstead, Herts. HP1 1PA   CONTACT: John Size TEL: 01442 251458   TEL. ANS. TIMES: 9-9 M-F, 9-12 Sa CAT COST: Free   CAT OUT:July   POSTAGE:77p for under £5 DISCOUNTS:£1 introductory voucher with first order WHOLESALE/ RETAIL: Both, wholesale on quotation CULTURAL NOTES:Some SEED COUNT:Some EXPORT:Yes SPECIALITIES: Cabbage, Marrow, Pumpkin, Squash, Lettuce, Cauliflower, Onions.   OTHER INFO:To sell seed in whatever quantity is required. 1350 veg, 3700 flowers listed

CODE-SUPPLIER INDEX

C Chiltern Seeds. Bortree Stile, Ulverston,Cumbria. LA12 7PB
TEL: 01229 5811   FAX: 01229 584549
CAT COST:50p in stamps   CAT OUT: Dec
POSTAGE:60p under £10, Europe £1 under £20, RoW £2 under
£25 DISCOUNT: Trade discount WHOLESALE/RETAIL: Retail
CULTURAL NOTES:Yes   SEED COUNT:If small no. of seeds
EXPORT: Yes CREDIT CARDS: A,AE,EU,MA,SW,V
OTHER INFO: Wide range
E-mail: 101344.1340@compuserve.com

CC Chris Chadwell. 81 Parlaunt Rd. Slough. Berks. SL3 8BE
TEL: 01753 542823   CONTACT:Chis Chadwell
OPENING TIMES: By appt. May-July
CAT COST: 3x 1st class stamps CAT OUT:Oct POSTAGE:50p
WHOLESALE/RETAIL: Retail mostly SEED COUNT:Some given
EXPORT:Yes SPECIALITIES: Himalayan, Japanese, N.American

CD Cotswold Grass Seeds Direct. The Barn Business Centre. Great
Rissington. Cheltenham. Glos. GL54 2LH
TEL: 01451 822055   FAX: 01451 810300
OPENING TIMES: M-F, 9-5   MIN. ORDER:£50
CAT COST: Free CAT OUT: Mar & July   POSTAGE:Free
DISCOUNTS: On lge orders WHOLESALE/RETAIL: Wholesale
SPECIALITIES:All grass seed   EXPORT: Yes
CREDIT CARDS: Yes   OTHER INFO:Grass seed in bulk
E-MAIL:caroline@cotseeds.demon.co.uk

CE Chesire Herb   ⌐ ⌐ ᴅ⌐ ⌐⌐ ⌐ᴛ⌐ᴍᴘ⌐rl⌐⌐ ⌐h⌐⌐ir⌐
CW6 9ES
TEL: 01829 7
OPENING TII
CAT OUT: J⌐
CULTURAL ⌐
OTHER INFC

CG Coombland
W.Sussex. R
TEL: 01403 ⌐
OPENING TI
CAT. COST:£
WHOLESALI

CH Craig House
9JW   C⌐
TEL:01704 ⌐
CULTURAL ⌐

CL Colegrave S
3EY
TEL:01295 ⌐
OPENING T⌐
DISCOUNT⌐
WHOLESAL
SEED COUN
CREDIT CA⌐

CO The Organi
Coombelan⌐
TEL:01932 ⌐
OPENING T
POSTAGE:
members, ⌐
WHOLESAI
CULTURAL
SEED COLLECTIONS:As gift packs   ᴄᴿᴇᴅ⌐⌐ ᴄᴀᴿᴅ⌐⌐⌐⌐⌐ ⌐
SPECIALITIES:Vegetables, herbs.Seed is untreated after harvest

CP Companion Plants. 7247 North Coolville Ridge, Athens, Ohio
45701. U.S.A   CONTACT:Peter Borchard
TEL: 614 592 4643 FAX: 614 593 3092
OPENING TIMES: 10-5 every day but Wed, no weekend hours
in Dec, Jan, Feb   CAT COST:$3 CAT OUT: Annually
POSTAGE ON ORDERS: Yes   WHOLESALE/RETAIL: Both
CULTURAL NOTES:Yes   DISCOUNTS:For W/sale bulk
EXPORT: Yes   CREDIT CARDS: MA,V
SPECIALITIES:Culinary, Medicinal, Herbs
E-MAIL: nHp://www.frognet.net/companion plants

CR Cravens Nursery. 1 Foulds Terrace. Bingley. W.Yorks.
TEL: 01274 561412   CONTACT: S.R.Craven
OPENING TIMES: Th-Su, please ring first   MIN ORDER:£5
CAT COST: £1   POSTAGE:Yes   DISCOUNTS:Yes
WHOLESALE/RETAIL:Retail   CULTURAL NOTES: Yes
EXPORT: Yes SPECIALITIES: Show Auriculas, Primulas,Alpines

CT CTDA. 174 Cambridge St. London. SW1V 4QE
TEL:0171 9765115
CAT COST:Free CAT OUT: May   POSTAGE:£1.50
WHOLESALE/RETAIL:Retail SEED COUNT: Yes EXPORT:Yes
SPECIALITIES: Aquilegia, Cyclamen, Hellebores

D Samuel Dobie & Son Ltd, Broomhill Way, Torquay. Devon. TQ2
7QW
TEL:01803 61628 FAX:01803 615150
CAT COST:Free   CAT OUT:Oct   POSTAGE: 75p under £5
DISCOUNTS:For Horticultural Societies
WHOLESALE/RETAIL:Retail   CULTURAL NOTES:Yes
SEED COUNT: Yes   CREDIT CARDS:Yes

DT D.T.Brown & Co. Ltd. Station Rd. Poulton Le Fylde. Lancs. FY6
7HX
TEL:01253 882371 FAX:01253 890923
OPENING HOURS:M-Th 8.30-5.30, F 8.30-4.30
CAT COST:Free   CAT OUT:Sept   POSTAGE:60p
DISCOUNT:For Horticultural Clubs
WHOLESALE/RETAIL:Both   CULTURAL NOTES:Basic
SEED COUNT:Yes   EXPORT:Yes
CREDIT CARDS:A,Sw,V   SPECIALITIES: Flower & Veg

E Elisabeth Goodwin Nurseries. The White Gate. 86, Cambridge
Rd. Girton. Cambridge. CB3 0PJ
TEL:01223 276013 OPENING TIMES:Th-Sa 10-1 & 2-5
CAT COST:50p coin or 2x 1st class stamps CAT OUT:Autumn
POSTAGE ON ORDERS:Yes   WHOLESALE/RETAIL:Retail
CULTURAL NOTES:Yes SEED COUNT:For large/scarce seed
SPECIALITIES: Plants for dry gardens
OTHER INFO: Moving, all orders will be forwarded for 1997.

F Mr.Fothergills Seeds. Kentford. Newmarket. Suffolk. CB8 7QB.
TEL:01638 751161 FAX: 01638 751624
OPENING TIMES: 9-5   CAT COST:Free   CAT OUT: Oct
POSTAGE: 50p under £5 WHOLESALE/RETAIL:Retail outlets
CULTURAL NOTES:Yes   SEED COUNT:Yes   EXPORT:Yes
CREDIT CARDS:A,MA,SW,V

FH Field House Alpines. Leake Rd. Gotham. Nottingham. NG11
0JN   CONTACT:D.Lockhead
TEL: 0115 9830278 OPENING TIMES: Every day exc. Th, 9-5
CAT COST: 4x 1st class stamps or 4x IRC (overseas)
CAT OUT: Jan   POSTAGE: EU 70p, £2 otherwise
WHOLESALE/RETAIL: Retail   CULTURAL NOTES: Brief
SEED COUNT:Min 20 SEED COLLECTIONS:Yes EXPORT:Yes
CREDIT CARDS:MA,V   SPECIALITIES:Primula & Alpines

CODE-SUPPLIER INDEX

G   Gesellschaft der Staudenfreunde e.V. Geshaftsstelle. Melensweg 1 65795.attersheim. Germany.
TEL: 0 61 90 36 42   FAX:0 61 90 71865
OPENING TIMES: Every day   CAT COST:Membership fee
CAT OUT:Dec   POSTAGE ON ORDERS:Yes
EXPORT:Overseas members   OTHER INFO:Seeds for members only. Seeds may change from year to year.

GC   Glenhirst Cactus Nursery. Station Rd. Swineshead. Boston. Lincs. PE20 3NX   CONTACT: S.A.Bell
TEL:01205 820314
OPENING TIMES:Th,F,Su 10-5 from 01/04 to 30/09
CAT COST: 2x stamps   CAT OUT: Early '97   POSTAGE: Yes
DISCOUNTS: On all seeds   WHOLESALE/RETAIL:Retail
CULTURAL NOTES:Yes   SEED COUNT:Yes
SEED COLLECTIONS:Yes   EXPORT:Yes
SPECIALITIES: Cactus & Succulents

GI   Pinks & Carnations. 22 Chetwyn Ave. Bromley Cross. Bolton. BL7 9BN   CONTACT: Tom Gillies
TEL:01204 306273   FAX:01204 306273
OPENING TIMES: By appt only   CAT COST: Stamp
CAT OUT: Aug   POSTAGE:Free in U.K, stamps for overseas
WHOLESALE/RETAIL: Both   SEED COUNT:Yes   EXPORT:Yes
CREDIT CARDS:A, V   SPECIALITIES:Carnations, Pinks

H   The Cottage Herbery. Mill House. Boraston. Tenbury Wells. Worcs. WR15 8LZ
TEL:01584 781575   FAX: 01584 781483
OPENIG TIMES: 11-5 Su only May-July & by appt.
CAT COST: £1   CAT OUT: Spring   POSTAGE ON ORDERS:Yes
WHOLESALE/RETAIL:Both   SPECIALITIES:Herbs   EXPORT:Yes

HA   Harvest Seeds. 325 McCarrs Creek Rd. Terrey Hills. NSW 2084. Australia.   CONTACT: B.Harrold
TEL: (02) 9450 2699   FAX:(02) 9450 2750
OPENING TIMES: M-F 8.30-4.30   MIN ORDER:$10.00
CAT COST:Free   POSTAGE:Yes   DISCOUNTS:Yes
WHOLESALE/RETAIL: Wholesale   CULTURAL NOTES:Yes
SEED COLLECTIONS: Gift packs   EXPORT:Yes
SPECIALITIES:Native grasses   OTHER INFO: Living cards

HD   HDRA. Heritage Seed Library. Ryton Organic Gardens. Ryton-on-Dunsmore. Coventry. CV8 3LG
TEL: 01203 303517   FAX:01203 639229
MIN ORDER: Max 6 pkts   CAT COST: Free to members
CAT OUT: Nov   CULTURAL NOTES:Yes   CREDIT CARDS:
For membership fees   SPECILIATIES:Unregistered vegetable seeds   OTHER INFO: Seed exchange scheme for members only.
E-MAIL: cog@hdra.demon.uk

JE   James Henderson & Sons. Kingholm Quay. Dunfries. DG1 4SU
TEL: 01387 252234   FAX:01387 262302
CONTACT: Mr. Henderson   OPENING TIMES:M-F 7.30-4.30
MIN ORDER: 3kg   CAT COST: S.A.E.   CAT OUT:Oct
POSTAGE:Yes   WHOLESALE/RETAIL:Both
CULTURAL NOTES:Yes   SPECIALITIES:Seed Potatoes only

HH   Hillview Hardy Plants. Worfield. Nr Bridgnorth. Shropshire. WV15 5NT.   CONTACT:Ingrid Millington
TEL: 01746 716454   FAX:01746 716454
OPENING TIMES: M-Sa, 9-5, Mar - Mid Oct
CAT COST:4x 1st class stamps   CAT OUT:Nov   POSTAGE:Free
WHOLESALE/RETAIL:Retail   CULTURAL NOTES:On request
EXPORT: E.U only   SPECIALITIES:Herbaceous and Alpines
OTHER INFO: Seed collected from nursery stock

HL   Henllys Lodge Plants. Beaumaris. Anglesey. Gwynedd.
TEL: 01248 810106   CONTACT:E.Lane
CAT COST: 2x 1st class stamps   CAT COST:Nov   POSTAGE:40p
WHOLESALE/RETAIL: Retail   CULTURAL NOTES: On request
SEED COUNT:For very small quantities
SPECIALITIES: Hardy Geraniums

HW   Holland Wildflower Farm. P.O.Box 328. Elkins. Arkansas 72727
TEL: 501 643 2622   FAX:501 643 2622   CONTACT:Julie Holland
OPENING TIMES: By appt.
MIN ORDER:$15 for credit card orders, otherwise no min.
CAT COST:Free   DISCOUNTS: On quantity
WHOLESALE/RETAIL:Both   CULTURAL NOTES:Extensive
EXPORT: Yes   CREDIT CARDS:Discover,MA,V
SPECIALITIES:Eastern US natives, prairie, wetlands & forest
OTHER INFO: Seed less than 1 ounce is sold by no. of sq.ft. coverage. E.g. I pkt covers 30 sq.ft.
E-MAIL: info@hwildfower.com

I   W.E.TH.Ingwersen Ltd. Birch Farm Nursery. Gravetye. East Grinstead. W.Sussex. RH19 4LE   CONTACT: M.Green
TEL: 01342 810236
OPENING TIMES:Every day 9-4, Mar-Sept. Rest of yr, 9-4, M-F.
CAT COST: Free   POSTAGE: S.a.e with order, 4 IRC (overseas)
CAT OUT: Early 1997   WHOLESALE/RETAIL:Retail
CULTURAL NOTES:Yes   EXPORT:Yes
SPECIALITIES:Alpines & Rock Garden Plants

IC   International Clematis Society. 115. Belmont Rd. Harrow. Middlesex. HA3 7PL.   CONTACT: F. Woolfenden (Secretary)
TEL: +44 181 427 5340   E-MAIL: clematis@dial.pipex.com
CAT COST: Free to members   CAT OUT:Feb/Mar
POSTAGE: Nominal   CULTURAL NOTES:Relevant articles in journal   EXPORT: Overseas members
SPECIALITIES: Clematis only
OTHER INFO: Seeds for members only.

J   Johnsons Seeds. London Rd. Boston. Lincs. PE21 8AD
TEL: 01205 365051   FAX:01205 310148
OPENING TIMES: M-F 8.30-5.30
CAT COST: Free   CAT OUT: Oct   POSTAGE:Free
DISCOUNTS: Yes   WHOLESALE/RETAIL: Both
CULTURAL NOTES: Yes   SEED COUNT: Yes
SEED COLLECTIONS: Yes   EXPORT: Yes   CREDIT CARDS:Yes
SPECIALITIES: Grass seed

JE   Jelitto Perennial Seeds. P.o. Box 1264. D-29685 Schwarmstedt. Germany.   CONTACT: Georg Uebelhart
TEL: 0049 5071 4085   FAX:0049 5071 4088
OPENING TIMES: M-F 8-4.45 CET   MIN ORDER:£32
CAT COST: Free   CAT OUT: Jan   POSTAGE:Yes
WHOLESALE/RETAIL:Wholesale. Happy to supply clubs/individuals provided the £32 min is met. CULTURAL NOTES:Yes
SEED COUNT:Gm needed to produce 1000 plants
EXPORT:Yes   CREDIT CARDS:Eu, Ma, V
SPECIALITIES: Perennials, Grasses, Herbs, Patio-plants. Pre-treated seed for fast germination.
OTHER INFO:Short plant description, over 50 col pics.

JM   J.E.Martin. 4 Church St. Mkt Harborough. Leics. LE16 7AA
TEL: 01858 462751   FAX:01858 434544
CONTACT:J.Martin-Proctor
OPENING TIMES:M,Tu,Th,F 8.30-5.30, Sa 8.30-5, Wed 8.30-1
CAT COST:Free   CAT OUT:Oct   POSTAGE:Yes
WHOLESALE/RETAIL:Both
EXPORT:Yes   SPECIALITIES: Potatoes

CODE-SUPPLIER INDEX

JV Jekka's Herb Farm. Rose Cottage. Shellards Lane. Alveston.
Bristol. BS12 2SY   CONTACT: Jekka McVicar
TEL: 01454 418878   FAX: 01454 411988
CAT COST:4x 1st class stamps   CAT OUT:Jan   POSTAGE:Free
WHOLESALE/RETAIL: Yes, will stock retail outlets & retail at
shows only.   SEED COLLECTIONS: 6 new collections
EXPORT:Yes   SPECIALITIES: Herbs
OTHER INFO:Full planting details on packets.

K Mr.K.Foster. Garden Cottage. Mulgrave Est. Lythe. Whitby.
N.Yorks.
TEL:01947 893315   FAX:01947 893315
CAT COST: S.a.e   CAT OUT: Sept   POSTAGE: Yes
DISCOUNTS: Yes   WHOLESALE/RETAIL: Retail
CULTURAL NOTES: Yes   SEED COUNT: Yes   EXPORT:Yes
SPECIALITIES: Leeks, onions, top grade veg seed
OTHER INFO: Specialist service aimed at gardeners growing
for show and kitchen use

KI E.W.King & Co. Monks Farm. Coggleshall Rd. Kelvedon. Essex.
CO5 9PG
TEL: 01376 570000   FAX: 01376 571189
CAT COST: Free CAT OUT: Sept POSTAGE: Free over £10, over
£35 trade WHOLESALE/RETAIL: Both CULTURAL NOTES:Yes
SEED COUNT: Yes   SEED COLLECTIONS: Yes   EXPORT:Yes
CREDIT CARDS: Ma, V   SPECIALITIES:Veg/flower, sweet pea

KS Kings Seeds. Kings Herb Heaven. 1660 Great North Rd,
Avondale, Auckland. NZ
TEL: 0-9-828 7588   FAX: 0-9-828 7588
OPENING TIMES: 9-5, daily except weekends
MIN ORDER: $7   POSTAGE: $3   CULTURAL NOTES:Yes

L Milton Seeds. 3 Milton Ave. Blackpool. Lancs. FY3 8LY
TEL:01253 394377 FAX:01253 305110
CONTACT:B.J.Robertson   MIN ORDER:£5
POSTAGE: 50p for under £10; £1 for orders containing peas
and/or beans   WHOLESALE/RETAIL: Retail
SEED COUNT:Yes   CREDIT CARDS:A,B,D,Ma,Sw,V

LA Landlife Wildflowers. The Old Police Station. Lark Lane.
Liverpool. L17 8UU   CONTACT: Ms.Watson
TEL: 0151 728 7011   FAX:0151 728 8413
OPENING TIMES: 9-5
CAT COST: Free   CAT OUT: Jan   POSTAGE:Yes
DISCOUNTS:Yes   WHOLESALE/RETAIL: Both
CULTURAL NOTES: Yes   SEED COUNT: Yes, seeds per gm
SPECIALITIES: Native wildflowers
E-MAIL: info@landlife.v-net.com

LG The RHS Lily Group. Rosemary Cottage. Lowbands. Redmarley.
Gloucester. GL19 3NG
CAT COST: Free to members   CAT OUT: Jan
SEED COUNT: Average 10-15 seeds per pk
OTHER INFO: Seed distribution for members only

M Marshalls. Wisbech. Cambs. PE12 2RF
TEL:01 945 466 711   FAX: 01 945 588 235
Phone lines: Jan-Apr 8.30-5.30 M-F, 9-4 Sa; May-Dec 9-4 M-F
CAT COST:Free   CAT OUT:Oct, June   POSTAGE:95p under £15
DISCOUNTS: Allotments, societies
WHOLESALE/RETAIL:Retail mail order   CULTURAL NOTES:Yes
SEED COUNT:No. of seeds/min no. of plants you can expect
CREDIT CARDS:Yes   EXPORT:Details on request
SPECIALITIES:Potatoes, veg   OTHER INFO:Pre-chitted potato

MA The Marches Nursery. Presteigne. Powys. LD8 2HG
TEL: 01544 260474   FAX:01544 260474   CONTACT:J.Cooke
CAT COST: S.a.e.   CAT OUT: Spring   POSTAGE:Free
WHOLESALE/RETAIL: Retail   CULTURAL NOTES:Yes
SEED COUNT: Yes   EXPORT: Yes
SPECIALITIES:Hardy Perennials

Sm/ S.M.McArd. 39 West Rd. Pointon. Sleaford. Lincs. NG34 0NA
Mc TEL: 01529 240765   FAX: 01529 240765
CONTACT: S.M.McArd   CAT COST: 2x 2nd class stamps
CAT OUT: Nov, Supplement each month   POSTAGE: 40p
WHOLESALE/RETAIL: Retail   CULTURAL NOTES:Some
SEED COUNT:Not on plain pks   EXPORT: EU only
SPECIALITIES: Unusual veg
OTHER INFO: Flower seeds free from all chemical treatment

MN Monocot Seeds. Jacklands. Jacklands Bridge. Tickenham.
Clevedon. BS21 6SG   TEL: 01275 810394
CAT COST: S.a.e. 50p stamps   CAT OUT: Oct
WHOLESALE/RETAIL: Retail   EXPORT: Yes
SPECIALITIES: Bulbous & tuberous rooted

MS Matthewman's Sweetpeas. 14 Chariot Way. Thorpe Audlin.
Pontefract. W.Yorks. WF8 3EZ   CONTACT: P. Matthewman
TEL: 01977 621381
CAT OUT: Autumn   POSTAGE: 50p under £10
WHOLESALE/RETAIL: Retail SEED COUNT: Yes EXPORT:Yes
SPECIALITIES: Sweet peas
OTHER INFO: Offer lecture/talk on sweet pea culture

N Andrew Norfield Seeds. Lower Meend. St. Briavels. Glos. GL15
6RW
TEL: 01594 530134   FAX: 01594 530113
MIN ORDER: No min for retail, £20 wholesale
CAT COST: 1st class stamp   CAT OUT: Dec
DISCOUNT:Free pkt for 8 pkts ordered
WHOLESALE/RETAIL: Both   CULTURAL NOTES: Yes
SEED COUNT: Yes   EXPORT:Yes
SPECIALITIES: Pre-germinated seed of hardy trees, shrubs,
palms & cycads.

NA Naturescape. Lapwing Meadows. Coach Gap Lane. Langar.
Notts. NG13 9HP   CONTACT:
TEL: 01949 851045/860592   FAX: 01949 850431
OPENING TIMES: See cat.   CAT COST: 4x 1st class stamps
POSTAGE: Free over £5   WHOLESALE/RETAIL: Both
CULTURAL NOTES: Yes   SEED COUNT: Yes
SPECIALITIES: Wild Flowers

NG North Green Seeds. 16 Witton La. Little Plumstead. Norwich.
Norfolk NR13 5DL
MIN ORDER: £   CAT COST: £1.25, 4x IRC (overseas)
CAT OUT: Late Autumn   POSTAGE:26p
WHOLESAE/RETAIL: Both   CULTURAL NOTES: General
EXPORT: Yes
SPECIALITIES:Helleborus, Fritillaria, Galanthus, choice bulbs,
trees & shrubs.

NP National Collection of Passiflora. Lampley Rd. Kingston
Seymour. Clevedon. N.Somerset. BS21 6XS
TEL: 01934 833350 FAX:01934 877255
CONTACT: John Vanderplank OPENING TIMES:9-1, 2-5 M-Sa
MIN ORDER: No min. U.K., £5 EU   CAT COST: £1
CAT OUT: Oct   CULTURAL NOTES: Yes
WHOLESALE/RETAIL: Both SEED COUNT: Yes EXPORT:Yes
SPECIALITIES: Passiflora only   CREDIT CARDS:Yes

CODE-SUPPLIER INDEX

NS Natural Selection. 1 Station Cottages. Hullavington. Chippenham. Wilts. SN14 6ET   CONTACT: M.J.Cragg Barber
TEL: 01666 837369
CAT COST: S.a.e   CAT OUT: Autumn   POSTAGE: 26p
WHOLESALE/RETAIL: Retail
SPECIALITIES:Obscure British natives

NT Native Gardens. 5737 Fisher Lane. Greenback. TN 37742. USA.
TEL: 423 856 0220   FAX: 423 856 0220   CONTACT:M.Bradforth
OPENIG TIMES: By appt.   CAT COST: £2
CAT OUT: Spring, fall/autumn update
WHOLESALE/RETAIL: Both   CULTURAL NOTES: Yes
SEED COUNT:Min 25 seeds   EXPORT:Yes
SPECIALITIES: Native seed of mid & eastern US
OTHER INFO: Min 25 seeds, usually 100.
E-MAIL:R.copallina@aol.com

O D.Orriell - Seed Exporter. 45 Frape Ave. Mt Yokine 6060. Perth. W.Australia   CONTACT: P.Orriell
TEL:+619 344 2290   FAX: +619 344 8982
OPENING TIMES: M-F, 9-5. Phone & fax 24hr service
MIN ORDER: Aus$25.00   CAT COST: US$6.00
CAT OUT: July   POSTAGE:Yes
DISCOUNT: Large orders   WHOLESALE/RETAIL: Both
CULTURAL NOTES:Some   SEED COUNT: Some
EXPORT:Yes
SPECIALITIES: Native Australian seeds, palms, cycads
OTHER INFO: Vice President, member of Fleuroselect group. Distributor of Kirstenbosch seed primer.

P Plant World. St. Marychurch Rd. Newton Abbot. Devon. TQ12 4SE
TEL:01803 872939   CONTACT:Ray Brown
OPENING TIMES:Gardens open 9.30-5 exc Wed, Easter- Sept
MIN ORDER: £8 UK, £20 overseas
CAT COST: 3x 1st class stamps or 2IRC (overseas)
CAT OUT: Oct   POSTAGE: 50p for under 10 pk, £1 overseas
DISCOUNT:Free pk for friend's name, or 10pks ordered
WHOLESALE/RETAIL: Both   CULTURAL NOTES: Brief
SEED COUNT: Some   EXPORT:Yes
CREDIT CARDS:A,Eu,Ma,V
SPECIALITIES: Primula, Hardy Geraniums, Aquilegias, Euphorbias, Mecanopsis

PA The Paradise Centre. Twinstead Rd. Lamarsh. Nr Bures. Suffolk. CO8 5EX
TEL: 01787 26944   FAX: 01787 269449
OPENING TIMES: Sa,Su & Bank Hols   MIN ORDER;£7.50
CAT COST: £1 or 4x 1st class stamps   CAT OUT: Jan
DISCOUNT: Several   WHOLESALE/RETAIL: Retail
CULTURAL NOTES: On request   EXPORT: Yes
CREDIT CARDS: Yes   SPECIALITIES: Unusual sp
OTHER INFO: Seeds suitable for growing abroad

PG Graysons Seeds. 34 Glenthorne Cl. Brampton. Chesterfield. Derbyshire. S40 3AR   CONTACT: P.Grayson
TEL: 01246 278503   FAX: 01246 566918
OPENING TIMES: By appt only   CAT COST: Free   CAT OUT: Oct
POSTAGE: 50p   DISCOUNT: For trade orders
WHOLESALE/RETAIL: Both   CULTURAL NOTES: Yes
SEED COUNT: Yes
SPECIALITIES: Alcea & Lathyrus
EXPORT:Yes
SEED COLLECTIONS: : Old-fashioned sweet peas & single hollyhocks
OTHER INFO: Producing our own cultivars

PH Phedar Nursery. Bunkershill. Romiley. Stockport. SK6 3DS
TEL: 0161 430 3772   FAX:0161 430 3772
CONTACT:Will McLewin
CAT COST: S.a.e   CAT OUT:Hellebores Jul, Paeonia Oct
POSTAGE: Nominal   WHOLESALE/RETAIL:Both
CULTURAL NOTES: Basic   EXPORT: Yes
SPECIALITIES: Hellebore & paeonia
OTHER INFO: Accurate, authentic seed, provenance not hybrid cultivated seed

PM Potterton & Martin. The Cottage Nursery. Moortown Rd. Nettleton. Nr Caistor. Lincs. LN7 6HX   CONTACT: R.Potterton
TEL: 01472 851792   FAX:01472 851792
OPENING TIMES: 9-5   CAT COST:1st class stamp   CAT OUT:Nov
POSTAGE: Free   WHOLESALE/RETAIL: Both
EXPORT: Yes   CREDIT CARDS:Yes

PR Prairie Moon Nursery. RR3 Box 163. Winona. MN55987. USA.
TEL: 507 452 1362   FAX:507 454 5238
OPENING TIMES:8-5 M-F Mail order only
CAT COST: $2.00 , $4 outside of USA   CAT OUT: Jan
POSTAGE: Yes   WHOLESALE/RETAIL: Retail
CULTURAL NOTES:Yes   SEED COUNT: Yes
SEED COLLECTIONS: Custom mixes   EXPORT: Yes
SPECIALITIES: 350 sp of native seeds
OTHER INFO: International customer are responsible for knowing their countries' customs regulations. Orders must be paid in US funds in advance.

PT Philip Tivey & Sons. 28 Wanlip Rd. Syston. Nr Leicester. LE7 1PA
TEL: 0116 269 2968   CONTACT:S.P.Tivey
SPECIALITIES: Dahlia Exhibition Seed only

R Range Nurseries. The Range. Clement St. Hextable. Swanley. Kent. BR8 7PQ
TEL: 01 322 661049   Phone, best bet 2-5   MIN ORDER: £3
CAT COST: Free   CAT OUT: Sept/Oct   POSTAGE: Free
WHOLESALE/RETAIL:Both, wholesale on quotation
CULTURAL NOTES: Some   SEED COUNT: Yes
EXPORT: Possible, postage payable

RE Rainforest Seed Co. Box 241, San Jose 1017, Costa Rica.
TEL: 506 232 9260
CAT COST: Free   SPECIALITIES: Rainforest sp
OTHER INFO: Seed mostly from our own 1,500 acre virgin rainforest. Portion of profits go to rainforest conservation organisations.

RH Royal Horticultural Society. RHS Garden. Wisley. Woking. Surrey. GU23 6QB
TEL: 01483 22423   FAX:01483 212343
CAT COST: S.a.e, members only
CAT OUT: Nov, details provided on membership uptake
POSTAGE: £4 UK members, free to overseas members
EXPORT: RHS members only   CULTURAL NOTES: Yes
OTHER INFO: List changes annually

RO W.Robinson & Sons Ltd. Sunnybank, Foron. Nr. Preston. PR3 0BN   CONTACT: I/E.Robinson
TEL: 01524 791210   FAX: 01524 791933
OPENING TIMES: Mar-Dec times vary   CAT COST:Free
CAT OUT: Sept   POSTAGE:Free   WHOLESALE/RETAIL: Both
CULTURAL NOTES: Yes   SEED COUNT: Yes   EXPORT: Yes
CREDIT CARDS: Yes
SPECIALITIES: Mammoth Strain veg

CODE-SUPPLIER INDEX

RS Richard Stockwell. Rare Plants.(REF SS), 64, Weardale Rd, Sherwood, Nottingham. NG5 1DD   CONTACT:R. Stockwell
TEL: 0115 969 1063 FAX: 0115 969 1063
OPENING TIMES: Mail order only
CAT COST: 4x 2nd class stamps or 2 IRC (overseas)
CAT OUT: Dec, updated July for Southern hemisphere
POSTAGE: Free UK, overseas £1 WHOLESALE/RETAIL: Both
CULTURAL NOTES: Detailed germination guide on all genera
SEED COUNT: If less than 10   EXPORT:Yes
SPECIALITIES: Rare climbers, dwarf sp

S Suttons Seeds. Hele Rd. Torquay. Devon. TQ2 7QJ
TEL: 01803 612011 FAX: 01803 615747
OPENING TIMES: 8.30-5, M-F
CAT OUT: Mid-Oct   POSTAGE:Free over £5
DISCOUNT: Trade/Associations WHOLESALE/RETAIL: Retail
CULTURAL NOTES: Yes SEED COUNT: pks of under200 seeds
SEED COLLECTIONS: Yes EXPORT: Yes CREDIT CARDS:Yes
OTHER INFO: Est. 1806

SA Sandeman Seeds. The Croft. Sutton. Pulborough. W.Sussex.
RH20 1PL CONTACT: JCP Sandeman
TEL: 01798 869315 FAX`: 01798 869400
OPENING TIMES: 8.30-5.30   MIN ORDER: £40
CAT COST: Free to trade customers only   CAT OUT: Sept
POSTAGE: Yes   DISCOUNTS:Over £1000
WHOLESALE/RETAIL: Wholesale   CULTURAL NOTES : Yes
SEED COUNT: On request   EXPORT:Yes
SPECIALITIES: Woody plant seeds and perennials
OTHER INFO: Info such as provenance etc. on request

SC Scottish Rock Garden Club. PO Box 14063. Edinburgh. EH10 4YE
TEL: 01786 824064
MIN ORDER: £2.50   CAT COST: Free to members
CAT OUT: Dec/Jan   POSTAGE: Free
WHOLESALE/RETAIL: Members only, mail order
CULTURAL NOTES: Yes
EXPORT: Overseas members
SPECIALITIES:Hardy plants & bulbs
OTHER INFO:List may be subject to slight changes from year to year. Seed exchange available to members only. Wild & garden sources from around the world

SE Seymour Selected Seeds. Admail 962 Farm Lane. Spalding. Lincs. PE11 1TD
TEL: 01481 65270 FAX:01481 64552 Answer machine 24hr
CAT COST: Free POSTAGE:Yes
DISCOUNT:Yes, also early order incentives
WHOLEALE/RETAIL: Mail order
CULTURAL NOTES: Yes   SEED COUNT: Yes
CREDIT CARDS:Yes
SPECIALITIES: Flower & veg

SG The Seed Guild. P.O. Box 8951. Lanark. ML11 9JH
TEL: 01555 664561 FAX: 01555 663636
CONTACT: D. McDougall
CAT COST: 3x 2nd class stamps   CAT OUT: Autumn
POSTAGE: Free over £10
WHOLESALE/RETAIL: Both
CULTURAL NOTES: On the internet
EXPORT: Yes   CREDIT CARDS:Yes
SPECIALITIES: Seeds from botanical gardens around the world
OTHER INFO: Seed list on Internet: http://www.
Gardenweb.com/seedgd
E-MAIL: 100104.346@compuserve.com

SH The Seed House. 9a Widley Rd. Cosham. Portsmouth. PO6 2DS
TEL: 01705 325639
MIN ORDER: £5
CAT COST: 4x 1st class stamps or 4IRC (overseas)
CAT OUT: On request with updated lists   DISCOUNTS:Trade
WHOLESALE/RETAIL: Both   CULTURAL NOTES: Yes
EXPORT: Yes
SPECIALITIES: Australian & N.Z seeds selected for European climate
SEED COUNT: Depends on cost, pks sold at unit price.

SI Silverhill Seeds. P.O.Box 53108. Kenilworth. 7745 South Africa
TEL: +27 21 762 4245 FAX: +27 21 797 6609
CONTACT: R.Saunders
OPENING TIMES: Mail order only
CAT COST: £1   CAT OUT: Jan   POSTAGE: Min £2
DISCOUNTS: Bulk discounts   WHOLESALE/RETAIL: Both
CULTURAL NOTES: Yes
SEED COUNT: Seeds normally sold by no., not by weight
EXPORT: Yes
SPECIALITIES: South African seeds
E-MAIL: silseeds@iafrica.com

SN Simpson's Seeds. 27 Meadowbrook. Old Oxted. Surrey.
TEL: 01883 715242 FAX: 01883 715245
OPENING TIMES: By appt, late Aug/early Sept
CAT COST: Free   CAT OUT: Late Oct
DISCOUNTS: Several
WHOLESALE/RETAIL: Both   CULTURAL NOTES: Yes
SEED COUNT: Yes   EXPORT: Yes
CREDIT CARDS: Yes
SPECIALITIES: Tomatoes, unusual veg, gourmet potatoes & peppers
OTHER INFO: M.A.F.F. registered growers & distributors No:2620. Newsletter & helpline for tomatoes. Organic seed

SO Southfield Nurseries. Boune Rd. Morton. Bourne. Lincs. PE10 0RH
TEL: 01778 570168   CONTACT: B.Goodey
POSTAGE: 60p   WHOLESALE/RETAIL: Retail
CULTURAL NOTES: Yes   SEED COLLECTIONS: Yes
SPECIALITIES: Cactus

SS Southern Seeds. The Vicarage. Sheffield. Canterbury. New Zealand 8173
TEL: 03 31 83 814 FAX: 03 31 83 814
OPENING TIMES: Mail order   MIN ORDER: NZ $25
CAT COST: NZ $5 or £2 sterling   CAT OUT: Mid year
POSTAGE: NZ $10   WHOLESALE/RETAIL: Retail
CULTURAL NOTES: Yes   EXPORT: Yes
SPECIALTIES: N.Z alpines/ South Island
OTHER INFO: Seed mainly collected from the wild

ST Stewarts (Nottm) Ltd. The Garden Shop. 3 George St. Nottm. NG1 3BH
TEL: 0115 9476338 FAX:0115 9410720
OPENING TIMES: 9-5.30, 6 days   MIN ORDER: 1 pk
CAT COST: 2x 1st class stamps   CAT OUT: Dec
POSTAGE: Yes
DISCOUNT: Early order incentive
WHOLESALE/RETAIL: Retail
CULTURAL NOTES: Some   SEED COUNT:Some
EXPORT: If necessary
CREDIT CARDS: Yes
SPECIALITIES: Seed potatoes, grass seed, veg

CODE-SUPPLIER INDEX

SU Suffolk Herbs, Monks Farm. Kelvedon. Essex. CO5 9PG
TEL: 01376 572456   FAX: 01376 571189
CAT COST: Free   CAT OUT: Sept
POSTAGE: Mail order free, trade free over £35
WHOLESALE/RETAIL: Both   CULTURAL NOTES: Yes
SEED COUNT: Yes   SEED COLLECTIONS: Yes
EXPORT: Yes   CREDIT CARDS: Ma, V
SPECIALITIES: Herb, oriental veg, wild flower, veg seed

SW Southwestern Native Seeds. Box 50503. Tuscon. Arizona
85703.USA.
CONTACT: J. Walker
OPENING TIMES: Mail order only   MIN ORDER: $13
CAT COST: $2   CAT OUT: Oct
POSTAGE; $1 US, $2 overseas
WHOLESALE/RETAIL: Retail   CULTURAL NOTES: Yes
EXPORT: Yes
SPECIALITIES: Wild collected native ornamentals

T Thompson & Morgan, Poplar Lane, Ipswich. Suffolk. IP8 3BU
TEL: 01473 688588 FAX: 01473 680199
OPENING TIMES: 9-5, M-F   CAT COST: Free
CAT OUT: Oct   POSTAGE: 70p
DISCOUNTS: Various throughout year. For horticultural socieies
& clubs.
WHOLESALE/RETAIL: Both   CULTURAL NOTES: Yes
SEED COUNT: Yes   SEED COLLECTIONS: Yes
EXPORT: Yes   SPECIALITIES: Wide range
OTHER INFO: Biggest illustrated seed catalogue in the world

TU Edwin Tucker & Sons Ltd. Brewery Meadow. Stonepark.
Ashburton. Newton Abbot, Devon. TQ13 7DG
TEL: 01364 652403 FAX: 01364 654300
CONTACT: Geoff Penton
OPENING TIMES: M-F 8-5, Sa 8-12
CAT COST: Free   CAT OUT: Oct
POSTAGE: For small orders   DISCOUNTS: Various
WHOLESALE/RETAIL: Retail   CULTURAL NOTES: Yes
SEED COUNT: Yes   EXPORT: Yes (some restrictions)
CREDIT CARDS: A, Sw, V   SPECIALITIES: Potatoes

U Unwins Seeds Ltd. Cambridge CB4 4ZZ
TEL: 01945 588 522 FAX: 01945 475 255
CAT COST: Free   CAT OUT: Summer, mid-autumn
POSTAGE: Free over £15   DISCOUNTS: See catalogue
WHOLESALE/RETAIL: Mail order, Retail stockists
CULTURAL NOTES: Yes   SEED COUNT: Yes
SEED COLLECTIONS: Yes   EXPORT: By agreement
CREDIT CARDS: Yes   SPECIALITIES: Sweet peas

V Vreeken's Zaden. Voorstraat 448, 3311 ex Dordrecht. Holland
TEL: 00-31-78-6135467   FAX: 00-31-78-312198
OPENING TIMES:Vary   MIN ORDER: £6
CAT COST: £3   CAT OUT: Nov POSTAGE: Free over £14
WHOLESALE/RETAIL: Both   CULTURAL NOTES: Yes
SEED COUNT: Most EXPORT: EU CREDIT CARDS: Eu, Ma, V
SPECIALITIES: Rare varieties veg & flowers

VH The Van Hage Garden Co. Great Amwell. Ware. Herts. SG12
9RP
TEL: 01920 870811 FAX: 01920 871861
OPENING TIMES: M-F 9-6, Sa 9-6, Su 10.30-4.30
CAT COST: Free   CAT OUT: Oct   POSTAGE: 50p
DISCOUNTS: Special offers. Discounts for allotment societies
WHOLESALE/RETAIL: Retail   EXPORT: Yes
SPECIALITIES: Dutch seed, giant carrot Flak

VS Samen Catalogue c/o Vreeken's Zaden. Voorstraat-West 448.
Postbus 182. 3300 AD Dordrecht. The Netherlands.
TEL: 00 31 78 6135467   FAX: 00 31 78 6312198
CAT OUT: Mar
WHOLESALE/RETAIL: Retail
EXPORT: Yes
SPECIALITIES: Rare veg seeds
OTHER INFO: Distributed through Vreekens.

W c/o National Auricula, & Primula Society (Southern), 67
Warnham Court Rd, Carshalton Beeches, Surrey. SM5 3ND
CONTACT: L.E.Wigley
OPENING TIMES: Mail order only
CAT COST: S.a.e. CAT OUT: Jan POSTAGE: S.a.e. with order
CULTURAL NOTES: Yes   EXPORT: Yes
SPECIALITIES: Auricula, Primula , Campanula, cottage garden
subjects
OTHER INFO: List contains hand-fertilised items from specific
crosses. Rare or uncommon items included whenever possible

X Rhododendron, Camellia & Magnolia Group (RHS), Whitehills,
Newton Stewart. DG8 6SL
TEL: 01671 402049 FAX: 01671 403106
CAT COST: £1, £2 overseas   CAT OUT: Jan
WHOLESALE/RETAIL: Members only
EXPORT: Overseas members
SPECIALITIES: Rhododendron
OTHER INFO: List includes collectors references and source of
seed plus wild-collected, hand and open-pollinated sp. Seed
available to members only.

Y Roy Young Seeds. 23 Westland Chase. West Winch. King's
Lynn. Norfolk. PE33 0QH
TEL: 01553 840867 FAX: 01553 840867
OPENING TIMES: Mail order only
CAT COST: Stamp UK, 2x IRC (overseas) each list
CAT OUT: Oct/Nov
POSTAGE: 65p UK, £1 EU, £1.50 elsewhere
WHOLESALE/RETAIL: Both   SEED COUNT:Yes
EXPORT: Yes
SPECIALITIES: Cactus & succulents
OTHER INFO: Over 1,500 varieties in retail catalogue.

YA Samuel Yates Ltd. Withyfold Drive. Macclesfield. Chesire. SK10
2BE
TEL: +44 (0)1625 427823 FAX: +44 (0)1625 422843
CONTACT: Charles Seddon
MIN ORDER: £50   POSTAGE : Free
WHOLESALE/RETAIL: Wholesale
CULTURAL NOTES:Yes
SEED COUNT:On request   CREDIT CARDS:
CWO or credit accounts only
SPECIALITIES: Sakata bred veg & flower seed
OTHER INFO: Subsidiary of Sakata Seed Corporation, Japan

Z Wild Seeds. Branas. Llandderfel, Gwynedd. LL23 7RF
CONTACT: Mike Thorne
OPENING TIMES: Mail order only
CAT COST: Free
POSTAGE: Free over £40
DISCOUNT: 10% over £100
CULTURAL NOTES: Yes
SEED COLLECTIONS: Yes
EXPORT: Yes
SPECIALITIES: Wildflowers

SUPPLIER- CODE INDEX

BOTANICAL- COMMON NAMES

Botanical	Common	Botanical	Common
Acanthus	Bear's Breeches	Carex	Ornamental Sedge
Acca	Fruit Salad Bush	Carthamus	Safflower
Acer	Maple	Catanache	Cupid's Dart
Achillea	Yarrow	Catharanthus	Periwinkle
Achimenes	Hot Water Plant	Centaurea	Cornflower
Aconitum	Monkshood	Centranthus	Pretty Betsy
Actidinia	Kiwi Fruit	Cercis	Judas Tree
Adansonia	Baobab	Cerinthe	Honeywort
Adenophora	Ladybell	Cimicifuga	Black Snake Root
Adonis	Pheasant's Eye	Cistus	Rock Rose
Agapanthus	African Lily	Clematis vitalba	Traveller's Joy
Agastache	Hyssop	Cleome	Spider Flower
Agave	Century Plant	Coccoloba	Sea Grape
Ageratum	Floss Flower	Commelina	Day Flower
Agrostemma	Corn Cockle	Convolvulus	Dwarf Morning Glory
Albizia	Silk Tree	Cordyline	Cabbage Palm
Alcea	Hollyhock	Cortaderia	Pampas Grass
Alchemilla	Lady's Mantle	Cortaderia	Pampas Grass
Allium	Garlic	Corydalis	Fumitory
Alonsoa	Mask Flower	Crepis	Hawksbeard
Alstroemeria	Peruvian Lily	Cryptomeria	Japanese Cedar
Althaea	Hollyhock	Cynara	Cardoon
Amaranthus	Love Lies Bleeding	Cynoglossum	Chinese Forget-me-Not
Amberboa	Sweet Sultan	Cytisus	Broom
Ammobium	Winged Everlasting	Datura	Angel's Trumpet
Anacyclus	Mt. Atlas Daisy	Delonix	Flamboyant Tree
Anagallis	Pimpernel	Dendranthema	Chrysanthemum
Anaphalis	Pearl Everlasting	Dianella	Flax Lily
Anemone	Wind Flower	Dianthus	Pinks
Antennaria	Pussy Toes	Dianthus barbatus	Sweet William
Anthemis	Golden Chamomile	Dianthus caryophyllus	Carnation
Antirrhinum	Snapdragon	Dicentra	Bleeding Heart
Aquilegia	Columbine	Dicksonia	Tree Fern
Arabis	Rock Cress	Dictamnus	Burning Bush
Araujia	Cruel Plant	Digitalis	Foxglove
Arctotis	African Daisy	Dionaea	Venus Fly Trap
Arenaris	Scotch Moss	Dipsacus	Teasel
Armeria	Thrift	Dolichos	Hyacinth Bean
Arnica	Mountain Tobacco	Dracaena	Dragon Tree
Artemisia	Sweet Annie	Eccremocarpus	Chilean Glory Vine
Aruncus	Goat's Beard	Echinacea	Red Cone Flower
Asclepias	Milkweed	Echinops	Globe Thistle
Asperula	Woodruff	Emilia	Tassel Flower
Astrantia	Masterwort	Epilobium	Willow Herb
Avena	Cat Grass	Eranthis	Winter Aconite
Banksia	Australian Honeysuckle	Eremurus	Foxtail Lily
Baptisia	False Indigo	Erigeron	Fleabane
Bellis Perennis	Daisy	Eryngium	Sea Holly
Berberis	Barberry	Erysimum	Wallflower
Bergenia	Elephant's Ears	Erythrina	Coral Tree
Betula	Birch	Eschscholzia	Californian Poppy
Bidens	Cosmos	Eucalyptus	Gum Tree
Borago	Borage	Euphorbia	Spurge
Brachyscome	Swan River Daisy	Eustoma	Prairie Gentian
Bracteantha	Strawflower	Foeniculum	Fennel
Brassica oleracea	Ornamental Cabbage	Francoa	Bridal Wreath
Buddleja	Butterfly Bush	Gaillardia	Blanket Flower
Bupthalmum	Yellow Ox Eye Daisy	Galanthus	Snowdrop
Calamintha	Catmint	Galega	Goat's Rue
Calceolaria	Slipper Flower	Gazania	Treasure Flower
Calendula	English Marigold	Geranium	Crane's Bill
Caltha	Marsh Marigold	Gerbera	Transvaal Daisy
Campanula	Bell Flower	Geum	Avens
Campanula medium	Canterbury Bells	Gilia	Birds' Eyes
Campsis	Trumpet Flower	Gillenia	Bowman's Root
Canna	Indian Shot	Ginkgo	Maidenhair Tree

278

BOTANICAL- COMMON NAMES

Botanical	Common	Botanical	Common
Glaucium	Horned Poppy	Ocimum	Basil
Globularia	Globe Daisy	Oenethera	Evening Primrose
Gloriosa	Glory Lily	Olea	Olive Tree
Grevillea	Australian Silky Oak	Onopordum	Cotton Thistle
Gypsophila	Baby's Breath	Origanum	Oregano
Hamamelis	Witch Hazel	Osteospermum	Star of the Veldt
Hedysarum	French Honeysuckle	Panacratium	Mediterranean Lily
Helenium	Sneezeweed	Papaver	Poppy
Helianthemum	Rock Rose	Paradisea	St.Bruno's Lily
Helianthus	Sunflower	Passiflora	Passion Flower
Heliotropium	Heliotrope	Pelargonium	Bedding Geranium
Helipterum	Everlasting	Peltiphyllum	Umbrella Plant
Helleborus	Xmas Rose	Penstemon	Beard Tongue
Hemerocallis	Day Lily	Periploca	Silk Vine
Hesperis	Sweet Rocket	Perovskia	Russian Sage
Heuchera	Coral Bells	Phacelia	Californian Bluebell
Hunnemannia	Mexican Tulip Poppy	Phaseolus	Snail Flower
Hypericum	St.John's Wort	Phormium	New Zealand Flax
Hypoestes	Polka Dot	Physalis	Chinese Lantern
Impatiens	Busy Lizzie	Physostegia	Obedient Plant
Ionopsidium	Violet Cress	Picea	Spruce
Ipomoea	Morning Glory	Pinus	Pine
Kniphofia	Red Hot Poker	Plantago	Plantain
Kochia	Burning Bush	Platycodon	Balloon Flower
Lathyrus	Everlasting Pea	Polemonium	Jacob's Ladder
Lathyrus odoratus	Sweet Pea	Polygonatum	Solomon's Seal
Lavatera	Mallow	Portulaca	Sun Plant
Lavendula	Lavender	Potentilla	Cinquefoil
Leonurus	Motherwort	Ptelea	Hop Tree
Leucanthemum	Chrysanthemum	Pulsatilla	Pasque Flower
Leucojum	Snowflake	Ramonda	Pyrenean Primrose
Liatris	Blazing Star	Rehmannia	Chinese Foxglove
Ligularia	Leopard Plant	Reseda	Mignonette
Lilium	Lily	Rhodochiton	Purple Bell Vine
Limnanthes	Fried Eggs	Ricinus	Castor Oil Plant
Linanthus	Mountain Phlox	Rosa	Rose
Linaria	Toad Flax	Rudbeckia	Cone Flower
Linum	Flax	Saintpaulia	African Violet
Liquidamber	Sweet Gum	Sanguinaria	Blood Root
Lithops	Living Stones	Santolina	Lavender Cotton
Lunaria	Honesty	Scabiosa	Scabious
Lychnis	Campion	Schizanthus	Butterfly Flower
Lysimachia	Loosestrife	Scilla	Blue Bells
Lythrum	Purple Loosestrife	Sedum	Stonecrop
Macleaya	Plume Poppy	Sempervivum	House Leek
Malcomia	Virginian Stock	Sequoia	Redwood
Malus	Flowering Crab	Silene	Catchfly
Malva	Mallow	Sisyrinchium	Blue-Eyed Grass
Matthiola	Stocks	Solanum	Winter Cherry
Mentha	Mint	Sophora	Japanese Pagoda Tree
Mentzelia	Blazing Star	Sorbus	Mountain Ash
Mimosa	Sensitive Plant	Sparaxis	Wand Flower
Mimulus	Monkey Flower	Specularia	Venus' Looking Glass
Mirabilis	Marvel of Peru	Stachys	Lamb's Ears
Moluccella	Bells of Ireland	Stokesia	Stokes Aster
Monarda	Bergamot	Strelitzia	Bird of Paradise
Morina	Whorl Flower	Streptocarpus	Cape Primrose
Musa/Ensete	Banana	Stylomecon	Wind Poppy
Myosotis	Forget-me-Not	Tagetes	Marigold
Myrtus	Myrtle	Thunbergia	Black-Eyed Susie
Nemophila	Baby Blue Eyes	Thymus	Thyme
Nepeta	Catnip	Tithonia	Mexican Sunflower
Nicandra	Shoo Fly Plant	Trachymene	Blue Lace Flower
Nicotiana	Tobacco Plant	Trollius	Globe Flower
Nierembergia	Cup Flower	Tropaeoleum	Nasturtium
Nigélla	Love-in-a-Mist	Ulex	Gorse

279

BOTANICAL- COMMON NAMES

Verbascum	Mullein
Veronica	Speedwell
Viola x wittrochiana	Pansy
Xanthisma	Star of Texas

SYNONYMS

Acca	Feijoa	Leucophyta	Calocephalus
Aeonium	Megalonium	Lobularia	Alyssum
Aethionema	Eunomia	Lotus	Dorycnium
Agastache	Brittonastrum	Lychnis	Silene
Agathis	Dammara	Lychnis	Viscaria
Albizia	Paraserianthes	Macfadyena	Doxantha
Allamanda	Allemanda	Mackaya	Asystasia
Amsonia	Rhazya	Macleaya	Bocconia
Androsace	Douglasia	Maclura	Cudrania
Anredera	Boussingaultia	Mammillaria	Mammilopsis
Arctostaphylos	Comarostaphylis	Mandevilla	Dipladenia
Arctotis	Venidium	Mauranya	Asarina
Arctotis	x Venidioarctotis	Melinis	Rhynchelytrum
Asarum	Heterotropa	Mimulus	Diplacus
Asarum	Hexastylis	Morina	Acanthocalyx
Aurinia	Alyssum	Neoregalia	Aregelia
Bignonia	Doxantha	Oreocereus	Borzicactus
Brachyglottis	Senecio	Parahebe	Derwentia
Bracteantha	Helichrysum	Paris	Daiswa
Buddleja	Buddleia	Parodia	Eriocactus
Calomeria	Humea	Parodia	Notocactus
Caralluma	Frerea	Parodia	Wigginsia
Cardamine	Dentaria	Paxistema	Pachistema
Centaurium	Erythraea	Persicaria	Bistorta
Chamaedaphne	Cassandra	Persicaria	Polygonum
Clarkia	Godetia	Photinia	Heteromeles
Consolida	Delphinium	Photinia	Stranvaesia
Corryocactus	Erdisia	Phuopsis	Crucianella
Corydalis	Fumaria	Poncirus	Aegle
Corydalis	Pseudofumaria	Potentilla	Comarum
Corydalis	Pseudofumaria	Probiscidea	Martynia
Crocosmia	Montbretia	Prunus	Amygdalus
Darmera	Peltiphyllum	Pulsatilla	Anemone
Dendranthema	Chrysanthemum	Retama	Lygos
Disporum	Prosartes	Rhodanthe	Acroclinium
Dorotheanthus	Mesembryanthemum	Rhus	Toxicodendron
Dregea	Wattakaka	Ruellia	Dipterocanthus
Drimys	Tasmannia	Saccharum	Erianthus
Elymus	Leymus	Schefflera	Brassaia
Emilia	Cacalia	Schlumbergera	Zygocactus
Ensete	Musa	Sclerocactus	Ancistrocactus
Epipremnum	Scindapsus	Sedum	Hylotelephium
Erysimum	Cheiranthus	Senecio	Cineraria
Eustoma	Lisianthus	Senecio	Kleinia
Fallopia	Bilderdyckia	Senna	Cassia
Fatsia	Aralia	Shortia	Schizocodon
Felicia	Agathaea	Solanum	Lycianthes
Gaultheria	Pernettya	Soleirolia	Helxine
Genista	Chamaespartium	Solenostemon	Coleus
Gladiolus	Aciderantha	Sphaeralcea	Iliamna
Hacquetia	Dondia	Stachys	Betonica
Hatiora	Rhipsalidopsis	Stenocactus	Echinofossulocactus
Helipterum	Rhodanthe	Stenomesson	Urceolina
Hepatica	Anemone	Stenotus	Happlopappus
Howea	Kentia	Stewartia	Stuartia
Hyacinthoides	Endymion	Stipa	Achinatherum
Hymenocallis	Ismene	Syagrus	Arecastrum
Incarvillea	Amphicome	Tanacetum	Balsamita
Ipomea	Mina	Tanacetum	Pyrethrum
Ipomea	Pharbitis	Tecoma	Tecomaria
Juniperus	Sabina	Tetrapanax	Fatsia
Kennedia	Kennedya	Thuja	Platycladus
Kitaibela	Kitaibela	Tradescantia	Zebrina
Lablab	Dolichos	Tweedia	Oxypetalum
Leucanthemopsis	Chrysanthemum	Verbena	Glandularia
Leucanthemum	Chrysanthemum	Veronicastrum	Veronica

SYNONYMS

Vitaliana	Douglasia
x Amarcrinum	x Crinodonna
Yushania	Arundinaria
Zauschneria	Epilobium
Zephyranthes	Cooperia

HAZARDOUS PLANTS

Aconitum
Actaea
Aquilegia
Caltha
Chelidonium
Colchicum
Daphne
Delphinium
Digitalis
Euphorbia
Gaultheria
Helleborus
Ipomoea
Iris
Kalmia
Laburnum
Lobelia
Lupinus
Narcissus
Ornithogalum
Polygonatum
Ruta
Zigadenus
Achillea
Acokanthera
Adenium
Aesculus
Agrostemma
Allamanda
Alocasia
Alstroemeria
Amsonia
Anemone
Anthurium
Arnica
Asclepias
Berberis
Brugmansia
Caladium
Calla
Colocasia
Cichorium
Cionura
Clivia
Codiaeum
Colutea
Consolida
Convallaria
Coriaria
Cornus
Cotoneaster
Crataegus
Crinum
x Cupressocyparis
Cyclamen
Cymbidium
Cytisus
Dendranthema
Dicentra
Dictamnus
Dieffenbachia
Dorstenia
Echium
Epipremnum
Eranthis
Euonymus

Ficus
Fremontodendron
Galanthus
Glaucium
Gloriosa
Gomphocarpus
Grevillea
Haemanthus
Hedera
Helenium
Helianthus
Hippeastrum
Hyacinthoides
Hyacinthus
Hydrangea
Hyoscyamus
Jatropha
Juniperus
Lagunaria
Lantana
Lathyrus
Lonicera
Mandevilla
Mandragora
Menispermum
Monstera
Nerine
Nerium
Nicotiana
Paeonia
Paphiopedilum
Parthenocissus
Pedilanthus
Periploca
Persicaria
Petteria
Phacelia
Philodendron
Physalis
Phytolacca
Pieris
Platanus
Podophyllum
Pulsatilla
Pyracantha
Ranunculus
Rhamnus
Rheum
Rhus
Ricinus
Robinia
Rumex
Ruscus
Scopolia
Sedum
Senecio
Skimmia
Solanum
Solenopsis
Sorbus
Spathiphyllum
Symphoricarpos
Symphytum
Synadenium
Syngonium
Tagetes

283

HAZARDOUS PLANTS

Tanacetumn
Taxus
Thevetia
Thuja
Tradescantia
Ulex
Veratrum
Viburnum
Vinca
Zantedeschia

The above is a list of hazardous plants, and I feel all growers should be aware of these. The majority of garden plants are safe. Children are at risk, as they can be tempted by seeds which may look like sweets and could cause stomach upset if ingested. Please keep all seeds out of reach of children.

Adverse reactions to plant substances can occur on contact or through ingestion. Many plants have yet to be scientifically screened. Foliage or sap may irritate, aggravate existing allergies, or cause photodermatitis (severe sensitivity to sunlight). Reaction can be delayed and may include itching, redness or blistering.

Seek medical attention immediately if you think you have an adverse reaction to a plant substance, take a sample of the plant with you if you can. Do not force the sufferer to vomit.

BIBLIOGRAPHY

The following is a list of useful books related to growing from seed and gardening in general. It is by no means exhaustive.

GENERAL

Brickell, C.D. (ed) 1992. The RHS Encylopaedia of Plants and Flowers. Dorling Kindersley, London.
Brickell, C.D. (ed) 1992. The RHS Encyclopaedia of Gardening. Dorling Kindersley, London.
Brickell,C.D. (ed) 1996. The RHS A-Z Encyclopaedia of Garden Plants. Dorling Kindersley, London.
Davis, B & Knapp, B. 1992. Know Your Common Plant Names. MDA Publications, Newbury, Berks.
The RHS Plant Finder. 1996/7. The Plant Finder Administrator. RHS Gardens. Wisley. Woking. Surrey. GU20 6QB.
Philip, C. The Plant Finder CDRom.1996/7. Lakeside. Whitbourne. Worcs. WR6 5RD.

JOURNALS
Van Der Werff, D. Plants, New, Rare & Elusive. A journal for New Plant Hunters. Aquilegia Publishing. 2 Grange Close. Hartlepool. Cleveland. TS26 0DU. (Available on subscription).

SEED REFERENCE BOOKS

Ashworth, S. 1991. Seed To Seed.Seed Saver Publications. Iowa.
Bubel, N. 1988. The New Seed Starter's Handbook. Rodale Press. Emaus. Pennsylvania.
Cherfas, J & Fanton, M & J. 1996. The Seed Savers' Handbook. Grover Books.
Deppe, C. 1993. Breed Your Own Vegetable Varieties. Little Brown.
F.A.O. 1961. Agricultural and Horticultural Seeds. Rome.
French, J. 1991. New Plants From Old. Aird, Melbourne.
Nabhan, G. 1989. Enduring Seeds. North Point Press, Berkley, California.
Whealy, K.1992. Garden Seed Inventory. Third Edition. Seed Saver Publications. Rural Route 3. Box 239. Decorah. Iowa 52101.

JOURNALS
Harvest Edition. 1987. The Seed Saver's Exchange, Rural Route 3, Decorah. Iowa. USA.
HDRA News. Ryton Organic Gardens. Ryton-on-Dunsmore. Coventry. CV8 3LG.
Seed News. Newsletter for seed savers. Heritage Seed Library. HDRA. Ryton Organic Gardens. Ryton-on-Dunsmore. Coventry. CV8 3LG.
Seedling. Quarterly Newsletter of Genetic Resources Action International (GRAIN), Girona 25 pral, E-8010 Barcelona. Spain.
The Seed Savers' Network Newsletter. Box 975. Byron Bay. NSW 2481.